UNLOCKING THE BIBLE

UNLOCKING
THE BIBLE

J. David Pawson, M.A., B.Sc

with Andy Peck

Collins

Collins is a division of
HarperCollins*Publishers*
77–85 Fulham Palace Road, London W6 8JB

www.collins.co.uk

First published in separate volumes in Great Britain
in 1999–2001 by HarperCollins*Publishers*
This edition published in Great Britain in 2003 by HarperCollins*Publishers*
Relaunched 2007

7

CONTENTS

INTRODUCTION

I suppose this all started in Arabia, in 1957. I was then a chaplain in the Royal Air Force, looking after the spiritual welfare of all those who were not C.E. (Church of England) or R.C. (Roman Catholic) but O.D. (other denominations – Methodist to Salvationist, Buddhist to atheist). I was responsible for a string of stations from the Red Sea to the Persian Gulf. In most there was not even a congregation to call a 'church', never mind a building.

In civilian life I had been a Methodist minister working anywhere from the Shetland Islands to the Thames Valley. In that denomination it was only necessary to prepare a few sermons each quarter, which were hawked around a 'circuit' of chapels. Mine had mostly been of the 'text' type (talking about a single verse) or the 'topic' type (talking about a single subject with many verses from all over the Bible). In both I was as guilty as any of taking texts out of context before I realized that chapter and verse numbers were neither inspired nor intended by God and had done immense damage to Scripture, not least by changing the meaning of 'text' from a whole book to a single sentence. The Bible had become a compendium of 'proof-texts', picked out at will and used to support almost anything a preacher wanted to say.

With a pocketful of sermons based on this questionable technique, I found myself in uniform, facing very different congregations – all male instead of the lifeboat-style gatherings I had been used to: women and children first. My meagre stock of messages soon ran out. Some of them had gone down like a lead balloon, especially in compulsory parade services in England before I was posted overseas.

So here I was in Aden, virtually starting a church from scratch, from the Permanent Staff and temporary National Servicemen of Her Majesty's youngest armed service. How could I get these men interested in the Christian faith and then committed to it?

Something (I would now say: Someone) prompted me to announce that I would give a series of talks over a few months, which would take us right through the Bible ('from Generation to Revolution'!).

It was to prove a voyage of discovery for all of us. The Bible became a new book when seen as a whole. To use a well-worn cliché, we had failed to see the wood for the trees. Now God's plan and purpose were unfolding in a fresh way. The men were getting something big enough to sink their teeth into. The thought of being part of a cosmic rescue was a powerful motivation. The Bible story was seen as both real and relevant.

Of course, my 'overview' was at that time quite simple, even naive. I felt like that American tourist who 'did' the British Museum in 20 minutes – and could have done it in 10 if he'd had his running shoes! We raced through the centuries, giving some books of the Bible little more than a passing glance.

But the results surpassed my expectations and set the course for the rest of my life and ministry. I had become a 'Bible teacher', albeit in embryo. My ambition to share the excitement of knowing the whole Bible became a passion.

When I returned to 'normal' church life, I resolved to take my congregation through the whole Bible in a decade (if they put up with me that long). This involved tackling about one 'chapter' at every service. This took a lot of time, both in preparation (an hour in the study for every 10 minutes in the pulpit) and delivery (45–50 minutes). The ratio was similar to that of cooking and eating a meal.

The effect of this systematic 'exposition' of Scripture confirmed its rightness. A real hunger for God's Word was revealed. People began to *come* from far and wide, 'to recharge their batteries' as some explained. Soon this traffic was reversed. Tape recordings, first prepared for the sick and housebound, now began to *go* far and wide, ultimately in hundreds of thousands to 120 countries. No one was more surprised than I.

Leaving Gold Hill in Buckinghamshire for Guildford in Surrey, I found myself sharing in the design and building of the Millmead Centre, which contained an ideal auditorium for continuing this teaching ministry. When it was opened, we decided to associate it with the whole Bible by reading it aloud right through without stopping. It took us 84 hours, from Sunday evening until Thursday morning, each person reading for 15 minutes before passing the Bible on to someone else. We used the 'Living' version, the easiest both to read and to listen to, with the heart as well as the mind.

We did not know what to expect, but the event seemed to capture the public imagination. Even the mayor wanted to take part and by sheer coincidence (or providence) found himself reading about a husband who was 'well known, for he sits in the council chamber with the other civic leaders'. He insisted on taking a copy home for his wife. Another lady dropped in on her way to see her solicitor about the legal termination of her marriage and found herself reading, 'I hate divorce, says the Lord'. She never went to the lawyer.

An aggregate of 2,000 people attended and bought half a ton of Bibles. Some came for half an hour and were still there hours later, muttering to themselves, 'Well, maybe just one more book and then I really must go.'

It was the first time many, including our most regular attenders, had ever heard a book of the Bible read straight through. In most churches only a few sentences are read each week and then not always consecutively. What other book would get anyone interested, much less excited, if treated in this way?

So on Sundays we worked through the whole Bible book by book. For the Bible is not one book, but many – in fact, it is a whole library (the word *biblia* in Latin and Greek is plural: 'books'). And not just many books, but many *kinds* of books – history, law, letters, songs, etc. It became necessary, when we had finished studying one book, and were starting on another, to begin with a special introduction covering very basic questions: What kind of book is this? When was it written? Who wrote it? Who was it written for? Above all, *why* was it written? The answer to that one provided the 'key' to unlock its message. Nothing in that book could be fully understood unless seen as part of the whole. The context of every 'text' was not just the paragraph or the section but fundamentally the whole book itself.

By now, I was becoming more widely known as a Bible teacher and was invited to colleges, conferences and conventions – at first in this country, but increasingly overseas, where tapes had opened doors and prepared the way. I enjoy meeting new people and seeing new places, but the novelty of sitting in a jumbo jet wears off in 10 minutes!

Everywhere I went I found the same eager desire to know God's Word. I praised God for the invention of recording cassettes which, unlike video systems, are standardized the world over. They were helping to plug a real hole in so many places.

There is so much successful evangelism but so little teaching ministry to stabilize, develop and mature converts.

I might have continued along these lines until the end of my active ministry, but the Lord had another surprise for me, which was the last link in the chain that led to the publication of these volumes.

In the early 1990s, Bernard Thompson, a friend pastoring a church in Wallingford, near Oxford, asked me to speak at a short series of united meetings with the aim of increasing interest in and knowledge of the Bible – an objective guaranteed to hook me!

I said I would come once a month and speak for three hours about one book in the Bible (with a coffee break in the middle!). In return, I asked those attending to read that book right through before and after my visit. During the following weeks preachers were to base their sermons and house groups their discussions on the same book. All this would hopefully mean familiarity at least with that one book.

My purpose was two-fold. On the one hand, to get people so interested in that book that they could hardly wait to read it. On the other hand, to give them enough insight and information so that when they did read it they would be excited by their ability to understand it. To help with both, I used pictures, charts, maps and models.

This approach really caught on. After just four months I was pressed to book dates for the next five years, to cover all 66 books! I laughingly declined, saying I might be in heaven long before then (in fact, I have rarely booked anything more than six months ahead, not wanting to mortgage the future, or presume that I have one). But the Lord had other plans and enabled me to complete the marathon.

Anchor Recordings (72, The Street, Kennington, Ashford, Kent TN24 9HS) have distributed my tapes for the last 20 years and when the Director, Jim Harris, heard the recordings of these meetings, he urged me to consider putting them on video. He arranged cameras and crew to come to High Leigh Conference Centre, its main hall 'converted' into a studio, for three days at a time, enabling 18 programmes to be made with an invited audience. It took another five years to complete this project, which was distributed under the title 'Unlocking the Bible'.

Now these videos are travelling around the world. They are being used in house groups, churches, colleges, the armed forces, gypsy camps, prisons and on cable television networks. During an extended visit to Malaysia, they were being snapped up at a rate of a thousand a week. They have infiltrated all six continents, including Antarctica!

More than one have called this my 'legacy to the church'. Certainly it is the fruit of many years' work. And I am now in my seventieth year on planet earth, though I do not think the Lord has finished with me yet. But I did think this particular task had reached its conclusion. I was mistaken.

HarperCollins approached me with a view to publishing this material in a series of volumes. For the last decade or so I had been writing books for other publishers, so was already convinced that this was a good means of spreading God's Word. Nevertheless, I had two huge reservations about this proposal which made me very hesitant. One was due to the way the material had been prepared and the other related to the way it had been delivered. I shall explain them in reverse order.

First, I have never written out in full any sermon, lecture or talk. I speak from notes, sometimes pages of them. I have been concerned about communication as much as content and intuitively knew that a full manuscript interrupts the rapport between speaker and audience, not least by diverting his eyes from the listeners. Speech that is more spontaneous can respond to reactions as well as express more emotions.

The result is that my speaking and writing styles are very different, each adapted to its own function. I enjoy listening to my tapes and can be deeply moved by myself. I am enthusiastic about reading one of my new publications, often telling my wife, 'This really *is* good stuff!' But when I read a transcript of what I have said, I am ashamed and even appalled. Such repetition of words and phrases! Such rambling, even incomplete sentences! Such a mixture of verb tenses, particularly past and present! Do I really abuse the Queen's English like this? The evidence is irrefutable.

I made it clear that I could not possibly contemplate writing out all this material in full. It has taken most of one lifetime anyway and I do not have another. True, transcripts of the talks had already been made, with a view to translating and dubbing the videos into other languages such as Spanish and Chinese. But the thought of these being printed as they were horrified me. Perhaps this is a final struggle with pride, but the contrast with my written books, over which I took such time and trouble, was more than I could bear.

I was assured that copy editors correct most grammatical blunders. But the main remedy proposed was to employ a 'ghostwriter' who was in tune with me and my ministry, to adapt the material for printing. An introduction to the person chosen, Andy Peck, gave me every confidence that he could do the job, even though the result would not be what I would have written – nor, for that matter, what he would have written himself.

I gave him all the notes, tapes, videos and transcripts, but these volumes are as much his work as mine. He has worked incredibly hard and I am deeply grateful to him for enabling me to reach many more with the truth that sets people free. If one gets a prophet's reward for merely giving the prophet a drink of water, I can only thank the Lord for the reward Andy will get for this immense labour of love.

Second, I have never kept careful records of my sources. This is partly because the Lord blessed me with a reasonably good memory for such things as quotations and illustrations and perhaps also because I have never used secretarial assistance.

Books have played a major role in my work – three tons of them, according to the last furniture remover we employed, filling two rooms and a garden shed. They are in three categories: those I have read, those I intend to read and those I will never read! They have been such a blessing to me and such a bane to my wife.

The largest section by far is filled with Bible commentaries. When preparing a Bible study, I have looked up all relevant writers, but only after I have prepared as much as I can on my own. Then I have both added to and corrected my efforts in the light of scholarly and devotional writings.

It would be impossible to name all those to whom I have been indebted. Like many others, I devoured William Barclay's *Daily Bible Readings* as soon as they were issued back in the 1950s. His knowledge of New Testament background and vocabulary was invaluable and his simple and clear style a model to follow, though I later came to question his 'liberal' interpretations. John Stott, Merill Tenney, Gordon Fee and William Hendrickson were among those who opened up the New Testament for me, while Alec Motyer, G. T. Wenham and Derek Kidner did the same for the Old. And time would fail to tell of Denney, Lightfoot, Nygren, Robinson, Adam Smith, Howard, Ellison, Mullen, Ladd, Atkinson, Green, Beasley-Murray, Snaith, Marshall, Morris, Pink and many many others. Nor must I forget two remarkable little books from the pens of women: *What the Bible is all about* by Henrietta Mears and *Christ in all the Scriptures* by A. M. Hodgkin. To have sat at their feet has been an inestimable privilege. I have always regarded a willingness to learn as one of the fundamental qualifications to be a teacher.

I soaked up all these sources like a sponge. I remembered so much of *what* I read, but could not easily recall *where* I had read it. This did not seem to matter too much when gathering material for preaching, since most of these writers were precisely aiming to help preachers and did not expect to be constantly quoted. Indeed, a sermon full of attributed quotations can be distracting, if not misinterpreted as name-dropping or indirectly claiming to be well read. As could my previous paragraph!

But printing, unlike preaching, is subject to copyright, since royalties are involved. And the fear of breaching this held me back from allowing any of my spoken ministry to be repro-duced in print. It would be out of the question to trace back 40 years' scrounging and even if that were possible, the necessary footnotes and acknowledgements could double the size and price of these volumes.

The alternative was to deny access to this material for those who could most benefit from it, which my publisher persuaded me would be wrong. At least I was responsible for collecting and collating it all, but I dare to believe that there is sufficient original contribution to justify its release.

I can only offer an apology and my gratitude to all those whose studies I have plundered over the years, whether in small or large amounts, hoping they might see this as an example of that imitation which is the sincerest form of flattery. To use another quotation I read somewhere: 'Certain authors, speak-ing of their works, say "my book" ... They would do better to say "our book" ... because there is in them usually more of other people's than their own' (the original came from Pascal).

So here is 'our' book! I suppose I am what the French bluntly call a 'vulgarizer'. That is someone who takes what the academics teach and make it simple enough for the 'common' people to understand. I am content with that. As one old lady said to me, after I had expounded a quite profound passage of Scripture, 'You broke it up small enough for us to take it in.' I have, in fact, always aimed to so teach that a 12-year-old boy could understand and remember my message.

Some readers will be disappointed, even frustrated, with the paucity of text references, especially if they want to check me out! But their absence is intentional. God gave us his Word in books, but not in chapters and verses. That was the work of two bishops, French and Irish, centuries later. It became easier to find a 'text' and to ignore context. How many Christians who quote John 3:16 can recite verses 15 and 17? Many no longer 'search the scriptures'; they simply look them up (given the numbers). So I have followed the apostles' habit of naming the authors only – 'as Isaiah or David or Samuel said'. For example, the Bible says that God whistles. Where on earth does it say that? In the book of Isaiah. Whereabouts? Go and find out for yourself. Then you'll also find out when he did and why he did. And you'll have the satisfaction of having discovered all that by yourself.

One final word. Behind my hope that these introductions to the Bible books will help you to get to know and love them more than you did lies a much greater and deeper longing – that you will also come to know better and love more the subject of all the books, the Lord himself. I was deeply touched by the remark of someone who had watched all the videos within a matter of days: 'I know so much more about the Bible now, but the biggest thing was that I felt the heart of God as never before.'

What more could a Bible teacher ask? May you experience the same as you read these pages and join me in saying: Praise Father, Son and Holy Spirit.

J. David Pawson
Sherborne St John, 1999

Yes I thought I knew my Bible
Reading piecemeal, hit or miss
Now a part of John or Matthew
Then a bit of Genesis

Certain chapters of Isaiah
Certain psalms, the twenty-third.
First of Proverbs, twelfth of Romans
Yes, I thought I knew the Word

But I found that thorough reading
Was a different thing to do
And the way was unfamiliar
When I read my Bible through.

You who like to play at Bible
Dip and dabble here and there
Just before you kneel all weary
Yawning through a hurried prayer.

You who treat this crown of writings
As you treat no other book
Just a paragraph disjointed
Just a crude impatient look.

Try a worthier procedure
Try a broad and steady view;
You will kneel in awesome wonder
When you read the Bible through.

Author unknown

I
OLD
TESTAMENT

THE
MAKER'S
INSTRUCTIONS

1.

OVERVIEW OF
THE OLD
TESTAMENT

God has given us a library of 66 books. The Latin word *biblia*, translated as 'bible', literally means 'books'. The 39 Old Testament books, which cover over 2,000 years, were written by a variety of authors and include many types of literature. It is no surprise, therefore, that many people come to the Bible wondering how it all fits together.

God did not arrange the Bible topically so that we could study themes individually: he arranged it so that we could read a book at a time. The Bible is God's truth about himself and how we should relate to him, set in the context of history. It tells how people, principally the nation of Israel, came to experience God for themselves and respond to his Word. Far from being a dry theological textbook, it is the vibrant story of God's redeeming work in the lives of his people.

Many fail to grasp the overall message because they have an insufficient understanding of the background to the Bible. This chapter aims to provide an overview of the Old Testament so that any particular portion of Scripture can be given its correct context.

Geography

If we are to understand the Old Testament there are two maps we need to appreciate first of all: those of the Promised Land and the Middle East.

The key area in the map of the Middle East is what geographers call 'the Fertile Crescent' – the band of fertile land which stretches from the River Nile in Egypt in the west, north-east through the land of Israel and then south and south-east to the plains surrounding the rivers Tigris and Euphrates in what used to be called Mesopotamia (which means 'the middle of the rivers', *meso* – 'middle' and *potamia* – 'rivers'). This fertile area comprised the centres of power in the ancient world, with Egypt located in the west and Assyria and later Babylon in the east. Israel was wedged between these two and much of the Old Testament is written with the struggles between these world powers in the background. There are also significant times when their threats or activities impinge directly on Israel.

Israel's geographical position made it significant as a trade route. The Syrian Desert to the east of Israel meant that traders and armies from the orient needed to cross Israel's border as they moved between Asia, Africa and Europe. A mountainous area of basalt rock to the south-west of the Sea of Galilee funnelled the travellers through Jezreel and on through to Megiddo. A great trunk road entered Palestine through the Syrian Gate, running through Damascus, across the Bridge of Jacob's Daughters and over a basalt dam to the Lake of Galilee. It then ran south-west via the Plains of Megiddo to the Coast Plain, through Lydda and Gaza to Egypt. Israel was a narrow corridor – to the east was the rift valley, which ran north to south down to the Dead Sea, and to the west was the Mediterranean Sea.

Israel, therefore, was at the crossroads of the world, with trade routes arriving from all directions and Megiddo the place

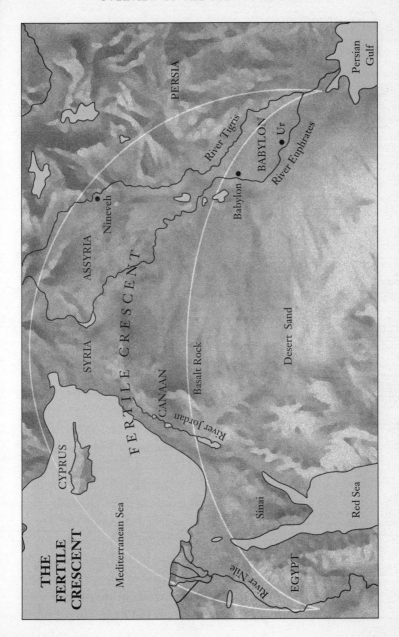

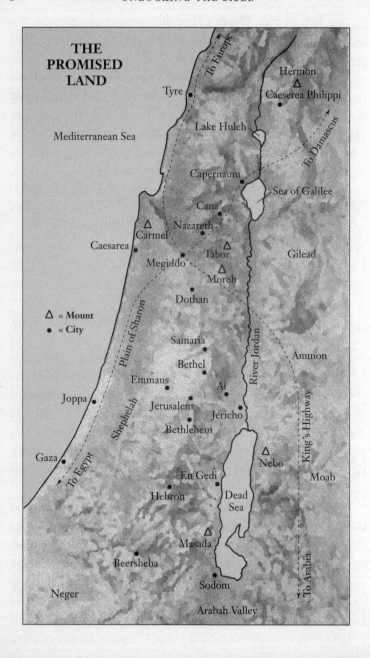

where they all met. Overlooking this 'crossroads' was the village of Nazareth, and doubtless Jesus would have sat on the hill there and watched the world go by.

This location has spiritual significance. God was planting a people at a crossroads where they could be a model of the kingdom of heaven on earth. The whole world could see the blessing that comes to people living under God's rule – and the curse that comes when they disobey. Israel's unique position is no accident.

Turning to the internal geography of the Promised Land, the northern part containing the crossroads of the world was called Galilee, or 'Galilee of the Nations' because of its international flavour. The southern part, Judaea, was more mountainous and isolated from the rest of the world, encouraging a more distinctively Jewish culture with the capital of Jerusalem at its centre.

The Promised Land is about the same size as Wales, but it includes every kind of climate and scenery. Wherever you live, there is somewhere in Israel that is just like home. The place most like England is just south of Tel Aviv. Carmel in the north is known as 'Little Switzerland'. Just 10 minutes from Carmel you can sit down among palm trees. Prominent in the land is the River Jordan, which rises on Mount Hermon and runs north to south within the rift valley mentioned earlier, through the Sea of Galilee and down to the Dead Sea. A fertile plain surrounds its course.

All the flora and fauna of Europe, Africa and Asia can be found in Israel. Scots pine trees grow next to palm trees from the Sahara. In biblical times the wild animals in the country included lions, bears, crocodiles and camels. It seems as if the whole world was somehow squeezed into one small country.

History

Having made ourselves familiar with the general geography of
the Old Testament world, we now need to consider an outline
of the history of the Old Testament. It may sound daunting to
have to cover 2,000 years or more, but a simple chart will help
us to grasp the basics (see p. 7).

The Old Testament covers over 2,000 years of history
before the time of Christ. Genesis 1–11 covers the 'prehistoric'
part – the creation of the universe, the Fall of man in the
Garden of Eden, the Flood and the Tower of Babel. The focus
here is on humankind in general, though including a 'godly'
line. But we can chart the history of Israel itself from 2000 BC,
when God calls Abraham (though it would be centuries before
the nation was formed).

The Old Testament period can be divided into four equal
parts of roughly 500 years each. Each period has a key event, a
prominent person and a type of leadership.

2000	1500	1000	500
Election	Exodus	Empire	Exile
Abraham	Moses	David	Isaiah
Patriarchs	Prophets	Princes	Priests

In the first period the patriarchs led Israel: Abraham, Isaac,
Jacob and Joseph. In the second period Israel was led by
prophets, from Moses to Samuel. In the third period they were
led by princes (kings), from Saul to Zedekiah. The fourth period saw the priests take the lead, from Joshua (a priest who
returned to Judah from exile under Zerubbabel's rule) to
Caiaphas in the time of Christ.

None of the leader types was ideal and each individual
brought his own flaws to the task. The nation needed a leader

— (O.T.) HEBREW HISTORY (BC) —

BIRTH, DEATH, RESURRECTION, ASCENSION | JESUS
MATTHEW, MARK, LUKE, JOHN

2000	1500	1000	500
Election	Exodus	Empire	Exile
Abraham	Moses	David	Isaiah
PATRIARCHS *(Abraham to Joseph)*	PROPHETS *(Moses to Samuel)*	PRINCES *(Saul to Zedekiah)*	PRIESTS *(Joshua to Caiaphas)*

MAN

			BEFORE
ABRAHAM		SAUL	JOEL JONAH
ISAAC		DAVID PSALMS	AMOS NAHUM
JACOB		SOLOMON S of S.	HOSEA OBADIAH
		PROV.	MICAH HABAKKUK
JOSEPH	EXODUS	ECCL.	ISAIAH ZEPHANIAH
GENESIS	LEVITICUS		
12–50	NUMBERS	'ISRAEL' (10)	DURING
(JOB?)	DEUTERONOMY	'JUDAH' (2)	JEREMIAH
	JOSHUA	ELIJAH	(LAMENTATIONS)
	JUDGES	ELISHA	EZEKIEL
	RUTH		
			AFTER
		1, 2 SAMUEL	HAGGAI
		1, 2 KINGS	ZECHARIAH
		1, 2 CHRONICLES	MALACHI

400 YEAR GAP			400 YEAR GAP
GOD SILENT INACTIVE			GOD SILENT INACTIVE
EGYPT			SOCRATES
INDIA			PLATO
CHINA			ARISTOTLE
			BUDDHA
			CONFUCIUS
		DANIEL	ALEXANDER THE GREAT
		ESTHER	JULIUS CAESAR
		EZRA	
		NEHEMIAH	

CREATION, FALL, FLOOD, BABEL
GENESIS 1–11

who was prophet, priest *and* king, and they found him in Jesus. Each stage, therefore, was a foreshadowing of the ideal leader who was to come.

This time line is broken by two 400-year gaps. The first comes between the patriarchs and the prophets around 1500 BC and the second after the priests at 400 BC. During these two sets of 400 years God said nothing and did nothing, so there is nothing in the Bible from those two periods. There were some Jewish books written in the second of these two periods, known collectively as the Apocrypha, but they are not part of the Bible proper because they do not cover the time when God was speaking and acting. Malachi is therefore the last book in the Old Testament of our standard English Bibles, then there is a 400-year gap before Matthew's Gospel.

It is especially interesting to note the events in world history which took place during these two gaps. The Egyptian, Indian and Chinese cultures developed during the first gap, while in the second Greek philosophy developed through Socrates, Plato and Aristotle. Other great figures of this time include Buddha, Confucius, Alexander the Great and Julius Caesar. So much happened which historians regard as important, but it was of little relevance to God. It was *his* history with *his* people which really mattered.

A brief overview of the books

Genesis 12–50 covers the first period of Israel's history when the nation was led by the patriarchs (see the table given above). It is possible that the book of Job was written at this time, since there are parallels with the sort of life the patriarchs would have lived.

Relatively few books cover the next quarter. Exodus, Leviticus, Numbers and Deuteronomy were all written by

Moses. The books of Joshua, Judges and Ruth continue the history of that period.

There are more books associated with the third quarter: Samuel, Kings and Chronicles, plus the poetic books: Psalms, Proverbs, Ecclesiastes and Song of Solomon. During this third quarter and after Solomon's time there was a civil war when the 12 tribes divided into two parts, the 10 tribes in the north calling themselves Israel, the two in the south Judah. This is the end of the united nation. There were prophets during that time – Elijah and Elisha – but they didn't have their own books.

Finally there are a large number of prophetic books associated with the Exile (the northern kingdom of Israel fell to the Assyrians, then the tribes in the southern kingdom of Judah were forced into exile by the Babylonians). Some contain prophecies from before the Exile, some during it, some after, and some have a mixture because the prophet overlaps more than one phase. This tells us something of the importance of this event to Israel's history. It meant the loss of the land God had promised them and struck at the heart of their identity as a nation.

Prophets warned the people that they were going to lose the land and prophets (sometimes the same ones) comforted them when they did lose the land. There were prophets urging them to rebuild the temple when they returned to Judah after 70 years away. The books of Daniel and Esther are written from Babylon itself. The prophets Ezra and Nehemiah helped to rebuild Jerusalem and renew the people once they had returned.

This brief outline is enough to demonstrate that the books of the Old Testament are not always in chronological order. The 'history books' are fairly accurately arranged, but the prophets are organized according to size not chronology. Hence it can be confusing to know who was speaking when.

The rise and fall of a nation

There is another aspect of the chart given on page 7 which is worth underlining. The chart shows a dotted line representing the fortunes of the nation, which reach their height under David and Solomon. The line's gentle rise indicates the progress up to this point, with a sharp drop once the peak is reached. Every Jew looks back to that period and longs for it to return. It was the golden age. They look for a son of David to restore their prosperity.

The last question the disciples asked Jesus before he ascended to heaven was about when he would restore the kingdom to Israel. They are asking the same question 2,000 years later.

The line continues its descent until Israel is exiled by Assyria in 721 BC and then Judah by Babylon in 587 BC.

Following the 400-year gap John the Baptist arrives, the first prophet for a long time. Then comes the life and ministry of Jesus. The New Testament covers 100 years compared to the 2,000-plus years of the Old Testament.

The order of the books

We have noted already that the chronology of Old Testament history is different from the order in which the books appear. There is also a big difference in the order of books as included in the English Old Testament compared with the Hebrew Bible. The English Bible is arranged in terms of **history**: Genesis to Esther, then **poetry**: Job to Song of Solomon, then **prophecy**: Isaiah to Malachi. The prophets are further split into the **major prophets**: Isaiah, Jeremiah, Ezekiel and Daniel, and the **minor prophets**: Hosea to Malachi. However, the descriptions 'major' and 'minor' are given because of the size

OLD TESTAMENT

HEBREW

LAW (TORAH, PENTATEUCH)
* In the beginning (Genesis)
* These are the names (Exodus)
* And he called (Leviticus)
* In the wilderness (Numbers)
* These are the words (Deuteronomy)

PROPHETS

Former:
* Joshua
* Judges
* Samuel
* Kings

Latter:
Isaiah
Jeremiah
Ezekiel
Hosea
Joel
Amos
Obadiah
Jonah
Micah
Nahum
Habakkuk
Zephaniah
Haggai
Zechariah
Malachi

WRITINGS
* Praises (Psalms)
* Job
* Proverbs
* Ruth
* Song of Songs
* The Preacher (Ecclesiastes)
* How? (Lamentations)
* Esther
* Daniel
* Ezra
* Nehemiah
* 1, 2 The words of the days (Chronicles)
'go up' (aliya) (last words)

[Luke 24: 37, 44]

ENGLISH

HISTORY (PAST)
* Genesis
* Exodus
* Leviticus
* Numbers
* Deuteronomy
* Joshua
* Judges
* Ruth
* 1, 2 Samuel
* 1, 2 Kings
* 1, 2 Chronicles
* Ezra
* Nehemiah
* Esther

POETRY (PRESENT)
* Job
* Psalms
* Proverbs
* Ecclesiastes
* Song of Songs

PROPHECY (FUTURE)

Major (4):
Isaiah
Jeremiah
* Lamentations
Ezekiel
* Daniel

Minor (12):
Hosea
Joel
Amos
Obadiah
Jonah
Micah
Nahum
Habakkuk
Zephaniah
Haggai
Zechariah
Malachi
'curse' (last word)

(The asterisks indicate books which appear in different sections of the Hebrew and English Bibles.)

of the book and nothing else. These divisions are generally highlighted in the contents page, if at all, so most readers are unaware of the change of category when they move from one section to the next.

The Hebrew Scriptures have three clear divisions. The first five books are not regarded as history but as **law**, and are known by the first words read as the scroll was unrolled. The next section goes under the title of **prophets**, a surprising title because it includes a number of books listed in the English Bible as history. Joshua, Judges, Samuel and Kings are called the **former prophets**, with the major and minor prophets (as they are called in the English Bible) listed as **latter prophets**. This is because the Jews see the history books as prophetic history – history according to how *God* perceived what was happening and what was important. All history is based on the principle of selection and connection – what is included and why it is included. The Bible's history is no exception, except that it is the prophets under God's inspiration who make the selection.

Ruth and the books of Chronicles are history within the English Bible but are not regarded as prophetic history within the Hebrew Bible. Indeed, there is no direct action of God mentioned in the book of Ruth, although the people in the story refer to him for blessings, and so on. Instead these books form part of the **writings**, the third and last division in the Hebrew Scriptures. There are more surprises here, for the poetry books are included, and Daniel, who we might expect to be included among the prophetic books.

This division may seem odd, but it is the division that Jesus refers to when he appears to the two on the road to Emmaus and the ten disciples, following his death and resurrection. We read about how he took them through the law, the prophets and the writings, and showed them everything concerning himself. This was the Old Testament division Jesus knew and accepted and I believe we could find it helpful too.

There are other Jewish history books which are not part of the Bible. The books of the Apocrypha are mostly 'history', although some contain other types of literature. They include fascinating stories, offering insights into the life of the Maccabees in their rebellion against the Greeks who occupied the land in the centuries before Christ. But these books were not judged to be records inspired by God and so were not included when the Old Testament canon was finally agreed. They have been incorporated into Roman Catholic Bibles.

In this volume the books have been re-arranged in chronological order, more or less, so that readers may hear the words of God in the order in which he spoke them and thus make more sense of the progressive revelation they contain

Conclusion

The Old Testament may seem confusing at first sight, but I hope this overview will help you to navigate successfully through its pages. There is no substitute, of course, for reading and re-reading the text itself. The exercise need not be academic. God has inspired the writing of the Old Testament and will meet with you through its pages. You only have to ask him.

2.

GENESIS

Introduction

The Bible is not one book, but many. The word 'Bible' comes from the plural word *biblia* which means 'library' in Latin. It consists of 66 separate books and is different from any other book of history in that it starts earlier and finishes later. Its first book, Genesis, starts at the beginning of the universe and its last, Revelation, describes the end of the world and beyond. The Bible is also unique because it is history written from God's point of view. A political history or a physical history of the universe has a focus determined by human interest, but in the Bible God selects what is important to him.

Themes

There are essentially two main themes in the Bible: what has gone wrong with our world and how it can be put right. Most agree that our world is not a good place to live in, that something has gone terribly wrong. The book of Genesis tells us exactly what the problem is, while the rest of the Bible tells us how God is going to put it right by rescuing sinful humanity from itself. The 66 books of the Bible form part of one great drama – what we might call the drama of redemption. The book of Genesis is vital because it introduces us to the stage, the cast and the plot of this great drama. Moreover, without the first few chapters of Genesis, the rest of the Bible would make little sense.

BEGINNINGS

The Hebrew title for this book is simply 'In the Beginning'. The Hebrew Scriptures were in the form of rolled-up scrolls and the name of each book was the first word or phrase written at the top of the scroll, visible to anyone seeking to identify which book it was.

When the Hebrew Old Testament was translated into Greek in about 250 BC, the translators changed the name of the first book to 'Genesis', which actually means 'origins' or 'beginnings'. It is a very appropriate title as the book includes the origin of so much – our universe, the sun, moon and stars, planet earth. Here we have the origin of plants, birds, fish, animals, humans. We have too the beginning of sex, marriage and family life, the origin of civilization, government, culture (arts and sciences), sin, death, murder and war. We also have the first sacrifices, of both animals and humans. In short, we have a potted history of humanity. The first 11 chapters of Genesis could be called 'the prologue to the Bible'.

THE NEED FOR REVELATION

Genesis not only deals with origins, it also deals with the ultimate questions of life. Where did our universe come from? Why are we here? Why do we have to die?

It is immediately obvious that these questions cannot be answered by any human being. Historians record what people have seen or experienced in the past. Scientists observe what is observable now and suggest how things may have begun. But neither group can tell us why it all began and whether the universe as it exists now has any meaning. Philosophers can only guess at the answers. They speculate about the origin of evil and why there is so much suffering in the world, but they do not actually know. The only person who could really answer these questions for us is God himself.

Who wrote it?

When we open the book of Genesis, therefore, we are immediately faced with the question: Are we reading the results of human imagination or a book of divine inspiration?

The question can be answered by adopting an approach similar to that used in scientific enquiry. Science is based on steps of faith: a hypothesis is produced and then tested to see if it fits the facts. So science progresses with a series of leaps of faith, as theories are posited and action is taken based on the theories. Similarly, in order to read Genesis properly we must take a step of faith before we even open the book. We must assume that it is a book of divine inspiration and then see if the answers it gives fit the facts of life and the universe as we see them.

There are two clear facts in particular which are perfectly explained by the answers in Genesis. Fact number 1 is that we live in a wonderful world of magnificent beauty and extraordinary variety. Fact number 2 is that the world has been ruined by those who live in it. We are told that 100 different species are becoming extinct every day, and we are becoming increasingly conscious of the damaging effects which modern production has on our environment. Genesis perfectly explains why these two facts can be true, as we will see later.

The place of Genesis

Genesis is not just the first book, it is the *foundational* book for the whole Bible. Most, if not all, biblical truths are included here, at least in embryo. This book is the key that unlocks the rest of the Bible. We learn that there is one God, the creator of the universe. We are also told that of all the nations, Israel were the people chosen for blessing. Scholars call this 'the scandal of particularity', that of all the nations, Israel should be especially selected. This is a theme which runs through the Bible to the very last page.

The importance of Genesis is confirmed if we ask ourselves what the Bible would be like if it began with Exodus instead. If that were the case, we would be left wondering why we should be interested in a bunch of Jewish slaves in Egypt. Only if we had a particular academic interest in the subject would we read any further. It is only by reading Genesis that we understand the significance of these slaves as descendants of Abraham. God had made a covenant with Abraham promising that all nations would be blessed through his line. Knowing this, we can appreciate why God's preservation of these slaves is of interest as we see how his unfolding purposes are achieved.

What sort of literature is Genesis?

Many readers of Genesis are aware of the considerable debate about whether the book is God's revelation. Some have suggested that it is a book of myths with little historical basis. I would like to make three preliminary points concerning this.

1. The whole of the Old Testament is built on the book of Genesis, with many references throughout to characters such as Adam, Noah, Abraham and Jacob (known later as Israel). The New Testament also builds on the foundations which Genesis provides and quotes it far more than the Old Testament does. The first six chapters are all quoted in detail in the New Testament, and all eight major New Testament writers refer to the book of Genesis in some way.

2. Jesus himself settles all questions concerning its historicity by his frequent references to the characters of Genesis as real people and the events as real history. Jesus regarded the account of Noah and the Flood as an historical event. He also claimed to be a personal acquaintance of Abraham. John's Gospel records his words to the Jews: 'Your father Abraham rejoiced at the thought of seeing my day; he saw it and was glad.' Later he said, '...before Abraham was born I am.' John also reminds us in his Gospel that Jesus was there at the beginning of time. When Jesus was asked about divorce and remarriage, he referred his questioners to Genesis 2 and told them they would find the answer there. If Jesus believed that Genesis was true we have no reason to do otherwise.

3. The apostle Paul's theological understanding assumes that Genesis is historically true. In Romans 5 he contrasts Christ's obedience with Adam's disobedience, explaining the results in life for the believer. This point would have no meaning if Adam had not been a real historical figure.

If Genesis is not true, neither is the rest of the Bible

Such considerations do not have implications for Genesis alone. If we do not accept that Genesis is true, it follows that we cannot rely on the rest of the Bible. As we have already noted, so much of the Bible builds on the foundational truth in Genesis. If Genesis is not true, then 'chance' is our creator and the brute beasts are our ancestors. It is not surprising that this book has been more under attack than any other book in the entire Bible.

There are two prongs to the attack: one is scientific and the other spiritual. We will examine aspects of the scientific attack when we look at the contents of Genesis in more detail later.

For now we merely need to note the claim that many of the details included in the early chapters do not square with modern science – details such as the age of the earth, the origin of man, the extent of the Flood and the age of people before and after the Flood.

Behind the scientific attack, however, it is possible to discern a satanic attack. The devil hates most the two books in the Bible which describe his entrance and his undignified exit: Genesis and Revelation. He therefore likes to keep people from believing the early chapters of Genesis and the later chapters of Revelation. If he can persuade us that Genesis is myth and Revelation is mystery, then he knows he can go a long way towards destroying many people's faith.

How did Genesis come to be written?

Genesis is one of five books which form a unit in the Jewish Scriptures known either as the Pentateuch (*penta* means 'five') or the Torah (which means 'instruction'). The Jews believe that these five books together form the 'maker's instructions' for the world and so they read through them every year, taking a portion each week.

It has long been the tradition among Jews, Christians and even pagan historians that Moses wrote these five books and there seems to be no good reason to doubt it. By the time of Moses the alphabet had replaced the picture language which prevailed in Egypt and is still used in China and Japan today. Moses was university educated and so had the learning and the knowledge to compile these five books.

There are, however, two problems to consider if Moses wrote these five books.

PROBLEMS OVER MOSES' AUTHORSHIP

The first problem is quite minor. At the end of Deuteronomy Moses' death is recorded. It is a little unlikely that he wrote that part! Joshua probably added a note about it at the end of the five books to round off the story.

The second, and major, problem is that the book of Genesis ends about 300 years before Moses was born. He would have no problem writing the books of Exodus, Leviticus, Numbers and Deuteronomy, since he lived through the events they record. But how could he have obtained his material for the book of Genesis?

The problem is easily overcome, however. Studies made of people in non-book cultures have revealed that those who cannot write have phenomenal memories. Tribes which have no writing learn their history through the stories passed on around the camp fire. This oral tradition is very strong in primitive communities and would have been so among the Hebrews, especially when they became slaves in Egypt and wanted their children to know who they were and where they had come from.

There are two kinds of history normally passed down in this memory form. One is the genealogy, since their family tree gives people an identity. There are many genealogies in Genesis, with the phrase 'these are the generations of' (or 'these are the sons of' in some translations) coming 10 times. The other is the saga or hero story – telling of the great deeds which ancestors accomplished. Genesis is composed almost entirely of these two aspects of history: stories about great heroes interspersed with family trees. With this in mind, it is easy to see how the book was composed from memories which Moses gleaned from the slaves in Egypt.

Nonetheless, this does not answer all the questions about Moses' authorship. There is one part of Genesis which he could not possibly have picked up that way, and that is the first chapter (or rather 1:1 through to 2:3, since the chapter division is in the wrong place). How did Moses compose the chapter detailing the creation of the world?

It is at this point that we must exercise faith. Psalm 103 refers to God making his ways known through Moses, including the creation narrative. It is one of the few parts of the Bible that must have been dictated directly by God and taken down by man, just as God clearly tells John what to write in Revelation when describing the end of the world. Usually God inspired the writers to use their own temperament, memory, insight and outlook to shape his Word (as with Moses in the rest of Genesis), and he so overruled by the inspiration of his Spirit that what resulted was what he wanted written. But he gave the story of creation in direct revelation.

A confirming detail is provided when we consider that there was no record of the Sabbath being observed before the time of Moses. We do not read that taking a day for Sabbath rest was part of the lifestyle of any of the patriarchs. Indeed, there is no trace at all of the concept of a seven-day week. Any time references are to months and years. Since we have Genesis 1 at the beginning of our Bible, we assume quite wrongly that Adam knew about it and observed a Sabbath as a model to everyone after him. But it seems instead that Adam looked after the Garden of Eden *every* day and had time with the Lord in the evenings. Likewise there is no suggestion that Abraham, Isaac or Jacob took a Sabbath, and their work as herdsmen probably offered little time for rest.

All this need not surprise us if, as suggested above, Moses received the first chapter – including the concept of Sabbath rest – from God himself. With this knowledge, he was then able to introduce the Sabbath concept into the life of Israel through the Ten Commandments.

To summarize, then, Genesis is clearly a book from God and should be read with this assumption. It is also a book written by Moses, using his education and gift for writing from his time in Egypt to record the extraordinary works of God as he reverses the effects of the Fall in the call of Abraham.

The shape of Genesis

It is instructive to note the overall shape of the book. The first quarter (Chapters 1–11) forms a distinct unit, covering many centuries and the growth and spread of nations throughout the 'Fertile Crescent' (the land stretching from Egypt to the Persian Gulf in the Middle East). The watershed comes with God's call of Abraham in Chapter 12. The next three-quarters of the book has a narrower focus, chronicling God's dealings with Abraham and his descendants, Isaac, Jacob and Joseph.

There are other divisions within this overall shape. In Chapters 1–2 everything is described as good, including human beings. In Chapters 3–11 we see the origin and results of sin as man drifts spiritually and physically away from Eden. We see God's character, his justice in punishing man, and his merciful provision even within this punishment.

In Chapters 12–36 six men are contrasted: Abraham with Lot, Isaac (child of promise) with Ishmael (child of flesh), and Jacob with Esau. We are faced with two kinds of people and asked which we identify with. God is tying his own reputation to three men, Abraham, Isaac and Jacob, flawed as they are. Finally the text focuses on Joseph, an altogether different character. We will see later how and why he is so distinct from his forefathers.

In the beginning God

Let us turn now to the book itself and to the amazing chapter with which it opens. It begins with the words, 'In the beginning God'.

Genesis is full of beginnings, but it is clear that God himself does not begin here. God is already there when the Bible opens, for he was already there when the universe came to be. Philosophical questions concerning where God came from are really non-questions. There had to be an eternal something or someone before the universe existed and the Bible is clear that this person is God. It is the fundamental assumption of the Bible that God exists eternally, that he has always been there, that he will always be there, and that he is the God who is. His very name, 'Yahweh', is a participle of the Hebrew verb 'to be'. An English word which conveys the nature of God contained in the word 'Yahweh' is 'always': he has always been who he is and will always be just the same.

While we do not need to explain the existence of God, we do need to explain the existence of everything else. This is the very opposite of modern thinking, which looks around at what is there and assumes that we need to prove the existence of God. The Bible comes at the question from the other direction and says that God was always there and we have to explain now why anything else is there.

Certainly when Moses was writing, every Hebrew knew that God existed. He had rescued his people out of Egypt, divided the Red Sea and drowned the Egyptian army, so their personal experience told them that God was there. Further 'proof' was unnecessary.

The need for faith

The New Testament suggests a useful approach to considering God which will help us in our reading of Genesis. In Hebrews 11 we read two things about creation. First that it is 'by faith we understand that the universe was formed at God's command, so that what is seen was not made out of what was visible'. Then, a little later in the same chapter, we read that 'anyone who comes to him must believe that he exists and that he rewards those who earnestly seek him'.

As far as the whole Bible is concerned, therefore – including Genesis – we must assume God is there and that he wants us to find him, know him, love him and serve him. Then we see what happens on the basis of this trust. We cannot *prove* whether God exists or not, but we can hold the basic belief that God wants us to know him and have faith in him.

A picture of the creator

Moving on from the first four words of the book, we come to a feature that may be surprising: the subject of Genesis 1 is not *creation* but *the creator*. It is not primarily about *how* our world came to be, but about *who* made it come to be. In fact, in just 31 verses the word 'God' appears 35 times, as if to underline that this is all about him. It is not so much the story of creation as a picture of the creator. So what does this picture tell us?

1. GOD IS PERSONAL

Genesis 1 depicts a personal God. He has a heart that feels. He has a mind that thinks and can speak his thoughts. He has a will and makes decisions and sticks to them. All this forms what we know as a personality. God is not an it, God is a *he*. He is a full person with feelings, thoughts and motives like us.

2. GOD IS POWERFUL

It is quite evident that if God can speak things into being by his Word, he must be enormously powerful. In all he gives 10 'commandments' in the first chapter, and every one is fulfilled just as he desires.

3. GOD IS UNCREATED

We have already noted that God is and always was there. He was always the Creator, never a creature.

4. GOD IS CREATIVE

What an imagination he must have! What an artist! Six thousand varieties of beetle. No two blades of grass the same. No two snowflakes. No two clouds. No two grains of sand. No two stars. An astonishing variety, yet in harmony. It is a uni-verse.

5. GOD IS ORDERLY

There is a symmetry in his work of creation, as we shall see. The fact that creation is mathematical has made science possible.

6. GOD IS SINGULAR

The verbs in Genesis 1, from 'created' onwards, are all singular.

7. GOD IS PLURAL

The word used for 'God' is not the singular *El*, but the plural *Elohim*, which means three or more 'gods'. So the very first sentence in the Bible, using a plural noun with a singular verb, is grammatically wrong but theologically right, hinting at a God who is 'Three-in-one'.

8. GOD IS GOOD

Therefore all his work is 'good' and he pronounces human beings as his best, his masterprice, 'very good'. Furthermore,

he wants to be good to all his creation, to 'bless' it. His goodness sets the standard for all goodness.

9. GOD IS LIVING

He is active in the world of time and space.

10. GOD IS A COMMUNICATOR

He speaks to creation and the creatures within it. In particular
he wants to relate to human beings.

11. GOD IS LIKE US

We are made in his image, so we must be in some ways like
him and he must be like us.

12. GOD IS UNLIKE US

He can 'create' out of nothing (*ex nihilo*), whereas we can only
'make' something out of something else. We are 'manufac-
turers'; he is the only Creator.

13. GOD IS INDEPENDENT

God is never identified with his creation. There is a distinction
between creator and creation from the very beginning. The
New Age movement confuses this idea by suggesting that
somehow 'god' is part of us. But the creator is separate from
his creation. He can take a day off and be quite apart from all
that he has made. We must never identify him with what he
has made. To worship his creation is idolatry. To worship the
creator is the truth.

Philosophies challenged

If we accept the truth of Genesis 1, then a number of alternative
viewpoints about God are automatically ruled out. These viewpoints could also be called philosophies (the word 'philosophy'

means 'love of wisdom'). Everyone has their own way of looking at the world, whether they consciously think about it or not.

If you believe Genesis, the following philosophies will not
stand.

1. **Atheism**. Atheists believe there is no God. Genesis 1 confirms there is.
2. **Agnosticism**. Agnostics say they do not know whether
   there is a God or not. Genesis 1 says we accept that there is.
3. **Animism**. This is the belief that many spirits control the
   world – spirits of rivers, spirits of mountains, etc. Genesis
   1 asserts that God created and controls the world.
4. **Polytheism**. Polytheists believe there are many gods.
   Hindus would be in this category. Genesis 1 states there is
   just one.
5. **Dualism**. This is the belief that there are two gods, one
   good and one bad, with the good god responsible for the
   good things that happen and the bad god for the bad
   things. Genesis 1 asserts that there is just one God, who
   is good.
6. **Monotheism**. This is the belief of Judaism and Islam –
   that there is one God, and just one person, thus rejecting
   God as a trinity. By using the word *Elohim* to describe
   God, Genesis 1 tells us that there is one God in three
   persons.
7. **Deism**. Deists see God as the creator, but argue that he
   cannot now control what he has created. He is like a
   watchmaker who has wound up the world and lets it run on
   its own laws. As such God never intervenes in his world,
   and miracles are impossible. Many Christians are, for all
   practical purposes, deists.
8. **Theism**. Theists believe that God not only created the
   world but is also in control of everything and everyone he

has made. Theism is one step towards the biblical philosophy, but does not in fact go far enough.

9. **Existentialism**. This is a popular philosophy today, where
   experience is believed to be God. Our choices and our own
   affirmation of ourselves is the 'religion' followed. There is
   no creator as in Genesis 1 to whom we have to give an
   account.

10. **Humanism**. Humanists reject the concept of a god outside
    the created world. Although Genesis 1 tells us that man is
    created by God, humanists believe that man is God.

11. **Rationalism**. Rationalists believe that our own reason is
    God, rejecting the indication in Genesis that the powers of
    reason were given when God created man in his image.

12. **Materialism**. Materialists believe that only matter is real
    and do not accept anyone or anything they cannot see for
    themselves.

13. **Mysticism**. In contrast to materialism, mystics believe that
    only spirit is real.

14. **Monism**. This philosophy underpins much of the New
    Age movement. It holds that matter and spirit are essen-
    tially one and the same thing. The idea of God as an inde-
    pendent spirit creating the world is thus ruled out of court.

15. **Pantheism**. This idea is similar to monism, in that every-
    thing is believed to be God. A modern version of it is
    called Panentheism: God in everything.

In contrast to all these philosophies, the biblical viewpoint
could be called **Triunetheism**: God is three in one, creator
and controller of the universe. This is the biblical way of thinking which comes right out of Genesis 1 and continues through
to the last chapter of Revelation.

Style

Let us move on to look more closely at the text of Genesis 1 and in particular the style of the chapter. The obvious point to make is that it is not written in scientific language. Many people seem to approach the chapter expecting the detail of a scientific textbook. Instead it is written very simply, so that every generation can understand it, whatever the standard of their scientific learning.

The account uses only very simple categories. Vegetation is divided into three groups: grass, plants and trees. Animal life also has three categories: domesticated animals, animals hunted for food and wild animals. These simple classifications are understood by everybody everywhere.

WORDS

This simple style is also demonstrated in the words used. There are only 76 separate root words in the whole of Genesis 1. Furthermore, every one of those words is to be found in every language on earth, which means that Genesis 1 is the easiest chapter to translate in the whole Bible.

Every writer has to ask about the potential audience for their work. God wanted the story of creation to reach everybody in every time and in every place. He therefore made it very simple. Even a child can read it and get the message. One of the results of this is the ease with which it can be translated.

The verbs are also very simple. One of the verbs used is especially important to our understanding of what took place. Genesis 1 distinguishes between the words 'created' and 'made'. The Hebrew word for 'created', *bara*, means to make something out of nothing and it only occurs three times in the whole of Genesis 1 – to describe the creation of matter, life and man. On other occasions the word 'made' is used instead, to indicate that something is made out of something else, rather in the way we may speak of manufacturing things.

The description of God's work of creation in seven days is also very simple. Each sentence has a subject, a verb and an object. The grammar is so straightforward that anybody can follow it. All the sentences are linked by one word – for example 'but', 'and' or 'then'. It is a remarkable production.

STRUCTURE

Genesis 1 is beautifully structured. It is orderly, spread over six days, and the six days are divided into two sets of three.

In Genesis 1:2 we read, 'Now the earth was formless and empty.' The development starts in verse 3 and there is an amazing correspondence between the first three days and the last three days. In the first three days, God creates a varied environment with sharp contrasts: light from darkness, sky from ocean, and land from sea. He is creating distinctions which make for variety. On the third day he also starts to fill the land with plants. The earth now has 'form'.

Then, on the fourth, fifth and sixth days, he sets out to fill the environments he has created in the first three days. So on day four the sun, moon and stars correspond to the light and darkness created on day one; on day five the birds and fish fill the sky and sea created in day two; and on day six animals and Adam are created to occupy the land created on day three. So God is creating things in an orderly and precise manner. He is indeed bringing order out of chaos. The earth is now 'full' – of life.

MATHEMATICAL PROPERTIES

It also fascinating to note that Genesis 1 has mathematical properties. The three figures that keep coming up in the account are 3, 7 and 10, each of which has particular significance throughout the Bible. The number 3 speaks of what God is, 7 is the perfect number in Scripture, and 10 is the number of completeness. If the occasions when the numbers 3, 7, and 10 occur are examined, some astonishing links emerge.

At only three points does God actually *create* something out of nothing. On three occasions he *calls* something by name, three times he *makes* something, and three times he *blesses* something.

On seven occasions we read that God 'saw that it was good'. There are, of course, seven days – and the first sentence is seven words in Hebrew. Furthermore, the last three sentences in this account of creation are also each formed of seven words in the original Hebrew.

And there are ten commands of God.

SIMPLICITY

The style of Genesis 1 is in marked contrast to other 'creation stories', for example the Babylonian epic of creation, which is very complicated and weird and has little link with reality. The simplicity of the Genesis account of creation has not been universally applauded, however. Some have suggested that this simplistic approach is proof that the Bible cannot be considered as serious in the modern era. But there is much to be said in defence of this simple approach.

Imagine describing how a house is built in a children's book. You would want it to be accurate but simplified so that the young readers would be able to follow the process. You might write about the bricklayer who laid the bricks, the carpenter who worked on the windows, the door frame and the roof joists. You might mention the plumber who put the pipes in, the electrician who came to put the wires in, the plasterer who plasters the walls and the decorator who paints them.

Written in this way the description has six basic stages, but of course building a house is far more complicated than that.

It requires the synchronizing and overlapping of different workers for particular periods of time. No one would say that the description given in the children's book is wrong or misleading, just that it is rather more complex in reality. In the same way there is no doubt that Genesis is a simplification and that science can fill out a whole lot more detail for us. But God's purpose was not to provide detailed scientific accuracy. Rather it was to give an orderly explanation that everyone could follow and accept, and which underlined that he knew what he was doing.

Scientific questions

Understanding the need for simplicity does not answer all the questions which arise from the Genesis account of creation. In particular we must consider the speed at which creation took place and the age of the earth, two separate but interrelated areas. Geologists tell us that the earth must have taken four and a quarter billion years to form, while Genesis seems to say it took just six days. Which is correct?

In terms of the order of creation there is broad agreement between scientists' findings and the Genesis account. Science agrees with the order of Genesis 1, with one exception: the sun, moon and stars do not appear until the fourth day, after the plants are made. This seems contradictory until we realize that the original earth was covered with a thick cloud or mist. Scientific enquiry confirms the likelihood of this. So when the first light appeared, it would just be seen as lighter cloud, whereas once the plants came and started turning carbon dioxide into oxygen, the mist was cleared and for the first time the sun, moon and stars were visible in the sky. The appearance of sun, moon and stars was therefore due to the clearing away of the thick cloud that surrounded the earth. So science does agree exactly with the order of Genesis 1. Creatures appeared in the sea before they appeared on the land. Man appeared last.

While scientists generally agree with the Bible on the order of creation, there are still areas of major conflict. These include the origin of animals and humans and a host of associated questions, including the age of the people who lived before and after the Flood, the extent of the Flood, and the whole question of evolution versus creation.

Before becoming involved in the detail of such questions, however, it is important to note that there are three ways of handling this problem of science versus Scripture. It is vital to decide how you are going to approach the problem before you do so. You must choose whether to repudiate, to segregate or to integrate.

REPUDIATION

The first approach offers a choice. Either Scripture is right, or science is right, but you must repudiate one or the other: you cannot accept both. Typically unbelievers believe science, believers believe Scripture and both bury their heads in the sand about the other.

The problem with repudiating science if you are a Christian is that science has been right in so many areas. We owe so much of our modern communication to scientific development, for example. Science is not the enemy some Christians seem to believe it to be.

The story of the discovery of 'Piltdown man' is a case in point. When a skull from a creature which seemed to be half-man half-ape was discovered at Piltdown in Sussex in 1912, many saw it as evidence of some form of evolution. When it was later found that the skull was actually a forgery, Christians were quick to pour scorn on science. They forgot that it was science which had discovered the skull to be a fake in the first place!

Choosing between science and the Bible thus has problems attached. We should not accept scientific truth unquestioningly, but neither should we be foolish enough to call people to commit intellectual suicide in order to believe the Bible. It is not necessary.

SEGREGATION

The second approach is to keep science and Scripture as far apart as possible. Science is concerned with one kind of truth and Scripture with another. This view claims that science is concerned with physical or material truth, whereas Scripture is concerned with moral and supernatural truth. The two deal with entirely separate issues. Science tells us how and when the world came to be. Scripture tells us who made it and why. They are to be kept entirely separate for there is no overlap to be concerned about. Science talks about facts; Scripture talks about values and we should not look to the one for the other.

This approach has become very common even in churches. It comes from a mindset shaped by Greek thinking, where the physical and the spiritual are kept in two watertight compartments. This kind of thinking is alien to the Hebrew mind, however, which saw God as Creator and Redeemer, with the physical and the spiritual belonging together.

If we take this segregated approach to Genesis we will be forced to treat the narrative as myth. Genesis 3 becomes a fable entitled 'How the snake lost its legs', and Adam becomes 'Everyman'. The book becomes full of fictional stories teaching us values about God and about ourselves, and showing us how to think about God and about ourselves – but we must not press them into historical fact.

Just as Hans Christian Andersen wrote children's books which taught moral values, according to this approach Genesis has stories with moral truths but no historical truth. Adam and Eve were myths, and Noah and the Flood was also a myth. This outlook extends beyond the Genesis narratives, of course, for once one questions the historicity of one section of the Bible it is a small step to question others also. This approach therefore leaves us with no history left in the Bible: plenty of values but few facts.

As with repudiation, then, the attempt to segregate science and Scripture also has its problems. In fact, Scripture and science are like overlapping circles: they do deal with some things that are the same and so apparent contradictions must be faced. And it undermines the whole Bible if we pretend that it is factually inaccurate but still has value. How then are we going to resolve the problem? Can the third approach help us bring science and Scripture together?

INTEGRATION

In trying to understand how to integrate the two, we need to remember two basic things, both equally important: the transitional nature of scientific investigations, and the changes in our interpretation of Scripture.

1. Science changes its views

Scientists used to believe that the atom was the smallest thing in the universe. We know now that each atom is a whole universe in itself. It was said until very recently that the X and Y chromosomes decide whether a foetus becomes a male or a female human being. Now this view has been overturned. The discovery of DNA has revolutionized our thinking about life, because we now know that the earliest form of life had the most complicated DNA. DNA is a language passing on a message from one generation to another – and because of that it must have a person behind it.

A generation ago most people would have understood that nature ran according to fixed laws. Modern science now asserts that there is a much greater randomness than we ever imagined. 'Quantum' physics is much more flexible.

Geology too is changing and developing. There are now many different ways of finding out the age of the earth. Some new methods are claimed to have revealed the age of the earth to be much younger, with 9,000 years at one end of the spectrum and 175,000 years at the other – much less than the four and a quarter billion years calculated previously.

Furthermore, anthropology is in a state of disorder. The prehistoric men thought to be our ancestors are now seen to be creatures which came and disappeared with no link with us. Biology has changed also, and today fewer people believe in the Darwinian concept of evolution.

All this means that while we should not discount the conflicts between scientific discovery and the biblical accounts, we would be foolish to try to tie our interpretation to a particular scientific age, given that scientific knowledge is itself always expanding.

2. Interpretation of Scripture changes

Just as developments occur in scientific understanding, so the traditional interpretations of Scripture can also change. The Bible is inspired by God, but our interpretation of it may not always be. We need to draw a very clear distinction between the Bible text and how we interpret it. When the Bible talks about the four corners of the earth, for example, few people today interpret that to mean the earth is a cube or a square. The Bible uses what is called *the language of appearance*. It talks about the sun rising in the east, setting in the west and running around the sky. But that, as we know, does not mean that the sun is moving around the earth.

Once we understand that scientific interpretation is flexible and that our interpretation of the Bible may change, we can then seek to integrate science and the Bible and make balanced judgements where contradictions seem to exist.

THE 'DAY' IN GENESIS 1

Such an 'integrated' judgement is much needed when we come to consider the arguments regarding the days in Genesis 1, a traditional battlefield in the science versus Scripture debate.

The problem of the days described in Genesis 1 and the real age of the earth was heightened by the fact that some Bibles used to be published with a date alongside the first chapter, namely 4004 BC. This was calculated by an Irish archbishop called James Ussher (another scholar went on to claim that Adam was born at 9 a.m. on 24 October!) All this despite the fact that there are no dates in the original until Chapter 5.

Ussher made his calculations based on the generations recorded in Genesis, unaware that the Jewish genealogies do not include every generation in a line. The words 'son of' may mean grandson or great-grandson. It is easy to discount Ussher's date, but we are still faced with a conflict between the apparent biblical assertion that creation took six days and the scientific assertion that it took much longer.

What was meant by the word 'day' in the original language? This is the Hebrew word *Yom*, which does sometimes mean a day of 24 hours. But it can also mean 12 hours of light or an era of time, as in the phrase 'the day of the horse and cart has gone'.

Bearing these alternative meanings in mind, let us consider the different views of the day in Genesis 1.

Earth days

Some take the word 'day' literally as an earth day of 24 hours. This conflicts with the scientists' assessment of the geological time it would take to create the earth, given its apparent age.

A gap in time

Some suggest a gap in time between verse 2 and verse 3. They argue that after we read that 'the earth was formless' in verse 2, there is a long gap before the six days when God brings everything else into being. So the earth was already in existence before God's work began in the six days. That is a very common theory, found in the Scofield Bible and other Bible notes.

A second way of finding more time is to explain it by reference to the Flood. There have been various books published, notably connected with the names Whitcome and Morris, which have said that the geological data we have all comes out of the Flood, the 'apparent' age of rocks the result of this inundation.

The illusion of time

Others suggest that God deliberately made things look old. Just as Adam was created as a man, not as a baby, so some believe that God made the earth to look older than it really is. God creates genuine antiques! He can make a tree look 200 years old with all the rings in it, and he can create a mountain that looks thousands of years old. It is a possible theory – God could do that.

The 'gap' and 'illusion' views both assume that we take the 'day' literally and therefore need to find more time to make sense of the geological record.

Geological eras

Another approach is to take a 'day' as meaning a 'geological era'. In this case we are not talking about six days, but about six geological ages, i.e. days 1–3 are not solar days (in any case there was no sun!). This is seen as an attractive theory by many, but it fails to account for the morning and evening refrain which is present from day 1, or for the fact that the six days do not correspond to geological ages.

Mythical days

We have already seen that some interpreters have no problem with the length of the days because they assume that the text is mythological anyway. For them the six days are only the poetic framework for the story – fabled days – and can be overlooked. The main thing is to get the moral out of the story and forget the rest.

School days

One of the most intriguing approaches has been put forward by Professor Wiseman of London University. He believes the days were 'educational' days. God revealed his creation in stages to Moses over a seven-day period, so the record we have is of Moses learning about the creative process in the course of a week's schooling. Others agree but suggest that the revelations took the form of visions, rather like the way John was given visions to record for the book of Revelation.

God days

The final possible interpretation is that these were 'God days'. Time is relative to God and a thousand days are like a day to him. It could be understood from this that God was saying that the whole of creation was 'all in a week's work' for him.

This serves to emphasize the importance God attaches to mankind in the scheme of creation, since human life can lose all significance if you take geological time as the only measure. For example, imagine that the height of Cleopatra's Needle on the Thames Embankment in London represents the age of the planet. Place a 10 pence piece flat on top of the needle and a postage stamp on top of that. The 10 pence piece represents the age of the human race and the postage stamp civilized man. Man is seemingly insignificant from a chronological perspective.

Maybe God wanted us to think of creation as a week's work because he wanted to get down to the important part, us living on planet earth. Out of all creation it is we who are most significant to him. He spends such little space in Genesis detailing creation and so much on mankind.

This theory can be extended. The seventh day has no end in the text, because it has lasted centuries. It lasted all the way through the Bible until Easter Sunday, when God raised his son from the dead. All through the Old Testament there is nothing new created; God had finished creation. Indeed, the word 'new' hardly occurs in the Old Testament, and even then is in the negative, as when in Ecclesiastes we read, 'there is nothing new under the sun'. So God rested all the way through the Old Testament.

There is, therefore, a strong argument for seeing the days in Genesis 1 as God days – God himself wanted us to think of it as a week's work.

Man at the centre

Turning to Chapter 2, it is immediately obvious that there is a great difference between this and Chapter 1. There is a shift in style, content and viewpoint. In Chapter 1 God is at the centre and the account of creation is given from his point of view. In Chapter 2 man is given the prominent role. The generic terms of the first chapter give way to specific names in Chapter 2. In Chapter 1 the human race was simply referred to as 'male' and 'female'. In Chapter 2 male and female have become 'Adam' and 'Eve', two particular individuals.

God is also given a name in Chapter 2. In Chapter 1 he was simply 'God' (*Elohim*), but now he is 'the LORD God' (as translated in English Bibles). When we read 'the LORD' in capital letters in our English Bibles it means that in the Hebrew his name is there also. There are no vowels in Hebrew, so his name is made up of four consonants, J H V H, from which the word 'Jehovah' has been coined. This is actually a mistake, because J is pronounced like a Y and V is pronounced like a W. In English pronunciation the letters would therefore be Y H W H, from which we get the word 'Yahweh'. In the New Jerusalem Bible that word is included just as it is – 'The Yahweh God'. We saw earlier how the English word 'always' conveys the meaning of the Hebrew (the participle of the verb 'to be') and it is a helpful word to bring to mind when thinking of God.

Chapter 2 explains more of the relationship between man and God. Chapter 1 included the reference to male and female being made in his image, but in Chapter 2 we see God interacting with man in a way which is unique among all the creatures he had made. There is an affinity between human beings and God that is lacking in every other part of his creation. Animals do not have the ability to have a spiritual relationship with God as humans do. In that sense, humans are like their creator in a unique way.

But we are also told of the differences between God and man, for although man is made in God's image, he is also *unlike* him. This is an important truth to grasp if we are to have a relationship with God. The fact that he is like us means that our relationship with him can be intimate, but the fact that he is unlike us will keep the relationship reverent and ensure that our worship is appropriate. It is possible to be too familiar with God on the one hand, or overawed by him on the other.

The importance of names

The name God gave to Adam meant 'of the earth' – we might call him Dusty. Later in the chapter the woman too is given a name: Eve, meaning 'lively'.

It was normal for names to be descriptive, or even onomatopoeic (like 'cuckoo'), so when Adam names the animals he uses descriptions which then become their name. Names in the Bible are not only descriptive, they also carry *authority* in them. The person who gives the name has authority over whoever or whatever receives the name. Thus Adam names all the animals, signifying his authority over them. He also names his wife, a feature still remembered today when the woman takes the man's surname when they marry.

This chapter also includes names of places. The land is no longer merely 'dry land': we are told of the land of Havilah, Kush, Asshur and the Garden of Eden. The water is named too. There are four rivers mentioned, and the Tigris and Euphrates are still known today. This puts the Garden of Eden somewhere near north-eastern Turkey, or Armenia, where Mount Ararat stands and where some believe Noah's ark is buried.

Human relationships

In Genesis 2 we see man at the centre of a network of relationships. These define the meaning of life. The relationships have three dimensions: to that which is below us, to that which is above us, and to that which is alongside us. Or, to put it another way, we have a vertical relationship to nature below, a vertical relationship to God above, and a horizontal relationship with other people and ourselves. Let us look more closely at these three dimensions.

Our relationship to nature. The first dimension is the relationship we have to the other creatures God has made. This relationship is one of subjugation – animals are given to serve mankind. This does not mean we have a licence to be cruel or to make them extinct, but it does mean that animals are further down the scale of value than human beings.

This is an important point to grasp in an age when more value seems to be placed on the protection of baby seals than on preserving the sanctity of the human foetus. Jesus was willing to sacrifice 2,000 pigs in order to save one man's sanity and restore him to his family. In Genesis 9 we read that animals were given to provide food for mankind after the Flood. In relation to nature below us, therefore, we are to have dominion, to cultivate it and control it.

It is interesting to note also in this context that human beings need an environment that is both utilitarian and aesthetic, both useful and beautiful. God did not put man in the wilderness, but planted a garden for him, just as old cottage gardens in England were a mixture of pansies and potatoes – the useful and the beautiful alongside each other.

Our relationship to God. The second dimension is the relationship we have to God above. The nature of this relationship is partly seen in God's command to man concerning two trees in the Garden of Eden: the tree of the knowledge of good and evil and the tree of life. One made life longer and one made life shorter. These trees are not magical trees, but they are what we might call 'sacramental' trees. In the Bible God appoints physical channels to communicate spiritual blessings or curses to us. So eating bread and wine at communion is for our blessing, but eating bread and drinking wine incorrectly or to excess can lead us to be sick or even die. God has appointed physical channels of both grace and judgement. The tree of life tells us that Adam and Eve were not *by nature* immortal, but were *capable* of being immortal. They would not have lived forever by some inherent quality of their own, but only by having access to the tree of life.

No scientist has yet discovered why we die. They have discovered many causes of death, but no one knows why the clock inside us starts winding down. After all, the body is a wonderful machine. If it is supplied with food, fresh air and exercise it could theoretically continue to renew itself. But it does not and no one knows why. The secret is in the tree of life: God was making it possible for human beings to go on living forever by putting that tree in the garden for them. Man was not inherently immortal, but was given the opportunity to attain immortality by feeding on God's constant supply of life.

The tree of knowledge of good and evil is very significant in relation to this. When we read the word 'knowledge', we need to substitute the word 'experience'. The concept of knowledge in the Bible is really 'personal experience'. This idea is present in older versions of the Bible which say, 'Adam *knew* Eve and she conceived and bore a son'. 'Knowledge' in this sense is a personal experience of someone or something. God's command not to touch this tree was given because he did not want them to know (experience) good and evil – he wanted them to retain their innocence. It is similar even today. Once we do a wrong thing we can never be the same as we were. We may be forgiven, but we have lost our innocence.

Why, then, did God put such a tree within their reach? It was his way of saying that he retained moral authority over them. They were not to decide for themselves what was right and wrong, but had to trust God to tell them. Furthermore, he was underlining the fact that they were not landlords on earth, but tenants. The landlord retains the right to set the rules.

The passage also underscores the importance of horizontal relationships, which we shall examine more closely below. Man not only needs to relate to those beneath him and God above him, but also to those alongside him. We are not fully human if we just relate to God and not to other people. We need a network. This understanding is reflected by the Hebrew word *Shalom*, which means 'harmony' – harmony with yourself, with God, with other people and with nature.

In Genesis 2 we have a picture of that harmony and God warns Adam that if he breaks this harmony he will have to die. This will not necessarily be with immediate effect, but his personal 'clock' will begin to wind down.

Some have questioned the severity of the penalty. Death seems a harsh punishment for one little sin. But God was saying that once man had experienced evil, he would have to limit the length of his life on earth, otherwise evil would become eternal. If God allowed rebellious people to live forever they would ruin his universe forever, so he put a time limit on those who would not accept his moral authority.

Our relationship to each other. Man needed a suitable companion. However valuable and valued a pet is, it cannot ever replace personal friendship with another human being. God therefore made Eve to be Adam's companion. We are told in Genesis 1 that male and female are equal in dignity – and we shall see later that they are equal in depravity and in destiny too.

In Genesis 2 we learn that the functions of men and women are different. The Bible talks of the responsibilities of the man to provide and protect, and of the woman to assist and accept. There are three points to note in particular, which are all picked up in the New Testament.

1. **Woman is made from man.** She therefore derives her being from him. Indeed, as we have already seen, woman is named by man just as he named the animals.

2. **Woman is made after man.** He therefore carries the responsibility of the first-born. The significance of that will become clear in Genesis 3, where Adam is blamed for the sin not Eve, since he was responsible for her.

3. **Woman is made for man.** Adam had a job before he had a wife and man is made primarily for his work, while woman is made primarily for relationships. This does not mean that a man must not have relationships or that a woman must not go out to work, but rather that this is the primary purpose for which God made male and female. The fact that man named woman also shows how the partnership is to work: not as a democracy, but with the responsibility of leadership falling to the male. The emphasis is upon co-operation, not competition.

Genesis 2 also deals with other areas fundamental to human relationships. It is clear that sex is good – it is not spelt S-I-N. It is beautiful, indeed God said it was 'very good'. Sex was created for partnership rather than parenthood (an important point which has a bearing on the use of contraception, which plans parenthood without proscribing partnership in intercourse.). Two verses, one in Chapter 1 and one in Chapter 2, are in poetry and both are about sex. God becomes poetic when he considers male and female created in his own image. Then Adam becomes poetic when he catches sight of this beautiful naked girl when he wakes up from the first surgery under anaesthetic. Our English translations of the Hebrew miss the impact. Adam literally exclaims, 'Wow! This is it!' Both little poems convey the delight of God and man in sexuality.

It is clear too that the pattern for sexual enjoyment is monogamy. Marriage is made up of two things, leaving and cleaving, so there is both a physical and a social aspect which together cement the union. One without the other is not a marriage. Sexual intercourse without social recognition is not marriage – it is fornication. Social recognition without consummation is not a marriage either and therefore should be annulled.

We are told that marriage takes precedence over all other relationships. There would be no jokes about parents-in-law if this had been observed throughout history! A person's partner is their first priority before all other relationships, even before their children. Husband and wife are to put each other as absolutely top priority. The ideal painted here in Genesis 2 is of a couple with nothing to hide from each other, with no embarrassment and a total openness to each other. This is an amazing picture and one to which Jesus points centuries later.

Genesis 2 depicts the harmony that should exist in the three levels of relationship between human beings and the created world, God above and our fellow humans. There are, however, some scientific problems to do with the origin of man which must be considered.

Where do prehistoric men fit in?

Evolutionary theory has developed the argument that human beings are descended from the apes. Geological finds suggest that there were prehistoric men who seem to be related to the modern *homo sapiens*. Various remains have been found, specially by the Leakeys, both father and son, in the Orduvi Gorge in Kenya among other places. It is claimed that human life began in Africa, rather than in the Middle East where the Bible puts it.

What are we to make of this evidence? How are we to understand the relationship of modern man to prehistoric man? Is it possible to reconcile what Scripture and science say about the origin of man?

THE ORIGIN OF MAN

Let us look first at what the Bible says. Genesis tells us that man is made of the same material as the animals. The animals were made of the dust of the earth. We too are made of exactly the same minerals that are found in the crust of the earth. A recent estimate indicates that the minerals in a body are worth about 85p! In contrast to the animal world, however, Genesis 2 also tells us that God breathed into the dust and man became a 'living soul'.

Soul

'Soul' is a misunderstood word. The exact phrase is also used of the animals in Genesis 1. They are called 'living souls' because in Hebrew the word 'soul' simply means a breathing body. Since animals and men are both described as 'living souls' they are both the same kind of beings. When we are in danger at sea we send out an SOS not an SOB – but what we want is for our breathing bodies to be saved.

Lord Soper was at Speaker's Corner in Hyde Park one day when he was asked, 'Where is the soul in the body?' He replied, 'Where the music is in the organ!' You can take an organ or a piano to pieces and you will not find the music. It is only there when it is made into a living thing by somebody else.

A special creation

The word 'soul' in Genesis 2 has misled many people into thinking that what makes human beings unique is that we have souls. In fact, we are unique for a different reason. To believe that man and the anthropoid apes came from common stock seems to be in direct opposition to the biblical account. Man is without doubt a special creation. He is made in the image of God, direct from dust and not indirectly from another animal. The Hebrew word *bara*, to create something completely new, is used only three times – of matter, life and man. This implies that there is something unique about man.

The Genesis account emphasizes the unity of the human race too. The apostle Paul told the Athenians that God made us of 'one blood'. Everything in history points to the unity of our human race in the present. I have studied agricultural archaeology a little and it is interesting to note that agricultural archaeology puts the origins of growing corn and domesticating animals exactly where the Bible puts the Garden of Eden, in north-east Turkey or southern Armenia.

SCIENTIFIC SPECULATION

What does science have to say on the matter? Many people would have us choose to accept one side and reject the other: either science has made false investigations into prehistoric man, or Scripture has given us false information.

There is no doubt that science has discovered remains that do look astonishingly like us. They have been given various names: Neanderthal Man, Peking Man, Java Man, Australian Man. The Leakeys claim to have found human remains which date back 4 million years. Among anthropologists it is almost wholly accepted that human origins are to be found in Africa, rather than in the Middle East.

Homo sapiens is said to go back 30,000 years; Neanderthal Man 40–150,000 years; Swanscombe Man 200,000 years; *Homo erectus* (China and Java Man) 300,000 years; Australian Man 500,000 years; and now African Man 4 million years. What are we to say about all this?

The first point which should be made very strongly is that nothing has yet been found that is half-ape and half-man.

There are prehistoric *human* remains, but there is nothing *half-and-half* as yet.

The second point to note is that not all these groups are our direct ancestors. This is now acknowledged by scientists – anthropology is in a state of flux today.

The third point of importance is that the remains do not follow a progressive order. Charts have been produced supposedly showing the development of mankind, starting with the ape on the left-hand side of the chart and moving through successive species to the modern human being, *homo sapiens*, on the right. But these charts are inaccurate: some of the earliest human remains have larger brains than we do today and walked more upright than some of the later remains. The consensus of opinion now is that none of these groups is connected to ours.

There are three possible ways of resolving the conflict. Here they are in very brief outline.

1. **Prehistoric man was biblical man.** What we are digging up was the same as Adam, made in the image of God. It has even been suggested that Genesis 1 portrays 'palaeolithic hunting man', and Genesis 2 portrays 'neolithic farming man'.

2. **Prehistoric man at some point changed into biblical man.** At some point in history this animal-like man or man-like animal became the image of God. Whether just one changed, or a few, or all of them changed at once is open to discussion.

3. **Prehistoric man was not biblical man.** Prehistoric man had a similar physical appearance and used tools, but there is no apparent trace of religion or prayer. He was a different creature, not made in the image of God.

It is unlikely that we need to plump for one explanation over another at this stage. Anthropology is itself in a state of change and development at present, and it is quite likely that the debate will raise other approaches in the future. It is sufficient for us to note the arguments and be aware that any conclusions we draw may well be provisional.

Evolution

Let us turn next to the question of evolution in general. Most people assume that evolution is Charles Darwin's theory. It is not. It was first conceived by Aristotle (384–322 BC). In modern days it was Erasmus Darwin, Charles' grandfather, who first propounded it. Charles picked it up from his atheist grandfather and made it popular.

If we are to grasp the basics of the theory, there are certain terms we need to know.

Variation is the belief that there have been small, gradual changes in form which are passed on to each successive generation. Each generation changes slightly and passes on that change.

From those variations there has been a **natural selection**. This simply means the survival of those most suited to their environment. Take the case of the speckled moth, for example. Against the coal heaps in north-east England the black moth was more suited in camouflage than the white. The birds were able to consume the white moths more easily and the black moths survived. Now that the slag heaps have gone in the area, the white moths are coming back again and the black moths are disappearing. Natural selection is the process whereby those species most adapted to their environment survive. This selection is 'natural' because it happens automatically within nature, with no help from outside.

The belief that there is only a slow, gradual process of variation and selection has now changed, however. A Frenchman called Lamarque said that instead of gradual changes there were sudden, large changes, known as **mutations**. In this situation, progression looks more like a staircase than an escalator.

The concept of **micro-evolution** is that there has been limited change within certain animal groups, e.g. the horse or dog group. Science has certainly proved that micro-evolution does take place.

Macro-evolution, by contrast, is the theory that all animals came from the same origin and that all are related. They all go back to the same simple form of life. This is not change within individual species, therefore, but a belief that all species developed from one another.

The final term to consider is **struggle**. In the context of evolution it refers to the 'survival of the fittest'.

I am not going to argue the case for or against evolution, except to point out that evolution is still a theory. It has not been proven and, in fact, the more evidence we get from fossils the less it looks like being an adequate theory to account for the different forms of life which arose.

1. In the fossil evidence, groups classified separately under evolutionary theory actually appear simultaneously in the Cambrian period. They do not appear gradually over different ages, they appear almost together.
2. Complex and simple forms of life appear together. There is not a sequence from the simple to the complex.
3. There are very, very few 'bridge' fossils that are halfway between one species and another.
4. All life forms are very complicated: they have always had DNA.
5. Mutations, the sudden changes which are purported to account for the development from one species to the next, usually lead to deformities and cause creatures to die out.

6. Interbreeding usually leads to sterility.
7. Above all, when the statistical probabilities are analysed, quite apart from the other objections, there is not enough time for all the varieties of life form to have developed.

The theory of evolution is not merely of academic interest, of course. How we each understand our origins has an effect on how we view mankind as a whole. Leaders infected by evolutionist philosophy have had a considerable impact.

Basic to the evolutionist theory is the concept of the survival of the fittest and the struggle which all species face to survive. This is found in some of the philosophies which have shaped our civilized society, and it has caused untold suffering. American capitalists such as John D. Rockefeller have said, 'Business is the survival of the fittest.' A similar outlook is found in fascism: Adolf Hitler's book was called *Mein Kampf*, 'My Struggle'. He believed in the survival of the fittest, the 'fittest' being in his view the German Aryan race. It is also found in communism. Karl Marx wrote about the 'struggle' between the bourgeoisie and the proletariat, which he believed must issue in revolution. The word 'struggle' could also be written across the early days of colonialism, when people were simply wiped out in the name of progress.

In short, the idea of the survival of the fittest when applied to human beings has caused more suffering than any other concept in modern times. But it has also faced us with two huge choices as to what we believe.

MENTAL CHOICE

It faces us first with a mental choice. If you believe in creation you believe in a father God. If you believe in evolution you tend to go for mother nature (a lady who does not exist). If you believe in creation you believe that this universe was the result of a personal choice. If you believe in evolution, you will argue that it was a random, impersonal chance. There was a designed purpose under creation, but under evolution only a random pattern. With creation the universe is a supernatural production, in evolution it is a natural process. Under creation the whole universe is an open situation, open to personal inter-vention by both God and man. In evolution we have nature as a closed system that operates itself. In creation we have the concept of providence, that God cares for his creation and pro-vides for it and looks after it. But with evolution we simply have coincidence: if anything good happens it is merely the result of chance. With creation we have a faith based on fact, with evolution a faith based on fancy (for it is just a theory). If we accept creation then we accept that God is free to make something and to make man in his image. If we accept evolu-tion we are left with the view that man is free to make God in whatever image he chooses out of his imagination. Accepting one or the other, therefore, has considerable ramifications.

MORAL CHOICE

There is also a moral choice behind accepting creation or evo-lution. Why is it that people seize on the theory of evolution and hold onto it so fanatically? The answer is that it is the only real alternative if you want to believe that there is no God over us. Under creation *God* is Lord, under evolution *man* is Lord. With creation we are under divine authority, but if there is no God we are autonomous as humans and can decide things for ourselves. If we accept God as creator we accept that there are absolute standards of right and wrong. But with no God under evolution, we only have relative situations. With God's world we talk of duty and responsibility, with evolution we talk of demands and rights. Under God we have an infinite depen-dence, we become as little children and speak to the heavenly father. With evolution we are proud of our independence, we speak of coming of age, of no longer 'needing' God. According to the Bible, man is a fallen creature. According to evolution he is rising and progressing all the time. In the Bible we have salvation for the weak. In evolutionary philosophy we have the survival of the strong.

Nietzsche, the philosopher behind the thought in Hitler's Germany, said he hated Christianity because it kept weak people going and looked after the sick and dying. The Bible teaches that you are powerful when you do what is right, but evolutionary philosophy leads to a 'might is right' outlook. One leads to peace, the other to war. Where evolutionism says you should indulge yourself, look after number one, the Bible says that faith, hope and love are the three main virtues in life. Ultimately the Bible leads us to heaven, whereas evolution promises little – fatalism, helplessness and luck – and leads to hell.

The Fall

When God finished creating our world he said that it was very good. Few today would say that it is a very good world now. Something went wrong. Genesis 3 describes for us what the problem is and how it arose.

There are three undeniable facts about our existence today:

1. Birth is painful.
2. Life is hard.
3. Death is certain.

Why is this? Why is birth painful? Why is life hard? Why is death certain?

Philosophy gives us many different answers. Some philosophers say there must be a bad God as well as a good one. More frequently, they say that the good God made a bad job of it and try to find in that some explanation for the origin of evil. Genesis 3 gives us four vital insights into this problem.

1. Evil was not always in the world.
2. Evil did not start with human beings.
3. Evil is not something physical, it is something moral. Some philosophers have said that it is the material part of the universe that is the source of evil, or in personal terms it is your body that is the source of temptation.
4. Evil is not a thing that exists on its own. It is an adjective rather than a noun. Evil as such does not exist, it is only persons who can be or become evil.

So what does Genesis 3 have to teach us on the subject? It is worth reminding ourselves that this is a real event in real history: we are given both the place and the time of it. At the dawn of human history a gigantic moral catastrophe took place.

The problem starts with a speaking reptile (more a lizard than a snake because it had legs, despite conventional wisdom; it was only later that God made the serpent slither on its belly). How are we to understand this extraordinary story of the snake speaking to Eve? There are three possibilities:

1. The serpent was the devil in disguise; he can appear as an angel or an animal.
2. God enabled an animal to talk, as he did with Balaam's ass.
3. The animal was possessed by an evil spirit. Just as Jesus sent the demons tormenting a man down the Gadarene cliffs into the bodies of 2,000 pigs, so it is perfectly possible for Satan to take over an animal. This would fool Adam and Eve, because Satan was putting himself below them. In fact Satan is a fallen angel, just as real as human beings, more intelligent and stronger than we are.

It is significant that Satan went for Eve. In very general terms, women tend to be more trusting than men, who are notoriously distrustful. Capitalizing on this, Satan subverts God's order and treats Eve as if she were the head of the house. Although it is clear that Adam is there with Eve, he says nothing. He should be protecting her, arguing with Satan. After all, it was Adam who had heard God's words of prohibition.

All told, there are three ways of misquoting the Word of God. One is to add something to it, another is to take something away, and a third is to change what is there. If you read the text carefully, you will find that Satan did all three. Satan knows his Bible very well, but he can misquote it and manipulate it too. Adam, however, who knew exactly what God had said, kept silent when he should have spoken up. In the New Testament he is clearly blamed for allowing sin to enter the world.

It is useful to note the strategy which Satan adopts in his approach to Eve. First he encourages doubt with the mind, second desire with the heart, and third disobedience with the will. This is always his strategy in all his dealings with humans. He encourages wrong thinking first, usually by misinterpreting God's Word. Next he entices us to desire evil in our hearts. After that the circumstances are right for us to disobey with our wills.

What is the outcome of sin? When God questions Adam he seeks to blame both Eve and God. He speaks of 'that woman you gave me', or 'the woman you put here with me'. He ceased to fulfil his role as a man by denying his responsibility to look after his wife.

God responds in judgement. This side of his character is seen for the first time: God hates sin and he must deal with it. If he is really a good God, then he cannot let people get away with badness. This is the message of Genesis 3. The punishment is given in poetic form. When God speaks in prose he is communicating his thoughts, from his mind to your mind, but when he speaks poetically he is communicating his feelings, from his heart to yours.

In Genesis 3 the poems reveal God's angry emotions (the wrath of God, in theological terms). God feels so deeply that Eden has been ruined – and he knows too where this will lead. The following paraphrase of Genesis 1–3 sheds a fresh light on this story.

A long time ago, when nothing else existed, the God who had always been there brought the entire universe into being, the whole of outer space and this planet earth.

At first the earth was just a mass of fluid matter, quite uninhabitable and indeed uninhabited. It was shrouded in darkness and engulfed in water; but God's own spirit was hovering just above the flood.

Then God commanded: 'Let the light in!' And there it was. It looked just right to God, but he decided to alternate light with darkness, giving them different names: 'day' and 'night'. The original darkness and the new light were the evening and the morning of God's first working day.

Then God spoke again: 'Let there be two reservoirs of water, with an expanse between them'. So he separated the water on the surface from the moisture in the atmosphere. That's how the 'sky', as God called it, came to be. This ended his second day's work.

The next thing God said was: 'Let the surface water be concentrated in one area, so that the rest may dry out.' Sure enough, it happened! From then on, God referred to 'sea' and 'land' separately. He liked what he saw and added: 'Now let the land sprout vegetation, plants with seed and trees with fruit, all able to reproduce themselves'. And they appeared –

all kinds of plant and tree, each able to propagate its own type. Everything fitted into God's plan. His third day's work was over.

Now God declared: 'Let different sources of light appear in the sky. They will distinguish days from nights and make it possible to measure seasons, special days and years; though their main purpose will be to provide illumination.' And so it is, just as he said. The two brightest lights are the larger 'sun' that dominates the day and the lesser 'moon' which predominates at night, surrounded by twinkling stars. God put them all there for earth's sake – to light it, regulate it and maintain the alternating pattern of light and darkness. God was pleased that his fourth day's work had turned out so well.

The next order God issued was: 'Let the sea and the sky teem with living creatures, with shoals of swimming fish and flocks of flying birds.' So God brought into being all the animated things that inhabit the oceans, from huge monsters of the deep to the tiny organisms floating in the waves, and all the variety of birds and insects on the wing in the wind above. To God it was a wonderful sight and he encouraged them to breed and increase in numbers, so that every part of sea and sky might swarm with life. That ended his fifth day.

Then God announced: 'Now let the land also teem with living creatures – mammals, reptiles and wildlife of every sort.' As before, no sooner was it said than done! He made all kinds of wildlife, including mammals and reptiles, each as a distinct type. And they all gave him pleasure.

At this point God reached a momentous decision: 'Now let's make some quite different creatures, more our kind – beings, just like us. They can be in charge of all the others – the fish in the sea, the birds of the air and the animals on the land.

> To resemble himself God created mankind,
> To reflect in themselves his own heart, will and mind,
> To relate to each other, male and female entwined.

Then he affirmed their unique position with words of encouragement: 'Produce many offspring, for you are to occupy and control the whole earth. The fish in the sea, the birds of the air and the animals on the land are all yours to master. I am also giving you the seed-bearing plants and the fruit-bearing trees as your food supply. The birds and the beasts can have the green foliage for their food.' And so it was.

God surveyed all his handiwork and he was very satisfied with it ... everything so right, so beautiful ... six days' work well done.

Outer space and planet earth were now complete. Since nothing more was needed, God took the next day off. That is why he designated every seventh day to be different from the others, set apart for himself alone – because on that day he was not busy with his daily work on creation.

This is how our universe was born and how everything in it came to be the way it is; when the God whose name is 'Always' was making outer space and the planet earth, there was a time when there was no vegetation at all on the ground. And if there had been, there was neither any rain to irrigate it nor any man to cultivate it. But underground springs welled up to the surface and watered the soil. And the God 'Always' moulded a human body from particles of clay, gave it the kiss of life, and man joined the living creatures. And the God 'Always' had already laid out a stretch of parkland, east of here, a place called 'Eden', which means 'Delight'. He brought the first man there to live. The God 'Always' had planted a great variety of trees in the part with beautiful foliage and delicious fruit. Right in the middle were two rather special trees; fruit from one of them could maintain life indefinitely while the fruit of the other gave the eater personal experience of doing right and wrong.

One river watered the whole area but divided into four branches as it left the park. One was called the Pishon and wound across the entire length of Havilah, the land where pure nuggets of gold were later found, as well as aromatic resin and onyx. The second was called the Gihon and meandered right through the country of Cush. The third was the present Tigris, which flows in front of the city of Asshur. The fourth was what we know as the Euphrates.

So the God 'Always' set the man in this 'Parkland of Delight' to develop and protect it. And the God 'Always' gave him very clear orders: 'You are perfectly free to eat the fruit of any tree except one – the tree that gives experience of right and wrong. If you taste that you will certainly have to die the death.'

Then the God 'Always' said to himself: 'It isn't right for the man to be all on his own. I will provide a matching partner for him.'

Now the God 'Always' had fashioned all sorts of birds and beasts out of the soil and he brought them in contact with the man to see how he would describe them; and whatever the man said about each one became its name. So it was man who labelled all the other creatures but in none of them did he recognize a suitable companion for himself.

So the God 'Always' sent the man into a deep coma and while he was unconscious God took some tissue from the side of his body, and pulled the flesh together over the gap. From the tissue he produced a female clone and introduced her to the man, who burst out with:

'At last you have granted my wish,
A companion of my bones and flesh,
"Woman" to me is her name,
Wooed by the man whence she came.'

All this explains why a man lets go of his parents and holds on to his wife, their two bodies melting into one again.

The first man and his new wife wandered about the park quite bare, but without the slightest embarrassment.

Now there was a deadly reptile around, more cunning than any of the wild beasts the God 'Always' had made. He chatted with the woman one day and asked: 'You don't mean to tell me that God has actually forbidden you to eat any fruit from all these trees?' She replied: 'No, it's not quite like that. We can eat fruit from the trees, but God did forbid us to eat from that one in the middle. In fact, he warned us that if we even touch it, we'll have to be put to death.'

'Surely he wouldn't do that to you,' said the reptile to the woman, 'he's just trying to frighten you off because he knows perfectly well that when you eat that fruit you'd see things quite differently. Actually it would put you on the same level as him, able to decide for yourself what is right and wrong.'

So she took a good look at the tree and noticed how nourishing and tasty the fruit appeared to be. Besides, it was obviously an advantage to be able to make one's own moral judgements. So she picked some, ate part and gave the rest to her husband, who was with her at the time and he promptly ate too. Sure enough, they did see things quite differently! For the first time they felt self-conscious about their nudity. So they tried to cover up with crude clothes stitched together from fig leaves.

That very evening, they suddenly became aware of the approach of the God 'Always' and ran to hide in the under-growth. But the God 'Always' called out to the man: 'What have you got yourself into?' He answered: 'I heard you coming and I was frightened because I haven't got any decent clothes. So I'm hiding in the bushes over here.' Then God demanded: 'How did you discover what it feels like to be naked? Have you been eating the fruit I ordered you to leave alone?' The man tried to defend himself: 'It's all due to that woman you sent along; she brought this fruit to me, so natu-rally I just ate it without question.'

Then the God 'Always' challenged the woman: 'What have you been up to?' The woman said: 'It's that dreadful reptile's fault! He deliberately deluded me and I fell for it.'

So the God 'Always' said to the reptile: 'As a punishment for your part in this:

Above all the beasts I will curse
Your ways with a fate that is worse!
On your belly you'll slither and thrust
With your mouth hanging down in the dust.
For the rest of the days in your life,
There'll be terror, hostility, strife
Between woman and you for this deed
Which you'll both pass along to your seed;
But his foot on your skull you will feel
As you strike out in fear at his heel.'

Then to the woman he said:

'Let the pain of child-bearing increase
The agony, labour and stress;
You'll desire a man to control
But find yourself under his rule.'

But to the man, Adam, he said, 'Because you paid attention to your wife rather than me and disobeyed my order prohibiting that tree:

> There's a curse on the soil;
> All your days you will toil.
> Thorns and thistles will grow
> Among all that you sow.
> With a brow running sweat
> You will labour to eat;
> Then return to the ground
> In the state you were found.
> From the clay you were made;
> In the dust you'll be laid.'

Adam gave his wife the name Eve (it means 'life-giving') because he now realized she would be the mother of all human beings who would ever live.

The God 'Always' made some new clothes from animal skins for Adam and his wife and got them properly dressed. Then the God 'Always' said to himself; 'Now this man has become as conscious of good and evil things as we have been, how could we limit the damage if he is still able to eat from the other special tree and live as long as us?' To prevent this happening, the God 'Always' banished the man from the Park of Delight and sent him back to cultivate the very same patch of ground from which he was originally moulded!

After he had been expelled, heavenly angels were stationed on the eastern border of the Park of Delight, guarding access to the tree of continuous life with sharp, scorching weapons.

THE RESULTS OF THE FALL

Chapter 3 is usually referred to as 'the Fall', when man fell from the beautiful state described in Chapter 2. It could all have been so different. If Adam had not tried to blame Eve, or even God, but had responded in repentance, God could have forgiven him on the spot. History might have been very different. Instead we have Adam's pathetic attempt at cover-up with fig leaves to mirror his folly.

The nature of the punishment is well worthy of note. Adam is punished in relation to his work, and Eve in relation to the family. The reptile becomes a snake (even today there are very small legs on the underside of a snake).

Their former relationship with God is destroyed. Their relationship with each other is also affected: they hide from each other and God pronounces a curse over them. In Chapter 4 the first murder takes place within the family, as envy gives way to defiance against God's warning.

Let us now focus on three areas in the subsequent story where God's reactions to the situation are especially seen.

1. Cain

Somebody has pointed out that the sin committed by the first man caused the second man to kill the third. Here we have Adam's own family. His eldest son kills his middle son, and for the same reason that they killed Jesus centuries later: envy. Envy was responsible for the first murder in history and the worst murder in history.

Cain means 'gotten' – when he was born, Eve said 'I have gotten' (in the King James translation) him from the Lord. Abel means 'breath' or 'vapour'. God favoured Abel, the younger child of the two, because he did not want anybody ever to think they had a natural right to his gifts and inheritance. Often in Scripture we see God choose a younger person over an older one (e.g. Isaac over Ishmael, Jacob over Esau).

The problem that divided them was that God accepted Abel's sacrifice and rejected Cain's. Abel had learned from his parents that the only sacrifice worthy of God was a blood sacrifice – the result of a life being taken. God had already covered the sin and shame of his parents by killing animals and providing a covering for Adam and Eve from their skins. A principle was being established: blood was shed so that their shame could be covered (it began there and continues through to Calvary). So when Abel came to worship God he brought an animal sacrifice. Cain simply brought fruit and vegetables.

God was only pleased with Abel's sacrifice, not with Cain's offering. Cain was angered by this. In spite of God's warning that he should master sin, Cain leads his brother away from his home on a false pretext, then murders him, buries him and totally disowns him ('Am I my brother's keeper?' he asks).

A clear pattern emerges here: bad people hate good people, and the ungodly are envious of the godly. This is a division that goes all the way through human history.

So God's perfect world is now a place where goodness is hated, and the evil people excuse their wickedness. Anyone who presents a challenge to the conscience is hated. We could say that Abel was the first martyr for righteousness' sake. Jesus himself said that the 'blood of the righteous has been spilled from Abel, right through to Zechariah'.

The narrative goes on to chart the line of Cain and it includes some interesting elements. Alongside the names of Cain's descendants are listed their achievements, most notably the development of music and of metallurgy, including the first weapons. Urbanization also came from Cain's line. It was Cain's line that began to build cities, concentrating sinners in one place and therefore concentrating sin in one place. It could be said that cities became more sinful than the countryside because of this concentration.

Thus what we might see as 'human progress' is tainted. The 'mark of Cain', as it were, is on these 'developments', and that is the biblical interpretation of civilization: sinful activity is always at its heart. Polygamy also came through Cain's line. Up to that point one man and one woman were married for life, but Cain's descendants took many wives, and we know that even Abraham, Jacob and David were polygamists.

There was a third brother, however, Adam and Eve's third son Seth. With him we see another line beginning, a Godly line. From the line of Seth, men began to 'call on the name of the LORD'.

These two lines run right through human history and will continue to do so right to the end, when they will be separated for ever. We live in a world in which there is a line of Cain and a line of Seth, and we can choose which line we belong to and which kind of life we wish to live.

2. Noah

The next major event is the Flood and the building of Noah's ark. The story is well known, both inside and outside the Bible. Many peoples have tales of a universal flood within their folklore. It has been questioned whether it was a real event and whether it literally covered the whole earth. The text does not indicate whether the Flood went right round the globe or just covered the then known world. Certainly the Middle Eastern basin, later called Mesopotamia, the huge plain through which the Tigris and the Euphrates flow, is the scene of all the early stories of Genesis and was definitely an area affected by flood.

The Bible's focus is not so much on the material side of this story as on the moral side. Why did it happen? The answer is staggering. It happened because God regretted that he had made human beings. 'His heart was filled with pain'. This is surely one of the saddest verses in the Bible. It communicates God's feelings so clearly, and these led to his resolve to wipe out the human race.

What had happened to cause such a crisis in God's emotions? To answer this we need to piece together the Genesis narrative with some parts of the New Testament and some extra-testamental material quoted in Jude and Peter.

We are told that between two and three hundred angels in the area of Mount Hermon sent to look after God's people fell in love with women, seducing them and impregnating them. The offspring were a horrible hybrid, somewhere between men and angels – beings not in God's order. These are the 'Nephilim' in Genesis 6 – the offspring of the union between the 'sons of God' and the 'daughters of men'. The word is sometimes translated as 'giants' in English versions. We do not know exactly what is meant – it is just a new term for a new sort of creature. This horrible combination was also the beginning of occultism, because those angels taught the women witchcraft. There are no traces of occult practices before this event.

The immediate effect of this perverted sex was that violence filled the whole earth; the one leads to the other when people are treated as objects and not as persons. Genesis 6 tells us that God saw that 'every imagination of man's heart was only evil continually'. He felt that enough was enough.

But God did not judge immediately, he was very patient and gave them full warning. He called Enoch to be a prophet to tell the human race that God was coming to judge and deal with all ungodliness. At the age of 65 Enoch had a son, and God gave him the name for the boy, Methuselah, which means 'When he dies it will happen'. So both Methuselah and Enoch knew that when Enoch's son died God would judge the world.

We know that God was patient, because Methuselah lived longer than anybody else who has ever lived – 969 years. When Methuselah died it began to rain heavily. Methuselah's grandson was called Noah. He and his three sons had spent 12 months building a huge covered raft according to God's specifications. Just one family, a preacher and his three boys, three daughters-in-law and his wife, were saved.

After the Flood, God promised never to repeat such a thing as long as the earth remained. He made a covenant, a sacred promise with the whole human race: not only would he never destroy the human race again, but he would support them by providing enough food. He would ensure that summer, winter, springtime and harvest came regularly. At a time when famine is common in various parts of the world, this promise may seem to have been ignored. But there is far more corn in the world than we need – it is just not evenly distributed. Everyone could be fed if the political will existed.

God put a rainbow in the sky to signify this covenant. The two things we need for life on earth are sunlight and water, and when they come together the rainbow is visible.

When God made this promise he also demanded something of mankind. He commanded that we must treat human life as sacred and therefore punish murder with execution. When a nation abolishes capital punishment, it says something about its view of human life.

3. Babel

The next incident that affected God deeply was the building of the Tower of Babel. People wanted to build a tower that reached into God's sphere of heaven, effectively to 'challenge heaven'. The text says that they wanted to build a name for themselves. We know roughly what the tower would have looked like: such a tower was called a *ziggurat*, a great brick structure with staircases extending heavenwards. On the top of such towers there were usually astrological signs. But it was not so much for worshipping stars that Nimrod (king of Babylon, or Babel) built that tower – it was more to express his own power and grandeur.

The Tower of Babel offended God very profoundly. He said that if he let them continue there was no telling where it would end. So God gave the gift of tongues for the first time, to confuse the people. They could no longer understand each other. From then on humanity split, scattering and speaking different languages.

There is an interesting footnote to the story of Babel. Among the people scattered at Babel were a group who climbed over the mountains to the east and eventually settled when they reached the sea. They became the great nation of China. Chinese culture goes right back to that day. They left the area of Babel before the Cuneiform alphabet replaced the picture language of ancient Egypt. All languages were pictorial right up to the time of Babel. The language they took to China they put down in picture form. The amazing thing is that it is possible to reconstruct the story from Genesis 1 to 11 by looking at the symbols which the Chinese use to describe different words.

The Chinese word for 'create', for example, is made up of the pictures for mud, life and someone walking. Their word for 'devil' is made up of a man, a garden, and the picture for secret. So the devil is a secret person in the garden. Their word for 'tempter' is made up of the word for 'devil' plus two trees and the picture for cover. Their word for 'boat' is made up of container, mouth and eight, so a boat in the Chinese language is a vessel for eight people, as was Noah's ark.

We can reconstruct the whole of Genesis 1–11 from the picture language in China. When these people first arrived in

China, therefore, they believed in one God, the maker of heaven and earth. It was only after Confucius and Buddha that they got involved in idolatry. The Chinese language is an independent confirmation from outside the Bible that these things happened and were carried in the memories of people scattered at Babel, who then settled in China.

JUSTICE AND MERCY

Two themes predominate in these chapters: from the Fall of Adam onwards we see both human pride and God's response of justice and mercy. He showed justice to Adam and Eve in banishing them from the garden and telling them that they would one day die, but also mercy in providing a covering for them. He showed justice to Cain in condemning him to be a wanderer, but mercy in placing a mark on him so that no one would kill him. He punished the generation of Enoch (although not Enoch himself), but we see his mercy in saving Noah and his family and his patience in waiting, as he gave Methuselah such a long life. What does the rest of Genesis tell us about God? Let us look further, and see what kind of relationship he had with his people through the generations and events which followed.

The sovereign God

There is a double thread running right through the portrayal of God in the Old Testament which requires an explanation. It is a juxtaposition which only becomes clear through reading the book of Genesis.

The God of the whole universe

On the one side the Old Testament claims that the God of the Jews is the God of the whole universe. In those days every nation had its own god, whether it was Baal, or Isis, or Molech, and religion was strictly national. All wars were religious wars, between nations with different gods. Israel's God (Yahweh) was considered by other nations to be just the national god of Israel. But Israel herself claimed that her God was 'the God above all Gods'. Indeed, the Israelites went even further, asserting that their God was the only God who really existed. He had made the entire universe. All the other gods were figments of human imagination. These claims were, of course, extremely offensive to the other nations. You can read of them in Isaiah 40, in the book of Job and in many of the psalms.

The God of the Jews

The other side of the picture painted in the Old Testament is that the God of the whole universe is the God of the Jews. They were claiming that the creator of everything had a very personal and intimate relationship with them, one little group of people on earth. In fact, they were claiming that he had identified himself with one family; with a grandfather, a father and a son. According to them, the God of the entire universe called himself 'the God of Abraham, Isaac and Jacob'. It was an incredible claim.

God's plan

This astonishing two-fold truth that the God of the Jews is the God of the universe, and the God of the universe is especially the God of the Jews, is explained for us in Genesis – indeed, without this book we would have no ground for believing it.

The book of Genesis covers more time than the whole of the rest of the Bible put together. The beginning of Exodus to the end of Revelation covers around 1,500 years, a millennium and a half, whereas Genesis alone covers the entire history of the world from its beginning right through to the time of

Joseph. So when we read the Bible we must realize that time has been compressed, and that Genesis covers many centuries compared to the rest of the Bible.

This time compression is also true within Genesis itself. We have noted already that Chapters 1–11 form a quarter of the book and yet cover a very long period and a considerable breadth of people and nations. The second 'part' of Genesis, Chapters 12–50, is a much longer section taking up three-quarters of the book, yet it only covers a relatively few years and a few people – just one family and only four generations of that family. This seems to be a huge disproportion of space if Genesis is claiming to tell the history of our whole world.

It is clear, however, that this difference in proportions is quite deliberate. There is a deliberate move away from looking at the whole world to focus in on one particular family as if they were the most important family ever to have lived. In one sense they were, for they were part of that very special line from Seth of people who called on the name of the Lord. As far as God was concerned, the people who called on him were more important than anyone else because they were the people through whom he could fulfil his plans and purposes.

This approach serves to remind us that the Bible is not God's answers to our problems; it is God's answer to God's problem. God's problem was: 'What do you do with a race that doesn't want to know you or love you or obey you?' One solution was to wipe them out and start again. He tried that, but even the father of the righteous remnant saved through the Flood (Noah) got drunk and exposed himself, demonstrating that human nature had not changed. But God did not give up. He was concerned about human beings; he had created them. He had one son already and he enjoyed that son so much he wanted a bigger family, so he was not about to give up on the problem of mankind.

His solution began with Abraham. Philosophers call this 'the scandal of particularity', suggesting that God was being unfair in choosing to deal only with the Jews. Why does he not save the Chinese through the Chinese, the Americans through the Americans, the British through the British? God's rescue programme is an offence to us – summed up by the poet William Norman Ewer:

> How odd
> Of God
> To choose
> The Jews.

Then Cecil Browne decided to add a second verse in reply:

> But not so odd
> As those who choose
> A Jewish God,
> But spurn the Jews.

We might explain God's approach by considering a simple domestic situation. A father decides to bring home sweets for his three children. He could bring three bars of chocolate and give them one each, or he could bring a bag of sweets, give it to one child and tell them to share. The first option is the most peaceful one, but treats the children as unconnected individuals. If he wants to create a *family* then the second approach would teach them more.

God's way, therefore, was to start a plan whereby his son would come as a Jew. He told the Jews to share his blessings with everyone else, instead of dealing with each nation separately. He chose the Jews, with the intention that all other peoples might know his blessing through them.

This is why he calls himself the God of Abraham, Isaac and Jacob in the Old Testament. Chapters 12–50 of Genesis are basically the stories of just four men. Three are classed together while the fourth, Joseph, is treated separately – for reasons which will become apparent later, when we focus on him in some detail.

Built into the stories of the first three men are contrasts with other relatives. The counterpoint to Abraham is his nephew Lot; the counterpoint to Isaac is his stepbrother Ishmael; the counterpoint to Jacob is his twin brother Esau. The relationships become progressively closer, from nephew to stepbrother to twin. God is showing that there are still two lines running through the human race in very stark contrast to each other. The stories invite us to line ourselves up with one side or the other. Are you a Jacob or an Esau? Are you an Isaac or an Ishmael? Are you an Abraham or a Lot?

ARE THESE STORIES REAL?

There are some who argue that these chapters are legends or sagas. They say that while there is a nucleus of truth in them, they cannot be confirmed as historically accurate. What such people forget is that 'fiction' is a very recent form of literature. Novels were totally unknown in Abraham's day. There would have been little point in writing invented stories. Indeed, if you were committed to inventing a story about a hero figure, you would doubtless ascribe miracles to them. The Genesis record includes hardly any at all. There are dozens in the book of Exodus, but Genesis has very few. Yet legend is usually full of miraculous or magical happenings.

Furthermore, nobody has found a single anachronism in these stories (an anachronism being the inclusion of material which could not have taken place in that time period). The cultural details that emerge in these stories have been shown by archaeology to be totally true.

The one feature that cannot be accounted for by natural explanation is the part which angels play, but they are involved throughout the Bible. If you have problems with angels you have problems with the whole Bible. Apart from that, these stories are very ordinary – they are about ordinary men and women who are born, fall in love, marry, have children and die. They keep sheep and goats and cattle and grow a few crops. They disagree, they quarrel, they fight; they erect tents, they build altars and they worship God. All these things are totally within the range of normal human experience.

WHY DID GOD CHOOSE THE JEWS?

What *is* different about these stories, however, is that God talks with the people in them and they talk to him. So we find that the God of the entire universe makes a special friend called Abraham. Indeed, God calls him 'Abraham my friend'. This is the scandal of particularity. People cannot cope with a God who makes personal friends. They feel that somehow it is inappropriate, and yet that is the truth of what happens here.

The big question is: Why should God choose to identify himself as the God of Abraham, Isaac and Jacob? What is so special about them? This has been the question asked by other nations, other peoples, down through the ages. What is so special about the Jews? Why should they be the chosen people and not us?

The answer lies in God's sovereign choice. These three men had no *natural* claim on God. He freely initiated the relationship with them and they could not claim that the relationship was due to them. Indeed, in each of the generations it is striking how the typical rights of inheritance are overturned. The first son would normally inherit the family wealth from the father, but in each generation God chooses not the eldest but the youngest son. He chooses Isaac, not Ishmael, and

Jacob, not Esau. He is thus establishing that no one has a natural claim on his love: it is just his love to give as he chooses. It was not, therefore, a question of a straight hereditary link through the eldest son. Neither Isaac nor Jacob were the first-born. What they inherited was a free gift.

More striking is the fact that none of these three men had a *moral* claim on God either, for they could not claim to be better than anyone else. In fact, the Bible states how each man lied to get himself out of a tricky situation. Both Abraham and Isaac lied through their teeth about their own wives to save their skins, and Jacob was the worst of the three. Not only were these men liars, they also took more than one wife. We are given a picture of very ordinary men like us who all had their weaknesses.

The only thing they had which did mark them out was *faith*. These men believed in God. God can do wonders when a person believes. God would rather have a believing person than a good person – he even said to Abraham that his faith went down in his book as 'righteousness'. Good deeds without a belief in God count for nothing.

Isaac and Jacob shared that faith, although they were very different in personality and temperament. The one common thing between the three men was that they had faith.

The faith of the patriarchs

Abraham's faith was especially evident when he left Ur of the Chaldees. The city was a very impressive, sophisticated place, one of the most advanced anywhere in the world, but God told Abraham he wanted him to live in a tent for the rest of his life. Not many of us would leave a comfortable city and live in a tent up in the mountains where it is cold and snows in winter, especially at the age of 75. God told him to leave a land he would never see again in order to go to a land he had never seen before. He must leave his family and friends (although in the event Abraham actually took his father and other members of his family halfway as far as Haran, from where he and his nephew Lot continued the journey). Abraham obeyed. He even believed God when he told him he would have a son despite his wife Sarah being 90 years old. (When the boy came they called him 'Joke'. *Isaac* is Hebrew for 'laugh'. When Sarah first heard that she was going to be pregnant at that age she just roared with laughter.)

Abraham's faith had considerable knocks along the way. Eleven years passed after God's promise and there was still no sign of a son. Abraham, at Sarah's suggestion, sought offspring through her maidservant Hagar. The Bible makes it clear that Ishmael was not a 'child of faith', but a 'child of the flesh' whom God did not choose (although God went on to bless him too with many generations of offspring which make up the Arab peoples today).

When Isaac eventually came, Abraham exercised faith when he was prepared to sacrifice him on an altar at God's request. The Bible tells us that Abraham was willing to kill Isaac as a sacrifice because he believed God would raise him from the dead after he had killed him. Considering that God had never done that before, this was some faith! He reasoned that if God could produce life (Isaac) from his old body, he could surely bring Isaac back from the dead if he wanted.

Most of the pictorial representations of the sacrifice of Isaac paint him as a boy of 12. But if we examine the text surrounding this event we see that the very next thing that happens is Sarah's death at the age of 127, which would make Isaac 37. So Isaac was probably in his early thirties at the time of the sacrifice. He could therefore have resisted easily, but he submitted in faith to his father Abraham, an old man. (The location is also significant, for the mountain of sacrifice was called Moriah, which later became Golgotha, or Calvary.) Isaac also demonstrates faith in other ways, principally in trusting Abraham's servant to find him a wife.

Jacob too had faith, but initially this was only faith in himself. The narrative records how he manipulated his father into passing on the blessing to him rather than Esau by scheming and deception. But at least it showed that he wanted the blessing, in contrast to Esau's disregard for what would have been his. Later in his life, God had to 'break' Jacob. He limped for the rest of his life after wrestling with God all night. But this was the turning point for his faith in God. From that moment on he believed God's promises that his 12 boys would become 12 tribes.

These three men, in spite of all their weaknesses and their failures, shine out as men who believed in God. They had faith, in sharp contrast to their relatives, who were people of flesh rather than people of faith.

Lot comes across as a materialist, choosing to go down into the fertile Jordan valley rather than live in the barren hills. He trusted his eyes, while Abraham, with the eyes of faith, knew that God would be with him in the hills. Esau decided he would rather have a bowl of 'instant soup' than the blessing of his father. The letter to the Hebrews tells us not to be like Esau, who regretted his bargain and afterwards sought the blessing with tears, though without genuine repentance. There is, therefore, a stark contrast between the men of faith and their relatives of flesh – a distinction which runs through many families today.

This contrast is also seen in the men's wives. Sarah, Rebekah and Rachel had one thing in common: they were all very beautiful. The three wives of the patriarchs had the lasting beauty of inner character and they all submitted to their husbands. The wives of the others are again a contrast. Lot's wife, for example, looked back to the comfortable life they were leaving but which was going to be judged by God, and having disobeyed God's word was turned into a pillar of salt.

Abraham

Let us look at those three men in greater detail. God made a promise to Abraham on which Christians still rely. God began creation with one man and he began redemption with one man. We are told that God made a covenant with Abraham, a theme which continues through the Bible to Jesus himself, who institutes a new covenant commemorated at the Lord's Supper.

It is important to grasp the meaning of 'covenant' clearly. Some confuse it with the word 'contract', but it is not a bargain struck between two parties of equal power and authority. A covenant is made entirely by one party to bless the other. The other party has only two choices: to accept the terms or to reject them. They cannot change them. When God makes covenants he keeps them and swears by them. Where a human being might say 'by God I promise to do that', God says 'by myself I have sworn', because there is nothing above God to swear by. So he swears by himself and he tells the truth, the whole truth and nothing but the truth.

In his promise to Abraham, God repeats the words of intention 'I will' six times in Genesis 12, rather like a husband marrying a bride. The truth is that the God of the universe married himself to this particular family and his first promise was to give them a place to live in (a little patch of land where the continents meet – the very centre of the world's land mass is Jerusalem and that is where the roads from Africa to Asia and from Arabia to Europe cross, near a little hill called Armageddon in Hebrew, the crossroads of the world). God said, in effect, 'This is the place I am going to give you for ever.' They hold the title deeds to that place, whatever any-body else says, because God gave the title deeds to them, to Abraham and his descendants for ever.

His second promise was to give them descendants. He said there would always be descendants of Abraham on the earth. And he said this in spite of both Abraham's and Sarah's advancing years.

The third promise was that he would use them to bless or to curse every other nation. The calling of the Jews is to share God with everybody. It is a calling that can cut both ways, for God said to Abraham, 'Those who curse you will be cursed, those who bless you will be blessed.' In return God expected first that every male Jew would be circumcised as a sign that they were born into that covenant, and second that Abraham would obey God and do everything God told him to do.

This covenant is at the very heart of the Bible and is the basis upon which God said, 'I will be your God and you will be my people', a phrase which is repeated all the way through the Bible until the very last page in Revelation. It tells us that God wants to stick with us. At the very end of the Bible God himself moves out of heaven and comes down to earth to live with us on a new earth for ever.

Isaac

We know less about him than about his father Abraham or his son, Jacob, but he is the vital link between them. His faith is to be seen in his accepting God's choice of a wife, staying in the land of Canaan when famine struck and leaving the land to his son even though he did not possess it in fact, only in promise. Sadly, his loss of sight in old age led to deception by his own family.

Jacob

Jacob is perhaps the most colourful of the three men. Even when he was being born he was holding the heel of his twin brother Esau, he was grasping from the very beginning. Esau went to live in a place we now call Petra, where it is still possible to view amazing temples carved out of the red sandstone. It was here that Esau formed the nation of Edom. The hatred between Ishmael and Isaac still exists in the Middle East in the tension between Arab and Jew, but the hatred between Esau and Jacob has disappeared. The last Edomites were known by the name of Herod and it was a descendant of Esau who was King of the Jews when Jesus was born. He killed all the babies in Bethlehem to try to get rid of this descendant of Jacob who was born to be King.

Inheritance

Abraham, Isaac and Jacob all showed their faith in one extraordinary, final way. They each left their sons what they did not actually possess. Abraham said to Isaac that he was leaving to him the whole land around them. Isaac also said to Jacob that he was leaving him the whole land, and Jacob said to his 12 boys that he was leaving them the whole land of Canaan. But not one of them possessed what they bequeathed. Only Abraham actually owned any land and this was just the cave at Hebron where Sarah lay buried. They each believed that God had given to them what they were bequeathing, and that one day the whole land would be theirs.

When we read about these men much later in the Bible in Hebrews 11, we discover that 'all these people were still living by faith when they died'. They were all commended for their faith, 'yet none of them received what had been promised. God had planned something better for us so that only together with us would they be made perfect'. Abraham, Isaac and Jacob are not dead. We can see the tombs of their bodies in Hebron, but they are not dead. Jesus said that God *is* the God of Abraham, Isaac and Jacob – not *was* but *is*. He is not the God of dead people: he is the God of the living.

Joseph

The final part of Genesis concerns a story which is familiar to many, the story of Joseph. It is a story that appeals to children as well as adults, a 'goody wins over the baddy' story. It has even been made into a musical, although the popular references to a multicoloured coat are probably inaccurate. It was more likely a coat specifically with long sleeves, rather than any kind of multicoloured garment – the major point being that Joseph was made foreman over the others and wore attire which emphasized that he did not have to do manual work. Such preference was odd since Joseph was not the eldest son, so it led to considerable resentment.

Joseph is the fourth generation, the great-grandson of Abraham, and yet again he is not the eldest. There is a clear pattern here: the natural heir does not receive the blessing. God chooses in his grace who receives it. The pattern has been for it to be one of the younger sons.

In one important way, however, the pattern does not continue. I noted earlier that there is a great difference between Joseph and the previous three generations. God never calls himself 'the God of Joseph'. Angels never appear to Joseph and his brothers are not rejected like those of the other three. His brothers are included in the Godly line of Seth, so there is not the same contrast to be seen in that respect. Furthermore, Joseph is never spoken to directly by God. He receives dreams and is given the interpretation of dreams, but he never actually receives communication from God as the other three patriarchs do.

So it seems that somehow Joseph stands on his own. Why is he different, and why are we told his story?

In part the reason is obvious, for his story links in naturally with the very next book in the Bible. In Exodus we find this family in slavery in Egypt and somehow we need to explain how they got there. The story of Joseph is the vital link, explaining how Jacob and his family migrated down to Egypt for the same reason that Abraham and Isaac had gone down to Egypt earlier: because of a shortage of food. (Egypt does not depend on rain since it has the River Nile flowing down from the Ethiopian highlands, whereas the land of Israel depends for its crops totally on rain brought by the west wind from the Mediterranean.) At the very least, therefore, the story of Joseph is there to link us with the next part of the Bible. The curtain falls after Joseph for some 400 years, about which we know nothing, and when it lifts again the family has become a people of many hundreds of thousands – but now they are slaves in Egypt.

If this is the only reason that the story of Joseph is included in Genesis, then it hardly explains why so much space is given to it. We are told almost as much detail as we are about Abraham and far more than we are about Isaac or Jacob. Why are we told about Joseph in such detail? Is it simply the exam-ple of a good man with the moral that good triumphs in the end? Surely there is more to it than that.

There are at least four levels at which we can read the story of Joseph.

1. THE HUMAN ANGLE

The first level is simply the *human* level. It is a vivid story told superbly with very real characters. It is a great adventure, stranger than fiction. There are some extraordinary coinci-dences in it, and you could summarize Joseph's life in two chapters: Chapter 1, down, and Chapter 2, up. He went all the way down from being the favourite son of his father to becoming a household slave, and he went all the way up from being a forgotten prisoner to being Prime Minister. In between we have the envy of his brothers which brought him low, and the key to a successful ending lying in the dreams. At the human level, therefore, it makes a good musical show for London's West End and thousands see it and enjoy it.

2. GOD'S ANGLE

You can also read the story from *God's* angle. Even though he does not actually talk to Joseph, he is there behind the scenes, the invisible God arranging circumstances for his purposes and plans and revealing them through dreams. It is clear in the Bible that sometimes God needs to speak to his people in this way, but it always needs an interpretation. Joseph said these dreams were from God and that the interpretation would come from God. Daniel would later be noted for the same gift. Joseph believed that his circumstances were overruled by God and that God was behind the things that happened to him.

The key verse in the story of Joseph is found in Chapter 45, verse 7, when he finally made himself known to his brothers after humbling and embarrassing them greatly. Having forgiven them for what they had done to him, he then said, 'But God sent me ahead of you to preserve for you a remnant on earth and to save your lives by a great deliverance.'

Joseph's brothers thought they had got rid of him by selling him to travelling camel traders as a slave and covering his special coat with the blood of a goat to trick their father into believing that his favourite son was dead. Yet Joseph could see that God's hand was in it. He could look back on his work in Egypt, having been elevated to high office following his interpretation of Pharaoh's dream (i.e. there would be seven fat years with good harvest, and seven lean years to follow). By advising that food should be stored during the plentiful years he had actually saved the whole nation of Egypt – and his own family when they also became short of food. He became their saviour.

God's providence can also be seen in the movement of Joseph's family down to Egypt. Although God had promised the land to them, he had told Abraham many years previously that he would have to leave his family in Egypt for 400 years 'until the wickedness of the Amorites was complete'. God would not let the family of Abraham take the promised land from those living in it until they became so dreadful that they forfeited their right to both their land and their lives. God is a moral God: he would not just push one people out and his own people in. Archaeology has indicated to us just how dreadful these people were. Venereal diseases were rife in the land of Canaan because of their corrupt sexual practices. Eventually they reached the point of no return, and only then did God say that his people could have their land. Those who complain about God's injustice in giving that land to the Jews are quite mistaken.

But there were other reasons too. God *wanted* his chosen people to become slaves. It was part of his plan to rescue them from slavery so that they would be grateful to him and live his way, becoming a model for the whole world to see how blessed people are when they live under the government of heaven. So he let them go through the evils of slavery, working seven days a week for no pay, with no land of their own, no money of their own, nothing of their own. Then, as they cried out to him, he reached down and rescued them with his mighty hand. God let it happen for his own purposes. He wanted them to know that it was God who delivered them and gave them their own land.

3. JOSEPH'S CHARACTER

We can also approach the narrative as a study of *Joseph's character*. The remarkable thing is that nothing said about Joseph is bad. We have already noted that the Bible tells the whole truth about Abraham, Isaac and Jacob, who certainly had their weaknesses and sins. Not one word of criticism is levelled at Joseph. The worst thing he did was to be a bit tactless and tell his brothers about his dream of future greatness, but there is no trace whatever of a wrong attitude or reaction in Joseph's character. His reactions as he sinks down the social ladder are first class: there is no trace of resentment, no complaining, no questioning of God, no sense of injustice that he should finish up in prison, on death row in Pharaoh's jail. Furthermore, even though he was far from home and totally unknown, he maintained his integrity when Potiphar's wife tried to seduce him. Even at rock bottom, languishing in jail, his concern seems to have been primarily to help others as he seeks to comfort Pharaoh's cup bearer and baker. Joseph is a man who seems to have no concern for himself, but a deep concern for everyone else.

His character is also flawless when he ascends to be second-in-command of Pharaoh's government. Note his reaction to the brothers who had sold him into slavery. He gives them food and refuses to charge them for it, putting the money back in their sacks. He forgives them with tears, intercedes for them with Pharaoh, and purchases the best land in the Nile delta so that they may live there. They had thrown him out and told his father that he was dead, but here he is providing for their every need.

Joseph is unspoiled either by humiliation or by honour. He is a man of total integrity and the only one so presented in the Old Testament. All the Old Testament characters are presented with their weaknesses as well as their strengths, but here is a man who only has strengths. There is only one other person in the Bible who is like this.

There is one chapter in the middle of the story of Joseph that comes as a shock. It is about his brother Judah. In the middle of the story about this good man there comes a stark contrast with his own brother Judah. Judah visits a woman he thinks is a prostitute, but who is actually his daughter-in-law with a veil on. He takes part in incest and the sordid story is told right in the middle of the Joseph narrative. Why is it there? It is there because it serves to highlight Joseph's integrity by contrast. Just as Abraham was contrasted with Lot, Isaac with Ishmael and Jacob with Esau, so Joseph is contrasted with Judah.

4. A REFLECTION OF JESUS

So far we have discussed this story at three levels: the human story of a man who was taken all the way down to the bottom and then climbed right up to the top, and who became the saviour of his people and the Lord of Egypt; the story of God's overruling of this man's life, using it to save his people; and finally the story of a man of total integrity, who all the way down and all the way up remained a man of truth and honest goodness.

Each level of the story reminds us of another: Jesus himself. Joseph becomes what is known as a *type* of Jesus. 'Type' in this sense means 'foreshadowing'. It is as if God is showing us in the life of Joseph what he is going to do with his own son. Like Joseph, his own son would be rejected by his brethren and taken all the way down to utter humiliation, then raised to be 'Saviour' and 'Lord' of his people.

Once we recognize the 'type', the comparisons are remarkable. The more we read the story of Joseph the more we see this picture of Jesus, as if God knew all along what he was going to do and was giving hints to his people. Jesus himself encouraged the Jews to 'search the Scriptures, for they bear witness of me', referring to the Old Testament. As we read the Old Testament we should always be looking for Jesus, for his likeness, for his shadow. Jesus himself is the substance, but his shadow falls right across the pages of the Old Testament, especially in Genesis.

Jesus in Genesis

Once we have seen that Joseph is a picture of Jesus, we can see Jesus in many other places throughout Genesis. Joseph is a model of God's response to faith in him, and his story demonstrates how God can take a person's life and use him to deliver his people from their need, lifting him up to be Saviour and Lord.

GENEALOGIES

The genealogies in Genesis are in fact the genealogy of our Lord Jesus Christ. If you read Matthew 1 and Luke 3 you will find in the genealogies there names from the book of Genesis. Jesus is of the line of Seth, which comes straight down to the son of Mary. Thus anyone who is in Christ is also reading their own family tree. These are the most important ancestors we have, because through faith in Christ we have become sons of Abraham.

ISAAC

When we examine the characters in Genesis we can see similarities to Jesus. We have noted Joseph already, but let us go back to the time when Abraham was told to offer Isaac as a sacrifice. He was told to go to a specific mountain called Moriah. Years later that same mountain was known as Golgotha, the place where God sacrificed his only son. Genesis 22 tells us that Isaac was Abraham's only beloved son – and we have seen already how Isaac was in his early thirties by then, strong enough to resist his father, but he submitted to being bound and put on the altar.

God stopped Abraham at the crucial point and provided another sacrifice, a ram with its head caught in thorns. Centuries later John the Baptist would say of Jesus, 'Behold the "ram" of God that takes away the sins of the world'. The word 'lamb' is often applied to Jesus, but little, cuddly lambs were never offered for sacrifice – the sacrifices were one-year-old rams with horns. Jesus is depicted in the book of Revelation as the ram with seven horns signifying strength – 'a ram of God'. God provided a ram for Abraham to offer in place of his son, a ram with his head caught in the thorns, and God also announced a new name to himself: 'I am always your provider'. At that same spot another young man in his early thirties was sacrificed with his head caught in thorns. Do you see there a picture of Jesus?

MELCHIZEDEK

It is also worth looking carefully at a strange encounter Abraham had with a man who was both a king and a priest. He was king over the city of Salem (which later became Jerusalem). When Abraham was on his way back from rescuing his family after they had been kidnapped, he arrived with the spoils from the enemy near the city of Salem. This was then a pagan city, nothing to do with Abraham's Godly line. He was met by the strange figure of Melchizedek, who was both a priest and a king, a very unusual combination, never found in Israel. This 'King Priest' brought out bread and wine as refreshments for Abraham and his troops and Abraham gave him a tenth of all the spoils of the battle, a tithe of the treasure. In the New Testament we are told that Jesus is a priest forever in the order of Melchizedek.

JACOB'S LADDER

And what about Jacob's ladder? When Jacob ran away
from home he slept outside at night with his head on a stone
and dreamt of a ladder (actually more like an escalator). The
Hebrew implies that the ladder was moving, and that there was
one ladder moving up and one ladder moving down, with
angels ascending and descending. Jacob knew that at the top
of the ladders was heaven, where God lived.

When he woke he promised to give a tenth of everything
he made to God. The giving of tithes was not part of the law
until the time of Moses. (Jacob's offer of a tenth of his possessions was more in the nature of a bargain with God: you bring
me back home safely and I will give you a tithe. It is not, however, possible to bargain with God – God makes a covenant
with you, not the other way round – and Jacob had to learn
that the hard way later.)

Centuries later, when Jesus met a man called Nathaniel, he
said to Nathaniel, 'I saw you sitting under the fig tree. I noticed
you and you are a Jew in whom there is no guile, no deceit.'
Nathaniel asked him how he knew this. Jesus replied, 'You
think that is wonderful, that I know the details of your life.
What will you think if you see angels ascending and descending
on the son of man?' He is saying, 'I am Jacob's ladder, I am the
link between earth and heaven. I am the new ladder.'

ADAM AND EVE

Further back, in Genesis 3, God made a promise in the middle
of his punishment of Adam and Eve. He said to the serpent
that the seed – or offspring – of the woman (seed is masculine
in the Hebrew) would bruise the serpent's head, even while the
serpent bruised the offspring's heel. Bruising a heel is not fatal,
but bruising a head is and this is the very first promise that

God would one day deal Satan a fatal blow. We now know who it was who bound the strong man and spoilt his goods.

In Romans 5, Paul tells us that as one man's disobedience brought death, so one man's obedience brought life, implying that Jesus is a second Adam. It was in the Garden of Eden that Adam said 'I won't' and it was in the Garden of Gethsemane that Jesus said 'not my will but yours be done'. What a contrast! They each began a human race: Adam was the first man of the *homo sapiens* race; Jesus was the first of the *homo novus*.

We are all born *homo sapiens*, and through God we can become *homo novus*. The New Testament talks about the new man, the new humanity. There are two human races on earth today: you are either in Adam or you are in Christ. There is a whole new human race and it is going to inhabit a totally new planet earth – indeed a whole new universe.

CREATION

One of the most remarkable things said about Jesus in the New Testament is that he was responsible for the creation of the universe. The early disciples came to see that Jesus was involved in the events of Genesis 1. As John said at the start of his Gospel, 'without him nothing was made that has been made'.

When we read Genesis 1, therefore, we find that Jesus was there. God said, 'Let us make man in our image'. Jesus was part of the plurality of the Godhead.

We have known for several decades now that the earth's surface is on flat plates of rock floating on molten rock, and that these plates are constantly moving, rubbing against each other to cause earthquakes. When it was discovered that these plates moved to form the land masses we have today, the scientists needed to coin a new word for the plates. They called them 'tectonic plates'. In Greek the word *tectone* means 'carpenter'.

The whole planet earth on which we live is the work of a carpenter from Nazareth – and his name is the Lord Jesus Christ!

So we finish our studies in Genesis where we began, with creation. God is indeed answering his problem of what to do when humans rebel. The solution is Jesus Christ, through whom the world came to be, for whom it was made, and by whom we discover the answer to all our questions.

3.

EXODUS

Introduction

Exodus is the story of the biggest escape in history. Over two million slaves escape from one of the most highly fortified nations in the entire world. It is humanly impossible, an extraordinary story, and it features a series of miracles, including some of the best known in the whole Bible. The leader of the Israelites at the time was a man named Moses. He saw more miracles than Abraham, Isaac and Jacob put together – in some places a number following one after another as God intervened on behalf of his people. Some of the miracles sound a bit like magic, for example when Moses' stick turns into a snake, but most of them are clear manipulations of nature, as God proves his power over all that he has made for the good of his people.

The original Hebrew title for Exodus was 'These are the names', these being the first words of the book to appear on the scroll when the priest came to read them. Our name 'Exodus' comes from the Greek *ex-hodos* – literally *ex*: 'out', *hoddos*: 'way' (similar to the Latin word *exit*), 'the way out'.

The whole event of the Exodus had a profound significance on two fronts.

1. National

First, it had national significance for the people of Israel. It marked the beginning of their national history. They received their political freedom and became a sovereign nation in their own right. Though they did not yet have a land they were a nation with a name of their own: 'Israel'. So central was this event that ever since then its celebration has been written into their national calendar. Just as Americans celebrate their independence on 4 July, so every March/April the Jews celebrate the Exodus. They eat the Passover meal and recount the mighty acts of God.

2. Spiritual

Second, it had spiritual significance. The Israelites discovered that their God was the God who made the whole universe and could control what he had made for their sake. They came to believe that their God was more powerful than all the gods of Egypt put together. Later they would come to realize that their God was the only God who existed (see especially the prophecies of Isaiah).

The truth that God was more powerful than every other god was made clear by the name which God gave to himself. His 'formal' title was El-Shaddai, God Almighty, but it is in the book of Exodus that the nation was given his personal name. Just as knowing a person's name enables a human relationship to become more intimate, when they discovered God's name Israel could enter into a more intimate relationship with him.

In English we translate the name as 'Yahweh', though there are no vowels in the Hebrew – strictly speaking it should simply be Y H W H. The name is a participle of the verb 'to be'. We saw in our study of Genesis that 'always' is an English word which communicates how the Jews would have understood it.

God is the eternal one without beginning or end – 'always'. This is his first name, but he has many second names too: 'Always my provider', 'Always my helper', 'Always my protector', 'Always my healer'.

In the book of Exodus we are also presented with the extraordinary truth that the creator of everything becomes the redeemer of a few people. The word 'redemption' includes the idea of releasing the kidnapped when the ransom price has been paid. This is how Israel was to understand her God. He was the creator of the universe and also the redeemer of his people. Both aspects are important if we are to learn to know God as he is revealed in the Bible.

The book

Exodus is one of the five books which Moses wrote. Genesis deals with events before his lifetime and Exodus, Leviticus, Numbers and Deuteronomy tell of events during his lifetime. These books are crucial to the life of Israel as they record the foundations of the nation. They are also foundational to the whole Old Testament. This group of slaves needed to know who they were and how they came to be a nation.

We saw in our study of Genesis how Moses collected two things from the people's memories: *genealogies* and *stories about their ancestors*. The book of Genesis is entirely made up of such memories. Exodus, Leviticus, Numbers and Deuteronomy are different, comprising a mixture of narrative and legislation. The narrative describes the Israelites' move from Egypt through the wilderness and into the land of Canaan. The legislation reflects what God said to them concerning how they should live. It is this unique combination of narrative and legislation that characterizes these other four books of Moses.

Exodus itself is part narrative and part legislation. The first half details what God did on the Israelites' behalf to get them out of slavery. The second half describes what God said about how they were to live now that they were free. The first half demonstrates God's grace towards them in getting them out of their problems. The second half shows that God expects them to show their gratitude for that grace by living his way. This emphasis is important. Too many people read the law of Moses thinking that it shows how they can be accepted by God. They get it the wrong way round. The people of Israel were redeemed by God, *then* they were given the law to keep as an expression of gratitude. This principle is the same in the New Testament: Christians are redeemed and *then* told how to live holy lives. To use theological jargon, justification comes before sanctification. We do not become Christians by living right first, but by being redeemed and liberated and then living right. *The liberation comes before the legislation*.

In Exodus the Israelites' liberation takes place in Egypt and the legislation takes place at Mount Sinai, as they travel to Canaan. Here they respond to God's covenant commitment to them. The covenant takes the form of a wedding service. God says 'I will' (be your God if you obey me) and then the people have to say 'We will' (be your people and obey you).

STRUCTURE

As well as there being two halves to the book of Exodus, there are ten different portions within it: six sections in Chapters 1–18 and four in Chapters 19–40. They can be arranged as shown in the following table.

Chapters 1–18
(people mobile)
Key themes
DIVINE DEEDS
GRACE
LIBERATION
FROM EGYPT
SLAVERY(men)
REDEMPTION

The sections
1. **1** Multiplication and murder

(ISRAEL)
2. **2–3** Bulrushes and burning bush
(MOSES)
3. **5–11** Plague and pestilence

(PHARAOH)
4. **12–13:16** Feast and first-born

(PASSOVER)
5. **13:17–15:21** Delivered and drowned
(RED SEA)
6. **15:22–18:27** Provided and protected
(WILDERNESS)

Chapters 19–40
(people stationary)
Key themes
DIVINE WORDS
GRATITUDE
LEGISLATION
TO SINAI
SERVICE (God)
RIGHTEOUSNESS

The sections
7. **19–24** Commandments and covenant
(SINAI)
8. **25–31** Specification and specialists
(TABERNACLE)
9. **32–34** Indulgence and intercession
(GOLDEN CALF)
10. **35–40** Construction and consecration
(TABERNACLE)

The first part (Chapters 1–18) details the events preceding and following their flight from Egypt. It includes many miracles, including the most famous, how the Israelites were protected when the first-born of Egypt were killed, and how they were able to pass through the Red Sea. It also includes the less famous but no less remarkable provision of God as they journey from Egypt to Sinai. During the Yom Kippur war of 1973 the Egyptian army was unable to last more than three days in the desert, yet in Exodus 2.5 million people survived there for 40 years.

In the second part the focus is on legislation. The Ten Commandments appear first, but there is also other legislation concerned with God's intention to live among his people. Just as they lived in tents, so God would join them in their camp. But his own tent would be distinct and separate from theirs. These people had never made anything but mud bricks until that point, but God gave them the skills to work with gold, silver and wood.

The second part does also include some narrative. Here we read the saddest part of the whole book, as the people indulge themselves and make a golden calf to worship. The book finishes with the construction of the tabernacle. God takes up residence and the glory comes down on his tent.

Chapters 1–18

Many perceive the first part of Exodus to be full of problems because it is such an unnatural story. There are so many extraordinary events that many people suggest that what we have here is a series of legends rather than truth. So, are the events described part of a myth or a miracle?

Myth or miracle?

1. NO SECULAR RECORD

The problem is not just with the nature of the events them-selves, but also with the fact that the events are not backed up by any secular, historical record. All we have is just one men-tion of 'the habiru' in Goshen – a possible reference to the 'Hebrews', as the 'children of Israel' were known. This lack of documentation should not surprise us, however. The Exodus of the Jews was one of the most humiliating events in Egypt's experience. They suffered severe plagues, including the death of their first-born. Their best charioteers were drowned in the Red Sea. This hardly made for comforting reflection.

2. THE NUMBERS INVOLVED

Many people find the story hard to believe due to the large numbers involved. We are told there were 2.5 million slaves who left Egypt. By any reckoning this is a huge number. If they marched five abreast, the column would be about 110 miles long, and that does not include the livestock. It would take months for them to move anywhere. It is also a huge popula-tion to keep fed and watered in a desert for 40 years.

3. THE DATE

There is also a question about the dating of the events. As we have no other record outside the Bible we cannot date the events with any certainty. So we do not know for sure which Pharaoh was involved and when it all took place. The choice seems to be between Rameses II, who had a powerful military force, who erected huge statues of himself and whose sons' tomb has only recently been discovered, and Dudimore, according to the 'new chronology' of David M. Rohl.*

(see footnote overleaf).

4. THE ROUTE

There is controversy concerning the route which the Israelites took when they left Egypt, too. There are three possibilities to consider: a route to the north, a route to the south, or one through the middle. We will come back to this question on page 113.

5. THE DIVINE NAME

Other scholars find problems with God's words to Moses in Exodus 6:3 where he says: 'I am the LORD. I appeared to Abraham, to Isaac and to Jacob as God Almighty, but by my name the LORD I did not make myself known to them.'

That last phrase may either be a statement ('...I did not make myself known...'), in which case Abraham knew him as 'God', but without a personal name distinguishing him from other gods; or a question ('...did I not make myself known...?'), in which case Abraham knew God by name as well as Moses. The latter is less likely.

THE FACTS

All these questions have made scholars doubt whether they are reading fact, fiction or perhaps 'faction'. Those who do not believe the events need to ask why they cannot. Is it prejudice or a so-called scientific view of the universe which prevents them believing? At the same time we can also try to look for the most understandable explanation for the facts which are indisputable.

1. Nobody can dispute that there is a nation called Israel in the world today. So where did they come from? How did

---

* See *A Test of Time* (BCA, 1996), and *Legend* (BCA, 1988) for this Egyptologist's remarkable claims to have discovered evidence for Joseph's time in Egypt, Moses' liberation and, even further back, the location of the Garden of Eden!

they get started? How did they ever become a nation if they were originally a bunch of slaves? We do know from secular records that they were a bunch of slaves. Something dramatic is needed to explain the existence of Israel.

2. Every year, every Jewish family celebrates the Passover. Why do they do it? This is a ritual which has survived for many thousands of years and also needs some explanation.

These two known facts at least need explanation, therefore, and it is the book of Exodus which provides the answers. So let us look at each section, following the structure laid out in the table above, and consider some of the questions surrounding the text.

1. Multiplication and murder

In this opening section we discover that the number of Hebrew slaves must have been around 2.5 million by the time the Exodus narrative starts. This may seem a large number given that they started with just the 12 sons of Jacob, their offspring and wider family. But if each family had four children (not a large number in those days) over 30 generations then this number could be achieved.

But why did they stay in Egypt for 400 years when they only went there for seven originally? They first arrived in the time of Joseph and Jacob following a famine in Canaan. (Egypt was the bread-basket of the Middle East thanks to Joseph's judicious storing of grain during the seven years of plenty.) They arrive voluntarily, are accepted as guests of the government and are given a fertile piece of the Nile delta called Goshen to live on together. So they remain a nation during the seven years of famine. But at the end of that time why did they not go back to their own land? This is a pertinent question, given that they are eventually forced to become slaves in Egypt.

The human reason is that they were very comfortable. It was much easier to make a living in the Nile delta than it was on the hills of Judea. The land was fertile, the climate was warmer, with no snow in winter as there was in the hills of Judea. The diet was good, they could eat fish from the Nile and look after themselves far better. So they stayed because they were comfortable. It was only when they were forced to become slaves that they remembered God and started crying out to him.

There is also a divine reason. God did not do anything to encourage them to go back to their own land for 400 years. If they had returned as soon as the famine was over, they would have been only a few people, far too small a number to accomplish what God intended. For it was God's intention to remove the people of Canaan from the land. He explained to Abraham that his descendants would stay in Egypt until the wickedness of the Canaanites was completed. God had to wait until they became so bad that it would be an act of justice and judgement to throw them out of the Promised Land and let the Hebrew slaves in. We read in Deuteronomy that it was not any virtue on the part of the Israelites which made God choose them. Indeed, if they behaved in the land like those they had expelled, they too would have to leave. To be instruments of justice they had to be righteous themselves.

But all that was to come later. As slaves in Egypt, the people of Israel faced three oppressive decrees:

1. Forced labour: the Pharaoh decided to use the Hebrews as labour for his building programmes.

2. Tougher conditions: they had to make bricks without straw (which meant the bricks were much heavier to carry). Archaeological digs within Egypt have discovered buildings made of three different types of brick: the foundations with straw, the middle with rubbish, as the Hebrews sought to continue making light bricks once denied the straw, and then on the top bricks made entirely of clay. The idea behind this harsh decree was that the extra weight of the bricks would make the Hebrews too tired for sex or mischief and so their population would decrease. It was a crude form of population control and it did not work, so the Egyptians had to introduce a third decree.

3. Death: all the baby boys born to the Hebrew slaves had to be thrown to the crocodiles in the River Nile.

2. Bulrushes and the burning bush

Most people know this story well. The River Nile was full of crocodiles and this form of genocide was considered necessary by the Egyptians if Israelite numbers were to be effectively reduced. The baby Moses should have died in this way. But we note that under God's providence Moses, like Joseph, was brought up at court and given the best education at the Egyptian university. This, of course, made him far better educated than any of the Hebrew slaves, and enabled him to write the first five books of the Bible. For the Jews Moses was the second greatest man in Old Testament – after Abraham. His time as an Egyptian prince came to a sudden end, however, when he lost his temper with one of the Egyptian slave drivers and killed him, after which he had to flee for his life.

The statistics of Moses' life make interesting reading. At the age of 40, he spent 40 years tending sheep in the very wilderness to which he would return to live for 40 years with the people of Israel! This was clearly God's hand at work.

Moses' meeting with the Lord through the burning bush is also intriguing, not so much for the bush as for Moses' excuses. God first told Moses to take off his shoes because he was on holy ground. Then he told Moses that he was going to be the man to draw God's people out of Egypt. Moses made five excuses as to why he should not do it.

First he said he was *insignificant*. God said he would be with him – he was the important one. Next he said that he was *ignorant* and had nothing to say. God told him that he would tell Moses what to say. His third excuse was that he would be *impotent* to convince the people that God had met with him and told him to lead them. God said that his power was going to be with Moses and he would perform miracles. Then Moses said that he was *incompetent* at speaking, having a stammer which would prevent him putting words together. So God provided his brother Aaron to be his spokesman. God would tell Moses what to say and he would relay it to Aaron. Finally Moses said that he was *irrelevant* – please would God send someone else? But God had provided Aaron as a partner: they would work together. Each time Moses' questioning focuses upon his weakness, and each time God has an answer.

3. Plague and pestilence

Ten plagues are mentioned in this section: the Nile turned to blood, the plague of frogs, the plague of gnats and mosquitoes, the plague of flies, the cattle disease, the boils, the hail storm, the plague of locusts, the darkness over the land and, finally, the death of the first-born.

There are a number of things to notice, and the first is that God is in total control of the insect world. God can tell mosquitoes and locusts what to do and where to go, just as he can tell frogs what to do. The plagues give a tremendous sense of God's control over what he has created.

It is also interesting to note how the plagues increase in intensity. There is a build-up from discomfort to disease to danger to death. There is also a movement from plagues affecting nature to plagues affecting people. The afflictions gradually get worse as Pharaoh and the Egyptian people refuse to respond to the warnings. Some see the final punishment as unfair – is the killing of the first-born not far too excessive and harsh? But the Egyptians had done worse to the Israelites, killing all their baby boys, so this retribution was thoroughly appropriate.

It is easy, too, to miss the religious contest that takes place during the plagues. Every one of those plagues was an attack on a particular god worshipped by the Egyptians:

Khuum: the guardian of the Nile
Hapi: the spirit of the Nile
Osiris: the Nile was believed to be the bloodstream of Osiris
Heqt: a frog-like god of resurrection
Hathor: a mother goddess who was a cow
Apis: a bull of the god Ptah, a symbol of fertility
Minevis: also a bull, the sacred bull of Heliopolis
Imhotep: the god of medicine
Nut: the sky goddess
Seth: the protector of crops
Re, Aten, Atum and Horus: all sun gods
Pharaoh was also said to be divine

The plagues were specifically directed against these Egyptian gods. The message was very simple: the God of the Hebrew slaves is far more powerful than all your gods put together.

Some see a problem with what we are told in this section of narrative about Pharaoh's heart. We read that God hardened Pharaoh's heart. Some have even erected a doctrine of predestination on this passage and verses in Romans 9 where Paul talks about God hardening Pharaoh's heart. They suggest that the passage teaches that it is up to God to choose whether he softens or hardens someone's heart. Advocates of this view argue that we do not know why God makes these choices, but whatever the reason, in the case of Pharaoh he decided he was going to harden his heart. It is as if God picks names out of a hat and decides to save some and send others to hell, to harden some and soften others.

This is not what the Bible teaches, however. If you study the text carefully you find that Pharaoh's heart was hardened ten times. On the first seven occasions Pharaoh hardens his own heart, in the next three God hardens Pharaoh's heart. So God only hardens Pharaoh's heart after Pharaoh has deliberately and repeatedly hardened his own heart. He confirms the choice that Pharaoh has made. This is the way God punishes: he helps people along the road they are determined to travel. In Revelation God says, 'Let him that is filthy be filthy still.' So there is no arbitrary choice about God's dealings with Pharaoh – he hardens his own heart first and then God hardens it for him. God responds to our choices. If we persistently choose the wrong way, God will help us along that route. He will demonstrate his judgement if we refuse to be a demonstration of his mercy.

4. Feast and first-born

The tenth plague was that every first-born boy in every Egyptian family would die. This was the pivotal plague to the whole drama. The tragedy would also happen to the Jews unless they followed God's instructions. They were to paint the blood of a lamb on their doorposts. The angel of death would come to Egypt that night and pass over the houses displaying the mark. For the other households, death would take place at midnight. Interestingly, blood is a scarlet/maroon colour, the hardest colour to see in the dark.

The blood had additional significance: the Jews were to slaughter a one-year-old ram, fully mature, and after they had put its blood on their doorposts they were to take it inside for roasting. So they were both covered by it and fed by it. When we call Jesus the 'lamb of God' it can suggest a softer, more docile image than the Bible intends, for he is actually the '*ram* of God', which gives a more robust picture. The Jews were to eat the meat standing up, dressed and ready to leave at a moment's notice. They were told to take emergency rations of unleavened bread. They were to leave Egypt that very night.

The Jews continue to keep the feast of the Passover to this day. At a particular moment in the evening, the youngest member of the family has to ask, 'What does all this mean?' The oldest member of the family replies, 'This is what God did on the night when every first-born boy died and we were saved because of the blood of the ram.' Thus they are reminded that the first-born needs to be redeemed in every generation.

5. Delivered and drowned

There are three possibilities for the route taken by the Israelites when they left Egypt, indicated on the map overleaf.

The first is known as the northern route. This suggests that they went through a row of sandbanks in a shallow part of the Mediterranean. Maps of Egypt show sandbanks marked at a place called Lake Sirbonis. Their route then takes them to Kadesh Barnea. But they could not have been followed by the Egyptian chariots across the sandbanks, so this seems unlikely.

The second theory is that they went straight across through the Mitler Pass to Kadesh. But there was a line of fortresses (where the Suez Canal is today) built across there, against any invasion from the east. So the Israelites would have

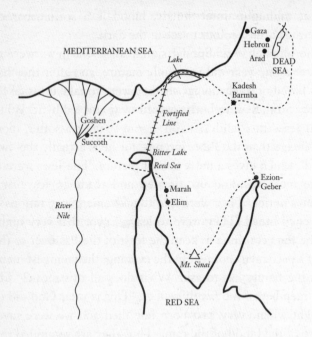

had to get through that line of fortresses. They were not armed and able to fight, so this route is very unlikely also.

The third possibility was the southern route down to Mount Sinai, where Moses had been a shepherd for 40 years. This is the most likely, for Moses knew this country. The location of Mount Sinai is uncertain, but all the tradition in the Middle East puts Sinai in the south. The Israelites left Goshen and came south. Pharaoh would only let them go into the desert, thinking that he could always bring them back from there. Having camped, they were hidden from the Egyptians by a cloud God had sent.

As regards the actual crossing of the sea, the Bible does not say that God divided the Red Sea, but that he sent an east wind which divided the water. But how could an east wind divide a sea?

If we were to examine the area in detail we would see that years ago the Great Bitter Lakes were actually joined up to what we call the Red Sea (see diagram below). They were joined up by a shallow, marshy channel called the 'Reed Sea' and in fact the Hebrew suggests the 'Reed Sea' is a more likely name than the 'Red Sea'. The fortified line came right down to the Bitter Lake.

If this was where the Hebrews crossed, there are two natural forces which could have divided the sea. A strong east wind could drive the water to the west end of the Great Bitter Lake, an ebb tide also pulling it south.

This does not explain the miracle at all. How did the east wind just happen to come at the right time? In looking at it in such a down-to-earth way, we are not trying to explain away the miracle. Rather we are showing that it is a miracle of 'coincidence'. In fact, the Bible tells us that there is no such thing as 'coincidence', but only 'providence'.

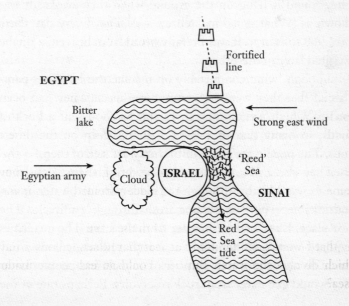

The most striking fact about this crossing of the Red Sea or Reed Sea is that it happened on the third day after the Passover lamb was killed. The Israelites' liberation came on the third day after the Passover lamb. Furthermore, the book of Exodus tells us the very hour when the Passover lamb had to be slaughtered: 3.00 p.m. On the third day after that the Israelites finally escape. They are free of Pharaoh and will never see him again. We will note later some parallels with events in the New Testament.

6. Provided and protected

The desert region over which the Israelites travelled was unable to support human life. It was not the ideal place to take 2.5 million people plus animals.

There were both external and internal problems for Moses, therefore, the most basic being the physical need for food and water. Every morning God provided food for them. They found it lying on the ground when they awoke. It was known as 'What is it?' in Hebrew – *Manna*. Every day there were 900 tons of it. It was literally bread from heaven, a theme revisited later in the Bible.

Though living comfortably on manna, the Israelites complained that they were not getting any meat. They had been used to a high-protein diet in Egypt. So God sent a flock of quails, so many that they lay 1.5 metres deep on the desert floor. The people ate quails until they were sick of them!

They also had a problem with water. The first oasis they came to was Marah. Although the place provided water, it was undrinkable – until it became fresh through a miracle. The next place, Elim, had fresh water from the start. The quantities required were considerable – at least 2 million gallons a day would be needed for that number of animals and people. Later they would get water from rock reservoirs. Perhaps one of the biggest miracles of their providential journey was that their sandals never wore out. Rocks even today wreck rubber tyres on vehicles, yet these sandals lasted 40 years!

Moses also faced internal difficulties. Given the enormous numbers, it is no wonder that one of the biggest problems Moses had was judging disputes between the people. We are told that this could go on all day, to the point where Moses became exhausted. It needed his father-in-law Jethro to suggest a delegation of responsibility, whereby Moses appointed 70 elders to assist in the work.

Chapters 19–40

After the narrative of the escape from Egypt, the second part of Exodus turns more towards legislation, the commandments God gave his people, telling them how they were to live, and the covenant he made with them.

7. Commandments and covenant

There are three 'legal' collections in the second half of Exodus. The best known is the 'Ten Commandments' (or decalogue, which means '10 words'), written with God's finger on two tablets of stone. (Most modern pictures of the event depict Moses returning from Mount Sinai with the Ten Commandments split between the two tablets, five on one and five on the other, but actually all 10 were on each stone.) This was a legal contract, in keeping with similar treaties agreed at that time. A conquering king might make a treaty with a vanquished nation, for example. Each party would have a copy. In the case of the Ten Commandments, one copy was God's and one copy was the people's. This treaty was special, however, known in the Bible as a 'covenant'. A covenant was not a *bargain* between two parties but a *contract* written by God which could be either accepted or rejected by the people.

The Ten Commandments formed the first legal collection and this was followed by what is known as the 'Book of the Covenant', which can be found in Exodus 20:23–23:33. This deals with laws relating to community life. The third collection is the book of laws in Chapters 25–31, which centre on the worshipping life of Israel and are concerned with the place of worship and those conducting worship. Overlap and expansion of these laws is found in Deuteronomy. Thus there are not just Ten Commandments, but a total of 613 rules and regulations about the way to live right before God.

It is crucial to underline the importance of the *context* of the laws in Exodus. The Ten Commandments and the Book of the Covenant are sandwiched between two links which refer to the past and the future.

1. In 20:2 God says, 'I am the LORD your God, who brought you out of Egypt, out of the land of slavery.'
2. In 23:20–33 God assures the people of his presence in the future and of the provision of land, providing they keep to his ways.

The first text refers back to Egypt and the second passage focuses on entering Canaan in the future. The context tells us that these laws from God are for people who have experienced his *past* and are expecting his *future* and who will therefore be able to live in his *present*.

King Alfred based the British legal system on the Ten Commandments, but it is hard to see how people can understand them if they have not experienced redemption. They must be seen in the proper context.

THE TEN COMMANDMENTS

A closer look at the Ten Commandments and the accompanying legislation reveals three basic principles which are enshrined there. First is the principle of **respect**. All the Ten Commandments are based on this – respect for God, respect for his name, respect for his day, respect for people, respect for family life, respect for life itself, respect for marriage, respect for people's property, respect for people's reputation.

The message is clear: a healthy, holy society is built on respect. So much of society today, especially the mass media, sets out to destroy respect. Television comedy often encourages an irreverent view of life so that nothing is regarded as sacred. Everything and everyone is a potential figure of fun. But it is clear that the loss of respect for God leads to idolatry, and the loss of respect for people leads to immorality and injustice.

Most of the Ten Commandments are about acts or words, but the last of the ten is about feelings – it is the only one about the heart. Perhaps this is why the apostle Paul said in Romans 7 that he had kept the first nine but he could not manage the tenth, the commandment about greed. For when we desire something we do not have, our problem is with our inner life. If you break one law you have broken them all. They all belong together like a necklace, and if you break a necklace just once the beads are all lost. In reality there are not ten separate commandments. They are all one law.

The second principle is **responsibility**. Increasingly we are taught that we are not responsible for our actions, even down to the claim that wickedness is due to genetics! We know that original sin is transferred through the genes, but the idea that some people are more wicked than others because they have a wrong gene leads to the view that people are not responsible for what they do. Exodus stands directly opposed to that view.

The Lord God says we are responsible before him for how we live with regard to his law.

The third principle is **retribution**. There are three reasons for punishment under the law. The first is *reformation*: punishment is intended to make the wrongdoer better. The second is *deterrence*: the idea being that observing others being punished works as a warning to other would-be malefactors. The third is *retribution*: the punishment occurs simply because the person deserves it, with no necessary concern for whether others heed the warning or the guilty party learns from his errors. This third principle of retribution is enshrined in the Exodus laws.

Capital punishment is applied to 18 different sins against God, from murder to breaking the Sabbath. These also include kidnapping, cursing or assaulting parents, and occasions when a person's uncontrolled animal causes death.

There is a very careful distinction in God's law between *intentional* and *accidental* death. There are two sorts of killing: intentional murder and accidental manslaughter. One carries the death penalty, the other a less severe punishment. In every case we are told that there is no sacrifice in the Mosaic law for continued deliberate, intentional sin. Indeed, if you read Hebrews you will find the same thing being said in the New Testament.

It is worth noting that the denial of personal freedom through imprisonment is not an option under the law. Nowhere in the Bible is this form of punishment argued. There was, however, a clear system of *restitution*, a system of compensation for those who had been injured. This is the *lex talionis*, known today by the shorthand expression 'an eye for an eye and a tooth for a tooth'. If, for example, a pregnant woman is attacked and the baby she carries is born with a deformity resulting from the attack, the guilty party will be handicapped in the same way as the victim. In other cases there was a system of repayment in kind or cash when property was damaged or stolen.

8. Specification and specialists

SPECIFICATIONS

Next we come to the extraordinary fact that God wanted to live with Israel. He had already made his holiness very clear. When the law was given on Mount Sinai, God wanted the Israelites to be sure what his holiness meant. God said that no one could touch his holy mountain and live. Moses erected a fence around the bottom. The giving of the law was accompanied by thunder, lightning and fire, indicating God's power and separateness from man.

But having emphasized his separateness, God then tells Moses that he wants to come down and live in the camp with them. Wherever they camp he wants to be there at the heart of his people. It will be in a tent in the middle of the camp and it must be a tent which communicates his holiness, so that the people will worship him respectfully.

This tent was called the 'tabernacle' and Exodus gives us the building specifications which God laid down, in the laws concerning the religious life of Israel (Chapters 25–31). Everything about the tabernacle was to speak of God and the right approach to him. It was to be located in the centre of the camp, with the 12 tribes arranged in sequence around it.

SPECIALISTS

To use it

Most importantly, the tabernacle was not readily accessible, despite being in the middle of the camp. To begin with there was a fence 100 cubits by 25, high enough to prevent an outsider looking in. The fence had just one opening situated

The Tabernacle

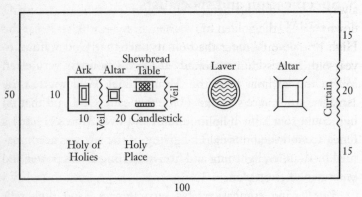

opposite the tribe of Judah. Inside the fence was a courtyard with an *altar* and a *laver*.

The first approach to God, therefore, would be through sacrifice: the animal would be slaughtered and then burnt on the altar in offering to the Lord. Then the worshipper would cleanse his hands in the copper laver between the altar and the holy place. Only then could God's tent be approached. The tent had two sections, the place where God actually lived being a smaller part of the larger tent, a place shut off from human view and visited just once a year by the High Priest.

The larger part was 10 yards by 20 yards and was known as the *holy place*. Only priests were allowed to enter and then only if they had sacrificed an animal and cleansed their hands in the laver. It had three pieces of furniture. There was a table with *shewbread*, 12 loaves representing the 12 tribes of Israel. There was also a seven-branch candlestick lit by holy oil burning continually, and another altar for sacrifice next to a veil.

The veil hid an area 10 yards by 10 yards, *the holy of holies*: the place where God dwelt. In the holy of holies was a chest and above the chest were two cherubim. In the Bible, cherubim are always angels of judgement. Here they are described as looking downwards to the golden top of the mercy seat. Once a year the High Priest would enter the holy of holies and sacrifice a one-year-old, spotless ram as atonement for the people. Also located in the holy of holies was the ark of the covenant, containing some manna and the books of the law. There was no natural light within the holy of holies, yet it was always radiantly bright. God dwelt there and his glory lit the place.

The beauty of the tabernacle must have been breathtaking, but most of it was hidden. There were beautifully embroidered curtains and coverings, but all were covered with a badger's skin, hiding the beauty from the people. Inside were golden pieces of furniture and curtains embroidered in blue (the colour of heaven), red (the colour of blood), silver and gold.

The whole structure indicated that if you wished to come to God you must make a sacrifice first in order to be clean. God said that this was a copy of where he lived in heaven.

Even when this tent was dismantled and moved, all the elements were kept covered up. The tent had to be carried by specified people and the 'ordinary' people had to keep a thousand paces away from it until it was erected again.

The holiness of God is also emphasized in the clothes of the priests. The High Priest was given specific instructions regarding what he was to wear. He wore 12 jewels on his chest representing the 12 tribes of Israel. These jewels are mentioned again on the last page of the Bible, which describes the New Jerusalem. The High Priest also wore a special girdle, turban, robe, ephod and coat.

The ordinary priests also had 'robes of office', but their requirements included only special coats, girdles, caps and

breeches. We can discern in these different robes a picture of
the one to come who would be the High Priest for ever on
behalf of his people.

To build it

Up to that point, the people's skills consisted only of construct-
ing and transporting bricks, so the task of building such an
elaborate tent would normally have been beyond them. We are
told that Bezalel, Oholiab and others were given particular
gifts by God to accomplish the building. This is the first mention of 'spiritual gifts' in the Bible, and it is interesting that it
should be in association with manual tasks such as these.

9. Indulgence and intercession

INDULGENCE

Moses was on Mount Sinai for a long time receiving the law.
Not knowing what had happened to him, the people asked
Aaron if they could worship a 'god' they could see. So with
Aaron's help they melted down their gold to make a bull calf
they could worship. The choice of animal was significant. As
we have already noted, these animals were one of many idols
used by the Egyptians. Bulls and calves were symbols of fertility and have been used as such down through history. It is a
clear principle of Scripture that idolatry leads to immorality:
loss of respect for God leads to loss of respect for people.
A wild orgy followed. When Moses came down and saw what
was going on, he smashed both copies of the law. He was symbolizing what the people had already done by their behaviour.

INTERCESSION

Moses went back up the mountain and told God that he was
fed up with the people, only to find that God was feeling just
the same. We reach a key moment in the history of Israel and a

pivotal moment in Moses' leadership. Moses told God that if he was going to blot Israel out of his book, he should be blotted out too, as he did not want to be the only one left. He was effectively saying, 'Take my life in atonement for them.' God explained that he only blots out of his book the names of those who have sinned against him, a theme picked up at various points throughout the Bible. The most important thing in life is to keep your name in the Book of Life. God said to Moses, 'I blot out of my book those who sin against me.'

Moses insisted that the people were punished and God told him to deal with the ringleaders. Three thousand died. This precise figure may mean little to us, but the details of the Exodus narrative have some amazing correspondences with events in the New Testament. The law was given on Sinai on the fiftieth day after the Passover lamb was killed. The lamb was killed at 3.00 p.m. and on the third day after that the slaves were liberated. On the fiftieth day after the Passover the law was given, a day the Jews then called Pentecost. Three thousand people died because they broke the law. It was on that same fiftieth day centuries later, when the Jews were celebrating the giving of the law, that God gave his Spirit – and this time 3,000 people were saved (see Acts 2).

10. Construction and consecration

Where did the Israelites get all the materials they needed to build the tabernacle? At least one ton of gold was needed, not to mention the cloth, linen, jewels, copper and wood. There was an average gift of a fifth of an ounce of gold from each man.

God had told Abraham many centuries before that not only would his descendants be in slavery, but when they left the land of their captivity he would bring them out with great possessions. The materials for the tabernacle and the priests' garments actually came from the Egyptians, who were so glad to see the back of the Israelites that they gave them all their jewellery. This tells us how they came to *have* the materials. They came to be *used* in the tabernacle because the people gave them, donated them for use in this way. Four words describe the nature of their giving: it was spontaneous, thoughtful, regular and sacrificial. This was not an enforced collection with penalties for those who did not give, but was purely down to the free decision of the people ('Everyone who is willing...').

At the end of Exodus we are told how God took up residence and consecrated the tent. The people saw his glory arrive and they saw the plume of smoke or cloud above the inner room. The inner room became filled with light as the glory of the Lord came into it. God was camping with his people. Thereafter, when they saw the cloud and the light move they knew it was time to move on.

Christian use of the Book of Exodus

The story of Exodus is compelling and the details of the Israelites' worship fascinating, but we must ask this: How should Christians read it today?

The first thing to say is that God has not changed. He deals with Christians in the same way as he did with the children of Israel. That is why so many of the words in Exodus are used again in the New Testament – words such as law, covenant, blood, lamb, Passover, Exodus, leaven. They are used in the New Testament but derive their meaning from the book of Exodus.

At the same time there are some significant differences. We are not now under the law of Moses but under the law of Christ. As we shall see, in some ways this makes things harder and in other ways it makes them easier.

The tabernacle is no longer necessary, for we know that Christ has provided direct access into the holy of holies. Neither are we dependent on God's provision of food and water from the sky and the rock.

There are two essential ways in which Christians need to apply Exodus today.

Christ

Christians are to seek Christ in the book of Exodus. Jesus said, 'Search the Scriptures, for they bear witness to me.' The Exodus is central to the Old Testament, and all the books which follow look back to it as the redemption on which everything else is based. In the same way the cross is central to the New Testament.

This is not a fanciful connection. Six months before Jesus died on the cross he was 4,000 feet high on top of Mount Hermon in the north of Israel, talking with Moses and Elijah. Luke's Gospel tells us that they talked about 'the exodus' which Jesus was about to accomplish in Jerusalem.

What is more, Jesus died at 3.00 p.m., the very time when thousands of Passover lambs were being slaughtered. So Christ is called 'our Passover lamb', the one who has been sacrificed for us so that the angel of death would pass over those who trust in him. He rose from the dead on the third day and his resurrection liberates us from death, just as the Hebrews were liberated from slavery on the third day after the Passover.

There are other links, too. We read in John's Gospel that Jesus is the bread from heaven. Paul says that Jesus is the rock from which Moses drew the water for the children of Israel. John also says in his Gospel that 'the word became flesh and "tabernacled among us"'. He literally pitched his tent, God in Christ dwelling in the midst of his people.

With all this in mind, we can understand Christ's words in Matthew: 'I did not come to destroy the law but to fulfil it'. In short, we cannot understand the New Testament without the Old.

Christians

The book of Exodus can also be applied to Christians. Paul, reflecting on some of the events in Exodus, writes to the church at Corinth: 'These things occurred as examples, to keep us from setting our hearts on evil things, as they did.'

The crossing of the Red Sea prefigures baptism. Paul says the children of Israel were baptized into Moses in the Red Sea and his readers had been baptized into Christ.

Christians also have a Passover meal regularly, for the Lord's Supper is a Passover meal, commemorating the liberation of Christ.

Paul speaks of keeping the feast and getting rid of the yeast or leaven because Christ the Passover lamb has been sacrificed. This seems a strange exhortation until we consider the context. He was writing to a church about the immoral behaviour of a believer who was sleeping with his stepmother. In this context the yeast stood for the evil that was taking place which needed to be got rid of if they were truly to 'keep the feast'. The Exodus account sees things in a material way, while the New Testament sees them in a moral context.

Many become especially concerned about how Christians should treat the laws given to Moses. It is true that we do not need to keep the law, but in many ways the 'Law of Christ' is much harder than the 'law of Moses'. The law of Moses says 'do not kill anybody', and 'do not commit adultery'. Many people are clear at that level, but the Law of Christ says 'do not even think about it'. It is much harder to keep the Law of Christ than the law of Moses.

On the other hand, it is much easier in some ways because now we do not need a great number of priests, rituals and special buildings. The apostle John wrote, 'For the law was given through Moses; grace and truth came through Jesus Christ.' Whenever we pray we can enter the holiest place of all unhindered in the name of Jesus.

There is a big difference, too, between the New Covenant and the Old. Under the law given at Pentecost 3,000 died, but with the Spirit given at Pentecost 3,000 lived. I would rather have the Spirit who writes the law on the heart than the old law.

The theme of glory also has a new meaning for Christians. Paul compares the fading glory of Moses with the Spirit's work in the New Covenant. Christians can know the same glory that Moses knew when he came down from the mountain. This glory, however, is not connected with altars, incense and robes but with the Spirit who indwells the believer. This glory increases day by day.

Finally, we must note the way in which the tabernacle speaks so powerfully of how we approach God today. We come first through sacrifice (the altar), justified through Christ, then we need cleansing by the Spirit (the laver). The colours of the tabernacle are significant: purple speaking of royalty, blue of heaven and white of purity. Today we have a High Priest who represents us before God, but one who needs no sacrifice for his own sins. He made the once-and-for-all sacrifice to which all the sacrifices under the Old Covenant point.

There is still to come a future deliverance for Christians equivalent to the Exodus. In Revelation we find that over half the plagues of Pharaoh are going to happen all over again. There is an astonishing correlation between the plagues at the end of history and the plagues which were visited on Pharaoh. Those who remain faithful to Jesus will come through these and be victorious. Chapter 15 of the book of Revelation says that the martyrs, and those who have overcome all the pressures of persecution outside and temptation inside, will sing the song of Moses. In Exodus 15 we have the first song recorded in the Bible, a song composed by Miriam to celebrate the drowning of the Egyptians in the Red Sea. This song will be sung when all this world's troubles are over and we are safe in glory. We will have a double exodus to celebrate – the Exodus from Egypt and the exodus of the cross.

4.

LEVITICUS

Introduction

Many people who resolve to read the Bible all the way through get stuck in Leviticus. It is easy to understand why. It is a very difficult book to read, for three main reasons.

The first is that it is quite simply a boring book – it is like trying to read the telephone directory. It is so different in content from other books of the Bible, especially the first two, which are full of stories. In these books there is a plot, there is drama, things are moving. When you get into Leviticus there is hardly any narrative at all and, since many regard the Bible as a collection of stories, it is a great disappointment to arrive at a book which has no stories of any kind.

The second reason is that it is so unfamiliar. It is from a different culture as well as having a different content. We are moving away from our present situation by 3,000 years and 2,000 miles. It is a totally different world and we read about things that we find very strange. For example, consider the way they deal with infectious disease in Leviticus. The poor person has to tear their clothes, let their hair grow long and unbrushed, cover the lower part of their face and go around shouting, 'Unclean! Unclean!'. In our society we deal with infectious diseases rather differently! It also includes other weird activities – we do not arrive at church today carrying a little lamb or a pigeon to give to the pastor, who then slits its throat in front of the whole congregation.

The third reason is that it seems to be so irrelevant. What has Leviticus got to say to me living today? At work on a Monday? Deep down we know instinctively that we are not under the law of Moses and, since this book is part of his law, we are not sure what – if anything – it has to do with us.

Context

Let us therefore consider the book with a view to overturning some of the misgivings we may have. Leviticus is one of five books that together make up what is called the Pentateuch (*penta* meaning 'five'). These comprise the law of Moses. The Jews call it the Torah, the 'Books of Instruction', and they read it through once a year. They start on the eighth day of the Feast of Tabernacles, sometime in September/October, and

'PENTATEUCH' – 5 books of Moses – 'TORAH' – instruction

Who?		Where?	When?	
GENESIS Beginnings	Universal	Chaldea	**CENTURIES** (Past)	
		Canaan		
EXODUS Going Out	National	Egypt	**YEARS** (300)	
LEVITICUS Levites	Tribal	S i n a i	**MONTH** (One)	
NUMBERS Statistics	National		**YEARS** (40)	
DEUTERONOMY Second Law	Universal	Negev Edom Moab	**CENTURIES** (Future)	

beginning with Genesis 1, they read it through the year to finish at the next Feast of Tabernacles the following autumn.

The interesting thing about the five books of Moses is that they have a distinctive and memorable shape. Noting this will help us put Leviticus in context. The diagram will make this clear.

ITS PLACE IN THE PENTATEUCH

Genesis is the book of beginnings: it is what the word 'genesis' means and it tells you how everything began, from the creation of our universe to Israel becoming the people of God. Exodus focuses on the Israelites going out from Egypt. Leviticus derives its name from the tribe of Levites, one of the tribes of Israel. The book of Numbers is precisely what it says: a book of statistics (600,000 men came out of Egypt, plus women and children, probably 2.5 million in all). Finally, Deuteronomy (*deutero* means 'second' and *nomus* means 'law') focuses on the second giving of the law (God gave his law twice, once at Sinai and once just before they crossed the Jordan into the Promised Land, so the Ten Commandments come twice – once in Exodus and once in Deuteronomy as a kind of reminder of the law just before they entered the Promised Land).

When we ask who these books are about, we begin to see the shape emerging. Genesis is a universal book – it is about everybody, the human race and the whole universe. Exodus is a national book – it zooms down on one people, the nation of Israel. In Leviticus the focus is even more narrow, on only one tribe out of the whole nation. Once past Leviticus, the focus opens out again and Numbers is about the whole nation once more. Deuteronomy puts Israel against the backcloth of the entire world and we are back to the universal viewpoint.

This shape helps to explain why so many people get stuck in Leviticus. While they are interested in universal things and even national things, they are less concerned when the focus is upon a particular tribe, other than their own.

ITS PLACE IN GEOGRAPHY

Genesis begins with the whole earth, then starts to focus in on the area of the Chaldees where Abraham lived, then on the land of Canaan to which he travelled, and then on Egypt where his descendants ended up. In the land of Egypt they became slaves for 400 years. In Leviticus the focus is once again very narrow, concentrating on just one place: Mount Sinai, where the law and regulations were given. The focus then expands with the journeys through the Negev, Edom and Moab, back into Canaan.

ITS PLACE IN TIME

Genesis covers centuries, all the past history of our earth. Exodus covers years, about 300. Leviticus only covers one month, while Numbers covers 40 years and Deuteronomy looks forward through the centuries to the future history of Israel. Once again we can see the shape of the five books of Moses. Leviticus is the hinge of the whole thing, focusing down to the most important month at the most important place with the most important tribe. The whole of the law of Moses hangs on this.

When the Jews read through the Pentateuch every 12 months, they spend about a fortnight to three weeks reading Leviticus.

Relation to Exodus

Having looked at Leviticus in the context of the Pentateuch, we should also relate it back to Exodus. It is very important to recognize how each book grows out of the previous book if we wish to understand it fully. In the second half of Exodus the

tabernacle is built, God's tent in which he lives among his people. If you imagine the camp in Exodus, God's tent would be
in the middle and hundreds of other tents all around it – the
divine tent and the human tents together. Leviticus is about
everything that goes on in God's tent and everything that
should go on in the people's tents. So it divides into two halves:
God's tent and the people's tents, with the rules and regulations for both.

Furthermore, when dealing with the tabernacle, Exodus
talks about God's approach to man, but Leviticus talks about
man's approach to God. Exodus is about the deliverance that
God brought to his people, but Leviticus is about the dedication of God's people to him. Exodus is about God's grace in
setting the people free, but Leviticus begins with thank offerings, explaining how the people can show their gratitude to
God for being set free.

We need both books and their complementary messages.
This book may not be as exciting as Exodus, but it shows that
God expects something from us in return for what he has done
for us. Once again we are reminded that we are saved in order
to serve. Exodus shows how God saved his people, but
Leviticus explains how they are to serve him.

'Be holy'

When we read the Old Testament it can be helpful to imagine
that we are Jewish. For a Jewish person the reason for reading
Leviticus is clear: it is quite literally a matter of life and death.
To the Jews there is only one God and that is the God of Israel.
All other so-called gods are figments of human imagination. It
was the same for the Israelites in Exodus and Leviticus. Since
there was only one God and they were his only people on
earth, there was a special relationship between them. On God's
side he promised to do many things for them: to be their

government; to be their minister of defence and protect them; to be their minister of finance, so there would be no poor among them; to be their minister of health, so that none of the diseases of Egypt would touch them. God would be everything they needed, their King. In return he expected them to live right and to do things right. The biblical word is 'righteous' – 'righteousness' means living right. The key text in the whole of Leviticus is one that is frequently alluded to in the New Testament: 'Be holy for I am holy'.

God expects the people he liberates to be like him and not like those around them. Many of the things which seem puzzling in Leviticus are explained by this fact. It is the key that unlocks the whole book. When God tells them that they must not do something, it is because the people around them are doing it but they are to be different, to be holy because he is holy. If God saves you he expects you to be like him; he expects you to live his way and to be holy as he is holy.

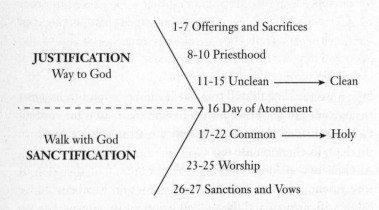

JUSTIFICATION
Way to God

1-7 Offerings and Sacrifices

8-10 Priesthood

11-15 Unclean ⟶ Clean

16 Day of Atonement

17-22 Common ⟶ Holy

Walk with God
SANCTIFICATION

23-25 Worship

26-27 Sanctions and Vows

The shape of the book

We have noted already that the book is in two halves. It builds up to a climax and then flows out from the climax. It is also like a multi-layered sandwich. The chart shows that the first section corresponds to the sixth, the second to the fifth, and the third to the fourth, leaving one right in the middle. There are clear correspondences between these sections, beautifully put together and worked out.

Remember that God is responsible for this pattern, not Moses. In fact, there are more words of God in the book of Leviticus than in any other book in the Bible! About 90 per cent of Leviticus is the direct speech of God – 'The LORD said to Moses...' There is no other book in the Bible that has so much of God's direct speech, so if you want to read God's Word this is a good book to start with. You will be reading the actual words of God.

The offerings and sacrifices of the first seven chapters are backed up by the sanctions and vows of the people in the last section. The details about the priesthood correspond to the details about the worship that they are to lead.

The climax of the book is the Day of Atonement, the day on which two animals were used to symbolize the sins of the people. They sacrificed one animal, a sheep, inside the camp. One after another they then laid their hands on the other animal, a goat, and confessed their sins. They pushed the goat out of the camp into the wilderness, where it would die with all their sins loaded on it. It was called the 'scapegoat', a word we still have in common use today.

The two sections of the book pivot around the Day of Atonement. The first half describes our way to God – what we call **justification** – and the second half describes our walk with God – what is known as **sanctification**.

Offerings and worship

Let us look first at the opening seven chapters, which deal with the rules for offerings. There are five offerings, of two different types.

Gratitude offerings

The first three offerings were the right way to say 'thank you' to God for blessing. They were not offerings for sin but offerings of gratitude. If we feel grateful to God he wants us to say 'thank you'.

For the **burnt offering**, an animal was brought, slaughtered and then burnt so that God could smell it. The sacrifice was said to be a sweet-smelling savour to him.

In a burnt offering the whole thing was burnt, but for a **meal offering** some was kept back so that the worshipper could have a meal with God. Part of the offering would be given to God and part would be eaten by the person making the offering.

The third gratitude offering was a **peace offering**, in which all the fat was burned.

Guilt offerings

The other two offerings were not to express gratitude but to deal with guilt. There was the **sin offering** and the **trespass offering** and these did two things.

First, they made atonement for sin. They offered God compensation for what the person had done wrong. The word 'atonement' does not mean 'at-one-ment' – that is a modern idea. It actually means 'compensation', so if you atone for something, you offer something as compensation. Both the sin offering and trespass offering are compensation offerings to God involving blood: as a compensation for the bad life the offerer has lived, they offer to God a good life that has not sinned.

Second, they only work for unintentional sins; they do not work for deliberate sins. In other words, nobody is perfect, we all make mistakes, we all fall into sin unintentionally. Even though we do not intend to do wrong, we do it. God provided offerings for unintentional sin, but there is no offering on this list for deliberate sin.

This is an important point which is picked up in the New Testament. The New Testament distinguishes between accidental and deliberate, wilful sin in Christians. Like the Old Testament, it says that if we deliberately sin after being forgiven, there is no more sacrifice for sin. Deliberate sin in those who have been forgiven is very serious, which is why Jesus said to the woman caught in adultery, 'Go and sin no more'. For accidental sin, however, there is full provision, because God knows we are weak, knows we fall, and knows we do not always intend to do what we do. As Paul says in Romans: 'The evil I would not, that I do.' This distinction between deliberate sin and accidental sin in God's people runs right through the New Testament as it does through the Old.

Worship calendar

As well as bringing offerings to God, the Jews had a calendar of worship to observe. There is no corresponding Christian calendar in the New Testament, no instructions about observing Christmas or Easter, but for the Jewish people a calendar was a vital part of their walk with God. They were being treated as children: adults do not need a calendar but children do, to remind them of things they would otherwise forget. Various types of feast are mentioned in Leviticus, and all had to be kept.

ANNUAL FEASTS

The calendar began in the first month of the year, which is roughly our March/April, with **Passover**, the Feast of Unleavened Bread. This took place on the fifteenth day of the first month, to remember how God brought the Israelites out of slavery in Egypt. On the day before the Passover began, a lamb had to be killed at 3.00 p.m.

Three days later (i.e. three days after the slaughter of the lamb) they had to offer the **Firstfruits** of the harvest to God. It is not difficult to discern the similarities in pattern with Jesus' death and resurrection.

Fifty days after that they were to hold the **Feast of Pentecost** (*pente* meaning '50'), or the Feast of Weeks. This was the day that the law was given on Sinai. They were to remember this and give thanks for it. When the law was given at Sinai on the very first Pentecost, 3,000 people were put to death because of their sin. Centuries later, when the Spirit was given at Pentecost, 3,000 were saved.

Next come the feasts towards the end of the year (the 'seventh month', or our September/October). At the **Feast of Trumpets**, the *shofar*, the old ram's horn, was blown. This signalled a whole new round of feasts.

Then came the **Day of Atonement**, the crucial day when the scapegoat was pushed out of the camp with all the sins of the people on its head.

The **Feast of Tabernacles** (also known as the Feast of Succoth) came after that, lasting eight days. For this feast they moved out of their houses and lived in shelters. They had to be able to see the stars through the roof to remind them of their 40 years of foolish wandering in the wilderness when they could have reached the Promised Land in just 11 days.

All these feasts will be fulfilled in a Christian way. The first three have already been fulfilled in the first coming of Jesus.

The second three will be fulfilled at his second coming. We cannot know the year that Jesus will return, but we do know that it will be around September/October, because he always does things on time. Indeed, this was the time when he was born: the evidence in Luke's Gospel points to the seventh month of the year, which corresponds to the Feast of Tabernacles. This is when the Jews expect the Messiah. Every time a trumpet is mentioned in the New Testament it is to announce his coming. When that happens, the last three feasts will be fulfilled, and on that Day of Atonement redemption will come to the whole nation of Israel.

WEEKLY HOLY DAY

In addition to the annual festivals, there was also to be a weekly rest, a particular blessing for people who had been slaves in Egypt. There is no trace of the **Sabbath** in the Bible before Moses. Both Adam and Abraham, for example, had no Sabbath day: they worked seven days a week. Moses introduced this weekly day of rest. It was not to be a holiday or a family day but a day for God, a holy day, and this was part of their calendar.

JUBILEE

But there were not only annual and weekly festivals – there was also to be a festival every 50 years, known as the **Jubilee**. Every 50 years everybody's bank balance was levelled up, debts were cancelled and all the property reverted to the family who originally owned it. So the leases would get cheaper the closer you came to the fiftieth year. Slaves were also set free in the jubilee year. Thus people looked forward to the jubilee, known also as 'the acceptable year of the Lord'. It was good news for the poor because they would be rich again, and it was a time when captives would be set at liberty.

Jesus proclaimed in Nazareth: 'The Spirit of the Lord is on me ... to preach good news to the poor ... to proclaim freedom for the prisoners ... to proclaim the year of the Lord's favour.' In other words, Jesus began the real jubilee to which every one of these people had been looking forward. Once again the Old Testament is needed to understand the New.

Rules for living

Clean and unclean

A crucial area to understand in Leviticus concerns the distinctions between holy and common, clean and unclean. Most

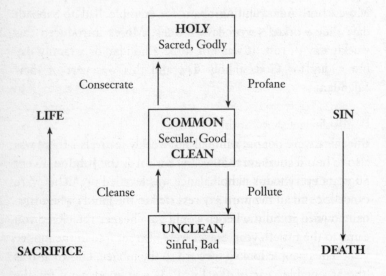

people think in terms of good and bad, but the Bible works with three categories, as the chart shows.*

There are two processes going on. The first process is when sacred, godly, holy things are profaned and become common. You can spoil a holy thing by making it common. When the Bible Society sent Bibles to Romania, the communist government allowed the pages to be used in toilet rolls. It sparked a revolution started by Christians who were scandalized by this action. What had happened in that situation according to the teaching of Leviticus? In using the Bible for such a mundane though necessary purpose, a holy thing had been made common. The second process is when a common, clean thing is made unclean and sinful.

The three words *sacred*, *secular* and *sinful* correspond roughly to these divisions of *holy*, *clean and common*, and *unclean*. Just as there is a process of profaning the holy to make it common, and polluting the common and clean to make it unclean, so there is a process of redeeming this situation. You can cleanse the unclean and make it clean, then you can consecrate it and it becomes holy.

What is holy and what is unclean must never come into contact. They must be kept rigidly apart. Things holy and things unclean have nothing in common. If there is a mixture of unclean and clean it will make both unclean. Similarly, if you mix holy and common things, that makes them all common – it does not make them all holy.

Hence the downward process shown on the chart leads to death, quite literally, whereas the upward process leads to life –

---

* For the illuminating distinction between holy, clean and unclean, I am indebted to G. J. Wenham, in his *New International Commentary on Leviticus* (Wm. B Eerdmans, Grand Rapids, Michigan, 1979).

but this involves sacrifice. Only by sacrifice can you cleanse what is unclean and bring it to life.

This has ramifications for our view of life. According to the Bible our work can be consecrated to God. Work can be any of these three things, holy, clean or unclean. There are some jobs that are illegal and immoral, which are therefore unclean. A Christian should not be in them. There are other jobs that are clean, but common. But you can consecrate your work and do it for the Lord, and then it ceases to be common – it becomes a holy vocation in the Lord. So it is possible for a printer to be doing holy work, just as it is possible for a missionary to do only common work. Your money can be unclean if it is spent on bad things, clean if it is spent on good things, or holy if it is consecrated to the Lord. Sex, too, can be any one of these three things.

Plenty of people are living decent, common, clean lives, but they are not holy people. God does not want us just to be living good lives: he wants us to be living holy lives. This is the emphasis in Leviticus.

Those outside the Church may claim that they can live lives as good as the lives of those within it, but they are not the holy people God is looking for.

Holy living

Living holy lives involves all kinds of very practical things.

■ The **health** of the body is just as important to holiness as the health of the spirit. What we do with our bodies does matter if we want to be holy to the Lord. Leviticus has instructions about haircuts, tattoos and men wearing earrings, as well as regulations on male and female bodily discharges and childbirth.

- There are a lot of regulations concerning **food** here, clean and unclean food especially.
- There is teaching in Leviticus about not getting involved in **occultism** or with spiritualist mediums.
- Instructions are given on the action to be taken when there is **dry rot** in the house. The house is to be torn down in love for your neighbour.
- There is teaching concerning **clothing**. There is to be no mixed material.
- **Social life** is covered: holiness means paying special attention to the poor, the deaf, the blind, and the aged. If you are a holy youth you will stand up when an older person comes into the room.
- **Sex** is also dealt with. Leviticus has things to say on incest, buggery and homosexuality.

If you ask what is a holy life, Leviticus says it is how you live from Monday to Saturday and not just what you do on Sunday. God is looking not just for clean people, but for holy people. That is a big difference and until you become a Christian you never even think of becoming holy; you just think of being good – and that is not good enough.

Rules and regulations

We need to be clear about our understanding of the law of Moses. It is called the 'law', not the 'laws', because it all hangs together. Holiness means wholeness, and all these rules and regulations fit together and form one whole. If you break any of them you have broken them all. (In the chapter on Exodus I likened the breaking of one of the Commandments to breaking a necklace, which causes all the beads to scatter.) This fact cuts across most people's view of the Ten Commandments. It is generally thought that if we can keep a high percentage of the laws we are doing well! This is not enough.

REASONS

God did not give reasons for all his rules. He did not tell us why we should not wear clothing of mixed materials, for example, or why we should not crossbreed animals or sow mixed seed. We can perhaps see a reason, however, in the fact that God is a God of purity – so he does not like mixed material for clothes, or mixed seed or mixed breeding. Although he does not always give the reasons for a prohibition, in some cases we can make an informed guess. The reason in some cases is undoubtedly hygiene. Some of the regulations about toilets are obvious, for example: there are hygienic reasons behind what God told them to do. Also it may be that some of the food forbidden as 'unclean' was also prohibited because of health concerns. Pig's flesh, for instance, was peculiarly liable to disease in that climate.

Where there are no reasons given, the people were simply to obey because they trusted that the law-giver knew why he had commanded it. In the same way, there are times in the family home when children need to be told that they are to do something 'because Daddy says so'. Sometimes to give the reason would be inappropriate, or it would be impossible to explain.

With many of the laws God is saying: Do you trust me? Do you believe that if I tell you not to do something I have a very good reason for that?

Too often we are only prepared to do something after we are convinced that it is for our good. We want to be God. Just like Adam and Eve, who took the fruit of the tree of the knowledge of good and evil, we want to decide, to experience and to settle it for ourselves. But God has no obligation to explain himself to us.

Sanctions

God may not give reasons, but he does give sanctions. There is a call for obedience, but the *cost of disobedience* is also spelt out. And the punishments are pretty severe. In Leviticus 26, therefore, a whole collection of positive reasons for being obedient is laid out, but by the same token there is also a curse on those who disobey. If a Jew reads the book of Leviticus, he finds that a number of things could happen if he disobeys God's law.

He could lose his home, he could lose his citizenship and he could lose his life. There are 15 sins mentioned in Leviticus for which capital punishment is the consequence. Maybe now we can see why understanding this book was so critical – it is literally a matter of life and death.

Furthermore, Leviticus makes clear that the nation as a whole can lose two things. They could lose their freedom, being invaded by enemies from outside (we see this in the book of Judges). Or they could lose their land, being driven out and made slaves somewhere else. In time, both these things happened to the nation of Israel. These were not empty promises and threats. There are rewards for trusting and obeying God, but there are also punishments for those who distrust and disobey him.

HAPPINESS AND HOLINESS

What God is actually saying through this combination of rewards and punishments is that the only way to be really happy is to be really holy. Happiness and holiness belong together and the lack of holiness brings unhappiness. Most people get it the wrong way round. God's will for us is that we be holy in this world and happy in the next, but many want to be happy in this world and holy later.

God is willing to let things happen to us which may be painful, but which will make us more holy as a result. Our

character tends to make more progress in the tough times than
the good.

Reading Leviticus as Christians

What has this book to say to us, living as Christians in the
modern world? Do we have to get rid of all mixed-fibre clothing? If we get dry rot in the house, do we have to burn it down?

One principle we can use as a guide is found in Paul's second letter to Timothy. Paul writes: 'From infancy you have
known the holy Scriptures, which are able to make you wise for
salvation through faith in Christ Jesus. All Scripture is God-
breathed and is useful for teaching, rebuking, correcting and
training in righteousness, so that the man of God may be thoroughly equipped for every good work'.

Paul is talking to Timothy about the Old Testament. The
New Testament did not exist when he wrote this, so 'the
Scriptures' referred to must be the Old Testament. When Jesus
said, 'Search the Scriptures, for they bear witness to me,' he
meant the Old Testament. We can learn about two things from
the Old Testament: salvation and righteousness. This goes for
Leviticus as well. It, too, can help us understand how to be
saved, and it will open our eyes to right living. Those two purposes just shine out.

Leviticus in the New Testament

It is always very illuminating to see what the New Testament
does with an Old Testament book. As somebody said: 'The Old
is in the New revealed, the New is in the Old concealed.' The
two belong together and each Testament outlines the other.

There are a number of direct quotations from Leviticus in
the New Testament, but two in particular come very frequently:

'Be holy, for I am holy' and 'You shall love your neighbour as yourself.' There are many other passages where parts of Leviticus are clearly in mind, and in particular we cannot understand the letter to the Hebrews unless we read Leviticus. These two belong to each other. Hebrews could not have been written unless Leviticus had been written first.

There are over 90 references to Leviticus in the New Testament, so it is a very important book for Christians to get to grips with.

THE FULFILMENT OF THE LAW

What, then, are we to make of the law of Moses today, remembering that there are not just 10 laws but 613 in total? We may have a hunch that we are not tied to them all, but how many *are* we tied to? For example, some churches teach their members to tithe. Others have strict rules about the Sabbath, even if for them the Sabbath is Sunday, not Saturday as observed by the Jews. Every Christian has to come to terms with this difficulty. It is complicated by the fact that Jesus said, 'I have not come to destroy the law, but to fulfil it.'

We must therefore ask how each law is fulfilled. It is obvious that some are fulfilled in Christ and finished with. That is why you do not have to take a pigeon or a lamb to church when you go to worship next Sunday. The laws about blood sacrifices have been fulfilled.

In a similar way the Sabbath law is fulfilled for us every day of the week when we cease to do our own works and do God's instead, thus entering into the rest that remains for the people of God. We are still free to keep one day special if we wish, but we are also free to regard every day alike. So we cannot even impose Sunday observance on other believers, never mind unbelievers, for we are all free in Christ.

It is very important to realize exactly what the fulfilment of each law is. Of the Ten Commandments, nine are repeated in the New Testament in exactly the same way, e.g. you shall not steal, you shall not commit adultery. The Sabbath one is not, being fulfilled in a very different way.

Other laws of Moses are fulfilled in different ways. One law in Deuteronomy says, for example, that when you are using an ox to thresh the corn, walking round and round, its hooves breaking the wheat from the chaff, you must not put a muzzle on it because it has every right to eat what it is preparing for others. This is fulfilled in the New Covenant. Paul quotes that law and gives it a completely different fulfilment, explaining that in the same way those who live for the gospel have a right to expect financial support from others. It is necessary to look at each law and see how it is fulfilled in the New Testament and given a deeper meaning.

There are, however, four crucial things that we learn from the book of Leviticus which are *unchanged* in the New Testament.

1. THE HOLINESS OF GOD

There is no book in the Bible which is stronger on the holiness of God than Leviticus and it is something we forget at our peril, especially in an age when people ask the question: 'How can a God of love send anyone to hell?' We know through Jesus that God is a God of love, and Jesus also spoke openly about hell. We cannot pick and choose: if Jesus told the truth about God being a God of love, we must also accept that he spoke the truth about hell.

Actually, God's understanding of love is a little different from ours. Ours is sentimental love, his is holy love. His love is so great that he hates evil. Very few of us love enough to hate evil. We learn about the holiness of God from the book of

Leviticus. We learn to love God with reverence, with holy fear. Hebrews says, 'Let us worship God with reverence and awe, for our God is a consuming fire.' This is a sentiment the writer got straight out of Leviticus. It is vital for Christians today to read Leviticus, in order to keep hold of this sense of God's holiness.

2. THE SINFULNESS OF MAN

Leviticus strongly underlines the sinfulness of man as well as the holiness of God. It is so realistic and down to earth. Here is human nature, capable of bestiality, incest, superstitions, and many other things which are an abomination to God. 'Abomination' means something that makes you want to be physically sick because you are so disgusted. The Hebrew word for it is a very, very strong expression; the English translations – abomination, loathsome, vile, revolting – are all just poor substitutes.

The Bible is about God's emotions. God's emotional reaction to sin comes because he is holy. The sinfulness of man is not just in polluting clean things, but also in profaning holy things. Common swearing is the profaning of holy words. There are only two sacred relationships in our lives – that between us and God, and that between man and woman. Ninety per cent of swearwords come from one of these two relationships. Mankind profanes holy things and pollutes clean things. We live in a world that is doing both, and the sinfulness of man is not only in making clean things dirty, but in making holy things common and in treating things as common when they are not.

3. THE FULLNESS OF CHRIST

Leviticus points towards the fullness of Christ and his sacrifice, once for all. God has provided a way of cleansing the sin from mankind. His problem is how to reconcile justice and mercy. Should he deal with this sin in justice and punish us, or should he deal with it in mercy and forgive us? Since God is both just and merciful, he must find a way of being just and merciful at the same time. It is impossible for us to find a way, but it has been possible for him – by the substitution of an innocent life for a guilty life. Only when that happens are both justice and mercy satisfied. The sacrificial laws of Leviticus begin to show us how that can happen.

There are particular words associated with this process which occur many times. 'Atonement' and 'blood' are frequently mentioned, because in the blood is the life. If a person's blood is taken away, their life is taken away. 'Offerings' are also frequently mentioned. The burnt offering speaks of the total *surrender* that is needed. The meal offering speaks of our *service*. The peace offering tells us of the *serenity* we can have with God. These are the three things that should characterize a grateful life, a life that has been saved.

Yet we note too God's side of the equation, his *sacrifice*. The only sacrifices we now have to bring to the Lord are the sacrifices of praise and thanksgiving, and these should be properly prepared and brought before him. But the sacrifices in Leviticus also speak of the sacrifice that Jesus made. The sin offering tells us about the *substitution* of an innocent life for the guilty, and the trespass offering brings home to us that this sacrifice *satisfies* divine justice, that there is some law that is being met by it. It all looks straight forward to the New Testament.

4. GODLINESS OF LIFE

Leviticus tells us to be holy in every part of our lives, even down to our toilet arrangements! Holiness is wholeness, which is why we can read of the incredible detail God goes into as he applies his holiness to every part of his people's lives. It tells you that a godly life is godly through and through or it is not godly at all.

It is important to note, however, that there are two major shifts between the holiness of the Old Covenant and the holiness of the New. In Leviticus there is the triple division between holy, clean and unclean. This still applies in the New Testament, but there are two major alterations to it.

First, holiness is moved from material things to moral things. The children of Israel *were* children and they had to be taught as children. They had to learn the difference between clean and unclean in matters of food, for example. Christians have no such rules, however. It took a vision to teach this to the apostle Peter. Jesus said that it is not what goes into your mouth that makes you unclean now, but what comes *out* of your mouth. Being clean or unclean is no longer a matter of clothes and food, but of clean and unclean morality. It has shifted from the material to the moral. Now we do not have all those regulations about clothes and food, but we do have a lot of teaching about how to be holy in moral questions.

Second, the rewards and punishments are shifted from this life to the next. In this world holy people may well suffer and not be rewarded, but the shift has happened because in the New Testament we have a longer-term view. This life is not the only one there is – it is only the preparation for a much longer existence elsewhere. So in the New Testament we read 'great is your reward in heaven', not on earth.

Given these two major shifts, Leviticus is a most profitable book for Christians to read. Above all, it gives us insight into those four vital things: the holiness of God, the sinfulness of man, the fullness of Christ, and godliness of life.

5.

NUMBERS

Introduction

Numbers is not a well-known book, neither is it widely quoted. Perhaps only two verses are well known. Samuel Morse quoted one of these after he sent the first telegraph message in Morse code to Washington DC on 24 May 1844. He expressed his amazement at what had happened with the verse, 'What hath God wrought?' (translated in the NIV as 'See what God has done.') The discovery of electronic communication was attributed to the God who had given the power.

The second verse is known by most people: 'Be sure your sin will find you out'. This was originally said by Moses as a warning to the people when he was telling them that they must cross the Jordan and fight their enemies.

Neither verse is generally known to come from Numbers. Very few people are able to quote verses from the book and I have found that few know what any one chapter contains. We need to remedy this situation, as Numbers is another very important part of the Bible.

'Numbers' is a strange title for a book. In the Hebrew the title is taken from the first words of the scroll, 'The LORD said'. When the Hebrew Scriptures were translated into Greek, the translators gave it a new title, *Arithmoi* (from which we get the word 'arithmetic'). The Latin (Vulgate) version translated this as *numeri*. So in English we know it as 'Numbers'.

It begins and ends with two censuses. The first was taken when Israel left Sinai one month after the tabernacle had been erected. The total number of people counted was 603,550. The second was taken when they arrived at Moab prior to entering the land of Canaan almost 40 years later. The number of people had dropped by 1,820 to 601,730 – not a very great difference. These were male censuses used for military conscription.

The book of Numbers tells us that there is nothing wrong with counting. King David was punished by God for counting his men, but this was because he was motivated by pride. Other parts of the Bible include examples of counting and taking stock – we are told, for example, that 3,000 were added to the Church at Pentecost. Jesus encouraged his followers to count the cost of following him by reflecting on how the leader of an army might evaluate his chances according to the relative strength of his army.

Three things can be said about the figures given in Numbers.

1. What a large number!

Many Bible commentators question the size of the numbers. The figures actually represent the military conscription – the men over 20 years old who were able to fight. We have seen already in our studies of Exodus that there were over 2 million people in total, so the 'large' number of 603,550 is actually a fraction of the whole population. There are a number of points to consider which indicate that the numbers given are, in fact, feasible and reasonable.

- In 2 Samuel we are told that David's army was 1,300,000, so a figure of around 600,000 is small in comparison.
- The number is also small in comparison to the Canaanites. The Israelites would need to be of a certain strength in order to fight battles (remembering, nevertheless, that God was on their side).
- Those who argue that it is impossible for the 70 families who came to Egypt to produce so many forget that the people were in Egypt for 400 years. If each generation had four children (a small figure for those times), the figure is possible.
- Some say it is too great a number to fit into the wilderness of Sinai. It is feasible, however: there was enough space. If they travelled five abreast, the column would be 110 miles long and it would take 10 days to pass!
- Some say these numbers mean that there were too many people to be fed successfully in the wilderness. That would certainly have been the case, but for God's supernatural provision.

2. What a similar number!

Given the magnitudes involved, a difference of 1,820 between the first and second censuses represents a very small percentage change. The tribe of Simeon had lost 37,100 and Manasseh had gained 20,500, but most remained about the same. Since numerical growth indicates God's blessing, we can note from the outset that this was not a period when God was pleased with his people. Considering the hostile environment and the length of time, however, maintaining such numbers was remarkable.

3. What a different number!

There were over 38 years between the two censuses, so a whole generation perished in the wilderness. (It was rare for men to reach 60; Moses was an exception to live until 120.) So although the number was similar, the people were not. Only Joshua and Caleb (2 out of 2 million) survived from those who left Egypt to enter the Promised Land. In some ways this is the biggest tragedy in the whole Bible. Numbers is a very *sad* book. Two-thirds of the book need never have been written. It should have taken 11 days to travel from Egypt to the Promised Land, but it actually took them 13,780 days! Only two of those who set out actually reached their home. The rest were stuck in an aimless existence, 'killing time' until God's judgement was complete. Over time they all died in the wilderness, and a new generation took up the journey.

Most lessons we learn from Numbers are negative. This is how *not* to be the people of God! Paul tells us how we should view it in 1 Corinthians 10: 'Now these things occurred as examples to keep us from setting our hearts on evil things as they did ... These things happened to them as examples and were written down as warnings for us, on whom the fulfilment of the ages has come.' Numbers is full of bad 'examples'.

Context

What, then, is the context for this book? The journey from Mount Sinai to Kadesh Barnea (the last oasis in the Negev Desert) and the beginning of the Promised Land of Canaan takes 11 days on foot. The route the Israelites took was to turn away from Kadesh and go across the Rift Valley, to the mountains of Edom. They finished up in Moab on the wrong side of the River Jordan. It took 38 years and a few months, not because it was a particularly difficult piece of country but because God only moved a little at a time. He stayed a very long time in each place and told them he would wait until every man among them was dead, except Joshua and Caleb.

What happened to bring God's judgement down on the people? At Kadesh the people refused to enter the land when God told them to. Today many Christians have been brought out of sin but have not enjoyed the blessing that God has set out for them. They too end up in a miserable wilderness.

Two-thirds of the book of Numbers is about this protracted journey. The Bible is a very honest book, telling us about failures and vices as well as great successes and virtues. When Paul told the Corinthians that Numbers was written down as an example and a warning to us, he meant this as a clear statement of the book's purpose. It may not be a popular book, but if you do not study history you are condemned to repeat it.

Even Moses was not permitted to go into the Promised Land, although he did enter it centuries later when he talked with Jesus. He too failed miserably at one crucial point, as we shall see.

Content and structure

Another of the five books of Moses, Numbers is a mixture of legislation and narrative. The author of the laws is not Moses but God. We are told 80 times in this book, 'God said to Moses...' God gives to Moses general laws and legislation, as well as regulations governing rituals and religious ceremony.

As for the narrative in the book, we are told that Moses kept a journal of their travels at the Lord's command. He also kept another book called 'the book of the Wars of the LORD', recording accounts of the battles. Numbers was written by Moses using these records, yet Moses himself is referred to in the third person

The mixture of narrative and legislation makes it seem rather like Exodus, but whereas in Exodus the first half is narrative and the second half law, in Numbers it is all mixed up. It is therefore much harder to find a connecting thread.

A pattern emerges more easily when we consider the narrative and legislation in context. The structure of the book is *chronological* rather than topical. We can see this best by putting the content of Numbers alongside that of Exodus, Leviticus and Deuteronomy.

Chronological context	Content	Duration
Exodus 1–18 *Egypt to Sinai*	Narrative	50 days
Exodus 19–40 *at Sinai*	Legislation	?
Leviticus 1–27 *at Sinai*	Legislation	30 days
Numbers 1:1–10:10 *at Sinai*	Legislation	19 days
Numbers 10:11–12:16		
Sinai to Kadesh	Narrative	11 days
Numbers 13:1–20:21 *Kadesh*	Legislation	?
Numbers 20:22–21:35		
Kadesh to Moab	Narrative	38 years
Numbers 22:1–36:13 *Moab*	Legislation	3 months, 10 days
Deuteronomy 1–34 *Moab*	Legislation	5 months

It is fascinating to note that all the laws were given to the Israelites while they were camped. The stories of their travels show how they broke those laws. While they were camped and stationary God told them what they *should* do, but while they were moving we hear the story of what they *did* do. They would learn lessons both ways, through the teaching from Moses and through the experience of journeying (rather as Jesus taught his disciples both in 'messages', such as the Sermon on the Mount, and as they travelled 'along the way').

The chart given above is like a multi-layered sandwich. Thus in Exodus 1–11 the Israelites are stuck in Egypt, then in Chapters 12–18 they move to Sinai. All this is narrative. However, in Exodus 19–40, Leviticus 1–27 and Numbers 1–10 they are still at Sinai. These three consecutive sections are full of legislation.

In Numbers 10–12 they move again, from Sinai to Kadesh, a journey of 11 days. The stay in Kadesh covers the crisis when the people rebel. God speaks to them at Kadesh from Chapters 13 to 20, again with legislation.

Numbers 20–21 covers the journey from Kadesh to Moab, the whole journey of 38 years covering just two chapters. Numbers 22–36 covers what God said to the Israelites while they waited to go into the Promised Land. The whole of Deuteronomy 1–34 belongs to that same, stationary time period.

Numbers has a lot of movement in it, Deuteronomy has none, and Exodus has movement in just the first half.

Legislation

As noted above, we are told on 80 occasions in Numbers that God spoke to Moses 'face to face'. This was unique: others would receive God's Word through visions when they were awake or dreams when they were asleep. The people would consult the priests' *urim* (the equivalent of 'drawing lots') when they wished to discern God's mind on a situation.

Moses first met with God on Mount Sinai, some distance from the rest of Israel, but now that the tabernacle was constructed God was dwelling with the people. The big danger now that God was 'with them', however, was that they might become overfamiliar, lose their sense of awe and respect, and forget his holiness. The laws in Numbers are not moral or social laws, but laws given to prevent the people from losing their reverence for God. The laws can be classified under three headings: carefulness, cleanliness and costliness.

1. Carefulness

WHEN CAMPED

They had to be very careful to camp in the right place (Chapter 2). Each tribe was allotted a specific place in relation to the other tribes and the tabernacle in the centre. The camp looked like a 'hollow rectangle' from above (see the chart below). The only other nation known to camp in this manner were the Egyptians – this was the preferred arrangement of Rameses II (the Pharaoh who may have been on the throne at the time).

The tabernacle in the centre was surrounded by a fence and there was only one entrance. Two people camped outside the entrance – Moses and Aaron. The Levites camped around the other three sides, and their three clans had special responsibility – Merari, Gershon and Kohath. No one else could even touch the fence and there were orders to kill anyone who approached. God was holy and could not be approached lightly.

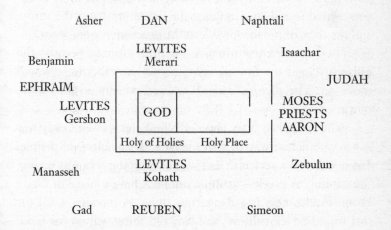

The other tribes were arranged around the tabernacle, each tribe with its own specific, allotted place in relation to God's tent and the entrance to it. The most important place was right in front of the entrance, and this was occupied by the tribe of Judah. It was from the tribe of Judah that Jesus would later come.

WHEN TREKKING

When the camp set out on a journey, everyone moved according to a fascinating pattern. There were specific instructions for the dismantling and transporting of the tabernacle. The priests would wrap up the holy furniture, then the Levites would pick it up. Everyone knew who had to carry which piece of furniture from the tabernacle, who had to carry the curtains, and what order they had to be carried in. Some tribes had to leave before the tabernacle pieces were carried. When the other tribes moved they 'unpeeled' like an orange. They marched in the same order every time, so that when they got to the next camp it was simple for each tribe to find their place and put their tents up. The whole thing is carefully detailed. The silver trumpets would sound to announce the departure from the camp, and the tribe of Judah would lead the procession with praise

They always knew when it was time to move because the pillar of cloud (or fire at night) above the tabernacle would move on. The picture is clear: when God moves, his people move.

Why is God so fussy about all these details? Not only was it a very efficient way to move such a vast quantity of people, but it was also a very efficient way of camping. He was saying, 'Be careful!' A careless attitude does not have a place in God's camp: carelessness is a dangerous thing. A modern word for this would be 'casualness', the 'any old thing will do for God' attitude.

In these detailed directions God is telling his people to be careful, for he is in the camp with them. He also outlines other areas where they would need to be careful. There are some sins mentioned in Numbers which are sins of 'carelessness'. Carelessness on the Sabbath was punishable by death. They were to have tassels on their clothes to remind them to pray. Vows had to be taken very seriously. If a vow was made to God it must be kept. (In Judges we have the story of a man who vowed to sacrifice to God the first living thing that he met when he came out, and he met his daughter!) If a wife makes a vow to God, then her husband has 24 hours to agree or disagree with it.

2. Cleanliness

As well as being carefully arranged, the camp had to be spotlessly clean, for these were 'God's people'. Even such things as the sewage arrangements were carefully detailed. They were told to take a spade when emptying their bowels so that they could keep the camp clean for the Lord. He was not just concerned with germs. God was interested in a 'clean' camp because he is a 'clean' God. The principle still holds today. A dirty, uncared-for church building is an insult to God.

Not only was the *camp* to be clean, we are also told of the cleansing of the *people* before they left Sinai.

There are further details of purification rites in Chapter 19. Death is an unclean thing. God is a God of life, so there was to be no taint of death in the camp. There was even a 'jealousy test' for adulterous wives. Even if there were no witnesses, God sees what happens and will punish the evildoer. This is *his* camp.

The expression 'cleanliness is next to Godliness' has some considerable support from the book of Numbers!

3. Costliness

SACRIFICES AND OFFERINGS

It is costly for a sinful person to live close to a holy God. Sacrifices were offered on behalf of the people on a daily, weekly and monthly basis. There were literally hundreds. Each sacrifice had to be costly – only the best animals were offered.

The daily sacrifice, weekly sacrifice and a special monthly sacrifice made it clear it was a costly matter to receive forgiveness from God. Blood had to be shed.

PRIESTHOOD

Furthermore, the priesthood had to be supported by means of offerings. The Levites were consecrated for service before they left Sinai. Some 8,580 served (out of the 22,000 in the tribe) and both priests and Levites were dependent on the other tribes for their financial support.

The upkeep of the priesthood, plus the regular sacrifices, therefore made up a considerable 'cost' to the people.

This teaches us that we still need to be very careful today about how we approach God. I may not need to bring a ram, pigeon or dove to be sacrificed when I come to God, but that does not mean I do not have to bring a sacrifice at all. There is as much sacrifice in the New Testament as in the Old. We read of the sacrifice of *praise* and the sacrifice of *thanksgiving*, for example. We need to ask ourselves whether we do make sacrifices to God. We too should *prepare* for worship.

Numbers also tells us about the Nazirite vow, a voluntary vow of dedication and devotion to God, although not part of the priesthood. The Nazirites vowed not cut their hair, not to touch alcohol (both were contrary to the social custom of the day) and not to touch a dead body. Some of these vows were temporary, others were for life. Samuel and Samson are the best-known Nazirites in Scripture. By the time of Amos the practice was ridiculed.

WHAT CAN WE LEARN FROM THIS?

Today there is a tendency towards an anti-ritual, casual approach to worship, forgetting that God is exactly the same today as he was then. We too are to approach him with awe and dignity. Hebrews reminds us that he is a consuming fire.

In the New Testament we read of how those gathered for worship may bring a song, a word, a prophecy, a tongue, an interpretation. This is the New Testament equivalent of preparing, approaching God in the right frame of mind.

Numbers also reminds us that we must worship God according to *his* taste and not ours. Modern worship tends to focus on the preferences of individuals, whether this be in favour of hymns or choruses, for example. We can forget that our preferences are quite irrelevant compared to the importance of making sure that our worship matches what God wants.

Our sacrifices of praise and giving are also mentioned in the New Testament: 'They [your gifts] are a fragrant offering, an acceptable sacrifice, pleasing to God.' In Leviticus and Numbers God loved the smell of roast lamb. In the same way, our sacrifice of praise can also be pleasing to God today.

Narrative

In turning to the narrative parts of Numbers, we move from the divine word to human deeds – from what the people *should* do to what they *did* do. It is a sad and sordid story. The wilderness becomes a testing ground for them. They are out of Egypt but not in the Promised Land, and this limbo existence is very hard for them to endure.

We need to remember that the people are now in a covenant relationship with God. He has bound himself to them. He will bless their obedience and punish their disobedience. The same acts of sin are committed in Exodus 16–19 as in Numbers 10–14, but only in Numbers is the law violated, so only in Numbers do the sanctions apply.

God's law can help you see what is right (and wrong), but it cannot help you *do* what is right. The law did not change their behaviour: it brought guilt, condemnation and punishment. This is why the law given on the first Pentecost day was inadequate and later needed the Spirit to be given on that same day. Without supernatural help we would never be able to keep the law.

Leaders

We will look first at the leaders of the nation and see how they tried and failed to live up to the law. They are all from one family, two brothers and a sister – Moses, Aaron and Miriam (the Hebrew version of the name Mary). We are told their good points and their strengths of character as well as their weaknesses.

STRENGTHS

Moses

Moses is the dominant figure throughout the book. In many respects he was a prophet, a priest and a king.

We have seen already how other prophets were given visions and dreams, but Moses spoke face to face with God in the tabernacle. He was even allowed to see a part of God – he saw his 'back'.

He also acted in the role of priest. There are five occasions when he interceded with God. Indeed, on occasions he was quite bold in the way he prayed for the people and urged God to be true to himself.

He was never called 'king', and of course this was some centuries before the monarchy was established, but he led the people into battle and ruled over them, and so functioned as a king, even if the title was not used.

One of the most notable things about Moses was that when he was criticized, badly treated or betrayed he never tried to defend himself. Writing about himself, he says he was the meekest of all the men on the earth – a hard thing to say if you want it to remain true! Of course, Moses was saying no more than Jesus when he said we should learn from him for he was meek and humble. Moses let the Lord defend him. Meekness is not weakness, but it does mean not trying to defend yourself.

Aaron

Aaron was Moses' brother, assigned to Moses as his 'spokes-man' when Moses had to face the Pharaoh in Egypt. He too was a prophet. He was also designated to be a priest, the chief priest. The Aaronic priesthood became the heart of the worship and ritual of the ancient people of God.

Miriam

Miriam was Moses' and Aaron's sister. She was known as a prophetess. She sang and danced with joy when the Egyptians were drowned in the sea.

So we have Moses as prophet, priest and king, Aaron as prophet and priest, and Miriam as prophetess. Note that the gifts are shared and that prophecy is a ministry for women as well as for men. Miriam's particular prophetic gift was expressed in song. There is a very direct link between prophecy and music. In later years King David chose choirmasters who were also prophets, and Elisha would often request music as a preparation for his prophesying. It seems that there is something about the right kind of music which releases the prophetic spirit.

Despite their strengths and gifts, however, each of these leaders failed in some way. It is instructive for us to examine their failings in detail.

WEAKNESSES

Miriam

Miriam's problem was jealousy: she desired honour for herself. She wanted to speak with God as Moses did. In addition she was critical of his choice of wife. Miriam was punished with 'leprosy' for seven days until she repented. She was among those who died at Kadesh.

Aaron

The next to drop out of the leadership picture was Aaron. Once again his problem was jealousy and desire for honour. Miriam and Aaron were together in criticizing Moses. Their excuse was that Moses had married someone of whom they did not approve (he married a Kushite woman who had come out of Egypt with them and who was not even a Hebrew). God did not criticize him for doing that, but Miriam and Aaron did.

Aaron thus died at Mount Hor, a little further on from Kadesh, when he was over 100 years old. Soon after they expressed jealousy and desire for honour, both Aaron and Miriam died.

Moses

Even Moses failed. He became very impatient with the people. The New Testament tells us that he put up with the people for 40 years in the wilderness. It was an amazing task of leadership to deal with over 2 million people who were always grumbling, complaining and having arguments that needed to be settled.

His big mistake came when he disobeyed God's instructions concerning the provision of water. Moses had provided water for the people by striking the rock with his rod. The limestone of the Sinai Desert has the peculiar property of holding reservoirs of water within itself. There are huge reserves of water in the Sinai Desert, but they are usually surrounded by rock and contained within the rock. Moses had released those reservoirs of water just by touching the rock with his rod.

On this second occasion when they were short of water God told Moses not to strike the rock but just to speak to it. A word would be sufficient to release the water in the rock. But Moses was so impatient with the people that he did not listen to God carefully and he struck the rock twice. God told Moses that because he was disobedient, he would not put a foot in the Promised Land. This is a poignant reminder of how important it is for a leader to listen carefully to God. Moses died at Mount Nebo in sight of the Promised Land, but unable to enter it.

Numbers tells us that it is a big responsibility to lead God's people. It must be done correctly and it must be done God's way.

Individuals

There were a number of individuals who let God down throughout the book of Numbers. The most outstanding was a man called Korah. We find Korah leading a rebellion because he was angry that the priesthood should be exclusively the right of Aaron and his family. Others joined him in this subversion, and soon there were 250 gathered together, challenging the authority of Moses and the priesthood of Aaron. The rebels said they could not believe that God had chosen Moses and Aaron and were critical of their failure to lead the Israelites into the Promised Land.

Then with great drama, Moses told the people to keep away from all the rebels' tents. Fire came down from heaven, struck their tents and destroyed them all. Korah saw it coming and ran away with a few of his followers, but they were swallowed up on some mudflats. (In the Sinai Desert there are mudflats which have a very hard crust but are very soft underneath, like thin ice on a pond. They are like a treacherous swamp or quicksand.)

Despite all this, some of the psalms are written by the sons of Korah. This man's family did not follow him in his rebellion, and his children later became singers in the temple. We do not need to follow our parents when they do evil.

Korah is mentioned in the book of Jude in the New Testament as a warning to Christians not to question God's appointments and become jealous.

Moses then announced that they needed to test whether God had chosen him and his brother for these positions. He told the leaders of the twelve tribes to get hold of twigs from the scrub bushes in the desert. They were to lay these twigs in the holy place before the Lord all night. In the morning Aaron's stick had blossomed with leaves, flowers and budding fruit. The other twigs were dead. From then on they put Aaron's rod inside the ark of the covenant as God's proof that Aaron was his choice and not self-appointed.

People

The people as a whole were problematic, as well as some individuals. Acts tells us that God *endured* their conduct for 40 years in the wilderness. Numbers says that the whole people failed except for two – two out of more than 2 million, not a high proportion. The people had one general problem and failed on three occasions of particular note.

GRUMBLING

The general problem with the people was 'grumbling'. You need no talent to grumble, you need no brains to grumble, you need no character to grumble, you need no self-denial to set up the grumbling business. It is one of the easiest things in the world to do.

The people thought that because God was in the tabernacle, he did not know what they said when they went to their own tents. What a big mistake! They grumbled about the lack of water, they grumbled about the monotonous food. It says they grumbled because they could not have garlic, onions, fish, cucumbers, melons and leeks as they had in Egypt. God heard their grumbling and responded accordingly. Soon he sent them quails to supplement their diet of manna – so many that they lay 1.5 metres thick, covering 12 square miles of ground! The people went out to gather the quail, but while they were still eating the meat, God struck them with a severe plague because they had rejected him.

Grumbling probably does more damage to the people of God than any other sin.

OASIS OF KADESH

The first particular occasion for failure was when they arrived at the last oasis, 66 miles south-west of the Dead Sea (today called Ain Qudeist) in the Negev Desert. They were told to send 12 spies, one from each tribe, to spy out the land and return to tell the whole camp what it was like. They spent 40 days in the south around Hebron and also travelled up to the far north, and they found it a very fertile land. But the conclusion of their report was negative. They spread the rumour that the land would devour them. They would rather go back to Egypt.

Two of the spies, Joshua and Caleb, said that God was with them and there was nothing to fear. They agreed that the land was well fortified and that it was inhabited by much bigger people. We know from archaeology that the average height of the Hebrew slaves was quite small compared to the Canaanites. They agreed too that the walls around the cities provided an obstacle. But they argued that God had not brought them this far to leave them in the desert. They told the people that God would carry them on his shoulders (just as a small boy might feel like a giant on the shoulders of his father).

The pessimistic arguments of the other 10 spies were more persuasive, however. The crowd actually wanted to stone Moses and Aaron for bringing them all this way. It had been just three months since they had left Egypt, but they were prepared to kill Moses and Aaron for bringing them out of slavery! They preferred to trust in what the 10 spies saw and said. They took the majority verdict, which in this case was contrary to God's intentions.

The contrast in the two reports is remarkable. The 10 men said they were not able to take the land and that was that; Joshua and Caleb said, 'We can't, but God can'. This was not merely positive thinking but a willingness to see the problems as opportunities for God.

As a result of the faithless outlook of the majority, God swore that not one of that generation would ever get into the Promised Land – except Joshua and Caleb. We are told that he swore by himself, because there is no one else higher by whom he could swear.

They had been spying out the land for 40 days, so God said that for every day they had spied out the land and come to the wrong conclusion, they would spend one year in the wilderness. He made the punishment fit the crime. This event becomes the hinge of the book of Numbers, just a third of the way through. Had they obeyed God, the rest of the events in the book would never have taken place.

THE VALLEY OF 'SCORPIONS'

The next time the people tested God and failed came after a magnificent victory over the Canaanite king of Arad.

They made their way back down into the deep valley of Arovar, also known as the 'valley of the scorpions'. It is just below Mount Hor and is well known for its scorpion and snake population. Once again the Israelites grumbled against God, returning to the theme of the poor diet, saying they would prefer to return to Egypt rather than remain in the desert.

This time God punished them by sending snakes so that many were bitten and died. Realizing their sin, they asked Moses to intercede for them. God did not stop the snakes, but he sent a cure for the snakebites. Moses set up a copper snake on a pole on the top of the mountain looking over the valley. If anyone was bitten by a snake, they could look at that copper snake on the pole and would not die. All they needed was faith to believe it would work.

PLAIN OF MOAB

The third and final crisis came when they got to the plains of Moab. They achieved a number of victories along the way. They wanted to use a main route through Edom. Their request was denied, despite their historical links (Edom was descended from Esau, Jacob's brother). A battle ensued and God gave them victory over Edom and Moab, so they were feeling confident. They camped by the Jordan looking across to the Promised Land.

But there was opposition to their advance on Canaan. The people of Ammon and Moab, owning land bordering the Promised Land, decided to disrupt their plans and hired a soothsayer from Syria to achieve their aim.

This soothsayer from Damascus was named Balaam. He had built a reputation for seeing the defeats of the armies he had cursed. But he had never been asked to curse Israel, for, as he actually explained to those who hired him, he could only say what God gave him to say! It was customary for a soothsayer to curse the opposition prior to a battle and so Balaam was asked to pronounce ill words upon the Israelites. His motive was purely the fee he would be paid. However, he proved to be unable to utter curses against Israel and ended up blessing her instead. He was unable to help himself!

Balaam announces that God will bless and multiply Israel – a prediction about King David and the son of David. So we have an amazing account of a non-believer prophesying a blessing upon Israel.

The account also tells the extraordinary story of the talking ass who refuses to advance when he sees an angel in his path. After Balaam beats the ass for refusing to move, the ass finally tells him why he is not moving! (Those who question whether this took place forget that animals can be possessed by evil spirits and good spirits. The serpent in the Garden of Eden and Jesus sending demons into the pigs are two biblical examples.) The message is clear: the animal has more sense than Balaam!

It is a sad story because of the sequel. Balaam finally realized how to obtain money from the kings of Ammon and Moab. He told them to forget about cursing but instead to send some of their pretty girls into the camp to seduce the Israelites. As this was prohibited by the law, most of the illicit sex took place outside the camp. But one man, Zimri, had the affront to bring a girl to the very door of the tabernacle.

Seeing this awful act, a man named Phinehas pinned the couple to the ground with a spear. Thereafter he was given a perpetual priesthood for himself and his family. He was the only man to defend God's house against what was happening in God's sight. The judgement may seem harsh, but remember that the Israelites were heading for the Promised Land. One of the worst features they would find there would be immorality. There were fertility goddesses, occult statues and phallic symbols, and all kinds of licentious behaviour. They needed to realize that such things were abominations before God.

What can we learn from Numbers?

Numbers was written for the Jews in order that later generations might learn to fear God. It was, therefore, written for Christians too, so that we might learn from their failures. We have seen already how Paul told the Corinthians that these events were recorded as 'examples', warning us not to live as the Israelites did. We can also fail to arrive, just as they did. The Bible is a mirror in which we see ourselves, according to James. We can live and die in the wilderness; we can look back on the 'pleasures of sin' but be unable to look forward to 'God's rest' in the Promised Land.

We can learn more about the character of God from Numbers, and the twin themes of kindness and sternness are taken up again at various times in the New Testament, in Romans, Hebrews, Jude and 2 Peter.

Jude also mentions both Korah and Balaam. Grumbling was as big a problem in the early Church as it was in Israel. When people grumble and complain it is called a 'bitter root' which can grow inside a fellowship and cause trouble.

In the New Testament we are reminded that we are names, not numbers. Even the hairs of our head are numbered. Our names are in the 'book of life', but there is also evidence that our names can be erased.

What Numbers says about God

In Numbers we are told very clearly that there are two sides to God's character. The apostle Paul draws them out when he says, 'Consider then the kindness and sternness of God...'

1. On the one hand we see his provision of food, drink, clothes and shoes. We see God providing his people with protection from their enemies, greater than them in size and number. We see his preservation of the nation despite their sinfulness.
2. On the other hand we see his justice. He is faithful to his covenant promises, punishing the people when they sin. This involves discipline, and ultimately disinheritance if they refuse to go on and follow his will.

We deal with the same God. He is holy and we must fear him.

What Numbers says about Jesus

1. As Israel went through the wilderness, so Jesus spent 40 days in the wilderness being tempted.
2. John 3:16 is well known, but the verse before it less so: '...as Moses lifted up the serpent in the wilderness, so must the son of man be lifted up.'
3. John also asserts that Jesus is the 'manna', the 'bread from heaven'.
4. Astonishingly, the apostle Paul speaks of the water being struck from the rock in the wilderness, suggesting that the rock was none other than Christ.
5. Hebrews says that if the ashes of a heifer could bring forgiveness, how much more will the blood of Christ achieve the same thing.

6. Perhaps the most amazing thing is that Balaam, the false prophet, actually made a true prophecy about Jesus! 'I see him, but not now; I behold him, but not near. A star will come out of Jacob; a sceptre will rise out of Israel.' From that time on, every devout Jew looked for the star of the king to come, and that is what led the wise men to Bethlehem.

Blessings of fellowship with God

Perhaps the best-known verse in Numbers is 6:24: 'The LORD bless you and keep you; the LORD make his face shine upon you and be gracious to you; the LORD turn his face towards you and give you peace.'

This was the blessing that God gave Aaron to give to the people when they set off from camp on the next part of their journey. It has every mark of direct inspiration from God because it is mathematically perfect. Whenever God speaks, his language is mathematically perfect. In the Hebrew there are three lines in the blessing:

> The LORD bless you and keep you
> The LORD make his face shine upon you and be gracious to you
> The LORD turn his face towards you and give you peace

In the Hebrew, there are 3 words in the first sentence, 5 in the second, and 7 in the third. There are 15 letters in the first, 20 in the second, and 25 in the third. There are 12 syllables in the first, 14 in the second, and 16 in the third. If you take the word 'LORD' out, you are left with 12 Hebrew words. We are left with the Lord and the 12 tribes of Israel! It is mathematically perfect. Even in English it builds up – there is a kind of crescendo through the lines. Each line has two verbs, and the second expands the first.

The blessing applies to Christians today, for the two things the blessing offers are **grace** and **peace**. This is the Christian blessing given in the epistles in the New Testament: 'Grace and peace to you from God our Father and the Lord Jesus Christ.'

We too can receive the blessings of fellowship with God that Israel enjoyed – if we heed the lessons of Numbers.

6.
DEUTERONOMY

Introduction

Every Jewish synagogue includes a large cupboard, usually covered with a curtain or a veil. Inside the cupboard are some scrolls wrapped in beautifully embroidered cloth. These scrolls are the law of Moses. They are called the Torah, which means 'instruction', and are regarded as foundational to the whole Old Testament. They are read through aloud once a year.

When a scroll was removed from the cupboard, the first part would be unrolled to reveal the opening words. The book became known by these words. The book of Deuteronomy is simply called 'The Words', because the first phrase in the Hebrew is 'These are the words'. When the Hebrew Old Testament was translated into Greek, they had to think of a more appropriate name. 'Deuteronomy' comes from two words in the Greek language, *deutero*, which means 'second', and *nomos*, which means 'law'.

The name gives us a clue to its content, for in Deuteronomy we find that the Ten Commandments appear again, just as in the book of Exodus.

A second reading

Why is it that the Ten Commandments need to be repeated a second time? Furthermore, there are 613 laws of Moses in total and many are repeated here. Why?

The clue lies in the book of Numbers. Deuteronomy was written 40 years after the book of Exodus. During those 40 years an entire generation died. These consisted of all the adults who came out of Egypt, crossed the Red Sea, camped at Sinai and heard the Ten Commandments the first time. By the time of Deuteronomy, they were all dead (with the exception of Moses, Joshua and Caleb). They had broken the law so quickly that God had said they would never get into the Promised Land. Their punishment was to wander around the wilderness for the 40 years until an entire generation had disappeared.

The new generation were only little children when they crossed the Red Sea and camped at Sinai. Most of them, therefore, would barely remember what had happened when their fathers came out of Egypt, and certainly would not recall the reading of the law at Sinai. So Moses read and explained the law a second time. Each generation must renew the covenant with God.

There is another reason for the second reading. This is to do with the timing. They were about to go into the Promised Land. They had been on their own in the wilderness and now they were facing a land that was already occupied by enemies. So the law was read and explained when the people were still on the east side of the River Jordan so that they might know what God required of them.

In addition, their leader Moses was not going to go in with them. He had forfeited his right to go in because he disobeyed God's Word concerning the provision of water from the rock. God had shown him that he was going to die in just seven days' time. So Moses wanted to ensure that this new generation were informed about the past and ready to face the future. Indeed, they would see the miracle of the parting of the water all over again, this time with the River Jordan. God wanted them to know his miraculous power, just as the previous generation had done.

It is important that we are clear about the context in which the law was given for the second time. God brought the Israelites through the Red Sea first and then made the covenant at Sinai. He did not tell them how to live until he had saved them. This is a pattern throughout the whole Bible: God first of all shows us his grace by saving us, and then he explains how we should be living.

This new generation were going to see God rescue them and take them through the Jordan, which at that time of year was in flood and impassable. Having seen that miracle, they would go on to their own equivalent of Mount Sinai (Mount Ebal and Gerizim) and hear a repetition of the blessings and curses of the Lord. It was a repeat performance at the end of 40 years for an entirely new generation.

Deuteronomy therefore, the last of the books of Moses, is written and spoken in the Israelites' camp on the east side of the River Jordan, while Moses is still alive and still leading them.

Land

There are certain key phrases in the book of Deuteronomy. One occurs nearly 40 times. It is **'the land the LORD your God gives you'**. The Israelites are reminded that this land is a gift, an undeserved gift. Psalm 24 states that 'The earth is the LORD's, and everything in it.' When we argue about who has the ownership of land, we should remember that ultimately God owns it all. He gives it to whomever he wishes. In Acts 17

Paul, addressing the Athenians on Mars Hill, explained that it is God who decides how much space and how much time a nation has on this earth.

The second phrase which occurs the same number of times is **'go in and possess the land'**. Everything we receive from God is a gift, but we have to take it. Salvation is a free gift from God, but we must 'go in and possess it' for it to be ours. God does not force it on us. Possessing the land would be a very costly thing for the Israelites: they would have to fight for it; they would have to struggle for it. Even though God gives everything to us, we have to make an effort to take it.

An important question arising from Deuteronomy concerns the ownership of the land. Was it to be theirs for ever, or was it theirs to keep or lose? There are two conclusions we can draw.

1. UNCONDITIONAL OWNERSHIP

God said he was giving the land to them *for ever*. This did not, however, mean they could necessarily *occupy* it for ever.

2. CONDITIONAL OCCUPATION

The occupation of the land was conditional. *Whether* they lived in it and enjoyed it depended on *how* they lived in it.

The Deuteronomy message is very simple: You can keep the land as long as you keep my law. If you do not keep my law, even though you own the land and I have given it to you, you will not be free to live in it and enjoy it.

There is a difference between 'unconditional ownership' and 'conditional occupation'. This distinction was one about which the prophets of the Old Testament needed to remind the people. The prophets could see that the people's behaviour would mean a forfeiture of their right to keep the land.

To this day the promises of God are conditional. They are gifts, but how we live in those promises determines whether we can enjoy them.

Covenant framework

The framework of covenant described in Deuteronomy was used throughout the ancient Near East. Whenever a king expanded his empire and conquered other countries he would make what was known as a 'suzerain treaty'. This was an agreement which in basic terms said that if the conquered behaved themselves, the king would protect them and provide for them, but if they misbehaved, he would punish them. Numerous examples of such treaties from the ancient world have been uncovered by archaeologists, particularly in Egypt. The pattern of the treaties is exactly the same in outline as the book of Deuteronomy.

Presumably Moses saw and studied these treaties when he was educated in Egypt. Moses presents the covenant to the people of Israel in the form of a treaty since the Lord was their king, and they were his subjects. The pattern of the suzerain treaty went as follows:

- **Preamble**: 'This is a treaty between Pharaoh and the Hittites…'
- **Historical prologue** summarizing how the king and his new subjects came to be related to each other
- **Declaration of the basic principles** on which the whole treaty would be based
- **Detailed laws** as to how the subjects were to behave
- **Sanctions** (i.e. rewards or punishments): what the king would do if they did behave properly, and what he would do if they did not

- **Witnessed signature**, normally calling on 'the gods' to witness the treaty
- **Provision for continuity**: what would happen if the king died and naming a successor to whom the people would still be subject

All would be settled in a ceremony when the treaty would be written down, signed and agreed by the king and his new subjects.

It is easy to see the parallels between this form and the form and content of the law given in Deuteronomy:

- **Preamble** 1:1–5
- **Historical prologue** 1:6–4:49
- **Declaration of basic principles** 5–11
- **Detailed laws** 12–26
- **Sanctions** 27–28
- **Invocation of divine witness** 30:19; 31:19; 32
- **Provision for continuity** 31–34

The sanctions are a key part of the book and concern our understanding of later events in biblical history. There were two things that God would do in terms of sanctions if the Israelites did not live the way he told them to.

NATURAL SANCTIONS

The natural sanction he could impose was the absence of rain. The land they were entering was between the Mediterranean Sea and the Arabian desert. When the wind blew from the west it would pick up rain from the Mediterranean and drop it on the Promised Land. But if the wind came from the east, it would be the dry, hot desert wind which dries up everything and turns the land into a place of desolation. During Elijah's day, therefore, God punished the idolatry of the people with a drought for three and a half years. This was a simple way of God rewarding or punishing the people.

MILITARY SANCTIONS

If the natural sanction failed, he would move on to something rather more fierce. He would use human agents to attack them. Amos 9 tells us something very significant in this regard. We read that when Israel was crossing the Jordan, God brought another people at the same time into the same land from the west. These people were called Philistines. Thus God brought a people who proved to be Israel's greatest enemy into the same land at the same time. Israel settled in the hills and the Philistines on the coastal plain (now the Gaza Strip). If Israel were faithful in keeping the laws they would enjoy peace. If they misbehaved God would send the Philistines to deal with them. It was as simple as that.

Corruption

The land of Canaan was inhabited by a mixture of Amorites and Canaanites. God told the Israelites to drive out these nations and possess the land. This point has given rise to a common objection to the Bible. Such apparent genocide seems barbaric to the modern mind. How can we reconcile a God of love with a God who tells the Jews to slaughter all the people living in the Promised Land? It seems immoral and unjust.

The answer is found back in Genesis. God told Abraham that he would keep his family and their descendants in a foreign country for 400 years until the wickedness of the Amorites was complete. God actually waited 400 years for those people to become so bad that they no longer deserved to live in Canaan – because they did not deserve to live anywhere on his earth. God does not allow people to go on occupying his earth regardless of what they do. He is very patient with them, but eventually he will act in judgement. Archaeology has revealed evidence of just how wicked the Amorites were. Sexually transmitted diseases were commonplace amongst them, for example. If the Israelites had mixed with these people it would have been like living in a land where everybody had AIDS, quite apart from the generally unhealthy influence of their corrupt lifestyle.

In Deuteronomy God says, 'It is not because of your righteousness or your integrity that you are going in to take possession of their land; but on account of the wickedness of these nations, the LORD your God will drive them out before you, to accomplish what he swore to your forefathers, to Abraham, Isaac and Jacob.'

Some ask why it was necessary for the *Israelites* to slaughter them. Could God not have destroyed them himself? The answer is very clear. He needed to teach the Israelites the importance of living the way he said. If they behaved like the Amorites, they would go exactly the same way.

When we read Deuteronomy we must realize that we are reading a *mirror image* of life in Canaan. Everything God tells the Israelites not to do is what was already happening in Canaan. We can build up a picture of what was happening in the Promised Land before they got into it. This can be summarized in three words.

1. IMMORALITY

We have noted already that there were sexually transmitted diseases in the land. There was fornication, adultery, incest, homosexuality, transvestism and buggery. There was also widespread divorce and remarriage. Deuteronomy outlines how all such behaviour was strictly prohibited.

2. INJUSTICE

Deuteronomy also addresses injustice. 'The rich were getting richer and the poorer getting poorer.' The age-old sins of pride, greed and selfishness were evident, leading to exploitation of the poor. Those with disabilities, the blind, the deaf, were not cared for. Many people were unable to break the shackles of poverty caused by usury. God said the Israelites were to be selfless. They were to look after the deaf, the blind, the widow and the orphan. People mattered.

3. IDOLATRY

Canaan was full of idolatry. There was occultism, superstition, astrology, spiritism, necromancy, and fertility cults. They worshipped 'Mother Earth', believing that sexual acts had links with the fertility of the land. In the pagan temples there were male and female prostitutes, and worship included sex. These practices were reflected in the monuments throughout the land: *asherah* poles (phallic symbols) were frequently seen on the hills as a witness to the pagan rituals which predominated.

Deuteronomy makes it clear how God viewed such behaviour. It was his land and it was now totally corrupt, defiled, debased. It was disgraced and God could not let it go on. Are things so different now?

The last work of Moses

Deuteronomy is the last of the five books of Moses, the Pentateuch. We have seen that it was written at a critical moment for the people of Israel. They were about to enter the Promised Land, but Moses was not going to lead them. He was by then an old man of 120, and was entering his last week of life (the book ends with his death). Having seen the weakness of the present generation's parents, he was afraid that they might go the same way. He saw ahead to the battles they would need to fight, both physical and spiritual.

In the last week of his life he spoke three times to them. The whole of Deuteronomy is made up of three long speeches, each of which must have taken the best part of a day to give. This spoken style comes across. It is a very personal and emotional book. Moses is appealing to the people, like a dying father to his children.

It is quite likely that during these last six days of the last week in Moses' life he spoke and wrote on alternate days. On days 1, 3 and 5 he gave these discourses, then on days 2, 4 and 6 he wrote down what he had said the previous day. He handed what he wrote to the priests, who placed it alongside the ark of the covenant, so that the people would never forget. This is his 'last will and testament', the greatest prophet of the Old Testament bringing the Word of the Lord to his people.

The book can be neatly divided into the three parts.

1. Past: Recollection (1:1–4:43)
a. faithlessness condemned (1:6–3:29)
b. faithfulness counselled (4:1–43)

2. Present: Regulation (4:44–26:19)
a. love expressed (4:44–11:32)
b. law expanded (12:1–26:19)

3. Future: Retribution (27:1–34:12)
a. covenant affirmed (27:1–30:20)
b. continuity assured (31:1–34:12)

First Discourse (1:1–4:43) Past

In the first discourse, Moses looks back to the days after Sinai when God had made the covenant with his listeners' parents. He reminds them that although it only takes 11 days to walk from Sinai to the Promised Land, their parents took 13,780. When they arrived at Kadesh Barnea on the border, they paused and at God's instruction sent one man from each of the tribes to spy out the land. The spies were positive about the quality of food in the land, but not about their chances of conquering it. The people were too big and the towns impregnable, they said. Only two, Joshua and Caleb, urged the people to trust God and go on.

Israel had everything in front of them and yet their morale failed. Although God had been faithful to them, they were faithless. The message of Chapter 4 is simply this: 'Do not be like your parents. They lost their faith and they lost the land. If you keep yours, you can keep the land.'

Second Discourse (4:44–26:19) Present

The legislation in the second part is not as easy to read. It is by far the longest section, probably given on the third day of that last week in Moses' life. It outlines the way the Israelites must live if they are to remain in the land God is giving them.

Summary

Chapter 5 Moses begins with the basic principles of God's righteous way of living, his upright way of living, namely the Ten Commandments. These are all about one thing, *respect*. Respect God, respect his name, respect his day, respect your parents, respect life, respect marriage, respect property, respect people's reputation. The quickest way to destroy society is to destroy respect.

It is very interesting to draw a contrast between the law of Moses and the laws in pagan society. If you contrast the standards in Moses' law with the worst practices of pagan society, as we have already done with the Amorites in Canaan, it is obvious what a pure, holy law is given in the Ten Commandments.

Chapter 6 The covenant law is expounded and expanded. We are told the *purpose* for the law: it is so that love can be communicated from one generation to the next.

Chapter 7 They are commanded to abolish all idolatry (i.e. the First Commandment) and exterminate the Canaanites, that they may not be led astray.

Chapter 8 They are encouraged to remember with gratitude God's dealings with his people. They are warned not to forget, especially when prosperity comes.

9:1–10:11 Moses reviews the sin and rebelliousness of the people. They are warned not to become self-righteous.

10:12–11:33 The theme in this section is obedience. If they are obedient they will be blessed; if they are disobedient they will be cursed – the choice is theirs. This is an emphasis throughout the book. The word 'hear' comes 50 times and the words 'do', 'keep' and 'observe' 177 times.

Alongside this, it is important to know that another common word in Moses' exposition is 'love'. It is used 31 times. If you love the Lord you keep his laws. In the New Testament Paul says that love is the fulfilling of the law. It is not a matter of legalism, but a matter of love. To love is to obey, because in God's sight love is loyalty. It means staying true to someone. Love and law are not opposed to one another – they stand together.

Chapters 12–26 A huge amount is covered in these chapters, sometimes in amazing detail. In this section of his speech Moses passes from the general to the particular, from the vertical (our relationship with God) to the horizontal (our relationship with others).

Contrasting standards

We can best observe these laws against a background of contrasts. What was so different, so special, about the law of Moses compared to other societies in the region?

1. STANDARDS IN THE PROMISED LAND

We have already seen how the laws in Deuteronomy are a *mirror image* of what was taking place in the land at that time. Some of the more puzzling laws relate to the practices of those already occupying the land.

2. STANDARDS IN NEIGHBOURING LANDS

There is also an interesting comparison to be made between the law of Moses and another law which has been discovered from the ancient world, the code of Hammurabi, an ancient Amorite King of Babylon (or Babel). These laws were written 300 years before Moses. They include prohibitions on killing, adultery, stealing and false witness. Furthermore, the famous law of *lex talionis*, or the law of revenge ('an eye for an eye and a tooth for a tooth'), is also included. All this should not surprise us. In Romans the apostle Paul says that God 'has written his law on the hearts' of pagans. He did not just write it on stone –

he has written it into the hearts of people so that everyone knows that certain things are wrong. For example, every society in the world has always thought incest was wrong.

There are, however, some big differences between Hammurabi's law and the law of Moses. There was just one punishment for any wrong done, and that was death. In the law of Moses the death penalty is quite rare. There are only 18 things in the law of Moses that deserve the death penalty. By comparison to Hammurabi's law, the law of Moses is not nearly so harsh.

Another huge difference is that in the law of Moses slaves and women are treated as people, whereas in the law of Hammurabi they are treated as property. Women have none of the rights and respect in the law of Hammurabi that they possess in the law of Moses.

The law of Hammurabi also includes class distinctions. There are nobles and common people, and a different law applies depending on the class. In the law of Moses there is no such thing as class. The same law applies to everybody.

A final point to note is that the laws of Hammurabi are *casuistic* laws – they are presented in the form of conditions. '*If* you do this, *then* you must die.' The laws of Moses are presented in what is called an *apodeictic* manner – not as conditions, but as commands. 'You *must not* do this.' The laws of Moses reflect God's right as king to say what should be. He makes commands because he sets the standard.

The commands and legislation fall into a number of different categories, detailed in the following sections.*

---

* For the following classification of the Mosaic laws I am indebted to my friend F. LaGard Smith, Professor of Law in Pepperdine University, Malibu, California, who has produced the New International Version without chapter and verse numbers, with the books in chronological order and with the laws arranged in convenient categories, as here. The hardback is entitled *The Narrated Bible* and the paperback *The Daily Bible* (both Harvest House, 1978).

1. Religious/ceremonial

IDOLATRY/PAGANISM

■ Israel is forbidden to follow other gods, or erect graven images. We are told that the Lord is a jealous God. Jealousy is an appropriate emotion for God, even if we might not think so at first. We are jealous when we want what is ours. Envy is when we want what is *not* ours. So just as it would be appropriate for a man to be jealous if another man took his wife, it is right that God should be jealous for his people when they follow other gods.

■ As a consequence of the First Commandment, *asherah* poles are specifically forbidden.

■ There are laws about cutting flesh and shaving heads when mourning.

■ If a relative seeks to entice their family away from the worship of God, they must be put to death – there should be no mercy.

■ When attacking idolatrous cities the Israelites are told to kill all the people and burn the city so that it could never be rebuilt.

■ Idolaters are to be stoned on the word of two or three witnesses, one of whom should be responsible for casting the first stone.

■ There is to be one place of worship. All 'high places' where the Canaanites worship are to be destroyed.

■ The Israelites are not to enquire about or get interested in other religions. They must shun child sacrifice, which is detestable.

FALSE SPIRITUALISTS

■ All false prophets, dreamers, and those who 'follow other gods' are to be put to death.

- All forms of spiritualism are punishable by death: consulting the dead, witchcraft, omens, spells, mediums.
- We are told that a true prophet like Moses will be raised up (a reference to Jesus).
- When false prophets speak in the name of other gods, or when they speak but the prophecy does not come true, they are to be put to death.

BLASPHEMY

- If the name of God is misused, the miscreant must be put to death.

DEDICATIONS

- All first-born animals must be dedicated to the Lord.

TITHING

- A tenth of all produce is to be set aside. Every three years produce would be passed on for the Levites, aliens, fatherless and widows.

CONQUEST

- Baskets of firstfruits are to be offered from any land the Israelites conquer.
- They are to declare their history when they arrive in the land, recounting their rescue from Egypt.
- Prayers of thanksgiving are also to be made.

SABBATH

- Up until the time of Moses, nobody had a Sabbath. It is a new provision for slaves who have previously worked seven days a week, but who are now given one day a week free from work.

FEASTS (ALL PILGRIM EVENTS)

- Passover.
- Weeks (Pentecost).
- Tabernacles.

SACRIFICES AND OFFERINGS

- If there is a murder, and the perpetrator cannot be found, a heifer is to be sacrificed to declare the innocence of the community.

EXCLUSIONS FROM THE ASSEMBLY

- Those with mutilated or castrated genitals are excluded from the assembly of the Lord.
- Children of forbidden unions (up to the tenth generation) are also forbidden to enter.
- Ammonites and Moabites are explicitly forbidden.
- Edomites (from the third generation) are permitted to enter.

VOWS

- Whatever we vow we must do. Vows are freely made, so should be followed through. If you make a vow to God you must keep it.

SEPARATION

- No mixing of seeds is allowed.
- A donkey and an ox should not be yoked together.
- Clothes of wool and linen may not be mixed.

These laws of separation may seem very strange, but they were connected to the old fertility cult which was widespread in the land. The pagans believed that by mixing such things they were producing fertility. God was emphasizing that *he* gives fertility: they did not need to practise such superstition.

2. Government

KING

There are laws here for a king, even though they were not to have a king for centuries.

- God is their king – kingship is a concession, not part of his plan.
- When a king comes to the throne he has to write out the laws of Moses in his own handwriting and read them regularly.
- The king is instructed not to have many wives, many horses, or much money.

JUDGES

- Rules for conducting law courts are given, including provision for a court of appeal. Interestingly, the penalty for contempt of court given here is death.
- There are also rules for justice: no bribes and no favouritism. An alien, an orphan and a widow must get exactly the same treatment as the richest businessman.
- There must be at least two or three witnesses who agree totally on what they have seen or heard. If they bear false witness they must suffer exactly what the person would have suffered if they were found guilty. If my false testimony in court gets someone fined £1,000, then when I am discovered to be a false witness I am fined £1,000. 'An eye for an eye, a tooth for a tooth.'
- There are regulations covering the administration of punishments. Floggings are to be a maximum of 40 strokes (they usually made it 39 to make quite sure they did not break the law). Excessive flogging is dehumanizing – the criminal is treated like a lump of meat. When a person is executed, the

body must not be left hanging on the tree after sunset. (The apostle Paul applies that to Jesus on the cross in Galatians.) There is no imprisonment.

3. Special crimes

AGAINST PERSONS

- Murder always carries the death penalty, unless it was manslaughter and unintended. Six cities of refuge, three either side of the Jordan, are to be set up where a man who has killed accidentally can run to escape the death penalty.
- Kidnapping also carries the death penalty.
- Death is the penalty for rapists if the attack took place in the country, but both parties are to be put to death if the attack took place in the town, because the victim could have cried out.

AGAINST PROPERTY

- There are laws against theft and the removing of boundary markers around land.

4. Personal rights and responsibilities

- Injuries and damages.
- Masters and servants: slaves have rights; workers should be paid on time.
- Credit, interest and collateral. Debts are to be cancelled after seven years by every creditor cancelling loans made to fellow Israelites. Interest must not be charged.
- Weights and measures. Properly weighted scales are to be used at all times.
- Inheritance. It is the responsibility of the next of kin to continue the family line.

5. Sexual relations

- Marriage. Strict instructions concerning the marriage bond, for those married, those pledged to be married, and those raped.
- Divorce. Divorce on the grounds of the husband 'disliking' his wife is prohibited. Remarriage to the original husband following a divorce is forbidden to protect the innocent woman.
- Adultery. Both parties should be put to death.
- Transvestism. Cross-dressing is detestable to God.

6. Health

- For leprosy there is a careful procedure to follow if anyone suspects they may have the disease, involving examination by the priest.
- There are laws against eating animals that are found dead.
- Strict rules govern 'clean and unclean food'. Camels, rabbits, pigs and certain birds must not appear on the menu.
- Meat and milk are not to be cooked together.

This last point is a law which has been misunderstood by almost every Jew: 'You shall not boil a kid in its mother's milk.' On the basis of this one verse the Jews have erected a 'kosher' system of diet whereby they have (effectively) two kitchens with two completely different sets of pots and pans and sinks to wash them in – in order that dairy products are kept separate from meat products, which Abraham never did, offering veal and butter to his visitors. They have totally misunderstood the purpose of the law, which once again was connected to a rite of the pagan fertility cult. The Canaanites believed that cooking a kid in its mother's milk caused it to have incest with its mother, which then promoted fertility.

7. Welfare

- Benevolence is not just encouraged, it is commanded. Sheaves of corn are to be left in the corner of the field for the poor to pick up.
- Parents should expect respect and support from their children: a stubborn, rebellious son is to be put to death.
- Neighbours whose animals have strayed are to be assisted.
- Animals are to be treated well: no one should muzzle an ox when it is treading out grain; it is permitted to take birds' eggs from the nest, but the mother should not be removed – she is to be left so that she can lay some more eggs.

8. Warfare

- Preparation is vital. War is not for the faint-hearted. Those afraid can go home.
- During a siege the soldiers must not cut down the trees around a city.
- A toilet area should be set up outside the camp and all waste covered up.
- A soldier who has recently been married can stay at home for a year before he has to go to war again. No one should go to war at the expense of a marriage at home.

What are we to make of all this?

1. SCOPE

God is interested in the whole of our lives. Living right is not just what you do in church on Sunday but concerns the whole of life. There is a right way to do everything. God wants people to be right in every area of their lives.

2. INTEGRATION

These laws show an amazing integration. We move, say, from a law about not eating camels to a law about observing a feast day. This is not pleasing to the modern western mind. We feel we must somehow classify all these laws. But God is saying that there is no division in life – there is no sacred/secular divide; all of life is for God.

3. PURPOSE

There is a clear purpose for all these laws. It was not to spoil the people's fun, or to hedge them about with restrictions. A recurrent phrase throughout the book is **'that it may be well with you and that you may live a long life in the land'**. God wants us healthy and happy, so he gave us laws. Some people picture God sitting in heaven saying 'don't' and 'thou shalt not'. But his purpose for prohibition is always for our good. He is concerned for our 'welfare'.

Third Discourse (27:1–34:12) Future

The third and last discourse given by Moses is in two parts.

1. Covenant affirmed (27:1–30:20)

In the first part he tells the Israelites that they are to ratify the law for themselves. After crossing the Jordan they are to stand below Mount Ebal and Mount Gerizim. The mountains are directly next to each other and form an amphitheatre with the valley in between. The leaders are to shout the blessings from Mount Gerizim and the curses from Mount Ebal. After each sentence they are to respond with an 'amen' – i.e. 'this is certain!' These curses and blessings are all included in Deuteronomy 28 (and, incidentally, in the Anglican Book of Common Prayer, to be recited every Lent).

Words are powerful. The rest of the history of the Old Testament hinges on Israel's response to these blessings and curses. When we read Deuteronomy 28, it is like reading the whole history of Israel for the last 4,000 years.

2. Continuity assured (31:1–34:12)

Joshua is appointed as Moses' successor at the age of 80. Moses then gives the written law to priests, who place it beside the ark. He commands that the whole law be recited every seven years.

Moses finishes his message with a song. Like many prophets he was also a musician. His sister Miriam sang following the crossing of the Sea of Reeds, and now Moses recites the words of a song before his death. The song details the faithfulness of God and his just dealings with Israel. He is a rock, utterly dependable, unchangeable, totally reliable. After the song is finished, Moses blesses the 12 tribes and includes prophetic glimpses into the future.

Finally comes the death and burial of Moses – the only part of the five books of Moses that he did not write! Presumably Joshua added the details. Moses died alone, with his back against the rock on the top of Mount Nebo, looking across the Jordan to the land that had been promised, but in which he would never set foot.

Centuries later, we read in the Gospels that Moses spoke with Jesus on top of one of the mountains, but he never entered Canaan in his earthly life. He was also buried on Mount Nebo, though not by his fellow people. In the New Testament Jude tells us that an angel came to bury him. When the angel got to Moses, the devil was standing on the other side of him. The devil pointed out that this man was his because he had murdered an Egyptian. But the archangel Michael said to the devil, 'The Lord rebuke you!' and so Moses was buried by the angel. It was an amazing end to an amazing life. The people mourned him for one month before preparing to cross the River Jordan.

The importance of Deuteronomy

Deuteronomy is the key to the whole history of Israel. Unable and unwilling to expel the Canaanites from the land when they first arrived, very soon they had intermarried and were involved in the same evil practices as the pagans. In fact it took them a thousand years, from the time of Abraham to the time of David, finally to inhabit the land promised to them. In the following 500 years they lost it all, as we shall see in the book of Kings. The whole history of Israel can be summarized in just two sentences. Obedience and righteousness brought them blessing. Disobedience and wickedness brought them curses. All this is made abundantly clear in the book of Deuteronomy.

Deuteronomy plays a huge part in the New Testament too. It is quoted 80 times in just 27 books.

Jesus

- Jesus was *the* prophet foretold by Moses in Deuteronomy.
- Jesus knew Deuteronomy very well. When he was tempted in the wilderness he used the Scriptures to defend himself, and each time he quoted from Deuteronomy.
- In the Sermon on the Mount we are told that not 'one jot or tittle' will pass from the law.
- When Jesus was asked to summarize the law of Moses, he summarized it in words from Deuteronomy: 'Love the LORD your God with all your heart and soul and mind and strength,' and Leviticus: 'Love your neighbour as yourself.'

Paul

- Paul used Deuteronomy when he wrote about the importance of our hearts being changed.
- He used Jesus' death as an example of one who was cursed.

■ He quotes the law about muzzling the ox as a principle to be
applied when supporting preachers.

Christians and Moses' law

How, then, should Christians today read the law of Moses?

Particular precepts

We are not under the law of Moses, but under the law of Christ.
We need to find out, therefore, whether each Old Testament
law is repeated or reinterpreted in the New Testament.

For example, out of the Ten Commandments, only the
Fourth concerning the Sabbath is not repeated in the New
Testament. And tithes are not enforced in the New Testament
either, although we are encouraged to give generously, cheer-
fully and liberally. Laws about clean and unclean food are
abolished.

General principles

We are saved *for* righteousness not *by* righteousness. This is an
important concept to grasp. The need 'to do' is just as common in the New Testament as in the Old, but the motivation is
also all-important now. Our righteousness must 'exceed that of
the Pharisees and the scribes', but now our righteousness is
inward as well as outward. Now we have the Spirit to enable us.
Thus we are justified by faith, but judged by works.

It is worth noting, too, that Deuteronomy is a warning
against syncretism. We can easily incorporate pagan practices
into our lives without realizing it. Hallowe'en and Christmas,
for instance, were originally both pagan festivals, which the
Church sought to 'make Christian' when they should have
avoided them altogether.

Conclusion

Deuteronomy is a crucial book within Israel's history, and not just because it was one of the five books of Moses. It reminds people of the past, teaches them how to live in the present, and urges them to look ahead to the future. It reflects Moses' concern that his people should not go astray. At the same time it states God's desire that his people, by honouring and respecting him, should be worthy of the land he was giving them.

A LAND AND A
KINGDOM

7.

JOSHUA

Introduction

A schoolteacher asked a classroom of children: 'Who knocked down the walls of Jericho?' There was a long silence before a small boy said, 'Please sir, I didn't!'

Later that day in the staffroom, the teacher recounted the incident to the headmaster. 'Do you know what happened in my classroom today? I asked who knocked down the walls of Jericho and that boy Smith said, "Please sir, I didn't."'

The headmaster replied, 'Well, I've known Smith some years and I know his family – they're a good family. If he says he didn't do it, I'm sure he didn't.'

The headmaster later reported the boy's answer to a visiting school inspector, whose response was: 'It's probably too late to find out who did it; get them repaired and send the bill to us.'

The joke, of course, is that everybody should know who knocked down the walls of Jericho. It is one of the better known stories in the Bible. If they do not know the story from the Bible, then they have heard the Negro spiritual song 'Joshua fit the battle of Jericho'. But this is the only part of the book many people do know. Joshua is not a well known book and a knowledge of the battle does not mean that everyone believes it actually happened. For even this story raises questions: How were the walls knocked down? Were they, in fact, knocked down at all?

It is clear that there are a number of preliminary questions for us to consider as we look at the book of Joshua. First of all we need to ask what sort of a book it is and how we should read the incredible stories it contains. We will then go on to look at the content and structure of the book, and how Christians can read it for maximum benefit.

What kind of a book is Joshua?

Joshua is the sixth book in the Old Testament. In our English Bible it is the book after Deuteronomy, with an apparently logical flow from the death of Moses at the end of Deuteronomy to the commissioning of Moses' successor Joshua at the start of the next book. To the Jews, however, the significance of the book's position is quite different. The end of Deuteronomy marks the end of the Torah, the law of Moses. These five books are read annually in the synagogue, with Genesis 1:1 beginning the New Year and Deuteronomy 34:12 being read at its end. Each of the five books is named after its first words, since these would be the words seen at the start of the scroll when the books came to be selected for reading. Joshua is the first book to be known by the name of its author.

Joshua is also a completely new type of literature. The first five books of the Bible set out the basic constitution of the people of Israel and are foundational to all that follows. By contrast, there is not a single law in Joshua, or in the books that follow. In Joshua we begin to see how the law is worked out in practice.

Joshua tends to be regarded as a history book because it comes in what is regarded as the history section of the English Bible. But it is more than just a history book. As we saw in the Overview of the Old Testament (pages 1–14), the Jews divide the Old Testament into three sections, rather like a library with books collected under three categories. The first five are the 'books of the law', also called the Torah or the Pentateuch. The 'books of the prophets' come next. Joshua is the first book of the 'former prophets', followed by Judges, 1 and 2 Samuel, and 1 and 2 Kings. The books of Isaiah to Malachi comprise the 'latter prophets', with a few exceptions. The third section is 'the writings', which includes Psalms, Job, Proverbs, Ruth, Song of Songs, Ecclesiastes, Lamentations, Esther, Daniel, Ezra, Nehemiah, and 1 and 2 Chronicles. So two books which are in the English Bible as prophets – Daniel and Lamentations – are part of 'the writings' in the Jewish Old Testament arrangement. Chronicles is the last book of the writings, although the English Bible includes it in the history section.

Joshua's inclusion as a book of prophecy under the Jewish arrangement surprises many, for most of it is in narrative form and reads more like straight history than the poetic prophecy of later books. There are, however, a number of reasons why we should concur with this 'prophecy' tag.

First, it is not widely known that Joshua was a prophet. It is true that he is better known as a military commander, but he was a prophet just like Moses in that he heard from God and spoke for God. Indeed, the last chapter of the book records Joshua, in the first person singular, delivering God's message to the people.

Second, biblical history is in any case a special kind of history. There are two principles which have to be followed when writing any history:

■ **Selection** – it is impossible to include everything, even when covering a short period of time. The Bible's history is highly selective, focusing largely on one nation and only on certain events within that nation's life.
■ **Connection** – a good historian takes seemingly disparate events and shows how they link together, so that a common theme is developed.

Using these two principles, we can see why the history in Joshua and the other 'history' books in the Bible is in fact *prophetic*. The author selects the events which are significant to God or are explained by God's activity. Only a prophet can write this kind of history, for only a prophet has insight into what to include and why. Seeing the book as prophecy reminds us that the real hero of the book is not Joshua but God (and this applies to any book of the Bible). We see God's activity in this world, what he says and what he does. Therefore, whilst it is genuine history, in that it describes what happened, we must see it as *prophetic* history, for it declares the reality of God and his work in the world.

The chart below shows the contrast between the books of the 'former prophets' and the books of the law.

FIRST FIVE BOOKS	**NEXT SIX BOOKS**
Genesis	Joshua
Exodus	Judges
Leviticus	1 and 2 Samuel
Numbers	1 and 2 Kings
Deuteronomy	
LAW (TORAH)	PROPHETS (FORMER)
PROMISE	FULFILMENT
GRACE	GRATITUDE
REDEMPTION	RIGHTEOUSNESS
LEGISLATION	APPLICATION
BLESSINGS	OBEDIENCE (LAND GIVEN)
CURSES	DISOBEDIENCE (LAND TAKEN)
COVENENT ESTABLISHED	COVENANT EXPRESSED
CAUSE	EFFECT

There are a number of things to note from this chart.

1 The law includes **God's promises to Israel**. The former prophets describe **how these promises were fulfilled**.

2 The law is **God's grace** expressed to the people. The former prophets show **how the people responded in gratitude** to what they heard (although, as we will see, this gratitude was often sadly lacking).

3 The books of the law describe **God's redemption of his people** from Egypt (Exodus). The former prophets explain **how the people were to respond** to God's initiative by living in righteousness.

4 The books of the law tell how **God would bless obedience and punish disobedience**. In Joshua we see **how an obedient response led to victory**, as in the battle of Jericho. Conversely, we also see the ramifications of disobedience to the law, as in the defeat at Ai. Continued disobedience meant that the land claimed in the book of Joshua was taken away in 2 Kings.

The former prophets tell the tragic story of how the people won the Promised Land through obedience to the law, but then forfeited it because of disobedience. To put it another way: the first five books are the cause and the next six books the effect.

How should we read Joshua?

Before focusing on the book of Joshua itself we need to deal with the scholarly debate which can undermine our reading of so much biblical history. Many scholars argue that biblical truth is not historical or scientific but moral and religious. They are quite happy to accept that miraculous events form part of the Bible – just as long as no one is expected to believe that they actually took place! They suggest that biblical history is 'myth' or 'legend', teaching spiritual truths or values but not describing actual events which took place.

We need not deny that parts of the Bible are fictional. Jesus' parables are technically 'myths'. It does not matter whether there was an actual prodigal son or not, since the purpose of the story was to communicate important truth to the hearers. However, admitting that the Bible contains stories is a long way from agreeing that events included in the Bible are fiction.

Questioning the truth of the Bible began in the nineteenth century, when scholars argued that Adam and Eve were not real people but mythological figures whose activities explain universal truths. They said that the Fall was not the entrance of sin into the world, with a real Adam and Eve eating fruit prohibited by God, but a story showing the universal truth that if you tell someone not to touch something, they will want to touch it!

This approach did not stop with the story of Adam and Eve. Noah's ark was next and eventually there were few biblical events which escaped this type of scrutiny. After this we were apparently left with a kind of biblical version of *Aesop's Fables*, which conveys spiritual truth but has minimal historical basis.

The process of reading the Bible from this standpoint was given a long name: *demythologization*. Put simply, this means that in order to obtain the truth, one must discard the story (myth), and with it any suggestion that the story is based on historical fact. Miraculous or supernatural elements can therefore be discarded as being part of the myth.

This demythologization did not stop with the Old Testament: the New Testament was also attacked. The virgin birth, the miracles and the resurrection were regarded as soft targets. This scholarly debate affected theological training, and before long there were church leaders who taught that it did not matter whether the resurrection actually took place, providing people *believed* that it did. They said that if Jesus' bones did still lie rotting in Israel, it made no difference to our 'faith'.

With this background in mind, it is no surprise to find that concerns have been raised regarding elements of the book of Joshua, not least the story of the fall of Jericho. Scholars reasoned that the miracles in the story could not be accepted as fact by readers in a sophisticated scientific age. They saw it instead merely as a tale teaching us that God wants us to win our battles.

However, demythologizing Joshua requires much of the book to be cut out, for there are many apparent myths within the book: the Jordan river dries up, the Jericho walls collapse, hailstones help win a battle, and the sun and moon stand still for a whole day.

How do we respond to such an attempt to undermine the historical value of Joshua?

1 If we were to accept that miracles do not happen, we would be left with a purely human history, with little or no spiritual benefit. **God's part would be totally excluded**. The 'values' or 'truths' would be of no more value than the sort of lessons gleaned, for example, from the secular history of China.

2 Mythical writings invent places and people to distinguish the genre from proper history, but biblical history is completely different. **Joshua includes real places** we can visit today: the River Jordan, Jericho and Jerusalem. **It also includes real people groups**, which secular historians acknowledge existed at this time: the Canaanites and the Israelites.

3 Joshua claims to be **written by contemporary eyewitnesses**. The first person plural 'we' is used, for the writers were reflecting on events they had seen. Furthermore, a common phrase in the text is 'to this day'. Contemporaries of the writer could check out the details. This is not a fable about mythical characters, but a sequence of historical events described by people who were there.

4 **Archaeologists confirm a great deal of information given in Joshua**. They have discovered that the entire culture of some of the cities included in the book changed over a 50-year period. There is evidence that cities such as Hazor, Bethel and Lachish were destroyed between 1250 and 1200 BC and the inhabitants reverted to a far simpler lifestyle. The date of this change fits with Joshua's account of how these cities were conquered.

5 Those who question the miraculous events in Joshua ignore the fact that the events in themselves are not necessarily miraculous. It is no problem for us to accept the miraculous, but it is interesting to note that such phenomena can be explained. For example, the River Jordan dries up during floods even today. The river meanders through the Jordan Valley and, because of the flood conditions, undercuts the banks on the curve. These banks can be so undercut that they collapse, causing the river to dam itself, sometimes for up to five hours. Similarly, in modern times, we know that large buildings collapse. Cathedrals and skyscrapers have fallen in the same manner as the walls described in Joshua. **It is not the events that are miraculous so much as the *timing***. The river dries up and the walls fall just when God said they would.

6 We have noted already that the Bible is not the history of Israel as such, for there is much that is excluded. Joshua covers 40 years, yet most of what happened in those 40 years is not recorded. The fall of Jericho fills about three chapters, which is out of all proportion if this is a history of Israel. **It is really the history of what the God of Israel did**. The writer records the periods when God was at work, for he is a living God, active in time and history, saying and doing things. If God had not intervened on their behalf, the Israelites would never have got the Promised Land. It was

an impossible task for a bunch of ex-slaves with no military training to go in and take a well-fortified land and replace a culture that was far superior to theirs in humanistic terms. If the subject of the book is God's activity, therefore, it should be no surprise when his work is beyond human understanding. If we seek to remove these parts of the story, or to 'demythologize' them, we undermine the whole nature and purpose of the book.

Questions about whether the Bible is myth or history boil down to a personal question: Do we believe in a *living* God? If our answer is yes, then we can go on to look at the Bible as a record of what he said and did and ask why he said and did these things.

The Bible is not just about God, or even just about the God of Israel. It is the history of God *and* Israel – the story of their relationship – and that is how we need to read every book of the Old Testament, including Joshua. It is not fanciful to see God's relationship with Israel as a marriage. The engagement took place with Abraham when God promised to be the God of Abraham and his descendants. The wedding took place at Sinai when the people heard the obligations and promises tied up with the law and agreed to play their part in the binding agreement God was introducing. The honeymoon was supposed to last for three months, as the people journeyed to the Promised Land. The bride, however, was not ready or willing to trust her husband, so it was 40 years before they finally entered the land. In Joshua we have the beginning of their life together in a prepared place, their new home. They were given the title deeds but still had to enter the land and take it. Sadly the marriage did not work out and there was even a temporary divorce, the faults being on the 'wife's side'. Since God hates divorce, however, he never left them.

The content of Joshua

It is important that we gain an overview of the content of Joshua before looking at the detail. This will save us from drawing inappropriate or unwarranted conclusions about what it means, just as we would refuse to judge a novel by selecting isolated pages without seeing the whole thing. Every sentence in a book takes its meaning from the context, so we need to see the book as a whole first.

The book covers the life of Joshua from the age of 80 to 120. This 40-year period matches exactly the length of Moses' leadership, also between the ages of 80 and 120, which is covered by Exodus, Leviticus, Numbers and Deuteronomy. The difference between the two is that Moses was a lawgiver and a leader while Joshua was just a leader, the period of lawgiving having been completed.

Structure

The book divides like a sandwich. There are three parts: two thin slices of bread and a lot of filling in the middle.

- The top 'slice' is **Chapter 1**, the prologue describing **Joshua's commissioning** as leader.
- The bottom 'slice' is **Chapters 23 and 24**, Joshua's **final sermon** and his **death and burial**.

The main section between these two outer 'slices' is the account of how Israel possessed the land that God had promised them, in spite of the fact that it was already occupied. This middle section can be further divided:

- **Chapters 2–5** cover the **entering** of the land of Canaan through the River Jordan.

- **Chapters 6–12** detail how they **conquered** the land, with a list of the 24 kings that Joshua defeated being given in Chapter 12.
- **Chapters 13–22** cover the **dividing** of the land between the tribes who had conquered it.

Joshua's commission

Joshua was 80 years of age when he received his call to serve as a leader. It is possible to identify two parts to the call: divine encouragement and human enthusiasm.

DIVINE ENCOURAGEMENT

God tells Joshua that he is his choice to replace Moses following his death. Moses had led Israel out of Egypt, and now Joshua would lead them into the Promised Land. God promises that just as he had been with Moses, so he would be with Joshua. He tells him to be strong, courageous and careful to obey the law. If he does this he will prosper.

It is an encouraging, if challenging, beginning to his leadership. The word 'prosper' has been misunderstood. It does not mean 'wealthy', and those claiming that the Bible promises financial rewards are mistaken. It means that Joshua will achieve what he sets out to achieve in God's name.

These words of encouragement were not merely for Joshua's wellbeing. God knew that his leadership would affect the morale of the whole people of Israel. And important as it was that Joshua's leadership should help morale, he was also to ensure that his own morality was of the highest standard. He was not just leading a group of individuals armed for battle who needed good pep talks, he was leading the people of God. Their standards of morality would affect their success in battle too, and Joshua was to set an example.

HUMAN ENTHUSIASM

When Joshua told the people of God's decision they were enthusiastic – indeed, their precise response echoes the commands God had given him privately, for they also urge Joshua to 'be strong and courageous'. Furthermore, they promise to obey him fully just as they had obeyed Moses. This may seem strange, as the Israelites' behaviour under Moses' leadership could hardly be described as obedient and this was one of the reasons why they had taken 40 years to travel to the Promised Land. But this new generation had learned from the disobedience of their forefathers. This generation had obeyed Moses whilst he had been alive, when they had conquered Moab and Ammon, and were now comfortable about reaffirming their support for the new man. They promise specifically to do what Joshua tells them and to go where he sends them. They ask that God may be with Joshua as he was with Moses.

This twofold aspect of Joshua's calling is instructive for calls to service today. Both aspects are required: a God-given sense that an individual is called to the work, and a heartfelt response from God's people that this is so.

Joshua's command

The heart of the book deals with Joshua leading the people as they enter the land of Canaan. There are three sections, all dealing fundamentally with the land.

1. ENTERING

(i) Before

Before entering, Joshua sends two spies into the land. When 12 spies had been sent out 40 years before, the negative report from 10 of them had contributed to Israel's faithless refusal to enter the land. This time just two are asked to go in, mirroring the number who had brought back a good report on that first occasion. Sending in spies may seem to be faithless – after all, had God not promised the land to them? But they were practising a principle Jesus used in a story when he was on earth: it is important to sit down and count the cost before you go to battle. It would have been foolhardy for the Israelites to enter Canaan without first obtaining the maximum amount of information about what they might face.

The place where the spies stayed tells us a lot about the moral state of Canaan. They ended up staying in a brothel with a prostitute named Rahab. It is clear from their conversation with Rahab that news of the Israelite victories over Egypt and the surrounding nations had made the locals fearful about their prospect of repelling an invasion. Indeed, Rahab was so convinced that God would give the land to Israel that she wanted to join them. The New Testament commends this amazing display of faith, for Rahab is included in the great heroes of the faith mentioned in Hebrews.

The means of her escape was reminiscent of the way in which the Jewish first-born escaped with their lives when the angel of death came to Egypt. They had painted blood from the Passover lamb on the door frames of their houses. Rahab was told to hang a scarlet thread out of the window so that she and her family would be spared the destruction that would come on the city of Jericho. It was as if she was marking her window with blood, so that death would not touch her home. Not only was she commended for her faith, but Matthew's Gospel records how this prostitute is included in the royal lineage which reaches to Jesus himself. It is an extraordinary and moving tale.

(ii) During

The River Jordan operated like a moat on the eastern edge of Canaan, especially at harvest times when floods could reach depths of 20 feet, with no bridges or fords to enable easy cross-ings. We have noted already that it is likely that a temporary natural dam upstream stopped the flow of the river to enable the people to cross. The timing was perfect: the river bed was dry at the precise moment when the priest at the front of the convoy entered the river.

The miracle enabled the crossing but also had an additional purpose. Many of the new generation of people who entered the land with Joshua had not witnessed the miracle of the crossing of the Red Sea recorded in the book of Exodus. God wanted his people to see his mighty power and to have confidence in the leadership of Joshua as he led them against the Canaanites and into the Promised Land. God was with him as he had been with Moses.

(iii) After

Their first camp in the Promised Land was at Gilgal, an open space near to the fortified town of Jericho which had been built to guard the eastern approach up to the hills. When the Israelites arrived they did three things:

1 They **took 12 stones from the bed of the River Jordan and made a cairn** as a reminder for future generations of how God had dried up the river. Remembrance was an important part of Old Testament piety. Israel had as part of their culture many reminders of what God had done for them in the past. A cairn of stones was a favourite method of marking a significant site, with the 12 stones represent-ing the 12 tribes.

2 They **circumcised all the men**. The new generation had not undergone this covenant rite, first introduced with Abraham. Joshua wanted to follow the law to the letter – the people's spiritual condition was important.

3 They **named the place Gilgal, which means 'rolled'**, because God had 'rolled away' the reproach or disgrace of Egypt.

God also did something when they entered the land: he stopped sending manna. For 40 years the Israelites had fed off this daily provision, but now they had reached the fertile land of Canaan, 'a land flowing with milk and honey', and the manna was redundant. Even today there are delicious grapefruits and oranges sold in Jericho.

(iv) The captain of the Lord's host

Jericho was the first city they were to attack, but before the battle Joshua had an unusual experience. He approached the city by night to see the fortifications for himself and was met by an armed man.

Joshua suspected this man was an enemy and asked whether he was friend or foe. He was surprised to receive the answer 'No', a nonsensical reply! But then the man added that he was not part of the Hebrew or Canaanite peoples, but belonged to God's forces, involved with heavenly rather than earthly troops. He was virtually asking Joshua whose side *he* was on! The person was none other than the captain of the Lord's host, i.e. a senior angel, an archangel or even the preincarnate Son of God himself. Joshua was being reminded that he was not the highest officer in the Lord's army, but only an under-officer. The experience also made clear to him that he did not fight alone, nor was he the true commander of Israel – he was a servant of God and the people.

2. CONQUERING

The military strategy for taking the land is clear – they were to divide and conquer. Joshua drove a wedge straight through the middle of Canaan and then, having divided the enemy into two halves, he conquered the south then the north. This strategy prevented the forces in Canaan from uniting, and meant that Israel could fight manageable numbers, dealing with each area in turn.

The view that Joshua is prophetic history is underlined by the space given to the first two cities attacked. Jericho and Ai were deemed the most significant. The moral lessons, both positive success and negative failure, learned from these two inital assualts, would be confirmed in later engagements; but the prophetic interpretation would not need to be repeated.

(i) The centre
Jericho

Ancient Jericho is a mile down the road from modern Jericho. Its ruins today are at Tel Es Sultan and reveal that Jericho is the oldest city in the world, dating from 8000 BC and containing the oldest building in the world, a round tower with a spiral staircase inside. These remains have been excavated and, of course, the key question was whether the walls which fell in Joshua's day could be found. In the 1920s the archaeologist John Garstang thought he had found them, only to be contradicted by Kathleen Kenyon, who asserted that Jericho was not even occupied in Joshua's day! However, the Egyptologist David Rohl has revised the dating and discovered fallen walls and burned buildings at another level in the diggings (see his remarkable book *The Test of Time*, Century, 1995, following the TV series of the same name, which includes his discovery of remains of Joseph's time in Egypt, and his even more remarkable *Legend: The Genesis of Civilisation*, Century, 1998, locating the Garden of Eden, still full of fruit trees - and he's not even a believer!)

When Jericho eventually fell, Joshua cursed anyone who sought to rebuild it. He said that their first-born would die when the foundations were laid, and their youngest would die when the gates were put in place. The book of Kings records an attempt to rebuild the city 500 years later, when the curse was enacted exactly as predicted. Although one would expect building work to take place on the ruins, therefore, the curse was a real deterrent. The remains of Jericho were left open to the weather and available to anyone wishing to remove stonework for other buildings. The absence of some walls thus helps to confirm the truth of the Bible's record.

Archaeologists have confirmed the size of the walls from similar constructions. They suggest that Jericho's walls were 30 feet high, with a 6-foot thick outer wall and a 12–15-foot gap between that and a 12-foot thick inner wall. The walls became a barrier as the city grew, so houses were perched on the top of the walls in close proximity to one another. It is easy to see how an earth tremor could send the whole lot toppling down. The text tells us that the sustained noise of the horns of 40,000 men was the trigger, so maybe this sound was sufficient – rather in the way that an opera singer can crack a light bulb if she sings at a certain intensity and pitch. The only house that remained standing was the one with the scarlet thread hanging from the window – the house of the prostitute Rahab, preserved because of her faith in the God of Israel.

The destruction was so great that no fighting was necessary – the Israelites simply walked in and took the city. But victory celebrations were conditional. God told them that this city was his, rather like the 'first fruits' of the harvest. They must recognize that this was God's victory, not theirs. The cities conquered in the future could be looted, but not Jericho. One man, however, disobeyed the command, and this fact links with the next story.

Ai

The flourishing city of Ai was farther up the hill from Jericho. But this time the battle was lost. Israel made two errors. The first was over-confidence: Joshua used fewer troops, believing that conquering this city would be as easy as it had been with Jericho. They learnt the important lesson that it is fatal to think that because God has blessed you once, he is going to do it again in the same way.

The man who took some of the loot from Jericho made the second error. Achan had taken a Babylonian robe, 200 shekels of silver and a wedge of gold weighing 50 shekels, thinking that these items' disappearance would not be noticed. When Joshua's troops first attacked Ai, they were routed and they fled. Joshua was distraught and asked God why he had let this happen, especially now that their reputation was growing. God explained that Israel had sinned; one of them had taken something devoted to God. So they drew lots to find the tribe, then the clan, then eventually Achan's family.

Lots may seem a strange way of deciding on an issue of this magnitude, but the Israelites believed that God was in control of every situation and would enable the person to be identified through the drawing of lots, and so it proved. A similar method was used throughout Israel's history. The priest carried a black stone and a white stone inside his breastplate, called the Urim and Thummim. People would use these to discern what they should do. When the white stone was drawn the answer was positive, and when the black one was drawn it was negative. This practice was continued among God's people right up until the coming of the Holy Spirit at Pentecost. From that moment the Holy Spirit guided his people instead and such methods were never used again.

Achan knew he was guilty. Had he owned up earlier, he might have been forgiven, but he had refused to come clean.

His family were also implicated in the crime because they had not exposed him, and so they were all stoned to death. It is frightening that one person's sin could cause a whole people to suffer such disgrace.

When the sin was dealt with, the Israelites fought against Ai again and this time they were victorious.

Mount Ebal and Mount Gerizim

Following the destruction of Ai, Joshua led the people of Israel to two mountains in the centre of the land. Moses had given clear instructions concerning the renewal of the covenant God had made with them at Sinai. They were to write the laws he had given them on uncut plastered stones and then they were to divide into two groups, one standing on Mount Gerizim shouting the blessings of the covenant and the other on Mount Ebal shouting the curses. The two hills form a natural amphitheatre, so that each group could hear the other and respond with an 'amen' to what was being called out.

(ii) The south

Despite this covenant affirmation, the people were still fallible, and they immediately made a big error in their dealings with the Gibeonites. The Gibeonites were a tribal group within the land of Canaan who realized that they were unlikely to be able to stand against an Israelite onslaught. They opted for deception instead. They visited Israel dressed in old clothes and shoes and carrying old wineskins, worn-out sacks and stale, mouldy bread. They claimed to be from a distant country and said they had heard of Israel and wanted protection.

The text says that the men of Israel took them at face value and did not enquire of God. Only later did they realize their error, but by then it was too late, and the four cities belonging to the Gibeonites had to remain untouched because of the oath the Israelites had taken to preserve their lives. The Gibeonites were protected by the treaty they had gained through trickery, and served as woodcutters and servants to the people of Israel. Thus Israel was unable to expel these people from the land.

Gibeon continued to be part of the picture. The King of Jerusalem, Adoni-Zedek, heard of the treaty that the Gibeonites had made with Israel and called on four Amorite kings to unite with him and attack Gibeon. The Gibeonites requested Israel's assistance and battle commenced. God assured the Israelites of victory, sending hailstones of such size that more died from the storm than by the sword. It was at this point that Joshua asked for an extraordinary miracle. He knew that he would not be able to continue routing the enemy when it was dark – at sunset all fighting stopped, whatever the state of the battle, since it was impossible to discern who was friend and who was foe. Joshua therefore made an unprecedented prayer request that the sun should stop in order that the battle could continue! This astonishing display of faith was rewarded, and we read that for a full day the sun stopped in the sky. Victory was complete.

I mentioned earlier that such stories have led to doubts about whether the events of Joshua actually happened. It does sound like a fable, doesn't it? Mr Harold Hill, the President of the Curtis Engine Company of the United States, was a consultant to the American Space Program. He wrote the following article in the *Evening World* newspaper in Spencer, Indiana, which later appeared in the *English Churchman* on 15 January 1971:

> I think one of the most amazing things that God has for us today happened recently to our astronauts and space scientists at Green Belt, Indiana. They were checking the position of the sun, moon and planets out in space where they would

be in 100 years and 1,000 years from now. We have to know this in order that we do not send up a satellite and it collides with something later on, on one of its orbits. We have to lay out the orbit in terms of the life of the satellite and where the planets will be so that the whole thing will not go wrong.

They ran the computer measurements backwards and forwards over the centuries and it came to a halt. The computer stopped and put up a red signal which meant that there was something wrong either with the information fed into it or with the results as compared with the standards. They called in the service department to check it out and they said, 'It's perfect.' The head of the operation said, 'What's wrong?'

'Well, we've found there's a day missing in space in a lapsed time.' They were puzzled and there seemed no answer. Then one man on the team remembered he'd been told at Sunday school of the sun standing still. They didn't believe him but as no alternative was forthcoming they asked him to get a Bible and find it – which he did in the book of Joshua 10:12-14 'And the sun stood still, and the moon stayed – and hasted not to go down about a whole day.' The space men said, 'There is the missing day.'

Well, they checked the computers going back into the time it was written and found it was close but not close enough. The elapsed time that was missing back in Joshua's day was 23 hours and 20 minutes – not a whole day. They read the Bible again and it said *about* a day! These little words in the Bible are important. But they were still in trouble because if you can't account for 40 minutes you will be in trouble 100 years from now. Forty minutes had to be found because it can be multiplied many times over in orbits. Then it was this same man who remembered somewhere in the Bible it said the sun went backwards. The space men told him he was out of his mind but they got out the Bible and found how Hezekiah on his death bed was visited by the prophet Isaiah who told him he was not going to die and Hezekiah asked what the sign should be. And Isaiah said 'This sign shalt thou have of the Lord, that the Lord will do the thing that he has spoken: shall the shadow go forward 10 degrees or go back 10 degrees?' And Hezekiah answered 'It is a light thing for the shadow to go down 10 degrees: nay, but let the shadow return backward 10 degrees'. And Isaiah cried unto the Lord: and he brought the shadow 10 degrees backward by which it had gone down in the dial of Ahaz. (2 Kings 20)

Ten degrees is exactly 40 minutes. So 23 hours and 20 minutes in Joshua plus 40 minutes in 2 Kings make the missing 24 hours which they had to log in the log book as being the missing day in the universe.

Those who disbelieve the Bible will no doubt have difficulty accepting this explanation!

The southern campaign continued with victories over Bethel and Lachish (which we know from archaeology were destroyed between 1250 and 1200 BC). The whole region was subdued.

(iii) The north

Having defeated the south, the people turned to concerns in the north. The northern kings were aware of the Israelites' success by then, and so united their forces for battle. Once again, however, God assured the Israelites of victory: their enemies' chariots were burned and their horses hamstrung.

The cities on the mounds were the only ones not totally destroyed, apart from Hazor which Joshua burned. Archaeologists confirm that that city was ruined by fire at this time, between 1250 and 1200 BC.

With the conquests over, we are given an interesting

summary of the Israelites' activity, including the statement that the Lord hardened the hearts of the nations so that they came against Israel in battle. Clearly their sins were so great that complete extermination was the only solution.

3. DIVIDING

Before progressing any further, we must establish the distinction between *occupation* and *subjugation*. Occupation refers to places; subjugation refers to peoples. Whilst the land was theirs, since the people were subjugated, the Israelites still had much land to occupy. Much of the rest of the book is taken up with this process.

The allocation of land was decided by national lottery, leading some to believe that God sanctions the sort of lottery which currently operates in many countries, including Britain. There is, however, an important distinction to be understood. Lotteries are arranged so that humans cannot influence the outcome. Israel chose the lottery specifically so that *God* could influence the outcome. After all, if God could control the sun, this was nothing to him.

(i) The east bank

The land itself is fascinating, and Joshua records how it was surveyed. The same size as Wales, it is the only green part of the Middle East. The Arabian desert lies to the east, the Negev desert to the south. The rain comes from the Mediterranean.

Moses had promised that the Reubenites, the Gadites and the half-tribe of Manasseh would be given fertile land east of the Jordan, providing they helped in the battle for Canaan. Joshua honoured this pledge.

Throughout the division of the land, the key word was 'inheritance'. The land was an inheritance for Israel, not just for a while, nor just for the lifetime of the victors, but as a permanent home to pass on to their descendants.

(ii) The west bank
At Gilgal: 2½ tribes
Caleb was one of the spies who had given a positive report about the land when the 12 spies were sent in 45 years before. Now, at the age of 85, we read that he was just as strong as he had been at 40. He approached Joshua and asked that he might be allowed to take the hill country that he had been promised all those years before. Joshua blessed him and gave him the town of Hebron.

The daughters of Manasseh reminded Joshua of Moses' promise to give them land too. The people of Joseph claimed to be too numerous for the land they were given and so were also allotted forested areas to clear.

The book outlines in considerable detail the towns and villages that were allotted to each tribe, with occasional reference to other matters. We read, for example, of the Israelites' failure to defeat the enemy when Judah could not dislodge the Jebusites in Jerusalem.

At Shiloh: 8½ tribes
Several tribes remained without allotted land, so each tribe selected men to survey the territory in order to divide it further.

(iii) Special cities
Refuge
There were six special cities of refuge, three on each side of the Jordan, where those guilty of manslaughter could flee when they were chased by those intent on revenge. Within Jewish law there was a distinction between accidental, unintentional killing and premeditated killing. These cities enabled the law to be applied.

Levites

When the land had been allotted, the text makes it clear that the Levites received no land as such, no specific territory. We are told that the Lord was their inheritance – serving God was sufficient for them. Of course, the individual Levites had to live somewhere and towns with pastureland were allotted to them, scattered amongst the other tribes.

(iv) The altar on the east bank

Towards the end of Joshua we are told how a potential tragedy was averted. When the two and a half tribes returned across the Jordan to their territories on the east bank, Joshua urged them to be careful to love God, walk in his ways and obey his commands. However, no sooner had they arrived home than they built an altar at Peor, by the Jordan. The other tribes regarded this as idolatry and immediately declared war. Fortunately, they decided to talk before the first blow was struck. The 'guilty' tribes claimed that the new altar was their way of remembering that they were still part of God's people on the other side of the river. This pacified the concerned tribal leaders and war was avoided.

Joshua's commitment

The last two chapters are a moving finale to the book. Joshua was conscious of his advancing years – at 120 he was the same age as Moses was when he died, and had served, like Moses, for 40 years. He knew he was going to die soon and so wanted to make provision for the future of the nation.

It is important to note that whilst Moses appointed Joshua as his successor, Joshua did not appoint a successor for himself. This may seem strange, but from then on the job of leadership could not be left to just one man. The leadership needs were different, the people were scattered across the land, and one man could not lead properly with so much ground to cover. So Joshua passed on his commission to them all.

Joshua's message was very firm: God had promised not only to bless them when they obeyed but to curse them when they disobeyed. God had brought them into the land as he had promised, but they must obey the law if they were to experience his continued favour.

Joshua gave all the credit for Israel's possession of the land to God. Although he had led the people, he recognized that God had fought for them and they should be grateful to him for their success. He concluded his speech by asking the Israelites to take an oath of loyalty to God.

The final chapter is in an altogether different style. Here Joshua speaks in the first person singular as he does in the previous chapter, but this time 'I' means God. His last message is prophecy and is understood as such by the people.

(i) Grace

First God reminds the people of all he has done for them. There is no mention of Joshua's role.

(ii) Gratitude

Now Joshua speaks, urging the people to fear God, serve him, be faithful and throw away any other gods. Then he speaks for himself and his household, saying, 'We will serve the Lord.'

The people agree to follow God with Joshua, who sets up a stone of witness. Three times the people declare, 'We will serve the Lord.'

The last verses of the book record three burials: the burial of Joshua, the burial of Joseph's bones and the burial of Eleazer. For 40 years they had carried with them a coffin containing Joseph's bones, because his dying wish was to be buried in the Promised Land. Now at last the bones could be laid to rest in the land Joseph had looked for.

So a triple funeral rounds off this book. We are told that as long as Joshua and his generation of leaders lived, the people were faithful to God. When the next generation grew up, however, things went badly wrong.

It is possible to sum up the lessons of the book of Joshua in two simple phrases:

- Without God they **could** not have done it.
- Without them God **would** not have done it.

These are two very important lessons. It is easy to put all the responsibility on God or to put it all on ourselves. The Bible has a balance: without God we cannot do it, but without us he will not do it. The change of verb is significant – it is not that without us he cannot, it is that without us he *will* not. If Joshua and the people of Israel had not co-operated with God, their entry into the Promised Land would not have happened, and yet without God and without his intervention, they could not possibly have done it.

Divine intervention

1. GOD'S WORDS

God's words are prominent in the book of Joshua as we hear of his solemn covenant to Israel which he could never break. He had sworn by himself that he would stay with them, and the land was his promised gift. God always keeps his Word – he cannot lie. So Joshua tells us that God gave to Israel all the land he had sworn to their forefathers that he would give them.

2. GOD'S DEEDS

God's deeds are linked with his words. We are told that God would fight for Israel. He would drive the other nations out of the land.

Joshua is full of physical miracles: the division of the River Jordan, the sudden cessation in the provision of manna, the collapse of the Jericho walls, the hailstones which help defeat the five kings, the lengthening of the day by making the sun 'stand still', and the drawing of lots to decide how the land is to be divided.

The book of Joshua is careful to give the glory to God for these amazing events. God was truly with Israel. The name *Immanuel* has four possible meanings or emphases:

1 *God* is with us!
2 God *is* with us!
3 God is *with* us!
4 God is with *us*!

The fourth version conveys the meaning of the biblical text. *Immanuel* means God is on *our* side – the emphasis is that he is going to fight for us, not them. Joshua is a testimony to this truth.

Human co-operation – positive

God works through human co-operation. He did not fight by himself: the Israelites had to go to the battlefield and face the enemy for themselves. Without them God would not have done it – they had to go into the land, they had to take action. God said that every bit of land they actually stood on he would give to them.

1. THEIR ATTITUDE

Not fear (negative)

In taking action and entering the land, the Israelites were not to be afraid. This was the command given to Joshua at the very beginning. This had been the cause of the people's failure 40 years before when they had refused to enter Canaan.

But faith (positive)

If they were to win every battle, their attitude had to be one of confidence and obedience. This faith showed itself in action as they obeyed the Lord's command to march around Jericho seven times in silence, when they doubtless would have preferred to get on and fight straight away. They also had to be prepared to take risks. Joshua took the risk of asking God publicly to stop the sun.

2. THEIR ACTION

Their confidence had to lead to obedience. They were to act on God's Word – they were to do what he said. This is a reminder to us that God's gifts have to be received. The Israelites were given every bit of land they put their foot on, but this meant they had to do something to make the inheritance theirs; it was not automatic.

There is a delicate balance to be reached between faith and action, summed up brilliantly by Oliver Cromwell, who once told his troops, 'Trust in God and keep your powder dry.' Or as C. H. Spurgeon said, 'Pray as if it all depends on God and work as if it all depends on you.'

If the Israelites' attitude was to become self-confident and their action was to become disobedient, however, they would lose every battle. That is why the two major parts of Joshua cover the story of Jericho and the story of Ai, one attack a success, one (initially) a failure. If we learn the lessons of those two towns then we are set for the conquest of the land.

Human co-operation – negative

The Bible is a very honest book. It deals with weaknesses as well as strengths. The book of Joshua tells us about three mistakes the Israelites made when they took over the land.

The first mistake was at Ai. They were defeated by superior troops because they had too much self-confidence. The previous generation had been under-confident, and thus guilty of fear, but this generation was over-confident and therefore guilty of folly. Both attitudes were equally damaging.

The second mistake was when the Gibeonites tricked them into making a treaty to protect them. Their refusal to first ask the Lord what to do is given as the reason for their folly on this occasion.

The third mistake was when the two and a half tribes put up an altar on the east bank of the Jordan and the tribes on the other side of the river accused them of treachery and turning away from the Lord. The misunderstanding that arose almost led to civil war.

Christian application

We are told in 1 Corinthians 10 and Romans 15 that everything in the past was written for our learning. How is the book of Joshua used in the New Testament, and how can we apply what we learn from it today?

Faith

In Hebrews 11 Joshua and Rahab the prostitute are used as examples of faith. They are part of the 'cloud of witnesses' with which we are surrounded.

James says that faith without action is dead; it cannot save us. Again Rahab is used as an example, for the way she hid the spies and said goodbye to the past in order to embrace the faith of Israel.

Sin

The book also gives us a graphic reminder of the problems which sin can cause amongst a whole people. In the New Testament an incident with Ananias and Sapphira exactly matches the sin of Achan. Acts tells the story of how this couple lie about money withheld from the church's common purse, while Achan deceives the people by not owning up to the goods he stole from Jericho. The result in both cases is the same – the judgement of God. Ananias and Sapphira are immediately struck down dead, as Achan was stoned to death by the people.

Salvation

The book is also a glorious picture of salvation. Joshua's name was originally Hoshea, which means 'salvation', but Moses changed it to Yeshua, which means 'God saves'. The Greek version of the Old Testament translates this as 'Jesus'.

Moses himself means 'drawn out', so his name and Joshua's together describe Israel's progress towards the Promised Land. Moses brought them out of Egypt, but it was Joshua the saviour who brought them into the Promised Land. Getting out of Egypt did not constitute salvation, but getting into Canaan did.

This illustrates an important truth: Christians are not just saved *from* something, they are also saved *to* something. It is all too possible to get out of Egypt but still be in the wilderness; to stop living the lifestyle of a nonbeliever but not enjoy the glory of the Christian life.

Applying the concept

Finally we must ask: How should a Christian apply the concept of the Promised Land?

HEAVEN

Some imagine that the Promised Land depicts 'heaven'. One hymn, for example, contains the line: 'When I tread the verge of Jordan, bid my anxious fears subside', as if the image of the river is depicting death, with Canaan (heaven) on the other side.

HOLINESS

The Promised Land, however, is not heaven but holiness.

The writer of Hebrews, commenting on Joshua's conquering of the land, says that the Israelites never entered 'the rest' under Joshua, despite entering Canaan. He goes on to say that there still remains 'a rest' for the people of God. This 'rest' means rest from battle – and the Promised Land is reached when we enjoy what God has for us. So whenever we overcome temptation we have a little foretaste of the rest that God has promised. The victories in Joshua should be replicated in the life of every believer as he or she lives for Christ and battles against sin. The 'rest' is that relief when our struggles with enemy forces are successfully behind us and our efforts have been rewarded.

8.

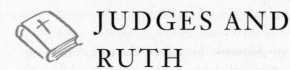

JUDGES AND
RUTH

Introduction

Judges and Ruth belong to each other, so we will consider
them together. The Bible is unique among sacred writings in
being mostly history. The Koran, for example, contains little
or no history, whereas the Bible displays a historical dimension
throughout. Furthermore, it includes history no human being
could have written, for it includes the very beginning of our
universe in Genesis and a description of its end in Revelation.
Either this is human imagination, or God himself has revealed
it – there is no other explanation.

When we looked at the book of Joshua, we saw how
prophetic history is a special type of history because it records
events in terms of what God says and does with his people
Israel. What we have in the Bible is no ordinary history book,
simply recording what a nation has done and experienced – it is
God's story of his dealings with his people.

There are four possible levels when it comes to studying
history:

1 **The study of personalities**: this approach involves
   detailed analysis of the individuals who made history –
   monarchs, military leaders, philosophers, thinkers. Their

lives control what is included; they are the reference point for all that happens.

2 **The study of peoples**: here the focus is on whole nations or people groups. We discover how nations grow stronger and weaker and how this affects the balance of power within the world.

3 **The study of patterns**: aside from the personalities and peoples, this approach looks for the patterns which exist across time frames, such as the way civilizations rise and fall. It is less concerned with the detail and more with themes.

4 **The study of purpose**: historians also ask where history is heading. They look for meaning and purpose. Marxist historians believe in dialectical materialism, i.e. the history of peoples includes conflict, especially between the workers and ruling classes. Evolutionary optimists believe in the ascent of man, i.e. humanity is making progress to a better world. Others look at war throughout history and predict doom and gloom.

The study of purpose can be divided into two strands: on the one hand there are those who see history as linear progression – things are moving forward with the present building on the past; on the other hand there are those who see history as a series of cycles where things tend to come full circle – to them there is little forward progression, just aimless and futile activity signifying nothing.

It is no surprise that a divine view of history includes a sense of purpose. It is not the optimism of the evolutionists, for not everything 'gets better', but biblical history does have a purpose, for God is in control and will bring things to the ending he intends. History is, indeed, 'his story'.

These two aspects of history – the linear and the cyclical views – will help us understand Judges and Ruth. The history in Judges is a classic case of a series of cycles: the same cycle is identified on seven occasions and, although the time line is there, it is largely in the background. Ruth, by contrast, is a time-line story with a beginning, a middle and an end, and a clear sense of progress.

The pattern of history in the book of Judges mirrors accurately the sort of lives many people live when they do not know God. They get up, go to work, come home, watch the television and go to bed again, ready to repeat the same cycle the next day. It is life on a large roundabout! You get nowhere and achieve nothing. The pattern seen in Ruth is more in keeping with the way God intends his people to proceed through life. Here there is purpose and meaning, a movement towards a goal.

The most important thing to establish about any book in the Bible is the reason why it was written. Some books reveal their purpose very easily, but Judges and Ruth require rather more investigation. We will need to examine each book in detail before we can come to any conclusions about the purpose behind them.

Judges

Most people have a Sunday school knowledge of the book of Judges – they only know the 'bowdlerized' version. Thomas Bowdler did not approve of certain parts of William Shakespeare's plays, so he revised them, omitting what he regarded as the 'naughty bits', and now his name has gone down in history. In the same way Sunday school stories from Judges omit some of the less palatable elements – concubines, prostitutes being cut up into pieces, rape, murder, phallic symbols, and so on. As a result many people are familiar with particular personalities within the book, such as Samson, Delilah,

Deborah and Gideon, but have no knowledge of the rest of it, let alone its overall theme and purpose.

Individual stories

The stories within the book are certainly gripping. There is an economy of words, but interesting detail is provided in vivid descriptions which make the characters live for the reader.

The amount of space given to each character is surprisingly varied. Samson has four chapters all to himself, Gideon has three, Deborah and Barak have two, but some have just a short paragraph. It almost seems that the more sensational they were, the more space they were given. Clearly the author's purpose is not to give a balanced account of each hero. It is easy, however, to get the impression that the book is about a series of folk heroes who saved the day in whatever situation they faced (and the book contains a selection of quite bizarre events), rather like Nelson or Wellington in British history.

We read early in the book of Caleb's younger brother **Othniel**. All we are really told is that he brought peace to his people for 40 years.

We read of **Ehud**, the left-handed leader who concealed his 18-inch swordblade by strapping it to his right leg. Since most people were right handed, it was customary to check the left leg for weapons. He was thus able to take his weapon into a private meeting with the King of Moab and plunge it into the King's belly!

We read of **Shamgar**, who killed 600 Philistines with an ox-goad.

We read of **Deborah** and **Barak**. Deborah was a prophetess, married to Lappidoth. Her name means 'Busy bee' and Lappidoth means 'Flash' in Hebrew! Deborah would settle disputes by hearing the answer from the Lord, and on an occasion recorded in Judges she told Barak to lead the people into battle. Barak refused to go into battle without her. Senior officers in Israel, then and today, always lead the troops into battle. God was angry with Barak's refusal and told him that the enemy Sisera would fall to the hand of a woman in order to humiliate him. And so it proved.

The next story concerns **Gideon**, one of the most fearful men in the Bible. He put some meat on an altar and fire from heaven burned up the meat. Then he asked the Lord for a sign from heaven, as if the fire was not enough! God graciously provided a further sign through a fleece which was dry one day and wet the next. Gideon had to learn that it is by God's strength and strategy that battles are won. God reduced his army from 300,000 to 300 so that Gideon would learn not to put his trust in human resources.

The next character we read of is **Abimelech** (more of him later); then comes **Tola**, who receives only the brief comment that he led Israel for 23 years. After him **Jair** led Israel for 22 years and had 30 sons who, we are told, rode 30 donkeys and controlled 30 towns. A little interesting detail, but nothing more!

There is a longer section recounting the story of **Jephthah**, the head of Gilead. He made the rash vow that he would sacrifice to the Lord whatever came to meet him when he returned from battle and ended up having to sacrifice his only daughter.

Ibzan of Bethlehem had 30 daughters and 30 sons who all married outside the clan of Judah. **Elon** led Israel for 10 years. **Abdon**, who came after him, had 40 sons, 30 grandsons and 70 donkeys! Again no more details are given.

When we come to **Samson**, however, we learn far more. His name literally means 'sunshine'. He was brought up as a Nazarene, which meant that he was not allowed to take alcohol or cut his hair. It is an extraordinary tale of a man who had trouble with women. He married, but his marriage broke up before the honeymoon. He moved on to a nameless prostitute before finally joining with a mistress called Delilah. Although having great physical strength, Samson was actually a weak man. His weakness was not primarily his relationships, but stemmed from a weakness of character. His charismatic anointing enabled him to accomplish many amazing feats of strength, but then the Spirit of the Lord departed from him. He was captured by the Philistines, blinded and put on a treadmill, the laughing stock of the Philistines.

Many years ago I preached a sermon called 'Samson's hair is growing again'. It became well known and one young woman who heard it wrote a poem about the blind Samson being led by the little boy to the pillars of the temple, where he pulled the whole temple down.

The boy who held his hand

They gouged them out,
At first
I could not bear to look:
    Empty and raw and cruel.
I would not look:
    The shock of emptiness,
    Knowing that he would not see.
I watched the shaven head bowed low
    Rocking with the rhythm of the grindstone.
    Round. Round. Round.
I watched the needless shackles:
    Heavy and hard,
    Biting the flesh that needs no binding.

Now
It does not matter that his eyes are gone:

I am his eyes,
   He sees through me.
He has to see through me, there is no other way.
And I have wept the tears he cannot weep,
   For all those careless years.
And I have learned to love this broken man,
While he has learned at last to fear his God.

So
I am not afraid to die:
Happy to be his eyes this one last time.
Taking his hand,
Leading with practised care,
Step by guided step
Into the place where he can pray,
'Lord,
O Sovereign Lord.'
And as the pillars fall, I cry
'Amen.'

In his last five minutes Samson did more for his people than he had done in all the years of his life.

HUMAN WEAKNESS

The Bible is always honest about the failings and weaknesses of the individuals it describes and Judges is no exception. The characters in the book reveal a number of flaws: Barak was not manly; Gideon was fearful, constantly asking for signs, and towards the end of his life made a gold ephod, a priestly 'pullover', which later proved to be a 'snare' to Israel, a relic which had become an object of devotion. Jephthah was the son of a prostitute who made a reckless vow; Samson treated his wife poorly, slept with a prostitute and took a mistress. They were not strong characters, nor were they holy people, yet God used them!

DIVINE STRENGTH

How did these less than perfect people manage to achieve so much? It was not through their own power. Their secret was that the Holy Spirit came on them – they were all 'charismatic' people.

Judges gives us vivid examples of divine strength working through weak people, as we read how these individuals were able to perform supernatural feats. Samson was perhaps the most graphic example of this, but there are many amazing stories. This is an especially important point to note, because the anointing of the Holy Spirit only comes on a *few* in the Old Testament. In Judges such anointing was experienced by just 12 people out of the 2 million who populated Israel at that time. We note too that the Holy Spirit comes on them *temporarily*, not permanently: for example, the text states that the Holy Spirit *left* Samson. In the Old Testament it was an anointing Spirit that touched them for a time rather than an indwelling Spirit who stayed with them.

WHAT WERE THE JUDGES?

Our consideration of some of the individual stories of the judges has omitted an important question. What exactly were the judges? Who were they and what did they do?

In English they are called 'judges', but this expression does not really capture the essence of the word originally used to describe them. When we read that Samson 'judged' Israel, or that Gideon 'judged' Israel, the idea behind the Hebrew expression is that they were 'troubleshooters' who saved the people of God from themselves and others. They are never given a title as such, but are described in terms of what they did. Indeed, the only person to whom the noun is applied in the book of Judges is God. He is *the* Judge, sorting out their problems. It would therefore be more correct to say that God is the rescuer or troubleshooter who operates through these heroes, by his Spirit, for the benefit of the people.

They are concerned with justice within the nation, but mainly with external problems, since the people are surrounded by hostile nations who attack them at various times: the Ammonites (three times), the Amalekites (twice), the Moabites (once) , the Midianites (once) and the Philistines (three times). There is also specific mention of the Kings of Jericho, Moab and Hazor.

The people of God had come into a highly populated area, to peoples largely hostile to their presence. They were perceived as invaders. The only justification for them being in that land at all was that God had given it to them, and they were to exact punishment on the resident population by wiping them out. Thus the book is not just about individual heroes – or the study of personalities, the first level of history described at the beginning of this chapter – but whole peoples too – the second level of history.

National history

If you add together all the years that the 12 people mentioned above judged Israel, they come to 400, but the book of Judges actually covers only 200 years. How can this be so?

GEOGRAPHICAL

This problem is easily resolved when we realize what the judges are actually doing. When we read about Gideon and Samson we tend to think that they were delivering the whole nation, but Israel was now divided into groups of tribes, spread over a wide area roughly the size of Wales. Therefore, when we read that a judge ruled for 40 years, it may only apply to tribes in the north. Another judge may have been saving a situation in the south at the same time. Samson, for example, delivered the southern tribes and Gideon the northern ones.

POLITICAL

At this time there was a leadership vacuum within Israel. Moses had led them out of Egypt, Joshua had led them into the Promised Land, but with both these great men dead, there was no figurehead for the nation – bearing in mind that this was before the days of the monarchy. Thus the judges were *local* leaders, commanding the loyalty of groups of tribes, but not uniting the whole nation.

MORAL

There was a moral reason why the tribes were continually facing opposition from other nations and people groups, and this is the heart of the book's message. The structure of the book makes this clear, as we shall see if we look at a brief outline of it. It divides very clearly into three parts.

1. **Inexcusable compromise (1–2)**
   (i) Allowances
   (ii) Alliances

2. **Incorrigible conduct (3–16)**
   (i) Sedition by the people
   (ii) Subjection by an enemy
   (iii) Supplication to the Lord
   (iv) Salvation by a deliverer

3. **Inevitable corruption (17–21)**
   (i) Idolatry in the north – Dan
   (ii) Immorality in the south – Benjamin

In Section 2, the four stages of the cycle are repeated seven times. The book finishes with a statement that has actually been the refrain throughout: 'There was no king in those days, every man did what was right in his own eyes.'

1. Inexcusable compromise

(I) ALLOWANCES – VULNERABLE VALLEYS

God sent Israel into the land to destroy the inhabitants totally. Archaeology confirms the wicked practices of the Canaanite people – sexual diseases were rife. Those who question the justice of this extermination forget God's Word to Abraham about the future of his descendants. He was told that the Jews would stay in Egypt for centuries until the wickedness of the Amorites reached its 'full measure'. God was tolerant of their wickedness, but they finally overstepped the mark and he used Israel as the instrument of his judgement on a most perverted society.

Instead of following God's commands, however, Israel were selective in their punishment. They captured the hills and mountains but allowed many of the peoples to remain, especially those living in the valleys. Israel thus became divided into three groups: northern, central and southern. Communication between the tribes was difficult and they were unable to respond speedily and unitedly when external threats arose. Furthermore, the valleys provided routes for invaders, who were only too keen to exploit such internal weakness.

(II) ALLIANCES – MIXED MARRIAGES

The lax standards of the valleys were too great a temptation for many Israelite men, and before long Israelites had married outside their faith in clear defiance of God's law which forbade 'mixed marriages'. This affected the spiritual life of Israel. If you marry a child of the devil you are bound to have problems with your father-in-law! Any designs on holy living were dashed and many Israelites in unequal marriages ended up serving Canaanite gods. The spiritual influence of the non-believer tends to be stronger in a mixed marriage, even today. The service of Canaanite gods led inevitably to immorality, for wrong belief always leads to wrong behaviour.

2. Incorrigible conduct

The bulk of the book of Judges consists of a series of cycles. With almost monotonous regularity the people of God repeat the same pattern.

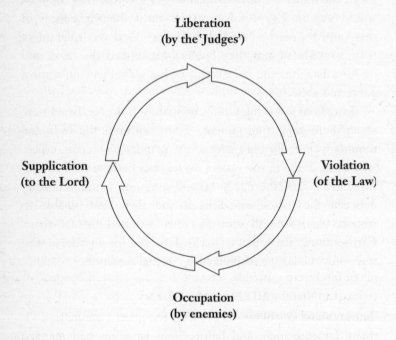

Liberation
(by the 'Judges')

Supplication
(to the Lord)

Violation
(of the Law)

Occupation
(by enemies)

- **Supplication**: It starts with Israel crying out to the Lord because they are facing oppression of some kind.
- **Liberation**: God sends a deliverer (e.g. Gideon, Samson) to rescue the people.
- **Violation**: In spite of their deliverance, the people slip back into sin.
- **Occupation**: God therefore sends a hostile people (e.g. Midianites, Philistines) to overpower Israel. Israel becomes a vassal state in a land they should have been freely owning.
- **Supplication**: In view of the hardship of the situation, they cry out to the Lord again and so the cycle continues. It seems they only pray when they are in trouble. It is hard to tell whether they are truly repentant or merely regretting the consequences of their behaviour. Clearly many were unaware that the oppression was their fault.

The cycle does not just apply to the whole nation: individuals also live in a similar routine of sin and forgiveness and further sin. It is not simply an endless cycle either, but a spiral going downwards. Things get steadily worse.

3. Inevitable corruption

The last part of the book of Judges is a most unedifying account of what happened to the people. There were two situations, one in the north in the territory of Dan and one in the south in the territory of Benjamin. On both occasions, the people of God were misled by a priest. It is a perfect illustration of the maxim mentioned earlier, that idolatry (wrong belief) leads to immorality (wrong behaviour).

(I) IDOLATRY IN THE NORTH – DAN

The story starts with a son, Micah from Ephraim, stealing 1,100 shekels from his own mother. He returns the money to her and she is so delighted that she uses it to make an idol which she gives to Micah for the private shrine he has set up in his home.

A young Levite comes to Micah's house in search of lodgings and is offered the opportunity to be his father and priest for a regular income, clothing and food. He accepts. Later the tribes of Dan, who failed to take the land God allocated to them in the south, migrate north. When their leaders lodge in this house with the idols and the priest, they offer the priest the chance to officiate for their whole tribe, for more money, and he accepts.

In clear violation of the law of God, therefore, the tribe of Dan slips into idolatry. Just as Judas Iscariot, one of the 12 disciples, went missing after his great sin, the tribe of Dan is missing in the book of Revelation. The sin starts with a man who steals money from his mother, then it is carried over to a Levite who becomes a private chaplain, first to a family and then to a whole tribe – without any proper appointment or authorisation.

(II) IMMORALITY IN THE SOUTH – BENJAMIN

This story is even worse. Another Levite from the tribe of Ephraim takes a concubine from Bethlehem in Judah. She leaves him and returns to her family home. After four months the Levite arrives in Bethlehem to seek her return. The father keeps urging the Levite to stay at his home before finally letting her go. They set off too late in the day and only get as far as Jerusalem, a pagan city at that time. The Levite refuses to stay with 'pagans', so they travel north to the tribe of Benjamin, arriving at Gibeah by nightfall. They are offered hospitality by an old man who welcomes them into his home. However, while they are eating, they are interrupted by 'wicked men of the city' who demand that the newcomer be given to them for sex. The old man refuses, but offers instead his daughter. Eventually the Levite gives them his concubine. The next morning the concubine lies dead on the doorstep, having been gang-raped through the night.

The Levite cuts his concubine up into 12 pieces and sends them to the other tribes of Israel. When the Israelites discover that men of the tribe of Benjamin committed the crime, they seek revenge on the perpetrators. The Benjaminites are offended by the accusation and refuse to hand the men over.

A civil war results which almost wipes out the tribe – only 600 men are left. Their towns are destroyed and all the women and children are slaughtered. The other tribes had vowed not to give their daughters in marriage to the tribe of Benjamin, but now the tribe is on the brink of extinction and the Israelites have pity on them and take action to prevent this happening. They find 400 virgins from Jabesh Gilead as wives for the Benjaminites, but they need more. They then concoct a clever plan. They hold a festival at Shiloh and allow the Benjaminites to kidnap their daughters – thus not technically 'giving' them away and so fulfilling the letter if not the spirit of their previous oath.

It is a dreadful tale in all aspects and, alongside the story of the tribe of Dan, it makes a depressing end to the book of Judges.

Theological or eternal purpose

After such a gloomy story we turn to a more uplifting subject: a consideration of the theological purpose of the book. Ultimately Bible history is not a human record but a record of what God has said and done, showing us who he is.

We have noted already that God is the judge or deliverer of the people, since he is the only person to whom the noun 'judge' is applied in the book. He is the real hero, and success is achieved when the human leaders co-operate with him.

However, when we ask the question, 'Who drove the Canaanites from the land, Israel or God?' we must reply, 'Both!' We can sum up the situation like this: Without him they could not; without them he would not. On the one hand God declared that he would give them the land and drive out the inhabitants, but on the other hand he needed Israel to respond to his direction.

Furthermore, we read that in some cases God did not drive out the opposition, but left them in the land to test Israel and teach them to fight. We learn from Amos that just as God brought Israel out of Egypt, he brought the Philistines from Crete as neighbours, to inflict injury on Israel.

Within the book of Judges, therefore, we find that God chastises his people. He delivers them *to* evil, demonstrating his justice, as well as *from* evil, showing his mercy.

This principle is also seen in the New Testament. There is, of course, the line in the Lord's Prayer: 'Lead us not into temptation but deliver us from evil.' The power of the Holy Spirit can heal the sick, but it can also bring disease; it can give sight to the blind, but it can also prevent good eyes from seeing; it can raise the dead, but it brings death too, as with Ananias and Sapphira. The ultimate sanction in church discipline is to hand over erring members to Satan, whose destructive power over the body may bring them to their senses and save their souls on the day of judgement.

Yet at the same time God hears the prayers of Israel and responds. He is grieved by their misery, he is patient and faithful, in spite of the people's repeated disobedience. So we read how God answered prayer, sending anointed leaders and directing operations, for example with Gideon and Barak. We see a dynamic relationship between God and man, each affecting the other.

Noting this important dynamic still does not explain the purpose of the book, however, but this will not become truly clear until we have looked at Ruth as well. At this stage all we see is the unedifying cycle of Israel getting into and out of trouble. We do not yet know where it is going.

The reasons for these problems within Israel can be explained in two ways:

1. SECOND-GENERATION MEMBERS

The people of Israel now occupying the Promised Land did not have the same knowledge of God and what he had done for them as the previous generation. They did not want to know God. Instead they did what was right in their own eyes, but wrong in his eyes. Everyone was a law to himself.

2. SECOND-GENERATION LEADERS

There was no seamless succession in the leadership. When a judge died, there was a gap before another judge appeared, and during this gap the people reverted to the type of behaviour which led to God's punishment. The pattern of the cycle is indicated by phrases such as, 'as long as the judge lived … but when the judge died…' This was very different from the dynastic succession which prevailed in other nations, ensuring continuity and stability – and the judges only ruled over a limited group, not a united nation.

This question of kingship crops up a number of times.

1 **Gideon** is offered the throne by his followers following his victory over the Midianites. The people ask him to start a dynasty. Some argue that he should have accepted, but clearly this is not God's time for a king to be chosen. Gideon tells the people their problem is that they have not looked to God as their king.

2 Following Gideon the leadership is in the hands of a number of people. **Abimelech** asks the people whether they

would prefer his sole leadership to leadership by Gideon's 70 sons as a group. He is duly installed and proceeds to murder his brothers. Things get steadily worse as his hunger for power demonstrates that he has little interest in the welfare of the people, and he is eventually killed in battle.

3 Throughout Judges we read the refrain, '**There was no king in those days**...' and the suggestion is that things would have been much better if there had been one.

We will return to this theme later. For now the important point to note is that Judges tells us there is a desperate need for a king. As we turn to the book of Ruth we are faced with the more positive message that a king will be provided. Ruth starts to address the question, 'Who will it be?'

Ruth

The book of Ruth was written at the same time as Judges but there could hardly be a greater contrast between the two.

■ Judges includes the stories of many people, Ruth just a few.
■ Judges is relatively large, while Ruth is one of the smallest Old Testament books.
■ Judges covers the whole of Israel, Ruth just one small town.
■ Judges spans 200 years, Ruth just one generation.

Ruth reads like a Thomas Hardy novel, with the sort of romance which would not be out of place in a magazine story. It is a breath of fresh air after Judges. In Judges we have mass killing, rape, a prostitute cut up into pieces, civil war, evil priests. It is just two miles from the Benjaminites' territory to Judah where Ruth is located, but it is a totally different atmosphere.

Ruth is only four chapters long. The first two chapters are about two inseparable women, and the second two chapters are about two influential men. These four people form the main characters in the drama.

1 Mother-in-law's loss
2 Daughter-in-law's loyalty
3 Redeemer kinsman's love
4 Royal king's line

1. Mother-in-law's loss

The story begins with a famine in Israel, which caused three men to leave for Moab. We can guess that the famine was a punishment from God, for this was a common sign of God's displeasure, and it provides a contrast with the location of the main drama – Bethlehem means 'house of bread' in Hebrew.

If the family had learned the lessons from Israel's history, they would have known that searching for food outside Israel always led to problems, as the stories of Abraham, Isaac and Jacob testify, but there is no record that they prayed to God for food. So Naomi and her husband travelled east across the hills on the far side of the Dead Sea to Moab. As time passed each of their two sons married a Moabite woman. Things went from bad to worse. Naomi's husband died and the two sons died also. The three widows were left alone. In those days a widow's future was bleak. The whole drama started from the men's refusal to rely on God. They sought a human solution to their situation instead of asking God what was happening and what they should do.

God would have told them that the famine was part of his punishment, and if only they would turn back to him they would have enough food again. But they did not even wait to ask him, let alone listen for an answer.

As a result of this crisis Naomi became bitter. Her name actually means 'pleasure', but when she returned to Israel she was unrecognizable to her old relatives and asked to be called 'Mara', meaning 'bitter', instead. She encouraged her two daughters-in-law to stay in Moab, knowing that returning to Judah would mean little prospect of remarrying. The men in Judah were not likely to marry outside their clan.

Orpah agreed and went back to Moab and is never heard of again. On the basis of her choice she had no more place in God's purpose. Ruth, however, went with Naomi and her name has gone down in history as an ancestor of Our Lord Jesus Christ.

The story carries the reminder that much can hang on just one decision. It is the choices we take that make up our character, and Ruth made the right choice at the right time.

At last we see someone whose actions break out of the endless cycle. Ruth became part of God's line instead. Her name is mentioned in the genealogy of Jesus in Matthew, despite the fact that she was both a Gentile and a woman.

2. Daughter-in-law's loyalty

Ruth was a beautiful character, both inside and out. She was full of humility and yet she had the sort of boldness that men find attractive. She was loyal, with a serving spirit, but she was not passive or an underdog by any means.

She not only chose to stay with Naomi, but chose Naomi's people and Naomi's God. God was evidently real to her, even though she had seen him punishing his people. On four occasions she said 'I will' to Naomi. In being so loyal to Naomi she demonstrated her love for her. 'Loyalty' and 'love' are almost the same word in Hebrew. Love that is not loyal is not true love. Likewise, God's covenant love for his people means that he sticks with them through thick and thin.

Furthermore, we read that Ruth found 'favour' in the eyes of the Lord. In Hebrew, 'favour' is the same word as 'favourite' – she became one of God's favourites. It is clear from the story that Ruth became the talk of the town in Bethlehem, for the Lord did not stop showing his kindness to Ruth.

3. Redeemer kinsman's love

The second half of the book includes two influential men, Boaz and the man who would become king.

Boaz was a man of great standing and great generosity. It was common for the poor to be allowed to collect any grain remaining in the field after harvest, but Boaz instructed his workers to make sure that Ruth especially received a large provision.

There are two other customs in the book of Ruth which we must appreciate in order to understand the unfolding drama. The first is the Levirate marriage. In the year of Jubilee, every 50 years, all the property was returned to the original family that owned it in the previous Jubilee year. It was imperative, therefore, that there was a male family representative to claim the property after 50 years. The Levirate law stated that if a woman's husband died before she had a son to pass on her inheritance, her husband's brother had to marry her and give her a son, thus keeping the property in the family. Ruth, of course, had been married to someone who was entitled to property, but now she had no husband or son, so a relative was under the obligation to marry her to keep her husband's name and line going and reinherit the property when it became available in Jubilee year.

The second law to understand was a social custom. A girl could not propose marriage to a man in those days, but she was free to indicate that she would like to be married to someone and could do that in a number of ways. One was to warm the man's feet! So when Ruth lay at Boaz's feet and covered them with her cloak she was indicating that she would not mind being married to him. These two customs explain how Boaz married Ruth.

When Ruth lay at Boaz's feet, it was a clear sign that she was interested. He was flattered that she had chosen him, as he was neither the oldest nor the youngest kinsman she could have chosen. However, his older brother was the one who should fulfil the legal duty, so he had to give him first option! His older brother gave his consent in the customary way, taking off his sandal and giving it to Boaz – the equivalent of shaking hands on a deal. Ruth and Boaz were free to marry.

4. Royal king's line

It is a beautiful story – a lovely rural romance. But we must ask what God was doing behind all this, for it is unlikely that the story would be included in Scripture merely as a light interlude. It becomes clear that God was preparing a royal line for a king of Israel. Ruth's right choice in joining with Naomi and returning to be part of her people was part of God's right choice, for he had chosen her to be part of the royal line.

Indeed, although God is not directly identified as being involved in the drama, he is frequently mentioned in the book, as the characters ask him to bless others. Naomi asked the Lord to bless Ruth for being with her. The harvesters asked God to bless Boaz and he returned the blessing to them. Boaz asked the Lord to bless Ruth for choosing him. When they spoke of God they used God's name, YAHWEH, a name which functions like 'always' in English – God is 'always' my provider, 'always' at my side, 'always' my healer.

It is interesting to note that Boaz was a direct descendent of Judah, one of the 12 sons of Jacob. He was also a descendant of Tamar, who had offspring after she was raped, which shows that God can use the most unlikely situations as part of his plan. Jacob gave a prophecy to Judah on his deathbed: 'The sceptre will not depart from Judah nor the ruler's staff from between his feet until he comes to whom it belongs.' This was several centuries before they thought of having a king, and yet Jacob promised Judah that a royal line would come from his house.

We learn too that Boaz's mother was not a Jew. Rahab the prostitute was the first Gentile in the land of Canaan to embrace the God of Israel. So we have a mixed family tree: Tamar was raped, Rahab was a Gentile and a prostitute, Ruth was a Moabite. And yet these are all ancestors of our Lord Jesus Christ.

Who wrote Judges and Ruth?

It is time now to examine why Judges and Ruth belong together, and also to answer the question: Who wrote them and why?

The end of a book of the Bible often reveals its purpose. The phrase, 'There was no king in Israel *in those days*' means that the book of Judges, and therefore Ruth as well, was written *after* they were led by a king. It is also obvious from the end of Ruth that David was not the king at the time of writing, for we read, 'Jesse was the father of David,' not 'Jesse was the father of David the King.'

These two facts strongly suggest that the book was written when there was a king, but before David's time. The only period when this was the case was when Saul was king, since David was king directly after Saul. So the book was written when Saul, the first king of Israel, was on the throne, the people's choice. He was chosen for his height and his physical appearance – not for his character or ability.

If we know when the book was written, we can also ask who wrote it. The speeches of the prophet Samuel in the first book of Samuel have been found to be identical in language to the book of Judges and Ruth. And it was his style to teach from the history of his people. It is most likely, therefore, that Samuel wrote Judges and Ruth as one book, when Saul was king.

More of the purpose for writing can be discerned when we ask which tribe King Saul came from. The answer is Benjamin. The whole message of the two books is that Benjamin is bad stock, in contrast to Judah and those in Bethlehem. In other words, the two-volume work was written to prepare the people to switch from Saul to David. Samuel had secretly anointed David but needed to prepare the people to accept him as king rather than their own choice of Saul.

He asks his readers to compare the degraded men of Benjamin with the delightful people in Bethlehem. At the very end Samuel mentions that Jesse was the father of David, knowing that he was God's appointed king and was going to change the whole situation.

This theory is backed up by a detail included in the first chapter of Judges. When the tribe of Judah entered the Promised Land the city of Jerusalem was assigned to the tribe of Benjamin. But the early part of Judges tells us that the city was in the hands of the Jebusites 'to this day', implying that Benjamin never conquered it. One of David's first acts as king, recorded in 1 Samuel, was to capture the city. This provides further clarification for the date of the book and confirms the likelihood that its purpose was to encourage people to be pro-David. The position of Ruth alongside Judges brings two cities into view: Bethlehem, the 'house of bread', David's home town, and Jerusalem, occupied by the Jebusites but soon to become the nation's capital.

How can we use Judges and Ruth today?

In the New Testament the apostle Paul tells Timothy that all Scripture is God-breathed and able to make us 'wise for salvation'. Jesus says that the Scriptures bear witness to him, so we must ask how a Christian should read Judges and Ruth.

Judges

Individual Christians can learn a great deal from the characters in the book of Judges. We can learn from the mistakes the judges made as well as from their correct choices. Each story has value to any believer. But we do not look to the judges to provide role models. Indeed, the New Testament discourages such a course. In Hebrews 12 we are told that those who have gone before, described in chapter 11 and including some of these judges, are watching to see how *we* run the race, looking to our only true model in Jesus, the author and perfecter of our faith, whose work of deliverance stands for all time.

The Church needs to study Judges because it could fall into the same spiral of anarchy today, doing what it feels is right in its own eyes. It could fall into error by looking for a visible 'monarchy', a human being whose viewpoint or leadership is valued more than that of Christ. Rule by democracy, oligarchy or autocracy depends on human leaders, but the Bible teaches that we should be led by a theocracy. Our leader is both human and divine; he was on earth and is now in heaven.

We must also remember that God is the same in character today as he was at the time of the events described in Judges and Ruth. He loves his people, and shows this by disciplining those who wander from his path. At the same time he works out his plans for our good. We need not be part of a cycle of despair. We can know real direction and follow God's purposes.

Ruth

Ruth was one of the earliest Gentiles to embrace the God of Israel. She is a picture of all believers who are in the royal line, brothers of Jesus through faith in him.

The book reminds us of Jesus, for if the Church is like Ruth, Boaz is like Christ – the kinsman redeemer. The Church has been brought into the line of the Old Testament people of God. We are the bride and he is the bridegroom. Ruth is not an isolated Old Testament book, but covers a theme which runs throughout the Bible. The whole Bible is a romance, finishing with the wedding supper of the Lamb in the book of Revelation. The Ruth–Boaz romance is a perfect picture of Christ and his Gentile bride.

9.

1 AND 2 SAMUEL

Introduction

The books which make up 1 and 2 Samuel in the English Bible are just one book in the Jewish Scriptures, and are included as part of the 'former prophets' section. Samuel covers 150 years of history, told from a prophetic point of view to record how God sees things and what he regards as important. The book is named after the prophet who dominates the story, and who probably wrote most of it. It covers great changes in Israel's history and the emergence of the great King David, whose fame is remembered to this day.

Context

Abraham, the father of the Jews, lived around 2000 BC; King David came to the throne around 1000 BC. God's promise to Abraham that he would have descendants and a land is therefore 1,000 years old when we reach the book of Samuel and the arrival of David. According to the Old Testament time chart given earlier in the Overview section (page 7), the book of Samuel records a third change in the pattern of leadership during the history of the people of Israel.

1 **From 2000 to 1500** BC Israel was led by *patriarchs*: Abraham, Isaac, Jacob and Joseph (though they were not a nation at this point).

2 **From 1500 to 1000** BC they were led by *prophets*: Moses through to Samuel.

3 **From 1000 to 500** BC they were led by *princes* (or kings): Saul through to Zedekiah.

4 **In the 500 years leading up to the time of Christ** they were led by *priests*: Joshua through to Annas and Caiaphas.

The dates are approximate, but this gives a helpful summary. Samuel describes the change from prophets to princes (or kings), the 150 years of the upward rise to the empire of David.

It is a highly significant period of Israel's history. The Jews speak of David's reign as the golden era of peace and prosperity when they conquered most of the land God had promised them. Even now, Jews long for a renewal of the days when a king reigned over a united and victorious nation. But it was not all good news, and we see in Samuel the beginning of a decline which continues through 1 and 2 Kings until Israel loses everything they gained in the previous 1,000 years.

Before examining how we should interpret them, we will look at the detail of the main stories in the books of Samuel, beginning with an overview of the content and structure.

Structure

1. **Samuel – last judge**
   - (i) Hannah – anxious wife
   - (ii) Eli – ailing priest
   - (iii) Israel – arrogant army
   - (iv) Saul – anointed king

2. **Saul – first king**
   (i) Jonathan – adventurous son
   (ii) Samuel – angry prophet
   (iii) David – apparent rival
   IN
   (a) Simple shepherd
   (b) Skilled musician
   (c) Superb warrior
   OUT
   (a) Suspected courtier
   (b) Stalked outlaw
   (c) Soldiering exile
   (iv) Philistines – aggressive foe

3. **David – best king**
   (i) Triumphant ascent
   UP
   (a) Single tribe
   (b) Settled nation
   (c) Sizeable empire
   (ii) Tragic descent
   DOWN
   (a) Disgraced man
   (b) Disintegrated family
   (c) Discontented people

4. **Epilogue**

In this structural chart, the lives of Samuel and Saul are each described in terms of their relationship with three individuals and one people group: Samuel with Hannah, Eli, Saul and Israel; Saul with Jonathan, Samuel, David and the Philistines.

David's life can be summarized very simply in four directional words, as the chart shows: in, out, up, down. The 'in' and 'out' refer to his changing favour with King Saul, the 'up' refers to his move towards the pinnacle of his power as king, and 'down' refers to his journey into the depths of despair.

Content

1. Samuel – last judge

(I) HANNAH – ANXIOUS WIFE

The book begins with the story of Samuel's mother, Hannah. Her husband, Elkanah, has two wives and Hannah, who is childless, has to bear the taunts of the other wife, Peninnah, who does have children. Years pass and Hannah's grief at her childlessness deepens. She visits the temple at Shiloh (where Israel kept the ark of the covenant) and prays that if God will at last grant her a son she will dedicate him to God's service. Eli the priest notices that she is muttering aloud and suspects that she is drunk. Hannah explains that she is deeply troubled and Eli sends her away with God's blessing. Later Hannah conceives and gives birth to a son, whom she names Samuel.

In gratitude she fufils her vow to the Lord and presents Samuel to Eli to serve at the temple. Hannah prays again, reflecting her confidence and joy in God. This prayer is clearly recalled by Mary 1,000 years later, when the angel tells her she is to give birth to Jesus. Her joy and praise in what is now called 'The Magnificat' contains echoes of Hannah's.

(II) ELI – AILING PRIEST

Samuel ministers under the priest, Eli. One night he hears a voice and runs to Eli, assuming that he is calling him, but Eli says he is not. This happens three times before the priest

realizes that it is God who wants to speak to Samuel. It is a significant moment, since the prophetic revelation, both verbal
and visual, was rare in those days.

Thus Samuel, aged 12, is given the responsibility of telling
Eli that God will act in judgement upon his family because his
two boys are misbehaving badly and Eli has been turning a
blind eye. The sons have been abusing their positions of
responsibility, eating consecrated meat and sleeping with some
of the women who bring offerings. From then on, God says,
no one in Eli's line will see old age.

This encounter was the start of Samuel's prophetic ministry, and it was not the last time that the word he gave would
be hard to receive.

(III) ISRAEL – ARROGANT ARMY

The next story concerns Israel's defeat at the hands of
the Philistines, the warring nation living on the west coast.
The Israelites assume that they lost the battle because they left
the ark of the covenant in the temple. Next time, therefore,
they take it with them into battle, but are again heavily defeated, with 30,000 foot soldiers killed, including Eli's sons (thus
fulfilling the prophecy concerning their early deaths). The ark
is captured by the Philistines and taken to the temple of
Dagon, the Philistines' god.

On hearing this news, Eli – an old, frail man by this time –
falls backwards off his chair and breaks his neck. The ark,
however, spells trouble for the Philistines. God sends terrible
illnesses upon them and they finally send it back to the
Israelites on a cart pulled by two cows. The Philistines follow
the cart to see where it goes, and they see it heading uphill in
the direction of Jerusalem.

Samuel gathers the Israelites at Mizpah and tells them
that the previous defeats have nothing to do with the ark and

everything to do with the pagan gods they are worshipping. Israel burns the idols, and this time is victorious in the fight against the Philistines. This demonstrates a principle described in Judges: whenever the Israelites disobey God an enemy comes to defeat them, but whenever they repent and put things right they defeat their enemies.

Samuel's fame grows from this time onwards, and his work as a judge and a prophet becomes greatly valued.

(IV) SAUL – ANOINTED KING

The last public thing that Samuel does as a prophet is to anoint Saul as king. The people ask Samuel whether they can have a king like the nations around them. They know that God is their king, but they want a king who is visible. At first Samuel is offended by their request, until God reminds him that he has no right to take offence, for it is God they have rejected.

God tells Samuel that if the nation has a king, they need to be prepared for the consequences. A king will want a palace and an army, so taxation and conscription will swiftly follow the coronation. In spite of these warnings, the Israelites still insist they want a king and they choose Saul, a man who is taller and more handsome than anybody else.

2. Saul – first king

Saul's selection is unusual. God tells Samuel that the one to be anointed as king will be a man searching for donkeys! So when Saul comes to his home asking for help Samuel knows what to do. Saul is given the gift of prophecy as a sign that he is the heir – though we have few details about what form this took. The people confirm Saul as king, aged 30, and Samuel, the last judge, hands over the leadership.

Saul makes a good start. The people are pleased with his appointment and he experiences early success in defeating the

Ammonites. But it is with respect to his relationships that things soon start to go wrong.

(I) JONATHAN – ADVENTUROUS SON

Saul's son Jonathan is instrumental in defeating the Philistines and Saul is initially very proud of him. Jonathan, however, makes the mistake of going into the next battle without telling his father. He wins, but Saul is jealous of his success and his relationship with Jonathan comes under strain.

In the next story, they are in battle again and Saul makes the rash vow that anyone found eating that day, before he has avenged himself on his enemy, will be put to death. Jonathan, ignorant of the vow, eats some honey. Thus we have the bizarre situation of Saul threatening to kill his own son for disobeying some instructions he did not hear. If the men under his command had not intervened, Jonathan would have lost his life.

(II) SAMUEL – ANGRY PROPHET

Saul's relationship with Samuel also deteriorates. As prophet, Samuel's job is to pass on to Saul the words God gives him. On one occasion Saul is instructed to await Samuel's arrival before offering the post-battle sacrifice. When Samuel is late arriving at the battlefield, Saul conducts the sacrifice himself. Enraged at this arrogant action, Samuel tells him his kingdom is about to be handed to someone else.

Saul's second major error also concerns disobedience to God's word. This time he is commanded to wipe out the Amalekites and their livestock, but Saul spares the king, Agag, and the best of the livestock. Once again Samuel arrives on the scene and finds that Saul has failed to obey all that God has said. Samuel becomes very angry, executes Agag before the altar of the Lord, and tells Saul that to obey is better than to sacrifice. Samuel further tells Saul that because he has rejected the word of the Lord, God has rejected him as king. From that day until Samuel's death, Saul would never hear from Samuel again. The story is a salutary reminder that ritual is no substitute for righteousness. It certainly marked the beginning of the end for the first king of Israel.

Deprived of Samuel's counsel, Saul has no way of finding out the Lord's will and so has no idea whether Israel's battles will be successful or not. Although he pleased God at the beginning of his reign by banning every medium from the land of Israel, at the very end of his reign, some time after Samuel's death, he manages to find one at Endor who is still in business. Saul goes to her and calls up Samuel's spirit for a final conversation. He is told that the imminent battle with the Philistines will be his last.

(III) DAVID – APPARENT RIVAL

Saul's story slips into the background with the arrival of David. The young David enters Saul's service, and we are told that Saul likes him very much, but after a good start Saul's relationship with David goes the way of Jonathan's and Samuel's.

IN

(a) Simple shepherd

David's arrival on the scene comes after God's rejection of Saul as king – although Saul is to remain king for some time. Samuel is sent to David's family home to anoint one of Jesse's sons as king, but finds that none receive God's approval. Only when the eighth and youngest son is called from the field does God indicate that this is the one who will be the next king. David is anointed secretly, pending the time many years later when he will eventually be crowned.

(b) Skilled musician

By this time Saul is deteriorating mentally as well as morally. We read that the Holy Spirit leaves him and an unclean spirit takes over. Saul becomes unpredictable, a man who can fly off the handle without a moment's notice. His advisors find that the one thing that can calm him down is music, so David, known as a skilled harp player, is brought to court and his music soothes Saul's spirit.

(c) Superb warrior

The story of David and Goliath is one of the best known in the Bible. It was the mismatch of the century, the sort of story Jews love: Goliath of Gath was 9 foot 6 inches tall, and David was just a little shepherd boy. It was customary for opposing armies to choose a champion each, who would fight each other. Whoever won would win victory for his side, which saved a lot of bloodshed.

By this stage in the story Saul has abdicated his own role as 'champion' for the nation and so, after some discussion, he allows David to fight Goliath on behalf of Israel. Despite the odds, David is convinced God will give him victory. He believes the battle is the Lord's and that his victory will show the whole world his power. He uses a sling, just as he had in his shepherd's work, and with just one stone from the five he has picked, Goliath is dead and the Philistines routed.

OUT

(a) Suspected courtier

If Saul could be jealous of his own son, what would he make of this new hero? He hears the people singing of how Saul had killed thousands, but David tens of thousands. David becomes a great national hero and Saul comes to hate him. From then on David's life is in danger. David continues to play music to soothe Saul's troubled mind, but there are times when Saul is so enraged that he flings a spear in David's direction.

Later Saul plots to kill him, first by offering him his daughter Merab in marriage in exchange for the defeat of the Philistines. David refuses to accept his daughter and Saul's plans are foiled when David defeats the Philistines unscathed. Later David does marry Michal, another of Saul's daughters.

Saul then asks Jonathan to be involved in David's death, but Jonathan and Michal are on David's side, and in the course of several plots warn him of Saul's intentions.

(b) Stalked outlaw

It becomes clear that David has to leave the palace, so he escapes and hides at Samuel's home in Ramah. Then comes an extraordinary event as Saul and his men try to take David prisoner, but the Spirit of the Lord comes upon them and they prophesy, unable to carry out the plan.

Jonathan continues to help David and they make a covenant whereby Jonathan promises to be David's subject, despite being Saul's son. He is a prince abdicating in favour of a shepherd boy. The Bible depicts a remarkable friendship. We are told that there had never been such love between two men as there was between David and Jonathan.

The priest Ahimelech at Nob feeds David with consecrated bread and gives him Goliath's sword. He flees west to Gath, where he is recognized by the Philistine king as the heir apparent and has to feign insanity in order to escape with his life.

At Adullam some 400 malcontents join with David. He sends his parents into Moab, the home of his great-grandmother for protection, and is told by a prophet to return to Judah.

While he is chasing David in the desert of En-gedi, Saul enters a cave to relieve himself, unaware that David is inside. David cuts off the bottom of his robe and when Saul leaves he shouts after him. Saul is so shaken when he realizes that David could have killed him in the cave that he repents temporarily. But before long the chase resumes.

In the desert of Maon David meets a woman he later marries. Nabal refuses hospitality to David and his men. His wife Abigail, however, brings food to them and saves her family from David's retribution. Nabal dies soon after this and David takes Abigail to be his wife.

(c) Soldiering exile

The most extraordinary part of David's story is one that is not often taught. David becomes fearful that Saul will eventually catch up with him, and so offers himself and his men as mercenaries to the Philistines, Israel's greatest enemy. Before long they become trusted allies.

(IV) PHILISTINES – AGGRESSIVE FOE

Saul's end comes when Israel fights the Philistines. Although David and his men are mercenaries with the Philistines, the Philistine leaders leave them out of this particular battle, concerned that David and his men may not remain loyal to them if they are sent into battle against their own people. In the event they are not needed anyway. The Israelites are heavily defeated, and Saul and Jonathan are killed just as Samuel predicted. The injured Saul falls on his own sword when he realizes his life is ebbing away. Thus the book of 1 Samuel finishes with the death of one of the most enigmatic characters in the whole Bible.

3. David – best king

(I) TRIUMPHANT ASCENT

UP

(a) Single tribe

We see the triumphant ascent of David in the first nine chapters of 2 Samuel. It begins with a lament at the death of Saul and Jonathan, which includes some moving words remembering the warmth of the loving friendship David had known with Jonathan.

There is, however, a war developing between David's house and Saul's house, with tales of murder and revenge abounding. Saul's chief commander Abner changes sides and brings Benjamin with him, but the nation is nonetheless torn apart.

(b) Settled nation

The tribe of Judah crowns David as king in Hebron in the south, where he remains for seven years. He eventually settles the nation as one unit, helped in part by the capture of Jerusalem from the hands of the Jebusites. The Jebusites are convinced that Jerusalem is safe from attack, but David takes the city by entering it via a staircase that runs from inside the city to a spring outside the walls.

It is worth noting that not only did Jerusalem have excellent fortifications for a capital city, with cliffs on three of its four sides, but it was also on 'neutral' territory between Judah (the tribe who supported David) and Benjamin (Saul's tribe). It was thus an appropriate political capital as neither Judah nor Benjamin could claim it was theirs.

(c) Sizeable empire

The book proceeds to chart David's successful campaigns against the Philistines, the Ammonites and the Edomites, whose lands became part of a vast empire. For the first (and last) time, most of the land God had promised was in Israel's hands. Israel was at the peak of her history.

Even at such a time of personal success, however, David is keen to remember Saul's house, and he honours Mephibosheth, the lame son of Jonathan, crippled in both feet.

(II) TRAGIC DESCENT
DOWN
(a) Disgraced man
David's decline begins one fateful afternoon. The army is away fighting against Ammon and David, who should be leading them, is at home looking out of a palace window. He notices Bathsheba, the wife of his next-door neighbour, bathing on the roof and likes what he sees. He proceeds to break five of the Ten Commandments. He covets his neighbour's wife, he bears false witness against the husband, he steals the wife, he commits adultery with her, and finally he arranges the murder of the husband. It is a terrible story and from that afternoon the nation goes downhill. Over the next 500 years they lose everything that God gave them.

Bathsheba becomes pregnant, David seeks to cover it up and eventually arranges for Uriah her husband to be killed in battle. The baby dies and David takes Bathsheba into the palace as his wife. She becomes pregnant again, but this baby survives and is called Solomon (meaning 'peace'). But David has no peace. A year later God sends the prophet Nathan to David to tell him of his sin through a parable and David realizes the gravity of his sin. Psalm 51 is a prayer of confession following this revelation.

(b) Disintegrated family
It seems as if David's immoral behaviour becomes a catalyst for unpleasantness throughout the family. His eldest son Amnon

rapes Tamar, one of his sisters. David's second son Absalom hears what happened and two years later exacts his own revenge.

Absalom gains such popularity with the people that David is obliged to leave Jerusalem. Once again he finds himself in exile.

In accordance with a prophecy made by Nathan, Absalom parades David's wives on the palace roof and has sex with them in public. A subsequent battle leads to the death of Absalom, but David is distraught, wishing that he had died instead.

(c) Discontented people

The rancour within David's family affects the people as a whole. Despite the vast empire they now control, they are not happy with David's leadership. The capital is in the south and the people in the north feel neglected. Concerns are brought to a head by a Benjaminite, Sheba, who refuses to recognize David as king and starts a revolt. David quells the uprising, but the feelings of anger remain.

4. Epilogue

The last chapters are arranged using a literary device, with the contents of the epilogue set out according to corresponding themes. The structure can be broken down into six sections, labelled A1, B1, C1, C2, B2, A2, and the sections A1 and A2, B1 and B2, and C1 and C2 cover similar themes.

A1 LEGACY FROM THE PAST

The whole of Israel faces a famine for three years. God tells David that the famine is a punishment on Israel for Saul's earlier slaughter of the Gibeonites, a group whom the Israelites had vowed not to touch. The Gibeonites request the death of seven of Saul's descendants as recompense for this outrage and David hands them over.

B1 DAVID'S MEN

There is a short account of David's 'giant killers' – the men who fought alongside him and gave him victory over the Philistines in a series of battles.

C1 DAVID'S PSALM

One of David's greatest psalms records how God delivered him from all his enemies. He writes of God as his rock, his fortress and his deliverer – the words of a man who can look back on God's extraordinary provision throughout his life and give thanks for it.

C2 THE LAST WORDS OF DAVID

These sayings read like a psalm as David reflects on God's Spirit, who inspired his writing of the songs which have been sung down through the ages and are perhaps David's greatest legacy.

B2 MORE CITATIONS FOR BRAVERY

David recognizes, records and honours the men who fought with him, including the three who crept back to Bethlehem to bring David some water when he was on the run.

A2 DIVINE JUDGEMENT AGAIN FALLS ON ISRAEL

At the end of his life, David is tempted by Satan to conduct a census of the fighting men of Israel. His motivation is pride and God punishes his action. Gad the prophet is sent to convey God's displeasure and David has three options: three years of famine, three months of fleeing from enemies, or three days of plague. He opts for the third and 70,000 people die of the plague.

David cries out to the Lord to stop the plague and is told to sacrifice at the threshing floor of Araunah the Jebusite, a flat area high above the city of Jerusalem. He offers a sacrifice and the plague stops. David sees the threshing floor as an ideal place to build a temple for God. He is offered the land free, but David says his offering to the Lord would be unworthy if it cost him nothing and insists on buying the land. The books of Kings describe the building of the temple on this very spot.

David was not allowed to build the temple himself because God said he had 'blood on his hands'. The temple had to be built by a man of peace. So the temple in Jerusalem, which means 'city of peace', was built by David's son Solomon. Although David drew up the plans, arranged the workmen and collected the materials, it was his son Solomon who saw the project through.

How should we read Samuel?

Our overview of Samuel has so far omitted any mention of how we should read the book. All readers approach the text with certain expectations, but it is important that we read the Bible as it was intended to be read if we are to understand and interpret it correctly. Samuel is no exception. There are six different levels at which we can read any series of Bible stories and it is important to choose the right one.

1. **Anecdotal (interesting stories)**
   (i) Children
   (ii) Adults

2. **Existential (personal messages)**
   (i) Guidance
   (ii) Comfort

3. **Biographical (character studies)**
   (i) Individual
   (ii) Social

4. **Historical (national development)**
   (i) Leadership
   (ii) Structure

5. **Critical (possible errors)**
   (i) 'Lower' criticism
   (ii) 'Higher' criticism

6. **Theological (providential over-ruling)**
   (i) Justice – retribution
   (ii) Mercy – redemption

1. Anecdotal

(I) CHILDREN

The simplest way is to focus on the most interesting stories. Sunday school teachers select the events that will communicate best with the children, and the story of David and Goliath, for example, is a particular favourite.

Maria Matilda Penstone expressed it like this:

God has given us a book full of stories
which was made for his people of old.
It begins with a tale of a garden
and finishes with the city of gold.
There are stories for parents and children,
for the old who are ready to rest,
but for all who can read them or listen
the story of Jesus is best.

There is some merit in using the stories in this way, but it is selective. Teachers can easily distort the true meaning of an event in favour of a platitude which they feel is of value and on a level which they think the children will understand.

(II) ADULTS

The stories in Samuel are superbly told, with an economy of words and a beautiful style. Since adults also enjoy a good story, many read the Bible purely for its anecdotal value. Film directors have enjoyed adapting stories such as David and Bathsheba for the silver screen.

While it is good that the stories are at least read, this approach ignores one fundamental point. At the level of anecdote, it does not matter whether stories are true or not. They could be fact, fiction or fable – whatever they are, the stories can still be enjoyed and the moral message can still be discerned. The big problem is, however, that it *does* matter whether the stories are true or not, because these smaller stories are part of the big story of the book of Samuel, which in turn has a crucial place within the Bible's overall story of redemption. If we doubt whether men did the things attributed to them here, how can we be sure that God did what is attributed to him in these pages? The human and the divine acts stand or fall together.

2. Existential

(I) GUIDANCE

I am tempted to call reading the stories of the Bible for guidance 'the horoscope method', because some people read the Bible each day hoping that something might leap out and fit them! There are rare occasions when people have testified to a particular verse or passage having played a significant role in their lives, but this says more about God's ability to use any means he chooses to guide us than it does about the legitimacy of the method. The method completely ignores the fact that most of the verses will mean nothing to a person's particular situation. There is a classic story about a man who was thumbing through his Bible looking for a verse and found, 'Judas went out and hanged himself.' Not satisfied, he looked for another and found, 'Go and do thou likewise'!

If we are reading the Bible for a personal message, what do we make of the verse in 1 Samuel where Samuel says to Eli, 'In your family line there will never be an old man'? It was appropriate centuries later for one of Eli's descendants, the prophet Jeremiah, who started his prophetic ministry when he was 17 since he would not live to old age. But there is no application for us. Or take another verse '...and Samuel hacked Agag to pieces before the Lord.' How would this be applied?

I am ridiculing this method because I am sure that this should not be the main reason for reading these stories. The books of Samuel will reveal relatively little if this is how we read them. We need to read the text in the *context* in which it is written if we are to extract the correct meaning. If we just look for texts relevant to our own situation, we will miss an enormous amount.

(II) COMFORT

In former days 'Promise Boxes' were used by the devout in order to find encouragement to face life. Each biblical 'promise' was printed on a curled up roll of paper and one was lifted out at random with a pair of tweezers each day. Needless to say, each was also lifted out of its biblical context and therefore often separated from the conditions attached to it. For example, 'Lo, I am with you always' is placed in the context of 'Go and make disciples', and we should not claim the promise if we are not fulfilling the command. Even without such a box, we can read the Bible in much the same way, looking for a verse we can lift out for ourselves. We shall find few like this in the historical books of the Bible, like Samuel and Kings. They yield up their treasures to those who read them whole, seeking to know just what God is like, how he feels about us rather than how we feel about ourselves, or even about him.

3. Biographical

(I) INDIVIDUAL

The third method is most common among preachers. One of the great features of the Bible is the honest way it records the failures and successes of the main characters. James says in the New Testament that the Bible is like a mirror that can show us what we are like through the people we read about. We can compare ourselves with Bible characters and ask whether we would have behaved in the same way.

With this in mind, we can note how the first two kings of Israel both started well and finished badly, yet Saul was seen as the worst king and David as the best.

We read of the character of Saul, a man who was literally head and shoulders above the rest, with many personal advantages. We read how the Spirit of the Lord came upon him and he turned into a different man. But we read, too, of the fatal flaws in his character, and how his insecurities led to poor relationships and jealousy of the gifted people around him.

We can contrast Saul with David, whom the Bible calls 'a man after God's own heart'. When Samuel chooses David we read, 'The Lord does not look at the things man looks at. Man looks at the outward appearance, but the Lord looks at the heart.'

Scripture describes David as a man of the outdoors, involved in manual labour, handsome and brave. He developed his relationship with God during the lonely days and nights as a shepherd, reading the law, praying and praising God for creation as well as redemption. These years were a preparation for him to become the most important person in the land.

We can note his skills as a leader, asking God's opinion before taking any decision. Even though he was anointed as king, he refused to take the throne too soon, but waited for God's timing. He was a magnanimous man even in victory, unhappy when his enemies were killed and furious because one of Saul's surviving sons was killed, even though Saul had been his enemy. He was a very forgiving man, and a man who could honour brave people – in the book of Samuel we have a list of those whom David honoured.

David was therefore the opposite of Saul: he had a heart for God and he loved honouring other people. Saul did not have a heart for God and did not like to have anyone else who was successful anywhere near him.

There are other comparisons: Samuel and Eli shared an inability to discipline their children. Jonathan and Absalom were both sons of kings but behaved very differently. Jonathan was an unselfish son of a bad king (Saul) who was willing to surrender to David's leadership. Absalom was the selfish son of a good king (David) who wanted to seize the throne from his father.

The women in Samuel also make a lovely character study. Hannah and Abigail both reveal interesting traits. We read of Hannah's devotion to God and her excitement when she became pregnant. Abigail courageously averted a crisis by making food for David's men when her husband had refused them hospitality. She so impressed David that he married her shortly after her husband's death.

(II) SOCIAL

We can also study the relationships between individuals.

Jonathan and David's friendship is one of the most pure and godly in the pages of the Bible.

The frustrating, even threatening, interaction between Saul and David is a classic example of how difficult personal relationships can be with unreliable temperaments, who alternate between welcoming and rejecting moods, especially when there is the added complication of influence by evil spirits.

The whole saga of David and the various women in his life is full of insights into gender relationships. Nor is his ability to win the affection and devotion of the various men in his life irrelevant to contemporary society.

The people's insistent choice of their first king and their reasons for it have something to say for the influence of image on contemporary elections.

So these stories have social as well as individual implications, from all of which we can learn valuable lessons. But this still falls short of the intended message of the text.

4. Historical

(I) LEADERSHIP

A fourth way of considering Samuel is to see it as a study of the history of Israel. Israel developed from a family to a tribe, then to a nation, and finally to an empire. It is this development into an empire that is outlined in the 150 years covered by the books of Samuel.

The request for a king came from the people, jealous of the unified and visible leadership which monarchies provided in other nations around them, and fed up with the federal relationship of 12 independent tribes which pertained at that time.

Samuel warned the people that there would be heavy costs associated with any move towards a centralized government through a king. The people went ahead with their request and the course of history was set. God acceded to their request, but insisted that Israel's king should not be like kings in other nations. Israel's king must write out the law and read it daily, and provide spiritual leadership for the people (this provision in Deuteronomy shows that God had anticipated this development). Thereafter the character of the nation would be tied to the king.

(II) STRUCTURE

The move from a federal to a centralized structure for the nation was not painless. We can study the book from this standpoint, noting the struggles David faced and his skill in overcoming them. We can note how his genius as an organizer and his skill as a commander under God led the nation to reach a peak of peace and prosperity under his rule. His selection of Jerusalem as the capital city was one of a number of brilliant master strokes. The city was captured from the Jebusites and so was not regarded as the preserve of any particular tribe.

The empire grew under David, previous enemies became satellite states and all the land which had been promised was conquered for the first and last time. The Philistines no longer bothered them. But centralized government proved to be the Israelites' downfall as well, for when power is in fewer and fewer hands, the character of those people who own the hands inevitably determines what happens.

5. Critical

(I) 'LOWER' CRITICISM

Lower criticism is the study of the Bible by scholars to see if there are any errors in the text. They study and compare manuscripts in the original languages, and note any discrepancies that may have occurred through errors of transmission by the copyists. This work gives us enormous confidence that the manuscripts which translators use are very close to the original and it is believed that the New Testament is 98 per cent accurate.

The earliest of the full Old Testament manuscripts is the Masoretic text dated at AD 900. There is a complete copy of Isaiah, one of the Dead Sea Scrolls, from 100 BC which is 1,000 years older than all the other copies available. This was discovered when the Revised Standard Version was being translated, so they held back the publication until the text had been checked against this older manuscript. In fact, the text they had been working on originally was very accurate and only a few things needed to be changed.

Whilst the Old Testament text does not have the same accuracy as the New Testament, we can still be assured that there is very little which is different from the original text. Furthermore, it is worth noting that any dilemmas regarding translation are on small details and not the central truths of the faith. In Samuel, for example, there are two accounts of the death of Goliath, but only one makes David responsible. If just one letter is adjusted, the discrepancy is solved. Clearly a copyist made an error in transmission.

(II) 'HIGHER' CRITICISM

Lower criticism is a necessary and welcome discipline, but higher criticism does a great deal of damage. It came originally from Germany in the nineteenth century and filtered into many theological colleges during the twentieth century.

The basic argument of higher criticism is that even if the original text accurately conveys what the writer meant, we can still be mistaken about what we should believe. The higher critics approach the text with their own presuppositions based on what they regard as reasonable. Those who argue that science has disproved miracles omit any miraculous events from the text, while those who cannot believe in supernatural foreknowledge omit any prophecy that accurately predicts the future.

These scholars work at a purely academic and intellectual level, with little concern for or understanding of personal faith. Their approach unavoidably leaves the text of Scripture in pieces, unrecognizable from the original.

6. Theological

A theological approach to reading the books of the Bible makes every page and every sentence of value. The levels of reading we have considered so far are concerned only with the human side of Bible study, but the Bible is primarily a book about God, with only a secondary interest in God's people. This type of study asks how we can read the text in order to get to know God.

We have already seen how Samuel is a prophetic book. The history recorded is history from God's perspective, recording what God believed to be important.

Taking the theological approach, therefore, we can look at a story and ask how this event related to God. How did he feel about it? Why did the event matter so much to God that it was included for us to read as part of Holy Scripture? We start to read the book from God's point of view and draw conclusions about who he is and what he is like. Confident that God does not change, we can then apply these timeless truths to our own day and generation.

JUSTICE AND MERCY

This is the best and most exciting way to read Samuel. The book describes God's intervention in the life of Israel, for he is the real actor in these stories, not Saul, David or Samuel. God both initiates historical events and responds to them. We see how Hannah is barren, she prays, and God gives her a son. We see how David, in God's name, kills Goliath with his first stone. We see how David, with God's help, escapes the clutches of thousands of men from Saul's army. God helps some folk and hinders others. He is just in punishing evil and sometimes merciful in not punishing when punishment is deserved.

He gives Israel the land, but when they disobey him he sends oppressors. When they repent he sends deliverers. He allows the people to choose a king, but when the king fails he gives them another, one after his own heart.

We can study the stories of Samuel, learn lessons from the history and compare ourselves with Saul or David, but the real reason to read the book is to learn about the character of God.

God's activity is seen especially at the heart of the book. He makes a covenant with David, confirming his commitment to Israel which had first been expressed in the covenants with Abraham and Moses centuries before. This is the most vital moment in 1 and 2 Samuel. It arises when David asks God if he can build a house for him. He is embarrassed that he has built such a grand palace for himself and that God is living in a tent next door.

When David tells God he will build him a house, three messages come from the prophet Nathan. The first message is, 'Do it.' The second message is, 'Don't do it.' God explains that a tent is good enough for him since he never asked for a palace of stone. The third message is that David must not build the temple because he is 'a man of blood', but his son can build it.

In the covenant God tells David how he will treat his son. He will discipline him but will never cease to love him. David's house and kingdom will endure before him for ever. His throne will be established for ever; there will always be a descendant of David on the throne.

From that moment on, the descendants of David always keep careful records of their family tree, wondering if their son might be the 'son of David' mentioned in the covenant. This promise becomes the focus of national hopes for the next 3,000 years as the Jews look for the Messiah.

This covenant is a crucial theme through the rest of the Bible. A thousand years later the promise was kept when Jesus was born to a humble couple who were in the royal line. Jesus was the legal son of David through Joseph his father, but also a physical son of David through his mother Mary. He was twice over the son of David. Throughout his life he was known as the 'son of David'. The disciples recognized his right to be known as 'Messiah' (the anointed one), and this theme continues in the later writings about him and his Church. The books of Acts, Romans, 2 Timothy and Revelation all use this title to refer to Jesus. They proclaim that all authority in heaven and on earth is given to the son of David and will always be in his hands. They rejoice that God has kept that covenant with David in his son Jesus.

In the fulfilment of the covenant we see that God's promise has wider implications, as the king on David's throne rules over the Jews and Gentiles who make up his Church.

It is only when we read Samuel from a theological point of view that we can appreciate the richness of the book in terms of its message and the part it plays in the themes developed in the Bible as a whole.

Conclusion

Samuel is a history book with a difference. It is prophetic history full of interesting, bizarre, romantic and cruel stories which, brought together, reveal God's ongoing purposes for his people. God wanted us to be ruled by one man – not King David I, but King David II. The books of 1 and 2 Samuel are part of Christian history. Jesus was king of the Jews in the past, he is king of the Church today, and he will be king of the world in the future, when he will reign in justice and righteousness, and the kingdom will finally be restored to Israel.

Thus the true significance of the book becomes clear as we understand how God is involved, acting behind the scenes, shaping history and assuring his people that his kingdom will grow and one day his own son, also the son of David, will be king.

10.

1 AND 2 KINGS

Introduction

My history teacher at school made the subject very dull. It was all about dates, battles, kings and queens and seemed to be complicated and irrelevant. My interest was revived by reading the spoof history book *1066 and All That*, which was certainly more amusing than my school history lessons, and where any historical event was summed up as either 'a good thing' or 'a bad thing' – there was nothing in between.

The book of Kings reads a little like *1066 and All That* (though without the humour). It describes the kings of Israel or Judah as either good or bad, depending on how they reigned. Unlike the school history many of us remember, however, biblical history is utterly compelling. It is not about irrelevant dates and battles, but is a record of God's people told from God's point of view. It is not for mere academic interest either: it is absolutely vital for the whole of mankind.

Context

The book of Kings focuses on the third of the four phases in the national development of Israel's leadership. As the Overview of the Old Testament explained (page 7), the first national leaders were patriarchs, from Abraham to Joseph, then came the prophets, from Moses to Samuel. Third came the kings, from Saul to Zedekiah, and finally the priests, from Joshua to Caiaphas.

The period of the kings is covered by four books in our English Bible:

1 Samuel: Samuel to Saul
2 Samuel: David
1 Kings: Solomon to Ahab
2 Kings: Ahab to Zedekiah

In the Hebrew Scriptures this leadership phase is covered by just two books, Samuel and Kings, with the break between Samuel and Kings cutting King Ahab's reign in two and separating the prophet Elijah's life and death. When the Old Testament was translated into Greek in 200 BC, the books became too long for one scroll. Hebrew words have only consonants, so the addition of vowels in the Greek made the books twice the length. Thus the breaks into 1 and 2 Samuel and 1 and 2 Kings were determined more by translation than by design.

Kingdoms

In Hebrew the book is called the 'Kingdoms' of Israel, not 'Kings'. The word 'kingdom' has a different meaning in Hebrew. In English it refers to a land over which a sovereign rules. Thus England is part of the United Kingdom under the reign of the Queen. In Hebrew, however, the word 'kingdom' refers to the reign of a monarch, so is defined in terms of authority not area, rule rather than realm.

Furthermore, the concept of a 'reign' in the Bible is very different from in the United Kingdom, where, under a constitutional monarchy, the Queen reigns but does not rule, the power residing in the elected government. The big advantage is that the armed forces and courts of law are not under the government directly, but are responsible to the Queen. The monarchy is valued not so much for the power it wields as for the power it keeps from others.

The kings of Israel, by contrast, had absolute power. They made the rules and commanded the armed forces. There was no parliament, no voting and no opposition parties. The king ruled by decree and not by debate. His influence over his subjects was total, and therefore his character and conduct shaped society during his rule. He stood as a representative of the nation before God, but also as a representative of God before the nation.

This meant a major change in the way the nation was evaluated. During the time described in Joshua, Judges and Ruth, there was a loose federation and the people were judged according to their actions. In Samuel and Kings, however, the king's character and conduct decided the fate of the nation.

Selected history

Although the book is about the kings of Israel, it is not even-handed in its allocation of space to each king. For example, Omri was a king in the north whom we know from other historical sources to have had an outstanding reign, creating an extraordinary economic turnaround for the nation. Yet the book of Kings dismisses him in eight verses, because he was deficient in the one area that mattered: he did evil in the sight of the Lord. Similarly, Jereboam II had a mini golden age in the north, yet he is given just seven verses for the same reason. On the other hand, Hezekiah, who was largely a good king, is given three chapters, a single prayer of Solomon covers 38 verses, and the stories of Elijah and Elisha, who were not kings at all, take up a third of the two books of Kings.

This apparently uneven treatment occurs because the writer is not driven by a conventional historical approach. We noted in our study of Joshua that any historian has to select what is important, make connections between the events or people he has selected, and then give an explanation as to why the events led on from each other. The writer of Kings is not interested in focusing on political, economic or military history, though he may mention all these in passing. Rather, he is concerned with two aspects of each king's rule or kingdom:

1 Its **spiritual** qualities – worship, either of the God of Israel or idols
2 Its **moral** qualities – justice and morality, or their opposites

Prophetic history

Kings is the last of a collection of books known as the 'former prophets' in the Hebrew Bible and follows Joshua, Judges and Samuel. This is history from God's viewpoint. Individuals and events are mentioned because God regards them as important and necessary for future generations. A man may be a brilliant politician or economist, but God is primarily interested in his belief and behaviour.

We could rightly term these books 'holy history', for they are a record with an abiding message and a story with an eternal moral. They offer us not just a lesson *from* history, but the lesson *of* history. Those who do not learn it are condemned to repeat it.

Universal truth

There are patterns in the history of Israel which can be universally applied. Take, for example, the length of the reign of each king mentioned in the book. A good king reigned on average for 33 years and a bad king on average for 11 years. From this we can derive the general principle that good rulers last longer than bad ones, since God is in ultimate control of history and can keep good kings on the throne.

There are exceptions – not every good king had a long reign and not every bad king had a short one – but the principle is generally true and can, indeed, still be seen in the length of time modern leaders rule.

The rise and fall of the nation

Kings covers some pivotal events in the history of God's people which we need to note if we are to grasp the message of the book and understand the books which follow. The book of 2 Samuel and the early part of 1 Kings describe the powerful position of Israel on the world stage, but most of the book of Kings is concerned with the nation's downfall. Under David and Solomon the nation was eventually united, and the empire stretched from Egypt to the Euphrates. At last the Israelites inhabited most of the land promised to Abraham 1,000 years before, and controlled more besides. But from Solomon's time onwards they headed downhill, through civil war and a divided kingdom to exile in a foreign land.

The national split meant that the name Israel no longer referred to the whole nation, but only to the 10 tribes of the north. The southern tribes of Judah and Benjamin were known by the name of the larger one, Judah. This distinction continues through the rest of the Old Testament.

The southern tribes of Judah and Benjamin became known as 'Jews', derived from the tribal name Judah. Before this point the people were known collectively as 'Hebrews' or 'Israelites'. This is an important distinction to bear in mind. In the New Testament John's Gospel distinguishes between the Jews in the south and the Galileans in the north. It was the Jews in the south who were largely responsible for the crucifixion of Jesus, not all the people of Israel *per se*.

A TALE OF TWO NATIONS

Kings covers the histories of these two 'nations'. The spiritual and moral standards of the 10 tribes in the north steadily deteriorated, until Assyria sent them into exile. In the south the progression downwards is less marked. There were good kings such as Hezekiah and Josiah, but eventually they went the same way as the north and were taken away to Babylon. Their forefather Abraham had been called out of Ur – now they finished up where Abraham had begun, though this time as displaced persons.

It is a salutary lesson about how easy it is to lose what has been gained. Often the duration of the demise is much less than the time it took to reach the pinnacle.

The kingdom of Israel

The kingdom of Israel went through three stages, summarized in the table below.

1. United kingdom

Saul	40 years
David	40 years
Solomon	40 years

2. Divided kingdom

10 tribes in the north – 'Israel'
2 tribes in the south – 'Judah'

War	80 years	Elijah
Peace	80 years	Elisha
War	50 years	Israel to Assyria, 721 BC

3. Single kingdom

140 years   Judah to Babylon, 587 BC

UNITY

The first stage was the 'United Kingdom', when three kings reigned in turn over the whole of Israel. The first king was Saul, who was largely bad; the second was David, who was mainly good; and the third was Solomon, who was both good and bad.

Each reign lasted exactly 40 years. The number 40 is often indicative of the length of time God tests people. Jesus was tempted for 40 days in the wilderness; the children of Israel were in the wilderness for 40 years. It is a trial period in God's sight, and all three kings failed the test. They started well, but finished badly. David received credit for being 'a man after God's own heart', but even he had a disappointing end.

The book of 1 Samuel covers Saul's 40 years, 2 Samuel covers David's 40 years and the first 11 chapters of 1 Kings cover Solomon's 40 years.

WAR

As soon as Solomon died, the north and the south became locked in a civil war that wrecked the 'United Kingdom'. The seeds of unrest had been sown when Solomon had taxed the nation heavily and confined the benefits to the south, causing the north to grow discontented. Solomon's death was the catalyst for this unrest to boil over into armed conflict.

The two southern tribes kept the capital Jerusalem and the royal line of David. The 10 tribes in the north lost both and set up their own centres of worship, at Bethel and Dan, complete with two golden calves as the focus of their worship. Since the royal line was in the south, they also elected their own king, Jeroboam.

Succession in the north proved to be rarely smooth. There were assassinations, coups d'état, takeovers. The kings were often self-elected.

For 80 years after the split, there was war between the north and the south amid increasing animosity, culminating with the tribes in the north making a treaty with Syria and Damascus to try to wipe out the two tribes in the south. Isaiah gives the details in his prophecy.

PEACE

The 80 years of war between the north and the south were followed by 80 years of peace, during which God sent two prophets who play a huge part in the book of Kings. Elijah's ministry is recorded in 1 Kings and the first two chapters of 2 Kings, and Elisha, who followed him, is a key figure in the early part of 2 Kings.

The respite did not halt the decline, however, and in 721 BC the Assyrians defeated the northern tribes of Israel and deported them from their land. They became the '10 lost tribes', never to return to the land as a nation.

After the exile of the northern kingdom of Israel, the book focuses exclusively on Judah and Benjamin in the south. It was a very small kingdom, with Jerusalem as its capital and a small amount of land surrounding it, but their kings were descended from the royal line and they knew about God's promise to David that there would always be one of his descendants on the throne.

When the northern tribes were deported, God sent prophetic warnings from Isaiah and Micah that the same would happen to the south, but this had little or no effect. The last event recorded in the book of Kings is that Judah was led into exile by the Babylonians just 140 years later.

Purpose

We come now to focus on the basic questions that should inform our reading of any book of the Bible: Who wrote the book? How did they write it? When did they write it? Why did they write it?

Who wrote Kings?

The writer of the book cannot be known with any certainty. Most Jews think it was Jeremiah and there are a number of reasons why the case for this is strong.

1 Parts of Kings are identical to Jeremiah's prophecy – even the wording is exactly the same.
2 Jeremiah is not mentioned in the book, despite being a contemporary of Josiah and at the heart of many of the events described. It would seem impossible for anyone to cover this period without mentioning Jeremiah, but if Jeremiah is the author it would be in keeping with other writers of the Bible for him to be self-effacing.
3 We know that prophets often wrote about kings. Isaiah wrote about Uzziah and Hezekiah, and God specifically instructed Jeremiah in his prophecy to write about Israel.
4 Furthermore, there was a time in Jeremiah's ministry when recalling the history of the nation would have been especially pertinent. His prophecy tells of the time when the people of God rejected his impassioned reminders that they should be obedient to the covenant and he had to pronounce curses on the nation. This would have been the appropriate juncture to write the book of Kings.

The one problem with this hypothesis is that Jeremiah was taken to Egypt in 586 BC, and he died there, yet the last part of

2 Kings exhibits remarkable knowledge of events in Babylon. It is difficult to see how these details could square with him writing the whole book. Perhaps the best solution is that Jeremiah wrote parts of Kings, with someone else finishing it. This might explain his own absence from the narrative.

Some suggest Ezekiel as another candidate. He was known to depend on Jeremiah and has a similar style. However, the date of his last prophecy is 571 BC, which argues against him being the writer. Jeremiah is the strongest candidate, but without further proof, we must leave the question open.

How was Kings written?

The book of Kings includes references to the fact that further information can be found in other sources: the Acts of Solomon, the books of the Chronicles of the King of Israel (mentioned 17 times) and the books of the Chronicles of the King of Judah (mentioned 15 times). These books are not the books of Chronicles included in the Bible. The writer is using national records woven together to communicate a lesson about history.

Parts of Isaiah are identical in wording to Kings, suggesting that either they used a common source or one borrowed from the other at certain points.

The writer covers events in the kingdoms of Judah and Israel simultaneously. It can be confusing to read about the king of Judah, followed immediately by a section on the king of Israel, but the order is deliberate. The writer wants us to understand how each kingdom was progressing in relation to its counterpart. This is vital for the narrative during the times when the two kingdoms were at war, or when intermarriage led to a time of peace.

The writer therefore used the same sort of historical methods employed today, taking material from other sources, gathering information from libraries, and so on. The difference is that his selection was divinely inspired, so that what we have in Kings is not simply history, but the Word of God.

When was Kings written?

A vital clue to the book's date is given by phrases suggesting the temple in Jerusalem was still standing, 'and still is to this day'. This suggests a date prior to the exile to Babylon in 586 BC, which was when the temple was destroyed.

However, another part of the book suggests a later date of writing. The Babylonians killed Zedekiah, the last king of Judah, having tied him up in chains and made him watch the execution of his sons before removing his eyes. The previous king, Jehoiachin, had given in to the Babylonians and was kept as a prisoner. The last thing we read in the book of Kings is that Nebuchadnezzar, King of Babylon, released Jehoiachin from prison and invited him to dine at his table. This suggests that the book was completed half way through the exile, especially as there is no mention of the people's return. It also means that someone from the royal line of David had his meals at the king's table in Babylon, and so Nebuchadnezzar unwittingly helped to keep the royal line secure.

Taking these two details together, therefore, it seems that the book was mostly written before the fall of Jerusalem, but was actually completed during the exile.

Why was Kings written?

The motivation of the writer follows naturally from the answer to the question of when the book was written.

Here is a nation that has lost its land and its capital, and has been taken away to another land. A whole generation will never see home again. They are slaves once more, their temple lies in ruins, so inevitably they have questions about their relationship with God. Where is he? Why has he allowed all this to happen? What about his promises?

The book of Kings provides the answers to these questions. It explains that the fault for the exile lies squarely with the people. God kept his promises: he promised that if the people misbehaved they would lose the land, but in spite of repeated warnings they did not listen. The history of Kings is thus a profound lesson to these people in exile.

Yet even in this dark book there is hope, because God promises never to break his part of the covenant. God says that although the people may break the covenant, he never will. He promises to bring his children back from exile. The punishment will be for a limited time only.

In fact, the people remained in the land of Babylon for 70 years. The number was not arbitrary. God had told them to let the land rest every seventh year, but they had ignored this law for 500 years, from the time of Solomon onwards. During that time, therefore, the land had missed 70 years of rest, so in one sense the 70-year exile provided the land with a chance to catch up on its holidays!

The book of Kings is saying that the exile was a disastrous time, but it was not hopeless. God had promised to keep the royal line of David going and he would do so.

Content

Solomon

As we look at the book in more detail we begin with the king who dominates the early chapters. Solomon's name means 'peace', which was appropriate since his reign benefited from the peace David had secured when building the empire. He was a good man who began well.

At the start of his reign God appeared to him in a dream and offered to give him anything he asked for. Solomon, knowing that he lacked experience, asked for wisdom. God promised Solomon not just wisdom, but many things he did not ask for besides: wealth, fame and power.

Solomon's gift of wisdom was demonstrated in the famous story of the two prostitutes who argued about a baby. Both had babies, but during the night one of the babies died, so its mother stole the other's baby and placed the dead one in its place. Solomon had to adjudicate on this most awkward situation. To whom did the live baby belong? Solomon asked for wisdom from God, and then told the women to cut the baby in half and keep half each. As soon as Solomon said this, the real mother pleaded that the baby be allowed to live and be given to the other woman. Solomon thus knew who was the true mother.

Perhaps Solomon's most memorable act was his building of the temple with the materials and the plans provided by his father David. God had promised David that he would allow his son to build the first permanent place for centralized worship, predicted in the book of Deuteronomy centuries before. It was a magnificent temple, and took seven years to build (it took 12 years to build Solomon's own palace, however).

We read that although the temple was built out of cut stone, the sound of hammer and chisel was never heard. This was a mystery for many years until someone discovered a gigantic cave the size of a large theatre at Mount Moriah near Calvary outside Jerusalem. The floor is covered with millions of little chips where the rock has been cut. The rock is so soft that it can be cut with a penknife, but when it is brought out into the open air it oxidizes and goes quite hard. All the stone for the temple came from this cave, where they cut the blocks to the exact shape needed to fit into the temple above ground.

Solomon was also responsible for the dedication of the temple. His dedicatory prayer, based on Leviticus 26 and Deuteronomy 28, is recorded at length in Kings. It mentions God's promise to bring his people back from exile if they turned back to him, a promise that became especially significant for those in Babylon when the book came out.

His reign brought great prosperity to the people of Israel. The empire stretched from Egypt to the Euphrates and included most of the territory which had been promised to them. Solomon's fame spread far and wide, even reaching the Queen of Sheba, who paid him a visit and was impressed by the splendour of his palace.

The time of peace meant opportunity for leisure and learning. Solomon collected 3,000 proverbs and wrote 1,005 songs. God chose to publish just six of these songs in the Bible. My theory is that Solomon wrote a song for each of his 700 wives and 300 concubines, but God picked only a few, including the one which appears in the Song of Solomon. Incidentally, it is at this point that we really must question whether Solomon's wisdom is demonstrated in taking so many wives. That meant 700 mothers-in-law! Like so many people, he had wisdom for everybody else, but not much for himself.

The Song of Solomon is written by a young man, so much in love that God is not mentioned directly. The book of Proverbs is mostly Solomon's work, written when he was middle-aged. Ecclesiastes was written at the end of his life, and there he shares the philosophy of an old man with the young. In that book we see Solomon's whole life, with time for philosophy, music, agriculture and architecture. Although he developed many interests, none of them satisfied him and Ecclesiastes is one of the saddest books in the Bible.

BAD

Solomon's main weakness has already been hinted at – he had too many wives. This was not just for sensual pleasure, but also revealed a lust for power. Many of the marriages were politically motivated, for example his marriage to the daughter of Pharaoh. As an Egyptian she could not live in the holy city of Jerusalem, so Solomon built her a palace just north of the temple, outside the city wall. Recent excavations there have uncovered the only Egyptian artefacts in the whole of Israel.

We are therefore presented with an interesting juxtaposition: on the one hand there is the magnificent temple, built to aid Israel's worship of the one true God; on the other there is King Solomon with many foreign wives, who all brought their own gods with them and dragged people away from the worship of the God of Israel. Solomon was not the only king to marry foreign women, but no other king could match him in terms of numbers.

The building of the temple also exacted a huge cost. Solomon used forced labour and heavy taxation which enraged the northern tribes, who were resentful at having to finance a southern building, so far from their own territories. In spite of the success of the temple, therefore, Solomon was laying the foundations for national catastrophe.

Solomon was a king with a divided heart who left a divided kingdom. Soon the empire would break up. Even in Solomon's time, Hadad the Edomite rebelled, and more would follow.

Divided kingdom

The reigns of the kings of Judah and Israel are recorded differently.

NORTH	SOUTH
Date of accession	Date of accession
Length of reign	Age at accession
Formally condemned	Length of reign
Name of father	Name of mother
	Summary of character
Reference to sources	Reference to sources
Death	Death and burial
Son or usurper	Son as successor

The kings of the north are all compared to the first northern king, Jeroboam, who was a bad king. So we read repeatedly of subsequent kings: '…and he did what was evil in the sight of the Lord, just like Jeroboam.'

In the account of the kings of Judah in the south, the writer uses different records and varies the order and the details. He starts with the date when they began to reign, but follows with the king's age – Josiah was just eight, for example. The length of the reign is given next, but then comes the name of the mother, not the father, for reasons which are not clear. (Today a person qualifies as a Jew if their mother is a Jew, but in the Bible it was the father who determined nationality.) Then comes the judgement as to whether they were good or evil. Whilst every king in the north was evil, the south had a mixture of good and evil, with David as the benchmark.

The kings

The north had 20 kings and the south had the same number, but the south survived for 140 years longer than the north because, as we noted earlier, good kings reign longer. Some of the bad kings survived only a couple of months before being killed.

As mentioned above, the northern kings were all bad, although some were not as bad as the others.

NORTH 'ISRAEL' (10) (tribes)		SOUTH 'JUDAH' (2) (tribes)	
Prophets	Kings	Kings	Prophets
AHIJAH	**Jereboam**	**Reheboam**	SHEMAIAH
	Nadab	Abijam	
JEHU	**Ba'asha**	*Asa*	
	Elah		
	Zimri		
	Omri		
<u>ELIJAH</u>	**Ahab**	*Jehoshophat*	OBADIAH
MICAIAH	**Ahaziah**	Jehoram	
	Jehoram	**Ahaziah**	
<u>ELISHA</u>	Jehu	ATHALIAH	
	Jehoahaz	*Joash*	JOEL
	Jehoash	*Amaziah*	
JONAH	**Jereboam II**	*Uzziah*	
AMOS	**Zechariah**		
	Shallum	*Jotham*	
	Pekah		ISAIAH
HOSEA	**Manahem**		MICAH
	Pekahiah	**Ahaz**	
	Hoshea	*Hezekiah*	
	721 BC	**Manasseh**	
		Amon	NAHUM
		Josiah	JEREMIAH
Very good		**Jehoahaz**	ZEPHANIAH
Good		**Jehoachim**	HABBAKUK
Bad		**Jehoachin**	DANIEL
Very Bad		**Zedekiah**	
QUEEN		587 BC	EZEKIEL

The south had six good and two very good kings (Hezekiah and Josiah), but also had one who was the worst of all. This is the exception to the rule about bad kings and short reigns, for Manasseh reigned for 55 years.

The south had just one dynasty, whereas the north had nine, with the succession changing hands due to assassination six times.

There was one queen. God had told David there would always be a *man* on the throne – women were not allowed to rule as monarchs. Athaliah had other ideas. She was Jezebel's daughter and married the king of Judah in the south. She wanted to be the first queen of Israel, so she systematically killed all the children of David's royal line, so that the way would be open for her to become queen. However, an aunt took the youngest boy, Joash, and hid him ready to take the throne when Athaliah died, so the royal line was spared.

The two very good kings of Judah were Hezekiah and Josiah. Hezekiah was contemporary with Isaiah and his story is included in Isaiah's prophecy. Hezekiah was a good king in many ways. It was he who ordered the digging of the tunnel to bring water into Jerusalem and make it safe against enemies. His big mistake occurred when he was taken ill and welcomed to his palace men from the (then) small and unknown city of Babylon. They brought a 'get well card' and Hezekiah was flattered that someone so far away knew and cared about his illness. He showed the men round the palace and the temple. It was Isaiah who pointed out the error. He told Hezekiah that the Babylonians would take away everything he showed them. Some years later they did just that.

The other good king came to the throne of Judah at just eight years of age. Josiah was born in the same year as Jeremiah the prophet. While they were cleaning the temple his men found the scroll of Deuteronomy, which had not been read for many years. When King Josiah read the curses God had promised if his people strayed from his laws, he was alarmed and began at once to put things right. He ordered a national reformation, destroying all the high places and calling a halt to the idolatry which had infected the land, in the hope that this would bring renewal. But people's hearts remained far from God. It is not possible to make people good by passing good laws.

Josiah also made a big mistake: he went to war with Egypt when he did not need to and he was killed at Megiddo. When he died the nation reverted to the evil practices he had stamped out.

Hezekiah was followed by Manasseh, a very bad king who took evil to new depths. He worshipped the god Molech, and this included sacrificing his baby sons in the valley of Hinnon, or 'Gehenna'. He also executed Isaiah the prophet for his preaching, ordering to him to be bound and put inside a hollow tree trunk, after which two carpenters with a big saw cut the tree in half.

One of the worst kings was Ahab, who married a Phoenician princess from Tia. Her name in Phoenician meant 'primrose', but the same name in Hebrew, Jezebel, meant 'garbage', and this was how she was known. It was clear that she used Ahab to achieve her own evil ends and that he needed little persuading. It was her scheming, for example, which arranged the death of a neighbour, Naboth, so that Ahab could take possession of his vineyard.

Elijah

It was this event which marked the start of the prophet Elijah's ministry. He was a Tishbite from Gilead, in the Trans-Jordan region, and was regarded as one of the finest of Israel's prophets. Although there is no book written in his name, Kings covers more of his life than most of the kings themselves.

He is best known for his confrontation with the prophets

of Baal on Mount Carmel. Mount Carmel is 12 miles long and juts out into the ocean in the north of Israel. At the eastern (inland) end there is a large depression just below the summit where 30,000 people could gather. This must be the place where Elijah challenged the prophets of Baal, whom Jezebel had introduced to the palace. There is a spring there that never runs dry, even in a drought. The text tells us that Elijah doused the sacrifice with water, even though there had been no rain for three and a half years.

The story is well known. Elijah built an altar and challenged the prophets of Baal to build their own altar alongside his and call on their gods for fire to burn up the sacrifice.

It was a very clever challenge. We now know that the altars of Baal had a tunnel underneath where a priest would be concealed to set fire to the wood when the people cried out to the god. Elijah cunningly asked them to build their altar in the open and promised to build his altar in exactly the same way, only he would also add water to make the challenge greater. His boldness led him to mock the priests in such a way that if his experiment had failed he would surely have been killed. He encouraged them to shout louder, suggested that their god was on holiday or relieving himself. It was a key moment in the history of the northern tribes. God sent the fire, Elijah's sacrifice was burned up and Israel knew who was truly powerful. The prophets of Baal were routed.

This amazing story has an unlikely sequel. When Jezebel heard about Elijah's victory and the death of her prophets, she threatened Elijah. Despite his victory over the 400 prophets of Baal, Elijah ran for his life to Horeb. The prophet was emotionally and spiritually exhausted, so God graciously sent an angel to cook him a meal, and later assured him of his presence and provision for the future of Israel. God had already set aside a colleague for Elijah to continue the work.

Elisha

Elisha, the ploughman, succeeded Elijah in the prophetic role. He asked Elijah for a 'double portion' of his spirit – a phrase that is frequently misunderstood. It does not mean that he wanted to be twice the prophet Elijah had been. It was actually a phrase taken from the inheritance customs. If a man had four sons, his estate was divided into five when he died and the double portion went to the eldest son, who became the heir of the family business, with the extra money to help with the responsibility. In asking for a double portion of Elijah's spirit, Elisha was asking to be his heir and successor to be allowed to 'take over the business'.

Elijah told Elisha that if he saw him leave the earth, he could be his heir. Elijah was one of the few people in the Bible who never died (Enoch was another). The text tells us that he rode in a whirlwind into heaven, and Elisha saw him depart. Elijah's robe fell on the ground, Elisha picked it up and walked to the River Jordan. Elisha's ministry was given an excellent start, with God parting the river for him, assuring Elisha that he was with him just as he had been with Elijah.

The work of Elijah and Elisha

The two prophets were very different. Elijah was the fighter, the preacher, the man who challenged the people. Elisha's ministry was more pastoral in nature. On one occasion he raised to life a widow's son, in the village of Shunem, just half a mile from the village of Nain where Jesus would do the same thing. Elisha also fed 100 people with a few barley loaves. Elijah's ministry seems similar to that of John the Baptist and Elisha's to the ministry of Jesus.

Elijah and Elisha were two of a number of prophets whom God sent to the northern tribes: Jonah was a prophet to Judah before he went to Nineveh, and he appears in the book of

Kings. Amos and finally Hosea were also sent. The prophecy of Hosea contains some of the deepest emotion of all the prophets, as he enacts within his own life the heart of love God has for his people.

The amount of space given to Elijah and Elisha in Kings reminds us that God gave the people frequent warnings about what would happen if they did not behave according to his law.

God's warnings

WORDS

Throughout the spiritual demise of the nation, the priests should have been reminding the people of their responsibilities. But they were too close to the establishment to provide an objective voice, so God sent prophets instead.

There were six prophets sent to the north: Ahijah, Jehu, Elijah, Elisha, Amos and Hosea. There were also a number who ministered to the south, before and during the exile: Shemaiah, Obadiah, Joel, Jonah, Isaiah, Micah, Nahum, Jeremiah, Zephaniah, Habakkuk, Daniel and Ezekiel.

It is important to note that God always gave his people a warning of his punishment if they continued in sin. The whole principle of the Bible is that God judges people for doing what they *know* is wrong. People who have not heard about Jesus will not be sent to hell because they have not heard about Jesus, but because they have done wrong against their own conscience.

Israel and Judah ignored the messages they received, preferring the false prophets who told them that all was well and gave them false reasons for the disasters that had befallen them. The true prophets were nonetheless prepared to tell the truth and pay the price of ridicule, beatings, punishment and sometimes death.

DEEDS

The warnings God sent were not just verbal, they were also visual. The people should have seen that God's blessings were being taken away from them. Note how the warnings increased in their severity:

1 They lost territory when Hadad led Edom out of the 'commonwealth'.
2 They lost independence when the Trans-Jordan tribes came under the control of Syria and one tribe, Naphtali, was lost totally to Assyria.
3 Judah saw the other nine tribes deported to Assyria.
4 Eventually they too faced deportation to Babylon, in three stages.

Apart from the spoken prophetic messages, therefore, there were a number of warning signs from events which were clearly heading for disaster, but the people ignored these too and did not change their ways.

Why read Kings?

Christians can be sure that all parts of the Old Testament are also intended for them. We are told in 1 Corinthians that the events in the Old Testament 'occurred as examples to us from setting our hearts on evil things as they did'. In 2 Timothy we read that 'all Scripture is God-breathed and useful for teaching, rebuking, correcting and training in righteousness'.

Individual application

THE PRESENT

We may not *be* kings, but we too are examples to others, at work, in the family, in the community. Like kings, we need to set the spiritual tone for the groups we are involved with, especially if we have a leadership role.

We can be tempted to have liaisons with people who have 'foreign' gods. We must beware of the dangers of marrying outside God's family.

Kings gives us the negative example of Queen Athalia, who sought to take up leadership against the will of God. All Christians can be tempted to seek leadership for the wrong reasons, or which is inappropriate for them personally.

Josiah's reign reminds us that we must be regular readers of the Bible. We can be negligent or ignorant of its truth and face similar consequences.

The book also provides key lessons for Christian leaders, for the king had a pastoral role to exercise for his people, a role he often abused.

THE FUTURE

We will *become* kings: we too are part of the royal family, preparing to reign with Christ. We can look forward to a bright future. Even if our lives have little opportunity for leadership now, there will come a day when it will be different.

Corporate application

THE CHURCH

Just as Israel put idols on the high places in the land, Britain has a tradition of pagan shrines being situated on the hills. Christian churches now stand on many of these sites, but the danger of compromise with paganism remains. Syncretism, the uniting of one religion with another, is still around and still popular.

When Elijah challenged the people of Israel, he asked them how long they would waver *between* two opinions. The same question could be asked of the Church today, for in Britain and elsewhere there are professing Christians who see nothing wrong in mixing their faith with pagan religion and contemporary materialistic and new age philosophies. Prince Charles says he prefers to be called Defender of Faith, not Defender of *the* Faith. We are into an era when it has become fashionable to say that all religions lead to God.

Furthermore, the Church has blessed pagan festivals, often unknowingly. Christmas is the most obvious example: it was originally a totally pagan midwinter festival celebrating the 'rebirth' of the sun. The people burned yew logs, sang carols, and ate and drank too much. When the first missionary, Augustine, came to England he sent word back to Rome saying that he was unable to get the people away from this pagan festival. Pope Gregory said that the best policy would be to turn it into a Christian festival, and that is what has happened, with questionable results. Today the Church universally celebrates this pagan festival, despite the fact that it is nowhere commanded or even encouraged in the Bible.

The book of Kings also demonstrates the principle that division leads to decline. Many church fellowships can testify to this sad truth. The nation reached its height in the unity it enjoyed under David and Solomon, and then lost everything in half the time it had taken to achieve it, once that unity had been destroyed. We must be vigilant if the same thing is not to happen to us in the Church.

THE WORLD

The book has a powerful message to offer about God's sovereignty in human history. Israel is the specific focus of his dealings as he intervenes in the lives of the kings, dispensing blessing and punishment, open to their cries for help. We see how, on the whole, good kings last longer than bad ones. In the same way, God rules over *all* nations. He chooses leaders and rulers and decides how much time and space each has. He can act in justice, giving the people the ruler they deserve, or in mercy, giving them the ruler they need. He still has the casting vote even in democratic elections.

His ability to overrule in no way reduces human responsibility. He can use even those who have no knowledge of him – a bad ruler like Nebuchadnezzar to take his people into Babylonian exile and a good ruler like the Persian Cyrus to restore them to their own land again.

News agencies only see the human side of history. Prophets discern the divine activity over and above this. That is why the Bible in general and the books of 1 and 2 Kings in particular are so different from other historical records. They give us the *whole* story, telling the whole truth about what happened in the events of Israel's saga.

CHRIST

Above all, we need to read Kings because of what it tells us about Jesus. A number of individuals who feature in Kings remind us of Jesus.

- **Solomon**: Matthew tells us in his Gospel that Jesus is greater than Solomon. Paul writes that Christ is our wisdom. John's Gospel tells us that Jesus likened his body to the temple. When Jesus died the temple curtain was split from top to bottom.
- **Jonah**: The prophet is mentioned in Kings. Just as Jonah was in the belly of the fish for three days and three nights, so Jesus would be raised after three days and three nights in the heart of the earth – in both cases a resurrection from the dead.
- **Elijah**: Jesus met and talked with him on the Mount of Transfiguration. Elijah was likened to Jesus' cousin John the Baptist, who had the same food and dress.

■ **Elisha**: Jesus indirectly linked himself to Elisha through the nature of the miracles he performed. Jesus raised a boy from the dead in the village of Nain, next to Shumen where Elisha had performed a similar miracle. He fed 5,000 people with bread and fish, mirroring Elisha's miracle in feeding the 100 with bread. When Jesus died, people came out of their graves, just as a dead man was revived after contact with Elisha's dead body.

There are also ways in which the life and ministry of Jesus fulfil the expectations of kingship. He is the king the Old Testament people longed for. He is in the royal line of David, and will one day restore the kingdom to Israel. He is the one who fulfils all the promises made about the descendants of David. Here is one king who will not disappoint, one even greater than David.

Conclusion

The book of Kings has a vital message for the world. God is Lord over all, and his people must learn the message of this book if they are not to mirror the decline recorded there, the disintegration of the people of Israel who ceased to listen to God and follow his laws. We can, however, be encouraged by God's power and ability to deal with his people in ways that are both just and merciful. No one can thwart his plans. His kingdom will outlast the years, and the book of Kings (or Kingdoms) gives Christians a longing for the day when Jesus will be seen by all as the final king.

POEMS OF WORSHIP AND WISDOM

11.

 INTRODUCTION TO HEBREW POETRY

Poetry is one of a number of forms of literature that are used in the Old Testament. It is found in the prophets and in the 'writings' or 'wisdom literature', notably in the Psalms, the Book of Job and the Song of Songs. But since Hebrew poetry is so different from English poetry, we need to consider it in some detail if we are to receive the full benefit from these parts of God's Word.

It is relatively easy to spot poetry in modern Bibles, since the print is arranged differently from prose sections. Prose has long sentences and full columns, poetry short sentences with larger spaces to set it apart. A cursory glance at a Bible shows that there is substantially more poetry in the Old Testament than in the New.

Prose is the more natural and spontaneous way to communicate. People speak and write in prose using a variety of sentence lengths to communicate their point. Poetry is an abnormal and artificial way of writing. It needs to be prepared beforehand, it requires considerable thought and the words used need to obey the rules of poetic style. We might ask why it is that poetry is used when prose is so much easier.

For example, imagine me coming home and saying to Enid, my wife,

I'm ready for my supper, wife.
Oh good, it's pies and peas.
You've given me a dirty knife –
I'd like a clean one, please!
And since there is no second course,
I'll have some more tomato sauce!

If I talked like that it would mean that I had thought about my words beforehand. But the artificiality of talking in poetry in such a setting would hamper clear communication!

A deeper effect

Why bother to compose poetry?

Poetry has a much deeper effect on people than prose. Poetry can penetrate parts of the personality that prose would leave untouched.

Deeper into the mind

Poetry is more easily remembered than prose, especially when set to music. It touches the intuitive and artistic part of the brain, that can be left unmoved by the ordered arguments of prose.

So poems from our school days may be remembered decades later, while lectures are forgotten by the next week. For this reason we generally learn our theology from hymns and choruses, which is why it's important to make sure that the songs used in worship have Bible-based content.

Deeper into the heart

Poetry is used in greeting cards because it is a more effective way of moving the heart of the recipient. It can evoke warm emotions, while the same sentiments expressed in prose would leave the reader unmoved.

Consider the following poem:

They walked down the lane together,
The sky was full of stars.
Together they reached the farmyard gate,
He lifted for her the bars.
She neither smiled nor thanked him,
Indeed, she knew not how,
For he was just a farmer's boy,
And she was a Jersey cow!

Whenever I have quoted this in a talk, the congregation has laughed. They expect romance but receive something ridiculous, which touches their sense of humour. If the same content were to be expressed in prose, I doubt if it would even raise a smile.

Deeper into the will

Poetry also affects our volitional powers. It moves us to the point where we are determined to act in a certain way. In schools poems have been used to instil values into pupils. War songs have been used throughout history to galvanize soldiers for action.

Consider this poem, entitled 'Indifference', by Studdert Kennedy, an army chaplain in World War I:

When Jesus came to Golgotha, they hanged him on a tree,
They drove great nails through hands and feet
        and made a Calvary;
They crowned him with a crown of thorns,
        red were his wounds and deep,

For those were crude and cruel days,
    and human flesh was cheap.

When Jesus came to Birmingham,
    they simply passed him by,
They never hurt a hair of him, they only let him die.
For men had grown more tender
    and they would not give him pain,
They only passed him down the street
    and left him in the rain.

Still Jesus cried 'Forgive them,
    for they know not what they do'
And still it rained the wintry rain
    that drenched him through and through.
The crowds went home and left the streets
    without a soul to see,
That Jesus crouched against a wall, and cried for Calvary.

There is something about the rhythm and the careful choice of words in that poem which compels us to examine our lives.

Beauty

Poetry touches the heart, the mind and the will by making words *beautiful* as well as meaningful. We are drawn to poems because the words are arranged in such a way that they appeal to our sense of beauty, balance, symmetry and proportion.

Just as a beautiful person has well-balanced features, so it is this balance that appeals to us in poetry.

There are three basic features of poetry that make the words beautiful for us: *rhyme*, *rhythm* and *repetition*.

Rhyme

Rhyme is a common feature of English poetry, but it is not generally found in Hebrew poetry. This classic nursery rhyme demonstrates a balance of rhyming words well:

> Jack and Jill went up the hill,
> To fetch a pail of water.
> Jack fell down and broke his crown
> And Jill came tumbling after.

It has a simple rhyme structure that is common to most nursery rhymes, and children have no trouble learning them.

Rhythm

The second feature of poetry that makes words beautiful is rhythm or metre, where the beat based on the syllables must fall on the correct words. For example:

> The boy stood on the burning deck
> Whence all but he had fled.
>
> *Mrs Hemans*

The poem has a 4/3 rhythm, a favourite for both Hebrew and English poetry, and often used in the metrical Psalms in Scotland. Take another example:

> The *Lord's* my *shep*herd, *I'll* not *want* – (4)
> He *makes* me *down* to *lie* (3)
> in *pas*tures *green* he *lead*eth *me* – (4)
> the *qui*et *wa*ters *by* – (3).
>
> *Francis Rous*

Good rhythm is dependent on the emphasis falling on the right syllable. When a hymn or chorus fails in this regard the effect is unpleasant. Take, for example, these two lines from a hymn:

> For *all* the *good* our *Father* does,
> God *and* king *of* us *all*.

The beat is placed on the wrong syllables and so emphasizes the wrong words. The hymn's beauty is lost.

Rhythm can also be used to shock the reader:

> Thirty days hath September,
> April, June and November;
> All the rest have thirty-one,
> Is that fair?!

The last line is startling because it breaks the rhythm and brings you up with a jolt.

Repetition

The third aspect of poetry that makes words beautiful is repetition. The repetition of a word or a line makes it poetic. There is a famous speech in Shakespeare's play *Julius Caesar* that repeats the line, 'And Brutus is an honourable man.' Or take this famous nursery rhyme that uses repetition:

> 'Baa, baa, black sheep, have you any wool?'
> 'Yes sir, yes sir, three bags full.'

The repetition may be of lines, phrases or even letters. Maybe you noticed how Studdert Kennedy uses words beginning with 'c' in his poem 'Indifference': 'crude', 'cruel', 'crouched' and 'cried'. They serve to emphasize the two 'c's that are the key to its theme: *cross* and *crucify*.

In other cases a refrain is used to emphasize a point. For example, Psalm 136 repeats the phrase, 'His love endures for ever.'

Other poems employ alliteration. In 'The Siege of Belgrade,' the first line of each verse is a consecutive letter of the alphabet, but this same letter is used for the main words in each verse. Psalm 119 is similar.

Wonder

Because poetry is partly about communicating pleasant sounds, the effect of poetry is often lost or diminished if it is just read silently. Poems are meant to be read aloud. There is something very satisfying about the sound of poetry. It brings a sense of wonder that isn't generally found in prose. It is no surprise, therefore, that poems are used in the worship of God. The Psalms (the Jews' hymn-book), are all in poetry. Prose is generally very difficult to sing, while poems lend themselves more readily to musical accompaniment.

Furthermore, poetry helps us to appreciate and express the sense of wonder that we feel as we worship. I will show what I mean by using a well-known poem:

Twinkle, twinkle little star,
How I wonder what you are.
Up above the world so high,
Like a diamond in the sky.

Jane Taylor

It's possible to kill the child-like wonder in this poem by reducing it to scientific terms:

> Twinkle, twinkle little star,
> I don't wonder what you are.
> You're the cooling down of gasses,
> Forming into solid masses.

Let's take it a step further:

> Scintillate, scintillate, globule prolific,
> Fain would I fathom thy nature specific.
> Loftily poised in ether capacious,
> Closely resembling a gem carbonaceous.

Note the contrast between the language of science and that of poetry. The former is exact and cold, while the latter is less precise but evokes wonder and awe. This is what makes poetry such a good medium for worship. Hymns, songs, psalms and choruses help us to express something of the wonder and glory of God in a way that scientific forms of expression cannot.

Poetry is visual as well as verbal. It paints pictures in the mind. Imagination is very necessary to writing poetry. It uses metaphors, similes and images. For example, 'Twinkle, twinkle little star … like a diamond in the sky' helps to conjure a picture of a shining star.

Let's take Psalm 42 as another example:

> As the deer pants for streams of water,
> so my soul longs for God.

We imagine an animal panting, with its tongue hanging out, and that makes us think of our own thirst for God.

Sound and sense

English poetry is based on Greek and Roman poetry, where the emphasis is on the sound. Although there are other forms and styles, English poetry generally rhymes, while in Hebrew poetry, the emphasis is on the sense.

This distinction is especially clear in the English tradition of 'nonsense verse', of which Edward Lear and Lewis Carroll were the masters. Carroll's 'The Jabberwocky' is a prime example of this sort of poetry:

> 'Twas brillig, and the slithy toves
> Did gyre and gimble in the wabe;
> All mimsy were the borogroves,
> And the mome raths outgrabe.

Reading such poetry is a little like enjoying Pavarotti singing Italian opera without knowing the language, or enjoying pop music when the words are inaudible or meaningless. We haven't a clue what it is about but we like it anyway.

Such poems may 'move' us but they don't take us anywhere. Reading them may help us to relax and to appreciate life, but they don't affect the way we live.

Hebrew poetry is very different from the English style. Even in the original language, the emphasis is upon the sense of the words rather than the sound of them, which is one reason why there is very little rhyme in Hebrew poetry.

Parallelism

While rhythm is not unknown (especially the 4/3 and the 3/3 rhythms), Hebrew poetry is mostly based on a form of repetition called *parallelism*. The word refers to the correspondence that occurs between the phrases of a poetic line. Parallelism is the basic 'building block' of Hebrew poetry. It is used for:

- *Emphasis*. If something is said twice, we know it is important.
- *Response*. A couplet enables 'antiphonal' singing, in which two choirs sing to each other. One choir sings the first sentence and the other choir echoes it.
- *Balance*. Just as there is balance in a human body – two hands, two eyes, two ears, two arms, two legs – so the couplet helps us to understand the beauty of a thought.

Usually the repetition is in the form of couplets but the Psalms also contain some triplets and just a few quadruplets. Here is an example of a couplet, from Psalm 6:

> O Lord, do not rebuke me in your anger
> or discipline me in your wrath.

To 'rebuke' is to tell someone they are in the wrong, while to 'discipline' is to punish, so the second line develops the first line's thought a little further. Or take the next verse in this psalm:

> Be merciful to me, O Lord, for I am faint;
> O Lord, heal me, for my bones are in agony.

In the first line the psalmist feels faint, but in the second line he is in agony and needs healing. So once again the second line has taken the first line a little further. But note that it is the *sense* that is repeated, not the sound.

I am concious of the fact that analysing poetry is like taking a flower to pieces and looking at its parts. Analysis destroys the beauty. Nevertheless, I want to help you to understand what's going on when you read biblical poetry – why it was written and how it was written.

There are three different forms of parallelism:

Synonymous

In synonymous parallelism the same thought is expressed twice in different words. Let's take Psalm 2 as an example:

> Why do the *nations conspire*
> and the *peoples plot* in vain?
> The *kings* of the earth take their stand
> and the *rulers* gather together
> against the *Lord*
> and against his *Anointed One*.
> 'Let us break their *chains*,' they say,
> 'and throw off their *fetters*.'
> The One enthroned in heaven *laughs*;
> The Lord *scoffs* at them.
> Then he rebukes them in his *anger*
> and terrifies them in his *wrath*.

Note how the words in italic type in each couplet have the same meaning, but generally the second word is 'stronger' or 'heavier' than the first.

Antithetic

Antithetic parallelism functions like synonymous parallelism, but the second line contrasts with the first line. So, in this example from Psalm 126:

> Those who *sow* in tears
> will *reap* with songs of joy.

Two pairs are contrasted: 'sowing' and 'reaping', 'tears' and 'joy'. In the next verse we have the theme expanded:

> He who goes out *weeping*,
> carrying seed to *sow*,
> will return with songs of *joy*,
> carrying *sheaves* with him.

These two lines add more detail to the contrast. We now have going out with seed and returning with sheaves.

Synthetic

In synthetic parallelism the second phrase complements or supplements the first. It doesn't say the same thing or the opposite thing, but something that follows from the first phrase. For example:

> When the Lord brought back the captives to Zion,
> we were like men who dreamed.
>
> *from Psalm 126*

> The Lord is my shepherd, I shall not be in want.
>
> *from Psalm 23*

In these examples the second phrase is the result of the first. Psalm 23 is built on the synthetic pattern:

> He makes me lie down in green pastures,
> he leads me beside quiet waters.

The shepherd has to know where there are green pastures and quiet waters. But those two things together create a picture of a shepherd who really knows his job and cares for his sheep.

* * *

So we have three forms of Hebrew poetry but many varieties within these forms. Parallelism is not just in thought and word, but also in grammar. For example, in these lines from Psalm 2 the order of the words in the Hebrew is:

> Then he rebukes them in his anger
> and in his wrath he terrifies them.

The order of the verb, the object and the prepositional phrase is varied in the second line.

Tricolon

These three types of parallelism are often interrupted by irregularities. Sometimes the rhythm and pattern are broken. Sometimes, instead of two lines there are three lines together. This is called a tricolon or triplet.

Take these three lines from Psalm 29:

> Ascribe to the Lord, O mighty ones,
> ascribe to the Lord glory and strength.
> Ascribe to the Lord the glory due to his name.

Here the lines build up a crescendo – 'Ascribe to the Lord' is the refrain – and then different words are added in three lines.

Or consider Psalm 3:

O Lord, how many are my foes!
How many rise up against me!
Many are saying of me, 'God will not deliver him.'

Here we have the repetition of 'many', and each line builds on the previous one: who he is complaining about, what they do, then what they say. Sometimes there's an omission and a word is not included or a phrase drops out.

Other features of Hebrew poetry

Simile

Hebrew poetry is full of similes – that is, pictures that show us how one thing resembles another. For example :

As a father has compassion on his children,
so the Lord has compassion on those who fear him.

from Psalm 103

Here a tender father's care for his children is likened to God's care for his people.

Chiasm

Here the second part of the first line becomes the first part of the second line. For example:

For the Lord watches over the way of the righteous,
but the way of the wicked will perish.

from Psalm 1

The second line reverses the first – 'the way' has swapped places.

Omission

In omission (or ellipsis), part of the second line is omitted. For example:

You have put me in the lowest pit,
in the darkest depths.

from Psalm 88

We are meant to read this as if the phrase 'you have put me' recurs in the second line.

Staircase

Sometimes the lines of a psalm resemble a staircase:

The voice of the Lord breaks the cedars;
the Lord breaks in pieces the cedars of Lebanon.

from Psalm 29

The second line expands on what the first line has already told us. We already knew that 'the Lord breaks the cedars'; now we are told that he breaks them 'in pieces' and that they are cedars 'of Lebanon'.

Acrostic

Here the poetry is based on the alphabet. In Psalm 119 – the longest of all the psalms, with 176 verses – each section (and every verse in that section) begins with a new letter of the Hebrew alphabet.

Refrain

Here the second line provides a refrain throughout. For example, in Psalm 136 the words 'His love endures forever' form the second line of every verse.

Poetry in God's Word

Our study of Hebrew poetry shows us how appropriate it is that it should be included within God's Word.

Modern chorus writers have found the Psalms rich in inspiration. But when psalms are used verbatim, it is rare that a whole psalm is included. Thus we do not have the words in their original context. This can mean that the balance of the psalm is lost and, in some cases, the meaning is changed.

Hebrew poetry is easy to translate into other languages because its emphasis is on content rather than sound. If I quote English poetry when preaching to a non-English-speaking congregation through a translator, the translation kills the poem dead, because English poetry is often based on sound, and those English sounds will not survive the translation process. But Hebrew poetry can be translated into any language, so it is easy to see why God chose such a medium.

Poetry in worship

Many people argue that we should be spontaneous in our approach to God and that it is artificial for us to plan what we are going to say. There is some truth in that, but there is enormous value in first thinking through what we wish to say. The Psalms give us a model of how to address God so that we are not over-familiar, and they powerfully reveal to us God's greatness and majesty. On the other hand, they also describe an intimate relationship with God that many people may not yet have enjoyed, and so they can spur us on to seek a greater experience of God's goodness.

The planned wording that we find in biblical poetry is a necessary part of our corporate worship. If we merely sang what we wanted to sing when we came to worship, it would be chaos – not to mention a dreadful noise! Corporate worship is made possible because choruses and hymns are designed for a congregation to sing them. Those who argue that we should only sing what we 'feel' forget that there is value in voicing responses that we may *not* feel, as an encouragement to respond genuinely and also to remember the truth for the future.

There used to be a family tradition in our house. Our three children used to come and wake me up at an ungodly hour on a certain day in the year, and then stand in a row at the foot of my bed and address me in a most artificial way with poetry. They finished by giving me a bag of their favourite sweets. The poem (or song) was 'Happy birthday to you'!

Of course, in a sense this was artificial – three children standing in a row, all saying the same thing. Wouldn't it have been nicer if each of them had come separately and told me what they really felt? No, because they would then not have been doing it together as my family. The fact that they came to me together and sang to me together – in a relationship with one another – made the little tradition much more special to me.

In a similar way, it pleases the Lord when we say something together, even though we have to use words that someone else has written. God loves to see us together. We may be standing in a row, singing to God in a somewhat artificial way, but we are corporately expressing our love for God. Poetry enables us to do this.

We noted earlier that psalms lend themselves to antiphonal singing, where choirs sing to each other. It is also possible to shout psalms as well as sing them. Psalm 147 is an example of this.

Psalms can also aid our sense of corporate identity. Psalms using the words 'I' and 'my' are best for private worship, but those using 'we' and 'our' remind us that we are praising together as the whole family of God.

Just as poetry touches the heart of man, it also touches the heart of God. We have noted that poetry is used in all the Psalms and also in many of the prophetic books. The Holy Spirit chose this form as a way of communicating the mind of God and as a means for us to respond to him. Those who are sceptical about the idea that poetry touches God's heart need to remember the bold language that Scripture uses to talk of God's feelings.

For example, Psalm 2 says that God 'laughs' when he views the futile attempts of humanity to defy him. Zephaniah 3 tells us that God 'rejoices' over us 'with singing'. So God is musical! Music is not something that modern people have invented but is part of what it means to be made in the image of God.

So when God addresses us with poetry we know that he is communicating his feelings from his heart to our hearts, and so we can ask what such biblical passages tell us about God's feelings. Understanding Hebrew poetry can be a key to understanding the very heart of God.

12.

PSALMS

Introduction

The Book of Psalms is the most loved and the best known part of the Bible. Individual psalms are popular with people who are not regular Bible readers and also with those who wish to praise the God whom they know and love. They have a universal appeal, translating easily into today's culture, despite being from so long ago. While most of the Old Testament needs to be understood in the light of the New Testament, most of the Psalms can be used directly. There is a timeless quality to the Psalms, and they can easily be applied to the Christian life. It is no surprise that hymn-writers throughout history have drawn their inspiration from them.

The Psalms have been valued throughout the history of the Church. Martin Luther said, 'In the Psalms we look into the heart of every saint.' John Calvin said that in the Psalms 'We look into a mirror and see our own heart.' A modern commentator put it this way: 'Every psalm seems to have my name and address on it.' It is the most human part of the Old Testament, which everyone can readily identify with.

The Book of Psalms is the hymn-book and prayer-book of Israel in the Old Testament. It is the longest book in the Bible and took nearly 1,000 years to write. Although most of the Psalms were written at the time of David (around 1000 BC), some of them were written at the time of Moses (about 1300 BC) and others at the time of the Exile (500 BC).

The word 'psalm' literally means 'twang' or 'pluck', referring to the stringed instruments that were used to accompany the singing of psalms. The Book of Psalms is placed in the Hebrew Bible at the start of the books of Writings – the third section of the Bible, coming after the books of the Law and the Prophets. In Hebrew the book is called *Tenillim*, which means 'Songs of Praise', which is probably a much better name for it (especially as the word 'Jew' comes from 'Judah', which means 'praise'). Psalms are most commonly spoken or sung, but they can even be shouted – a form that doesn't go down well in some cultures!

There are various kinds of psalms, as we will see later. The simplest division is between the personal psalms, using the pronoun 'I', and the collective psalms, using 'we'. Thus some psalms are most suited to private worship and others to public worship. However, the division must not be too strict, as Jesus encouraged his disciples to use the words 'Our Father', implying that they should have a corporate responsibility even when they prayed privately.

Emotions

Some psalms express deep grief. I am especially moved by Psalm 56, which says that God 'puts our tears into his bottle'. When Jewish people wanted to express their sympathy at the death of someone they loved, they didn't send flowers or wreaths to the funeral, but instead they had glass bottles, about four inches high, which they would hold under their eyes and weep into. They would then send the bottle of tears to the bereaved relatives as an expression of sympathy. The psalm tells us that God is able to do the same for us, even when our tears are about things not nearly as serious as death.

The Psalms cover the whole gamut of human emotions. They include what we might term the 'negative' emotions of anger, frustration, jealousy, despair, fear and envy. The psalmist expresses exactly how he thinks and feels, including cursing men and complaining about God. They also reflect the more 'positive' emotions of joy, excitement, hope and peace.

David wrote most of the personal psalms. They cover many of the things that people might want to say to God. Later we shall look at three particular kinds of psalms, which I call 'please psalms', 'thank-you psalms' and 'sorry psalms'.

In spite of their strong worship focus, the Psalms were not intended to be used only by priests. There is an almost complete absence of altars, priests, vestments and incense. The Psalms are intended for common people to use in their worship of God.

Biblical themes

The Psalms not only cover every human emotion; they are also comprehensive in their treatment of biblical themes. Luther said the Psalms are 'the Bible within the Bible' – the Bible in miniature. They cover the history of Israel, creation, the patriarchs, the Exodus, the monarchy, the Exile and the return to Jerusalem.

The Psalms are the most quoted Old Testament book in the New Testament. The most quoted verse in the New Testament is Psalm 110:1: 'The Lord says to my Lord: "Sit at my right hand until I make your enemies a footstool for your feet."'

Not all the psalms in the Old Testament are in the Book of Psalms. Moses and Miriam wrote one (see Exodus 15). Deborah and Hannah also composed psalms (see Judges 5 and 1 Samuel 2).

Since the authors of most of the Bible were male, it is interesting that women too wrote psalms, perhaps reflecting the naturally intuitive side of the feminine nature. Job wrote three psalms, while Isaiah and King Hezekiah each wrote one.

Other Old Testament characters also used psalms. Jonah's prayer while he was inside the whale is a classic example. He said he was praying from Sheol, the world of departed spirits, and quoted five different psalms in that prayer. Habakkuk quotes from the Psalms three times in his prophecy.

All the Psalms employ poetry as their sole means of expression. So do the Song of Solomon, Proverbs and Lamentations. Other Old Testament books (e.g. Ecclesiastes and the Prophets) are a mixture of poetry and prose. Parts of the historical books are also in poetic form (e.g. Genesis 49; Exodus 15; Judges 5; 2 Samuel 22).

Five books in one

The Book of Psalms is actually five hymn-books grouped together. Some commentators have seen parallels with the five books of the Law, but the reason why there are five books may be more mundane than that – perhaps the psalms were originally written down on five scrolls.

There is enormous variety in length among the Psalms. The shortest, Psalm 117, has only three verses, while the longest, Psalm 119, has 176 verses.

Since they were all written in Hebrew poetry, they are best read aloud. They can't be analysed in the way one might read one of Paul's epistles, focusing on each verse. Indeed, over-analysis of the Psalms serves to destroy their beauty. It is far better to read the whole psalm, meditate on it, let it sink in and, if necessary, repeat the process.

Each of the five books ends with a doxology, (see Psalms 41, 72, 89 and 106). The last book ends with Psalm 150, which is a doxology that rounds off all five books. The size of the books varies because of the different sizes of the psalms themselves, but the first book and the last book are the biggest.

Divine names

Many commentators have looked for distinguishing features in each book. There is an interesting pattern in how God is addressed within the five books. Two names are used – *Yahweh* and *Elohim* – names that appear throughout the Old Testament.

Elohim simply means 'God', though being plural it contains within it the idea of God's trinitarian nature. *Yahweh* was the personal name for God that God told Israel to use, and it is derived from the verb 'to be'. The English word 'always' conveys its meaning very well.

Yahweh is the name for God that is used mainly in Book 1. It is used on 272 occasions and *Elohim* is used on only 15. But in Book 2 the opposite is the case: – *Elohim* is used on 207 occasions and *Yahweh* on just 74. Book 3 also favours *Elohim* (36 occasions) rather than *Yahweh* (13). Books 4 and 5 switch back in favour of *Yahweh* again, with 339 *Yahweh* references and only 7 for *Elohim*.

It is not difficult to discover why this is so. King David's psalms are mostly in Books 1 and 2, with a few in Book 5. We will see later that his psalms are more personal and so use God's personal name.

The name *Elohim* communicates to us the transcendence of God. He is far removed, completely different to us; he is the Most High God. The name *Yahweh* conveys a greater sense of intimacy with God. God is both transcendent and immanent, and we need to keep both these aspects of God's nature in tension. The Psalms reflect this in the names that they ascribe to God. They begin and end with the intimate name that he revealed to his people.

Groups of psalms

Aside from the divine names, scholars have searched in vain for any system of classification in the Book of Psalms. There are groups of psalms that seem to fit together, but there is no logical order and no apparent reason why particular psalms are arranged as they are in a particular book.

The groups of psalms are as follows:

- Psalms 22–24: Saviour, shepherd and sovereign.
- Psalms 42–49: by the sons of Korah.
- Psalms 73–83: by the sons of Asaph.
- Psalms 96–99: God is king.
- Psalms 113–118: the 'hallel psalms' (sung at Passover).
- Psalms 120–134: the 'songs of ascents' (as pilgrims went 'up' to Jerusalem).
- Psalms 146–150: the 'hallelujah psalms'.

Some psalms contain parts that are repeated in other psalms (see, for example, Psalm 108 and Psalm 57:8–12).

Who wrote the Psalms?

David wrote over half the Psalms: 73 of them have his name attached to them, and the New Testament also attributes Psalms 2 and 95 to him. It is likely that others too came from his pen.

He had many roles – shepherd, warrior, king and musician – but it was this latter role that meant the most to him, for when he died he thanked God that he had been Israel's 'sweet singer'. It was the composition and singing of psalms that was closest to his heart. This ministry of David had been used in his early life to soothe Saul's troubled mind. The prophet Amos, writing centuries later, selects this image of David strumming on his harp to make a point about the complacency of Israel (see Amos 6:5).

Solomon also wrote some psalms: Psalm 72 and Psalm 127. The former was composed when the Temple was being built. He recognizes that unless the Lord builds the house, the labourers labour in vain. Without God's glory the Temple is nothing.

The sons of Korah wrote 10 psalms. A man named Korah features in a story recorded in the Book of Numbers. God punished him with death when he led a rebellion against Moses and Aaron. But generations later, his descendants were engaged in Temple worship. Their psalms appear in Book 2.

The sons of Asaph wrote 12 psalms, found in Book 3. Both they and the sons of Korah were part of the choir that served in the Temple. Since choir-masters were thought of as seers or prophets, it is no surprise that they composed some of the Psalms.

Quite a lot of the Psalms are anonymous, but they are all in Books 4 and 5. It is thought that Ezra the priest may have been responsible for Psalms 49 and 50.

A personal experience

Many of the Psalms were inspired by a personal experience, rather in the way that songs and choruses come to be written today. David had learned to sing and to play musical instruments while working as a shepherd in the countryside, and so he was used to turning his daily experiences into song.

In fact, the main parts of David's life are depicted in the Book of Psalms. For example, Psalm 3 was written after his humiliating flight from his son Absalom, who had seized the throne and forced David to flee from the palace. Psalm 7 was written about a Benjamite called Kush. Psalm 18 was written when David was delivered 'from the hand of all his enemies and from the hand of Saul'.

David wrote two penitential psalms after committing specific sins. One of them is Psalm 51, written after he had seduced Bathsheba, another man's wife, breaking five of the Ten Commandments in the process. The other was written after he had numbered his troops, an activity designed purely to boost his ego. When he realized the sin he had committed he wrote the very moving Psalm 30.

Other psalms are associated with particular places. For example, many were written by David when he was on the run from Saul at En Gedi. He often describes God as his 'rock' and 'fortress', perhaps because he hid at the huge outcrop of rock known as Masada.

Fourteen psalms have historical titles linking them to events in David's life:

- Psalm 3: When David fled from the army of his son Absalom.
- Psalm 30: David's sin prior to the dedication of the Temple area.
- Psalm 51: After Nathan exposed David's sin with Bathsheba.
- Psalm 56: David's fear at Gath.
- Psalm 57: At En Gedi, when Saul is trapped.
- Psalm 59: David's jealous associates.

- Psalm 60: The dangerous campaign in Edom.
- Psalm 63: David's flight eastwards.
- Psalm 142: David at Adullam.

Furthermore, many of the Psalms, while not including any particular details, clearly come out of David's varied experiences as musician, shepherd, fighter, refugee and king. For example, Psalm 23 is based on his daily life as a shepherd. Psalm 29 was clearly inspired by a violent thunderstorm, which reminded David of the voice of God.

David is refreshingly honest in his writing. He curses men, complains about God and asks for revenge on his enemies. But each negative comment is made to God. He tells God exactly how he feels and what he thinks, however inappropriate the emotion may seem. It is no surprise that his psalms have had such universal appeal, as people of all nations and all generations have identified with his words.

For the whole people of God

Not all the Psalms are personal; some are for the whole people of God. David wrote Psalm 2 for Solomon's coronation. It expresses David's hopes for his son, and the fulfilment of the promise that God had made to David: 'You are my Son; today I have become your Father'.

Other psalms express how a group or nation may be feeling. The 'songs of ascents' (Psalms 120–134) are appropriate for those who are on pilgrimage to Jerusalem.

Many of the Psalms are meant to help people in their personal walk with God. For example, Psalm 119 is written to encourage us to read the Bible. In every verse of that psalm there is a synonym for the Scriptures. It speaks of 'the law of the Lord', or 'the commands of the Lord', or 'the precepts of the Lord', or 'the decrees of the Lord', or 'the statutes of the Lord'.

Psalm 92 encourages the observance of the Sabbath. It teaches worshippers to proclaim God's 'love in the morning' and his 'faithfulness at night', which was the origin of morning and evening worship on a Sunday. (This has largely disappeared – now it's an hour and a half in the morning, and the rest of the day is your own!)

Actually, of course, we are not under the Sabbath law now – that is part of the law of Moses. For us every day is the Lord's day, though we are free to make one day 'special' if we wish (see Romans 14).

A 'psalm sandwich'

Psalms 22–24 form a very important group. They are like a sandwich, though people tend to lick the jam out and leave the bread! Let me explain. These psalms really belong together – I call them the cross, the crook and the crown. They present us with a Lord who is first of all Saviour, then Shepherd, and then Sovereign. If we just extract the well-known Psalm 23 from the middle of the 'sandwich' and claim that Jesus is our shepherd, we miss the lessons of the two psalms on either side of it.

Psalm 22 begins with the cry that Jesus would later quote from the cross: 'My God, my God, why have you forsaken me?' Whereas Psalm 23 begins: 'The Lord is my shepherd.' The order of the two psalms implies that until we have been to the cross and found the Lord as our Saviour, we are not able to regard him as our Shepherd.

Psalm 24 then says: 'Who is this King of glory? The Lord strong and mighty, the Lord mighty in battle. Lift up your heads, O you gates; lift them up, you ancient doors, that the King of glory may come in' (verses 8–9). Or, to paraphrase: 'Open up the gates – the Lord is coming as our Sovereign, our King of Kings, our Lord of Lords.' So we only have Jesus as the Good Shepherd because he was first our Saviour and is our coming King.

Those three psalms fit so beautifully together. In a book that I produced called *Loose Leaves from the Bible* I translated them into modern English:

My God, my God, why?
Why have you left me all alone – me, of all people?
Why do you seem so distant,
    too far away to help me
    or even to hear my groans?
O my God, I shout in the daylight,
    but there's no reply from you;
I howl in the dark,
    but no relief comes.
It doesn't make sense,
    because you are utterly good,
    lauded to the skies by this nation.
Our ancestors trusted you to the hilt;
    and when they did,
    you got them out of trouble.
They appealed to you –
    and reached safety;
when they relied on you
    they were never let down.
But I am treated more like a worm than a human being,
    with no consideration from men
    and only contempt from the mob.
Everyone looking at me makes fun of me;

they put their tongues out,

shrug their shoulders and jeer:

'He said the Lord would prove him right;

see if he gets him out of this!

If the Lord is so fond of him,

let him set him free.'

If they only knew –

you were the one who brought me safely through
childbirth

and you kept me safe while I was still being breast-fed.

I have had to depend on you

since my life began;

and you have been my very own God

since my mother brought me into the world.

Don't leave me now when I'm in such peril,

for there is no-one else who can possibly help.

I'm in a bull-ring,

surrounded by the most ferocious beasts in the whole
country;

they bare their teeth, like a fierce, famished lion.

My strength is draining away,

my joints are being dislocated,

my heart beats like putty in my chest,

my body is as dry as baked clay,

my tongue is stuck to the roof of my mouth.

You're letting me disintegrate into dead dust.

A gang of crooks circle me like a pack of hounds;

they've already torn my hands and my feet.

My bones stand out clear enough to count,

but they just stare and gloat over me.

They've grabbed my clothes

and they're gambling for my shirt.

What do you think you're doing, Lord?

Don't remain aloof!
You're my only support!
Hurry back to my side!
Save my dear life from this violent end –
from the fangs of the dogs,
from the jaws of these lions,
from the horns of these bulls …
You've given me your answer!

I'll tell my brothers you've lived up to your name again;
I'll be among them when they meet and share my testimony.
Each one of you who fears this God Jehovah,
tell him how much you think of him.
Everyone who claims to be descended from Jacob,
give all the credit to him.
All who belong to the nation of Israel,
hold him in deep respect.
For he was neither too haughty or too horrified
to get involved with the suffering of the underdog;
he didn't turn his back on him,
but listened to his cry for help.
You will give your praise to me
in the large congregation;
and I will keep the promises I made to you,
as reverent eyes will see.
Those who suffered will be satisfied;
those who have been seekers will become singers.
May this thrilling experience last for ever.
In every corner of the world,
people will think about God again
and come back to him.
Different races and nations
will be really united

in worshipping him.
For the Lord controls the world
    and is in charge of all international affairs.
Yes, even the top people will bow to his superiority,
        for they are but mortals heading for the grave
        and nobody can hold on to his life indefinitely.
Future generations will take over his work,
        for men will talk about this God who really exists
        to their children who come after them.
His liberation will be announced
        to those whose lives haven't even started yet;
they will be told that God has worked it all out
        and it is finished!

Psalm 22

This Psalm was clearly in Jesus' mind as he died on the cross.

The only God who really exists,
    the God of the Jews
cares for me as an individual,
    like a shepherd for his sheep;
so that I'll never lack anything
    that I really need.
He forces me to rest,
    where there is abundant nourishment;
then he moves me on,
    making sure I have constant refreshment.
He puts new life into me
    when I'm exhausted.
He keeps me on the right track,
    to maintain his good reputation.
Even if I travel through a deep, dark ravine,
    where danger lurks in the shadows,

I'm not afraid of coming to any harm,
    because you are right there beside me.
With your cudgel to guard and your crook to guide,
    I feel quite safe.
You lay the table for me,
    in full view of my helpless foes;
you treat me as an honoured guest
    and put on a lavish spread.
For the rest of my days nothing will chase after me –
    except your generous and undeserved kindness
and I'll be at home with this God,
    as long as I live.

Psalm 23

The God of the Jews owns this planet,
    with everything in it
    and everyone on it;
because he built up the land from the bed of the ocean
    and sent down the water that flows in its rivers.
But who could scale his holy height?
    And who could stay in his perfect presence?
Only one whose conduct was faultless
    and whose character was flawless;
who had not based his life on things that don't ring true
    and who had never broken his word.
Such a man would be given attention and approval
    by the God who saved him.
For people like this really want to find God
    and meet him face to face, as Jacob did.

(Pause for a moment and think about yourself.)

Fling wide the city gates!
  Open up the old citadel doors!
His magnificent Majesty is about to enter!
Who is this marvellous monarch?
  The powerful God of the Jews,
  the undefeated God of Israel!
Fling wide the city gates!
  Open up those old citadel doors!
His magnificent Majesty is about to enter!
Who is this marvellous monarch?
  The God who commands all the forces of the universe –
that's who this marvellous monarch is!

(Be quiet for a while and think about him.)

Psalm 24

God is King

We can deal with the other groups of psalms with greater brevity.

Psalms 96–99 have a common theme: God is King. This is the nearest we get in the Old Testament to the concept of the kingdom of God.

Psalms 113–118 are known in Hebrew as the 'hallel psalms' and are sung together at the Passover.

Psalm 118 provided the inspiration for a well-known modern chorus: 'This is the day that the Lord has made,/We will rejoice and be glad in it.' However, 'the day' being referred to is actually the Passover day in the Old Testament, not the sabbath, much less Sunday.

Also in Psalm 118 is the cry, 'O Lord, save us', or literally, 'liberate us'. The Hebrew for 'liberate us' is *ho shanah*, from which we get the word 'hosanna'.

Unfortunately, we now think of it as a kind of heavenly 'hello'! It is actually a demand for freedom. When Jesus rode into Jerusalem on a donkey the people saying 'Hosanna!' were actually calling for him to liberate them from the Romans. The crowd fell silent because he took a whip and drove out the Jewish businessmen from the Temple instead of attacking the Romans.

Psalms 120–134 are called the 'songs of ascent', meaning 'songs of going up'. Jerusalem is, of course, right up at the top of the hills (actually, it is in a little hollow at the top), so all the pilgrims had to go up to Jerusalem.

Psalm 121 means a great deal to my wife and I, because some years ago she had cancer in her eye and was in danger of losing her life. The surgeons were battling for her life, and I was wondering what to preach on that Sunday while she was in hospital. The Lord directed me to Psalm 121, and I found that every verse is about eyes. The first line is 'I will lift up my eyes to the hills.' When walking up to Jerusalem it is a very danger- ous thing not to keep your eyes on your feet, but the psalmist says, 'I will lift up my eyes to the hills.' So I preached on that psalm and took a tape recording of it to her in hospital. However, a young nurse, who had only been a Christian for two months, had already beaten me to it. She had visited my wife and had given her a word from the Lord: 'You will lift up your eyes to the hills.' A few weeks later we were in Canada and climbing the Rockies together. She has had no trace of cancer since then.

The final group is Psalms 146–150. They are all 'Hallelujah!' songs. *Hallelujah* is Hebrew for 'Praise the Lord' (*hallel* means 'praise' and *yah* is a short form of *Yahweh*).

Types of psalm

Although it is not possible to classify the books of psalms, there are a number of types of psalm that we can identify.

Lament psalms

First, there are the lament psalms or 'please psalms'. They are sad songs written out of the personal unhappiness of the psalmist. In some he is ill; in others he has suffered injustice; in a few he feels his own guilt. Many people are surprised to discover that, with 42 lament psalms, this category is larger than any other.

There is a lot of self-pity in these psalms, but the feelings are presented to God, and healing is found.

They all have the same form and would have been sung to slow funereal music. They each have five parts:

1 A cry to God.
2 A complaint about what is wrong.
3 A confession of trust that God will deliver.
4 A petition calling on God to intervene.
5 A promise to praise God when deliverance comes.

All the lament psalms follow this five-fold pattern. This is why it is necessary to read the whole psalm – just a few verses from a psalm don't give the whole form.

If you just took the first bit, then you would wallow in self-pity. But the psalmist always finishes by promising to praise God when he is out of the situation.

While most of these are individual psalms, some were written on behalf of the nation (see Psalms 44, 74, 79, 80, 83, 85 and 90). Interestingly, none of these were written by David.

Psalms of gratitude

Secondly, there are the psalms of gratitude. These 'thank-you psalms' are the largest group after the lament psalms. They have a particular form and almost all of them are anonymous. Four things are said in every one of them:

1 A proclamation: 'I am going to praise ...'
2 A statement about what he is going to praise God for.
3 A testimony of deliverance.
4 A vow of praise: he continues to praise God for what has happened.

These psalms say a lot about God's attributes and activity. They contain thanks for God's kingly rule, for the creation, for the Exodus, for Jerusalem, for the Temple, and for the opportunity to engage in pilgrimage. There is also gratitude for God's Word, seen supremely in the 176 verses of Psalm 119.

Psalms of penitence

Thirdly, there are the psalms of penitence or 'sorry psalms'. They are few in number but reflect the deep contrition felt when the psalmist is made aware of his sin. Note especially Psalms 6, 32, 38, 51, 130 and 143.

Special psalms

There are also certain other special categories of psalm.

Royal psalms

Just as David wrote about his experiences as a shepherd, he also wrote from his experiences as a king. Psalms 2, 18, 20, 21,

45, 72, 89, 101, 110, 132 and 144 fit into this category.

The British national anthem is based on a number of these psalms. Psalm 68 focuses on the king's victory in battle, which is the background to the line 'Send her victorious' in the anthem. The big difference, of course, is that a British monarch is not the ruler of the Lord's people, so many of these statements are inappropriate. There is only one nation that God chose to be his nation, and that is Israel. We must never forget that any non-Jewish nation is a Gentile nation, and so cannot be special in the same way as Israel.

There is, however, a wonderful psalm about a queen. Psalm 45 reflects on how unworthy the queen felt to be the king's wife. This is a good picture of how we ought to feel as the bride of Christ. We are going to sit on thrones with Jesus, and live like royalty.

Many nations have thought that they were the chosen nation, and so used the Psalms wrongly. The lion and the unicorn in the English coat of arms come from Psalm 22. One of the earliest English translations of the Bible includes the unicorn, even though the word was not in the original.

Canada is the only nation in the world with 'The Dominion' in its name. The name 'The Dominion of Canada' is based on Psalm 72: 'He shall have dominion ... from sea to sea' (AV). Canada stretches from the Pacific to the Atlantic and so was called the Dominion of Canada by its founding fathers.

Messianic psalms

Some of the royal psalms are also messianic or prophetic psalms. David was a model of the ideal king, and these psalms reflect the desire for a king who is truly worthy of God's honour.

The word 'Messiah' means 'anointed'. Every king of Israel was anointed with oil at his coronation as a symbol of the Holy

Spirit. Even the kings and queens of England have what is called 'the unction', the anointing with oil (a special blended oil made from 24 different herbs and oils).

The word 'Messiah' (meaning 'anointed one', as does 'Christ' in Greek) occurs only once in the whole of the Old Testament, in Psalm 2. But if the Psalms are examined for their prophetic element, we find that 20 of them are quoted in the New Testament. It is astonishing to note what is prophesied about Jesus, the Son of David, in these psalms:

- God will declare him to be his Son.
- God will put all things under his feet.
- God will not let him see corruption in the grave.
- He will be forsaken by God and scorned and mocked by men; his hands and feet will be pierced; his clothes will be gambled for; but none of his bones will be broken.
- False witnesses will accuse him.
- He will be hated without a cause.
- A friend will betray him.
- He will be given vinegar and gall to drink.
- He will pray for his enemies.
- His betrayer's office will be given to another.
- His enemies will be his footstool.
- He will be a priest after the order of Melchizedek.
- He will be the chief cornerstone and will come in the name of the Lord.

David called himself a prophet because he could see someone else as he wrote. It is amazing how David was able to enter into the sufferings of Jesus on the cross, without ever having experienced them himself.

Psalm 22 begins, 'My God, my God, why have you forsaken me?' (the words that Jesus cried from the cross).

It speaks of pierced hands and feet centuries before the Romans used crucifixion as a method of execution. One of the greatest 'I am' statements of Jesus occurs in this Psalm, and is very unexpected: – 'I am a worm and not a man'.

Wisdom psalms

The 'wisdom psalms' are the result of quiet reflection and meditation. They resemble the Book of Proverbs, and are full of practical wisdom for life.

Wisdom in the Bible is concerned primarily with two things: – the conduct of life and the contradictions of life.

The Book of Psalms begins with a wisdom psalm about the conduct of life. There are two ways in which we can walk: 'the way of the wicked', or 'the way of the righteous'. Towards the end of Matthew's account of the Sermon on the Mount, Jesus uses similar words: 'For wide is the gate and broad is the road that leads to destruction, and many enter through it. But small is the gate and narrow the road that leads to life, and only a few find it'. So Psalm 1 implies that this Book of Psalms is for those who are walking in the right way. It is not for those who sit, walk or stand with the evildoers. If we walk with someone, we pick up something from them. If we stand around with them, the relationship is getting deeper. If we sit with them we become friends. We read that we must not walk, stand or sit in the way of sinners, because the company we keep is probably the biggest influence in our life.

The wisdom psalms also focus on the contradictions of life. The biggest contradiction is that bad people often get away with their evil behaviour while good people suffer.

Psalm 73 tackles this problem head on. The psalmist feels as if he has cleansed his heart in vain, that it is a waste of time trying to live a good life, because wicked people die in their beds in peace, having made plenty of money.

The psalmist says he is troubled all the day and can't sleep at night. His solution is to go to the Temple and reflect on God's glory and the end that the wicked will face. It is one of the few psalms that mention the afterlife. The concept of the afterlife isn't explained as thoroughly in the Old Testament as it is in the New.

Imprecatory psalms

In these psalms the psalmists ask God to visit their enemies with judgement.

For example:

> Let the heads of those who surround me
> be covered with the trouble their lips have caused.
> > Let burning coals fall upon them;
> may they be thrown into the fire,
> into miry pits, never to rise.

from Psalm 140

One of the best known imprecatory psalms is Psalm 137, which was composed in Babylon:

> By the rivers of Babylon we sat and wept
> when we remembered Zion.
> There on the poplars
> we hung our harps,
> for there our captors asked us for songs,
> our tormentors demanded songs of joy;
> they said, 'Sing us one of the songs of Zion!'
>
> How can we sing the songs of the Lord
> while in a foreign land?
> If I forget you, O Jerusalem,

> may my right hand forget its skill.
> May my tongue cling to the roof of my mouth
> if I do not remember you,
> if I do not consider Jerusalem my highest joy.

> Remember, O Lord, what the Edomites did
> on the day Jerusalem fell.
> 'Tear it down,' they cried,
> 'tear it down to its foundations!'

> O Daughter of Babylon, doomed to destruction,
> happy is he who repays you
> for what you have done to us –
> he who seizes your infants
> and dashes them against the rocks.

This is not pleasant. There is no forgiveness for the enemy and certainly no recognition that what is being said might be inappropriate. It is understandable that some people should ask whether Christians should use these psalms at all.

Can Christians use imprecatory psalms?

First, we must remember that the Jews only had the Old Testament. Hence, we mustn't expect the Old Testament to feel fully Christian. They had no knowledge of Jesus, who said, 'Father, forgive them, for they do not know what they are doing'.

Secondly, these psalms are good models of honesty in prayer. If we feel a certain way, then it is appropriate to tell God how we feel. It is just as bad to feel the way the psalmist does and not say it, as it is to say it. In fact it is worse, because we are trying to hide it from God.

I remember a Christian lady who had been in a terrible car crash. For 20 years afterwards she was dreadfully handicapped; she could only stagger around on crutches and was in constant pain. One night, as she was going into her bedroom, she cursed God for her agony. But then she caught her foot on the carpet and fell over, knocking herself out. She was unconscious for many hours, and when she woke up it was morning, and sunlight was coming through the window and shining directly into her eyes. She was convinced that she had died and was now facing the Lord, and with horror she remembered that the last thing she had done in life had been to curse God. She assumed that she would have to go to hell because of this. But then she realized that the bright light was in fact just sunshine and she was still in her bedroom. The relief was enormous. Then she suddenly noticed that she had no pain. She got up and discovered that she was totally healed. She could move every limb! She dashed out into the street and told everybody she met that she had cursed God but he had made her well! Of course, this is not a good model to copy, but the point is that because she was honest with God, this lady received healing from him. How gracious he is!

Thirdly, the enemies of Israel were also God's enemies. The imprecatory psalms do not just ask for vengeance on the psalmists' personal enemies; they also remind God that the psalmists' enemies are His enemies. For Christians today, the enemies of God are not flesh and blood, but the principalities and powers. If we really love God, we will hate the devil and all evil. The Old Testament saints did not have the knowledge that we have about the Day of Judgement and heaven and hell, so they had to pray that the wicked would be punished in this present world. They believed that after death everyone went to a place called Sheol – a kind of railway station waiting-room where no trains arrive. They had to pray for God to be vindicated in this life. They were crying to a good God for justice.

Fourthly, in every case the psalmists refuse to take revenge themselves, but leave it to God. This is a principle that Paul teaches in Romans 12: 'Do not take revenge, my friends, but leave room for God's wrath'. He will take vengeance on the wicked.

Finally, it is important to note that in this matter the New Testament is no different from the Old. There are also imprecatory prayers in the New Testament. In Revelation 6 the souls of the martyrs in heaven are praying, 'How long, Sovereign Lord, holy and true, until you judge the inhabitants of the earth and avenge our blood?'. These prayers are no different from the imprecatory psalms, even though they are made 'in heaven'. The Christian martyrs are asking God to vindicate himself and to bring justice.

So if we do it in the right spirit, we have no problem using these psalms today. One day every sin will be punished, the righteous will be vindicated and the martyrs will sit on the very thrones that condemned them to death.

The Psalms' view of God

The Psalms are remarkably balanced in their view of God. We have already seen how his transcendence (*Elohim*) is balanced by his immanence (*Yahweh*).

The Psalms encourage us to magnify God, not because we can make him bigger, but so that our view of him may be enlarged.

The Psalms tell us about God's *attributes* – that is, what he *is*. Psalms 8, 9, 29, 103, 104, 139, 148 and 150 are good examples of this. Psalm 139 describes his omnipotence (i.e. he is all-powerful), his omniscience (he is all-knowing) and his omnipresence (he is everywhere).

The Psalms also tell us about God's *actions* – that is, what he *does*. Psalms 33, 36, 105, 111, 113, 117, 136, 146 and 147 are good examples of this. In particular we learn about his two major acts:

> *creation* (e.g. Psalms 8 and 19) and
> *redemption* (e.g. Psalm 78, which tells the story of the Exodus).

The Psalms tell us that God is Shepherd, Warrior, Judge, Father and, above all, King.

In view of these attributes and actions of God, it is no surprise that in the Psalms theology very quickly becomes doxology. Truth leads inevitably to praise.

Using the Psalms today

It is clear from the New Testament's use of the Psalms that it is legitimate and desirable for Christians to use them. The songs in the New Testament are modelled on the Psalms (e.g. Luke chapters 1 and 2). The apostles turn to the Psalms when they are under pressure (e.g. Acts 4), and they often use them when they are preaching (e.g. Acts 13).

The writer of the Letter to the Hebrews quotes the Psalms extensively. Each of the first five chapters of Hebrews includes a reference to one or more psalms.

Jesus quoted from the Psalms in his public teaching (e.g. the Sermon on the Mount), in answering the Jews, while cleansing the Temple and at the Last Supper.

So how should the Psalms be used today?

It is best if they are read aloud or sung. Some of them explicitly encourage shouting! Their impact and value is greatly diminished if they are read silently. Many psalms also encourage bodily movement such as lifting hands, clapping, dancing and looking upwards.

We are commanded in the New Testament to use the Psalms in corporate worship (e.g. Ephesians 5). They can be sung or read aloud to the congregation by singers or readers, or the whole congregation can read, sing (or even shout!) them together.

Clearly the Psalms are meant to be sung to musical accompaniment. As we have already seen, the Hebrew word that we translate as 'psalm' literally means 'pluck', implying that stringed instruments normally accompanied the singing of psalms (though other instruments are also mentioned in the Book of Psalms). In many psalms the word *Selah* occurs. It is probably a musical direction to the choir-master meaning 'pause' or 'change key' or 'play louder' or even 'lift up your voices at this point'.

How should we sing psalms today? I think they should be sung 'whole'. Too many songs, choruses and hymns use only parts of a psalm, and in doing so they violate its original sense and context.

Some psalms can be sung in metrical verse (as is often done in churches in Scotland). Some psalms are well suited to being sung by a choir. The Psalms are also well suited to private use. Here are some guidelines:

- Reading one psalm per day is a good habit.
- Some psalms are ideal bedtime reading. They can be a help against destructive emotions and bad dreams.
- Read psalms even when they don't seem to be relevant to your circumstances, because there will come a time when they will be.
- Try giving a title to the psalm – this will help you to concentrate on its content.
- Translate the psalm into your own words. (See my examples earlier in the chapter.)

■ Some psalms are a great comfort when you are ill – or even
  when you are dying.

While there is great value in studying the Psalms, we derive
the greatest benefit from them as we *use* them in our lives.
We discover their true beauty and power when we read them
aloud, sing them, and shout them. The Psalms are meant to
lead us into a passionate praise that glorifies God.

13.

SONG OF SONGS

Introduction

Many people are surprised to find the Song of Songs included in the Bible. It is one of only two books in the Bible where God is not mentioned even once (Esther is the other). There is no mention of anything obviously spiritual in it from beginning to end, and its graphic description of human sexuality means that it's one of the books of the Bible that are generally avoided during Sunday school!

The very title 'Song of Songs' sounds strange. Hebrew writing does not include any adjectives, so phrases such as 'fantastic song' or 'brilliant song' are not possible. So instead of 'the Greatest Song', the expression 'the Song of Songs' is used, just as 'the Highest King' is known as 'the King of Kings' and 'the Greatest Lord' is called 'the Lord of Lords'.

But accepting that it is a lovely song gives us no clear understanding of why it is in the Bible, for not only is it unspiritual, but it is also very sensual. It touches all five senses – smell, sight, touch, taste and hearing – and gives an erotic description of the bodies of the young man and the young woman in the drama. So although it is not taught at Sunday school, it becomes something of a favourite with young people!

For many years I didn't preach from this book because I didn't know how to handle it. But I found that the Jewish Rabbis treated it as a very holy book. They called it 'the Holy of Holies' and even took off their shoes when they read it. Furthermore, I learnt that some Christian devotional writers raved about it. I determined to get to grips with it for myself, and so I bought commentaries and devotional expositions of the book in order to gain some understanding of it. But this just increased my sense of guilt. I was told that the book was written in a hidden code and that none of the words meant what I thought they meant. I reached rock bottom when I read one commentary's explanation of a verse in chapter 1 where the woman in the drama speaks of her lover resting between her breasts, and the commentator said that this means between the Old and the New Testaments! I confess that this was the last thing in my mind when I read that verse, and so I concluded that God must have put this book in the Bible as a kind of 'Catch 22' to find out whether you were spiritual or carnal. It was many years before I was able to explore the book in any depth.

What sort of literature is it?

Allegory?

An allegory is a fictional story that is intended to communicate a hidden message. For example, *The Pilgrim's Progress*, the seventeenth-century classic by John Bunyan, is an allegory in which each part of the story is intended to depict a spiritual truth. Many have interpreted the Song of Songs as an allegory, but each commentator seems to invent his or her own code, often with little reference to the text itself. It seems that the commentators see what they want to see and are reluctant to take the plain meaning of the text, because they don't believe that the book, with its graphic descriptions of sexuality, is acceptable as it stands.

One reason for this is that Christians have generally been

more influenced by Greek thinking than by Hebrew thinking. The Greeks believed that life was divided between what they termed 'the physical' and 'the spiritual', with the latter regarded as more important. By contrast, the Hebrews believed in one God who made both the physical and the spiritual, and they saw no difference in value between the two. If a good God made this material world, then material things are good; and if this same God made us male and female, with the capacity to fall in love and become man and wife, this too was good.

Affirmation

This Hebrew way of thinking can help us in our interpretation of the book, for, rather than seeing the book as an allegory, we should see it instead as affirmation. Here in the middle of the Bible, God is affirming the love between a man and a woman. His inclusion of the Song of Songs within the Bible reminds us that sexuality is God's idea. He thought it up. Indeed, one of the biggest lies that the devil has spread around the world is that God is against sex and Satan is for it. The truth is the exact opposite. God is saying that sex is a clean and legitimate part of a married couple's love for one another. Indeed, when conducting a marriage service, I always read part of the Song of Songs and tell the couple to read the rest of it on their honeymoon.

Analogy

But the Song of Songs is more than affirmation – it is also an analogy. This is clearly distinct from the fanciful allegorical interpretations that we have discounted. An allegory is a work of fiction with a hidden meaning, whereas an analogy is a fact which is like another fact. Jesus used analogies in his teaching. For example, he would describe the Kingdom of Heaven in terms that his hearers could grasp. The Song of Songs functions in a similar way. The love between a man and a woman is like the love between God and human beings. Both are real, and the former helps to explain the latter. The Song of Songs is saying that our relationship to God can be like that. We should be able to say, 'My beloved is mine and I am his', in the same way that lovers speak of one another.

The book's author

The book was written by King Solomon, who had a gift for writing lyrics. In 1 Kings we learn that he wrote 1,005 songs in all, though only six were included in the Bible. My theory is that Solomon wrote a song for each of his 700 wives and 300 concubines, but of all these 1,000 women, only one was God's choice for him, and so the song that he wrote for her was the only love song that was published as part of the Bible. The Song of Songs tells us that by the time he wrote the song he already had 60 wives.

Three people or two?

Scholars are divided about the plot. Some argue that it involves three people – a triangular tug of war between a shepherd boy, a king and the girl, who is torn between the two. It makes an interesting story and a good sermon, because you can finish it with a moving appeal: '*You* are that girl! Will you choose the prince of this world or the Good Shepherd?' But unfortunately this plot does not fit the text – why would Solomon compose a song depicting the king (himself) as the villain? Furthermore, the atmosphere is one of innocence, not guilt. This is not an evil king seducing a simple girl. It's a pure love song all the way through.

So it is more likely to be a plot featuring just two people, which means that the king and the shepherd are the same person. This may seem improbable until we remember that some of the kings of Israel were once shepherds – David being an obvious example. Moses too was a shepherd before he became a leader of God's people. It is not an unusual combination.

But even assuming that the king and the shepherd are one and the same, it is still not easy to understand exactly how the story fits together. It is a little like taking the lid off a jigsaw box and seeing all the different coloured pieces mixed up inside. We despair of ever finishing unless we have the picture on the lid to help us.

So let me give you the picture on the lid so that when you read the story for yourself, all the little bits will fit together.

The story

Solomon had a country estate on the slopes of Mount Hermon. He used it as a retreat from the pressures of being King in Jerusalem. He could relax, go hunting and forget for a while that he was the King. On occasions he would lead sheep to find green pasture and water amid the rocky terrain. He might typically travel 15 miles in any one day.

On Solomon's country estate a tenant farmer had died. The farm passed to his sons, though we don't know exactly how many there were. There were probably three or four sons and two daughters. One of the daughters is a child; the other is grown up and is the subject of the song. Her life lacks any excitement. Her father divided the estate, giving vineyards to the sons and daughters, but the sons make her do all the work in the house and a lot of the work on the farm. She complains that she had to look after their vineyards so much that she

neglected her own. Furthermore, because she had been working outside, her skin had become dark. Although bronzed skin
is an attractive feature in our culture, the reverse was true for
her – indeed, a bride would be kept out of the sun for 12
months before her wedding. So she was conscious of the fact
that her dark looks meant that she would probably remain a
slave to her brothers for the rest of her life.

One day she is working in the fields and meets a young
man. They enjoy conversation and arrange to meet the next
day. After a few occasional meetings, they agree to meet every
day. The meetings become the highlight of the day, and after a
fortnight they are deeply in love. The one thing that troubles
the woman is that she doesn't know who the young man is. She
keeps pestering him, asking which farm he comes from and
where he rests his sheep at midday. But he evades her questions
and will not tell her who he is.

She is deeply in love with him and he with her, and finally
he asks if she will marry him. She has waited years for this! She
is overjoyed and says 'Yes' immediately. He tells her that he has
to leave the next day to return to work in the south in the big
city. He leaves her to get ready for the wedding and promises
to return.

The next few months are the most exciting of her life. She
never thought it would happen, but now at last she is to be
married. But she begins to have nightmares. It doesn't take a
very deep knowledge of psychology to interpret her dreams.
All the dreams are centred on one theme: 'I've lost him and I'm
looking for him.'

One night she dreams that she is running through the
streets, looking for her lover. She meets the watchman and asks
whether he has seen him. But he hasn't. She runs around the
streets, frantically searching for him. When she finds him, she
gets hold of him, drags him back to her mother's bedroom and

tells him she will never let him go. When she awakes, she finds that she is holding the pillow.

Another time she dreams that her lover is at the door and puts his hand through the hole in the door to lift the latch on the inside. But he is unable to open it because it is bolted further down. She is paralysed and can't move. She can't get off the bed, and he's trying to open the door, and she becomes frustrated. Then his hand disappears and she finds that she can move. She runs to the door and – he's gone!

The nightmares have a simple explanation: she's afraid that he won't come back to marry her. She thinks this is only a holiday flirtation, and her lover won't keep his promise.

Then one day, she's out in the fields and notices horses and chariots and a great cloud of dust approaching. She asks her brothers who it is.

The brothers say it is the landlord, King Solomon from Jerusalem, who has come to visit his estates. They get ready to bow down low before the King. She has never seen him, and so she takes a look – only to find that the King in the big chariot is her young man!

Since everyone knows that he has got 60 wives already, she realizes that she must be number 61!

So she leaves the farm and travels south to live in the palace. They are married, and she appears at the first banquet, held to honour her. She sits at the top table next to the King, and feels distinctly inferior to the 60 beautiful, fair-skinned queens in their robes all around her.

When a man has more than one woman, each woman begins to feel insecure and asks whether he loves her more than the others. So she asks Solomon if they can go back north. 'Can't we just lie on the grass under the trees? Couldn't we go and live on your estate up there?' He explains that because he is the King he must live and reign in Jerusalem. Finally she asks about the beautiful women all around her. She says with a tone of real inferiority, 'I'm just a rose of Sharon, I'm a lily of the valley.'

We assume that these are beautiful flowers, but in Israel they are tiny little flowers which you would walk on like daisies in a lawn. The lilies of the valley grow in the shadows, and the rose of Sharon is a tiny little crocus that grows on the flat plain next to the Mediterranean Sea.

The King's reply, that she is a lily among thorns, delights her, for lilies among thorns, by contrast, are the most beautiful flowers in Israel. This lily is white with a graceful form, and this is how her beloved sees her. So she sings a little song to rejoice, and the song is: 'He brought me into his banqueting hall and his banner over me is love.'

This, then, is the outline of the story – the picture on the jigsaw box.

Why should we read this book?

There are two reasons why we should read it and study it. First, at the heart of Christianity is a very personal relationship. Being a Christian is not going to church, reading a Bible or supporting missionaries; being a Christian is being in love with the Lord. The only point of singing hymns is that we are singing love songs. If we miss this, we miss everything.

So at the heart of the Bible is the very intimate, loving relationship between Solomon and a country girl.

The book adds a wider dimension to the portrayal of the relationship between God and his people. Sometimes in the Bible, God is spoken of as a husband and Israel as a wife. He courts her and marries her at Sinai when the covenant is established. When Israel goes after other gods, she is described as an adulteress.

This theme underlies the prophecy of Hosea. The Lord asks the prophet to find a prostitute in the street. He protests and asks God why. He is told to marry her, and she will have three children. She will love the first child, but not the second, and the third child, who won't even be Hosea's, is to be called 'Not Mine'. God tells Hosea that she will return to life on the street in her old profession, leaving the three children with him. He is to find her, buy her back from the pimp who is controlling her and bring her back home, and then he is to love her again. Finally, God tells him to tell Israel that this is how God feels about them.

In fact, the whole relationship in the Old Testament between God and Israel is that of a husband whose wife behaves appallingly. He woos her, wins her, loses her, still loves her, and wants to get her back home again.

When we move to the New Testament, this same theme continues. Jesus is depicted as the bridegroom looking for a bride. On the last page of the Bible the bride is eager for the wedding and says 'Come!' She has made herself ready with white linen, which is righteousness. So the whole Bible is a love story from beginning to end.

The Song of Songs expresses this relationship. The words of the young man to the bride are the words that God says to us. Her replies are the sort of responses we can make. So it's not an allegory, nor is it full of hidden meanings. 'Pomegranates' means 'pomegranates' and 'breasts' mean 'breasts'. God means what he says, but it's an analogy of the relationship that we can have with God.

We need to be careful in our interpretation. Our relationship with the Lord is not erotic, but it is emotional. Even though the song includes sexually explicit language, there is appropriate restraint. It doesn't enter into the physical details that modern literature would.

Nevertheless, it is an emotional relationship. The story reminds us of the conversation between Jesus and Peter in Galilee after Jesus' resurrection. Peter had denied the Lord at a charcoal fire in a courtyard, and the only other charcoal fire mentioned in the New Testament is a few weeks later, in Galilee. So Peter sees the fire and he remembers those awful moments. Yet Jesus doesn't say how disappointed he is with him, nor does he exclude him from future service. No, he tells Peter that he can cope with him, provided that he is sure of one thing – that Peter loves him.

In the same way, the Lord doesn't ask us how many times we have been to church or how many chapters of the Bible we have read this week. He asks us: 'Do you love me?' Jesus said that the law could be summarized as: 'Love the Lord your God with all your heart and mind and strength, and love your neighbour as yourself.' Love really is as important as this.

Secondly, not only is your relationship with the Lord a very personal one; it's also a very public one. Most people fall in love with the Lord because they see him as their Shepherd, the One who will be with them in the valley of the shadow of death, the One who will lead them by the still waters and the green pastures. But at some stage after we have fallen in love with Jesus as our Shepherd, we discover that he is also a King! He's the King of Kings, and we are his bride. We are going to reign with him and become his queen. So we are in very public view, which puts an extra responsibility on us. It would be nice if we could keep it private and return to the forests of Hermon, keeping our relationship with the Lord secret. It would save a lot of unpleasantness, criticism and exposure. But he wants us to remain in the spotlight, forever pointing to him as the source of our life and sharing with him the responsibility of reigning over the earth.

14.

 PROVERBS

Introduction[1]

Proverbs seems at first to be a strange book to be included in the Bible. It contains humorous observations and pithy sayings that seem to be little more than common sense.

The book doesn't seem very spiritual. It says little about private or public devotions, and some of its themes seem distinctly mundane.

Some of the proverbs make points which are obvious to everyone. For example: 'Poverty is the ruin of the poor'; 'A happy heart makes the face cheerful'; 'Better to live on a corner of the roof than share a house with a quarrelsome wife'; 'Like one who seizes a dog by the ears is a passer-by who meddles in a quarrel not his own'.

Some of the proverbs seem more entertaining than edifying, and others seem downright immoral. For example: 'A bribe does wonders, it will bring you before men of importance'.

Many of the proverbs have found their way into everyday speech:

---

1 For Proverbs (and Ecclesiastes) I am deeply indebted to the superb commentaries of Derek Kidner in the 'Tyndale' series published by IVP. Readers wanting to study these books in greater detail are warmly commended to obtain these models of their kind.

'Spare the rod and spoil the child';
'Hope deferred makes the heart sick';
'Pride goes before a fall';
'Stolen food is sweet';
'Iron sharpens iron'.

The Book of Proverbs describes life as it really is – not life in church, but life in the street, the office, the shop, the home. The book covers all aspects of life – not just what you do on Sundays in church. It considers how you should live throughout the week in every situation.

So the characters who are found in the Book of Proverbs can be easily recognized in all cultures. There is the woman who talks too much, the wife who is always nagging, the aimless youth hanging around on street corners, the neighbour who is always dropping in and staying too long, the friend who is unbearably cheerful first thing in the morning.

Indeed, the 900 proverbs cover most of life's important subjects, often presenting them as contrasts: wisdom and folly, pride and humility, love and lust, wealth and poverty, work and leisure, masters and servants, husbands and wives, friends and relatives, life and death. But there are significant and surprising omissions. There is very little which is 'religious', no mention of priests and prophets, and very little about kings – all people who figure prominently in the rest of the Old Testament.

It is important that from the outset we are clear about the way in which we should view the subjects that are covered. Some people would make the mistake of claiming that Proverbs focuses upon 'secular' life, but the so-called 'secular/sacred divide' is not one that the Bible endorses. Indeed, as far as God is concerned, the only thing that can be described as 'secular' is sin itself.

The idea that only the 'religious' is 'sacred' comes from the Greek philosophers and has filtered into much modern thinking, even among Christians. The Bible knows of no such division. Any activity can be sacred if it can be devoted to God. He would rather have a good taxi driver than a bad missionary. All legitimate jobs are at the same level.

So Proverbs is interested in where most of our waking life is lived. This book tells us how we can make the most of life and warns us that many people waste it. It is about the 'Good Life'. Its wisdom enables us to arrive at the end of our days pleased with all that we have accomplished.

How is Proverbs related to the message of the rest of the Bible? The apostle Paul, in his second letter to Timothy, said that the holy Scriptures are able to make him 'wise for salvation through faith in Christ Jesus'. But a reading of Proverbs may leave us wondering where 'salvation' appears, since the themes of redemption that are common in other biblical books are strangely absent.

But the theme is there. The word 'salvation' is very close in meaning to words such as 'salvage' or 'recycling'. God is in the business of recycling people so that they become useful. Christians are changed from sinners into saints, but also from being *foolish* to being *wise*. The message of the Bible is that the real cause of pollution on the planet is people. Jesus himself likened hell to the rubbish dump in the valley of Gehenna outside Jerusalem, where all the garbage was thrown. He spoke of people being 'thrown' into hell as if they were good for nothing. God recycles people who are heading for hell, turning fools into wise people.

So in that sense Proverbs is full of 'salvation', since it tells us the sort of life we are saved for and reminds us about the sort of life we have been saved from. It thus corrects an imbalance that is common in the preaching of many churches. Too much attention is paid to what we are saved *from* and not enough to what we are saved *to* and *for*.

What about wisdom outside the Bible? Many would argue that there is a lot of wisdom that is not included in the Bible. What about the wisdom of Plato, Socrates, Aristotle and Confucius? It need not surprise us that there is wisdom outside the Bible, for all men and women are made in the image of God, and so they are able to make sense of life. But this is not to say that they have enough sense to make the *most* of life. Only when Christ redeems us do we grasp the real meaning of life and live as God intends. So in this respect the world's 'wisdom' will always be folly, for it lacks eternal perspective.

So Proverbs is affirming the truth that God is 'the All-Wise God', the source of all wisdom, and that it is his wisdom that created the whole universe, with all its complexity.

Why was Proverbs written?

Proverbs is unusual among the books of the Bible in that it tells us why it was written. The prologue says that learning from proverbs will lead us to wisdom, and it tells us that the very first step in becoming wise is to 'fear God' (that is, Yahweh, the God of the Jews). If we come to understand that he hates evil and that, as the all-seeing Judge, nothing escapes his attention, then we will see our folly and our need for help in order to live life as he desires. Wisdom comes from fearing him, asking him for wisdom and learning how to handle the affairs of this world in a shrewd and sound way.

The book also tells us that wisdom comes from God via other people. God has chosen to pass on his wisdom especially through parents, grandparents and other people who are more experienced than us. So Proverbs contains many references to the family relationships that form the context in which wisdom is shared.

The author

The man who is most associated with wisdom in the Bible is the man who wrote the Book of Proverbs, King Solomon. On his accession to the throne God offered him anything he asked for, and he asked for wisdom to govern others. God gave him wisdom, along with other things that he didn't ask for, such as fame, power and wealth. His wise words were legendary, although he seemed to have more wisdom for others than for himself. After all, collecting 700 wives (and presumbably 700 mothers-in-law!) was hardly wise, not to mention 300 concubines.

But there was an important condition attached to God's promise of wisdom. He told Solomon in 1 Kings: 'I will give you a wise and discerning heart … *if* you walk in my ways and obey my statutes and commands'. So we must conclude that the evident folly of his latter years was the result of neglecting these conditions.

In his prime, Solomon became so famous for his wisdom that the Queen of Sheba made a long journey not just to see his wealth but to hear his wisdom. Modern philosophers look back to the wise men of Greece such as Plato, Socrates and Aristotle, who lived around 400 years before Christ, but they forget that back in the Bronze Age, about 1,000 years before Christ, there was a wise man who was just as famous. Solomon wrote many of the proverbs in the Book of Proverbs, and he collected many others. He also wrote the Song of Songs and Ecclesiastes.

He wrote the Song of Songs when he was a young man, so much in love that he forgot about God altogether. It is a book of the heart. He wrote Proverbs when he was middle-aged. It is a book of the will. His last book, Ecclesiastes, was written in old age. It's a book of the mind, as he meditates on his life and wonders whether he has achieved anything with it. So we have

Solomon as a young lover, a middle-aged father and an elderly philosopher, writing these three books of wisdom.

One of the most intriguing things about the Book of Proverbs is that some of the proverbs in it come from outside Israel. There are some proverbs from Arabic philosophers, and a whole chapter from Egypt, probably collected through one of his wives, who was the daughter of Pharaoh. Solomon recognized that God had given wisdom to people outside the land of Israel, and so he was happy to include it in his work. These sayings were brought into the framework of a life lived under God.

But that is not to say that the Book of Proverbs does not have a strong reverence for God. God is mentioned 90 times in the book as *Yahweh*, the God of Israel – not some god that other nations might believe in. There is certainly no suggestion that the Arabic or Egyptian gods have any value.

Part of the collection was completed by King Hezekiah, who collected many of Solomon's unwritten proverbs some 250 years later, and these too are included in the book. So Proverbs as we have it today was not completed until about 550 BC.

The book's style

Before examining the content of the book, we need to consider some background points about its style and intention.

Proverbs, not promises

First, it is crucial to realize that this is a book of proverbs, not a book of promises. We should never quote a proverb as if it is a divine promise.

The English word 'proverb' comes from the Latin *proverba*. *Pro* means 'for' and *verba* means 'word'. The two combined mean 'a word for a situation'. A proverb is an appropriate word that fits the situation. It is thus a timeless truth that can be used in different situations in life.

The Hebrew word that we translate as 'proverb' is *maschal*, which means 'to resemble or to be like something'. Jesus began a number of parables with the phrase, 'The Kingdom of Heaven is like this …'

So a proverb is a general observation on life, whereas a promise is a particular obligation.

Let me illustrate. Here is a proverb: 'Pawson has a passion for punctuality.' How is that proverb applied? It means that Pawson likes to be on time, but that is not the same as saying that Pawson makes a promise to be at a certain place by a certain time. I am not morally to blame if the proverb breaks down, but I am to blame if a promise breaks down. So a proverb is only *generally* true. We shouldn't apply a proverb to every situation and expect it to work. We must not assume that God is making promises to us when we read proverbs.

Thinking that a proverb is a promise has caused problems to many people. For example, 'honesty is the best policy'. This is generally true, but not always true. I know people who have lost a fortune through being honest!

Furthermore, proverbs can contradict each other – for example, 'more haste, less speed' and 'he who hesitates is lost'.

Turning to the Book of Proverbs, we find the same features. In chapter 26 we read, 'Do not answer a fool according to his folly', but the very next verse says, 'Answer a fool according to his folly'!

Two proverbs that have frequently been used as promises have caused Christians great consternation. One of them is 'Commit to the Lord whatever you do, and your plans will succeed'. Christians have started all sorts of business ventures on the basis of this verse. Although it is generally true, it doesn't mean that every business venture that is committed to the Lord is bound to be a success.

The second proverb that has caused problems is this: 'Train a child in the way he should go, and when he is old he will not turn from it'.

Many parents with children who are not believers have a problem with this verse. They say they trained their children in the way they should go, but are disappointed that they seem to have departed from it.

Once again, the proverb is not a promise – it is only generally true. Children are not puppets, and we can't force them to go our way. They will reach an age when they will make their own decision, and they are free to do so. Both these proverbs are guidelines, not guarantees. If the users of the proverbs had realized this, much heartache would have been averted.

Poetry

The second thing that we need to be aware of is that proverbs are poetic. They are presented in a form that is easy to remember.

Let me translate a familiar proverb for you:

In advance of committing yourself to a course of action, consider carefully your circumstances and options.

Or, to rephrase:

There are certain corrective measures for minor problems which, when taken early on in a course of action, forestall major problems from arising.'

Those are both translations of 'Look before you leap'! Which is easier to remember?!

We noted in Part I that Hebrew poetry is a unique form. It is not based on rhyme, as most English poetry is, but on rhythm. The rhythm is not only a matter of beat or metre; it is also a rhythm of thought. So Hebrew poetry often consists of pairs of lines (called parallelism) in which one line relates to the other in one of three different ways. In synonymous parallelism the thought in the first line is repeated in the second. For example:

> Pride goes before destruction,
> *and* a haughty spirit before a fall.

In *antithetical parallelism* the second line contrasts with the first one:

> He who oppresses the poor shows contempt for their Maker,
> *but* whoever is kind to the needy honours God.

In *synthetic parallelism* the thought in the first line is advanced by the second:

> Stay away from a foolish man,
> *for* you will not find knowledge on his lips.

In the examples above, the words *and*, *but* and *for* give a clue as to which type of parallelism is being used.

All the proverbs fit into this kind of pattern, but they are not as easy to remember in English because the rhythm is lost in translation. But Jewish parents passed on values to their children in this way, and we still do so today.

There are other devices that are used in Proverbs. Chapter 31 is arranged as an acrostic – that is, each line begins with a new letter of the Hebrew alphabet. On other occasions the structure is numerical: 'there are three things … and four things ...' or 'there are six things God hates ...' and so on. These forms enable the reader/hearer to commit the proverb to memory.

Patriarchy

The third thing that we need to bear in mind is that this book is patriarchal. It is presented as a father's advice to a youth. It offers no advice at all to women! Such an approach is common throughout the Bible. For example, the letters in the New Testament are not addressed to 'brothers and sisters', but to 'brothers'. This apparent chauvinism is the result of one of the fundamental assumptions in Scripture – that is, that if the men are right, the women and the children will be right also. The Bible is deliberately addressed to men – precisely because it is their responsibility to lead their families, by teaching and example.

Wisdom and Folly

So in Proverbs we have Solomon, a middle-aged father, desperately trying to prevent a young man from committing the same errors as he did himself. He presents his son, and his readers, with the choice that they must make about how they will live their lives. Do they want Wisdom or Folly as their companion for life? He symbolically portrays both these options as women.

Wisdom personified

Chapters 8 and 9 describe Wisdom as a wonderful woman. The son is advised to love her like a sweetheart, to make her a beloved member of his family, to go after her, to court her. She says, 'I love those who love me, and those who seek me find me'.

Wisdom personalized

In chapter 31 (the acrostic chapter) a mother advises her son on what to look for in a good woman. She is to be a good wife, mother, neighbour and trader. Such a woman is vital to good, stable family life. She is 'more precious than rubies'.

Folly personified

The same pattern is used with Folly, which is personified in chapter 9. Folly seduces men with her smooth talk, enticing her prey with tempting offers. But for all who fall for her charms the end is death: 'She will destroy you, rob you of your manhood'.

Folly personalized

In chapter 6 Folly is depicted as a prostitute who reduces her victim to 'a loaf of bread'. To her he is no more than a meal ticket.

A biblical theme

This use of women as symbols is not unique to Proverbs. In the Book of Revelation there are two women – a filthy prostitute and a pure bride. The prostitute is called Babylon and the bride is called Jerusalem. So this theme runs through the whole Bible. Which woman is going to be your companion and your partner – folly or wisdom?

The Bible often presents us with choices, and this is the case in Proverbs. Will we choose life or death, light or darkness, heaven or hell?

Moral or mental?

Furthermore, Proverbs depicts wisdom and folly in another way: it tells us that they are *moral* choices rather than *mental* ones. When the world speaks of fools, it means people whose IQs aren't very high. But in the Bible someone who is very intelligent can be very foolish. Someone can be mentally clever and morally silly.

I once heard of a country yokel down in Somerset many years ago who had a strange reputation. If you offered him a sixpence or a £5 note, he always took the sixpence. Thousands of tourists heard about this man and tried the trick on him. The poor, foolish man always took the coin, never the note. But really he was no fool – he made a fortune out of it!

Folly and wisdom have nothing to do with qualifications. In Psalm 14 the psalmist said, 'The fool says in his heart, "There is no God"'. The devil told Eve that eating the fruit would lead to wisdom, but in fact it only led to independence from God, the source of all wisdom. Worldly wisdom seeks to find the most profitable option, but biblical wisdom seeks what is best for your character. It is based not on knowledge of the world, but on knowledge of God.

This idea is backed up by a verse from chapter 29 that is often misunderstood: 'Where there is no vision the people perish' (AV). It is used when church leaders want to convince the congregation that their particular scheme should be followed. But in more modern translations the Hebrew word translated as 'vision' is more correctly translated as 'revelation', and the word 'perish' as 'cast off restraint' or 'become a fool'. So the verse is actually saying, 'If God isn't revealing things to you, you will become a fool.' So wisdom is practising God's presence in every area of life. We will need his Spirit's help if we are to understand his mind.

The book's structure

We turn now to consider the structure of the Book of Proverbs. The book has an amazing symmetry. Indeed, the only passages which don't really fit are the prologue at the beginning and the Arabic wisdom in chapter 30. Here is an outline of the book's structure:

PROLOGUE (1:1–7)
ADVICE TO YOUTH (1:8 – 9:18)
SOLOMON'S PROVERBS (10:1 – 22:16)
WISE WORDS (22:17 – 23:14)
ADVICE TO YOUTH (23:15 – 24:22)
WISE WORDS (24:23–34)
SOLOMON'S PROVERBS (25:1 – 29:27)
(AGUR [30:1–33])
ADVICE TO YOUTH (31:1–31)

It is arranged like a multi-layered sandwich. So 'Advice to Youth' provides the outer two layers, then the 'Proverbs of Solomon' are the next two layers, and then the 'Words of the Wise' sandwich 'Advice to Youth' in the middle.

Having seen the structure of the book, let us fill in some details:

PROLOGUE
Why the Proverbs were collected

ADVICE TO YOUTH (1:8 – 9:18)
From a father about bad women

1. *DO:*
   Obey your parents
   Seek and get wisdom
   Keep your heart
   Be faithful to your spouse

2. *DON'T:*
   Get into bad company
   Commit adultery
   Take out loans
   Be lazy
   Befriend foolish women

SOLOMON'S PROVERBS (**10:1 – 22:16**)
Collected by himself

1. *CONTRAST:* godly and wicked lives
2. *CONTENT:* godly life

WISE WORDS (**22:17 – 23:14**)
Egyptian (princess?)

ADVICE TO YOUTH (**23:15 – 24:22**)
More *DO's* ('get wise') and *DON'Ts* ('get drunk')

WISE WORDS (**24:23–34**)
Arab (numerical)

SOLOMON'S PROVERBS (**25:1 – 29:27**)
Copied by Hezekiah

1. *RELATIONSHIPS*
   with kings

    neighbours
    enemies
    yourself
    fools
    sluggards
    gossips

2. *RIGHTEOUSNESS* (**27:1 – 29:27**)
    humility in self
    justice for others
    fear of the Lord

ADVICE TO YOUTH (31:1–31)
From a mother about a good woman

1. *KING OF A NATION*
2. *QUEEN OF A HOME* (**31:10–31**)

The structure and content of the book make a number of things clear:

1 This is one of the few Bible books to spell out its purpose clearly – see the prologue.
2 These proverbs are especially pertinent for the royal family. There are 10 exhortations addressed to 'my son'. These are applicable especially to Solomon's own son, telling him the sort of company that he should keep and the sort of woman he should marry.
3 Most of the proverbs in chapters 10–15 use antithetic parallelism, whereas chapters 16–22 use synonymous parallelism.
4 Whilst we can discern a structure to the book as a whole, the proverbs themselves are not listed in a topical arrangement. They read like the advice that parents would give to a son

leaving home. They are disconnected and disorderly, but they cover the major areas. No parent would prearrange his or her advice into sections with a neat conclusion!

So for the purpose of analysis we will rearrange the proverbs and consider particular themes.

The wise man

In Proverbs a number of synonyms are used to describe wisdom: 'prudence', 'sensible', 'judicious', 'appropriate', 'careful to avoid undesirable consequences'. A wise man is contrasted with the fool, who is reckless, rash, careless and wasteful.

A wise man is able to discern between good and evil, and he knows how to respond to and deal with a situation. He is discreet and realistic, with power to make plans. He makes the most out of life.

The wise are open to correction and reproof, keen to turn away from their own independence and self-reliance towards the light of God's truth. Instead of fearing men, they fear God. The wise man values truth at any price, whether about himself, others or God.

The fool

There are over 70 proverbs about what a fool is like. A fool (always male) is described as ignorant, obstinate, arrogant, perverted, boring, aimless, inexperienced, irresponsible, gullible, careless, complacent, insolent, flippant, sullen, boorish, argumentative. He wants everything on a plate; he doesn't think for himself; he prefers fantasy to fact, illusions to truth. At best he is disturbing; at worst he is dangerous. He is a sorrow to his parents, yet he despises them as old-fashioned.

There are two particular fools in this fools' gallery. One is the *scoffer*, the debunker who is cynical and critical of everybody but himself. The other is the *sluggard*, the lazy man who is hinged to his bed. He is described as throwing his life down the drain.

Words

Another key subject in Proverbs is the tongue. Chapter 6 records seven abominations to the Lord: snobbery, lies, murder, conspiracy, mischief, perjury and gossip. The tongue figures in four of those. So sins of speech are a major topic throughout the book, for what is in the heart comes out of the mouth.

Words are powerful

Words cut deep. They can be cruel, clumsy and careless. Self-esteem can be ruined by words – they can make it too high or too low. Even bodily health can be affected. Our beliefs and convictions are formed by words. A timely word can have an enormous effect.

Words can spread like a prairie fire, causing strife, discord and division. They may be subtle hints, suggestions and innuendoes. But good words can reach many people as their benefit spreads across communities.

Words have their limits

Words are no substitute for deeds. The tongue can't alter facts. Brazen denial and the strongest excuses won't stand.

Words can't compel people to respond. Even the best teacher can't change an apathetic pupil, and even the worst gossip won't hurt the innocent. Only the malicious will pay any attention.

Healthy Speech

There are four categories of words that should be on our lips:

- Honest words – the straightforward 'yes' or 'no'.
- Few words – the less said, the better. Reticence to speak is a virtue.
- Calm words – words should be spoken from a cool spirit. A hot temper is rarely of benefit.
- Apt words – a word matched to the occasion, shaped for the benefit of the hearer or reader, can bring great joy.

Such speech needs time for reflection first. We need to know what we are talking about and to think through the implications before we speak.

Such speech also flows from a person's character, for what a person says comes from what they are. A person's words are worth what he or she is worth.

In the New Testament, James says that if anyone does not sin with his tongue, he is a perfect man.

Family

Proverbs is full of advice about relationships – both family relationships and friendships. The family unit is the pivot of society. Three of the ten commandments that God gave to Moses relate to the family, including the only commandment with a promise – 'Honour your father and your mother, so that

you may live long in the land the Lord your God is giving you'.
Proverbs holds before the reader the following ideals about the
family:

Husband and wife: parents happily united

Proverbs teaches monogamy, despite the fact that it is written
by Solomon! Parents should share their children's training and
should speak with one voice. The man is to be loyal, but a
woman can make or break her husband, bringing blessing or
rottenness to his bones.

The book teaches a very high view of marriage and takes a
serious view of any sin that would break a marriage up, especially sexual infidelity. A person who strays from the marriage
bed loses honour and liberty, throws away their life, courts
social disgrace and physical danger. In short, they commit
moral suicide.

Parents and children: children faithfully trained

We are told that parents are fools if they don't discipline their
children. 'Spare the rod and spoil the child' is one of the
better-known proverbs. The book also says that discipline is a
loving act. There is no suggestion that this is a cure-all for
parents. We also learn that foolishness is bound up in the heart
of a child. They are free to welcome or despise the instruction
they are given. Proverbs teaches that children are naturally
foolish and need encouragement to be wise. This is diametrically opposed to today's humanistic philosophy that says that
the child is basically good and will turn out well if given the
right environment. The Bible is so blunt as to say that if you
don't punish your children quickly when they are doing wrong,
you don't love them.

There is teaching on the need to train children in righteousness from an early age, seeking to foster wise habits, so

that they think and act in ways that will bring joy and pride and not shame and disgrace. Even the best teaching cannot force obedience; it can only encourage wise choices. Even sons of the best parents may still be too rebellious, lazy, indulgent or proud to take advice. They can use up a family fortune and neglect a greedy parent in old age.

Brothers (including cousins and other relatives)

Not many of the proverbs are directly concerned with the horizontal relationships in the family. The book describes the kind of relationship where the brother is helpful and faithful, and also the kind which brings discord, injury and bitterness.

Friendships

The Hebrew word that is translated 'friend' also means 'neighbour'. It refers to all non-relatives who live within the immediate circle of one's relationships. The advice of the book contrasts with today's depersonalized world where true friendship is rare.

Good neighbours

Good neighbours promote peace and harmony, are reluctant to quarrel and are disarmingly kind. They are generous in their judgements and always willing to give help when needed. They appreciate the importance of silence and privacy. They say 'No' to unwise agreements.

Good friends

Proverbs teaches that a few good friends is better than a host of acquaintances. A good friend can be closer than a relative.

A good friend has four qualities:

- *Loyalty* – will stick with you, no matter what.
- *Honesty* – will be frank with you and tell you the truth.
- *Consultancy* – will give you advice. An opposite viewpoint may be what is required.
- *Courtesy* – will always respect your feelings and refuse to trade on your affection.

Conclusion

What should we make of the Book of Proverbs? Let us begin by asking whether it achieved its objective. Israel was now in a position of peace and prosperity. Solomon realized that they could lose all this so easily (although he didn't realize that he himself would cause that loss).

In chapter 14 we are told that 'Righteousness exalts a nation, but sin is a disgrace to any people'. Solomon collected the proverbs into a book because he knew that without wisdom it would be impossible for Israel to remain in peace and prosperity. But Israel largely ignored the wisdom they received; they moved further away from God. Indeed, even Solomon didn't live by his own wisdom.

There is a great deal in the New Testament that builds on the Book of Proverbs and focuses on the theme of wisdom. The book is quoted 14 times directly, and there are many other occasions when it is alluded to.

In Luke 1 we read that John the Baptist came 'to turn ... the disobedient to the wisdom of the righteous'. Jesus spoke with such wisdom that his hearers asked where he got this wisdom from.

Most people are familiar with the Wise Men who followed a star to Bethlehem. Whilst they have been commonly regarded as Gentiles, it is more likely that they were descendants of the Jews who had been left behind in Babylon after the Exile. They had remembered the prophecy of Balaam, that a star would arise out of Israel to be the King of the Nations (Numbers 24), so when they saw it they followed it. Their presence in Matthew's birth narrative says much about the importance of Christ's incarnation.

Jesus was said to be 'filled with wisdom' as a child (Luke 2). In his public ministry he said that the Queen of Sheba came from the ends of the earth to listen to Solomon's wisdom, but now One greater than Solomon had come (Luke 11). When Jesus was criticized for eating and drinking, he replied that 'wisdom is proved right by all her children' (Luke 7).

Reflecting on the life of Jesus, the apostle Paul wrote in 1 Corinthians 1 that 'Christ is our wisdom. He has become for us wisdom from God'.

The wisdom of God is seen supremely in the cross. The world says that dying on a cross is sheer folly. But Paul says that what was foolishness to the world was the wisdom of God.

Within the New Testament epistles there are many direct quotations from the Book of Proverbs. Paul writes in Romans 12: 'If your enemy is hungry, feed him; if he is thirsty, give him something to drink. In doing this, you will heap burning coals on his head'.

Peter frequently quotes from Proverbs. For example, in 2 Peter 2 he quotes from Proverbs 26: 'As a dog returns to its vomit, so a fool repeats his folly.' Peter's exhortation to his readers to 'fear the Lord and honour the King' comes straight out of Proverbs 24.

In Hebrews 12 the writer quotes from Proverbs 3 with respect to God's discipline of his children: 'My son, do not make light of the Lord's discipline, and do not lose heart when he rebukes you, because the Lord disciplines those he loves, and he punishes everyone he accepts as a son'.

In Proverbs 30, Agur asks the question, 'Who has gone up to heaven and come down?' Jesus answers this very question in John 3, when he speaks of his own journey from heaven to earth.

But the Letter of James is where the Proverbs are especially used. This epistle has been called the New Testament version of Proverbs, since it is so similar in style. It moves swiftly from topic to topic with little sense of order, just like its Old Testament counterpart. Some of the themes in James come from Proverbs, not least a devastating analysis of the evils of the tongue and a description of the benefits of wisdom.

Proverbs may seem a strange book to be included in the Bible, but closer inspection shows that its place is thoroughly justified. It deals with some of the major themes of Scripture, it is quoted and alluded to by other parts of the Bible and is an important part of the Christian's arsenal in his or her fight against foolish living. But it is not an easy book. Care must be taken in reading it, and many of its lessons will find us out.

15.

ECCLESIASTES

Introduction

The Book of Ecclesiastes includes some statements that many would regard as debatable. Consider which of the following you would agree with:

- Generations come and generations go, but the world stays just the same.
- A man is no better off than an animal, because life has no meaning for either.
- It is better to be satisfied with what you have than to always want something else.
- A working man may or may not have enough to eat, but at least he can get a good night's sleep. A rich man has so much that he stays awake worrying!
- Don't be too good or too wise. Why kill yourself? But don't be too wicked or too foolish either. Why die before you have to?
- I found one man in a thousand that I could respect, but not one woman!
- Fast runners do not always win the race, and the brave do not always win the battle.
- Put your investment in several places – in many places, even – because you never know what kind of bad luck you're going to have in this world!

There's a saying which is especially true for our study of this book: 'A text out of context becomes a pretext.' In other words, we must see how the text functions within the book in which it is found before we quote it. The above statements were part of the writer's reflections, but they must not be taken out of the context of the book as a whole.

Ecclesiastes is probably the strangest book in the Bible. Although it is easy to understand, it says the most outrageous things. In places it reads like the mottoes on slips of paper that we find in Christmas crackers. In other places it has a poetic quality. These lines from the English poet, Alfred Lord Tennyson, could easily have been written by the author of Ecclesiastes:

> 'Tis better to have loved and lost
> Than never to have loved at all.
>
> *In Memoriam*

> For men at most differ as heaven and earth,
> But women, worst and best, as heaven and hell.
>
> *Pelleas and Ettare*

> Authority forgets a dying king.
>
> *Morte' d'Arthur*

> Our little systems have their day,
> They have their day and cease to be.
>
> *In the Valley of Cauteretz*

> Because right is right, to follow right
> Were wisdom in the scorn of consequence.
>
> *The Revenge*

But despite its strangeness, Ecclesiastes has a very contemporary ring to it and features many of the philosophical ideas of our own day:

■ *Fatalism:* whatever will be, will be.
■ *Existentialism:* live for the present moment – who knows what the future will bring?
■ *Chauvinism:* men are better than women.
■ *Hedonism:* living for pleasure.
■ *Cynicism:* even good things aren't what they seem.
■ *Pessimism:* things are bound to get worse.

The book's author

This book of philosophical speculation comes from King Solomon, who has reached the end of his life and is disappointed, disillusioned and hopeless. When we read Solomon's three books, it is easy to tell how old he was when he wrote them. The Song of Songs was written when he was a young man, deeply in love. Proverbs is the book of a middle-aged man trying to stop his son from falling into the same errors that he himself succumbed to. But in Ecclesiastes we have the writings of an older man. Confirmation of this is found in a verse towards the end of the book, in chapter 12: 'Remember your Creator in the days of your youth, before the days of trouble come and the years approach when you will say, "I find no pleasure in them"'.

As an old man, he has reflected deeply upon life. He is fond of the phrase, 'I saw …' The insights in this book are the result of his observations.

The book's style

Solomon gives himself the Hebrew title *Qohelet*, a word that is translated in various ways: 'preacher', or 'philosopher' or 'lecturer'. But the best translation is 'speaker', particularly as this is also the title of the person who presides over the debates in the House of Commons, and so conveys very well the way in which the book is written. For it is written in the style of an old man presiding over a debate – a debate that is going on in his mind. Like every good speaker, he allows the pros and the cons to be given equal opportunity. So the motion that life is not worth living is followed by a motion proclaiming that it is.

As such, the book is contemporary for all centuries, as people have always engaged in similar debates, especially as they reach their forties and ask, 'What is it all about?' Some people make radical changes in their lifestyle because they feel that they are missing out on life.

In Ecclesiastes, Solomon is asking some big questions. What is life about? Is life worth living? How can we make the most of life? He is asking the right questions, even if he hasn't found the right answers. His concerns and answers oscillate throughout the book. His *message* is sometimes optimistic, sometimes pessimistic. His *mood* is at one time uplifting, then depressing. The book's *merit* switches from the profound to the superficial and back again.

Negative statements

Solomon's opening statement is a profoundly negative one: 'Meaningless! Meaningless! … Everything is meaningless!'. The word translated as 'meaningless' could also be rendered as 'emptiness'. Here's a man who gets to the end of his life and says that it's all been pointless and useless.

It is important to remember that Solomon was a king who had the power to do anything he wanted and the wealth to indulge every whim. The book mentions the huge range of activities in which Solomon engaged in an attempt to find the happiness that eluded him.

He tried science and agriculture, even breeding his own cattle. Then he moved on to the arts. No doubt he inherited a love of music from his father. He built some great buildings. He gathered pictures from around the world and placed them in a gallery. Then he turned to entertainment, with court comedians visiting him in his palace. But none of this satisfied him. He was involved in business, and amassed a fortune in the commercial world. He tried pleasure – food, wine and women. Still dissatisfied, he turned to philosophy and bought many books, including some from Egypt. They stimulated him but failed to meet his deepest needs.

There was nothing wrong with these interests in themselves, but they failed to provide what he was looking for. His life was filled but not fulfilled, and at times he wished that he was just an ordinary man.

We can explain his failure to make sense of life. The nub of his problem was that he has *observed* so much but had *perceived* so little. He had tunnel vision – he was looking at life through one eye, as in a telescope, but he had no depth and no perspective.

There were two limitations in particular:

1. Space

On 28 occasions he uses a phrase to describe the location of everything he saw: it was 'under the sun', a phrase that occurs nowhere else in the whole Bible. If our vision is limited to this earth and this life, we will never understand what life is all about and what makes it worth living. We will have to depend upon finding fulfilment in the fleeting pleasures that the world can offer.

2. Time

Solomon also uses the phrase 'while we are still alive'. He assumes that death is the end of meaningful, conscious existence. He has no thought of the afterlife, which can give perspective and meaning to the years of life that we are allotted.

Our modern age shares some of Solomon's tunnel vision. It often observes the world in scientific terms that assume that there is no God and no life to come. Science can tell us how the world came into being, but not why. Solomon needs to look at life from a different angle, but this will only come if he looks at it from God's viewpoint.

Positive statements

The unresolved questions of the book sometimes give way to optimism. Our ignorance need not lead to despair; it may be that we are ignorant because no one knows, or because God knows but we don't yet see it ourselves. Whenever Solomon brings God into his thinking, he becomes more positive. There are two passages in Ecclesiastes where this is especially true.

The first is in chapter 3. This is the best known and most frequently quoted section of the book. Its verses have often been used as titles for novels and films. It is a poem with a lovely rhythm, reminding us that there is a time and place for everything.

God is sovereign,
Sets the seasons:
Date of birthday,
Day of death.
Time for planting,
Time for reaping;
Time for killing,
Time to heal.

Time for wrecking,
Time for building;
Time for sorrow,
Time for joy.
Time for mourning,
Time for dancing;
Time for kissing,
Time to stop!

Time for finding,
Time for losing;
Time for saving,
Time for waste.
Time for tearing,
Time for mending;
Time for silence,
Time to talk.

Time for loving,
Time for hating;
Time for fighting,
Time for peace.
Have your fun, then,
But remember ...

God is sovereign;
HE decrees.[1]

Most readers miss a key verse when the poetry ends and the text returns to prose. We read that God himself 'has made everything beautiful in its time'. So the overall emphasis is not upon human decision but divine decree. The New English Bible translates the verse as follows: 'Everything that happens in this world happens at the time God chooses.'

It is this perspective that brings light to our pessimism about life. When we believe that our lives are in God's hands and that he knows the right time for us to dance and to weep, then we see that the things that happen to us are not chance, but part of God's choice for us. He is weaving a pattern out of our lives.

Some believe that this approach is fatalistic, that it suggests an impersonal fate that nobody can affect. But this is quite different from God freely choosing what he allows to happen to us. Our free will never overrides God's. He will be at work in all things to achieve his purposes. He calls us to choose his way, surrendering our wills to his sovereign control. We are both accountable and responsible for the lives we live.

This approach to life is reflected elsewhere in the Bible. We are encouraged to see all the plans we make in the light of God's sovereign will. All plans are made 'God willing'. My father had a favourite saying: 'Life is long enough to live out God's purpose, but it's too short to waste a moment.' This is the message of chapter 3. Our times are in his hands, and he will decide what is best for us in the future.

The other passage that has a strong sense of the presence of God is in chapters 11 and 12. The Living Bible translates it as follows:

1 This may be sung to the popular tune, 'I am sailing'.

It is a wonderful thing to be alive! If a person lives to be very old, let him rejoice in every day of life, but let him also remember that eternity is far longer, and that everything down here is futile in comparison.

Young man, it's wonderful to be young! Enjoy every minute of it! Do all you want to; take in everything, but realize that you must account to God for everything you do.

So banish grief and pain, but remember that youth, with a whole life before it, can make serious mistakes.

Don't let the excitement of being young cause you to forget about your Creator.

Honour him in your youth before the evil years come – when you'll no longer enjoy living. It will be too late then to try to remember him, when the sun and light and moon and stars are dim to your old eyes, and there is no silver lining left among your clouds. For there will come a time when your limbs will tremble with age, and your strong legs will become weak, and your teeth will be too few to do their work, and there will be blindness, too. Then let your lips be tightly closed while eating, when your teeth are gone! And you will waken at dawn with the first note of the birds; but you yourself will be deaf and tuneless, with quavering voice. You will be afraid of heights and of falling – a white-haired, withered old man, dragging himself along: without sexual desire, standing at death's door, and nearing his everlasting home as the mourners go along the streets.

Yes, remember your Creator now while you are young, before the silver cord of life snaps, and the golden bowl is broken, and the pitcher is broken at the fountain, and the wheel is broken at the cistern; and the dust returns to the earth as it was, and the spirit returns to God who gave it. All is futile, says the Preacher; utterly futile.

But then, because the Preacher was wise, he went on teaching the people all he knew; and he collected proverbs and classified them. For the Preacher was not only a wise man, but a good teacher; he not only taught what he knew to the people, but taught them in an interesting manner.

The wise man's words are like goads that spur to action. They nail down important truths. Students are wise who master what their teachers tell them.

But, my son, be warned: there is no end of opinions ready to be expressed. Studying them can go on forever, and become very exhausting!

Here is my final conclusion: fear God and obey his commandments, for this is the entire duty of man. For God will judge us for everything we do, including every hidden thing, good or bad.

There are some helpful points to note in this last passage of the book:

Remember

Solomon urges his hearers, especially those who are young, to remember God. This advice probably came from his own experience – the Song of Songs has no mention of God, for example. He is saying that he would not have faced the trauma of wondering what life was all about if he had only remembered God earlier in his life.

Fear

He urges his hearers to fear God. The wisdom literature of the Bible constantly tells us that the fear of the Lord is the beginning of wisdom. If we truly fear God, we are not afraid of anything or anyone else. We must fear God, because he is going to ask us for an account of the life he has given us.

Jesus told his followers not to fear those who can kill the body but rather to 'Fear him who, after the killing of the body, has power to throw you into hell' (Luke 12). If people outside the Church don't fear God, it's because people inside it don't fear him either.

Obey

Solomon knew that he had not obeyed God as he should. Nevertheless he tells his readers to be careful to obey God. He now knows that God's laws are given for our good, not to spoil life but to help us to make the most of it. He talks of this as 'the whole duty of man' (chapter 12). Our responsibilities are more important than our rights.

Conclusion

Solomon had collected and collated proverbs, but he had delved into too many other philosophies as well. Here was a man who had read too much and had become disillusioned in the process. So much of the emptiness in the Book of Ecclesiastes comes from these other philosophies. The book shows the limits of human wisdom and is a salutary reminder of the sort of person we will become if we don't discover God's way to live.

God has included this strange book in the Bible because it allows us to examine the wrong ideas alongside the good and true ones. It faces us with the pessimistic and fatalistic view of life, showing us the best that human thinking can provide.

It tells us that if we don't understand the meaning of life from heaven's angle and from the angle of the next world, we finish up disillusioned, disappointed and depressed.

Of course, the Bible doesn't leave us with the pessimism of this book. The New Testament tells us that Christ is our wisdom. Through him we find out both *why* and *how* we should live life.

John 17 tells us that true life is to know him. He is the Alpha and the Omega, the One who ensures that life really does have meaning and purpose.

16.

JOB

Introduction

Many common phrases in the English language come from the Book of Job. Someone who shows fortitude in the face of great suffering is said to have 'the patience of Job'. People whose words make the sufferer feel worse are called 'Job's comforters'.

The Anglican funeral service uses a line from the early part of the book: 'the Lord gave, and the Lord hath taken away; blessed be the name of the Lord' (AV). Music lovers will be familiar with the refrain, 'I know that my redeemer liveth' (AV), which Handel used in the *Messiah*. But despite people's familiarity with a few verses from Job, the book as a whole is not well known. Most people fail to understand the purpose of the book, and are thus unable to put the parts that they do know into an appropriate context.

The Book of Job may be one of the oldest books that we possess today, though it is not easy to date it. We know that it comes from Abraham's era, because so many details in the book could only fit that period. The author uses the name 'Yahweh' to refer to God, just as Moses does, but there is no trace of the Exodus, the Covenant of Sinai or the Law of Moses, which were so fundamental to the Old Testament.

Readers of Job are immediately faced with a question that determines the way in which they read the book. Is it fact, fiction or a mixture of the two – 'faction'?

Fact?

Those who believe it to be fact emphasize that other biblical writers treat Job as a real person. Ezekiel lists him with Noah and Daniel as one of the three most righteous men who ever lived. In the New Testament, James refers to Job's perseverance as an example for his readers.

Furthermore, the opening chapter tells us that Job lived 'In the land of Uz'. Although the whereabouts of Uz is uncertain, we can be confident that Job lived in the Mesopotamian Basin, around the Rivers Tigris and Euphrates beyond Damascus.

In addition, the story line suggests a real person. His reactions to the disasters that he faces are realistic and the descriptions of his personal feelings seem authentic. His discussions with his wife are what we might typically expect, and the comments of his friends and the arguments that follow seem true to life. His ownership of significant numbers of livestock is normal for a wealthy farmer.

Fiction?

Many are unconvinced by these arguments. Despite the plausibility of so much of the book, the reader has a sense that there is something that doesn't seem to ring true to life.

For example, take the events of the first chapter. There are four consecutive disasters, with each leaving one survivor who returns to Job to describe the incident. It is stretching credulity to think that all four disasters have just one survivor and that each would choose the same words: 'I am the only one who has escaped to tell you!'

Also the happy ending seems contrived. Job loses all his children in the first scene, yet in the last he has exactly the same number of new children – seven boys and three girls. We are clearly supposed to rejoice in the happy ending, almost as if the loss of his former children is insignificant to him. It makes us ask the question, 'Is this too neat for reality? Are we supposed to take this as fact?'

Questions about the factual basis of the book are also raised when we consider the speeches, for each one is written in Hebrew poetry. We have already noted in Part I that poetry is an artificial form of speech. It would not be used in conversation, and certainly not to discuss the weighty issues considered by Job and his friends. Yet all Job's 'comforters' speak in superbly crafted poems, which begs the question, 'Who committed the poetry to paper?' Either all his friends were brilliant poets with outstanding memories, or we will have to think of an alternative explanation.

'Faction'?

The only solution that makes sense is to say that the Book of Job is *faction* – that is, it is based on fact, but the facts have been enlarged and embroidered. So Job is a real person who has to make sense of disaster and ongoing suffering, alongside a belief in the God of the Bible.

So the Book of Job is similar to some of the plays of William Shakespeare, who took the basic historical facts about people such as Henry V and produced plays that emphasized the inner motivations of the characters. A more modern example would be Robert Bolt's play, *A Man for All Seasons*, based on the life of Sir Thomas More. Bolt captures the essence of the issues that the man faced, but the audience knows that the end product is not the same as the real events.

Literature

The Book of Job is written in Hebrew poetry that depends upon sense and repetition and not upon sound for its beauty. It is a great work of literature and defies strict classification. It combines epic poetry, drama and debate with an intriguing plot and profound dialogue. Not surprisingly, the book has been much admired by some of the greatest minds. Thomas Carlyle said, 'It is a noble book', Alfred Lord Tennyson described it as 'the greatest poem of ancient or modern times' and Martin Luther said, 'It is most magnificent, sublime, as no other book of Scripture.' It has been placed on a par with the works of Homer, Virgil, Dante, Milton and Shakespeare as one of the greatest pieces of literature of all time.

Philosophy

But Job is more than a great work of literature – it is also a work of philosophy. It asks the questions that philosophers have pondered throughout the history of mankind: Why are we here? What is life about? Where did evil come from? Why do good people suffer? What is God's involvement in the world? Is he interested and does he care?

Job covers all these themes, but especially the question, Why do good people suffer? Job was clearly a good man, but experienced the most appalling tragedy. The book addresses the issue of why this should be.

Theology

Job is also a book of theology. Philosophy can deal with the big questions in an abstract manner, but theology relates these questions to God. It is important to note from the outset that only those who have a particular view of God have difficulties with the fact of suffering. If you believe that God is bad, then there is no problem about suffering, because you would expect a bad God to make you suffer. Only if you believe that God is good do you have a problem. Furthermore, you may believe that God is good but weak, and so is unable to do anything to help you. Again, on the grounds of logic, you should then have no problem with suffering, since a weak God can sympathize but cannot help. Only when we believe that God is both *able* to help and *good* in his nature do we have a problem with suffering.

Many 'modern theologians' try to avoid the problem of suffering by denying one or the other of those two things: they reason that either God is bad and is playing tricks on us, or he is too weak to affect anything. But it is clear that the author of the Book of Job believes:

1 that there is one God.
2 that he relates to his creatures.
3 that he is the almighty, all-powerful Creator.
4 that he is good, caring and compassionate.

Yet at the same time the book describes Job's situation, which seems to fly in the face of such beliefs. The reader is left to see how Job deals with this conflict and how God makes himself known in the midst of it.

Wisdom literature

It is important that we also understand that the Book of Job is part of the 'wisdom literature' in English Bibles, along with Proverbs, Psalms, Ecclesiastes and the Song of Songs. In the Hebrew Bible these books are called the 'Writings', a miscellaneous collection of texts which came out of the prophetic period but which are not regarded as prophecy. Understanding the Book of Job in this way should help us to interpret it correctly, because some statements in wisdom literature can be misleading. Let me explain in more detail.

First, not everything in wisdom literature is right. It includes passages where men wrestle with questions. Their statements do not always reflect God's mind, but they are included to show the argument being made, and providing that we see their purpose, we can interpret them without any problem. Job's friends make many statements based on a limited understanding. They are given to show us examples of how people come to terms with suffering, but to take any of their statements out of context, as if they expressed God's mind on the matter, would be the height of folly. Every statement in the Bible must be seen in the context of the book in which it appears. The message of the book as a whole determines the meaning of any statement within it.

Secondly, it is important to note that wisdom literature is general and not particular. This means that words of wisdom are not always true in every situation. The Book of Proverbs, for example, is not a list of promises but includes sayings that are generally true most of the time.

If you try to claim that they are true in every situation, you will be disappointed. This gives the clue to the problem that Job and his friends faced. They were aware of proverbs indicating that if you live a bad life you suffer for it. This is often true, but not always, and Job is part of the 'but not always'. The Book of Job is trying to deal with the exceptions to the rule.

A Jewish perspective

We must bear in mind one acute difference between a Jewish understanding of this book and a Christian one. The Jew of Old Testament times was unable to see the problems of temporal life in the light of eternity. He felt that the justice of God must be seen in this life, since both good and bad people went to the same destination – *Sheol*, the place of shadowy existence where departed spirits slept.

Christians, of course, have a totally different perspective on present suffering. In the light of Christ's work, they see the bigger picture of heaven. Suffering in this world is small compared to the life that will be enjoyed in heaven.

So throughout the Book of Job there are only hints about life after death. Job declares at one point that he will see God when he is dead, but this is not a common theme, and he certainly does not understand how this might take place.

The book's structure

The introduction creates a marvellous tension that underpins the whole framework of the book. God makes a wager with Satan, and that wager is settled in Job's body. But at no point does Job know that the wager has taken place. So this secret, known by the reader, helps to keep us guessing as Job faces the dilemmas of his situation.

Such a plot is extremely risky, as it makes suggestions about God's character and activity, in particular, his relationship with

Satan, which would be the height of blasphemy if it were not true – that God himself was responsible for Satan's attack on this good man.

Let us now consider how the book is structured:

THE PROLOGUE (**chapters 1–2**) (prose)
Two rounds: God versus Satan.

THE DIALOGUE (**3:1–42:6**) (poetry)
1. *Human* (**3–37**)
   (a) Eliphaz, Bildad, Zophar (**3–31**)
     (i)   Round One (**3–14**)
     (ii) Round Two (**15–21**)
     (iii) Round Three (**22–31**)
   (b) Elihu (**32–37**) – a monologue

2. *Divine* (**38:1–42:6**)
     (i) Round One (**38–39**)
     (ii) Round Two (**40:1–42:6**)

THE EPILOGUE (**42:7–17**) (prose)
Final rounds: God versus Job.

The Book of Job is arranged like a sandwich. The prose is the 'bread', providing the story and the background at the beginning and the end, while the poetry is the 'filling' in the middle, consisting of the debate that Job has with his three friends and a youth who appears when the friends have left.

The epilogue provides the resolution to what has gone before. It is a happy ending, with a difference.

Two plots

There are two plots skilfully woven together – a heavenly plot and an earthly plot. The events that happen on earth are the result of something that has already happened in heaven – just as in the Book of Revelation there is war on earth directly after a war in heaven.

The divine plot

The book begins with the heavenly plot – God's meeting in heaven with Satan. Satan was an angel whose job was to report sins. He was God's counsel for the prosecution who travelled across the earth to report to God what human beings were like. By the time of Job, Satan had reached such a point of cynicism that he couldn't believe that anyone would love God for his own sake. He thought people only loved God for what they could get out of him.

So there is a debate between God and Satan, with Satan arguing this very point. God asks Satan whether he met Job when he visited the earth. God argues that Job loves him because he loves him, and not because of any blessing he has received.

Satan continues to be cynical in his reply, claiming that if God were to take away his blessings, Job would curse God just like all the others. And so the heavenly wager takes place.

The key to every good drama is tension. While the reader is aware of the heavenly wager, Job is not. If he knew, the test would not be valid.

This interaction teaches us important lessons about Satan. First, it implies that he cannot be in more than one place at once. He does not have God's omnipresence. So when people say that Satan is troubling them because something trivial has gone wrong, they are mistaken. He generally has more important work to do with other people! What some people call 'satanic attack' should be more properly called 'demonic attack'. Satan's forces are at work all over the world, but that is not to say that Satan himself is personally involved.

This wrong thinking about Satan has arisen partly because we follow the error of the ancient Greeks and divide the world into the 'natural' and the 'supernatural'. We assume that Satan must be supernatural, and so we place him alongside God, as if he is equal in power and authority. Instead we should divide the world as the Bible does, with the Creator on one side and his creatures (including Satan) on the other. Satan is not omnipotent, omniscient or omnipresent; he is a mere creature.

Secondly, Satan needs God's permission to attack Job. Satan cannot touch a person who belongs to God unless God gives him permission. In the New Testament, God promises all believers that they will never be tempted above what they can bear, because he controls the tempter.

The human plot

The larger part of the book describes the debate between Job and his friends. The key question that is addressed is, 'Why is Job suffering more than other people?'

There are two viewpoints:

a the friends are sure that the suffering has come because Job is sinning;

b Job is quite sure that he's not sinning and protests his innocence.

Since the reader knows that Job is correct, the dialogue is alive with tension.

The two-plot structure of the book reminds us that none of us knows the whole picture when it comes to understanding the reason for suffering. Beyond looking for reasons, everyone is faced with a bigger question: Can I continue to believe in a good God when everything's going wrong? The Book of Job gives an answer to this question.

The importance of this issue is clarified by asking, 'What was Job's greatest pain?' Was it

- *physical*? He was afflicted with sores from head to toe, he was tired and weary, and was in considerable physical pain.
- *social?* His physical appearance and the local community's knowledge of his recent tragedy made him a social outcast. He sat on the ash-heap at the end of the village, and people walked on the other side of the street rather than talk to him. Even the teenagers laughed at him.
- *mental?* He faced the mental pain of not knowing why these distressing things were happening to him, especially as there seemed to be nothing in his past to point to.
- *spiritual?* His spiritual pain was far greater than any other, for he felt that he had lost touch with God. He cried out, asking that he might find him, talk to him, even argue with him! This was the real, the deepest pain. The agony of suffering is compounded if we feel that God is far away and no longer cares. (However, when Job was finally able to speak with God, it didn't turn out as he had imagined.)

The prologue

The prologue introduces us to the characters in the story:

God

God (who is called *Yahweh*) initiates the whole series of events by challenging Satan.

Satan

Satan is the counsel for the prosecution. In the Hebrew text he is called '*the* satan', which means 'the accuser'; 'satan' is not yet a proper name.

Job

Job is described as 'blameless and upright; he feared God and shunned evil'. Those two things belong together: the fear of God leads to the shunning of evil. If you lack the fear of God, then you're not so worried about sin. God is clearly pleased with Job's piety and has blessed him with children, property and good health.

Job's wife

It is difficult to write about Job's wife without appearing negative! The text describes her as 'a foolish woman', meaning that she is insensitive to Job's plight. She urges him to 'Curse God and die!'. Just when he needs support and help, she is the first one to bring him pain. She tells Job that God has deserted him and proceeds to do the same.

Job's friends

Job's three friends are older than him. They begin by sitting with him and not saying a word for seven days.

The human dialogue

Job eventually breaks the silence by cursing the day he was born. He wishes he had been stillborn and had gone to *Sheol*, which was the unconscious, shadowy afterlife that the people of Old Testament times believed in. At least then he would be at peace instead of in constant pain. It is gloomy, self-pitying talk, though never for one moment does he think of taking his life.

Each of the three friends speaks three times, but for the purposes of analysis we will put their speeches together.

Eliphaz

Eliphaz's speeches suggest that he is an elder statesman – a pious, mystical man. Unlike Job's other friends, he is gentle in his approach. He believes that Job is being punished because he has sinned. He bases his view on the orthodox doctrine of reward and punishment, on history itself, and on the cumulative wisdom of the age. In short, if Job has not sinned, then why is he being punished?

Furthermore, he makes reference to a vision he has had, which has confirmed to him that Job's punishment is thoroughly merited by his behaviour. He explains that because human nature is inherently evil, nobody can say that they are innocent before God. Since we are all sinners, Job should just admit that sin is the reason for his pain. When Job asks why he suffers more than others, Eliphaz tells him that suffering is God's way of making him a better person.

Although the advice is very gentle, Job doesn't take it, so Eliphaz becomes more impassioned in his argument, claiming that Job is obstinate to insist on his innocence, and also that he is irreverent and keen to undermine religious belief. Eliphaz clearly resents Job's antipathy to his views, and eventually his sympathy gives way to sarcasm. He argues that since we are all totally depraved, we can't grumble about suffering. The wicked won't prosper, and even if they do, they won't be happy – they will only seem to be happy.

Finally, when Job still doesn't respond, Eliphaz speaks of God's transcendence. He claims that God is too big to be concerned, so Job shouldn't expect God's attention.

A transcendent God can't be bothered with every individual life.

Bildad

Bildad's name actually means 'God's darling', but his words fail to match his name. Traditionally, the older person would speak first in such a situation, and Bildad is clearly a bit younger than Eliphaz – probably around 50 years of age.

Bildad is the 'theologian' of the three and a traditionalist *par excellence*. He is full of clichés, jargon and formulas, and has very little patience or compassion for Job. He tells Job that he has lost his children because they were sinners who deserved God's wrath. He believes in a moral universe, with the law of cause and effect applying to our moral life as well as to our material life.

As far as Bildad is concerned, if you sin, you suffer, so Job must be a pretty bad sinner. It is not surprising that in the course of the dialogue his relationship with Job becomes increasingly strained.

Eventually he tells Job that he is talking nonsense. He takes refuge in God's omnipotence, asking Job if he has forgotten that God is all-powerful. Since God is bigger than we are, we can't argue with him, so why not just accept it?

His bottom line is similar to the argument that Eliphaz made: God's omnipotence is the answer.

Zophar

The next man to speak with Job is the most dogmatic of the three. He is younger than the first two, but still middle-aged. We might call Zophar 'Joe Blunt', because he accuses Job of talking to cover up his guilt. He claims that even if Job isn't consciously sinning, he must be sinning unconsciously. He insults Job and tells him to choose between the broad way and the narrow way – that is, the wicked way and the righteous way. He admits to being puzzled by the prosperity of the wicked, but claims that it is short-lived. Since Job's prosperity has gone, he must be wicked. Zophar reminds Job that God is omniscient, and so he knows the sins that Job is not conscious of.

***

The arguments of Job's three 'friends' have much in common. They all assume that we live in a cause-and-effect moral universe, and they try to force the facts to fit their beliefs. They take refuge in doctrine and they try to force it upon Job insensitively. Indeed, their arguments are examples of how *not* to apply biblical doctrine! We need to hold firmly to clear doctrines, but we also need to be careful about how we apply them to individual cases. For example, it is sometimes true to say that someone is not healed because they don't have faith, but one would need considerable wisdom to know when this maxim should be applied to a particular person. Great damage can be done if we aren't wise.

Having noted all this, the three friends' speeches are not all bad, and they contain hints of the ultimate answer that God will bring.

Job

Job makes ten speeches: three to Eliphaz, three to Bildad, three to Zophar and one to Elihu. In these speeches Job is basically saying that God is responsible for his suffering. He explains that he can't repent because he's not conscious of any sin. He has sought to live rightly in God's sight.

There seems to be a clear *progression* or development in his speeches. We can detect an increasing boldness, both in what he says to his friends and in what he would like to say to God.

There is a definite *alternation* between despair and hopelessness on the one hand and confidence and hope on the other. Such mood swings are often characteristic of people who are ill. Sometimes he hopes that things will turn out better, and at other times he fears that they are going to turn out worse. He asks God to leave him alone, and yet he talks frankly and honestly with him. He wants to put God in the dock and claims to be able to win a case against him. He hints at a belief in life after death, but it is hard to tell whether this is part of a buoyant mood swing or a settled belief.

There are two outstanding chapters in Job's speeches. The first is chapter 28, a song about *wisdom*. Wisdom is described as a woman to be desired, rather as Solomon describes wisdom in the Book of Proverbs. Job talks nostalgically about the days when he was respected and his words were valued.

The other outstanding passage is chapter 31, a protest about Job's *innocence*. He recounts the areas where his behaviour was above reproach. He agrees that if he had violated these standards, the punishment would be just; but he protests that he has not. He claims there is no reason for his punishment.

This final speech brings stalemate. Eliphaz, Bilbad and Zophar leave him, to be replaced by a youth named Elihu, who has been listening to Job's arguments.

Elihu

Elihu has the arrogance of youth. He claims to be hesitant to speak, but he seems unable to stop. He gives Job what he claims are the latest ideas, but in the end he has nothing new to say. He refutes Job's arguments, but his approach is the same as that of the three earlier speakers – he tries to convince Job of his sin.

He says God uses different ways of saving people from themselves – visions, dreams in the night, and sometimes sickness. The suffering that Job is enduring is God's chosen method for him. He is helping him to mend his ways before he dies. Job doesn't dignify the speech with a reply, so finally Elihu leaves too.

We noted earlier that wisdom literature must be carefully interpreted. Some of the statements made by the four 'comforters' are clearly not true, because they are talking about things they do not fully understand. But in other respects what they say is true; their error is in the way that they apply their wisdom. They take the proverb, 'Whatever a man sows, he will also reap', and they assume that it must apply to Job's situation.

Furthermore, their appeal to God's character is inappropriate. They misread how it might apply to Job. Eliphaz appeals to God's transcendence, saying that he's bigger than we are and is too far away to be concerned about us. Bildad appeals to God's power and Zophar to God's knowledge of everything.

So the friends were half right, as Job would find out, but taken as a whole, the answers they offered him were inadequate.

The divine dialogue

Round one: – the Creator

During his speeches, 36 times Job asked God to speak with him. Now he gets his wish. On both occasions when God speaks to Job, it is out of a storm. There is much humour in the way that God addresses him. God reminds Job that he is the Creator of all things. He runs through his awesome activity of creating and sustaining the world, asking Job whether he could match this work. He finishes by asking whether Job is in a position to judge, telling him that it is impertinent for Job to believe that God should explain himself to him. Job is made to feel very small.

Eventually Job replies, 'I am unworthy – how can I reply to you? I put my hand over my mouth. I spoke once, but I have no answer – twice, but I will say no more'.

Round two: creatures

In the second round God doesn't talk about himself as Creator, but about two of his creatures. Once more the dialogue is full of humour. He asks Job for his thoughts about the hippopotamus ('behemoth') and the crocodile ('leviathan'), as if the answer to the great questions about life can be found in these extraordinary creatures!

Job is being reminded that he can't understand God. He can't understand the animal world, never mind the moral world. So the point of God's speech is, 'Why are you trying to argue with me?'

Job replies that God knows all things, that no plan of his can be thwarted. He now realizes that his questioning of God was totally inappropriate, and he despises himself and repents in dust and ashes.

Although the encounter with God is humiliating for Job, the heart of his problem is dealt with, for he is back in touch with God again. The dialogue provides a magnificent, if unexpected, climax to the book.

The epilogue

When Job has accepted that he should not reproach God for his dealings with him, the text changes from poetry to prose. God gives him back his children (seven sons and three daughters), his property and his flocks of camels and sheep, so that

Job becomes far wealthier and happier than he ever was before. He is vindicated as God's servant.

God is, however, deeply critical of Job's three friends. He says they have not spoken accurately about Job, which tells us that we shouldn't quote their speeches as if they were truth.

The fascinating thing about the two 'rounds' with God is that God still doesn't give Job any answers to his questions, and neither does he tell Job about his wager with Satan. God had his reasons for allowing Job to suffer, and it wasn't good for Job to know what had gone on in heaven.

Conclusions

It is useful for us to note the different conclusions that can be drawn from the Book of Job.

Jewish conclusions

A Jewish reader would draw the following conclusions from the book:

1 There is no strict correlation between sin and suffering in this life.
2 God allows all suffering.
3 We may never know the reason why. Some suffering can be sent to us as punishment. But even if it is not, it can be purposeful even if the reason is hidden from us.
4 If sin and suffering were directly related, we would be forced to be godly for purely selfish reasons. Love for God and people would not be voluntary.

Christian conclusions

For Christians the Book of Job can be seen in the context of the New Testament:

1 Job knew the God of nature, not the God of grace. The cross of Jesus puts a different value on human suffering. Job is a 'type' of Christ, foreshadowing the One who suffered innocently centuries later. Jesus was a righteous man, yet he suffered as if he were a guilty man. Through the cross we begin to see that God can use any situation for good. All human suffering must be seen against the background of the pain of the cross.

2 God allowed Satan to bring about Jesus' death on the cross, with his own Son asking the question, 'My God, why?' As with Job, God didn't explain why. This suggests that under the pressure of the pain of crucifixion, even the Son of God lost touch with the reason for his suffering.

3 The Christian knows that there is life after death. The problems of suffering do not have to be resolved in this life. It is interesting to note that in the Greek version of the Book of Job an extra verse has been added: 'and it is written that he [Job] will rise again with those whom the Lord raises up.'

4 This hope of resurrection reminds us that there will be a final vindication of Job. Christians believe that Jesus is coming again to judge the living and the dead. One day there will be a courtroom scene in which Jesus will be the judge and all the wicked and righteous people who have ever lived will stand before his throne to receive according to what they have done in the body. So what Job longed for is actually going to come true. There will be a public vindication of justice, with God's righteousness applied to the entire human race.

DECLINE AND FALL OF AN EMPIRE

17.

INTRODUCTION
TO PROPHECY

This section focuses on the pre-exilic prophets – that is, prophets whose ministry came before the two exiles of God's people. The people of the northern kingdom (Israel) were deported to Assyria in 722 BC and those of the southern kingdom (Judah) were led off to Babylon in 587 BC. Most of the prophets in this section are concerned with warning the people that God would send them into exile if they did not return to the covenant. Such a disaster seemed inconceivable, for the people could not imagine that God would let his Temple be destroyed and his people removed from the land he had promised them.

This was not the only focus of the prophets' message. Some also had things to say to the nations surrounding Israel and Judah, and some were given messages exclusively directed to another nation.

There is much confusion regarding the nature of prophecy both in the Bible and today, so a few words of explanation are needed before we examine the books themselves.

Prophecy had been part of the life of the people of God from their beginning as a nation. Moses was described as a prophet, and the Old Testament books that we think of as history in our Bibles are called prophetic books in the Jewish Scriptures. The pre-exilic prophets begin what are known as the 'book prophets' (i.e. whole Bible books consisting solely of one prophet's message, whereas the 'earlier prophets' were embedded in historical narratives, often more than one in each), though their order in the Bible does not reflect the order in which the books were written.

They were very ordinary men, but they had the very extra-ordinary function of speaking for God. They received their messages from God in both words and pictures. The words became 'heavy within them', so that they felt a burden which was only eased when it was passed on.

The 'pictures' were called visions when they came while the prophet was awake, and dreams if they came during sleep. It is important to realize when reading prophecy that when the prophets describe their visions they usually do so in the past tense, as if the things they have seen have already happened. We would put it in the future tense and say, 'I have seen what is going to happen', but the prophet either puts it in the present tense – 'I see it happening' – or in the past tense – 'I have seen it happening'. In both cases, the prophecy predicts the future. The descriptions are very detailed. Nahum, for example, actu-ally saw the red uniforms of the soldiers who would destroy Babylon. No known enemy in Nahum's time wore red, but the Persians, newly on the scene, destroyed Babylon wearing red coats.

The prophetic gifting had two sides to it. The ability to speak for God depended on the ability to hear from God. The message had to be received before it could be given. It came to the prophet through different channels, physical, mental or spiritual.

God may speak in an audible voice. God is not often recorded as doing this in the Bible – when he did, many people thought it was thunder – as, for example, when he said to Jesus at his baptism, 'You are my beloved son.'

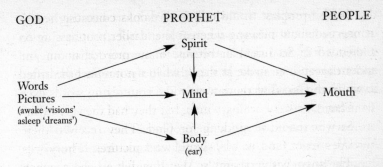

God can also put words into the mind so that the prophet knows he is hearing God's voice. Over time the prophet will learn to distinguish thoughts implanted by God from those of his own mind.

Also, God can speak to the prophet's spirit and implant words or impressions that his mind doesn't understand. For example, when someone prays in tongues, God speaks to the person's spirit and puts words into their mouth, although their mind doesn't understand what has happened.

Of course, God can also speak to the body and then straight to the mouth, bypassing mind and spirit altogether – as he did with Balaam's ass in the Book of Numbers. But this is very rare.

Regardless of the means of reception, words from God must ultimately come out of the prophet's mouth and be delivered to the people.

Two categories of message were common: messages of challenge, when people were sinning, and messages of comfort, when they were doing right. If the messages generally seem more negative, this is because God usually needed to speak when there were problems. So many of the prophetical messages are challenge rather than comfort. In the Book of Isaiah the first half is challenge and the second half is comfort.

A false prophet would only give comfort because he was concerned about pleasing the people and not about passing on God's word. So Jeremiah became a byword for doom and gloom because he spoke at a time when the people had drifted away from God (but there were some comforting words even from him).

So why should we study the prophets?

We are not Jews, so why should we study their history?

The answer is very simple. We should study the prophets so that we may get to know God better, because God has not changed. The prophets reveal God – the God who revealed himself as the great 'I am' or 'Always'.

There are three major things that the prophets seem to focus on, as the chart shows:

1. God's activity – powerful
Nature: miracles
History: movements

2. God's integrity – predictable
Justice: punishment
Mercy: pardon

3. God's flexibility – personal
Man: repents
God: relents

1. The prophets focus on the activity of God – what he has done, what he is doing, what he is going to do. When we recite the Apostles' Creed in church, we begin with the words, 'I believe in God the Father Almighty, Maker of heaven and earth.' That is how the prophets present him – as a God who is so powerful that he is in total control of both nature and

history. Therefore he can make miracles happen in nature and he can cause movements to happen in history. This is a concept of God that we must keep hold of in our modern, scientific age, in which most people regard nature as a closed system and history as the result of economic forces. It is not easy to remember that God is in total control of both nature and history. Reading the prophets regularly keeps in our minds this picture of a mighty God who can make anything happen in nature and history.

2. The prophets focus on God's integrity – they show us that God is consistent. He is always the same; he does not change in character. He is a unique combination of justice and mercy. If you stress one more than the other, you will get an unbalanced view of God. If you only think of God's justice, you get too hard a view of God. If you only think of his mercy, you get too soft a view of him. In the one case there will be fear but no love, and in the other case there will be love but no fear. The prophets provide a wonderful balance. God's justice means that he must punish sin, and his mercy means that he longs to forgive it and pardon it. This tension for God is only resolved at the cross, because only at the cross do justice and mercy meet. Sins are both punished and pardoned at the same place and at the same time – Jesus takes the punishment and we get the pardon. The integrity of God's character means that you can predict how God will behave. He will exercise mercy as long as he can, but when it is persistently refused he must exercise justice. That's the message of Jonah and Nahum, for example.

3. The prophets emphasize God's flexibility. I believe this is a most important insight into God's character. He can change his plans – they are not fixed for all eternity, but they change depending on how people respond to him. This is especially seen in a section of the prophecy of Jeremiah, where the prophet went to the potter's house and saw the potter trying to

make the clay into a beautiful vase. But the clay would not run well in the potter's hands to make this vase, so the potter pushed it back into a lump and made a crude, thick pot with it. God said to Jeremiah, 'Have you learned the lesson of the potter and the clay?' Most of the preachers I've heard preach on this passage misunderstand it. They say that the potter decides what shape the clay will be and that this implies predestination – if God decides your destiny, you are stuck with it. Actually the clay decides whether to be a beautiful vase or a crude pot, for it decides on whether it responds to the potter's hands. God said he wanted to make Israel a vessel of his mercy, but they wouldn't have it, so he made them a pot full of his justice.

So the prophets speak of a God who is personal, who is alive and who calls us into a living relationship with him. Things are not fixed – that's fatalism. God is flexible – he adjusts to his people. Where his people respond rightly, he makes us into a beautiful vessel. But when we respond wrongly, he will still make a vessel of us, but it will be a vessel full of his justice, and we will be a demonstration of God's justice to the rest of the world. The choice is ours. What sort of clay do we want to be? Do we want to demonstrate his mercy to the world or his justice?

The flexibility of God is a very precious truth to me, but sadly, it's a picture of God that most Christians have not grasped. The future is not fixed; it's not predetermined; it's open, because God is personal. The one thing that God cannot change is the past, but he can and will change the future. The Bible even dares to say that God repents when we repent. This need not alarm us. The word 'repent' simply means 'to change one's mind'. So when we change our mind, God changes his! But he doesn't change his character, so we can always rely on him.

So it is a good thing to read the prophets and get to know God better. He is a powerful God and can do anything in nature and history. He's a predictable God – he will act according to his integrity of character – and therefore we can know how he will respond. But he is also a personal God who wants a living relationship with us so that he can respond to us and we can respond to him. That's the God we worship.

The pre-exilic prophets include some of the best and least known of the prophets, but together they give us a good range of the style and focus of prophetic ministry.

18.
JONAH

Introduction

This introduction to Jonah encompasses Nahum as well, for there were significant similarities between these two prophets. Jonah and Nahum both went to the same place and they both had the same sort of message.

Jonah was born near Nazareth. He was a local hero to the people of Nazareth, and Jesus must have heard about him when he was a little boy. Of all the prophets, Jesus compared himself to Jonah.

Nahum came from Capernaum. *Caper* means 'village', so *Caper-Nahum* is named after the prophet. This village was Jesus' main base on the Sea of Galilee, so he had a very close connection with these two prophets.

It is especially significant that they came from the north, because this was the international part of Israel. It was called 'Galilee of the nations' because the crossroads of the world was in Galilee. A road from Europe came down the coast and crossed through the region before heading east to Arabia. The road from Africa came up from Egypt and crossed through Galilee and north to Damascus. So everyone going from Asia to Africa or from Europe to Arabia came through this crossroads. At the crossroads there was a little hill called Megiddo. 'The Hill of Megiddo' in Hebrew is 'Armageddon', where the last battle of history will be fought. So Nazareth was on a hill overlooking the crossroads. As a boy Jesus must have seen many coming and going, rather like travellers passing through an airport lounge.

Galilee was very international, whereas up in the hills of Judea in the south the people were nationalistic, isolated and right off the main routes.

So there were two locations within the nation which affected the ministry of Jesus. He was very popular in the international place in the north, but he was very unpopular in the nationalist centre in the south, where he was eventually crucified.

Jonah and Nahum were northerners and were therefore very much aware of international affairs, and they were both sent by God to Assyria.

The threats to the Holy Land came from the big western and eastern powers. Israel was continually being squeezed between these two power blocs as each tried to overcome the other. Somebody has said about Israel that if you live in the middle of a crossroads you're bound to get run over, and that's exactly what happened. In the days of Jonah and Nahum, Assyria, with its capital at Nineveh, was the problem.

Jonah went to challenge Assyria in 770 BC and Nahum went in 620 BC, so they were 150 years apart. They were both sent because of the sheer wickedness of the Assyrian people. The Assyrian empire lasted for about 750 years and at one stage even managed to take over Egypt. It started as a small power in about 1354 BC and gradually expanded. But it expanded by means of great cruelty. Indeed, the Assyrians were one of the most cruel, brutal nations that history has seen. They invented the hideous practice of impaling their enemies on wooden spikes until they died. They used to execute thousands of people at once in this way. They ruled their empire by terror.

Nahum called the capital Nineveh a 'bloody city', and the name was well deserved. If a nation thought that the Assyrians had their eye on their country they were mortally afraid of what would happen.

Zephaniah also spoke about the Assyrians, but Nahum finally went to them and said, 'You're finished! God's going to wipe you out.' And, sure enough, Nineveh fell in 612 BC, and the whole Assyrian empire disappeared five years later, immediately after Nahum's warning.

Fact or fiction?

Turning to the story of Jonah itself, we must first respond to the huge debate about whether it is fact or fiction. Most people know the book because of the story of 'Jonah and the whale' and most people's impressions of the book depend on whether or not they believe that the story is true.

Some say that the incident in which the whale (or big fish) swallows Jonah is like the story of Pinocchio, who also lived inside a whale. They argue that no one could be expected to take such a fantastic story seriously. Therefore they take it to be a parable with a moral and offer various options as to the meaning. Some say it was told to challenge the hearers to greater missionary endeavour – it was a reminder to Israel that they had a missionary responsibility to the rest of the world. Jonah's running away from his mission is a moral for Israel to learn from.

But when there is a parable in the Bible, it is usually very clearly indicated. Jonah, however, is treated as history. Also, when Jesus told parables they never contained miracles, and yet there are eight miracles in this story.

Other scholars believe that the Book of Jonah is an allegory, with every incident corresponding to real life. So Jonah is a personification of Israel, rather as John Bull is of Britain or Uncle Sam is of the United States. They say that Jonah being swallowed by the whale is a metaphorical picture of Israel being swallowed up in exile.

But there are serious objections to treating Jonah as fiction.

1   The style of the book is exactly the same as all the historical books. Its wording, style and grammar are identical to those of 1 and 2 Kings.

2   The book deals with real places and real people mentioned elsewhere in the Bible. Jonah is mentioned in 2 Kings, and so we know that he was a prophet during the reign of Jeroboam II. His father was Anatai and he is treated as a real person in the historical books of the Bible.

3   More importantly, Jonah treated Jonah as a real person. He believed in Jonah and the big fish. Jesus said of himself that 'a greater than Jonah is now here', and he likened his own period of death to Jonah's time in the whale.

4   But above all, the theories claiming that Jonah is a parable or an allegory do not do justice to chapter 4. The main question that opens up the message of the book is 'Why did Jonah run away?' Many people never even bother to ask the question! Why, then, are people so eager to treat Jonah as the man who never was? Why are they so reluctant to accept this book as fact?

The first objection is that what happened to him was physically impossible. The second is that it was psychologically improbable that one Jewish preacher could convert a huge pagan city. Could we imagine a Jew arriving in the middle of London, preaching in Trafalgar Square and bringing the city back to God? It seems very unlikely that the whole of London would repent.

As for the physical impossibility, we must first ask, 'Could it happen?' Secondly, we must ask, 'Could God make it happen?'

Is it possible for a man to be swallowed by a great fish or whale?

When I was a pastor in the village of Chalfont St Peter, Buckinghamshire, the local blacksmith had a son who worked with marine mammals in California. He trained a whale and a dolphin who were friends and played together in a large tank. When the dolphin died the whale wouldn't allow the keepers to touch the body of his dead friend, and kept the body of the dolphin in its mouth for three days. It would periodically bring the dolphin above the water to try to get it to breathe again. The blacksmith's son showed us a film he had taken of these three days, and the dolphin was just about the size of a man.

This incident links with an unusual newspaper story about a whaler named James Bartley who was working off the Falkland Islands. He and three other men were thrown into the sea when a whale came up under their boat. The other men were rescued, but not Bartley. The captain wrote in his log, 'Swept overboard, presumed drowned, James Bartley.'

Later they happened to catch the whale that had capsized the boat. As they were cutting it up they saw something moving inside the whale's belly. They cut it open to find James Bartley in a deep coma. But it was clear that he was still breathing. After a few days he recovered consciousness and went on to live a normal life. His only handicap was that where his skin had not been covered by clothing, it had been bleached by the digestive juices of the whale, so he had a very unusual appearance for the rest of his life. So this true story proves that it is physically possible to survive within the belly of a whale.

Some Christians seem eager to believe anything. A Salvation Army officer once said that if the Bible said that

Jonah swallowed the whale he'd believe it! But this kind of blind faith just draws ridicule from the world. All things are possible with God, but the Bible doesn't ask you to believe the absurd.

DEAD OR ALIVE?

The key question for me is whether Jonah was dead or alive.

I had never asked myself that question until I saw the film of the whale with the dolphin in its mouth trying to get it to breathe again. But when I re-read the Book of Jonah, to my astonishment I found that all the evidence points to the fact that the whale picked up a dead body.

If you read chapter 2 you discover that Jonah was actually drowned. We read that when the sailors threw him into the sea he sank to the bottom of the sea and lay there at the roots of the mountains, with his head in the seaweed. It takes only about a minute and a half to drown, and it takes much longer than that to reach the bottom of the sea! Sunday school materials mistakenly picture the whale floating around on the surface with its mouth open when the sailors threw him overboard. None picture him, as the Bible does, lying in the seaweed at the bottom of the Mediterranean.

Furthermore, the prayer which he prays tells us that he is in Sheol, the abode of the dead. He describes his last moment of consciousness, when his life was ebbing away and the waters engulfed him. He says that at that time he remembered the Lord.

So all the evidence points to Jonah having died. It seems that the whale does not lead to Jonah's survival but to his resurrection. When the whale spewed him up, God reunited his spirit and body. This ties in with Jesus' statement that, just as Jonah was in the belly of the whale, so he would be in the heart of the earth.

Worldly sceptics would find it easier to believe that Jonah was swallowed and remained alive in the whale than the idea that he died and was resurrected! I believe that Jonah is the most outstanding example of resurrection in the Old Testament.

MIRACLES

The interpretation of the Book of Jonah leads us to face bigger questions about our belief in God. In this book it is not just the swallowing of Jonah by a whale that we have to come to terms with, but a total of eight physical miracles, including a far bigger miracle than the one that most people associate with the book.

For in the last chapter God tells a worm to do something. The blacksmith's son in California could train whales quite easily – they are highly intelligent mammals – but I've never seen anyone train a worm! But God tells a worm what to do. If anybody says to me, 'You don't still believe that story about Jonah and the whale, do you?' I say, 'That's nothing – I believe the story about the worm too!' They usually look quite blank because they have no idea what I'm talking about.

Let us briefly consider the miracles in this book:

1 God sends a wind that causes a storm, and the ship is in danger.
2 When the sailors cast lots to find out who is the cause of divine anger, they identify Jonah. God has controlled the outcome of an apparently random selection.
3 When the sailors throw Jonah overboard, God calms the sea.
4 God sends the great fish to swallow Jonah's body.
5 God makes the great fish vomit the body on to dry land.
6 God makes a vine (a castor plant, from which we get castor oil) grow overnight.

7 God sends a worm to eat the roots of the plant so that it dies.

8 Finally God sends a hot, scorching desert wind.

So on eight occasions God controls nature.

How we react to these events tells us a lot. There are three philosophies that are widely held in the UK:

1 *Atheism* says that God didn't create the world and therefore he doesn't control it.

2 *Deism* is a more common philosophy which holds that God created the world but that he can't control it now. I would say that many people in British churches are Deists, which means that they can't believe in miracles. So they go to church and thank God that he is the Maker of heaven and earth, but they won't pray about the weather!

3 *Theism* is the biblical philosophy which says that God not only created the world in the past but also controls it now.

Of course, there are some Christians who combine two of these philosophies. They believe in miracles in the Bible but they don't believe that they happen today. They are practical deists and theoretical theists.

Converting Nineveh

Let us turn next to the psychological improbability that an enormous city like Nineveh would convert. Here are some arguments in favour of this being an historical fact:

1 First, they were religious and even superstitious. They actually believed in God.

2   Secondly, they were guilty. Guilt makes cowards of us all, so when they were accused of what they had done, they knew it and were prepared to own up.

3   Thirdly, the revival started at the bottom among the ordinary people and worked its way up to the palace.

4   Fourthly, they had the sign of Jonah. If Jonah's skin was white from his time in the whale, he must have been quite a sight. No doubt his explanation of what had happened to him made a big impression on them.

5   Fifthly, above all, when the Holy Spirit works, things happen.

I don't have any difficulty in believing that the whole city repented. Jesus certainly believed it when he said that the people of Nineveh will rise up on the Day of Judgement, because they repented when they heard about God and his hearers did not.

Why did Jonah run away?

But there is a big question that we have not yet considered in detail. Why did Jonah run away from his task? This is the subject of chapter 4, which is rarely taught, preached or even read. Yet it is the very heart of this little story. Why was Jonah so reluctant? Who was he thinking about?

Some people say he was thinking primarily of himself. He was just scared to go to Nineveh – he feared being impaled as an enemy of Assyria. But this doesn't explain why he suggested that the sailors throw him into the sea. He wasn't afraid of death as such.

Secondly, people say he thought that the Gentiles had no right to hear about the God of Israel. It was a kind of reverse of anti-Semitism – we might call it 'anti-Gentilism'. But this doesn't explain why he fled away to the Gentiles in Tarsus.

Others say that he was thinking of the Assyrians, the wickedest people on earth. And yet, more than that, he was really thinking of Israel, because Assyria was the biggest threat to little Israel, and he didn't want to have anything to do with this potential invader.

None of these solutions take into account the words of Jonah in the last chapter. He had told the people of Nineveh that in 40 days God would wipe out their city. The result of his preaching was that the people all repented. Disaster was averted.

An evangelist would be thrilled if a whole city repented, but Jonah was disappointed. He sat on a hill outside the town and said to God, 'I told you this would happen! I know what you're like. I knew you'd let them off. I knew you would just threaten them with destruction, but then fail to go through with it!' Doesn't Jonah want people to be saved? Is he so narrow-minded and so bigoted that he doesn't want people to repent?

The key is his reference to what he had said to God in his own country: 'O Lord, is this not what I said when I was still at home? That is why I was so quick to flee to Tarshish. I knew that you are a gracious and compassionate God, slow to anger and abounding in love, a God who relents from sending calamity' (4:2).

We must look to 2 Kings 14:23–25 to find out what had happened to Jonah in his own land.

When he was called to be a prophet he was sent to the King Jeroboam II of Israel – a notoriously bad king who did evil in the sight of the Lord. When God told Jonah to go to the king, Jonah responded positively at first, expecting to be able to deal with the king's wickedness. But the message that Jonah was given was not what he had expected. The Lord said, 'Go and tell the king that I want to bless him, that I'm going to enlarge his borders and make him great.' Jonah protested that he was a wicked king and that this was the wrong approach.

He was saying to the Lord in his heart, 'It'll never work, Lord. If you bless bad people they just get worse.'

Indeed, the king did get worse. The more the Lord blessed him, the worse he got. So Jonah came to the conclusion that mercy doesn't change wicked people. Jonah is telling God that he knows God's business better than God himself does.

God's compassion

So this past episode coloured Jonah's attitude as he went to Nineveh. He said, 'Let's just see what happens, Lord. I'm going to watch this city and see whether your letting them off will cure them or not, whether they get better or worse.'

Underlying all this is Jonah's jealousy for the Lord's character and reputation. He could not cope with anyone taking advantage of divine mercy. He believed their repentance was superficial and would not last. He thought that if God was too soft with them, they would conclude that he never carries out his threats of judgement. Jonah's warning would be doubted, even ridiculed, and eventually forgotten.

When the plant grew up alongside him, he was very thankful for it, since it gave him shade from the sun. But when the worm ate the roots it died, and Jonah was very angry again. He asked God why he had caused it to die. God told Jonah that it was legitimate for him to be angry about the plant, but did he have a right to be angry about Nineveh? There were over 120,000 children in the city and many cattle too. Didn't God have a right to have a heart for them?

So although Jonah was jealous for the Lord in not wanting to see the Assyrians escape punishment, he did not understand God's compassion, his desire to postpone punishment as long as possible. That was why he ran away to sea, and that was why, for him, the success of his preaching was so hollow. We too sometimes forget how patient God is and how full of mercy he is and how many chances he wants to give people.

There is a time, of course, when God's patience runs out. This is ultimately the message of the prophets – Jonah just got the timing wrong. In his day it was still the time of God's mercy and patience with Nineveh. But that patience would not last for ever, as we shall see when we study the prophecy of Nahum.

19.

JOEL

Introduction

We know nothing about Joel except his name and the name of his father, Pethuel. As both names contain the Hebrew word *el* ('God'), we may assume that they were from a godly family, but we can say little about them with any certainty.

Joel's prophecy was given 10 years after Obadiah's (see p. 600). The prophecy of Obadiah was almost exclusively directed at other nations and held out a prospect of good things for Israel. Joel, however, picked up on the concept of the 'Day of the Lord', which Obadiah had used, but said that judgement would fall not only on 'the nations' but on Israel too. This came as a considerable shock to the people of Israel, who assumed that they were all right in the sight of God.

Similarly, many Christian people today complacently assume that they will safely arrive in heaven, however they live. In fact, sin among God's people is more serious than sin outside of God's people. In Romans 2 Paul reminds his readers that if they do the same things that they criticize unbelievers for, they will not escape the wrath of God. God has no favourites. The idea that once you belong to God you can sin freely is totally unbiblical. He has not given a blank chequebook for us to use whenever we sin. It would be totally unfair of God to condemn an unbeliever to hell for adultery but, in the case of a believer guilty of the same behaviour, to say, 'Here is your ticket to heaven.'

So the prophets had to correct that idea in Israel first, because the people of Israel thought they were all right. Elijah had challenged them strongly, but Joel was the first to say that the Day of the Lord could bring darkness, not light.

I find it helpful to analyse the whole Book of Joel before interepreting it. The three chapters coincide with the three sections of the prophecy, though we are not told if they were delivered separately or all at once.

An outline of the Book of Joel

The plague of locusts (chapter 1)
The ruin of the land (1:1–12)
The repentance of the people (1:13–20)

The Day of the Lord (chapter 2)
A terrible repetition (2:1–11)
A true repentance (2:12–17)
A timeless recovery (2:18–27)
A total restoration (2:28–32)
   (a) Spirit, men and women (2:28–29)
   (b) Signs, sun and moon (2:30–31)
   (c) Salvation, calling and called (2:32)

The Valley of Decision (chapter 3)
Vengeance on the nations (3:1–16a)
Vindication of Israel (3:16b–21)

The plague of locusts (chapter 1)

The ruin of the land (1:1–12)

The prophecy of Joel was sparked off by a natural disaster. A plague of locusts had hit the country. It must have been an extraordinary sight. Locusts are like big grasshoppers. In a swarm of locusts there may be up to 600 million insects covering 400 square miles. They can eat up to 80,000 tons of food a day, so when they descend on an area all vegetation disappears. They travel 2,000 miles per month at a speed of between 2 and 10 miles per day for 6 weeks and lay 5,000 eggs per square foot. Their appetite is voracious and their heads look like those of horses.

My only experience of them was in Kano in northern Nigeria. Although it was midday, it suddenly became dark. I thought it was an eclipse of the sun until I saw a huge black cloud approaching that had blotted out the sun, and soon we were in darkness as if it were midnight. I estimated that the locusts were moving at 12 miles per hour, and it took an hour and a half for them to pass. After they had passed we saw that the trees had been stripped of their bark as well as their leaves. Every living piece of vegetation was destroyed. I will never forget it. It was an horrific experience.

Although they are common in Africa, swarms of locusts are comparatively rare in Israel. So when they arrived, Joel told the people that God was behind it. He told them that it was the first of God's warnings that if they continued living as they were, something even worse would happen.

As a result of the locusts the people didn't have enough grain to make a grain offering in the Temple. Public worship ceased. The vineyards, orchards and olive groves had all been destroyed. The nation faced drought, bush fires and starvation, and the economy was at a complete standstill. Some have speculated that Joel's message was given at the Jewish harvest festival known as the Feast of Tabernacles – the very time when they should have been celebrating the harvest of their crops.

There was biblical precedent for understanding the plague as God's judgement. In Exodus 10 the eighth plague (of locusts) in Egypt was sent by God, and in Deteronomy 28 God said he would send plagues if the people were disobedient.

This raises an interesting question for us today: How do we know when a disaster is from God?

We should look for three things:

1 it is directed against his people;
2 it has been prophesied beforehand;
3 it is unusual in either its scale or its detail.

So, to use a fairly recent example, I believe that the fire in York Minster was an example of God at work. It is its unusual character that convinces me in particular. The lightning that struck York Minster came from a small cloud that circled York Minster for 20 minutes in a blue sky. The cloud wasn't big enough for rain, yet it discharged a lightning bolt (without any thunder) that burnt the cathedral from the top down, just after they had renovated it and installed the latest smoke-detection and fire-fighting equipment. Choir boys marching through the cathedral saw it happen, but they heard nothing because there was no thunder at all. I obtained a map of that cloud from the Meteorological Office, and 16 non-Christian meteorologists said that it had to be from God. It was the most unusual thing they had seen in a long time.

People asked me if it was God's judgement. I said I believed it was God's mercy. He waited until everybody had left the cathedral after that degrading consecration of a bishop who denied the faith. He could have done it while they were all still in there. So I believe that the incident expressed his mercy rather than his judgement, but I also believe it was a warning.

So one of the signs that an event is from God is its unusual nature. The unnatural often demonstrates the supernatural. Another sign is the discernment of God's people, and there were many people with prophetic gifts who saw God's hand in the York Minster disaster. Although none had prophesied beforehand, many wondered what God might do if a bishop were consecrated with such errant beliefs.

But disasters, whether they are direct from God or not, are always a reminder of God's judgement. It is important to realize this, lest we make inappropriate assessments about everything that takes place. In Luke 13 Jesus is asked to comment upon the tragic deaths of some labourers when the Tower of Siloam fell down. He is asked if they were greater sinners than anybody else. Jesus replies that they weren't, but unless those who saw the disaster repent of their sin, they too will perish. Every earthquake, typhoon and flood is a reminder to us of the frailty of life and the need to get right with God.

The repentance of the people (1:13–20)

In the second half of chapter 1 Joel tells the elders to call for a national act of repentance, warning them that if they do not repent there will be a terrible repetition of God's judgement, though he is not specific about what they should repent of. We are left to research the historical background in 1 and 2 Kings to find out what was happening at the time which required that the nation should receive such a warning.

We cannot be definite about the period when Joel prophesied, but it was probably during the ninth century BC, which may tie in with particular events in 1 and 2 Kings. A clue may be the fact that there is a reference to the priests in Joel, but no reference to a king. In the books of Kings there is a period when there is a queen on the throne (841–835 BC) – the only time in the history of God's people when this was the case. God had promised King David that as long as the kings kept the statutes and commands of God, they would never lack a son to sit on the throne of Israel. He allowed them to have a king, but not a queen.

Furthermore, the female monarch in question was Queen Athaliah, who had behaved treacherously. She had been the queen mother, and when the king died she seized the throne and murdered all of his sons, so that she could be queen. Her mother was the infamous Jezebel, who had wrought havoc in the northern kingdom. But one son of the king was saved by the High Priest and hidden in the Temple. Had she managed to kill every boy, the royal line of David would have ended. But despite her despicable behaviour, the people accepted her as their ruler. Even the High Priest didn't object – though at least he had the courage to hide the boy. The boy's name was Joash, and shortly after Joel had preached, the people gained the courage to depose Athaliah and put Joash on the throne, even though he was only seven years old.

So Joel's prophecy was possibly given against this background. National sin had been committed and therefore national repentance was required.

The Day of the Lord (chapter 2)

A terrible repetition (2:1–11)

But the people did not repent. They continued to sin, so at the beginning of chapter 2 Joel describes what is at first sight a repetition of the plague of locusts. But when you look at the text more closely it becomes clear that this time this plague of

locusts is actually just a picture of thousands of soldiers marching into the land and destroying everything, rather as locusts
would. It is a far more alarming picture than even the first one.
Indeed, given the total destruction, it is very likely that Joel
was describing the Babylonians, who, alone among all the
ancient peoples who conquered others, had a terrible scorched-
earth policy. They not only killed all the people and their
children, but also destroyed every living thing, including trees,
sheep and cattle. The Babylonian army left nothing alive, and
that is a very similar picture to a locust plague. There are parallels here with Revelation 9, where, once again, a plague of
locusts is described followed by an army from the East of 200
million soldiers. Whether Joel is describing soldiers or another
plague of locusts, it is clear that God was capable of sending
both and that his judgement was still necessary.

A true repentance (2:12–17)

Again Joel repeats the message that what God is looking for is
true repentance. After his first call for repentance most of the
people just went out and got drunk. People have twofold reactions to coming disaster. Some prepare and repent, others get
drunk.

So Joel issues a second call for true repentance. One of the
memorable phrases in this second call is 'Rend your hearts and
not your garments.' Watching someone tear their clothes can
be impressive, but that isn't good enough for God. It is our
hearts that matter, not what we do to our clothes. It is interesting to note that Joel does not list the sins. We can only assume
that the people were only too aware of what God was concerned about.

We do well to remember that God says he is willing to
change his mind concerning their punishment. They are in a
dynamic relationship with God – he will respond to them. So

God tells them how to pray: they must plead for mercy and call on God to demonstrate his love and faithfulness to them as his people in the land he has given them.

A timeless recovery (2:18–27)

Some speculate that this part of the prophecy was not given at the same time as the earlier parts. Here Joel urges the people to be glad rather than afraid. He promises Israel that if they really repent from their hearts, God will restore the years that the locusts have eaten. This is a principle that applies today. Many regret the wasted years in their lives, but God says he will restore those years to them. But he will only restore the years that the locusts have eaten if there is true repentance.

The root of repentance is that we 'change our minds'. So it is appropriate to say that if they repent, God will change his mind. God assures them three times that never again will he act in this way, and that then they will know him.

A total restoration (2:28–32)

Joel moves on to some wonderful promises. God says that if they truly repent, never again will he punish them with such action. Instead, there will be a total restoration – not just a physical restoration of the crops that the locusts ate, but also a spiritual restoration.

(A) SPIRIT, MEN AND WOMEN (2:28–29)

One of the greatest promises given in the Book of Joel is that God will pour out his Spirit on all kinds of people, regardless of sex, class or age. Young men will see visions and old men will dream dreams. Also, maidservants and menservants will prophesy. God promises to put his prophetic Spirit in all kinds of people. This promise was picked up by the apostle Peter on the Day of Pentecost eight centuries later. He explained that

Joel's prophecy was coming true as the Spirit came upon the 120 disciples.

(B) SIGNS, SUN AND MOON (2:30–31)

The second part of the promise is that the sun will be darkened and the moon will be turned to blood. Some say this was fulfilled when Jesus died and the sun was darkened for three hours, but this sign actually remains to be fulfilled at the end of the age, for Jesus himself mentions it as a sign of his second coming in Matthew 24:29.

It is interesting that there will be signs in the sky, because the sky responds to significant events on earth. People foolishly tell me that the fact that the Wise Men followed the star proves that astrology is all right. But I tell them that they have got it totally wrong. Astrology believes that the position of the stars influences a baby at the moment of birth, but at Bethlehem it was the position of the baby that influenced the stars! So when Jesus died the sun went out. The universe responds to significant events down here. That's amazing, isn't it? We are not governed by the heavens; they are governed by God.

(C) SALVATION, CALLING AND CALLED (2:32)

Joel also promised salvation for everyone whom the Lord called and who responded to the Lord. Salvation was not automatic, as if the nation as a whole was 'saved' through some mystical process. There is a double call in salvation. God calls people to be saved, through human preachers, and people in turn call on God.

I don't like telling people to repeat the sinner's prayer – I just tell them to call on the Lord themselves. We are told that 'Whoever calls on the name of the Lord shall be saved.' It is very important that people themselves should call on his name.

Whoever does that will be saved. Peter picked that up at Pentecost, and 3,000 people called on the name of the Lord and were saved that day.

So Joel's promise of total restoration is not just about crops, wine and corn, but about human hearts.

Joel said that all this would happen on the Day of the Lord. We don't need to believe that it is literally a day of 24 hours; the word 'day' is flexible in Scripture. The Hebrew word *yom* can mean a whole epoch. If I say, 'The day of the horse and cart is over', I don't mean a period of 24 hours. I mean that an historical era is finished and we are in the day of the motor car. That is the meaning of the word 'day' in 'the Day of the Lord'. The point is this: man has had his day, and the devil has had his day, but one day God is going to have his day. There is coming the Day of the Lord when he will have his say, when he will bring the world under his rule.

Joel mentions the Day of the Lord five times in his prophecy, always referring to it as a time of judgement. The phrase is also picked up by later prophets such as Isaiah, Jeremiah, Ezekiel, Amos, Zephaniah and Malachi. The Day of the Lord is also a prominent part of the New Testament (see 1 Corinthians, 1 Thessalonians, 2 Thessalonians and 2 Peter). There is a day coming when the Lord will have his day, and that will be the last day.

So the order of judgement is: first, God's people, and then his enemies later. We have a choice: do we want judgement now or later?

We are now in the 'last days', which began when Joel's prophecy came true and the Spirit was poured out on the Day of Pentecost. From that day we have been living in the last days. The next great event is the return of Jesus Christ to planet earth.

The Valley of Decision (chapter 3)

Vengeance on the nations (3:1–16a)

Where? The final chapter has a vision of the Valley of Decision. It is the Kidron Valley on the eastern side of Jerusalem, and to this day it is called the Valley of Judgement. It is full of Jewish graves because it is believed to be the place of resurrection when God will make his decision about our eternal destiny. It is also called the Valley of Decision, but I have heard that name misused by preachers. Joel says there are multitudes in the Valley of Decision, and so preachers use this to encourage unbelievers to make up their minds about God. Actually it is the valley in which God decides who goes to heaven and who goes to hell. It is the valley of his decision, when he will have the last word. It is his decision that decides our eternal destiny.

Why? God's decision will depend on how people have treated his people, his purpose and what he has done in the world. The nations of Tyre, Sidon and Philistia are especially singled out as ripe for judgement. The last word is that God will vindicate his people and restore them to their land.

How? The nations are called to come and fight, though there is a certain amount of sarcasm in the call, for who can 'fight' against God? The nations are told to beat their plough-shares into swords and their pruning-hooks into spears (note the very opposite in Isaiah 2:4 and Micah 4:3). Zephaniah speaks of the meeting of the nations in his prophecy.

Vindication of Israel (3:16b–21)

The final section focuses upon the restoration of Judah. She will be inhabited and fertile but, by contrast, Egypt will be desolate and Edom will be a desert, because of the violence which they have committed against Judah.

This raises a very big question upon which there are deeply divided opinions in the Church today. Obadiah, Joel and many other prophets end their prophecies with promises for the future of Israel. Since many of these remain unfulfilled, we must ask when they will be fulfilled.

There are four different opinions in the Church today, and although mine is not that of the majority, I believe it is the one that is most faithful to Scripture.

The opinions divide upon whether the promises should be taken literally or spiritually. Are we to assume that Israel will literally recover the land that God promised, or do we see the land as being symbolic of spiritual blessings, now applied to the Church, as the new Israel. This latter view is called 'replacement theology' and is probably the view of the majority of preachers in the UK.

My problem with this view is that, while they claim all the old blessings for the Church, they don't apply the curses also – these stay with Israel! God told Israel that she would be blessed if she was obedient and cursed if she was not.

The blessings included life, health, prosperity, fertility, respect and safety. The curses were disease, drought, death, danger, destruction, defeat, deportation, destitution and disgrace.

With replacement theology, the old Israel has lost the land because she was not obedient. But the blessings are applied to the Church, the new Israel, without any mention of the curses if the Church is not obedient.

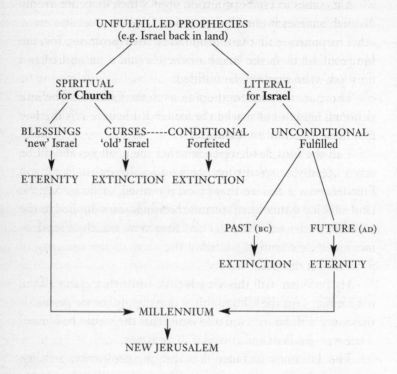

UNFULFILLED PROPHECIES
(e.g. Israel back in land)

SPIRITUAL
for **Church**

LITERAL
for **Israel**

BLESSINGS   CURSES-----CONDITIONAL   UNCONDITIONAL
'new' Israel   'old' Israel   Forfeited   Fulfilled

ETERNITY   EXTINCTION   EXTINCTION

PAST (BC)   FUTURE (AD)

EXTINCTION   ETERNITY

MILLENNIUM

NEW JERUSALEM

Those who believe that the promises apply to Israel literally
are also divided into two groups. One group say the promises
were all conditional and have been forfeited by Israel, and so
there is no future for Israel as the people of God. We can evangelize Israel, but just as we would any other nation. They are
now just a nation – they are no longer God's people.

But this argument does not fit in with the New Testament.
Of the 74 New Testament references to 'Israel', none refer to
the Church. Furthermore, there are references to the continuing throne of David, the house of Jacob and the 12 tribes of
Israel. The assumption is that Israel is very much alive and well

when it comes to God's promises, even if their rejection of the Messiah has meant punishment.

The promises that God made to Israel were unconditional. He promised them the land for ever. He told them that even if they lost it, he would always bring them back again, because he had sworn it to them. So there is a future for Israel. I believe that Paul held this view when he said in Romans 9–11 that they may have rejected his God, but God had not rejected them. After all the Gentiles have been saved, then 'all Israel' will be saved. God doesn't divorce people; he hangs on to them. Furthermore, I believe that Jesus is coming back to reign on this earth, and then the Jew and the Christian will be brought together into one flock under one Shepherd, and the Kingdom will finally be restored to Israel.

The last question that the disciples asked Jesus is recorded in Acts 1: 'When will the Kingdom be restored to Israel? Will it be now?' Jesus didn't say this was a silly question; he said it was not for them to know the date that the Father had fixed. They just got the timing wrong. The Kingdom is going to be restored, but not yet. Then he told them to go and preach the gospel to all nations.

So you have to face the fact that there are all these different views and all of them finish up with the old Israel becoming extinct – apart from the one I accept. I believe that the promises of God can't be broken. Indeed, if God can't hang on to Israel, he can't hang on to us either.

Conclusion

The prophecy of Joel teaches us important things about the character of God and the nature of his activity with his people and in the world around us. Joel's prophecies have been partially fulfilled, but we await their final fulfilment, when God will wind up this phase of history and bring his people to himself, as he promised.

20.

AMOS AND HOSEA

Introduction

Amos and Hosea prophesied during the eighth century BC and the two books named after them are among the earliest included in the Bible. Although their focus was upon the northern kingdom (i.e. Israel rather than Judah), it is useful to set their preaching within the context of what was happening elsewhere in the world, especially since aspects of modern society can be traced back to this era. We will then look at the situation in Israel before examining the work of the prophets separately.

What man was doing

History records that Rome and Carthage were founded in the eighth century BC. Great rivalry between the two cities led to the Punic Wars, in which Rome was finally triumphant. From this victory came the foundations of the Roman empire. Roman law was gradually established, soon followed by the vast road-building projects which were to characterize the Romans' reign and would enable the gospel to spread some 700 years later.

Also during this century, the Olympic Games began in Greece – man's obsession with sport has ancient roots! But more significant was the spread of the Greek language throughout the Mediterranean, with Homer being one of the best-known Greek writers. The Greeks established many city-states and developed a new form of government known as democracy (though their approach was some way short of the emancipation that we associate with the word today).

In the East the Chinese and Indian civilizations were also emerging, so that there is a sense in which Israel and Judah were located at the centre of the growth of civilization, with developing cultures to the east and to the west and many travellers passing through the land.

What God was doing

God's relationship with his people had reached a difficult phase. His intention was that they should be a model to the world of what a relationship with him was like. This was why he had placed them at the 'crossroads' of the world. His covenant with them, made at Sinai in the time of Moses, stated that if they obeyed him he would bless them more than any other people, and if they disobeyed him they would be cursed more than any other people. So they were faced with a privilege and a responsibility. But by the eighth century God was faced with the dilemma of what to do with a people who were far from him.

Two kingdoms

A brief outline of their recent history will help to explain God's concerns. By the eighth century BC the people of God had been split into two. They had become a kingdom with a visible king, as they had wanted some 200 years before, but they had to endure all that went with kingship – taxation to finance the king's lavish lifestyle and conscription to defend the land.

But this kingdom had just three kings before it split. The first, Saul, was the 'people's choice' – good-looking, handsome and tall, but with some serious weaknesses of character.

When he failed to live in obedience to God's word, God gave the people a man of his own choosing – David – who is described in 1 Samuel as 'a man after God's own heart'. Despite an excellent start, he too was led into sin. One lustful look led him to break five of the Ten Commandments and he was never the same afterwards. The decline in Israel's power began on that afternoon.

The third king was Solomon, David's son. He brought great glory to the kingdom – during his reign Israel's empire was at its height – but he did so by heavy taxation and forced labour. He left the legacy of a magnificent Temple but a divided people. The northern tribes were unhappy about the fact that the kingdom's resources had been concentrated on Jerusalem in the south.

Civil war ensued as soon as Solomon died. The north rebelled against the south, and eventually the kingdom was divided, with the ten tribes in the north taking the name Israel and the two tribes in the south, who stayed loyal to Jerusalem and to the royal line, taking the name Judah.

This meant, of course, that the north was without a temple and without a royal line. They established their own holy shrines at Bethel and Samaria and their own royal line, independent of the bloodline of David that God had promised to bless.

The history of Israel in 1 and 2 Kings tells the desperate story of the reigns of these northern kings. The average length of their reigns was three years. Many of them were assassinated, and there were a number of coups. It was an unstable government, but this is not surprising, for this was not a government based on God's chosen royal line.

The south fared better, its kings reigning for an average of 33 years. (Interestingly, Jesus is believed to have been this age when he died.)

Social conditions

Peace

It is important that we understand the social conditions of the north as we seek to understand the messages that Amos and Hosea spoke. It was an era of peace and prosperity. Assyria was the superpower of the day, but Jonah's visit to Nineveh had effectively postponed their threat to Israel for some time. That generation of Assyrians had repented of their evil warmongering, and so the fear of Assyrian invasion was over, for the time being.

Prosperity

As a result, Israel now enjoyed a time of great prosperity, especially under King Jeroboam II, whose rule for a time stabilized the nation. Its economy benefited from being on the trade routes between Europe and Arabia, and a number of merchants and bankers became very wealthy.

'Haves' and 'have nots'

Although the standard of living rose, society became divided between the 'haves' and the 'have nots'. Many enjoyed the consumer society with its luxury goods. The height of fashion was to have a second home – what they called a 'summerhouse' – to which you would go in the heat of the summer, usually up in the hills. A new aristocracy developed – the 'get rich quick' boys. But housing became a problem, because as the rich got richer the poor got poorer. The rich had second homes but many people didn't even have one at all.

Moral effects

Morally the effects of all this affluence were very clear. There were financial scandals, bribery and corruption, with even the judiciary being corrupted. There was no justice in the courts without bribing the judges. They were soon into seven-days-a-week trading because they could make more money that way. Avarice led to injustice and affluence led to permissiveness. Sexual laxity was the order of the day and alcohol consumption rose sharply. Although this was 2,700 years ago, the parallels with our modern Western culture are all too easy to see.

Religious life

Religious life was also booming, but it was not the religion of Israel. Rather, the people had become interested in the faiths of the other nations, and in particular they had turned to those of the indigenous peoples of Canaan. This included the faiths of the East and the West that arrived with the travelling merchants and the Canaanite peoples' cult of 'mother nature'. Indeed, at the temples at Bethel and Samaria the worshippers had sex with male and female prostitutes, believing that this would persuade God to bless their crops. They even set up a golden calf at Bethel in a direct contradiction of God's laws against graven images. So God's holy people, who were supposed to be a royal priesthood and a holy nation, had become just like everybody else.

God would have been justified in washing his hands of them and trying to start again with another people. But God is not like that. He was married to the people of Israel, and he hates divorce. Having made a covenant with them, he was determined to stay with it. However, he couldn't turn a blind eye to their behaviour. In the giving of the Law at the time of Moses he promised that he would be forced to curse them if they were disobedient, and the Books of Amos and Hosea relate the ways in which he brought discipline to his people.

God's discipline

A food shortage

Since the people were embracing fertility cults, it was appropriate that God should demonstrate that their sexual promiscuity did not have a positive effect on the harvest. Instead a number of harvests failed. God was saying, 'Wake up! You're dependent on me, not on the fertility goddesses'. But after this disaster, as with the others, came the refrain, 'Yet you did not return to me.' In spite of the food shortage, they carried on with their pagan rituals.

A water shortage

Next, God sent a shortage of fresh drinking water, which was, of course, a great calamity in a land that was dependent upon regular rain.

Diseased and ravaged crops

An attack of mildew and locusts destroyed the crops, which led to food shortages for the animals. It may seem obvious that a people who were in covenant relationship with God should turn to him to ask what had gone wrong, but Israel refused to do so.

Plagues and raids

The crops and animals had already suffered. Now God sent plagues upon the people, and enemy raids took away their livestock. We can see that each discipline was more severe than the last. Now people were being directly affected. But still they didn't return to God.

Storms bring fire

God also allowed lightning to strike some of their cities, resulting in the destruction of vast areas of housing. But none of this had any effect. As long as they could keep their money and enjoy their holiday homes, they didn't care.

On top of God's warnings came two further disasters. It was as if God was desperate to get their attention.

An earthquake

This was much more than a little earth tremor. Some 250 years later it is mentioned in Zechariah as *the* earthquake. It demonstrated God's power over the natural realm and reminded the people of the fragility of human life. Yet still the people refused to return to God.

Exile

Eventually God's final sanction was for them to be invaded and deported by the Assyrians, never to return again. This happened in 721 BC, 30 years after Amos and 10 years after Hosea. This may seem a heavy price to pay for disobedience, but God had warned Israel about it time and again, not just through the discipline and the disasters but also through the ministries of these two prophets, who underlined and explained what God was doing and what he might be forced to do.

Indeed, Amos 3:7 says, 'Surely the Sovereign Lord does nothing without revealing his plan to his servants the prophets.' God is so amazingly merciful that he never punishes without sending a prophet first to explain to the people what will happen if they continue in their behaviour. In the New Testament the Book of Revelation is a warning of what God is going to do with the whole world, but still people don't turn to him. How much more can God do?

The 'last chance' prophets

So Amos and Hosea were the 'last chance' prophets sent to Israel, warning them of what God would be forced to do if they failed to turn back to him. The two prophets were very different. Amos was tough; Hosea was tender. Amos came with strong accusations of what they were doing wrong; Hosea came with a strong appeal to return to the Lord. If Amos spoke to their minds, Hosea spoke to their hearts. Amos majored on the justice of God, Hosea on God's mercy. Amos communicated God's thoughts to the nation, but Hosea communicated God's feelings. There is some overlap between the two prophets, but these broad characteristics shine through their messages. It is interesting that God's very last words in Hosea are a very tender, emotional appeal, hoping that Israel would repent and allow him to refrain from the judgement that he would have to execute.

AMOS	HOSEA
Rural southerner	Urban northerner
Warning	Wooing
Tough accusation	Tender appeal
Justice of God	Mercy of God
Divine wrath	Divine love
His purity	His pity
Social sin	Spiritual sin
Injustice	Idolatry
International	National
'Seek God'	'Know God'

The Book of Amos

In the year 750 BC a man appeared in Bethel, stood on the temple steps and preached. His accent betrayed him as a southerner, so he was guaranteed to receive a hostile reaction because of who he was and what he was saying.

By profession, Amos was the poorest kind of farmer. He was a herdsman and also looked after sycamore trees, which was regarded as the very lowest job because sycamore figs tended to be the food of the poor. So he had no religious training and was not an obvious candidate for preaching, but under God's hand and by God's grace he was exactly the right man for the job.

His home town was Tekoa, 12 miles south of Jerusalem, in the heart of the southern kingdom, on the borders of the desert. God spoke to this man from the bottom rung of the social ladder, saying, 'You're the man to go and tell the northerners what is going to come to them.'

Chapter 7 of the Book of Amos gives us a remarkable insight into his personal life and his reaction to what he encountered. This chapter shows us two remarkable things:

1 His praying affected God;
2 His preaching angered men.

His praying affected God

On one occasion God showed him two pictures: the first was of locusts devouring everything in the countryside, and the second was of a fire destroying everything in the towns. He was profoundly shocked by the vision and so he said to God, 'Sovereign Lord, I beg you not to do that!' He asked God how Jacob (i.e. God's people) could survive such an onslaught. He pleaded with God not to do it, and so God drew back from what he had said he would do.

Two things are remarkable about the conversation. The first is that prayer can affect God in that way. God seems to change his course of action according to the pleading of Amos. Moses had the same experience and, of course, Jesus on the cross prayed, 'Father, forgive them. They don't know what they're doing.' The lesson of the conversation between Amos and God is clear. Our praying will never change his character but it can change his plans. This is not an impersonal God who sets things in stone, but a God who listens to us, a God who is willing to be persuaded.

The second thing is that Amos speaks of the nation as 'Jacob' rather than 'Israel'. In so doing he refers to the corrupt

schemer, the man who deceived his own father to get a blessing, who was renamed Israel. It is as if Amos is deliberately
reminding God of the ambiguous past of the man who gave the
nation its name. It is a perfect way of saying in one word that
Israel had gone back to being what Jacob had been before he
met God and wrestled with the angel.

Also in chapter 7 Amos has a vision of the Lord standing
alongside a wall with a plumb line in his hand. God was showing Amos that he was measuring Israel against his standards,
not their own, and that judgement must follow.

His preaching angered men

Predictably, the preaching of Amos angered the religious leaders. Prophets are not popular with priests or pastors. Prophets
are typically against the status quo and hence are a threat.
Amaziah the priest is especially concerned about the effect that
Amos was having and ended up opposing him. But, undaunted,
Amos preached on, predicting the demise of Jereboam, his wife
and his family.

God gave Amos his messages in two ways. He had visions
while he was awake and dreams while he was asleep. An Old
Testament prophet was known as a 'seer' because he saw things
that other people didn't see. He could see what was really
going on; he could see into the future.

The biblical text frequently tells us about what Amos saw.
One of the most telling pictures, forming a climax to his
prophecy, is a basket of fruit that is so ripe that it is on the
verge of going bad. The message was clear: Israel was ripe for
rottenness.

He also pictured God himself, invariably as a lion. In those
days there were still lions in the land of Israel. They lived in

the jungle along the Jordan River and came up into the hills looking for lambs, so lions were familiar to the people.

Amos says, 'God the lion has roared. Who will not tremble?' He gives a graphic picture of what will happen to Israel. He says it will be like a lamb caught by a lion. The shepherd may rescue an ear and a couple of legs from the lion's mouth. This is all that will be left of Israel – an ear and a couple of legs. It is vivid picture language that catches people's interest and imagination. God was known as the shepherd of Israel, so it must have been a shock for them to hear him being depicted as a lion.

Themes in Amos

The prophecy of Amos is a collection of sermons, with no clear structure. For this reason it is difficult to analyse the book as a whole. It is as if the book plants time bombs in people's hearts, ready to go off at an appropriate time in the future.

A number of themes can be identified:

Eight sentences (chapters 1:1–2:16)

1 Damascus
2 Gaza
3 Tyre
4 Edom
5 Ammon
6 Moab
7 Judah
8 Israel

Three sermons (chapters 3–6)

1 'Yet you have not returned'
2 'Seek me and live'
3 'Woe …'

Five symbols (chapters 7–8)

1 A plague of locusts
2 Fire devours the deep
3 A plumb line
4 A basket of ripe fruit
5 The destruction of the ripe fruit

Three surprises (chapter 9)

1 The rebuilding of David's house
2 The return of the people
3 The fertility of the land

A poetic book

Although there is little structure, the choice of genre is quite deliberate. Throughout the Bible a distinction can be made between poetry and prose. The former gives us God's feelings about a situation, the latter God's thoughts. Many are unaware that the Bible is full of God's emotions. God is full of feelings. We need to understand what makes him angry, what makes him sad, what makes him feel sick, what makes him happy. People become obsessed with their feelings about God, but actually our future depends on his feelings about us.

Some poetry is very light and lifts you, but some is very heavy, and is called a dirge. The poetry in Amos falls into the latter category.

Repetition

Amos also uses repetition, which is especially effective when speaking. He wants his hearers to remember the message that although God has sent troubles, they have not returned to him. So he repeats the refrain: 'You did not return to me.'

But let's look at chapter 1 and see how skilfully he structures his words. His refrain in this section is 'For three sins, even for four'.

The inhumanity of Israel's neighbours

He starts by condemning Israel's neighbours. He focuses on Damascus and how they deserve God's punishment. Damascus was not part of the people of God, so it was dealt with for inhumanity and cruelty in particular. Then he rails on Gaza, which was noted for its brutality, then on Tyre for its treachery. No doubt Amos' audience agreed with the message so far.

The infamy of Israel's cousins

Then he moves on to the ethnic cousins of Israel – Edom, Ammon and Moab. He says God will deal with Edom for their ruthlessness, with Ammon for their barbarity, and with Moab for treating sacred things profanely. His audience are still with him at this point in his talk.

The infidelity of Israel's sister

Next he moves a little closer to home, condemning Israel's sister Judah. God will deal with Judah for rejecting the laws of God and accepting the lies of men.

The insensitivity of Israel's children

Then comes the shock. Just when he has the audience with him, he tells them that God will deal with them too. He tells them that they have become so used to sin that they have forgotten how to blush. What is worse, they don't seem to realize it. The main message for Israel is that past redemption means future retribution. Since God chose them out of all the families of the earth, he must punish them more severely. The terms of the Sinai covenant were divine blessings on obedience and divine curses on disobedience, which the people had voluntarily, even eagerly, accepted. Israel could be blessed more than other nations – or cursed more. It is a divine principle that of those who are given much, much is expected. Extra privileges bring greater responsibility.

This is a principle that runs through even to the New Testament. Christians are among those who have heard the gospel, who know the commandments, and therefore God will deal with them more severely.

Another sermon that uses repetition is full of the word 'woe'. It is a series of curses upon those who have been disobedient. Amos tells them that many of those who long for the Day of the Lord are mistaken about what that Day will mean. They are presuming that all will be well. They are complacent in their decadent lifestyles. But they must realize that ritual is no substitute for righteousness and sacrifice is no substitute for sanctification.

The theme 'Seek me and live' is the basis for another sermon. They are told to stop seeking comfort in the land and instead to seek the Lord. They are to seek righteousness. If they do, the Lord will hear them and forgive.

Amos' final message

The last message sounds especially fierce. The vision of the fruit suggests that Israel is 'ripe for judgement'. God says he will never forget them – he records everything. He only forgets what he has forgiven, but the rest he never forgets. Amos tells them that the 10 tribes of Israel will be scattered among the nations, never to rise again. But in the midst of this terrible permanent sentence, it's as if the sun breaks through the clouds, for God says, 'But not all of you. Only the sinners in Israel will disappear. There will be a remnant. I will build again the tabernacle of David and bring Gentiles in to take your place in the people of God.' So a remnant that will keep true to God will survive and will be part of an enlarged people of God that will include Gentiles.

Indeed, these words of prophecy were quoted 800 years later in Acts 15, when the Council of Jerusalem met to consider the grounds for the admission of Gentiles into the Church. The leader of the church in Jerusalem reminded the council of the prophecy of Amos, in which God had promised that he would restore the tabernacle of David and bring the Gentiles in.

The Book of Hosea

Ten years after Amos had preached in Bethel, another prophet came on the scene. He was to be God's last prophet to the northern 10 tribes of Israel. We have already noted that Hosea's ministry was a real contrast to that of Amos. This time it's affection rather than accusation, wooing rather than warning, tender rather than tough, mercy rather than justice. It is God's final appeal before the 10 tribes disappear.

A key word unlocks the whole prophecy. It is the Hebrew word *chesed* (the *ch* is pronounced like the 'ch' in 'loch'). The word has no exact English equivalent. It is essentially a covenant word, used to describe those with whom you have a covenant relationship. It does mean 'love', but it has an awful lot of the word 'loyalty' in it too. True love is not true love unless it is loyal.

Chesed is often translated as 'loving kindness' or 'faithfulness'. 'Faithfulness' is used 60 times for this word in our English Bibles, while 'kindness' is used 9 or 10 times. It means unswerving love and undying devotion – it means we're so committed to someone that we go on loving them, whatever happens.

The old English word 'troth' is close (the word 'betrothed' is still used by some). It may be very significant that the word 'troth' itself has died out, because this kind of loyalty has died out too. Love is too often known without loyalty. People enjoy love with someone for a while, then drop them for someone else.

A covenant love

The whole relationship between God and Israel is a covenant love and therefore a *chesed*, stay-with-it love. Indeed, the Book of Hosea depicts the covenant love of God for his bride, Israel.

On God's side

God covenanted to look after them, protect them and provide for them. He had rescued them from Egypt and at Sinai had offered them the opportunity to be his people, which they had accepted. He was looking for glad, eager obedience – for a bride who wanted to live the way he wanted her to live.

On Israel's side

Israel was to respond joyfully to God's demands, knowing that because they were given for their good, they would be a delight to obey. David's Psalms express his delight in the Law of God. The longest Psalm in the Bible (119) is entirely about the benefits of the Law. But as a whole, the people of God did not obey and, by the time of Hosea, their failure was most pronounced.

God had to say through Hosea's messages, 'What's happened to our marriage?' He assured them of his loyal love but was certain that he was receiving very little back.

In order for Hosea to understand God's feelings, God took him through an extraordinary experience. God often prepared a prophet through his relationships or lack of them. God told Jeremiah that he must not marry, because he had to tell Judah that God too was now a bachelor. From the loneliness of not having a wife Jeremiah learned how God was feeling without Israel. Ezekiel was told that his wife would die but he must not weep for her, in order to show Judah that God too had been bereaved of his wife. In the same way, Hosea was taught how God felt by obeying some unusual instructions with regard to his marriage situation.

The background (chapters 1–3)

Chapters 1–3 give the background to the story. They are autobiographical and, indeed, are so fantastic that scholars argue whether it's fact or fiction, or whether the order of the chapters is different from the order of the events. But I believe we are safe to take it in its plainest, simplest meaning.

The first three chapters give us the storyline of the prophecy.

Chapter 1: the children

Hosea was told to marry a prostitute – something as shocking then as it would be today, especially for someone whom God intended to be his spokesman. They had three children, at least one of whom was not Hosea's. Then his wife returned to her old occupation. Hosea found her, brought her home and put her through a period of discipline when he didn't know her as a wife. He then courted her and started all over again with her as his wife.

The names of the children carry their own message. The first was a boy called Jezreel, which means 'God sows it'. He was a very rebellious, unruly child who had to be disciplined.

The second child was a girl called Lo-Ruhamah, which means 'not pitied'. This was a deprived child who didn't have love from her mother.

The third child was a boy called Lo-Ammi, which means 'not my people'. He was the child whom Hosea didn't father, and so the boy was disowned. So we have: disciplined, deprived and disowned. The children summarize how God was dealing with his people Israel. The names of the children were important to the message, though I haven't met any Christian parents who have used any of those three names!

Chapter 2: the wife

Chapter 2 tells us three things about Hosea's wife. First, she was reproached by her own children for what she was doing. They knew she was doing wrong. Secondly, Hosea punished her for her behaviour, and finally she was restored as his wife. The alliteration once again is clear: reproached, requited, restored.

Chapter 3: the husband

The pattern of threes continues with Hosea himself. We are told three things about him in chapter 3.

First, he was faithful to his wife even when she was faithless to him.

Secondly, he was firm with her, and for a period he did not treat her as his wife. He brought her home but didn't share the bed with her – representing the period of discipline in the exile that God was going to put the Jews through.

Thirdly, he was feared. His wife had a healthy fear of him, and trembled when she was with him. It meant that respect and loyalty were slowly being brought back into her life.

The message (chapters 4–14)

Chapters 4–14 give us the message that grew out of this relationship. Like the Book of Amos, Hosea is a collection of the prophet's sermons, presented in no particular order. Nevertheless, we can put it together under various headings, which give us the main themes and enable us to read it with understanding.

We must realize that everything Hosea says centres around these two headings: *Israel's unfaithfulness* and *God's faithfulness*. It is the contrast between the *chesed* that comes from God and the lack of response from the people that forms the theme of his whole prophecy.

This sums up God's argument with Israel, and his compassion for them comes out of this dilemma: What do you do with a people whom you love but who are unfaithful to you?

Israel's unfaithfulness

Hosea identifies seven sins, which we will call the 'seven deadly sins of Israel'. Their record shows God's detailed knowledge of what was going on.

1 **Infidelity** The people had become unfaithful in their marriages as well as unfaithful to God.

2 **Independence** God's chosen government was in Jerusalem, but they had created their own royal line with their own independent kingdom. And independence is, of course, the essence of sin. They effectively said they would not have God to rule over them. They preferred their own kingdom and were in active rebellion against God's chosen king in the south.

3 **Intrigue** The lack of loyalty towards God was mirrored in the people's disloyalty towards each other. This was seen in

people talking behind each other's backs, secret agreements being concocted and many people being upset.

4 **Idolatry** The golden calf of Samaria figures large in Hosea's prophecy. The people were openly accepting the Canaanite gods and engaging in pagan worship. The high places of Canaanite religion were being revered.

5 **Immorality** The bull was a symbol of fertility, and sexual immorality became common. The laws regarding sexual practices in the books of Moses had been jettisoned in favour of the lax morality of the surrounding nations. We have noted already that such immorality was even regarded as 'religious', in spite of its opposition to God's holy Law.

6 **Ignorance** The response to Hosea's prophecy made it clear that Israel was largely ignorant of the ways in which God's holy Law was being ignored. But it wasn't just that they didn't know about God – they didn't *want* to know about God.

7 **Ingratitude** God underlines the ingratitude of their behaviour by giving Hosea a series of pictures which would stick in their minds.

In chapter 7 Hosea uses a variety of images to describe the character of Israel, and none are complimentary. He said their evil passions were like a heated oven ready to bake the dough. He also compared them to an unturned cake that's getting all burnt on one side but uncooked on the other. Such a cake is completely inedible – a picture of the compromise of the nation. Its half-heartedness makes it effectively useless.

Hosea continues with the image of the fluttering dove trapped in a net. Israel has kept faith with no one, least of all God. She turns to Egypt one moment and Assyria the next – but never to God. So he must capture and discipline her.

The guilty parties

Hosea follows his list of deadly sins by identifying four groups of people whom he believes are responsible for this condition.

1 **The priests** They should have known God and should have been reminding the people of the Law of God so that if they sinned, sacrifice was available. But they had abrogated their responsibility. Those who should have been an example were just as bad as the rest.

2 **The prophets** Israel was not without a large number of prophets. But they were all false prophets. They would tell the people of God not to worry about their behaviour, claiming that God wouldn't do the dreadful things he had promised – which, of course, was exactly what they wanted to hear. But God needs men who will tell the people what they don't want to hear, even when it's costly.

3 **The princes (or kings)** Although God had not chosen the northern royal line, they were still responsible for the people. In some respects the kings were like pastors to the people, responsible for ensuring that they were obedient to God's Law. However, few of the kings were at all concerned with how the nation had responded. Many of the people would take their lead from the kings. When they saw immorality at the head of the nation, they assumed it was OK for them to do likewise.

4 **The profiteers** Many were making big money out of the housing market, and the poor lost out every time. The Law of God was clear on the evils of charging interest and exploiting the poor. Hosea singles out the profiteers as the corrupters of society.

The judgements

Hosea tells them that suffering is coming in three areas.

1 **Barrenness** He says there will be miscarriages, and some women will not even be able to conceive. Others will lose their babies when they are born.
2 **Bloodshed** Next God predicts that an enemy will attack and kill many of them. He will not defend them.
3 **Banishment** Ultimately this enemy will be victorious and will evict them from the land.

God's faithfulness

These punishments are the severe side of Hosea's prophecy. Although he is more tender than Amos, he is not without a hard-hitting challenge. But it's not his main thrust. The major theme is that, in spite of their widespread disobedience, God is still faithful.

There's a statement in 1 Timothy about our relationship to Jesus. It says that if we deny him or if we disown him, he will disown us, but if we are faithless to him, then he remains faithful. That might have been lifted straight out of Hosea.

For the good news is that God has compassion on the people of Israel. This is the real heart of Hosea's word.

We can use the letters ' G-O-D' as an aid to memory (though not in the right order).

Because of his love for them God cannot let them *Off*, he cannot let them *Go* and he cannot let them *Down*.

GOD CAN'T LET THEM OFF (5:10–6:6)

This passage depicts God's hatred of their professions of repentance. He says, 'I will tear Ephraim and Judah as a lion rips apart its prey. I will carry them off and chase all rescuers away. I will abandon them and return to my home until they admit their guilt and look to me for help again.' He says that as soon as trouble comes they typically talk about returning to the Lord who will help them, without any real intention of changing their hearts. So God has to say, 'What shall I do with you? For your love vanishes like morning clouds. It disappears like dew. I sent my prophets to warn you of your doom. I have slain you with the words in my mouth, threatening you with death. I don't want your sacrifices – I want your love. I don't want your offerings – I want you to know me.'

GOD CAN'T LET THEM GO (11:1–11)

God makes his appeal to them, reminding them of the time when Israel was a child. God loved him as a son and brought him up out of Egypt. But the more God called to him, the more he rebelled, sacrificing to Baal and burning incense to idols. Although God had trained him from infancy, taught him how to walk and held him in his arms, Israel treated God with considerable scorn.

But God cries, 'How can I give you up, my Ephraim? How can I let you go? My heart cries out within me! How I long to help you! No, I will not punish you as much as my fierce anger tells me to. For I am God and not man, I am the Holy One living among you, and I didn't come to destroy.'

We see here a powerful expression of God's feelings. Whatever happens, he knows he cannot let them go.

GOD CAN'T LET THEM DOWN (14:1–9)

This passage is an impassioned appeal by God for the people to return to him and allow him to cure them of their idolatrous behaviour. It is not that Israel has mistakenly sinned – she has been defiant in her pursuit of evil. But God tells them that if they repent, he will forgive them. He will never let them down.

The passage finishes with a statement: 'Whoever is wise, let him understand these things, and whoever is intelligent, let him listen. For the paths of the Lord are true and right, and good men walk along them, but sinners trying it will fail.' It is one of the strongest appeals in the whole of the Bible to people who don't want to know about God's love, and it finishes the prophecy. Israel is given a final choice – to follow the ways of the Lord or to continue in waywardness.

How do we apply Amos and Hosea today?

First, we must concede that neither Amos nor Hosea succeeded in bringing Israel back to God. Their messages went unheeded, and God was forced to judge the people in the way he had promised. In 721 BC, Assyria defeated them and took them into exile, never to return.

Next, we must note that there is a big difference between our situation and that to which Amos and Hosea spoke and prophesied. In Israel there was a theocratic government; the Church and the State were one and the same thing. But this does not apply in the New Testament, where Church and State are clearly separated. The New Testament situation is summed up by Jesus' words, 'Render to Caesar the things that are Caesar's and to God the things that are God's.' So Christians today live in two kingdoms. I am a citizen of the United Kingdom, according to my passport. I am also a citizen of the Kingdom of God. So we have to be careful when applying Old Testament prophecies to our modern situation.

We suffer from a complication brought about by the Emperor Constantine in the fourth century AD. Europe has tried to combine Church and State. Constantine tried to create a Christendom in which the Kingdom of God and the kingdoms of man are one and the same thing, and the legacy remains in many European nations. So to be born into England is to be born into the Church, and we have centuries of an established Christianity behind us. But as far as God is concerned, the Church and the State are separate. We can make applications from Old Testament prophecies, but we must bear in mind that the two situations are not directly comparable.

So we cannot take a message from Amos or Hosea and say that the nation must obey in the way that God expected Israel to obey. But where the prophecy is directed to the people outside Israel, a legitimate application can be made. God's accusations to the other nations were based on conscience, not on the Law of God. In the same way, a secular nation will be judged on the basis of whether they lived according to what they intrinsically knew to be right.

So some of the sins that Amos and Hosea condemn in non-Israelite nations do apply. This includes inhumanity, riding roughshod over human rights, and legislation that makes the rich richer and the poor poorer. These are areas that we can apply validly.

However, this is not to say that the rest of prophecies to Israel are irrelevant. They do carry a powerful message to the Church today. For the Church too often behaves in a fashion similar to that of the people of Israel. There are plenty of New Testament passages that reinforce the messages of Hosea and Amos. We too must return to God, lest we come under his judgement. So when we read these prophecies, we must apply them to the people of God first, and then we are in a position to tell society what God says to them about the way they are living.

21.

ISAIAH

Introduction

Isaiah is a fascinating book to study. For a start, the documents of the prophecy of Isaiah are among the best attested of all the books in the Old Testament. The Dead Sea Scrolls, found in 1948, included a copy of the book that dated from 100 BC, which was around a thousand years older than the next oldest copy, which dated from 900 AD. At the time translation work on the Revised Standard Version of the Bible was being completed, but the work was stopped while these documents were checked. But very little needed changing.

Isaiah is also fascinating because of the way the book has been arranged in our Bibles. The chapter headings in the Bible are not inspired. (I wish we had a Bible without chapter and verse numbers, because then we would know our Bibles according to the flow of thought, and not in an artificial way according to 'texts', as we do today. For at least 1,100 years the Christian Church had Bibles without any chapter and verse numbers.)

But whoever divided Isaiah into chapters did a rather interesting thing, though I doubt whether it was deliberate. They divided the book into 66 chapters, the same number as the books of the Bible. Furthermore, they divided Isaiah into two distinct parts of 39 chapters and 27 chapters. It just happens that the Old Testament has 39 books and the New Testament 27.

Also, the message of the first 39 chapters summarizes the message of the Old Testament, and the message of the last 27 chapters summarizes exactly the message of the New Testament! The second part of Isaiah (i.e. chapter 40) begins with the voice crying in the wilderness, 'Prepare the way for the Lord' – words later used by John the Baptist. It moves on to a servant of the Lord who is anointed by the Holy Spirit, dies for the sins of his people, and is raised and exalted after his death. It then moves on to the declaration that 'You shall be my witnesses to the ends of the earth', and it finishes up with God saying, 'I am making all things new. I create a new heaven and a new earth.'

In other words, if somebody took the whole Bible and squeezed it into one book, you'd finish up with the prophecy of Isaiah. It is the Bible in miniature.

Even more remarkable is the fact that chapters 40–66 divide very clearly into three sections, each of nine chapters. So in chapters 40–48 the theme is comforting God's people; in chapters 49–57 the theme is the Servant of the Lord, who dies and rises again; and chapters 58–66 are about the future glory.

Furthermore, each of these sections of nine chapters divides into three sections of three chapters. If you take the middle three there are three very clear sections; 49–51, 52–54 and 55–57. If you take the middle section (chapters 52–54), and the middle verse of the middle chapter of that middle section, you come to the key verse in the book: 'He was pierced for our transgressions, he was crushed for our iniquities; the punishment that brought us peace was upon him, and by his wounds we are healed' (53:5). None of this is inspired as such, but it is remarkable that even the central verse of the second section should sum up the central theme of the New Testament.

The Book of Isaiah is very well known in parts. I remember someone's comment after reading one of Shakespeare's plays.

He said he didn't like it because it was too full of quotations and he was sure that Shakespeare had taken a lot of his material from somewhere else, not realizing that it was Shakespeare who had originated those quotations! The same is true of the Book of Isaiah. There are many texts from it that are well known to those who have been brought up in church circles.

For example:

> Though your sins be as scarlet, they shall be as white as snow.
>
> **(1:18, AV)**

If wool has been dyed it is impossible to make it white again, but this is what God says about our sins.

> They shall beat their swords into plowshares, and their spears into pruninghooks.   **(2:4, AV)**

This verse is on a block of granite outside the United Nations headquarters in New York. It is a pity that they didn't quote the whole verse, for it starts, 'He shall judge among the nations ...' Without God to judge between the nations, there is no way that anyone will ever manage to complete the second half of the verse.

Other well-known quotes include:

> A virgin shall conceive, and bear a son, and shall call his name Immanuel.   **(7:14, AV)**

> For unto us a child is born, unto us a son is given: and the government shall be upon his shoulder: and his name shall be called Wonderful, Counseller, The mighty God, The everlasting Father, The Prince of Peace.   **(9:6, AV)**

The spirit of the LORD shall rest upon him, the spirit of wisdom and understanding, the spirit of counsel and might, the spirit of knowledge and of the fear of the LORD.   (11:2, AV)

Thou wilt keep him in perfect peace, whose mind is stayed on thee.   (26:3, AV)

They that wait upon the LORD shall renew their strength; they shall mount up with wings as eagles; they shall run, and not be weary; and they shall walk, and not faint.   (40:31, AV)

How beautiful upon the mountains are the feet of him that bringeth good tidings.   (52:7, AV)

The Lord's hand is not shortened, that it cannot save; neither his ear heavy, that it cannot hear.   (59:1, AV)

Oh that thou wouldest rend the heavens, that thou wouldest come down.   (64:1, AV)

Another well-known section is the call of Isaiah in chapter 6, when he has a vision of God in the Temple, though his difficult mission, described in the next verses of the same chapter, is less well known. Chapter 35 describes the desert blossoming as a rose. Chapter 40 starts with the familiar words, 'Comfort ye, comfort ye my people, saith your God.' We have already mentioned 53:5, 'he was wounded for our transgressions, he was bruised for our iniquities'. Most Christians recognize 55:1, 'Come ye, buy, and eat; yea, come, buy wine and milk without money and without price.' Chapter 61 includes the text for Christ's first sermon in Nazareth: 'The Spirit of the Lord God is upon me; because the Lord hath anointed me to preach good tidings unto the meek.'

Having said that people know certain parts of the book if Isaiah, it is also clear that the book as a whole is not known at all well. This is a shame, for it is the book that both Jesus and the apostle Paul quote more than any other part of the Old Testament. The New Testament is full of quotes from it, especially from the second part.

Few Christians seem to be aware that phrases such as 'grieving the Holy Spirit', 'God shall wipe away all tears', 'a voice crying in the wilderness', 'you shall be my witnesses to the ends of the earth' and 'every knee shall bow and every tongue confess' all come straight out of the second section of Isaiah.

So it is clear that if you really want to know the Bible, you need to get to know Isaiah. It will provide you with insights into the New Testament as well as the Old.

The man

Like most biblical writers, Isaiah was a self-effacing and God-centred man, so he was loath to talk about himself. What we do know about him comes from his writings and from other Jewish historical books, in particular from the historian Josephus, who says quite a lot about Isaiah. So it is possible to piece together a picture. He must have had godly parents, for his Hebrew name, *Yesa-Yahu* ('Isaiah' is the anglicized form of this), means 'God saves'. This has a similar root to the names Jesus and Joshua. It was an entirely appropriate name, because he has been called the evangelist of the Old Testament. He is the one who brings the gospel, the good news, especially in the second part of the book. The word 'new' rarely occurs in the Old Testament, but it does occur frequently in this second part of the Book of Isaiah. He grew up to be the greatest prophet of all time, classed by the Jews in the same category as Moses and Elijah.

From a human point of view he had a head start, having been born in a palace and brought up in court. He was the grandson of King Joash and was therefore a cousin of King Uzziah, which is one reason why he was so devastated by Uzziah's death. Isaiah had wealth, rank and education. This gave him some advantages, but it also made it hard to be a prophet. But he had such an encounter with the Lord in the Temple that the path he should follow was made crystal clear.

He moved freely in court circles and counselled kings, so many of his prophecies deal with political issues, especially the false security of making alliances with powers such as Assyria or Egypt.

As far as his own family life is concerned, his wife was a prophetess, but we do not have a single prophecy from her. It is quite likely that he checked his prophecies with her before delivering them.

He had at least two sons. One of them was named *Maher-Shalal-Hash-Baz*, which means 'haste the booty, speed the spoil' – not the sort of name that most parents would choose for their offspring! But it was a prophetic name pointing to the day when Jerusalem itself would be looted by an enemy and all the treasures would be taken. The other son was called *Shear-Jashub*, which means 'a remnant shall return'. So the two sons' names sum up the two focal messages of Isaiah. The bad news (mainly in the first half of his book) is that Jerusalem will be sacked and looted and spoiled. The good news is that a remnant shall return – Israel still has a future, even after losing everything.

There is speculation that he had a third child called Emmanuel. Certainly, there was a little boy born around that time who was the subject of prophecy. Nevertheless, I think it was another man's child, not his. The child Emmanuel – whose name meant 'God with us' – was a sign to the king. He was, in fact, a double sign, which was also fulfilled centuries later in Jesus.

His call

Isaiah's call came during a visit to the Temple. He had a vision and was overcome by the holiness of the Lord. His age is not given in the text, but he was probably in his late teens or early twenties. From this moment on, Isaiah used a name for God that was not used by anyone else – 'the Holy One of Israel'. This name occurs nearly 50 times all the way through his book and in both parts of it. As soon as he caught a sight of God's holiness, he felt unclean and wanted to leave the Temple. It is interesting that he felt that his lips were unclean. He had the remarkable experience of an angel flying with a live, red-hot coal to cauterize his lips. Some think this was an imaginary vision, but it really happened. Throughout his life Isaiah would tell people that his scarred mouth was the result of God burning his lips.

The call of Isaiah gives us an unexpected reference to the Trinity. Isaiah was asked by God, 'Whom shall I send? And who will go for us?' The plural 'us' indicates that the whole Godhead would be sending him. Then comes the shattering news that, although he is being commissioned to preach to the people, they will not listen to his preaching. God will make them hard of hearing and they will not receive the word or make any response. So God is saying to Isaiah at the start of his ministry, 'Don't think you're going to be a successful preacher. The more you preach, the harder they will get! Indeed, I'm going to use your preaching to deafen them and blind them, lest they should be converted and healed.'

It's an extraordinary statement, underlining a truth found in other parts of the Bible, that the word of God not only opens people's hearts, but can also close them. It can push people further away. After we have listened to the word of God, we are either harder against it or softer towards it. But we can't remain neutral.

The verses outlining Isaiah's experience of preaching are quoted in the New Testament more often than any other verse in Isaiah. Jesus used it of his own ministry. He said he spoke so that 'they may be ever seeing but never perceiving, and ever hearing but never understanding; otherwise they might turn and be forgiven!' (Mark 4:12). In other words, he spoke in parables to hide the truth and to harden those who weren't really interested. Paul quoted the same verse when he preached to the Jews and they wouldn't listen.

So the hardening impact of the word of God is a key theme, and it is no wonder that Isaiah asked: 'How long do I have to go on preaching and hardening them with no response?' The Lord's reply came: 'Until the land is utterly forsaken.' Isaiah had one of the toughest assignments of all the prophets. But, of course, if he hadn't gone through with it, we wouldn't have this amazing book. He didn't know that centuries ahead, this book would be an inspiration. But in his lifetime he was a failure. Nobody listened – they just got harder and harder for 40 years.

The location of Judah

Our understanding of the book is aided by appreciating that Judah was surrounded by a number of nations – smaller ones close to her borders, with the larger, super-power nations further away. In Isaiah we find that God first used the small nations to discipline his people, but when they wouldn't listen, he used the bigger ones. The small nations included the

Syrians in the north and the Ammonites, the Moabites and the Edomites to the west and the south. Then to the west were the Philistines, whom God had brought from Crete, and down in the desert were the Arabs. The bigger powers were, in the east, Assyria and then Babylon, though the latter did not reach its full power until Isaiah had died. His references to Babylon speak prophetically of the power and prominence that she will one day enjoy. In the west was Egypt.

There were a number of alliances against 'little' Judah in Isaiah's day. Perhaps the most surprising was the one between the 10 tribes of Israel (i.e. the northern kingdom) and the Syrians. This was a serious moment in the history of God's people. It was at this time that Isaiah assured the king of Judah that they would win, in spite of being just two small tribes. Isaiah said, 'Behold, a virgin will conceive and bear a son and call his name Emmanuel.' This would be a sign that God would bring victory.

Emmanuel means 'God is with us', but there are four different ways of reading the phrase 'God is with us', depending on which of the four words are stressed. The emphasis should actually be on the word 'us'. God is with 'us' – not with 'them'! In other words, it means that God is on our side. So when the boy was conceived and the name was given, the king knew that the alliance between the 10 tribes and the Syrians wouldn't win.

On another occasion the Philistines linked up with the Arabs. Once again, this was a serious threat against little Judah. But again God was on their side.

In the time of Isaiah, Assyria, with its capital Nineveh on the shores of the Tigris, was the big power to the east. Egypt was the big power in the south-west. But there was also a new power growing called Babylon (in the region known today as Iraq), which would become even more powerful in the future.

Isaiah prophesied during four reigns. He began in the year when King Uzziah died and Jotham came to the throne. Ahaz, Hezekiah and finally Manasseh were also on the throne during his ministry.

The kings of Judah

In noting how Isaiah needed to preach, it is useful to note the pattern that develops when we examine the success of the kings of Judah. The Books of Kings tell us whether the king in question was good or bad in the eyes of God. The good kings won the battles and the bad kings lost. If they were good, God was with them and no one could defeat them.

Uzziah (792–740 BC) was a case in point. He was a good king to begin with and had a long reign of 52 years. But in the last years he became a bad king – he did evil in the sight of the Lord and died of leprosy. This was his punishment for changing from a good king to a bad king.

During the early years of Isaiah the first enemy attack came from the Philistines and the Arabs in a formidable alliance. But Judah won because the king followed God's ways. But when the king became disobedient, the Assyrians defeated Judah.

Jotham (750–740) was a good king who reigned for 19 years (10 of those as regent). Whoever came to attack Judah during his time was defeated. The Ammonites and also an alliance between Israel and Syria were defeated.

Ahaz (735–715) was a bad king who was defeated by the Edomites, the Philistines and the Assyrians.

Hezekiah (715–686) was a good king who reigned for 29 years and defeated the Philistines. It was during his reign that the Assyrians besieged Jerusalem with 185,000 troops, but God sent an angel to wipe them out completely. Until a few years ago many people thought that was a legend, but a British archaeologist has found human skeletons lying at the foot of the city wall, and they are believed to be the remains of this very army.

The siege of Jerusalem was the reason for an engineering work in the city that lasts to this day. Concerned about the need for water during the siege, Hezekiah dug a tunnel to bring water from a spring outside the city. It is still possible to walk through this very tunnel.

But it wasn't all good news. Hezekiah made a big mistake towards the end of his life when he fell ill. He cried to the Lord and was given 15 more years of life, but he did not use the time well. On one occasion messengers arrived with a 'Get well' card from the son of the king of Babylon – at that time a small but growing state. Hezekiah was pleased that somebody so far away was thinking about him, so he showed the visitors around his palace so that they would tell their king what a wonderful king Hezekiah was. But when Isaiah heard what had happened, he was horrified. He told Hezekiah that one day the king of Babylon would take everything that the Babylonian visitors had been shown. It's a very dramatic little narrative right in the middle of the Book of Isaiah, and it came true just as Isaiah had said.

Manasseh (695–642) was one of the worst kings of Judah. He was involved in devil worship and even sacrificed his own son to the demonic god Molech, who was the centre of the satanic worship in Judah. Most bad kings lasted just a short time, but his reign, at 53 years, was one of the longest that Judah had known.

Manasseh hated Isaiah so much that he forbade him ever to speak. This is one reason why we have the prophecy of Isaiah written down. But finally Manasseh could stand it no more and resolved to kill the prophet. It was a particularly nasty death. According to Jewish history, Manasseh ordered a hollow tree-trunk to be brought. Isaiah was tied up, pushed into the hollow

tree and sawn in half. He is mentioned in Hebrews 11 as one of
the 'heroes of the faith'. The words 'some were sawn in two'
refer to him.

The table below outlines the different reigns in Isaiah's time:

KING	REIGN	CHARACTER	VICTORIES	DEFEATS
UZZIAH	52 years	GOOD then BAD	ARABS PHILISTINES	ASSYRIANS
JOTHAM	19 years	GOOD	AMMONITES SYRIANS ISRAELITES	
AHAZ	20 years	BAD		EDOMITES PHILISTINES ASSYRIANS
HEZEKIAH	29 years	GOOD	PHILISTINES ASSYRIANS	
MANASSEH	53 years	BAD		ASSYRIANS

The book

The first thing that strikes the reader of the Book of Isaiah is
the contrast between its two parts. Like the other prophetic
books, it is a collection of different messages given at different
times. It is not in chronological order; sometimes it is in topical order and sometimes it is in no order at all. So it is a bit of a
mixture, but on the whole one type of prophecy predominates
in the first part of the book and another type predominates in
the second part.

The first 39 chapters are quite different from the last 27 –
so much so that many scholars think that the second part was

written by someone else, referred to as 'Deutero Isaiah' ('Deutero' means 'second'). The differences between the two parts can be summarized as below:

PART 1	PART 2
More bad news than good	More good news than bad
Human activity	Divine activity
Sin and retribution	Salvation and redemption
Justice	Mercy
Confronting	Comforting
God of Israel	Creator of the universe
National	International
God = fire	God = father
God's hand	God's arm
upraised to strike	outstretched to save
Curses (woe)	Blessings
'Strange work'	Good tidings
Jews	Gentiles
Assyria	Babylon
Before the exile	After the exile
Present	Future

Since the second half is largely focused on the post-exilic period, sceptics feel that the events are given in such detail that someone else must have written it. They say that Isaiah couldn't have predicted that Babylon would be defeated by a man called Cyrus, because it happened 100 years after Isaiah had died.

So scholars suggest that 'Proto Isaiah' wrote chapters 1–39, then 'Deutero Isaiah' wrote chapters 40–56, and 'Trito Isaiah' apparently wrote the last 10 chapters. So now we have three Isaiahs! This is taught as gospel truth in some Bible schools. The reason given is that there is such a difference in style, content and vocabulary that a different author must have been responsible for each section.

The unity of the book

It is argued that whether there were three Isaiahs or one doesn't really matter. But these scholars forget that Isaiah gave many messages over a period of many years, and with a different aim – either to confront or comfort. So he would naturally use a different style and different vocabulary. It is not necessary to saw the book in two or three.

In addition, there are a number of reasons for believing that the same writer wrote all of the Book of Isaiah.

First, the two parts have so much in common. Isaiah's description of God as the 'Holy One of Israel' occurs 50 times – 25 times in Part 1 and 25 times in Part 2. While there are some themes that are covered in one part and not the other, all the major themes straddle the two parts.

Secondly, it would be amazing if the writer of Part 2 of the book, which includes what many regard as the greatest prophetic section in the whole Bible, should be forgotten. If the names of the other biblical prophets – including the minor prophets – are known, it hardly seems likely that the name of the author of the second part of Isaiah would be lost.

Thirdly, both Jesus and Paul quote from Part 2 and accredit Isaiah as the prophet. This is enough for me. I can't believe that either Jesus or Paul would lie about the authorship of Isaiah if it were uncertain.

Lastly, the key argument concerns whether or not God knows the future. If he does, then he has no difficulty in communicating that future to Isaiah. Once we settle this central issue, many of our problems are solved.

Part 1 (chapters 1–39)

The Book of Isaiah is a collection of different prophecies made over 40 years, so it is not very ordered. But there is a broad shape to it which will help our understanding as we read it. We will give a brief overview of Part 1 before looking at some of the themes in more detail.

Chapters 1–10 are a reproof for Judah and particularly for Jerusalem. The nation was wealthy, but just as Amos preaches against the inappropriate use of wealth in the northern kingdom of Israel, so Isaiah does the same in Judah. He criticizes the women of Jerusalem for the money they spend on jewellery and clothing, while neglecting the poor and disadvantaged.

Then in chapters 13–23 there is a section about judgement on other nations. God used them to discipline his people, but they overstepped God's permission in their actions. They were malicious and cruel and did more to Israel than God had intended them to do.

In chapters 24–34 there is a mixture of good and bad news. There is judgement for the northern tribes and Judah, but the coming glory is described twice. So there is a rebuke, but the people also get a little glimpse of a brighter future.

Chapters 36–39 tell the story of King Hezekiah's illness, which we looked at earlier. They are really a transitional story to show how Assyria gave way to Babylon as the main threat to Judah, through Hezekiah's foolishness in welcoming the envoys from Babylon.

Judah (chapters 1–12 and 24–35)

BAD NEWS

Disobedience

The prophecies of Isaiah were given against a backdrop of peace and prosperity. Indeed, the nation had not known such wealth since the days of Solomon, when the country was at its peak. But alongside the prosperity came pride and indulgence. There was an 'every man for himself' attitude. The poor were oppressed and injustice was common.

The religious life of the nation had become ritualistic. The people went through the routine of worship, but their hearts remained cold towards God. As a result they drifted in their allegiance to God and tolerated pagan idols, worshipping the Canaanite gods Baal and Asherah in the superstitious belief that doing so would make their crops grow and their lives flourish.

Discipline

So a pattern develops similar to the one seen in the Book of Judges. God allows foreign attacks to teach Judah that they should trust in him. As we have seen, these attackers included Syria and Israel, Arabs and Philistines, Edom, Ammon and Moab, and the superpower of Isaiah's early ministry, Assyria (which was eventually defeated by Babylon). But instead of trusting God, they made alliances with whichever power seemed able to provide the most protection at the time. God did not get a look in.

Disaster

God had promised in the time of Moses that if the people did not keep his commands and heed his warnings they would lose the land he had given them. So with Isaiah's warnings falling on deaf ears, in 587 BC the people eventually followed their northern neighbours Israel into exile, though this time at the hands of Babylon.

Dejection

Isaiah predicted that the people's journey and sojourn in Babylon would not be a pleasant one. But he said that it was in exile that many would return to God. As a nation they never again followed after foreign gods. Syncretism and idolatry were banished from their national life.

GOOD NEWS

Remnant

The good news of Part 1 is that from the exile a remnant will return, and that there will be a king who will bring peace to the nations. From the remnant of the people will come a king like David who will be an Everlasting Father, a Counsellor, a Prince of Peace with the government on his shoulder.

Return

It is also clear that despite the disobedience of Judah, God will never break his covenant. So the promise throughout is that they will one day return to the land they had lost. They returned 70 years later, just as Jeremiah would predict.

Reign

Isaiah prophesied that a king would come who would reign like no other. Details of his reign are given: his birth; his ministry in 'Galilee of the Gentiles'; his lineage, from the line of Jesse; his anointing to do God's work. Anyone who doubts the validity of Christ's claim to kingship need only look back to the accuracy of the predictions in Isaiah.

Rejoicing

Throughout the chapters there are times of rejoicing at God's goodness amidst the bad news. See 2:1–5; 12; 14:1–2; 26; 27; 30:19–33; 32:15–20; 34:16–35. Of all the prophetic books, it is Isaiah that is full of joy.

THE NATIONS (CHAPTERS 13–23)

Isaiah mentions a number of nations which had dealings with Judah: Assyria, Babylon, Philistia, Moab, Syria (Damascus), Cush, Egypt, Edom, Arabia and Tyre. There are three points that we should notice:

1 God used them to discipline his people.
2 They exceeded his limits. They were inhuman and unjust, and mocked the God of Israel.
3 God punished them with fire and eventually extinction.

But in spite of this punishment of the nations, Isaiah predicts that the whole earth will share in Judah's blessings (see chapters 23–24).

Part 2 (chapters 40–66)

A picture of God

The second half of Isaiah gives us an incredible picture of God all the way through.

HE'S THE ONLY GOD THERE IS

God says, 'There are no gods beside me.' We are told that the so-called gods don't really exist. God is the only God. Other gods have been invented by the peoples. God also says, 'There are no gods like me.' Isaiah mocks the other gods, pointing out that they have ears but they can't hear, they have eyes but they can't see, they have feet but they can't walk.

This view is, of course, a profoundly offensive statement in our modern world, where we are asked to accept all religions. But there is no God beside the God of Israel.

THE ALMIGHTY CREATOR

The nations are as a drop in the bucket or dust on the scales. It is God who names the stars. Man was commanded by God to name the animals but never to name the stars, and we are wise to remain ignorant of the star sign we were born under. Opinion polls suggest that six out of ten men and seven out of ten women read their horoscope every day. Man should instead look to the Almighty Creator for wisdom about the future.

GOD IS THE HOLY ONE OF ISRAEL

This title for God occurs 25 times in the second part of the Book of Isaiah. Amos focuses on God's righteousness, Hosea on God's faithfulness and Isaiah on God's holiness. It is clear that he never forgot his initial vision of God in his splendour, and so this description becomes a key motif in the book.

THE REDEEMER OF HIS PEOPLE

God is described as the 'kinsman redeemer'. Just as the kinsman redeemer would step in to help a family, so God has the power and is willing to help because of his covenant commitment to his people.

THE SAVIOUR OF THE NATIONS

This title was applied to God in the Book of Isaiah before it was applied to Jesus in the New Testament. It is Isaiah who emphasizes God's concern for all peoples and his desire that there should be an international gathering in the new heaven and earth.

THE LORD OF HISTORY

Isaiah says that the nations are but a drop in the bucket. God begins, controls and ends history. He foretells and controls the future. (See 41:1–6, 21–29; 42:8–9, 10–17; 44:6–8, 25–26; 46:10–11; 48:3.)

ALL FOR HIS GLORY

This focus on God throughout the book is in order that his glory might be made known. The word 'glory' is a key word in the book. God wants his splendour to be displayed for the world to see.

The servant of God

A series of songs are especially significant in the second part of the book and are among its best-known chapters. They are called songs because they are very poetic. They mention a 'servant of God' (20 times), and to this day the Jews don't know who he is.

The meaning of the 'servant' seems to change. On nine occasions the servant seems to be the whole people of Israel (eg. 49:3), but then on other occasions it becomes clear that he is an individual. Furthermore, the title is also given to specific people in other parts of the Old Testament: Uzziah, Josiah, Jeremiah, Ezekiel, Job, Moses and Zerubbabel are all called by this name at various times.

But four things can be said about this servant of the Lord:

1 His faultless character. This servant is perfect; he has no faults. This statement can't be applied to any other person.
2 He is a deeply unhappy man, a man of sorrows who is acquainted with grief.
3 He is executed – killed as a criminal – and yet he is sinless. He is killed for others' sins, not his own. He is accused falsely and his grave is with the rich.
4 After he has been killed for the sins of others, he is raised from the dead and exalted to a very high position.

There is no indication that Isaiah or any other prophet made the connection between the servant of God and the coming king motif earlier in the book. Obviously this is no mystery to the Christian, but to the Jew it is. They can't integrate this servant in the second half of Isaiah with the promised king in the first half. It simply doesn't make sense to them.

The first Jew to make the connection between these two was Jesus, and the connection came at his baptism when God said, 'You are my Son whom I love; with you I am well pleased.' God was putting together something that had been said about the king – 'You are my son' – and something that had been said about the servant – 'With you I am well pleased.' Jesus knew that he was to combine those two figures in one.

Not only did Jesus make the connection, but Peter made it often in his preaching. In the Book of Acts, Peter makes the connection between the king and the servant. Many priests became Christians in the early days because they knew the Book of Isaiah and saw the connection between the king and the servant.

Philip also made the connection when he met the Ethiopian eunuch in the Book of Acts and found that he was reading Isaiah 53.

Paul made the connection supremely. In Philippians he talks about the one who was equal with God and yet took the form of a servant. The Jews don't feel that a king could suffer like that and be put to death as a common criminal. The cross is an offence to the Jewish people – a king nailed to a cross is not the kind of king they want. Jesus doesn't look like the king with the government on his shoulder. They are looking for a victorious king to come and reign, not to die.

The Spirit of God

Perhaps surprisingly, the Holy Spirit is also very prominent in Isaiah. The phrase 'grieving the Holy Spirit' comes from Isaiah 63:10–11. We read that the Spirit anoints this servant for his task (61:1–3). 'I will pour out my Spirit on your offspring' (44:3) – a reference, of course, to Pentecost. We have already noted the reference to 'us' in Isaiah 6, as in 'Whom shall I send and who will go for us?'

So the Trinity is in the Old Testament for those with eyes to see. Here is the mighty God who created the world, here is his suffering servant and here is the Holy Spirit – all three Persons are present in the second half of Isaiah.

Prophecy

It is important to grasp a principle about understanding prophecy, especially as prophecy comprises a third of the Bible, including 17 books from Isaiah to Malachi. This is especially important with a relatively complicated prophecy such as Isaiah.

All the prophets spoke to their own age and also to the future.

1 **To their own age** It was as if they had a microscope for the present day. They saw their own day clearly through God's eyes and spoke accordingly. But the word's application was not limited to their own day. The abiding moral principles can speak to any culture in any age. For God's character does not change, and his moral standards remain the same for all time.

2 **To the future** They also had a telescope on the future. They spoke of what would happen one day. But this is where it gets complicated, for it was impossible for the prophet to gauge the distance in time between the events he saw, just as someone gazing at mountain peaks from a

long way off would be unable to grasp how much distance there was between them. So what many of the Old Testament prophets (and we as readers) thought was one mountain with two peaks was in fact two mountains spaced far apart. So two future events are described as if they are next to each other, when actually there are thousands of years between them. (see diagram, p.652)

Christians today live between the two peaks. One peak is the past and the other peak is the future, because we know something that the prophets didn't know. They looked for the coming of the King, but we know that the King is coming twice.

Not only is this the case, but sometimes the fulfilment of the prophecies does not occur in the order they are given. So we know, for example, that the suffering servant of the second part of Isaiah is fulfilled before the reigning king of the first part. Christ has come as the servant who goes to the cross, but not yet as the king who reigns over all.

So it is not surprising that the Jews who know Isaiah very well are still looking for the first coming. The Jews' expectation that the Messiah would come only once as king caused them to be disillusioned with Jesus, and to disqualify him as their Messiah. When Jesus rode into Jerusalem on Palm Sunday, it seemed that at last he was coming as king, in the way that the crowds wanted him to. They went wild with excitement, thinking he was about to throw the Romans out. But he was riding on a donkey, symbolic of the fact that he hadn't come to fight.

Revelation tells us that when Jesus comes a second time, he will come to fight, for then he comes as a man of war on a white horse. But on Palm Sunday his mission was peace, not to fulfil Isaiah's prophecy of a reigning king. To everyone's amazement, when he came through the gate, he turned left instead of right. To the right was the Roman fortress where the occupying force was based. But Jesus turned to the Temple and whipped the Jews out of it. His priorities were different from those of the Jews.

So we can perhaps imagine why, a few days later, the same crowd said, 'Crucify him!' and chose to save Barabbas, the guerrilla fighter, instead. They thought he was coming to take the throne, but all he did was clean up the Temple – how very disappointing! So when Pilate placed a plaque above his head reading 'This is the king of the Jews' they couldn't believe it. The only man in that whole nation who believed it said, 'Lord, remember me when you get your kingdom.' For the dying thief saw in the suffering, dying man One who was the coming king.

The ultimate future

INTERNATIONAL

We have noted already that the message of Isaiah, especially of the second part, is that the whole earth would know God's blessings, not just the Jews. He mentions that 'distant islands' will know God. It is likely that this is a reference to Britain, since this land was referred to as a 'distant island' by the Phoenicians, who shipped tin from the Cornish mines.

NATIONAL

Yet this worldwide focus does not mean that Judah is forgotten. Jerusalem, Zion and the mountains of the Lord are to be the location of God's activity too. We know that one day he will come on a horse and take over the governments of the world. The kingdoms of this world will become the Kingdom of our God and of his Christ. So the Church today is getting people ready for the king to come and reign. We are preparing subjects in all nations now so that he can come back. When the good news is preached to all the nations, then the end shall come, because God wants all ethnic groups to be represented.

In the second part of Isaiah it seems as if he is constantly switching from the future of Jerusalem to the future of the nations. But we also find in Isaiah 4 that the house of the Lord will be established on the mountains, and all the nations will come to it. It's a future for a 'united nations', but it is centred on Jerusalem. Just as the suffering servant element has happened, so will the reigning king element.

So why do we read Isaiah?

1 It's part of God's word. The study of any part of the Scriptures is able to make us 'wise unto salvation'. In Isaiah the key words are 'save' and 'salvation' (the name Isaiah itself means 'God saves').

2 The book is a good introduction to the whole Bible. It is a summary of all the themes of both Testaments, brought into one book by the Spirit's inspiration. So if you think the Bible is too big a book for you to read through, read Isaiah for a start, and it will introduce you to all the themes of Scripture.

3 It is a very good introduction to prophecy. It is in one of the three Major Prophets, placed first in the section of the prophets in our Bible. It is typical of most prophecy in being a combination of protest about the present and prediction about the future. It is easy to see the ways in which certain parts are fulfilled by Christ's coming in the New Testament.

4 Isaiah helps us to link the Old and New Testaments by showing us how they illuminate each other. We can understand the New Testament much better if we know Isaiah.

5 We read it to get to know Jesus. Jesus said, 'Search the Scriptures, for they bear testimony to me.' He's talking about the Old Testament. Isaiah helps the reader to understand the Lord better than almost any other Old Testament book. If you read through Isaiah 53, you are at the foot of the cross. 'By his stripes we are healed.'

6 We gain a bigger view of God. 'O magnify the Lord with me' means 'Enlarge your understanding of God himself.' The second half of Isaiah gives us a bigger view of God, the Holy One of Israel, the Creator of the ends of the earth.

Thus, although Isaiah is the largest prophetic book, and will take time and effort to be understood, there are many reasons why Christians should make it the one prophetic book that they definitely read.

It is the Bible in miniature. It will aid their understanding of the Old Testament, illuminate their understanding of the New and, most importantly, enlarge their vision of God.

22.

MICAH

Introduction

The prophetic books from Hosea to Malachi are called the 'Minor Prophets' in our Bibles. But this is a misnomer, for it suggests that one group is lesser than the other. In fact, they were so called to distinguish the smaller books from the larger three – that is, Isaiah, Jeremiah and Ezekiel. This misnomer is never more so than with the prophecy of Micah. For he has a memorable message – one that still reverberates around the world today.

Micah was a contemporary of Isaiah, and one section of the Book of Micah is identical to a section in the Book of Isaiah. It concerns beating swords into plough-shares and spears into pruning-hooks, and the reign of peace that will come when Christ returns. Who copied whom, or whether the Holy Spirit gave them an identical message is unclear, but they were both speaking to the same situation, so it's clear that God wanted the same message to be given again.

There is a passage from Micah which you will have heard read at carol services: 'But you, Bethlehem Ephrathah, though you are small among the clans of Judah, out of you will come for me one who will be ruler over Israel' (5:2). The prediction was made 700 years before Jesus was born.

There is a classic verse: 'He has showed you, O man, what is good. And what does the Lord require of you? To act justly and to love mercy and to walk humbly with your God' (6:8), and there is a statement right at the end of the book which has been made into a number of hymns: 'Who is a pardoning God like you?' (7:18).

These are all memorable, but they are usually taken out of context and used as pretexts. We must put the whole book into context, into time and place. God always expressed his word at a particular time and to a particular place. That is why the Bible, unlike all other holy books in the world, is full of history and geography. If you read the Koran or the Hindu Vedas you will find that they are more books of thoughts and words. But the Bible is a book of history and geography, because God unfolded his total revelation at particular times and in particular places, and this is very important for Micah.

Where?

The promised land was a very narrow strip between the Mediterranean on the one hand and the Arabian Desert on the other. It was a corridor through which all the traffic from Europe, Asia and Africa had to pass. It usually passed down the coast along a road called the Way of the Sea. The crossroads of the world was at the hill of Megiddo (Armageddon in Hebrew). All the world's traffic passed through it, and there was a little village called Nazareth on a hill overlooking the crossroads. For this reason Galilee, the northern part of Israel, was called 'Galilee of the Nations', because international traffic went through it. The south was far more culturally Jewish. It was up in the hills with far fewer international visitors.

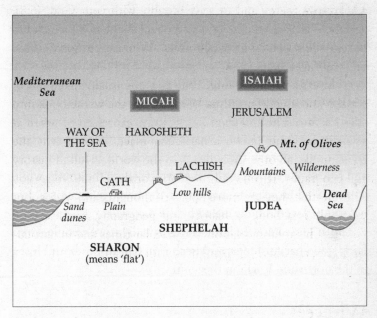

If you take an east-west cross-section in the south, we have the Mediterranean Sea at one side and the Dead Sea at the other. The Dead Sea is a lot lower than the Mediterranean.

Micah came from the Shephelah, a district of hills 20 miles inland on a 3,000-metre shelf. He lived between the Philistines and the Jews. As such he could look up to the corrupt city of Jerusalem and down to the Gaza Strip.

A key detail to appreciate is that Isaiah and Micah were contemporaries. They were preaching at the same time, but Isaiah was born in the royal palace. He was a cousin of the king and so was comfortable conversing with the government. Micah, by contrast, lived in the Shephelah, a poor region. So Isaiah came from an upper-class, wealthy background, but Micah was a simple country man with a heart for the ordinary people who were being exploited. By reason of his background, Isaiah was not so conscious of this, so they complement each other very neatly.

When?

It is possible that Micah prophesied during the reign of three kings, the bad King Ahaz, the good King Jotham, and the very good Hezekiah (see chart, p. 309).

By this time, of course, Israel was divided, following the civil war that had broken out after the death of Solomon. The 10 tribes of the north had separated, calling themselves Israel, and the two tribes in the south were known as Judah. So Isaiah and Micah were speaking to the two tribes in the south, while a man called Hosea was speaking to the tribes in the north, just before they were finally exiled by the Assyrians.

Both Hosea and Isaiah were essentially town people, from fairly good backgrounds, so Micah is in contrast to both Hosea in the north and Isaiah in the south.

Why?

King Jotham (750–731) and King Ahaz had led the country astray. Jotham was regarded as a 'good' king, but he failed to remove the 'high places' from the land. These high places encouraged the worship of the Canaanite gods. The king should have upheld the Law of God and made sure that the people did the same. Ahaz, however, was a 'bad' king and failed to stop the evil practices that were spreading from the northern ten tribes to the southern two, and from the cities to the country. In the Bible cities are always seen as dangerous environments. The concentration of sinners accentuates the spread of sin. So vice and crime are normally worse in the city than in the surrounding country.

In the case of Judah, the corruption in Jerusalem was beginning to touch the country towns in the Shephelah. Micah could see the effect that the bad influence was having, and it hurt him. He observed bribery among the judges, the prophets and the priests. The very people who should have upheld the Law of God were being paid to say things that the people wanted to hear. There was exploitation of the powerless. Covetousness, greed, cheating, violence and cruelty became all too common. Crime was on the increase; landlords were stealing from the poor, evicting widows and orphans and putting them out on the streets; merchants and traders were using inaccurate scales and weights, so that business was corrupt. Sin was infiltrating every level of society. Above all, the rich and powerful were abusing the poor. Social and political power were being used to line pockets. It is a sad picture – a complete breakdown of respect and trust. Family relationships, the mainstay of any nation, were disintegrating. But Micah had a passion for social justice and was horrified that such things were happening among God's people – a people who were intended to be a light to the nations.

Amidst his concern about the situation, Micah had a vision from God that touched Judah, the north and the surrounding nations. His vision seemed to go out in ripples. His first vision was really for the tribe of Judah, and then his vision went further afield and he had a vision for the whole nation – even those 10 tribes in the north, though they would now have nothing to do with the south. His heart was enlarged to carry the burden of the lost world, though it started with a burden for his own people.

He saw God coming down to deal with Judah. He would judge them and take away from them even their little bit of land in the south. It was a painful thing to see, and it affected him very deeply.

There were two factors which made him feel all this: one was the Holy Spirit and one was his own spirit. Every prophet had a dynamic encounter with the Holy Spirit that led him to preach. But often his human spirit also felt the pain. Micah said that he howled like a jackal and cried like an ostrich and tore off his clothes, so great was his anguish. He realized that the situation was hopeless.

He was especially concerned about three problems: idolatry, immorality and injustice. It was injustice that was really getting to his heart. He couldn't bear to see what God's people were doing to each other. Idolatry is when people insult God and worship something else. Immorality is when people indulge themselves. But injustice is when people injure each other, and this was the biggest burden in his heart. As 'one of the people', his heart went out to the widows and orphans who were on the street because they couldn't pay the rent. There is a strong cry for social justice throughout his prophecy.

I always find it helpful to see the structure and shape of a book, especially if it is as well ordered as the Book of Micah. It is in three quite distinct parts. I have given them different titles to indicate the main thrust of each part.

Chapters 1–3 simply talk about crime and punishment – the bad things that are happening which God is going to punish. Chapters 4–5 focus on peace and security. Justice and mercy are the themes of chapters 6–7.

Crime and punishment (chapters 1–3)

In these chapters Micah is urging the people to grasp that sin has now spread from the city even to the country villages and towns in the Shephelah where he came from. The content of his message cleverly grabs their attention. He pronounces judgement on them by using the name of each village in a way that means they would never forget his message.

The places

If Micah were preaching in London, he would say something like this: 'Hackney will be hacked to pieces. Hammersmith will be hammered flat. Battersea will be battered for all to see and Shoreditch will be thrown in a ditch near the shore. Crouch End will crouch with fear at the end and there will be no healing for Ealing. Harrow will find itself under a harrow and Church End will see the end of the Church. Barking will be set on by wild dogs and sheep will graze over what is left of Shepherd's Bush. Vultures will feed on the corpses at Peckham.'

It may sound a bit odd to write in this way, but that is exactly how Micah speaks about local places. He takes every village name in the Shephelah and he twists that name to be a message of judgement. It is a brilliant bit of preaching to show that God won't let them get away with their behaviour. Sooner or later he will do something about it.

The people

It is clear that God held the influential leaders responsible for the situation. He pointed the finger at the king, the priests and the false prophets who had allowed the spiritual decay to develop unhindered. But he was especially concerned about the profiteers whose ruthless exploitation of the weak meant that the rich got richer and the poor got poorer.

Peace and security (chapters 4–5)

Chapters 4–5 are a surprise, for they contain mostly good news. Chapter 3 ends with Jerusalem in ruins. Micah says that the instigator of the sin – the big city – will be laid waste. But in chapters 4–5 we have a different picture. He is saying that the present corrupt state is not the end of the story.

The Kingdom

A Kingdom is coming in which there will be multilateral disarmament – all disputes will be settled by a King in Zion. The headquarters of the United Nations should not be in New York, but in Jerusalem, for that is where disputes will one day be settled. When 'the Lord reigns in Zion' he will settle all the world's disputes. The Kingdom is going to be established on earth. When we pray the Lord's Prayer, we pray for this to happen: 'Your Kingdom come on earth, as it is in heaven.' Of course, it can't come until the King comes, because you can't have a Kingdom without a King. Micah went on to say that the King is going to come from the little village of Bethlehem. *Beth* means 'house' and *lehem* means 'bread', so the name literally means 'house of bread'. It was this little village that supplied corn to Jerusalem, as well as lambs for sacrifice.

The King

Micah looks ahead, not just to Jesus' first coming, but to his second. The description is of his second coming, when he comes to reign on earth over the nations. The wording is identical to Isaiah 2:1–4, raising the question of which came first. Did one copy the other, did they both copy from someone else, or did they receive identical messages from God? It is impossible to tell with any certainty.

So the whole of the second part of Micah is good news. The city of David will supply the King who will come to rule the world and bring peace and prosperity.

Justice and mercy (chapters 6–7)

The last section of Micah is in the form of a court scene. God is the counsel for the prosecution and Micah is the counsel for the defence. The people of Judah, now corrupted by sin, are standing in the dock and God is vindicating himself.

God speaks in the personal pronoun, 'I', and so does Micah. They have an argument about who is in the dock. God explains that what he really wanted from them was not sacrifices (the blood of thousands of lambs), but righteousness. He said he required them to 'act justly, love mercy and walk humbly before God'.

Justice is giving people what they deserve, but mercy is giving them what they don't deserve. A man was having his portrait painted and said to the artist, 'I hope this will do me justice.' The artist said, 'It is not justice you need, it is mercy!'

Justice and mercy are not contradictory; they travel the same road together. The difference is that justice can only go so far, but mercy takes over and goes further, and God is the supreme master of both. God will always do justly. No one will ever be able to say that God is unfair.

But all that God received was the blood of thousands of lambs. Judah kept up the ritual and the religious side, but God was looking for more than that. The one thing that matters is how men stand with God, and the one test of that is how they stand with man. If you are in relationship with God, then you will find yourself acting justly and showing mercy, because that is exactly how he acts towards you.

Micah is miserable in the court scene, and then his misery gives way to rejoicing when he realizes that the judge in the courtroom is going to show mercy as well. So we get this lovely balance at the end of the book, with the covenant of mercy that God makes.

When a child is naughty a parent has a problem. Are you going to show them justice and give them what they deserve or let them off? It is very hard to be just and merciful, except under one circumstance, and that is where an innocent person is prepared to suffer the justice on behalf of the guilty. Then sin can be punished and pardoned at the same time. That is why the cross was necessary. As the hymn 'Beneath the Cross of Jesus' puts it:

> O safe and happy shelter,
> O refuge tried and sweet,
>   O trysting place
> Where heaven's love and
>   Heaven's justice meet.

Elizabeth Cecilia Clephane (1830-65)

At the cross we see God's perfect justice (the death penalty for sin is exacted) and also God's perfect mercy (that the guilty can go free), because the innocent has paid the price. If God forgave us without the cross, then he would be merciful but not just. If he refused to forgive sin and punished it all, he would be just but he wouldn't be merciful. This is why the Old Testament background is so important. We learn that the Israelites knew forgiveness of sin through the sacrifice of an innocent life. Without shedding of blood there can be no forgiveness of sin, because if there is no shedding of blood, then God cannot be both just and merciful.

Micah also writes of the need to 'walk humbly'. This third requirement is just as important as the other two. It is possible to do the first two and feel proud, but you are only doing it because God first did it for you, and you walk humbly with him.

In the New Testament Matthew picks up the prediction that a ruler would come from Bethlehem. A decision made by the Roman Emperor in his palace in Rome, thousands of miles away, brought Joseph and Mary to Bethlehem to pay their poll tax. It was amazing timing.

But the New Testament also tells us that when that King comes, he will take over the government of the world and bring peace to all the earth. This has yet to be fulfilled, but it will happen when Christ comes again.

It is important to note that there are many prophecies explaining what will happen when the Messiah comes which were not fulfilled when Jesus came the first time. This is a great offence to the Jewish people. They believe that the Messiah will bring worldwide peace, and so because Jesus failed to do this, he cannot be the Messiah. But a secret hidden from all the prophets of the Old Testament and only revealed in the New was that the Messiah would come twice – first to die for our sins and secondly to rule the world.

Theological themes

Before leaving Micah we would do well to highlight some of the theological themes present in the book.

Two sides of God's character

It depicts two sides of God's character: he is just and so must punish, but he is merciful and so can pardon. He hates sin, but loves sinners. This theme permeates the book. Each section begins with condemnation and ends with consolation. So justice comes before mercy. Sin must be punished before it is pardoned.

Micah reminds us that we should leave the work to God. We must reflect God but not replace him. But our job today is still to 'act justly, love mercy and walk humbly before God.' That requirement will never change.

Where Christ will come

The prophecy tells us clearly that the King will come to Bethlehem, a most unlikely place. It was small and insignificant, apart from its provision of bread for the Jerusalem market and lambs for the Temple sacrifices. But the prophecy was fulfilled, and all through the poll tax of Caesar Augustus.

Why Christ will come

The prophecy also points forward to Jesus' second coming, when he will rule over the whole world. So prophecies that were not fulfilled in his first coming will be fulfilled when he comes a second time.

Social action

The prophecy also gives Christians a charter for our life in society. The Church should have a prophetic voice, alerting people to the evils of exploitation where they occur and providing a voice for the poor and disadvantaged. In so doing we are preparing for the time when we will reign with Christ when he returns.

Social rejection

In view of this, Christians should not be surprised when those around them, even those close to them, dislike what they stand for. Micah himself said that 'a man's enemies are the members of his own household.' Jesus told his disciples that just as some people hated him, so they would hate his disciples also. Christians today must be prepared to walk as he did and face the consequences.

23.

NAHUM

Introduction

The prophet Nahum is closely linked with his better-known colleague Jonah, so when we looked at Jonah we noted the similarities between them. They both came from the 10 tribes of the north and were both sent to Nineveh, the capital of Assyria, the major world power. However, Nahum's message of destruction came 150 years after Jonah's time, when the circumstances were very different.

The recent history was as follows: after Jonah went to Nineveh, Assyria's empire expanded. They tried to invade the 10 tribes of the north during King Ahab's reign, but they failed. They came back during the reign of the Assryian king Ashurbanipal III and took the tribe of Naphtali away completely, only to return later under Shalmaneser to deport the other tribes into exile. From that point on, all that was left of the land was little Judah in the south. It was a catastrophic time for the people of God.

During Hezekiah's reign Sennacherib came and besieged Jerusalem, but was repulsed when an angel killed 185,000 Assyrians. But they were not deterred and continued their expansion. They conquered Thebes in Upper Egypt and became a mighty empire.

Following Jonah, two prophets were given messages for Assyria. First Zephaniah, as part of his message to Judah, predicted that God would destroy Assyria and make its great capital Nineveh a desolate wasteland. The once-proud city would become a pastureland for sheep and a variety of wild animals would make their homes there. Once-great palaces would lie in ruins, open to the elements.

But Zephaniah spoke of this destruction without specifying when it would happen. It was Nahum who finally told the Assyrians that they were finished. In his prophecy we have the record of their final warning. The one big difference between Jonah and Nahum is that on this occasion, God did not let them off. It is interesting that they both describe God as slow to anger, but the difference with Nahum was that time had run out. Once God's anger is aroused, you cannot turn it away. While his wrath is simmering it can be turned away, but when it boils over, nothing can stop it. There is, of course, a day coming when the whole world will face God's wrath. We read in Revelation of a day when people would rather be swallowed in an earthquake than look at the anger on the face of God.

The king of Nineveh prayed and fasted again, as at the time of Jonah, but God would not accept it. It was too late to change. The last verse of Nahum has the stern words: 'There is no remedy for your wound; your injury is past healing.'

Amazingly, this is described as good news – though not, of course, for the Assyrians. It is good news for Israel and for Nahum, who was born under Assyrian rule in the Holy Land. Nahum is telling the Assyrians that everyone who hears the news about their downfall will clap their hands, 'for who has not felt your endless cruelty?' It is a vivid prophecy.

As with the prophecy of Jonah, there is a question that underlies the Book of Nahum which has troubled Christians down through the generations. The prophecy of Jonah asks,

'Does God control nature?' Nahum asks, 'Does God control history?' The Bible says it is God who draws the atlas of history. When the apostle Paul preached to the Greeks on Mars Hill at Athens, he said that God allots every nation its place in time and space. God allows a nation to rise and become an empire, and it is God who brings it to an end. I believe that God brought the British empire to an end when we washed our hands of the Jewish people in 1947 and said we wanted nothing more to do with the Jews. Within five years the empire had gone.

God not only controls all of nature, he also controls all of history. It is he who raises up princes and brings them down. God is in charge of history, and therefore history is predictable. Part of the prophets' task was to predict history – to write history before it happened. Nahum is saying that Nineveh is finished, which seems unbelievable when you look at the power and might of Nineveh.

An outline of the book

Below is an outline of Nahum's prophecy. It has only three chapters and divides easily between them. Their focus is the fall of Nineveh.

Proclamation – Who? – Intervention (chapter 1)
Disaster for his enemies
Deliverance for his friends

Description – How? – Invasion (chapter 2)
A day of looting
A day of lions

Explanation – Why? – Inhumanity (chapter 3)
Conquest by force
Corruption by finance

Proclamation (chapter 1)

First of all there is the proclamation that God's enemies are going to be punished by him. Divine intervention means disaster for God's enemies, and deliverance for his friends. God's intervention always has this dual character. When he steps into history and acts, it means disaster for all those who defy God and who trust themselves. God is a jealous God. He is not envious – God doesn't envy anybody anything, because it's all his anyway – but he is jealous. Envy is wanting what someone else has; jealousy is wanting what's rightfully yours. You may be envious about someone else's wife, but you would be jealous about your own. So God is jealous for his name, his reputation, his people, and his world. God says, 'It's my name, it's my reputation, it's my world, and I won't allow people to behave like this in my world.'

Alongside God's jealousy is his vengeance. These are not popular attributes of God, but we need to understand them if we are to gain a proper appreciation of who he is. Nahum concentrates almost exclusively on God's jealousy and vengeance against those who defy him and trust themselves.

The first chapter is an acrostic poem, where each verse begins with the next letter of the Hebrew alphabet, and so is easily remembered by the people of Israel. It was good news for them – something to store in their hearts.

Chapter 1 alternates between a statement to Nineveh and a statement to Israel – bad news for one and good news for the other. It is a marvellous literary work. Nahum could put words together in a memorable way, by the inspiration of the Holy Spirit.

Description (chapter 2)

If chapter 1 is a proclamation that Nineveh will fall, chapter 2 is a description of how it will happen. It is absolutely astonishing in its detail – almost as if Nahum was watching the events unfold on television.

The fascinating thing is that the people who came to destroy Nineveh wore scarlet uniforms, just as Nahum had prophesied, even though such uniforms were unheard of in Nahum's day. He saw too how they entered through the river gates and described the city of blood:

> Listen, I hear the crack of the whips as the chariots rush forward against her. Wheels rumbling, horses' hooves pounding and chariots clattering as they bump wildly through the streets. See the flashing swords and glittering spears in the upraised hands of the cavalry. The dead are lying in the streets – bodies, heaps of bodies, everywhere. Men stumble over them, scramble to their feet and fall again.
>
> All this because Nineveh sold herself to the enemies of God.

It is vivid writing, and we can imagine the prophet preaching it. Nahum was calling Nineveh a toothless lion – an aptly chosen picture, because the lion was the emblem of Assyria. But they are no longer a threat to anyone and are in terror themselves. So there's a kind of poetic justice in this.

Explanation (chapter 3)

In chapter 3 Nahum moves from description to explanation. The reason for judgement is the sheer inhumanity of Assyria. We see here God's justice. He doesn't judge the Assyrians for breaking the Ten Commandments, because they don't know them. When God sends a prophet to pronounce against people who are not the people of God, he accuses them of the crimes against humanity that they know instinctively are wrong. Those who have never heard of the Ten Commandments still know that it's wrong to be barbaric and cruel.

So God judges people by what they know. This is a principle that goes right through Scripture. If a person doesn't know the Ten Commandments, they will not be judged for breaking them. If a person has never heard of Christ, they will not be judged for not having heard of Christ. But everybody has some knowledge of God through the creation around them and their conscience inside them. God will judge everyone by what they know instinctively to be wrong. So the United Nations document U144, the Declaration of Human Rights, wasn't written by Christians, but it includes the sort of things that all would acknowledge as just and right.

So God was judging the Assyrians' evil practices. In their chariots they would ride all over a country, slaughtering all the inhabitants and taking it by force. They were also corrupted by money, and bribery was common among them. Nahum said they knew that these two things were wrong, and because of them God was going to destroy their city.

I find that remarkable, because our world is not a stranger to either of these sins, and people know they are both wrong.

What happened to Nineveh?

Today Nineveh is a desert. The once-great palace is completely gone. In its place live owls and hedgehogs and all the wild beasts, just as predicted by Zephaniah. It was lost for centuries, but was found by an Englishman called Layard in 1820 on the west bank of the Tigris.

What happened to Nahum?

We know that the prophet never returned from Nineveh. His tomb can be found on the west bank of the Tigris today. It is revered by the Arabs, who recognize Nahum as one of the holy men of God.

Capernaum, a town in Galilee, was named after him (*Caper* = 'village', *naum* = 'Nahum'). It was this village, among others, that received the condemnation of Jesus. As with Nineveh, they too refused to hear the word of the Lord. Like the once-great city, Capernaum also lies in rubble today.

24.
ZEPHANIAH

The messenger (1:1)

The prophetic books focus more on the message than on the messenger, and this is never more true than with Zephaniah. We know very little about him. The only biographical details are in verse 1 of chapter 1, where we are told his name and his genealogy. The name Zephaniah in Hebrew is *Sephenjah*, which means 'hidden God'. It is uncertain whether this means God had hidden himself or if Zephaniah had been hidden by God. His genealogy gives us a clue, for he is the only prophet who traces his ancestry back four generations. Hezekiah, the last 'good' king of Judah (see Isaiah 36–39), was his great-grandfather. So Zephaniah was of royal blood. During Manasseh's reign, royal offspring were being sacrificed to the god Molech under the king's direction, so it is my theory that Zephaniah was hidden by his mother so that he would avoid the slaughter. Hence his very name is a reflection of God's preservation of him to be a prophet for the people.

The genealogy gives us the era in which he lived and preached. Since the time of Hezekiah, the nation had drifted away from God. In addition to child sacrifice and the worship of Molech, Manasseh reinstated the phallic symbols and asherah poles on the high ground and encouraged the people to go back to the fertility cults, with their sexual overtones. The site for child sacrifice was Gehenna, a valley just south of Jerusalem, cursed by Jeremiah and used as a picture of hell by Jesus. Throughout the early years of Manasseh's reign Isaiah tried to stop the decline in national morality and warned Manasseh of the dire consequences of his evil ways. But the king refused to listen and forbade Isaiah to preach, so that he had to write down his prophecies and circulate them in written form. Eventually Manasseh ordered Isaiah's execution.

That wasn't all, for Manasseh was also involved with astrology and spiritualist mediums, in further defiance of the Law of God. This spiritual confusion led to moral chaos, for idolatory always leads to immorality. God's verdict on Manasseh in 2 Chronicles was that he was more evil than the original Canaanites – a staggering statement, given that God had instructed his people to expel the Canaanites because of their corrupt lives. So we can imagine how God felt at this point. He had removed the evil Canaanites to make room for his holy people, and now they were worse than the people they had replaced.

Manasseh died after reigning for 55 years and was succeeded by Amon, a very weak character who did nothing to put the situation right, and Judah continued to slide. Amon was assassinated after only two years on the throne. The whole nation was in moral chaos.

Then an eight-year-old boy named Josiah became king, though the real ruler in the early years was Hilkiah, the High Priest. With good and bad kings in his family tree, it was not clear who this boy king would follow – Hezekiah, his great-grandfather, or Manasseh, his grandfather. So God sent Zephaniah the prophet to prevent the nation from being exiled for their sin, as their northern brothers had been.

The message (1:2–3)

The voice of prophecy had been silent for 70 years. Ever since the death of Hezekiah and the murder of Isaiah there had been no word from God. So Zephaniah spoke into a vacuum with a very strong message.

The prophecy has been called the compendium of all prophecy, because it includes so many elements also found in other prophets' work. His whole message revolved around the 'Day of the Lord', which is mentioned 23 times in the prophecy. This 'Day' is not a 24-hour period but means an era of time, as in 'the day of the horse and cart'. It was the day of God's judgement, of putting things right; the day of the vindication of righteousness, when wrongs were righted and wickedness was punished.

There is a parallel in the English calendar. Historically, there are four quarter days for settling accounts: Lady Day (25 March), Midsummer Day (24 June), Michaelmas Day (29 September) and Christmas Day (25 December). All accounts were examined, audited and settled, and fraud was punished. They give us a picture of the Day of the Lord.

Zephaniah uses an interesting word to describe God's emotions. He says that God is 'irritated', though with none of the selfish petulance that humans exhibit. The Day of the Lord is the day when God has had enough and his anger boils over.

There are two sorts of anger in the Bible. One is the inner anger that a person keeps inside and doesn't let out. It simmers away and is not obvious to other people. The other is the anger that erupts suddenly so that everyone knows. So it is this inner anger that is demonstrated in the Book of Zephaniah. The prophet is saying that God's anger is simmering now, and the day of wrath will come, when God can't hold it in any longer.

Although simmering anger is often missed, the signs that God is angry can be seen. The symptoms of the simmering are there for all to see in a society going downhill (compare Romans 1). But one day God's anger is going to boil over. We must put off this day by repenting and getting things put right. This is one of the themes of the prophecy.

An outline of the Book of Zephaniah

Foreign religion (1:4–2:3)
Deserved (1:4–6)
Declared (1:7–9)
Described (1:10–16)
Deflected (2:1–3)

Foredoomed regions (2:4–15)
The west – Philistia (2:4–7)
The east – Moab and Ammon (2:8–11)
The south – Egypt and Ethiopia (2:12)
The north – Assyria (2:13–15)

Future redemption (3:1–20)
Curses – divine justice (3:1–8)
  (a) National obstinacy (3:1–7)
    (i) Rebelling (3:1–4)
    (ii) Resisting (3:5–7)
  (b) International obliteration (3:8)

Blessings – divine mercy (3:9–20)
  (a) International godliness (3:9)
  (b) National gladness (3:10–20)
    (i) Rejoicing (3:10–17)
    (ii) Returning (3:18–20)

These three sections are very clear, but as is often the case, the chapter headings don't divide the book appropriately.

Foreign religion (1:4–2:3)

In the first section the prophet is concerned with the foreign religions which have become part of Judah's national life. He announces judgement and makes four basic statements about the Day of the Lord that is coming.

Deserved (1:4–6)

There had been considerable drift away from a proper relationship with God. Many had abandoned their allegiance to the God of Israel in favour of other gods. The priests, who should have been ensuring that the covenant was kept, were themselves leading people astray. Superstition was common and many followed Manasseh's evil worship of Molech.

Declared (1:6–9)

Zephaniah describes what will happen to them when God judges them. When we read the prophetic books we may feel we are reading exactly the same message. But God needs to repeat himself, especially as there have been 70 years between these words and his last ones. Zephaniah is warning the people that the Day when the Lord will judge is coming very close.

Described (1:10–17)

The judgement will be catastrophic for the people. They are largely complacent about their behaviour and how God feels about it. Zephaniah warns them that when the judgement comes, everyone will know.

Deflected (2:1–3)

He then offers them the possibility that even at this stage, judgement can be deflected from Israel and turned away by repentance. It is the same message that all the prophets have. If they will humble themselves, God will hear and forgive and show them mercy in return. Indeed, the need for meekness is a key requirement in the prophets' messages (see Isaiah 2:9 and Micah 6:8).

Foredoomed regions (2:4–15)

Zephaniah addresses the nations threatening Judah from every point of the compass. On the west side of Judah was the land of Philistia, from which modern 'Palestine' claims to be descended. On the east side were Moab and Ammon, and to the south were Egypt and Ethiopia. To the north-east was Assyria, the world power of the day, on the Tigris and Euphrates rivers. Few nations were unaffected by the Assyrians. They had taken away the 10 tribes in the north. Babylon at this stage was still a small and insignificant power.

Zephaniah is given a message that these nations will be judged by God. God is the judge of the whole world, and they will be judged for their attitude to Judah. But this interaction with Judah is a two-way one. Not only does God judge foreign nations for their attitude to Judah, but he also uses them to discipline Judah. We are told in the Book of Amos that God brought the Philistines from Crete to inhabit the land west of Canaan at the same time as the children of Israel invaded Canaan. It is God who moves nations around and draws the map to dictate where people will be.

So the Philistines became a real thorn in the side of Israel, right through to the time of King David (about 700 years later).

Indeed, the name 'Philistine' has become proverbial in the English language to describe someone who is hostile to other cultures. In Deuteronomy God explains the situation: 'I have brought them to test you. If you keep my word, you will keep them at bay and they will be no problem to you. But if you disobey me, I have brought them to be an instrument of discipline for you, and when you are doing wrong they will overcome you.'

This action demonstrates God's concern. God is a Father to his people, and a good father disciplines his children when they go wrong. In fact, Hebrews 12 says, 'If the Lord doesn't discipline you, then you are not a true son of God.' This principle is not always grasped by Bible readers. If you become a child of God, then God will discipline you when you sin. But God does this so that you won't need to be punished after death. So Christians can expect life in this world to be tough. I can never believe the testimonies in which people claim that after they came to Jesus all their troubles disappeared. I believed them once, but it depressed me, for my testimony was so different. I came to Jesus, and my troubles began! When I was baptized in the Spirit my troubles became even worse. I have been in more trouble in the last five years than in the previous 40! But I am glad, because it fits the promises of Jesus. He said, 'In the world you will have big troubles. But cheer up – I am on top of them!'

Future redemption (3:1–20)

In the last section there is a strange tension between cursing and blessing. It is almost as if Zephaniah is saying, 'Choose what you really want to have. Do you really want God's justice?' He is full of mercy and wants to have mercy on us, but he can't give it without our cooperation, because he only gives to those who ask for it.

I listen to many prayers for all kinds of things, but it thrills me to hear people ask for mercy, for they have understood a key law of the Kingdom. We only ask for mercy if we think we are bad. If we think we are fine, we ask for health, strength, guidance, all sorts of things – but we never ask for mercy.

Curses – divine justice (3:1–8)

(A) NATIONAL OBSTINACY (3:1-7)

(i) Rebelling (3:1–4)

In the first half of chapter 3 Zephaniah faces the people with the possibility of a day of divine justice, when he tells them how obstinate they are. They have rebelled against God quite deliberately and are resistant to God's appeal.

(ii) Resisting (3:5–7)

He also accuses them of resistance. The rulers, officials, priests and prophets are all implicated. They are an obstinate people. A while ago, having read the verse in Zephaniah, 'Morning by morning he dispenses justice', I composed a song of my own, to the tune of the hymn 'Great is thy faithfulness':

> Great is thy righteousness,
> O God all holy.
> There is no error of judgement with thee.
> Thou changest not, thy commandments
> They fade not.
> As thou hast been, thou for ever wilt be.

> Great is thy righteousness,
> Great is thy righteousness,
> Morning by morning thy justice I see.
> All that is merited
> Thou has requited.
> Great is thy righteousness –
> Lord, hear our plea.

We love to sing pleasant songs about God's positive attributes such as faithfulness, but we must accept that there is another side to God, and we should be grateful for that too. Paul says in his Letter to the Romans that we should 'Consider the kindness and sternness of God – sternness to those who fell but kindness to you, providing you continue in his kindness.'

Zephaniah is telling the people that if they continue rebelling and resisting there will be a national disaster. God's anger will boil over and the Day of the Lord will come.

(B) INTERNATIONAL OBLITERATION (3:8)

What is true of God's anger towards Judah is also true of the whole world. He says that this same anger will boil over towards the nations and wipe them out. They will all stand before him and the wicked will be consumed by his jealous anger.

Blessings – divine mercy (3:9–20)

The book concludes with a note of hope, in common with many of the prophets. For example, Amos preached a message of God's justice, as the penultimate prophet to the 10 tribes in the north before they disappeared, but the last word to the north was the prophecy of Hosea, a message of God's mercy and love. It is almost as if God's last word to us is 'Won't you have my mercy?' Zephaniah finishes in the same way. God doesn't want to punish – he has no pleasure in the death of the wicked. He wants to show mercy, and so finishes on a note of hope for the future.

(A) INTERNATIONAL GODLINESS (3:9)

His note of mercy for the nations is that out of every nation he will draw people who love him. We are told that people will come out of every kindred, tribe, tongue and nation. God doesn't want a single ethnic group on earth to be missed out. This is why he told us to preach the gospel to all ethnic groups and to make disciples of them.

(B) NATIONAL GLADNESS (3:10-20)

But then he finishes up with the possibilities of blessing for Israel itself. Nine times in this last little section God says 'I will ...' Judah may break his covenant, but he will never break it.

(i) Rejoicing (3:10–17).

In that day no one will be proud or haughty; they will do no one wrong and tell no lies. No one will be able to make them afraid. He talks about a wonderful future when he will quiet them with his love. He even says God will sing about his people: 'he will rejoice over them with singing'.

(ii) Returning (3:18–20).

God will gather those who have been scattered and bring home a remnant who will revere his name. Though they have been despised, they will be exalted in the eyes of the world. God will give them 'praise and honour in every land where they were put to shame'. So at the end of the book there is a note of extraordinary hope. God's people have the opportunity to be judged now and to get right with God now.

Conclusion

We are left with one question about Zephaniah. Was Zephaniah's prophecy effective? Did Josiah take any notice?

Josiah came to the throne at the age of eight in 640 BC and reigned for 31 years. At first he was heavily influenced by the High Priest, Hilkiah, who tended to keep the status quo, but then he began to be influenced by Zephaniah. At the age of 16 he destroyed the altars in Jerusalem. At the age of 20 he ordered all the pagan altars to be destroyed throughout the whole country. At the age of 28 he noticed that the Temple of God was in bad repair and so he ordered it to be put right. While they did this, someone found a copy of the Law of Moses in an old, dusty cupboard. They realized that they hadn't been studying it or reading it for years. When Josiah read it, he was horrified. He realized why God was warning them. So at the age of 28 he ordered the Law to be read again and carried out throughout the nation.

So the signs up to this point were good. But Josiah didn't realize that you can't make people good by an Act of Parliament. Many people today think that if only our government would pass good laws, then people would behave in a Christian way. But righteousness can't be imposed from above – it must be expressed from within, as God works in the human heart.

Josiah's life ended following an ill-advised attack on the Egyptian army, who were passing through the Holy Land to attack Assyria. He was killed in the ensuing battle, despite being in disguise.

So while having some influence, Zephaniah failed to turn the nation around. The people didn't listen. But his work was not wasted. There was a young man the same age as Josiah whom God told to pick up the prophetic burden. Jeremiah was charged with telling the people that the reform wasn't working and they needed to return to God.

Making use of Zephaniah

The key application for the believer today concerns judgement.

(a) The Day of Judgement for the whole world will come after death. Judah's condemnation is a foretaste and foreshadowing of what will happen to the world. Jesus alludes to Zephaniah in connection with the Second Coming (see Matthew 24:29 and Zephaniah 1:15). So most people will face God's wrath after Jesus returns.

(b) The Day of Judgement for God's people will come before it does for other people. 1 Peter 4:17 reads: 'For it is time for judgment to begin with the family of God; and if it begins with us, what will the outcome be for those who do not obey the gospel of God?'

Zephaniah is a powerful reminder for Christians that they should expect God's discipline, but not lose heart. Discipline in this life is a sign of God's care and assures us that we won't be judged along with the world.

Zephaniah and Revelation

In closing, we must also note the remarkable correlation between the prophet Zephaniah and the outline of the Book of Revelation.

Both Zephaniah and Revelation start with judgement on God's people – Israel and the Church respectively. They both move on to judgements on the nations (see Zephaniah 2; Revelation 4–15). Finally, they move on to the Day of Judgement (Zephaniah 3:1–8; Revelation 20).

But the last word is the final bliss of God's giving a place to his people where they can live for ever (Zephanaiah 3:9–20; Revelation 21–22). In Zephaniah the location is the old Jerusalem, but in Revelation it is the new Jerusalem. In Zephaniah God comes as King, but in Revelation Jesus comes again as King.

In all there are over 400 allusions to the Old Testament in the Book of Revelation, but the closest connection is with the prophet Zephaniah. So a seemingly obscure Old Testament book is actually a central book for our understanding of the future.

25.

HABAKKUK

Introduction

The prophecy of Habakkuk is unusual among the prophetic books. Firstly, in most prophecies God addresses the people through the prophet, but in Habakkuk the prophet addresses God directly, the people not being involved at all as the conversation takes place. There are elements of this in other prophecies, notably Jonah and Jeremiah, but no other prophetic book starts in this striking way.

Secondly, in chapter 2 the prophet is instructed to write his message in large letters on a wall.

Then thirdly, chapter 3 is a prophecy set to music, which was fairly rare. It was the earlier leaders such as Moses, Deborah, Samuel, Saul, Elijah and David who had found music to be an inspiration for the prophetic word, although later Ezekiel too made use of music.

We know very little about Habakkuk. We know that he prophesied 20 years after Zephaniah, around 600 BC, and that his name literally means 'someone who embraces'. It was a wrestling term put into colloquial language. We might call him 'Clinger' – not an especially flattering name!

But though his name is not especially pleasant, it accurately describes his relationship with God as it unfolds in the book.

Habakkuk was a man who clung to God, who dared to argue with God, and who insisted on getting answers from God, even if he didn't like the answers when they came. So although we don't know much about the prophet's background, we learn something of his mind, heart and will through his conversations with God recorded in the book. We also gain insights into the key dimensions of his prophetic ministry – his praying (ch. 1), his preaching (ch. 2) and his praising (ch. 3).

The book has great relevance to us today, for it deals with some very basic questions that all thinking believers ask. If God is good and all powerful, why do the innocent suffer and the guilty go free? Why doesn't God do something about the mess that the world is in? Most wrestle with these issues by themselves or with other people. But the best way of dealing with such big questions is to wrestle with God and cling to him until he gives you an answer. Habakkuk gives us a wonderful example of a man who did just that. His boldness and sheer honesty come through in the prophecy, and the book is both challenging and delightful as a result.

In contrast to Zephaniah, Habakkuk is full of 'quotable quotes'. For example, 'Your eyes are too pure to look on evil' (1:13) is a popular verse, though, as we shall see later, we must be careful how we interpret it. Here are some other well-known verses:

> For the earth will be filled with the knowledge of the glory of the Lord, as the waters cover the sea.   **(2:14)**

> The Lord is in his holy temple; let all the earth be silent before him.   **(2:20)**

> In wrath remember mercy.   **(3:2)**

Though the fig-tree does not bud and there are no grapes on the vines ... yet I will rejoice in the Lord, I will be joyful in God my Saviour. **(3:17–18)**

The most famous verse from Habakkuk, which has become the 'Magna Carta' of Protestantism, is 'The just shall live by faith' (2:4). Martin Luther made this one verse ring around northern Europe at the time of the Reformation, though, as we shall see later, it wasn't properly understood.

An outline of the Book of Habakkuk

The prophet (1:1)

Complaining prayer (1:2–2:20)
Complaint: God does too little
Question: Why don't the bad suffer?
Answer: The bad will suffer (the Babylonians will come)
Complaint: God does too much
Questions: Why use the bad to punish the bad?
Why do the good suffer?
Answers: The good will survive!
The bad will suffer!

Composed praise (3:1–19)
He trembles at God's past action (3:1-16)
He trusts in God's future protection (3:17–19)

The Book of Habakkuk divides clearly into two parts. Chapters 1 and 2 form the first part and chapter 3 is the second part. The contrast between the first and second parts is enormous, as we can see in the table below:

Chapters 1–2	**Chapter 3**
Wrestling with God	Resting in God
Miserable	Happy
Shouting	Singing
Prayer	Praise
Impatient	Patient
Asks for justice	Asks for mercy
Down in the dumps	On a high
God is inactive (in the present)	God is active (in the past and future)

The table demonstrates the enormous change between the first and second parts, leading to the inevitable question: What has happened to Habakkuk for this contrast to be so apparent? We will need to go into the prophecy in detail to find out what has changed him.

Complaining prayer (1:2–2:20)

God does too little (1:2–11)

Habakkuk told God exactly what he was thinking. At first he complained that God was doing too little and then he complained that God was doing too much – God couldn't win!

He believed in interrogatory prayer. Intercessory prayer is when you ask God for things, but interrogatory prayer is when you ask God questions. It is a very important type of prayer, which I find most helpful. I simply ask God a question, and if something comes into my mind – especially if it is something very unexpected – I accept it as from God. Nine times out of ten it proves to be so.

For example, when our daughter died, we were astonished to find out how much she had been doing for the Lord. She never talked about it, but she had been in regular touch with missionaries in China, Africa and Haiti, to name just a few. Furthermore, she was a worship leader in the church, and was so loved that the whole church mourned her. When I was talking to the Lord about her I said, 'Lord, I am very proud of our daughter, but how do you feel about her? What is your opinion?' Immediately the words came to me: 'She is one of my successes.' So at her funeral I preached on the theme, 'Are you one of the Lord's successes or one of his failures?' If you have never heard from the Lord in your life, then try asking this question: 'Lord, is there anything in my life that you don't like?' If you really want to hear from God, just ask him that question.

The social setting of Habakkuk helps us to understand his questions. There had been no word from God in the 20 years since the time of Zephaniah. The nation had continued its downward slide, in defiance of Zephaniah's message. King Josiah had not achieved what he had hoped for with his reforms and met a premature death at Megiddo in 608 BC. Habakkuk prophesied during the time of his successor, Jehoiakim, who became a very worldly, selfish king. His palace was extended but the poor became poorer under his reign. Bribery, corruption, lawlessness and oppression filled the streets of Jerusalem. It became so dire that it wasn't safe to walk the streets at night alone. The Assyrians, who had taken away the 10 tribes, were now in decline, so there was no strong world power as such.

Why don't the bad suffer?

This feeling that nothing was happening while Jerusalem deteriorated was at the heart of Habakkuk's concern. When he addressed God he built his case very carefully. He knew that God's nature must be reflected in his attitude and actions and that he wouldn't wipe his people out, but he also knew that God must execute punishment and ordain judgement on sin. So he complained to God that he was doing nothing about the violence and corruption in his holy city. He wanted God to reverse the trends, to change society and to restore law and order.

God does too much (1:12–2:20)

God was gracious in responding to Habakkuk's anger, but Habakkuk was surprised and dismayed by the five responses that God gave:

1 Open your eyes a bit wider – watch.
2 You are in for a very big surprise.
3 I have planned something that will happen in your lifetime.
4 I haven't told you what I am doing because you wouldn't believe it.
5 I have already begun to do something and you have missed it.

In short, God tells Habakkuk that he has noticed the evil in Jerusalem and has already acted by raising up the Babylonians to punish the people of Judah. At this time Babylon was just a growing city on the Tigris River. Few had heard of it, and it had barely been mentioned in the Bible up to this point. But when two messengers from Babylon visited King Hezekiah and were shown around his palace, Isaiah realized the danger and predicted that one day Babylon would take away everything from the palace and Temple that the king had shown the two men.

At the time Babylon was too small for the prophecy to have seemed likely, but in Habbakkuk's day this prophecy was nearing fulfilment, and Habakkuk was understandably shocked.

It was just as if God had said he was going to bring Nazi
Germany to punish England. But we can see throughout history that this is how God typically deals with nations. He raises
up one nation to deal with another. So such activity need not
surprise us.

THEY ARE WORSE THAN WE ARE

But Habakkuk is surprised and dismayed. He now complains
that God is doing 'too much', for he knows that the Babylonians have a worse reputation than the Assyrians, who had
eventually overpowered Israel (the 10 tribes) and taken
them to an exile from which they never returned. But the
Babylonians would be even worse. They were the first nation to
introduce a scorched-earth policy whereby they removed every
trace of life from the land of the peoples they conquered.
Habakkuk realized that if the Babylonians came to Jerusalem
there would be nothing left. This explains the meaning of the
well-known words at the end of the book: 'Though the fig tree
does not blossom, and there are no grapes on the vine, and
there are no sheep or cattle in the pen ...' This is how the land
would be after the visit of the Babylonian army.

THEY WILL NOT DISCRIMININATE BETWEEN GOOD
AND BAD

Habakkuk also reminds God that there are some righteous
people in the city of Jerusalem who would die along with the
wicked. Although he doesn't say so directly, the implication is
that he is among them. He is angry that God is using people
who are more wicked than Judah to execute the punishment. In
Habakkuk's reasoning this is immoral, so he utters the much-
quoted words, 'Your eyes are too pure to look on evil' (1:13).
Habakkuk was trying to suggest that God's very character was
impugned by what he had promised to do. But in so doing he

says something about God that isn't true. God is pure and holy, but that does not mean that he cannot look on evil, for he has to watch evil being committed every day. He watches every rape, every mugging, every act of cruelty. Habakkuk has his own view of what God will or won't look upon, but he is wrong.

When Habakkuk has finished arguing with God, he goes up to the watchtower in Jerusalem and sits on the wall. He says he is going to watch to see if God will really do what he has said. He is almost saying, 'I am going to call your bluff. I dare you to bring them, Lord.'

WRONG PLACE

In reply God tells Habakkuk that he is achieving nothing by sitting on the watchtower. He should go down into the street and write what God has told him on the wall so that passers-by can read it – the first advertising hoarding in the Bible! Habakkuk should be warning the people, not sitting at a distance to see whether God will do what he has promised.

When God reveals to us what he is going to do, he does it so that we can tell people to get ready, not so that we can wait around to see if he does it.

WRONG TIME

God also tells Habakkuk that if he stays in a tower he won't see anything for quite a time. He might jump to the wrong conclusion about what God is doing. God says, 'The revelation awaits an appointed time.' So he needs to take a long-term view and warn the people of what will come.

The good will survive

It is during this interchange that God tells Habakkuk that 'the just will live by faith' (2:4b), which became the most famous verse in the book, because of its use by Luther during the time of the Reformation. But as we hinted earlier, although much good was accomplished through the Reformation, the verse itself was misunderstood.

If we look at the verse in context, Habakkuk is saying that the Babylonians will kill the righteous as well as the wicked. God is saying in the verse that he will protect the righteous (or 'the just') – they will survive, provided that they remain faithful to him. When the Babylonians arrive there will be many who will lose faith in God, believing that he has let them down. But God says that those who go on believing in him will survive that coming judgement.

So this is the real meaning of the verse. The word 'faith', both in the Hebrew and in the Greek languages, includes the idea of faithfulness. It is faithfulness that saves; they must *go on* believing and *keep* faith.

This intrepretation fits in with the way that faith is some-times used as a noun in the Old Testament. It is used about faithfulness in marriage. Faith in marriage is to stay together till death parts the couple. It is also used of Moses when he kept his arms outstreched while the children of Israel won the battle against the Amalekites. He was faithful in praying for the people.

The principle is the same in the New Testament. Believing in Jesus on one occasion isn't faith. True faith is continuing to believe in him, whatever happens. This is why we read in the Gospels, 'He who endures to the end shall be saved.'

The rest of the New Testament also uses the verse in this way. Three different passages quote Habakkuk 2:4 and interpret 'the just will live by faith' as referring to people *continuing* to believe.

In Romans 1:16–17 Paul writes: 'I am not ashamed of the gospel, because it is the power of God for the salvation of everyone who believes: first for the Jew, then for the Gentile. For in the gospel a righteousness from God is revealed, a righteousness that is by faith from first to last, just as it is written: "The righteous will live by faith."' In other words, it begins with faith and it ends with faith. Salvation is enjoyed by *going on* believing.

In Galatians 3:11 Paul contrasts faith with the self-righteous keeping of the law. He says that no one is justified by the law, and quotes Habakkuk 2:4 as the reason, because 'The righteous will live by faith.' Living by faith is not a single act but a continuing attitude for a whole lifetime. Only *ongoing trust* in Christ saves.

The writer of Hebrews also uses the verse to back an argument about the need for *ongoing trust*. In 10:39, having quoted Habakkuk 2:4, he adds, 'But we are not of those who shrink back and are destroyed, but of those who believe [i.e. go on believing] and are saved.'

So it is clear that these passages underline a most important correction to the way in which the text was used during the Reformation and since. The verse must not be interpreted as saying that if a person has believed for just one minute – that is, if they have made a 'commitment to Christ' – their life is safe. This is a gross misuse of the text. The just shall live by 'keeping faith' with the Lord. There is complacency amongst some Christians, who use an unscriptural phrase – 'Once saved, always saved' – as if a moment or short period of trusting will ensure that they escape God's wrath. But it is those who keep faith with the Lord who survive the worst that happens.

The bad will suffer

But having used the Babylonians to judge, God does not let them get away with their evil. In the second half of chapter 2 there is a series of woes addressed to Babylon. The word 'woe' in Scripture is a curse and should never be used by a Christian unless they are sure what they are doing. When Jesus said 'woe', awful things happened, and he said 'woe' as often as he said 'blessed'. For example, there were 250,000 people living on the shores of Galilee in Jesus' day in four major towns. Jesus pronouced a curse on three of the towns. He said, 'Woe to you, Capernaum', 'Woe to you, Bethsaida', 'Woe to you, Korazin', but he didn't say 'Woe' to Tiberias. If you go to Galilee today you will have to stay in Tiberias, for it is the only town there is. The towns that Jesus said 'Woe' to have all disappeared.

Habakkuk lists five reasons why the Babylonians will incur God's wrath:

1 **Injustice** They plundered the nations that they overran, with little regard for their people.
2 **Imperialism** They dictated how the nations that they conquered should live, with little concern for justice and little pity for the people's plight.
3 **Inhumanity** God condemned their bloodshed, their use of slave labour to build Babylon, and their callous treatment of their enemies. They even took babies by the legs and bashed their heads against rocks.
4 **Intemperance** They were an ill-disciplined people when it came to alcohol, and did terrible things when they were drunk. This included the destruction of animals and even trees. When Israel went to war God forbade them to cut down a single tree unless they needed it for the war.
5 **Idolatry** They worshipped lifeless wood, stone and metal idols, ignoring the true God of Judah. At this stage, of course, Babylon had not reached the height of her powers, but even so Habakkuk was instructed to announce the doom.

So the rebuke is for actions that violate the conscience. At no point are the Babylonians judged for failure to keep God's Law. They don't have a covenant with God. But they are judged for doing things that they know in their hearts are wrong. God's judgement of them is a reminder to the people of God that he is concerned about their behaviour in these areas too.

So God answers Habakkuk's argument by saying that the good will survive and the bad will suffer. God is not blind to what has been going on, nor is he impotent, nor is he unjust. He is the living God, in contrast to the dead, lifeless idols fashioned by men.

Having given Habakkuk the answer he sought, God then adds, 'Let all the earth be silent.' God is effectively saying, 'You have your answer. Now shut up!'

Composed praise (3:1–19)

It was while he was quiet that Habakkuk saw the light. He stopped arguing with God and thought about what God had said, and his whole mood changed. He understood that God had a much greater picture than he did, and also a longer-term view. Although he couldn't see God at work now, God would act when the time was right.

The last chapter is set to music, composed in his own mind with his own hand, reflecting this change of heart. The musical instructions as to how the singing should be accompanied – 'with stringed instruments' – are included at the end of the chapter. So when we come to chapter 3 we have a completely different outlook expressed. Indeed, the text is so different here that scholars claim that chapter 3 was an addition.

He trembles at God's past action (3:1–16)

In chapter 3 Habakkuk changes his focus on three occasions. He starts with 'he', moves on to 'you', then finishes with 'I', as if he gets more personally involved as the chapter progresses.

HE (3:2–7)

Habakkuk now focuses on God's power in the period covering the exodus, the wilderness and the conquest of Canaan. He asks God to do it again. What he has heard about, he wants to see. This time there is no request for a change of plan, no questioning of God's activities. He only asks that in his wrath, God might remember to be merciful.

So if chapter 1 focused on Israel's violence and chapter 2 on the Babylonians' violence, chapter 3 calls for God's violence.

YOU... (3:8–15)

In these verses Habakkuk is involved in the vision. He is still asking questions, but this time they are right ones. He reflects on God's majesty and power in creation. He knows that God has the power to do whatever he pleases. He is now content to 'wait patiently for the day of calamity'.

He trusts in God's future protection (3:17–19)

I (3:16–19)

The change from 'you' to 'I' gives an important insight as Habakkuk reflects on his own reaction to the news of the Babylonian invasion. He is 'walking by faith', even if there is no visible evidence of God's word coming true. He speaks of the pressures from inside – how his emotions are artificially lifted by his vision of the future. But at the same time he faces pressures from the outside that are depressing him. He doesn't look forward to the disaster that is about to come on the people, but nevertheless he is able to 'rejoice in the Lord'. In chapter 1 his argument came from a mind that was concentrated on the present. But now he looks back into the past and sees that God has always intervened. He looks into the future and sees that God will intervene again, and so he is prepared to wait. In our age we focus so much on the present that we have little or no time for the past or the future. But it is this perspective that will help us when injustice overwhelms us.

I have put chapter 3 into verse, to the tune of Beethoven's 'Ode to Joy'. It seems a fitting way to end our study.

Lord, your fame has gone before you from the time your
    arm was bared,
Tales of deeds so overwhelming, even listening makes me
    scared.
Now today, O Lord, repeat them, prove that you are still the
    same –
But in wrath remember mercy for the honour of your name.

Look, this Holy God descending spreads the sky with
    glorious rays,
Trailing from his hand of power, earth is filled with sounds
    of praise;
But the guilty nations tremble, plague and pestilence their
    fears:
Even ancient mountains crumble when the infinite appears.

Are you angry with the rivers? Is your wrath upon the
    streams?
Do you rage against the ocean with your horse and chariot
    teams?
Writhing hills and flooded valleys, sun and moon stand still
    in fear
At the glint of flying arrows, lightning of your flashing spear.

Striding through the earth in vengeance, threshing nations
    till it's done,
All to save your chosen people, rescue your anointed one.
You have crushed their wicked leader, stripped him bare and
    split his head;
So his storming, gloating warriors scatter to the wind
    instead.

Having heard the final outcome, knowing all and not just
    part,
Great emotion grips my body, quivering lips and pounding
    heart,
Trembling legs give way beneath me, yet with patience will
    I wait,
When the foe invades my country, certain of his dreadful
    fate.

Though the fig tree does not blossom and the vine is void
    of grapes,
Though the olive trees are barren and the fields produce
    no crops,
Though no lambs are in the sheepfold and no cattle in the
    stall –
Yet will I enjoy my saviour, glad that God is all in all.

Joyfully I face the future with my failing strength restored
And my angry questions answered by this marvellous
    sovereign Lord.
See my heart and feet are leaping like a deer upon the
    heights –
Set my words to holy music, voices and stringed
    instruments.

26.

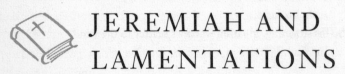

JEREMIAH AND LAMENTATIONS

Introduction

Jeremiah is a key figure in the Old Testament and is one of the best known of all the prophets. But his book is not one of the most popular. Here are three reasons why people don't like it. It is daunting, difficult and depressing.

Daunting

It is 52 chapters long, second only to Isaiah's 66 chapters. Legend says that Jeremiah visited Southern Ireland and kissed the Blarney Stone and received the gift of the gab! The length reflects both the number of prophecies in his 40-year career and the dedication of his secretary in writing them down. But for many readers it is too long a book to tackle with any enthusiasm.

Difficult

The book is in neither chronological nor topical order and so it is hard to follow. The writings have been bunched together in what seems to be an arbitrary fashion. We might call it a collection of collections. This is compounded by the fact that Jeremiah seems to change his viewpoint. Critics take particular delight in finding contradictions in his preaching. He is totally against Babylon in the early years, but then later advised people to submit to Babylon. It is one of the reasons why he was called a political traitor. The truth is that over 40 years his message changed according to the circumstances and the course that God had intended him to follow.

Depressing

The most popular reason for disliking Jeremiah is that it is one of the most depressing parts of the Bible. There seems to be nothing but bad news for Judah, with Jeremiah sharing the pain he felt at what was happening to the nation and in his own ministry. The very name 'Jeremiah' in the English language has come to mean being a wet blanket. In literature a 'jeremiad' is a mournful poem or dirge. So Jeremiah has got a bad press. Once again, this is not the whole picture. There is good news in his prophecy, but it is hidden among so much bad news that it is easily overlooked.

But in spite of these difficulties, it is a wonderful book. Of all the characters in the Bible, I identify most with Jeremiah. I once preached my way through the whole book and had to stop twice because I was getting so emotionally involved. It was almost too much to share it. It was as a result of that series of sermons that the prophecy came that I was to leave that church and travel, and so the book means a lot to me personally.

It is fascinating because there is a lot of human interest in the book, which draws the reader into understanding Jeremiah and empathizing with his situation. The prophet reveals his heart and his inner struggles more than any other prophet. But there is also a divine interest because it is packed with information about God. If you study Jeremiah seriously you will understand God much better.

The moment

Jeremiah began preaching in the seventh century BC, almost at the end of the life of the two tribes in the south, who went into exile in 586 BC (though some were deported even earlier). He lived during the reigns of seven different kings of Judah: Manasseh, Amon, Josiah, Jehoahaz, Jehoiakim, Jehoiachin and Zedekiah. His 40-year prophetic career was during the reigns of the last five.

He spoke at a traumatic time for the people of God. The 10 tribes in the north had been taken into exile by Assyria, leaving the two tribes of God's people living in and around Jerusalem. Isaiah and Micah had now gone, their messages largely unheeded. Jeremiah is the last prophet to speak to the people and warn them that it was almost too late to stop the disaster from coming.

His birth was in the reign of Manasseh, the evil king who had sawn the prophet Isaiah in half inside a hollow tree for prophesying against him. If this evil wasn't bad enough, he also sacrificed his own babies to the devil and filled Jerusalem's streets with the blood of innocent people. Two boys of significance were born in his reign – Josiah, who became king, and Jeremiah. Manasseh was replaced by another wicked king, Amon, who lasted a few years before Josiah found himself on the throne at the tender age of eight. It was during his reign that the Book of Deuteronomy was found in a dusty old cupboard in the Temple. Josiah was horrified to read that the curses of God were on the land and the people. So he tried to reform the people but failed.

It is interesting that although Jeremiah was one of Josiah's contemporaries, he was silent about the reforms. Jeremiah doesn't mention Josiah and the Books of Kings don't mention Jeremiah. It is almost as if Jeremiah realized that a reform ordered by the king did not change people's hearts. While it looked good, outwardly the situation hadn't changed. Josiah's ill-advised battle with the Egyptians, in which he was killed at Megiddo, proved in part that problems still remained.

Josiah's death lead to a succession of evil, weak kings. It was during the reigns of the last four of these bad kings that Jeremiah did the bulk of his work, which is one reason why he is seen as being so negative. At times he expresses the hopeless feeling of 'It's too late!' but also has this tiny hope that if they repent, God will yet change the situation.

This tension came from an illustration that Jeremiah was given by God. In chapter 18 God tells him to visit the potter's house and observe the potter as he makes vessels, depending upon the clay at his disposal. Many assume that the message concerns God's ability to choose to do whatever he wants with us. Choruses have been written to this effect with lines such as 'You are the potter, I am the clay'. But this is not the lesson that Jeremiah picked up. He saw the potter's intention to make a beautiful vase but, because the clay would not run in his hands, he put it back into a lump, threw it on the wheel again and made a thick, crude pot. God asked Jeremiah if he had learned the lesson. Who decided what the clay would become? The answer is that the clay decided, because it wouldn't run with the potter's original intention. So the message was that God wanted to make the clay into a beautiful shape, but if the clay would not respond, he would make an ugly shape instead. So in the context of Jeremiah's times, God was saying that even at this late stage his people could repent and change and become the beautiful vessel that he had intended. So there is a dynamic relationship between God and people in the Bible. God is not dealing with puppets and decreeing what shall be. Rather, he wants a response from us and will make us what he wants us to be if we cooperate.

But the parable of the potter had a further lesson. The ugly clay pot was baked and became hard so that it couldn't be changed, and then Jeremiah was to take that hard pot, break it and throw the pieces into the valley of Hinnom where the rubbish was thrown. God is saying that if we harden our hearts we will reach the point where we cannot be changed into a beautiful state. So at that point God will break us. God prefers our life to be beautiful, and if we will respond to him he will make it so.

At this time Jeremiah demonstrates that all is not doom and gloom. He tells them that there is a little hope. But eventually the book ends with Zedekiah, the very last king of Judah, who was finally taken away by the Babylonians. He was forced to watch his sons being killed and then had his eyes put out, and was taken away blind. It is a tragic episode in the life of the people of God. It seemed to be an end, but there was still more to come.

The man

Jeremiah is a most unusual name. In Hebrew it can mean either 'to build up' or 'to throw down' – a bit like the English words 'raise' and 'raze', which sound the same but have opposite meanings – 'to make higher' or 'to destroy completely'. The name perfectly described his ministry. His basic message for 40 years was that God pulls down those who disobey and builds up those who obey.

He was born at Anathoth (modern Anatah), three miles north-east of Jerusalem looking down on the Dead Sea. He was appointed a prophet by God before he was born. Like John the Baptist, he was set aside while he was still in his mother's womb. He became a very diffident, sensitive, shy youth.

He was born into a priestly family but the family line was under God's judgement. A curse had been placed on the house of Eli – none of his descendants would see old age because of his sins. Therefore God had to get this man started early if he was going to get 40 years out of him! A lover of nature, he often used nature to illustrate God's messages, particularly birds.

He was probably about 17 when he began to preach and he was very, very nervous. God reassured him that he would make his forehead like brass, so none of the hostile looks or comments of the people would intimidate him. Anyone who has spoken in public will know what that means.

His life as a prophet was exceedingly tough. He had to move to Jerusalem, three miles away, because his family were going to assassinate him. His 40-year career ran alongside Habakkuk, Zephaniah, Ezekiel and Daniel, and he was in the thick of the political world. He advised his people to surrender to the Babylonians, and the people hated him. No one likes a policy of appeasement. The Babylonians gave Jeremiah the choice of going to Babylon with his people or staying in Judah – which was really no choice, for he didn't like the Babylonians and his people didn't like him.

In the end he finished up in Egypt. Some Jews kidnapped him and took him a long way up the River Nile to the Elephantine Island, where the Ark of the Covenant had already been taken. (It is probably now in Ethiopia.) This is where he died, alone. It is a sad story.

The method

Speaking

Although he was a speaker, most of his speaking was in poetry – distinguished in many Bibles by shorter lines, as opposed to prose, which looks more like a newspaper column. As a rule, when God speaks in prose he is communicating his thoughts from his mind to the mind of the reader, but when God speaks in poetry he is communicating his heart to the reader's heart. Poetry is, of course, heart language, and most of Jeremiah's prophecy is in poetry. Unfortunately, too many people treat the Bible purely as a source of understanding God's thoughts and fail to notice that it is a very emotional book. I believe the finest translation from Hebrew into English, which communicates the emotions of the Hebrew language, is the Living Bible. It is the most accurate translation of God's feelings, though not the most accurate translation of his thoughts.

Acting

Sometimes Jeremiah's message was delivered through drama in order to provoke comment. On one occasion he buried some dirty old underwear. When asked why, he replied that the underwear depicted the inner lives of the people. We have already noted the important lesson gained from observing the potter. Another time he wore a cattle yoke as a burden to demonstrate the need to submit to the Babylonians. When everyone in Jerusalem was trying to sell their property because they knew that when the Babylonians came it would be worthless, God told Jeremiah to buy property. He bought a field from his relative who was desperately anxious to sell. Jeremiah knew that one day the people would return from Babylon, and this investment enabled him to 'put his money where his mouth was'.

Other dramatic illustrations included hiding stones, throwing books into the river Euphrates and carrying a jar on his head round the city like a woman. They seem bizarre, but they got the message across.

Writing

Jeremiah's prophecies were preserved by Baruch, one of God's 'backroom boys', who was like a secretary to Jeremiah. At one point the prophecies enraged King Jehoiakim so much that he cut them up with a knife and burned them. After 23 years of ministry, Jeremiah was not allowed to speak publicly, so it was Baruch who ensured that his voice was still heard. Here was a man who would never, in one sense, do great things himself, but who made it possible for others to hear the word of God. In fact, God rewards those who work in secret more than those who work publicly. Without that work, his words would have been lost.

The message

We have noted that the Book of Jeremiah is not in chronological or topical order and so it can be difficult to read, but there is a general pattern that will aid comprehension:

Prologue – Jeremiah's personal call (1:1–19)

The sinning nation (2–45)

627–605 BC Immediate retribution (2–20)
(mostly poetry)
Babylon destroys Assyria (612 BC)
Babylon defeats Egypt (605 BC)
605–585 BC: Ultimate restoration (21–45)
(mostly prose)
Babylon deports Judah

The surrounding nations (46–51)

Epilogue – national catastrophe (52)

The prologue in chapter 1 is about how Jeremiah was called by God as a young man, and how he was terribly shy and afraid of public speaking.

Chapters 2–45, 'The sinning nation', includes Jeremiah's prediction that Judah's punishment is coming very quickly. It covers the years 627–605 BC. It is mainly poetry, which means that Jeremiah is communicating God's feelings to them – in particular his regret and his anger. God has a conflict of emotions. He loves them but he cannot let them go on as they are. The prediction that Babylon will destroy Assyria and defeat Egypt comes here. The kings of Judah had mistakenly assumed that if they made a treaty with Egypt they would be protected.

Chapters 21–45 contain good news as Jeremiah looks beyond the despair of exile to the ultimate restoration. After he knew that the situation was hopeless, he gave them a longer-term view of the ultimate restoration of the people. This section is mainly prose, for it conveys mainly thoughts rather than feelings from God. In the long term, after Babylon has deported Judah and Jerusalem is devastated, some of the people will come back and rebuild Jerusalem, so the situation is not totally lost.

Chapters 46–51 cover God's judgement on the nations that surround Judah. The restoration will be accompanied by the judgement on those who have caused her troubles. That's how the God of justice operates in history.

Chapter 52 is a kind of epilogue about the dreadful national catastrophe that was breaking on Jeremiah's people. It describes how Jeremiah was taken away to Egypt, and Jerusalem was left empty and devastated. It is not a happy ending.

Like the other prophets

A lot of Jeremiah's message is the same as that of the other prophets. In fact, if you read through the prophets one after the other, you could easily get bored. For it is the same old story of idolatry, immorality and injustice. The prophets were observing the same decline. Jerusalem was filled with violence so that children couldn't even play in the streets and old people dared not come out.

There are four major thrusts of his message which we find in all the other prophets. Indeed, when Jeremiah was nearly put to death, somebody remembered that Micah had said exactly the same thing years before, and this saved Jeremiah's life.

1. APOSTATE PEOPLE

The people were totally corrupt. Idolatry and immorality were the two main problems. Some of the awful practices of the surrounding nations were being practised by the people of God, including child sacrifice in the Valley of Hinnom and idols being brought into the Temple of God, in direct contravention of the second commandment. There was also moral rottenness and broken marriages.

God calls Jeremiah to preach that certain people were responsible for the situation.

The prophets

Jeremiah's ministry was bedevilled by people around him who claimed that they were prophets too but gave the opposite message to Jeremiah. In chapter 23 he attacks these false prophets, accusing them of never having stood in the counsel of God and listened to what God was telling them. Instead they copied their messages from each other or invented them from their own minds, telling people what they wanted to hear.

In particular they were saying, 'Peace, peace' when there was no peace. They claimed there was no need to worry. After all, Jerusalem was God's city and he would look after the Temple. But Jeremiah was scathing of those who put their security in the Temple. He tells them that they have turned it into a den of thieves, and warns them that they can't assume that just because they are God's people, they won't be judged.

There is a similar lesson in the New Testament. The majority of Jesus' warnings about hell were given to born-again believers! Yet I meet many believers who have no fear of hell because they assume that it can never happen to those who call themselves Christians.

But Jesus teaches that we must continue in our faith if we are to escape the wrath to come. The apostle Paul reminds born-again believers that all will appear before the judgement seat of Christ. We are justified by faith, but judged by works.

The priests

Jeremiah blamed the priests for the nation's sin because they were supporting what we would call today 'inter-faith festivals'. They were holding pagan religious services in the name of tolerance – just as in the UK today there are services that include non-Christian religious groups, in the misguided belief that we are all on different roads leading to the same God.

The princes

The princes (or kings) were condemned for their failure to uphold God's laws. Jeremiah prophesied that Jehoiakim would die without mourning and would be buried like an ass – and his death took place just as Jeremiah had promised. Zedekiah, the last king, was weak and vacillating, a mere puppet of the politicians.

Jeremiah's images describing this apostate people are full of sexual metaphors, some of them quite obscene. He likened the people, who were going after foreign gods, to a faithless, adulterous wife going after other men. Hosea had been the first prophet to use this metaphor. Jeremiah asked the people to imagine how God felt with an unfaithful wife. Their integrity in other relationships was also poor. Jeremiah claimed that there was 'not one honest person in Jerusalem'.

One of the most dreadful things he said to them was that they were unable to blush. They had no shame. Their apostasy doesn't even trouble them. God had already divorced the 10 tribes – did they want him to divorce the two tribes as well?

2. IMPENDING DISASTER

The second major thrust of his message that is also shared with other prophets is the theme of impending disaster. When God made promises to Israel at the time of Moses, he made two kinds: 'I bless you when you are obedient' and 'I curse you when you are disobedient.' These were reaffirmed in the Sinai covenant. So when God punishes, he is keeping his promise. Most people think of his faithfulness as keeping on doing good things for us, but his faithfulness is seen in punishing as much as in pardoning.

Jeremiah was specific about what would happen. He received a vision of a boiling pot tilting from the north, and told the people that the danger would come from that direction – not from Assyria, which had taken the 10 tribes away, but from Babylon, whose armies would also invade from the north. He warned them that the danger would come soon. He had a vision of an almond branch bursting into blossom – the sign of spring, and it happens so quickly with an almond tree. In the same way, Judah would suddenly see the Babylonians coming.

3. ULTIMATE RESTORATION

But beyond this doom and gloom comes a ray of hope. Some of the most positive prophecies about the future of the people of God are found in Jeremiah. He prophesied a restored nation with a new covenant with God. The old covenant of Moses wasn't working, because the commandments were written outside of people and not inside them. They were written on stone but needed to be written on the heart. So in chapter 31 we have one of the loveliest predictions in the Old Testament. We are told that God will make a new covenant with the house of Israel and the house of Judah, based on the fact that God will write his laws in the people's hearts. They won't need to be taught about God because they will all know him, and God will forgive them and not remember their sins any more.

Many readers in church stop there, but I want to read on. God also says:

> This is what the Lord says, he who appoints the sun to shine by day, who decrees the moon and stars to shine by night, who stirs up the sea so that its waves roar – the Lord Almighty is his name: 'Only if these decrees vanish from my sight,' declares the Lord, 'will the descendants of Israel ever cease to be a nation before me'   **(31:35–36)**

So the Lord says that only if the heavens above can be measured and the foundations of the earth below can be searched out will he reject all the descendants of Israel because of all they have done. God guarantees that he will keep his side of the covenant. There will always be an Israel and there still is. The fact that the name 'Israel' is back on the map today is proof that God keeps his promises.

Here Jeremiah promises the ultimate restoration of his people. He writes of God bringing them home again with rejoicing, singing and dancing, and states that it will be in 70 years. (This figure later encouraged Daniel when he read the prophecy in the exile and realized that the 70 years were nearly up. The figure may seem arbitrary, but it was carefully calculated as the time required for the land to get its rest, since they had missed the one-year-in-seven rest for the land in the previous 500 years [2 Chronicles 36:21].)

Jeremiah also promised Judah a new leader. He gave him the titles 'the good shepherd', 'the righteous branch', 'the messianic prince', 'the shoot from David's tree', 'the fountain of life'. He promised that this man would come and would restore the throne to them, and the Gentiles would share in Judah's blessing.

4. PUNISHED ENEMIES

Although God would allow the Babylonians to take Judah into exile, he would make sure that they were punished for their cruelty. Habakkuk had majored on this in his prophecy. So Babylon would later be conquered by the Persians in fulfilment of this prophecy (which, in turn, led to the return of the Jews through the decree of Cyrus, the Persian king). Other enemies will also be dealt with: Egypt, Philistia, Moab, Ammon, Edom, Damascus (Syria), Kedar, Hazor and Elam. There's a section at the end of Jeremiah's book which predicts what will happen to all the nations who have attacked Israel or have been unkind to them, and it is God who will exact vengeance, not Israel. Only Egypt and Babylon received any positive comment.

Unlike the other prophets

Having looked at the things that Jeremiah says that are in common with the other prophets, we will now look at the three things he says which are quite unique to him.

1. SPIRITUAL

Jeremiah has been called 'the spiritual prophet', because he is the one prophet who says that religious ritual is worse than useless if your heart isn't in it. In fact, his condemnation of hypocrisy in worship has led some to mistakenly assume that Jeremiah thought the whole system of sacrificial offerings to God was a waste of time. Actually, he was saying that the outward ritual of worship was not all that important, for God was really looking for heart motivation. Did the worshipper really engage in spiritual activity? The body may be circumcised, but is the heart also? The priests were falsely encouraging the idea that religious observance was somehow a substitute for godliness. So Jeremiah needed to put a tremendous emphasis on the spiritual aspect of religious life.

At the same time, Jeremiah was preparing the people for the day when they would lose the Temple and not be able to offer sacrifices. In Babylon they would meet in what became known as 'synagogues'. The word 'synagogue' is a Greek word which means 'to come together'. The people of God would assemble for three things: praising God, praying and reading the Scriptures. In fact, this resembled the New Testament Church situation, when the priesthood had been made redundant by Christ's once-for-all sacrifice. The Church has no temple, altars, incense, priests or sacrifices. The New Testament Church simply came together to celebrate communion, to pray, to praise and to read and study the Scriptures. So the early churches were effectively Christian synagogues. The temptation of the Christian Church from the beginning has been to go back to the ritual of the Temple and to have priests, altars, incense and vestments. But it's a reversion to the Old Testament pattern and not what God intended at all.

Jeremiah was one of the men who liberated the Jews from a dependence on ceremony, so that they could survive without it and still meet together in Babylon. He was the only prophet who could foresee that they would have to find a form of religion without the Temple and all its paraphernalia.

2. INDIVIDUAL

The next unique thing in Jeremiah's prophecy is that he predicts that in the new covenant God will deal with individuals. The Sinai covenant was collective rather than individual, with the whole people, not each person. One of the striking features of the new covenant as it comes in the New Testament is the emphasis on each individual. Jesus was constantly talking about individual followers. Jeremiah describes the contrast: 'In those days people will no longer say, "The fathers have eaten sour grapes, and the children's teeth are set on edge." Instead everyone will die for his own sin; whoever eats sour grapes, his own teeth will be set on edge' (Jeremiah 31:29–30).

In the New Testament, the new covenant is an individual covenant with each person separately. So it is impossible to inherit a place in the Kingdom. God deals with everyone as individuals who need to make their own decisions. So in the New Testament individuals were baptized on their personal confession of Christ.

So in the New Testament we read that on the Day of Judgement each person stands alone and is answerable for their own sins, not anyone else's. So this great switch from God dealing with the people to God dealing with the individual is first sounded in Jeremiah and is then picked up by Ezekiel, and the whole New Testament is based on that understanding.

In many respects Jeremiah's life embodies this principle. He was shut out of the Temple, rejected by his local congregation and so had to survive on his own with God.

3. POLITICAL

Jeremiah gives more political advice to the rulers of Israel than any other prophet. When Judah was shrinking in size, it tried to play off one superpower against another. But Jeremiah warned them not to go to Egypt, because Babylon would defeat them too. His political advice was to give in to Babylon, to cooperate, and to seek to get the best possible terms for surrender. He even describes Nebuchadnezzar, the king of Babylon, as God's servant – which would be like someone from the Church in 1939 telling the British Government to negotiate with Adolf Hitler because God had sent him. It sounded like treason to suggest giving in to a tyrant without even trying to defend Jerusalem.

But the kings of Judah turned down his political advice. He was called a traitor. When he advocated surrender to the Babylonians he put a yoke on his shoulders and walked around Jerusalem as a visual aid of what the people should do. When the king of Babylon arrived in Jerusalem he actually offered to put Jeremiah on his honours list (see chapter 39). We can imagine how the other Jews would feel about this. But this was merely the last episode in a long story of maltreatment and misunderstanding.

The maltreatment

Jeremiah had been persecuted from the very beginning of his ministry. Indeed, the first attempts to kill Jeremiah came from his own relatives in his home area, the village of Anathoth. They plotted to assassinate him because it injured their family pride that this teenager was going around upsetting the whole of Jerusalem. God had a little word for him then: 'I'm only training you for worse things.' What a comfort!

From then on, he was branded a traitor. He was rejected by the other prophets because they were false prophets. He was shunned by the priests because he spoke against the priests' job, the Temple and the sacrifices. The kings regarded him as a political traitor and the people hated him, hatching various plots to end his life.

Not only was Jeremiah threatened with death; he was also close to death on a number of occasions. He was beaten and imprisoned by the priest Pashhur and flung into a dimly lit dungeon. On other occasions he was put in the stocks with his hands and feet locked, and he was pilloried with an iron collar. Finally he was put in a cistern (a kind of deep well shaped like a flask, with a narrow neck so that the water didn't evaporate). When empty of water, it would typically have four or five feet of soft mud in the bottom. So Jeremiah was up to his neck in the slime, with just a little daylight coming through a small hole above his head. He had, of course, to remain standing, or he would have drowned in this mud. He was eventually released by a foreigner who took pity on him, lowered a rope into the cistern and pulled him out.

He was often in hiding because of attacks on his life. There were few remaining in Jerusalem who would seek his advice, and finally he was forcibly removed by the Jews who fled to Egypt. It was here that he died. His death is not recorded in Scripture. One tradition suggests that he was stoned to death (see Matthew 21:35). Whatever happened, it is clear that he died in obscurity, little dreaming that he would become famous throughout the world and that we'd be talking about him 2,500 years later.

The misery

Jeremiah is known as 'the weeping prophet'. The Book of Lamentations shows the pain in his heart for his people, for the land lost and for the city of Jerusalem destroyed. But even in the Book of Jeremiah itself his misery comes out, because he wasn't afraid to let us know how he prayed in those situations.

Physical sufferings

We have seen already some of the physical pain that Jeremiah felt at the hands of those who despised his message. He was certainly not afraid to bare his soul and reveal his feelings. Here was a man deeply hurt by what his people said and did to him, especially when regarded as a traitor by his own family. He hated the notoriety that went with the faithful proclamation of God's message, and also found his ministry extremely lonely.

Mental sufferings

His physical sufferings were bad enough, but he also felt trapped by God. The particular pain was that God had given him no choice. God had called him to the prophetic ministry and had somehow trapped him so that he could do nothing else. His prophecy includes his resentment and the mental and emotional suffering that came out of this loneliness and rejection.

One of the worst things was that marriage could not relieve the burden of his loneliness. God forbade him to marry. This way Jeremiah would not have to see his own children starve when the Babylonians came. His own life thus became a powerful message, just as Hosea's marriage to a prostitute and God's command to Ezekiel not to mourn the death of his wife were messages to the people they spoke to.

We have intimated already that the book gives real insight into Jeremiah's pain, and at the same time provides help for those going through trauma.

On one occasion he said, 'I know, O Lord, that a man's life is not his own, and it's not for a man to direct his steps.' A well-known quote is: 'If I decide that I'll never talk about God again, there is a hidden fire burning in my bones. I am weary with forbearance and I cannot contain it.' The poor man is effectively saying, 'I'm never going to preach another sermon.' And then he says, 'But I can't stop. It's burning in my bones. I've got to let it out.'

He had no choice about preaching, because his heart was burning for God. Even when he made a decision never to preach again, he just found himself out on the streets preaching. In fact, God hadn't really forced him into it – God never forces people. But we can understand his feelings about being trapped.

Jeremiah knew that the people would never listen, and at various points he concludes that he is involved in a hopeless task. God even forbids him to pray for the people (7:16).

Despite this, however, the prayers of Jeremiah are a significant part of the prophecy and include some of the most moving passages (e.g. 1:6; 4:10; 10:23–25; 11:20; 12:1–6; 15:15–18; 17:14–18; 18:19–23; 20:7–18). These nine prayers of Jeremiah are among the most honest of any in Scripture. He tells God exactly how he feels, and as such provides a good example for our prayers.

Lamentations

The Book of Lamentations was written by the prophet Jeremiah, so it is appropriate that we should consider it alongside the Book of Jeremiah. It is one of the saddest books in the whole Bible. Many would compare it with the Book of Job, but Job is sad because of a personal tragedy, whereas in Lamentations Jeremiah is weeping over a national catastrophe. As you read Lamentations you can almost see the tears dropping onto the page and making the ink run. Here's a man weeping his heart out.

In the Greek translation of the Old Testament this book is simply called 'Tears'. In the Hebrew translation it's called 'How', because that was the first word that was read when the scroll of the book was opened. The English title, 'Lamentations', comes from the Latin word for tears.

It was written as Jeremiah saw the desolated city of Jerusalem. He knew too the pain of his people – prior to the destruction of the Temple and the city the people had been under a terrible siege. Mothers were eating their own babies and even eating the afterbirth of women in labour. They were desperate. The whole thing is so, so sad, and so he weeps. It must have been like Hiroshima following the atom bomb, or war-torn Kosovo in recent years.

The fact that the book is written as a series of laments need not surprise us. We know that Jeremiah was a poet, because most of his prophecies were in poetic form. We also know that he was musical and wrote songs, again because of what we find in his book. This highlights the astonishing relationship between prophecy and music. The spirit of prophecy inspires both poetry and music, and vice versa. A number of Old Testament saints who were blessed with the gift of prophecy would ask for music to be played to them before prophesying. Zechariah, Ezekiel and, of course, David were prime examples.

These are not the only laments composed by Jeremiah. He also composed a lament (mentioned in Chronicles) for the boy king Josiah, who mistakenly thought he could defeat the Egyptians and was killed at Megiddo. Just as David lamented over Saul and Jonathan when they were killed in battle against the Philistines, so Jeremiah composed a lament for the whole nation to sing when King Josiah died and the promise of his reign was brought to an untimely end.

Structure

In spite of the passion that Jeremiah feels for the ruined city and the exiled people, he has composed the lament using strict guidelines. For once the chapter divisions are in the right place, with each chapter comprising one of the five songs that are beautifully and carefully put together.

The device he uses is an acrostic whereby the letters of the alphabet are a framework for the song or poem. Since the Hebrew alphabet has 22 letters, each section has 22 verses.

Four of the laments work on this pattern. The third lament is slightly different, comprising 66 verses, but again the acrostic method is used.

The first poem has 22 verses – one for each letter and three lines to each verse. The second poem starts again with the first letter of the Hebrew alphabet. Then comes the third poem, once again with three verses for each letter. The fourth goes back to 22 verses, with two lines to each verse. The only poem that doesn't follow the letters of the alphabet is the last one, though it too has 22 verses.

WHY USE THIS DEVICE?

1 It's easier to remember. Jeremiah was concerned that the people who were left in the land and the people who were sent to exile would hear his laments and take them to heart. An acrostic helps to achieve this.

2 This method helps to express Jeremiah's complete grief – his 'A to Z' of grief. It has symbolic significance. He is telling a story of grief all the way from alpha to omega, from the beginning to the end.

3 But I think the third reason is most telling. I tried a little experiment. I took a piece of paper and I wrote down the 26 letters of the English alphabet and asked if it would help me to pour out the teachings of Lamentations. I found that's exactly what it does. It took me less than two minutes to write out Jeremiah's Lamentations. I don't claim that it is a great piece of writing, but I do think it summarizes the whole book:

Awful is the sight of the ruined city,
Blood flows down the streets.
Catastrophe has come to my people,
Dreadful is their fate.
Every house has been destroyed,
Families are broken for ever.
God promised he would do this –
Holy is his name.
I am worn out with weeping,
Just broken in spirit,
Knowing not why.
Let me die like the others –
My life has no meaning.
Never again will I laugh
Or dance for joy.
Please comfort me, Lord;
Quieten my spirit,
Remind me of your future plans.
Save your people from despair,
Tell them you still love them.

Understand their feelings,

Vent your anger on their destroyers.

We will again

eXalt your name,

Yield to your will,

Zealous for your reputation.

So the alphabet can be a very useful tool for expressing feelings.

Why did he write a lament at all?

Even given that there was wisdom in using a lament, it is not immediately obvious why he would choose to write in such a way, especially given the size of his other work.

I believe it was because he wanted others to weep with him and sing the songs. Maybe he wanted to send them to the people taken away in exile so that they might express their feelings too. It makes eminent sense, for when people go through tragedy it is vital that they express their feelings. If grief is called for, it must be allowed to be expressed. It is cruel to tell the bereaved to be brave and not to cry. The Jews and the Catholics are two of the best groups in this regard, because they have a tradition of wakes, when they actively encourage tears. Throughout the Bible tears are encouraged. Our Western tendency to admire people who don't weep comes from Greek rather than Hebrew thinking. In modern Israel a man can never get to be Prime Minister unless he can weep over the grave of an Israeli soldier. In Hebrew thinking it takes a man to weep – it's not a sign of weakness.

She, he, I, they, we

The next thing we must notice about the poems is that the personal pronoun changes with each chapter.

In the first poem the personal pronoun is 'she', referring to the city and to the people of the city, called 'daughters of Jerusalem'. In the Old Testament cities and their people are seen as feminine – a tradition also followed in English texts.

Then, in the second poem, the personal pronoun is 'he'. It is a poem about the person who has caused the disaster. It's about God.

The third poem is the longest and becomes very personal, for it is about Jeremiah himself. The chapter focuses on 'I, me, my'.

The fourth poem and chapter is almost impersonal by contrast, with a detached description of 'those, they, theirs'.

The fifth returns to 'we, us' as Jeremiah identifies with his people again. God is no longer 'he', but is directly addressed as 'you, yourself'.

When we study the Bible carefully we do well to notice these little words as clues to the meaning. So the five very different themes require very different titles, reflecting the way Jeremiah has chosen to see the situation.

The five poems

1. THE CATASTROPHE – 'SHE'

The first poem looks at the ruined city and her daughters.

It wasn't just that the whole city had been besieged and then destroyed, nor just that the Temple had gone. What really upset Jeremiah was the fact that this was God's city. He knew that sin was the reason, and this pained him even more. It is clear that Jeremiah was an eye-witness to the events he described. He sees the wrecked buildings, the deserted streets after the exile to Babylon. It is easy to imagine him remonstrating with the few people still left: 'Is it nothing to you, all you who pass by? Aren't you touched by such a dreadful sight?' So the description of the empty, desolate city is vivid, demonstrating the anguish Jeremiah felt when viewing the scene.

2. THE CAUSE – 'HE'

The second poem focuses on the fact that the disaster wouldn't have taken place if Judah had surrendered to the Babylonians, as Jeremiah had suggested. It was painful to know that he could have helped them to avoid it all. Jeremiah knew that God had to allow the exile because he had promised that he would deal with them in this way if they were disobedient, but his frustration at the opportunities they had wasted was no less real. This comes out especially in the second poem, where the anger of God is mentioned five times. Jeremiah knew that there comes a time when God's anger boils over. There are two kinds of anger in the Bible: slow anger that simmers, and the quick temper that blazes away and is over with. Both cause problems at a human level. At a divine level, God is both slow and quick in his anger – though, of course, without the selfish element that characterizes human anger.

The whole emphasis in the Bible regarding God's anger is that if we do not watch God carefully and if we fail to see his anger simmering, we probably won't notice it until it boils over. In Romans 1 we are told that God's anger is already simmering. We are given signs to look for, including exchanging natural relationships for unnatural ones. Another sign is anti-social behaviour and the breakdown of family life. Sadly, in the Western world these things are all too common.

3. THE CURE – 'I'

The third poem is the personal one. Jeremiah realized that God could have wiped out all the people in his anger, but instead he had sent them to Babylon. So they were still alive, the people had not been extinguished and the nation was still a nation. Jeremiah believed that it was because of God's mercy that they had not been entirely consumed. He says, 'Your mercies are fresh every morning.'

It is good to have such an attitude, whatever our problems. We can always look to God's mercy. There is a fundamental difference between the way the world lives and the way the people of God should live. The world lives by *merit* – we live in a 'meritocracy'. You get what you work for. But in the Kingdom of Heaven the basis of life is *mercy*. The world demands rights, but Christians know that they have no rights.

4. THE CONSEQUENCES – 'THEY'

Jeremiah moves on to recall the consequences of not repenting. He even goes back to Eden and God's righteous punishment of Adam and Eve. He wants everybody to know that this desolation does have a purpose. The people need to know that God is involved in dealing with sin, but will also be involved in deliverance.

5. THE CRY – 'WE'

The last poem is simply a prayer, a plea for God's mercy. Jeremiah knows that God is their only hope, and so turns his despair into a prayer that God will indeed restore his people once more to the land.

One theme that appears in all five poems is the word 'sin'. Almost every page of the Old Testament has sin on it – sometimes just the word, sometimes sinful deeds. By contrast, there is salvation on almost every page of the New Testament.

Jeremiah acknowledges honestly that the people's sin deserves this judgement, but at the same time he cries out to God for the mercy that will restore them. That's why we call this book 'Lamentations' – plural. It's really five different songs of lament and sorrow.

To this very day the whole of Lamentations is sung once a year in every synagogue on the ninth day of Abib (July), because that is the exact date on which the Babylonians destroyed the Temple.

Every year to this day Jews remember the exodus in the Passover, and the loss of the Temple on the ninth of Abib. Every July you can go to the synagogue and you will hear them mourn. The amazing thing is that the ninth of Abib is not only the day when they lost the First Temple – on that very day in AD 70 Titus came and smashed the Second Temple.

On the exact date when they were lamenting the loss of the First Temple, they lost the Second Temple – and Jesus, of course, predicted that. Just as Jeremiah came to warn them about the loss of the First Temple, Jesus came to warn them about the loss of the Second. This is why Jesus and Jeremiah have been bracketed together so often.

When Jesus said to the disciples, 'Who do men say that I am?' they replied that he had been likened to Jeremiah. This prophet may not seem an obvious choice, but his life was a perfect parallel to Jesus' life. So just as Jeremiah could say, 'A man's foe shall be there of his own household', so Jesus too had problems with his own home area. The people tried to throw Jesus off a cliff in his home town of Nazareth. Indeed, Jesus escaped five assassination attempts in all. Also, some of Jesus' acts were in the same spirit as those of Jeremiah. When Jesus cleansed the Temple and used a whip against the Jews who were turning the Temple into a greedy money-changers' centre, he quoted Jeremiah, 'How dare you make my Father's house into a den of thieves!'

Jesus was a Jeremiah in the popular mind. Jeremiah himself at one stage said, 'I feel like a lamb led to the slaughter.' Jesus, for his part, reminded the people that their ancestors had stoned and rejected the prophets who had been sent to them.

Links with Jesus

On the north side of Jerusalem is a cave which in Jewish tradition is known as 'Jeremiah's Grotto', because they believe that it is where Jeremiah went to pray when he was lonely and hurt and in pain. The grotto is a cave in a hill called Golgotha, where we believe that Jesus died on the cross.

One of the things that Jesus said on his way to Calvary was, 'If they do these things in the green tree, what shall be done in the dry?' He was telling the people of Jerusalem not to weep for him but for themselves, for the days were coming when things would be much worse. He was pointing to AD 70, just 40 years ahead. Forty years was the period of testing. God gave the Jews 40 years to respond to his crucified and risen Son. But as a people they remained hard-hearted, so 40 years later the Temple was pulled down again.

Destinies

There are two destinies held before believers in the New Testament – one is weeping and wailing and gnashing of teeth. Whenever Jesus used these words, he was talking to his own disciples, though many assume they should have been directed at unbelievers. The other possible destiny for us as the people of God is that God will wipe away all tears from our eyes. So in a sense the two destinies facing us both involve tears – either we are weeping for ever or having God wipe away the tears.

Not only that, but the world is facing the same prospect. The book that quotes Jeremiah and Lamentations more than any other is the Book of Revelation, which focuses on the end times. Half of the New Testament quotes from Jeremiah are in Revelation and are applied to the city of Babylon. Babylon in Revelation is the final world finance centre – the city that is going to be destroyed. When Babylon is destroyed the world will weep over it, but according to Revelation, Christians will sing the 'Hallelujah Chorus'. Very few people listening to Handel's *Messiah*, with its magnificent 'Hallelujahs', realize that it's a celebration of the world's stock exchange going bust! The world banks will become bankrupt and the whole financial system that man has built up will collapse.

Revelation 18 finishes with quote after quote from Jeremiah. Lamentations talks about the ruin of Jerusalem. But God will bring a new city down from heaven to earth – the new Jerusalem, like a bride adorned for her husband. This is where believers will live, on a new earth in a new Jerusalem for ever.

27.

OBADIAH

Introduction

Obadiah was the first of the pre-exilic prophets and his book is the shortest in the Old Testament, at just 21 verses. He spoke in 845 BC, and this opened a period of 300 years during which prophet after prophet after prophet warned the people of God not to continue in their present course of action.

We know that Joel came soon after Obadiah because he quotes him, reminding the people of what God had already said to them. In particular he picked up one phrase that Obadiah introduced – 'the Day of the Lord' – a phrase used in other Old Testament prophecies and in the New Testament. It is the day when God comes to put wrongs right, and we looked at it in detail at the end of Joel.

The Book of Obadiah is included at the end of this section because its focus is on the events at the very end of the pre-exilic period, when the people of Judah were exiled into Babylon.

Some prophets had two messages – one for God's people, Israel, and one for the nations around Israel. Obadiah spoke to Edom, one of Israel's neighbours, a region to the south-east of the Dead Sea. It is the only prophecy by Obadiah that we possess today, and it may have been the only one he gave.

We know very little about Obadiah except that his name means 'the worshipper or servant of Yahweh'. Most of his message is a prediction about the future which came as a vision. It is a visual rather than a verbal message. The state of Edom was located in what we call trans-Jordan, the territory to the east of the Jordan valley. It was part of the land that had been promised to the people of Israel but had never actually been occupied by them. Under King David, Edom had become a satellite state, in much the same way as Poland and Latvia became satellite states of Russia. As soon as David's empire began to break up, Edom sought its own freedom and rebelled against Israel. They had two cities, Bosrah and Sela (known today as Petra), situated on one of the most important roads of the Middle East, from Europe to Arabia.

Petra is a most unusual place. It includes what looks like a cathedral carved out of red sandstone and hundreds of temples carved out of the rock, all round a huge empty circle in the middle of the mountains. Towering above Petra is Mount Seir, around 2,000 feet high. The prophecy of Obadiah is about that mountain.

The architecture of the temples is superb, and the view from the top of the mountain takes in the Red Sea and the Dead Sea. It provided an impregnable fortress for the Edomites who lived in the caves. But they were a godless people. Archaeologists have found altars where they offered humans alive to their gods.

Obadiah says they were full of pride. They believed that nothing could defeat them – not even God. So it was God himself who did just that, and that is the essence of Obadiah's message.

It is significant that the God of Israel is seen here as the God of other nations. This theme is constant throughout the Bible, but it must have sounded radical in a day when every nation had its god, and today as well when many believe that each person should be left to worship the god they prefer without having to worry anyone else.

But Christians believe there is just one God, who will judge people of every other religion too. The God of Israel is the God with whom every nation will have to deal and to whom every nation will have to give account.

This is also the message of the New Testament. When Paul spoke at Athens on Mars Hill, he told them that God allots every nation its time and space. He draws the map. For example, I believe it was God who brought the British Empire to an end. When I was a boy the school atlas was largely red. It was possible to travel right round the world and never leave British soil. What happened to this great empire? The answer is that Britain washed its hands of God's people, Israel. So God said, 'If Britain can't look after Israel she can't look after anybody,' and within five years the empire went. I believe that was one of the clearest examples of the hand of God.

So it is clear through reading the prophets that God judges other nations by their attitude to his people. I believe the same principle applies today to the Church. God judges people by how they treat the Church. What we do to God's people we do to God. Jesus picked up the same principle, saying that at the final judgement God will say to the nations: 'Whatever you did for one of the least of these brothers of mine, you did for me' (Matthew 25:40). By 'brothers' he means 'my people'. In the same way, when Saul of Tarsus met Jesus on the road to Damascus, he learned how the Lord saw his people. He said, 'Saul, why are you persecuting me?' – when in fact Saul had been persecuting Christians. He was horrified to learn that in persecuting them he was persecuting Christ. But as far as Christ was concerned, persecuting Christians meant persecuting him. So the people of God are the apple of God's eye. Just as the iris of your eye is the most sensitive part of your body, so God is especially sensitive when his people are persecuted.

Now that God's people are in every nation of the world, every nation is having to decide their attitude to God's people. On the Day of Judgement that will be a major factor. This principle comes out in prophet after prophet when they speak to other nations, and that is why most of their prophecies are addressed to the nations that lived around Israel and so had taken up an attitude towards Israel.

So although Obadiah may seem a small and obscure book, it is actually dealing with some fundamental issues of judgement that will affect all the nations of the world.

An outline of Obadiah

The book can be divided into two parts. In the first part (verses 1–14) Obadiah says that one nation is going to be judged – namely, Edom. In the second part (verses 15–21) the prophet sees all the nations being judged.

One nation will be judged (1–14)
The nations destroy Edom (1–9)
Edom despises Israel (10–14)

All nations will be judged (15–21)
Yahweh punishes the nations (15–16)
Israel possesses Edom (17–21)

One nation will be judged (1–14)

The nations destroy Edom (1–9)

Edom literally means 'red'. The city is made up of red sandstone, but that is not why it is called 'red' (Edomites were descended from red-headed Esau). Its location is on the eastern side of the rift valley of Arabah. Its two major cities are Petra and Bosrah, both monuments to man's ability to build.

But Obadiah tells the Edomites that the nations are going to destroy them, and that unlike burglars, who just take the things they are interested in, they will take everything, including their territory. He tells them that God hates pride in men. Pride is almost an invitation to God to bring that man low, for to be proud is to have a very high view of yourself and a low view of everyone else. If you put yourself up, you have to put others down, even God himself.

Edom despises Israel (10–14)

So Edom's location at the top of Mount Seir was symbolic of its attitude to the nations that surrounded it, and to Israel in particular. The Edomites were direct descendants of Esau who, of course, had sold his birthright to Jacob and was in conflict with his twin brother for most of his life. Esau's descendants had settled on the east side of the rift valley and Jacob's descendants settled on the west side. In Deuteronomy God forbade Israel to have a wrong attitude to Edom because Esau was Jacob's brother. This is why Obadiah tells Edom that she should not have treated her brother as she did. But Edom's attitude to Israel was aggressive. We read in Numbers and Deuteronomy that they refused to allow Moses and the Israelites safe passage through their land.

This antipathy was also seen when the empire of Israel began to crumble in King David's day. The Edomites rose up and joined in with anybody who attacked Jerusalem or Israel – whether Philistines, Arabs, or later, the Babylonians. The Babylonians were a very barbaric people. But the Edomites joined in and egged them on. When the Arabs attacked Jerusalem, the Edomites joined them. The hatred and jealousy and resentment of centuries came out. When the Philistines came against Jerusalem, the Edomites joined them. They took every opportunity to support others, perhaps because they weren't strong enough themselves.

On three occasions God says 'You should not' concerning their behaviour (12, 13, 14) and tells them that their disobedience will be punished.

An obvious question arises. Did the Edomites hear what Obadiah said? And if they heard it, did they heed it?

The first part of the prophecy is about Edom, but halfway through Obadiah changes from the third person to the second. So it seems that he had the courage to go to Petra to give the message in person. But there is no record of their having heeded the words – in fact, just the opposite. When the Babylonians attacked Jerusalem in 587 BC, they were egged on by the Edomites (Psalm 137:7).

Furthermore, other prophets also spoke against Edom. Isaiah 11, Jeremiah 49 and Ezekiel 25 all condemn Edom, with Isaiah using language similar to that of Obadiah to underline God's determination to judge. So since the message of Obadiah and the other prophets was ignored, God's judgement fell.

History records that in the sixth century BC the Arabs attacked them and they had to flee their cities and move across the rift valley into the Negev Desert to live as Bedouins. By 450 BC there were no Edomites left in their former land, and by 312 BC Petra was in the hands of the Nabateans. The Negev was renamed Idumea after the arrival of the Edomites. The Edomites were forcibly Judaized by Hyrcanus, so that Judaism became their official religion, though they retained their distinctive racial characteristics.

Edomites reappear in the New Testament. Herod the Great (featured in the infancy narrative in Matthew's Gospel) was from Idumea. He asked Julius Caesar if he would sell him the throne of Israel in 37 BC, and so the king of Israel was an Edomite! His people's heritage of great buildings became the inspiration for the building projects for which he was famous. This is why he built so many palaces, including one on Masada, as impregnable as the great temples of Petra.

So when the Wise Men came asking where they could find the new-born King of the Jews, Herod was angry. He didn't want a Jew on his throne, for Edom had conquered! So this was behind his slaughter of every boy under two years of age in Bethlehem.

It was his son who killed John the Baptist and to whom Jesus had nothing to say at his trial. His grandson was the Herod who was responsible for the death of James and was eaten by worms (see Acts 12). His great-grandson was a man called Agrippa who died in AD 100 without children.

So the Edomites disappeared. There isn't a single Edomite in the world today, thus fulfilling Obadiah's prophecy. God takes his time judging people. It was over 600 years from the time of Obadiah to their final disappearance. From this we can learn two clear lessons concerning God's judgement.

IT TAKES TIME

> Though the mills of God grind slowly,
> Yet they grind exceeding small;
> Though with patience he stands waiting,
> With exactness grinds he all.
>
> *Friedrich von Logau (1604–55)*

God takes his time. He is slow to anger, but when he says he will do it, he will do it – maybe a thousand years later, but he will do it. Where is Edom today? Gone. Where is Israel today? Back in her land.

GOD JUDGES THOSE WHO HURT HIS PEOPLE

God had said to Abraham, 'I will bless those who bless you, and whoever curses you I will curse' (Genesis 12:). God has two peoples in the world today: Israel and the Church. To attack either is to hurt him.

All nations will be judged (15–21)

Edom is an example of the type of godless nation that has always been hostile to God's people.

Yahweh punishes the nations (15–16)

The reasoning behind the punishment is clear: 'As you have done, so it will be done to you.' The punishment fits the crime. The Philistines are also mentioned as deserving God's wrath.

Obadiah saw that one day all nations would be judged. The God of Israel will hold every nation responsible, especially for their attitude to his people.

Israel possesses Edom (17–21)

One day, Israel will possess Edom. Edom is specifically included as a part of the land that God promised to his people – so one day they must have it, and Obadiah saw that. He saw that there would be no survivors from the house of Edom, and that their land would be possessed by its true owners. He saw Israel expanding to the north into Ephraim and Samaria, to the south into the Negev, to the east into the Edom hills and as far as the Mediterranean coast in the west.

What has all this got to do with us?

First, we must note that there is a Jacob and an Esau in every one of us. In the Epistle to the Hebrews Christians are told not to be like Esau, who sold his birthright for a pot of soup, and wept afterwards. He was full of regret and remorse, but he was never able to repent.

Instead we must be a Jacob. He wrestled with God until God made him lame. But he got the blessing, and it is from Jacob that God's people Israel came. Esau lived for the present, for the immediate satisfaction of his physical desires, and he lost his future. The Esaus of this world live for this world only. They don't care about the future; they are only concerned about the satisfaction of their desires in the present. The Book of Obadiah encourages us to be a Jacob – the man who was broken by God and became a prince, and whose name Israel is now on the map again, after 2,000 years.

Secondly, we learn from this book that when God speaks, he keeps his word. When he says he will do something, he may not do it by next Tuesday, and we may have to wait a thousand years, but if God says he will do it, he will do it, and this is why we can trust his word. So little Obadiah may be called a minor prophet, and certainly he wrote a small book, but everything he said will come true.

THE
STRUGGLE TO
SURVIVE

28.

EZEKIEL

Introduction

The Book of Ezekiel is the most neglected and the least favourite part of the Old Testament. The first half of it (chapters 1–24) is almost unrelieved doom and gloom. This depressing text leads many readers to give up and move to another book in the Bible! The book is long and repetitive, and 20 years of preaching are squeezed into it. Much of it is not relevant to our situation – it's in another world at another time, and we're just not familiar with it. Language that is at times crude and even offensive gives further reason for dislike. Few would say it is their favourite book.

Furthermore, Ezekiel shows a side of God's character that few find appealing. The prophet speaks of the severity of God's judgement. The typical radio or television religion focuses on God's goodness but rarely on his judgement, and that's how people like it.

So at first sight there seems to be little encouragement to read the book! But books like Ezekiel challenge us to ask two questions: 'Why do you read your Bible?' and 'How do you read it?' The two questions are related, because the reason why you read your Bible will actually determine how you read it. Method will flow from motive.

How to read Ezekiel

On the whole there are three approaches to reading a book like Ezekiel:

The verse-centred approach (self)

There is the verse-centred approach, in which people look for a word for themselves. I'm tempted to call it 'the horoscope method of Bible reading', where we read through until a verse fits our situation. But this is not how God intended the Bible to be read. Indeed, you would have to go a long way through Ezekiel before you found a personally relevant verse that leapt off the page! Devotional Bible reading can be useful and is better than nothing, but it's not the right way to read the Bible. It is an essentially self-centred way of reading.

The passage-centred approach (others)

Next, there is the passage-centred approach. Some Christians read the Bible mainly for the sake of other people. This is especially the case for preachers and teachers, who are wondering what they should preach about. Four passages in Ezekiel are special favourites with preachers.

Perhaps the most popular is chapter 37, made famous by the Negro spiritual 'Dem bones, dem bones, dem dry bones ... hear the word of the Lord'. The themes of death and life are too good to resist, and the extraordinary image of bones joining together, covered with flesh, makes for dramatic effect.

Another favourite is chapter 34, especially used at the induction of a new pastoral minister. The subject-matter is good shepherds and bad shepherds. The good shepherds search for the lost sheep while the bad shepherds feed themselves. It is easy to use this passage as a basis for preaching about the responsibility of the pastor.

Chapter 47 is another preaching favourite, though it tends to be taken out of context and used in an allegorical way. In the chapter a man finds a river flowing from the temple. He steps into it up to his ankles, and then up to his knees, and then up to his waist, and then it is deep enough to swim in. So preachers use the water as a picture of the Holy Spirit. They ask: 'How deeply are you into the Spirit? Are you swimming in the Spirit yet, or are you just paddling?' But geographical details in the context (fishermen at En Gedi by the Sea in the Arabah Valley) surely intend the prophecy to be taken literally. The Dead Sea becoming full of life with the influx of desalinating fresh water is a miracle of nature, but preachers find it easier to 'spiritualize' such events and apply them to human nature, especially if they have problems with supernatural intervention in the physical realm. And the allegorical treatment of the Old Testament has a long history in church pulpits, emanating from the Greek disdain for the literal and physical in the teaching of Clement and Origen of Alexandria in the third century AD.

Finally, chapter 18 focuses on the personal responsibility of each individual for his or her own sin. There was a saying in Israel that 'the fathers ate sour grapes and the children's teeth were set on edge' because God had said that he punished sin to the third and fourth generation. But Ezekiel introduces the very important principle that, on the Day of Judgement, each person will be responsible for his or her own sin. This idea that each person is accountable to God is a favourite theme of preachers. But the popularity of these chapters means, of course, that most preachers leave the rest of the book alone.

The book-centred approach (God)

This is the best approach to Ezekiel, and it involves getting a grasp of the whole book rather than just parts of it. Only by doing this can we really understand what God is saying to us through it. Ultimately the main reason for reading the Bible is that we might know God. Bible reading teaches us what kind of a God he is – how he responds to us, how he feels about us and what he will do with us. So if we avoid Ezekiel we avoid a crucial part of God's revelation about himself and we miss out on what it teaches us.

When Christians read the Bible book by book for the first time, I always recommend using the Living Bible. As I mentioned earlier, some years ago the church I served in Guildford read through the whole Bible non-stop in this version. *The Living Bible* is the most accurate translation of the feelings expressed in the Bible, but since it is a paraphrase, it is not the most accurate translation of the thoughts and the precise wording of the biblical text.

The Bible is, of course, the word of God and the word of man. So we can look at it for both inspiration and interest. There is a great deal of human interest in it. God chose to communicate his word through people, in all their complexity, at particular times and in particular situations. These are not 'ivory tower' speculations but words that made a difference to the world and to people's perception of it.

By understanding the real-life situations portrayed in the Bible we can appreciate the way in which God's word came to real people in real history. When speakers take the divine word out of its human context, boring preaching and teaching is the result.

The background to Ezekiel

So it is vital that we grasp the historical background before we look at the major themes in Ezekiel's prophecy. A century before, the 10 tribes of Israel had been carried off to Assyria. They had ignored the warnings of the prophets Amos and Hosea, and so they had been deported from their own country.

Ezekiel was concerned with the two tribes in the south, who turned out to be even worse. Despite the warning from their northern brothers, they had fallen into godless behaviour and had ignored prophets such as Isaiah and Micah, who had warned them of judgement to come. When Jeremiah came a little later, they ignored him too. The little prophecy of Habakkuk warned them of their impending doom at the hands of the Babylonians, but his message also fell on deaf ears. So finally the worst happened and they were deported into Babylon.

There had been some bright spots in their recent history, but these had not been enough to turn the nation around, and the spiritual situation was generally bleak. When King Josiah discovered the book of the Law during a spring-clean of the temple, he was horrified to see how far the people had drifted from the Law of God. They were even sacrificing babies to the pagan god Molech in the Valley of Hinnom. (In his teaching Jesus used this place as a picture of hell.) So Josiah attempted to reform the nation, removing the 'high places' from the land and tackling the moral corruption in society, but it was in vain. The people's hearts had drifted far from God.

Then came a succession of 'bad' kings. Jehoahaz reigned for just three months, after being elected by the people. He failed to stand up to Egypt, and the Pharaoh took him away to Riblah and chained him up. Then came Jehoiakim. Although he was the son of the upright Josiah, he was unconcerned

Josiah ..

about the spiritual state of the nation. In fact, Jehoiakim was just a puppet king chosen by the Egyptians to replace Jehoahaz.

So at this stage in her history Judah was at the mercy of the big superpowers – Egypt to the south-west and Babylon to the north-east. God could have held those big powers off, as he had done in the past, but he had promised that if the people drifted away from him, they would not know his protection any more.

So Nebuchadnezzar of Babylon invaded and controlled the country for three years before finally leaving. Judah suffered a series of attacks from various nations – the Arameans, the Moabites and the Ammonites. The result was that by Ezekiel's time all that remained of Judah was the city of Jerusalem, now totally under foreign domination.

The final blow came when the Babylonians returned and besieged Jerusalem for two-and-a-half years. Finally the city was taken and all the treasures were removed, just as Isaiah had prophesied.

All the top people were taken away. This was a favourite trick to reduce a conquered people to helplessness. So the first deportation took away 7,000 army officers and soldiers, about 1,000 craftsmen and around 10,000 artisans, leaving behind only the very poorest people. (Incidentally, the prophet Daniel was among those deported at that time.) It looked as if the whole purpose of God was being brought to nothing.

Zedekiah was the very last puppet king of Judah. He was allowed to rule in Jerusalem with just a small army. Once again the city was besieged and Zedekiah was captured by Nebuchadnezzar's army. They killed each of his sons before his very eyes so that he would see that the royal line had come to an end. Then they removed his eyes, so the last thing he saw was his sons being killed. Then Nebuchadnezzar ordered Jerusalem to be totally destroyed. This sad tale can be found in 2 Kings 22–25.

Handwritten margin notes:
Ch 4 – word — speaking for God
Ch 3 – vision — proclaiming of God
pictures a future
visions of the future

Ezekiel's preaching

It was around this time that Ezekiel was called to preach, although he was thousands of miles away from Jerusalem in the land of Babylon.

From the start, God told Ezekiel that he would make his forehead like flint – nothing would be able to discourage him. When the people got harder and harder and didn't want to hear, he would need to be single-minded in following through with God's commission.

His message came in part through what is known as 'apocalyptic language' (the word means literally 'unveiling' – of that which has been previously hidden, particularly the future, which must necessarily be described in figurative, even highly symbolic terms). It is a form of prophecy, but it's more visual than verbal, very symbolic and very dramatic. Ezekiel and Daniel are the best examples of this kind of prophecy in the Old Testament, and Revelation is the only example in the New.

Like all prophets, Ezekiel had supernatural sight. This involves insight, foresight and oversight. He was able to look down on the world from God's perspective and see the unfolding of his purposes.

Space

Ezekiel saw things happening in Jerusalem when he was hundreds of miles away in Babylon. Modern scholars imagine that he must have kept going back to Jerusalem to see what was happening. But through the Holy Spirit Ezekiel could actually see events in his homeland. On one occasion while he was preaching in Babylon he had a vision of a man in Jerusalem dropping dead, and weeks later he heard that the man had indeed died in Jerusalem at the exact moment when he had seen him drop dead in his vision.

Time

Ezekiel was also able to see into the future. The Bible is a book full of predictions about the future. Around 27 per cent of the verses in the Bible contain predictions, with Ezekiel having a higher percentage than most other biblical books. Ezekiel and Daniel have the highest percentage of predictions about the future in the whole Old Testament. Around three quarters of the predictions in Ezekiel have already come true to the letter. The statistical chances of such a thing happening are 1 to 75 million. There are 735 separate events predicted in the Bible. Some are predicted only once or twice, one over 300 times. Of those 735 events, 593 (81 per cent) have already happened. The Bible has been 100 per cent accurate so far. The remaining 19 per cent of its predictions have yet to be fulfilled, but we can be sure that they will be.

Three periods

Ezekiel's prophecies were given in three separate phases, and in each period of time he dealt with different subject-matter. In the first period (chapters 4–24), the most depressing of the three, he was aged between 30 and 33. It made the dreadful announcement that Jerusalem would be totally destroyed. Understandably, this is the section of his book that nobody quotes (indeed, very few people could quote any part of the book). This first period of prophecy was before the first siege of Jerusalem, after which the city was under Babylon's control without being destroyed.

The second time Ezekiel prophesied was in the eleventh or twelfth year of his exile, when he was 36 or 37 years of age. This period of prophecy can be found in chapters 25–32. This time Ezekiel prophesied not about Jerusalem but about the nations around her, who had taken advantage of the fact that she was now under Babylon's control and who were glad to see Israel finished. Even today Israel is completely surrounded by peoples who would love to see her destroyed.

The next major event came in 587 BC, when Jerusalem was totally destroyed and, at exactly the same time, Ezekiel lost his wife in Babylon. But the prophet was instructed not to weep, because at the very minute when she died, Jerusalem would also fall. His refusal to weep was symbolic of how Israel should feel about what had happened to Jerusalem – that is, completely numb. He was told to record the date of his wife's death in his diary so that he could match it with the news from his homeland. Of course, the dates were exactly the same.

Three years after his wife had died and thirteen years since he had last prophesied, Ezekiel started to prophesy again when he was 50 years of age. During the intervening period of silence God had told him that his tongue would stick to the roof of his mouth, preventing speech until God released it. This time he prophesied for one year, but now the whole of his message focused on the return home. For example, he said that one day the Valley of Dry Bones would come together and be a mighty army. It's all positive optimism, looking forward to a good future (chapters 33–39).

Chapters 40–48 talk about the restoration of the temple in Jerusalem. However, Ezekiel died without ever seeing the temple or Jerusalem again. He was buried in a tomb in Babylon, at a place called Kifi in modern Iraq.

A refrain

There is one phrase that appears 74 times in Ezekiel's prophecy – '*then you will know that I am the LORD*'. It is a refrain repeated with slight variations in sections B, C and D of the book (see the outline below).

In section B (chapters 4–24) the wording is: '*you* will know that I am the LORD'. But in section C, which deals with God's revenge on the neighbours of Judah, the refrain is: 'then *they* will know that I am the LORD'. When, in section D, Ezekiel moves on to the good news about the return from the exile in Babylon, the wording is: 'then *the nations* will know that I am the LORD'. In other words, when God brings the Jews back to the land, the whole world will know that God is the Lord, because, humanly speaking, it is absolutely impossible to re-establish the state of Israel.

So the three variations of this refrain tell us, first, that the people of Israel were not very sure of God – hence the phrase, 'then you will know …'; also that the neighbours of Judah were not very sure that the God of Israel existed – hence 'they will know …'; and finally, that the whole world was not very sure whether there was a God – hence 'then the nations will know …'

An outline of the book

A. Redeployment of the priest (1–3)
B. Retribution for Jerusalem (4–24) – first phase
The siege of Jerusalem
C. Revenge on the neighbours of Judah (25–32) – second phase
The fall of Jerusalem
D. Return from the exile in Babylon (33–39)
E. Restoration of the temple in Jerusalem (40–48) } **third phase**

Redeployment of the priest (chapters 1–3)

Ezekiel was born into the priestly family of Zadok in 622 BC and so would have been reaching the age of his Bar Mitzvah when King Josiah was killed. He was taken away from his home country when he was aged 25, as part of the first deportation, along with Daniel and the cream of Jewish society. Once they had been deported, they were allowed to live in their own settlements with relative freedom. Ezekiel settled with his family at a place called Tel Aviv (it is now the name of the largest city in Israel), by one of the canals that joined the Tigris and Euphrates rivers.

The name Ezekiel means 'God strengthens', but in the prophecy he is more commonly referred to (83 times, in fact) as 'Son of man' – a title that Jesus used for himself. No other prophet is known by this title.

I am fascinated to note that at the age of 30, when he should have started his priesthood, he was called to be a prophet. But he was far from his home country, and knew he couldn't ever be a priest in Babylon, for there was no temple there. The prophetic call came through an amazing vision of the Lord. So from the age of 30 to 33 this prophet, who was called 'Son of man', performed miracles and preached. Clearly, Ezekiel was a forerunner of Christ, who was, of course, prophet, priest and king. Jesus began his ministry when he was 30, for that was the age at which a Jewish man could begin to serve as a priest.

But although Ezekiel could not officiate in the temple, he could still take part in worship. In the absence of the temple, the Jewish synagogue (the word means 'meeting-place', literally: 'come together') became the place for praise, prayer and Scripture reading. Indeed, it was the model that the early Christians adopted as the Church moved away from a temple focus in the early days of overlap between the Old and New Covenants.

The call of Ezekiel was most unusual (see chapter 1). It came as part of a strange vision – a vision so odd that some modern scholars have speculated that he had a fit, went into a trance or took drugs! It would need a surrealist artist to do it justice. In fact, the favourite interpretation today is that he saw a UFO (Unidentified Flying Object).

First of all, he saw four creatures, which were a combination of animals, humans and angels. They had the wings of angels, parts that were human and parts that were animal. These four creatures are clearly symbolic of all the living beings that God has created in his universe, whether animal, human or angel. These are the three main orders, reminding us that human beings are not the peak of creation.

Above the four creatures he sees the Creator on his throne – majestic, mysterious, covered in glory. Wherever God is, there is glory. Indeed, the phrase 'the glory of the LORD' recurs throughout the book. 'Glory' means the radiance or brightness of God.

Clearly, the throne can travel in any direction. This symbolizes the omnipresence of God, who is able to be anywhere and everywhere. He is a mobile God. This is significant because, until this point, every vision of God's throne in the Bible had portrayed it as static, fixed in Jerusalem. So it was a comfort for Ezekiel to learn that God's throne was mobile, for it meant that he could move to Babylon. This was an important truth to communicate to the exiles, who may have believed that God lived in one place, hundreds of miles away in Jerusalem.

Furthermore, the 'eyes' on the rims of the wheels tell us that God can see everything, everywhere. It's a very meaningful picture. No wonder Ezekiel was overwhelmed with the vision and fell to the ground.

It is interesting that he fell face down. In the Bible the reaction to the divine presence is to fall forwards. The apostle Paul at his conversion and John on the Isle of Patmos fell on their faces.

God then gave Ezekiel a scroll on which to write the prophecies that he was to deliver, and God told him to eat the scroll. The words on the scroll were words of lamentation, mourning and woe – curse words. Yet he found it sweet.

Retribution for Jerusalem (chapters 4–24)

Prophet after prophet had foretold two disasters: (1) Jerusalem would be destroyed by the Babylonians, and (2) the people would be deported to Babylon. Isaiah, Jeremiah and Habakkuk had all said the same thing.

When Jerusalem was taken by the Babylonians and the top people in society were deported, the city itself remained standing. Some of the people of Judah claimed that the judgement was not as bad as Jeremiah had made out. God had apparently said he would destroy the city, but in fact it still existed and it still had Jews living in it. They admitted that they were now under a foreign power, but they still had the city! So the inference was that maybe Jeremiah had exaggerated the problem of sin. If he was wrong about the extent of the disaster, maybe he was wrong about other things too. So the word of God was being watered down, rather as Satan had done in the Garden of

Eden when he had questioned Eve's understanding of God's prohibition.

But it was important that the people of Judah understood what God was doing. The exile was not merely punishment, but was also meant to reform the people. So someone had to persuade them that God meant what he had said. Ezekiel had to point to the destruction of Jerusalem as the time when they would know that God was the Lord. Their sin was as bad as the prophets had said, and therefore the judgement would also be as bad as the prophets had said.

Jerusalem will fall

Ezekiel had to communicate this message not only verbally, but also visually. He had to teach them in six different ways that Jerusalem was finished:

1 He was told to take a slab of clay, draw a picture of Jerusalem on it and lay siege to it with model battering-rams and so forth. He did this in total silence, watched by the crowds who were doubtless asking, 'What's the old prophet doing now?'

2 As if this wasn't odd enough, God told Ezekiel to lie on his left side for 390 days and then to lie on his right side for another 40 days. He had to do that to symbolize how long the house of Israel and the house of Judah had been disobeying God (390 years and 40 years respectively). God said that to make sure that Ezekiel did this properly, he would be tied up with rope!

3 Ezekiel also had to go on a meagre diet, to symbolize the shortage of food during the siege of Jerusalem. He was allowed 0.2 kilograms of bread and 0.6 litres of water per day, and he had to live on that diet for a long time. He was to cook his bread over a fire fuelled by his own dried

excrement. (Actually, he protested to God and was allowed to use cow dung instead – a wonderful example of God's flexibility!) This was all meant to show that things would be desperate in Jerusalem during the siege.

4 God told Ezekiel to shave his head and his beard with a sharp sword and then to put the hair in three piles. He was to burn the first pile when the siege of Jerusalem came to an end. The second pile was to be struck with a sword all round the model city, depicting slaughter. Then the third pile was to be thrown up into the air so that it was scattered – which was to be the fate of the people of Jerusalem.

5 For the fifth drama Ezekiel had to put all his clothes in a bag, dig a hole in a wall and creep out through the wall at night. By doing this he was predicting what would happen when Jerusalem fell – and indeed, King Zedekiah had to leave the city in just this way.

6 Perhaps the hardest drama of all concerned the death of Ezekiel's wife. He was not even allowed to mourn, because when Jerusalem finally fell the people would be so stunned that they wouldn't be able to believe it and wouldn't even cry.

One of the most telling visions in the book is the one describing the glory of the Lord in the temple. The glory went up to the top of the Mount of Olives and then disappeared. This was exactly what happened to Jesus when they rejected him.

How will Jerusalem fall?

Ezekiel says that the city will fall to Nebuchadnezzar, who is described as having 'the sword of the Lord'. There is the chilling description of Nebuchadnezzar standing at a fork in the road, casting lots. Will Jerusalem or Rabbah of Ammon be crushed first? The destruction would be utterly ruthless and would involve cutting off the ears and noses of the inhabitants. Ezekiel writes of sword, famine, wild beasts and plague as four dreadful judgements on the people. We read that at this time, the glory of the Lord will leave the temple.

Why will Jerusalem fall?

There are three major reasons for the judgement against the people – idolatry, immorality and ingratitude.

IDOLATRY

The people of God were worshipping the goddess Asherah in the temple. Pictures of animals had been painted on the walls of the temple ruins. The women had started worshipping a goddess called Tamus at the very gate of the temple. Ezekiel even saw 25 men in the temple worshipping the sun. It was an extraordinary and dreadful time. In short, the people of God were behaving even more badly than the surrounding nations.

IMMORALITY

Ezekiel calls Jerusalem 'the bloody city' because of its ruthless exploitation of widows, orphans and strangers and because of the murders that were taking place in the city. This title had also been given by Nahum to the evil city of Nineveh, capital of the Assyrian empire. In Jerusalem there was lying, sexual immorality and contempt for parents – all in disobedience to the Ten Commandments. How low Jerusalem had fallen.

INGRATITUDE

God criticizes the people for their ingratitude and uses five parables to drive his points home:

1 *A wild vine.* Judah is depicted as a useless and worthless vine. The wood had no value other than as firewood. In John 15 Jesus uses a similar parable.

2 *A girl.* In chapter 16 Ezekiel tells the story of a deserted baby girl who becomes a queen and then a prostitute.

3 *Two sisters.* Their names are Oholah and Oholibah, representing Samaria (i.e. the ten tribes in the north) and Jerusalem (the two tribes in the south). They are both prostitutes, depicting how both kingdoms had drifted away from God. The language here is extreme, and was intended to shock the people into realizing what they had become.

4 *A lioness and her two cubs.* The cubs are taken captive, depicting King Jehoahaz being taken to Egypt and King Jehoiakim being taken to Babylon.

5 *Two eagles* – one representing Pharaoh and one Nebuchadnezzar.

The parables were a way of communicating truth to those who wanted to know – just as another 'Son of man' also used parables as a way of speaking to those who truly wanted to hear. In these parables Ezekiel was telling the people that their true situation was far worse than they realized.

He says, firstly, that each individual is responsible for their *personal* state. It is no good blaming one's predecessors. Each one must stand alone on Judgement Day to give account. Secondly, he says that each person is responsible for their *present* state. It is not what someone *was* that matters, but what they *are*. The righteous may become wicked and the wicked may become righteous. It is important to die in a state of grace.

But he does also blame three groups of people for allowing the national situation to become so bad: the prophets, the priests and the kings. He says they are all partly responsible for the condition of Jerusalem. Things were so bad that God couldn't save Jerusalem even if Noah, Job and Daniel (three of the best men in history) were living in it – which came as an enormous shock to the people.

So this section of the book is largely gloomy. The only glimpses of hope come in 16:60–62, 20:40–44 and 21:24–27, where the prophet hints at an everlasting covenant that God will make with his people. His kindness will shame them to the point where they loathe themselves.

Revenge on the neighbours of Judah (chapters 25–32)

The middle section of the book contains the prophetic message that Ezekiel delivered when he was 36 or 37 years of age. The background is important. When Jerusalem fell, all the neighbouring countries were thrilled. (The phrase 'Hip! Hip! Hooray!' comes from the delighted cry 'Hip! Hip!', which is made up of the three initial letters of 'Jerusalem is fallen!' in the Latin language, so the phrase was originally an anti-Semitic celebration.) So many people were delighted and tried to take advantage of the Babylonian invasion. The Edomites and the Ammonites did horrible things to the Jewish people who were left, and that explains the bitterness expressed in some of the Psalms of this era.

For example, Psalm 137 begins sadly, reflecting on the difficulty of singing about God in a foreign land, but it finishes with a bitter cry: 'Happy shall he be who dashes your little ones against the stones.' The Edomites took babies by the ankles and smashed their brains out against the walls of Jerusalem. The Psalm is a cry from the heart: 'We want you to suffer in the same way as we have suffered.'

So the middle section of Ezekiel is not an arbitrary rant at non-Jewish peoples but, rather, is a description of God paying back these surrounding nations for exploiting the fall of Jerusalem.

Some of the predictions are remarkably detailed. Let's just take one, where Ezekiel predicts the downfall of the fishing port of Tyre, located on the eastern coast of the Mediterranean Sea. Ezekiel predicts that one day Tyre will be razed to the ground, the whole city will be thrown into the sea, and the place where Tyre stood will be a place for fishermen to dry their nets. It is an extraordinary prophecy, because no other city has ever been thrown into the sea, either before or since.

But it came true. When Alexander the Great came marching down towards Egypt with his great army, the people of Tyre simply got into their fishing boats and went out to the island that lay half a mile from the shore, knowing that Alexander had an army but not a navy. But Alexander wasn't called 'the Great' for nothing. When he saw all the people on the island, thinking they were safe, he commanded that every brick, every stone and every piece of timber in the city should be used to build a causeway out to the island. After this was done, his army went across and defeated the people of Tyre. Their city had literally been thrown into the sea.

If you look at a map of the area today, you will see that modern Tyre is out on the island and sand has silted up against Alexander's causeway. If you go to the site of old Tyre on the mainland, you will find that it is just bare rock, with fishermen's nets spread on it, just as Ezekiel prophesied.

Chapter 25 includes predictions about Ammon, Moab and Edom to the east of Judah, and others about Philistia to the west. Chapters 26–28 focus on Tyre and Sidon to the north, and chapters 29–32 deal with Egypt in the south.

This middle section of the book is fairly straightforward to understand, except that one man is singled out as an example of supreme pride – the king of Tyre. Many people see a picture of Satan's pride in the description of the king of Tyre, for he actually said, 'I am a god.' The Egyptian Pharaoh did much the same, even making the absurd claim, 'I made the Nile.' He may have dug some of the irrigation channels, but he did not make the Nile itself. God will not stand human pride. It is the ultimate sin to set yourself up as if you are God. It's what Adam and Eve did in the Garden of Eden when they wanted to be like God. Although they had been made in the image of God and so were already like him in character, they wanted to be like him in power and authority too.

It is significant that Babylon is not mentioned even once. Maybe this was because it was treasonable to write anti-Babylonian literature; or perhaps, since the people of God were now in Babylon, comment on that nation was not appropriate. What is clear is that after their exile the people of God never again entered into worship of foreign gods. God's judgement had achieved its purpose.

Return from the exile in Babylon (chapters 33–39)

After Jerusalem was destroyed in 587 BC there was a complete change in Ezekiel's preaching from pessimism to optimism. In chapters 33–39 – the most pleasant section of the book – he predicts and anticipates the people's return from exile.

Chapter 33 talks about watchmen who stand on the walls of a city, day and night, to warn the inhabitants of danger. If a sentry did not spot an enemy coming, he forfeited his life – it was a capital crime. God tells Ezekiel that he has been appointed as a watchman. God was saying to him, 'If you don't warn my people, you will pay for it with your blood. But if you warn them, there is no more responsibility on you – they will pay for it with their own blood.'

One of the best-known passages in Ezekiel is the one where God bemoans the fact that he has looked for even one man who would 'fill the gap' between himself and the people, but he has been unable to find one. But Ezekiel was such a man. Now, of course, Ezekiel was not in Jerusalem – he was far away in Babylon – but he was still a watchman, and when he saw trouble coming, it was his responsibility to warn the people. If he didn't he would pay for it personally. So in a sense he had no choice but to go through with this costly ministry – he would be held responsible if he didn't.

Chapter 34 deals with the 'good shepherds' and the 'bad shepherds' within Israel. The bad shepherds were the prophets, priests and kings who should have been caring for Israel but were failing to do so. At the end of this chapter God promises that he himself will be their good shepherd. Of course, Jesus had this chapter in mind when he said that he was the good shepherd, in contrast with the bad ones who did not look after the sheep.

Interestingly, the Bible never blames the sheep for the state of the flock. This is a principle that applies to churches as well. The shepherds are responsible for the state of the flock, not the sheep.

In chapter 35 Edom is singled out for special mention, partly because of the ancient rivalry between the two nations stemming from the friction between Esau and Jacob.

Chapter 37 is well known because of the Negro spiritual about the dry bones. But very few people go on to read the parable of the two sticks, and this is just as important. Ezekiel was told to take two sticks and hold them in one hand, side by side. God told him to write 'Ephraim' on one stick (the popular name for the northern ten tribes) and 'Judah' on the other (the name for the two tribes in the south). Then he was instructed to hold them together in his hand so that they became one stick. Some people think this was a vision, but I think it was a straight miracle, rather like the miracle of Moses' rod in Egypt. God was saying, 'I'm going to make the two kingdoms into one people again, and I'll be their shepherd.' This is echoed by Jesus' words: 'I have other sheep that are not of this sheep pen. I must bring them also'.

In chapter 38 there is a strange prophecy concerning the future. It's about 'Gog' and 'Magog', though we are not exactly sure what is meant by those names. They are picked up again right at the end of the Book of Revelation, making it clear that this prophecy has not yet been fulfilled. A great conflict is going to come out of the north, though we don't precisely know where it will come from or who will cause it. Ezekiel was looking through a telescope into the distant future. He never saw this prophecy fulfilled and neither have we. But one day it will happen, in the final conflict before history winds up.

These chapters include a most interesting refrain – 'I will'. It occurs 77 times. These covenant words appear in such phrases as 'I will bring you home', 'I will be your God' and 'I will give you good shepherds'. Here is God the husband talking to his wayward wife and saying, 'We're still married and I will still keep my side of the covenant – I will, I will, I will.'

When God made his covenant with Israel he told them that even if they broke the covenant he never would. In Deuteronomy we read that there will be times when he will have to throw them out of the land, but he will always bring them back. So when God brings them back home after throwing them out, then the nations will know that he is the Lord, because it will have happened so publicly and everybody will know that they are back. The surrounding nations may not like it, but they will have to acknowledge that God has brought his people back. They are still his people. Romans 9–11 says that although they may have rejected God, he hasn't rejected them.

Restoration of the temple in Israel (chapters 40–48)

The most serious loss to the people and Ezekiel was the loss of the temple. They had always assumed that, whatever else might be lost, God would never let his own dwelling-place on earth be destroyed. This section that focuses on the temple is the most difficult part of the book to understand.

According to the text, the prophecy was given in the twenty-fifth year of Ezekiel's exile, when he was 50. As a rule, if the Bible gives dates for a prophecy, they mean that you must fit the text into its historical context in order to understand it.

Ezekiel was not allowed to finish preaching to the exiles without filling them with the hope of something to look forward to. They may have been disciplined, but they had not been destroyed. God will never allow his people Israel to disappear. Jesus said that heaven and earth may pass away, but the Jewish 'race' will never pass away (Matthew 24:35; NIV margin). Its continued existence is one of the proofs that the God of Israel is real. God communicates his eternity to whatever he touches, so you can't destroy what belongs to him.

The plan for the building of the temple is given in chapters 40–42. The building is described in great detail, as in an architectural plan. Its dimensions would be large enough for 13 English cathedrals! But it is quite different from Solomon's temple. It is bigger, it has no holy of holies, no ark of the covenant, and no table of the shewbread.

In chapter 43 Ezekiel has a vision of the glory of the Lord returning to the temple and lighting it up, just as it did following Solomon's prayer of dedication 600 years before. The glory was so bright that it was necessary for it to be covered by the veil so that it would not blind people. Ezekiel has earlier seen the glory depart, and now he sees it return.

There is an altar and there are sacrifices, but chapter 44 says there is no high priest. This is significant for our interpretation, because when the Jews returned from exile they *did* have high priests, up to and including the time of Jesus. In this chapter the place of the high priest is taken by a 'prince of priests'. Interestingly, the only priests in the vision are sons of Zadok – Ezekiel's family.

The description of the temple is especially intriguing because it has *never been built*. When the people of Judah returned from exile they built a temple that looked so poor that Haggai had to tell them not to despise the day of small things. Furthermore, they didn't have a king when they returned. A man called Joshua was the high priest and Zerubbabel was the governor.

At the time of Jesus, King Herod, an Edomite (a descendant of Esau), was rebuilding the temple on grander lines in order to impress the Jews. He did incorporate some of Solomon's ideas into it, but it was quite different from Ezekiel's vision. This temple was of enormous size and was still being built when Jesus began his ministry. Some of the stones were 40 feet long, 3 feet high and 3 feet deep, weighing 100 tons. It was a magnificent sight, but Jesus said not one stone would be left standing on another. It was hardly finished when the Romans pulled the whole thing down in AD 70, and so Jesus' prediction came absolutely true.

So is Ezekiel's temple ever going to be built?

Not literal

Some people say it was not intended to be built literally. It was a prophetic vision that was provided to give the Jews hope. The detail in the vision makes it seem realistic, but it is a parable that should be read for its spiritual value. But this does not explain why Ezekiel is told to tell such detail to the people!

Others argue that it was a description of a heavenly temple. They point to certain biblical passages (e.g. Exodus 25:40; Hebrews 8:2, 5; 9:11f., 24; Revelation 9:11) as evidence.

Literal

PAST

Another possibility is that God wanted them to build this temple, but the people ignored Ezekiel's plans and built their own version, which they thought they could afford. This would explain why the glory did not return, the prince did not come and the river did not flow. Supporters of this view point to the fact that here in chapter 43 the refrain that recurs throughout the book, 'then you will know', does not appear.

FUTURE

Another possibility is that the temple will be built in the future. Many Christians are convinced that it will be part of the New Jerusalem. The 12 gates will be named after the 12 tribes. The New Jerusalem will be called 'The Lord is There'.

Others speculate that the temple will be rebuilt by the Jewish people before Jesus returns or that it will be rebuilt in the Millennium. The problem here is that other prophets mention sacrifices, altars and priests, all of which are absent from this vision (see Isaiah 56:6–8; 66:21; Jeremiah 33:15–18; Zechariah 14:16).

Some Christians point out that the New Testament makes it clear that God does not dwell in temples (Acts 7:48; 17:24). Jesus referred to himself as 'this temple' (John 2:19, 21), and Christians are also described as temples (1 Corinthians 3:16; 2 Corinthians 6:16, 19; Revelation 3:12). Therefore (so the argument goes), whether the temple is rebuilt or not doesn't really matter.

It is hard to be definite about whether the temple will be rebuilt. This is one of those areas where we are going to have to wait and see! The good news is that God's plan was that he himself would come and dwell on earth, in the person of Jesus Christ. All believers are the temple of God now – he dwells in us. So however uncertain we may be about Ezekiel's vision of the temple, we can rejoice in this.

The final chapters

In chapter 45 the whole land is divided between the tribes, but in a way very different to that prescribed in the Book of Joshua. It is allocated in horizontal strips from east to west. Also we have the restoration of offerings and holy feasts and holy days, with the exception of Pentecost.

Then chapter 47 includes the vision of a new river in the Middle East. Most rivers that run through the Promised Land flow into the Mediterranean from the Judean Hills. But there is one amazing river called the Jordan which runs along the longest crack in the earth's surface, from Syria to Africa. The deepest point of the crack and the lowest point on the surface of the earth is Jericho.

In Ezekiel's vision the source of the new river is right under the temple up in Jerusalem. Any river that starts there has to flow into the Dead Sea. Jerusalem is surrounded by hills, but there is one opening in those hills to the south-west of the city, which heads straight down to the Dead Sea. Ezekiel sees a river going down that valley and more and more tributaries joining the river, so that it gets deeper and deeper, and a man wading down the river will soon find himself out of his depth and having to swim.

Ezekiel sees the new river entering the Dead Sea in the region of En Gedi, which is half-way down the West Bank. This is the place where David hid from Saul in the caves. He sees this river freshening the sea and the fishermen of Galilee coming down to the sea to fish. It's no longer the Dead Sea – it's a fresh, live sea. The whole vision is a dream to fill the people with hope that the future is going to be better.

Finally, in the last chapter of the book Ezekiel sees the gates of the city being re-erected and the land enjoying peace and prosperity. Everything is wonderful. So what began as a gloomy book finishes with great hope.

Why should Christians read Ezekiel?

First, the book tells us that God judges his own people – judgement begins at the house of the Lord. God is holy and so he must judge. A judge has two functions – to punish the wicked and to vindicate the righteous. God is the perfect judge, because he knows everything, can do anything and can be everywhere. His name was tied to the Jewish nation, so he had to punish them for their sin, but because of his mercy he also rescued them from their enemies. Too many Christians think that as soon as you have believed in Jesus, judgement is finished. But this is far from the case. We must all appear before the judgement seat of Christ. God judges his own people, and he judges them by a higher standard than others.

Secondly, we need to remember that God takes vengeance. If people mistreat us, it is not necessary for us to try to pay them back; we can safely leave this to God. So when someone is treating you badly, feel sorrow rather than anger, for God is going to pay them back.

Thirdly, God will always restore his people. Just as Israel will never disappear from history, the Church will never disappear either. We belong to the people of eternity, and there will always be an Israel and a Church, and one day there will be one flock under one shepherd. God is the God who restores his people.

Fourthly, we must note that a great deal of what we've looked at in Ezekiel is picked up in the Book of Revelation. One of the reasons why Christians don't understand Revelation is that they don't know enough about the Old Testament, and Ezekiel in particular. Revelation alludes to the Old Testament 300 times. It picks up the symbols of Ezekiel and uses so much from this Old Testament book that if you don't know Ezekiel, you will be puzzled by Revelation.

Above all, Ezekiel gives us a view of God – of his omnipotence, his power, his omnipresence. There is a tremendous sense of his holiness in the book – a sense that he has tied his name to a nation, that his name rests in their hands. The one thing we can appeal to is God's name and God's reputation, for we know that his name is linked to us. We either give God a good name or a bad name. God will always vindicate himself in the long term.

The book reminds us that God's reputation is at stake in his people. This is why he will restore them, because he has to vindicate his name. He will never let the earth and the nations think that he is finished as God because his people are finished. Many of them may perish, but his people will continue, because they are the people of God.

29.

DANIEL

Introduction

The Book of Daniel is a mixture of the best-known and the least-known parts of Scripture. Everyone knows about Daniel in the lions' den; many people know about Shadrach, Meshach and Abednego in the fiery furnace; and the story of Belshazzar's feast is known by some, in part because it is the origin of the phrase, 'the writing on the wall', meaning the judgement that is coming.

The best-known chapters of this book are easy to understand, but there are other chapters that are among the most difficult in the whole of Scripture. The language is unusual and the symbols and figures are obscure.

The book is also a mixed picture when it comes to interpretation. There is a lot in it that can be explained on a human level. The fact that Daniel was healthy when he avoided red meat and stuck to vegetables and fruit would be no surprise to anyone who understands nutrition. But there are also events that clearly have a supernatural explanation, and those who are sceptical about the miraculous struggle to accept them. For example, three men are thrown into a fiery furnace which has been heated seven times hotter than usual. Not only do they survive, but their hair is not even singed! Natural explanations will not work here.

Some of the book makes sense to our modern Western culture. We can understand accounts of the experiences of displaced people far from home. But there is also a great deal in this book that is distinctly unfamiliar to us. The focus on dreams and angelic beings seems odd, and even if such a focus is becoming more popular, in the main it is not thought credible.

Human or divine?

So reading Daniel raises questions about the nature of the Bible. What *is* the Bible? Is it a human book or a divine book?

At one level it is written by humans about humans, so many people simply treat the Bible as they would treat any other book – they read it as a work of history or literature or religion. But this approach misses the obvious. For the Bible – and the Book of Daniel in particular – includes events that are impossible without supernatural intervention, with patterns of prediction and fulfilment that point to a divine hand behind it all.

So the Bible must have been inspired by God, and it is definitely *about* God. Only God can do miracles, suspend natural laws, interfere with natural processes, and intervene in the laws of cause and effect which govern most events on our earth. In the Book of Daniel, God performs signs and wonders on many occasions. And only God knows the future.

This supernatural dimension is demonstrated when we examine the content of the book. It covers 75 years of Daniel's life but 440 years of history. The astonishing thing is that Daniel predicted future events with remarkable accuracy. Furthermore, there are parts of the book that still await fulfilment. The Bible as a whole predicts 735 events (27 per cent of its verses focus on the future), and 593 (i.e. 81 per cent) of these predictions have already been fulfilled. The Book of Daniel contains 166 predictions, many of them symbolic.

Whereas at one time prophecies and miracles were perceived to be proofs of the divine inspiration of the Bible, today they are considered a handicap. People want to remove the miracles and prophecies to make the Bible more 'credible'. They are seen as fiction rather than fact, as sagas of ancient literature rather than historical truths. So, for example, Daniel in the lions' den is explained away. Either the lions had just been fed, or they didn't eat Daniel because most of him was backbone and the rest was grit!

Those who treat the Bible in this way say that its lack of historical content does not also mean a lack of genuine spiritual and moral value. Just as Aesop's fables convey meaning to the readers without factual basis being necessary, so many Bible commentaries by modern liberal scholars take the miracles as fables, and assume that the predictions about the future were added later, after the predicted events had occurred.

As we shall see, chapter 11 of Daniel is an amazing account of a series of events which took place centuries after Daniel's lifetime. There are 27 specific predictions in this chapter, every one of which was fulfilled centuries later. Either people must have written these predictions after the events happened, or the book was inspired by God beforehand.

It is extraordinary to me that the many people who want to treat the miracles and prophecies in this humanistic way still want to keep the Bible. They believe they can keep it for its moral and spiritual values. In other words, they seek to live by the Ten Commandments or the Sermon on the Mount but they ignore the miracles and the prophecies. However, this means that there is very little of the Bible left. It ceases to be a book of salvation; it becomes a mere set of guidelines on what man must do for himself, rather than what God can do for us.

But this attitude towards the Bible actually exposes people's feelings towards God. They don't want the supernatural side of Scripture because, if they believed it, then they would have to live differently. God is only too real in the supernatural, and so belief in that would mean having to come to terms with him.

For example, the evidence for the resurrection is so strong that any jury in any court would be totally convinced that it had happened as an event. The eye-witness testimony plus the circumstantial evidence is far stronger than the evidence that Julius Caesar invaded England in 55 BC. But the problem is that if Jesus rose from the dead, then people know they have to change their lives. If the resurrection of Jesus really happened, then it follows that Jesus' claims about himself must be true, and therefore his claims on us must also be valid.

You can't ignore Jesus, but you can ignore Julius Caesar. You can believe in Caesar without doing anything, but you can't believe in Jesus Christ without changing your whole way of life. So scepticism about the Bible is usually linked with a reluctance to accept the supernatural dimension of Scripture, because if we accept that dimension there are practical repercussions.

A book of contrasts

The Book of Daniel can be divided into two parts. The first half (chapters 1–6) is mostly miracles and the second half (chapters 7–12) is mostly prophecy. So those who have a problem with the supernatural parts of the Bible won't know what to do with this book! Chapters 1–6 are easy to understand and are favourite texts in Sunday schools. But chapters 7–12 are so difficult that even adults rarely study them.

CHAPTERS 1–6	CHAPTERS 7–12
mainly miracles	mainly prophecies
third person: 'he'	first person: 'I'
written about Daniel	written by Daniel
during Daniel's life	after Daniel's life
the present	the future

There is also a contrast in language between the two parts of the book, though the division is not as simple as those listed above. In the first part, the first chapter is written in Hebrew and the next five are in Aramaic, the official *lingua franca* of the time. In the second part, the first chapter is in Aramaic and the other five are in Hebrew. It would seem, therefore, that the chapters were directed towards particular readers. The Aramaic chapters were written for a world audience and those in Hebrew were meant especially for Jews.

Historical background

The book is set in Babylon, the nation ruled by Nebuchadnezzar – a proud, cruel tyrant who took delight in torturing his victims. He was the Hitler of the ancient world. He conquered Assyria and then wanted to defeat his main rival, Egypt. Judah was in the way, so it would have to be removed if his ambition of ruling a large empire was to be fulfilled.

It is important to realize that the children of Israel were taken into exile to Babylon in three stages and also returned in three stages, though those who returned were far fewer than those who went. In fact a whole Jewish community remained in Babylon (now Iraq) until the 1940s. It is likely that the 'wise men' who followed the star to Bethlehem came from this Jewish community, and were not the Gentiles that many preachers make them out to be. They would have known of Balaam's prophecy of a 'star' rising out of Judah to be king of God's people.

Three deportations

The first deportation happened in 606 BC. The Babylonians took the top layer of Jewish society – that is, the royal family and the court officials – together with the temple vessels. This was in part to make sure that the conquered Jews were unable to rebel against Babylonian rule. Jehoiakim was left as a puppet king. Those who were exiled at this time included four young men named Daniel, Hananiah, Mishael and Azariah (the Babylonians renamed them Belteshazzar, Shadrach, Meshach and Abednego). Handsome and intelligent youths from the Jewish nobility, they were chosen to be trained to serve the Babylonian king. They are the heroes of the first part of the book. We know that Daniel never returned to his homeland.

The second deportation occurred in 597 BC. This time the upper classes were removed, including the politicians, and so too were the craftsmen. Ezekiel was among those who were deported. King Jehoiachin was left in charge.

The rest of the people were taken in 586 BC, when the city and the temple were destroyed. The Babylonians took away King Zedekiah but left Jeremiah the prophet.

Three returns

The first return came in 538 BC, when the Persians overthrew the Babylonians, and Cyrus allowed exiled peoples, including the Jews, to return to their homelands. Around 50,000 Jews came back in the first wave, led by Zerubbabel. Then a second group returned under Ezra in 458 BC, when the rebuilding of the temple was begun. The last wave came in about 444 BC, when the city walls were rebuilt and the city of God was made secure from its surrounding enemies.

Daniel's story dovetails with the Book of Esther. She lived in Susa, the capital of the Medo-Persian empire, while Daniel played a major role in both the Babylonian and the Medo-Persian empires. He was popular under successive conquerors. His was an amazing career, quite apart from the significant way in which he represented God.

Part 1 (chapters 1–6)

Chapter 1

Chapter 1 focuses on Daniel's deportation in 605/606 BC and his selection for the royal court of Babylon. He was given the name of a Babylonian god, Belteshazzar, as were his three companions. They did not object to the names, but they did remain faithful to their God when it came to diet. They were being fed to look fat, for obesity was a sign of prosperity. They were being fattened up for senior positions. But Daniel and his three friends did not wish to violate God's dietary laws, and so they asked the man in charge of their training at the university of Babylon whether they could go on a Jewish diet for 10 days and then be compared with those on the Babylonian diet.

So Daniel began his stand for principle in the relatively small matter of diet, but this gave him the resolve to face the lions later. There's a profound lesson here. If you can stand your ground over a little issue, you're likely to stand your ground over a big one. Your character is formed in small decisions on little issues, which enables you to stand later when the big crunch comes.

In the event Daniel and his friends were not only better in health but were much better in their studies than the other students. So they were permitted to continue with their kosher diet.

So this opening incident introduces us to young men with real character who were laying a foundation for a lifetime of service to God. In spite of doing what many would call a 'secular' job, Daniel and his friends were in 'full-time service' for God. Indeed, any job can be a sacred vocation if it is sanctified to God. All believers should be in 'full-time service'.

Chapter 2

Chapter 2 begins the more mysterious part of the book with a dream of a monster. It is the only part in the first six chapters that puzzles people. This kind of symbolic writing is known as 'apocalyptic' – a genre that is used in other biblical books such as Revelation.

In 606 BC Nebuchadnezzar had a dream, and sent for all his wise men to tell him the meaning of the dream, or lose their lives. But he had forgotten the dream itself, so he was asking for a description of the dream as well! It was a tall order and was beyond the abilities of Nebuchadnezzar's wise men. But Daniel was able not only to interpret the dream but to recount it too.

The dream was of a giant made of different materials from head to foot, starting with a gold head, through silver and iron, down to feet made from a mixture of clay and iron, which, of course, gives us the familiar phrase 'feet of clay'. The interpretation of the dream was that the golden head was Nebuchadnezzar, but the rest of the body was an unveiling of future empires that would follow Babylon. The Medes and Persians under Cyrus would replace Babylon, but not with the same grandeur or glory as Babylon. They would be followed by the Greek empire under Alexander the Great, who would obliterate the Medes and Persians. The Greeks would be replaced by the Romans, symbolized by legs of iron – a fitting picture of what Rome became. It was her armies that established Roman law. Rome would be followed by feet of mixed clay and iron, a brittle and unstable mixture of weakness and strength. A 'stone' would end it all.

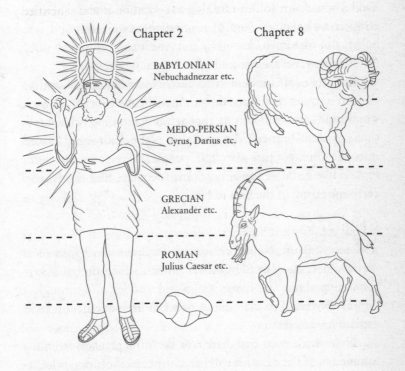

So this dream was God's first warning to Nebuchadnezzar. God was effectively saying: 'I'm in charge of kingdoms. I cause kingdoms to rise and fall, and I will bring these other empires after you.'

Chapter 3

Chapter 3 is the famous story of the fiery furnace. Nebuchadnezzar, probably because of this dream, ordered a gigantic gold-covered statue to be erected. It was 90 feet high and 9 feet wide. This statue dominated the flat landscape of Mesopotamia. He made a decree that whenever the state band played, everybody had to bow down to this idol. It was a kind of established state religion and a quick way of uniting the empire around one belief. But Shadrach, Meshach and Abednego refused to obey (interestingly, we are not told what Daniel was doing).

Reports of this rebellion reached Nebuchadnezzar, and so the three young men were thrown into the fiery furnace, which was heated seven times more than usual. Even those who threw them in were burned. We read that Nebuchadnezzar looked into the furnace and saw four people there, one of whom looked like a son of the gods. Some speculate that this was an early appearing of the Son of God.

Chapter 4

The story about Nebuchadnezzar's madness in chapter 4 is my favourite story in the Old Testament, which probably says something about me! It was a sign and wonder, and through it he was converted to the God of Israel. A little background will explain my fascination.

Nebuchadnezzar had married a beautiful princess from the mountains of Persia, where Tehran, the capital of Iran, is located today. She came to the palace of Nebuchadnezzar but was soon homesick. She missed, in particular, the mountains, the trees and the wild animals. When Nebuchadnezzar heard the source of her complaint he promised to deal with it. He built a huge mountain of brick and covered it with trees, shrubs and plants. It was so outstanding that it became one of the seven wonders of the world. Tourists flocked to see the 'Hanging Gardens of Babylon'. Then on top of the gardens he placed a private zoo of wild animals, all to please his wife, unused to the flat plains around Babylon.

One day he was on the roof of his magnificent palace and was struck by what he had achieved. He said, 'Is not this great Babylon which I have built by my power and my glory?' He fell asleep and had a dream of a huge tree that reached the sky. The animals found shelter under it and there were birds in its branches. The tree was cut down and bound in iron, and then began to grow again.

Once again he asked Daniel for an interpretation and was told that he was the tree, who would be driven out from among men for seven years until he acknowledged that the Most High ruled the kingdoms of men and gave them to anyone he wished. A year later God told Nebuchadnezzar that the prediction would be fulfilled. Sure enough, he went mad for seven years, so that his own people had to lock him up in his zoo. He ate grass for seven years. His hair grew like the feathers of an eagle, and his nails became like the claws of a bird – just like the millionaire recluse Howard Hughes in his last days.

At the end of seven years he lifted his eyes to heaven and said, 'God, you're God,' and God restored him to his throne and made him greater than before. It's a terrific story, though the ending is mixed. He made the mistake of forcing everyone to bow down to the God of Israel – worship should be an act of free will. But nevertheless, he was converted.

Chapter 5

Chapter 5 is the story of the end of Babylon. Belshazzar had succeeded Nebuchadnezzar by this point. At a big feast he made a mistake that would cost him his life. He took the holy vessels which had been stolen from the temple in Jerusalem and used them for an orgy. But God was watching, and during the feast Belshazzar saw a finger writing these words on a wall: 'MENE, MENE, TEKEL, PARSIN'. When he saw the disembodied finger writing this message, he was understandably scared stiff. Once again Daniel was the interpreter. He explained that the writing meant, 'Your reign is over, you don't measure up and your kingdom is divided.' That very night the Persians attacked Babylon, the empire was finished and Belshazzar was killed.

Chapter 6

Chapter 6 covers the well-known story of Daniel in the lions' den. What is less well known is that there was now a different king and a different empire, and that Daniel was around 90 years of age. Darius the Mede was the king, and once again anti-Semitism was rife. The people of the empire were forced to worship the king himself and were forbidden to pray to any other deity for a month. The scheme was set up by Daniel's jealous colleagues to trap him, and it worked. He continued his habit of opening his upstairs window to pray towards Jerusalem. Those seeking a flaw in Daniel now had the ammunition they required, and they forced Darius to apply the penalty for disobedience. He threw Daniel into the lions' den as punishment, but the angel shut the lions' mouths and he was delivered from disaster. So once again Daniel proved himself to be a man of integrity and God proved his ability to keep his servant.

Part 2 (chapters 7–12): Daniel's legacy

When we come to the second half of the Book of Daniel, we're in a totally different atmosphere. We move from the third person to the first person, so from now on Daniel is writing the book himself. We also switch from Aramaic to mostly Hebrew, so we are moving to a section that is primarily for God's people. Certainly, one would not advise a non-believer to read Daniel 7–12.

In this section Daniel makes unique predictions that are so detailed, so dated in sequence and so accurate in the light of historical events that it's simply history written down before it happened. So every reader is faced with the question of whether the future is known by God.

The Bible makes it clear that God not only knows the future but also shapes it. However, this doesn't mean that everything is predetermined and planned. There's a very delicate balance in Scripture between divine sovereignty and human responsibility. So we must not say that everything is predetermined, as if we are robots. But it does mean that God can shape events. If I were playing against a master chess player, he would win, but I would be free to make the moves I wanted to make. So every move I make, he can match, and he can still win. God has more free will than us, so our freedom is limited by his. There's a flexibility in God's sovereignty that we really must hold very precious, lest we slip into the idea that God has predetermined everything, and we do not matter.

There are a number of points to be made about the visions of the future in chapters 7–12.

On the negative side, they are not continuous; not a series of events following each other. Nor are they consecutive, in the sense of being in the correct order. Nor are they co-terminous, i.e. starting or finishing at the same time.

On the positive side, the visions do vary in duration, some brief and some covering a longer period of time. They do overlap each other, and some are simultaneous. Above all, they cover two periods of time, one leading up to the first coming of the Messiah and one leading to the second. It's as if Daniel

DANIEL'S VISIONS OF THE FUTURE

① NOT CONTINUOUS

7   12

② NOT CONSECUTIVE

7   8   9   10   11   12

③ NOT CO-TERMINOUS

START   (Same Year)   FINISH

④ DO VARY IN DURATION

⑤ DO OVERLAP EACH OTHER

⑥ DO COVER TWO PERIODS

BC   AD   GAP

Prophetic 'Telescoping'

seen

hidden

Foresight   Foreshortening

looked through a prophetic telescope and saw two 'peaks' of history, a lower in front of a higher, without realizing the length of the valley between them.

So Daniel can see right up to the first coming of Christ, but then he can't see anything else until the events leading up to the second coming. Like most Old Testament prophets, he didn't realize how much time there would be between these two peaks. He saw it all as one thing coming, and he called it 'the kingdom'. He didn't realize that the kingdom would come in two stages, because the King would come twice.

So these chapters predict the events leading up to the first coming of the King and also the events leading up to his second coming, and the astonishing thing is that these two series of events are almost identical. In the first period there is a man called Antiochus Epiphanes. In the second period there is a person called the Antichrist, and the descriptions of these two figures are remarkably similar. In other words, as we study the events that lead up to the first coming of Christ, we have an insight into the events leading up to the second coming.

Predictions already fulfilled

When we considered Nebuchadnezzar's first dream in chapter 2, we noted the series of human kingdoms of decreasing quality, from the golden king at the head, through the silver, down through the iron, to the feet of clay. This series of human kingdoms will lead to the inauguration of the divine kingdom. So we have the Babylonian, Medo-Persian and Greek kingdoms, followed by the Roman empire, during which Jesus, the divine king, came into the world. Daniel expected that the divine kingdom would completely take over from the human kingdoms, but he didn't realize that the divine kingdom would go through a period in which it was on earth alongside the human kingdoms. He was seeing this second peak as almost part of the first and didn't realize that there would be a gap of at least 2,000 years, in which we live. We live in the divine kingdom, and yet there are still human kingdoms in the world such as Russia, China and the USA.

So the rock from a mountain which had not been touched by man struck the colossus at its feet, and the whole thing collapsed. This rock was the kingdom of God breaking in on human kingdoms – replacing them all, sending them all tumbling, and establishing God's divine kingdom in their place. Daniel assumed from the vision that this would happen all at once, but we know that it's happening in two stages, for the kingdoms of this world have continued alongside the divine kingdom.

Another prophecy that has been fulfilled is chapter 8, where the focus is on a ram and a goat with one horn. These two beasts correspond to two parts of the giant in chapter 2 – the Medo-Persian empire and the Greek empire. The ram signifies the Persian empire, which stretched from India down to Egypt, including the whole of Turkey. Everything that chapter 8 says about the Persian empire came true.

The goat stands for the Greek empire that followed the Medo-Persian empire. Alexander the Great was given the nickname 'the Goat' because he was always charging ahead. He was only 31 when he died, but he had conquered the entire 'civilized' world and is revered as one of history's great conquerors. But he was a self-indulgent man, and his sinful lifestyle contributed to his downfall. When he died, his empire was divided between his four generals. Lysinicus was given Turkey, Cassander had Greece, Ptolemy had Egypt and Seleucid had Syria. So Israel was trapped between Seleucid and Ptolemy, and faced considerable difficulty as a result.

Chapter 9 contains a prediction of how long it would be before the divine king arrived. Bible scholars call this passage 'Daniel's seventy weeks', and much ink has been spent on conjecture about its meaning. Pet theories abound. Daniel is told that 'seventy sevens' are decreed for Israel. But it is important to realize that the word 'seven' means not a week but seven years. So it isn't seventy 'weeks' at all but seventy sevens – that is, 490 years. So from the time of the decree to go back from Babylon to Jerusalem until the coming of the king would be 483 years (i.e. sixty-nine sevens).

It is not clear which decree Daniel is referring to, nor is it clear whether he is using the Babylonian calendar (based on the solar year of 365¼ days) or the Jewish calendar (based on the lunar year of 360 days). There were actually four decrees. The decree of Cyrus began the return of the exiles in 536 BC. Then Darius made another decree, allowing more of them to go back. Artaxerxes made two decrees, which enabled Nehemiah to return and rebuild. But whichever decree you count from, the allotted years end at the birth or baptism of Jesus! Either way, just under 500 years later Jesus came – which is near enough for me, for it is truly amazing that Daniel should predict Christ's coming 500 years before it happened.

There are details about chapter 9 that we need to explore. Although he predicts the exact time for the coming of Christ, Daniel was told it would be a long time until the end of the sixty-ninth seven, when the king would come. But crucially, he left the seventieth 'week' out of these events. I believe that in the seventieth week he was looking right past the first coming, to the second coming. So there was a huge gap in time between the sixty-ninth seven and the seventieth seven. Thus this 'week' equals a seven-year period that has not yet taken place, when the Antichrist will appear. According to the text, a pact will be enforced and a treaty with Israel will be under threat. During this time persecution will be especially fierce. Sacrifices will cease and the temple will be desecrated in the same manner as at the time of

Antiochus Epiphanes, which implies that it must have been rebuilt at some point.

Chapter 10 covers a further revelation which caused Daniel great consternation. It shows that all earthly conflicts are matched by a heavenly conflict between angelic and demonic forces. This is a remarkable insight, though many Christians exaggerate its importance. The chapter tells us that behind every earthly power and every growing kingdom there is a demonic prince. There is demonic influence behind people who want to take over or devastate other countries. This chapter mentions 'the prince of Persia' and 'the prince of Greece'. God sends his angel Michael to overcome them.

It is interesting to note that Daniel isn't involved in that battle; it is left entirely to the angels. Some Christians have built a whole strategy of prayer and evangelism on Daniel 10. They believe that in an evangelistic campaign they must identify the evil demon over the city and bind him before they can start preaching the gospel. But Jesus did not say, 'Go into all the nations, find the demon and bind him', but rather, 'Go and make disciples of all the nations.' We should leave spiritual warfare to the angels until demons make themselves manifest. I notice that Jesus and the apostles never went looking for demons, but when a demon came and attacked them, they dealt with it. I believe that's the model for us. We should not go looking for demons and trying to bind them, but we should get on with our job of making disciples for the kingdom. On one occasion Paul waited for three days before he cast out the demon from a girl who had been disturbing their meetings.

Chapter 11 is the most astonishing prediction of the future in the whole Bible. In 35 verses 135 major events are predicted, covering a total of 366 years (see the table at the end of this chapter). Liberal scholars cannot handle this chapter. They say

Daniel couldn't possibly have written it – it must have been written 400 years later. But God knows the beginning and the end, and he enabled Daniel to write it all down.

In chapter 11 there is also mention of Antiochus Epiphanes IV, the greatest scourge against the Jewish people before the divine King comes. He became the regent in the Greek empire just north of Israel, and he was the guardian of a young boy who was in fact the king. But he killed the boy and took the throne for himself. He was a terrible tyrant and was determined to wipe out the Jewish religion. He desecrated the temple by sacrificing a pig on the altar, and he filled the temple rooms with prostitutes. He even erected an image of Jupiter in the temple. He massacred 40,000 Jews and sold an equal number into slavery. It was so dreadful that the Jews could not stand it, and the result was the Maccabean revolt. He is, in a sense, the parallel to the antichrist at the end of history. They belong together; the one foreshadows the other. If you want to know about the antichrist, read about this man.

The division between chapters 11 and 12 is especially unhelpful, since chapter 12 continues to focus on the antichrist and is concerned with events associated with the second coming of Christ, including the resurrection of both good and bad people.

Predictions not yet fulfilled

While we can identify many ways in which Daniel's prophecies have been fulfilled, there are many aspects that still await fulfilment.

Even though the King has come once, he has not yet taken over the kingdoms of the world. For that we await his return.

Chapter 7 contains some extraordinary pictures. Some people try to line up chapter 7 with chapter 2 and say that the four strange beasts of chapter 7 are the same as the four empires in the giant in chapter 2, suggesting therefore that most of the events depicted by the vision have already taken place. There are five reasons why this is unlikely:

1 History does not fit the details. Greece did not start with four heads, neither did Rome have four horns. It is hard to see the parallel.

2 In chapter 8 Persia and Greece are a ram and a goat. It seems unlikely that they should now be depicted differently.

3 Daniel is told that all four beasts 'shall arise' in the future, so the first cannot be Babylon, which has died out.

4 The four beasts cannot be the Babylonians, the Persians, the Greeks and the Romans, for we are told that the first three beasts will still be around when the fourth appears. When Rome arose, the other three empires had already gone, though the nations were still around.

5 In chapter 7 the beasts ascend in strength, but the colossus depicts declining empires – Rome is not as strong as Babylon, for example.

So what do we make of the beasts – the lion with wings, followed by a big bear, followed by a leopard with wings and four heads, followed by what I can only describe as a griffin or a dragon, followed by a kingdom? The kingdom is clearly God's kingdom, which is established on earth by a figure 'like a son of man, coming with the clouds of heaven' to reign with the saints of the Most High. The second coming of Jesus is clearly in view here. My speculation is that the lion with wings is the USA and the UK, the bear is Russia and the leopard is the Arab world. So they will still be around right at the end, but they will be replaced by the kingdom of God, but I could not be dogmatic about this identification.

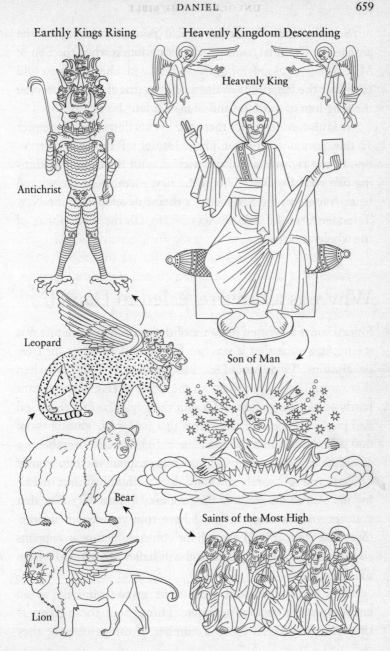

Earthly Kings Rising

Heavenly Kingdom Descending

Antichrist

Heavenly King

Leopard

Son of Man

Bear

Saints of the Most High

Lion

So in chapter 7 the last world powers give way to the antichrist. The final coming of the kingdom is when the Son of Man comes in clouds of glory to deal with the antichrist and take over the kingdoms of the world, so that they may become the kingdom of our God and of his Christ.

It is also evident that there are events described in chapter 12 that have not yet taken place. Daniel talks of the resurrection of the righteous and the wicked, with the righteous shining like stars for ever. This is the first mention of the wicked being 'raised' in the Scriptures, a theme developed in the New Testament (see John 5:29; Acts 24:15). It's the final climax of the whole of history.

Why was all this revealed to Daniel?

Since Daniel was often unaware of the meaning of what he was seeing, it is clear that it was not for Daniel's sake but for later generations. There would soon be a period of 400 years when there would be no prophets, so the Book of Daniel was meant partly to aid the people of God in the gap. The fact that God had predicted some of the events that took place during those 400 years helped to make his silence slightly more bearable.

Here are some other scriptures that explain the importance of forewarning: 'Surely the Lord does nothing without revealing his plan to his servants the prophets' (Amos 3:7); 'See that you are not alarmed … See, I have told you ahead of time' (Matthew 24:6, 25); 'I am telling you now before it happens so that when it does happen you will believe that I AM' (John 13:19).

The prophecies in Daniel were given primarily as an encouragement to God's people. Throughout these chapters they are encouraged to do a number of things because they know the future: to stand firm, to do exploits, to bring under-standing, to endure suffering, to be refined, to resist evil and to find rest.

Some people just want to know the future out of sheer curiosity. They want to be in the know and to have it all tied up. The essential reason for God revealing the future to us is so that we can handle it properly, be ready, and stand firm and do what God wants us to do. We can endure suffering, know-ing that the end will be glorious.

The other reason why God has revealed the future is to warn unbelievers, especially those who want to be powerful people and to build human empires. Ultimately the Son of Man will replace them all. We belong to the future King of the whole world. The Son of Man will come in clouds of glory and establish the kingdom of heaven here on earth, and we shall reign with him. So we had better get ready to be good, respon-sible governors of the world with him.

We will consider the benefits of the Book of Daniel for Christians when we look at it again alongside the Book of Esther at the end of the next chapter.

Historical Events Predicted in Daniel 11:2–35

v. 2 Persia

The three rulers after Cyrus were:

- **Cambyses** (529–522 BC), who conquered Egypt
- **Pseudo-Smerdis** (522–521 BC), who got the throne by impersonating the King's murdered brother and was assassinated by
- **Darius I Hystapes** (521–486 BC), mentioned in Ezra 5–6.

The fourth ruler was **Xerxes I** (486–465 BC), the Ahasuerus of Esther 1. He was the acme of Persian wealth and power. He invaded Greece in 480 BC but was disastrously defeated at Salamis.

vv. 3–4 Greece

v. 3 Alexander the Great (356–323 BC) avenged Greece by defeating Persia and in 12 years established a vast empire of Greek culture, bringing Asia under Europe. He is the 'he-goat' of Daniel 8. He died in Babylon at the age of 32.

v. 4 Alexander's son by Barsina was murdered, and his son by Roxana, born posthumously, was also murdered, so the empire was divided between four generals:

- **Lysimacus** (Thrace, Bithynia and Asia Minor)
- **Cassander** (Macedonia and Greece)
- **Ptolemy** (Egypt)
- **Seleucis** (Syria to Babylon)

The last two became 'south' and 'north' in the rest of Daniel 11 (i.e. in relation to God's people, Israel, now back in Palestine).

vv. 5–35 Egypt and Syria

This passage covers 162 years, with Israel 'caught between the door and hingers' (Luther) of two inter-related dynasties. The name 'Syria' had not appeared in Daniel's day, so this area is referred to as 'the north' only.

v. 5 Ptolemy I Soter (meaning 'Saviour') (323–246 BC) ruled Egypt and a close relative, **Seleucis I Nicator** (312–281 BC), ruled Syria. Both took the title 'King' in 306 BC. The latter became stronger, ruling the area from Asia Minor to India, and so became a rival and a threat.

v. 6 Ptolemy II Philadelphus ('brotherly love') (285–246 BC) of Egypt persuaded Antiochus II Theos ('God') to divorce his wife Laodice and marry his own daughter, Berenice. The union was unsuccessful, both as a marriage and as an attempt to unite the two royal families. When Ptolemy died, Antiochus took Laodice back as his wife, but she murdered him, Berenice and their son.

vv. 7–9

A 'see-saw' period of battle between the two nations.

v. 7 Berenice's brother, **Ptolemy II Euergetes ('benefactor')** (246–221 BC) attacked **Seleucis Callinicus** (247–226 BC) and killed Laodice in revenge. He was victorious throughout the northern kingdom as far as Persia and Media.

v. 8 Ptolemy II returned with Egyptian idols carried away 280 years previously and the populace called him 'benefactor' thereafter.

v. 9 Seleucis returned the attack, lost his fleet in a storm, was ignominiously defeated and died after a fall from his horse.

vv. 10–20

v. 10 Two brothers in the north – **Seleucis III** (226–223 BC), who was assassinated by mutinous troops during battle in Asia Minor, and **Antiochus III 'the Great'** (223–187 BC), who came to power at 18 and spent his life fighting to avenge his father's humiliation. He swept like a flood as far as Gaza, Egypt's fortified line.

v. 11 Ptolemy V Philopater ('love father') (221–203 BC) met Antiochus the Great with an army of 70,000 soldiers, 5,000 cavalry and 73 elephants at Rahpia in 217. Antiochus was totally defeated, with 10,000 dead and 4,000 taken prisoner and narrowly escaped capture himself.

v. 12 Ptolemy V, through indolence and indulgence, failed to follow up his advantage. Antiochus recovered and went east to India and the Caspian Sea, gaining wealth and strength.

v. 13 When Ptolemy and his queen died mysteriously, Antiochus attacked Egypt again and defeated its army (under General Scopas) at Panias, near the source of the Jordan, later Caesarea Philippi. Scopas fled to Sidon.

v. 14 Others now formed alliances with Antiochus (e.g. Philip of Macedon), including some Jews who thought they were making prophecy come true in seeing Egyptians routed, and expected national independence to follow. Many perished in battle.

v. 15 Sidon was besieged and taken, in spite of an unsuccessful attempt by three Egyptian generals to break the siege.

v. 16 Antiochus made the mistake of occupying Israel as a military base and laid waste the country to support his troops.

v. 17 Threatened by the growing might of Rome, Antiochus sought to unite with Egypt by giving his beautiful young daughter, Cleopatra, as wife to the seven-year-old **Ptolemy V Epiphanes ('glorious')** (204–181 BC). His hope that she would bring Egypt under his control was foiled when she sided with her husband against her father.

v. 18 Antiochus became scornful of growing Roman power – 'Asia does not concern them [the Romans] and I am not subject to their orders.' He refused their ambassadors, decided to conquer Greece himself and was humiliatingly defeated by the Roman consul Lucius Scipio Asiaticus at Thermopylae in 191 BC and at Magnesia on the Maeander River in 189 BC.

v. 19 Harsh conditions of peace with Rome sent Antiochus home broken and he was killed while trying to plunder a temple at Elym. He had opened Asia to Rome.

v. 20 Seleucis IV Philater ('love father') (187–175 BC) wanted only peace and quiet but had to raise huge taxes to pay tribute to Rome. His finance minister, Heliodorus, came to take treasures from the Temple in Jerusalem, was halted by a supernatural apparition and returned to poison the king.

vv. 21–30

Antiochus Epiphanes ('Glorious') (175–164 BC). The 'little horn' of Daniel 7. The worst tyrant of the Old Testament period. Syria's power was declining and was soon to give way to Rome. His frustration was to result in bitter persecution of Israel and an attempt to wipe out her religion by desecrating the Temple and imposing Greek culture.

v. 21 His vileness included association with prostitutes and public copulation, avaricious indulgence, cunning and intrigue. His titles 'Ephipanes', meaning 'glorious' was converted into the nickname 'Epimanes', meaning 'madman' behind his back. The direct heir to the Syrian throne, Demetrius, was being held as hostage in Rome, so Antiochus seized power in Syria by posing as the guardian of the second in line to the throne, Seleucis IV's baby son Antiochus, whom he later killed. He gained popularity by promises of less tax and easier laws, which were not kept.

v. 22 At first his military activity was very successful. He gained peace with Rome by paying tribute in arrears and with bribes, then invaded Egypt in 170 BC and defeated Ptolemy V Epiphanes between Gaza and the Nile delta. On the way south he called at Jerusalem and murdered Onias, the High Priest, the virtual ruler of Israel.

v. 23 Though Syria was not a large nation, Antiochus was now able to control Egypt, using two nephews, **Ptolemy VI Philometer** (181–145 BC) and **Ptolemy Euergetes** as pawns.

v. 24 He now systematically robbed the richest areas in his grip (e.g. Galilee), using the wealth not for himself (as had previous rulers) but as bribes for favours and in extraordinary prodigality (scattering money in the streets, laying on lavish spectacles etc.). He was also making plans to capture Egyptian cities such as Alexandria.

v. 25 He made another expedition to Egypt with chariots, cavalry and elephants. He corrupted Egypt's court and they conspired against their king.

v. 26 This led to Egypt's defeat.

v. 27 Antiochus and Ptolemy Philometer sat round the table, each aiming to outwit the other while making a treaty. Both failed.

v. 28 When Antiochus returned north, he turned to Israel, coveted the wealth of the Temple, massacred 40,000 Jews and sold the same number into slavery. Jason, the High Priest, fled to Ammon.

v. 29 During another expedition to Egypt, he captured his nephew Philometer, but was forced to retreat from Alexandria.

v. 30 During his final expedition to Egypt, Egypt sent an embassy to Rome, who sent ships from Cyprus. Consul Gaius Popilius Laenas demanded Antiochus' withdrawal from Egypt and Antiochus left in anger, realizing that this was the end of his hopes.

vv. 31–35

Antiochus now turned his frustrated anger against the people of God.

v. 31 Jews became his scapegoat and he began a savage persecution (recorded in 1 and 2 Maccabees), using sympathizers within Israel. He forbade worship and sacrifice, erected an image of Jupiter in the Temple and sacrificed a pig on the altar on 25 December 168 BC (this 'abomination of desolation' is mentioned in Matthew 24:15).

v. 32 This precipitated the revolt of Mattathias' priestly family of the Maccabees ('hammerers'). Under the

leadership of Judas, there were many heroic deeds
(mentioned in Hebrews 11). Israel was freed and the
Temple rededicated on 25 December 165 BC.

vv. 33–35 The surprising effect of persecution was spiritual revival, because of purging and the separation of
true from false believers.

30.

ESTHER

Introduction

The Book of Esther is unusual for two reasons: along with Ruth, it is one of only two books in the Bible named after women; and along with the Song of Solomon, it is one of only two books in the Bible that never mention God's name directly. So for these reasons many people have been puzzled by Esther. It is an interesting and romantic story, but why is it in the Bible? Why do we have to read it? What can we possibly learn from it?

Esther, along with Ezekiel and Daniel, was written during the Jewish exile, and so is one of the few books in the Bible set entirely outside the Promised Land (though Esther was written much later than the other two books). These books tell us how the Jews behaved when they were in Gentile society, and so they can give us a good guide on how to behave in non-Christian society.

Historical background

Babylon was defeated by a coalition of Medes and Persians. Darius the Mede was the first ruler of the new empire, followed by a Persian, Xerxes I (otherwise known as Ahasuerus). Daniel rose to be prime minister and was known by his Babylonian name, Belteshazzar. Hadassah rose to be queen and was called Esther (a pagan name, short for Ishtar, a Babylonian goddess). So both Daniel and Esther were promoted to positions where they could help their people.

God didn't force the Jews to go back to the Promised Land. Certainly, if they had all returned, this book would never have been written. Many thousands chose to return, but even more chose not to.

The Book of Esther is probably the best historically attested book in the Old Testament. Records other than the Bible, such as the *Histories* by Herodotus (a contemporary Greek historian, born in 480 BC), confirm that Esther is a late book. There are many other outside records that confirm what we read in Esther. In 1930 archaeologists excavating Persepolis, the capital of the Persian empire, dug up a stone tablet bearing the name 'Marducha'. The prime minister in the book is Mordecai, so it is highly likely to be the same person.

A romantic story

It is a most romantic story. Esther was young and beautiful, the queen of an empire. Only one man knew her secret – a secret that could mean death! That's the stuff of women's magazines.

Here is an outline of the story: Xerxes ruled over a kingdom that stetched from India in the east to Egypt in the west. But there was trouble ahead, so he held a conference for 180 days to decide how he was going to deal with the threat posed by the Greeks. At the end of the conference they held a seven-day feast in the palace garden. When they had had too much to drink, the king sent for his wife, Vashti, to come and dance for them, for she was young and pretty and he wanted entertainment for his generals. But Queen Vashti refused to come, and that begins the whole story. This refusal put the king in a really embarrassing situation. If he didn't deal with his wife, you can guess what all the wives of the generals were going to do. If he couldn't control his household, they were going to be in trouble as well, so something had to be done. He told her she must never enter his presence again!

But he found his bed a bit cold and he grew increasingly lonely. So somebody suggested that he should hold a beauty contest, and that the winner could become his wife.

It was a serious business. Esther had a full 12 months of beauty treatment before entering the contest. She duly won, and so became Xerxes' new queen.

She was from the tribe of Benjamin, which is amazing, considering the difficult history of that tribe. Mordecai was her cousin, but she had been left an orphan, so he had adopted her as his daughter. At Mordecai's request, she kept their relationship secret – because of anti-Semitic attitudes, the Jewish communities in the empire were in a precarious position. Despite being new to the harem, she became the king's favourite wife.

As we set the scene, we also note the position of another man who was exalted in the court at that time. He was called Haman and is the 'baddie' in the story. He was descended from Agag. Saul, the first king of Israel, had been told by Samuel the prophet to go and defeat Agag. But Saul wouldn't kill him, and so Samuel took over and hacked Agag to pieces before the altar of the Lord. This set up hatred between the Agagites and the Jews, and so Haman had a hatred of the Jews because of that bit of history – a hatred which makes the story especially highly charged. We have an intriguing situation – a Jewess who hasn't revealed that she's a Jewess is the queen of the Persian kingdom, and Haman is a high-ranking courtier but hates all Jews.

The flash-point came when Haman insisted that everyone must worship the emperor. Mordecai refused, and so Haman told the king. He explained that they should really annihilate the Jews living in the empire. They were different, with their own laws, their own customs, and their own religion. They were misfits and they really must go. He also offered a large bribe to the treasury if the king would agree to annihilate the Jews. They actually drew lots to decide the day on which all the Jews would be secretly killed. Interestingly, the lots cast the thirteenth day of the month for the annihilation of the Jewish people. This is one of the reasons why the thirteenth day has been regarded with superstition ever since.

When the Jews heard what was going to happen they mourned, fasted and put on sackcloth and ashes. Mordecai sent a message to Esther to beg the king for mercy. He suggested that God had brought her to the kingdom for such a time as this. She was the queen, through a rather unlikely chain of events, and so was in a position to help her people.

So Esther faced a real battle. Should she reveal that she was Jewish? If she did, her life would be at stake too. But she decided that if she perished, she perished.

So how was she to make the request known? The queen was not allowed into the king's presence unless sent for, but she knew she had to see him. So she boldly walked into his presence and suggested a banquet, with Haman as the guest of honour. The king acceded to the request and the banquet was duly arranged.

Meanwhile, Haman had become so angry with Mordecai that he built a gallows 23 metres high to hang him on. But he didn't tell anybody who it was for.

The night before the banquet, the king had insomnia, and so got up to read. He came upon his old diaries and read the account of how Mordecai had saved his life years before from an assassination plot involving two of his officers. He was reminded that he had never rewarded him. So as soon as he woke the next morning he made arrangements to reward Mordecai. It was an extraordinary coincidence – clearly the hand of God.

Before the banquet, the king said to Haman, 'I'm trying to think of a reward to give to someone who really pleases me. What would you suggest?' Haman thought it must be him, and so he replied, 'Have a procession in his honour and give him a robe and a horse.' The king agreed with the suggestion, but it was Mordecai who was sent for and rewarded – an unbelievable turnaround.

At the banquet Esther plucked up courage to speak to the king about her people. When the king heard that Haman was behind such an evil plot, he ordered Haman to be hanged on his own gallows, and the Jews were saved. A new edict was issued overturning Haman's dispatches and giving the Jews the right to defend themselves and the right to assemble and annihilate any armed force that might attack them. It was a staggering intervention, for there were assassins all over the empire ready to kill all the Jews.

So when the day arrived for Haman's edict to exterminate the Jews, the Jews were ready and proceeded to overrun their adversaries and execute Haman's family. Such was the danger to the Jews that if this hadn't happened, there would be no Jewish people left because the Persian empire stretched from India to Egypt. If the original edict had stood, Jesus could never have been born. So Esther saved the day. It's no wonder that the Jews every year celebrate the Feast of Purim in memory of these days.

Everyone loves a story like this and it is superbly told. As a literary structure it is superb. A good storyteller will build up to a point of real tension and then relieve the tension, with everybody living happily ever after and the baddies coming to a sticky end. The story of Esther is a masterpiece in that regard.

An outline of the book

Danger (1–5)
1: The prologue
2–3: The king's first decree
4–5: Haman's exasperation with Mordecai
The king's insomnia (6)
Deliverance (6–9)
6–7: Mordecai's exaltation over Haman
8–9: The king's second decree
The epilogue (10)

There is a beautiful symmetry to the book. We have the king's first decree that everybody had to worship him, and the king's second decree that the Jews must never be touched again. We have Haman's exasperation with Mordecai, and then we have Mordecai's exaltation over Haman. And the whole story hinges on one man being unable to sleep – truth is genuinely stranger than fiction!

Why is this book in the Bible?

But there surely needs to be more than just a good story. Why is this book in the Bible? Is it just to give us an example of having courage when we find ourselves in a public position?

Certainly, the annual Feast of Purim is a secular rather than a spiritual feast. There is no religious ceremony. Martin Luther said of Esther and 2 Maccabees, 'I wish they did not exist at all; for they Judaize too much and have much heathen perverseness.'

So of what value is the Book of Esther to the Christian? Are we to see in Esther an example of obedience, humility, modesty and loyalty? What do we make of the less pleasing aspects of the book, such as the vindictive slaughter of the Persians?

We must note the spirit of anti-Semitism in these pages. Firstly, the Jews were *different*. They observed their own laws and followed their own customs; their practice of circumcision, their Sabbath observance and their diet were especially distinctive. Secondly, the Jews were *independent*. They refused to be under control and so were seen to be a threat to totalitarian authority.

Satan is determined to destroy the Jewish people because salvation is of the Jews. Satan was behind the slaughter of the boys in Egypt. Moses was saved by the little basket of bulrushes. Satan was trying to destroy the Jews before the Messiah could be born. It was the devil who was behind the slaughter of 200 babies in Bethlehem, but Jesus escaped to Egypt.

So there is something demonic about anti-Semitism. Pharaoh tried to destroy the Jews, Haman tried it, Herod tried it and Hitler tried it. It keeps popping up in history, because salvation is of the Jews. We ought to be very grateful to the Jewish people. Everything we know about God came through them, and the Saviour was and is a Jew.

Forty different authors wrote the Bible over a period of 1,400 years in three different languages. Only one of those writers was a Gentile – Dr Luke – and he got all his material from Jews. Without the Jews we wouldn't have a Bible at all. No wonder they are hated more than any other people.

But there is another, unseen actor in this drama. God must be behind it all. For when so much hangs on an apparently minute detail or circumstance, it is clear that we are watching God at work.

I see God at work in this story, in the preservation of the people from whom his Son would be born. I see it in the people's prayer and fasting when they first hear of Haman's foul plot against them. I see it in Mordecai's belief that God would preserve the people. He even told Esther that if she wasn't prepared to be God's channel, somebody else would. He didn't use God's name as such, but it was implied. This was incredible faith in God's overruling. I see it in the chance events which all fitted in together: that Mordecai had saved the king's life years earlier; that Artaxerxes had written it in his diary. I see it in the fact that Artaxerxes couldn't sleep and read the very page in his diary on which Mordecai was mentioned. If the name of God is not in the Book of Esther, his finger certainly is. One scholar called Esther 'the romance of providence', and he was absolutely right.

Why, then, is God never mentioned? Well, here's the biggest surprise. He is mentioned, five times, but few are able to spot it! He is actually mentioned in the form of an acrostic, using the initial letters of either his name or his title. Sometimes it's forward, sometimes it's backwards. I've tried to put it into English for you so that you can see it, but bear in mind that it's in the Hebrew.

The Jews, who loved playing with words, were very fond of acrostics (the use of initial letters of words or sentences as a 'hidden' message, e.g. FAITH means 'Forsaking All I Trust Him). You'll find them all the way through the Psalms, especially in the longest of them, Psalm 119. The description of the ideal wife in Proverbs 31 is another acrostic. In the Book of Lamentations four out of five chapters are alphabetic acrostics, each line beginning with the next letter of the alphabet. It is a very skilled literary device, and it can be used to convey coded or secret messages.

In the Book of Esther there are five acrostics, and the first four follow a remarkable pattern (see 1:20; 5:4; 5:13; 7:7).

Acrostics in Esther

1:20	5:4	5:13	7:7	7:5
Due	**L**et	Yet	For	Wher **E**
Respect	**O**ur	I	He	Dwellet **H**
Our	**R**oyal	Am	Saw	The Enem **Y**
Ladies	**D**inner	Sa **D**	That	That Daret **H**
Shall	This	Fo **R**	There	Presume
Give	Day	N **O**	Was	In
To	Be	Avai **L**	Evi **L**	His
Their	Graced	Is	T **O**	Heart
Husbands,	By	All	Fea **R**	To
Both	King	This	Determine **D**	Do
To	And	To	Against	This
Great	Haman	Me	Him	Thing
And			By	?
Small			The	
			King	
HVHJ	JHVH	HVHJ	JHVH	EHYH
Backward	Forward	Backward	Forward	= 'I Am'
Gentile speaks	Jew speaks	Gentile speaks	Jew speaks	(Exodus 3:15)
About queen	By queen	By Haman	About Haman	
Overruling by God	Ruling by God	Overruling by God	Ruling by God	

Now the first two use the first letters of four consecutive words, whereas the second pair use the last letters. The first acrostic is backwards, the second is forwards, the third is backwards and the fourth is forwards.

We must realize that these acrostics are actually in the Hebrew text and therefore in the Hebrew language. In English, the four letters are actually 'J-H-V-H', the four letters of God's name, pronounced 'Jehovah' in English and 'Yahweh' in Hebrew. To understand how it works, let us take an English equivalent version in which we use the word 'Lord' as a substitute for 'Jehovah' or 'Yahweh'. The translation has had to be twisted a bit to show you how it works.

Let's take the first, 1:20: 'Due respect our ladies shall give to their husbands, both great and small.' The initial letters of the words 'Due respect our ladies' are D-R-O-L, which is the word 'Lord' backwards. Then in 5:4 we see the same thing forwards: 'Let our royal dinner' also spells L-O-R-D.

Why is it sometimes backwards and sometimes forwards? When it is backwards the words are being spoken by a Gentile, but when it's forwards it's a Jew speaking. It may be that the Jews are saying that the Gentiles can never say the word right, or it may be that they don't want to put the sacred name on Gentile lips.

There's an acrostic in Esther which stands on its own. The letters are slightly different and spell out 'I AM', though the spelling is backwards again. The writer has carefully worked it all out and then worked it into the text so that no Gentile would notice it.

There are various explanations of why this method was used, but the one that fits best is very simple. It was written in a time when it was dangerous to mention the Jewish God (Xerxes died in 465 BC), and therefore, presumably, it was written a bit later than the events, when such a document would be deemed subversive.

At first people would have passed on the story of Esther verbally, so that it would be remembered as a folk tale. But there came a time when it was imperative to write it down, because the people celebrated the deliverance annually and so needed to hear the true story of what lay behind the feast. Furthermore, anti-Semitism was rife, and it was thought dangerous to be caught with a document about the Jewish God. So Esther was written without mentioning God, but using an acrostic was a typically Jewish answer to the problem.

What can Christians learn from Daniel and Esther?

They lived during the same period and faced the same exile. They were two people far from home, and yet they were used by God in positions of influence in pagan society, without compromising their principles. They were thus able to make great advances for the kingdom of God. The stories encourage us to go as far as we can to get a good position in the world, providing we remain true to our faith. God can use us for the kingdom in high places, so we can let him put us where we can make advances.

God uses individuals

One person can make all the difference. God uses men and women, and we are all in exile. Christians don't belong in this world. We are misfits, because our citizenship is really in heaven. We are gradually being weaned away from attachment to the world to being at home in heaven.

But God can use individuals in the kingdoms of this world who keep their principles and remember who they are. God can use people who are willing to be promoted but who are not willing to be assimilated. Jews always have the temptation to allow themselves to be assimilated in order to avoid persecution, and Christians face the same temptation.

In Germany at the beginning of this century, the Jews were so assimilated to German culture and language that when Theodore Hertzl called the first Zionist Congress in 1897 to discuss the idea of the Jews having a country of their own again, the German Jews didn't want to know. Hertzl wanted to have the conference in Munich, but the German Jews said, 'Don't have it in Munich. We are now Germans – we're not Jews any more. So don't embarrass us.' So Hertzl held the conference in Basle, in Switzerland.

Christians have a temptation to behave like everybody else so that we're not singled out and regarded as odd. But God uses the individuals who are willing to be different. We used to sing in Sunday school, 'Dare to be a Daniel – dare to stand alone'. Daniel and Esther were both willing to die rather than compromise their faith in God.

God preserves his people

God preserved Daniel in the lions' den and Shadrach, Meshach and Abednego in the fiery furnace. He also preserved the Jews in Susa through Esther. If you want to wipe out God's people, you will need to wipe out God first! God preserves his people. We may die for him, but we're still preserved. So we can be confident that there will always be an Israel and there will always be a Church.

God rules the world

The one word that is common to both these books is the word 'kingdom'. The Christian gospel is the gospel of the kingdom. For both Daniel and Esther, the kingdom of God came first.

From these two books we learn that the human kingdoms of the present are in God's hands. God raises rulers up and he puts them down. Nebuchadnezzar had to learn that the Most High rules over the kingdoms of men and gives them to anyone he wishes. So it is God who redraws the boundaries of the atlas and decides who has power and who doesn't. It is God who decides every election – he has the casting vote – sometimes in justice and sometimes in mercy. If he votes in justice, he gives us the government we deserve; if he votes in mercy, he gives us the government we need. In my lifetime God has removed from office six prime ministers within a short time of them breaking a promise to Israel – from Neville Chamberlain to James Callaghan. When George Bush, the US President, turned against Israel and withdrew money from them, he lost power shortly afterwards. God is the God of Israel. He rules the human kingdoms of this world; they only rule by his permission. He is in charge.

There's another use of the word 'kingdom'. There are the human kingdoms of the present, but there is also the divine kingdom of the future, when God will take over world government. The kingdoms of this world are going to be replaced by the kingdom of God. So we must realize that Daniel's and Esther's jobs have not yet finished. They were faithful in government in a pagan empire and will be raised from the dead to rule in the kingdom that God will inaugurate. So when Jesus comes back to earth, Daniel and Esther will both be with him.

So we shouldn't merely read the Bible as history, but as an introduction to people we are going to meet one day. We shall have all eternity to get to know these great saints of God. We shall be reigning with the saints of the Most High, with the Son of Man on the throne. All those people who have proved faithful will be used again on this earth to share the government in the kingdom of Christ.

31.

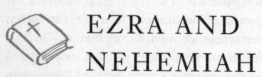

EZRA AND NEHEMIAH

Introduction

When we study the history of God's people, Israel, we see how God stepped up the punishments for their sins. Each punishment seems to be a little harder than the previous one. He started by sending aggressors such as the Philistines from surrounding nations to raid them, so their first punishment was loss of property. But they didn't take any notice of this, so the punishment became a little more serious: drought, famine and shortage of food. When they still didn't listen, God sent disease and loss of health. But the ultimate punishment for them was to lose the Promised Land and to be taken away into another country. They had been brought out of Egypt into the Promised Land, but God promised to exclude them from it if they continued in sin.

Two exiles

There were two exiles. The first involved the ten tribes in the north, known by this time as Israel, when Assyria conquered and deported them in 721 BC. The second exile involved the two tribes in the south, known as Judah, after the largest of the two. This time Babylon was the conqueror in 586 BC. It is this second exile that concerns us when we look at Ezra and Nehemiah.

Three deportations

When the Babylonians overran Judah they did not wipe out everything, as the prophet Habakkuk had expected them to do. They were actually much gentler. They deported the people in three groups, at three separate times, each when Nebuchadnezzar was on the throne of Babylon.

The first group left in 606 BC. It included the royal court, in the belief that if the rulers departed, it would be easier to subdue the nation of Judah and keep it under Babylonian control. Included in that top layer was Daniel, who was taken away as a teenager with the royal court to Babylon and was to be an important figure in the exile.

But those who were left still attempted to gain their freedom from Babylon, so the aggressors came a second time in 597 and took away all the craftsmen and merchants in the hope that if they removed the people who made the money they could impoverish the people and finally bring them under control. Among the craftsmen was a priest called Ezekiel, who, like Daniel, figures large in the exile as well.

But still the remaining people rebelled, so finally armies from Babylon came in 587, razed the temple to the ground and destroyed everything. Jerusalem was left as a deserted ruin, Judah was virtually empty and the tribes of Judah and Benjamin were taken away to Babylon.

The exile of Judah lasted for 70 years, a time Jeremiah the prophet had prophesied to the exact year. His words were an encouragement to Daniel to pray that God would fulfil his promise.

Three returns

The exile ended just as God had promised, though there were in fact three returns to match the three deportations. The first was of 50,000 people in 537, when Cyrus was the Persian leader and Zerubbabel was leader of the Jews. He was one of the royal line, stretching back to King David, and so as such was part of the fulfilment of God's promise that there would always be a descendant of David on the throne. Indeed, he is one of the ancestors in Jesus' family tree listed in Matthew 1, which helped to legitimize Jesus' claim to be the Messiah.

Just over 90 years later, in 458, there was a second return when Artaxerxes I was on the Persian throne. This time just 1,800 returned under Ezra. He was a priest who, for the first time, brought back the Levites to restore the structure of worship for the people of Israel. It wasn't easy to persuade them to come. It was only after repeated appeals that Ezra was able to find 1,800 to join him on the long trek back to restore religious life.

Then, around 14 years later in 444, Nehemiah returned with a few craftsmen. His chief concern was to rebuild the walls of Jerusalem which had been destroyed by Babylon and without which the city was vulnerable to attack.

So in the three returns there is the rebuilding of the social life, the rebuilding of the religious life and the rebuilding of the physical life. It is important to note that the second exodus was quite unlike the more famous first one in the time of Moses. It seems to have been done in bits and pieces. It is very evident that relatively few made the 900-mile, four-month journey back. They had a much better time in Babylon than their forefathers had in Egypt at the time of Moses. This time they weren't slaves, but had become involved in business, and when Jews become involved in business it is not easy for them to leave it behind. I heard a lovely story about a Jewish man in New York who bought a little shop that was squeezed in between two gigantic department stores. He wondered what to call his little shop, and after much deliberation decided to call it 'Entrance'!

Two books, one author?

The Books of Ezra and Nehemiah are named after the second and third returns, though in fact the two books cover all three returns, with the Book of Ezra covering the first two and the Book of Nehemiah covering the third. The people were no longer known as Hebrews or Israelites but were now called Jews, after the word 'Judah', meaning 'praise'. In some ways this was symbolic of the sort of people they aimed to become on their return.

The first thing that strikes you about these two books is that they are so like each other. They each follow exactly the same pattern. Furthermore, the writing is very similar to that in 1 and 2 Chronicles. In the Hebrew scriptures Ezra and Nehemiah were bound together in one book, and later they were called '1 and 2 Ezra' and were bound together with 1 and 2 Chronicles. One suggestion, which I think has a lot going for it, is that Ezra wrote the whole lot. He was a careful man who was able to keep records, and it looks as if he wrote Ezra, Nehemiah and 1 and 2 Chronicles.

Ezra and Nehemiah are both written in two different languages – part in Hebrew and part in Aramaic. Aramaic was the common language that everybody could speak, just as Greek was the common language at the time of the New Testament. Aramaic was a Semitic language used throughout the Fertile Crescent in the Middle East. The Jews had been exposed to it and used it in their exile in Babylon and when doing business with people from other nations. Thus many of the records they brought back from the exile were written in Aramaic. The only other book in the Old Testament that is in two languages is Daniel.

The structure of the books

Ezra and Nehemiah are each written in four sections, with the second and fourth sections identical in theme. They focus on rebuilding the state and reforming the people:

EZRA	NEHEMIAH
Return I (1–2)	Return III (1–2)
a, b	a, b
Rebuild (3–6)	Rebuild (3–7)
a, b, c	a, b, c
Return II (7–8)	Renew (8–10)
a, b, c	a, b, c
Reform (9–10)	Reform (11–13)
a, b	a, b

Return number I, under Zerubbabel, focuses on the rebuilding of the temple, though this was sporadic. It took the prophets Haggai and Zechariah to get it going again. Return number II focuses on the reform of the people. Return number III led to the rebuilding of the walls, renewing the covenant and again, the reform of the people. Every time it seems as if the people forgot about the sins that had lost them their land.

It is even more remarkable to notice the structure of the two books. The first section in each book has two sub-sections, the second has three, the third has three, and the fourth has two (listed as 'a', 'b' and 'c' in the chart above). It is a remarkable structure. It has been planned very carefully and is beautifully composed and balanced, strongly suggesting that one man, probably Ezra, was the author of both.

There is one other remarkable parallel. Chapter 9 in both cases is an amazing prayer, when both Ezra and Nehemiah confessed national sins. The two chapters are especially important in both books.

Ezra – the book

An outline of the book

Return I (chapters 1–2)
Cyrus: The decree to build the temple (1)
Zerubbabel and co. 'go up' (2)

Rebuild (3–6)
Joshua: The altar and the temple foundations (3)
Artaxerxes: A letter is received (4)
Darius: Letters are received and sent (5–6)

Return II (7–8)
Ezra and co. 'go up' (7)
Artaxerxes: A letter is sent (7)
The Levites 'go up' (8)

Reform (9–10)
Private intercession (9)
Public confession (10)

Historical background

The historical background to Ezra is as follows. Cyrus was the Persian ruler who had conquered Babylon. He was the ruler of the major world power in the eastern end of the Fertile Crescent. But he was a very benevolent man and he had a policy of kindness towards conquered peoples. It is interesting that as far back as Isaiah, God had said that his anointed servant Cyrus would bring his people back from exile. Many scholars can't believe that Isaiah could possibly have known the name, and insist that the text was written up after the event. But God knew the name of the man. From archaeological records we know that Cyrus told all the captive peoples in Babylon that they could return to their lands and rebuild their religions, providing that they prayed to their gods for him. So we see God's hand in the timing, for the 70 years are now up.

Return I (chapters 1–2)

In the Book of Ezra you have the first return under Zerubbabel and a rebuilding of the temple. There is then the return under Ezra and the reform of the people. One of the saddest features of both books is that when the people got back, they quickly returned to their sinful practices. Isn't it tragic! It had cost them their land, they had been away from home for 70 years, and yet when they got back they started ignoring the commandments of God. How quickly people forget.

As we have noted, Zerubbabel was the grandson of Jehoiachin and therefore in the royal line of David. Although he was known as the Governor rather than the King, he was chosen to lead the people back. He took with him a High Priest called Joshua.

Rebuild (chapters 3–6)

JOSHUA

Under Joshua the people erected an altar and offered sacrifices when they arrived back in their homeland. During the whole of their exile they had not been able to offer sacrifices because they didn't have a temple or an altar, so this was their first priority on their return. Incidentally, this was also the first thing their forefather Abraham did when he pitched his tent. He would invariably erect an altar for worship.

ARTAXERXES

Having arrived back and begun sacrifices, they immediately faced trouble. Artaxerxes replaced Cyrus and received a letter from the Samaritans who inhabited Judah before the return. The Samaritans were half Jewish and half Gentile, the product of marriages between the few Jews who had managed to escape deportation and people from other nations. As 'half-breeds', their relationships with the pure Jews were rarely cordial – apart from anything else, they had escaped deportation. From this time on the Jews and the Samaritans were unable to live alongside each other. The letter suggested that the rebuilding of the temple masked evil intent, and so it managed to stop the work. But they had made a big mistake, because Artaxerxes was the step-son of Esther and was therefore very sympathetic to the Jewish people.

DARIUS

Later, another letter was sent back from Babylon by another emperor, Darius I, who encouraged them to get on with the rebuilding again. It was under Darius that Daniel was thrown into the lions' den and Darius was forced to realize how great God was. So the rebuilding was very patchy. There were times when the opposition from the Samaritans stopped the rebuilding and there were times when they just became tired of working on the temple and concentrated instead on building their own homes. Haggai the prophet asked, 'Is this a time for you to live in panelled houses when the house of the Lord still is not built?' and the words stung them back into action. It was a real problem to keep their morale up, because they were just a little group of people in a barren land doing a bit of rebuilding when they could.

Return II (chapters 7–8)

After 50 years a group under Ezra's leadership returned. By this time law and order was a problem, so Ezra returned with a magistrate's commission to enforce the rule of law. Artaxerxes sent another letter at that point and encouraged the Levites to return, which is when Ezra managed to find another 38 who were willing to go with him. The text of the Book of Ezra is now in the first person singular, as he recounts his experience of this time.

Reform (chapters 9–10)

PRIVATE INTERCESSION

The reform is one of the saddest parts of the story. Ezra prayed privately, asking God to have mercy on the people when he saw how quickly they were returning to their old ways. Ezra insisted that the people make a public confession of what they were doing. He made a blacklist of all the people who were drifting back into breaking the commandments. One of the most common sins was marrying outside the people of God – a practice forbidden to Israel and also forbidden to Christians in the New Testament. Someone has rightly said that if you marry a child of the devil, you are going to have problems with your father-in-law!

PUBLIC CONFESSION

Ezra insisted on breaking those marriages up because they were unlawful in God's sight. The New Testament doesn't tell us to do that, but Ezra took this matter very seriously, and so wives and children were put away so that the people of God might be the pure people of God. He even went into the pedigrees of some people who had come from Babylon but weren't true Jews.

Ezra – the man

Ezra was a fascinating character. His name literally means 'help' (Nehemiah's name means 'comfort'). This little group of returned exiles certainly needed help and comfort. Ezra was a direct descendent of Aaron through Aaron's son Eleazar, and later Phinehas and Zadok the priest, so he had priestly heritage.

The Book of Ezra tells us that he brought the Scriptures with him – probably the books of the Law (i.e. Genesis to Deuteronomy). He was described as a 'Scripture man' because he did three things with the Bible: he studied it, lived it and taught it. It is comparatively easy to do the first and the third, but he realized that it was very important that his life as well as his lips spoke the Scriptures. Ezra's devotion to the Scriptures led to a tender heart that wept over other people's sins. It is easy enough to weep over your own sins when you are found out, but to weep over other people's sins indicates a depth of spirituality that few share.

Tradition says that Ezra was the president of the council of 120 Jews who collected the books together and formed the Old Testament. We can't be sure whether this is true, but certainly his focus on the Scriptures laid the foundation for the next 400 years, since during that period there would be no prophets and the only word from God would be the word which had been given in the past – including, of course, Ezra and Nehemiah.

Few realize that Ezra laid the foundation of the Bible-based synagogue. From that time on, the order of service in the synagogue would follow Ezra's directions, even today. In fact, every synagogue service is the exact opposite to the order of nearly every Christian service. Their order was the word first, worship second. You listen to God before you speak to him, then your worship is a response to what he says to you.

This way worship becomes far more meaningful and far more varied. Sometimes you feel like dancing and singing, and other times you are serious and in a penitent mood. Instead of having to work people up to worship, you allow the word to set the course. People who are full of God's word are ready for worship. If you go to a synagogue, they spend an hour reading and expounding God's word and then they respond to it in worship.

So Ezra laid out that order. He set up a wooden pulpit in the market-place and he read and explained the Scriptures to them, and their worship came as a response. This was the order of worship in the early church, according to a document called 'The Didache'. When I served a church in Guildford we would have an hour in the word and then half an hour's worship, and it worked very well.

Nehemiah – the book

An outline of the book

Our outline of Nehemiah confirms the similarity with the outline and structure of Ezra, demonstrating that both came from the same pen. It has the same fourfold division, with two subdivisions, then three, then three, then two.

Return III (1–2)
Sad information (1)
Secret inspection (2)
Rebuild (3–7)
Erecting defences (3)
Encountering difficulties (4–6)
  External opposition,
  Internal exploitation
Enlisting descendants (7)

Renew (8–10)
Scripture communicated (8)
Sins confessed (9)
Submission covenanted (10)
Reform (11–13)
Sufficient quantity(11)
Spiritual quality (12)
   Mixed marriages
   Misappropriated funds
   Desecrated Sabbaths
   Neglected duties

Return III (chapters 1-2)

BAD NEWS FROM JERUSALEM

The third return from exile began when Nehemiah, still in Babylon, received bad news from Jerusalem. He was the cupbearer to King Artaxerxes. My guess is that he got the job through Queen Esther, because Artaxerxes was her stepson. It was not an especially pleasant job to taste the wine, literally wondering if your next drink would be your last, but it was a very responsible one. It made him a confidant of the king, and he would share things in the relaxed atmosphere of that relationship. When Nehemiah heard the news that the rebuilt walls of Jerusalem had been pulled down again and that the local people around Jerusalem were angry about the rebuilding of the city, he looked so unhappy that the king asked him what was the matter. Nehemiah explained his concern to the king, fearful that his sad countenance may lead to punishment. He was astonished at the response. Artaxerxes not only gave him authority to return to rebuild the walls, but also wrote letters of introduction for the people who had the necessary materials to ease Nehemiah's project.

A NIGHT-TIME INSPECTION OF THE GATES

So in the second part of the first section Nehemiah is back in Jerusalem, making a secret inspection of the walls by night to assess the damage. Here is a wise leader who counts the cost of the enterprise before he does anything – a man who doesn't rush in a foolhardy fashion. He is a man of faith, but he sees exactly what the task is before he starts.

Rebuild (chapters 3–7)

THE WALLS ARE ERECTED

Nehemiah found that the walls and gates needed repair – most of the walls having been completely destroyed and others requiring significant repair. Visitors to Jerusalem today often look at the old walls of the present old city and imagine it must be the Old Testament city. Actually, the present walls are only a few hundred years old, built by Sulamein the Magnificent after the crusades. The old city was located outside the present wall on a tongue of land south of the temple area. The present temple area, with the Mosque of Omar and the Mosque El Aqsa, is about 13 acres – a big stone platform at the top of a hill. However, excavations of the Old Testament city have revealed the wall of Nehemiah's day.

Nehemiah demonstrated great leadership qualities in his building. He shrewdly asked people to build a section of the wall opposite their own home. The astonishing fact is that he got the entire city wall built in 52 days. With the addition of gates, for the first time the city was secure.

FACING PROBLEMS

But they faced many difficulties during that time:

External opposition. The first was ridicule. The Samaritans mocked the work, claiming that a fox would be able to push the wall over. But when these taunts fell on deaf ears, they tried threats that became a bit more serious. They even had a conspiracy and tried to lure Nehemiah away from the job. They offered to be friends, seeking to entice Nehemiah away for negotiations. But he wisely refused – nothing would deflect him from the task.

Internal exploitation. They also had internal difficulties. Within the walls, the rich were getting richer and the poor were getting poorer, primarily because of the way that the financial transactions contravened the Mosaic Law. Interest was being charged on loans in such a way that the people became crippled by debt. Nehemiah bravely addressed the issues and sought to equalize the economic levels among the people.

THE CITY IS EMPTY

Furthermore, very few people wanted to live in the city. They feared attack and preferred to live in the country, where it was easier to hide. So Nehemiah had to compel people to come and live in the city. He had lists of the descendants of Jerusalem's pre-exilic inhabitants, and he persuaded people to come and live where their families used to live. He also took a census so that he knew where everybody was. There were 42,360 Jews, 7,337 servants and, interestingly, 245 singers. The fact that he lists the singers demonstrates his interest in restoring the worship of God at the temple.

Renew (chapters 8–10)

EZRA READS THE LAW

Next we find Ezra reading the law publicly from his wooden pulpit from daybreak until noon. It says that he not only read it, but he gave the sense of it so that they could understand. The reading took place at the Feast of Tabernacles, which is the Jewish harvest festival. It was intended to be a joyful occasion – in fact, the rabbis say that if someone is not full of joy at the time of Tabernacles, they are sinning!

AN ACT OF CONFESSION

The people were so moved that they broke down and wept, confessing their sins and the sins of their forefathers to God. This represents a crucial difference between Ezra and Nehemiah. Ezra saw the situation as a time to weep, but Nehemiah was telling them to have a party. Ezra wept over the sins that the word of God was revealing, but Nehemiah focused on the rebuilding of the walls and said it was a wonderful occasion. Nehemiah said they were to enjoy themselves, cook really good meals and have a celebration. There is a time to weep and a time to rejoice, and we are wise if we know the right time.

A COVENANT IS MADE

At the end of the prayer of confession, Ezra arranged for the people to renew their covenant with God. The leaders, the Levites and the priests made a binding agreement. Chapter 10 lists the people who signed it.

Reform (chapters 11–13)

INHABITING THE CITY

Part of Nehemiah's work was to encourage the people to move into the city, now that the walls had been rebuilt. Chapters 11 and 12 list the people who were commended for living in the city.

CORRECTION

Mixed marriages

In the last chapter Nehemiah really gets to work. First he had to break up mixed marriages which were polluting the nation. He called curses on those who had married outside Israel.

I often say the difference between Ezra and Nehemiah is that Ezra pulled out his own hair, but Nehemiah pulled out other people's! Nehemiah literally pulled the hair out of the sinning Israelites.

Misappropriated funds
He also had to deal with misappropriated funds. Some had been misusing the money they had been given charge of. Nehemiah sought to bring justice and fairness into the financial dealings.

Desecrated Sabbaths
The Sabbaths were not being kept as they should. Businessmen who came back from Babylon found that they didn't have the same lucrative market, and so to build up their businesses they opened their shops on the Sabbath. Nehemiah actually insisted on shutting the gates every Sabbath so that commerce couldn't take place.

Neglected duties
The religious world was little better. Priests were neglecting their duties in the temple, and so Nehemiah had to put this right too. The Levites and singers had not been paid for their temple functions and had returned to farming for their living.

So both Ezra and Nehemiah not only had to be rebuilders of things, but they had to be reformers of people. They exercised their authority courageously and even ruthlessly in order to turn the nation around.

Nehemiah – the man

On the whole most people warm to Nehemiah rather than Ezra, and it is easy to see why. There is something a bit nicer about Nehemiah, not least because he was a happy man and encouraged others to be happy. It was Nehemiah who said, 'The joy of the Lord is your strength.' I don't think Ezra would ever have said that – he was too busy weeping over the people. In many ways they make a perfect couple. The 'help' and the 'comfort' belong together.

But there are unique characteristics about Nehemiah that impress me deeply. We feel we know him. He is much more candid about his feelings than Ezra. He talks more about himself, he is more autobiographical. In particular, there are more 'I' passages, and this tells us four things about him.

Prayerful

If Ezra is the Bible man, Nehemiah is the prayer man. Before he did anything, he prayed. We have examples of both long and short, public and private prayers. It isn't the length of your prayer that matters, it is the depth of it. Here is a man who talked to the Lord naturally about everything – a man of prayer. He asked God to punish those involved in evil, and he boldly asked that God would remember him and reward him for his good deeds.

Practical

He was very well organized. Some people are so heavenly minded that they are no earthly use, but not this man. He didn't mind putting his hand to cementing. He could organize well, he studied the gates and the walls and assessed the needs of the people. He wasn't up in the clouds, he was a practical man. Isn't it wonderful when you get a combination of a practical man and a prayerful man?

Emotional

He was an emotional man with deep feelings, showing both deep sorrow and great happiness. He encouraged others to enjoy the Lord, to rejoice and to have the strength of joy, but he could also be angry and pull people's hair out. He was rarely dull!

Social

But above all he was a social man. I don't think Ezra could have done what Nehemiah did, because Nehemiah got on with people. He was brilliant at personnel management. He was able to draw alongside people and exhort them to complete the task. He could boost morale and help them to be re-energized when they flagged. There is always something attractive about a man like that, and it is interesting that when he talks about the work, he always says 'we'. On one occasion he refused to have the food allotted to the Governor in order to identify with the people. He had his private moments when he inspected the wall, but as for the building, he said, 'and *we* built the walls'. He gave credit to everybody: 'We got on with the job, we had a mind to work and we got it done in 52 days.' He didn't say, 'It was *my* achievement.' We read, 'they perceived that this work was done by our God.'

There is such a balance in his character – prayerful and practical, joyful and sorrowful, tough and tender, sensitive to God and sensitive to people. Here is a good example of a character we can emulate.

God and his people

God

A common question when studying biblical history is: Why study history from so long ago? What has all that got to do with us – 2,000 miles away and 2,500 years later?

For one thing, we are looking at interesting events and inspiring personalities. The Bible describes people warts and all, and is never dull. But we are really reading the story of God and his people – a God who bound himself by a covenant to one people and one nation, and now binds himself to us with a new covenant. Notice how Nehemiah talks about 'my God'. We have a picture of a God who keeps his promises.

He promises his people two things – to bless their obedience and to curse their disobedience. The same God who keeps the one promise will keep the other, and the fact that he sent them into exile means he was keeping his promise to them.

HE SENT THEM INTO EXILE

In Leviticus 26:44 God promised to take the people out of the Promised Land if they misbehaved, and he kept his promise. The reason for the exile lasting 70 years is rarely appreciated. It is explained at the end of 2 Chronicles.

The laws of God stated that the land needed its Sabbath rest as well as the people. God had commanded that every seventh year they should not take crops from the land, but give it a fallow rest. But the land had missed its holiday for 500 years – which, of course, equals 70 years (every 7th year for 500 years). At the end of 2 Chronicles God said, 'If you won't give the land its holiday, I will. The land is 70 years behind in its rest, so out you go for 70 years.'

God keeps his word. He has promised to reward the righteous and to punish the wicked. He will do both, because he is covenanted to do both, and that will apply to his people as much as to anyone else. Paul, writing to Christians, says, 'We must all appear before the judgement seat of Christ, that each one may receive what is due to him for the things done while in the body', whether good or bad.

HE BROUGHT THEM OUT OF EXILE

Just as God promised to punish, he was also keen to bless (see Jeremiah 29:10). So after the allotted time he brought them back – a second exodus, though this time there was no sea to cross and no pursuing army.

GOD'S SECRET WORK

In both Ezra and Nehemiah, I notice that God works secretly. There are no prophetic words in these books, there are no miracles, and yet we see God working in an amazing and quiet way.

Leaders inside his people. We see how he raised up individuals from within the people of God to accomplish his work. Zerubbabel became the leader. Ezra and Nehemiah each had a specific task and were raised up at just the right time.

Leaders outside his people. God is not limited to the people of God. He also works in leaders who don't know him – men like Cyrus, Artaxerxes and Darius. Some were sympathetic to God's people; others, like Nebuchadnezzar, were unsympathetic, at least to begin with.

God's people

God is behind the scenes, protecting his people, but he also expects the people to play their part in effecting change. He had shown himself to be a covenant-keeping God, but they in return were called on to keep their side of the covenant and be the holy people God demanded. But the majority of the people failed in their task. The one lesson we get from these books is that the people quickly returned to the sins they had committed before. The only sin they didn't fall back into was idolatry. To this day Jews have such a horror of idolatry that they have never again gone back to worshipping idols, and never will.

Winston Churchill wrote a magnificent history of World War II in six volumes. I have read them and they are fascinating reading, but the sixth has a very interesting title. It covered the very end of the war, and he called it *Triumph and Tragedy*. The subtitle was this: 'How the great democracies triumphed and thus were able to resume the follies that had so nearly cost them their lives.' That was the ultimate verdict of the great wartime leader: people return to their folly.

ONLY SOME WENT HOME

In spite of the chance of returning to their homeland, only 50,000 out of two million actually did so (that's 2.5 per cent). The main reason was that life was prosperous and comfortable in Babylon, while it would be rough and uncertain in Judah. Those returning faced the difficult 900-mile journey and the prospect of poverty once they returned to the land.

THOSE WHO DID SOON FELL INTO SIN

We have noted already that in spite of the exile, the people still fell into sin. They didn't fear God as they should and were soon violating the Law as badly as they had prior to their sojourn in Babylon. This is evidenced by a failure to keep marriage within the faith, and a willingness to exploit their fellow countrymen whenever they could. Indeed, Nehemiah talks of 'the filth of the nations of the land'.

So it is no wonder that in chapter 9 in both books, Ezra and Nehemiah are distressed by what has happened. They had to rebuild the people, to be saved from their sins and themselves.

The result

God stopped speaking to them for 400 years – there were to be no miracles or messages for four whole centuries. So Ezra, Nehemiah and the two prophets Haggai and Zechariah are concerned with the rebuilding.

Daniel made one amazing prediction which is especially relevant to a study of Ezra and Nehemiah. He said: 'Know and understand this. From the issuing of the decree to restore and rebuild Jerusalem until the Anointed one, the ruler, comes, there will be seven "sevens" and sixty-two "sevens" … After the sixty-two "sevens" the Anointed one will be cut off and will have nothing.' When we studied Daniel, we saw that these 62 'sevens' or 490 years brought us right up to the public ministry of Jesus, whether we take the 'decree' as that of Cyrus or Artaxerxes.

So right from the exile through to Jesus there is a direct line of prophecy. I believe God showed that to Daniel so that we should know that even though the children of Israel coming back from exile went back into sin, all was not lost. God knew what to do about it. God wasn't surprised; he had already planned what he would do to put the situation right. He would send the Saviour to get them out of their sin, and that is why Jesus came.

32.

1 AND 2 CHRONICLES

Introduction

When people try to read through the whole Bible they tend to get stuck either in Leviticus or in Chronicles. Leviticus is difficult to read because there is no storyline and the religious rituals described seem to have no connection with modern life. Chronicles is difficult because the first nine chapters are nothing more than genealogies, with names that are mostly unpronounceable. Furthermore, having just completed the Books of Kings, people are puzzled to find that so many of the same stories are repeated in Chronicles, and so they decide it's not worth reading it. So we must begin our study of Chronicles by asking why these two books seem to cover the same ground as 1 and 2 Kings.

Our first clue to the answer is found by noting the different order of the books in the Hebrew Bible, which is quite different from the order of books in the English Bible. The position of Chronicles within the Jewish canon suggests, as we shall see, that its connection with Kings is not as great as we may think, even though it covers broadly the same period of time. The chart on page 15 will make the situation clear.

Firstly, we note that the books are grouped differently. In the Hebrew Bible there are three groups of books: the Law, the Prophets and the Writings. Indeed, when Jesus spoke with the two men on the road to Emmaus after his resurrection,

Luke records that he took them through the Law, the Prophets and the Writings, and explained how they related to him. This was, after all, his Bible (Luke 24:37,44).

So in the Hebrew Bible, the first five books are the Law (also known as the Torah or the Pentateuch) – what we call Genesis, Exodus, Leviticus, Numbers and Deuteronomy. But in the Hebrew Bible they are known by the first words on the scroll. Genesis is called 'In the beginning'; Exodus is called 'These are the names'; Leviticus is 'And he called'; Numbers is 'In the wilderness'; and Deuteronomy is 'These are the words'.

The Hebrew Bible then lists what are regarded as prophetic books. There are two sub-groups of Prophets. The first is Joshua, Judges, Samuel and Kings. Both Samuel and Kings are just one volume in the Hebrew Old Testament, the major reason being that the Hebrew language uses consonants and not vowels, so they only took up half the space. When these books were translated into first Greek and then English, they took up more space, so were divided into two books, because the vowels doubled the length of the words.

But these four books are classified not as history but as prophecy, because they are prophetic insights into history. Samuel was the prophet who dominated that early period, and during the period of the kings there were dozens of prophets. It was the prophets who wrote the history and interpreted it and showed the people what God was doing. The later prophets were placed into a second sub-group, which is much the same as in the English Bible.

The Writings are a kind of miscellaneous box in which everything else goes. It includes the Psalms (the word literally means 'praises'), Job and Proverbs. Ruth is not considered a prophetic book, so it goes into the Writings, which is not the case in the English Bible. The Song of Songs, Ecclesiastes,

Lamentations, Ezra, Nehemiah, Esther and Daniel are also included. It is especially surprising that Daniel is not put among the prophets, but he speaks of other nations.

As the chart shows, the last book in the Jewish Old Testament is Chronicles, only it is called 'The Words of the Days'. So it is clear that the book is regarded in a totally different light to Kings. One book is prophetic and the other is not.

This is a much better arrangement than the English one, not least because the last word in the English Old Testament (at the end of Malachi) is 'curse'. In the Hebrew Bible the last words are 'go up', as in 'let us go up to Jerusalem' (Heb: aliya).

In the English arrangement we have three quite different groupings. We treat Genesis, Exodus, Leviticus, Numbers and Deuteronomy as history, and lump them in with Joshua and Judges, as if it just carries on. We include Ruth because we think it is also part of the history. Then Samuel, Kings and Chronicles come in order. This is why we tend to get the impression that Chronicles is just saying the same thing over again.

The result of this is that 1 and 2 Chronicles are very little known in church circles. There are only two verses that are widely quoted. The first is from 2 Chronicles 7:14: 'If my people who are called by my name will humble themselves and pray and seek my face, and turn from their wicked ways, then I will hear from heaven, and will forgive their sin, and will heal their land.' There was a musical called *If My People* based on that one verse, and yet the verse was taken right out of context. It was used as if 'I will heal their land' applied to England or America, but the land in question was, of course, the land of Israel. And there is nothing to allow us to apply it to any other land.

The other well-known verse is from the reign of King Jehoshaphat, when he was attacked by three separate nations who became allies against Judah. They marched on Jehoshaphat, who, in response, prayed and sought the Lord.

The prophets told him, 'You are going to win the battle', but he was told to send singers ahead of the army. So the choir led the army into battle and sang praises to God, and the enemy fled. This only happened on one occasion and hardly provides a precedent for singing in the streets to drive demons out of a city, as some Christians have thought. Both of these verses have been taken right of context. But sadly, apart from these two verses, people don't know Chronicles at all.

Duplication?

The Books of Chronicles and Kings are, of course, not the only parts of the Bible where the same period is covered twice. There are two accounts of creation in Genesis, in chapters 1 and 2 – one from God's point of view, one from man's point of view. There are four accounts of Jesus' life in the New Testament. Even though the books seem the same, they each come from a different angle, because each Gospel was written for a different kind of person.

The writing of Chronicles and Kings reminds us that all history has an angle. You cannot write history without betraying your personal interest, because, from all that happens, you select the things that you are interested in and that you think are important. Having given that selection, you then connect them up to show how one thing led to another, and then you evaluate what you have written.

So a historian goes through the steps of selection, connection and evaluation, and moral judgements are being made about what should be included. Even in the spoof history book *1066 And All That*, moral judgements were being made all the way through about whether a thing was good or bad. In the same way, you find that the moral judgement in Kings is quite different from that in Chronicles.

Comparing Samuel, Kings and Chronicles

Samuel and Kings were only two books in the Hebrew Old Testament (they are four books in ours), and they cover a period of 500 years only. But when we read Chronicles we find that the book starts much earlier and finishes later. It mentions Adam, returning through the centuries to the very beginning of the human race. Samuel and Kings finish in the exile, but in Chronicles we have the return, 70 years later. 'Let us go up to Jerusalem' is the last word in Chronicles. And therefore these two writers had quite a different task in front of them, and they met that need quite differently.

SAMUEL / KINGS	CHRONICLES
500 years	Starts earlier, finishes later
Written soon after the events	Written long after the events
Political history	Religious history
Prophetic viewpoint	Priestly viewpoint
Northern and southern kings	Southern kings
Human failings	Divine faithfulness
Royal vices	Royal virtues
Negative	Positive
Moral – righteousness	Spiritual – ritual
PROPHET	PRIEST

In Kings, the people needed an explanation for why they had been sent into exile, but in Chronicles they knew why – they just needed to be encouraged and sent back to the land to re-establish the walls of the city and rebuild the temple. Kings is written quite soon after the events, Chronicles long after. Political history dominates Kings, while Chronicles is mostly religious history. So Kings is written from a prophetic viewpoint, and Chronicles from a priestly viewpoint. Kings covers the north and the south; Chronicles, covering the same period, never mentions a single northern king. The writer is not interested in the north at all. That's a huge difference. Kings concentrates on the human failings of the kings that led to disaster. But the Chronicler wants to concentrate on divine faithfulness. So in Chronicles the royal vices are played down in favour of the royal virtues, so that Chronicles has a more positive view of the kings.

It is not that the Chronicler is trying to change history; rather, he selects mostly good things that the kings did. The emphasis is moral, and the key word is *righteousness*. Kings answers the question of whether the kings were righteous or not. But in Chronicles the interest is more in ritual, the temple and the sacrifices, with the emphasis on spiritual rather than moral issues. So in Kings we have a prophet writing, and in Chronicles a priest. The difference of viewpoint is enormous.

It has already become clear that one of the best ways of assessing the focus of Chronicles is to ask what material is omitted that is included in Kings and Samuel. A mere glance at the contents gives a clue. In Samuel, Saul has about a sixth of the book, with the life of David accounting for two thirds. Solomon's life accounts for about half of 1 Kings and the divided kingdom also has about half. So what is going on? What is the Chronicler leaving out?

Omissions

1 There is no mention of Samuel's part in choosing kings.
2 Saul barely receives a mention. We have Saul's death, but it is only mentioned to introduce David. There's nothing about the rest of Saul's life. The writer wants the readers to see the kings in a good light, and so most of Saul's reign is ignored.
3 David is mentioned at some length, but even then it is interesting to note what is omitted. His struggles with Saul are ignored, and there's no mention of his seven-year reign in Hebron or his many wives. Absalom's rebellion is missed out, and the whole episode with Bathsheba – the turning-point in David's reign – does not receive a single line.

This selection of material is very significant. The Chronicler is including positive stories and leaving out anything that is unsavoury. So with the absence of the episode with Bathsheba, David appears in a wonderful light, as does Solomon. There is not a word here about his many wives, the idols that were brought into the palace, his faulty relationship with God, or his failure to deal with the high places and the presence of pagan temples.

This positive focus continues throughout the book. After the division of the kingdom, the Chronicler omits the kings in the north in favour of the kings of the south. He gives a lot of space to the good kings like the boy king Josiah and Hezekiah, but the bad kings receive hardly any coverage at all.

Unless the Chronicler is prejudiced, he is quite deliberate in his editing decisions. He has certain interests – there are common themes that were not prominent in Saul's reign but were in David's and Solomon's, and in the reigns of some of the kings of Judah.

An outline of the books

Book 1: The godly king
1–9:   Adam to Saul
         First king of Israel
10–29:   David and the Ark
         Best king of Israel
Book 2: The godly kings
1–9:   Solomon and the temple
         Last king of Israel
10–36:   Jereboam to Zedekiah
         Best kings of Judah
         Last king of Judah
         Throne and temple

Inclusions

First of all, the Chronicler is only concerned with the royal line of David. None of the kings of the north were in the royal line, so they don't receive a mention. Chronicles is specifically a history of the royal house of David, and nothing else. So Saul is not included because he was not in the royal line of David, but was from the tribe of Benjamin. One man is included at some length who receives little mention in Kings – namely, Zerubbabel. He was of the royal line of David and came back from the Babylonian exile. It was in him that the people's hopes for the Messiah lay, because he was the only one to return from David's line. So when the Chronicler gets to the genealogy there is half a chapter on Zerubbabel's family tree. He is painting the royal line in a very favourable light.

Religious focus

Chronicles is especially concerned with the king's attitude to the Ark and the temple. He concentrates on any records about the people's treatment of the Ark of the Covenant and the temple in which it was housed as the place where God would live among his people. So we are told how David brought the Ark to Jerusalem, of his desire to build the temple, his preparation for it, the gathering of the materials, drawing the plans, and how he arranged the services of worship and the choirs and the choirmasters. The great detail in Chronicles is almost skipped over in Kings and Samuel.

Furthermore, six of the nine chapters focusing on Solomon are almost exclusively concerned with his part in building the temple that his father David was not allowed to build. The Chronicler records Solomon's prayer when it was dedicated, and how the glory of the Lord came. It is Chronicles that contains the account of the underground quarry from which materials for the temple were brought.

So this focus suggests a priest's view of history. A prophet would concentrate on the bad things the kings did which brought judgement on the land. But the priest is pleased to record the building of the temple, the arrangement of choirs and the establishment of worship. He knew David as the man who was the worship leader, the Psalm writer and the man who wanted the temple built. David and Solomon are thus seen in a different light from Kings.

After Solomon's time, when the kingdom was divided, the Chronicler is only interested in the south, because that's where the temple and priests of God are, and where the royal line is kept. He picks out eight kings – five of them good – and, in accordance with his principle, ignores the twelve very bad kings in the south. We have already noted his focus on David and Solomon. Let us look briefly at the other six kings.

Six kings

Asa

He selects Asa, who put away the idols in Judah and Benjamin and removed his mother from the palace, because she was secretly worshipping an idol in her bedroom. It was Asa who made a covenant with the Lord and enriched the temple with silver and gold so that, in a priest's eyes, he was a good man.

Jehoshaphat

Then we have the account of Jehoshaphat, Asa's son, who sent the Levites to teach the Law of God in every city. He was victorious over Ammon and Moab. We saw earlier that he sent the singers into battle at the head of the army, and he was instrumental in restoring a stronger focus upon God.

Jehoram

One bad king who is mentioned is Jehoram, but his mention is crucial to the plot. His big mistake was in marrying Ahab's daughter, Athalia, whose parents had been steeped in the worship of foreign gods. She came south and made a bid for the throne, killing most of the royal princes. But a priest named Jehoiada kidnapped the youngest prince, Joash, hid him for six years and later produced him as the rightful king. Once again a priest plays a crucial part in preserving the royal line of David.

Joash

Joash was also mixed in character. He restored the temple by encouraging the people to give money towards its upkeep. But he slew the godly Zechariah, son of Jehoiada, in spite of the kindness that Jehoiada had shown to him.

Hezekiah

Hezekiah reopened and repaired the temple. The people celebrated the Passover with great joy. His reforms are covered in just a few verses in Kings, but are given three chapters in Chronicles. He reformed the worship and re-established the temple in people's thinking.

Josiah

The Chronicler also spends much time on Josiah, the boy king who, during a spring cleaning of the temple, found the book of the Law. He returned proper services and feasts to the temple and attempted to reform the nation at a time of pagan worship.

All these kings opposed idolatry, which is why they were good kings in the eyes of the priests. The interesting thing is that although idolatry was prevalent before the exile, when the Jews returned from exile, they were never tempted as a nation to return to idolatry, and they haven't to this very day.

Crucial to our understanding of Chronicles is to note that it ends with Cyrus the Persian overcoming the Babylonians and sending the Jews back to their land to rebuild the temple. So the readership comprises those who are returning from exile. They have never seen a Jewish temple and aren't ruled over by a king in David's line. The Chronicler tells them three things – I call them 'the three Rs'. He wants to give them *roots*, *royalty* and *religion* again. So Chronicles has a clear purpose. He is preaching, not just teaching history.

Who they were	a *rooted* people
What they were	a *royal* people
Why they were	a *religious* people

Identity

The returning exiles needed to know who they were. They had roots that stretched back to Adam, for God himself had been controlling their history. They belonged to God, and he had singled them out from the whole human race, selected Abraham and preserved them as a people. Thus they were not merely inhabitants of a land, but a people whose identity was tied up in God's purposes. Hence the lengthy genealogies.

Leadership

The second thing they needed to know was that they were a royal people, with their own king. The Chronicler wanted them to start thinking about the king again and to restore the kingdom of Israel. He was telling them, 'You're not just a group of people – you're a royal priesthood, a royal people. You have a king and the royal line has been preserved, and you're going to be a kingdom again.' So as the people faced the temptation to sink into a slave mentality, the book was to be a great inspiration.

Purpose

The third thing he wanted to convey was the purpose for which they existed as a people. The most important thing that made them what they were was the fact that they were God's chosen people. Their worship of God was absolutely central to their identity as a people. So when they returned, their priority was to get the temple rebuilt and for worship to be re-established after the pattern of Moses.

We have noted already that over 10 per cent of those who returned were priests, which is a far higher proportion than the number of priests in the whole people. They were committed to re-establishing Israel as a religious nation, so rebuilding the temple was the top priority. The name 'Jew' literally means 'praise God'. They were keen to live up to their name.

So Chronicles was a sermon for a returning remnant, to encourage them to persevere amidst the difficult times. It wasn't a very exciting business, and they had to struggle to make a living. They were very poor, and building the temple was slow work. It needed two prophets – Haggai and Zechariah – to urge them to keep going. But the Chronicler had to get the truth instilled in them that God must come first in their life as a people.

Israel exists today largely because its people wanted a home of their own where they could be safe, though I am sad to say that they did not really go back to establish themselves as God's people.

I'll never forget the 45 minutes I spent with a President of Israel in his residence. At the end of the talk he said, 'Well, I'm an agnostic. I don't really believe in God.'

I replied, 'But this is the land where God did his greatest miracles.'

He said, 'Well, I can't believe it.'

I was very sad. It was so important that they went back as God's people and that the temple should be the very centre of their return and their hopes. They have returned to their land but not to their Lord.

Christian application

Christ

The themes of Chronicles were picked up in the life of Christ.

ROOTS

Matthew begins with the genealogy of Christ, and Luke takes the genealogy right back to Adam. It was important that the reader was convinced about the veracity of Christ's roots. Christ was and is a Jew, not a rootless person dropped arbitrarily into history, but sent to fulfil the expectations of a particular people.

ROYALTY

Furthermore, Christ was born in the royal line, so he could claim to be the Son of David. Indeed, he could inherit the throne twice over. Through his father he had a legal right to the throne and through his mother a physical right, because they could both trace their family tree back to David. And though he is not yet openly a king, he is the One who is on David's throne forever.

RELIGION

He was also the fulfilment of Israel's religious hopes, because he actually became the temple. We are told in the early part of John's Gospel that 'The Word was made flesh and "tabernacled" among us.' Referring to his body, Jesus said, 'Destroy this temple, and I will raise it up in three days.' He saw himself as the focus of their worship, as one who fulfilled the symbol of the temple. He would make many of the Jewish practices obsolete, for many of them had been brought in to serve as pointers to him.

Christians

ROOTS

The apostle Paul explains that Christians have been 'grafted into' God's people, so that even as Gentiles we can say that we have Jewish roots. Their genealogy is ours. So when I read 1 Chronicles 1–9, I am reading my family tree, because I am now a son of Abraham. Such roots are even more significant to us than our own family tree. Our family tree will disappear at death, but it's the Jewish family tree that is now our genealogy. In Christ we inherit the blessings of Abraham.

ROYALTY

Peter reminds us in his first letter that we are now royal people and a royal priesthood. We are princes and princesses, who should walk down the street like royalty, for we are going to reign over this world with Christ. Revelation tells us that God has redeemed people from every kindred and tribe to reign on the earth. Therefore, like the ancient Jews, we can live with dignity, knowing who we are and what our position is.

RELIGION

In addition, we have become the temple. Paul asks, 'Don't you know that your bodies are the temple of the Holy Spirit?' We are to reflect this in the way we live.

The three things that the people returning from the exile needed to be taught, we need to claim too. The one big difference for us is that we are still in exile. We haven't come home yet; we're strangers and pilgrims in a foreign land. I live in England but I don't belong here. Our citizenship is in heaven, and that can cause tension with those with whom we mix. After all, Jesus said to his disciples, 'They hated me, so they're likely to hate you also.'

Consequently, we have to work hard to keep our relationships with unbelieving relatives and friends, because now we belong to a new family. We must remember that what we do to our body, we're doing with the temple of God. This is one reason why so many people give up smoking when they become Christians. There's nothing in the Bible against smoking. As I often say, it won't take you to hell – it only makes you smell as if you've already been there! But many Christians come to realize that by smoking they are abusing the temple of God – making it smell, making it dirty and shortening its life.

So Chronicles is not just a dull old bit of history duplicating what has already been said. It is a message of hope for the future, showing us what we're here for and how to find our true identity as the people of God in a strange land. It is a vital book with a vital message, both for the people at the time and for us today.

33.

HAGGAI

Introduction

Haggai is the first of the last three Minor Prophets in our Old Testament. After these three God didn't bring further revelation for over 400 years. So for four centuries the Jews had to tell their children, 'Some day God will speak to us again.' It was not until John the Baptist came that his voice was heard again.

These three are very short books because the prophets spoke for a very short time. Haggai only spoke for three months, and then he was finished. Only Obadiah is shorter within the Old Testament. Zechariah spoke for just two years and overlapped slightly with Haggai. So these brief prophecies were in contrast with Isaiah and Jeremiah, who preached for 40 to 50 years and whose books are therefore much longer.

Haggai and Zechariah are known as post-exilic prophets, because they came after the exile. Before the exile, the prophets were full of warnings about coming disasters, but afterwards the mood was quite different. They are full of encouragement and comfort, as the people try to repair the damage to the nation.

There are many similarities between Haggai and Zechariah:

1 They spoke at the same time. Both of them carefully dated their prophecies, which few of the earlier prophets had ever done. They generally give the day, the month and the year when the word was given. Each of Haggai's five prophecies

have an exact date, so we can see just how many days or weeks there lay between each of them. The same is true for Zechariah. They overlapped by just one month in 520 BC.

2 They spoke in the same place – the rebuilt city of Jerusalem in Judah.

3 They spoke to exactly the same situation. The historical background is key to grasping their message.

Historical background

The Persian king Cyrus conquered Babylon in 538 BC. He was a benevolent dictator and told the peoples who had been displaced that they could return to their homelands, provided that they built a temple in which they would pray to their God on his behalf. In the event, only 50,000 Jews decided to return. The rest, having mostly been born in exile and having established themselves as merchants in Babylon, decided to stay. Babylon was on a major trade route and many of the Jews had become quite wealthy. Jerusalem did not have the same advantages and seemed a bleak prospect.

Those who returned were led by two men: a prince named Zerubbabel (the name means 'seed of Babylon') and Joshua the High Priest. Zerubbabel had been born in exile and had never seen the Promised Land, but he was the only surviving member of the royal line of David, being the grandson of the last legitimate king, Jehoiachin. So he had to return if God's promises that there would always be a son of David on the throne of Israel were to be fulfilled. The name Joshua means 'God saves' or 'God our Saviour' and is a form of the name Jesus. He was a descendant of Ido and re-established the priesthood – though this was not difficult, because two out of every fifteen who returned were priests, so there was plenty of choice. Spiritual interests primarily motivated those who returned, for they knew they were not going to be wealthy. It was going to be a hard struggle in a land that had not been cultivated for 70 years, and in a city with no walls.

On returning to the land, Zerubbabel's and Joshua's first concern was to build an altar, and their second was to build a temple around it and re-establish themselves as God's people. There were distinct similarities with their forefather Abraham, for in returning they were tracing the exact same route. Abraham's home town, Ur, was down the river from Babylon, and so they were going to have to repeat the whole story of Abraham again and leave their home, their relatives and their businesses and go to a country they had never seen. The first thing that Abraham did when he got to the Promised Land was to pitch his tent and raise an altar and give a sacrifice of thanksgiving to God that he'd safely arrived. The returning exiles did exactly the same. They gathered a few stones and made an altar and thanked God for bringing them back.

We must not underestimate the great sacrifice they had made. They left friends, relatives and brick-built homes. They exchanged prosperity for poverty, fruitful trading for land that had not been cultivated for 70 years. But they had their dream from the Book of Chronicles of re-establishing a royal kingdom with their own king – to be the people of God in the land God had promised their forefathers.

But the task of building the temple was daunting. There were so few people and they had no resources. So they decided to build a much smaller temple than Solomon's, but even this seemed beyond them. They faced opposition from the Samaritans and, when Darius replaced Cyrus, they lost the subsidy that Cyrus had given them to rebuild the temple. Darius cut the subsidies that had been given to returning peoples to build temples, to help finance military campaigns.

So fantasy gave way to reality, the size of the task discouraged the people and their hearts sank. They stopped building after only two years, and for 14 years didn't put another stone on the temple, leaving just the foundations and low walls. On top of scratching a living, building temples was a luxury they couldn't afford. Their concern now was mere survival.

Then the economy went into severe recession. Food became scarce and very expensive, inflation rocketed and droughts and disease reduced the supply of food. They had no savings, having spent all the money they had saved in Babylon on food and clothing. It was a huge anticlimax. They had returned with hopes of rebuilding a nation, and found instead that they could hardly stay alive.

Inevitably, they asked 'Why?' They came to the conclusion that they had been correct to return but had chosen the wrong time. They began to ask whether they should have stayed longer in Babylon, built up more money for themselves and waited until they were fit enough to come back in strength and greater wealth. Abraham may have been content with a tent and an altar, but they wanted to rebuild. They'd been back for 18 years and had so little to show for it.

It was into this depressing situation that Haggai spoke. He'd come back with them from exile, probably as a priest, though we don't know for sure. His father is not mentioned, so his family was probably not prominent. His prophecy is written in prose, which is very significant, for in Scripture God's thoughts are more often communicated by prose, and his feelings by poetry. So there is little of God's feelings in the book. It's as if God is fed up; he doesn't feel any more.

It is also significant to note how the word of the Lord is described in Haggai. We are told it did not come 'to' Haggai, as to other prophets, but 'by' Haggai. So this is a word of insight rather than a revelation that he saw. He was given insight regarding what was wrong and, on 26 occasions in just 38 verses, he prefaces his words with 'thus says the Lord'.

An outline of the book

A depressed people: 1:1–11
Your houses decorated
My house devastated
A determined people: 1:12–15
Feared the Lord
Obeyed the Lord
A discouraged people: 2:1–9
Former house – glorious
Latter house – greater
A defiled people: 2:10–19
Clean doesn't make dirty clean
Dirty does make clean dirty
A designated prince: 2:20–23
Other thrones overturned
This throne occupied

In total, Haggai brought 26 words from the Lord over five days. He came asking questions from the Lord intended to make the people think. Let's look at the main themes of his message.

A depressed people (1:1–11)

The real reason why the people were depressed was that their thinking had gone wrong. They needed to revise their thoughts, and their feelings would follow. It's amazing that God's people don't like to think. The most common comment I get after I've preached is, 'Well, you gave us something to think about', always said in a tone of mild rebuke, implying that they didn't come to church to think! Sometimes preachers and prophets need to make people think – to provoke them to think again and to ask questions.

The people failed to realize that God had caused the disaster they were suffering from. They themselves had taken the first steps into this depression. Haggai explained that they had not assessed the situation correctly. They thought it was the wrong time to build the temple because they couldn't afford the energy or the money. But Haggai said that the crop failure and the rapid inflation came because they stopped building the temple. As soon as they stopped putting God and his house first, things began to go wrong, but they didn't notice. So the cause and effect were the wrong way round in their thinking.

Haggai's solution was to challenge them about the quality of their housing compared to the temple. Their houses were panelled with wood at a time when wood was very scarce (after the trees had been chopped down by the Babylonians), and they had to import cedar wood from places like Lebanon. A person with a wood-panelled house was spending unnecessary amounts on his own home, rather than simply using the plentiful supplies of stone. It's a very simple message: 'Just compare your own home with God's home, and this will tell you where your priorities have been.'

A determined people (1:12–15)

The people responded positively, and returned to the task of rebuilding. The exile had taught them to listen to prophets, and so they moved fast. It took just three and a half weeks to get the builders organized and to find more material for the temple.

A discouraged people (2:1–9)

The second message came just 27 days after they had begun building. Morale was declining, largely because older people were making odious comparisons with Solomon's temple: 'Call this a temple!? You should have seen the temple we had.' It was devastating criticism and it hit the workers hard.

Present

Haggai had a word from the Lord to keep them building. He told them not to be depressed by the small size of the rebuilt temple. Better to begin small than not at all. God is not worried about the size of his house. He is just keen to have a house to live in where he can dwell among his people.

In this section God gave them precepts and promises. The precepts (commands) were twofold: 'Be strong' (three times) and 'Don't fear' (once). The promise was: 'I am with you; my Spirit remains with you.'

Future

But Haggai also focuses upon the future. He predicts that God will shake the heavens and the earth and all nations. Here God is confirming that he is in control of nature and history.

Then comes an enigmatic phrase: 'The desired of all nations will come.' The Hebrew wording is hard to translate, but I think it is unlikely that it refers to the Messiah. The word 'desired' is usually translated in the Old Testament as 'valuables or treasures which you desire' (see 2 Chronicles 32:27; 36:10; Daniel 11:18, 43). This is a promise that further silver and gold will come and help restore the temple to its original condition. It's saying that God will shake the nations and they will send their treasures. This is exactly what happened, because shortly after the prophecy a whole wave of silver and gold came from Persia to help with the rebuilding (Ezra 6:4). So we read too much into this verse if we think it refers to the Messiah.

God also said he would fill this temple with his glory, and the glory would be greater than the glory of the former house. Clearly, this cannot mean that God's glory would be greater, for that would suggest that his *shekinah* glory had been dimmed when it filled Solomon's temple. Instead it refers to the splendour of the building itself. This is connected to the promise that the wealth of the nations would come. Furthermore, God promised that the temple would know great peace and harmony.

A defiled people (2:10–19)

The next crisis came two months later. December had arrived, and there was no rain. Haggai had said that the people had caused the drought and famine by stopping the temple reconstruction. But having recommenced building for two months, the rain expected in October still hadn't arrived by December. It seemed there would be another bad harvest.

So Haggai had a theological problem. Although God hadn't promised to respond immediately, the people expected him to. So he asked God what the problem was. God's remedy was for him to return to the people with another set of questions. On three occasions he asked them to give careful thought.

He first asked, 'If you put dirty and clean things together, do the dirty things make the clean things dirty or do the clean things make the dirty things clean?' The priests replied that the dirty defiles the clean.

Next he asked the priests, 'If a thing is consecrated to the Lord and you put it with something unconsecrated, does the consecration pass over from the consecrated to the uncon-secrated?' The answer was no.

Haggai explained that God had delayed the rain because they were building a consecrated temple but were unconsecrat-ed as they were doing it. Dirty people building a clean temple made the new temple dirty in God's sight. They thought they were godly because they were building a temple, but they were actually contaminating the temple in God's sight because they were not putting their lives right.

Haggai didn't specify the sins, but from their reaction we can see that they knew what he was talking about. They put it right, and the rain began the next day. The word from the Lord was, 'From this day I will bless you', because they had got the message.

A designated prince (2:20–23)

The next message was for Zerubbabel. It was simple: 'You are the signet ring of God.' A signet ring was always worn by roy-alty, and God was saying that from Zerubbabel the royal line would be re-established. He was the prince in David's line – but, of course, he couldn't ever be king, because Darius the Persian was king. Instead Zerubbabel was made the governor of Judah.

A further promise was made to Zerubbabel: 'But there will come a day when I will shake the universe and the nations. When I shake them, I will overthrow their thrones and I will establish the throne of Israel, and your line will be on it.' God was promising Zerubbabel that he would shake Persia, Egypt, Syria, Greece and Rome and would re-establish the kingdom of Israel from Zerubbabel's line. This would take place 'on that day', which probably links in with the prophecies concerning Jerusalem in Zechariah 12–14.

Christian application

Christ

The prophecy was never actually fulfilled for Zerubbabel himself, but the genealogy of Jesus suggests a way in which it came true. Zerubbabel has a very important and perhaps surprising place in the history of our salvation. God fulfilled his promise to that man by putting him on both sides of the genealogy of his Son. Jesus could have traced his legal line back to David through his father, or step-father, Joseph (in Matthew), and he traced his physical line back to David through Mary (in Luke), so he had this double claim to be the Son of David. Zerubbabel figured in both lines.

Christians

Haggai's central message was the importance of putting first things first. Jesus repeatedly takes up this theme in his teaching. In Matthew 6 Jesus tells his hearers to seek *first* God's kingdom and God's righteousness, and matters like food and clothes will be dealt with. The best welfare state ever is the kingdom of heaven, because Jesus said that if we put God first, all these other things will look after themselves. God doesn't promise us luxury, but that everything we need will be supplied. Too often we tend to put making a living or keeping alive first, and we give God what is left. But that's not the way it works, and Haggai's message comes through to us very clearly.

There's a more important aspect too. God is not so much concerned about what we do for him, but whether we're clean to do it. This is why Jesus said in the Sermon on the Mount that when we bring an offering to the Lord and realize that there's someone we need to be reconciled to, we had better go and put that right first, before bringing the offering to the Lord. Once again, Haggai's message is coming through. Dirty people can make clean things dirty. Get things right, put God first, and then God can welcome what you do for him and bless you and look after you.

It's really quite a simple message, but it's a message that perhaps still needs to be brought. Life is not about staying alive or making a living, but about living right and living for God.

34.

ZECHARIAH

Introduction

The Book of Zechariah has a great number of similarities with Haggai. Indeed, Zechariah 8 could easily have come from the earlier prophet's mouth. This is not surprising, because Haggai and Zechariah overlapped by one month, with Zechariah beginning exactly where Haggai left off. From the outset we must note that if Haggai is one of the easiest of the Minor Prophets to understand, then Zechariah is one of the hardest. There are three main differences to point out:

1 Zechariah was later than Haggai and continued his prophecy for much longer. It was like a relay race – as if Haggai passed the baton to Zechariah, who then ran with it, but ran very much further.
2 The Book of Zechariah is much longer than Haggai. In our Bible, it has 12 chapters instead of just a couple.
3 Zechariah looked into the far distant future, while Haggai dealt with the present and its immediate problems. Zechariah seemed to be able to look to the end of time. Some of his more immediate future predictions are mixed with some of his very distant future predictions, which leaves us in confusion as to the time period that is being considered.

Also there is a lot more poetry in Zechariah than Haggai. His style is markedly different in places. It is what we call an 'apocalyptic' book. Apocalyptic prophecies are a strongly visual form of communication, full of symbols and weird pictures. Animals and angels tend to be especially prominent, with the latter involved in explaining the pictures to people. This is reminiscent of the Book of Revelation, the second half of Daniel and a few parts of Ezekiel. The reason why the prophecy is in this strange form is very simple – it is very difficult to imagine the distant future. You can imagine the near future quite easily, because it is just the present trends continuing. But the distant future is much more difficult. After all, how would you describe life today to somebody living a thousand years ago? A description of television would sound extraordinary. They would have little or no understanding. The only way you can describe the distant future to people is to try and give it in the form of a picture or a symbol, and then explain the symbol to them.

So Zechariah is a very different kind of prophecy. We understand the message of Haggai very easily. He tells the people to finish the temple, and God will bless them. Who needs any explanation of that? But Zechariah is a very different proposition.

The prophet

His name means 'God remembers'. It is a very common name in the Old Testament, belonging to some 29 people. He was a priest, so here is a priest who is also a prophet – though this is not especially surprising, because around two out of every fifteen of the people who returned from Babylon were priests. It was a religious return, for the people came back to re-establish

God's name in Jerusalem. They certainly didn't come back because the land was going to be more fertile or because trading would be better, for life in Babylon was much better. They returned for spiritual reasons, and so a high number of priests returned.

There are two extraordinary developments which Zechariah highlights. The first is that priests would replace prophets as the spiritual leaders of the community. For the next 400 years there would be no prophets, just priests. So Zechariah being a priest and a prophet marks a kind of transition. Indeed, he predicts that there will come a day when nobody will want to claim to be a prophet.

The second startling development is that the priests are going to take over from the kings as leaders. Zechariah made a crown of silver and gold to put on the head, not of Zerubbabel, but Joshua the priest. For the first time in Israel's history the office of priest and king would be united. This had happened only once before in the Old Testament, in the Book of Genesis, when a man called Melchizedek, who was the king of Jerusalem, was a priest as well – but this was long before the birth of Israel as a nation. We know from the New Testament that this is the line from which Jesus comes. He is from the order of Melchizedek, not Eli. He is a priest, a king and a prophet. So Zechariah marks a kind of fusing of these three positions of leadership. The priest takes over from the prophet and the priest takes over from the king. By the time Jesus came there were only priests. John the Baptist was the first prophet they would get after 400 years. But the rulers were two high priests, Annas and Caiaphas. So Zechariah is a very significant book in marking this transition.

There is an easy way of dividing the different periods of leadership in the history of Israel. If you take the 2,000 years of Israel's history from Abraham to Jesus, you can divide them very neatly into four periods of 500 years. During the first 500 years, from 2000 to 1500 BC, they were led by patriarchs – Abraham, Isaac, Jacob and Joseph. During the next 500 years, from 1500 to 1000 BC, they were led by prophets – Moses to Samuel. From 1000 to 500 BC, they were led by kings or princes. But from 500 BC to the coming of Jesus, priests led them. So God had given them a sample of every kind of leadership. Each kind of leadership failed Israel. What they really needed was one leader who would combine all these offices in one – which is, of course, what they got with Jesus.

An outline of the book

Present problems (chapters 1–8)
(Carefully dated. All prose.)
Rebuke and rebellion (chapter 1)
Encouragement and enthronement (chapters 1–6)
   Four horsemen among myrtle trees
   Four horns and four craftsmen
   A man with a measuring line
   The cleansing of Joshua
   A golden lampstand and two olive trees
   A flying scroll
   A woman in a basket
   Four chariots
Fasting and feasting (chapter 7–8)
Future predictions (chapters 9–14)
(Undated. Some poetry.)
National (chapters 9–11)
   Vanquished enemies
   A peaceful king
   A mighty God

   A gathered people
   Deforested neighbours
   Worthless shepherds
International (chapters12–14)
   An invading army
   Grieving inhabitants
   Banished prophets
   Reduced population
   Plagued attackers
   Universal worship

The book divides into two parts. He received the word from God in pictures, and so that is how he passes it on. But the whole of chapters 1–8 are concerned with the situation as it is now, and that is why, like Haggai, he dated his three prophecies.

The first prophecy doesn't include the day, but does give us the month and the year. The next was three months later, and the third two years after that. It is not clear why Haggai stopped prophesying or why God sent someone else to carry on. Maybe Haggai died or was taken ill and couldn't continue. Zechariah simply took over just a month before Haggai finished.

Present problems (chapters 1–8)

Rebuke and rebellion

The prophecy is given as they are still building the temple. Although it is not finished yet, they have at least listened to Haggai. The one striking thing about the prophets who came after the exile is that the people listened to them and did what they told them. I am sure this is partly due to their being away from home for 70 years. Indeed, Zechariah began with quite a pointed sermon. He reminded them that it was precisely because their forefathers wouldn't listen to the prophets that the exile happened. It was a very timely reminder.

It is a very simple sermon. Their forefathers not only knew they were doing wrong but were told they were doing wrong. They had no excuse whatever. 'So,' said Zechariah, 'don't make the same mistake. If you don't do what Haggai has told you, you will be in trouble too.'

Encouragement and enthronement

Then Zechariah stopped preaching for three months, and began again using a very unusual sort of approach. He gave them eight pictures, which had all come to him in the night as visions. The simple difference between a vision and a dream is that you are awake when you see a vision, and asleep when you dream a dream. These visions came during the night, and we are told that God had to keep waking him up to give him the next one. So on this occasion God preferred to use visions rather than dreams, even though they were given at night.

The eight visions seem quite unconnected with each other, but are generally addressed to the rebuilding of the temple – especially the first two. As we look at these cryptic pictures, there is a particular refrain which comes four times: 'Then you will know that the Lord Almighty has sent me to you.' Zechariah is saying that the test of a prophet is whether what he says happens. One of the laws of Moses stated that if a prophet says something is going to happen and it doesn't, you should stone the prophet, for he is false. This should make anyone hesitate before they make a prediction about the future. Fortunately, we are not under the Law of Moses, but we do have false prophets around, and it is very important that they are tested. If their predictions do not come true and it doesn't happen, they should be rebuked for misleading the people and misusing God's name.

FOUR HORSEMEN AMONG MYRTLE TREES (1:7–17)

There were two red horses, one brown and one white, each with riders on them. According to the angel, they are God's press reporters – messengers of God who ride through the earth and report back to God and tell him what is happening. If it had been a vision today, they would doubtless have been on motorbikes. They report that there is peace in every part of the world, which was precisely the situation after Cyrus had defeated Babylon. For Cyrus was a man of peace, and the whole earth knew peace during his reign. Zechariah is telling the people to take the opportunity of peace to rebuild Jerusalem and complete the temple. Indeed, it was not long afterwards that they were invaded by Egyptians, Syrians, Greeks and Romans. God also adds that he is angry with those who took his people away and treated them badly. He was angry with his own people for 70 years, but now he is angry with the people who treated them so disgracefully. But for now there is going to be this time of peace, when God doesn't send war to any nation.

FOUR HORNS AND FOUR CRAFTSMEN (1:18–21)

Zechariah must have had some farming background, for there are many agricultural pictures here. Here he sees four craftsmen or blacksmiths de-horning. Throughout apocalyptic prophecy a horn is a symbol of the strength of an army. A horn is an aggressive weapon, and therefore he is now seeing a picture of de-horning going on in the four corners of the earth. God is de-horning the aggressors. Babylon is no longer a threat, and soon God will de-horn other nations that have threatened Judah, though it is not clear which they are. They can get on with building the temple and put all their resources into that, rather than worrying about imminent attack.

A MAN WITH A MEASURING LINE (2:1–13)

The attention shifts to the city of Jerusalem, where he sees a man measuring out the walls. Zechariah realizes that the city is going to be far too small, and that eventually it will outgrow the walls. Jeremiah had predicted this, and it is a fascinating prophecy. I have a series of maps of Jerusalem through the ages, from when it was the little city of David, showing how it expanded and stretched. Jeremiah has accurately predicted the extension of the city – both the direction and where the suburbs would be. Now, of course, the problem with a rapidly expanding city is, how do you defend it? As soon as you make walls, the space inside the walls gets more and more crowded. The man with the measuring line said, 'It is going to be too small for all the people who will come and live here.' Then there is a lovely promise given. God says, 'I will be the wall. You won't need a wall when the city expands – I will defend it.'

In part, this vision is intended to be an encouragement to other Jews to return from Babylon, especially if their reluctance to move is because they believe that Jerusalem is not safe.

There are two predictions about Gentile nations here:

1   *Those who attack Israel will have to face God.* There is a lovely phrase: God says, 'Whoever touches my people touches the apple of my eye.' The 'apple' of the eye is the iris, the middle part that looks just like an apple on end with a stalk in the middle. It is the most sensitive part of your body, and as soon as even a speck of dust touches it, your eyelid slams down. Jesus himself used the saying, 'As much as you have done it to the least of these my brethren, you do it to me.' It is the same principle. God's people are the most sensitive part of God.

2   *Many of the Gentiles will become part of Israel* (see chapters 12–14). History has proved that the God of Israel exists – the history of the Jewish people is proof. Whoever has

dared to attack Israel pays for it later, and yet people from other nations have joined Israel and have been grafted into their olive tree. Both the judgement on the nations harming Israel and the incorporation of nations into Israel show that the God of Israel is the universal God of all peoples.

THE CLEANSING OF JOSHUA (3:1–10)

The next vision concerns Joshua's change of clothes. Zechariah is now looking at the leadership of Zerubbabel and the priest Joshua. What is going to happen now? The first thing is that Satan comes into the picture. Interestingly, the devil hardly ever appears in the Old Testament. He appears in Genesis 3 in the Garden of Eden, at the end of Chronicles, when he tempted David to number Israel, and in the early chapters of Job. Of course, he is behind a lot of things, but he becomes far more prominent when Jesus arrives. But he does appear here.

Whenever something really significant is going to happen, the devil tries to stop it. He tried to kill every male Jew in Egypt so that Moses would not survive and the people would never get out of Egypt. He killed all the babies at Bethlehem when Jesus was born, because he didn't want that baby to grow up and rescue God's people. On this occasion, he says that Judah cannot have Joshua to lead them, because he is a dirty man, having shared in Judah's past sins. Zechariah saw Joshua standing in filthy clothes and realized that the devil was right. The devil does seem to have the function of the counsel for the prosecution in heaven. In Job he is there in heaven in the council of God, accusing the people.

In the vision Zechariah hears that Joshua is like a brand plucked from the burning, like a half-burnt stick pulled out of the fire. So they take the dirty clothes off Joshua and clothe him in clean ones, with a clean turban on his head. It is a beautiful picture, for he saw that by God's grace Joshua, in spite of having shared in the sins of his people earlier, was now clean in God's sight and could be the priest, though he would need to keep clean. God promises that what he had done for this one Jew, he would one day do for the whole nation. He said he would remove the sin of this land in a single day. God can clean a person up and make him a priest. He also promises that in that day, each person will invite his neighbour to sit under his vine. These words foreshadow Jesus finding Nathaniel and telling him that he saw him under his fig tree.

A GOLDEN LAMPSTAND AND TWO OLIVE TREES (4:1–14)

Next, Zechariah is awoken to see a seven-branched golden lampstand in the temple. He also sees a vessel higher than the lamp with a tube running down into the lamp, and realizes that the vessel is full of oil and that nobody will ever need to replenish the oil in the lamp, because there is a reservoir of oil flowing through the lampstand. This symbolizes Zerubbabel as someone who has a reservoir of the Holy Spirit pouring through him. Oil is always a symbol of God's Holy Spirit in the Bible. This is why the word 'anointing' is used when the Holy Spirit comes on someone – anointing with oil. The Queen of Great Britain was anointed with oil when she was crowned in 1952. So Zerubbabel is God's anointed, and the word for 'anointed' in Hebrew is 'Messiah' – God's Anointed One ('Christ' in the Greek language).

But then comes a text that has been quoted by so many: 'Not by might, nor by power, but by my Spirit,' says the Lord. In context, this means not by military might, nor by political power. In other words, the royal line of David must achieve what it achieves not by having an army, or by gaining political authority, but by the Spirit. What a tragedy that the Church has often got this wrong, with such dreadful episodes as the

Crusades. You cannot establish the kingdom of God by military or political power, but only by God's Spirit. But the proof that this power was given to Zerubbabel is most unusual. When those building the temple got to the top, the builders held the ceremony of the capstone – that is, the last stone to go on a gable that joins the two sides as they have been built. The text says that Zerubbabel would actually lift that capstone into place with his hands. It is usually quite a heavy stone, but the prophecy says that he would carry it and put it in place, single-handed, with no aid, no ropes, no pulleys. We are told, 'Then you will know that I, the Almighty Lord, have sent my prophet to you.' Samson carried the gates of the Philistine city away, and now the same Holy Spirit is giving Zerubbabel the power to lift that big stone and get it up. It's an exciting little picture.

In his next vision Zechariah sees two olive trees which stand for Zerubbabel and Joshua. There is to be a dual leadership; the lampstand speaks of the Spirit resting on them both. Zerubbabel is necessary to the future, though not as a king. My feeling is that since they were not allowed a king of their own in Persia, they decided to crown the priest, thinking that the Persians couldn't object to a priest, despite the fact that he wasn't really the king. In so doing they avoided trouble with the Persian empire. Whether this is the case or not, the temple would be completed in their lifetime, and then they would know that the Lord Almighty had sent Zechariah to them. There was no need to despise the day of small things, when looking at the temple compared to Solomon's.

A FLYING SCROLL (5:1–4)

The scroll is ten by five metres in size, and it flies through the air, over the land. The words on the scroll read, 'Curses on all who steal and lie.' As it travels over the homes of the people, it hovers when it comes to the house of someone who is stealing or lying. A curse drops from the scroll on the house and the house is destroyed. Zechariah is saying very simply that God will curse whoever has been stealing or telling lies.

A WOMAN IN A BASKET (5:5–11)

Zechariah sees a woman who looks like a prostitute in a 35-litre measuring basket. Two women with storks' wings come flying down, pick up the basket in their beaks with the woman in it, and fly to the east. This is a picture of God taking their sins away to Babylon. God is saying, 'I took sinners there, now I want to take your sin there, because that is where it belongs.' Babylon, as often in Scripture, is the place of sin.

FOUR CHARIOTS (6:1–8)

Finally, we have the picture of four chariots with red, black, white and dappled-grey horses which go out throughout the whole earth to do God's will. They have already finished their work in the north in Babylon, so one chariot is having a rest. But the other three go everywhere in the world to do his will. God has a world-wide control of history. His agents can be sent anywhere speedily.

It is at this point that three wise men arrive from Babylon. They were merchants, bringing silver and gold as a gift for the temple. But Zechariah was told to take some of it and make a crown and then have a coronation for Joshua in the temple. The refrain comes again, 'Then you will know that I am the Lord.' But this is a crucial point. As I said earlier, the priest and the king were never united in Israel. They had been united in Jerusalem, long before the Jews took it, in the days of Melchizedek. But now the two are once more combined. But there is a condition attached to this: 'if my people diligently obey'. God is saying he will give them a king again, but not from the royal line of David this time. Joshua was chosen because he was a priest, and so Persia wouldn't think that the leader would be a problem to them. It is a neat device to encourage them to be the kingdom of Israel again, and yet it is not yet the true fulfilment of the promises of the Messiah.

Fasting and feasting

Two years later two men came to Zechariah from Bethel in the north. (This suggests, incidentally, that within two years they had begun to spread out over the old country and were re-establishing other towns than Jerusalem.) The men represented a group of people in Bethel who were seeking guidance about their religious life. They came to see a priest, but found a prophet. Their questions concerned two practices, fasting and feasting, because these were the two practices that they observed as part of their religion. They wanted to ask first of all about the fasts they were regularly observing. They had two per year, in the fifth and seventh months, to remember how Jerusalem had been destroyed, to mourn for the loss of the city. They were asking how much longer they were supposed to continue doing this, especially now that Jerusalem had been returned to them.

Zechariah's answer was interesting. He told them that the fasting was actually a self-centred ritual. They fasted because they were sorry for themselves, sorry that they didn't leave their sins alone. He told them the kind of fast that God would like by quoting Isaiah 58. They must fast from dishonesty and cruelty, and instead be generous and kind, and help the helpless and succour the needy. The fast that God really wants does not involve doing without food but doing without sin. This is a relevant word for those who practise Lent, but never deal with the sin in their lives. Furthermore, he said that it was precisely for these reasons that the exile came. They had become selfish and greedy instead of being generous and kind.

As for the questions about the feasts, there had been certain festivals which had been kept up in the exile but were more holidays than holy days. They celebrated these in the fourth, fifth, seventh and tenth months, so that in total there were two fasts and four feasts per year during their time in exile. But once again Zechariah tells them that their feasts are far too self-centred. They were having a good time with food, friendship and fun, but God was not given the central place of celebration. They should make them truly holy days instead of holidays, and be thankful that God had brought them back to the land to praise him. 'Don't just have a holiday or a bank holiday – have a celebration of the fact that God has been faithful to you, that you are back in the holy mountain, that the streets are full of young people and elderly people again. Rejoice that God is going to bring more back and repopulate the whole land. That is what you should be doing with your feasts.'

Zechariah also tells them that they need to be ready for the fact that many more people are going to come to them because, as Jews, they know God. He is saying there will come a time when people will come and seize the robe of a Jew and ask him to explain who God is.

Future predictions (chapters 9–14)

The second half of the book is more complicated, because now Zechariah turns away from the present situation and looks into the distant future. What he says could fit any time centuries ahead, and it is not in any particular order – rather like a jigsaw, with pieces of different shapes and sizes. You don't know where they fit and, without a picture on the lid, you are really lost. It reminds me of the beginning of the Letter to the Hebrews, where it says, 'God spoke to our fathers in the old days through the prophets in various ways (or in bits and pieces), but now he has spoken to us through his Son.' Jesus is the picture on the lid. Through him we can begin to fit all the pieces together and know how it is all going to turn out. This is why the Book of Revelation alludes to Zechariah so extensively, because it is able to fit these pieces into the picture of the distant future or 'the end times', the time when history reaches its final countdown. It is Jesus who will break the seals on the scroll at the countdown of history, and so we have a great advantage over the Jews who read this book but can't see how it comes together.

There is a distinct change in style and content in the second half of the book. And for the first time in the prophecy, part of it is written in poetry. There is no mention of the contemporary situation or the temple or Joshua or Zerubbabel. There are no visions and even God's name changes, from 'the Lord of Hosts' ('Yahweh of heaven's armies') to just 'Yahweh'. It has a totally different feel – so different that some scholars say it must have been someone else who wrote it. Some scholars are very rigid in their ideas. But in fact the second bit is different because God gave it to Zechariah in a different way. These passages are not dated, so we don't know when they were given to him; it may have been years later.

As for the content, the prophecies are called 'oracles'. The Hebrew word is literally 'heavy' or 'weighty', but it is usually translated as 'oracle', though I don't think that quite conveys the true meaning. It is a 'heavy burden'. If the Lord has given you a heavy burden, you will know what I am talking about. Something is heavy on your heart until you share it, and once you have shared it, it lightens. You know when the burden is delivered.

The second half of the book includes two such burdens. One is covered by chapters 9–11 and the other by chapters 12–14, and they are very different.

National (chapters 9–11)

In chapters 9–11 the focus is on the people of Israel. There is no indication as to when these things will happen or even if they are in the right order. It is interesting that Ephraim is also mentioned. This was the name given to the 10 northern tribes, and suggests that they are not forgotten by God, even though they never returned from exile in Assyria.

There are six pictures that are part of this future, though it is impossible to relate them to each other.

VANQUISHED ENEMIES (9:1–8)

The first picture is that Israel's enemies will be vanquished. Syria, Tyre, Sidon and the Philistines all receive specific mention. God will deal with all those who have come against Jerusalem. He will not allow Jerusalem ever to be wiped off the map. It is his city, and it's where he has put his name. Therefore I can guarantee that even if New York, Beijing, Washington DC and New Delhi are wiped off the map, Jerusalem will still be there. There will always be Jewish survivors to be integrated into the land. He even says that some Philistines will join them. Since modern-day Palestinians call themselves descendants of the Philistines, it is an intriguing promise, and there will come a day when never again will there be an oppressor to run over God's people. It is just a piece of the picture, and we don't know at what date it will be fulfilled, but God keeps his promises, even if he waits centuries to do so.

A PEACEFUL KING (9:9–10)

The second picture is of a king of peace riding to Jerusalem on a donkey. We know how this fits the picture, because Jesus did exactly that, though the tragedy is that when Jesus fulfilled this prophecy they didn't notice the donkey. They thought he was riding on a donkey because he couldn't get a horse, and so they completely missed the symbolic message. When Jesus rode in on a donkey the people waved their palm leaves and threw their coats down, shouting 'Hosanna! Hosanna!' It is not a kind of heavenly 'Hello', as some seem to think, but rather it means 'Liberate us now!' It is a cry of people who have been oppressed for centuries, but see political autonomy coming near. They even call him 'Son of David' in the expectation that he will set them free.

But he wasn't coming to fight for them. Had he wanted to come and fight for their liberation, he would have ridden a horse, as he will at his second coming. So they received the biggest shock of their lives when he went through the gate in Jerusalem and turned left instead of right. Instead of heading to the Fortress Antonia where the troops had their headquarters, he grabbed a whip and turned left into the temple, where he whipped the Jews out of God's temple. I am not surprised that a few days later they said, 'You can crucify that man – we prefer the freedom fighter!' The big irony of history is that the freedom fighter whom they chose had a most unusual name – Jesus Bar-abbas, which means 'Jesus, Son of the Father'. So on that day there were two men called Jesus, Son of the Father. Pilate said, 'Which Jesus, Son of the Father do you want? The man who won't fight for you or the man who will?' They preferred the fighter. But Malachi says that one day this Prince of Peace will come in judgement. He will bring righteousness and peace, and will have dominion from sea to sea.

A MIGHTY GOD (9:11–10:7)

Here we have a picture of the Lord appearing visibly to fight for Israel. It is a change from the previous picture, which depicts peace. We have here a Lord who will come for his flock and be a good shepherd to them, unlike the bad shepherds they have had. The picture includes the glorious description of a redeemed people who will sparkle like jewels in his crown.

The next oracle focuses on Greece. It would be centuries before the Greeks would come to conquer the land, headed by the evil Antiochus Epiphanes IV. He raised the statue of Zeus in the temple in Jerusalem, slaughtered a pig on the altar and filled the vestries with prostitutes. It was one of the worst periods in history and lasted exactly three and a half years – that is, 42 months or 1,260 days, which is exactly the period predicted concerning the antichrist in the New Testament. Under Antiochus Epiphanes the Jews suffered what Christians will suffer under the antichrist. It is intriguing that the rise of Greece should be predicted in this third little piece of the picture. We can grasp what is going on now, but it is hard to see what they must have made of it at the time.

A GATHERED PEOPLE (10:8–12)

The next picture is of gathered people – a reversal of the Diaspora, with Jews brought from every nation to their land. Indeed, the present-day people of Israel have come from over 80 nations, so they have brought the music and dances of 70 nations. This is a picture of the gathered people coming home, and Zechariah says there will not be enough room for them. It even says that a highway will be built between Egypt and Assyria.

DEFORESTED NEIGHBOURS (11:1–3)

The next picture is a puzzling one. The neighbours of Judah are being deforested – the cedars of Lebanon, the oaks of Trans-Jordan or Bashan and even the jungle of Jordan. Today, the jungle of Jordan has largely gone and there is just a small area of cedar trees in Lebanon. The oak trees of Bashan have also gone. It is unclear why this oracle is given.

WORTHLESS SHEPHERDS (11:4–17)

The picture of worthless shepherds is even more puzzling. It is conveyed by an acted parable, with Zechariah taking a job as a foreman shepherd. He has to sack three shepherds for not looking after the sheep. They throw their wages back at him – 30 pieces of silver. The text says, 'When the shepherd is smitten, the sheep are scattered.' Once again we have parts of a picture, and yet we can see where they fit in when we read the Gospels. Judas threw his 30 pieces of silver back into the temple because he was a bad shepherd, though he had been both a preacher and a healer. Jesus used the quote of the shepherd being smitten and the sheep being scattered to refer to himself when his disciples fled at his arrest in the Garden of Gethsemane.

The shepherds' staffs are broken, the first 'favour' revoking the covenant that God had made with the nations, and the second 'union' breaking the brotherhood between Judah and Israel.

International (chapters 12–14)

The second series of pictures is international. They show us what will happen on an international basis, with Jerusalem at the heart of the action. On 21 occasions we find the name Jerusalem in this section. It is as if Jerusalem is going to be the focus of the future. This is where the United Nations headquarters will have to be moved to – here is a picture of Zion as the centre of world government.

One phrase is used frequently in this section: 'on that day' occurs 18 times, with 'day' itself another two times, though it has not been used before in the prophecy. The word also occurs frequently in the New Testament, especially on the lips of Jesus. This 'day' is not a 24-hour day. The Hebrew word *yom* can mean anything from a 24-hour period to a whole era.

We use the word 'day' in the same way in English. If I say, 'The day of the horse and cart has gone and the day of the tractor has come', I am not talking about 24-hour days at all, but about an era. There will come a day of the Lord when the whole world will see that it is God's day, that the day of man's pride and greed is over, that the day of God's holiness is here.

Only one section in chapter 13 is poetry, and the word 'day' doesn't appear in that part, interestingly enough. Once again the order of the prophecies is not in sequence, and 12:3 and 14:2 probably refer to the same event.

AN INVADING ARMY (12:1–9)

The first is a picture of an international United Nations force attacking Jerusalem. An army gathered from the entire nations of the world is sent to the Middle East. This hasn't happened yet, but it is a piece of the jigsaw. Jerusalem has yet to be attacked in that way, so it is clear that the difficulties that Israel is facing on the international stage will continue. We may live to see this United Nations force sent to attack the Jews. They have very few friends left at the United Nations, and America, their major friend, is now beginning to turn against them.

GRIEVING INHABITANTS (12:10–14)

The next picture is of grieving inhabitants. There will come a day when the people of Jerusalem are so desperate that they will not try and make peace treaties with Palestinians or anyone else, but will cry to God. God's answer will be to send 'him whom they pierced' – Jesus Christ. Can you imagine how the Jews will feel when they realize that Jesus was their Messiah and they killed him? They will weep as if their eldest son had been murdered.

It is Zechariah who first said that the Jews will actually see 'him whom they pierced'. In fact, that very phrase is taken up in the first chapter of the Book of Revelation, where we are told that when Jesus comes back, those who pierced him will see him. The only thing needed to convert a Jew is to know that Jesus of Nazareth is alive. That was all it took for Saul of Tarsus, and that is all it takes today.

It will be painful for them to look back on 2,000 wasted years, when they could have been leading the world and yet have been hounded from one country to another, as the Book of Deuteronomy said they would be. No wonder they will weep.

BANISHED PROPHETS (13:1-6)

Zechariah has a vivid vision of false prophets. They have been amongst the greatest dangers that Jerusalem ever faced. Jerusalem is going to be cleansed of all such people, along with the idolatry and false gods. It says they will be cleansed of sin and washed from all impurity by a fountain of water. He goes on to talk about Zion being cleansed from sin, and the false prophets then will be so ashamed and so disgraced that they will disown their profession. Prophets with visible wounds, previously seen as a badge of honour, will claim that they were made in a pub brawl! It is a vivid story of people ashamed of giving false teaching.

A REDUCED POPULATION (13:7-9)

The next picture is of a reduced population. But this passage is clearly not in order, for here Jerusalem is said to be reduced to one third of its population, while in the next section (14:2) it is reduced to a half! It seems to be a throwback to the text about the shepherd being smitten and the sheep scattered. I am not sure where this fits; it could be future or past. We will have to wait and see. What is clear is that the third who are left will be a remnant refined by God.

PLAGUED ATTACKERS (14:1–15)

In chapter 14 we return to this international attack on Jerusalem. It is not clear whether this is the same attack as in 12:1–8, but I believe this is definitely in the future. God will gather this huge military force, and yet he will also fight for the Jews. It is clearly linked closely to the second coming and probably to the battle of Armageddon, because here we have the statement, 'and his feet shall stand on the Mount of Olives'. God hasn't got feet, but Jesus has, and this is interpreted by all Jews as the coming of the Messiah.

We are told there will be a great eruption, which will cause amazing geophysical changes to the whole area. I assume we have to take it literally, even though it boggles the imagination. Jerusalem is down in a hollow surrounded by mountains; there are eight peaks around Jerusalem. It is an amazing geometrical landscape – the east face of the Dome of the Rock faces the Mount of Olives, the north-east faces Mount Scopus, the south faces the Mount of Condemnation. We read that when his feet stand on the Mount of Olives, the peaks will shake and go down, and Jerusalem will be left on the peak! Jerusalem will at last be the high place.

This is all part of the picture. Our imagination finds it quite difficult to fit it all in, but the main point of this picture is that the United Nations force around the city will be dealt with. Those who have come to attack Jerusalem in the final battle will be held, 'their eyes will rot in their sockets and their tongues will rot in their mouths, and in panic they will kill each other.' Not surprisingly, the people of God will then say, 'The Lord is our God.'

UNIVERSAL WORSHIP (14:16-21)

Finally, there is a picture of all the nations seeing Jerusalem as the place of God's name, with all the nations of the world observing the Feast of Tabernacles. It is the one feast that Christians ignore. We observe Passover, in a sense, with Easter. We observe Pentecost with Whit Sunday, but Tabernacles? For the Jew this is the greatest feast, celebrated in September/October. It is their Harvest Festival. They live in little booths open to the sky so that they can see the skies and remember how God brought them through the wilderness. It is an eight-day feast, and the final day is a wedding day. On this day they 'get married to the Law'. There is a wedding canopy and a rabbi with a scroll of the Law of Moses standing under the canopy. They all dance round and they get married to the Law of Moses for another year. They start reading Genesis 1 the next morning, and they read through until they read the last verse in Deuteronomy, 12 months later. Then they get married to the Law again. But they have got the wrong bridegroom, because that eighth day of the Feast of Tabernacles looks forward to the marriage supper of the Messiah, the marriage supper of the Lamb.

This reminds us that the whole Bible is a romance. It tells how a father found a bride for his son, and it finishes up with them getting married and living happily ever after. All good romances finish with a marriage, and the Bible is no exception! This marriage is on the eighth day of this feast, referred to in Revelation as the marriage supper of the Lamb. Jesus was born during the Feast of Tabernacles – the clues are all there in Luke's Gospel. He was born in September or early October in the seventh month, the month of the Feast of Tabernacles. We read in John's opening chapter that 'the Word became flesh and tabernacled among us.' In John 7 Jesus' brother sarcastically asks him whether he was attending the Feast of

Tabernacles, because that is when they were expecting the Messiah. They didn't believe in him and they were teasing him, but he said, 'My time has not yet come.'

Therefore of one thing I feel quite sure – I know the month when Jesus will come back. I don't know the year, but he must come back on time. It will be during the Feast of Tabernacles. Indeed, many Jews believe that the Messiah will come during the Feast of Tabernacles, on the basis of Zechariah 14. From then on nations will celebrate the feast annually and will send representatives to Jerusalem. We are told that if they don't attend, their country will get no rain. So the Feast of Tabernacles has become for Jews, and now for an increasing number of Christians, a focal point of the hope for a universal reign of the Messiah over the whole world.

Christian fulfilment

Having looked at the pieces of the jigsaw, we must now build the picture. We must remember that what the prophets saw may bear no relation to the timing of events. Things that looked close to one another may well be hundreds or thousands of years apart. It is clear that many of the events described refer to the two comings of Jesus Christ.

The first coming

Jesus was born at the Feast of Tabernacles. He came to Jerusalem for the last time riding on a donkey. He was betrayed for 30 pieces of silver, and when the disciples fled at the trial of Jesus, the Gospel writers quoted the verse, 'When the shepherd was struck, the sheep were scattered.'

The second coming

There is a close link with the Book of Revelation. We are told that the feet of Jesus will stand on the Mount of Olives. There are strong indications that his return will be at the Feast of Tabernacles. Revelation reminds us that when Jesus comes again, the Jewish nation will 'look upon him whom they pierced'.

Unfulfilled prophecy

Zechariah, along with other Old Testament prophecies, contains predictions that have not been fulfilled. The chart below gives the three broad explanations for this.

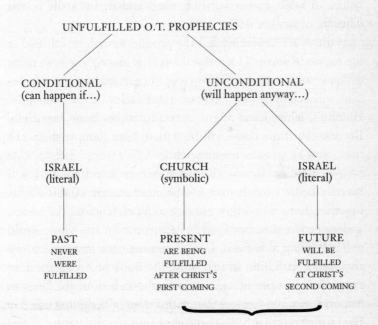

UNFULFILLED O.T. PROPHECIES

CONDITIONAL
(can happen if...)

UNCONDITIONAL
(will happen anyway...)

ISRAEL
(literal)

CHURCH
(symbolic)

ISRAEL
(literal)

PAST
NEVER
WERE
FULFILLED

PRESENT
ARE BEING
FULFILLED
AFTER CHRIST'S
FIRST COMING

FUTURE
WILL BE
FULFILLED
AT CHRIST'S
SECOND COMING

CONDITIONAL

Some say that the fulfilment was dependent upon the obedience of Israel. The key word was 'if'. Since Israel was disobedient, the prophecies are obsolete and are never going to be fulfilled. Hence there is no point in studying them because they are of no relevance today.

UNCONDITIONAL

Others see the prophecies as fulfilled in the Church. They see them fulfilled 'spiritually' – so the Church is the new Israel, victorious now and participating in the victories predicted for Israel. The problem with this view is that while the blessings are applied to the Church, the curses are not. So there is a failure in logic. Either both blessings and curses apply to the Church, or neither do.

Others are expectant that the prophecies will be fulfilled in the future. Romans 11 speaks of a revival among the Jews prior to the second coming. In this view, the survivors of the tribulation will celebrate the Feast of Tabernacles in the millennial kingdom, when Jesus reigns over all nations from Jerusalem. Beyond that time there will be a New Jerusalem, with the 12 tribes and 12 apostles prominent.

My opinion is that the prophecies not yet fulfilled will literally come true. It may not be clear exactly how it all fits together, but we do know enough to be clear about the basics, and we can be sure that God has a purpose for the whole world and it is going to happen. Jesus is coming back to reign and we shall reign with him. In that sense the Book of Zechariah does not end on a note of sadness with the failure of the Jews to respond, as some suppose, but with a note of hope that one day God will do all that he has promised.

35.

MALACHI

Introduction

The background to the Book of Malachi is very similar to that of Haggai and Zechariah. It was written 100 years after the return of Judah from exile in Babylon. Things were not good; Jerusalem was still relatively deserted and the farmland was largely barren and uncultivated. Recent harvests had been poor and swarms of locusts and lack of food made life hard and precarious. The temple had been finished in 520 BC, but it was so small compared to Solomon's that it had done little to lift morale. Although Nehemiah had repaired the walls, the people still preferred living out in the country, where they could more easily hide from attack. They had not built a palace because they didn't have a king – although Zerubbabel, their governor, was a rightful heir in the royal line of David. So Judah now comprised a small hill town and some surrounding villages – a pale reflection of the kingdom of David in its heyday. The people were disappointed, disillusioned and even despairing. They were beginning to ask whether it had been worthwhile returning to Judah at all. They said, 'We've been back 100 years, and where's this kingdom we were going to build?'

There was just one piece of good news – they had learned their lesson about idolatry in the exile. Never again did they go after other gods or seek to change their religion. But having said that, the practice of this religion had become a formality.

The people attended the temple, but it was largely out of tradition – a ritual without reality, and certainly no longer a priority. They were now asking what was the minimum amount of time they needed to spend on religious activity, and what was the minimum amount of money they could get away with. Furthermore, the priests were like the people. They were not bothered about how many people came to attend the services, as long as they just got through it and made their living. The services were conducted in a casual and careless manner, as if anything would do for God.

With this attitude in the religious life, it was no surprise that it affected their moral life too. When people question the purpose of bothering about God, it's not long before they stop bothering to be godly. Or to put it more simply, when one generation is asking, 'Why bother about God?' the next generation will be asking, 'Why be good?'

So, for example, even though they knew that trading on the Sabbath was wrong, they built their equivalent of out-of-town supermarkets just outside the gates so they could open them on the Sabbath. Consumerism took over, with a devastating effect on family life. The question, 'Why be faithful to God?' soon became 'Why be faithful to your wife?' – especially when your wife gets older and loses her sex appeal. Why not trade her in for a newer model?!

Furthermore, the nation was short of women following the return from Babylon, so they were marrying outside of the people of God. Not only were they divorcing and remarrying, but also they were remarrying non-Jewish women, in contravention of the Law of God. The city of Jerusalem was being filled with abandoned wives and, since there was no welfare state, widows, orphans and abandoned wives had an especially hard time.

They didn't have a government to blame but they did have a God to blame, which is precisely what they did. They said,

'God's not bothered about us, so we're not bothered about him.' It sounded very impressive. 'God has stopped loving us, so we've just stopped loving him. We can't believe in a God of love – just look at the situation we're in. We have to look after ourselves. He's abandoned us, so we might as well just look after number one.'

Their criticism of God had two sides to it. On the one hand they said, 'God doesn't reward good living', and on the other hand, 'He doesn't punish bad living. So why bother?'

This was the situation that Malachi had to deal with. His whole prophecy was in prose, not poetry – an indication that God had lost his feelings for his people – so much so that he wouldn't talk to them again for another 400 years! This was his last word, and a very cool word at that.

Unique features

The Book of Malachi has five unique features:

1 There is more of God's speech in Malachi than in any other of the prophetic books. Of its 55 verses, 47 (i.e. 85 per cent) are the direct words of God.

2 This prophecy is anonymous. Most people think that 'Malachi' is the name of the author, but it's not actually a name at all. It simply means 'messenger'. 'Malachi' is never used as a name anywhere else in the Old Testament, but it's frequently used to mean 'messenger'. So he's just an anonymous messenger, a 'nobody' who brings God's last word to his people in Israel. The Jews suspected that the author was Ezra, but we have no evidence to decide one way or another.

3 Malachi is unusual in that he is the one prophet who had dialogues with people. It is clear that he spoke the prophecy

and was heckled, because he reports the heckling. His hearers were offended by his preaching because his basic message was, 'You started all this! It was not God who stopped being bothered about you. You did it first. If you stop bothering about God, he won't be bothered about you.' In Romans in the New Testament, the apostle Paul explains that men gave God up, so God gave men up. In the same way, when a nation gives God up, he gives them up. So the prophecy takes the form of sharp exchanges between the prophet and the people. On 12 occasions he says, 'But you say …' – implying interruption of one sort or another.

4 This is prose, not poetry, because God's feelings have dried up. God feels exhausted by his people and therefore won't talk to them for another 400 years. So we see God's heart here. Wouldn't you be fed up if, having taken them to exile and brought them home, they now can't be bothered about you?

5 The fifth feature is that this is God's last word. Perhaps the Christian order of the books in the Old Testament is right after all. (The Hebrew Scriptures finish with Chronicles.) This was God's last message to them, and the last word in it was 'curse'. To this day, whenever the Jews read Malachi in the synagogue they do not read the last verse: 'lest he smite the land with a curse'. Instead they return to verse 5 so that they don't end with the word 'curse'. They refuse to end with God's last word.

An outline of the book

Past survival (1:1–5)
Jacob – Israel – loved – persevered
Esau – Edom – hated – destroyed

Present sins (1:6–3:15)

Priests (1:6–2:9)

Cheap sacrifices

Popular sermons

People (2:10–3:15)

Mixed marriages

Heartless divorces

Doubtful questions

Unpaid tithes

Slanderous talk

Future separation (3:16–4:6)

Right choice

Righteous – healing in the sun

Wicked – burning in the fire

Last chance

Moses – lawgiver – remember

Elijah – forerunner – recognize

Past survival (1:1–5)

To understand the first verses in the book we must go back 1,500 years. Malachi announces that God loved Jacob and hated Esau – the twins whose attitudes towards each other had not been good. It seems a strange statement to our ears. It is important to realize that in the Bible the words 'loved' and 'hated' do not mean what they mean in English. To love someone is to care for them and seek their highest good. To hate someone in biblical language is not to care for someone and not to seek his or her good. So when Jesus said, 'You're not worthy to follow me if you don't hate your father and mother', he wasn't meaning that his hearers must have bitterness and resentment towards them, but rather that they should care for him more than them.

Furthermore, God is not just talking about Jacob and Esau in the past but about the two nations of Israel and Edom in Malachi's day. He's reminding them that over the previous 100 years he has done nothing but good for Israel and has punished Edom. When the Babylonians came to take the Jews into exile, the Edomites – the descendants of Esau living over the Jordan – were delighted and joined in. Their cry was, 'Hooray! They're finished!' They joined in the horrific destruction, taking the babies of the Jews by the heels and bashing their brains out against the Jerusalem wall.

Since that day Edom had been under God's judgement. It came over a long period of time. God threw them out of their home city of Petra by bringing the Arabs against them. They were forced to scratch a living in the Negev desert, where there were no crops.

So in Malachi, God told Israel that he had done all this to Edom because of what they had done to the Jews. 'I have loved you and I haven't cared for them.' Malachi is asking them to think about their survival in comparison to Edom, and to be grateful to God. The lesson is clear. When we complain to God, we should think about what he's done to other people and reflect on what he's done for us, and be grateful.

Behind all of Malachi's preaching there is a particular idea of God that we do well to grasp. He sees God in three functions, as the whole Old Testament does – areas easily forgotten by those who don't read the Old Testament. We read the New Testament and think God is the loving Father, but these three dimensions of God as seen in the Old Testament are vital. He is the Creator in our past, the King in our present and the Judge of our future. We must remember this framework when we approach issues concerning God.

Present sins (1:6–3:15)

Priests (1:6–2:9)

The first people whom Malachi attacks are the priests. God is seen as Father and as Master and should be respected. Instead, they were treating God with contempt. Too often in church services God is treated with familiarity rather than with reverence and respect. Here he tells the priests that they are bringing God into disrepute and dishonour. Once again the people respond by asking 'How?' He replies with two instances:

CHEAP SACRIFICES

Firstly, the people were offering cheap sacrifices. Instead of choosing the best lamb, as detailed in the Law of Moses, they were choosing the worst – blind and crippled animals – to offer to God. Malachi points out that in not offering to God the best, they were doing less than they would for the Persian governor. 'You give God what's left over. You give someone else the best you can give!'

Secondly, he tells them that God's name is great among the nations but not among them, so that the Gentiles have more reverence for God than they do. The message is quite devastating.

POPULAR SERMONS

Next he condemns the priests for telling the people what they want to hear rather than teaching them the Law. They were supposed to be God-fearers, not men-pleasers. Here again is a fundamental temptation and pressure on those who serve God in the Church. It's so easy to give people what they want to hear and not to disturb them. If they are disturbed, you know you won't be invited back!

Malachi reminds them of God's covenant with Levi back at the time of Moses, when the priests were told that they wouldn't need to work for pay, but would be supported by the others, provided that they taught people to fear the Lord. But now they were not teaching people to fear the Lord. The Levitical priests were told that people must be able to see godly lives and not just hear their words. Their lips and their lives must be giving the same message. So he tells them they are already under a curse and there is worse to come. Many of their children will die and the priesthood will come to an end if this behaviour continues.

People (2:10–3:15)

Next Malachi focused on the people. There were five things which showed that both their belief and their behaviour were slipping.

MIXED MARRIAGES

The young people were marrying outside of the people of God. Throughout Israel's history as a nation, God had insisted that the people must marry from within the nation. This practice is also happening in the Church. If you marry a child of the devil, you're going to have problems with your father-in-law! – quite apart from a lifetime of great unhappiness.

HEARTLESS DIVORCE

The second problem was what we might term 'heartless' divorce. Some practised consecutive polygamy. Simultaneous polygamy is where men have more wives than one at the same time; consecutive polygamy is where they have as many wives as they want, provided they have them one at a time. This is another practice that has become all too common within the Church. But it hurt God, because every marriage is made in

God's sight – whether it's in a registry office or a church. So every marriage comes under the Law of God. God's Law, according to Jesus, is that consecutive polygamy amounts to adultery – though it would seem that most preachers today are frightened of saying so. Malachi had faced this, and we have to face it too, but it's probably the most unpopular thing to face in today's Church. God simply says, 'I hate divorce.'

DOUBTFUL QUESTIONS

When God accused the people of breaking the covenant, they replied, 'But how are we breaking it?' He replied that they were breaking the covenant with each other by marrying outside the people of God.

They thought they were innocent and didn't like this preacher accusing them. People don't mind you making general statements, but when you spell it out in particular ways, it hurts. Malachi explained that this was wearying God. He was effectively saying, 'You're saying, "How can you believe in a God of love when this is happening?" How dare you ask such questions! You ask, "Where is the justice of God?" How dare you ask that question. Judgement will come, although it may not come immediately, because God is patient with us. But don't ever accuse God of being unfair and of being indifferent to bad things going on.'

As if this wasn't bad enough, Malachi shocked the people by telling them that when God came to punish bad people, he would start in his temple. They were crying out to God to deal with bad people, but when he came it would be them that he would deal with! The priests would be the first to be judged, and then the people.

He lists the people who don't fear God: sorcerers, adulterers, perjurers, those who are defrauding labourers of their wages, those who deliberately withhold payment of bills, those who oppress widows and the fatherless, and those who deprive foreigners of justice. It's pretty direct talking.

At this point there's a definite change of tone. It is as if God speaks from his heart. He explains that the fact that the people are not destroyed is part of his mercy. While Judah has a long history of unfaithfulness, he still remains faithful. They may break his covenant, but he will remain committed to them. God is saying, 'Return to me and I will return to you.' It is true that when we get away from God he gets away from us, but when we return to him he returns to us! God is in a dynamic two-way relationship with his people, and he responds to them all the time. God is constantly meeting us where we are, responding to us, reflecting our attitude to him. Some people think of God as sitting way up in heaven far away, and making decrees and pushing us around like puppets – but that's not the Bible picture. The Bible shows God as one who is responding to us all the time, who changes his mind when we change, who repents when we repent, who returns to us when we return to him. It's a dynamic relationship.

UNPAID TITHES

Next Malachi tells them that they are stealing from God. Once again the people question the suggestion, asking 'How? We've never stolen from God.' Again the reply is sharp: 'You have left unpaid tithes and offerings.'

Malachi effectively pins them to the ground and they object. He explains that they have not kept up the 10 per cent tithe to God or the voluntary offerings, and so are under a curse because of the law of tithing. The Law of Moses says that if you pay, God blesses you, and if you don't, he curses you to the third and fourth generation.

Christians are not, of course, under that law. I have never preached tithing in my life! I've preached *giving*, because in the

New Testament we're to give out of gratitude – the Lord does not want your gift if you don't want to give it! But in the Old Testament they had to tithe. Preaching tithing today will always cause problems. My wife and I once listened to a young man in a church preaching on tithing. Most who do this focus on the blessings and miss out the curses, but at least he was consistent. But the message was appalling. He told the congregation that if they didn't tithe, their grandchildren and great-grandchildren would suffer; that God would punish those who broke the tithing law to the third and fourth generation. They would be under a curse.

So when they came to take up the offering, they took the largest amount for years – which was hardly surprising. But afterwards I told the leaders of that church that it was wicked teaching, for it makes people give out of fear. The Lord loves a cheerful giver, and we give under the new covenant of grace. For some people tithing would be far too little and for others it would be far too much, and we need to be much more flexible.

But Malachi could legitimately say that the people were already under a curse because they hadn't brought the tithes. If they wanted to know blessing again they would need to bring all the tithes into the Lord's storehouse, and God would open the windows of heaven and pour out such a blessing as could not be contained. The context of this promise suggests that he literally meant clouds and rain to end the drought.

SLANDEROUS TALK

Malachi continued his condemnation by accusing the people of slanderous talk. Once again they responded by asking how they had slandered God. Malachi said that it was the way they had denigrated the service of God, claiming that there was no point, because even evildoers prospered. In so doing they claimed that God wasn't Lord and didn't know what he was doing.

Did all this have any effect? Was Malachi as effective a preacher as Haggai and Zechariah had been? Did the people respond? The answer is that some did – they discussed the message and they repented. They owned up to their responsibilities and put things right. God even wrote down in a book the names of those who were fervent in their response.

Future separation (3:16–4:6)

In the final section Malachi outlined the separation within the people of God. He said that within Israel there was coming a day when they would be divided into two. The prophets called it 'the day of the Lord'. It is mentioned in other prophets such as Zechariah, Amos and Joel. It's a day of reckoning, of settling accounts and of judgement. On that day there will only be two groups: those who serve God and those who don't.

This passage includes a lovely description of life for the righteous. I used to get up at four in the morning to milk 90 cows on a farm in Northumberland. During the winter we kept the cattle indoors and fed them on cake and hay for months. Then came the day when we let them out for the first time in the spring. If you know anything about country life, you know what happened next. Even the oldest cow gambolled like a lamb. Large, lumbering cows would jump around the field for joy. Malachi says this is how it will be for the people of God. They too will leap for joy on the day when God comes to bring final salvation to his people.

Those who are rejected on that day are described as 'like stubble burned after harvest'. In the days when this was legal in the UK, all that would be left was ash. Just as the calves leaping in a green field under the sun is a picture of the righteous, the ashes of stubble is a picture of those who have not responded to God. There are three things we must note at this point.

1 Israel as a people will survive. Malachi said on behalf of God, 'I don't change. I don't go back on my word.' So we can be sure that there will always be an Israel.
2 But it is also clear that some in Israel will be lost. Obviously, not every Jew who has ever lived will be saved, nor does it mean that the Jews do not need the gospel.
3 There are statements that some outside Israel will be saved. Malachi says there will be those among the nations who will be part of the righteous, so we have hints of what would come in the New Testament.

Postscript (4:4–6)

The last three verses are built around the two greatest men in the Old Testament – Moses and Elijah. This is God's last appeal to his people of Israel in the Old Testament – his last word for 400 years, before the opening of the New.

God calls the people to remember Moses and return to the Law, for God is their great king. Then he says that God will give them another chance. He will send one more prophet to them – an Elijah figure who will come to challenge them. Elijah was the first major prophet to challenge the idolatry and immorality of Israel, while Moses was the prophet who led them out of Egypt and who gave them the Covenant and the Law.

So the Old Testament closes with these words: 'If they don't listen to Elijah, then the land will be smitten with a curse.' They would get one last chance before the day of the Lord – one more prophet to prepare the way of the Lord. For over 400 years they waited for that to happen. They were occupied by Persians, Egyptians, Syrians, Greeks and Romans, and finally the chance came. Suddenly there was a man dressed like Elijah, eating locusts and wild honey, just like Elijah. The country flocked to hear this man who preached the message that Malachi said he would preach. He called people back to wisdom and back to family life. But he'd only come as a fore-runner to prepare the way for the Lord Jesus.

When you turn to the New Testament you find that there was a great debate about whether John the Baptist was Elijah. On two occasions, Jesus said that Elijah was his cousin John (Matthew 11:7–14; 17:9–13). So Malachi and Matthew go side by side in our Bible. Matthew tells us how Elijah did come in the person of John the Baptist. He deliberately wore the clothes of Elijah and ate the food of Elijah. This was the revelation of God's next move. When Jesus reached a watershed after two and a half years of his ministry and took the disciples to the foot of Mount Hermon and asked, 'Who do people think I am?' they said, 'Well, some think you're a reincarnation of Jeremiah or somebody else.' But Jesus asked who they thought he was. Peter saw the truth and said, 'Well, you have lived before, haven't you? But not down here – you've lived up there. You're the Christ, the Son of the living God.' Then Jesus took Peter, James and John up the mountain, and Moses and Elijah appeared and talked to Jesus. Malachi promised it, and it all came together.

Christian application

1 We are told in 1 Corinthians 10 that all these Old Testament examples are written for the use of Christians. What happened to the Jewish nation can easily happen to us. Apathy, disbelief, immorality and heartlessness can afflict the Christian believer too.

2 We must let the New Testament interpret the Old. We are not under Sabbath or tithing laws, but we are under the Law of Christ, which is stricter than the Law of Moses on divorce and remarriage, and on many other issues.

3 On the other hand, we must not be libertine in the way we treat God's grace. Too many Christians effectively lose the fear of God – if we do that, we have not fully grasped the gospel of Christ.

4 We must remember that judgement begins at the house of God. The New Testament writers follow the same pattern as Malachi when it comes to judgement. When God comes to judge, he first judges his people and then he judges everybody else. There will be a separation even of people in church. We mustn't be complacent, assuming that because we made a decision for Christ in the past we are OK. We must be eager to 'make our calling and election sure' and to persevere in the things of God, if we do not want to face the judgement that came on the people of Malachi's day.

II
NEW
TESTAMENT

THE
HINGE OF
HISTORY

36.

THE GOSPELS

Introduction

The Bible is a library of books written by 40 different authors over 1,400 years. God did not choose to give us a compendium of texts with chapter and verse numbers, nor did he provide books of doctrine arranged systematically. Instead he gave us a library of **different types of literature**, as diverse as poetry and history, letters and revelation, in three different languages – mainly Greek and Hebrew, with a little Aramaic.

Variety

This library reflects the **unique personalities and perspectives** of the various authors, just as any two books in a public library would be unique according to the personalities of the writers. It is important to remember that the Holy Spirit, the divine 'editor' of the Bible, did not treat the authors as word processors, communicating his truth but bypassing their minds and hearts. He was the ultimate author, yet at the same time the individuals themselves were free to communicate in their own way. Indeed, few of the authors knew that what they wrote would one day be declared part of Holy Scripture.

With this in mind, apparent contradictions within the Bible can be often settled by examining the **authors' intentions**.

Take, for example, the controversy concerning Paul's assertion that we are saved by faith and not works, and James' teaching in his Epistle on the need for works. When Paul dealt with the subject of faith in Romans he anticipated a different set of questions and concerns than James. Paul is concerned that we do not seek to be saved by our works, James that works accompany faith and thus show it to be genuine.

Unity

In spite of this variety, the Bible demonstrates at the same time its divine authorship. There is one overall theme: the **unfolding drama of redemption**, which runs from Genesis to Revelation. Genesis 1–3 and Revelation 21–22 have remarkable similarities, despite being written 1,400 years apart, wonderfully reflecting God's hand. It is possible to recognize the unity of the Bible without assuming that this must also mean uniformity. Just as God is one but three persons, so his Word reflects both unity and diversity.

Approaches to Bible study

We need to bear these aspects in mind whenever we come to study the Bible. Two approaches are equally important:

1. Variety: analysing a book and seeing its **differences** from other books.
2. Unity: noting its **similarities** with other books, and how it fits into the whole.

Those with a liberal view of the Bible tend to focus on the variety, denying claims to unity. Those with an evangelical view focus on the unity, fearful that to focus on variety may reveal contradictions.

It is necessary to retain a balance between acknowledging the divine authorship and inherent unity of the Bible, and at the same time looking at each book as the work of a human being writing for a particular purpose. If we just focus on the divine authorship, we may unwittingly gain a wrong perspective on a vital area of truth, failing to notice the way in which different authors have treated a theme. We mistakenly treat the texts on any theme as if there is just one book with one message and one style, forgetting that God has used the unique situation of book and author to communicate his truth. On the other hand, if we just focus on the individuality of the book, we may forget that it is part of a library which God has put together, exhibiting a wonderful unity of theme and purpose.

The value of this approach is especially clear when we come to study the **Gospels**. At one level, there is a unity of theme as each writes of the good news of Jesus. They have the same time period, people and places on which to report, but each has a **particular focus and audience** in mind. This is especially the case with John's Gospel, as it stands apart so distinctly from the other three 'synoptics', which hold so much in common. As we look specifically at these differences, John's particular flavour will become apparent.

The Gospels

The Gospels are the nearest thing we have to a biography of Jesus, covering his life, death and resurrection. What few realize, however, is that they are written in a unique style, one which was previously unheard of in the first century and which has no modern literary counterpart. Careful readers will know that to interpret the Gospels properly they will need to see each verse in its immediate context *and* in the context of the

book as a whole. This creates problems if they do not understand the *style* of literature they are reading. We need to clarify
what kind of a book a 'Gospel' is before looking at them in
individual detail.

What is a Gospel?

A Gospel is certainly not an autobiography, since Jesus never
wrote any books, but it is not a straight biography either,
because over one-third of the pages of each Gospel describe
the death of Jesus. No biography would spend a third of its
pages on its subject's death, however spectacular or tragic that
death may be. Perhaps the best comparison with modern life is
not from the literary world at all, but from the world of the
media. A Gospel is like a **news bulletin**.

The English word 'gospel' is an Anglo-Saxon version of
the Greek word *evangelion*, which was used in New Testament
times to describe the announcement of shattering news by an
emissary sent around the towns and villages of an area. The
defeat of an enemy or the death of an emperor would be typical
examples. In the same way a Gospel is a news announcement
which conveys straight away that this is exciting news to share.
The implication is that the world will never be the same again
once this news is heard.

Just as news is generally read aloud to hearers, so the
Gospels were intended to be read aloud (in common with the
rest of the New Testament). We can derive much benefit today
if we too read them aloud (even just to ourselves) as well as
silently.

Why were they written?

The reason for the Gospels being written in the form we have
them is clear. In the early decades following Christ's ascension
the Church grew in numbers and spread across the Roman

world as the apostles spread the gospel message. Thus many people wanted the 'news' from those who had seen the events of Jesus' life first-hand. It became imperative that the **witnesses** to what Jesus did and said wrote down **reliable accounts** of his life and times.

Why are there four?

The first thing that strikes many people is that there are four Gospels which overlap considerably in content and wording. To some people it seems superfluous that there should be four, especially if they are saying the same thing, as they appear to do. Would it not have been much more convenient if we only had one? Why could someone not get them together and produce just one volume, with each writer contributing their part?

This may seem a logical and sensible approach, but something important is lost whenever people attempt to harmonize the Gospels into one volume. God had a good reason for inspiring four Gospels, just as he had a good reason for duplicating other parts of Scripture. For example, there are two accounts of creation in Genesis 1 and 2 – one from God's viewpoint, one from man's. And there are two accounts of the history of Israel in Kings and Chronicles, written from completely different perspectives although covering the same time period. In the same way we have four accounts of Jesus' life and death because God wanted to give us a number of **different angles** in order for us to grasp the full picture.

If you wanted to take photographs to show someone the shape of the aeroplane Concorde, you would have to take at least four or five, otherwise they would never understand the whole concept because it looks so different from every angle. Similarly Jesus is the most amazing character who ever lived and so God inspired four people to look at him for us and to write down what they saw. The writers of the Gospels each wrote independently, with their own perspective on Jesus.

INSPIRATION

This perspective on how the Gospels came to be written shows us something important about the inspiration of Scripture. It underlines that the writers of the Bible were not 'word processors', writing words dictated directly from the mouth of God.* God intended to use individuals who could bring their own understanding of Jesus and convey his message with a particular aim in view. Yet at the same time, what they wrote is no less the Word of God, each word being inspired. It is both the words of man and the Word of God. Inspiration therefore includes the individuality of each author.

How are the Gospels different from one another?

When a famous figure dies there is typically a series of different types of writing which follow his death.

1. The first publications usually tell us **what the person did**; early obituaries fulfil this aim.
2. Later people become more interested in **what the person said**, and so begin to publish collections of letters and speeches.
3. Then comes the third stage, which looks behind the words and deeds to discover **what the person was**, examining character, motivation and what they were really like.

The four Gospels follow these three stages quite markedly, as the table on pages 786–787 demonstrates. Mark is most concerned with what Jesus did, focusing on his actions, miracles, death and resurrection. Matthew and Luke both include far more about what Jesus said, recording more of his preaching

---

* Some parts of Genesis and Revelation are an exception to this and bear the marks of having been given directly in verbal form.

than Mark does. John, however, is not just interested in what Jesus did, nor does he focus on what he said. His supreme concern is with Jesus' identity, with who he was. While the Gospels are distinctive as forms of literature, they do encompass a wide range of reflection on Jesus, providing an all-round view and giving the reader a comprehensive understanding.

How to study the Gospels

Having noted the distinctiveness of the Gospels as a form of literature, there are two levels on which we can approach them in order to unlock their meaning. The first has already been indicated, namely the need to examine each Gospel from the point of view of the **writer's insight**, looking at what he saw and understood about Jesus from his angle. The other is to look at the Gospel in terms of the **writer's intention** and how he wanted readers to respond. The two levels overlap, but will help us enormously when we come to look at each book.

The writer's insight

Each Gospel writer wanted to convey a particular insight about Jesus and so organized his material accordingly (see the table on pages 786–787). He wanted to do more than just convey remembered words and deeds of Jesus – he also wanted to give a context in which the life of Jesus could be understood. His viewpoint is not necessarily unique to his Gospel: there is overlap between the writers, but it is clear that each writer has a primary insight.

- Mark wrote the first and shortest Gospel, seeing Jesus as the Son of Man.
- Luke wrote the second Gospel and saw Jesus as the Saviour of the World.

- Matthew wrote the third Gospel, depicting Jesus as the King of the Jews.
- John wrote the fourth Gospel, with Jesus as the Son of God.

The writers chose and structured their material in the way that would best convey their particular perspective.

The writer's intention

However, we also need to consider each Gospel from the point of view of the reader. Each writer has a particular audience in mind and is concerned to convey his message about Jesus to them.

Careful study indicates that Matthew and John are written for believers:

- Matthew is concerned for new believers and his book is arranged in order that we will know how to live as disciples.
- John is written for older believers, to encourage them to hold on to their faith in Jesus and also to counteract heresies about John the Baptist and Jesus himself.

On the other hand, Mark and Luke are written primarily for unbelievers.

- Mark is concerned to excite his readers with the news about Jesus so that they might have faith in him.
- Luke, as the only Gentile author in the Bible, is concerned that fellow Gentiles might know about Christ.

The different audiences govern what the writers include and how they arrange their material.

Similarities

We have already noted that there is overlap between the Gospels' content and their wording, with the first three being especially similar. In fact, 95 per cent of Mark is included in Matthew and Luke, in some cases with very similar or identical wording. These first three are known as **'synoptic' Gospels**. The word 'synoptic' is made up of two Greek words, *syn*, which means 'together', and *optic*, which means 'see' or 'view'. The first three Gospels reflect a common view of Jesus, as opposed to John, who writes more independently. There is an enormous change when you finish reading Matthew, Mark and Luke and start reading John.

Much material is common to all three Gospels. A few things are found only in Mark, but both Matthew and Luke used most of his material, though in different ways. Matthew split Mark into little bits and mixed these up with his own material, whereas Luke took blocks of Mark, using whole chunks at once.

Of course there has been some debate: did Matthew and Mark use Luke, or did Matthew and Luke use and expand Mark, or did Mark abbreviate Matthew and Luke? It is most likely that Matthew and Luke expanded Mark, working with his Gospel in front of them. Matthew has some material which is unique to him, which he did not get from anyone else, and Luke also has some of his own.

MARK AS THE BASIS

Not surprisingly, the three synoptics have a clear literary connection, based on Mark. Although placed second in our New Testament, Mark was almost certainly written first. He divides his Gospel very carefully into two parts with an interval in between. The first covers Jesus' ministry in the north, in Galilee. The second part covers Jesus' move south to Judaea.

Apart from one incident in Nazareth when the villagers tried to throw him off the cliff, Jesus was very popular in the north, where thousands followed him. But he was very unpopular in the south, where he had frequent problems. The Jewish authorities were hostile, and few followed him. With this division, Mark builds up to a climax as Jesus leaves the friendly north for hostility and eventual death in the south.

This two-part framework is one that Matthew and Luke both use as their basis. Luke is the next Gospel to be written. He rewrites Mark, adding both his own material and other content shared to Matthew. This probably comes from a separate source, written or oral, known to both Matthew and Luke, and designated by New Testament scholars as 'Q' after the German word for 'source' (*Quelle*). Matthew then composed his Gospel, adding material from his own research, including material from 'Q', but arranging it differently to suit his own particular purpose.

Conclusion

If we are to grasp its message fully, it is important that we understand what a Gospel is and for whom it is written. The table below summarizes what has been said about the Gospels.

FOUR GOSPELS
Mark – Son of Man
Matthew – King of Jews
Luke – Saviour of the World
John – Son of God

THREE STAGES
What Jesus did – Mark
What Jesus said – Matthew/Luke
Who Jesus was – John

TWO ANGLES
Writer – insight
what? how?
Reader – intention
who? why?

In the Gospels we have four news bulletins, conveying to us the person and work of Christ, with unique first-hand accounts of his life and times, written with the purpose of building up believers or convincing non-believers to put their faith in the one whom God has sent. They are best read through in one sitting, preferably aloud, as they were preached before they were written down.

They are extraordinary books, for they describe 'the hinge of history'. The world will never be the same again. Christ has come, a man yet at the same time God, to be the Saviour of the world. Because of this, time has been divided into two epochs: BC (before Christ) and AD (*anno domini*, Latin for 'year of our Lord').

37.
 MARK

Introduction

We saw in the general introduction to the Gospels (pages 777–787) that Mark was the first of the four to be written, although it is placed second in our New Testament. It is written primarily for **unbelievers**, and you quickly notice its vivid, dramatic and emotional style. It is a gripping page turner, hard to put down once started.

Who was Mark?

The author of Mark's Gospel, like the authors of the other three Gospels, does not name himself. He refuses to draw attention to himself, although there are clear hints telling us who the writer is. It is almost as if he is saying that he wants the whole of our attention to be on Jesus, not on him.

He is a man with three names, each giving a clue to his background.

1. 'Mark' comes from the Latin name **Marcus**, telling us that although he was Jewish he did have official Roman connections in some way. We do not know for sure what these were, but his family had quite a big house in Jerusalem and must have been of some standing, with at least one maidservant.

2. His Hebrew name was **Johannan**, or John, which means 'Yahweh (God) has shown grace', and he was often known as John Mark.

3. His third name is unusual: **Colobodactolus**, a Greek name which means 'stubby fingered'. The first Gospel ever to be written was by someone with stubby fingers!

So Mark had three names, a Greek nickname, a Latin name and a Hebrew name.

HIS FAMILY HOME

Mark's mother was Mary, which is Miriam in Hebrew. There is a strong possibility that his family home was the location of the Last Supper. This is understood because of an unusual incident following Jesus' arrest in the Garden of Gethsemane, directly after the Last Supper which took place in an 'upper room' in Jerusalem.

We read that as Jesus was arrested the soldiers grabbed hold of a young man who was dressed in nothing but a bed sheet. He struggled clear, leaving the sheet in a soldier's hands, and fled naked into the night. This is an unusual detail to include unless this was John Mark himself, who had left his house in a great hurry to follow the disciples into the Garden, then had hidden behind one of those old olive trees, heard Jesus praying and saw his arrest. It would explain how we know the details of Jesus' prayer, which took place out of earshot of the disciples he had taken with him.

This is speculation, but it is very likely that the location of the Last Supper was John Mark's home and that this incident provides support for his authorship.

How did he get his information?

John Mark was not part of the apostolic band. As a youth he would have seen Jesus, but he was never a leading figure in the unfolding events. Although he is mentioned elsewhere in the New Testament, it is always as a 'number two', someone's personal assistant. So it is perhaps surprising that of all people John Mark should write the first Gospel.

He was personal assistant to three very great Christian leaders in the early Church and this gives us a clue to his source material. First he assisted his older cousin, **Barnabas**, a Levite from Cyprus. It would seem that Barnabas trained him in Christian service.

Next, Mark became an assistant to the apostle **Paul**, accompanying Paul and Barnabas on their first missionary journey. It was not a complete success, with John Mark backing out when they reached the coast of Asia Minor. Luke does not record for us in Acts exactly why he left. Maybe he was homesick. Some speculate that he struggled to accept Paul's leadership because he felt that his cousin Barnabas should have been the leader. Others suggest that the dangers of attack from bandits put him off. We do not know for sure. We do know, however, that when Paul and Barnabas set out on their second journey, John Mark became the focus of an argument, with Paul insisting that John Mark be left behind following his previous desertion and Barnabas arguing that he should come. In the end Paul and Barnabas parted company over this.

Finally, Mark became personal assistant to the apostle **Peter**, who arrived in Rome after Paul. It was from this relationship that Mark received the information for his Gospel. His initial task was to act as interpreter for Peter's messages, translating them into Latin as Peter travelled around the churches in Rome. An early Church document tells us that some members of the congregation of the church in Rome asked if they could have Peter's sermons recorded in a more permanent form. They were afraid that Peter's boldness would lead to his arrest, especially as this was the time of the feared Emperor Nero, and they were anxious that his memories of Jesus should not be lost. The record says that Peter was not especially enthusiastic about the idea, but that 'he neither hindered nor encouraged Mark to do this'.

Style

As a result of his close connection with Peter, the Gospel of Mark has also been known as the **'Gospel of Peter'**. Indeed, a close examination of Peter's sermons in Acts reveals a close correlation with Mark. Peter's own temperament shines through the pages of this Gospel. We could nickname him 'Action Man', since he was so impetuous, frequently speaking before thinking and often prepared to act when others were more cautious. We know from other Gospels that Peter was the one who wanted to walk on the water. He was the one who grew tired of waiting for Jesus to appear after the resurrection and said, 'I'm going fishing.' He was the one who jumped into the water when John said it was Jesus on the shore.

Peter could not sit still and this Gospel conveys this breathless excitement throughout. The word 'immediately' comes many times, summing up Peter's zest for life. For this reason Mark's Gospel is the most vivid and the most alive of the four and the most exciting to read aloud. The actor Alec McCowen packed a London theatre for months with a simple recital of Mark's Gospel.

In the first part of Mark relatively little time is spent on the first two and a half years of Jesus' ministry. It is written in a fast-moving style as Mark seeks to excite the reader with what is happening. But in the second part he spends more time on subsequent months, then even more time looking at Jesus' last weeks, until he focuses right down on the last week and the last day, when every hour is described. It is like an express train slowing up and coming to a halt – and it halts right in front of the cross.

In his structure Mark is building everything up towards Jesus' death, and slowing everything down to stop before the cross. It is a masterly piece of journalism, and is probably the best Gospel to give to a complete outsider who knows nothing about Jesus and wants to read about this exciting person who is our Saviour and Lord.

The content of Mark's Gospel

Peter's weaknesses

Mark's Gospel typically places Peter in a bad light, for there is far more emphasis on his weaknesses than his strengths – almost as if Peter was concerned that readers should know about his **mistakes**. So Mark includes Jesus' words to Peter: 'Get behind me, Satan!' when he protests against Jesus' explanation of his future suffering. By contrast, in Matthew we read, 'You are Peter, and on this rock I will build my church and the gates of Hades will not overcome it.' Mark also includes the moving account of Peter's denial of the Lord, but fails to include his reinstatement, which appears in John.

Miracles

Peter was far more impressed with **what Jesus did** than what he said, and so the Gospel displays a great enthusiasm for Jesus' miracles. This reflects an evangelist's heart, keen on anything which would interest unbelievers in the message. This is borne out by the relative proportions of Mark devoted to the miracles and the discourses. Mark includes 18 miracles, which

is similar to Matthew and Luke. He includes only four parables, however, compared to 18 in Matthew and 19 in Luke, and
only one major discourse, in Chapter 13.

Omissions

Peter's own ignorance is also reflected in the Gospel. It
would seem that Peter did not know how or where Jesus was
born. Never once in his speeches in Acts or in his letters does
he indicate any knowledge whatever of Jesus' birth. Peter's
knowledge began at the River Jordan, where he and his brother
Andrew were baptized and John introduced them both to
Jesus. In Mark, therefore, there is no Christmas story or tales
about Jesus' boyhood. The Gospel gets going where Peter's
knowledge began – with John preaching and baptizing.

Shape

The Gospel covers the three years of Jesus' public ministry, but
its shape is reflected in both time and space, **chronology** and
geography. The narrative builds up over the first two and a
half years to a watershed moment (see below, pages 793–794),
and then everything flows down from that, covering the last six
months of Jesus' life on earth. Mark focuses on Jesus' Galilean
ministry, omitting his visits to Jerusalem in the early years. (See
diagram overleaf.)

CHRONOLOGICAL STRUCTURE
There are three phases in the ministry of Jesus.

- **The first phase**: Jesus was very popular. Thousands came to
  be healed and he was the talk of the whole country.
- **The second phase**: The opposition begins. Starting with a
  difference of opinion over the Sabbath, it extended to other
  areas and soon Jesus had made more enemies than friends.

■ **The third phase**: Jesus concentrated on his 12 disciples, out
of the thousands who flocked to hear him.

The Gospel covers three distinct periods of time. The first
two and a half years are covered in Chapters 1–9, Chapter 10
covers the next six months, and Chapters 11–16 cover Jesus'
last week.

GEOGRAPHICAL STRUCTURE

The geographical structure of the Gospel parallels the time divisions. The story starts at the River Jordan, which is the lowest
point on the earth's surface, and moves from there to Galilee,
where Jesus conducted the bulk of his ministry. The diagram
indicates an ascent up to the highest point in the Promised
Land, Mount Hermon, at the foot of which is the town of
Caesarea Philippi. It is here that the Gospel reaches its **watershed**. As soon as that point is reached Jesus sets his face towards

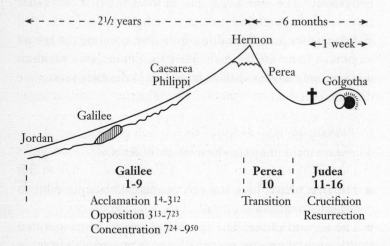

Jerusalem and it is downhill all the way – literally down from that high point to Judaea, through Perea, which is on the east side of the Jordan, and eventually to Jerusalem, where Jesus dies on the cross and rises again three days later.

So what happened at Caesarea Philippi after the first two and a half years that changed the direction of Jesus' ministry so totally, and which Mark is so keen to highlight for his readers?

THE WATERSHED MOMENT

A little background will help us. Caesarea Philippi is located at the source of the River Jordan, which emerges at the foot of Mount Hermon and measures 30–40 feet in width. The source of the water is the snow on the top of Mount Hermon, which melts and filters down a crack inside the mountain, flowing out through a hole beneath the actual surface of the river.

This strange natural phenomenon became the focus for superstition and religious cults and the centre of pagan worship for centuries. In the cliff face above the river there are carved alcoves, in which were placed statues of gods. One statue was of the Greek god Pan and to this day the place is called Paneas or Baneas. There was also a statue of Caesar, put there by one of Herod the Great's four sons, Philip, who was given that part of the land when Herod died. Philip called the place after himself and after the Roman Emperor, hence the name Caesarea Philippi.

So here we have a statue of the Greek god Pan, a god who was supposed to have appeared on earth as a mortal man, and a statue of Caesar, a man who was called a god. It was to this location that Jesus took the 12 disciples and asked, 'Who do people say I am?'

The disciples replied with the various views of the day: mostly reincarnations of great men from their history – Jeremiah, Elijah, even John the Baptist.

Then Jesus asked them pointedly who *they* thought he was. It was Peter who had the right answer. He realized that Jesus had lived before, but not down here on earth. '**You are the Christ**,' he said, '**the son of the living God.**'

This was the first time that any man had grasped who Jesus was (the first woman was Martha, whose confession is recorded in John's Gospel). It is this answer which is the pivotal point in the Gospel. Jesus had waited two and a half years to ask the question, and now he was able to talk to Peter about two things he had never mentioned before:

1. He spoke about being able to **build his Church**, a subject never mentioned before, even amidst all his preaching, healing and miracles. The reason is evident: Jesus cannot build his Church until people know who he is, for the Church can only be made up of people who know his identity. At this point Jesus renames Simon (which means 'reed') and he becomes Peter. The name is a play on words, for 'Peter' is very close to the word for 'rock' in the original language, as in our word 'petrified'.

2. He also spoke for the first time of his **intention to go to Jerusalem and die on the cross**. The disciples had been with him for two and a half years and he had never before given a hint that he was going to die. Now he explains that he must go to the cross and nothing will stop him. Peter is alarmed and announces that he must not go, only to be rebuked by Jesus. From this point on, the cross is the focus for the Gospel.

This, then, is the **watershed** of Mark's Gospel. We can easily miss the real flow and development of the story if we do not realize this, assuming things about the disciples because we know how they turned out, but missing the progressive revelation portrayed in the Gospel.

Now that the disciples have understood who Jesus is, the next incident follows on quite naturally. Jesus takes Peter, James and John up to the top of the mountain, above the snow line, where he is transfigured before them. In describing the event, Peter says that Jesus' clothes became brighter than any bleaching agent on earth could make them. He actually uses the word 'detergent' (or 'fuller', which was the equivalent in those days). The light was shining through Jesus' clothes from the inside and they 'saw his glory'. He met with Moses and Elijah to discuss his 'exodus', whereby he would accomplish a release for his people, as Luke records.

The key point of the Gospel, therefore, is the realization by the disciples of who Jesus is: he is the Christ, the Messiah. This is the key point for the readers too. This is the **good news** Mark is communicating through the shape of his Gospel. It is picked up by Matthew and Luke, who then build on it.

Mark's value to us

1. A clear picture of the person of Christ

Mark is primarily concerned with what Jesus did, but he is not unconcerned about the person of Christ. Indeed, it is Mark who makes it clear that **Jesus revealed himself to his followers gradually**. It is a puzzling feature of a Gospel that reveals the person of Christ that it also highlights the fact that Jesus himself seemed to want his identity kept quiet.

A number of references emphasize this point most markedly.

- In 1:25 and 1:34 Jesus would not let the demons speak because they knew who he was.
- In 1:43, having healed a man with leprosy, Jesus sent him away at once with a strong warning: 'See that you don't tell this to anyone.'
- In 3:12, again speaking to demons, 'he gave them strict orders not to tell anyone who he was'.
- In 5:43, having raised Jairus' daughter to life, 'he gave strict orders not to let anyone know about this'.
- Other incidences along the same lines occur in 7:24, 7:36, 8:26, 8:30, 9:9 and 9:30. Even on Mount Hermon Jesus asks his disciples to keep quiet about his identity.

This special feature of Mark is known as the 'Messianic secret' and reflects Jesus' concern to complete his mission without interruption. He wanted the disciples to understand from his Father who he was, and he restrained their thinking so that they would arrive at the conclusion the right way. He also kept his identity hidden because early recognition of his Messiahship would lead to premature adulation and a demand that he become a political messiah, which would hinder his ministry and could conceivably prevent his death.

2. Teaching on the work of Christ

The second great theme of Mark's Gospel is the work of Christ. He emphasizes the **death of Jesus**: one-third of the Gospel is concerned with the cross – a fact often lost on those who make plays and films about Christ's life. This underlines how unusual a Gospel is as a form of 'life story'. We could scarcely imagine the writings on famous public figures like Mahatma Gandhi or John F. Kennedy giving so much attention to their deaths, in spite of their assassinations.

The cross dominates the content throughout the Gospel. It is clear from Mark that people plotted to kill Jesus from the very beginning. He made enemies as well as friends through his teaching. His challenges to the religious status quo were unpopular with the religious and political leaders and aroused considerable hostility. The Pharisees in particular hated his attacks on their traditions.

HUMAN AND DIVINE ASPECTS OF JESUS' DEATH

Mark's emphasis on the cross includes both the human and the divine aspects of Jesus' death.

Human

On the human side, **Jesus was charged with blasphemy for saying that he was God**, which in Jewish law was a capital crime deserving death. We are told, however, that the accusers could not agree on the words he had used in order to confirm the validity of such a charge. Eventually the judge asked Jesus himself who he was. Of course, Jesus as a Jew had to speak when questioned by the High Priest, so he acknowledged that he was the Christ. The judge tore his clothes and said, 'You heard it! What is your verdict?' and the Sanhedrin, the ruling council of 70 men, said that he deserved to die.

Despite this verdict, they could not officially put someone to death, since the land was occupied by the Romans and was under Roman law when it came to the death penalty. They needed the Romans' approval for the death sentence, therefore, but in Roman law blasphemy was not a crime. The only hope was to *change* the crime and by the time Jesus came before Pilate he was being charged with **treason**, not blasphemy. It is Mark's Gospel which is the clearest on this point. In the end the offence they charged him with was not that he said, 'I am God' (blasphemy), but that he said, 'I am king, the king of the Jews' (treason).

The human side of the death of Christ was unjust from beginning to end. Although he was guilty of neither blasphemy nor treason, that is how he was charged and condemned.

Divine

The divine side of Christ's death, however, is also brought out in Mark, for **Jesus was sure from the very beginning that he had come to die**. He predicted his death, and his resurrection, more than once. We also read of Jesus taking the 'cup', an image which – used metaphorically – always speaks of God's wrath against sin. Mark no doubt heard Jesus use the word in the Garden on the night of his betrayal.

From the time that Jesus first mentions his future suffering, we have the sense that he had to be betrayed, that God had planned it that way, Jesus was aware of it, and there was no avoiding it. Peter must not try to tempt Jesus to run away from the cross.

This combination of the human and the divine is most compelling, confronting readers with the stark realities of Christ's mission. It makes this a very suitable Gospel to give to unbelievers.

3. People's reactions to Jesus

Mark frequently records people's reactions to the teaching and miracles of Jesus. There are two key words all the way through – **fear** and **faith**. From beginning to end of the Gospel, it is as if those who meet Jesus are faced with a choice between the two. Mark seems to be asking: What is your response to this story, fear or faith?

In the account of the stilling of the storm, for example, Jesus is in the boat and the disciples ask him, 'Don't you care if we drown?' Jesus answers, 'Why are you so afraid? Do you still have no faith?' One of his favourite sayings given throughout the Gospel is, 'Don't be afraid.' Fear and faith are incompatible responses to any circumstance or situation.

A basis for belief

In Mark's Gospel, therefore, we are presented with a clear picture of the person and work of Christ, and an encouragement to respond in faith rather than fear when the supernatural element enters in. These are further reasons why Mark is such a good Gospel to give to unbelievers. It gives them a very basic knowledge of Christ's person and his work, and encourages their right response to both.

The ending

Mark's Gospel has a very peculiar ending. It actually **finishes in the middle of a sentence**. In the early manuscript copies we have of the Gospel it ends right in the middle of verse 8 in Chapter 16, with the strange phrase 'for they were afraid of...' English translations usually tidy up the language with 'for they were afraid' or 'they feared'. But nothing can hide the fact that the Gospel ends suddenly, and ends with this note of fear.

Reasons for the ragged ending

That the Gospel should end in this way is surprising, as Mark's whole theme is to get people switching from fear to faith, and it raises a series of important questions: What happened to the rest of the story? Why is Mark not nicely rounded off? Why are there no accounts in Mark's Gospel of the appearances of Jesus after his resurrection? There is only the empty tomb and the finding of that empty tomb, but there is no mention of Jesus actually meeting the disciples, which is very strange when it is compared to the other three Gospels.

There are at least three possibilities to explain all this.

1. Mark **intended** to finish on this uncertain note and to leave the ending open.
2. Mark was **prevented** from finishing – i.e something interrupted his writing. He may have been suddenly arrested or taken off, or perhaps he dropped dead, and the manuscript was never completed.
3. The ending has been **lost** in some way. Either the manuscript was mutilated by persecutors, or it is even just possible that *Peter* tore the end off! As this is really 'Peter's Gospel', it is meant to be a record of his preaching about Jesus. We know from 1 Corinthians that one of the most important resurrection appearances was to Peter on his own, but we have no record of this in the Gospels. Maybe it was originally included by Mark, but Peter wanted it removed because he thought it was so precious, so intimate and so personal that he did not want any account of it to be published. Some argue that although we do not have the actual ending to Mark's Gospel, much of it is included in Luke and Matthew's versions anyway, as they drew so heavily on Mark's work.

We do not know what happened, but argument 1 is highly unlikely, for it would mean that Mark deliberately ended in the middle of a sentence, with the words, 'the women said nothing to anyone, for they were afraid of...' This would be an extraordinary ending for a Gospel intended to convey *good* news, especially one directed at unbelievers.

Another ending added

What we do know is that other endings have been added, both a shorter and a longer version. Somebody else has completed Mark's Gospel so that we do have the complete story.

The long version, which is the one usually included in Bibles today, runs from verse 9 to verse 20, and balances fear with faith – though it does tell us that the disciples did not believe Jesus had risen even when they saw him. It includes some remarkable statements by Jesus, many of which are not appreciated by sections of the Christian Church today. Jesus talks about tongues (the only recorded instance where Jesus mentions that his followers would speak in tongues), and says that his followers would cast out demons, heal the sick, and pick up snakes and not be harmed (which happened to Paul in Malta). There is also a statement here in which Jesus makes baptism in water essential to salvation. He says, 'Whoever believes and is baptized will be saved'.

We do not know who wrote this ending, but it does reflect what the early Church believed about Jesus' actions between his resurrection and ascension, and it includes items from the other Gospels. There is a little bit about the road to Emmaus and a short section similar to Matthew's Great Commission. It seems as if somebody has picked out various elements from the other Gospels, put them together and rounded off Mark that way. We need not worry about the authenticity of the longer ending. It is a valid part of the Word of God and does reflect the early Christian understanding, even if it does not deliver Mark's actual words.

Conclusion

The Gospel of Mark focuses on what Jesus did, as Peter conveys his appreciation of his master and is keen that non-believers should come to faith in him. It presents the basis for belief in a clear and vivid way. The Gospel also has significant value for those who are already followers of Jesus, reminding us of Christ's person and work, and of the need to respond to this 'news bulletin' with faith and trust. Its fresh and enthusiastic tone is a good antidote for those whose Christian walk has become stale because they have lost the wonder of the Christ event. Being the shortest, it is the easiest Gospel to read in one sitting. If you can, read it aloud for the best effect – either to yourself or, better still, to someone else.

38.

MATTHEW

Introduction

Who was the writer?

It is commonly agreed that the author of this Gospel was
Matthew, also known as Levi, although his name does not
appear on the original document. His name means 'gift of
God' and he was one of the twelve apostles. He was a tax collector at Capernaum and the Gospels of Matthew and Luke
both record that he left everything to follow Jesus, and threw a
party so that his friends and colleagues could meet Jesus for
themselves. Although one of the Twelve, he is not one of the
more prominent and is rarely mentioned in any of the Gospels.

How was the Gospel written?

We have already noted that Matthew was written using the
content and framework of Mark's Gospel. There are considerable similarities, including identical wording in some places.
Matthew follows Mark's broad arrangement of two distinct
phases, whilst adding his own distinctive structure. So he
includes 'phase one', the two and a half years in which Jesus
ministers in Galilee, and 'phase two', the final six months in
the south amongst the more nationalistic Jews of Judaea. He
also sees the watershed of Christ's ministry coinciding with

Peter's confession of Christ at Caesarea Philippi and the subsequent movement of Jesus towards the south and the cross.

We have also noted the importance of getting to grips with the *writer's insights* – what he saw and understood about Jesus from his particular point of view – and with Matthew these can be highlighted by asking why he felt he needed to rewrite Mark. It is in examining the differences between his Gospel and Mark's Gospel that Matthew's purpose becomes clear.

The differences between Matthew and Mark

Insights

Matthew was one of the Twelve, and had time to reflect on the three years he spent living close to his master. While Mark stresses his humanity (the Son of Man), Matthew sees Jesus as the **King of the Jews**, the one who fulfils the promises of the prophets. No one had been on David's throne for 600 years – the current King Herod had no ancestral claim to it. Now at last one was coming who would be the rightful king.

From the very beginning Matthew focuses his readers' attention on Christ's ancestry in the royal line of David, describing how his birth fulfils prophecy and has the marks of God's involvement, heralded by archangels and welcomed by an angelic choir. While Luke includes the shepherds, it is Matthew who records the worship of the child by wise men from the east. This theme of Jesus as the King of the Jews is also seen in his passion, as Matthew records the crown of thorns, the 'sceptre' and the title given to Jesus, all mocking his pretensions – but to Matthew appropriate for a royal person.

Intentions

Matthew writes for a completely different audience from Mark. Mark is written for unbelievers, Matthew for **new believers**, many of whom at that time were converted Jews.

His intentions can be seen clearly at the end of the Gospel, where he records Christ's final words to his apostles, commanding them to 'make disciples of all nations'. Matthew certainly fulfils that aim, providing a manual of discipleship for those who enter the kingdom. Indeed, this was how the Gospel came to be used within the early Church and is one of the reasons why it is included first in our New Testament.

While Mark's Gospel was appropriate for someone interested in Christ but not yet persuaded, therefore, Matthew's rewrite of Mark accomplishes a very different purpose.

An earlier start

Matthew starts his account much earlier than Mark, with the birth of Jesus set in the context of his ancestry. Mark starts with his baptism and is less interested in, or even ignorant of, his birth. Thus well before we hear Jesus' teaching and see his miracles, Matthew has set the scene for us, creating a sense of expectation as the Jewish messiah arrives on the scene of history.

A longer account

Matthew is the fullest and most systematic account of Jesus' life, reflecting perhaps the orderly mind of an accountant. He includes material from his own observations as one of the Twelve, as well as some research of his own. Both Luke and Matthew apparently use a common source unknown to or ignored by Mark. Not only does Matthew add the birth of Jesus, he has more discourses and collected sayings, and more detail concerning Christ's death, with 14 extra sayings of Jesus included in the narrative of his death.

Alterations

Matthew has made a number of alterations to Mark's text in order to bring out aspects he feels are important. Matthew's accounts are often shorter, omitting harsh or vivid detail to produce a smoother story which clarifies any misunderstandings and spares the blushes of the disciples. The 'feel' of Matthew therefore is more sober, less enthusiastic and less emotional than Mark. This is an older man reflecting on his own first-hand experiences, and he comes across more as a teacher than a preacher.

Collected sayings

Matthew collects the sayings of Jesus into five 'sermons' (see the table below), forming summaries of his teaching on discipleship. The Sermon on the Mount is best known, but there are four others on the connected theme of the **kingdom**. This is by contrast to Mark, who has very little in the way of discourse, and to Luke, who spreads the sayings of Jesus all the way through the narrative.

Given the Jewish readership, it is highly likely that Matthew has a special reason for presenting exactly *five* sermons. Their place at the heart of his Gospel parallels the five books of the law of Moses which begin the Old Testament (Genesis to Deuteronomy). Matthew is telling his readers that Jesus brings a **new law** – not the law of Moses any more, but the law of Christ. Hence throughout the Sermon on the Mount we have Jesus' restatement of the law: 'You have heard it said in the law of Moses, but I say to you…' Things will never be the same again.

Structure

Matthew uses Mark's basic framework, as we have already noted, but he adds his own structure. Alongside the two-phase division of Mark he adds two motifs prefaced by the phrase 'From that time...' So we read, 'From that time on Jesus began to preach, "Repent, for the kingdom of heaven is near",' and 'From that time on Jesus began to explain to his disciples that he must go to Jerusalem and suffer many things...' The first appearance of the phrase captures the sense of his ministry in the north, and the second the inevitability of his death in the south. Matthew also uses the words, 'When Jesus had finished...' to change direction in his narrative.

The most marked and telling structural change, however, concerns the way in which he alternates the five blocks of Christ's teaching with four blocks of his deeds. We can lay this out as follows:

THE STRUCTURE OF MATTHEW

Introduction: birth, baptism, temptation

Word	Chapters 5–7
Deed	Chapters 8–9
Word	Chapter 10
Deed	Chapters 11–12
Word	Chapter 13
Deed	Chapters 14–17
Word	Chapter 18
Deed	Chapters 19–23
Word	Chapters 24–25

Conclusion: death and resurrection

So we have five sermons, four of them followed by accounts of the deeds of Jesus which serve to illustrate his sermons. The purpose for this will be examined in more detail later, but for now we should simply note that Matthew is keen to demonstrate that Jesus communicated in word *and* deed, giving us a model to follow. Mark invites us to come and see what Jesus did, but Matthew invites us to come and see what he did *and* hear what he said.

Narrative on the cross

Matthew has a considerably fuller ending than Mark. In view of Mark's abrupt ending, some have speculated that the last part of Matthew may actually have been Mark's original ending. We have no way of knowing, but can list his particular distinctives in the last two chapters.

1. **Details of the arrest**: Matthew is concerned with Christ's innocence, so he emphasizes that these things happened so that Scripture might be fulfilled.

2. **The end of Judas**: Matthew records the warnings of Jesus to the disciples and the remorse of Judas as he returns the money, though by then it is too late.

3. **Events immediately after Jesus died**: It is Matthew who records the opened tombs and the sightings of previously dead people in the city of Jerusalem.

4. **The tomb**: Matthew records the guarded tomb and the report by the soldiers that the body was stolen.

5. **After the resurrection**: Matthew says much more than Mark about events following the resurrection. He records Jesus' return to Galilee, and his meeting with the 11 disciples (and about 500 others, some of whom 'doubted'). There is great significance in the location. Galilee was at the crossroads of the world, with Mount Megiddo a crossover point where roads from the east, north, south and west converged. The population here was cosmopolitan, 'Galilee of the nations'. Jesus was on a mountain, reminiscent of Moses on Mount Nebo. It is at this point that

the Great Commission is given: they must make disciples of all nations (literally all ethnic groups).

The special features of Matthew

A. His interest in Jews

As well as drawing on Mark for material, Matthew adds a number of special features of his own, and the reader is immediately struck by the Jewishness of Matthew's Gospel. It is obviously aimed at Jewish readers, though not exclusively so. His sensitivity to Jewish concerns and interests can be seen throughout.

1. GENEALOGY

The Gospel begins with a genealogy, of little interest to Gentiles but fascinating for Jews keen to know about **Jesus' ancestry**, for in their mind the family tree establishes the person. Furthermore, the arrangement of the genealogy alerts Jewish attention. Jesus' ancestors are arranged in three groups of 14, the first group from Abraham to King David, the second from David up to the exile, and the third from the exile to Jesus. These periods represent the eras when God's people were governed by a particular style of leadership: prophets, princes (kings) and priests.

The significance of the three groups may be lost until we realize that every Jewish name has a numeric value, with each letter assigned to a number and the total forming the number of the name. David in Hebrew (which has no vowels) is DVD and comes to 14. So immediately we see Matthew's concern to convey a pattern: Christ's ancestry is Davidic, and he has come at just the right time.

Matthew chooses to give the genealogy of Joseph's ancestors. We may think there's nothing unusual about that – until we recall that Jesus was not *physically* related to Joseph. Why not follow Luke in giving Mary's ancestry? Because to a Jewish mind it was the *legal rights* that mattered, and they came through the father, though through mothers today.

One further point of interest is that a Jew carefully versed in his Old Testament would note that if Jesus was a *physical* descendant of Joseph, his rights to the throne of David would be questioned, since Jeconiah is listed as one of Joseph's ancestors. God had said through Jeremiah that no descendant of Jeconiah (also known as Jehoiachin) would ever sit on David's throne. Matthew's purpose was to establish Jesus' *legal* claim to be a 'son of David'.

2. TERMINOLOGY

Matthew's sensitivity to Jewish readers is further seen in the language he uses. Most marked is his reference to the 'kingdom', a key theme of Jesus' message. Matthew writes of the **'kingdom of heaven'**, not the 'kingdom of God' as in the other Gospels. Jews would avoid using God's name in speech for fear of speaking irreverently and so Matthew uses the phrase 'kingdom of heaven', even though his meaning for the phrase is the same as for the phrase 'kingdom of God' used by the other writers.

3. OLD TESTAMENT USE

Matthew refers to the Old Testament more than any of the other Gospels. One of his favourite sayings is 'that it might be fulfilled, which was spoken by the prophets'. This is one of the reasons why Matthew is placed first in the New Testament, even though it was not written first. It provides **continuity** with the Old Testament better than all the others. Altogether there are 29 direct quotations from the Old Testament and an additional 121 indirect references or allusions.

This is seen in particular in Matthew's birth narrative. He seems to Gentile eyes to take a long time explaining why Jesus was born in Bethlehem – because the prophets had predicted that Bethlehem of Judaea would be the birthplace of the king. Yet this would be crucially important for Jews wondering if this was the Messiah God had promised long ago. Matthew is keen for readers to understand that the prophets spoke of the birth to a virgin, the slaughter of the innocents, the flight into Egypt and the return to Galilee. The phrase 'that it might be fulfilled, which was spoken by the prophets' occurs 13 times in the story of Jesus' birth, where Matthew quotes Micah, Hosea, Jeremiah and Isaiah.

4. MESSIAH

In addition, Jewish readers would have a particular problem believing that Jesus was the Messiah in the light of his **crucifixion**. How could the Messiah be condemned as a criminal and sentenced to death? So Matthew stresses that Jesus was actually innocent of all the charges. It was the Jews who were guilty of unjust accusation, illegal trials, and changing the charges in order that the Romans might convict and execute him. Matthew spells out why the Jews did not receive their Messiah and includes a list of woes against the Pharisees, the most religious of all Jews.

5. THE LAW

Linked with the Jewish emphasis is Matthew's concern that we understand the law correctly in the light of Jesus' teaching. Matthew emphasizes as no other Gospel that Jesus did not come to abolish the law, but to **fulfil** it. Matthew records the words of Jesus, that 'not one jot, or one tittle of the law will pass away'. Many Jews thought Jesus had come to destroy the law, but Matthew states clearly that this was not his purpose.

He came that it might be 'fulfilled' – achieved rather than annulled.

To keep the door open for Jews

By the year AD 85, just after Matthew wrote his Gospel, Jewish believers were being excommunicated from the synagogues. The Church as a whole was becoming more and more Gentile. Consequently a deep gulf was opening up between the Jews and the Church. Matthew wanted to keep the door open for Jews, to help them realize that the followers of Jesus were not abandoning the Old Testament, nor had they forgotten their Jewish roots. He was a Jew, they were his people and, like the apostle Paul, Matthew had a longing that Jews should come to believe in their own Messiah.

To remind Gentiles of their roots

Secondly, Matthew wrote a Gospel that was Jewish in character because he wanted Gentile Christians never to forget their Jewish roots. Matthew, more than the other Gospels, roots Jesus in Judaism, putting him in the context of God's purposes for Israel, with a genealogy reaching back to Abraham and David.

He is saying to Jews on the one hand, 'Don't run away from Christians,' and to Christians on the other hand, 'Don't run away from Jews.' This Gospel intends to bring Jew and Christian together.

B. His interest in Gentiles

Matthew's purpose is not exclusively Jewish. He is careful to mention **Christ's concern for Gentiles** too.

- At the very beginning wise men from the east, possibly Gentiles, come to see the baby in Bethlehem.
- In the genealogy of the first chapter, Ruth and Rahab, both Gentiles, are listed.
- We are told that Jesus ministered in 'Galilee of the Gentiles'.
- Matthew records the faith of the Roman centurion, hailed as extraordinary by Jesus.
- We read of people of the east and west coming to sit in the kingdom.
- The gospel is good news to the Gentiles who will trust in his name.
- We read of the Canaanite woman's faith.
- Matthew records that Jesus is the cornerstone rejected by the builders and that the kingdom will be taken away from the Jews and given to the Gentiles.
- At the end of the Gospel Jesus commands his followers to go and make disciples of all 'nations', and the word he uses means all the ethnic groups, i.e. Gentiles.

Furthermore, Matthew does not hesitate to record the **negative words Jesus used when referring to the Jews**. He includes a whole chapter devoted to 'woes', as well as other scattered comments. A 'woe' was a curse word. Chapter 23 is a collection of his sayings against the Pharisees and religious leaders. It is stern stuff.

We tend to be rather more keen on the blessings, forgetting that Jesus uttered curses as well. In Jesus' day there were 250,000 people living on the shores of Galilee in four major cities. Today there is just one town. Why? Jesus said, 'Woe to you, Chorazin ... Woe to you, Bethsaida ... and you, Capernaum...', and they have all disappeared. The only town he never cursed was Tiberias and it is still there.

C. His interest in Christians – Jewish or Gentile

A MANUAL FOR DISCIPLESHIP

We have seen already that Matthew wrote his Gospel with new converts in mind, and that his purpose can be gleaned from Jesus' command at the very end of the Gospel, when he leaves his followers with a job to do before he returns: 'Go and disciple all ethnic groups, baptizing them and then teaching them to observe everything I have told you to do.' These words provide the basis for our understanding of Matthew's aim: **to help disciples** by teaching them what Jesus commanded. We might call his Gospel a 'manual for discipleship'.

It is by far the best book of the New Testament to give to new converts. It is carefully designed to teach them how to live now that they are disciples of Jesus. The Christian life may start with a *decision* for Jesus, but it takes years to make a *disciple*. A key element in discipleship is learning **how to live in the kingdom of heaven on earth**, and Matthew wrote his Gospel precisely for that purpose: so that we could make disciples.

THE CHURCH

Such a purpose explains why Matthew is the only Gospel to record Christ's words about the Church. The word is used in two very different senses – the **universal Church** and the **local church**.

The first use comes following Peter's confession that Jesus is 'the Christ, the Son of the living God', a key turning point in the Gospel. Once his followers had realized who he was, Jesus could build his Church. And having built his Church, he could die on the cross. Here the word 'church' refers to the universal Church, the whole Church of Jesus. There is only one Church of Jesus Christ and he is building it.

The second meaning of the word comes in Chapter 18: 'If your brother offends you go and tell him. If he repents of it you have won your brother. If he refuses to admit he was wrong, take two or three witnesses. If he still refuses to confess it tell it to the church'. This cannot mean the universal Church, but rather the local community of which the offended person is a part.

In these sayings Matthew outlines the two meanings of the word 'church' in the New Testament: there is the Church of Jesus, which he is building, and the local church, which is part of that universal Church and to which you can take your complaints when necessary.

Not only is Matthew the only Gospel to speak of the Church, it is also clear that some of the teaching is specifically intended for the later age of the Church, post-Pentecost. Matthew records teaching which was not immediately relevant to its hearers. For example, of the 37 verses in Chapter 10 dealing with Jesus' instructions to the Twelve, only 12 verses were immediately relevant. The chapter speaks of Gentile persecution, but at this stage Gentiles were not involved in any persecution, so Matthew is including material from the lips of Jesus which was specifically meant to be of *future* relevance. Similarly, the 'church' discipline of Chapter 18 must have been given for a later period, since the disciples could not have understood it at the time.

THE KINGDOM

If teaching on the Church is unique to Matthew, his teaching on the kingdom covers themes also included in the other Gospels. But 'the kingdom' is a *particular* interest of Matthew. None of the other writers give it the same prominence. We saw earlier that he arranges Jesus' teaching into five blocks. These are all on kingdom themes. Furthermore, his parables often commence with the words, 'The kingdom of heaven is like...' This dominant theme reflects the preaching of Jesus and is one which runs through the whole story of the Bible as God sets about the re-establishment of the kingdom of heaven on earth. It is, of course, a theme that unites both Jew and Christian as both look for the kingdom of God. This fits in with Matthew's aim of uniting Jew and Gentile.

There is, however, a crucial difference between the *Jewish expectancy* of the kingdom and the *Christian experience* of the kingdom, which explains why so many of the Jews failed to understand that Jesus was their Messiah. It is important to understand this if we are going to grasp Jesus' teaching on this theme. (See diagram below.)

To the Jew the kingdom is wholly future – it is something that has not yet come and therefore they call it 'the age to come'. Today, when the Jewish nation celebrates the Feast of

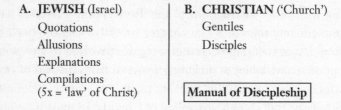

A. JEWISH (Israel)	B. CHRISTIAN ('Church')
Quotations	Gentiles
Allusions	Disciples
Explanations	
Compilations	
(5x = 'law' of Christ)	**Manual of Discipleship**

KINGDOM OF HEAVEN (= God)

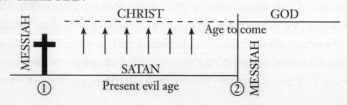

Tabernacles every September or October, they look expectant-ly for the coming Messiah to bring the kingdom of heaven here on earth. That is the centre of their hope. They see the present time as the 'present evil age', the world being ruled by Satan. The devil is the prince of this world, the ruler of this world, the god of this world. These are titles which both Jesus and Paul gave Satan, but they were already familiar titles to the Jewish people.

The difference in the Christian hope for the future is this: **Christians believe the Messiah has already come, but also that he is due to come again**. In Matthew Jesus speaks of this as the secret of the kingdom, namely that the Messiah is com-ing twice, not once. So the 'age to come' which the Jews look for has already begun – it has broken in with Jesus. The king-dom of heaven has come in a very real sense and is now here, but it overlaps with the 'present evil age', rather than replacing it as the Jews expect. Between the two visits of the Messiah the two ages overlap. The reason why Christians are in tension is that we are living in the 'overlap of the ages'. The kingdom is both now and not yet, inaugurated but not consummated. Not yet established, it can still, however, be entered now.

With this understanding of the *coming* kingdom we can better understand why the message of the Gospels was such an affront to Jews who thought they were all good enough to enter the age to come. John the Baptist told them they had to get cleaned up and be baptized in the Jordan, so that their sins might be washed away, ready for the coming kingdom. Many were completely oblivious to the need. Once we grasp this very different idea concerning the kingdom, we will understand much better the teaching of Jesus and the conflicts he encountered.

Matthew is keen that the theme of the kingdom should be balanced appropriately with other teaching, for this focus on the kingdom – with believers as subjects of the king – can lead us to think of our relationship with God solely in those terms. The frequency with which a word is used is often a key to a writer's emphasis, and Matthew mentions 'Father' 44 times altogether, compared to just 4 times in Mark and 17 times in Luke. He is stressing that as we live as subjects of the King of Heaven, we can also call him 'Abba, Father'. We are sons as well as subjects. If we were merely subjects seeking to obey a king, we could start to think that our obedience somehow saves us and forget the filial relationship into which God calls us. So this is a powerful antidote to legalism and a life based on rules and regulations.

Given the understanding of the kingdom outlined above, it is possible to identify the main theme of Matthew's Gospel as this: **How do you live in the kingdom now?** Let us take a brief look at the five 'sermons' into which Matthew has gathered Jesus' teaching about the kingdom.

1. The lifestyle of the kingdom (Chapters 5–7)

This compilation is better known as 'the Sermon on the Mount' and is often badly misunderstood. It is not Jesus' advice to non-believers on how to live. It is tough enough for a believer to seek to live this way, never mind a non-believer. No, the sermon teaches us **how believers are to live, now that they are in the kingdom**.

It starts with a remarkable series of statements: 'Blessed are the poor in spirit, for theirs is the kingdom of heaven ... Blessed are the meek, for they will inherit the earth ... Blessed are the pure in heart, for they will see God...' Jesus is describing a new kind of person, a changed character.

After the opening 'beatitudes', the commands in the sermon are wide ranging and intensely practical. Here are just a few examples:

- If you have called somebody an idiot, you are a murderer.
- The law of Moses said, 'Do not climb into bed with a woman you are not married to,' but Jesus says, 'Do not even look at a girl and wish you could.'
- He also says, 'Do not divorce and remarry.'
- We are told not to worry, for if we worry we libel the King of Heaven, who looks after his own creation and so will look after us.

This is the lifestyle of the kingdom and these chapters provide excellent material for someone who is recently converted. The vital point to grasp is that they are not saved *by* but *for* such a lifestyle.

2. The mission of the kingdom (9:35–10:42)

This 'sermon' follows logically on from the first. Matthew indicates that when a person enters the kingdom they have a mission to go and bring others in. A large amount of Jesus' teaching on **evangelism** therefore comes in Chapters 9 and 10.

Jesus instructs his disciples to demonstrate the reality of the kingdom by raising the dead, casting out demons and healing the sick, and then to tell those who have observed that the kingdom is coming. So the *actions* should precede the *words* about the kingdom. The passage also gives considerable detail about how they should travel, what they should take and how they should respond to opposition.

3. The growth of the kingdom (13:1–52)

We move next from mission to growth. What should we expect concerning the **spread of the kingdom**? Here the teaching is through a series of parables.

- The sower: we should not worry if three out of every four seeds come to nothing. From the one seed in good ground you can get a yield of 30-, 60- and 100-fold, so it will be worth it.
- The wheat and the tares growing together: the kingdom of Satan will grow alongside the kingdom of God, until they are separated at the final harvest.
- The grain of mustard: Jesus describes a seed which becomes a big tree, depicting the growth of the kingdom from very small beginnings and paralleled accurately by the growth of the Church. Jesus started with 11 good men and now has 1,500 million!
- The pearl of great value: we are told how to value the kingdom, for it is like a precious pearl. We should be prepared to give up all we already have in order that we may possess it.
- The net: Jesus tells us not to worry about bad converts, because the kingdom of heaven is like a net which is full of all kinds of fish, both good and bad. His message is that we must wait until the 'fish' are finally brought to shore on the last day, rather than trying to sort them all out as soon as we have caught them.

4. The community of the kingdom (18:1–35)

Matthew includes here some of the teaching Jesus gave concerning the **relationships of those within the local church**. He speaks of how we should deal with those who drift away from the faith, and how we should handle those who sin against others within the community of believers.

5. The future of the kingdom (Chapters 24–25)

By the time Matthew wrote his Gospel, many Christians were asking when Jesus would be returning. So Matthew (as do Luke and Mark) includes a section helping his readers to know what they should look for by way of **signs of his coming**.

The location for this 'sermon' is significant: Jesus and the disciples are sitting on the Mount of Olives overlooking the temple and the disciples are asking Jesus about the end of the age. Matthew links the disciples' questions about this with Jesus' prophecy that one day the temple would be destroyed.

Jesus gives them four signs to look for before his coming:

1. Disasters in the world: wars, famines, earthquakes, false Christs.
2. Developments in the Church: universal persecution, falling numbers, false prophets, completed mission.
3. Danger in the Middle East: sacrilegious dictator, un-equalled (but limited) distress, false Christs and false prophets.
4. Darkness in the sky: sun, moon and stars gone, sky-wide lightning, the coming of the true Christ and Christians gathered 'from the four winds'.

Of these four signs, the first is already to be seen; the second is well on the way; the third has yet to appear, and when it does the fourth will quickly follow.

Matthew continues the section with a series of parables focusing on being ready for the King when he gets back. In every parable there is the phrase 'he was a long time coming', emphasizing the need for faithfulness in the face of consider-able delay.

MAJOR THEMES

We have seen already a number of themes which are part of Matthew's particular concern. There are three others which we also need to consider, all of them fundamental to discipleship in the kingdom.

1. Faith

The first that comes up repeatedly is the theme of faith. It is not unique to Matthew, but is certainly a special interest of his. His message is that a subject of the kingdom who is also a son of the Father lives by faith. This does not refer to a one-off decision of faith, but to someone who, having believed, goes on believing. Often in Matthew, Jesus asks people, 'Do you believe what I have told you? Do you believe that I can do this?' Jesus looks for a **continuing trust** in him and in his Word. He reserves his highest commendation for the centurion who came to him for healing, contrasting his great faith with the lack of faith in some parts of Israel.

2. Righteousness

One theme which you will not find in the other Gospels is that of righteousness – the need for **doing as well as believing**. It is made quite clear that the order is important: you believe first, but you believe in order to do. Take one of the shortest parables in the whole Gospel, for example, about a man who had two sons and asked them to go and work in his vineyard. One said 'yes', but did not go; the other said 'no', but went. Jesus went on to ask which of the two did the will of his father, implying that we can profess to be obedient, but we lie when we do not actually do what he tells us. Being a disciple is not just believing in him but actively 'doing righteousness'.

This is made clear in many places in Matthew's Gospel. It is the underlying reason for the baptism of Jesus, and explains the meaning of it, which is often misunderstood. Why was Jesus baptized? He had no sins to wash away, nothing to be cleansed, and yet he came to John to be baptized. When John protested that it was Jesus who should be baptizing him, Jesus still insisted, because 'it is right for us to fulfil all righteousness'. It was not an act of repentance for him as it was for everybody else, but it was an act of righteousness. His Father had told him to do it, so he did it. At the very start of the Gospel, Jesus demonstrates the importance of doing by modelling himself the very activity he would expect from his followers.

It is not surprising, therefore, that his teaching is full of this theme. He says that, 'unless your righteousness exceeds the righteousness of the Scribes and Pharisees, you will not enter the kingdom'. The Pharisees were a group who were excessively religious. They fasted twice a week; they gave tithes of all they possessed; they traversed sea and land to make proselytes; they were great missionaries; they read their Bibles; they prayed. And yet Jesus said that the righteousness of his followers must exceed all that.

Just as it is important that we understand exactly what is meant by faith, so we must make sure we come to terms with the concept of righteousness as Matthew presents it. Jesus is not saying that we are saved *by* righteousness, but that we are saved *for* righteousness. It is an important distinction. If Matthew's Gospel is given to an unbeliever, they may get the impression that being a Christian means doing good, but in fact it is *after* you become a Christian that – having been saved and forgiven – you are called to display the righteousness of doing as described in Matthew.

3. Judgement

This third theme may seem surprising: it seems to contradict the thesis that Matthew wrote a Gospel for believers. Yet there is in Matthew a considerable volume of teaching on judgement from the lips of Jesus himself. What is more, a close examination of the context of each warning about hell will reveal that all but two were given to born-again believers.

Matthew is **warning disciples against complacency**. Starting to follow Jesus is no ticket to heaven. Followers must fear hell themselves if they are to remain 'on the way'. So while two of the warnings of judgement are given to the Pharisees, the rest are directed at those who had left all to follow Jesus. Most strikingly, he never warns sinners in this way.

This truth becomes especially clear when we consider the context of one of Christ's most famous statements about hell: 'Do not fear those who can kill your body and after that do nothing; rather fear him who can destroy body and soul in hell.' Who is he talking to? He is actually addressing Christian missionaries (the Twelve) just before he sends them out to declare and demonstrate the kingdom. He does not say that the fear of hell should be part of their message to sinners, but rather that they should fear it themselves, for when they fear hell, they will not fear anyone or anything else, even martyrdom.

If we had only the Gospel of Matthew in the whole New Testament we would have enough to know that Christians should fear finishing up on God's rubbish heap, which Jesus called 'Gehenna', the valley of Hinnom outside Jerusalem where everything useless was thrown to be burnt up. Matthew is a sobering Gospel for disciples, teaching them to be serious, to press on, to go on believing, and to go all the way with Jesus.

HOW MATTHEW'S MESSAGE IS TAUGHT

Given Matthew's aim of providing a discipleship manual, we might ask why he put all this teaching into the framework of Mark's Gospel. Why did he not just call it a manual for discipleship and record the teaching which a disciple needs? The answer to this question gives a profound insight into the way Jesus and Matthew intended that their hearers and readers should learn.

Context

Matthew is being true to the way the teaching was originally given by Jesus. Jesus gave his teaching in the context of his deeds and he performed his miracles in the context of his teaching. Teaching needs to be given in this practical context. We need the **balance of word and deed**.

A two-way process

We also need to be told the *indicatives* of the gospel: **what Christ has done for us**, and then be faced with the *imperatives*: **what we are to do for the Lord**. We are led astray if we focus on one and not the other. If we concentrate on what God has done, we might imagine that we need do nothing, and this can lead to licence (i.e. how I live does not matter). If we focus only on what we do for the Lord, we might imagine that it is all down to us, and this can lead to legalism (i.e. my works earn my salvation). Instead, our behaviour needs to follow from our belief – we work out what he works in. The power of the kingdom releases us from sin so that we may live in the purity of the kingdom. The kingdom is both an offer and a demand. So what God does for us and what we do for him are all part of the gospel, the good news of the kingdom.

The need to balance the indicative and the imperative is especially true when we consider the cross of Christ, for it is particularly dangerous to divorce Christ's teaching from all that he achieved there. We cannot teach people how to live the Christian life *without* giving them the teaching in the framework of what Christ achieved for them on the cross. Matthew's order helps us to be continually grateful to Jesus for all he has done. He wisely decided to present the disciples' teaching in the framework of the good news that the Jesus who demanded all this from his followers was the Jesus who healed the sick, raised the dead, and died and rose again for us.

Conclusion

Matthew's Gospel was a firm favourite with the early Church. They were concerned with the Great Commission, to go into all the world and make disciples of all nations, teaching them to observe all that Jesus had commanded. Matthew's Gospel enabled them to do just that, as a manual of discipleship for both Jewish and Gentile believers, uniting the Old and New Testaments and telling the world that the Christ has come, the King of the Jews, fulfilling the promise to Abraham that through him and his seed all the nations of the world would be blessed. Here is the son of David come at last – and here is how we should live today as subjects of the King.

39.

LUKE AND ACTS

Introduction

The Bible is made up of the words of man and the Word of God – many human authors but one divine editor. Most of the authors were responding to an immediate need and had no idea that what they were writing would one day be part of the Bible. We can therefore study the books of the Bible at two levels: the historical and the existential. On the historical level we ask: Why was it written? What was the human reason behind it? On the existential level, we ask: Why is it in our Bible? Why does God want us to know about this? This will be our method as we consider both the Gospel of Luke and the book of Acts later on. The two books have the same author, and together they make a rather special case. So who was Luke and why did he write these two volumes?

Who was Luke?

1. A GENTILE

Luke is unique amongst all the authors in the Bible because he is the only Gentile. His 'English' name comes from the original Loukas and he was a native of Antioch in Syria, which was the Paris of the ancient world at the eastern end of the Mediterranean Sea, well north of the Promised Land.

It was at Antioch that the first Gentile church was established and the followers of Jesus Christ were first called 'Christians' – a somewhat disparaging nickname given to them by the locals who noted that they sought to follow 'Christ'. While this name has become popular today and has a wide range of definitions, in Acts the words 'believer' or 'disciple' were commonly preferred.

Luke was well placed as a Gentile to show through his writing how the gospel spread from Jerusalem to Rome. We can easily forget that it is a unique thing for a religion to jump ethnic barriers, especially from being essentially Jewish to becoming largely Gentile. Most people are born into their national religion and stay there. Here is a religion which has jumped from one people to another. This focus on Gentile readers is demonstrated in a number of ways. For example, Luke avoids the Hebrew and Aramaic expressions like 'rabbi' and 'Abba' used in Matthew and Mark, preferring to translate such words into Greek for his readers, to make sure that they understand.

2. A DOCTOR

Luke was a doctor by profession – the apostle Paul refers to him as 'the beloved physician' when writing to the Colossian church. Medicine had been developing for 400 years and doctors received careful training. Luke needed to be observant, analytical and careful in his records – skills which he also uses in writing his Gospel and the book of Acts.

There are many incidents which betray Luke's medical background. The birth of Jesus, for example, is told from Mary's angle. We have the details of Jesus' circumcision, mention of the swaddling clothes or diapers – all the kind of things a doctor would be interested in. (Incidentally, Luke gives us Mary's genealogy to trace Christ's physical ancestry, while

Matthew gives us Joseph's line.) When Mark describes the sickness of Peter's mother-in-law he calls it simply a fever; Luke writes of a 'high fever'. Of the miracles which Luke records, five out of six are miracles of healing.

God uses a doctor to report the supernatural! The virgin birth, the miracles of Jesus, and the signs and wonders in the book of Acts all come from Luke's pen. Some doctors are sceptical about anything which is outside the natural, physical realm, but Luke is able to bring his considerable skill as a writer and physician to record what actually took place, even when it was outside medical knowledge or ability.

3. A HISTORIAN

Luke was meticulous in his detail, wording and grasp of cultural nuances. Not an apostle himself, he was dependent for his knowledge of Jesus on those who were close to him. Some modern historians have criticized his writing, claiming that he was mistaken, but subsequent archaeological findings have always found in favour of Luke, to the point where he is now recognized as one of the finest historians of his day. Indeed, if we treat 'Gospel' as a different genre from 'history', as suggested earlier (page 780), then Luke is the only *history* writer in the New Testament. His primary objective was to provide an accurate and reliable account of what had been said and done in the life of Jesus, rather than announce the good news of salvation, though there was bound to be an overlap between the two.

4. A TRAVELLER

Luke was also a very experienced traveller. It is Luke who refers to the 'Sea' of Galilee as a 'lake' – it is only 13 kilometres long and 8 kilometres wide. To a seasoned traveller, this would certainly be merely a lake! He travelled with the apostle Paul, indicated by the so-called 'we' passages in Acts. Luke remains anonymous, similar to other New Testament writers, seeking to divert attention away from himself, but the use of 'we' betrays the fact that he was there. Luke was Paul's travelling companion, especially when Paul was at sea – on the voyage from Troas to Philippi, Philippi to Jerusalem, and Caesarea to Rome. Maybe Paul felt the need of a physician when he sailed? Some of Luke's finest writing depicts the voyages towards the end of Acts and the eventual wreck on the shores of Malta.

This willingness to travel is a significant factor in our understanding of how Luke's Gospel and Acts came to be written. We know that Paul was under arrest for two years in each of two places – in Caesarea and Rome. We will see later that it was probably during these times that Luke composed his two-volume work – the Gospel in Caesarea, and Acts in Rome, where of course he could interview Paul at his leisure.

5. A WRITER

Luke writes in an educated, polished Greek similar to that of Hellenistic historians. His skill as a writer will be examined when we consider Luke and Acts in more detail. His account of the shipwreck in Malta has been acclaimed as one of the masterpieces of literature from the ancient world. He has a good vocabulary, an excellent style, and an ability to hold the reader's interest, with a smooth and speedy switch from one plot to the next. His skill as a historian is also evident; his research is thorough and he knows what to include and what to leave out.

6. AN EVANGELIST

Luke was an evangelist – with his pen rather than his voice. 'Salvation' is a key word in both books. That word and its cognates are used repeatedly. As a Gentile Luke is especially concerned that salvation comes to 'all flesh'. In his Gospel he records John the Baptist's quotation from Isaiah, 'and all flesh shall see the salvation of God', and many have seen this as the key theme of the Gospel of Luke.

We will see later, in our study of the Gospel, how Luke has particular interest in various groups of people who can and will see the salvation of God. Similarly, the theme of Acts is the Holy Spirit poured out on all flesh – on Jews, on Samaritans, unto the ends of the earth. This 'Jewish' religion is for everybody in the whole wide world: Luke portrays Jesus as the Saviour of the world.

History records that Luke died at the age of 84 in Boeotia in Greece, having never married.

The audience

Having looked at the writer, let us turn now to the audience he was writing for in his two-volume work. Luke wrote these volumes for one man, Theophilus, which literally means 'Mr God-Friendly'. It seems strange that he should spend four years researching in order to write for just one person, even if he did think there might be a wider audience one day. Who was this man Theophilus?

One theory is that Theophilus is a fictional figure, just as an author might write a book for an imaginary representative of a group – 'Dear Mr Sincere Enquirer'. So Theophilus is a made-up name, 'God-Friendly' meaning somebody who is interested in the faith and wanting to find God. However valid the theory, however, it does not fit all the facts.

Others argue that he was a real person, probably a publisher interested in Christianity – an intriguing idea, certainly. It is indeed better to see Theophilus as an individual who really did exist. He was obviously a man of some importance, in some public office, because Luke gives him a title as well as a name: 'Most Excellent' Mr God-Friendly. This is precisely the same title used for Festus and Felix when they presided over Paul's trials, strongly suggesting that Theophilus was in the legal profession, either a lawyer or a judge. Why, though, would Luke want to give a lawyer such a full account, first of Jesus and then of Paul?

Paul's defence lawyer

If we imagine that Theophilus is Paul's defence lawyer, or even his judge at the trial in Rome, then it becomes clear. Either would need to have a full brief, detailing the circumstances leading to the trial.

How did this new religion start? Who was the founder? How did Paul come to be part of its propagation? Furthermore, the lawyer would be especially interested in how this faith was viewed by the Roman authorities. So when Paul was imprisoned in Caesarea, Luke researched the life and death of Jesus, and when Paul was moved to prison in Rome, he did all the research and recording of Paul's contribution to this new religion.

His work includes traces of him having interviewed a number of people we know to be important in the New Testament Church: James, probably Matthew, and certainly John (there are some things in Luke that are only otherwise found in John – for example, he and John are the only two to record the cutting off of Malchus' ear during the arrest of Jesus).

Compilation of the books

Luke had certain disadvantages when it came to collecting the necessary material for the 'defence brief'. He was not one of the Twelve, he had never met Jesus, and he was not an eyewitness of his life and ministry. But he overcame these difficulties by visiting those who *were* eyewitnesses. He collected the accounts about Jesus while he was waiting for two years in

Caesarea until Paul was shipped to Rome. When Paul arrived in Rome, there were another two years during which Luke could write up the story of Paul in his second volume, the 'Acts of the Apostles'.

If the notion of the 'defence brief' is correct, it would explain so much in both volumes. It would explain why the Romans are portrayed as entirely sympathetic to this new religion throughout the two books. Both in the trial of Jesus and in the trial of Paul, Luke includes three statements that the men are totally innocent. Pilate says three times that Jesus is innocent, and three times Roman authorities say Paul could have gone free if he had not appealed to Rome. So in both volumes the trouble surrounding the Christians is not caused by Romans, but by Jews seeking to cause problems for this new faith.

Eyewitnesses

A lawyer would require first-hand testimony, eyewitness accounts, and **carefully researched facts** presented in an orderly fashion. Both of Luke's volumes include careful dating by Roman events (e.g. Luke 2:1 and 3:1) and his introduction to Theophilus in his first volume confirms his purpose: 'Many have undertaken to draw up an account of the things that have been fulfilled among us, just as they were handed down to us by those who from the first were eyewitnesses and servants of the word. Therefore, since I myself have carefully investigated everything from the beginning, it seemed good also to me to write an orderly account for you, most excellent Theophilus, so that you may know the certainty of the things you have been informed about.' This wording certainly fits in with the type of material a lawyer would require.

FOCUS ON PAUL

This theory also explains the unusual features of the second volume. Acts is known as the 'Acts of the Apostles', but it centres on just two of them, barely mentions others and omits any reference to the majority. In addition, while Peter is the main character in the first 12 chapters, he disappears almost as soon as Paul is converted. The book then focuses almost exclusively on Paul, accounting for two-thirds of the account. This would seem an unusual proportion, unless the whole work was primarily intended to defend Paul and explain to the Roman authorities that there was nothing seditious or subversive about the new religion. Paul is thus depicted as a Roman citizen, innocent by Roman law and deserving a 'not guilty' verdict at his trial.

There is also an interesting difference to be noted from Jesus' trial in Jerusalem. He was innocent by Roman law, yet was crucified because of Jewish pressure. Paul, by contrast, is on trial in a place where the Jews could not influence the verdict. His appeal to Caesar precluded their interference.

It explains too why Paul's testimony is given three times in the book of Acts – a little excessive (none of the other apostles give their testimony) unless it is because Paul is on trial and it is vital that the lawyer hear what he said at every one of his previous trials, so that all of it can be used in evidence for him and not against him.

In addition, seeing Acts as a defence lawyer's brief helps explain why Acts finishes so abruptly. It stops with Paul awaiting trial. This also discredits other arguments for the purpose of Acts. If it was purely an account of Paul's life, this would be an odd place to finish. We know that Luke himself lived to the age of 84, so he was alive to record Paul's death if that had been his purpose with Acts. If, on the other hand, the purpose was legal, then the brief finishes as we would expect, with Paul awaiting trial.

One final anomaly could clinch the matter. Why would Dr Luke give so much space to such a detailed account of the shipwreck on Malta if he was aiming to write a history of the early Church? And why would he describe only this disaster at sea, since Paul had been through at least three others? Surely it was because he wished to highlight Paul's exemplary behaviour in not attempting to escape in the confusion, but instead saving the lives of all on board, including his Roman captors, who were responsible for delivering him safely to the Roman court. After recounting this heroic and patriotic effort, I can imagine the defence lawyer at Paul's trial concluding with the words, 'I rest my case, your honour.'

WAS THIS BRIEF SUCCESSFUL?

All the evidence points to Paul being acquitted at his first trial in Rome. The letters he wrote to Timothy and Titus contain details which do not fit into his life before that and so imply that he was freed. There is even a strong tradition that he achieved his ambition of reaching Spain. Some of the ancient churches in Spain claim that Paul was their founder.

We cannot say for certain, but the evidence of tradition points to the fact that Paul was released at his first trial, but later re-arrested and then beheaded. Despite that ultimate outcome, it looks as if Luke's work was not wasted: if he wrote the two volumes primarily to save Paul's life in that first trial, and thus free the apostle for more ministry, then he succeeded.

Conclusion

We have focused here on Luke's concern for Paul, but it is also clear that the trial had repercussions for Christianity everywhere. It was not just Paul but *Christianity* that was on trial: what happened in Rome spread everywhere, so this was an important test case.

Luke's two volumes could be called *The History of Christianity, Parts 1 and 2*. They comprise a superbly written account covering a period of 33 years, from the beginning of Jesus' public ministry through to Paul's imprisonment or house arrest in Rome. It is full of unique information, so that the original reader and also later readers would know for sure what took place and how they should respond.

Luke was doubtless aware that his work would interest a **wider audience** too, with the general public in Rome becoming aware of the amazing spread of Christianity. Soon it would no longer be seen as a sect of Judaism, but as an advancing, universal and international faith, and it was becoming important news in Rome itself. Luke's work, therefore, was not just a defence brief, but a **declaration of the faith** and as such was a crucial contribution to the mission among the Gentiles.

His Gospel, therefore, is a piece of unique material. In the opening he tells Theophilus that many others have drawn up accounts of what happened. He would have known about Mark, maybe Matthew and possibly other records. But his own Gospel is the fruit of **wide-ranging, original research**, including interviews and verbatim accounts from eyewitnesses, all set within the context of the Roman world. He portrays the wide vista and then zooms in to focus on individuals. Despite the fact that Luke was not himself an apostle, there was never any doubt that Luke–Acts should be included in the New Testament 'canon'. That is truly a mark of how the early Church regarded this outstanding work, 'apostolic' in content and authority if not in authorship.

40.

LUKE

Introduction

Luke is the best loved but the least well known of all the four Gospels. This may seem a surprising observation. Most people know the parts **unique** to Luke extremely well: the parable of the Good Samaritan is a favourite of many, with the very words now included in our language; most people know what is meant by 'the prodigal returns' from the story of the 'prodigal' son; the accounts of Jesus meeting with Zacchaeus, Mary and Martha, the dying thief and the two on the road to Emmaus are also very familiar.

But where Luke's material **overlaps** with the other Gospels, we tend to know their accounts much better than his. For example, what is meant by the description of disciples as 'salt', recorded by Matthew and Luke? Most people assume that this refers to the work of the believer in being a preservative and a flavouring in society, taking the meaning from the uses of salt in food preparation. But Luke records further details, saying that if salt loses its saltiness it is fit neither for the soil nor the manure heap. This implies that the metaphor is actually to do with the land and not the kitchen. Salt came from the Dead Sea and was full of potash and other salts. It was used as a fertilizer in farming and as a disinfectant for human waste. As such, salt made good things grow and stopped bad things spreading: the disciples, Jesus said, should do the same. Most people fail to notice Luke's additional details and read their own meaning into Matthew's 'salt of the earth'.

Another example of our neglect of Luke comes in the saying, 'For if men do these things when the tree is green, what will happen when it is dry?' On speaking engagements I have often teased my hearers by taking a vote on whether they think this comes from the Old Testament, the New Testament or William Shakespeare. The majority are usually wrong! Actually, Jesus said these words as he carried his cross to Calvary. Only Luke records these words, which few seem to have read.

Elements unique to Luke

The structure of Luke's Gospel is based on Mark's arrangement, with the key watershed moment happening at Caesarea Philippi, after which Jesus made for Jerusalem. But it can also be seen as falling into five sections:

1:1–4:13	The first 30 years of private life
4:14–9:50	Galilean ministry
9:51–19:44	Journey to Jerusalem, with teaching greatly expanded
19:45–23:56	Last days in Jerusalem (this part is radically different from Mark's approach)
24	Resurrection and ascension

Let us consider the parts which are unique to Luke.

Birth stories

The birth stories are all from **Mary's angle**, in contrast to Matthew's focus on Joseph. It gives a very different feel to the narrative. Luke has more human interest and gives intimate details of the conception and delivery, even mentioning the swaddling clothes. Luke includes a genealogy of Jesus as Matthew does, but his is drawn from Mary's side and goes back further, to Adam. Legally, Jesus is a descendant of David through Joseph, but his physical descent is traced through Mary, also to King David. So Jesus is a royal prince twice over.

Luke's birth narrative also indirectly gives us the **month of Jesus' birth**. We are told that Zechariah belonged to the priestly tribe of Abijah. We know from 1 Chronicles which month this tribe was called on to serve in the temple: in the one-year cycle they were the eighth tribe out of 24. So Zechariah was there in the fourth month of the Jewish calendar. We know that Elizabeth became pregnant at that time, and that this was six months ahead of Mary, so we can calculate that Jesus was born 15 months later, in the seventh month of the following year at the Feast of Tabernacles (late September or early October to us). The Jews expected the Messiah to come at that feast and still look for him then to this day.

Boyhood story

Luke records the only story about the first 30 years of Jesus' life. At the age of 12 Jesus had his Bar Mitzvah, which means 'able to do good deeds'. When a Jewish boy reaches this age he becomes responsible for his own behaviour. Up to the age of 12 the parents are punished when the boy does wrong, but from then on he is responsible for his own behaviour and for keeping God's commandments. He is taken to the synagogue and he reads a portion of the law of Moses. From that time on he is considered a man. At that point he becomes a partner with his father in whatever trade or profession his father has.

This explains the story of **Jesus' visit to Jerusalem with Joseph and Mary**. In those days the women went ahead, walking 15 miles a day and then putting the tents up and cooking the meal for the arrival of the men. The children under 12 travelled with their mothers, and the boys over 12 travelled with their fathers. Jesus may have travelled there with Mary, as he had always done before, but as he was now 12 it would have been normal for him to have come back with Joseph. It is understandable that each thought Jesus was with the other.

It also sheds further light on the reply Jesus made when Mary found him in the temple. 'Didn't you know that I was in my father's house [or business]?' These are the first recorded words of Jesus. The most amazing thing is that it then says he came back to Nazareth and was subject to his parents. The story reveals that Jesus knew who he really was, even at the age of 12. It is also clear that Mary had never told him who he was (she refers to Joseph as 'your father').

Baptism

At the baptism of Jesus Luke also includes unique information. It is Luke who tells us that **Jesus received the Holy Spirit** after his baptism **as a result of prayer**. Matthew and Mark record him receiving the Spirit as he came up out of the water, but it is Luke who mentions his prayer: 'And as he was praying, heaven was opened and the Holy Spirit descended on him in bodily form like a dove.' Indeed, Luke tells us more about baptism in the Spirit than any other writer in the New Testament. This is a theme we will consider in more detail later (page 849).

The teaching of Jesus

UNIQUE TEACHING BLOCKS

Luke's treatment of Jesus' teaching is also different. Matthew's Sermon on the Mount becomes the Sermon on the Plain and every beatitude is matched with a woe. So, for example, 'Blessed are you who mourn' is coupled with 'Woe to you who laugh now'. This need not suggest that Matthew and Luke conflict in any way. It is clear that Jesus preached that sermon more than once and in varied forms. Luke has simply given us a very different and shorter form of the sermon.

UNIQUE PARABLES

A number of Jesus' stories we owe entirely to Luke:

- The parable of the good Samaritan
- The parable of the prodigal son (or rather prodigal father and two lost sons – see the paraphrase on pages 854–857)
- The parable of the persistent widow
- The parable of the Pharisee and the tax collector
- The parable of the friend at midnight, banging on a neighbour's door to get some bread for an unexpected visitor
- The parable of the barren fig tree
- The parable of the crooked manager
- The parable of Lazarus and the rich man who finished up in hell – the only parable to have the name of anyone in it ('Lazarus' may even refer to an actual person; see paraphrase on pages 859–860)
- The parable of the two debtors

UNIQUE INCIDENTS

Among the unique events are:

- The miraculous catch of fish
- The mission of 'the Seventy' (given as 72 in some versions)
- The ascension. This is the only Gospel to include an account of the ascension, apart from the brief mention in Mark's 'longer' ending, and Luke also records an account of it at the start of Acts, thus linking the two works and emphasizing the significance of this event.

Luke also includes particular incidents about **people** who especially interested him.

- The prostitute who anointed Jesus' feet in the house of a Pharisee
- The woman touching the hem of his garment in the middle of a big crowd
- The meal at the home of Martha and Mary
- The tax collector up a tree (Zacchaeus)
- The healing of the man with dropsy
- The crippled woman
- The ten lepers
- The widow's offering
- The dying thief
- The two on the road to Emmaus

These stories underline that Luke had more interest in people than any other Gospel writer – not an unexpected feature from someone who was a family doctor.

Interest in people

There are at least six groups of people in whom Luke had a special interest.

1. SAMARITANS

Samaritans were a group **regarded as outcasts by the Jews**, because they were the result of Jewish intermarriage with Gentiles during the exile. There was so much antagonism that Jews travelling between Judaea and Galilee would make a longer journey east of the Jordan rather than travel through Samaria.

Only Luke tells us that the one leper who returned to say 'thank you' after 10 were healed was a Samaritan. The rest were Jewish, and they took the blessing of healing for granted.

Luke also records how James and John wanted to call down fire from heaven on the Samaritans because they were rude to Jesus. He then continues the story in Acts, where we read how John comes back to Samaria with Peter, to pray that the Samaritans might receive the fire of the Holy Spirit!

He also, of course, tells the story of the Good Samaritan, 'good' not being an adjective normally regarded as appropriate for these people. In playing on the Jewish hearers' astonishment that such a person might be so caring, Luke reveals his concern that this story of Jesus be preserved – as an encouragement to Samaritans, no doubt, and as an aid to healing the rift between the two peoples.

2. GENTILES

As a Gentile himself, it is natural that Gentiles should figure large in Luke's story, and the label itself is made prominent. Luke betrays this theme early on, when Simeon says that Jesus would be 'a **light to the Gentiles**'.

He records Jesus' mention of the widow of Zarephath and Naaman the Syrian in his sermon at Nazareth. It was the suggestion that these Gentiles had more faith than the people of Israel that caused local people to attempt to take Jesus' life.

Luke also tells us of the sending out of the Seventy, a number which Jews regarded as symbolic of the nations, based on

Genesis 10, and he includes the ministry of Jesus east of Jordan in Perea. The other Gospel writers include Jesus' journey from the north to Jerusalem, but omit the work he accomplished on the journey through non-Jewish territory.

3. OUTCASTS

Luke has a great interest in all outcasts, in **any people whom others treated with contempt**. He records the healing of the 10 lepers, and the calling of Zacchaeus the tax collector. This profession was despised on two counts: first because of the tax collectors' collusion with the Romans, who gave them the responsibility to collect the taxes, and second because their wages came from whatever they could acquire on top of the taxes themselves. Yet not only does Jesus meet with Zacchaeus, a member of this unpopular profession, but we are also told that on that day 'salvation' came to his house.

Luke also records the involvement of the shepherds in witnessing and broadcasting news of the birth of Jesus. In those days shepherds had a reputation for being untrustworthy parasites on society, living on what they could pilfer from others. As a result, a shepherd's testimony was not regarded as legitimate in a court of law.

It is also noteworthy how Luke includes the story of the ex-prostitute who anointed Jesus' feet, her model response to his forgiveness being an object lesson to the self-righteous.

4. WOMEN

Luke shows a particular interest in women. Martha and Mary have been mentioned already. In addition Luke writes of the woman touching the hem of Jesus' cloak, and the healing that then took place. No other writers comment on the women weeping for Jesus as he carried his cross. Furthermore, Luke names the wealthy women who supported Jesus' ministry financially. The Gospel includes **10 women who are not mentioned anywhere else** and another three in parables.

5. POOR

Luke seems almost **biased towards the poor**. For example, he records Jesus' words, 'Blessed are you who are poor' and 'Woe to you who are rich', whereas Matthew says, 'Blessed are the poor in spirit' and includes no reference to the rich. In Luke's Gospel poverty is seen as a blessing, in contrast to the way it was viewed by the people of Israel, who thought it was a sign of God's disapproval. He records that Mary and Joseph brought pigeons to the temple for sacrifice at the birth of Jesus. This was the cheapest possible sacrifice allowed under Levitical law.

He also includes a number of other sayings reflecting aspects of Jesus' teaching which touch on poverty:

■ 'Give to everyone who asks you, and if anyone takes what belongs to you do not demand it back.'
■ Jesus said to his host, 'When you give a luncheon or dinner, do not invite your friends, your brothers or relatives or your rich neighbours; if you do, they may invite you back and so you will be repaid. But when you give a banquet, invite the poor, the crippled, the lame, the blind, and you will be blessed. Although they cannot repay you, you will be repaid at the resurrection of the righteous.'
■ At the parable of the great banquet: 'Go out quickly into the streets and alleys of the town and bring in the poor, the crippled, the blind and the lame.'
■ In the parable of the rich man and Lazarus: 'The time came when the beggar died and the angels carried him to Abraham's side. In hell where the rich man was in torment, he looked up and saw Abraham far away, with Lazarus by his side...'

6. SINNERS

The last category of people in whom Luke shows a special
interest may seem surprising. But did Jesus not come to save
sinners? A 'sinner' in those days was a special term for Jews
who had **given up trying to keep the law of Moses**. There
were 613 laws of Moses, which was hard enough, but the
religious leaders had added even more. A high proportion of
the population had just given up. Luke records stories and
incidents highlighting that these were the very people Jesus
had come to reach. He highlights how the Pharisees hated
Jesus because he mixed with people who were not keeping
the laws. How could he be close to God yet be so close to
'sinners'?

Luke is a very **humanitarian Gospel**. People mattered to
Luke as they did to Jesus. He was concerned for those who
could not help themselves, and whom others *would* not help. He
was clearly fond of the word *splanknidzomai*, which means
'compassion', depicting Jesus as a man living not for his own
power or popularity but so that the powerless might be
touched by God. This is summed up in a statement at the end
of the story of Zacchaeus: 'He came to seek and save the lost.'
Similarly, we read: '...and the people all tried to touch him,
because power was coming from him and healing them all'.

Other emphases in Luke

1. ANGELS

Luke has a particular interest in angels, especially at the start of
his narrative. Heavenly beings announce the birth of John to
Elizabeth, tell Zechariah what to name his son and announce
the birth of Jesus to Mary. Then later, when Jesus is tempted in
the wilderness, Luke records the ministry of angels, and as
Jesus prays in Gethsemane we read: 'An angel from heaven
appeared to him and strengthened him.'

It is said that members of the medical profession are the most sceptical about the supernatural. Luke the medic and careful historian not only sees no difficulty in including angels in his narrative, but is keen to stress their **vital role**.

2. THE HOLY SPIRIT

Luke has been called the '**charismatic Gospel**'. There is more about the Holy Spirit in Luke than in Matthew and Mark combined.

- Luke records how the Holy Spirit is responsible for the conception of Jesus: 'The Holy Spirit will come upon you, and the power of the Most High will overshadow you.'
- Both Elizabeth and Zechariah are said to have been filled with the Holy Spirit and it was prophesied that John the Baptist would be filled with the Holy Spirit within the womb.
- The Old Testament concept of anointing by the Spirit is also seen in Anna and Simeon. Simeon is moved by the Spirit to meet the baby Jesus and Anna is described as a prophetess.
- The Holy Spirit came upon Jesus at his baptism. Then we are told: 'Jesus, full of the Holy Spirit, returned from the Jordan and was led by the Spirit in the desert.'
- After the time of temptation in the desert, 'Jesus returned to Galilee in the power of the Spirit...'
- Luke records Jesus' teaching on praying for the Spirit: '...how much more will your Father in heaven give the Holy Spirit to those who go on asking him'.

The Gospel finishes with Jesus telling his followers to wait in Jerusalem until they are 'clothed with power from on high'. Luke's interest in the Holy Spirit continues into his second volume, and Acts includes even more frequent references.

3. PRAYER

a) By Jesus

Luke writes about Jesus' prayers far more than any other Gospel author. As noted earlier, the giving of the Spirit at his baptism was in response to prayer from Jesus and this was his first recorded prayer. His last is uttered on the cross: 'Father, into your hands I commit my spirit.'

In between these two, Luke records nine occasions on which Jesus prayed. Seven of these are unique to Luke. Jesus seems to have been **constantly praying to his Father** for direction.

b) By disciples

Luke is also concerned that we should understand the **importance of prayer for every disciple**. Chapter 11 especially includes extensive teaching on this. In addition, the parable of the persistent widow gives encouragement that God is willing to answer prayer, and the parable which follows, contrasting the tax collector and the Pharisee, encourages humility in prayer. Prayer is no less essential for those who would follow Jesus than it was for Jesus himself.

4. JOY

Luke has **more words connected with the root word 'joy' than any other book in the New Testament**. Luke is the only author, for example, to use the word for laughter. He also records the joy in heaven over one sinner who repents. And on one occasion, Jesus was 'full of joy through the Holy Spirit'.

This theme is linked with that of praise and worship. The birth narrative opens with the song of the angels, 'Glory to God in the highest', and finishes in the temple with people 'praising God'. Luke continually **lifts his readers up to heaven**. Some of the most beautiful songs of praise are in

Luke, such as the 'Magnificat' (Mary's song) and the 'Nunc Dimittis' (Simeon's song).

5. THE UNIVERSAL GOSPEL

Luke is the universal Gospel, showing Jesus to be the **Saviour of the whole world**. It is a theme which can be seen throughout the book, as this Gentile writer impresses on his largely Gentile readers how this good news can be for them.

- He does this first with the genealogy of Jesus. He does not stress his Jewish roots as Matthew does, but goes back to Adam, highlighting the humanity of Jesus and the fact that the gospel is for all: God has always been concerned with *all* peoples.
- From the very beginning the angels' song includes the words 'peace on earth, good will towards men'.
- Luke quotes Isaiah, telling us that 'all flesh will see God's salvation'.
- The Seventy are sent out not to the 'lost sheep of Israel', as the Twelve are directed in Matthew, but to 'every city and place'.
- We read that 'people will come from east and west and north and south, and will take their places at the feast in the kingdom of God'.
- At the end of the Gospel Jesus predicts that 'repentance and forgiveness of sins will be preached in his name to all nations'.

So here, faithfully recorded by Luke, is a faith with strong Jewish roots, based in a Jewish context, and which reaches its climax in Jerusalem – all in readiness for the story of Acts, when the faith spreads across the empire, even reaching Rome itself. As such, it is the least Jewish of all the Gospels, as we might expect given Luke's concern to convince the Gentiles of the certainty of the events he records.

How are we to read Luke's Gospel?

A human Gospel

This is a Gospel **for humans lost in sin**. Jesus is the Saviour. Alone of all the Gospels 'salvation' is used as a noun in Luke. Luke wants his readers to know the salvation of Christ, based on the historical events he has described. The verb 'to save' is used more here than in any other New Testament book.

Luke tells us that 'today' is a day of salvation (this is said 11 times, compared to 8 in Matthew and once in Mark), and 'now' salvation has come (14 times, compared to 4 in Matthew and 3 in Mark). He underlines that mercy, forgiveness and reconciliation are available here and now. This salvation comes through the cross of Christ – it is like another baptism for Jesus. Just as the Jewish people were liberated from captivity in Egypt, so his cross provides a new 'exodus' for his people. This, therefore, is a saving Gospel. Luke wants his readers to find salvation in Jesus.

A happy Gospel

The themes of **praise and rejoicing keep recurring**. It is the Gospel that mentions laughter and it has more words connected with joy than any other. In the popular parables in Chapter 15 we see the joy of those who find what was lost, depicting the joy in heaven over the sinner who repents. The response of the disciples to the risen Lord is joy, and the Gospel concludes with rejoicing. In this sense it is attractive and 'user-friendly', an ideal Gospel for the outsider who wants to learn more about Jesus.

A heavenly Gospel

Luke keeps the **focus on heaven**. He stresses the supernatural birth of Jesus, the involvement of the Holy Spirit, and the importance of prayer. He wants those who read it, whatever their background, to be in heaven. The words of Jesus in the parable of the great banquet sum up his concern: 'Go out to the roads and country lanes and make them come in, so that my house will be full.' Luke knows that God has people from all nations he intends to bring into heaven – for Jesus truly is the Saviour of the world.

A most readable Gospel

Luke was able to put the elements of his story together with great skill. We often name the story in Luke 15 the 'parable of the prodigal son', for example. But this is because we fail to see Luke's **abilities as a writer**, and we also fail to appreciate the parable in its context within the Gospel. It is actually the parable of the prodigal *father*, who wasted his money by giving it to his two boys. When you read Chapters 15 and 16 straight through, you can see how the themes flow – and how Luke has carefully composed a most readable Gospel.

Chapter 15 begins with tax collectors and sinners, eating inside a house with Jesus, while Pharisees and scribes murmur outside. The rest of the two chapters all flow out of this setting and explain it. Jesus tells the story of a sheep which is lost; it is far away from where it should be and knows it. Then he speaks of a coin that is lost at home, but does not know it – one story for the men, one for the women, but two 'lost' items.

Then we come to the major story of two lost sons, with the emphasis not on the younger, but the older son. He is more 'lost' than the younger one, but he does not know it. The younger son is therefore like the lost sheep, lost far away and knowing it. The older son is like the lost coin, lost at home but not knowing it.

The parallels do not end there, however, for when we move on to Chapter 16, we again see two characters, corresponding to the two sons in Chapter 15. The first is a puzzling story about a rogue whom Jesus commends for dishonesty. Interestingly, exactly the same word is used to describe the younger son *wasting* his substance in the far country, and for the rogue *wasting* his master's substance. So we have the same word and the same character. Likewise, just as the elder son claimed he did everything right – 'I never broke a commandment of yours' – so the rich man in the second story in Chapter 16 is not described as guilty of any sin, vice or crime, yet he finishes up in hell because of his indifference to others, his indulgence of himself and his independence from God.

A **unified theme** flows through these parables, therefore, carefully presented by Luke. Sadly our chapter and verse divisions have served to separate what Luke so skilfully and deliberately brought together. The following paraphrase of the stories Jesus told is designed to re-emphasize Luke's unified theme.

Paraphrased parables

Two men and their money (Luke 15–16)

Some time later the spiritual outcasts, some simply irreligious and others downright immoral, gathered around Jesus to hear what he had to say. But the Pharisees and the legal scholars criticized him for associating with them and muttered among themselves, 'This fellow seems to enjoy the company of those who don't even *try* to keep God's laws – he actually has meals with them!' So Jesus defended his action by telling them a story.

'Which of you men,' he began, 'owning a flock of 100 sheep and losing one of them, wouldn't leave the 99 in the open field where they were and search everywhere for the lost one until he has found it again? And when he does find it, he's so happy he thinks nothing of carrying it all the way back on his shoulders. When he gets it home, he invites all his friends and neighbours: "Come and celebrate with me – I've found that sheep I'd lost!" I'm telling you, it's exactly the same in heaven; there's more excitement up there over a single sinner who's brought back from his wilful wandering than over 99 respectable citizens who never put a foot wrong!

'Or what woman owning a valuable pendant with 10 silver tokens, and losing one of them, wouldn't get a torch and brush and search every nook and cranny until she has found it again? And when she does find it, she's so happy she invites all her friends and neighbours, "Come and celebrate with me. I just found that coin I'd lost!" I'm telling you, it's exactly the same among God's angels; they also celebrate every time just one sinner has a change of heart.'

Then Jesus added, 'There was once a man with two sons. The younger one went to his father and demanded, "Dad, I want my share of the business now, before you die." So the father divided his assets between the two brothers. Not long afterwards the younger son turned his capital into cash and went abroad. There he squandered his fortune on an extravagant lifestyle. Just when he had spent all his money, that country was hit by a bad harvest which led to a severe shortage of food. Prices rocketed and he soon felt the pinch. To stay alive he hung around a local landowner who let him cart swill to the pigs. Often he longed to stuff his own stomach from the same trough, but no one even thought of giving him anything.

'When he finally came to his senses, he said to himself, "Just think – all those hired hands on my father's farm have more than enough to eat, while here I am, starving to death. I'd better get back to my father again. I'll just say to him,

'I realize I've done a terrible wrong, both against God and against you. I'm not fit to be regarded as your son again, but how about taking me on to the payroll with the other employees?'"

'So he set off home. But while he still had some way to go, his father spotted him coming. He was moved to the depths of his being and ran out to meet his son, threw his arms around his neck and kept kissing him. The son began his prepared speech: "Dad, I realize I've been terribly wrong, from God's viewpoint as well as yours – I just don't deserve to be regarded as your son any more..."

'But his father interrupted him, turned to his servants who had come to see what was happening, and ordered them, "Bring my best suit and get him properly dressed, put my signet ring on his finger and get some shoes for his feet. And slaughter that calf we've been fattening up. We must have a big meal to celebrate such an occasion. My son was as good as dead to me and he's come back into my life again. I thought I'd lost him, but we've found each other again!" So the festivities got under way.

'All this time the elder son had been out working in the fields. As soon as he approached the family home at the end of the day, he heard sounds of a party – people were singing and dancing to a band. So he summoned one of the lads standing around and asked what it was all in aid of. The lad blurted out, "Your brother's back and your father has slaughtered the calf you were fattening because he's home safe and sound."

'The elder brother was furious and refused to go anywhere near. So out rushed the father for the second time that day, to appeal to him to change his attitude. But he exploded in anger, "Look at all the years I've been slaving for you here! Never once have I disobeyed your orders or gone against your wishes. Yet you have never even let me kill a baby goat to have a good time with my pals. But as soon as this son of yours turns up, having swallowed up your hard-earned savings in brothels, then you go and kill the best animal on the farm in his honour!"

'But the father gently replied, "My dear boy, you were the one who stayed here by my side and you know that the remaining estate is already made over to you. Don't you understand that we just had to have this celebration? For here is your brother, who's been as good as dead to us, and now he's living with us again. I thought we'd lost him for ever, but now we've found each other again."'

Jesus went on to tell another story to his own followers. 'Once upon a time there was a wealthy man who employed an agent to manage his estate, and reports reached him that this man was embezzling his capital. So he sent for the man and faced him with it. "What's all this I keep hearing about you? I'm going to have your accounts audited right away. I can't keep you on as manager."

'So the agent considered his future prospects. "What can I possibly do for a living," he said to himself, "now that the boss has given me the sack? I'll make sure that when I'm out of a job there'll be plenty of my former clients who want to help me out."

'So he sent for every tenant who had an outstanding debt to his employer. To the first one who came, he said, "How much do you owe my boss?"

'"Four thousand litres of oil," he replied.

'Then the agent said, "Here is the original contract. Quick, sit down here and alter the figure to two thousand." Later he said to another, "You there. How much did you agree to pay?"

'He replied, "Two hundred sacks of wheat."

'So the agent said, "Here's your agreement; you can cut the figure down by a fifth."

'When the landlord heard about those revised contracts, he couldn't help congratulating the dishonest agent for his quick thinking and shrewd move.

'Sadly it's often the case that those who live for what this world offers show more sense in their business dealings with other people than those who have been enlightened about the other world. So my advice to you is this,' said Jesus. 'Use the world's dirty money to make sure you have plenty of friends, so that when you finally leave all your assets behind, they will welcome you with open arms into heaven itself.

'The man who is trustworthy in trifling matters will have the same integrity in big deals too. And the man who cheats over small amounts will be just as crooked in big business. So if you can't be trusted to handle a corruptible commodity like money, who is going to let you look after anything of lasting value? And if you are unreliable in looking after other people's assets, who will ever think of giving you some of your own?

'No employee can ever work wholeheartedly for two employers. He is bound to make comparisons and will like one better than the other, or be more loyal to one, while being less concerned for the other. That's why you can't devote yourself to making money and serving God at the same time.'

Some Pharisees overheard these remarks of Jesus to his disciples. They managed to be both rich and religious and they sneered at his statement. But he knew what they were thinking and told them, 'You may convince your colleagues, but God sees right through you! Men may be impressed, but God is disgusted.

'The commandments of Moses and the accusations of the prophets were in force right up to the arrival of John the Baptizer. Since then the rule of God has been inaugurated and people are seizing the opportunity to live under it. In fact, it would be easier for planet earth and outer space to disappear than for one iota of divine legislation to be annulled.

'To give you just one example: in God's sight, whoever divorces his wife and marries someone else is living in adultery, and whoever marries a divorced woman also commits adultery.

'There was once a wealthy man, who used to wear the most expensive suits and enjoy lavish meals every day of his life. And there was a poor beggar who sat in the gutter just outside his drive gates, appropriately named God-help-us. His wretched body was a mass of ulcers and he would have given anything just to eat what was thrown into the wastebin up at the house. Stray dogs in the neighbourhood used to lick the matter oozing from his sores. In the course of time, the beggar died and his spirit was escorted by the angels into the loving embrace of Abraham. Shortly after that, the wealthy man passed away and a very impressive funeral took place. But he himself did not attend it. He was already suffering in hell.

'In his agony, he glanced up and spotted Abraham in the far distance, and he was hugging that old beggar, God-help-us! "Father Abraham," he shouted, "have pity on me. I'd even suck that beggar's finger if he'd dip it in some water first! This heat is unbearable!"

'But Abraham solemnly replied, "Just recall how comfortable your life was and how miserable was the lot of my friend God-help-us. Now it is time for him to have a bit of comfort and for you to know what it is to suffer. In any case, there's a huge canyon between us. No one can cross from here to there and no one can get from there to here."

'So the poor rich man thought of another possibility. "I plead with you, then, Father Abraham. If you can't send anyone over here, please send someone to my home on earth. At least my five brothers could be warned about this dreadful place."

'But Abraham shook his head and pointed out, "They have a Bible in the house. If they just read what Moses and the prophets had to say, they'll have all the warning they need."

'But the condemned man disagreed. "That's not enough to convince them, Father Abraham. But if someone came back from the grave to tell them what really happens, they'd surely change their ways."

'But Abraham simply said, "If they won't pay attention to the words God gave through Moses and the other prophets, they are hardly likely to believe someone who tells them he's returned from among the dead."'

41.

ACTS

Introduction

When we study any book of the Bible we need to engage with it at two levels. First, we examine the **human level**, considering who was writing and why, aware that each book is rooted in a particular situation with a particular audience in mind. At this level we look at the historical situation, seeking to make the Word of God *real* in its original context.

Second, we consider the book at the **divine level**, asking why the Holy Spirit intended the book for us and seeking to determine the way in which it is *relevant* to us today.

We might term these two levels the **historical** and the **existential**. The historical level asks why was it written, what was the human reason behind it? The existential level asks why is it in our Bible and why does God want us to know about this? This two-fold approach will prove especially helpful as we look at the book of Acts.

Acts on a historical level

Who wrote it and why?

THE AUTHOR

The author was Luke, a doctor by profession from Antioch, Syria, and the only Gentile writer in the Bible. He was a companion of Paul, often travelling with him, and had a keen interest in researching the events surrounding the life of Jesus and the growth of the Church. It was probably in Caesarea and Rome that he wrote Luke and Acts respectively (see pages 829–33 for more details on Luke as the author of these two books).

DEFENCE BRIEF

We have seen already that Acts is the second volume of a two-volume work written by Luke, to prepare Paul's defence as he awaited trial in Rome (see pages 833–7). Acts commences by addressing the same man who is referred to at the beginning of Luke's Gospel as the 'most excellent' Theophilus, a title suggesting a lawyer or judge and used elsewhere in Acts of Felix and Festus, both governors who met with Paul. Luke was doubtless aware that his 'brief' might be more widely circulated as people in Rome asked questions about the faith for which Paul stood trial.

Had this been a history of Paul's life, then at the very least Luke would have included the outcome of his trial, if not details of how he died. If this was a history of the Church we would have expected far more details about the church in Rome. But it was not Luke's intention to provide full biographical details about Paul, nor to cover Church history for its own sake, but to give enough information for Theophilus to understand how the Christian faith had developed and why the apostle Paul was now unjustly accused. Hence the readers of Acts are left at the end with the situation which prevailed when Luke had completed the brief for Theophilus.

Structure and outline

Having understood why it was written, the next question concerns the outline of the book, since this also sheds further light on its purpose. There are three commonly held theories concerning Luke's intended structure for Acts.

1. TWO SECTIONS

The simplest theory is that Luke structured Acts around the **two main apostles**. Peter is the apostle to the Jews and dominates Chapters 1–12, and Paul is the apostle to the Gentiles and dominates the rest of the book. There is much to support this theory, since there is a remarkable parallel between what Luke says about Peter and what he says about Paul. It may be that this was intended to counter the threat of two separate churches developing, a Jewish church and a Gentile church, with each claiming their apostle as the one to follow. Luke's account emphasizes that the lives of Paul and Peter were comparable in many respects, so that we should not see one as more important than the other. Here are some of the similarities:

■ They both performed miracles.
■ They both saw visions.
■ They both suffered for their faith.
■ They both made long speeches.
■ They were both filled with the Spirit.
■ They both preached with boldness.
■ They both preached to Gentiles and Jews, though Peter primarily preached to Jews and Paul primarily to Gentiles.
■ They were both imprisoned and miraculously set free.

- They both healed the sick.
- They both healed a congenital cripple.
- They both exorcised demons.
- They both had extraordinary means of healing, Peter with his shadow and Paul with his handkerchief.
- They both raised the dead.
- They both declared judgement on false teachers.
- They both refused worship.
- They both died in Rome (though Luke does not include this in his account).

This analysis strongly suggests that amongst Luke's reasons for writing is this concern to ensure that both men were equally honoured and valued as apostles in the Church. One way of approaching the book of Acts, therefore, is simply to divide it into two sections.

2. THREE SECTIONS

In Acts 1:8 we read, 'You shall be my witnesses beginning in Jerusalem, Judaea and Samaria and to the uttermost parts of the earth.' Some see this statement as the structure Luke follows in developing his themes. The witness for Christ **starts in Jerusalem**, in Chapters 1–7. Chapters 8 to 10 take the witness further **into Judaea and Samaria**, and then finally it spreads from there **to Europe and the heart of the Roman empire**. Thus Luke is seen to be demonstrating how Jesus' words at the beginning had been fulfilled by the end of the book, as the gospel reaches Rome with Paul, the witness of Christ to the Emperor himself. But Rome is hardly 'the ends of the earth'!

3. SIX SECTIONS

The three-stage structure may be compelling in some ways, but there is a better and more detailed way of understanding

Luke's approach. This understanding comes directly from noticing a **literary device** which Luke seems to be using to underline his theme. He includes a **series of similar phrases** at various points in his narrative. Note the following:

- **Acts 6:7.** 'So the *word of God spread*, the number of disciples in Jerusalem increased rapidly and a large number of priests became obedient to the faith.'
- **Acts 9:31.** 'Then the *church* throughout Judaea, Galilee and Samaria enjoyed a time of peace. It was strengthened and encouraged by the Holy Spirit, it *grew in numbers*, living in the fear of the Lord.'
- **Acts 12:24.** 'But the *word of God* continued to increase and *spread*.'
- **Acts 16:5.** 'So the *churches* were strengthened in the faith and *grew daily in numbers*.'
- **Acts 19:20.** 'In this way the *word of the Lord spread* widely and grew in power.'

These five statements in Acts about growth in either the Word of God or the Church provide a summary which marks the end of a section. Luke tells us what happened and then he summarizes that because of what happened the Church grew and spread.

In the light of these divisions, the suggestion given above that Luke organizes geographically is partly correct, as these marker verses suggest the following six sections:

1–6:7	Jews in Jerusalem
6:8–9:31	Hellenists and Samaritans
9:32–12:24	Gentiles and Antioch
12:25–16:5	Asia Minor
16:6–19:20	Europe
19:21–28:31	Rome

Luke is describing the 'irresistible force' of this new religion throughout the Roman empire. It is as if the death and resurrection of Jesus are like a stone thrown into a pond. Luke shows how the ripples have spread, with each summary statement underlining that the ripples are continuing, until eventually they reach Rome itself. It is clearly a selective description – the expansion is only depicted in one direction, north-west. The only hint of expansion to the south is the conversion of the Ethiopian on his way home to Africa.

Significant events

Let us now consider some of the events which Luke regarded as significant within this expansion, as he shows the way in which the Christian faith spread from being a rural Jewish movement to an international and cosmopolitan faith.

THE DAY OF PENTECOST

Luke begins with the **first great event in the spreading of the gospel**: the Day of Pentecost (Chapter 2). The Holy Spirit came on 120 disciples in the temple as they gathered for morning prayers at 9 o'clock in Solomon's porch. The gift of tongues accompanying the outpouring was the reversal of God's judgement at the Tower of Babel (in Genesis 11) and enabled the various nationalities gathered at the feast to hear Peter's sermon. Some 3,000 people responded in repentance and baptism and were added to the Church. Many would later return to their home countries to spread the message, including Rome itself.

THE COMPLAINT OF THE WIDOWS

Surprisingly, Luke records at the beginning of Chapter 6 how the Gentile widows' complaints about not getting a fair share of the food was a key event in the spread of the Church, for it comes directly before the first summary statement in 6:7. The apostles were keen to ensure that there was **no distinction made between the Jews and non-Jews** when it came to aid. A Jewish/Gentile split at this stage was to be avoided at all costs. As a result the apostles selected seven deacons to assist with food distribution. Two of these men, Philip and Stephen, were to make their own impact.

STEPHEN'S MARTYRDOM

Stephen was preaching when he was seized and brought before the religious rulers, accused of spreading anti-Jewish propaganda. We know very little about him from Acts, yet his final sermon is included as one of the longest chapters in the whole book (Chapter 7). His words underline Luke's purpose of describing how Christianity changed from being a Jewish, national religion to being a **Gentile, international faith**.

To the horror of his accusers, Stephen outlines before the Jewish leaders how much of God's activity took place outside their land, before there was a temple. The covenant with Abraham, the rescue from Egypt and the giving of the law were all outside the Promised Land. Their accusations that he was speaking against this holy place and the law were false, therefore, for God's Word and presence transcend national boundaries.

This speech is a theological explanation and justification for the spread of the message to the Gentiles, and within the unfolding drama of Acts it shows how the death of Stephen and subsequent persecution thrust believers out from Jerusalem into Samaria and up as far as Antioch, Luke's birthplace.

PHILIP IN SAMARIA

Luke then records how Philip, another of those seven deacons, went to Samaria and saw many respond to his preaching.

There was a great deal of antipathy between Jews and Samaritans and the disciples themselves had not been altogether generous. The last time John was in Samaria with Jesus, he and his brother James asked if they could pray that God would send fire from heaven to burn all the Samaritans up. Now **many Samaritans came to faith**, and later on Peter and John arrived to pray that the Samaritans would be baptized in the Holy Spirit, asking for fire from heaven for a rather different reason!

Philip was then transported to preach to an Ethiopian eunuch on his way home from Jerusalem. It would seem a curious incident to include, were it not for Luke's purpose of showing how the gospel spread. This is how the gospel came to Ethiopia, brought by that eunuch, the **first African convert**.

THE CONVERSION OF SAUL

Saul's conversion is also a pivotal moment in the whole narrative (Chapter 9). Indeed, this testimony is recorded three times, so that Theophilus might know the evidence given to the other adjudicators. Saul was later known as Paul, and we learn how he was **commissioned to serve Christ** and how he was united with the Jerusalem believers so that they could work to an agreed strategy. Once Barnabas and Paul have been sent out from the church at Antioch, the focus of the book moves from Peter to Paul.

PETER IN CAESAREA

The expansion of the gospel faced a significant stumbling block: the **Jewish food laws** forbade Jews to eat with Gentiles. Luke therefore includes an account of how God taught Peter that eating 'non-kosher' food was permissible and sent him to a Gentile home to preach the gospel.

Acts 10 is a pivotal chapter, showing Peter's astonishment that the **Holy Spirit came upon non-Jews** exactly as he had come upon Jews elsewhere. So crucial was this that Peter had to explain what happened to the apostles in Jerusalem in order that they might be apprised of the way in which God was at work.

THE JERUSALEM COUNCIL

Peter's conversation with the Jerusalem believers is a forerunner to the meeting of the Jerusalem Council in Chapter 15. Paul was sharing the way in which his ministry among the Gentiles had caused the Church to grow. But he was conscious of the danger of a rift developing between the Jewish church and this influx of Gentiles into the kingdom. They had, of course, little or no understanding of the Jewish heritage. The subsequent letter sent to the Gentile churches ensured that the **Gentile church could grow freely** with the encouragement of the 'mother' church in Jerusalem.

COHERENT PURPOSE

It is clear that Luke has selected particular events in order to show Theophilus not just **the fact of the Church's expansion** but also **how it took place**. These are not just haphazard stories. They depict how the Christian faith came to spread across the Roman world and how it remained united despite the cultural pressures it faced. Luke does not tell us of many individual conversions, nor what became of the majority of the apostles, but instead picks out particular events which serve his purpose.

Acts on an existential level

Having looked at the human or historical aspects of Acts, we now need to focus on why the divine editor wanted us to have this book. We must not leave our study in the past, but must also seek to hear its message for today. So we move from the historical significance to the existential meaning of the book, asking what it has to say to us about God now.

Links

Acts is a **vital link between the Gospels and the Epistles**. Imagine the New Testament without it. Many things would be very difficult to understand. People and ideas are mentioned in the Epistles without explanation. Some key people and places cannot be understood without this book.

1. PAUL

Most of the letters in the New Testament are written by Paul, but who was Paul? He was not one of the twelve apostles, so he is not mentioned in the Gospels. Without the book of Acts we would know very little about him or his ministry, or how he came to be writing to churches and individuals and why these letters are important.

2. BAPTISM IN WATER

The baptism of believers is another matter with an important link in Acts. **Only in Acts is it described as being in water**. So while Paul frequently refers to baptism in his *letters* – for example, 'Don't you know that when you were baptized you were baptized into his death?' – he never actually links the word 'baptized' with the word 'water'. This has led some scholars to argue that Paul did not teach water baptism and that 'baptism into Christ' means something purely spiritual. But in Acts you find that Paul was himself baptized and had his converts baptized. So we know that when he talks about 'baptism' in his letters he is talking about baptism in *water*.

3. BAPTISM IN THE SPIRIT

The phrase 'baptized in Holy Spirit' occurs in all four Gospels, but none of them tells you what it actually means, or what happens when somebody is so baptized. If you looked for a meaning in the Epistles you would also be disappointed. Paul uses the phrase in 1 Corinthians – 'For we were all baptized in one Spirit into one body' – but he does not say what that means in practice. It is only the book of Acts which explains **what it really means to be baptized in Holy Spirit**, for only there is the event actually described.

4. THE LAW OF MOSES

Acts also helps us when we consider our approach to the law of Moses today. How do we know that we Christians are not bound by it? The law of Moses had 613 different requirements, so we need to be clear whether we are free from these laws or not. How do we know whether or not these are still binding? The answer comes as we read about the great argument concerning circumcision which reached a climax in Acts 15, when it was settled once and for all that **Christians are free from the law of Moses**, though still bound by the law of Christ.

5. THE CHURCH

It is surprising to discover that even the word 'church' could be misunderstood, were it not for Luke's record in Acts. In the Gospels only Matthew mentions the word at all, and his two references are not descriptive of what a church should be like. The Epistles are generally addressed to churches and give us hints as to what they were, but it is only in Acts that we learn **what a church actually was**, including how it was planted, how the apostles appointed elders and what the relationship was between the apostles and the churches they founded.

6. CONVERSION

Acts is crucial to us also because we learn so much about **the proper way in which people were born again**. The Gospels record events before the coming of the Holy Spirit and the Epistles are written to people who are already established in their faith. Neither provides an appropriate model of how people come to faith in Jesus in the Church age. So we go to Acts to see how the apostles brought people into the kingdom, and we read of the normal pattern of *repentance*, *faith*, *baptism in water* and *baptism in Spirit*. (For further explanation of this process, see my book *The Normal Christian Birth*, published by Hodder and Stoughton.)

A model for today

Acts is therefore an important source of information and explanation – but it is clearly much more than that too. Many would see it as a model for church life everywhere, and pine for the day when **modern churches will exhibit the same qualities Luke describes**. This seems a reasonable assumption. After all, it is the only Church history we have in Scripture. Presumably the Holy Spirit wanted it included so that we would know what God intends for his people.

1. BAD AS WELL AS GOOD

Valid though this 'model' approach is, problems do arise if we assume that it is always an *adequate* model. Luke's portrayal is far from idealistic and includes the difficulties as well as the blessings. Acts records **arguments, divisions and mistakes as well as extraordinary growth**.

■ Few would want to hold up the story of Ananias and Sapphira and their deception as model behaviour.

- Simon's flagrant desire to profit by receiving the Holy Spirit does not provide a good model for a young convert wanting to make progress.
- Even the apostle Paul has a 'sharp disagreement' with Barnabas. No blame is attached to either party, but the wording used suggests that it was certainly not ideal preparation for a missionary endeavour.
- Luke describes the attitude of Gamaliel to the new movement. He counsels his fellow leaders to wait and see what happens rather than declare their hands for or against the Christians. But Luke's description does not mean such detached objectivity was an appropriate response and this fence-sitter is not mentioned again.
- By contrast Saul of Tarsus, Gamaliel's student, opts for an aggressive stance. Rather than 'wait and see' he prefers to seek to stop the new faith in its tracks and persecutes the Church. His hostility is overturned on the Damascus road, and this leads him to become a great, perhaps the greatest, apostle.

The account of the community of believers in Acts is therefore a mixture of good and bad. There are rivalries, arguments, hypocrisies, immoralities and heresies. We are given examples of how *not* to do things, as well as models to follow.

2. ABNORMAL AS WELL AS NORMAL

When it comes to understanding events in Acts, there is a distinction to be made between the abnormal and the normal. There were certain things that happened in Acts which were abnormal and **should not be expected to happen continually**.

Take Paul's conversion, for example. He hears the voice of Jesus and is blinded by a light. This was a clearly a one-off experience. If we use this as a paradigm or pattern for modern conversions, not many will pass the test. Indeed, Paul himself claimed it was a unique commissioning for him to be an apostle.

Consider also the death of Ananias and Sapphira. Have believers today not done worse things yet not been slain? Or is the replacement of Judas by casting lots a model for today? Clearly not.

Furthermore, if events are to be repeated, one would be hard pressed to decide which precedent to follow in certain cases. The apostle Peter was saved from Herod, but the apostle James was not. Which outcome should we expect to happen today? We must beware of taking one event or one experience of the early Church and making that a norm for the whole Church in any period.

This discussion brings us to a key question: **How do we distinguish between what is abnormal and what is normal?** Has the Church not often assumed that some phenomena are abnormal and not for today, only to be proved wrong? A series of questions will help us in this kind of decision.

a) Is the event only mentioned once?

If an event is only mentioned once and never repeated, it is likely – though not certain – to be abnormal. On the Day of Pentecost, for example, some things happened which were unique. We do not expect to see wind and flames every time someone receives the Spirit. On another occasion we read that the building shook when the believers met for prayer. This would be an inaccurate guide for us today as to whether genuine prayer had taken place. **Some of the early events were necessarily one-offs**. If something is only mentioned once, therefore, it *may* happen again, but it would be wrong to say that it *must* be repeated.

b) Is the event repeated?

In the descriptions of baptism in the Spirit in Acts, however, we can see some similarities. On the Day of Pentecost the wind and flames are clearly unique, but other phenomena are repeated. When those at the house of Cornelius (10:46) and the disciples of John receive the Spirit, they speak in tongues – suggesting that this may be a repeatable phenomenon, even if the wind and flames are not. Indeed, whenever someone is baptized in the Spirit in Acts, there is always something that happens to make it clear to recipients and onlookers alike that the Spirit has come. **A repeated event increases the likelihood that what we are reading is to be normal for the Church today**.

c) Is there independent confirmation elsewhere in Scripture?

If the Gospels or the Epistles give **independent attestation that the happening in question was a normal part of Christian life at that time, it is pretty certain that we can accept it today**. It is not, for example, just Acts 2:33 that speaks of the Spirit being 'poured out'. Joel 2:17 from the Old Testament and Titus 3:5 in the New confirm this as a term of general validity.

The appointment of elders in Acts is another example. Was this a one-off event? No, it was not just a temporary office in Acts: Titus, 1 Timothy and Hebrews all include references to the universal necessity for this sort of leadership.

3. PRESENT AS WELL AS PAST

Once we have asked the three questions given above, we are better placed to distinguish between the one-off events which were merely part of Luke's historical account and those things which God intends us to recognize as what *should* always happen, even if in the average church today it is a long way from what *does* happen.

It is important that we use these questions and that we use Acts as a model, for if we do not we can fall into the error of believing that another period of Church history is the one we want to duplicate. Many denominational groupings effectively take their cue from such a period, be it the Reformation, the age of the Puritans, the Methodists or the early Pentecostals. They forget that **the Bible provides a sufficient model and is the ultimate standard by which to judge all other ages**.

Acts gives us a model of what the early Church members did and what they were.

What they did

Acts tells of their warm fellowship together, the centrality of the apostles' teaching, the importance of the prayers, and their spontaneous evangelism as the Spirit empowered them and sent them out to tell others about Christ. It also tells of their fearless declaration of the gospel when they faced opposition from Jews and Gentiles alike. It is a vibrant book full of the action of God and the growth of the kingdom.

What they were

They were a people filled with the joy of knowing God, even praising him when they were in prison. They were people who feared God. And they were people of hope and courage: Peter and John were willing to disobey the Jewish leaders and refused to stop preaching. Stephen was also prepared to confront them, even though it meant losing his life.

Acts as a missionary manual

Accepting that Acts is a model for us today, how are we to read it? One of the most helpful approaches was provided by a man writing early in the twentieth century, Roland Allen. He wrote three books which have shaped the thinking of many who seek to understand how Acts should be used today. They are entitled *Missionary Methods – St Paul's or Ours?*, *The Spontaneous Expansion of the Church* and *The Ministry of the Spirit*.

His thinking was far ahead of his time, and I owe much to his insights. He argues that **Acts is not just a model for Church behaviour but a missionary manual for Church expansion**. Acts tells us how to fulfil the Great Commission and spread the gospel. From this one book we can identify a seven-fold strategy which we can follow today.

1. SEND APOSTLES

The word 'apostle' literally means 'sent one'. It was the understanding of the early Church that certain individuals were commissioned by God to spread the gospel. There are five kinds of apostle in the New Testament:

1. Jesus the *Chief Apostle* – there is no one else like him.
2. The 12 apostles, *witnesses of the resurrection* – there is no one like them today.
3. Paul, apostle number 13, the 'last of all born out of due time' – no one is like him today, *writing inspired Scripture*.
4. A *pioneer church planter* who builds new churches with new converts – the apostle Paul would be among this kind too, as would Barnabas and others, who were always sent out in a team.
5. *Any Christian sent from A to B to do anything* is an 'apostle', e.g. Epaphroditus, who was sent to be Paul's housekeeper in Rome – in this sense anyone could be an 'apostle'.

It is the fourth and fifth definitions which apply today. The Church of Jesus Christ needs **church planters and those**

willing to be sent out to accomplish particular tasks in God's name.

The initiative and backing should properly come from the local church. It is clear in Acts that it was the Holy Spirit who set apart the people for the work. The sending out did not come from a decision made by the people, but by the direction of the Spirit. So it was the Spirit who said that Paul and Barnabas should be set aside for the work he had for them. The Church was prepared to send out its best people in order that Christ would be made known.

It is also noteworthy that the apostles were sent out in teams. There was always a minimum of two travelling together (just as Jesus had sent his disciples out two by two). There is no sanction for the 'lone-ranger' missionary in Acts.

2. REACH CITIES

It was common for the apostles to commence work in highly populated centres, so that growing churches could have a ripple effect throughout the surrounding area. So, for example, when Paul went to Ephesus and taught daily in the lecture hall of Tyrannus, we read that 'all the Jews and Greeks who lived in the province of Asia heard the Word of the Lord'. It is likely that a man named Epaphras came to faith through these lectures and planted the church at Colossae. Paul wrote to the church, although he had never visited it himself or been involved in its growth.

It was therefore a sensible and effective strategy to go to the **major urban areas as a bridgehead for further expansion**, and this is something which we need to bear in mind today.

3. PREACH THE GOSPEL

Paul would typically focus first on the synagogue. 'As his custom was, Paul went into the synagogue and on three Sabbath days he reasoned with them from the Scriptures.'

When Paul was with the Jews he would use the Old Testament. But note, too, how **his approach changed according to the audience**. When Paul preached to Jews he quoted the Bible, but when he preached to Gentiles he sought to establish some common ground before introducing biblical concepts. Take, for example, the account in Acts 17 of his address to the Athenians. This was not an especially successful message, though there were some notable converts. Luke includes it so that we might see how Paul addressed a pagan audience.

In his message to the Athenians Paul refers to incidents which took place in their past and to poets whom they knew. He knew that there had been an earthquake in Athens many years before which devastated the city and destroyed their buildings. Being polytheistic, the Athenians assumed that they had upset one of their gods, and were anxious to know which one. So they decided to let some sheep loose in the main street. Whichever idol the sheep lay down nearest to would indicate which god the Athenians had upset. However, the sheep refused to follow the plan and ended up lying down in the middle of a field. So the council met and concluded that if they still did not know which god they had upset there might be a god they had forgotten, who was upset at the absence of an altar for him. So they erected an extra altar, inscribing upon it the words 'To the unknown god'.

Paul, viewing this altar on his visit to the city, uses it as a base from which to tell them of the God they did not know. Immediately he has an audience. From that common ground he can go on to tell them about a God they should and could know, and about Jesus, whom this God raised from the dead and appointed a judge of the human race.

This concentration on preaching the gospel is seen on almost every page of Acts as the Holy Spirit gives the Christians boldness and power to declare their message.

4. MAKE DISCIPLES

The apostles were concerned that people should become 'disciples'. They were not interested in our modern methods of responding: raising a hand, coming to the front of a public meeting or signing a card. They realized that **disciple-making took time** and so Paul would stay in a place for a considerable time to make sure that the believers were established. In Ephesus he taught about the kingdom of God every afternoon from 12 until 4 o'clock (the siesta time) for two years in order that young converts might learn and new people come to faith. Hence, while Luke records how the word 'Christian' was originally coined at Antioch, those who came to faith were more commonly known as 'disciples', or followers of 'the way'. It was **perseverance on the journey** that mattered, not a one-off decision that had little effect on daily life.

5. PLANT CHURCHES

Acts records how the preaching of the gospel established groups of believers and how the apostles revisited these groups later on, so that each missionary journey bore fruit in the **establishment of ongoing communities of believers**. This aspect of the missionary strategy can be easily overlooked if we live in a country where there are already many churches. We fail to see that some churches cater for just one sector of society, perhaps of a relatively narrow sociological type. There are often no existing churches which can reach other groups. This style of church planting ensures that existing churches need not feel that the newcomers are encroaching on their territory, since they will be **reaching an entirely different sociological group**, even if they are geographically very close.

6. APPOINT ELDERS

We read how Paul and Barnabas returned to Lystra, Iconium and Antioch and 'appointed elders for them in each church, and with prayer and fasting, committed them to the Lord, in whom they had put their trust'.

The newness of the churches meant that the 'elders' could only have been 12 months old in the faith, but this was no problem. As long as the candidates were ahead of the others and maturing, they could be **trusted to lead**. This pattern of appointing elders to lead the flock is seen throughout Acts, as the apostles sought to find local leadership so that the communities could become self-governing and not dependent on their founder. It would seem that the elders were appointed by the whole church, with local believers confirming apostolic nominations. (The word for 'appointed' is literally 'hand-raised', so the elders were voted in by a raising of hands.)

In some ways, therefore, the work of an apostle was clearly defined:

- Reaching key cities
- Preaching the gospel whilst adapting it to the hearers
- Making disciples rather than decisions
- Staying with them and training them
- Planting churches so that they left a community behind
- Appointing elders to lead that community

7. APOSTLES LEAVE

This seventh and final stage in the missionary model is also crucial. Once the church was established, the apostle moved on. Further contact may have happened through a letter, a visit, or the sending of an apostolic 'delegate'. **Once a fellowship had local leaders, the apostle could leave them to continue the work**. The churches were self-propagating, self-governing and self-supporting. As such, the ministry of true apostles was mobile. Typically they would also support themselves through a trade and thus not be a financial burden to anyone while the church was being established.

OMISSIONS IN THE PLAN

This analysis of the 'missionary' methods used in Acts has some notable omissions which are often considered essential today.

- There were no church buildings – the believers met in homes or hired buildings.
- Investment in property was not considered necessary.
- There were no clergy–laity distinctions.
- All offices in the church were based on gift and function – and every believer was considered to have a ministry.
- There was no hierarchy.
- There were no headquarters.
- There was no infant baptism.
- There were no churches based on national or denominational lines.
- There were no orders of worship – while we have hints as to how the churches worshipped, we have no set patterns to follow from that time.
- The apostles did not set up hospitals, schools, clinics or aid organizations.

So much of what we regard as a normal part of Church or Christian activity today was not normal for the early Church.

The theological angle

Our consideration of Acts has focused on many areas. We have noted the purpose of the book, the identity of the recipient, the way in which Luke structured his book to achieve his purpose, and how the book can be used as a 'missionary manual'. There is one final way of looking at the book which dovetails with the analysis we have already made, and that is to look at the book from a theological angle. How are we to view it on this level?

Whose acts?

Let us begin with the title. The book was originally called simply 'Acts'. It comes from the Greek word *praxis*, from which we get the word 'practice'. Acts thus describes **the practice of Christianity**, but who is it the practice of? Whose 'acts' are they? There are four possible answers to this.

1. APOSTLES

The book is usually called 'the Acts of the Apostles' which, as we have seen, is quite misleading since **most of the apostles do not appear in it!** James is beheaded in the early chapters, John is mentioned alongside Peter, but only Peter receives much space and more than half the book focuses on Paul, who was not one of the original Twelve. So it is not strictly about the 'Acts of the Apostles'.

2. JESUS

The book begins by saying, 'The former treatise, Theophilus, was about all that Jesus *began* to do and to teach,' thus clearly implying that the present volume is about **all that Jesus *continued* doing and teaching**. Therefore we could call it the 'Acts of Jesus continued'. The name of Jesus is mentioned 40 times in the first 13 chapters. He was the subject of the apostles' preaching and it was in his name that healing was done. So a case can be made for the 'Acts of Jesus'.

3. THE HOLY SPIRIT

Closer study reveals, however, that **the most prominent person in Acts is the Holy Spirit**, who is also mentioned 40 times in the first 13 chapters, and 70 times in all. So perhaps we should call it the 'Acts of the Holy Spirit'. Certainly this would do justice to his role. It is the Holy Spirit who empowers the 120 disciples for witness on the Day of Pentecost and is often described as filling the believers. Some of the big decisions in Acts are due to the direction of the Holy Spirit, and Peter's message at the home of Cornelius is interrupted by the Spirit falling on those present. It was the Spirit who prevented the believers from entering Asia and Bythinia, sending them instead to Troas. He provides the dynamic for the missionary expansion. So it would certainly be valid if we understood the book as the 'Acts of the Holy Spirit'.

4. GOD

This would make sense but for a more important person who is also mentioned prominently in the book. While the Holy Spirit is mentioned 40 times in the first 13 chapters, someone else is mentioned 100 times: God himself. If we make Jesus or the Holy Spirit the focus, this could make us unwittingly 'unitarian' in theology, a trap into which some groups have fallen. **The Holy Spirit focuses us on Jesus, and Jesus brings us back to God**.

The Trinity

So Acts is really Trinitarian in its theology. The word 'Trinity' is not actually in the Bible, but is a short-hand expression for the three persons who make up our one God. Acts is about three things, therefore:

1. The kingdom of God the Father
2. The name of Jesus the Son
3. The power of the Holy Spirit

Thus the best comprehensive title for the book would be **the 'Acts of God through Jesus Christ by the Holy Spirit in the Apostles'**.

Conclusion

Acts is the remarkable account of the spread of Christianity from Jerusalem to Rome. Luke sifts the evidence and selects the events which chart this expansion, providing a model for church life and a missionary manual to enable the expansion to continue. Simultaneously he achieves his overall goal of briefing Theophilus so that his friend the apostle Paul might be declared innocent at his trial. At the same time God intended that we should understand how he is at work in building his kingdom, so that whoever we are and wherever we live we might be clear about the ideals for which we should work and pray.

42.

JOHN

Introduction

In the introduction to the Gospels (pages 777–787) we saw that there are three identifiable phases of interest in a great man who has left this world: an interest in what he **did**, in what he **said** and in **what or who he was**. It is clear that John's interest is primarily in this third area. He is looking at Jesus from the *inside* and asking: Who was he?

Matthew, Mark and Luke focus more on what Jesus did and said, rarely tackling questions concerning his inner motivation. It is John who gives us a portrait of **Jesus' inner life and self-identity**. We will see later that this is not his sole reason for writing, but it is an important aspect to grasp if we are to understand the Gospel.

In all there are five major differences from Matthew, Mark and Luke.

1. Omissions

The way John differs from the synoptic Gospels is especially evident when we consider the **content of his Gospel**. It is not just that John writes with a special viewpoint on Jesus, but he omits a number of areas considered significant by the other Gospel writers:

- the conception and birth of Jesus
- his baptism
- his temptations
- the casting out of demons
- the transfiguration
- the Last Supper
- Jesus' struggle in prayer in Gethsemane
- the ascension

These are surprising omissions, especially if we note the prominence which the other writers give to some of these events. The transfiguration, for example, is seen as a pivotal event in the synoptic Gospels. And John was asked by Jesus at the cross to look after his mother, so perhaps he omitted the birth story to save Mary from more publicity. The main reason for these omissions, however, is simply that **such details did not suit John's purpose**. He set out to tell us something quite different from the other Gospels and there was no point in including what he regarded as unnecessary material.

Not only are there omissions, but there is also an **under-playing of some themes** regarded as important or worthy of more space in the other three Gospels. Miracles proliferate in the Gospels of Matthew, Mark and Luke, for example, but in John there are just seven. John also makes little mention of one of the major themes of the preaching of Jesus: the kingdom of God. The word only occurs twice, when Jesus tells Nicodemus that unless he is born again he cannot see the kingdom of God, and when he tells Pilate that his kingdom is not of this world. Again, this does not mean that miracles or the kingdom are unimportant, but just that John has a different purpose from the other writers, and a different way of achieving it.

2. Additions

MIRACLES

Just as there are omissions, there are also some very important additions. Of the seven miracles that John mentions, **five are completely new**:

- the water into wine at the wedding at Cana
- the man by the pool at Bethesda
- the healing of the nobleman's son
- healing the man blind from birth
- the raising of Lazarus

Only two, walking on water and feeding the 5,000, are repetitions.

Furthermore, John uses a **different word for miracles**, referring to them as 'signs'. A sign always points to something beyond itself. So he does not record fewer miracles because he believes them to be less important, but in order to highlight the way in which the miracle or sign points to Jesus. We will note the full impact of this for John's purpose later.

INDIVIDUALS

John includes more stories about individuals and a number of these are unique to his Gospel. Peter's initial refusal to have his feet washed, the conversation with the Samaritan woman at the well, and the conversation with Nicodemus are all included. Indeed, these **one-to-one dialogues** are given more prominence than the meetings with crowds which seem to dominate the other three Gospels. The words of John the Baptist in this Gospel are all in private conversations, not public proclamations.

STATEMENTS ABOUT JESUS

There are also seven big statements about Jesus himself which appear in John, known as the **'I am' sayings**:

■ I am the living bread
■ I am the light of the world
■ I am the door
■ I am the good shepherd
■ I am the resurrection and the life
■ I am the way, the truth and the life
■ I am the true vine

These statements only occur in John's Gospel and they serve to emphasize his purpose as he gives us an insight into how Jesus viewed himself.

3. Emphases

The synoptic Gospels are based on the outline of Mark and tend to use his framework of 30 months in the north in Galilee, followed by six months in the south in Judaea, focusing especially on Jerusalem. But John is quite different. Almost all of his Gospel is **in the south** and includes material from Jesus' early ministry. He chooses to emphasize the occasions when Jesus went to Jerusalem for the **feasts** (maybe as often as three times a year). Much of John therefore surrounds the Feast of Tabernacles, the Passover and the dedication of the temple, and ignores much of Jesus' ministry in the north.

4. Style

The style differences in John can be seen especially in two areas.

LANGUAGE

The language of John is different from the other Gospels. They have considerable overlaps, with identical wording being used in places. John's language suggests that his work is **completely independent**. For example, when the synoptic Gospels describe the feeding of the 5,000 they have 53 words in common with each other but just 8 in common with John. Even the word for 'fish' is different.

DISPUTES

The synoptic Gospels major on the parables of Jesus. Longer teaching sections are rare. In John, however, Jesus seems to be involved in **endless arguments**, with **long discourses focusing more on issues of belief than behaviour**. Since these are largely from his southern tours, it does seem that when Jesus went south he changed his style of teaching, probably because he was involved in more arguments with the Judaeans about his identity.

Take the long discussion in John 8, for example. Jesus has been speaking of his relationship to his Father, God. The Pharisees ask Jesus, 'Where is your father?' – the inference being that Jesus could not speak confidently about his parentage and was rumoured to be illegitimate.

'You do not know me or my Father,' Jesus replies. 'If you knew me, you would know my Father also.' So Jesus tells them that he does know who his father is, and turns the argument back on the Pharisees. They should know him too, but are far from him.

This raises an interesting issue concerning Jesus' opponents, which is often not understood. When we read in John's Gospel that the 'Jews' hated Jesus, that Jesus was always arguing with the Jews and that the Jews crucified him, we make a very big mistake if we apply the name 'Jews' to the whole nation. Indeed, this misunderstanding has stimulated anti-Semitism for 2,000 years. When John refers to 'the Jews' he means the southerners, the Judaeans, as distinct from the Galileans in the north, whose attitude (with a few exceptions) was altogether different and more positive towards Jesus.

5. Outlook

John's outlook is very different from that of the synoptics. John was conscious of **the need to communicate to a Greek world as well as a Hebrew one**. He was writing his Gospel in Ephesus in Asia (western Turkey today), where there was a meeting of Greek and Hebrew thought. An understanding of the difference between them is necessary if we are to grasp some of the approaches John uses in arranging his material.

Put simply, the Hebrews used a *horizontal time line* in their thinking, holding the common ideas of past, present and future. They knew God as the One who was, who is and who is to come. All their thinking was on such a time line, where time has both purpose and progress. The Greek mind, by contrast, thought of a *vertical line in space* and was concerned with life above and below, in heaven and on earth.

If you think in Hebrew terms, therefore, you have a concept of time travelling in one direction, with God deciding where things are heading. The first three Gospels assume this sort of time line, and John does not abandon it entirely. After all, he is Jewish himself. He includes, for example, the concept of the 'hour' five times.

However, he also uses the Greek approach, with a vertical line between heaven and earth, above and below. Therefore he sees Jesus as the **one from heaven**, quoting Jesus' words in 3:13: 'No man has ever gone into heaven except the one who came down from heaven – the Son of Man.' And in 6:33: 'For the bread of God is he who comes down from heaven and gives life to the world.'

We saw earlier that there is little mention of the kingdom of God in John's Gospel. Whereas the synoptic Gospels emphasize the kingdom breaking into this present evil age and awaiting the consummation, John focuses more on the *vertical* aspect of God loving the world and sending Jesus down to earth. We could say that John is primarily an 'up and down' Gospel, whereas the others are 'now and then' Gospels.

Understanding John's Gospel

Having considered the ways in which John's Gospel stands apart from the other three, we should take a closer look at John himself.

Who was John?

A FISHERMAN

Before being called to follow Jesus, John was a fisherman involved in both sides of the business, both catching and retailing. We know he had connections in Jerusalem and it is likely that these included a retail business for selling the fish which had been caught in Galilee. So he was **a man of two worlds**, the rural north and the urban city of Jerusalem in the south. As such, he stood out from most of the apostles, who were exclusively northerners – the only native southerner being Judas Iscariot.

A RELATIVE OF JESUS

He was a **cousin** of Jesus and the brother of James, one of the other disciples. Indeed, at least five, and probably seven, of the Twelve were Jesus' relatives, though his own brothers remained sceptical until after the resurrection, when James and Jude not only became believers but penned two of the books of the New Testament. This closeness was evident at the cross, when Jesus asked John to look after his mother.

JESUS' CLOSEST FRIEND

John, however, was not just close to Jesus because he was a cousin. He was also part of an **inner circle**, along with James and Peter, of those who were particularly close to Jesus. He refers to himself as 'the disciple whom Jesus loved', intending to deflect attention from himself by not actually giving his name, but nonetheless providing us with the insight that, of all the Twelve, John was nearest to Jesus. At the Last Supper it was John who was seated next to Jesus as they reclined to eat their meal. Jesus wanted his good friend at hand as they shared this momentous event together.

THE LAST APOSTLE

Not only was John the closest to Jesus, but he was also the last surviving apostle. He writes his Gospel **as an old man**, reflecting on Jesus with unique insight. At the end he records the story of how Peter learned from Jesus that he would be crucified, and how Peter asked Jesus about John's death. Jesus replied that it was none of his business and that if Jesus wanted to keep John alive until he returned, that was up to him. From that day a rumour went round that Jesus would come back before John died, but that is not what Jesus said, and John makes this clear at the end of his Gospel.

The closeness of John to Jesus is reflected in the way in which he **feels free to expand Jesus' actual words**. John paraphrases some of his discourse to bring out the full meaning, because he believes he knows Jesus' mind well enough to explain what he meant. So, for example, if you read John 3:16, 'For God so loved the world that he gave his only begotten Son...', it is not clear who is speaking. Is it Jesus in conversation with Nicodemus, or John expanding the section with reflection of his own? It is certainly a strange thing for Jesus to say, and sounds more like a third person talking about Jesus, in a rather indirect way. This is typical of John throughout the Gospel. He expands what Jesus said because he really understands what he meant. He draws out the implications **under the guidance of the Holy Spirit**. For this reason Eusebius, one of the early Church Fathers, called it 'the spiritual Gospel', and it is easy to see why.

John's purpose

What exactly was John's purpose in writing? Looking at this question will really open up our understanding of the book. Already we have seen John's concern to look at Jesus' inward being, but this was all part of a wider concern which he makes explicit at the end of his Gospel. He tells us that he selected the material **so that readers might believe that Jesus is the Christ, the Son of the living God**, and that by believing this, they might have life in his name. This is a clear enough statement, but it is important that we grasp the *full* meaning of what John says.

EXACT MEANING

We need first of all to understand the precise wording in the original Greek language. Greek has a 'present continuous' tense for verbs which is not easily translated into English, but is so often crucial to a proper understanding of the text. It means to be **continually doing** something. To translate the sense into English it is necessary to add the two little words 'go on'. For example, Jesus did not say, 'Ask and you will receive, seek and you will find, knock and it will be open to you', implying that each action need only be done once. He actually said, '*Go on asking* and you will receive, *go on seeking* and you will find, *go on knocking* and it will be open to you.' So if someone does not receive the Holy Spirit when they first ask, they should not panic: they should go on asking.

This present continuous verb is used by John in 20:31, so that the verse is more properly translated: 'These are written that you may *go on believing* that Jesus was the Son of God and by *going on believing* you will *go on having* life.' This same construction illuminates the best known verse in the Gospel. John 3:16 is better understood as, 'For God so loved the world that he gave his only begotten Son, that whoever *goes on believing* will never perish, but *go on having* eternal life.'

FOR NON-BELIEVERS OR BELIEVERS?

John was not written so that his readers might *start* believing that Jesus is the Son of God. It was written that they might *go on* believing it. Much of the content of John is inappropriate for people who come to the Gospel with no prior knowledge of Jesus. The book is written **for mature Christians**, to help them hold on to their faith so that they do not depart from their understanding of who Jesus is, but go on believing and therefore go on having eternal life.

This was John's principle for the selection of his material. The Gospel was not intended to be comprehensive, but aimed to provide readers with what they needed to know in order that they might continue to have life through constant believing. Put simply, the end for which John was writing was **life** – and the means to that end is **ongoing trust and obedience**.

LIFE IS THE END

John describes the life which Jesus offered as a **present continuous life**. Eternal life includes quantity – it is everlasting; but also quality – it is abundant. It is not just an insurance against death, but a life we are to enjoy here and now. John's statement of purpose in 20:31 implies that this life is something we possess but may lose if we do not continue to have faith. So the themes of life and belief are pivotal to John's overall purpose. Life is the end for which he is writing – that his readers may go on having life – whereas belief is the means to having this life. If we go on believing, we go on having life.

FAITH IS THE MEANS

That John was concerned with believing is confirmed by the frequency with which he uses the word – 98 times. This is far more than the other three Gospels put together. But we need to be careful, for he does not mean the same thing every time. For John there are **three stages or phases of belief**.

a) Credence

To give credence means **to believe that something is true**. The operative word is 'that'. So we believe *that* Jesus died, *that* he rose again. It is believing in certain historical facts, accepting the credibility of the gospel, accepting its truth. Credence is based on the words and works which establish Christ's claims.

This is not by itself saving faith, for at this stage anyone can say they believe that something is true. It is only the *beginning* of saving faith to accept the truth. (The devil believes the truth too; he accepts it and he trembles, but he is not a believer.)

b) Confidence

Confidence is the second stage of belief: having accepted the truth, we then put our confidence *in* Jesus by **trusting and obeying** him. It means taking the truth and acting on the basis of what we say is true. Jesus said to Peter towards the end of the Gospel, 'Follow me' – an activity of confidence, based on trust and obedience. We may claim to believe in someone, but if we do not have confidence in them, own 'faith' is superficial.

c) Continuance

This third dimension of belief concerns the ongoing aspect that we considered above when looking at John's main purpose. We are to **go on believing**. In both the Greek and the Hebrew languages 'faith' and 'faithfulness' are the same word, and sometimes we do not know which is meant. If you really trust someone you will go on trusting them. If you are really full of faith then you will be faithful. You will go on believing in someone whatever happens and whatever it costs. Faith, therefore, is not a single *step* (instantaneous) but a *state* (continuous).

Jesus makes this explicit when teaching his disciples in John 15. He uses the imagery of the vine to describe himself and tells them that they are the branches of the vine. He warns them that they must stay, abide, remain in him. If they do not, they will become unfruitful, be cut out and burned. So while John teaches that no one can come to Jesus unless the Father draws him, he also teaches the necessity of the believer *abiding in Christ* if he or she is to enjoy eternal life. This life is in the vine, not the branches (cf. 1 John 5:11).

To summarize what we have noted about John's purpose, therefore: his aim is that readers continue to believe in Jesus so that they will continue to have eternal life. This belief involves the three stages of accepting the truth, acting on the truth and holding on to the truth. Jesus himself is the Truth.

The truth about Jesus

There is a further aspect to John's purpose which will help us understand some of the details of the text. By the time John was writing, around AD 90, there was **considerable speculation concerning Jesus**, even about his early life. A number of 'non-canonical' gospels were written purporting to describe Jesus' childhood. One describes Jesus as a little boy playing in the street in Nazareth. Someone pushed him over into the mud and Jesus cursed him with leprosy. There is also a story of the boy Jesus fashioning little birds out of clay, blessing them and watching them fly away.

Actually Jesus did not do a single miracle until he was 30, because he could not do them without the power of the Holy Spirit. Jesus did miracles not as the Son of God but as the Son of Man, filled with the Spirit. Given the erroneous teaching which was being spread about, John was concerned to silence once and for all speculation concerning Jesus' identity. **Just who was he?** There were in particular two notions circulating in Ephesus which John felt the need to correct.

1. TOO HIGH A VIEW OF JOHN THE BAPTIST

We know from Acts 19 that there was a group in Ephesus who were followers of John the Baptist but had not believed in Jesus until Paul corrected them. In John's day, it seems, there were still those who venerated John the Baptist to the point where there was a danger that they would become a sect of Christianity, **focusing on repentance and morality as John had but without the emphasis on the Holy Spirit which Jesus brought**.

The apostle John set out to write a Gospel that would correct this exalted view of John the Baptist. Every time he mentions John the Baptist he puts him down. He says that John was not the light of the world – he only pointed to the light. He says that John did no miracles. He records John's own words that he must decrease and Jesus increase, that Jesus was the bridegroom while he was just the best man.

John the Baptist said two vital things about Jesus:

■ He will be the **Lamb of God** who takes away the sins of the world.

■ He will be the one who **baptizes in the Holy Spirit**.

Both these things need to be taught if followers are to get a proper balance in their understanding of Jesus. John the Baptist made it clear that *only* Jesus could take away sin and baptize in the Holy Spirit. But in spite of what John had said, his followers had not remembered much of this and Jesus was not given his special place.

2. TOO LOW A VIEW OF JESUS

Much more serious was the fact that in Ephesus they were already holding too low a view of Jesus. This can be understood in part by reflecting on the strong influence of Greek philosophy. As noted earlier, Greek philosophers divided life into two spheres. Various terms are used interchangeably for this: above and below, the physical and the spiritual, the temporal and eternal, the sacred and secular. Not only did they divide these two, they exalted one above the other. Plato said that the spiritual is more real, Aristotle said that the physical is more real.

This being so, the Greeks had a real problem with the teaching that Jesus was both physical and spiritual, earthly and heavenly, human and divine. In their thinking **physical and spiritual could not be put together** like this, and so they developed a number of variations in order to decide which side of reality Jesus was.

1. **More divine than human?** Some said Jesus was more divine than human, that he was never truly human but just *appeared* as a human being. This heresy was known as 'docetism', from a word meaning 'phantom' – i.e. Jesus was only seemed to be human. According to this view Jesus never really experienced humanity, for his deity always overshadowed his human side.

2. **More human than divine?** Others said he was more human than divine, a man who responded perfectly to God and developed fully the capacity of the divine that is in all of us. This is termed 'adoptionism' – i.e. Jesus was only *adopted* as God's Son, usually thought to have happened at his baptism when he was filled with the Spirit. Sadly, this is a heresy still being taught today.

3. **Partly human, partly divine?** Some argue that he was partly divine and partly human without saying he was more one than the other. This view is still current today. The Jehovah's Witnesses argue that we must view Jesus as a demi-God, semi-human, the first *created* being. Since the first verse of John explicitly states that he was God, and was with God in the beginning, the Jehovah's Witnesses translate the passage to say that he was *a* God, inserting an indefinite article that is not in the original Greek.

4. **Fully human, fully divine?** John's Gospel clearly asserts that Jesus is both fully divine *and* fully human. It was crucial for this to be demonstrated if John's purpose was to be achieved. Only one who was fully divine and fully human could save mankind from sin – his *humanity* enabling him to die on our behalf and his *divinity* ensuring that he would conquer death and offer life to those who would believe in him. If John's readers were to have life in Jesus' name, they must know the *same* Jesus the apostles knew.

John therefore wanted people to know the truth about Jesus and so he deliberately focused on these two areas, on Jesus' humanity and divinity.

1. HIS REAL HUMANITY

Jesus is actually 'more human' in the fourth Gospel than in the other three. Take, for example, the shortest verse in the Bible:

'Jesus wept.' It shows Jesus as fully human, standing at the grave of one of his best friends, knowing that soon he would be calling him from the grave, yet weeping at the situation. John records Jesus being hungry and thirsty, tired and surprised, all thoroughly human characteristics. Pilate unwittingly sums up what John was portraying with the words, 'Behold, the man!' In Jesus John shows us **what humanity is really like**, or what it should be.

This humanity is also seen in John's emphasis on Jesus' **prayer life**, where more detail is given than in the other Gospels. John depicts a truly human Jesus who needed to pray, depending on his Father to direct what he said and what he did. Some of his most beautiful prayers are in this Gospel.

Furthermore, the Gospel's focus on the **death of Jesus** emphasizes as no other that he really died. John records how one of the soldiers pierced Jesus' side with a spear, bringing a sudden gush of blood and water. Then John adds the sentence, 'He knows that he tells the truth, and he testifies so that you also may believe.' It was important to John that his readers should know that Jesus was really dead. Incidentally, this extra-ordinary symptom indicates a ruptured pericardium, a 'broken heart'.

By the same token, John also provides eyewitness evidence of the **resurrection**, recording his observation of the strips of linen and the head cloth in the empty tomb. Not only was Jesus really dead, but he was really raised from the dead.

2. HIS DIVINITY

The main emphasis in John, however, is on the **full divinity of Jesus**. This takes us back to John's purpose for his Gospel, and gives us the opportunity to look closely at the intriguing way in which John develops this. We have seen already how John recognizes that faith begins with credence, the belief that something is so. John makes the case for belief that Jesus is fully divine by organizing his evidence around the figure seven, the perfect number in Hebrew thinking. John includes in his Gospel **three complete bodies of evidence for Jesus' divinity**: seven witnesses, seven miracles and seven words.

a) Seven witnesses

The word 'witness' is used 50 times in the fourth Gospel. John stresses that we have **personal testimonies** to the truth about Jesus. There are seven people who attribute divinity to Jesus in this Gospel:

- John the Baptist
- Nathanael
- Peter
- Martha (the first woman to do so)
- Thomas
- John, the beloved apostle
- Jesus himself

In Jewish law two or three witnesses would be enough to establish the truth, but here John includes the perfect number of people to testify that Jesus really is the Son of the living God.

b) Seven miracles

We noted earlier how John records just seven miracles in all, and he calls them 'signs' because they point to who Jesus was. He actually includes the seven miracles (signs) which were the most supernatural and sensational works that Jesus performed. He does not include casting out demons, because there were plenty of people doing that in the ancient world, including the Pharisees. Instead he highlights **miracles no one else could do**:

- Turning water into wine – an unmistakable miracle.
- Healing the nobleman's son while miles away from the sick person, without seeing or laying hands on him.
- Healing the man by the Pool of Bethesda who had been there for 38 years, clearly suffering from a chronic condition.
- Feeding the 5,000, a miracle which all four Gospels include – a creative miracle, producing a lot from a little.
- Walking on water.
- Giving sight to the man blind from birth.
- Raising Lazarus from the dead – not the resuscitation of a corpse soon after death, as with Jairus' daughter or the widow of Nain's son, but the raising of a man whose body would already have started to rot.

John is saying that these are 'signs' pointing to the divinity of Jesus. As Nicodemus said, no man could do the things Jesus was doing unless God was with him.

c) Seven words

John uniquely records for us seven 'words' which Jesus gave about himself, mentioned earlier. To Jewish ears his claim was unmistakable, for each time he began with the Hebrew word for God, YHWH, meaning 'I am'. John carefully includes these sayings **in settings which demonstrate that Jesus' claim was legitimate**.

- 'I am the bread of heaven' was delivered following the feeding of the 5,000 with five loaves and two fish.
- 'I am the light of the world' followed his giving sight to the man born blind.
- 'I am the resurrection and the life' was said as he brought Lazarus out from the grave.

He also said, 'I am the door', 'I am the good shepherd', 'I am the way, the truth and the life', and 'I am the true vine'. This is a man who knew himself to be God in human flesh and these seven words, placed deliberately throughout the Gospel, are crucial to John's case that Jesus is worthy of the readers' trust.

Open relationship to the Father

In John's Gospel, Jesus' relationship to the Father is far more open than in the synoptics. John records that Jesus was **sent** by the Father, **one** with the Father, and **obedient** to the Father in the words he speaks and in the works he does.

So much of Jesus' controversy with the Jews concerned his identity and this was what created the greatest animosity, especially when he claimed to be God: '"I tell you the truth," Jesus answered, "before Abraham was born, I am!" At this they picked up stones to stone him, but Jesus hid himself, slipping away from the temple grounds.'

In fact, John is the only Gospel directly to describe Jesus as God, though the implication is there in the other three. John begins with the statement 'the Word was God' and towards the end Thomas confesses Jesus as 'my Lord and my God'.

Themes

We come finally to consider the themes which are integral to John's overall purpose that faith in Christ might be continued.

1. Glory

'Glory' is a key word in John, for it was a word which the Old Testament reserved for God himself. In the very first chapter, John uses the same word for the Word dwelling among men as is used of the *shekinah* glory of God when he revealed himself through the tabernacle at the end of Exodus. John saw this splendour of God in Jesus throughout his whole life, death, resurrection and ascension. Even the cross was a place where Jesus was glorified. From the very start, therefore, we are introduced to a man who is **utterly distinct** from his contemporaries and set apart from all other men of God.

2. Logos

John starts his Gospel in a unique way. When Mark wrote his account of Jesus, he began when Jesus was 30 years of age, since this was when he first sprang into public view. Matthew was the author of possibly the next Gospel to be written, but decided to go further back, arguing that it was necessary to include Jesus' conception and birth, and because he was a Jew, the genealogy had to go back to Abraham. Luke felt that, since Jesus was the Son of Man, he must be seen as a human being belonging to the whole human race, and so he started his genealogy with Adam.

In contrast to the other three, John decides to begin even earlier, emphasizing that Jesus existed before creation. So he takes the words from Genesis 1:1 as the basis for his opening to the Gospel: 'In the beginning was the Word, and the Word was with God, and the Word was God' (see the paraphrase of John's opening on pages 912–914).

JESUS' NAME

An interesting question arises here which will help us to understand what John wrote. **What do you call Jesus before he was born?** We are so used to speaking of 'Jesus' that we forget this was a brand-new name, given when he came to earth. So what was he before? If John is to write of one who existed at the very beginning, what should he call him?

John chose a unique name: 'the Logos', translated as 'the Word' in most Bible versions. He chose it because it expresses so well who Jesus was, in a way which would make sense to those who were reading. We generally think of 'a word' as an expressed thought that comes out of the mouth and into the ear. A word is expressed by one person and affects another. In this sense Jesus is a **communication** – a word from God to us.

BACKGROUND TO 'LOGOS'

A little history will help explain why John chose to call Jesus the Logos. This concept had particular meaning in Ephesus, where John was writing. Six hundred years before there lived in Ephesus a man called Heraclitus, acknowledged as the founder of science. He believed in the necessity of **scientific enquiry**, probing the natural world, asking how and why things were the way they were. Was it merely chance? Were we in a chaotic universe or was there an order?

He looked for patterns or 'laws' to see if he could deduce some logic behind the operation of the natural world. He used the word *logos* to stand for 'the reason why', **the purpose behind what took place**. When he looked at life (*bios*) he looked for the *logos*; when he studied the weather (*meteor*) he sought the *logos*. This concept now appears in our words for the study of different areas in science: biology, meteorology, geology, psychology, sociology, etc.

So Heraclitus said that the *logos* is 'the reason why'. Every branch of science is looking for the *logos*, the reason why things are as they are. John, realizing that **Jesus is the ultimate reason 'why' everything happened**, took up this idea and called Jesus the *logos*, 'the Word'. The whole universe was made for him. He was the Logos before there was anyone else to communicate with. That is the reason why we are here. It is all going to be summed up in him. He is the 'Reason Why'.

The word has another phase in its history too, this time across the Mediterranean Sea from Ephesus in Alexandria, Egypt. Alexandria had a school which combined Greek and Hebrew thinking, in part because there were many dispersed Jews living in the city. This school, or university, was the location for the translation of the Old Testament into Greek by 70 scholars known as the 'Septuagint' or 'LXX'. One of the Jews involved was a professor called Philo. In seeking to interpret Hebrew thinking into Greek, Professor Philo seized on the word *Logos* and said that the Logos was not to be spoken of as 'it', but as 'he'. He was **'personifying'** the Logos, rather in the way that in Proverbs wisdom is personified as a woman.

THE LIVING WORD

John combines the thinking of Heraclitus and Philo. There is an organizing principle, a 'why' at the root of everything, and this Logos is not just to be personified: he is a person and his name is Jesus. He is the Word, with a capital 'W', the one and only living Word.

On the first page of his Gospel, John says four absolutely vital things about the Logos.

1. **His eternity**. In the beginning the Logos was *already* there. We cannot go further back in our imagination than the beginning of the universe. He was not created, but has equal status with God as creator of the world.

2. **His personality**. 'The Logos was *face to face* with God.' That is the literal translation. It is the word used of two people looking into each other's eyes and loving one another. Christians are the only people on earth who can say that God is love, because they are the only people who believe that God is three in one. The Jews and the Moslems cannot say that he *is* love, because they believe he is just one

person, and love is impossible for just one person. God is more than one person, and if he is father and son loving each other, you can say that he is love and always was love.

3. **His deity**. In the beginning the Logos was already there, face to face with God in a personal relationship, and he '*was God*'. The Logos was not created, nor was he any less than God: he was totally equal to God. When Thomas exclaimed, 'My Lord and my God!' he stated the truth about Jesus. He was there at the beginning involved in creation. Scientists today speak of the earth's crust as being made up of 'tectonic plates'. The word relates to the Greek word *tecton*, which means 'carpenter'! Jesus, the carpenter from Nazareth, made our planet. He is the source of light and life. Everything exists for his pleasure.

4. **His humanity**. A little later in the first chapter we read the amazing words: 'The Logos *became flesh* and pitched his tent amongst us, and we beheld his glory, glory such as you would only see in the begotten Son of the Father.' It is possible to know God personally. Jesus is God with a face. God is Jesus everywhere.

With this staggering first chapter John is declaring from the outset that there are valid reasons for believing.

- Since Jesus is eternal, he can give us everlasting life.
- Because of his personality we can experience a personal relationship with him.
- In his deity he and he alone can forgive sins.
- In his humanity he can make atonement for us.

3. Life

If the Logos theme commences the Gospel, 'life' is an important theme which runs throughout, mentioned 34 times. As we saw earlier, the Gospel is written so that Christians might go on believing and go on having life in Christ. We noted too that this life is *abundant* and *present* as well as *everlasting*. John draws a series of contrasts as to what this life will mean for the believer.

LIFE/DEATH

He explains that having this life means that **believers will not see death**. Life will just continue beyond death. Death cannot touch it. So he contrasts those who are certain to die with those who will never die. 'For my Father's will is that everyone who looks to the Son and believes in him shall have eternal life, and I shall raise him up on the last day.'

LIGHT/DARKNESS

John also uses the contrast of light and darkness. When Jesus speaks of 'never walking in darkness', he is referring to **moral darkness**. He says that if we walk with him we will not have things to hide, for we are walking in the light with everything above board and no secrets. Darkness, however, is the metaphor for death and an absence of God. Jesus says, 'I am the light of the world. Whoever follows me will never walk in darkness, but will have the light of life.'

TRUTH/LIES

We have noted how John highlights the three stages of accepting the truth, doing the truth and holding to the truth, if faith is to be genuine. But he also contrasts truth with lies and includes a whole section in Chapter 8 where this theme dominates a discussion between Jesus and his opponents. The word for 'truth' and the word for 'real' are the same in the Hebrew and Greek languages. **If we live in the truth, we are also living in reality**. Jesus says, 'If you hold to my teaching, you are really my disciples. Then you will know the truth, and the truth will set you free.'

FREEDOM/SLAVERY

This was a discussion point between Jesus and the Pharisees, who claimed never to have been slaves to anyone but had clearly forgotten the slavery in Egypt! Jesus said that whoever sins is a slave to sin, because every time you sin you help to strengthen the chain of habit that will be your master. He had come to set them free. True life, therefore, meant **freedom from spiritual bondage**. 'So if the Son sets you free, you will be free indeed.'

LOVE/WRATH

John is clear in his understanding of two contrasting aspects of God's activity. A person is either in God's love or under his wrath. There is no middle way. The **eternal consequence** of one as opposed to the other is made very clear. Jesus says, 'Whoever believes in the Son has eternal life, but whoever rejects the Son will not see life, for God's wrath remains on him.'

REAL LIFE

Real life, therefore, is a **personal relationship with Jesus and his Father**. It is life in the light and the truth, in freedom and love. Praying to his Father, Jesus says, 'Now this is eternal life: that they may know you, the only true God, and Jesus Christ, whom you have sent.'

4. Holy Spirit

No Gospel tells us as much about the Holy Spirit as John. As such, it is well placed before the book of Acts, in spite of Acts having such strong links with Luke's Gospel. It is through the

Holy Spirit that we can enjoy the life which John describes. The teaching on the Holy Spirit is therefore prominent in John's writing.

- In Chapter 1 John the Baptist testifies that Jesus received the Holy Spirit and that he will **baptize** others in Holy Spirit.
- In Chapter 3 Jesus talks about the necessity of being **born of water and Spirit**, before we can enter the kingdom.
- In Chapter 4 Jesus speaks of the Spirit as **living water** and says we must worship God **in Spirit and in truth**.
- In Chapter 7 Jesus goes to the Feast of Tabernacles in Jerusalem, the feast being held in September or October at the end of the dry season. On the last day of Tabernacles the Jews enacted a ceremony in which the priests filled up a great pitcher with water at the Pool of Siloam, carried it to the temple and poured the water on the altar, while praying for the early autumn rains. On this occasion Jesus stood up and called out, 'If anyone is thirsty, let him come to me. I will give him a **spring of living water**, gushing up in his innermost being.' The text tells us that he was speaking about the Holy Spirit, whom those who already believed in him were later to receive.
- Chapters 14 to 16 are full of the new '**Comforter**' who is going to come, the Spirit of truth. The Greek name for the Holy Spirit is *paraclete* (*para* meaning 'alongside', *cletus* meaning 'called') – the one who stands by you, or the one who is called alongside. The Holy Spirit is also described as one who is just the same as Jesus. He will continue the work of Jesus after he has left, convicting the world of sin, righteousness and judgement, empowering believers and reminding them of everything Jesus said.
- In Chapter 20 Jesus prepares his followers for the **Day of Pentecost** by giving them a sign and a command. The sign

was Jesus blowing on each of them, and the command was, 'Receive the Holy Spirit.' They did not receive anything at that moment, but it was a rehearsal for Pentecost a few weeks later. That day, when they were seated in the temple, they heard the sound of the wind, reminding them of what Jesus had done. Then they obeyed his command and received the Holy Spirit he had promised.

John's opening paraphrased

John's opening statements are crucial to the purpose in his writing a Gospel. Yet they are so profound that even believers can feel out of their depth – another confirmation that this is not the most helpful Gospel to distribute amongst unbelievers. The following paraphrase is intended to make the passage more 'user-friendly', translating 'Logos' as earlier defined ('the reason why').

At the very first moment of its existence, the whole reason for our universe was already there and had been there from all eternity. Both the purpose and pattern of it all were to be found in a person, someone who could look God in the face because he too was fully divine. From the start of what we call 'Time', he was working alongside the creator. It was through this partnership that everything else came into being. In fact, not one thing was made without his personal involvement. Even life itself originated in him and his own life sheds light on the meaning of life for every member of the human race. His light goes on shining through all the gloom of human history, because no amount of darkness can ever extinguish it.

In the course of time a man appeared with a special commission from God himself. His name was John and he came to announce the imminent appearance of this light of life, so that everyone could put their faith in God by getting to know this person. John himself could not enlighten anyone, but God sent him to point out the one who would. The real illumination was already entering the world at that very time and was going to show everybody up by shining among them. He came right into this world, the world he himself had brought into being – yet the world did not recognize him for who he was! He arrived at his very own place, but his own people would not give him a welcome. Some did accept him, however, using his name with utter confidence, and these were given his authority to regard themselves as God's new family – which, indeed, they were now by birth, not because of their physical beginnings (whether that was a result of impulsive urges or deliberate choice), but by the direct act of God.

So this divine person, who was the reason behind our whole universe, changed into a human being and pitched his tent among ours. We were spectators of his dazzling brilliance, which could only have radiated from God's very own Son, shot through with generosity and integrity.

John was a reliable witness and shouted to the crowds: 'This is the person I've been telling you about. I told you that my successor would take precedence over me, because he was around before I was even born.'

And we also have benefited so much from all that he had in such full measure, receiving one undeserved favour after another. All we got through Moses were strict rules which we had to try to keep, but the help and the honesty we needed to live right came through Jesus, the real Messiah. Nobody had ever before had the chance to see God as he really is; now God's very own Son, who has been closer to his Father than anyone else, has shown us everything we need to know about him.

Conclusion

John is a remarkable Gospel, utterly different from the other three. It reflects the unique insights of the man who was closest to Jesus while he was on earth, and is full of a concern that we should not just know about what Jesus did, but should also realize who he was. It reflects, too, John's burden that believers in Jesus should not be side-tracked by erroneous teaching, whether concerning Jesus' identity or the veracity of his claims. He wanted believers to be absolutely sure that eyewitnesses, Jesus' own words and his astonishing works all point to one who was truly God come in the flesh, the living Word, the very glory of God among man. John's collected evidence and proof all make the most compelling testimony to Jesus' right to demand our ongoing trust and obedience.

THE
THIRTEENTH
APOSTLE

43.

PAUL AND HIS LETTERS

We know more about Paul than any other apostle. A third of the New Testament is either by him or about him. This includes the second half of Acts and the 13 letters that he wrote to churches and individuals. He has had more influence on 2,000 years of Church history than any other person, except Jesus himself. Indeed, there have been few people who have had a greater influence on the history of Europe. If we are to understand Paul's letters it is important that we understand his background and how he came to occupy such a key position.

Paul's early life

Paul's original name was Saul, named after Israel's first king – Paulus or Paul was his Latin name, used following his conversion, but we will refer to him as Paul only. He was born in Tarsus, a city in the north-eastern corner of the Mediterranean, on the coast of what is today south-eastern Turkey. The university at Tarsus was the third most famous in the Mediterranean world, after Athens and Alexandria.

Paul was brought up with three major influences on his life. First, his parents were Jews, and so from childhood he was taught about God from the Old Testament Scriptures. He was born into the tribe of Benjamin – a tribe famous for producing Saul, the first king of Israel, and for nearly being wiped out following a dreadful episode described in the Book of Judges. It would seem that the family moved to Galilee at some point during his childhood and sent Paul to Jerusalem to study under a very famous liberal rabbi called Gamaliel.

This Jewish academic is mentioned in Acts 5 where, concerning the growing Christian movement in Jerusalem, he said that if it were of human origin, it would die out, but if it were from God, the Sanhedrin would be unwise to fight it. In other words, he nailed his colours firmly to the fence! But Paul did not share his professor's detached attitude, believing that the Christians were the greatest threat to Judaism there had ever been. He was determined to fight for the Jewish faith and, if possible, to remove this new sect.

Following Stephen's speech to the Sanhedrin (see Acts 7), they stoned him to death for his 'blasphemous' views, and Paul agreed to his execution. He even looked after the coats of the men who threw the stones. Stephen was the very first man to die for his faith in Jesus.

Stephen's death may well have made a deep impression on Paul, for Acts 7 tells us that Stephen's face lit up with glory and he exclaimed that he could see Jesus at the right hand of God. But at the time, the martyrdom only served to make Paul more determined to be the first anti-Christian missionary, and he was even prepared to leave his own land to persecute Christians elsewhere.

The second influence on Paul's life was his learning of the Greek language. Living in Tarsus, he spoke Greek, which was the *lingua franca* of the ancient world, operating rather as Swahili does on the eastern coast of Africa. So when, after his conversion, Paul was called to missionary service, he was able to preach anywhere, knowing that he would be understood.

Thirdly, Roman law influenced Paul. His father had been made a Roman citizen, also making Paul a citizen by inheritance. This gave him privileges that he sometimes used in his missionary work. On one occasion he used his citizenship to avoid a pre-trial flogging, and when he was accused of violating the Jewish temple laws he appealed to Caesar, which was the legal right of all Roman citizens. When he was executed he was not crucified, as Peter was, but was instead beheaded – the swift method of execution reserved for citizens. His Roman citizenship did not make Paul's life free from suffering – far from it – but it was a significant factor in some of the most important moments in his ministry.

This unique combination of Jewish, Greek and Roman influences provided Paul with an ideal background for working as a missionary for Jesus to the Gentile world. This underlines the truth that God often prepares people for service even before they come to faith in Jesus.

Paul's conversion

It is interesting to note that Paul's conversion took place near a little town called Kuneitra in the Golan Heights, just a few miles from Damascus. He was a man who was proud of his Jewish roots, fighting for the purity of the Jewish faith, but as soon as he travelled beyond the borders of Israel he met with the risen Jesus of Nazareth, who told him that he would be sent to the Gentiles. Incidentally, this happened below the mountain where Jesus had been transfigured before Peter, James and John, though this time Jesus was much brighter, for he had now ascended and recovered the glory that he once had.

The conversion was dramatic. Paul came to understand that Jesus was truly the Messiah and that repentance and faith was the only response he could make. This process of new birth took three days and was not complete until a local believer named Ananias prayed with him. Ananias was well aware of Paul's reputation as a persecutor of Christians but obeyed God's command to go to him. After Ananias had prayed for him, Paul was filled with the Holy Spirit and was baptized. In my book *The Normal Christian Birth* (Hodder & Stoughton, 1989) I explain why I believe that the four elements of repentance, faith, baptism and receiving the Spirit are essential parts of being born again into the Kingdom, and they are demonstrated here in Paul's 'start' in the Christian faith.

After his conversion

It is fascinating to note that Paul did not immediately start work as a missionary. He started preaching where he was, however, and very quickly aroused hostility among the Jews. On one occasion he had to be let down in a basket from a window in the city wall in order to escape with his life.

It was to be at least thirteen years before Paul would begin to do what God had called him to do on the day of his conversion. He went to Arabia and spent three years alone with God, rethinking his theology in the light of his meeting with Jesus. He was the last person to be commissioned by the risen Lord and was to be the thirteenth and last apostle of this kind. Some have argued that Paul should be thought of as the twelfth apostle, filling Judas Iscariot's place, but Paul always recognized the Twelve and never counted himself as part of them. Nevertheless, he was keen to assert that he was a special apostle, and it was this special calling that gave him the authority to write so much of the New Testament.

We can only speculate about how he arrived at such a profound theology during his three years in Arabia. It is clear that finding out that Jesus was, after all, the Messiah who had been promised to the Jews would have had a significant impact upon his understanding of the Old Testament. Also Jesus had asked Paul why he was persecuting Him when, of course, Paul had actually been persecuting Christians, not Jesus as such. So he would have realized that whatever is done to Christians is also done to Christ. This was no doubt foundational to his thinking about the Church as the body of Christ on earth.

Paul's arrival in Jerusalem to meet the apostles led to great consternation. After all, he had been responsible for imprisoning the family members of those whom he was visiting. However, Barnabas was prepared to take the risk of befriending Paul and checking his credentials so that he could be introduced to the Christian Church in Jerusalem. The Jews in Jerusalem regarded Paul as a traitor: he had been one of their best trainee rabbis, and now he had joined the hated Christians. So he was sent back to Tarsus for ten years. This period is often overlooked. We think of Paul's conversion, and we imagine that his missionary journeys followed on immediately. But in fact he spent three years in Arabia thinking it all through, and ten years back in his home town waiting for that call to be confirmed. It was only when Barnabas invited him to help the church at Antioch and they then recognized his call to be a missionary that he was able to begin his work. We can compare Jesus' 18 years as a carpenter.

Paul's missionary work begins

The city of Antioch in Syria figures a great deal in the New Testament. It is likely to be the place that Jesus had in mind when he spoke of the Prodigal Son's journey to a 'far country'.

Antioch was the 'far country' for the Jews; it was the Monte Carlo of the ancient world. But despite its reputation, it was here that the first Gentile Christian church began. The word 'Christian' was first coined by the people of Antioch as a nickname for the members of that church.

The confirmation of Paul's earlier call to missionary service came during a prayer meeting at Antioch (see Acts 13). A prophecy was given which said that the time had come for Paul and Barnabas to be separated from the rest of the church so that they could begin the work to which God had called them. So Paul received a call to service from Jesus at his conversion, and that call was confirmed through a prophecy in the Church. This pattern is worth noting. Too many people believe that they have a call from the Lord but don't wait for this to be confirmed by the Church.

Barnabas and Paul had already been involved in a task that we today might regard as beneath the dignity of missionaries. There was a severe famine in Judea, so the church in Antioch made a collection and asked Paul and Barnabas to look after the funds and ensure that they reached their destination. But this wasn't the last time that Paul was involved in collecting money.

The map indicates how first Jerusalem and then Antioch were bases for missionary activity. Antioch was now the epicentre, with ripples spreading out even to Rome itself. Paul's first ambition was to evangelize the whole of the north-eastern part of the Mediterranean world, as far as the capital of the empire. So they set off to Cyprus first, and then they went back to the mainland. They planted churches in Antioch, Lystra and Derbe, and then returned to report to their home base in Antioch. The names of the areas further afield are better known to us today, as most of Paul's letters were written to the churches around the Aegean Sea. In his third and last journey

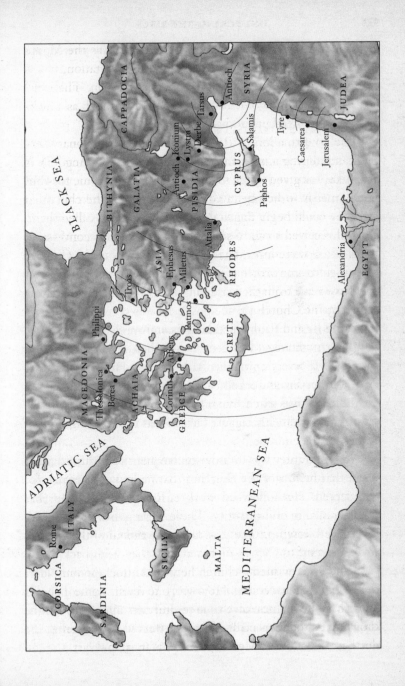

he left Crete, was shipwrecked in Malta and finally arrived, as a prisoner, in Rome.

Paul's mission strategy

Paul's strategy was to plant a community of the Kingdom in every key city and then to move on as quickly as possible. Sometimes he would be in a city for just three weeks. In other cases he would stay much longer. For example, he was in Corinth for 18 months. Sometimes he had to leave, and sometimes he chose to leave, but he invariably left behind a church to evangelize the whole district. He did not attempt to cover every town and village, preferring to focus on the key city in each province. So as a true apostle he was constantly mobile, exploring fresh territory, breaking new ground.

But the strategy was costly, and Paul faced many grave dangers. He was shipwrecked three times. He came close to death on numerous occasions, once even being stoned and left for dead. He was often hungry and tired. Furthermore, as he says in his letters, his biggest burden was the responsibility of caring for the churches.

So his strategy was to move on frequently, but this did not mean that he forgot the churches that he had already planted and served. His follow-up work ensured that the churches grew in quality and quantity. There were two ways in which he could follow up. One was to revisit and the other was to write letters.

When he revisited a church he would often appoint elders to carry on the leadership. However, one revisit was not always enough, as he did not have time to deal personally with all the issues that arose, especially as he also wanted to evangelize the northern coast of the Mediterranean as far as Spain.

So Paul's letters were his main means of ongoing follow-up while he continued his evangelistic work. They were not theological treatises written in a library by an academic. Rather, they reflect the concern of an apostle who wanted his converts to continue in the faith.

He eventually arrived in Rome, but not in the way he had expected – he arrived as a prisoner, and his missionary work was to preach the gospel to the Roman soldiers who guarded him. He was a prisoner on trial for his life, and his friend Dr Luke wrote his defence for the judge or defence lawyer Theophilus – we know this as the Gospel of Luke and the Book of Acts. Paul was acquitted and released, and there is strong evidence that he continued his missionary work, possibly travelling as far as Spain. He revisited areas such as Crete and Necapolis and went to a number of other places that he had not been to before. Then, having been betrayed by a metalworker called Alexander, Paul was arrested a second time during Nero's reign. He was taken away so quickly that he couldn't even pick up his notebooks or his overcoat.

What kind of man was Paul?

We have just one possible description of Paul's appearance, which is not very flattering. He was short (Paulus means 'little'), bow-legged, hook-nosed and balding. His eyebrows met in the middle, his eyes looked odd and he had very rough hands. Imagine a church that is considering Paul to be their pastor; what would they think on hearing this description?! Then add the facts that he never stays in one place very long, he often upsets people, he has been in trouble with the police, he has spent time in prison, and is a very dogmatic preacher. Furthermore, he is not married, he is a part-time tent-maker, he divides his congregations and speaks in tongues. But God has a habit of choosing the people whom we think are most unlikely!

Paul also had many positive qualities, such as dedication, enthusiasm, single-mindedness and extraordinary concentration. He believed that his singleness enabled him to focus totally on the one thing that he had been called to. He met danger with great courage, and he opposed his adversaries with appropriate anger. Indeed, some of his letters are red hot! He could be blunt and fierce, and yet he could also show tremendous concern, care and compassion.

Paul's key themes

But the secret of Paul's success is not to be found in his human qualities – admirable though they are – but in the three fundamental themes that permeate his letters.

In Christ

There is no doubt that this man absolutely lived for Christ. He said in his letter to the Philippians, 'to me, to live is Christ'. From the day when he met Christ on the Damascus road he was totally absorbed with Jesus. So as far as he was concerned, if he died he would be better off. He said, 'I desire to depart and be with Christ, which is better by far'.

He called himself 'the slave of Christ'. A slave in the ancient world was someone who was despised, totally owned by somebody else, with no spare time and no money. Yet in 2 Corinthians Paul also called himself an ambassador for Christ, which is a more impressive image. He was proud to be an ambassador, and yet also proud to be a slave.

The phrase 'in Christ' contrasts with the way in which many Christians speak of their relationship with Jesus today.

Paul very rarely used the phrase that most modern believers use, 'Christ in me'. When we speak of 'Jesus in me', we are in danger of reducing Jesus in size to a little Jesus inside our hearts, but the lesser is in the greater. Paul would speak of 'the Holy Spirit in me', but when he talked about Christ he said, 'I am in Christ'. It is in Christ that we are blessed with every blessing; it is in him that everything is ours. So wherever Paul was in the Roman empire, his true address was 'in Christ'.

For the gospel

Paul lived for the gospel. He would do anything to spread the gospel message. So even when in prison, he found that the gospel was something to rejoice in. So although he was chained to a Roman soldier for eight hours at a time, he rejoiced that he had three captive congregations per day! According to his letter to the Philippians, he saw some of these men become believers. On hearing that some preached Christ out of rivalry and jealousy of him, he said he was delighted that the gospel was being preached, whatever the motives of those preaching it. He said he would go anywhere to tell anyone what God had done in Christ.

There are two words that qualify his gospel message. First, it was an *eschatological* gospel. The word 'eschatology' comes from the Greek word *eschaton*, meaning 'the last things'. Paul believed that the future had invaded the present. If we forget that future dimension of the gospel, we forget the gospel itself. The gospel is not just good news about life here and now; it is good news about a new world that is coming, about the new bodies that we will receive when we see Christ.

Secondly, it was an *ethical* gospel. Paul was not interested in 'saving souls' whose lives remained unchanged. The gospel had ethical implications for all of life, and he was concerned to impress this upon his converts.

By grace

Paul was constantly amazed by the fact that Jesus had claimed him when he was on his way to put Christians in prison. He could not get over the fact that his salvation was totally undeserved, that if Jesus had given him what he *had* deserved, he would have been in hell. So the word 'grace', which means receiving what you don't deserve, sums up the way Paul felt. In Romans he says, 'While we were still sinners, Christ died for us'. This grace produced gratitude in Paul, and gratitude is the motivation behind so much of this man's labours.

Paul's letters

Paul is the most famous letter writer in history, and yet letter writing was very rare among the Jews. Jews in the ancient world seldom had cause to write letters, since they lived in a small country, so it was fairly easy to visit friends and relatives.

Writing and sending letters was an expensive way to communicate and was used only when necessary. In the Roman empire quite a lot of letters were written, but usually by officials or by wealthy people who could afford to pay a postman to deliver the letter to its destination. So in the absence of a public postal service, there would have to be an important reason for writing a letter, such as a crisis or a major problem.

In the ancient world letters were often very short, generally written on just one sheet of papyrus and probably no more than 20 words in length. Longer letters would require several sheets to be stuck together. Paul's epistles are some of the longest letters that we have from the ancient world. His average length was about 1,300 words, and Romans runs to 7,114 words – possibly the longest letter written in that period!

Paul followed the same format in every letter. His name

was always at the start, so that the recipient, by unrolling the first part of the scroll, could see who had sent the letter. He then added the address, so that the postman knew where to take the letter. The next thing Paul did was to greet the recipients. This was a pattern typical of most letters written at the time, but Paul used it to encourage the church or individual to whom he was writing. (The seven letters to the churches of Asia in the Book of Revelation follow exactly the same pattern, with the ascended Jesus commending each church before criticizing it.)

Next came the subject that was on Paul's mind, which normally made up the bulk of the letter. At the end of the letter there would be a brief summary covering the main points in the letter. Finally there would be some more greetings and a signature.

In the ancient world most people composed their letters with the assistance of an amanuensis (i.e. someone to whom they dictated the words), and Paul was no exception to this rule. Silas, his travelling companion on his later missionary journeys, was one of the people who helped him in this way. So Paul did not write his letters while sitting at a desk, but more likely dictated them as he strode around the room, or was chained to a Roman soldier. The letters have a conversational style and, like the Gospels, were spoken before being written down. Paul would add his own signature at the end of the letter, out of courtesy and because some letters had circulated falsely claiming to be written by him. So at the end of 2 Thessalonians Paul is careful to confirm that he is the author. It is possible that the act of letter writing would have been physically difficult for Paul. At the end of Galatians he explains that the large letters of his signature are due to poor eyesight.

Three kinds of letter

Paul wrote three kinds of letter. First, there are the four *personal* letters to individuals. He sent such letters to Philemon, Timothy (twice) and Titus.

Then there are the eight *occasional* letters written to churches. They are called 'occasional' because they were occasioned by something that had happened in the church in question, not because they were written 'occasionally' (i.e. 'now and then').

Then there is Ephesians, the only *general* letter by Paul that we have today. It has no particular connection with any individual or church, nor was it written because of any specific need or crisis associated with the recipient. Some people mistakenly believe that Romans is also a general letter, but careful study reveals that a situation in the church in Rome had prompted Paul to write the letter.

Ephesians is relatively easy to apply to our lives, but the personal and occasional letters present more of a challenge. It is like overhearing a phone conversation. We have to try to piece together the theme while only hearing one person's words. For example, someone might answer the phone and say the following:

'Hello? ... It's come? Congratulations! ... How much does it weigh? ... What colour is it? ... Don't let your wife get her hands on it! ... You'll find that it's very thirsty ... For a caterpillar, it moves quite quickly ... Mind you, you are on clay, aren't you? ... I might get one myself ... Cheerio!'

Few would guess that this conversation concerned the delivery of a new tractor!

Sometimes we have to work like a detective to try to reconstruct the other side of the 'conversation'. For example, Paul wrote two letters to the Christians at Thessalonica. The first was a very warm letter, but the second was very cool. Something must have happened to change his tone, so we need to read the two letters very carefully to discover what it was.

In addition to having just one side of the correspondence, we also have the problem of the culture gap between ourselves and Paul, for we are 2,000 miles and 2,000 years away from the background of these letters. We need to find the principle behind the practice and then apply it to life today. For example, does Paul's instruction to the Corinthians about head-covering mean that women should wear hats in church services today?

Thank God that the New Testament churches were not perfect! It can encourage us to discover that the New Testament churches had problems too. We should also note that without these problems, we would not have a single letter by Paul! For example, it is only because the Corinthian church was so charismatic and so carnal that we have the exposition about love in 1 Corinthians 13. It is because some people in the church at Corinth got drunk during the services there that we have the words of institution of the Lord's Supper. Because Paul dealt with a multitude of issues in his letters, we are able to gain a better understanding of what following Jesus is really about.

Letters, not lectures!

It is interesting to note that no other religion uses letters for divine revelation. Not only were letters rare in the ancient world, but it was unheard of for letters to be seen as a means through which God could speak. Although Paul knew that he wrote with the authority of an apostle, he had no idea that his letters would be regarded as Scripture. But very soon they were being widely circulated within the churches across the Roman empire. Eventually they were collected together and arranged according to size, rather in the manner of the prophetic books at the end of the Old Testament. The nine letters to churches come before the four to individuals. Even before the New Testament canon was completed, Peter referred to Paul's letters as 'Scripture'. Paul was regarded as a special apostle, and his work was quickly acknowledged to be part of divine revelation.

The nature of the letters means that they are not systematic statements of belief or behaviour. They include only what is directly relevant to the situation in hand. For example, Colossians does not mention the term 'justification', even though it is a feature of many of Paul's other letters.

We can note two reasons why God chose to use letters. First, they make God's word *personal*. The letters are addressed to ordinary people like us. They contain the personal and emotional elements that we would expect in such communication. So although there is a cultural gap to bridge, the humanity of the letters makes them easy to relate to.

Secondly, the letters make God's word *practical*. They are related to real life, to real needs, to marriage, to slavery, to children in the home, to daily work. God wanted us to have his word in a practical and personal form, so that we would never become philosophical or esoteric in our thinking. God chose to give us his word in letters rather than lectures!

Conclusion

This overview has aimed to fill in some of the background to the apostle Paul and his letters, but there is no substitute for spending time reading them yourself. It's a good idea to read each letter in one sitting. When reading a letter from a friend, we would not just pick out isolated sections of it; we would want to read and understand the whole letter. Similarly, in reading one of Paul's letters, we must grasp the whole if we are to understand the detail. In the following chapters you will find overviews of each letter that are designed to help you to do just that.

44.

1 AND 2 THESSALONIANS

Introduction

Paul's two letters to the Thessalonians were written within a few months of each other and are easier to understand than some of Paul's other writings. They were sent by Paul, Silas and Timothy, the team who visited Thessalonica, though clearly Paul was the author. Although written to the same people at the same place within a short span of time, the two letters are totally different in atmosphere, temperature and tone. They deal with the same subjects, but they do so in entirely different ways. The first letter is very warm and personal, reflecting Paul's concern for the church at Thessalonica. However, in the second letter Paul's manner is cool, sharp, detached and distant.

We are helped in our understanding of Paul's letters by examining the particular background of each letter, especially when he wrote it and the location of the recipients.

The map shows the position of Thessalonica at the top of the Aegean Sea. It was then a major port, but the harbour has now silted up and the city is not quite so near the sea.

Thessalonica was a key city in the region. It was on the Ignatian Way, the main Roman road from Rome to Asia, and

its port was the terminus of some major north-south trade routes. The city produced more coinage than any other town around the Aegean Sea, so it was an important financial centre. It was ideal as a location for business and, of course, Paul saw that it could be of strategic importance for the spreading of the gospel.

The city had a large and mixed population, including a number of Jewish traders. Archaeology has shed considerable light on the Thessalonica of Paul's day. Excavations have revealed a Roman forum, a sports hippodrome, a Hellenistic market and a Samaritan synagogue. Indeed, recent finds have confirmed Luke's description of the local leaders as 'politarchs'. It had formerly been assumed that Luke was mistaken, since this title was not known in other cities. But archaeologists have found 41 inscriptions including this very title in and around the Thessalonica of this period.

Paul at Thessalonica and Berea

Paul arrived at Thessalonica during his second missionary journey in around AD 49. He had been trying to evangelize first in Asia and then in Bithynia, but each time he had sensed the Holy Spirit preventing him from going to those regions. While they were at Troas (ancient Troy) Paul had a dream of a man beckoning him to come over to Macedonia to help the people there. So they crossed the Aegean Sea, reaching a port called Neapolis. Paul preached in Philippi but was thrown out of the city, so eventually he arrived at Thessalonica.

As was his custom, Paul preached to the Jews in their synagogue. Although he was an apostle to the Gentiles, he had a special responsibility to the Jews. He believed that once they were converted, they would form a church that would reach out to the Gentiles in the neighbourhood.

However, the most fruitful group in the synagogue turned out to be not the Jews but the fringe people who were called 'God-fearers'. They had not become Jews and had not been circumcised, but they were interested in Judaism because they felt that the God of the Jews was the true God.

But this policy of visiting the synagogue led to sharp disagreement in Thessalonica, and some of the Jews made it impossible for Paul to do any further work there. They were especially angry about Paul's claims that God-fearers could belong to God without becoming Jews. An ugly riot was stirred up in Thessalonica by these Jews, and so Paul voluntarily left after about three weeks and, undaunted, moved on to Berea. So he was only at Thessalonica for a very short period, but he left behind a solid church, among whose members were a number of high-society women.

Paul at Athens and Corinth

At Berea he was once again forced to leave, and travelled south to Athens, leaving behind Silas and Timothy to carry on the work at Berea. In Athens the opposition to Paul's message came from a different quarter. Greek philosophy taught that the human spirit is gloriously released from the body at death, so Paul's belief in bodily resurrection was laughed at. There were a few converts, but not enough to form a church.

From Athens Paul went on to Corinth, and it is clear that by this stage he was thoroughly demoralized.

He had been forced out of Philippi, then Thessalonica and then Berea. In Athens he had been laughed at and saw just a handful of converts. When he arrived in Corinth he was in a depressed state. Indeed, we read in his first letter to the

Corinthian church, 'I came to you in weakness and fear, and with much trembling'. It was almost as if he had lost his nerve, and it's easy to see why. We think of Paul as the most successful missionary ever, but there are not many people who could endure such a sequence of hard experiences.

So imagine how Paul must have felt when Timothy and Silas caught up with him at Corinth and brought the news that the church in Thessalonica was generally doing well. It lifted Paul's spirits. He was unable to leave his work in Corinth, so he decided to write a letter to the Thessalonians.

Furthermore, Timothy and Silas had also brought some money from Philippi. Paul had arrived at Corinth penniless and had been forced to return to his former tent-making trade, but he had made friends with a Jewish married couple named Priscilla and Aquila. They too were tent-makers and had just escaped from Rome. So Paul was doubly encouraged as he dictated his letter to the believers in Thessalonica.

Their receptivity (1 Thessalonians 1)

Paul's positive mood is reflected in the opening chapter of 1 Thessalonians, where he says he is delighted to hear that the believers in Thessalonica are standing firm in their faith. He uses the word 'receive' many times. He is clearly thrilled that they didn't just *hear* the word of God but *received* it too. Let's now try to get an overview of the content of 1 Thessalonians by looking at four groups of three words.

Word, deed and sign

Paul says he gave them the gospel in three ways: by word, by deed and by sign. Many Christians seem to believe that if you give people the words of the gospel, you have given them the gospel. But the people who have heard those words have as yet been given no proof that those words are true. They need to *see* the gospel as well as *hear* it. Of word, deed and sign, two are for the eye and only one is for the ear. If such a balance made for effective communication in Paul's time, it surely must do so in our televisual age.

Paul didn't assume that people were waiting to hear the gospel, but he did assume that they were waiting to see it. The deeds were the human proof that the words were true, and the signs were the divine proof that the words were true.

Too often we focus almost exclusively on word-based evangelism. Preaching the word of God is vital, but it must be backed up by the way we live and by signs and wonders from God.

When Jesus sent out his disciples two by two, he said to them (I'm paraphrasing here), 'It's really very simple. All you've got to do is go to a town, raise the dead, heal the sick, cast out demons, and then tell them that the Kingdom has come to them. In other words, *demonstrate* the gospel before you *declare* it.'

Faith, hope and love

The next triplet of words is one that was often used by Paul. It is better known to us at the end of 1 Corinthians 13, but he also used it in 1 Thessalonians. It is clear that the Thessalonians were stronger in faith and love than they were in hope. Faith showed them what God had done in the past, and love showed them what he was doing in the present. But the Thessalonians had a weaker understanding of what God would do for them in the future.

We should note that faith, hope and love are not meant to be merely attitudes. They are all meant to have an active dimension too: faith acts, love toils and hope grips.

God, Jesus and the Spirit

Paul says that the Thessalonians' experience of God has been fully trinitarian. They have not focused upon one member of the Trinity to the exclusion of the other two. They repented towards God, they believed in Jesus and they received the Spirit.

Turn, serve and wait

The final triplet gives us Paul's definition of a good Christian. He uses three verbs to describe their faith: they *turned* from idols to *serve* the living God and to *wait* for his Son from heaven. Christian living involves repenting of the past, ongoing service in the present, and waiting for Christ's return in the future.

His integrity (1 Thessalonians 2–3)

The first problem to be addressed in 1 Thessalonians comes in chapter 2. Paul faced opposition wherever he went – human opposition, largely Jewish in origin, and the satanic opposition that was behind the human element. Both were due to jealousy, for both the Jews and Satan were jealous of losing followers. The devil is the father of lies, and in order to undo a new work of God, he will either defame the messenger or destroy the message. The first thing he does is to impute bad motives to the man who started the work and tell lies about him.

This had already begun to happen in Thessalonica. We can get some idea of the nature of the defamation by looking at the way that Paul defends himself in chapters 2 and 3. Nine times he defends his integrity against lies. He is not doing it for his own sake, but because he knows that if his reputation is destroyed, then the Christians at Thessalonica will not have any confidence in the gospel that he gave them.

These are the nine accusations that were brought against Paul:

1 *Paul is a bungler.* He left the situation at Thessalonica in confusion, being unable to sort it out to everyone's satisfaction.

2 *Paul is a coward.* He left Thessalonica because he is a criminal on the run. (Actually, we know that he left so that the converts in Thessalonica would not have to come up with bail money for him.)

3 *Paul is a fanatic.* He is so single-minded that he is mentally unbalanced.

4 *Paul is lecherous towards women.* There were many wealthy women in the fellowship, and Paul was rumoured to have given them inappropriate attention.

5 *Paul is a trickster.* They accused him of being a con man, of associating himself with the Thessalonian Christians because he thought he could use them to his own advantage.

6 *Paul is a flatterer.* They claimed that he played to the gallery, that he actually had very little to say that was worth hearing, and that he was not genuinely concerned for the Thessalonian church.

7 *Paul is an opportunist.* They said he was only preaching for the money that the church would give him.

8 *Paul is an idler.* They said he didn't do any real work and had an easy life.

9 *Paul is a dictator.* They said he was harsh and lorded it over his converts.

None of these accusations were true, but, of course, things that are said tend to stick. They stay in people's minds, however convincing the rebuttal may be.

The devil was behind these accusations, but in fact they are all things that are true of the devil himself. The enemy was imputing his own satanic motives to Paul.

Paul defended himself in 11 ways, appealing to the Thessalonians and to God as two separate witnesses to the fact that not one of those accusations was true.

1 *He points to the effectiveness of his ministry.* He says to them, 'You are a solid church, full of faith and love, and you are evangelizing others. Is that the work of a bungler?'

2 *He emphasizes his boldness.* He had been thrown into jail in Philippi, and yet when he came to the very next town, Thessalonica, he started preaching all over again. Was that cowardly behaviour? A coward would have run away to another country.

3 *He claims to be without guile.* He says that he means what he says and says what he means. He doesn't try to fool anyone.

4 *He appeals to his godliness.* God approves of him, even if no one else does.

5 *He appeals to his humbleness.* He chose not to stand on his rights or his dignity.

6 *He appeals to his gentleness.* He says he treated the Thessalonians as a nurse treats a baby. No one could have cared for them more.

7 *He appeals to his selflessness.* He reminds them that he gave them time, money and his very self.

8 *He appeals to his busyness.* Far from being lazy, he laboured from dawn to dusk every day.

9 *He appeals to his holiness.* He says, 'You are witnesses, and so is God, of how holy, righteous and blameless we were among you'. Indeed, he is almost repeating the defence of Jesus, for he is effectively saying, 'Which of you convicts me of sin?'

10 *He appeals to his earnestness.* He claims that he was not just a mother to them, but a father too. He was motherly when they needed comfort and fatherly when they needed discipline.

11 *Finally, he appeals to his strictness.* He says he never compromised his standards with them and never tried to trick them into anything.

The situation that Paul faced regarding the Thessalonian church gives us a salutary insight into the way in which the devil uses criticism to undermine Christian work. He loves to make Christians suspicious of their leaders and tries to impute false motives to them.

But Paul is not surprised by such opposition. He tells the Thessalonians that they should expect it too. For a Christian, suffering for Christ is a proof of election, a mark of honour and a seal of faith. The people who should really worry are those who never suffer for the gospel, never have it rough, never make enemies, and never have to pay the price of following Jesus. For Paul, suffering was normal. He was willing to accept imprisonment, or flogging, or stoning, and would always fight against anyone who imputed unworthy motives to his ministry in order to destroy it.

Their maturity (1 Thessalonians 4–5)

In 1 Thessalonians 4 and 5 Paul tries to help the Thessalonians to grow in spiritual maturity. There are two issues that he is especially concerned about: *holiness* and *hope*.

Holiness

This is central to Christian living, for it is God's will that every believer should be holy. Paul is aware of two areas where the Thessalonians are struggling.

WOMEN

The first of these is *women*.

The Greeks had a permissive and promiscuous lifestyle, rather like the gods they worshipped. Wives could be changed regularly and mistresses were common. A man called Demosthenes said this about the Greek way of life: 'We keep prostitutes for pleasure, we keep mistresses for the day to day needs of our body and we keep wives for the begetting of children and for the faithful guardianship of our homes.'

Seneca said: 'Women are married to be divorced and divorced to be married.' Chastity was almost unheard of.

So against this backdrop, Paul told the men in the Thessalonian church that they had to give up their prostitutes and mistresses, and shun the promiscuous attitudes that prevailed.

They were to honour their marriages by keeping the marriage bed pure. A wife was not to be treated like a prostitute or mistress.

WORK

The other area of struggle for the Thessalonians was *work*.

This is often seen as an unmentionable four-letter word! We tend to hear very few sermons on work, perhaps because most of the preaching in churches is done by people who don't do nine-to-five jobs. They may work 16 hours a day for the church, but they don't have a 'job' in the usual sense of the word. Few discipleship courses ever mention work. They explain how to be a Christian in your spare time – how to pray, how to read your Bible, how to witness, how to serve the church. This gives people the distinct impression that they are meant to serve the Lord out of working hours, and can leave Christians with very itchy feet, wanting to get away from work and into Christian service.

They forget that a Christian is already in full-time service for the Lord. The way we work is meant to be part of our holiness. Our working lives should express our love for the Lord and for our neighbour. Glorifying God should be our motivation in our work. Our working life is lost to the Lord until it is seen as part of our holiness.

Some of the Thessalonians had abandoned regular employment and were idly awaiting the return of the Lord. This outlook was not untypical of the surrounding culture. The Greeks as a whole lived for leisure. They believed that work (especially manual work) was evil and degrading, and so wherever possible they used slaves to do it for them. Hebrew thinking, based on the Old Testament, saw work as part of worship. There was no distinction between working with one's hands and any other form of labour. All work had equal dignity before God and should be used to please him.

So Paul has to tell these people to earn their own living and to make it their ambition to be dependent on no one. Able-bodied Christians should not live on the charity of other people, but should earn their own living so as to support their families and give help to those in genuine need. Paul is not talking about those who *cannot* work, but those who *will* not.

Hope

Paul also found it necessary to teach the Thessalonians about hope. It is a key theme in the New Testament – the return of Christ is mentioned over 300 times. So Paul regarded hope as fundamental teaching for new Christians. Although the Thessalonians were strong in faith and love, they were weak in hope, partly because of the Greek world's attitude to death.

Iscillus said: 'When a man dies, there is no resurrection.' Theocrates wrote: 'There is hope for those who are alive, but those who have died are without hope.' Another philosopher said: 'When once our brief life sets, there is one perpetual night through which we must sleep.' A tombstone from ancient Greece reads: 'I was not, I became, I am not, I care not.'

So the Thessalonian Christians assumed that when members of their church died, they would miss out on Christ's return. We are not sure whether this was because they did not believe that the dead were resurrected at all or because they believed that the dead would not be resurrected until later. So Paul needed to reassure the Thessalonians that they should not grieve as other people did, for when Jesus returns, the dead will actually be the very first to meet him. They will rise first, followed closely by those who are alive.

This means, of course, that Christians will return to earth after their death. Having met Jesus in the air, they will come back to earth with new bodies. Heaven is, as it were, only a waiting-room – temporary accommodation for those who have died and are awaiting Christ's return to earth, when they will be with him forever.

It is clear that the Thessalonian church had also misunderstood the teaching they had received concerning when Jesus would return. Paul quotes the phrase that Jesus first coined, that he would come like a 'thief in the night' – the implication being that it would be a total surprise, with no warning. Many assumed that Jesus could come at any minute. But Paul corrects this assumption, saying that he will only come unexpectedly to those who are not watching for him. The words 'a thief in the night' are not directed at Christians, but at those who are not ready. By contrast, the Thessalonians are not living in the night, they are living in the day. If they keep watching, they will not be surprised. Indeed, it is clear from other parts of Paul's teaching and other parts of the New Testament that the Second Coming will be preceded by certain signs. This is a theme to which he returns in 2 Thessalonians.

Final exhortations (1 Thessalonians 5:12–28)

The themes become far more compressed at the end of the letter, as if Paul wants to preach a dozen sermons to them. Chapter 5 is packed with a number of unrelated issues.

Leaders and members

The city of Thessalonica operated with a democratic form of government. One positive result of this was that the women there had a degree of emancipation that was not enjoyed by women elsewhere in Greece. But a negative result of this democratic system was that the church membership had little or no respect for their leaders. So Paul tells the Thessalonians to respect their leaders, since they cannot lead if they are not respected. The Church is not a democracy but a theocracy, for it is ruled by the Holy Spirit. This rule is demonstrated through Spirit-filled leaders and Spirit-filled followers. The leaders are not dictators, nor are the members part of a democracy.

Paul tells the members three things that they must not be and five things that they must be: *don't* be idle, timid or weak; *do* be patient, forgiving, joyful, prayerful and thankful.

The trinity

Paul finishes the letter with some teaching about each person of the Trinity:

The *Holy Spirit.* The church is told not to quench the Spirit or despise prophecies, but to test everything. They were to hold on to what was good and to avoid what was evil.
God. Paul prays that God will sanctify them amidst the surrounding culture that is so opposed to God.
Jesus. Paul prays that Jesus will keep them blameless until the day when he returns. The Second Coming should be a motivation towards godly living.

Their tenacity (2 Thessalonians 1)

Paul's second letter to the Thessalonians, written just a few months after the first one, has a completely different tone. In it he is cold and distant, horrified and upset. It would seem that he has heard some bad news about the church, and so he feels the need to write again and cover some of the ground that he has already dealt with in the first letter.

He begins by complimenting them on the fact that their faith remains strong despite severe persecution. The hatred that was formerly directed against him is now being directed against them. He tells them that their suffering should be seen as part of living for the gospel.

Although they are suffering great injustice now, he assures them that in the future, the God of justice will deal with those who are troubling them. He uses six words to describe what God will do with those who persecute Christians: 'destruction', 'exclusion', 'judgement', 'tribulation', 'vengeance' and 'everlasting'.

So when we hear of people troubling Christians, we should tremble for the persecutors. We need to remember that there are only two destinies facing all people: one is to be with God for ever; the other is to be in hell for ever.

Their stability (2 Thessalonians 2–3)

In 2 Thessalonians Paul is still concerned with the two big issues that he dealt with in the first letter – their holiness and their hope – but this time he covers them in reverse order.

Hope

Despite Paul's careful teaching on the return of Jesus, the church remains confused about the subject. Their hope has changed from being too weak to being too strong. Some of them believe that the Lord's return has happened already or is imminent, so there is no point in doing anything else except wait for him. Consequently some of them have given up their jobs.

It would seem that this wrong thinking has been caused by a fraudulent letter that they have received. Claiming to be from Paul, it suggests that the Second Coming is about to take place. In 1 Thessalonians we saw how the devil attacked Paul, God's messenger. Now the devil is attacking the gospel message itself. He knows that it is so easy to get Christians unbalanced about the Second Coming, either by ignorance or fanaticism.

Paul gives an extraordinary response to this perversion of the gospel message. He tells them that the Second Coming cannot be imminent because there is at least one big thing that still has to happen before Jesus can come. He writes of the coming of 'the man of lawlessness', who will have no regard for law and will set himself up as God. Elsewhere in Scripture he is called 'the beast' or 'the antichrist'. Since this man has not yet arrived, the idea that the Second Coming is just around the corner must be false.

Paul's perspective helps us to appreciate the difference between the New Testament view of history and that of other philosophies.

Greek philosophy believed that history moves in cycles – empires come and empires go, but it never leads anywhere. A common variant of this today is the view that history does go forward, but the cycles are up and down. There are good times, then bad times; war, then peace; inflation, then deflation. Once again, there is no positive progression.

The progressive view of history was very common at the beginning of the twentieth century. It was believed that life was getting better, that the future would be brighter than the present. However, here at the beginning of the twenty-first century, I would say that the opposite view of history is the more common. Many people feel that things are getting worse, and the key word now is survival, not progress.

But the view of history shared by Jews, Christians and Communists is the *apocalyptic* view of history – that is, that things will become much worse until they hit rock bottom, and then they will suddenly get better and stay better. In the Bible we find this view especially in Jewish prophets such as Daniel.

The Jewish, Christian and Communist variations of this view of history differ concerning who is going to *cause* the change. The Communists believe that man will do it, though this dream is fading rapidly. The Jews say that God will do it. Christians say that Jesus will do it and that this will happen at his Second Coming. So this New Testament view of history, seen in detail in the Book of Revelation, is behind what Paul is saying in his letters to the Thessalonians.

Paul says that although the Lord's return is not imminent, the influence of 'the man of lawlessness' is already in the world. There is lawlessness, and yet it is restrained. One day God will remove the restraint, but Jesus himself said that it will only be for a very short time (from the Book of Revelation we can assume that that time will be three and a half years), after which Jesus will return. In the meantime, the Thessalonians should wait patiently and remain busy.

Holiness

Paul's teaching on work sounds very harsh, for he says, 'If a man will not work, he shall not eat'. According to Paul, Christians should not feed a believer who throws in his job, for he is being lazy. Paul is not here addressing the question of unemployment – that is a social evil which we must fight; he is not talking about those who *cannot* work, but those who *will not* work.

When the Lord comes, he wants us to be doing our job faithfully and working for him. The parables about the Second Coming all have this emphasis. Jesus told parables about masters who were delayed in coming back. The delay will test the dedication of Jesus' servants. God is not so interested in *what* job you do as he is in how *well* you do the job that you have. He would rather have a conscientious taxi driver than a careless missionary, because he is more interested in character than in achievement. Too often we have a hierarchy of valued activities, with missionaries, evangelists and pastors at the top, then doctors and nurses, then schoolteachers and so on. But nothing could be further from the truth. In the Bible manual labour is at the top! Jesus was a carpenter, Paul was a tentmaker and Peter and John were fishermen – these activities were part of their work for God.

People who have been in the same office for 40 years and wish they had been able to serve the Lord have misunderstood this point. When Jesus comes back, he will be running the world with us and will be looking for people whom he can trust to run the law courts and the banks and everything else. Paul rebukes the Corinthian Christians for taking one another to court, explaining that they will be judging the nations one day. Christians should live and work now in such a way as to prepare themselves for the job they will have when Jesus comes back.

Prayer

Prayer is a theme that features strongly in both of Paul's letters to the Thessalonians. He tells them that he is praying for them and asks them to pray for him. He even says that his prayers for them can be as big a help to them as preaching to them. So he is quick to thank God for them, and he asks God to perfect them in grace and goodness, to protect them from Satan and to direct them in love and loyalty.

He also values their prayers for him. In spite of being the greatest missionary of all and the thirteenth apostle, he knows that he needs their prayers. He asks them to pray that the gospel message will spread rapidly, since he is conscious that every moment is valuable. He also asks them to pray for his own safety, since he is aware that, as a messenger of the gospel, he is involved in a battle on enemy territory.

Conclusion

Paul's two letters to the Thessalonians remind us of two key aspects of the Christian life:

1 *Walking*. When we come to Christ, it is the beginning of a journey with him. We must make sure that we keep walking with him, in holiness. Salvation is a process – we are saved *from* hell and *for* heaven. Seeking holiness is an essential part of our lives.

2 *Waiting*. Towards the end of every chapter of these two letters there is some reference to the Second Coming. We would do well to recover this theme in our preaching and worship today. Just as Jesus will return to this world, so will we. He is looking for a people who will govern with him.

For Paul, living in the light of the Second Coming was a fundamental part of Christian discipleship, and these two letters emphasize the dangers of incorrect thinking on this important issue.

45.

 1 AND 2 CORINTHIANS

Introduction

Many Christians imagine that the Christian life would be much smoother if only we could recover the conditions of a previous era. Some think fondly of the Welsh Revival of 1904; others go back even further to the Methodist Revival of the eighteenth century; and even the Puritan era has become a favourite in recent years. But perhaps the most popular choice would be the days of the New Testament. It is assumed that if we could only return to those times, all would be well. People forget, of course, that the Church of New Testament times had problems too. There were external pressures from those Jews and Gentiles who reacted with hostility to the gospel message, and there was also strife within the Church.

When we turn to Paul's letters to the Corinthians, we find a church with problems that threatened to wreck its life and ministry. No church founded by Paul had more problems than the one at Corinth, but let us be thankful to God that as a result of their difficulties, we have these two marvellous letters. They include the matchless description of love in 1 Corinthians 13, and in 1 Corinthians 15 we have the earliest account of the resurrection appearances of the Lord in the New Testament.

The problems were certainly severe. The church was deeply divided, with cliques of people following different leaders. They had immorality of the worst kind – a man living in sin with his mother (or possibly his stepmother), a practice that even pagans would have condemned. Some of them had been drunk at the Lord's table. Others practised an aggressive form of feminism. Furthermore, they had misunderstood basic Christian doctrine. It must have been tempting to write off such a church, but Paul did not. He wrote to them and visited them in the hope that they would see their errors and return to a better way of life.

The city

An examination of the location of the church helps us to understand why it faced such great difficulties.

The city of Corinth was on a narrow isthmus of land that joined the mainland of Greece to the Peloponnese. The isthmus became an important destination for merchants wishing to avoid the more hazardous southern route between the southern coast of Achaia and Crete. Cargo from large vessels would be carried over the isthmus and put on another ship to travel on. Smaller boats would be pulled overland on rollers and would then be relaunched for the next leg of the journey.

Corinth itself was two miles from the sea but had its own port, Lechaeum. A double city wall stretched all the way from the city to the port. Just outside Corinth was Mount Acrocorinthus, which rose to 2,000 feet, with views of Athens 40 miles away. Corinth and Athens were rather like Edinburgh and Glasgow today. Athens was the university city where philosophers lived and arts festivals were held, and Corinth was the bustling port. Rivalry between the two was intense.

The first city

Archaeologists have discovered a great deal in Corinth, especially since the earthquake of 1858, which uncovered some of the ruins. They found the judgement seat where Paul was put on trial and a Jewish synagogue. All the evidence concurs with Luke's account in the Book of Acts. In modern times a deep ravine known as the Corinthian Canal has been cut through the isthmus, so that an ocean-going liner can just squeeze through. Nero had tried to cut a canal during Paul's lifetime but failed. The first city was destroyed by the Romans in 146 BC and was rebuilt and repopulated as a Roman colony in 44 BC by Julius Caesar. From 29 BC it was the capital of the senatorial province of Achaia. It had a cosmopolitan population including Jews, who built their synagogue, and Greeks, who influenced the architecture and philosophical outlook. But it was founded on Roman laws and largely practised Roman religion. There was no landed aristocracy, so any class distinctions came purely through the wealth that was generated by the market and port. Very soon the immorality of the former city returned, with the snobbery that comes through wealth and intellectual arrogance.

The second city

The city that Paul visited was very wealthy and terribly pagan. The inhabitants worshipped the gods of Greece and Rome, including Poseidon, god of the sea, and Aphrodite, goddess of love. The huge temple of Aphrodite housed 2,000 priestesses who were effectively prostitutes, since the worship there involved intercourse with a priestess. Indeed, 'to Corinthianize' became a verb in the Greek language, meaning 'to have promiscuous sex'. So this background explains in part why Paul needed to concentrate on male-female relationships in his Corinthian letters.

The church

The social context

The city was mostly populated by freedmen – ex-slaves who had either bought their freedom or earned it in some way. Hence Paul's remark in his first letter that not many of the church members were of noble birth. They were very ordinary people, but at the same time they were quite wealthy, having worked their way up the social ladder. This may account for the tendency to prefer one church leader over another – those who work hard to become wealthy are used to being able to choose, and they like to have their own way when it comes to church politics.

The moral context

In 1 Corinthians 6:9–10 Paul lists the sort of sins that were part of the Corinthian believers' former way of life. They had been 'sexually immoral … idolaters … adulterers … male prostitutes … homosexual offenders … thieves … greedy … drunkards … slanderers … swindlers'. It is clear that such behaviour was typical of the people of Corinth. And among the church members some of these practices were still a problem.

The spiritual context

Idolatry was part of the Corinthian culture. But at the same time, the church itself displayed evidence of the work of the Holy Sprit. Its members had been baptized in the Spirit and exhibited many gifts of the Spirit in their worship.

Cultural influences

The two biggest battles for any church concern how to keep the church in the world (i.e. evangelism) and how to keep the world out of the church (i.e. holiness). Most pastoral problems can be put under one of these two headings, and this was especially true of the Corinthian church.

In particular, there were some background problems that affected the believers.

Pagan morality

Corinth was a typical seaport when it came to sexual permissiveness. Almost anything was acceptable in Corinth, and it is clear that the church was not immune to the port's influence in this regard.

Roman law

Though it was in Greece, the city had considerable Roman influence. In particular, it enjoyed Roman law and order. This in itself was not a bad thing – Paul himself used his privileges as a Roman citizen throughout his ministry. But the church had taken things too far. They would take each other to court rather than settle matters amicably, and Paul felt the need to address the issue.

Greek philosophy

Greek philosophy was the background of the Corinthians' outlook, and this explains many of their problems. Indeed, since Western civilization is based on Greek thinking, it also explains much about church life and practice today, so we would do well to consider it in some detail.

The word 'democracy', for example, is Greek in origin. Democracy was a Greek political idea. Although there is no democracy in the Bible, many Christians assume that it should govern church life. To take another example, sport was important to the Greeks, but apart from some illustrations in Paul's letters, there is nothing about sport in the Bible. But sport is the religion of the men of this country, and it often dominates the lives of Christians.

Body and soul

However, the worst aspect of Greek thinking is the separation of the physical and the spiritual. To the Greeks the body and the soul were two separate things, and this is often common in Christian thinking too. The Hebrews thought of the 'soul' as a breathing body. The signal 'SOS' ('save our souls') actually comes from Hebrew thinking – it really means 'save our bodies', even though the word 'soul' is used instead.

The Greeks believed that the body was not integral to the soul. They thought that when the body disintegrates at death, the soul is set free. They spoke of an immortal soul in a mortal body, believing that only what happens to the soul is really important.

In this respect Hebrew thinking is the exact opposite of Greek thinking. In the Hebrew view of things, we have a mortal soul and we need an immortal body. The body is very important. So the Christian should side with Hebrew thinking as outlined in the Old Testament, rejecting the Greek belief in the immortality of the soul and, with the Jews, believing in the resurrection of the body.

This difference in beliefs explains why the Corinthians struggled to grasp what was acceptable behaviour for a Christian. The

Greeks did one of three things with their bodies: they either indulged them, since what is done to the body does not affect the soul; or they ignored them and tried to live an ascetic life, free from physical desires; or they idolized them, making statues of the perfect body. Their sports were performed nude for this very reason.

So Paul has to remind the Corinthians that their body is the temple of the Holy Spirit. What we do with our bodies *does* affect our souls. He tells them that getting drunk at the Lord's table does affect one's spiritual life, and if they visit a prostitute, in effect they are joining Christ to that prostitute, because their body is actually part of Christ.

This incorrect attitude to the body also causes problems today, because many evangelicals are essentially Greek in their thinking. Many are unwilling to accept the use of the body in worship, believing that worship should be inward. So using the body – for example, raising one's hands – is regarded as inappropriate, even though such practices are commended in Scripture. The only part of the body that we are expected to use is the mouth, despite the fact that Romans tells us to present our (whole) bodies as a living sacrifice.

The correspondence

Paul actually wrote four letters to the Corinthian church, though we have only got two of them. 1 Corinthians is actually his second letter to the church and 2 Corinthians is actually his fourth letter. The other two were probably lost, but some commentators believe that they may have been included in 2 Corinthians. One was a very hasty letter which Paul perhaps later regretted writing, and the other was a very hot letter which, he acknowledges, was very severe.

A brief outline of Paul's movements as found in Acts and the Corinthian letters will help us to grasp how the letters came to be written.

Paul arrived in Corinth for the first time alone, having faced opposition in Thessalonica, Berea and Athens. He returned to his former trade of tent-making, at one time working with a Jewish couple named Priscilla and Aquila, who had been thrown out of Rome, along with many other Jews, during the reign of Claudius. He preached in the synagogue, and his ministry was later helped by Timothy and Silas, who arrived with a gift of money from Philippi that enabled him to devote more time to preaching. He was eventually expelled from the synagogue, so he moved his operation next door to the home of Titius Justus. In a dream God assured him that many people in the city would come to faith, so he was encouraged to continue his work. The synagogue ruler Crispus and his family, among others, were converted. By the time Paul left Corinth 18 months later, a church had been established.

Paul went from Corinth to Ephesus, then to Jerusalem, and then back to his home church in Antioch. On returning to Ephesus he was disturbed to learn about sexual immorality going on between family members in the Corinthian church.

So he sent his first letter – a hasty one telling them to put things right. But then a verbal report came from Chloe's household, possibly from Stephanas, Fortunatas and Achaicus, who visited Paul in Ephesus. They told him that the first letter had had a negative reception. Some suggest that this letter is in fact 2 Corinthians 6–7, since these chapters sound like the sort of approach that Paul may have used. Chloe's family also brought a letter asking a number of questions about spiritual gifts and about marriage and divorce, though it ignored the issues that concerned Paul. So when we read 1 Corinthians we have to decide whether each section is a response to the verbal report from Chloe's household or to the questions in their letter.

Paul sent Timothy to deliver his letter to the Corinthians, intending to cross over to Macedonia himself after he had spent more time with the Ephesians, for his ministry with them was fruitful. He would then work his way southwards to spend the winter in Corinth. But he changed his plans when he received a report from Timothy saying that despite his letter, the Corinthians were worse than ever. So Paul went to Corinth immediately.

But Paul's second visit was a disaster, and he soon had to leave. He later describes it as a distressing confrontation. The church's self-designated leaders, who even called themselves 'apostles', didn't want Paul in Corinth and insulted him.

So he sent a severe and tearful third letter demanding that the church should deal with the ringleader. The letter is believed to be lost, though it may be 2 Corinthians 10–13, for the tone of this part of the letter would certainly fit the circumstances.

Titus was collecting relief money from the churches established in Macedonia and Achaia, and so he took the letter with him. He was competent in sorting out problems, and it seems that he was able to give verbal backing to Paul's request for firmness.

In the meantime, Paul was facing a difficult time in Ephesus – possibly the riot referred to in Acts 20. He travelled to Troas, hoping to hear good news about Corinth from Titus, but he was dismayed to find that Titus was not there. He eventually found him in Macedonia and was delighted to hear that the crisis was over. Paul was so pleased that he sent a fourth letter (2 Corinthians) with Titus. Paul's third and last visit to the Corinthian church was a happy one.

The contrast between the content of the two letters is quite marked, as can be seen below:

1 CORINTHIANS	2 CORINTHIANS
Practical issues	Personal insinuations
What he thought was wrong with them	*What they thought was wrong with him*
Church members	Church ministers

1 Corinthians – the 'filling'

1 Corinthians is like a sandwich, with lots of 'filling'. The two slices of 'bread' are the Corinthians' problems concerning belief about the cross and the resurrection. The 'filling' is the problems concerning their behaviour.

Let us look first at the 'filling'. Paul was dealing firstly with the report that he had received from Chloe's household about what was going wrong, and secondly with the questions arising from the letter brought by Chloe's family. So this large section of 1 Corinthians is a mixture of the two. These were the problems that beset the church at Corinth:

1 *Division.* Cliques had arisen centred on individual leaders. Some of the people were followers of Paul, some of Peter, some of Apollos – rather as today, some Christians focus their loyalty around church leaders of the past or the present.

2 *Immorality.* There was incest and prostitution taking place in the church, without any discipline being exercised.

3 *Litigation.* Church members were taking each other to court rather than settling matters among themselves.

4 *Idolatry*. Some of the Christians in Corinth were mixing worship of God with pagan practices.

5 *Men and women*. 'Feminist' beliefs had led some people to seek to abolish gender distinctions.

6 *Food offered to idols*. They were wondering whether it was appropriate for them to buy meat at the market that had been offered to idols.

7 The *Lord's Supper*. In those days the Lord's Supper was celebrated as a full meal, the bread and wine being consumed as part of a larger meal. But in the Corinthian church the Lord's Supper was being abused – some people were overeating and others were getting drunk. A love feast at which they were meant to remember Jesus had become something of a farce.

8 *Spiritual gifts*. The exercise of spiritual gifts had made the church gatherings chaotic. Paul told them that if unbelievers entered one of their meetings and heard people speaking all together in tongues, they would conclude that the church members were mad.

When considering the problems of the Corinthian church, it is helpful to distinguish between those that had been raised in the letter to Paul and those that Paul had picked up from verbal reports. In some cases the distinction is made clear by Paul's wording: 'Now concerning …' But in other cases it is not clear whether Paul is quoting the Corinthians or speaking himself. For example, in 1 Corinthians 7:1 is Paul really saying that it is not good for a man to marry, or is he quoting their understanding of the issue? In 1 Corinthians 14:34 he says that women should remain silent, but is this his view or theirs? For this reason it is vital to study the context and not just the text.

Some questions are clear. They asked about meat offered to idols because most of the meat that they bought had already been involved in a pagan religious ceremony. The slaughter-house was a religious place, and the meat was offered to idols before it was put on sale in the marketplace, so this created a conscience problem for Christians. They also asked about marriage and divorce and about spiritual gifts. Paul thanked God that they were such a charismatic church but told them that they were also a carnal church. They had all the spiritual gifts, but they lacked the necessary character to handle them properly.

Applying 1 and 2 Corinthians to life today is fraught with problems. Some Christians try to apply them literally and legalistically, as they do other parts of the Bible. It is amazing how many Christians think that Jesus wanted us to have a feet-washing ceremony in church just because he once washed the feet of his disciples. This is a clear case of the legalistic applica-tion of Scripture. Jesus washed the disciples' feet because they were dirty – it's as simple as that! Walking on dusty roads in open sandals made their feet hot, sticky, smelly and filthy.

Hats in church?

So let us take an issue that arises in 1 Corinthians 11:2–15. Should women wear hats in church? Many believers have insisted that they should, on the basis of the teaching in these verses.

But in the whole passage there is nothing at all about hats – the word doesn't even occur. The word for head cov-ering that Paul uses is 'veil', and this word only occurs once in the whole chapter, in a context that explains how women have been given long hair instead of a veil. So there is not a single sentence that says that women should wear a veil, much less a hat!

The section is actually about men's hair being shorter than women's hair. In simple terms, the principle is that the person sitting behind you in church should know whether they are sitting behind a man or a woman. The deeper principle is that men and women are different, because the real message is not about hats or about hair, but about the head. So when we look at a man, we should think of his head, but when we look at a woman, we should think of her hair. This tells us the difference between men and women and reminds us that God is the head of Christ, Christ is the head of every man, and man is the head of woman. So the passage argues that men should have short hair so that their head can be visible and women should have longer hair so that their head can be invisible.

The underlying principle is that in Christ we are still male and female – we have not been neutered. We are still what God created us to be, so when we worship God we do so not as persons, but as men and women, willing to accept how God made us. So transvestism is condemned in the Bible, for when men want to be like women and women want to be like men, there is a rebellion against how God has made us. When we worship God as Creator, we come to him as his creatures, and so we need to let that difference be clearly seen.

Western culture is generally saying the exact opposite. It argues for the removal of many differences between men and women, and this belief is creeping into the Church. But men and women *are* different. We are complementary, of equal value and dignity and status in God's sight, but with different roles, responsibilities and functions before God.

There are two wrong ways of applying this teaching in 1 Corinthians 11:2–15:

1 *Apply the passage to the body, but not to the spirit.* Here a woman wears a hat, but she 'wears the trousers as well'. I

have seen women who wear hats faithfully in church, in apparent obedience to their interpretation of this passage, but they dominate their husbands, thus proving that they have not grasped the right idea at all! They have applied the passage to their body but not to their spirit.

2 *Apply the passage to the spirit but not to the body.* Some say that as long as their spirit acknowledges the headship of men, it doesn't matter whether or not they reflect this in their outward appearance. But because the body is part of us and we worship God with our body, this position also misses the point of the passage. It is appropriate that women should identify themselves as women by the way they wear their hair and by the way they dress.

The importance of love (1 Corinthians 13)

Not only were gender distinctives a problem, but the Corinthians also failed to grasp what Scripture teaches about love. The English word 'love' doesn't do us any favours at this point, for it covers a multitude of concepts, so that we often have the same problem in understanding love in our day.

The famous chapter on love is actually part of a larger section focusing on spiritual gifts (chapters 12–14). Chapter 12 is about spiritual gifts by themselves; chapter 13 is about spiritual gifts without love; and chapter 14 is about the true, excellent way – spiritual gifts *with* love. So chapter 13 is not really a love poem to be used at weddings, however apt it may seem!

In the New Testament there are three Greek words that are translated into English as 'love':

Eros	Philadelphia	Agape
lust	*like*	*love*
attraction	*affection*	*attention*
body	*soul*	*spirit*
emotional	*intellectual*	*volitional*
reactive	*reciprocal*	*regardless*
dependent	*interdependent*	*independent*

Eros was the word used for sexual attraction. Closely allied to *eros* but less common was *epithumia*, a dustbin word for the worst kind of lust. Eros is not necessarily a bad word, but *epithumia* certainly is, meaning promiscuous attraction between the sexes or in same-sex relationships. Eros is essentially a thing of the flesh, an emotional love, a dependent love. It is dependent on the object of your affection continuing to attract your lust. As soon as this stops, the relationship struggles.

The word *philadelphia* comes from *philo*, 'to love', and *adelphia*, 'brother'. It means to like someone. It is a word of affection rather than attraction. It is essentially a word of like-mindedness. Friends generally have similar tastes and outlooks; they have sympathy and empathy with each other, and so a bond of affection grows. It is essentially an intellectual thing, as opposed to an emotional bond, and it is interdependent.

The Greeks very rarely used the word *agape* to describe love, probably because they rarely saw it demonstrated. This is a love that gives attention to people. It is not a love that is attracted by them, nor is it a mutual, interdependent affection. It is therefore primarily an act of the will. When a person loves in this way, it is because they see that someone needs it. Since it is an act of the will, it is the only love that can be commanded. It is impossible to tell someone to fall in love or to have affection for someone else, but it is possible to tell someone to love a person with *agape* love.

Agape love is the love of God. God does not love us because we are attractive or lovable. The Bible says he loves us because he loves us. In the Old Testament, we discover that God did not love the Jews because they were a great nation, but because he is love and he chose to care for a bunch of slaves whom nobody cared about. This kind of love is sacrificial – a love that is willing to pay any price to care for someone. This is the love that God has for us – while we were still sinners, God loved us.

The reason why so many churches have been divided over charismatic issues is that there has been a lack of *agape* love. This sort of love can bring together people who may have very different views on a matter. They can choose to love one another despite their different points of view.

The 'bread' of the 'sandwich'

At the beginning and the end of 1 Corinthians Paul deals with two very fundamental matters of belief.

The crucifixion

The word of the cross is an offence to the Greeks, in part because they reject the notion that the body has any value. So they sneer at the idea that a body on a cross can bring spiritual salvation. It is largely because they have failed to realize the importance of the cross that they are divided into cliques over other, less important matters. Paul has to remind them that none of their church leaders was crucified for them – only Jesus. So why are they following human leaders?

The resurrection

At the end of 1 Corinthians Paul deals with their doubts about the resurrection. As Greeks, they would have believed in the immortality of the soul and would not have seen any value in the resurrection of the body. Paul has to correct their thinking and help them to perceive the future in bodily terms. Just as Jesus had a new body after the resurrection that could eat fish and cook breakfast, so Christians will have a bodily existence in the future. Paul's words in 1 Corinthians 15, possibly written around AD 56, are the very first written record of the witnesses of the resurrection body of Jesus.

2 Corinthians – a personal letter

This is the least methodical of Paul's letters, but also the most personal. It is nearly all autobiography, for Paul talks almost exclusively about himself and his ministry. If 1 Corinthians is for church members, 2 Corinthians is for church leaders and ministers. If the first letter is what Paul thought about the Corinthians, the second letter is what they thought about him – and the relationship was pretty bad by this point.

We can divide their attitude into two phases.

The first phase concerned other leaders who were good men – both Apollos and Peter were well regarded. But people began to compare one leader with another, and so divisions developed, as we have already noted in looking at the first letter.

In the second phase they had some bad leaders. Leaders came into Corinth who claimed to be special apostles. They criticized their predecessors, building themselves up and pushing Paul down. We should be wary of leaders who behave in this way. Many of the things that they said about Paul were not true.

In 2 Corinthians Paul responds to those who were criticizing both his message and his ministry. Their criticisms were numerous – it was a thorough character assassination.

- They accused him of fickleness, of always changing his plans.
- They said he was cowardly, preferring to write to them rather than visit them.
- They said he was timid when he was with them in person.
- They criticized him for not having any letters of recommendation. The false apostles had come with qualifications that they could frame and put up on the vestry wall. This is why Paul says in 2 Corinthians that he doesn't need any such letter, since the Corinthians themselves are his letter of recommendation. The acid test of a man's ministry is not his academic qualifications or his training, but the kind of people he produces.
- They accused him of being secretive and less than frank.
- They said he was distant, aloof, unfeeling and uncaring.
- They accused him of not being a polished speaker.
- They criticized him because he didn't charge a fee. In Greece, entertainment was provided by travelling philosophers, and the bigger the fee charged, the greater the reputation of the speaker.

So much for the criticisms. How did Paul defend himself?

Paul's defence – (2 Corinthians 1–9)

The earlier part of the letter is Paul's sincere response to the accusations. He didn't charge a fee because he wanted the Corinthians to receive the gospel for free. He says that every man's work will be tested, so those who follow him must be careful how they build. He rejects the accusation that he was timid, reminding them of his second visit, when he was anything but timid.

It is just pouring out – a defence of himself. Some of his greatest statements are in this second letter:

> *We are hard pressed on every side, but not crushed; perplexed, but not in despair; persecuted, but not abandoned; struck down, but not destroyed … We put no stumbling-block in anyone's path, so that our ministry will not be discredited. Rather, as servants of God we commend ourselves in every way: in great endurance; in troubles, hardships and distresses; in beatings, imprisonments and riots; in hard work, sleepless nights and hunger; in purity, understanding, patience and kindness; in the Holy Spirit and in sincere love; in truthful speech and in the power of God; with weapons of righteousness in the right hand and in the left; through glory and dishonour, bad report and good report; genuine, yet regarded as impostors; known, yet regarded as unknown; dying, and yet we live on; beaten, and yet not killed; sorrowful, yet always rejoicing; poor, yet making many rich; having nothing, and yet possessing everything.*
>
> 2 Corinthians 4:8–9; 6:3–10

Paul's attack (2 Corinthians 10–13)

Chapters 10–13 are very different to the earlier part of the letter. Instead of defending himself, he now attacks others. He resorts to irony and sarcasm as he deals with the false apostles who have come in and taken over.

This passage must be read aloud if its passion is to be truly appreciated. Let us look at one especially powerful passage:

I hope you will put up with a little of my foolishness; but you are already doing that. I am jealous for you with a godly jealousy. I promised you to one husband, to Christ, so that I might present you as a pure virgin to him. But I am afraid that just as Eve was deceived by the serpent's cunning, your minds may somehow be led astray from your sincere and pure devotion to Christ. For if someone comes to you and preaches a Jesus other than the Jesus we preached, or if you receive a different spirit from the one you received, or a different gospel from the one you accepted, you put up with it easily enough. But I do not think I am in the least inferior to those 'super-apostles'. I may not be a trained speaker, but I do have knowledge. We have made this perfectly clear to you in every way.

Was it a sin for me to lower myself in order to elevate you by preaching the gospel of God to you free of charge? I robbed other churches by receiving support from them so as to serve you. And when I was with you and needed something, I was not a burden to anyone, for the brothers who came from Macedonia supplied what I needed. I have kept myself from being a burden to you in any way, and will continue to do so. As surely as the truth of Christ is in me, nobody in the regions of Achaia will stop this boasting of mine. Why? Because I do not love you? God knows I do! And I will keep on doing what I am doing in order to cut the ground from under those who want an opportunity to be considered equal with us in the things they boast about.

For such men are false apostles, deceitful workmen, masquerading as apostles of Christ. And no wonder, for Satan himself masquerades as an angel of light. It is not surprising, then, if his servants masquerade as servants of righteousness. Their end will be what their actions deserve.

I repeat: Let no-one take me for a fool. But if you do, then receive me just as you would a fool, so that I may do a little boasting. In this self-confident boasting I am not talking as the Lord would, but as a fool. Since many are boasting in the way the world does, I too will boast. You gladly put up with fools since you are so wise! In fact, you even put up with anyone who enslaves you or exploits you or takes advantage of you or pushes himself forward or slaps you in the face. To my shame I admit that we were too weak for that!

What anyone also dares to boast about – I am speaking as a fool – I also dare to boast about. Are they Hebrews? So am I. Are they Israelites? So am I. Are they Abraham's descendants? So am I. Are they servants of Christ? (I am out of my mind to talk like this.) I am more. I have worked much harder, been in prison more frequently, been flogged more severely, and been exposed to death again and again. Five times I received from the Jews the forty lashes minus one. Three times I was beaten with rods, once I was stoned, three times I was shipwrecked, I spent a night and a day in the open sea, I have been constantly on the move. I have been in danger from rivers, in danger from bandits, in danger from my own countrymen, in danger from Gentiles; in danger in the city, in danger in the country, in danger at sea; and in danger from false brothers. I have laboured and toiled and have often gone without sleep; I have known hunger and thirst and have often gone without food; I have been cold and naked. Besides everything else, I face daily the pressure of my concern for all the churches. Who is weak, and I do not feel weak? Who is led into sin, and I do not inwardly burn?

If I must boast, I will boast of the things that show my weakness. The God and Father of the Lord Jesus, who is to be praised for ever, knows that I am not lying.

2 Corinthians 11:1–31

Paul believes that such a defence is necessary, not because he is concerned for his own reputation but because he is concerned for the reputation of the gospel. He is jealous for the Corinthians; he doesn't want them to wander away from the truth. He fears that if they believe the false teachers, they may well be deceived and drift from the truth that is in Jesus.

There are no apostles today of the same kind as Paul, so we might think that these passages have little relevance to us. But there are parallels today, for servants of God are still attacked as Paul was, whether they be pastors, evangelists or prophets. They should note the importance of standing firm on the gospel and, like Paul, they should seek to be sure that their motivation is correct.

Famine relief (2 Corinthians 8–9)

Finally, we must note that the middle chapters of 2 Corinthians deal with a different issue. Paul had a real heart for famine relief, and perhaps he wondered if turning their minds to caring for others might help them to put their problems into perspective. So in chapters 8–9 he gives some wonderful teaching about Christian giving, urging the Corinthians to know God's blessing as they give generously to others. It is a masterful piece of writing, revealing the pastoral heart of the apostle and the strength of his convictions regarding the correct use of money.

Conclusion

So, despite the fact that the Corinthians were Paul's most difficult church, these two letters are rich in teaching for the Church today. They give us practical teaching on how to live in a hostile environment and how a church should discipline its members and regulate its activities. They also give us a rare insight into how the apostle Paul coped with opposition, and so they provide an excellent model for God's servants to follow, wherever they may be serving and whoever their opponents may be.

46.

 GALATIANS

Introduction

Paul's letter to the Galatians tends to divide people into two camps: those who think highly of it and those who do not.

Some notable Christians in the past have been very positive about Galatians. Luther said it was the best book in the Bible. He said, 'This is my epistle. I am married to it.' John Bunyan, the author of *Pilgrim's Progress*, said, 'I do prefer Luther's commentary on Galatians, except the Holy Bible, before all the books that I have ever seen as most fit for a wounded conscience.' Clearly, Galatians had a profound effect on Bunyan. The letter has had a deep influence on Christian history, and many Christians love it.

However, some people dislike Galatians intensely. It has been called 'a crucifixion epistle' and 'a thorny jungle'. Some say that every sentence contains a thunderbolt. Here are five reasons why people dislike it so much:

'It's too emotional'

It is a highly charged letter. It is written in white heat, perhaps on asbestos papyrus! It is full of emotion, and this makes some people uncomfortable. Many people, particularly in Britain, have tried to keep emotion out of religion, but when they read Galatians they find a man burning with anger, and this disturbs them.

'It's too personal'

Some people argue that Galatians is too personal. Certainly, Paul has put more about himself into this letter than into any other. He talks about his physical handicaps at one point, pleading with his readers on the basis of his own weakness. He mentions a public argument that he had with the apostle Peter, where he had to stand up to Peter in front of a whole congregation and tell him that he was wrong – a reminder that even in the early Church the apostles had their public differences. We are sometimes too anxious to agree rather than differ, too anxious to avoid confrontation. When truth was at stake, even Peter and Paul would face up to each other and fight for it.

'It's too intellectual'

In Galatians, Paul is using all his Rabbinical background and training to argue the case he is making, and it is a very tight intellectual argument. None of the translations that I have ever read has really got to grips with the thread of the argument, so I confess that I have actually translated it myself (the translation appears at the end of this chapter). The argument is quite subtle and there are some very fine points in it, requiring some hard thinking. Do not let this deter you. We are to love God with all our mind. One of the most frequent comments I get after preaching is a kind of mild rebuke that says, 'Well, you gave us something to think about today.' It is said in a tone of 'I didn't come to church to think, you know.' Well, I make no apologies for stretching minds, and Paul stretches your mind too. We need to study Galatians very carefully and go through it again and again to see what Paul is saying.

'It's too spiritual'

Galatians strips off spiritual veneers and strikes at an individual's pride. If you have got any pride left, then don't read Galatians, because you will have none left by the time you have finished. It really does go to the root of the matter, beyond your mind and your heart, through to the marrow. It is the sharp, two-edged word of God that penetrates deeply.

'It's too controversial'

Above all, people have found Galatians too argumentative. The modern mood is that we do not want to argue about religion. We do not want to quarrel, but to be comfortable with each other. Galatians is not that kind of a letter. Paul argues with other Christians, not with unbelievers, and his message in the letter has in turn caused many arguments.

Arguments can be good. If Luther had not been willing to get into an argument, the Reformation would not have occurred. So argument has benefited us greatly. The reason why it is not popular today is that we fear that differences will lead to division. The two prime virtues considered today are tolerance and tact, though neither is a virtue in the Bible. Jesus was neither tolerant nor tactful.

Is this unwillingness to face our differences a good thing or a bad thing? I believe it depends on whether the issues are primary or secondary. The trouble is that we tend to get so heated over secondary issues that we are not really confronting people over primary things. Does it really matter whether we use alcoholic or non-alcoholic wine for the Lord's Supper? Yet people get so upset about this.

Take the Sabbath issue, for example. I do not believe this is an issue that Christians should be making too much of. Paul says that each should be fully persuaded in his own mind. If one wants to regard Sunday as special, that is his privilege. If another wants to regard every day as the Lord's day, that is his privilege. We do not have the right to impose Sunday on each other as believers, never mind on unbelievers.

But when we come to Galatians, we are handling some of the biggest issues of all. There are fundamental issues without which you lose the Christian gospel, so, I am afraid, fighting is involved. Many of the biggest battles that Christians have to face are inside the Church, not outside it. That is painful. Who likes a family that is arguing? Whenever the devil attacks the Church from the outside, the Church gets stronger and bigger. His attacks are much more successful when they come from the inside, and one of the quickest ways to do that is to pervert or corrupt or erode the gospel. If he can do that, he knows that he has destroyed the Church from the inside.

In Galatians we see two leading men, Peter and Paul, involved in a public confrontation on a fundamental issue. I believe that God has given to Christian men the responsibility of fighting for and protecting the doctrine of the Church, and it is a tragedy that we don't have more strong men of conviction who will fight to protect the gospel. There are many women who want to and who try to, but I believe there are not enough men who are prepared to stick their necks out and confront error when they hear it or see it.

Peter and Paul did fight it out. Peter was in the wrong and Paul was in the right, and the Bible has been honest enough to share that with us. Clearly, God wanted us to know about that confrontation.

Reading New Testament letters

It is important to read a New Testament letter all the way through, especially if it is addressing one particular issue, which is the case with Philemon and Hebrews, for example. Only then can you get the sense of what the writer is saying. You must remember that you are only hearing one side of a conversation. It is rather like being in a room when the telephone has rung and somebody else has answered the phone, and you only hear what they say. In this situation it is easy to get the wrong idea about what the person at the other end of the line has been saying, because you will have listened with preconceived notions. When you read an epistle, somehow you have to reconstruct the situation about which it was written and read between the lines. You must ask yourself, 'What was happening that motivated Paul to write this letter?' You will find that this is a helpful way of studying the letters.

This is the method we are going to use to look at Galatians. We will be asking key questions such as:

Why was it written?
What questions was it answering?
What problems was it solving?

There may be only one issue being discussed, as with Philemon, or many issues, as with 1 Corinthians, but you need to ask these questions if the meaning of the letter is to become clear.

Paul the enthusiastic Jew

There is no doubt that the author of Galatians was Paul. It may have been the first letter that he ever wrote to a church. By any standard, Paul was one of the greatest men who ever lived. He was born in Tarsus in what is today southern Turkey. Tarsus had the Roman world's third most important university, after

Athens and Alexandria. He was Jewish, but was also a Roman citizen and spoke the Greek language – an ideal background for the task that God had in mind for him. God prepares us for ministry even before we are born, but he also prepares us through our experiences long before we know him. He is putting things into us that he can use later.

Paul was taught a trade, as every good Jewish boy was. His trade was tent-making. However, in Greek society, if you worked with your hands you were lower down the social scale than those who worked with their heads and were 'pen-pushers' – an attitude that, sadly, we have inherited. But in the Bible jobs such as tent-making and fishing were well respected. Paul says, in one of his letters to Thessalonica, that the believers should all work with their hands, for he had given them an example to do that. So the Bible attaches dignity to manual labour. After all, the Lord Jesus himself had worked as a carpenter.

So Paul worked as a tent-maker, probably for the Roman army, and then studied at the university in Jerusalem under Professor Gamaliel. He became an ultra-orthodox, fanatical Jew – a 'Hebrew of the Hebrews', a 'Pharisee of the Pharisees', as he called himself. His attitude was: If you are going to keep the Law, you must keep all of it. Just obeying the Ten Commandments was not enough. He does admit that he struggled with the tenth commandment, 'Do not covet.' (It is interesting that this is the one commandment that deals with inner motivation; the others deal with outward behaviour.) However, Paul believed that he had succeeded in keeping the whole of the Law. He was blameless. There were not many Jews who could say that.

He had achieved a great deal of self-righteousness and attacked everybody who attacked Judaism, especially the Christians, who claimed that Jesus was God. Paul thought this claim was the ultimate blasphemy. He set out to destroy this new faith and watched Stephen being stoned to death. But from then on he began to be pricked in his conscience. As Stephen died, he said, 'I can see Jesus on the right hand of God. Into your hands I commit my spirit.' This stirred Paul to attack the new faith even more fiercely, because now he was also fighting his own conscience. He finally lost the fight when, on the Damascus road, he met Jesus.

Paul the fervent missionary

The man who wrote Galatians had become one of the most enthusiastic followers of Jesus ever, an ardent propagator of the faith he had once tried to destroy. He knew both Judaism and Christianity inside out, having switched from one to the other. During his missionary journeys he planted churches throughout the known world, constantly pioneering fresh territory. He called it 'colonizing for Christ'.

The readers

There were two geographical places called Galatia, and scholars expend a lot of ink in discussing which of these was the Galatia of Paul's letters. In what we now call Turkey there was a group of cities in the north called North Galatia, and there was a group of cities in the south called South Galatia. North Galatia is especially interesting to us in Britain because it was originally colonized by people from Gaul (France), who were related to the Celtic peoples of the British Isles. However, I believe that Paul's letter was in fact written to Christians in South Galatia rather than North Galatia. South Galatia comprised a group of cities – Lystra, Derbe, Antioch and Iconium – which Paul had already visited. So it is understandable that he would write a letter like this, having himself planted the churches and entrusted them to new elders and to the Head of the Church in heaven.

Alternative teaching

Unfortunately, what happened to them has happened to many new fellowships today. Other men came in and took over the work. We should beware of men who come and seek to take over, for they are often dangerous men, building their empires by taking possession of fellowships that other people have planted. Often such leaders lead new churches down the wrong path, and Paul faced this with the Galatians. The people who did it were Jewish believers, who followed Paul around everywhere. They were his biggest problem. They said to the Gentiles, 'Don't listen to Paul – he has only given you half the story. He has brought you to faith, yes, but he didn't bring you fully into the faith, because you need the Law of Moses as well as Christ.'

This focus upon the Law is still with us today. I am amazed how often I go into churches in this country and see the Ten Commandments displayed on the wall. The first church in England that I became pastor of in 1954 had the Commandments up on the wall behind my head in the pulpit in chocolate-brown Gothic lettering! I decided that the first thing I was going to do was to paint it out, and so I got a pot of paint and painted all over it. There was a great outcry. Somebody complained that there was nothing to read during the sermon! They said they had to have something there, so I put a cross up on the wall instead.

Everywhere Paul went and brought the full gospel of Christ, these Jewish believers followed up and said, 'Of course, he hasn't told you everything, and we have now come to give you the whole story.' That is exactly how some leaders talk today when they try to take over other people's fellowships. They claim that the Pastor's teaching is good, but that they have more wisdom.

Bad news

Paul has heard some very bad news about his young churches – the ones that he laboured to bring into being. His work was being undone, and two things were happening.

Additions to Paul's message

As in many modern cults, the new leaders were adding to the gospel – what we might call 'the gospel plus'. So many sects and cults around today add to the gospel, and they usually add another book to the Bible, such as Mary Baker Eddy's *Science and Health*, or Joseph Smith's *Book of Mormon*. Beware of anyone who insists that you need another book as well as your Bible, for it is the 'gospel plus' argument again. Something is being added on, and you can only put so much luggage in a canoe before it overturns. Or to use another analogy, rot starts in the pulpit – dry rot. It is essential to be on our guard against bad teaching.

An attack on the messenger

It was not just that these teachers were adding to Paul's gospel – they were attacking the messenger too. They claimed that Paul was not preaching the full gospel, that he was not a true apostle, that his version of the gospel was second-hand and that he was not approved by the Church. In undermining Paul's authority they sought to establish their own.

What was the issue?

On a first reading of the letter you would think it is about circumcision, for this seems to be the thing that Paul is focusing on. The question arises: Was he making a mountain out of a molehill? Why get so concerned about this little thing? If people want to be circumcised, surely that is acceptable. Was he justified in making such a song and dance about this Jewish custom of circumcision?

Circumcision is a minor operation – the removal of part of the reproductive organ of the male. It is not practised on females in Judaism, though it is in certain tribes in Africa. It is still a widespread habit in the Semitic world, largely for hygienic reasons in that climate. But to the Jews it had a religious significance. It was the mark of a Jew. Of course, only males were circumcised, because in the Jewish world it is the male who inherits, and the promises pass down through the male line. Circumcision was a sign of eligibility to inherit the blessing promised to Abraham. It was even said by God to Abraham that if any Jewish male was not circumcised, he had to be thrown out of the people of God because he had broken the covenant. Part of the covenant with Abraham was that every male descendant would bear this mark.

So to a Jew circumcision is of crucial importance. There are things that mean everything to the Jew: the Passover, kosher diet, the Sabbath and circumcision. Whatever else they may do or not do – they may be liberal or non-practising Jews – those four things still apply.

It is important that we grasp Paul's argument concerning God's promise to Abraham. He argues in Galatians 3 that the promise made to Abraham was only intended for one male descendant of Abraham. The word that God used for 'seed' was singular, so when God said 'to Abraham and his seed' he did not mean to all his male descendants, but to one of them. Paul argues that when that one male seed came, which was Jesus, circumcision became obsolete, because now the promise had been inherited. The one to whom it was promised had received the inheritance, so there was no point in circumcising anybody now. So circumcision was a sign of inheritance, and Jesus had that sign. He was circumcised and he was the one who inherited.

Now, of course, Paul had been circumcised as a Jewish male, and it seemed strange, in the light of his argument, that he did actually circumcise Timothy, who came from Galatia. This may seem contradictory, but it was because he was going to accompany Paul in his missionary work, and Paul always went into the synagogue first and preached to Jews. Timothy would never have managed to get into the synagogue with him if he had not been circumcised, so Paul did it purely as an act of accommodation for evangelism. In the same way, C. T. Studd and other missionaries to China grew pigtails, in order to get alongside the people. But Paul, who had circumcised Timothy for that same reason, was now saying to the Galatians, 'How dare you consider it!' Circumcision was clearly very important, but behind it was something else.

Paul's very strong language in Galatians reminds me once again that the Bible is not a book for children – it is a book for adults. (The tragedy is that most people stop reading it when they become adults.) He says, 'I just wish that those who would cut off your foreskins would go the whole hog and castrate themselves.' Then they wouldn't be able to reproduce themselves. Strong language indeed!

Why is he so against circumcision?

The answer is that behind circumcision lay Judaism. Judaism can easily become a religion of works. It is a religion of saving oneself by keeping the Commandments. It is an impossible task, but so many people try it. This is the danger of putting the Ten Commandments up on a wall. It is communicating to people that you have got to live by these laws in order to get right with God. An outsider coming in is faced straight away with a list of 'Thou shalt nots', which gives the impression that we are against everything, that we are negative, and that if you come anywhere near God he will stop you having fun.

Judaism

Christianity is rooted in Judaism, which is in turn rooted in the Old Testament. But how much of the Old Testament should come through to the New? How many of those 613 laws actually apply to us? That is one of the biggest questions you have got to face when you study the Old and New Testaments.

Let me give you an example. I do not ever tell Christians to tithe, because it belongs to the Law of Moses and is never mentioned in the New Testament with respect to Gentile believers. Jews did it, but no Gentile believer was ever told to tithe. We are, however, told to *give*.

I once listened to a young man preaching on tithing. Clearly, he had used his computer to search for the word 'Tithing' and had got all the biblical references on the subject. He said there were blessings attached to tithing, and he gave them all. God says in Malachi, 'Prove me now herewith if I do not open the windows of heaven and pour out a blessing on you.' He then said that there are also curses attached to tithing.

He proceeded to tell us about a curse in the Old Testament, that our grandchildren and great-grandchildren will suffer if we do not bring our tithes. I looked at the faces of the congregation and could see their fear of causing their great-grandchildren to suffer. It is no wonder that the offering was pretty big the following Sunday! But I was horrified. In the New Testament giving works on an altogether different principle. The Lord loves a cheerful giver, which doesn't mean grin and bear it. You should give because you *want* to give, not because you are forced to, in case your great-grandchildren suffer. That belongs to the old covenant.

Another example is the Sabbath law. We must think about what we are doing before we apply old covenant laws to Christians, because if you apply some of them you must apply all of them, and if you apply the blessing, you must apply the curse. Now, are we prepared to do that? I am not. So Paul is saying, 'If you get circumcised, that is just the camel's nose in the tent, and you will soon have the hump and all. If you go the way of circumcision for the reason these teachers are giving, then all the other 613 laws will follow.'

That is why Paul is so anxious. The problem is not circumcision itself, but the way in which it opened the door to Judaism. He had tried Judaism, and when he considered the commandments he had kept (not just the ones he felt like keeping), he said he thanked God that he was delivered from it all. In the same way, if we tell people to keep the Law of Moses, we are consigning them to hell, because they cannot do it.

It is important to put people under grace, rather than under law. There is a law we are under, but it is the law of Christ, not the Law of Moses. That Law is obsolete; it has been done away with. But one of the biggest problems in the Church today is that we are giving people a mixture of the law of Christ and the Law of Moses. Why do you think churches have vestments, altars, incense and priests? We don't need any of those things – they belong to the Law of Moses, but they have crept back in.

Throughout the Book of Acts we see a loosening of the ties between Judaism and Christianity. Stephen, the first martyr of the Church, was stoned for this particular issue. When Philip baptized the Ethiopian eunuch, he took it a little further, and then Peter was sent by God to Cornelius, a Gentile, at Caesarea. Soon the Jewish believers in Jerusalem were very, very suspicious about this new faith being taken to Gentiles. It didn't seem Jewish enough for them, and so finally Paul went up to Jerusalem to challenge the very heart of the Church, that was sending out these anti-missionaries who were saying it was not enough just to believe – you had to be circumcised as well. The real issue was not circumcision, but whether Gentiles had to become Jews when they became Christians.

Salvation

The real issue was salvation itself – the whole question of how salvation is obtained. People offer several different answers to this question, and all are assumed to be Christian.

Works alone

Most religions of the world are about salvation by works. You must pray, you must fast, you must give alms and so on, and then, at the end of it all, you will get right with God. You save yourself by your own efforts. Do-it-yourself religion appeals to people because it leaves them with their pride, for they feel that they have achieved salvation. It is self-righteousness, and that is something that God hates. He would rather deal with sin than self-righteousness. Jesus just couldn't get on with self-righteous people. He was a friend of sinners, but with the self-righteous, such as the Pharisees, he couldn't get on at all.

Works plus faith

The belief about the need for works is very common. I used to be an O.D. (Other Denominations) chaplain in the Royal Air Force. When a new bunch of men arrived the Anglican chaplain would walk off with 70 per cent of them, then the Roman Catholic chaplain would take everybody with an Irish accent, and I would be left with the Baptists, Methodists, Salvationists, Buddhists, Hindus, Muslims, agnostics and atheists. It was fascinating to be a chaplain to atheists.

When the men were seated before me, I would ask how many were Methodists, how many were Baptists and so on, and each group would put their hands up. In the same tone of voice I would ask how many were Christians. Dead silence! Occasionally a lad would put his hand up and smile, but usually they would all look around to see if anybody else had put their hand up.

'Come on,' I would say. ' You told me how many of you are Methodists and Baptists and so on. Well, how many of you are Christians?'

'But what do you mean by "Christian", Padre?' they would reply.

'What do you think I mean?' I would ask.

'Someone who keeps the Ten Commandments', would be the usual response.

'Okay, I will accept that a Christian is someone who keeps the Ten Commandments. How many Christians are there here?'

There would be real uncertainty, and then somebody would say, 'But Padre, you can't keep them all!'

'Well, how many do you have to keep to be a Christian?'

'Six out of ten.'

'Okay, I accept that a Christian is somebody who keeps six of the Ten Commandments. So how many Christians are there here?'

It led to a tremendous discussion of what a Christian is. You see, works plus faith implies that we keep as many commandments as we can, and then we ask God to forgive us for the commandments that we are not able to keep. That is the most common understanding of Christianity in our country. We might call it 'do-gooding Christianity'.

Faith plus works

Some believe that you start with faith and then you go on to works. After you have believed in Jesus, you have got to keep the Law. This is what the Judaizers of Paul's time were saying.

Faith alone

Paul was saying to the Galatians, 'Having started in the Spirit, are you going to continue in the flesh? The Law belongs to the flesh – it is your effort, it is not the Spirit doing it in you.' Paul was fighting for faith alone, faith from first to last, as he often puts it – faith from beginning to end. He said, 'I am not ashamed of the gospel. It is the power of God that saves everyone who goes on believing,' faith from first to last.

In other words, we cannot compromise on this – you must go on believing. That is the heart of it. You do not believe at the beginning and then work for it. There is a big difference between telling people they need to go on believing and telling them they need to keep the Law now. What Paul is fighting for is Christian freedom. To introduce the Law at any stage is to put people under a curse, because the only pass-mark that Jesus will accept for the Law is 100 per cent. You either keep all the Law or you have broken the Law.

The same thing is true even with human laws. If I drove through a red light and I was stopped by a policeman, and I said to him, 'But, Officer, I stopped at every red light on the way here,' he would reply, 'I don't care if you stopped at every red light – you have broken the law!' That is what God says. The Law is not just a string of individual pearls – it is a necklace, it is a complete thing. If you break it at any point, the pearls all fall on the ground. You have broken the Law, so it doesn't matter whether you have broken one commandment or all of them.

Imagine that three men are stranded on a rock when the tide is coming in, and there is a three-metre channel of water between the rock and the beach. If the first man manages to jump a third of the way, he will drown. If the second man is a better jumper and manages to jump two thirds of the way, he will still drown. The third man only misses by six inches, but he is lost too.

God's word says, 'Cursed be he who does not continue in all these laws, to go on doing them.' This is the curse you are under if you try to keep the commandments to get to heaven under your own steam. But the gospel has a different way of righteousness altogether.

The obvious question that arises is, Why did God give the Ten Commandments? Why did he give the Law of Moses at all? The answer is in Galatians.

First, God gave the Law *to restrain sin*. It helps to make life livable. At least some will be kept and others attempted.

Secondly, God gave the Law *to reveal sin*. It is by the straight edge of the Law that we realize how crooked we are. In other words, it is only the Law that tells you that you are a sinner. You don't find out how wrong you have been until you have studied the Law of God. The Law was introduced to prepare us for Christ by showing us that we couldn't keep that Law. That is why preaching the Ten Commandments can bring a person to conviction of sin, because they know there is no way they can keep them – especially in the way that Jesus reinterpreted them.

A key theme

Liberty is a key theme in Galatians. The longing for freedom is universal, but the question is, freedom from what? The message of the Bible is that Christ came to set us free, to turn slaves into sons and heirs. So just as the Jews were liberated from Egypt, we are freed through Christ from bondage to sin. But freedom is so easily lost. As J. P. Curran put it, 'The condition upon which God hath given liberty is eternal vigilance.' The problem is not just getting freedom but *keeping* it. Liberty can be lost.

The picture overleaf depicts the whole of Galatians. It is a very simple picture, but I need to explain it. It shows three key concepts in Galatians: legalism, liberty and licence. Legalism is clearly an enemy of liberty, but what people don't always realize is that licence is too. Galatians 1–2 talks about our liberty in Christ under the favour of the Father and in the sunshine of his love. We are in the freedom of the Spirit, and the foundation is faith in the Son. So Father, Son and Spirit are giving us the freedom of standing up here on top of the mountain.

The picture shows that there are two ways of losing that freedom. One is to slip back into the Law, depicted as a cage. We are trapped in it – we try to climb out, but we can't. If you get back under the Law, you are under the wrath of God again,

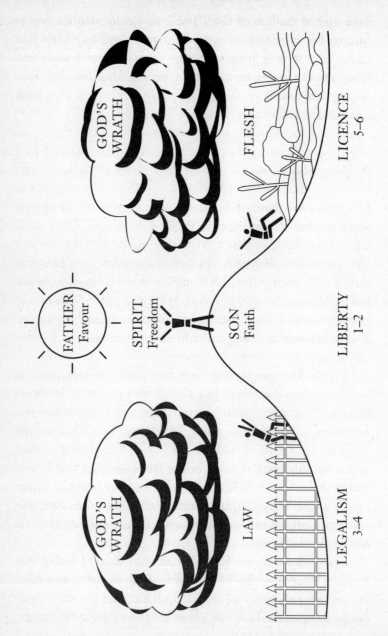

because you can't keep the Law. But there is another way to lose your liberty, and that is to slip down into the swamp of the flesh. That also is bondage, but it is bondage to your own desires, and you are under the wrath of God again. You have lost your freedom.

Striding Edge on Helvellyn in the Lake District is a perfect illustration, because it is a very narrow path right along a ridge. On either side of it are two huge hollows called corries. In the last ice age they were hollowed out by two great balls of ice revolving, thus leaving this very sharp edge. The Matterhorn in Switzerland was the result of three balls of ice revolving, leaving a three-pointed peak.

It is a delicate edge that we walk in the liberty of the Spirit. It is so easy to slip one way or the other. I would say that the biggest danger to Christians in their liberty is legalism. This may surprise you. Licence is pretty obvious, but when churches start making extra rules and regulations, you get too easily into legalism, and that kills liberty. A legalistic fellowship can be easily identified – everybody has pursed lips, and there is a kind of set expression on people's faces. Trying to keep the Law makes people tough and hard. Legalism makes the Christian faith a matter of rules rather than relationships. People think they are Christians because they are keeping the rules – don't smoke, don't gamble, don't drink, don't do this, don't do that – but the relationship with God has gone.

The liberty of the Spirit is not doing what you *want*, and it is not doing what others *tell* you, *it is letting the Spirit guide you*. As Paul says in Galatians, it is not the freedom to sin, it is the freedom *not* to sin. That is real freedom. No unbeliever has that freedom – that is the freedom that God wants for us. But it is so easy to try to stop people sinning by putting them under Law, and that is how some churches operate. They try to protect their members from doing this and that, without realizing that legalism is just as much an enemy of liberty as licence is.

That is the whole argument of Galatians. Chapters 1 and 2 talk about this liberty, chapters 3 and 4 talk about the legalism that can spoil it, and chapters 5 and 6 talk about the opposite danger, licence. So Paul is actually fighting on two fronts, and that is the real problem. To keep liberty and avoid both legalism and licence is quite a delicate operation.

Let us look at legalism, licence and liberty in more detail.

Legalism

Circumcision is the first link in the chain for those Galatians. It would be the beginning of legalism. It is not part of the gospel, and they would also have to keep all the rest of the Law.

Some say, 'But won't people take advantage when you tell them they are not under Law? Won't they become lawless? If you don't give rules, won't people go and indulge themselves?'

When I was a Methodist minister there was a book half an inch thick called *The Constitutional Practice and Discipline of the Methodist Church*. It is now three and a quarter inches thick! Many loose-leaf pages are added every year. So, if rules and regulations could bring revival, the Methodists would leave us standing! But it doesn't happen that way. How easy it is to try to regulate and give rules for this, that and the other, and think that somehow our organization will bring life. It doesn't. Liberty brings life, and God set us free to be free. We must watch legalism like a hawk. If you slip into it, you invariably become hard and hypocritical, because you dare not tell other people if you are breaking the Law.

Licence

There is a real danger in what Paul calls 'the works of the flesh'. Beware of them. They are another form of slavery. They are like a swamp which it is easy to slide into and very hard to get out of. The works of the flesh are listed by Paul in Galatians. Some are obvious, such as promiscuity and occultism. But there are also some more subtle ones, such as quarrelling, rivalry, jealousy, envy and prejudice.

'Now what happens,' asks Paul, 'when somebody slips into this?' There are a lot of banana skins on the Christian road. He says that if someone has slipped into sin, pick them up quickly, get them back into the fellowship and get them healed. But if someone deliberately and wilfully goes on wallowing in sin, he solemnly says that they will not inherit the Kingdom. They may say, 'I'm all right – I've got my ticket to heaven,' but Paul says, 'You're not all right – you won't inherit the Kingdom.' Now that is a very serious warning.

You can slip into legalism, you can slip into licence, and you need to be pulled quickly out of both. But if you deliberately and wilfully choose to live either in the cage or in the swamp, then you won't inherit the Kingdom.

Liberty

Liberty is the freedom not to sin. Isn't it a lovely freedom? You are free now, in Christ, not to sin. You don't need to say yes to it. As Paul puts it in his letter to Titus, 'We have been given the grace to say no.' Isn't that beautiful? Let us look at what happens by referring to the picture again. Imagine a path at the top of the mountain, stretching away beyond the person on the path. We need to walk in the Spirit, along the striding edge –

avoiding the pitfalls of licence and legalism. As you walk in the Spirit, something beautiful happens. Fruit grows in your life – the fruit of the Spirit. There is only one fruit of the Spirit, with nine flavours, whereas there are many works of the flesh.

There is a fruit in the Mediterranean called the *Mysterio Deliciosus*. If you take one bite, it tastes like an orange, and if you take another bite, it tastes like a lemon! It has got many different flavours in it. In the Christian you will find all the flavours of the fruit of the Spirit. You see some of the flavours in unbelievers, don't you? Some unbelievers have joy, others have peace, but you will never see all nine together except in Christ and in those who are filled with the Spirit and walking in the Spirit. The nine flavours relate you to God, other people and yourself. Three of those flavours – love, joy and peace – bring you into perfect harmony with God. The next three – patience, kindness and goodness – bring you into harmony with other people. Then faithfulness, meekness and self-control bring you into a good relationship with yourself. What a lovely fruit it is!

The fruit of the Spirit is limited, of course, without the gifts of the Spirit, just as the gifts are inadequate without the fruit. If I went to hospital to visit a sick person, I could show them all the fruit of the Spirit – I could show them love by visiting them, and joy by cheering them up, and peace by calming them down, and patience by listening to all the details of their operation, and kindness by giving them a bunch of grapes, and goodness by offering to look after their children, and faithfulness by visiting them every day, and meekness by leaving when the nurse tells me to, and self-control by not eating the grapes! I have demonstrated all the fruit of the Spirit in that visit, but I haven't healed them, because that is the gift of the Spirit. We need both the gifts and the fruit. We must never set these against each other.

Paul says that as you walk in the Spirit, the fruit grows. He uses the word 'walk' here in two different ways, using two different Greek words. Your English translation probably has 'walk' both times. In chapter 5, verses 16 and 25 he says, 'walk in the Spirit'. In the Greek verse 16, 'walk' is peripatetic walking – what the Australians call 'walkabout'. It means to go for a walk by yourself. But in verse 25 the word 'walk' really means 'march in the Spirit, in step with others'. So there are two kinds of walking in the Spirit. There is walking in the Spirit when we are by ourselves, and there is walking in step with the rest of our Christian brothers and sisters, and we need both. True liberty is walking along that height in step with your brothers and sisters, walking in the Spirit together.

So this is the message of Paul's letter to the Galatians. It is one of the most relevant letters, although not one of the most comfortable, and I would share the opinion of those who say that this letter is the Magna Carta of Christian liberty. I really believe that is a wonderful title for it. Many people are standing for other kinds of freedom, good or bad, but the freedom we stand for is the freedom not to sin, the freedom to keep out of that cage called legalism and out of that swamp called licence, and the freedom to keep up there on the heights, enjoying the blessing of God's favour.

Legalism is still with us

Legalism is all over the place. People are trying to get to heaven by their own works. Or, having started in faith, they are going back to works, which is tragic.

The late Dr W. E. Sangster went to visit a dying woman in hospital. He said to her, 'Are you ready to meet God? What will you say when you meet him?'

She held up her worn hands and said, 'I am a widow. I have brought up five children, so I have no time for church or the Bible or anything religious. But I have done my best for my children, and when I see God I will just hold up these hands, and he will look at them and he will understand.'

Now, what would you have said to a woman like that? Well, Dr Sangster just said to her, 'You are too late, my dear, you are too late.'

She said, 'What do you mean?'

And he replied, 'Well, there is somebody who has got in front of you, and he is holding up his hands in front of God, and God has eyes for no other.'

She said again, 'What do you mean?'

He told her, 'Don't put your trust in your hands – put your trust in his hands.'

Legalism is still with us and it is rife. The average Briton thinks that being a Christian is being kind to their grandmother and their cat. They think, 'I am as good a Christian as anybody who goes to church.' When they say that, they are trapped in legalism. We need to tell them that only 100 per cent is good enough for heaven, and if they go there as they are, they will ruin it for everybody else!

We find legalism in churches too. They are so prone to add their own rules to their membership. There are four steps up to the front door of a church: repent, believe, be baptized and receive the Holy Spirit. There should be no additional steps to the front door. The staircase is inside. There are a lot of steps to climb up inside, as we find in 1 Peter and 2 Peter, but there are only four steps outside. But unfortunately churches tend to say, 'You have got to be confirmed by a bishop', or 'You have got to be this or that', or, 'You have got to be committed', or, 'You have got to accept the leadership', and so on. Those steps all belong inside the church, not outside.

Licence is still with us

There are still those who think that adultery by an unbeliever will take them to hell, but adultery by a believer is acceptable. There are still those who believe that certain kinds of sin in believers are excused, that you may lose a bit of blessing or reward, but you cannot lose your ticket to heaven. Galatians deals with that very firmly and says that you will not inherit the Kingdom of God if you deliberately go back to sin.

Liberty is still with us

We must stay and walk with others along the narrow path, the wind of the Spirit blowing in our faces and the blessing of God's grace upon us. We are free not to sin and free to be bold, if we will only walk in the Spirit.

Galatians is one of the most powerful letters you will ever read. Above all, read the letter and heed its message. Here is my paraphrase of it:

> *From: Paul, the Lord's emissary (not appointed by any group of human officials or even by divine guidance through a human agent, but personally sent by Jesus the Messiah and God his father, who brought him back to life after his burial). All the Christian brothers here have read and approved my letter.*

To: The gathering of God's people in the province of Galatia.

May you all enjoy the undeserved generosity and total harmony of God our Father and his Son Jesus, our Lord and Messiah. Our bad deeds cost him his life, but he gave it willingly to rescue us from the immorality of our contemporary scene. The plan of escape was decided by our Father-God, who should never cease to get the credit. So be it.

I am shattered to discover that already all of you are deserting this God who picked you out for his special offer of Christ's free gift and swinging to a different gospel, which is not even 'good news'. You are being muddled by certain people who aim to turn the gospel upside down. But listen – if we ourselves, or even a supernatural messenger from the other world, should bring a message to you that contradicts what I have delivered, may we be damned! We told you this before, but I must repeat it – if anyone at all preaches a gospel that varies from the one you first accepted, then to hell with him!

Now does that sound like someone who is trying to get on the right side of men, or of God? Am I being accused of seeking popularity? If I still wanted to please people, the last thing I would be is one of Christ's workers.

My dear brothers, I must make it quite clear to all of you that the Good News I tell is no human tale. I neither heard others relating it, nor did anyone pass it on to me. I got it direct from Jesus the Messiah, as the events of my life prove.

You must have heard about my earlier career in the Jewish religion. In my extreme fanaticism I was hunting down God's company of Christian believers and playing havoc with them. As an ardent supporter of Judaism, I forged ahead of many fellow-nationals of my own age, because I was so enthusiastic about the established customs of my ancestors.

Then God took a hand. He had marked me out before I left my mother's womb and generously chose me of all people to show others what his Son was really like, especially those I used to call foreigners. At once I decided not to seek anybody's advice. So I did not go to Jerusalem to consult those who were already working as emissaries of the Lord. Instead I went off alone into the Arabian desert to think it all over; and from there I returned straight to Damascus.

It was not until three years later that I finally got to know Peter in Jerusalem. Even then I only stayed two weeks and saw none of the other apostles, though I did meet James, our divine leader's own brother (as God watches what I write, I'm not making any of this up). After that I went to various places in Syria and Cilicia, so the Christian gatherings in Judea would still not have recognized my face. All they knew of me was hearsay – that their bitter enemy was now spreading the very beliefs he had tried so hard to wreck – and they thanked God for the transformation.

Another fourteen years passed before I paid another visit to Jerusalem. This time Barnabas and Titus went with me. It was God who prompted me to go and have a private discussion with the reputed leaders of the Jewish Christians. I intended to check with them the gospel I had been spreading among other nations, lest all my efforts were being wasted. I took Titus as a kind of test case, for he was a Greek Christian. But they never once insisted that he go through the initiation rite of being circumcised. In fact, the question would never have arisen but for some interlopers who had no right to be in the meeting at all. They sneaked in to spy on the freedom we enjoy in our relationship with Christ; they were looking for some way of getting us back under the control of their system. But not for one minute did we give way to their demands, or you would have lost what is truly good news. As far as the apparent leaders were concerned (their exact position doesn't bother me, for God pays no attention to status; I mean those who were obviously looked up to by the others), they added nothing whatever to the teaching I had outlined. On the contrary, they could see that I was as qualified to take the good news to uncircumcised people as Peter had been to the circumcised. For the same God who was

*working so effectively through Peter's outreach to the Jews was
obviously doing the same through mine to the Gentiles. James, John
and Cephas (Peter was using his Hebrew name) seemed to be the three
mainstays and when they realized how much God was blessing my
work, they shook hands with Barnabas and myself as a token of full
partnership, on the understanding that they would concentrate on the
Jews and we on the non-Jews. The only plea they made was that we
should not forget to send financial aid to poor Jewish Christians and I
was more than ready to go on with this.*

*But a serious crisis arose when Peter returned our visit and came to
Antioch. I had to oppose him to his face, for he was clearly in the wrong.
When he first came, he was quite happy to eat with the Gentile
converts. Then some colleagues of James arrived and Peter was afraid
of what they might think, so he began to have his meals separately. The
other Jewish believers pretended to agree with him and even my friend
Barnabas was swept into the hypocrisy. When I saw that such
behaviour could not be squared with the reality of the gospel, I said to
Peter in front of everybody, 'You are a Jewish national, but you dropped
your scruples and adopted the lifestyle of Gentile foreigners. Why all of
a sudden are you now trying to make them accept Jewish customs?'*

*We were born within God's chosen people and not among the lawless
outsiders of other nations. Yet we know perfectly well that a man cannot
be innocent in God's sight by trying to obey the commandments but only
by trusting Jesus Christ to take away his sins. So even we Jews had to
get right with God by relying on the work of Jesus the Messiah rather
than on our own attempts to live up to God's standards. Our sacred
writings freely admit that 'judged by God's laws, no man living could
ever be acquitted' (Psalm 143:2). But suppose our quest to be right
with God through Christ does find us living outside the Jewish law.
Does that make Christ an anarchist, deliberately encouraging
lawlessness? Never!*

*What would really make me a lawbreaker would be to erect again
the whole legal system I demolished. I discovered long ago that trying to*

keep God's laws was a deadly business. The failure killed my ego – but that gave me the very break I needed to live as God wanted me to. For when I realized that Jesus died on the cross for me, the person I used to be died as well. I know I'm still around, but it's not really me; it's Christ living his life in me. So the real life I'm now living in this mortal body springs from continual trust in God's Son, who loved me so much he sacrificed his life for me. Whatever anyone else does, I'm not going to be the one to make God's generosity redundant. For if I could get to heaven by keeping the commandments then Christ's death is utterly meaningless.

You stupid Galatians! Who has hoodwinked you, so that you no longer act on what is true? Your eyes were fastened on Jesus Christ by our vivid description of his death by crucifixion. Just answer me one simple question – when you first experienced God's Spirit, was that because you had done what the law demands or because you believed what you heard?

Right! Then have you gone out of your minds? Having got started by the supernatural power of God's Spirit, do you think you can reach the finish by the natural energy of your own constitution?

Have you learned nothing from all you've been through? Surely you won't throw it all away now. Tell me, when God went on giving you a liberal supply of his Spirit, so that real miracles were happening among you, was this while you were trying to obey his laws or while you listened to what he said with complete trust?

Your experience is identical with Abraham's, for he 'believed that God could do what he promised, and because of this trust he was listed in God's records as a good man' (Genesis 15:6). You realize, then, that the true descendants of Abraham are those who have this same trust in God. And the Bible, looking forward to the days when God would accept other races on exactly the same basis of faith, includes the announcement of this good news to Abraham himself – 'Through you all the peoples of the world will enjoy God's blessing with this man Abraham, who was so full of faith'.

But those who rely on keeping the commandments are actually under God's curse, not his blessing. For the law of Moses states quite clearly that 'anyone who fails to keep all the rules of this book all the time will be cursed' (Deuteronomy 27:26). It is patently obvious that nobody could possibly reach such a standard, if this is how God looks at us. So even the Old Testament points to another way to get right with God – 'The good man will live by trusting' (Habakkuk 2:4). The law never mentions this matter of believing, its emphasis is all on achieving – 'The man who obeys these rules will live well' (Leviticus 18:5).

Christ has ransomed us from this binding curse of the law and the price was to be cursed in our place. Quite literally, he paid the supreme penalty of the law – 'The body of a man under God's curse is to be hanged on the bough of a tree' (Deuteronomy 21:23). By removing the curse in this way, Jesus our Messiah released the blessing of Abraham to non-Jews. So we could now receive the promised power of the Spirit, simply by believing.

Brothers, all this is nothing out of the ordinary: I can illustrate what has happened from everyday human affairs. Once a man's will has been sealed, it cannot be cancelled nor can any other provisions be added. Now God made his testament in favour of Abraham 'and his issue' (Genesis 22:18). Just note that the word is singular rather than plural, indicating one surviving descendant rather than many; actually, it referred to Christ. But my main point is this – an agreement already ratified by God cannot be cancelled by a legal code introduced four hundred and thirty years later, or else the promise was worthless. The two are incompatible. If the blessing is now inherited by keeping the commandments, it is no longer available on the original terms. But God generously gave that first promise to Abraham and he will always stand by it.

Then what was the point of the law? It was a temporary addition to deal with human lawlessness! Until Abraham's 'issue' arrived to inherit the promised blessing, wrongdoing had to be exposed for what it was and kept under some control.

Unlike the promise, the law was not given direct to men. God communicated it through heavenly messengers and an earthly intermediary handed it on. Normally a middleman is used to negotiate between two parties; and in a sense the law was a mutual contract, in that the conditions had to be accepted by the people. But our belief is that God stands alone. He is not an equal to be bargained with, but can act entirely on his own terms, as he did in giving the promise direct.

Do these differences mean that God introduced two rival religious systems, the law as an alternative to the promise? Never! If passing a law could make people live good lives, then legislation would be the answer. But the laws of the Bible simply shut down this possibility by proving that everybody does wrong, leaving the only way out that of believing God's promise by trusting in Jesus the Messiah.

Until the opportunity of faith came, we had to be remanded in custody and kept under the strong guard of the law, waiting for the day when we would be shown how to believe. Putting it another way, we were like children and the law was a strict guardian, keeping us under firm discipline until Christ could take over and put us right through our trust in him. Believing in Jesus Christ brought the full status and freedom which belongs to grown-up sons of God.

All of you who were initiated into the Christian life by immersion in water are now wrapped up in Christ. So you are no longer separate individuals – one a Jew and another a Greek, one a slave and another free, one male and another female. All of you make up just one person inside Jesus. As parts of Christ you belong to him, which makes you that single descendant of Abraham who is entitled to claim the blessing promised to his 'issue'.

Look at it like this – a child can inherit a business, but as long as he is under age he is no better off than one of the employees, even though he owns the whole lot. He is supervised by guardians and his affairs are managed by trustees, until the date set by his father. In much the same way, when we were spiritual infants, our behaviour was governed by the world's childish superstitions.

But God had appointed a time for our coming-of-age and when it was ripe, He sent his Son into our world. He came in the same way as we did, from a woman's body. She was a Jew, so he was born subject to the law. This enabled him to purchase the freedom of those who lived under its tyranny and give us the full status of grown-up sons.

Because you too have been recognized as God's sons, he sent the Spirit of his Son into our inmost beings, so that we call out instinctively, 'Abba! Dad!' (which is exactly how Jesus addressed his heavenly Father). This proves that each of you is a son of God and no longer his servant; and if you are his son you are also his heir, and he will make sure you get the estate.

There was a time when you had no personal relationship with God. But your religion bound you to do so much for 'gods' who weren't even real! But now that you know God as he is (or rather, now that he has introduced himself to you) how can you possibly go back to those feeble and needy superstitions? Do you really want to be in their grip again? Already you're observing a calendar of so-called 'sacred' days and months and seasons and years. I am beginning to have a horrible fear that all my efforts to help you have been wasted.

My brothers, I beg you, please stand with me. After all, I was willing to identify with you. You've never hurt me before. You know it was because of physical illness that I first came to tell you the good news. My condition must have been a real trial to you, but you never made fun of it, nor were you disgusted with me. Indeed, you gave me a welcome fit for a heavenly messenger or even the Messiah Jesus himself. You were so pleased and proud to have me. Where have all those feelings gone? I recall vividly that you wished it was possible to donate your eyes for transplanting in me. Now you seem to suspect me of being your enemy. Is that because I have been so honest with you?

I know these others are so keen to make a fuss of you; but their motives are not good. They want to have you all to themselves, so that you will make a fuss of them.

Don't get me wrong – special attention is always fine, provided the intentions are right. You are my special concern, even when I am not actually with you. My own children, I feel like a mother struggling with the pains of childbirth until Christ is brought right out in your lives. I just wish I could be with you at this moment so that you could hear the change in my tone of voice. I really am at my wit's end to know what to do about you.

Tell me this – you seem to have such a strong urge to be governed by the law of Moses, but have you really listened to everything it says? Take this one recorded incident:

Abraham was the father of two sons by two women, one a slave-girl and the other free. The slave-girl's boy was the natural result of a physical act; but the child of the free woman only came as the supernatural result of a divine promise. This contrast is intended to picture spiritual realities, for the two sons represent two very different kinds of relationship with God.

One stems from Mount Sinai and its children are born into bondage. Their symbolic mother is the slave-girl Hagar, whose connections were with Arabia, where Mount Sinai stands. She corresponds to the present Jewish capital of Jerusalem, whose leaders and subjects are under oppression. But there is another 'Jerusalem' of heavenly origin, represented by the free woman, and she is the mother of all of us who believe. The Bible says of her, 'Celebrate, you barren woman who never had a child; burst into cries of joy, you who never knew the pain of labour; for the lonely wife will have a far bigger family than she who has her husband' (Isaiah 54:1).

My brothers, we are like Isaac, for our life was brought into being by a divine promise. As in his day, the child born in the normal course of nature bullied the one born by the power of God's Spirit, so it is today. But look what the Bible says about the outcome of this: 'Throw out the slave-girl and her son, for he will never share the father's property with the son of the free woman' (Genesis 21:10). So, brothers, get this quite clear in your minds – we are not the children of a slave-girl but of a free woman.

When Christ set us free, that was real freedom! So hang on to it and don't get tied up again in the chains of slavery. Listen! I, Paul, a Jewish Christian, make this serious statement – if you get circumcised, Christ himself will be of no more value to you. Let me repeat that. I give my solemn assurance to anyone who submits to the initiation ceremony of circumcision, that he has put himself under an obligation to obey every single statute of the Jewish law. The operation will not only cut off part of your body; it will cut you off from Christ! Any of you who tries to get right with God by keeping the commandments will find you have slipped beyond the range of God's undeserved mercy.

We Christians build our hopes on a very different basis. By the help of God's Spirit we wait expectantly for that right standing and state which result from trusting in Jesus the Messiah. Once we are part of him, it doesn't count for anything whether we are circumcised or uncircumcised. The only thing that matters is the kind of believing that is expressed in loving.

You were racing ahead in the Christian life. Who caused an obstruction and stopped you from putting the truth into practice? That kind of plausible persuasion never comes from God, who always calls you to press on. As they say, 'It doesn't take much yeast to taint a large lump of dough'. Yet somehow the Lord gives me the confidence that you are not going to change your outlook. As for the person who is disturbing you, he will one day have to take his punishment, whatever his position is now.

Regarding myself, brothers, I gather I am supposed to be preaching the need to be circumcised, even after all this time. If that were really true, how can anyone explain the violent opposition I encounter at the hands of other Jews? If I was advocating their laws, they wouldn't be so offended when I speak about the cross. I just wish that those who are agitating to cut off your foreskins would go the whole hog and castrate themselves!

So, my brothers, God meant you to be free. On the other hand, don't make this freedom an excuse for indulging your old self. Use it to show your love for others by putting yourselves at their service. For the whole law can be expressed in just one principle, namely 'You are to care for your fellow-man as much as you do about yourself' (Leviticus 19:18). But if you snap at each other and pull each other to pieces, watch out that you don't end up exterminating each other altogether!

The approach I'm advocating is to let God's Spirit decide each step you take. Then you just won't try to satisfy the desires of your old self, whose cravings are diametrically opposed to what God's Spirit wants – and vice-versa. The two are incompatible, which is why you find that you can't always do what you really want to. If the Spirit is leading your life, you have nothing to fear from the law.

When the old self is at work, the results are pretty obvious. It may produce promiscuity, dirty-mindedness or indecency. It is behind occultism and drug addiction. It shows up in hatred, quarrelling, jealousy, temper, rivalry, prejudice and envy. It leads to binges, orgies and things like that. I've warned you before, people who go on doing this sort of thing will have no share in God's coming reign.

When God's Spirit is at work, a fruit appears in the character. Each cluster includes loving care, deep happiness and quiet serenity; endless patience, practical kindness and unstinted generosity; steady reliability, gentle humility and firm self-control. No law has ever been passed forbidding such virtues! They have room to grow because those who belong to Christ have nailed their old self to the cross, together with all its passions and appetites.

If God's Spirit is leading our lives, let the same Spirit keep us in step with each other. We get out of step when our hollow pride wants a reputation of being ahead, regards others as rivals and is envious of their progress.

Brothers, if anyone slips up and is caught doing wrong, those of you who are spiritually mature should get him on his feet again. But handle him gently and humbly, keeping an eye on yourself, for sudden temptation could just as easily hit you.

When the strain is too much, help to carry each other's burdens; this is simply carrying out Christ's instructions. If anyone thinks he is too important to stoop to this, he really isn't worth anything and only fools himself.

Let everyone weigh up his contribution, to see whether he is doing enough. Then he can take pride in his own work, without making odious comparisons with what others are doing. For each must shoulder his own load of responsibility.

A person who is being taught to understand God's Word should give his teacher a share in the material things in life.

Don't be under any illusion – no one can turn their nose up at God and get away with it. It is a universal law that a man must reap exactly what he has been sowing. If he cultivates his old self, he will harvest a character that has gone rotten. If he cultivates God's Spirit, that Spirit will produce life of a lasting quality.

So let us never get fed up with doing good. One day there will be a grand harvest, if we don't give up. So whenever we get the chance, let's give as much help as we can to everybody, and especially to our immediate family of fellow-believers. Look what sprawling letters I use in my own handwriting!

It is those who are concerned about outward appearances and like to show off who are pressurizing you into being circumcised. Their real object is to avoid the unpopularity associated with the cross of the Messiah. Even though they observe circumcision, they don't seem to bother about the rest of the Jewish law. They only want to get you circumcised so that they can brag about the number of converts to their ritual.

Never let me boast about anything or anybody – except the cross of Jesus the Messiah, our Lord. Through that execution I am dead to society and society is dead to me. Our standing in Christ is neither helped by being circumcised nor hindered by remaining uncircumcised. What really matters is being made into a new person inside. All who live by the simple principle will receive the undisturbed harmony and undeserved help of God, whether Gentile or Jew.

From now on, let no one interfere with my work again. I have the marks I want on my body; I am branded with scars gained in the service of Jesus.

May the generous love of Jesus, our divine Master and anointed Saviour, fill your inmost being, my brothers. So be it.

47.

ROMANS

Introduction

The best way to study the Bible is book by book. The Bible is a library of books, and so each book of the library needs to be seen as a distinct unit, with its own author, in its own time period, in its own literary genre, and written for a particular audience. Attention to this would help the many people who approach Romans forgetting that it is a letter, and so fail to ask the sort of questions that will unlock its meaning and purpose.

Although letters were very expensive and difficult to send in Roman times, about 14,000 letters have been discovered by archaeologists from this period. A letter would typically range from 20 to 200 words, the length being governed in part by the fact that letters were carried and delivered by the same person, so the weight was important. Longer letters were rare. Cicero's longest letter was 2,500 words, and Seneca's 4,000-word letter was an all-time record. Paul's average letter was 1,300 words long, but his letter to the Romans, at over 7,000 words, is his longest. Indeed, it is the longest letter that we have from the ancient world.

An unusual letter

The letter is also unusual for a number of other reasons. The opening and closing greetings are exceptionally long. Indeed, the last chapter is a long list of people sending their love. It is highly unusual to spend such a long part of a letter just passing greetings from friend to friend. Furthermore, Romans reads more like a lecture than a letter. This is not a chatty letter in which the author tells his readers about his life. It is more like a lecture, with occasional dialogue, as if the writer is answering a heckler.

It is also set apart from Paul's other letters because he is writing to a church with which he has had no contact. Paul made a point of looking after his own churches very faithfully, and not interfering with anyone else's work, so it seems strange that he should write his longest letter to a church that he didn't start and had never visited. Yet it is clear from his tone that, although he does not have any personal relationship with them, he wants to meet them and wants them to know him.

Furthermore, this letter is more intellectual than his others, with no particular mention of any crisis or controversy that requires his correction (although, as we will see later, there are problems that need to be addressed). Most of his letters contain a scent of battle, but there is none of that here.

Given its unique style, Bible commentators have sought to explain the purpose of Romans in a variety of ways. We can group them under three basic headings.

Some start with Paul and say that his reason for writing is to be found in him. Some say the reason is to be found in both the writer and the readers and the relationship between them. Others say the reason for writing is to be found in the readers only.

The writer

The first explanation runs like this: The year is about AD 55, and Paul has been preaching for 20 years. His strategy has been to plant a self-supporting, self-governing, self-propagating colony of the Kingdom in every major centre of population. This has now been achieved in many major cities in the eastern Mediterranean.

His final act in the east was to make a big collection for the poor in Jerusalem. The Jerusalem church was facing a famine and was desperately poor, so Paul taught the churches that he founded to share what they had and made a collection of money for the poor believers in Jerusalem. He has three months in Greece, awaiting good weather to sail, before he takes the money to Jerusalem. Since he has the time, he writes this long letter during the winter as a permanent record of the gospel he preached. There are two versions of this theory:

A statement

Some argue that Romans is a statement of the gospel he had preached – his last will and testament. He didn't know how much longer he would be able to travel and speak, for he had been warned that persecution and prison would come. So Romans is a circular letter summarizing Paul's teaching. Those who believe this theory point to Paul's words, 'I am not ashamed of the gospel' as evidence.

An argument

Others adapt this theory to argue that he is putting in written form the objections to the gospel that he has encountered, rather as Josh McDowell has published books explaining how to answer the objections that people make when confronted with the gospel message today. Paul was used to arguing and discussing the gospel and had used it to good effect, notably when using the lecture hall in Ephesus. So he knew the main questions and objections and so wished to produce a handbook on objections to the gospel.

Problems

But there are significant problems with these two approaches.

Firstly, if this is the summary of his gospel, why send it to just one church? Why not circulate it to many? Wouldn't Jerusalem or one of the churches he had planted be a more appropriate destination?

Secondly, Romans does not include all the elements of Paul's gospel. For example, there isn't a single thing about the Kingdom, yet we know that Paul preached the Kingdom of God. There are other glaring omissions: there is very little about the resurrection of Jesus or his ascension; there is almost nothing about the Church; there is no mention of the Lord's Supper; and there is no clear explanation of heaven or hell. Repentance is almost absent, and the concept of being born again is completely missed. There is a glaring absence of references to God as Father.

So these gaps tell us that this is not a summary of Paul's preaching, for this is not the whole gospel as we read it in his other letters and as we hear it preached in Acts. Those who build their gospel preaching on Paul's letter to the Romans are going to be deficient in a number of areas. Also, some themes seem to be more prominent than they need to be. Why is there so much time spent on the subject of the justification and actions of Abraham?

The third reason why we can't believe that Paul is writing a definitive statement of the gospel is that chapters 9–11 simply don't fit. In these chapters Paul lays bear his heart for the Jewish people, saying he would go to hell if it would get them to heaven. If this was a summary statement, it is an unusual theme to include. The scholars tell us that chapters 9–11 are a parenthesis, and not really part of the general argument. I studied Romans at Cambridge under a brilliant Bible teacher to whom I owe a great deal, John A. T. Robinson, Bishop of Woolwich (though he subsequently moved from his evangelical stance for a while). Despite his brilliant grasp of the book, he only taught Romans 1–8, claiming that chapers 9–11 were not directly related to Paul's purpose in writing.

But a theory that doesn't account for chapters 9–11 cannot be correct, for the simple reason that Paul didn't divide his letters into chapters as we do. His thoughts run straight from chapter 8 to chapter 9 and from chapter 11 to chapter 12, with no break at all. These chapters are not a parenthesis. So at the end of chapter 8 he says that nothing can separate us from the love of God in Christ Jesus, and goes on to list the things that could not separate the believer. Then the thought continues in chapter 9, as he answers a possible rejection of this view: if this is so, what about the Jews? Didn't God cut them off? There is also a consistent sequence of thought from the end of chapter 11 to the beginning of chapter 12. Chapter 11 finishes with a glorious description of praise to the mercy of God and is followed immediately in chapter 12 by 'I beseech you by the mercies of God ...'

The writer and the readers

The second theory examines the relationship between Paul and the Romans and looks for a reason why Paul sent the letter.

Capital of the empire

It notes that Rome, as the capital of the empire, would be a natural place for Paul to want to minister. This would be a strategic place for the gospel, since in those days all roads really did lead to Rome.

There is an element of truth in this. It would mean that he is writing an introduction to them, instead of asking someone to write to them on his behalf, to show that he is not a controversial preacher but preaches the gospel they had already heard.

Gateway to the west

The next theory is an adaptation of the one above and is far more compelling. This argues that for Paul, Rome was the gateway to Spain in the west. Now that he has evangelized the eastern half of the Mediterranean, he wants to go west and so needs a new base that is nearer to his intended mission field. Jerusalem was his first base and Antioch was his second, but Antioch was a long way from Spain, so Rome would be his third base for missionary activity.

There may be elements of truth in both these theories, but it is not the whole truth.

1 Both these theories assume that Paul is trying to get something from the readers for himself. But the tone of the letter is the exact opposite. He says he wants to give to them, not to get anything from them. He actually says he wants to minister to them.

2 Also, neither theory explains chapters 9–11. Why should he mention Israel so much, if he just wants their support for his missionary work in the west? In fact, these puzzling chapters, which are a problem to many of the theories, are the most important of the letter.

3 Furthermore, these theories also fail to explain chapters 12–16, which focus on some particular areas in which the Romans are to live out their faith. Why does Paul not give a general talk about Christian ethics and behaviour? Why does he single out just a few practical problems?

The readers

Let us come now to the theories that approach the letter from the point of view of Rome. Here we are asking why the church in Rome needed this letter.

External – the city

POLITICAL

Paul is quick to affirm the value of government which, he says, God has placed over the Church. In chapter 13 he tells them to respect the political leaders and to pay their taxes. Indeed, the leader wields the sword as the servant of God himself. So if they are persecuted as a church, they must make sure that it is not because they have done wrong and deserve it.

SOCIAL

Rome was a huge metropolis, and the behaviour of people in the city comes through in the letter. Chapter 1 reads like a Sunday newspaper published in Rome. In particular, Rome was a hotbed of homosexuality. Out of the first 15 Roman emperors, 14 were practising homosexuals. If the emperors were like that, can you imagine what the court was like? He mentions various sinful practices typical of the city at the time: the outbreak of antisocial behaviour; children being disobedient to parents; people throwing away law and order; uncontrollable violence and crime. It is a remarkable picture of the ancient capital city of the empire, and it has a number of parallels with our day. They had a big problem collecting taxes, since moonlighting and tax evasion were rife. So he is especially concerned that the church does not become corrupted by the society around. The lifeboat functions best when it is in the sea, not when the sea is in the boat!

Internal – the church

So some would argue that the letter is Paul's ministry before he arrives in Rome, because he wasn't sure whether he would arrive. The Holy Spirit had revealed that he might be arrested and put on trial at any moment. He doesn't know whether he will be able to achieve his ambition and preach in Rome, so he is determined to preach through a letter before he gets there, leaving them in no doubt that the gospel is the answer to this situation. So there is a thread running through the letter of ministering to Christians who have to live in this city riddled with vice, crime and violence.

We know very little about the church in Rome. We know that Peter and Paul visited the city, but these visits came after the church was founded. We know there were people from Rome in Jerusalem on the day of Pentecost, and no doubt some of them were converted that day. Some must have carried the gospel back to Rome, because there was a colony of 40,000 Jews in Rome at that time.

So the first Roman church was Jewish and began in a ghetto with Hebrew believers in Jesus who were filled with the Holy Spirit. It grew and was no doubt fostered by evangelism among Jewish merchants and traders coming in and out of the city.

The Roman emperor Claudius was anti-Jewish and expelled all 40,000 Jews from the city. Acts 18 tells us that a couple named Priscilla and Aquila met Paul following their expulsion.

So the Christian church in Rome would have become solely Gentile at this time.

In AD 54 Claudius died and the Jews returned, because the next emperor, Nero, realized that the Jews were good for business and invited them back. But, of course, they returned to find that the Gentiles were running the church. The Jews were not made especially welcome, and so there was tension.

This background helps to unlock the letter to the Romans. As we read the letter, we find that almost every part of it is dealing with this situation. As a Jew who was called to the Gentiles, Paul was uniquely equipped to reconcile them.

Chapters 1–8

Sin

He starts the letter by looking at sin in the city of Rome and reminds both groups that they are sinners. Jews are no better than Gentiles, Gentiles are no better than Jews. He says that since Christ's death avails for Jew and Gentile, we must go to the Spirit for life.

Justification

He covers the way in which guilty sinners can be declared innocent saints before God. Then he moves on to consider how Jew and Gentile can get right with God and explains that both are 'justified' in the same way, by faith. The same blood saves them, so there is no need to argue about who is more important.

Licence and legalism

In chapters 6–7 Paul deals with two particular problems that Jews and Gentiles have with the gospel. Gentiles were prone to licence and Jews were prone to legalism. Licence

occurs when Christians mistakenly believe that their freedom in Christ allows them to ignore divine laws, whereas
legalism causes Christians to believe that keeping the Law
gives them merit before God. So in chapter 6 Paul deals
with licence and reminds them that when they were baptized
they recognized that sin had no more dominion over them.
In chapter 7 Paul deals with legalism and relates his own
difficulties in keeping the Law, especially the command not
to covet.

Then in chapter 8 Paul writes about the liberty of the
Spirit and explains how it unites both Jew and Gentile.

Chapters 9–11

The discussion about the place of the Jews in chapters 9–11 is
crucial to the whole letter. The Gentiles were tempted to think
that they were the new Israel, having replaced the Jewish people, who were now out of God's purposes. So chapters 9–11
deal with the tension between Jew and Gentile.

Many British churches believe what is known as 'replacement theology'. In fact, the name Israel was never given to the
Church in the New Testament, and Paul has to remind his
readers that God has not finished with the Jews, just because
they rejected him. He tells the Gentiles not to be proud
because the Jews were cut off and they were grafted in, for they
will also be cut out if they do not continue in God's kindness.
Furthermore, he explains that one day all Israel will be saved.
Indeed, for the last 2,000 years there have always been a few
Jewish believers in Jesus.

The gulf between Jew and Gentile came in part because
the temple in Jerusalem included a great barrier between the
Gentile court and the other courts. The notices on the barrier

said 'No Gentiles', and Paul was arrested because he was falsely accused of taking a Gentile beyond the barrier. So although both Jews and Gentiles were now believers in Jesus, there was a certain amount of tension.

So Paul seeks to deal with any problems by telling them that they are all sinners and justified by faith, whether Jew or Gentile. Indeed, he describes Gentiles as sons of Abraham by faith, using a term previously reserved for the Jewish people.

Chapters 12–16

This theme of Jew and Gentile tension continues in chapters 12–16. Although dealing with more practical issues of conduct, he focuses on those issues that will cause tension between Jewish and Gentile believers. Food was the most obvious problem, for Gentiles were comfortable eating food that was non-kosher or had been offered to idols. Then he deals with a special day in each week, for Gentile believers didn't have Sabbath observance. Paul is able to explain that whether a believer recognizes Sunday as special is up to them.

In fact of course, Sunday is not a Sabbath. We should worship God on Sunday because it is the eighth day of creation, not because it replaces the Jewish Sabbath. It is the first day of the second week of creation and the first day of God's working week. If we are commemorating his rest, we would worship on Saturday, but we are celebrating the fact that he has gone back to work, which is what he did on Easter Sunday, when he started recreating the entire universe. However, whereas on the first six days of creation he created the heaven and the earth first and the people last, he is now creating new people first and the new heaven and earth last.

Sunday is the busiest day for God. More people become a new creation in Christ on Sunday than any other day of the week. The Spirit was poured out on Sunday, so Sunday is a day of celebration for Christians. But it was never a day of rest in the early Church. For 300 years Christians could not worship at 11 a.m. or 6.30 p.m. but had to worship very early in the morning or late at night, because Jewish believers only had a day's holiday on Saturday. The Gentile believers had the Roman holiday, which was every tenth day, and slaves had no holiday at all. Since most of the early Christians were slaves, they could not observe Sundays for 300 years.

But in a church made up of Jewish and Gentile believers, the tension regarding days was intense. The Jews kept a Sabbath (Saturday) as their special day and the Gentiles didn't keep a special day at all. Paul explains that it is entirely a matter of choice.

When we face similar issues today we need the same kind of flexibility. The Lord may lead us to a course of action, but that doesn't mean we have to tell everyone that this is what they should do.

It should be clear from the outline given below that Romans is not primarily a doctrinal treatise. Rather, Paul uses doctrine for practical purposes.

Having considered the reason for the letter, let us turn to consider some of its main themes. It is not my aim to give a commentary on the letter, but I can give you some pointers as you read it.

Key words in Romans

An analysis of the key words shows us what the important themes are.

God

The word 'God' is mentioned 153 times, more than any other word. Paul stresses that the believers in Rome are God's people (whether Jews or Gentiles). It is God who is at the centre of their church. The titles 'Christ' and 'Lord' appear 65 times and 43 times respectively.

Law

The word 'law' occurs 72 times in Romans. We have already noted that Paul needed to focus upon the Jews' legalistic tendencies.

Sin

'Sin' is also a frequently used word and comes 48 times. Paul addresses the problem of sin in the city of Rome, and also sin among believers. He is saying it doesn't matter where it is – God is against sin, whether it is in believers or unbelievers. Christians are justified by faith, but they will be judged by works, because works are the fruit of faith. Sin in the Christian does matter.

Faith

'Faith' is mentioned 40 times. It is faith that unites the Jews and Gentiles. They were united in sin before, but now they are united in faith, for they are all sons of Abraham through faith.

Righteousness

The key concept flowing from Paul's focus on faith is righteousness, and particularly the righteousness of God. The man largely responsible for the Reformation, Martin Luther, came to understand the vital importance of justification by faith through this letter. He was frightened by the phrase, 'the righteousness of God', only to discover later that this was something that God wanted to give us by faith. We must never forget that the cross was a double substitution. Jesus not only took our sins but also imparts his righteousness to us. It is not merely a transaction whereby we escape hell.

This righteousness from God can be a hard thing to grasp. When most people hear the word 'repentance', they think of all the bad deeds they should repent of, but the hardest thing is to repent of good deeds. Paul said that when he considered his righteousness, he felt it was human dung. The prophet Isaiah was equally blunt. He said the righteousness of Israel was like a menstrual cloth – not something they would want to parade in public. Paul is saying that *our* righteousness can be the biggest barrier between us and a relationship with God. When we preach this, it is the 'good' people who struggle with it most. Those who know they are bad will be the first to respond.

It is rare to hear a preacher urge the congregation to repent of their good deeds, but good deeds are more likely to keep people out of heaven than anything else. Also it is rare in a prayer meeting to hear anyone ask for mercy – which is tragic, because God is so full of it that anyone who asks for it will receive it.

Paul's concept of righteousness is far more than just being concerned that his hearers are safe when they die. The nearest English word to 'salvation' is 'salvage', not 'safe'. An awful lot of people want to be safe, as if we have a ticket to heaven, but the process of recycling takes time. The word 'saved' occurs in three tenses in the New Testament. We have been saved, we are being saved, and we will be saved. Paul uses theological terms to describe the process which correspond to the different tenses – justification, sanctification and glorification. Let us consider their meaning.

Justification

There is a New Guinea Bible in pidgin English. Instead of 'justification' it has 'God – 'e say 'im alright', which is a marvellous translation. Justification means to be in God's good books. It is a beautiful blessing, but only the beginning of salvation. In justification God sets us free from the penalty of sin, which is a result of our broken relationship with God. God declares that we are in the right. Most other religions argue that we should put ourselves right before we can be right with God. But with Christianity, God says we are all right first.

But many people think that is all there is. They think they have arrived when they are justified, when actually they have just set off from the right platform.

Sanctification

This is the second part of being saved. Having been set free from the penalty of sin and with the broken relationship now restored, we are now set free from the power of sin. The grip of sin is broken, and sanctification comes as much by faith as justification. We are justified by faith and we are sanctified by faith. We don't have to produce it ourselves, but we do need to go on trusting every moment of every day.

Glorification

'Glorification' describes the end of the whole process, when we are set free from the presence of sin altogether – the time when we will live in a world where there is nothing that we can't enjoy, in which there is no temptation. It is at this point that we can finally say with great confidence, 'once saved, always saved'.

Imputed and imparted

These considerations link with the theologians' distinction between imputed righteousness and imparted righteousness. We are justified on the basis of faith in Christ so that his righteousness covers our unrighteousness. The picture is used of us 'putting on' Christ, like a new set of clothes, when we are baptized into Christ. We are clothed with him, so that God can only see him when he looks at us. We are hidden in Christ. It is imputed. God wants to impart his righteousness to us, not just credit it to us. This is the process of sanctification.

So the moment we believe, we are justified, but God wants us to become righteous as well (i.e. sanctification). Ultimately that process will be completed when we stand in glory and see him as he is (i.e. glorification).

It is interesting to observe that although Paul begins the letter by focusing on his message, when we get to the end of the letter he doesn't talk about his message, but about his method of evangelism. He says, 'The Gentiles heard my message, they saw how I lived and they witnessed signs and wonders, all by the Holy Spirit, so I have fully communicated the gospel to them.' The lesson for us is clear: we must demonstrate the gospel as well as declare it.

Outline of the letter

When it comes to analysing the letter itself, my main advice is to read it and keep reading it. There are various ways of dividing the letter up. The simplest is to split it very neatly into 'faith', 'hope' and 'love'. Chapters 1–4 are all about faith. Then, in chapter 5, Paul starts talking about hope. Faith looks to the past and what God has done in Christ. Hope looks to the future at what God is going to do, not just with Gentiles but with Israel as well.

Then, in chapters 12–16, the third word appears – love. Paul is concerned with the present and how the believers work out their faith within society and in the church.

Having recognized this broad outline, we can now analyse the letter in more depth:

Prologue – Paul's message – from Jew and Gentile

Saved in the same way
1. Righteousness from God
(a) Judgement for the sinner under wrath
(b) Justification for the saint through faith
2. Reconciliation through Christ
(a) Death as sin's penalty – he died for sinners
(b) Dominion of sin's power – we died to sin
3. Renewal in the Holy Spirit
(a) Bondage of Law in the flesh – defeat and despair
(b) Freedom of life in the Spirit – conquest and confidence

Belong to the same God
1. In the past Israel was selected.
2. In the present Israel is stubborn.
3. In the future Israel will be saved.

Live in the same world
1. Their personal bearing – in service and suffering
2. Their public behaviour – in state and society
3. Their practical brotherhood – in scruples and song

Epilogue
Paul's method – word, sign, deed

Individual greetings

Israel

Although it is not my intention to provide a commentary on the letter, Romans 9–11 cause readers considerable confusion, so we will expand on Paul's teaching about Israel.

Israel's past selection (Romans 9)

He expresses his deep sadness for his people. He even writes that he would be willing to go to hell if it would mean them getting to heaven. He explains that, although they had everything going for them, they had still rejected the one whom God had sent. But this was not a reflection upon God. He didn't expect all of them to trust Jesus, because he didn't elect all of them. Paul uses examples from Israel's history to explain his point.

1 *Ishmael and Isaac*. Isaac was selected above the older Ishmael. Abraham had tried to arrange his own future through his union with Hagar, but God's promise of a son still stands.
2 *Jacob and Esau*. Once again, the younger inherited the blessing, rather than the older, despite the fact that he was the rogue of the two.

3 *Moses and Pharaoh*. Paul explains God's hand in the hardening of Pharaoh's heart – implying that God chose to do so,
   in response to Pharaoh's own reluctance to go God's way.
4 *Gentiles and Jews*. In the same way as God had chosen one
   and not another in the Old Testament examples, so God
   had also chosen the Gentiles and, for a time, had 'rejected'
   the Jews. He is not 'disappointed' with the current state of
   affairs – this is what he had decided.

Paul's teaching on predestination is implicit within his argument and can be summarized as follows:

1 God is under no obligation to be merciful to anyone.
2 God chooses for a purpose – that he may display his wrath
   and his judgement.
3 Those chosen for justice deserve it (e.g. Pharaoh was given
   repeated chances to change his mind). Those chosen for
   mercy don't deserve it.

Israel's present stubbornness (Romans 10)

On the human side, Paul teaches that we have a responsibility to
live in a right relationship with God. But we have two choices:

1 Works (the Law) – Trust by the Law. By this method we
   seek to produce our own righteousness. It is, of course,
   doomed to failure – but this was the general approach of the
   Jewish nation.
2 Words (the Gospel) – Trust in the Lord. By this method
   God's righteousness is provided for us. We accept our
   inability to keep the Law, and we look to the one who has
   kept the Law in its entirety.

Israel's future salvation (Romans 11)

Paul seeks to answer the question of whether God has rejected his people by pointing out that God has always reserved a remnant. It is true that some Jews have been hardened, but this does not mean that the people as a whole have fallen beyond recovery. Therefore the Gentiles should not be smug about their welcome into the covenant people of God, for just as the Jews have been 'broken off', so can they, and just as they were grafted in – so can the Jews be once again. And one day they will be. That is a 'mystery', which in Scripture means 'a secret that can now be revealed.'

Conclusion

While many have imagined that Romans is a theological tome far removed from Paul's missionary activity, our analysis indicates that the letter is intensely practical. In addressing the vexed questions surrounding Church unity, it provides insights into how the Church should develop from its Jewish roots, while at the same time providing clarity on key issues of faith for God's people in every generation. As such it is a masterpiece of clear, logical thinking, and many people feel that it is the finest of Paul's writings. Many Christians have memorized Romans – such is the esteem in which it is held. It is thus a key book for any believer to grasp. I urge you to read it and re-read it until you grasp its message.

48.

COLOSSIANS

Introduction

When the apostle Paul was unable to visit churches he would generally write a letter. At various times, he would hear of a situation but would be unable to leave his work to give it his attention. Towards the end of his ministry letter writing became his only means of communication, for he spent a lot of time in prison – two years in Casaerea awaiting trial and a further two years in Rome. He was under house arrest in Rome, chained to a Roman soldier, but he was able to receive visitors, and it was through a visit from a man named Epaphras that the letter to the Colossians came to be written.

Paul wrote three kinds of letters: to individuals, known in the Bible by the name of the individual; occasional letters, to address a particular situation in a church; and general letters, which were for general circulation and did not deal with particular problems. When Paul wrote Colossians, an occasional letter, he also wrote an individual letter to Philemon, and a general letter known as Ephesians, though it was intended for use in a number of churches. They were sent at the same time and sent with the same postman, Tychicus, to the same area.

As we have seen, Paul's letters follow the pattern that was common in the ancient Greek world. They begin with the name of the sender, then comes the address of the receiver, then greetings, then a compliment, then the substance of the letter, then a summary, then a closing greeting and finally a signature. But despite the inclusion of a summary, the 'occasion' warranting a letter is not always immediately clear. It is like listening to one side of a telephone conversation. We need to read between the lines to understand why the letter was written.

Colosse

The geographical background of the letter provides our first clue to understanding it. Colosse is in the western part of Turkey, situated in a valley close to the towns of Hierapolis and Laodicea. By Paul's time the town had diminished in importance compared to its two neighbours, but the valley in which it was situated was highly regarded. There were hot springs in the surrounding mountains, made white by mineral deposits. Today they are called the Cotton Castle Spa Waters. Tourists go there to bathe in the hot, salty water and sunbathe on the white cliffs, though the town itself no longer exists.

Colosse was situated on the south bank of the River Lycus, a tributary of the River Meander, whose winding path gives the name to the geographical feature of a river's typical pathway in its middle course. It was on a major trade route from Ephesus to the Euphrates and so had a very mixed population. Travellers from all over the Europe made their home there. Natives of Colosse were called Phrygians, and were joined by Greeks, who settled at the time of Alexander the Great. Jews had arrived to make the most of trading opportunities and, of course, the Romans' influence had strengthened as their empire grew. In the seventh century AD the Saracens made it a Saracen town, but whoever was in control, it retained its international flavour.

The mixed population meant that the town had many different religions. We would call it a pluralistic town today, with no one faith dominant. This religious culture helps to explain Paul's approach, as we will see. We can identify six main areas of religious belief.

Animism and superstition

The native Phrygians believed in the power of what were known as primitive (elemental) spirits, who exercised their powers in and through the natural world. So a spirit might control the river, or a tree, or might reside in a mountain – the white mountains served to foster this belief. It led to superstition and fear as the worshippers sought to appease the spirits and ensure that life went smoothly. It was very similar to the sort of beliefs that are held by jungle tribes today. Some sections of the modern Green Movement have similarities with this outlook.

Astrology

A belief that stars and planets can influence people's lives was also prevalent. It probably arrived via travellers from the East who found the locals only too willing to add another pattern of belief to their outlook. Once again, there are modern parallels. Six out of ten men and seven out of ten women in Britain read their horoscope every day. Some even take business decisions based on what their stars purport to tell them.

Greek and Roman gods

All the gods and goddesses of Greece and Rome were in Colosse, along with the associated pagan practices. Some people believed that the gods welcomed a rigid abstinence from bodily desires such as food and sex; others thought the gods smiled on the lax sexual behaviour which had become characteristic of Roman life.

Mystery religions

These were Eastern in origin and are often described as Gnostic religions, from the Greek word *gnosis*, meaning 'to know', which is the opposite of 'agnostic'. An agnostic is someone who doesn't know, but a Gnostic is someone who believes they are 'in the know', often because they understand special secrets through spiritual experience. Sometimes there were initiation rites to enter, and there was a belief that you could make progress through special rites to spiritual perfection. Gnosticism was to bedevil the Church in its early centuries and, though given different names, it remains with us today.

Judaism

The style of Judaism in Colosse was very different to that in the Holy Land. It was more philosophical, less moral and more mystical than the Judaism of Israel, in part due to Gnostic influence. This Judaism was full of speculation, and as such was very compelling and interesting for people. It gave a high place to angels, as agents both in creation and in the giving of the Law. It was thought that angels controlled the communication between God and people. But there was also the more traditional reverence given to the Jewish calendar and food laws.

Christianity

The Christian faith had not come to Colosse from the apostle Paul. There is no evidence that he ever passed through the town. The man who had visited Paul in prison, Epaphras, had planted the church. Acts tells us that Paul had spent two years in Ephesus preaching and discussing daily at the lecture hall of Tyrannus. Luke records that the word of God had become known throughout Asia. Epaphras was converted through Paul's preaching and took the gospel to his home town, Colosse. So Paul wrote to the church on the basis of the report he had received from Epaphras, which is one reason why there are so many greetings. He mentions Aristarchus, Mark, Demas, Luke and Epaphras himself, writing of Epaphras as a hard worker who continues to pray for them. But his lack of personal knowledge means that he has no authority over them, and so his tone is fairly cool and gentle all the way through.

False teaching

Bible scholars and students have argued endlessly about what was happening in Colosse. It is clear that wrong teaching was affecting the church, but scholars are unable to agree on the precise problem, because when you look at Paul's counter-arguments, they don't suggest any particular religion or cult.

It is clear that he wasn't facing the strict Jewish teaching that he encountered in other churches. It is clear too that he wasn't just encountering mystery religions or astrology. Yet his arguments seem to respond to a mixture of religions and philosophies, so that the only solution that fits the evidence is to conclude that Paul is arguing against all the ideologies of the culture in which Colosse was placed. There are many similarities with what we know as New Age today, for there was a mixture of ideas and philosophies, with no particular code of doctrine. Like New Age, it was more of a mood than a distinct faith. This mixing of Christianity with other ideas is known as syncretism, and Paul knew that it could destroy the faith of the church, for when the Christian faith is mingled with other faiths, the message of Christ is no longer prominent.

So Paul writes against hollow and deceptive philosophies that claimed to offer fullness and freedom, that sought to overcome evil powers and exalted fasting. He said the church was hoodwinked into believing that Christ was not enough. In this respect, the letter has a very important message for the Church at the turn of the Millennium, for it reminds us of the dangers of religious practices entering the Church, whether these have apparently biblical or pagan roots. Christianity for many people in the UK is a religion – I call it 'Churchianity', for it is merely a ritual, with little attention paid to the Jesus of the Bible. On the other hand, practices associated with pagan religion are also slipping into the Church. Some Christians advocate reflexology and yoga, for example.

The effects of syncretism

As Paul's response to syncretism is a major feature of the letter, we must consider the two main effects that it had on the church at Colosse.

The immanence of God

The believers had lost their sense of the immanence of God. Christians believe that God is both transcendant and immanent, meaning that he is both far above us and also near to us. This truth is a paradox. If you forget either side of the paradox, you lose the Christian belief in God. God is both greater than the universe and nearer than breathing. So the Colossians saw God as a distant being, regarded as almost beyond reach. So they filled the gap between with beliefs in angels and spirits, believing it was necessary to use an intermediary to communicate with God. They had thus overstated their belief in God's transcendence, and as a result were in danger of missing out on an appreciation of his gracious presence with them.

The pre-eminence of Christ

This belief in the need for intermediaries came in part because, by contrast with their high view of God, Jesus was too low in their thinking. So although Paul could commend the church for their signs of faith, he was not impressed with what Epaphras told him about their doctine. They had lost a belief in the pre-eminence of Christ, who was being placed alongside other beings. They had failed to realize his position as Lord of creation and head of the Church – rather as Jehovah's Witnesses today see Jesus as a created being rather than God himself.

Regulated behaviour

Paul mentions two essentially non-Christian practices that had become part of their lives.

Observance of a calendar

The Colossians had begun observing annual, monthly and weekly festivals, despite the fact that there is no trace in the New Testament of Christian observance of a calendar – indeed, the calendar that the Church observes is largely a pagan one mixed into Christianity.

This observance of calendars provides an outstanding example of syncretism from an unlikely source – the celebration of Christmas. Most Christians are hostile to the idea that Christians should not observe Christmas, but not one verse in the New Testament commands Christians to do anything special at Christmas. In fact, the Christmas season is based on a pagan mid-winter festival celebrating what they saw as the 'rebirth' of the sun on 25 December. This ritual was made 'Christian' when Augustine was sent from Rome by Pope

Gregory to evangelize Britain in 597, and he found that the locals would not change their celebrations. They included yuletide logs, carols and orgies. Every village elected a 'Lord of misrule' for 12 days, who was able to have any young girl he wanted for the '12 days of Christmas'. So the Pope's advice was to 'Christianize' the festival. The legacy of this decision is that Christ is reduced to a baby in a manger, and is often dismissed as such.

Furthermore, there is no specific instruction to celebrate Easter either. Christ is risen 'every day', and his life should be enjoyed and celebrated as such. Even Sunday observance is never actually commanded in the New Testament. We are free to keep Sunday special if we want to, and we are free to count every day as the Lord's day if we want to. We are not under any law about Sunday, Christmas or Easter, and yet so many Christians seem to think that we are.

Abstinence

The Greek practice of abstaining from legitimate bodily pleasures was also popular in Colosse. Some forbade marriage, arguing that celibacy was preferable. Others had a list of things they must not touch or taste. Paul had to say that God has given us all things freely to enjoy. A Christian is free to both fast and feast, according to their own desire and conscience.

It is clear from Paul's teaching in Colossians and other letters, notably Galatians and Romans, that Christianity is not about giving up sweets for Lent (in the Church of England calendar) but is about giving up the attitudes and practices that displease God, such as pride, lust and envy. It means living consistently in Christ every day of your life. So in that sense every day is special.

This theme of the abstinence of the body is especially

demonstrated in the life of Martin Luther. In his days as a monk, he sought to save himself by following what he understood to be the appropriate practices. He prayed to three saints every day and flogged himself until he fell unconscious on the cell floor. He went on a pilgrimage and climbed the holy steps in Rome on his knees. But he found no peace. His Father Superior asked him, 'If you take away relics and pilgrimages and prayers to saints and all these devotional practices, what will you put in their place?' Martin Luther replied, 'Christ, man only needs Jesus Christ.' This is how the Protestant Reformation began. It removed the unnecessary practices of religion and put Christ back in his place.

All the divine fullness in the eternal Christ

Paul plays the false teachers at their own game. They were focusing on how 'fullness' could be found through their practices, so Paul uses the same word to describe Christ. He tells them that 'all the fullness of God dwells in him'. Charles Wesley wrote these sentiments in a hymn: 'Our God contracted to a span, incomprehensibly made man.' Paul is explaining that when we have Jesus, we have all of God.

In particular he is:

Creator of the Universe

According to Paul, the elemental powers of nature that were so revered are under Jesus' control. This was accomplished on the cross when Jesus cancelled our debt and disarmed our debtors. So the cross was far more than an example of self-sacrificial living, but was a means of real and lasting victory.

Conqueror of the powers

He is the conqueror of the powers, for all the principalities and the powers in the universe are under Jesus. Indeed, all the treasure of wisdom and knowledge are found in him. He is all in all.

Controller of the Church

As conqueror of the powers, it follows that he is the head of the Church too. The Church has only one head, not many. It has no human head, but one divine head. The head of the Church is Jesus, and this headship is not delegated to anyone else. If a local church is not properly related to the head, it becomes spastic, for the channels of communication between the head in heaven and the body on earth break down.

All human focus on the exalted Christ

In view of Christ's exaltation, our focus should properly be upon him. Paul describes how believers are identified with Christ, and are undergoing an inner renewal. Outward practices that ignore this inner work are redundant.

Purity in the passions

So the believer's life in Christ must be worked out in many practical areas. Paul teaches that natural passion for evil must be 'put off' and Christ must be 'put on' in an act of the will. Lust, greed, anger and malice are to have no part in a Christian's life. Paul speaks of putting to death such behaviour.

Charity in the church

Furthermore, the Christian's focus on Christ means a change in relationships. We are to be like God in the way we behave towards one another – in humility, compassion, kindness, forgiveness and love. The Christian is to live as one whose mind is set on things above, and God's character provides the perfect model.

Harmony in the home

Paul is concerned to demonstrate that Christlike living extends to the home, so he outlines the key relationships for the household – between husbands and wives, between parents and children, and between masters and slaves (for these too were part of the household). There is to be a mutuality of relationship, with each party playing their appropriate role within the relationship. He uses the word 'submission' to describe the way people should respond – submission of wives to husbands, of children to parents and of slaves to masters. But at the same time, the responsibility is on husbands and parents and masters to love sacrificially those who submit to them.

Conclusion

We can draw two conclusions from Colossians.

Negative

The first is that Paul states in Colossians that it is possible for someone, having started on the road to salvation, never to reach the end. This conclusion is not exclusive to this letter or to Paul, for it is found elsewhere in the New Testament, notably in Matthew and Hebrews. In referring to their hope of heaven, Paul says this will hold true, 'if you continue in your faith'. He warns them that if they give way to unchristlike passions, they will forfeit the right to escape God's wrath on the last day. There is urgency in his teaching, for he is concerned that they will be led astray by the myriad of ideas that are afflicting the believers. At one point he uses the word 'kidnapped' to describe what may happen, for it is as if they allow themselves to lose their freedom in Christ. If they lapse back into religion, they lose everything.

Positive

The positive side of the letter is that, once we have come to faith in Christ, we must continue to trust him. The letter is full of exhortations to continue in him. Just as Jesus promised that if we remain in the vine we will bear much fruit, so Paul is urging the Colossians to remain focused on Christ if their lives are to please God. So he urges them in chapter 2 that, as they had received Christ, so they must continue to live in him.

It is not enough just to come to Christ. We need to be rooted and built up in him, established in him. We need to continue in Christ all the way. Paul's teaching is similar to that of Jesus himself, who said, 'I am the true vine. Abide in me, stay in me. Branches that abide in me will be fruitful. Branches that don't abide in me will be cut off and burned' (John 15). So although Paul didn't know the members of the church, he was nevertheless concerned for them in case they lost what they originally had in Christ.

49.

EPHESIANS

Introduction

Paul's letter to the Ephesians was almost certainly written at the same time as his letter to the Colossians. There are a number of reasons why this is likely.

First, the themes of Ephesians are so similar to those of Colossians that it has been suggested that Ephesians was modelled on Colossians. Colossians is written as a defence against syncretism and provides a clear exposition of Christian belief and behaviour. Ephesians also covers this ground. In both letters the Church is pictured as the body, household relationships are addressed with similar wording, and the subject of slavery is dealt with. (This theme is also covered in his letter to Philemon, which was probably written at about this time).

Secondly, Paul said he wanted the Colossian letter to be read not only at Colosse but also at Laodicea and Hierapolis, two other churches in the Lycus valley, suggesting that the problems he was addressing also existed there. Since Ephesus was only 120 miles away, it is not unreasonable to expect that similar problems might have been affecting the church there as well, especially as Ephesians is written as a general letter, not specifically to Ephesus. The word 'Ephesians' is missing from some early manuscripts.

Furthermore, the lack of personal greetings in the Ephesian epistle is surprising if the letter was directed exclusively at the Ephesian church, since Paul spent two years there and would be likely to mention individuals, as he does in his other letters.

But, having noted the similarity to Colossians, we must also be aware that Ephesians is set apart from Paul's other epistles because it is far less dominated by the readers' concerns. In a general letter such as this, Paul doesn't deal with any false teaching as in his other letters, nor does he deal with any problems or questions.

The city

The city of Ephesus was situated at the intersection of major roads running east-west and north-south. Ephesus stood at the doorway to the Asian interior, with travellers from Persia, Egypt, Greece and Rome meeting within its walls. It was a big port in Paul's day, though the port has now silted up and the modern location of Ephesus is some way inland at a place called Ayasohuk, and the old city is now a ruin. One of 12 cities in the Ionian League, it was a centre of commerce and finance, with a theatre that held 24,000 and an enormous pagan temple, measuring 420 feet by 240 feet. The temple was dedicated to a black meteorite that fell on Ephesus. It was a big, shiny, black block of material, covered in bumps, each shaped like a female breast. This was regarded as a sign from the goddess Diana (Artemis in Greek), and so a cult of the female breast, the temple to 'page three,' was developed in Ephesus. This many-breasted meteorite was set on the altar and little silver reproductions of it were sold. People would come as tourists and would take home one of these little silver reproductions to put on the mantlepiece at home.

The church

We know more about the church at Ephesus than any other church in the New Testament. We first read of it in Acts 18–20 when Paul visits it. There is a great deal of correspondence concerning the church: in addition to this letter, we find that 1 and 2 Timothy were both addressed to Timothy in Ephesus, and were about the Ephesian church. In Revelation a letter is addressed to the church at Ephesus, and the three letters of John and the Gospel of John were written in Ephesus, because John the apostle settled there with Mary the mother of Jesus.

We also have evidence from extra-biblical material that the church became well established. It was an important city in the history of the early Church, with the Council of Ephesus being held there in AD 431. A visitor today can view the ruins of the church of St. John and his grave. It is fairly certain that this is where the aged apostle died.

Paul stayed in the city on two occasions for a total of two years, during which time the church grew. The faith was so popular and the response to the claims of Jesus so immediate that the trade in Diana trinkets suffered. So many Diana worshippers switched to the true God that Paul faced trouble from the silversmiths. The trade in silver meteorite statues virtually disappeared.

The structure of the letter

It seems clear that Paul felt that the best thing he could do to prevent the heresies in Asia from ruining the Church was to send a letter with a summary of Christian belief and behaviour. It is the closest we have to a statement of his gospel, especially as Romans is not the statement of his gospel that many believe it to be. Ephesians is more systematic than any other letter, and many regard it as Paul's finest, calling it 'the Queen of the epistles'.

The structure of the letter is very clear. Put simply, the first half is about our relationship to God in Christ, and the second half is about our relationship to others in the Lord. When Paul writes about our relationship to God, he uses the word 'Christ', but when he writes about our relationships with each other he uses 'Lord'. It is Christ who gives us our relationship to God, and he is the Lord who governs our relationships with each other.

Part 1:	Part 2:
His purpose and power	Our walk and warfare
Relationship to God (in Christ)	Relationship to others (in the Lord)
Salvation worked in	Salvation worked out
Doctrine	Duty
What we are saved by	What we are saved for
Adoration	Application
Forgiveness	Holiness
Justification	Sanctification
Our release	Our response
Divine sovereignty	Human responsibility
Inside the Church	Outside the Church

So in the first half of the letter, Paul outlines how salvation comes to believers, and in the second half he shows how they should behave once they have become believers. It is important to note that we are not saved *by* good deeds, but we are saved *for* good deeds.

The world thinks that being good saves us. The gospel actually states that we are being saved in order to be good, and the two ideas are totally different!

The two key words in the first half are *purpose* and *power*. We see what God intends to do and we note the power that he has to achieve that purpose. The key words for the second half are our *walk* and our *warfare*. We are to walk in the light, walk in love, walk as children of the light, and we are to fight in spiritual warfare.

So the first half is really concentrating on what happens inside the Church and the second half on what happens outside the Church. The first half is dealing with the vertical dimensions of the gospel, and the second half is dealing with the horizontal dimension of the gospel.

It is vital that we keep the two elements together. If we believe we are saved and have a ticket to heaven regardless of how we live, we have not understood the gospel.

The structure of the epistle tells us something important about salvation, for the order is vitally important. There are some people who think that Christianity is just about 'being good'. But it is equally distorted to say that Christianity is just about 'being saved'. We must have both, but we must have them in the right order. Most religions in the world put sanctification before justification – they require people to attain goodness (however that is defined) before God can accept them. Christianity is unique. It says we are accepted by God first, just as we are, in order that God may make us what he wants us to be. Justification must come before sanctification, for we cannot live the Christian life until we are in right relationship with God. Christian behaviour is built on Christian belief. Christian duty flows from Christian doctrine.

An examination of chapters 1–3 shows that Paul is explaining the doctrine of salvation in the context of a service of worship. The 'order' is praise, prayer, preaching, prayer, praise, and the theme of the whole service is the power and purpose of God.

Praising – purpose: to sum all things up in Christ.
Praying – to know purpose and power.
Preaching – power and purpose.
1. *Christ*: – raised up to reign.
2. *Gentiles*: – raised up to rejoin.
3. *Paul*: – raised up to reveal.
Praying –to know power and purpose.
Praising – power: to do exceeding abundantly.

The apostle places great emphasis on Jew/Gentile unity. Paul is keen to stress that God has broken down the wall between Jew and Gentile, so powerfully demonstrated by the wall in the temple, which barred Gentiles from the inner courts on pain of death. The legacy of this sharp division plagued the early Church, and Paul was especially aware of the implications. He was writing from prison because he had been falsely accused of taking a Gentile named Trophimus (from Ephesus, no less), into the exclusively Jewish area of the temple.

But Paul's emphasis upon the Church as the 'new building' replacing the temple should not lead us to assume that God has finished with the old Israel. The so- called 'replacement theology', whereby the Church is seen as the replacement for Israel, is an incorrect reading, for as Paul explains in Romans 9–11, God still has purposes for his people.

Walking in the Spirit

Chapters 4–6 are concerned with our response to what God has done. The Revised Standard Version uses the word 'walk', throughout these chapters, and it is a helpful verb to describe the way we should respond. We can jump in the Spirit and leap in the Spirit, but God wants people to walk in the Spirit.

Walking is not so spectacular as leaping and jumping, but it is taking one step at a time in the right direction.

Paul lists eight areas we are to walk in.

Humility

We walk in humility because that is the secret of unity. We cannot have Christian unity if we don't have humility, because wherever there is pride, unity is broken. So we mustn't be too upset when people say things about us – after all, we need to remember that it would be much worse if they knew the truth!

One of my favourite poems highlights this very well:

> Once in a saintly passion I cried with desperate grief,
> 'Oh Lord, my heart is black with guile, of sinners I am chief.'
> Then spoke my guardian angel, and whispered from behind,
> 'Vanity, my little man, you're nothing of the kind.'

False modesty is not humility. Real humility realizes that we are what we are by the grace of God, and if it weren't for his grace we would be nowhere.

Unity

We are encouraged next to walk in unity. Paul reminds us that there is *one* body, *one* Spirit, *one* faith and *one* baptism. There is only *one* God and Father of us all. So we walk in unity, because we were all saved by the blood of Jesus, whatever our disagreements. Keeping the unity of the Spirit means being active -- we must not assume that just because we all attend the same church, all is necessarily well. We must work at it.

Maturity

Paul encourages the church to walk in maturity. He says that we move from unity to grow up to the full stature of Jesus

Christ and explains that this is why God has given us apostles, prophets, pastors, evangelists and teachers, to build us up so that we might mature and grow up. Christian fellowship begins with unity of the Spirit and ends with unity in *the* faith. The unity of the Spirit is maintained until unity of *the* faith is attained. Too many evangelicals have made extensive doctrinal agreement the basis of unity, and therefore they criticize some of us who have fellowship with, say, Catholic charismatics. But the basis of unity is one Spirit. If we meet someone who has been baptized in the same Spirit we were baptized in, we have fellowship with him or her. It is true that we may not yet have achieved full unity of *the* faith, but that will come with maturity. The goal is to believe the same thing, but the beginning of this is the unity of the Spirit. So whenever we meet someone in whom the Holy Spirit dwells, they are part of the one body of Christ. We may not have got it all right either!

Integrity

In chapter 5 integrity comes to the fore. We are urged to ensure that our life matches what we say, and that what we say is in keeping with being a child of God. We are told not to crack dirty jokes – it is as practical as that.

Charity

We are to be charitable with one another. We should forgive each other as Christ has forgiven us. Christians are tolerant of each other while remaining intolerant of error and sin. It is a difficult balance but an important distinction to make.

Purity

We are to go on being filled with the Holy Spirit. The verb suggests a continuous filling. We must walk in purity of motive and of heart if we are to please the God who called us.

Docility

Many of Paul's words have a negative connotation in modern language. But docility, or submission to one another in Christ, is a beautiful sign of maturity.

He mentions three areas:

Wives should submit to their husbands;
Children should submit towards their parents;
Slaves should submit towards their masters or employers.

In each case the former is to 'put themselves under' the latter out of reverence for Christ. Their submission is to be a human example of their submission to Christ.

Responsibility

Those who are submitted to, have a responsibility to be worthy of their role. This is quite a challenge. Husbands are to love their wives as Jesus loves the Church – no less. My wife has said to me more than once that when I submit to Christ, she is happy to submit to me. So husbands, parents, and employers have a responsibility towards those who put their lives in their hands. In no way does teaching about submission excuse over-bearing or domineering behaviour.

Spiritual warfare

The section on spiritual warfare is a very popular part of the letter. We are told to put on the whole armour of God, for we are not fighting human beings. It is much easier to fight human beings – some Christians seem to prefer it. But Paul explains that we are not wrestling against flesh and blood, but against principalities and powers in the heavenly places.

Indeed, we are wrestling in precisely the place where we have been placed in Christ. Chapter 1 tells us that we sit with him in heavenly places.

It is clear that the one thing we should never do is retreat, for in Paul's description of the armour there is no mention of protection for the back. You may not be able to walk forward at times, but you are to stand, and never take a backward step. The reference to the shield of faith extinguishing fiery darts almost certainly refers to the Roman soldier's shield that was covered with very soft wood. Fiery darts that plunged into the wood went out. So all the fiery darts that the evil one fires can be absorbed by our faith.

Predestination

A study of Ephesians would not be complete without looking at predestination. It is a theme that is especially prominent in the first chapter. Predestination is a subject that is often misunderstood. Some speak as if we are just robots or puppets who cannot resist whatever God chooses to do.

This understanding comes in part from an interpretation of a passage in Jeremiah 18 in which people are likened to clay in the hands of a potter. Many argue that God is the potter who does what he chooses with the clay. The clay has no choice. But Jeremiah 18 may be making the opposite point. For in the parable, the potter had every intention of making the clay into a beautiful vase, but the clay would not run in his hands, so he made it into a lump again and put it back on the wheel and made a crude, thick cooking pot. So God is actually teaching Jeremiah that we should choose to co-operate with the potter and allow him to make something beautiful out of us. The application in Jeremiah's day was that God wanted to make Israel a beautiful vessel holding his mercy, but instead he had to make an ugly vessel holding his judgement.

This parable helps us to answer the view that we cannot resist God. It shows that if we respond to God, the destiny which he planned for us from the foundation of the world will be ours. But there is nothing to suggest that if he predestines us to be something, we cannot resist his will.

To use a personal illustration, my father knew I wanted to be a farmer. I spent every holiday on the farm and when I left school at 16 I went to work on the farm, milking 90 cows every morning at 4 o'clock. I loved farming. I didn't know that my father had planned for me to take over a farm in Scotland when I was 21. The farm was in the family and he was able to arrange this. But when my father told me that the farm was ready for me, I had to tell him that God was leading me in another direction. Had I accepted that farm, I could always have said that my father predestined me to be on this farm, that he planned it before I even knew about it.

In the same way, 'to predestine' means literally to decide a destiny beforehand. But the idea that God simply treats us as puppets and makes us do what he has predestined is false, just as my father did not force me to do what he had predestined for me. God predestines us to glory. We can resist and refuse that predestined way, or we can accept it. If we accept it, we can say forever afterwards that he planned this for us before the foundation of the world.

The two views of predestination

The common view is that to predestine means that individuals are chosen to be saved by God, whereas others are chosen not to be. In this understanding, God decides before we are born whether we will be saved. God's grace is said to be irresistible, for once God has decided we will be saved, nothing can stop it. So it is entirely God's choice whether a person ends up in heaven or hell, for without his grace at work in our lives, it is impossible for us to respond to God in repentance and faith. Having been chosen, we are assured of a place in heaven. This view of predestination is often associated with the French theologian John Calvin – although while Calvin did teach electing grace, he taught in his *Institutes* that believers can lose their salvation.

However, this view has been challenged. First, if we study the references to predestination in the Bible, we find that believers are not so much chosen for salvation as for service. Secondly, the emphasis is not on the choice of individuals but on the choice of a people, a chosen or elect people. Thirdly, the Bible does not say that God's grace is irresistible. It can be resisted. In his sermon in Acts, Stephen criticizes the Sanhedrin for always resisting the Holy Spirit. Grace is conditional on faith. Only if we continue to believe, do we continue in the faith.

Furthermore, our destiny is not dependent on God's choice but on ours, on whether we choose to respond to his grace or choose to resist it. It is clear that we are born again after repenting and believing, not before. It is because we have repented and believed that God can give us new life in Christ.

Finally, our perseverance is something that is required rather than guaranteed. The Bible speaks of persevering, abiding in the vine, overcoming, remaining in Christ, going on believing. These are all words reflecting continuing faith on our part. This is not salvation by works, but salvation by continued faith, and that's an important emphasis to make. This argument against Calvin's view of predestination is often called Arminianism, named after a Dutch theologian called Arminius.

So I believe in predestination. I believe that God predestined me to be what I am. I believe that he decided that he wanted me in heaven before I even knew he existed. He loved me before I loved him, and he chose me rather than me choosing him. Having said all that, I believe that it was because I didn't resist his grace and received it and continue believing that I will finish up in the celestial city.

This chart illustrates the different approaches to predestination:

Calvin	Arminius
to salvation	to service
individual	corporate
persons	a people
irresistible	conditional
grace	faith
destiny determined by God's choice	destiny dependent on our choice
lost – so not chosen	lost – so wrong choice
born again before repentance and faith	born again after repentance and faith
perseverance guaranteed	perseverance required

Once saved, always saved?

Our consideration of predestination has a bearing on a cliché which has been widely used. People say, 'once saved, always saved.' The biggest problem here is that the word 'saved' is ambiguous. What does 'once saved' mean? I'm being saved, but I have a lot more to be saved from. Salvation is a process, not an instantaneous miracle and therefore, like others, I'm waiting for Jesus' Second Coming, when he will bring salvation to those who are waiting for him. It is at that point that I will be 'once saved', because all of me will be saved then, including my body.

It is my equally firm belief that the discussion about predestination should not spoil Christian fellowship. Regardless of our viewpoint, we can unite around Christ.

Conclusion

This letter to the Ephesians is probably the clearest presentation of Christian doctrine and duty, belief and behaviour, theology and ethics, in all Paul's epistles. Little wonder that it is the favourite for many believers and among many denominations. Probably its emphasis on unity is a major factor in its popularity in this ecumenical era, though it is important to note the parallel concern for truth and integrity.

50.

PHILIPPIANS

Paul's letter to the Philippians was written during his first imprisonment in Rome while under house arrest. Philippi was the first city he had visited in mainland Europe and the location of his first church plant. It was a special place for Paul and, as we will see, the church had a special place in his heart.

In Paul's day Philippi was a large and prosperous city due to its location on a major east-west trade route called the Ignatian Way. The city lay in a large gap in the mountain ranges stretching from the Black Sea to the Adriatic. Gold and silver deposits in the mountains nearby added to its wealth. In the early 1990s an archaeologist found a tomb in Philippi full of golden treasures – a find second only to Tutankhamen's tomb in Egypt. It was the tomb of Philip, the king of Macedonia (the northern part of Greece), after whom the city was named. His more famous son was Alexander the Great, who built a vast empire before his death at the age of 31.

The area was the scene of some key ancient battles. In 168 BC the Romans came and conquered the people. In 42 BC Anthony beat Brutus and Cassius at Philippi. In 31 BC Anthony and Cleopatra were defeated and killed there. Having been such a key battleground, the Romans made it a colony. The emperor Augustus gave it a pompous name: 'Colonia Julia Augusta Philipensis', but people called it 'Philippi' for short. It was a mini metropolis and it was given exactly the same rights as if it were on Roman soil, and so many Romans felt able to settle there.

A colony of heaven

Philippi's location meant that it had a strategic role as a base for the gospel. It was a gateway to Europe. It is clear from Luke's account of the expansion of the Church in Acts that God intended it to be a 'colony of heaven'. In Acts 16 we read how Paul was prevented by the Holy Spirit from going into Bithynia in Asia. Paul and his companions travelled west, uncertain of their final destination until Paul had a dream of a man dressed like a native of Macedonia beckoning them to come to his country. So Paul and his companions sailed over to the port of Neapolis and then moved on to Philippi. His preaching recorded in Acts is the first clear record of the gospel's arrival in mainland Europe. It may have been brought by natives of Europe who had visited Jerusalem and were converted when the Spirit came at Pentecost, but we have no evidence of this.

The Philippian church

The church started from a handful of people around AD 52. Paul's strategy for evangelizing an area was to begin his work in the Jewish synagogue in the city he was visiting. But there was no synagogue in Philippi, for there were less than the required 10 male Jews to form one, and so Paul met with a Jewish ladies' prayer group instead. Among the women was one who was to be instrumental in the work of the Philippian church – a businesswoman named Lydia. Originally from Asia, she sold purple cloth for a living. Acts tells us that she had slaves and a household and that the whole household was baptized. Advocates of infant baptism are disappointed to discover that the word 'household' doesn't mean 'family', but includes slaves and all kinds of relatives. So there is no suggestion that young children were included.

But not everyone was pleased that Paul had come, and his preaching soon met with opposition. It came in the unlikely form of a girl who followed Paul and his team around, telling the listening crowds: 'You must listen to these men! They are from the high God! They are telling you the truth!' (Acts 16). But what seemed to be good publicity was the exact opposite, for the girl was a clairvoyant employed by businessmen who owned her and used her powers to make money. So Paul cast the demon out of the girl, and she stopped troubling their meetings. But the owners were horrified and stirred up trouble for Paul. It wasn't long before he found himself in jail, accused of advocating laws against the law of Rome – which was a change, as it was normally the Jews who were accusing Paul.

Acts recounts how Paul and his companions turned the cell where they were placed into a worship service. They were in jail in total darkness at midnight and yet they were praising God! As if in response to their worship, God sent an earthquake, bringing the cell walls down, and the whole prison was thrown open. The jailer, knowing that the penalty for losing prisoners was crucifixion, yelled out, 'What must I do to be saved?' Paul's reply was immediate: 'Believe in Jesus!' We must assume that Paul preached to him and his household for hours through the night, for by the morning they were ready to be baptized. So with Lydia, the jailer and his household, and possibly other Jewish women from the prayer group, the church at Philippi began.

But Paul was still in jail, and he knew his rights as a Roman citizen in Philippi, a Roman colony. He told the authorities that they had treated him unjustly. The authorities, realizing that they would face the penalty of imprisonment if their treatment of Paul was found to be unjust, begged him to leave town. He said, 'Well, if you come and get me out of jail and accompany me out of town, I will go!' And so the leaders of the town came and escorted him out. So he was in Philippi for just a short period – a matter of days or weeks at the very most, and yet he left behind the first 'colony of heaven' in Europe.

The letter was written many years later. Paul continued his missionary work for many years before being arrested in Jerusalem. The charge was unjust – he was falsely accused of taking a Gentile into a prohibited area in the temple. He appealed to Caesar, was eventually sent to Rome in chains, and for two years awaited trial. It was during those two years that Dr Luke wrote Luke's Gospel and Acts, the two volumes that would be Paul's defence at his trial and would lead to his acquittal.

Paul's reasons for writing

Paul's desire to write the letter springs from two things he received from Philippi.

Financial support

The first was a gift of money. The church were so grateful to Paul for bringing them the gospel that they decided to support Paul financially, despite the fact that Paul never asked for anything. They were the only church that wanted to demonstrate their concern for Paul's ongoing ministry in this way.

Physical support

The second gift was even more welcome. A man arrived not just with money but with his domestic skills to serve Paul while he was under house arrest. Clearly, the church had asked themselves, 'How can we help him?' and decided that physical aid was their best contribution. The man they sent was called Epaphroditus. He is called an 'apostle'. The word literally means 'a sent one' (from a Greek verb, *apostolos*, meaning 'I send'). An 'apostle' is someone who is sent from A to B to do something.

Five kinds of 'apostle'

There is a lot of confusion surrounding the term 'apostle'. In fact there are five kinds of 'apostle' in the New Testament.

1 Jesus is called an apostle because God sent him from heaven to earth to save us, so he is the Chief Apostle.
2 The second kind of apostles are 'the Twelve' who were witnesses to the resurrection of Jesus and were sent out to the world by him. Their qualification was that they knew Jesus before and after his resurrection.
3 Paul is himself a special apostle. He was not one of the Twelve because he had not known Jesus before he died. But he was nevertheless called by the risen, ascended Jesus on the road to Damascus, so he was a third kind of apostle.
4 The fourth category is Paul wearing his other hat as a pioneer missionary sent out to plant churches in unreached territory. Indeed, the word 'sent' in Latin is *mitto*, from which we get our words 'missionary' and 'missile'. A missionary is an intercontinental ballistic missile filled with the

dynamite of the gospel! We still have these church-planting apostles today.

5 Epaphroditus is in the fifth category of apostles – someone who is sent from anywhere to anywhere to do anything. So it's a very broad group and doesn't necessarily indicate the high status that we might expect.

Epaphroditus becomes ill

While Paul appreciated the visit of Epaphroditus, we are told in the letter that he also brought sadness, for it was not long before he became ill. Interestingly, Paul's prayers did not lead to his healing. This need not surprise us. Healings in the New Testament are usually associated with evangelism and not with healing Christians. A number of Paul's associates had physical problems that were not healed. Timothy was told to take a bit of wine for his stomach's sake, and Trophimus was described as being left 'sick'. The healing ministry of the New Testament was not to keep Christians fit, but to demonstrate the gospel in evangelism.

But the rumour went back to Philippi that the man they had sent was desperately ill and about to die. So Paul decided that the best thing to do was to send Epaphroditus back to Philippi with a letter to the Philippians, to thank the church for the money.

The letter

The letter is quite different from Paul's others. It doesn't concentrate on problems or crises but on the relationships between Paul and the Philippians, and gives us a window into how Paul felt about one of the churches he had planted. We get to know Paul as a person and a friend rather than as a preacher or missionary, and we gain a glimpse of what a profound relationship there was between him and his converts.

One intriguing feature of this letter is that he doesn't seem to know how to finish it. He keeps saying 'and finally'. This need not surprise us – in many ways this is just typical letter writing. He keeps remembering something else, just as in a letter to a friend we keep saying, 'Oh, I must mention that etc. ... Oh, there's just one other thing ...' So it has a spontaneous feel, reflecting the momentum of his thinking as he dictated it.

Koinonia

Before considering how Paul arranges his main teaching, we will examine two key themes that he develops.

One word that figures quite prominently in the letter is *koinonia*, translated as 'fellowship' in most of our Bibles. It is actually a far more profound word than the meaning it is often given. We talk about 'a bit of fellowship over a cup of tea in the hall after the meeting' – as if a cup of tea creates fellowship! It creates a bit of friendship, but fellowship is far more than a cup of tea.

Actually *koinonia* was a word that could be used of partners in a business. But the strength of meaning is probably seen best by the way the word was used in New Testament times. Siamese twins born in the ancient world were said to have *koinonia* in blood, for if one died the other would die too. In the same way, our fellowship with one another is to be of that quality – what happens to one will happen to the other – that's *koinonia*.

The church in Philippi was free of the sort of major problems that Paul faced in other churches that he wrote to, but there were some concerns. The *koinonia* in the Philippian church was being affected by two women called Euodia and Syntyche – though from the way they behaved, 'Odious' and 'Soon Touchy' might be more appropriate! They had worked with Paul but their disagreements were causing problems. Their behaviour was indicative of a problem of disunity that Paul addresses elsewhere in the letter. It wasn't the kind of disunity that troubled Corinth, where they were following different ministers or leaders. It was the kind of disunity where people become proud – more concerned about themselves than about each other. Paul had to say, 'When each of you cares more for others' interests than for your own, you will be united.'

Joy

Another word that characterizes this letter is *joy*. In spite of the situation Paul is in, the letter is filled with rejoicing. He is facing a lonely future and a trial which could lead to death, and people who are against him are preaching while he languishes in prison – and yet his favourite words in the letter are 'joy' and 'rejoice' and 'thanksgiving'. Bengel said: 'The main point of the letter is "I rejoice, you must rejoice."' Von Hugel called the letter 'radiance amid the storm and stress of life'.

Paul lists the sources of joy in the letter: prayer, Christ preached, faith, suffering, news of loved ones, hospitality, receiving and giving. But deep down there were two reasons for his joy:

Because of what he lived for

Such a joy-filled perspective was possible because he lived so that the gospel might be made known. This was true on two counts. The whole palace guard had heard the message, presumably because he had a captive audience. And even though some preached out of rivalry while he was in prison, Paul was delighted that Christ was being made known.

This ability to know joy in God was illustrated in the Second World War. Paul Schneider was a pastor of a church in Berlin who was imprisoned by Hitler because of his preaching against Fascism. As a result he never saw his wife and two-year-old boy again. Despite beatings and torture and finally execution, the letters that he wrote from Dachau concentration camp to his wife were full of joy. Again and again he wrote, 'I'm so happy' and 'I'm so grateful to the Lord.' He lived for Christ and therefore he had nothing to lose.

If you live for Christ, to die is profit! Paul is eager to go, but willing to stay. He says to the Philippians, 'You are worried about me. Actually it's the other way round – I'm worried about you. I'm not worried about me at all!' He says, 'I am willing to be let off and restored to my ministry, but I am eager to go.'

When David Watson found he had serious cancer, I wrote a letter to him, which he quotes in his book *Fear No Evil*. I told him there is a difference between 'willing to go to be with the Lord, but eager to stay' and 'eager to be with the Lord, but willing to stay'. The words spoke to him, and he prayed his way through until he was 'eager to go but willing to stay'. This is the ideal position for the believer, exemplified by Paul, who was able to say that he was 'willing to stay around if needed a bit longer, but very eager to go'.

This focus upon the gospel is further emphasized by noting how often Paul writes about Jesus. There are 38 occasions in this little letter when he talks about Jesus. We tend to talk about Christ being in us – but in this letter Paul writes about being in Christ. Christ is the greater one, Paul is found 'in him'.

Because of what he lived on

The Philippians' financial contributions were the only ones that Paul received. Even Antioch, the church that sent him out as a missionary, is not known to have provided support. So towards the end of his letter Paul thanks the Philippians for the money, but does so in an interesting way. He actually says, 'I didn't need it, but you needed to give, so I am thrilled with the gift – not for my sake but for your sake, because that makes you rich.' He's congratulating them on giving it rather than being excited to receive it.

When I give preaching classes I test speakers on quoting texts out of context, using the text, 'I can do all things through Christ who strengthens me.' I ask: 'Now, what does that text mean? What things do you think you can do through Christ who strengthens you?' I receive all sorts of answers, but no one mentions money. But in context the statement is about money. He is saying, 'I can manage with whatever income I have, whether it be large or small. If I've got a lot of money coming in, I can manage through Christ who strengthens me.'

There are two opposites in Scripture when it comes to money: 'coveting' is one extreme and 'contentment' is the other. Paul says elsewhere, 'Godliness with contentment is great profit' and 'I have learned to be content.' This is remarkable, given Paul's testimony in Romans 7 that the one commandment of the ten that he found he couldn't keep was the tenth, 'Thou shalt not covet'. Paul was a typical Pharisee, and the Pharisees' weakness was that they liked making money. They were religious and rich at the same time. Jesus told them, 'You can't be both, you can't live for making money and live for God, you can't worship God and Mammon together.' The Pharisees laughed at him, saying, 'That's just because you're poor!' But Jesus knew what he was talking about. So it's amazing that this covetous man Paul – a Pharisee, a man who liked money and liked making money – said, 'I have learned to be content.'

A controversial passage

Any study of this letter must consider one of its better known passages: Philippians 2:5–11.

Despite being a beautiful passage, it has been a source of great controversy. The biggest question is: Why is it in Philippians, and why is it so different from the rest of the letter?

It has a double theme, which is very clear – emptied/exalted or down/up. There is a beautiful balance, with Jesus coming all the way down to the cross and then going all the way up to the very top. He empties himself, and God exalts him.

Liturgical

Some people suggest that Paul is quoting a hymn which the early Church sang and which suited the point he was making. But we have no evidence for that – it may even be that Paul is composing a hymn here. After all, when something touched Paul's heart deeply, he often lapsed into poetry. In the Bible prose is used to communicate God's thoughts, but poetry is used to communicate his feelings.

Theological

Although it is possible that Paul is quoting a hymn or maybe even composing a hymn himself, the biggest controversy about this passage occurs when people treat it as a theological passage – as if it's discussing the nature of the person of Christ.

Some use this passage to support what is called the Kenotic theory of Christ. The word 'kenotic' comes from the Greek word *kenosis*, meaning 'emptied'. They debate how much of

God Christ emptied himself of when he became a man. What did he let go?

From this thinking comes a very dangerous theological assumption – that Jesus was not 100 per cent God when he was on earth, but emptied himself of part of his divinity in order to become a man.

It's certainly obvious that he left his glory behind. – At Christmas we sing,

> Mild, he lays his glory by,
> Born that man no more may die.

He also left his omnipresence behind – he could no longer be everywhere. Jesus could only be in one place at any one time – that was certainly a limitation.

It's also clear that he did not now know everything – he confessed that there were some things he didn't know. He didn't know the date of his return – only the Father knew that. He was sometimes surprised, which means he didn't know what was going to happen. He left behind his omnipotence too, because he could only do miracles after the power of the Holy Spirit had come upon him. He didn't do miracles as the Son of God but as the Son of Man baptized in the Holy Spirit.

So there is no doubt that he did empty himself of many of his privileges and his powers. But the key is that he did not in any sense cease to be God; he remained 100 per cent divine and 100 per cent human – he was fully both.

So it is crucial to realize that the things he gave up were not of his nature but of his privileges. 'The fullness of the Godhead still dwelt in him bodily', even though he laid aside his privileges. If I gave up the house we live in and the car I drive and other privileges that I have, that doesn't mean I cease to be me. I may have chosen to give up my privileges but I am still 100 per cent David Pawson. So in the same way, although he emptied himself of his equality with God, he did not empty himself of God.

Ethical

Actually, this whole passage is neither liturgical nor theological, but from the context in the letter, it is an *ethical* passage – it is about Christ's attitudes and choices. You can tell a man's character from his choices, and we see here the extraordinary choices that Jesus made.

The choices that Jesus made

Becoming a man

His first choice was to become a man. An illustration I use with children may help at this point. I say, 'Look at those tropical fish in that tank. Supposing you saw them fighting and killing each other and you knew that you could save them if you became a fish and went to live in the tank, knowing that they would probably kill you – would you do it?'

They are not too sure at this point. I continue: 'Don't worry – we would lift your body out of the tank and give you the kiss of life and bring you back to life. But there is one catch. We can't bring you back to where you were – you'd have to stay a fish for the rest of your life!'

God the Son was equal with God, with all the glory of heaven. He chose to be a man, knowing that he would be killed when he came to earth. He knew too that even after God raised him from the dead, he would have to remain a man for the rest of eternity. So he is still 'one of us' and always will be – one person of the Trinity will always be a human being like us.

His social status

The second choice concerned his birth. If you had the pick of any standard of living, what would you choose? Imagine choosing your parents, the house you would be born in, and the level of society in which you would live – where would you choose? Jesus chose to be at the bottom of society, born to a poor couple. Above all, he chose the role of a servant.

His early death

But his biggest choice came when, at the age of 33, he chose to die a horrible, humiliating, painful death – the worst ever devised for human beings – crucifixion. Paul writes of the mind of Christ and explains that our mind should be like his. This 'mind' has nothing to do with intellect, but refers to our character. Paul says that these choices fitted Jesus perfectly to be given authority and power, because God looks for people whom he can trust. He can only trust those who have no interest in their own power or status or wealth. So we read: 'Therefore God exalted him and gave him a name which is above every name' (2:9). He could trust Jesus with the control of the universe because he knew he would never have any self-interest.

It is important to be clear about what Paul means by 'Have this mind among you'. He is not saying 'Imitate Christ' but 'Have this mind among you, which you already have in Christ.' So he is not saying, 'This was the mind of Christ, therefore be like Christ.' Rather, 'You have already got the mind of Christ if you are in Christ. Therefore, let that mind of Christ be expressed in your relationships with each other.' It's a much deeper thing than just saying, 'Imitate Christ's attitude.'

As always, the context of the passage gives us the meaning. Paul is urging his readers to not look after their own interests, but to have the same attitude as Jesus has. They should make the choice to go down instead of trying to go up. Only then can God trust them with authority.

So the passage is not about theology, liturgy or hymn singing, but about ethics and unity. Paul is saying, 'If we have the mind of Christ, we will have unity in our fellowship.' He explains that they must have unity in order to be able to demonstrate the gospel to those outside the church. He says, 'I long to hear that you stand fast together for the sake of the gospel.' Disunity in a church is the quickest way to stop that church's influence on society, but unity within a church is the strongest demonstration of the one God and the one Christ.

Working out their faith

The major teaching of the letter follows this poem about Jesus. Paul tells the Philippians how to work out their faith in practice.

Redemption – an experience to apply

  a God works it in.
  b You work it out.

Paul explains that just as they have experienced redemption in Christ, so they must demonstrate what they believe. Salvation is never something we experience passively – the truth must be made a reality in all that we do.

Righteousness – an end to pursue

  a Not ours,
  b but his.

We work out our salvation by seeking righteousness. But there are two kinds of righteousness – our own and Christ's. Despite having been a strict Jew who followed the Law rigidly, Paul knew that his good works would not save him. Most people find it difficult to understand that we must repent of our good deeds as well as our bad. In this respect it's much easier to convert outright sinners than religious and respectable people who think they are not bad enough to need 'saving'.

Paul says, 'When I consider my righteousness, I feel like a child who has just emptied his bowels and is holding up the potty and saying, "Look what I've done, God".' The illustration may seem crude, but the word used in the Greek is the word for human excreta. So Paul says, 'I want Christ's righteousness, not mine.'

Resurrection – an event to desire

a Out from the dead.
b With a new body.

Paul says, 'I press on, I share his sufferings and his resurrection that I might attain the resurrection out from the dead.' In fact he uses the word 'out' twice. The Greek reads, 'that I may attain the out-resurrection out from the dead'. It sounds nonsensical, but the Book of Revelation explains that there will be two resurrections at the end of history: the first is the resurrection of the righteous, and the second is the resurrection of everybody else for judgement, with a long gap between the two.

The first one is the resurrection out from among the dead, the second is the resurrection of the rest of the dead, and Paul says, 'I want to be in the first resurrection. My goal is to be raised from the dead when Jesus gets back' – a resurrection out from the dead.

Responsibility – an effort to make

a Forgetting the past.
b Straining towards the future.

The Christian life requires effort – which is news to some people. It is not just singing choruses at the bus stop until the bus comes to take you to heaven, but making every effort after holiness. He tells the church to forget the things that are behind and to press on towards the goal for which they were called.

Paul says he doesn't feel that he's arrived but is pressing on to embrace all that God has planned for him.

Reproduction – an example to follow

a Bad – earthly minded.
b Good – heavenly minded.

I have a row of books on holiness on my shelves, but I have learned more about holiness from people I know who walk with the Lord than I have from reading them. There are those who convey Christ just by being with us. They drive us on to want to be better. In the same way, Paul was concerned that the Philippians should follow the correct sort of person. He said there are both in the church – there are those 'whose God is their belly', who dig their grave with a knife and fork, and then there are those who have set their minds on things above. Make sure you follow the correct model.

So this is the goal he is still working for. He isn't saying that he's bound to be in heaven but that he wants to be in that first resurrection.

The peace of Christ

At the end of the letter Paul gives the church a promise about anxiety. He says that the peace of Christ will guard their hearts and minds (4:7). But there's a condition attached – namely, that they control their thoughts and only think about things that are honest and good and pure and true. So the promise and the condition must go together.

Conclusion

We have seen that the major thrust of the letter is not what the Lord does in the believer but what the believer needs to do in response. Many of the promises of the letter are conditional, and it is clear that we must play our part.

The absence of conflict and the warmth of relationship make Philippians one of the most pleasant of Paul's letters to read, and with the exception of a few passages, one of the easiest to understand. Of all the letters, it gives the clearest insight into the level of partnership that Paul's ministry generated – a partnership that was to be not only a compelling witness to the world but was to sustain Paul himself in his hour of need. At the same time, it is clear that here is an apostle utterly content, in spite of his circumstances. He is content with everything except himself! He knows he can receive strength through God, and so he urges his readers to do the same. He is keen that they should rejoice together.

51.

PHILEMON

The letters of Paul have been arranged on the same principle as the prophets in the Old Testament – the longer the book, the earlier the place it gets in the Bible. So the letters of Paul are arranged in two blocks – his letters to churches and his letters to individuals – and within those two blocks the longest comes first and the shortest comes last. So they are not in chronological order. Philemon comes last simply because it's short. It's the only letter that is purely about one individual – a runaway slave. It is the most obviously private of all the correspondence in the New Testament.

Two questions require an answer as we approach the letter: 'Why was it written?' and 'Why has God put the letter in the Bible if it's a private letter about one individual?'

The answer to the first question is fairly obvious, for the story behind the letter is quite simple. It's a personal drama about a slave named Onesimus who was sullen, lazy, rebellious, and resentful. He ran away to Rome, thinking that the large metropolis would be a good place to hide. It is not clear how he met Paul, especially as Paul was under house arrest, chained to a Roman soldier.

In those days the normal punishment for a runaway slave was crucifixion, but if his master was particularly kind he would merely brand him on the forehead with the letters 'FF', meaning '*fugitilis*' (or 'fugitive'). He would have to wear that brand forever afterwards but would at least keep his life.

Paul tells Onesimus to return to his master, Philemon, whom Paul knew as a Christian in Colosse. He writes the letter to smooth the reunion. Since the penalty for desertion was so strict, the tone and content of the letter were important. But Paul knew that it was also important so that Onesimus did not run away from his past. An important part of repentance involves putting the past right.

Paul said to Onesimus, 'You realize I have got to send you back.' But God must have had his hand on this situation, for his master was a Christian at Colosse known to the apostle Paul. So Paul said, 'I'll send you back with a letter to him, and I'll explain everything.'

We can appreciate Paul's tone by noting how he uses a deliberate pun on Onesimus' name. The name means 'useful' – presumably it was given to him by his master. But Paul wrote to Philemon, 'You may have found him useless in the past, but I am sending back a "useful" slave to you.' More than that, he was sending him back as a brother in Christ. Paul even says that he would repay any money that Onesimus had stolen.

We can easily forget that letters were rare in Roman times, especially ones sent over a distance as great as that between from Rome to western Turkey. So it is very likely that when sending the letter to Philemon, Paul also sent the letters to the Colossians and the Ephesians with the same postman, Tychicus.

The story can be considered from a number of angles:

The personal angle

There are three main characters:

1 *Paul.* Despite being in prison, he still has time for individuals like Onesimus. It is clear from his tone that he is fond of this slave, though it has to be said that Paul lays on the appeal a bit thickly. He says, 'I am an old man and a prisoner' – it's a bit of a sob story, but it shows that this is a very human document.

2 *Philemon.* Has a church meeting in his house, and a wife and a son. Paul explained that it would be hard for all three of them – hard for Paul to let Onesimus go, because he had come to value him; hard for Onesimus to go back, because he has run away; and hard for Philemon to accept him and forgive him. 'Nevertheless,' says Paul, 'let's all do the hard thing!'

3 *Onesimus.* The useful servant who is soon to be restored to his master's household, back in work.

The letter shows that Paul knew some of the other people involved in Philemon's house church – Apphia and Archippus are addressed along with Philemon. Epaphras, Mark, Aristarchus, Demas and Luke all send their greetings to the church.

If we ask, 'Did the letter achieve its objective?', the answer is almost certainly 'Yes.' We would not have the letter if it did not – Philemon would almost certainly have torn it up, and it certainly would not have been included in the New Testament canon.

The social angle

We can also study the letter from a social angle, considering the question of slavery. Some are shocked that Paul made no attempt to abolish slavery. They argue that although he writes about it in his letters, he never suggests that it should be stopped. How can treating people as property be in keeping with the Bible's teaching about the value that God places on our lives?

But this view is misinformed. In fact, Paul does condemn slave trading (along with murder, adultery and lying in 1 Timothy 1:10). His unwillingness to seek the abolition of slavery can be explained by the fact that about two-thirds of the population of the Roman empire were slaves – to have argued for its abolition would have been to argue for chaos in society. Paul preferred to be known as a preacher of the gospel rather than as a champion of social causes.

Instead, he just broke slavery from the inside by changing the relationships and attitudes involved. So he urges Philemon to see Onesimus as a brother, not as a piece of property. He writes about Onesimus as 'my son'; who is 'dear to me'. In his letters to the Colossians and the Ephesians he also suggests that masters and slaves should have new attitudes to each other. He knew that eventually such a perspective would undermine the very foundations of slavery.

The spiritual angle

But there is a spiritual side to this letter that we must look at. I believe it is in our Bible because it is a perfect picture of our salvation. We are the slave who ran away from God. We were no use to God, but Jesus came and paid our debts and presented us back to God as a useful servant again. So we have a picture of justification – Onesimus is to be received as a son – and we have a picture of sanctification – now he is useful to his master.

The ethical angle

Paul was simply doing for the slave Onesimus what Jesus had done for him. He was saying to Onesimus, 'Jesus paid for you and rescued you and recycled you and sent you back to serve the Father. Now you go and do that to others.' In other words, our relationships to others are conditioned by what Christ has done for us. We must recycle people and send them back to the

Father. We must be willing to pay the price for them, as Christ paid the price for us.

Conclusion

So our behaviour towards others is to be based on the way that God has treated us.

We are to accept as we are accepted, forgive as we are forgiven, show mercy as we have received mercy, love as we are loved. If we don't do this, it means that we demonstrate we have not really understood God's grace (see the parable of the unforgiving servant).

Paul is showing here that his personal salvation in Christ became the way he chose to live. All that Christ did for him, he now did for others. It's a beautiful example of 'working out your salvation.'

52.

1 AND 2 TIMOTHY AND TITUS

Introduction

Paul's letters to Timothy and Titus tend to be seen together for two quite different reasons. On the one hand, they are different from the other letters that Paul wrote, while on the other hand, the three letters themselves are so similar to each other. So commentators regularly deal with the three at once. As we shall see, this makes eminent sense, though the assumptions made by the scholars are not always correct.

Unlike the other letters

The letters stand out because, with the sole exception of Philemon, Paul's letters are directed to churches, and also, while not without theological comment, the letters are primarily practical. Most of his other epistles focus in the first half upon doctrinal matters, with practical issues being covered in the second half, but in these letters the practical advice is given throughout. Paul gives brief comments upon a number of issues, refraining from the more detailed treatments that he gives in his other letters.

Like each other

Scholars have long recognized that the three letters form a distinct group. The same author writes them at the same time for the same reasons, even though their destinations are varied.

Authorship

But these features of the epistles have led to doubts concerning Paul's authorship. The reasons given are listed below:

Style – internal differences

Their content, style and vocabulary make them stand apart from his other work. Word searches have suggested a low correspondence between his vocabulary in these letters compared with that in his earlier work.

Content – external differences

Other scholars suggest that Paul describes a different sort of Christianity in these epistles compared to his other work. Whereas the Paul of the other letters wrote of faith, here the author adds the definite article – *the* faith. He seems to describe a more structured ministry than previously. His battles with the Gnostic heresy seem more developed, and in the outworking of his faith he appears to favour pagan rather than Christian ideals – for example, 'moderation in all things'.

Itinerary

Other scholars suggest that Paul cannot have written the letters because they don't fit into the itinerary of the end of Paul's life as described in Acts.

The differences explained

In fact the differences between these letters and some of Paul's other work can easily be explained.

First, they are written much later. Any author will change his style over time, and this can easily account for the changes observed. We need not assume that there is a different author.

Secondly, not only is Paul older, but the churches are older too. Many will be 'second-generation' Christians, and the church structures may indeed have changed. Paul's writings merely reflect this.

Thirdly, it is no surprise that the details about Paul's journeys don't fit in with Luke's account in Acts, because Acts does not include the last years of Paul's life. It finishes with Paul under house arrest in Rome, but much happened after he was released, as reflected in the epistles. He was acquitted, released and was able to continue his ministry, visiting Crete and possibly Spain before being arrested again after he was betrayed by Alexander the metalworker. 2 Timothy is written during Paul's second imprisonment.

So I am quite convinced that Paul wrote these three letters. They were written in the last months of his life. He wrote to his young friends and colleagues, Timothy and Titus, to help save the churches they had been sent to from dying.

Pastoral epistles?

These letters are commonly known as the 'Pastoral Epistles' – a title coined in 1703 by D. N. Berdot. But in spite of its popularity, it is a misleading description. First, these letters are no more 'pastoral' than any other letters of Paul. Every letter he wrote was pastoral, for they dealt with pastoral problems, including Romans, which is mistakenly said to outline Paul's theological outlook.

Secondly, these letters are not addressed to pastors. Timothy and Titus were not 'pastors' as such, and the letters were not intended for the settled, permanent church leadership that we find today. We must be careful not to read later developments back into the New Testament.

The danger of calling these letters 'pastoral' is that they tend to be treated as a handbook for pastors, as if they describe 'how to organize the local church'. It is true that they include instructions, but they focus upon the need for elders and deacons, not pastors, and they expect a number of men to be appointed as elders. These letters are not a mandate for one-man leadership, as we shall see.

Furthermore, as a manual for pastors they are very inadequate, since there is no advice on areas that one would expect to be included. There is no mention of how to choose elders, what their duties are, how many there should be, and what the length of their term of office should be. The letters mention preaching, but omit leading worship, apart from small references to prayer. Although we can glean some details, it is clear that providing advice for pastors is not their purpose. We have to assume that Timothy and Titus already knew all they needed to know on such matters.

Evangelistic epistles?

To label the letters 'pastoral' suggests that they are inward looking, but Paul's concern is not confined to the local church. In Paul's thinking, leadership is important because it affects the membership, and membership is important because the quality of the believers determines the effectiveness of their witness to the outside world. In fact, the whole thrust of the letters is to get the church right in order for the world to be evangelized. So some would argue that 'evangelistic epistles' would be a more apt description. After all, this concern for evangelism runs throughout the letters. Paul writes of the importance of good deeds that 'adorn the gospel', thus making the gospel attractive to unbelievers. Reputation with unbelievers is crucial and is a measure of a man's suitability for eldership. Timothy is specifically told to do 'the work of an evangelist'.

At the same time, Paul urges his colleagues to deal with what makes the gospel repellent. The false teachers were wrecking the character of the church and creating barriers for the gospel. The relationships between members did not adorn the gospel – rather, they discouraged outsiders from wanting to hear what the church believed. Paul believed it was crucial to sort out the church, if the gospel was to make headway in the neighbourhood. He tells Timothy that God 'wants all men to be saved', and therefore they must make sure that God's people are a positive witness to his reality.

Apostolic epistles

But to call the letters 'evangelistic' would not be strictly accurate either. The best description is that they are apostolic epistles, because Timothy and Titus were actually what we might call 'apostolic delegates'. When we read between the lines of the letters we find that their function is not to be pastors to the churches they were sent to, nor to be evangelists. Rather, Paul has sent them with his authority as apostolic delegates.

When Paul and his team saw a group of believers established in an area, their follow-up would include one or more of four forms. Paul would return to the church to see how they were getting on; or he would send letters to them; or he would send one of his team back to the church for a period; or he would leave one of the team there to help the church become established. So this is where the role of the 'apostolic delegate' is seen.

The title 'apostle' requires some explanation, for it is a much-misunderstood term. It literally means 'sent one' and is used with reference to several groups in the New Testament.

'Apostle' is one of a number of titles for individuals involved in Christian ministry in the New Testament. The Greek word *episcopos* is also used, from which we get the word 'episcopal'. An *episcopos* is someone who is an overseer of a church. The word 'elder' is also used, taken from the Greek word *presbuteros*, from which we derive the word 'Presbyterian'. In fact *presbuteros* and *episcopos* were interchangeable – they simply meant older, more mature Christians who oversaw the work. One word describes their character, the other their function.

Finally, we have the word *diaconos* which means 'servant', someone who looks after the practical side of a church.

So in the New Testament, the apostle planted the church, made sure it was firmly rooted, and handed it on to the overseers/elders and deacons.

The key thing is that all these ministries were always plural. There is no such thing as one-man ministry in the New Testament. There was a team of apostles, there was a team of elders, there was a team of deacons. In those days they had many bishops to one church, not many churches to one bishop – that's a complete reversal of the New Testament situation.

Only one man in the New Testament was an apostle, an overseer and a deacon at the same time – his name was Judas Iscariot! – If you read Acts 1 carefully, you will see that Peter said, 'We'll have to replace Judas – we'll have to find another apostle/overseer/deacon to replace him.' So I don't think that's a good precedent for combining these three ministries!

Normally these ministries are separate and different. An apostle should plant a church, reach the point where it has elders and deacons, and then leave it, his work having finished. For example, in Paul's letter to Titus, we read that Paul left Titus in Crete to complete the job by appointing elders in every city and then meet with Paul in Rome. Unfortunately, ever since the first century AD, the roles of apostles and elders/bishops have got confused, and we finished up with one bishop over many churches or a person in a church calling himself an apostle. This is very different from the New Testament situation.

The apostolic team

So it was in the context of the apostolic team that Timothy and Titus operated. Paul had planted churches, and their job was to sort out problems that arose later. Timothy was sent to Ephesus and Titus was left behind in Crete, both in the capacity of apostolic delegates (or 'trouble-shooters'), to sort things out on a short-term assignment. In both cases Paul urged them to do the job as quickly as possible before joining him in Rome.

This was not the first time they had been given this role. Both men had been sent to Corinth at different times and with different results. Timothy had struggled, but Titus had been rather more successful. The different outcomes to their work can be accounted for in part by their differing approaches to conflict. Timothy was a timid man needing a lot of encouragement. Titus, by contrast, was tougher in his approach. So Titus simply needed to be told what to do, while Timothy needed a great deal of encouragement to stir up the gift that was in him. Paul had to remind him that God had given him a spirit of power and of love and of a sound mind.

A study of the way Paul communicates in the two letters suggests that he was especially fond of Timothy. He calls Timothy 'my dear son'. It seems likely that Timothy was the nearest Paul ever came to having a family of his own. There was a relationship with Timothy that was special, and it is probable that Paul saw Timothy as his deputy, in spite of their difference in temperament and background.

It is not clear exactly how much authority the two men had to carry out their work. Timothy is frequently told to 'command' the church, but this was according to the apostolic doctrine that Paul taught, not according to his own ideas.

What is clear is that the authority was not hierarchical, nor was it successive. The apostolic delegates' job was completed when they handed the leadership of the church to elders and deacons who could continue leadership under Christ's direction. They did not 'create' further apostles.

In these three letters, Paul wants his two friends to ensure that the churches in both places have sound leadership and a sound membership. As always, Paul was not after quantity but quality. He wanted quality leaders and quality members, because he knew that this would lead to a large quantity of converts.

It is interesting to note what Paul doesn't ask. He makes no reference to the size of the church or its leadership, but seems more concerned with the quality of the leadership and the membership. He left Titus in Crete to improve the quality of the membership, but in Ephesus it was the quality of the leadership that was not right. The letter to Titus tells you what kind of members an apostle should leave behind, but the letters to Timothy consider the kind of leadership that is necessary.

We can look at the letters in three ways: from the point of view of the writer, from the point of view of the readers, Titus and Timothy, and finally from looking at the situations in Crete and Ephesus that needed the guidance of these apostolic delegates.

I find it amazing that anyone can question whether Paul is the genuine author, since we can construct the whole of Paul's life from these letters. There is more personal information about Paul in these letters than in any other, so it is hard to imagine that they are not from Paul.

The pattern of Paul's life

Past changes

Paul writes of the changes in his life, reflecting on how, as a blasphemer and violent man, he had persecuted the Church of God and put himself on the wrong side of Christ. He calls himself the worst of sinners and is full of thanks to God, who apprehended and appointed him as the apostle to the Gentiles. When God forgives us, he forgets what we once did, but we never will, and Paul's reflections demonstrate this.

Present circumstances

Paul tells his younger colleagues about the difficulties he was experiencing and his recent history. In 1 Timothy we read that he had visited Ephesus, Crete, Nicopolis, Corinth, Miletus, Troas and Spain for the first time. In 2 Timothy he reflects on his situation in prison in Rome – he doesn't have the same freedom he had previously enjoyed when under house arrest. Now he's in a condemned cell, having been betrayed by Alexander the metalworker and having packed in such a hurry that he left his overcoat and his notebooks behind. In this letter he asks Timothy to come quickly and bring these items before winter. He knows that he could be there some time and that Nero was unpredictable and couldn't be relied on to be just and fair.

Future prospects

So it is with this moving backdrop that Paul writes to Timothy, his young friend. We might call it his 'last will and testament'. He is over sixty and is aware that his life is drawing to an end. During his first imprisonment, Luke wrote the Book of Acts, mainly as a defence to prove to the Roman authorities that Paul did not deserve death. But in this second imprisonment, Paul knew that such defence would not be of any help, and he feared the worst. The letter reflects his sadness that Demas had deserted him and others had been cowardly, refusing to support him. Now it is time to hand on the baton to Timothy, who is still young and can carry on with this work. He writes of his work done, a course run, a fight won.

The purpose of Paul's life

As well as the pattern of his life, we also see the purpose of his life. It is clear from his letters that Paul lived for the gospel (also described as 'the faith' and 'the truth' in these letters) and urged his young colleagues to have the same attitude. This was the compelling motivation for all that he did. As a result he wanted to outline God's activity and man's response so that his young companions in the work, and ultimately the churches, would receive teaching that was 'sound'. The Greek word he uses means 'healthy', and Paul saw this as the perfect antidote to the poisonous words offered by false teachers and ungodly men in the congregations.

Objective (divine)

GOD

In parts of each letter Paul focuses upon what God has done. He writes of God's personality, his love and grace, and calls him 'the Saviour'. God is more commonly known as the Judge, with Jesus as 'the Saviour', but calling God the Saviour fits in with what we know of God the Father taking the initiative in sending his Son and committing all judgement on the Last Day to the Son.

Other titles describe the majesty of God's character in these letters. He is the King of Ages (i.e. eternal), immortal, invisible, whom no one has seen or can see and who dwells in unapproachable light. He is the only wise God, the Living God, the King of Kings and the Lord of Lords.

JESUS

Jesus is seen as both Judge and Saviour. His work on the cross is described in various ways. We are told that 'Christ Jesus came into the world to save sinners', that he 'destroyed death and brought immortality to light' and that his death was atonement for everyone. Furthermore, we are given a short outline of his life: 'He appeared in a body, was vindicated by the Spirit, was seen by angels, was preached among nations, was believed on in the world and was taken up in glory' (1 Timothy 3:16).

THE HOLY SPIRIT

Paul also mentions two aspects of the Holy Spirit's work. First, he writes of the experience of the Spirit, reminding Timothy of the time when he received a gift of the Spirit, when Paul and others laid hands on him. He is reminded that the Holy Spirit is a Spirit of love, power and self-control.

Secondly, he writes about the exercise of the spiritual gifts, urging Timothy to use what he was given when hands were laid on him. We don't know the gift(s) he received at this point, or whether the two references to 'laying on of hands' in 1 and 2 Timothy refer to his conversion or ordination. But either way, he is encouraged to use what he has received.

Subjective – (human)

We move next to consider what man's response should be to God's initiative.

Throughout his writings Paul makes it clear that there are three dimensions to salvation for the believer, and these letters are no exception. Salvation is not instantaneous or automatic, but three tenses are used to describe the process of salvation.

PAST (JUSTIFICATION) – EXPERIENTIAL

Paul teaches that salvation is past, in that we look back to a starting point when we first trusted Christ. The prepositions used are vital. Salvation comes by grace, not by good deeds or 'works of the Law'. Believers are saved from bad deeds, not primarily from hell, as some would argue. Finally, salvation comes through the Holy Spirit.

In Titus, Paul writes of the 'bath of regeneration', which speaks of the baptism by water and baptism in the Holy Spirit. Both are needed for a proper initiation into the Kingdom.

PRESENT (SANCTIFICATION) – ETHICAL

The present aspect of salvation is Paul's major concern, though not his primary focus. Paul is clear that doctrine is to be done. He has no time for academic debate, intellectual gymnastics and speculative arguments that don't change lives.

The gospel leads to good deeds. It leads to separation from evil and the grace to say no to ungodliness. Positively, we are set apart for good. We are like vessels for noble use, cleansed from dirty uses.

Good deeds lead to the gospel. The letters remind us that good living by Christian believers can draw people to seek God for themselves.

FUTURE (GLORIFICATION) – ESCHATOLOGICAL

But that is not the end of salvation, for none of us is fully saved yet. We are simply on the way of salvation, travelling a road called The Way. Indeed, I am worried when someone tells me, 'Seven people were saved on Sunday night.' My standard reply is, 'You mean that seven people *began* to be saved on Sunday night.' They are not completely saved yet.

And for Paul, future salvation was the primary focus of the three. Eternal life is something we inherit, but in the meantime we need to keep persevering in our faith. Paul writes of those who have wandered away from the faith. He warns Timothy that he must watch his life and doctrine closely, for he will save himself and his hearers.

In these letters Paul includes 'five faithful sayings', and one of these, in 2 Timothy 2:11, serves to illustrate this point. Let us take it line by line.

Positive:
'If we died with him, we will also live with him' (referring to conversion/baptism and not martyrdom)
'If we endure we will also reign with him.'

Negative:
'If we deny/disown him, he will also disown us.'

But the final line changes the pattern: 'If we are faithless, he will remain faithful, for he cannot disown himself.' Some argue that this means a believer can never be lost. But all that God is promising is that he will remain true to himself. Paul contrasts God's stability with our instability. It is true that no believer can be lost, but someone who is faithless actually ceases to be a believer, because they are literally faith-less. In these letters, Paul writes of those who 'wander' from the faith, implying that while they used to believe, they no longer do.

Part of Paul's understanding about future salvation is that we will win a crown. We must continue to persevere so that we may receive all that God has for us.

John Calvin, the influential French theologian, is often quoted as teaching that once a person trusts Christ, their future salvation is secure. But he actually wrote:

> *Still our redemption would be imperfect if he did not lead us ever onward toward the final goal of our salvation. Accordingly, the moment we turn away even slightly from him, our salvation which rests firmly in him gradually vanishes away. As a result, all those who do not repose in him voluntarily deprive themselves of all grace.*

I rarely use the word 'salvation' today, preferring instead the word 'recycled'. If someone asks me what job I'm in, I tell them I'm in the recycling business. Their look tells me that I am in a favourable occupation. It's only when I tell them that I don't recycle paper and metal, but that people are my raw material, that they begin to look alarmed. But I believe this picture is thoroughly biblical. After all, it is people who need to be recycled. They need be restored to the original purpose for which they were made. Indeed, the word 'Gehenna' in the New Testament was borrowed from Jerusalem's rubbish dump.

An important verse for our understanding of salvation is Titus 3:5, which reminds us that God has saved us through water baptism and Spirit baptism. The words are very similar to John 3:5, which tells us we are born again out of water and Spirit. In fact, as I show in my book, *The Normal Christian Birth* (Hodder & Stoughton, 1989), Paul saw water baptism and Spirit baptism as essential to salvation. It is only because we have thought of being saved as getting a ticket to heaven that we get into the false thinking that those two baptisms are not essential to salvation. Once we see salvation as a recycling process, these two things become an essential part. Paul says God has saved us through the bath of regeneration and the renewal of the Holy Spirit, which he poured out upon us generously. So recycling starts in our baptism and it continues as we are bathed in the Holy Spirit.

Timothy and Titus

The contrast between Timothy and Titus is striking. Titus was an uncircumcised Gentile from a pagan background. Timothy was born in Lystra, one of the first towns Paul evangelized in Galatia. The fellowship in Lystra recommended Timothy to Paul as a good understudy, and so their relationship began.

Timothy had a Jewish mother and a Jewish grandmother who taught him the Scriptures when he was a child. He was not circumcised, because his father was not a Jew, but later Paul did circumcise him, not because he thought circumcision did anything for Timothy but because he thought it would help when he visited a synagogue. Paul was keen that his teams did not give unnecessary offence.

The New Testament includes reference to three special assignments for Timothy before visiting Ephesus. He was sent to Thessalonica, to Corinth and to Philippi as Paul's delegate. He also collaborated with Paul in writing at least six letters: the two letters to the Thessalonians, the two to the Corinthians, the letter to the Philippians and the one to Philemon. However, Timothy was not generally healthy. He had recurring digestive trouble, so that Paul told him to take a little wine for his stomach's sake. Indeed, Paul felt it necessary to urge Timothy to be like a soldier or an athlete in practising the self-discipline required for Christian ministry. We don't know if Timothy managed to arrive in Rome before Paul was executed, but we can see how eager Paul is for him to come in his second letter to him.

In contrast to his letters to Timothy, Paul's letter to Titus contains few personal references. Titus is clearly an excellent worker who achieved great results in Corinth, and it seems Paul has total confidence in him. But we can glean relatively little about him from the letter. Paul doesn't give Titus the same sort of exhortations as Timothy.

Most of Paul's letters hint at the crisis or difficulty needing to be addressed in the opening section, and Titus is no exception. Although there were churches in every city in Crete, there were *no elders* to lead them, and so it was urgent that somebody appointed local leaders who could help them to grow. Titus' task was to see that such elders were appointed.

The letters to Timothy were written because the church in Ephesus had the wrong elders. So Timothy was given the task of getting rid of the *wrong elders* and putting the right ones in place. In fact, the job in Ephesus seems more suited to Titus than Timothy!

Paul was concerned about the quality of membership in Crete. From his comments it seems that their pagan background was still influencing them and, in turn, their life as a church. Cretans had a reputation for poor behaviour, and this influence was being felt in the churches on the island. In Ephesus, by contrast, it is the leadership who require attention. In both cases there was false teaching. In Crete this was peripheral to the life of the church, whereas in Ephesus the bad teaching was given by these wrong leaders. So it was absolutely essential to the health of the church to do something about it.

We can split the work that Paul gives to both Timothy and Titus under three headings.

Complete the transition

The first task for them is to complete the transition from churches that are dependent on apostles to ones that are led by local leaders. They needed to become independent in the right sense of the word so that their contact with the founding workers could diminish.

Quality leaders

ELDERS

Paul impresses upon his two friends the sort of elders they should look for. He emphasizes character, with a particular focus upon the way the elder functions as head of his family, especially as the elder would often be the head of the home in which the church met. He mentions payment, arguing that someone who preaches and teaches is worthy of a 'double honorarium'.

It is interesting to note that Paul mentions the need for an elder to have a good reputation with outsiders. When a church chooses its elders, it can be very useful to consult with those outside the church for a recommendation. A good report can be a good sign.

Paul teaches that elders are male. If anyone asks me if a woman can be an elder, I reply that this is possible as long as

she's married to one wife! This is, after all, one of the qualifications for an elder. The weight of other passages convinced me
that eldership is a male responsibility, just as discipline in the
home is the father's ultimate responsibility.

Leaders often grumble that their problems would be
solved if only the members would follow them. My suspicion is
that the real problem is that most of them do! Inevitably people subconsciously follow their leaders. They may not follow
what the leaders say, but they do follow what the leaders do.
One of the awesome and frightening responsibilities of being a
church leader is that you see your own strengths and weaknesses appearing in the church. Of course, this is a particular
danger in a one-man ministry, where his character will become
the character of the fellowship. With a plurality of elders, individual leaders' strengths and weaknesses will tend to balance
each other out much better. It is partly for this reason that the
qualifications of church leaders (i.e. elders and deacons) focus
on character and not gift. It is not so much what a leader can *do*
that makes him a leader, but what he *is* both at home and in
public. The only ability required of elders is that they should
be able to teach, whether one-to-one or to a congregation.

DEACONS

The qualities required in a deacon are very similar, though there
is the suggestion that women also may be deacons. Paul writes
about women, but there is some dispute concerning whether
this is deacons' wives or female deacons (deaconesses). Anyone
who serves the church in a practical capacity must exhibit
godliness, however able they may be. The important thing in
working for the Lord in the church is relationships, not ability.

It is clear that there is no hierarchy. Appointment as a
deacon is not the first step on the ladder towards eldership,
even if it is sometimes seen that way. Deacons were concerned

with the temporal needs of the church, while the elders focused upon the spiritual needs.

Quality members

The letters also outline the importance of quality members on a whole array of practical matters. Paul writes of the importance of modesty within the church and of respectful behaviour within society, shown through their prayerful concern for their political leaders. He is also concerned that appropriate provision should be made for those in need within the household.

He teaches the importance of older women helping younger women, of respect being given to the elderly, and of deserving widows being provided for.

The letter to Titus focuses especially upon the quality of membership. Paul writes that godly character is to be seen in the church, in the home, in the workplace. In fact the letter is a wonderful church membership training class curriculum, showing how a member adorns the gospel. Paul's constant concern in these letters is that the church looks right to the world. It is interesting to note that the catalogue of virtues that Paul uses in this letter is not a Christian list but a Greek one. The Greeks did have a list of what they considered to be good in people, and Paul actually uses this pagan list and challenges Christians to live up to it.

This is not to suggest that the Church should ape the world's standards of morality, but it does mean that at the very least we should be what the world calls good. This implies, of course, that non-believers have discernment. They often keep Christians up to scratch!

The role of women

Perhaps the most controversial teaching in these epistles concerns women. Paul apparently imposes strict limitations on the ministry of women.[1] Feminist theologians dislike these letters. They make a number of claims:

1 *Pseudepigraphical.* Some say the letters are not by Paul but are a second-century forgery in his name. Thus they should not be part of the canon.

2 *Rabbinical.* Others argue that if these letters are from Paul, the teaching on women is a throwback to his rabbinical days before his conversion. As an old man he is returning to prejudices from his Jewish childhood.

3 *Cultural.* They argue that this teaching is purely cultural. If Jesus were alive today, he would have chosen six men and six women as apostles. The favourite phrase that sums up this position is to say that Paul was culturally conditioned. So Jesus' choice of 12 men to be his apostles was tactful, because in his day it would have been offensive to have women apostles – an argument which fails to realize that Jesus never did anything merely because it was 'diplomatic'! One of the compliments that the Pharisees paid him was, 'You pay no attention to any man.' If it had been right for him to do it, then he would have done it.

4 *Heretical.* Others claim that women were barred from teaching because women led many of the cults. The Church needed to distance itself from these practices, so it barred women from teaching. There is, however, no evidence to support this theory.

---

1 For a full discussion on this and related issues, see the author's *Leadership is Male* (Eagle, now Bethel, 1988).

5 *Educational*. The next argument suggests that the lack of education for women in Paul's day made it unwise for them to be in a teaching/leadership role. But if this was true, Paul should not have let uneducated men lead the Church. In Acts, the Sanhedrin describe the 12 apostles as uneducated men, and so they were.

But it is clear that Paul teaches that the gender differences between men and women still apply in the Church. We are not neutered in Christ; God wants us to be manly men and womanly women. Paul's teaching stands out against the modern descent towards 'personhood', where distinctions are minimized or obliterated altogether.

God made us men and women, and we need each other. He made us for different roles and responsibilities. When men behave like women and women behave like men, we are distorting God's creative beauty. So men are given the responsibility of leading. Although this is not popular teaching today, it's there in Scripture. We can't get round it.

Confront the trouble-makers

The second great task was to confront the trouble-makers. When Paul left the Ephesian elders for the last time, he told them that after his departure wolves would come in sheep's clothing into the very flock he had served. So in Timothy's day, that prophecy was coming true, which is why Paul sent Timothy to get rid of the wolves.

This false teaching is a common thread in these epistles. It is in the background in Titus and in the foreground in the letters to Timothy. Indeed, it was the precise reason why Paul wrote to Timothy. If you neglect a problem it just gets worse, but if you are willing to face up to it as soon as it appears, then the cure can be swifter in the long run.

The error they propagated

It is difficult to discover the precise nature of the teaching. Some argue that it was similar to second-century Gnosticism.

1 *Greek elements*. They believed that the body was evil and therefore taught that sex was wrong, and that a person needed to obey certain food laws to be acceptable to God. They also incorporated a dualistic understanding of the world and an over-realized eschatology (i.e. that the resurrection had already taken place).

2 *Jewish elements*. Their belief in food laws and their focus upon genealogies suggest a Jewish background. Paul's remarks suggest that they had their own interpretation of the Old Testament.

Paul was probably wrestling on two fronts – fighting a Hellenistic Judiasm that combined Greek and Jewish strands to form a potent attack against the gospel.

The example they promoted

We noted earlier that Paul tells Timothy that a good elder is 'worthy of double honour'. The text has been badly translated in most English versions, but the meaning is clear. An elder who labours in preaching and teaching is worthy of double honorarium. This implies a paid ministry and refers to those who preach the gospel to unbelievers and teach it to believers. By contrast, Timothy should not be paying bad elders anything at all, especially if they are lovers of money.

We can discern the character flaws in the elders by noting what Paul writes against. He says they had a form of godliness, but denied its power. They looked good on the outside, but inside their motivations were self-serving. Although seeming legalistic, they were licentious, proud about what they had achieved, and greedy for money, believing that somehow money was a reward for their piety.

The effect they produced

The effect of these leaders upon the church was catastrophic. Their false teaching operated like a gangrene in the body. They argued for a strange mixture of legalism and licence. Either will kill the liberty of the Spirit, and both together are especially serious. Leadership must spring from a pure heart, a good conscience and sincere faith, and these bad elders didn't have any of those three things. They were not only propagating errors, they were presenting a bad example.

Communicate the truth

The third important task when laying the foundation in a church is to communicate the truth. Ultimately the most important aspect of a church's life is good, consistent Bible teaching. Churches that are not receiving constant systematic teaching of God's word become very vulnerable to all kinds of mischief, but constant confrontation with the word of God – communication of the truth of the gospel – is going to enable growth in the lives of those who are taught.

Timothy had to confront the trouble-makers, face them with what they were doing, deal with it quickly, get them out of the way, and replace them with good elders. A church can stand anything from outside, but when it is attacked from the inside, that's a very dangerous situation.

Teaching included verbal instruction, exhortation and admonition. It was teaching with authority, not merely education or the imparting of information. But it also included the visual demonstration of the truth – Timothy and Titus were to expound the truth and be examples of the truth.

The message to be declared

Their message was to be based on what Paul calls 'the faith' and 'the truth'. There were three sources for them to use.

1 *The Scriptures.* The Old Testmanent was to be read publicly, as well as being preached and taught.
2 *The apostles' doctrine.* In Acts 2 we read of the new believers devoting themselves to the apostles' doctrine. Paul was among those whose reflections upon the coming of Christ were to be regarded as authoritative for the believers in the churches of the New Testament.
3 *Trustworthy sayings.* There were a number of sayings, almost credal statements, that were known to reflect the truth of the Scriptures. Five are mentioned in the letters.

To be faithful communicators, Timothy and Titus must show integrity in their handling of truth, and be prepared to do so 'in and out of season'. Paul describes the doctrine that should be taught as 'sound', which comes from a Greek word meaning 'healthy'. By contrast, the deviations from the apostles' doctrine are a disease, like gangrene in the body.

This teaching should not be limited to the members of the Church, but has a wider focus. Timothy is urged to 'do the work of an evangelist'.

The model to be demonstrated

The visual aspect of truth is also encouraged in these letters. Paul reminds Timothy that he has been a model to him in a number of areas; he writes of 'my teaching, lifestyle, purpose, faith, patience, love, endurance' (i.e. persecution and suffering) and being prepared to die. He is emphasizing that what you are says more than what you say. We must practise what we preach.

In the same way, he urges Timothy to be a good model to those whom he seeks to lead. Timothy's life before the church family and in the eyes of outsiders must be above reproach. Though this sounds daunting, the focus is not upon 'being perfect' but 'making progress'.

He is urged to flee from evil and pursue godliness. In this way his model of godly living can become a magnet to outsiders.

How do we apply these letters today?

1 *Purity is internal rather than external.* Any legalistic interpretations of the faith are by their nature external.

2 *Distinctions of age, sex and class still apply in Christian fellowship.* The verse used by some as a proof text for the obliteration of these distinctions (Galatians 3:28) only applies to our vertical relationship with God – that is, as far as God is concerned, these distinctions do not have any bearing on our eligibility for salvation.

3 *A church's goodness must equal and exceed the world's idea of what is good.* That's a very important principle, because the world is not fooled. The world knows what a good person is, and they expect to see good people in church. We have a responsibility to live good lives.

4 *Character is more important than ability.* Church leadership is about being a good model as well as a good manager; about being visible as well as audible.

5 *Shepherds are responsible for the state of the flock, not the sheep.* The Bible never blames the sheep for the state of the flock, only the shepherd. I speak to a lot of pastors who are only too ready to blame their people for the state of their churches, but God always holds the shepherds responsible for the state of the flock.

6 *Sound, healthy doctrine covers how we behave as well as what we believe.* In the Scriptures sound doctrine means belief translated into behaviour.

7 *The Church is a family but it has no father on earth.* It has a divine Father. All the people in the Church – leader and member alike – are brothers. That is very important. We are not to call anyone 'father'.

8 *Welfare within the Church must be discriminating.* We must not take on the responsibility of others. We are told that if the family of a widow is capable of looking after her, the Church should not undertake that responsibility. There is a misguided philanthropy that takes on too much welfare. The Church was told to take on the care of those widows who had no one to care for them. The Church has got to be sensible in the way it looks after the needy.

9 *A church's character is a reflection of the character of its leaders.* Members follow the leaders of a church, whether they like it or not.

10 *If the letters to Timothy and Titus teach us anything, it is that the biggest battles we face are inside the Church.* We need to contend for the truth of the gospel against some subtle distortions, four in particular today. The gospel is in danger of being:

- *Politicized* – the kingdom of God as a social programme for this world only
- *Feminized* – God as a doting mother rather than a disciplining father
- *Relativized* – without any absolute distinctions between true and false, right and wrong
- *Syncretized* – blended with other faiths in the name of world religion.

This requires a two-fold task: to explain the truth and expose error.

THROUGH
SUFFERING TO
GLORY

53.

 HEBREWS

Introduction

Difficult or delightful?

Among modern readers opinion about the Letter to the Hebrews is very divided. Some find it one of the most difficult letters of the New Testament. This is partly because, to Gentile eyes, it is a very Jewish letter, describing sacrifices, altars and priestly matters in some detail. A proper understanding of Hebrews requires a familiarity with the Old Testament Scriptures, especially the Book of Leviticus, which most Gentiles don't have. In addition, some of the arguments in Hebrews don't touch the modern mind. Who cares about angels and genealogies? They are hardly a major topic of conversation, even among Christians.

Furthermore, the Greek of the Letter to the Hebrews is very complicated, though it is widely regarded as the best Greek in the New Testament. The New Testament was written not in classical Greek but in *koine* Greek, the language of the streets as opposed to the language of the university. But Hebrews is nearer to the classical language than any other part of the New Testament. Even in English translation the language is refined and sophisticated, and for some this represents a barrier.

But Hebrews has its supporters. Some say it is the most delightful book in the whole Bible. They love it and revel in it, usually for one of three reasons.

1. THE MAGNIFICENT CHAPTER ON FAITH

This chapter is like taking a walk through a mausoleum, as the reader looks back into the past to the lives of the great heroes of faith. To those who find the detailed argument of the earlier chapters a bit tough, chapter 11 is something of a relief. At last there is something that registers with them.

2. THE LIGHT SHED ON THE OLD TESTAMENT

Hebrews deals with the question of how the Old Testament and the New Testament relate. It explains how we should treat the Law of Moses, as it unfolds the relationship of our Christian faith to the ritual of the temple and shows how the people of God have entered a new era of relationship with God. As such it provides many interpretive models for our understanding of the Old Testament as Christians.

3. WHAT IT TELLS US ABOUT CHRIST

Those who love Jesus love Hebrews, because it throws a light on him that no other part of the New Testament does. A favourite word of the writer of Hebrews is 'better'. Jesus is described as 'better' rather than 'the best' (though that is also true), because he is being compared with lesser alternatives that were attractive to the original readership. Jesus is better than the angels, better than the prophets, better than all other intermediaries.

The opinions that this is a difficult or a delightful book are really both extreme positions that miss the main point of the letter. The real key to Hebrews is the question, 'Why was it written?' Though it is a little complicated to find the answer, once you have found it, the whole letter opens up.

Who was the author?

But before we look at why the letter was written, we need to consider who wrote it. One scholar called this 'the riddle of the New Testament', for it is the only New Testament book whose authorship is definitely unknown. There have been all sorts of guesses. Some older versions of the King James translation of the Bible call it 'the Epistle of Paul to the Hebrews', but this is sheer guesswork. I don't think Paul wrote it. It is not his style or his language. Others have suggested that it might have been written by Barnabas, in part because of the large amount of encouragement within its pages. Some say Stephen, others support Silas or Apollos. One suggestion is that the author was Priscilla, and the lack of a name was to conceal the fact that a woman wrote it, though I think this is very unlikely. Ultimately I have to say – with the great church Father, Origen of Alexandria – God alone knows who wrote it!

Where was the letter sent to?

We are also uncertain where the letter was sent. The only address on it is 'to the Hebrews', which is hardly specific! Once again there are many suggestions. Some say it was sent to Alexandria, others say Antioch or Jerusalem or Ephesus. We cannot be certain, but there is a big clue right at the end. The writer says that 'everyone *from* Italy sends greetings'. So I think it is a sensible deduction to say it was sent *to* Italy, which suggests that it was meant for the church in Rome.

Yet we can clearly see that the Letter to the Hebrews was written a bit later than the Letter to the Romans, because Hebrews refers to certain things that had not yet happened when Paul wrote Romans. So I am assuming that Hebrews was written to the Christians in Rome and, in view of the title, to that half of the church that was Jewish. But this raises the question, 'Why would a letter be needed for half the church?'

When was the letter sent?

Clearly, the first leaders of the church in Rome have died, because near the end of the letter the writer says, 'remember your leaders'. The temple and its sacrifices were still in operation, because the writer talks about them in the present tense. So he must have written the letter before AD 70, when the temple was destroyed and the sacrifices ceased. So Hebrews was written after Paul wrote to the Romans in AD 55 and before AD 70.

Nero

The reason for the writing of the letter becomes clear when we consider what happened during this period. The situation had changed considerably since the time of Paul's Letter to the Romans, largely because of Nero's accession to the imperial throne. We noted in our study of Romans (see *ch. 47*) that under Claudius some 10,000 Jews were banished from Rome in the early AD 50s, before Paul wrote his letter. (It was at this point that Priscilla and Aquila fled to Corinth, as mentioned in Acts.) The church in Rome became increasingly Gentile as a result, so that when the Jews returned after the death of Claudius in AD 54, tensions were developing between the Jewish believers and those with a Gentile background, who were now leading the fellowship. We saw in our study of Romans that Paul wrote to help the Jews to reintegrate alongside their Gentile brethren.

But Nero's reign was a time of great suffering for the church. Nero, like Hitler, did some good things in the beginning. If you read the life of Hitler, you will find that he saved Germany from unemployment and inflation, built great roads, and ordered the production of the Volkswagen Beetle as 'the people's car'. In the same way, when you read the history of Nero, you find that he did a lot of good things for Rome in the beginning. He listened to other people's advice and was able to rule wisely. But there came a point when Nero stopped listening and became a dictator. Just as Hitler wanted to rebuild Berlin, so Nero wanted to rebuild Rome. He had big ideas for pulling everything down and building the grandest buildings that had ever been built. In short, he became a megalomaniac, and the people who began to suffer more than anybody else were the Christians, and many of them were killed by Nero.

In the Letter to the Romans there is no trace of persecution. The church has to fight immorality in Rome, but there isn't yet any direct persecution. But in the Letter to the Hebrews there is one section which tells us the kind of persecution they were already suffering. None of them had yet been martyred, which means we are in the middle of Nero's reign. Their homes were being vandalized. Their possessions were being confiscated. Some of them had been in prison – hence the reference towards the end of the letter to visiting 'those who are in prison'. Timothy is mentioned as one of those who had been imprisoned and released. So it was getting pretty tough to be a Christian. It wasn't costing them their lives at this point, but it was costing them pretty well everything else.

Jewish believers

Of course, this was happening to all the believers, whether they were Gentiles or Jews, so why was this letter written only to the Jewish believers? The answer is very simple and explains the whole letter. The Jews had a way of escape from suffering that was not open to the Gentile believers. The Jewish believers could get out of trouble by going back to the synagogue. At this time Christianity was illegal, but Judaism was still legal, with synagogues officially 'registered'. The church was an underground church, rather as in the Communist era in Russia and China, and in some parts of the Muslim world today.

So the Jewish believers could return to the synagogue and so take their families out of persecution. They could even claim to be going back to the same God. But the cost of doing it – indeed, the only way for them to get back into the Jewish synagogue – was to publicly deny their faith in Jesus. It was a great dilemma. They had heard about Jesus and believed he was the Messiah. But having joined the church, they now found their children being persecuted at school, their windows being smashed and their property being confiscated. They knew that if they took their families back into the synagogue they would be safe. But they would have to say in front of the synagogue, 'I deny that Jesus is the Messiah.'

So the letter is written primarily to Jewish believers against the background of persecution. The writer uses sailing metaphors to urge them to stand firm – 'don't pull up your anchors, don't drift away, don't lower your sails' – which may suggest that he had a sailing background.

Exhortation and exposition

At the end he says he has written a 'short letter of exhortation'. It is certainly a letter of exhortation, but it is not very short! An exhortation is very practical. He is not trying to teach them doctrine, but is trying to stop this drift back to the synagogue. Everything he says from beginning to end is aimed at that problem. He throws everything at them. He appeals to them, warns them, speaks tenderly yet strongly. He uses every argument he can, because he fears they will lose their salvation if they go back to Judaism.

Appreciating this passionate appeal will save us from seeing the book as a doctrinal exposition. Many preachers I have heard expound this letter as if it were purely a study of Christ, and they miss the practical element. According to the *Oxford English Dictionary*, the word 'exhort' means 'to admonish urgently, to urge someone to a course of action'. The whole letter is urging people to a particular course of action. The appeal is both negative and positive: 'Please don't go back, but do go on.'

There's a true story of someone who died in the potholes of Yorkshire. This is what the coroner said at the inquest: 'If he had just kept moving he would be alive today.' Instead he sat down and stayed in one place, and hypothermia set in. This is the message of the Letter to the Hebrews: 'Keep moving!'

But this is not the language of rebuke. The author identifies with his readers. He says, 'Let us go on', putting himself alongside them. Indeed, he calls himself a paraclete (which is also the title given to the Holy Spirit in John's Gospel and means 'standby, strengthener'). We might think of him as a climber going back for someone at the end of the rope and climbing with them to help them reach the summit.

The pattern of the letter is unusual for the New Testament, as the writer constantly alternates between exposition and exhortation. (Most of the New Testament books have doctrine first and application second.) He is constantly arguing and appealing, and the proportions of the argument and the appeal change as we go through the letter.

In chapters 1 and 2 we have a long argument and a short appeal. But gradually, as you read the book there are shorter arguments and longer appeals, until chapter 11 gives a short exposition, followed by a long appeal in chapters 12 and 13. So the writer presents more argument and less appeal at the beginning, and less argument and more appeal at the end. This is one reason why the earlier part is a little more difficult to understand than the later.

The appeal sections are replete with the phrase 'Let us ...' For example: 'Let us lay aside every handicap and keep running, looking to Jesus'; 'Let us go on'; 'Let us go for the finish'; 'Let us go for the prize'. 'Let us' occurs thirteen times in the whole letter, but eight times in this last section. It is a great build-up to a personal appeal, which would move all but the most hard-hearted.

Most of the arguments are taken from the Old Testament, which was the only Scripture they then had (apart from Paul's Letter to the Romans). So these arguments would have been readily accepted by the Jewish believers. The writer treats the Old Testament in two ways: negatively, contrasting the inferior life under the Old Covenant with that enjoyed by the New Covenant believer; and positively, noting the continuity between the Testaments and the many examples we can emulate. To quote Augustine, 'The New is in the Old concealed, the Old is in the New revealed.'

Language and structure

Many find the language and structure of Hebrews difficult to grasp. The diagram opposite will help us. It gives us an outline of the shape of chapters 1–2, showing the division between heaven and earth. God in heaven spoke his words through angels and to the prophets in bits and pieces. You can piece together the whole of the life of Jesus from the Old Testament. It is like a jigsaw puzzle when the box is first opened. The prophets gave the word to men, but in fact that word brought death to them, for the word of the Law brought death.

Next we see how 'in these last days he has spoken to us through his Son who died.' The Son has spoken to us through the apostles. We hear the words of the prophets in the Old Testament and the words of the apostles in the New Testament.

Jesus became a man, died and then returned to heaven as our Pioneer. 'Pioneer' is a favourite title for Jesus in the Letter to the Hebrews. It means 'the Trailblazer', the one who went

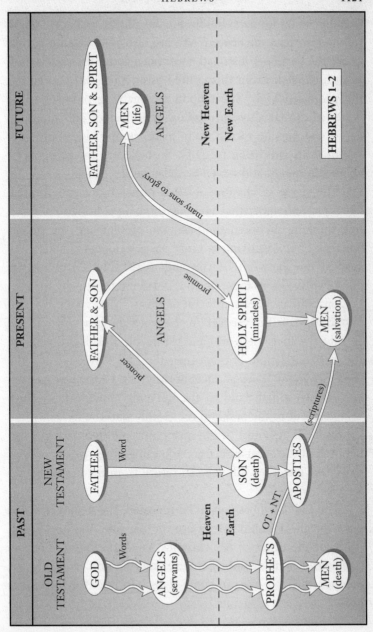

PAST — PRESENT — FUTURE

OLD TESTAMENT / NEW TESTAMENT

HEBREWS 1–2

ahead in order for us to follow. He did all this so that we might follow him back to heaven. We are also told that he is now above the angels. A man had never been above the angels until Jesus ascended. From this exalted position he has poured out the promised Holy Spirit upon us, enabling miracles to be done. Men may therefore follow the Pioneer and finish up above the angels, taking their place among the many sons whom Jesus will bring to glory. So believers are going to be above the angels, and served by the angels.

The shape of chapters 4–10 is rather more complicated. We must remember that Hebrew thinking is horizontal time-line thinking, between the past, the present and the future, whereas Greek thinking is more space-oriented thinking – a vertical line between heaven and earth. The Letter to the Hebrews combines these two outlooks, and this is why the outline opposite may seem difficult to grasp.

So we have the vertical line between the heavenly and the earthly, the invisible world and the visible world, and we have the horizontal time-line between the Old Covenant and the New Covenant. They all meet at the cross. Faith takes us from the earthly and the old to the heavenly and the new. Faith brings us out of the past and the earthly into the heavenly and the future. The bottom-right quadrant reminds us that you can fall back in the other direction. You can go back from the New Covenant into the Old; you can return from the heavenly into the earthly again.

The old sacrifices had to be repeated; the new sacrifice is once for all. The old priests are on one side; the one Priest, Jesus, of the order of Melchizedek, is on the other. The old sanctuary has its closed tabernacle, and the new sanctuary has its open throne – we can come right into the Holy of Holies now.

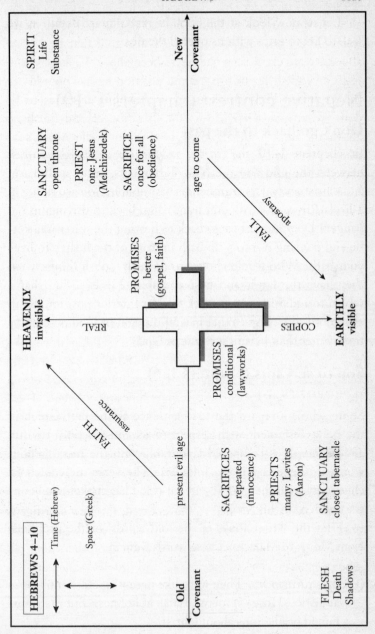

HEBREWS 4–10

Time (Hebrew)
Space (Greek)

Old Covenant

New Covenant

HEAVENLY invisible

EARTHLY visible

REAL

COPIES

FAITH
assurance

FALL
apostasy

present evil age

age to come

SPIRIT
Life
Substance

SANCTUARY
open throne

PRIEST
one: Jesus
(Melchizedek)

SACRIFICE
once for all
(obedience)

PROMISES
better
(gospel, faith)

PROMISES
conditional
(law, works)

SACRIFICES
repeated
(innocence)

PRIESTS
many: Levites
(Aaron)

SANCTUARY
closed tabernacle

FLESH
Death
Shadows

Let us now look at the book in rather more detail, as we seek to get to grips with its overall themes.

Negative contrast (chapters 1–10)

Don't go back to the past

In chapters 1–10 the writer is drawing a sharp contrast between the Old and the New Testaments, between Judaism and Christianity. His argument is very simple. You are riding in a Rolls-Royce now; do you want to go back to driving an old banger? Do you want to go back to heating the water in a kettle and pouring it into a tin bath in front of the hearth to have your bath? Who would choose to do such foolish things when they have the latest and best available? He is saying that a return to Judaism is to go back to a far inferior position. So in chapters 1–6 he argues that having the Son of God is so many times *better* than having servants of God.

Son to servants (chapters 1–6)

1. PROPHETS (1:1–3)

Some scholars regard the first sentence as the best Greek in the New Testament with respect to its construction, rhythm and beauty. It is compared favourably with the more famous words in Genesis 1:1 and John 1:1. The verse includes both continuity with the Old Testament (God has spoken) and contrast with it (by his Son).

First the writer looks at the 'old words' of the prophets, from Moses to Malachi. These words were in:

(a) *Many fragments*. They were like jigsaw pieces. Amos looks at justice, Hosea at mercy, Isaiah at holiness. But each contained predictions about Christ.

(b) *Many forms.* The picture on the lid of the 'jigsaw' varied too. There was prose, poetry, prediction, history, parable, law, love-songs and visions. The communication was through ordinary men and women from a wide range of social backgrounds.

Then the writer compares these previous methods with the 'new words'. He says that in these 'last days' (i.e. in the final period of history, since the coming of Christ) God has given us a final means of communication. This 'Word' has been given to us as believers. This time it was not fragmentary but 'by a Son'. He goes on to give us a three-dimensional view of Jesus.

(a) Creation

(i) *He gets it all in the end.* God has made Jesus the heir of all things. So the Son will one day have it all. Psalm 2:8 speaks of the nations being his inheritance. So the One whose own clothes were gambled for at the end of his first visit will return and reign over all kingdoms and peoples.

(ii) *He made it all in the beginning.* This Son started it all. He was not just a humble carpenter, but was there at the very beginning as the Creator, initiating and deciding upon creation.

(iii) *He keeps it all going meanwhile.* While he was on earth he demonstrated his power to 'still the storm'. In his risen life, he is at the helm of the universe, holding it all together.

(b) Creator

(i) We see a *reflection of his brightness.* Just as sunshine is to the sun, so his glory is to the Son. Glory is part of his intrinsic being.

(ii) He is the *stamp of God's likeness.* Just as a seal is made by an impression, so Christ is the exact impression of God. When we see Jesus, we see the Father.

(c) Creature

(i) *Saviour on a cross.* Despite all we have said, this glorious Son died on a cross. In so doing he made purification for sins. This time it was not by a word, but by his action, allowing himself to be a sacrifice. This was his work. Not even his Father, God, could share it with him.

(ii) *Lord with a crown.* But he did not remain dead. He was raised and glorified. He is the Lord, ascended above all and at the helm of the universe – the Prince of Peace, the Prophet, Priest and King at the right hand of God. This exalted position of Jesus leads the writer naturally on to the next section, where he looks at the Son with respect to angelic beings.

2. ANGELS (1:4–2:8)

Scripture depicts angels as heavenly, spiritual and supernatural beings above man and below God. They are the highest created order. Although they were revered within Judaism, the writer argues that they are just ministering servants. He is asking his readers, 'Do you want to go back to the stage where the only contact you have got with heaven is through angels? You have got the Son – you can't get closer to the Father than that.'

The Jews gave the angels an exalted status as intermediaries or messengers. Christians, however, tend to think too little of angels. Therefore it was necessary for the writer to compare Christ with the angels, so that the readers would see both in their true light.

(a) Present – he didn't sit with angels (1:4–14)

Christ had a superior position to angelic beings. The writer demonstrates this with a series of questions and quotations from the Old Testament.

(b) Past – he didn't speak by angels (2:1–4)

The old angelic words were binding, for they came with divine authority. This new communication is even more serious.

(i)   Direct communication. It comes at the horizontal level. The word is given by the apostles, who are eye-witnesses to Christ. They saw and heard the message that they proclaim.

(ii) Divine confirmation. At the same time, this was not merely 'human' communication, but signs, wonders and miracles confirmed the word. So there is an urgency about receiving and responding to the word. It provides the moorings we need if we are not to drift away.

(c) Future – he didn't suffer for angels (2:5–18)

(i)   The world subject to man (2:5–9). Man was placed on earth to rule the universe. In Genesis 1:28 we read that he was given dominion over all the creatures of the earth, the air and the sea. Psalm 8:4–6 reinforces this position. But in reality we do not see mankind in general ruling over all – except that Jesus became a man and fulfils in himself the design of God for mankind.

(ii) Man subject to death (2:10–18). We are reminded that man is subject to death and that this fear of death is used by Satan to keep us in bondage. Jesus knows what it is like to be human, having lived on earth as a 'flesh and blood' man, and continuing to be a human, though now in his exalted state. As such he can sympathize with men and women who face struggles similar to those that he faced.

3. APOSTLES (3:1–4:13)

An apostle is someone 'sent' by God to fulfil a task, as were Moses and Joshua. But Jesus was a 'better' apostle than both of them, 'sent' for a greater purpose.

(a) Moses – out of Egypt (3:1–18)

Moses is generally regarded by Jews as one of their greatest leaders, but Jesus is even greater. At the Transfiguration in the Gospels, Jesus meets with Moses and Elijah, but he is clearly the superior one.

(i)   Faithful house. In Hebrew the word 'house' means both 'building' and 'family', rather as 'the House of Windsor' means the generations that belong to the royal family. Jesus is described as 'builder of a faithful house'. We are the stones who are part of the building. But the writer asks whether we are as faithful in our faith as Moses and Jesus were.

(ii) Faithless hearts. Sadly, Israel failed in their task of being faithful to God. Only two people out of 2.5 million got into the Promised Land. The leaders were good but the followers were not.

The problem was unbelief, which led to disobedience and finally to apostasy and destruction. They failed to 'enter the rest'. The history of Israel represents a warning to New Testament believers. The people rebelled at Massah (Exodus 17:1–7) and gave in to testing at Meribah (Numbers 20:1–13). In both cases the problem was lack of water.

The writer warns that the readers can do the same thing themselves. They can become hardened by sin. The same fate will befall them that befell the people in the Old Testament, for God will be angry with all who are disobedient (cf. Romans 11:22).

(b) Joshua – into Canaan (4:1–13)

The 'land of rest' was to be a land of rest from disease, slavery, invasion and poverty. They would also have a day of rest and celebration every week – the Sabbath. They were also supposed to know rest from spiritual struggle (Deuteronomy 12:9; Joshua 1:13). But that last rest was never entered into, so remains to be claimed.

(i) The work of God (4:1–10). On the seventh day of creation, God was no longer at work in creation. The description of this day is different to the other six in that it omits evening and morning, leaving some to speculate that there may be a special significance attached to it, beyond the fact that it is a day of rest. The Sabbath day, when God ceases from his work, portrays a God who is always at peace and rest in himself.

(ii) The word of God (4:11–13). Faith can be defined as the right response to the word of God. The word is living, like the God who speaks it; it is active, in that its blessings and curses affect people; it is sharp, like a Roman two edged sword; it is piercing, able to divide joints and marrow; it is discerning, able to get to the truth of a matter.

Jesus is like Moses in that he brings his people out, but also like Joshua in that he leads his people into the Promised Land. This is a reminder that it is important not only to remember what we have been saved from, but also to consider what we have been saved for.

Substance to shadows (chapters 7–10)

Having argued that the Son is better than the servants, the writer then changes his approach, and in chapters 7–10 we have the remarkable argument that the substance is better than the shadows.

This is perhaps best illustrated by the story of *Daddy Long Legs*, originally a book by Jean Webster and now a film. It is the story of a little girl in an orphanage. She knows that there is a wealthy man who provides for the orphanage. One day she sees his shadow on a wall, and, because it is an elongated shadow with tremendously long legs, due to the position of the light, she calls the shadow 'Daddy Long Legs'. For years she dreams of this shadow. But one day she meets him and falls in love with him. He too falls for her and their relationship develops.

The point is this. Once she has got him, she stops thinking about the shadow altogether, because the substance is better than the shadow. What would you think of her if she went back to the shadow on the wall and tried to kiss it, now that she knows the real man?

In the Old Testament there are many 'shadows' of Jesus. Some people call them 'types', but I prefer to call them shadows. It is as if Jesus cast his shadow back into the Old Testament, but since a shadow is always distorted, it never quite gives you the clear picture that you want.

When we read the Old Testament there is a sense in which we are reading about the shadows of Jesus. Here are three examples of what I mean.

1. PRIESTHOOD (MELCHIZEDEK)

In the Book of Leviticus we are looking at many shadows of Jesus. The sacrifices are the shadow of the sacrifice he made for sin at the cross. The animal sacrifices are shadows of Jesus, who is described in the New Testament as the Passover Lamb. The priesthood of Aaron and his family is a shadow of Christ's priestly work of intercession for us.

Jesus is also clearly shadowed in the Book of Genesis by Melchizedek – the mysterious priest-king who reigned over Jerusalem centuries before it was taken by the Jews, and who gave bread and wine to Abraham.

2. COVENANT (NEW)

But there is also the shadow of God's covenantal relationship with his people through Christ. The writer asks why they were considering going back to the Old Covenant now that they were in the New. The New Covenant was, after all, based on forgiveness and what I call 'forgetness'. I think the most amazing miracle is that when God forgives, he also forgets.

When I was a Pastor at the Millmead Centre in Guildford, there was a Sunday when everyone had gone home after the service, but there was a little old lady sitting in the church all by herself, crying her heart out. I went and sat by her and asked what her problem was. She explained that years ago she did a dreadful thing, and that if her family and friends knew about it they would never speak to her again. She said that for 30 years she had been asking God to forgive her, and he never had. I told her that the very first time she asked him, he forgave it and he forgot it. So for 30 years he hadn't known what she was talking about! She told me she didn't believe it. I took her through some scriptures which spoke of the New Covenant and how God would no longer remember her sins. It took 20 minutes to convince her that God had forgotten all about it. She got up, and I couldn't believe my eyes – she danced around the church! She was about 70, and here she was, dancing around the church for sheer joy. God had forgotten it! Our trouble is, we can't forget it, and so we struggle to forgive ourselves.

3. SACRIFICE (CROSS)

We also see a shadow when Abraham offered Isaac as a sacrifice. Many assume that this incident took place when Isaac was a young boy, but he was actually in his early thirties. Every Jewish picture of the scene shows a full-grown man who could easily have overcome his father, but instead submitted to him.

Our failure to realize his age is caused partly by chapter divisions. We miss the next incident in the next chapter, which talks of Sarah's death and tells us how old Isaac was when she died. So Isaac was around 33, and the mountain – Mount Moriah – was the very mountain on which Jesus died on the cross. The parallels are very clear. In the event, of course, an angel stopped Abraham, and a ram with its head caught in thorns was sacrificed on that mountain. Centuries later, the Lamb of God had his head crowned with thorns and was offered on Mount Moriah.

So the writer impresses upon them the inferiority of a return to Judaism, with its repetitive sacrifices and its inferior covenant. If they returned to Judaism, they would be rejecting the once-for-all sacrifice of Jesus.

Positive continuity (chapters 11–13)

Go on into the future

We now turn to the positive side in the second half of the letter, where the author draws a contrast between the Old and New Testaments. He emphasizes the continuity between the Old and the New. There are good things in the Old that are not obsolete – some things follow straight through.

Faith in God

One common theme is the theme of faith. When we consider the resources that the Old Testament heroes had, their faith leaves us standing. They didn't have any of the revelation we have in Christ. They didn't have the pouring out of the Holy Spirit. And yet those men went on believing, even though they never saw what they believed in. So we have a kind of double relationship to the Old Testament. There are some things we leave behind, because they are shadows and we now have the substance. But there are some things we need to emulate, particularly in this area of faith. The writer goes through group after group in the Old Testament:

- Abel, Enoch and Noah.
- Abraham, Isaac and Jacob. (God has tied his name to those three human names. He will always be known as the God of Abraham, Isaac and Jacob.)
- Joseph and Moses.
- Joshua and Rahab. (Rahab is the first woman in the list. She was a prostitute and a Gentile, but she staked her whole future on God's people, hiding the spies in Jericho. She is held up as an example of faith, not only in the Letter to the Hebrews, but also in the Letter of James. She appears in the genealogy of Jesus, for she was the great-great-grandmother of David.)
- Gideon, Barak, Samson and Jephthah.
- David.
- Samuel and the prophets.

There are two things we must note about this list of believers:

1 Their faith was shown in what they did. By faith Noah built an ark; by faith Abraham lived in tents for the rest of his life; by faith Moses gave up the ease of Egypt, and so on. As James puts it in his epistle, 'Show me your faith by your works.' Real faith shows itself in action.

2 The second thing that is important to note is that all these men were still living by faith when they died, yet they never saw what they believed in. Faith to them wasn't just a one-off decision at a crusade, but an on-going trust that

continued until they died, even if they never saw what was promised.

At the end of chapter 11 there is a tremendous reminder that these great heroes of the faith are waiting for us to catch up with them. Then we will join them in seeing what they were believing for! So, for example, Abraham left a very comfortable two-storey home, with heating and running water, to obey the voice of God. Archaeologists have dug out the houses of Abraham's home area, Ur of the Chaldees, and they were the most up-to-date, comfortable homes you can imagine. Abraham was 80 when God told him that he must leave his house to live in a tent for the rest of his life. Imagine how you would feel if you had a nice, comfortable, centrally heated bungalow by the sea, and God said he wanted you to leave your relatives and friends and live in a tent in the mountains for the rest of your life! Yet Abraham did it, by faith. And one day we will join him in enjoying all that God has for his people.

Focus on Jesus

But our attention must not be on Abraham, or any of the other great heroes of faith. We must fix our eyes on Jesus! In the closing chapters the writer focuses on three areas in which we should focus on Jesus.

1 Pioneer and perfecter of our faith. Forget about the spectators – there is somebody standing at the finishing-post who actually fired the pistol at the starting-line. He is the one who started us off, and he will be the one who will see us finish. The message is, 'Keep your eyes fixed on Jesus and run!'

2   Mediator of a New Covenant. Valuable though the Old Covenant was, it was inferior to the one that God brought in through Jesus.

3   Sufferer outside the camp. Jesus needed to be prepared to die a criminal's death in order for our salvation to be secure, literally an outcast among his own people.

'Problem passages'

Having taken an overview of the book, let us now look at what are considered to be the 'problem passages' of Hebrews – though it is worth noting that the label 'problem passage' is generally given to passages that don't fit in with what the readers already believe! I am constantly being asked, for example, 'What do you think about Paul's problem passages on women?' I don't think there are any problem passages on women. They are only 'problems' to those who disagree with them!

The so-called 'problem' in Hebrews concerns the suggestion that believers may fall away from faith in Jesus and not be saved on the final day. The best known of these warnings is found in Hebrews chapter 6. But the letter also includes several other severe warnings to those who drift away (see 2:1–2; 3:5–6, 12–14; 6:4–8, 11–12; 10:23–30, 35–39; 12:14–17). These verses represent a thread running all the way through the letter, which starts in chapter 2 with the words, 'How shall *we* escape if we neglect so great a salvation?' Every time I have heard that quoted, it has been quoted against sinners who are neglecting the gospel. But the 'we' here refers to Christian believers. The writer is saying that all we need to do to get into danger is to neglect our salvation. Most churches have members who have drifted away.

This theme continues with two passages in chapter 3, the long one in chapter 6, and another in chapter 10, which says, 'If we deliberately keep on sinning after we have received the knowledge of the truth, no sacrifice for sins is left …' This has led some commentators to conclude that the people in question were not believers at all. He must have been writing about non-believers who became interested in Christianity but didn't continue. After all, what about 'Once saved, always saved'? But the description in chapter 6 of the people who are in danger is surely a description of those who have been born again! The writer is talking to those who have been 'enlightened', who have 'tasted the heavenly gift', who have 'shared in the Holy Spirit', who have 'tasted the goodness of the word of God and the powers of the coming age'. I cannot fit any unbeliever into that description. In any other letter, these phrases would not even be questioned as a description of Christians.

There is a passage in 1 Peter which uses almost identical language to describe Christians: 'Like newborn babes, crave pure spiritual milk so that by it you may grow up in your salvation, now that you have tasted that the Lord is good.' This is clearly about believers, yet it is using similar language to Hebrews chapter 6. The whole of 1 Peter is addressed to believers. Even calling them 'spiritual infants' implies that they have been born again.

The warnings given involve two phases. Phase 1 is neglecting the faith and drifting away. Phase 2 is denying the faith. There is a difference, therefore, between Phase 1 (what is known as backsliding) and Phase 2 (what is called apostasy).

Backsliding is a recoverable condition, but according to Hebrews 6 we can get to a point of no return where there is no possibility of recovering our salvation. So Hebrews 6 doesn't discuss whether you can lose your salvation, but whether having lost it, you can find it again. The answer is that you can't.

We must warn those who are backsliding and drifting of the danger they are in, because there can come a point where they can't find their way back. I wish Hebrews didn't say that! But I cannot get round chapter 6 and other parts of the epistle, which are so urgent in their pleading from beginning to end. This terrible danger looms down the road for those who 'pull up their anchor', 'lower their sails' and 'drift away'.

Some suggest that these are hypothetical warnings – that this severe danger could never happen. But this argument does not hold. I believe there is hypocrisy in threatening people with something that could never happen. The Bible is the word of truth, not a book that plays games with people. Hebrews alone convinces me that it is possible to reach a point of no return in drifting away from Jesus, even without other passages in other New Testament books. The ultimate point of apostasy for these Hebrews believers would be standing in front of the synagogue and denying that Jesus is the Messiah. In so doing they would be crucifying Jesus afresh. The writer warns that if you crucify him afresh, he can do you no more good, which is a solemn warning.

It's important to add that this doesn't mean that believers should wake up every morning wondering if they are saved or not. There is an assurance in the New Testament that comes from a believer's walk with the Lord. Assurance in the New Testament is not based on a decision made at a point in time, but on one's present relationship with God. Paul reminds us in his Letter to the Romans that the Spirit goes on witnessing with the believer's spirit that he or she is a child of God (Romans 8:16; cf. 1 John 4:13).

To put it another way, you can have a present assurance that you are on the way to heaven, but I don't believe there are any guarantees that you will get there. So if you keep on that way and keep on believing in Jesus, you are certain to arrive. The teaching of Hebrews does not produce neurotic Christians wondering whether they are saved or not, but it does produce serious Christians who don't play games with God, who don't backslide and who don't neglect their faith and drift away.

Throughout the New Testament there are some very solemn warnings to Christians about backsliding. In John 15 Jesus says, 'I am the vine; you are the branches. If a man remains in me and I in him, he will bear much fruit.' But then he says, 'If anyone does not remain in me, he is like a branch that is thrown away and withers; such branches are picked up, thrown into the fire and burned.' I can't twist that! Common sense tells you what it says.

It is interesting that the failure of over two million of the Jews who had left Egypt to make it to Canaan is used by three different New Testament writers as a warning to Christians that they might have started well in their Christian lives, but they need to make sure they arrive. We may have left Egypt, but we need to make it to Canaan. This is used by Paul in 1 Corinthians 10, by the writer of Hebrews in chapter 4 of his letter and by Jude as a warning to Christians. It is not those who start but those who finish who make it.

I remember seeing Billy Graham being interviewed on television. The interviewer asked him a question he had not been asked before: 'What will be your first thought when you get to heaven?' Billy immediately replied, 'Relief! Relief that I made it.' Now there is a humble man who isn't cocksure, but knows he is on the way. I am sure right now that I am on the way to heaven – the Spirit tells me I am on the right road. But I can't tell you more than that. I intend to keep on travelling till I make it.

John Bunyan's *Pilgrim's Progress* pictures the Christian life as a journey, from the sinful city to the celestial city. At the end, the main character 'Christian' and his companion face the crossing of the River Jordan – the dark, deep, black river of death. They don't like it one bit. Christian's companion says he is unwilling to go through that river, and turns off to the left down a side path, hoping for another way over. Bunyan writes, 'So I saw in my dream that there is a way to hell, even from the gates of heaven.' The companion had been on the right path, but he left it just before he arrived at the celestial city.

This theme is also clear in the Book of Revelation. The whole book is a message for people under terrific pressure. The promise to those who overcome is that God will not blot out their names from the Lamb's Book of Life. What does that mean? If you want to keep your name in the Book of Life, then overcome, go right on to the end, never go back, keep your eyes fixed on Jesus. There is a warning on the last page of the Bible that if you play around with the Book of Revelation and start taking things out of it or adding things to it, God will take away your share in the tree of life.

So, you see, there is this thread of warning alongside the glorious scriptures which tell us of God's keeping power. If you have the Father, Son and Holy Spirit on your side, you have got everything going for you. Just keep on believing, and you will make it.

Conclusions

1. It is possible for us to 'lose our salvation'

The book is a warning to us all that we should continue trusting and not think that a one-off decision for Christ will necessarily mean that we will be saved on the final day. (See also my book, *Once Saved, Always Saved?*, Hodder & Stoughton, 1996.)

2. Once you are lost it is impossible to recover

This is the message of Hebrews 6. Such teaching is found elsewhere, notably in 1 John 5:16. It is a solemn message, but I don't believe we can interpret these scriptures any other way.

3. Predestination requires our continued co-operation

It is not automatic. God did predestine us. He chose us before we chose him, but he requires our co-operation. It is as if someone threw a rope to a drowning man, and the man throwing the rope said, 'Grab hold of this, and hold on until I have got you to the shore.' Would the drowning man say, when he got to the shore, that he had saved himself by hanging on? Never! He would say that someone had saved him. The idea that you saved yourself because you held on is just not true, but you have your part to play. That is why Peter, in his Second Letter, urges his readers to make their calling and election sure (2 Peter 1:10–11). God has elected us and chosen us, so we make that sure by pressing on, by going on for maturity, so that we may have a rich welcome into heaven.

I believe in predestination. God predestined me to be his son; God elected me, chose me; he was after me long before I was after him. But I need to make that calling and election sure by holding on to the rope until I am safely on the shore.

So I want to be both a Calvinist and an Arminian. These two schools of thought have tended to be set in opposition to each other, Calvinists stressing the electing work of God, among other things, and Arminians stressing our need to persevere.

Hebrews is the one book that I don't think we can twist on this issue and say it is full of problems. It is full of clear statements that we need to hear.

4. Holiness is as necessary as forgiveness

We have seen that it is not just those who accept the forgiveness of God who make it, but those who press on. This implies that holiness is as necessary as forgiveness. It is no good claiming to be forgiven if we are not prepared to acknowledge the lordship of Christ and live a godly life. The verse in Hebrews which encapsulates this teaching is 12:14: 'Make every effort to live in peace with all men and to be holy; without holiness no-one will see the Lord.' I find that far too many Christians today want forgiveness but not holiness; they want happiness from Jesus in this life and holiness in the next. But the will of God in my New Testament is clearly holiness in this life, even if it makes me unhappy. Our hedonistic generation just wants pleasure, not pain.

Hebrews 12:7 says God is prepared to chastise us, to cause us pain, if that will make us more holy. The one thing he is after is our holiness, and he can make it tough for his children. Hebrews even goes so far as to say that if the Lord has never chastised you, you are a bastard and not a true son. The full gospel is that forgiveness and holiness are both gifts of grace. They are both offered on the same basis – faith. But you need both.

5. God is a holy God

Following the publication of my book *The Road to Hell* (Hodder & Stoughton, 1992), in which I outlined the Bible's teaching on hell, I had a number of BBC radio interviews. Every interviewer asked the same question: 'How can a loving God send anyone to hell?' What interests me is that no one ever asks, 'How can a holy God send anyone to hell?' Yet God is holy, and his love is holy love, which means he will never be content with less than holiness for the ones he loves. Hebrews emphasizes this point repeatedly. Note the following passages:

- Without the shedding of blood there is no forgiveness (9:22).
- Without faith it is impossible to please God (11:6).
- It is a dreadful thing to fall into the hands of the living God (10:31).

■ Let us be thankful, and so worship God acceptably with reverence and awe, for our God is a consuming fire (12:28).

What value does Hebrews have for believers?

1 It aids our Bible study. It helps us to understand the relationship between the Old and New Testaments. The shadow concept is most helpful for understanding the Old Testament; we can note the ways in which hints of Jesus are found there.

2 It is Christ-centred and so helps to keep our eyes fixed on Jesus. The writer constantly makes Jesus his focus. In particular, it is the only New Testament book to major on his priesthood. His present work in heaven is to intercede for us. Some have even called Hebrews the 'Fifth Gospel' because of its emphasis on Christ's present work.

3 It is faith-building. It is an inspiration to think of the many people who have gone before us and who are watching us (see especially chapter 11).

4 It warns us of the danger of backsliding. We are given severe warnings about the two stages: the drifting away, whereby we stop meeting with other believers and neglect our faith; and the deliberate, wilful apostasy whereby we deny our faith in Christ altogether.

5 It emphasizes the importance of church membership. It stresses that safety lies in fellowship when we are under pressure. The devil will pick off Christians on their own. So when the pressure is on, stay close to the family. The book urges the readers to remember their leaders (13:7) and to co-operate with them. It also reminds them of the

need to keep on loving, visiting those in prison and spurring one another on towards good deeds.

6   It helps in times of persecution. The book also reminds us of the way the believers were treated in the early days of persecution at the hands of Nero. In view of such threats and difficulties, it is important to stay focused on Christ. Such passages are especially valuable to believers facing persecution today.

54.

JAMES

Introduction

There are two particular difficulties in studying Scripture. One is mental difficulty, when you don't understand what you are reading, and the other is moral difficulty, when you do understand it! More people have moral difficulties than mental difficulties, and if ever a book is likely to give the former, it is James. It is a frightening book, because once you have read it, you can't plead ignorance. It is one of the easiest books in the Bible to understand and one of the hardest to undertake.

How practical!

Most people's first impression of the book is that it is extremely practical. This is no-nonsense Christianity for daily life – where the rubber hits the road. It is realistic, with very little focus on doctrine and an awful lot on duty.

On my bookshelf at home I have a number of commentaries on James, all with 'action' titles: *Truth in Action*, *Faith that Works*, *Behaviour of Belief*, *Belief that Behaves*, *Make Your Faith Work*. They all emphasize that the key word of the Letter of James is 'do' – a word that is also important in the rest of the Bible. Unfortunately we tend to overlook the little words, preferring to just underline theological terms like 'justification' and 'sanctification', but the word 'do' is also common in the Bible and just as important.

In Matthew's Gospel there is a short parable about the father who told his two sons to work in his vineyard. One said no initially, but went nevertheless. The other said yes, but never arrived. Jesus asks which of the two *did* the father's will, not which of the two *said* the right thing. It was the doing that was important.

It is the same in James. We have this challenge to be 'doers of the word' and not just hearers of it.

How illogical!

As well as seeming simple, the book also seems illogical. It's full of practical counsel that can't be put into order. I tried to make a diagram of James and failed totally. I even tried to get a structured outline, but was unable to do so because of the way he wanders around from one subject to another. He starts a subject, then he leaves it, then he comes back to it later. They are pearls of wisdom that haven't been strung. Yet in some ways this serves the purpose of the book, for it is a book urging us to action rather than analysis.

The practical and illogical elements added together give strong reminders of the Book of Proverbs in the Old Testament. It too has little structure and focuses on the day-to-day issues in life. This is what is known as Jewish wisdom literature. The Rabbis have different forms of preaching, but there is one form where they simply 'muse aloud'. It is called *charaz*. There is no prepared address, but just an elderly Rabbi in the synagogue sharing pearls and gems of wisdom.

James was clearly taught by such a Rabbi when he was a young man, because he is a master of *charaz*, and he is just doing the same thing for his readers.

Who is James?

There are five people called James in the New Testament. Perhaps the best known is James the son of Zebedee and the brother of John, who was the first martyred apostle, beheaded by Herod in AD 44. Next there is James the son of Alphaeus, another of the Twelve. There is James the father of Judas (not Iscariot). There is James the little (mentioned in Mark 15:40). Finally, there is James the half-brother of Jesus. It was this final James who penned the epistle.

James was one of four half-brothers of Jesus who, together with a number of sisters (we don't know how many), formed the family circle. Few realize that at least five, and possibly seven, of the twelve apostles were Jesus' cousins, which explains why so many of them were present at a private wedding at Cana in Galilee (see John chapter 2). The disciples would not have just turned up uninvited.

So Jesus found quite a number of apostles from his wider family circle. But his immediate family didn't know what to make of him. When you have lived with someone for 30 years and they suddenly go around saying they are the Messiah, it can't be easy! At the beginning of his public ministry he seems to disown Mary (most assume that Joseph had died by this time). He didn't call her 'mother' any more – he called her 'woman'. 'Woman, what have I to do with you?' was his first recorded comment to Mary, at the wedding at Cana.

Furthermore, there was clearly tension between Jesus and the rest of the family. At one time his family came to take him home and lock him away, because they thought he was out of his mind (Mark 3:21). Finding a large crowd surrounding him, they sent a message through to Jesus: 'Your mother and brothers and sisters have come to take you home.' He replied, 'My mother – who is my mother? My brothers and sisters – who are my brothers and sisters? Anybody who does the will of my Father in heaven is my mother, my brother and my sister.' His family thought this was crazy talk, and no doubt Mary felt hurt by the implications.

It seems that Jesus almost dissociated himself from his mother until the cross, where he said to John, 'That is your mother' – in effect asking John to be Mary's son in his place. Apart from her being mentioned as one of those who were at the prayer meeting before the day of Pentecost, that is the last we hear of Mary in the Gospels. You never hear her name again. She had played her role, and it was now over. She was a remarkable woman. I am happy to call her 'blessed', because she prophesied that all generations would call her blessed. I am not prepared to call her a virgin now, because she had other children after Jesus by Joseph (Mark 6:3).

Things were not smooth between Jesus and his brothers. In John 7:3–5 the brothers reminded him that it was the time of the Feast of Tabernacles, and teased him that he really ought to go, because the Jews expected the Messiah to come at that Feast. What an ideal time to declare himself!

Yet in spite of this suspicion and disdain, two of these brothers became writers of the New Testament – Jude and James. It is said that when Jesus died on the cross, his brother James was so deeply upset and full of regret about what he had said about him and how he had teased him, that he said he would never eat food again. He would have fasted until he died, except that three days later Jesus appeared to his followers and to James personally. From that moment on, James called himself a bond-slave of Jesus.

Although these two brothers wrote two books of the New Testament, they never took advantage of their relationship to Jesus. They never said, 'Listen to me – I am a brother of Jesus.' Jude actually says, 'I am the brother of James.' So his own brothers were persuaded by the resurrection that Jesus, who had lived with them in the carpenter's cottage in Nazareth, was none other than the Son of God. James is mentioned as a member of the little prayer group that waited for the coming of the Spirit at Pentecost. So Jesus' cousins followed him, and his immediate family believed in him. That tells you something about the quality of Jesus' character.

The next mention of James comes in Acts 15, where he is the presiding elder of the fellowship in Jerusalem. He wasn't one of the Twelve, and yet clearly by unanimous consent, he was recognized as the leader of the mother church in Jerusalem.

His role in Acts 15 was especially crucial. He faced a most difficult and delicate crisis – the biggest in the early church's life. It concerned the whole question of circumcision, and whether Christianity would remain a Jewish sect or would become a universal faith. James presided over the meeting that could have split the church right down the middle if agreement had not been reached. But James saved it by appealing to the Spirit and to the Scriptures. Peter reported what the Spirit had done with Cornelius and his household, and then James said, 'Well, that ties in with what Scripture says', and quoted from the Old Testament. It is important to note that rather than giving his flock a command – since, as Christians, they were not under the Law – he encouraged them to choose a loving response to this issue.

If there is one thing I long to see, it is people who understand the Spirit and people who know the Scriptures getting together. We are in danger of diverging. I have been part of the charismatic renewal in this country, but my greatest concern is that it is drifting away from its scriptural bearings.

I have an equal concern for those who know the Scriptures inside out, but don't know the dynamic of the Holy Spirit.

I have written about this theme in *Word and Spirit Together* (Hodder & Stoughton, 1993).

So on the basis of this understanding from the Spirit and the word, James gave a judgement upon which everybody agreed. What could have been a catastrophe turned into a beautifully uniting moment, under James.

After this council, a letter was sent out to the Gentile believers everywhere, which explained that the Gentiles should not have any burden from the Law of Moses, but should be sensitive to the scruples of Jewish Christians when eating with them. The letter promoted a position similar to that set out by Paul in Romans concerning disagreement among Christians over issues not directly dealt with in Scripture. Paul said that those who have liberty in disputable matters must be prepared to forgo their liberty for the sake of the weaker brother. It is true, of course, that the more you mature in the Christian faith, the freer you are from scruples, but while a person still has them, more mature believers should give way.

Scruples can be very awkward. Often we feel guilty about doing something because we were told as a child that it was wrong. I was taught as a child that we shouldn't ride bicycles or use cameras on a Sunday. Well, it was years before I found out that there was no verse in the Bible about cameras and bicycles! When I worked on a farm I had to cycle five miles to get to church, and it was such a strange position feeling guilty about cycling to worship God! But as you grow up in Christ, you feel more and more free to enjoy things that God has freely given you.

Others may feel awkward about certain practices which are all right in themselves but which would be a stumbling-block because of their association with the person's pre-Christian past. The classic example is drinking wine at a meal with a former alcoholic. If you know that someone would find this a problem, it is loving to forgo your liberty for the sake of the Christian brother or sister's conscience. If I am with a Jew, I stick to a kosher food diet, just as the apostle Paul did. We need to be adaptable and sensitive to other people's consciences and not flaunt our own freedom.

When James sent this letter from Jerusalem to the Gentile believers, he also wrote another letter to go to the Jewish believers, and this is the Letter of James. It is a letter telling the Jews how to behave in the Gentile world. The advice corresponds almost exactly with the letter in Acts 15 to the Gentiles about how to behave towards the Jewish world. So it is a mirror reflection of that letter, albeit a much longer one.

Other historical documents tell us that James stayed in Jerusalem and was given the nickname 'James the Just', which was a wonderful quality for a presiding elder. He also had a second nickname, 'Oblias', which means a bulwark, a really reliable person.

James came to a tragic but glorious end. Following the death of Festus, the Roman Governor, and before Albinius took up office, there was a gap of about two months in AD 62 when there was no Roman Governor. The Jewish rulers seized the opportunity to attack Christians, because there was no Roman government to say, 'You can't put anyone to death.' At that time they captured him, took him to the pinnacle of the temple and said, 'Now blaspheme Christ, or we will throw you off!' This was the very pinnacle where the devil took Jesus in Matthew chapter 4. James the Just simply replied: 'I see the Son of Man coming on the clouds of glory!' So they threw him off.

But the fall didn't kill him, so they started to stone him. As he lay there, with his bones broken and the stones being thrown at him, he said, 'Father, forgive them, for they don't know what they do.' The crowd watching cried out, 'James the Just is praying for us!' What an end! Finally someone, out of sheer mercy, got a big wooden club and clubbed his head, and he died. Of course, he was only one of the many who perished for Jesus in those early years.

When his fellow Christians came to pick up his body and give him a decent burial, they were astonished, because for the first time they saw his knees, which looked like the knees of a camel. Here was a man who spent more time on his knees than on his feet!

He was well regarded within the church. Eusebius, one of the early church fathers, said of him:

> *The philosophy and godliness which his life displayed to so eminent a degree, was the occasion of a universal belief in him as the 'most just of men'.*

Hence the nickname, James the Just. One of the writers at the time, Hegessipus, said:

> *James was a Nazirite. He was in the habit of entering alone into the temple, and was frequently found upon his knees begging forgiveness for the people, so that his knees became hard like a camel, in consequence of his constantly bending them in his worship of God, and asking forgiveness for the people. Because of his exceeding great justice he was called 'the just'.*

Authorship

James was so well known that further identification at the start of his letter was unnecessary – 'James' was sufficient. Interestingly, he includes a number of Jesus' sayings from the Sermon on the Mount (23 quotations). As far as we know, James wasn't there to hear them, so he must have picked them up either directly from Jesus, or later from the Twelve as the collection of Jesus' sayings circulated.

However, in spite of the historical evidence linking James with this letter, doubt has been cast upon his authorship, because the style of the letter is so unlike what might be expected from a Galilean. Other Jews despised the Galileans in part because of their distinctive dialect. They were regarded as illiterate. In Acts the Chief Priest reflects on the courage of the apostles: 'How can these uneducated men challenge us like this?' But the Greek style in which the letter is written is much more polished than might be expected.

Style

James uses a number of the best devices of public speaking. Let me run through them.

1 He uses rhetorical questions – that is, questions that don't require an answer but make the hearer think. See 2:4–5, 14–16; 3:11–12; 4:4, 12.

2 He uses paradoxical statements to gain attention. For example: 'Count it all joy, my brothers, when you face trials of various kinds' (1:2). 'Joy' and 'trials' don't seem to go together, so this gains attention. See also the irony in 2:14–19; 5:5.

3 He has imaginary conversations in which he creates a dialogue with someone. Once again this raises people's interest levels. People are always fascinated to overhear conversations. See 2:18; 5:13.

4 He also uses questions to introduce new subjects. See 2:14; 4:1.

5 He includes many imperatives in the letter – there are 60 of them in just 108 verses!

6 He personifies things. He talks of sin as if it is an animal, and he uses pictures and figures from everyday life. He talks about ships' rudders, forest fires, and bridles and

horses in a farmer's life, all of which gain attention.

7   He uses famous men and women such as Elijah, Abraham and Rahab as examples.

8   He particularly uses a direct form of address – 'you' – which is a great way of getting attention.

9   He is not afraid to use harsh language. See 2:20; 4:4.

10 He sometimes uses vivid antithesis (contrasting opposites). See 2:13, 26.

11 He often uses quotations. See 1:11, 17; 4:6; 5:11, 20.

So how did such speaking devices find their way into the letter? I think the answer lies in what we find in 1 Peter 5:12. Many of the writers of the New Testament didn't actually write but dictated the text. They used an amanuensis – what we would call a shorthand typist or a secretary today.

Both Paul and Peter, for example, used Silas quite a lot in this capacity. So it looks as if James delivered all this verbally, and got someone to write it down for him, knock it into shape and send it off as a circular letter. This explanation would solve all the 'problems' that some scholars have. So we have got Greek rhetoric and Hebrew wisdom combined in this letter.

The readers

The letter is not addressed to a church, or a group of churches, or an individual, like most of the New Testament letters. It is addressed to the 12 tribes scattered among the nations, which makes it quite clear that it is addressed to the Jewish Dispersion – to the churches started among the dispersed Jews around the Mediterranean. It mentions the Lord Jesus Christ in the first verse, and 'my brothers' on 12 occasions.

The Jews were dispersed twice: once to Babylon in the involuntary exile of 586 BC, and again just before Jesus came, when many opted to settle all over the Mediterranean world.

There were more Jews outside than inside Israel, with as many as 10,000 Jews in Rome itself. Many would return three times a year for the Jewish festivals, but they quickly imbibed the culture around them, so much so that the Jews became a byword for hypocrisy.

So Christ came at the ideal time for the spread of the gospel. The Jews had been scattered around the Mediterranean, the Roman roads had been built and the Greek language was spoken everywhere – it was absolutely perfect. God had prepared the whole situation for the rapid spread of the news about Jesus. When the apostle Paul arrived in a new place on his missionary journeys, he went first to the synagogue, believing that the first converts would be from the God-fearing people there.

It is clear that the Jewish disciples in the Dispersion around the Mediterranean faced a totally different situation to the Jewish believers at home. The Jerusalem church was made up almost entirely of Jewish believers. They were isolated and segregated, and so became too strict. Legalism and the pride that goes with it were their biggest problems. But in the Dispersion, the Jewish believers faced the problem of assimilation. Many were embarrassed to be known as Christians and were too lax in their behaviour. Their problem was greed, because most of them had left Israel for business reasons in search of riches elsewhere. They were becoming too much like the Gentiles.

Content

Wealth

Our introduction has touched on a number of themes picked up by James, with business being one of the major ones. It is a key concern for any Jew. They have been hounded from one country to another, so they have needed a trade or profession that is easily portable. That is why so many of them have become tailors, for they only need to take a needle and thread with them, and they are in business. Others have become jewellers, because a jeweller's goods can be easily packed into a small suitcase. They have also become moneylenders, of course. In medieval Europe Christians were not allowed to be moneylenders, so the Jews became bankers, with the Rothschilds among the most famous.

But the focus on business has its own snags. Jesus said, 'You cannot worship God and money' – you can't devote yourself to God and to money-making at the same time. The Pharisees laughed when Jesus said that, because they were both rich and religious. But Jesus said, 'It is impossible.' They said, 'He doesn't know how to make money, so he is just against the rich.' But Jesus constantly warned us that it is hard for rich people to get into the Kingdom – and, of course, by New Testament standards, most Western Christians are rich. Money itself is neutral and can do a lot of good. But Paul writes, 'The *love* of money is the root of *all kinds* of evil.'

It is clear from the Letter of James that wealth had corrupted some of his readers. They were exploiting their employees, holding back their wages to help the cash-flow of the business. They were indulging themselves, spending their money on needless luxuries. They were flattering the rich people who came into their assemblies, telling the poor people to sit at the back, but showing the rich people to the front seats. Others were insulting and despising poor people.

It is the same the world over – when you make money, you regard yourself as successful, and others as failures who haven't made it. Snobbery goes with wealth.

This attitude prevails in some churches today, where the few rich people in the fellowship effectively control what happens. Staff are reluctant to be unpopular, for fear of angering major donors who have an unhealthy authority.

Being wealthy actually gave false security. Godliness is life lived in reference to God. Money wreaks havoc with godliness, because when you have got plenty of money, you make plans without reference to God. James said they should always add 'God willing' to any plans that were made. My father always used to put 'D.V.' (*Deo volente* – Latin for 'God willing') in his letters to acknowedge that any plans he made were made in reference to God. James preached against the wealthy who left out the 'D.V.'

The neglect of God and the neglect of the poor tend to accompany money-making. James lists other sins common to the rich: envy, because the more you have, the more you want, and the more you envy those who have got more; selfish ambition; pride; boasting and bragging; presumption; impatience; anger; covetousness; arguments; quarrels; fights and litigation. Litigation is one of the pastimes of the rich. You could take the Letter of James into the City of London and preach on it.

I was once asked to go and speak to the members of the Stock Exchange. They asked me for a sermon title before I went, and so I told them it would be 'You can't take it with you, and if you did it would burn'. They absolutely refused to publicize the title! So I changed it to 'How to invest beyond the grave', and they were quite interested!

The tongue

James also focuses on the tongue as a major cause of problems for the believer. We might speculate that he could recall his own idle words when teasing Jesus (in John chapter 7).

The Jews love words, but there was an inherent danger in speaking too much. A particular weakness for expatriates was gossip. People far from home gossip within their little community. James understands this only too well, and he has a lot to say about the tongue and words.

He says things such as, 'You use the same tongue to bless people and curse them. It is like bitter and sweet water coming out of the same fountain.' James says that the tongue is the hardest part of your body to control. If you can control it, you are perfect. So the tongue is a ready reckoner for how holy you are. Consider your speech, because it is 'out of the abundance of the heart that your mouth speaks.' You are entirely sanctified when you always say the right thing, when you keep silent when you should, and when you speak up when you should. Jesus said we shall be judged on the Day of Judgement for 'every careless word', because it is the careless words, spoken when you are tired or busy, that reveal your real heart, not your careful speech, when you are thinking about what to say.

Other images are used to describe the tongue: it has been set on fire by hell; it is like a little ship's rudder, and it can turn the whole ship. The effects are like a forest fire that was started with just one match. Sins of the tongue, such as grumbling, cursing, lying and swearing, are all mentioned in this little letter.

Important though the themes of wealth and words are, the two words that open up the letter are 'world' and 'wisdom'.

The world

James explains that 'friendship with the world is enmity with God' – you can't be popular with the world and with God. Jesus wasn't, and if he couldn't manage it, neither will we. In fact, the apostle Paul taught that the godlier we are, the less popular we are likely to be. Paul actually said to Timothy,

'Whoever would live a godly life in Christ Jesus will suffer persecution.' Non-believers may respect you, but they will try to knock your faith out of you.

James said that 'pure religion before God' meant two things: 'to keep yourself untainted from the world and to visit widows and orphans in their distress'.

It is often said that Christians should be 'in the world but not of it'. This is true, but it does not mean that we should stay away from non-believers. When my good friend Peter was a car dealer in Australia, he would sack any member of his staff who became a Christian. (Don't worry – he found them a job elsewhere first!) He did so on the principle that he couldn't be a witness at work if he was surrounded by Christians!

James teaches us the difference between being tested and being tempted. God will never tempt us, but he will test us. The difference is this: you test people in the hope that they will pass the test, but you tempt them hoping they will fail. God will test you, so we should count it all joy when things get tough, for we know God is moving us up a class. It is the devil who tempts us and wants us to fail. However, he can only tempt us if there is something in us that he can use to make us want to take the bait. But God has promised us that we will never be tempted more than we can cope with – which means, of course, that the devil is totally under God's control. The devil can't touch us unless he gets permission from God first. (See the early chapters of Job for a prime example of this.)

So you will never, ever be able to say as a Christian, 'I couldn't help it.' So in the world we face testing and temptation. One comes from God in the hope that you will pass the test; the other comes from the devil in the hope that you will fail. We need the wisdom to discern which is which. When the missionary Hudson Taylor's wife suffered greatly towards the end of her life, and became totally blind, somebody asked: 'Why should God do this to you when you have served him so faithfully?' 'Oh,' she said, 'he is putting the finishing touches to my character.'

So life won't get easier as we get older. I find that guidance gets harder. In the early years of being a Christian, God has mercy on us, giving us such clear guidance that we have no doubt about what we should be doing. But then he puts us in a situation where we have really got to begin to work things out for ourselves. He doesn't spoon-feed us as we mature, but gives us more responsibility, and trusts us to make judgements instead of giving us a clear line.

Wisdom

We noted earlier the similarity between James and Proverbs, so it is no surprise to learn that wisdom is another key theme of the letter. James isolates two categories of wisdom. Just as there are two sorts of trial – testing and temptation – so there are two sorts of wisdom – wisdom from above and wisdom from below.

The wisdom from below comes from human experience through having tried things out – we call it the school of experience. But there is another way to get wisdom, which doesn't take so long. We simply ask for it! James says that if anyone lacks wisdom, they shouldn't assume that they must stay that way. He explains that wisdom comes by asking God, without double-mindedness and without doubting.

Wisdom is far more available than we realize. James says it is a lovely wisdom because it is pure and it is peaceable – it solves the problem. All divine wisdom is available to you at any moment. When you are in difficulty, all you have got to say is, 'Lord, I need wisdom.' And you will be astonished at the response.

Problems

We need to look now at the so-called 'problems' posed by the Letter of James.

Its general tone

It doesn't seem to be a very Christian letter. There is not much about Christ or the gospel in it. There seems to be more emphasis on man's activity than God's, on deeds rather than doctrine, on law rather than gospel, on works rather than faith. It does not mention key events, such as Jesus' death, resurrection and ascension, or the ministry of the Holy Spirit. It seems to be about doing good deeds.

So some have questioned whether the book describes Christianity as it is found in the rest of the Bible. Notable thinkers have written it off. The Protestant reformer Martin Luther said he was disgusted with the letter, that it contained nothing evangelical and failed to show Christ. (In fact Christ is only mentioned twice in the whole letter.) Luther called it a 'right strawy epistle', meaning that there is no corn in it, just straw, which is just about as insulting a remark as you can make. He said, 'I do not believe it is apostolic. It would be better not to have it in the New Testament.' When he translated the Bible, he put James in an appendix at the end, together with Hebrews, Jude and Revelation. He didn't quite have the courage to cut it right out, but he shifted it out of the main text.

Indeed, there is very little in this whole letter that an orthodox Jew couldn't accept. It talks of the Law, the synagogue, brothers and elders, and addresses God as 'God Almighty'. If you were to remove the two mentions of Christ, and the words 'born', 'name', 'coming' and 'believers', an orthodox Jew would agree with everything.

Its specific teaching

In addition to these problems, there is a more specific concern, which has caused great consternation among Bible readers. In 2:24 James says, 'You see that a person is justified by what he does and not by faith alone.' This seems to undermine the teaching of the New Testament, and of the apostle Paul in particular, about how we can be right with God. Luther said it undermined the fundamental gospel truth of 'justification by faith alone'.

The general tone of the letter and the specific concern about its teaching on faith meant that it had a hard fight to get into the New Testament and a hard fight to stay there. It was one of the last letters to be included (in AD 350).

So how do we deal with this apparent contradiction? A number of points can be made:

1   James died in AD 62 and so couldn't have read Paul's letters on the subject, though he knew Paul and persuaded him to observe the Nazirite law to show he was still Jewish (see Acts 21:18–25). So if there is a contradiction, it can't be deliberate.

2   Paul was writing for Gentiles, whereas James was writing for Jewish believers, so their purpose was different. Paul was defending Gentiles from Jewish legalism, while James was defending Jews from Gentile licence. It is not surprising, therefore, that there is a difference in emphasis.

3   When we come to the specific 'problem' passage, we find that the word 'works' has several different meanings. Paul writes of the works of the Law, while James writes of the works of faith – that is, *actions*. What James is saying is, 'Faith without actions is dead.' He is not commenting on the works of the Law. He uses an illustration to show that love without actions is no use. Suppose someone says to a

brother, 'Oh my, you don't have any clothes or food, do you? Well, God bless you, brother, God bless you!' James asks, 'What use is that?' That is love without action, love without the works of love.

So when he talks about faith, he is talking about faith without action. And unless you act in faith, you don't have faith. Professing faith can't save you. Faith must be practised. He says that even the devils believe in God, and they tremble!

But then he gives illustrations of faith with action, using Abraham and Rahab, a good man and a bad woman. They both acted in faith, one prepared to take life and the other to save it. Abraham acted in faith when he prepared to kill his son, his only hope of descendants. Rahab the prostitute acted in faith when she looked after the spies and asked them to save her from the coming invasion.

James is saying that faith is not something you profess. You have got to show you believe in Jesus by acting. You will fall flat on your face if he doesn't catch you. That is faith. So James is absolutely right when he says faith without actions cannot save you, for such faith is as dead as a corpse. Faith is not reciting the Creed, it is acting in faith, demonstrating trust in the Lord.

So with Paul and James, God is giving us two different angles on this crucial issue so that we get it in balance and get the whole truth. Legalism says we are saved by works; licence says we are saved without works; but liberty (the Christian position) says we are saved for works, but they are good works, works of love.

Even Paul, the apparent champion of justification by faith, says in Ephesians 2: 'For we are God's workmanship, created in Christ Jesus to do good works, which God prepared in advance for us to do.' So we are not saved by good deeds, but we are saved for good deeds, and we will be judged by our deeds.

James, the apparent champion of works, says in 2:5 that believers should be 'rich in faith'.

Legalism says, 'We are going to make sure that you are not free to sin, by making rules and regulations.' Licence says, 'We are free to sin.' Liberty says, 'We are free not to sin.' These may sound like neat clichés, but nevertheless they are true. It is the most important thing in the Christian life to get a clear grasp of the differences between those three statements, because this is the heart of the gospel, and we need both Paul and James to get this right. So on the general question of 'faith versus works', I believe that the Letter of James needs the rest of the New Testament, and the rest of the New Testament needs James.

In his assessment of the letter, Martin Luther completely missed the point. He said it contradicts Paul and all the other Scriptures, but Luther was no more infallible than the Pope he opposed. He was too focused on the doctrine of justification by faith to see how important James' emphasis really was. Faith must act and be worked out. What God has worked in has to be worked out in the world, in an alien atmosphere.

Conclusion

We are not dispersed Jews, so is the letter relevant to us? It is very relevant to us, because we are dispersed Christians. Some Christians are so wrapped up in church life that they are more like the Jews in Jerusalem. Their problem is pride, caused in part by being isolated from the world.

But most Christians are like the Jews in the Dispersion, working in the everyday world, tempted to become assimilated into the world and to adopt its moral standards. We are citizens of heaven but strangers on earth, part of the dispersed people of God, awaiting our future dwelling where we will be finally home. We are in the world but not of it.

Our position is best summed up by the Epistle to Diognetus, written at the end of the first century AD. The Epistle is a response to the question: 'What's different about the Christians?' He said:

> *Christians are distinguished from other men neither by country nor language. Living in such places as the lot of each has determined and following the customs of the natives in respect to clothing, food and the rest of their ordinary conduct, they display their wonderful and confessedly striking method of life. They dwell in their own countries, but simply as sojourners. As citizens, they share in all things with others, and yet endure all things as foreigners. Every foreign land is to them as their native country, and every land of their birth as a land of strangers. They pass their days on earth, but they are citizens of heaven. They obey the prescribed laws, and at the same time, surpass the laws by their lives. They are reviled and they bless …*

Christians today need to live in that fashion – to make sure that the world remains external to them. The world's motives, methods and morals are still a challenge. The pressures on Christians today remain essentially the same as they were back in the first century. In this regard, the Letter of James is right up to date and of great value to any believer seeking to follow Christ. It focuses on how to behave in the world and in the church. James is particularly interested in what we do, not what we say. Bible knowledge is useless unless we do something about it.

55.

1 AND 2 PETER

1 Peter

On 2 September 1666 there was a great fire in London. It began in a baker's oven and caused tremendous damage. Two hundred thousand people lost their homes, since most of the houses were timber-framed and so were unable to withstand the flames. It was estimated that the fire did £10 million worth of damage. Altogether 90 churches were destroyed, although many of them were later rebuilt by Christopher Wren, including St Paul's Cathedral. Of course, when there is a disaster, it is one of the unfortunate sides of human nature that people look round for a scapegoat. Often the innocent are accused, and in the case of the great fire of London, the French Catholics were blamed.

On 19 July AD 64 a fire began in the city of Rome which lasted for three days, devastating much of the city. It engulfed the centre of Rome, destroying temples and houses. The citizens looked for a scapegoat, and found one in the Emperor Nero. They knew he had ambitions to pull down old buildings and put up new magnificent structures, so they assumed he was behind it. Nero, in turn, shifted the blame onto the Christians, and so began a serious persecution of the church.

They faced awful times. They were tortured, sewn into the skins of wild beasts and made to crawl round the amphitheatres on all fours, while they were set upon by lions and other wild animals. They were hunted by dogs and some of them were crucified.

I remember standing with my back to the Colosseum in Rome and looking at a low, green hill which used to be Nero's palace garden. I thought of the day when he held a barbecue in that garden. He had some Christians coated with tar and bitumen, tied them to posts around the garden and set them on fire. They were burned alive to provide lighting for his party.

The news of this barbarism against God's people spread through the whole Roman Empire from church to church. But as the news spread, so too did a letter from the apostle Peter. He wrote it to the Christians with whom he had a special connection and interest in what we now call north-west Turkey, to warn them and prepare them for persecution.

Peter himself would eventually die in that period – crucified in Rome at the hands of Nero. Jesus had predicted that he would die in this way, though when he came to be executed he requested that the cross be turned upside down, because he didn't feel worthy to be the same way up as Jesus.

Although there is no direct mention of it in Scripture, Peter had probably been ministering in that area. Paul had ministered in southern Turkey, but Peter seems to have gone to northern Turkey, and so it is to this area that he sends his letter.

The writer

We know a lot about Peter, and his first letter is a favourite among Christians. It is a warm, human letter that touches the heart. In the first chapter he tells his readers that even though they hadn't seen Jesus, they loved him and had an unspeakable joy in doing so. This love for his Saviour continues throughout the letter.

His first name was Simon or Simeon or Simone. It was a common name, though not especially complimentary – it meant 'reed'. But when Jesus met Simon, he gave him the name 'Peter', a less common name meaning 'rock', indicative of the change of character that Jesus expected. He started as a man easily swayed, like a reed in the wind, but when Jesus left him he was solid rock.

Peter was a fisherman from Bethsaida in Galilee, the brother of Andrew. They were the first two whom Jesus called to follow him. Peter is the first in every list of the Twelve and was the unofficial spokesman for the group.

Peter's character comes across very clearly in the Gospels. He has considerable strengths: he is charming, eager, impulsive and energetic. But these strengths are balanced by weaknesses: he could be unstable, fickle, weak, cowardly, rash and inconsistent. He was an impulsive man with foot-and-mouth disease – opening his mouth and putting his foot in it! But that also meant that he sometimes said wonderful things about Jesus. Many believers identify with Peter, because he is so like them.

Perhaps the most moving moment in his life came after he denied Jesus three times before Jesus' crucifixion, and then met him on the shores of Galilee after the resurrection. Jesus cooked breakfast for the disciples and Peter suddenly found himself looking into a charcoal fire. There are only two charcoal fires mentioned in the whole New Testament – the first was in the courtyard of the High Priest, when Peter was warming his hands over the fire, and denied that he knew Jesus three times. Now he is looking at a charcoal fire again, and no doubt the memory of his cowardice was still strong.

Jesus didn't say to Peter, 'I rather hoped you would be the first pastor, but I'm afraid now you will just have to give out the hymn-books.' Nor did he say, 'I am going to put you on probation for a year and see if you have pulled your socks up, and after a year we will review your case and reconsider your position.'

He actually said: 'Peter, I can cope with you, provided I am sure of one thing. Do you love me?'

This is the most important thing for any believer. Do you love him? Jesus asked Peter this same question three times, and somehow that put Peter back on track. A short time later it was Peter who was preaching at Pentecost when 3,000 were baptized. It is not surprising that the importance of love for Jesus is included in this epistle.

Peter is, of course, mentioned elsewhere in the New Testament, and was strongly involved with John Mark in the compilation of Mark's Gospel. Mark was not one of the Twelve and gleaned all his information from Peter – which is why, of all the Gospels, Mark includes Peter's weaknesses, and why Peter's own impulsive personality shines through the Gospel. In Mark, Jesus is seen as the 'man of action', not unlike Peter.

The first half of the Book of Acts is all about Peter, although because Luke wrote the book as a lawyer's brief at the trial of Paul, Peter disappears once Paul arrives on the scene.

He receives a brief, though less complimentary mention in Galatians, when Paul reflects on his heated exchange concerning Peter's refusal to have table fellowship with Gentiles in the presence of Jewish believers. Peter was wrong in his behaviour and Paul told him so.

We know he was married because Jesus healed his mother-in-law, and the apostle Paul mentions in passing that Peter took his wife with him on his missionary journeys. So we know more about Peter than any other of the apostles, with the exception of Paul.

The letter was written while Peter was in Rome. It is clear that both Peter and Paul spent some time there (Paul was under house arrest awaiting trial and was later executed at the hands of Nero), but there is no evidence that Peter was the first bishop of Rome – this is pure speculation by those who wish to believe in apostolic succession.

The readers

We are not sure how the church in Asia Minor (north-west Turkey) began, but Acts 2 records that on the day of Pentecost at Jerusalem there were people from the provinces of Cappadocia, Bithynia and Pontus, which made up Asia Minor. Maybe some people from that area were converted by Peter's first sermon, were baptized, went back home and later asked Peter to visit them.

Peter gives his readers a Jewish title, 'the Dispersion', even though they would have included many Gentiles. Just as the Jews were dispersed all over the world, so Christians were a dispersion. The name emphasizes that they were misfits. He calls them 'aliens and strangers'. The lack of specific details indicates that the letter is meant to be a circular letter for the believers in that region.

This 'misfits' label is apt, even today. One of the problems when you become a Christian is that you become a misfit. I can't stand testimonies that go like this: 'I came to Jesus and all my troubles were over.' I don't believe them, for a start, and they are so misleading. My testimony is rather different: 'I came to Jesus at 17, and my troubles began! Some years later I got filled with the Spirit, and my troubles got much worse!'

From time to time I am asked what is the evidence of being filled with the Spirit, and I always say, 'I will tell you in one word – trouble!' The reason you get into trouble is that one of the immediate effects of being filled with the Spirit is that you have a boldness of speech. This is even more common in Acts than tongues. The Greek word is *parrhesia*, meaning that you become bold to speak out. This is not the way to win friends and influence people!

Christians are misfits and no longer belong in the world. They are actually part of a new species – no longer *homo sapiens* but *homo novos* – 'new men and women', no longer in Adam, but in Christ.

This difference between a believer and those around them becomes particularly difficult, of course, when a husband or a wife is converted before their partner. Here are two people living in two different worlds. This is why the Bible teaches that a believer must not marry an unbeliever, otherwise there will be a whole area of life that they can't share.

Therefore Christians should expect trouble. Jesus was honest in telling his followers what to expect. Paul told the southern Galatian churches in Acts that 'through much tribulation we must enter the kingdom of God.' So evangelists should be honest, promising people who come to Jesus that they are in for trouble. But they can cheer up, because Jesus is on top of it.

Major themes

Turning to look at the major themes covered in 1 Peter, the first surprise is that Peter doesn't tell the believers how to escape persecution, but rather, how to endure it. The focus is on conducting themselves in a godly fashion in a hostile world, not on avoiding trouble. So suffering is at the heart of the letter and is one of the most frequently used words in it.

But Peter has two other themes. He wants to remind his readers of the salvation which is the foundation of their attitude to suffering, and then he wants to explain how to deal with suffering. Memory is a vital part of Christian living. Peter is urging them to think back to the central truths of their faith. So God's grace is a key element at the start and the end of the letter.

1. SALVATION – THROUGH CHRIST

Peter says there are two aspects of our salvation that we must
be sure of – the individual and the corporate. Both are a part of
being saved, though the former is more often discussed. We
are saved as individuals, but we are being saved into a family
which will stand us in good stead, especially when the pressure
is on. We won't be able to cope by ourselves. We need to be
part of a fellowship that is going to stay together.

(a) Individual – the word of God

The first focus is upon our vertical relationship with God. The
individual side comes through the word of God, for it is
through the word that we are born again. Peter lists the three
things that follow – faith, hope and love – a triad better known
at the end of 1 Corinthians 13, but which occurs all the way
through Scripture. Faith is primarily relating us to what God
has done in the past. Hope relates us to what he is going to do
in the future, and love relates us to what he is doing in the present. Let's look at these three in more detail:

(i) A living hope. Peter says hope is crucial as an anchor,
     because when the storm of persecution comes, hope will
     hold the believers firm. These days hope is the most
     neglected of the three. But the future hope is a key
     theme of the New Testament, and so it should be for us
     today.

     It was certainly key for Peter's readers, for if you know
     that Jesus is coming back for you, it is easier to face trou-
     ble. Peter's first letter is the epistle of hope. He tells them
     that 'God has given us a living hope by the resurrection
     from the dead.' Even if you are killed, death won't touch
     you! We have a living hope for the future, and the hope of
     a new body and a new planet earth on which to live. Hope

is not wishful thinking. We know we will receive our inheritance.

The real difference between a Christian who has got hope for the future and one who hasn't is this: a Christian who doesn't have hope is willing to depart and be with Christ but wanting to stay here, but a Christian with real hope wants to go but is willing to stay. Paul said, 'I am wanting to depart, but if God wants me to stay around here a little bit longer, I am willing to stay.' That's the attitude we should have.

(ii) A tested faith. Peter knew the readers would very soon be undergoing the severest test. He said that our faith would be tested just as gold is refined in a fire. The fires test it, and it comes out purer. In the days when gold was purified by hand, they used a big vat. The refiner would keep stirring it over the fire until he could see his own face in it perfectly, and then he stopped refining it. This is what Peter has in mind as a picture of what God is doing with us! Our faith is tested so that we become increasingly Christlike.

(iii) A joyful love. Salvation includes a new devotion to God and to people. Peter mentions the joy in the believers' hearts in knowing that Christ is risen and alive – a joy he had experienced himself on that first Easter Sunday.

Peter is clear that salvation is both past, having been accomplished in Christ (1:10; 4:10; 5:5), and future (1:13; 3:7; 5:10). We still await the final salvation that God will bring.

(b) Corporate – the people of God

In addition to the concern for an understanding of individual salvation, Peter wants the readers to grasp the corporate dimension. Through the word of God we find individual salvation for ourselves, but that also introduces us to the people of God, an important theme for Peter.

He uses Jewish titles to describe God's people:

(i)   A spiritual house. He tells them they are a living temple, with Christ as the cornerstone and themselves as living stones. They are God's dwelling-place on earth – his holy temple. When people touch them, they are touching God's holy temple. Whenever the phrase 'you are God's temple' occurs in Scripture, 'you' is always plural, and 1 Peter is no exception. He urges the believers not to feel a sense of inferiority because of the trial they will face, but to remember who they are and whose they are.

(ii) A royal priesthood. He also describes the believers as a royal priesthood. I remember giving a lecture on the priesthood of all believers at a seminar in Zurich in Switzerland. A man came to me afterwards and said, 'That was wonderful!' – he had never heard such a thing before. But when I asked him whether he was a priest, he immediately denied it – 'No, I'm a layman'! Only after repeated questioning about whether he was a priest did he realize that according to the New Testament, the answer was yes!

      Peter encourages his readers to bear their priesthood in mind when facing persecution. They must see themselves as priests, who can go to God on behalf of the people who are persecuting them. They may be the only priest their enemies will ever have.

(iii) A holy nation. Peter also urges the believers to 'be holy'. It is almost as if he has lifted the command straight out of the Book of Leviticus. Just as Israel was to be a model and example for the world of what it is like to live for God, so these believers were to do the same in the face of the persecution that would come to them. Understanding their exalted position would be a help as they sought to respond in a godly manner to the difficulties of life.

So Peter sees this discussion of salvation as a foundation. They must be absolutely sure they have the individual side of it – the faith, the hope and the love – and the corporate side, that they belong to the people of God.

2. SUFFERING

According to Peter, suffering is the inevitable result of salvation. Indeed, it is astonishing how much of the New Testament was written to Christians who were suffering, or about to suffer, persecution. Like Peter's letters, Hebrews and Revelation are written against this backdrop. Both Jesus and Paul were concerned to warn believers that they would face persecution. Western Christianity, where persecution is minimal, is actually abnormal. Peter says three things about the suffering:

(a) Make sure you don't deserve it

If you go to prison for a crime, then you certainly can't say that you are suffering for Jesus. Often we offend people with our manner or our awkwardness, and we pretend that their negative reaction is the offence of the gospel, when it is nothing of the kind. We must make sure that the only offence is the offence of the gospel. So Peter is concerned that his readers should not be deserving of any punishment they receive.

(b) Don't take revenge

When the readers suffer, Peter says they must not retaliate. The natural instinct is, of course, to hit back. Someone once told me that he didn't mind turning the other cheek as taught in the Sermon on the Mount, providing he could also bring the right knee up sharply! We smile because we know how he feels.

When somebody harms us, we instinctively want to take revenge. Peter says that Christians must never do that. When Jesus suffered he did not retaliate, even when they spat on him. When a lamb was slain in the Old Testament, it was not tortured beforehand – its throat was cut quickly with a minimum of pain. But when the Lamb of God was slain, they mocked him, flogged him, jammed thorns into his forehead, dressed him up and spat on him. Yet his response was to ask his Father to forgive his enemies because they didn't realize what they were doing.

Peter says that in the same way, we should never think of getting our own back. We should repay evil with good. As Jesus said, we should 'bless those who curse us' rather than seeking to get even.

(c) Don't let it get to you

The persecutors were trying to wear down the believers, so Peter's advice was not to allow them to. He reminds the readers that although their bodies may be harmed, the persecutors are unable to touch their spirits. 'Let them do what they like with your body, but keep your spirit intact – that way, even though you seem to be losing, you will, in the end, gain the victory.'

Suffering is only for a little while, after all – a lifetime is nothing compared to eternity. Furthermore, the devil is behind all persecution, so don't see it in purely human terms.

3. SUBMISSION

As hinted earlier, Peter urges his readers to learn to submit to suffering rather than seek to avoid it. He applies this unusual advice in a number of areas. It is not blind submission, as we shall see, but it is learning to have a submissive spirit.

One of the things that astonished the world when the Jews were being carted off to extermination camps was how quietly they walked into the cremation chambers. It was an astonishing fact, because they knew what was going to happen to them. Peter is saying that the Christian must have a similar attitude.

Such behaviour is against all human instinct, the very opposite of how we normally respond to injustice. When something is unfair we generally say so. One of the earliest things children learn to say is 'It's not fair!' You hear the same sentiments expressed on picket lines outside a factory on strike.

Yet Peter is saying that Christians have no rights. They need to prepare for suffering by learning to give in and accept it. Peter perfectly exemplified this attitude when he came to be crucified himself. He didn't fight it, but insisted on being crucified upside down.

Peter covers four areas where submission is especially appropriate:

(a) Citizens

First, the readers should learn to submit to the civic authorities (a theme also developed in Paul's writings). They should be honest citizens, they should honour the Emperor, and they should pray for their rulers. Christians should be known as people who are glad to pay their taxes. They should not grumble about the government, but should be known as loyal subjects.

This does not mean, of course, that they are to do everything they are told. There is a limit on obedience to civic authorities. When the authorities told the apostles to stop preaching Jesus in the streets, it was Peter himself who said, 'We must obey God rather than men.' The limit comes when the authorities tell us to do something that is against the law of God. But providing this is not the case, Christians must be loyal subjects and should not be arrested because they are rebellious or aggressive towards the authorities.

(b) Slaves

It is no surprise that Christian slaves of unbelieving masters also faced suffering. The slave was the total property of his master. He had no money, time or rights of his own. Many of the masters treated their slaves abominably, and when the slaves became Christians, the masters treated them worse because they thought the slaves were getting above themselves and needed to be kept down. But in the face of this provocation, Peter urges the slaves to submit to their masters, to learn to give in and not be aggressive or resentful towards them.

(c) Christian wives

Another group that faced great suffering were Christian wives of unconverted husbands. This is a very difficult situation which causes great heartache. Peter tells wives to be subject to their husbands, which includes even the unbelieving ones. Peter gives advice on how wives can win their unconverted husband for Christ, which is totally contrary to what tends to happen. When a wife is converted before a husband, she thinks the two things she must do are preach at him and pray for him (preferably praying with all the other converted wives of all the unconverted husbands!).

Peter says neither – in fact he says that if you preach, it is the worst thing you can do. He says you have got to win him without a word. So he would have no time for the Christian wife who goes home after church and tells her husband how the sermon was ideal for him! Sadly, when the wife is converted, too many non-believing husbands say, 'Jesus ran off with my wife! She doesn't belong to me any more.'

It is very important that wives learn to go along with their husbands, but far too many women go to coffee mornings and Bible studies and become spiritual racehorses, while their husbands are still at the starting-post and feel less and less like the head of the house.

Most Christian wives later regret having preached to their husbands. By contrast, Peter says, 'Become more attractive to look at and more attractive to live with.' That is a simple pro-gramme for Christian wives. In chapter 3 Peter explains how the wife should become beautiful, though it's worth noting that he does not explain how to be glamorous. The beauty is to be inward first; the outward will follow.

(d) Young people

There is a fourth area of submission, though Peter separates it from the other three because it is not to do with suffering. He says that younger people should submit to older people, give way to them and look to them for leadership. One of the pun-ishments the prophet Isaiah had to announce to Israel was that their failure to go God's way meant they would be ruled by women and exploited by youth – which is not irrelevant to the situation in the church today.

In all this Peter is not saying that they should blindly sub-mit. But what Peter is saying is that whether they are young wives, or employees, they should develop the attitude of not being aggressive, of not asserting themselves or insisting on their rights.

If the devil is ultimately behind all suffering, then God needs to be behind all submission. It takes a Christlike spirit to endure suffering silently and submit to those over you. Yet in so doing, believers follow the way of their Master, who didn't retaliate when sent to the cross, but was able to say, 'Father, forgive them – they don't know what they are doing.'

A problem passage

Although 1 Peter is generally straightforward, there is one problem – an unusual passage in chapter 3 which has at least 314 different interpretations! The passage says that Jesus was put to death in the body and made alive in the spirit, in which he went and preached to those who were disobedient in the days of Noah's flood. A few verses later Peter says, 'This is why the gospel was preached even to those who were dead, that they might be saved in their spirit.'

Liberal preachers have based their doctrine of a second chance for salvation after death on this passage, despite the fact that every other scripture says it is impossible. Death seals our fate. There is a great gulf fixed beyond death. But here, apparently, Jesus did preach to those who had died.

How should we understand it? I find that the trouble with the many interpretations is that people try to get round the simple, plain meaning of it, because it is an awkward passage to fit in with the general teaching of Scripture that death is the end of your opportunity of salvation.

I always start by taking Scripture in its simplest, plainest sense, and only change it if it really is difficult. It clearly says that between his death and resurrection Jesus was active, conscious and actually communicating with others, who were also fully conscious and communicating with him.

Now, of course, you never hear about this in church because all Holy Week services finish on Friday and start up again on Sunday, so you are never told what Jesus was doing on the Saturday! It also raises, incidentally, interesting questions about the precise events of that week. The Gospels talk of Jesus being in the tomb three days and three nights, but traditional Friday-to-Sunday interpretations leave us with one day and two nights! In fact, I believe that Jesus died on the Wednesday afternoon – all the evidence points to that. We have assumed that Friday was the day he died, because the text tells us he died on the day before the Sabbath. But in the year in question, it was not the Saturday Sabbath. John's Gospel tells us that the Sabbath was a special High Sabbath. The Passover began with a Sabbath and, in the year AD 29, which was almost certainly the year Jesus died, the first day of the Passover was a Thursday, with the Wednesday being the eve of the Passover. This fits all the evidence better than all the other theories. So if he died at 3 o'clock on the Wednesday and he rose between 6 p.m. and midnight on the Saturday, every bit of the Gospel evidence fits.

To return to Peter's passage, we tend to think of Jesus doing nothing between his death and resurrection, being just unconscious, inactive in the tomb. But it says only his body was dead. His spirit was very much alive. He went to the world of the dead and he was preaching. I can imagine Peter meeting Jesus on the first Easter Sunday and saying, 'Jesus, where on earth have you been?'

Jesus replies, 'I haven't been on earth, I have been in Hades, the world of the departed.'

'What on earth (or what in Hades!) have you been doing for three days and three nights?'

So Jesus tells Peter that he was preaching to those who were drowned in Noah's flood. This means, of course, that those who were drowned in Noah's flood were also conscious and that we will be fully conscious one minute after we have died. We will know who we are, we will have our memory. It is only our body that dies, not our spirit. Death separates body and spirit. Later, spirit and body will be reunited in the resurrection.

But Jesus went through all three phases in less than a week. He was an embodied spirit until he died on the cross. Then he commended his spirit to God, and his body was put in the tomb. Alive in the spirit, he went and preached to those disobedient people from Noah's flood. And then his body and spirit were reunited on Easter Sunday morning. But he was fully conscious and able to communicate all the way through.

If we take that at face value, it does mean that Jesus went and preached the gospel to that particular generation, and *only* to them. It does clearly imply that it was a gospel that could save them and redeem them, so isn't this a second chance after death?

I believe it was a second chance for them and for them only. There is no hint in the Bible that anyone else would ever have such an opportunity. But it seems that this was one generation who could accuse God of being unjust and unfair. They could say, 'You wiped us out and then promised never to do it again.' I believe that God wanted to make it clear that his justice and his righteousness were pure, and so he said, 'Son, go and tell them the gospel. I won't have anyone on the Day of Judgement accusing me of treating anyone unfairly.' God is righteous, and bends over backwards not to be unfair or have favourites. So maybe that is why this unusual and extreme incident arose.

So rather than to try to twist Scripture to fit our system, it is better to accept it at its simplest, plainest level. But there is no ground here for a second chance for anyone else – that is universalism, and that is not taught in Scripture.

Conclusion

Although the United Kingdom is generally free of persecution, I can anticipate increasing pressure, not least over such things as the Sex Discrimination Act, where churches will face pressure to liberalize their stance on homosexuality in the church and female elders. I can forsee the day when it will be considered an offence either to criticize another religion or even to say that your religion is better than any other. 1 Peter may one day be especially relevant to us.

The first words of Jesus that Peter heard were 'Follow me.' It is this following of Jesus that shines through in the letter. We must stand up to suffering as Jesus did. Christ was the Cornerstone, Christians are described as living stones. Christ is the Chief Shepherd, Christian leaders are under-shepherds. Just as he was hated and experienced suffering, so too will Christians. They must live as he lived.

2 Peter

This letter was written in AD 67, three years after Peter's first letter, just before he was crucified in Rome. In John's Gospel Jesus had predicted that Peter would die violently when he was old. So for 40 years he lived with the knowledge that he would be killed, though he did not know when. He says in the letter that he believes the time will be soon.

It is so different in style to 1 Peter that some scholars say it could not have been written by Peter. Its Greek is more laboured, almost as if someone was translating from one language to another using a dictionary, but with little knowledge of the grammar. Also, there are no greetings at the end or addressees at the beginning.

Indeed, 2 Peter was one of the books that were not readily accepted into the canon of the New Testament by the early church. This was partly because there were many forged documents which purported to be written by the apostles but which were in fact nothing of the sort, and partly because of the difference in style.

But the similarities are all there. Peter's favourite words still appear in the second letter as well as the first. If you go through the two letters you will find he keeps talking about our 'precious' faith and our 'precious' Jesus. Everything is 'precious' to Peter. He uses the word five times in his first letter and twice in the second.

Furthermore, he refers to his former letter (see 2 Peter 3:1). He writes of himself as an eye-witness of the Transfiguration. He knew the apostle Paul personally and spoke with him as an equal. There are words that occur in 2 Peter that are only found in 1 and 2 Peter and in Peter's speeches in Acts. So there is good reason to believe that the author of 2 Peter is indeed Peter.

So how do we account for the difference in style between Peter's two letters? I believe that Peter wrote 2 Peter, but without using Silas as a secretary, as he did with the first letter. He knows he needs to write urgently, but he doesn't know Greek well, so the grammar is more clumsy, though the meaning is clear. This would account for the difference of style quite comfortably. In some ways 2 Peter is Peter's last will and testament, just as 2 Timothy was Paul's.

Content

The letter deals with a totally different situation from his first. The readers are the same, but it's a few years later, and he feels the urgent need to address dangers inside the church. There are two kinds of pressures that churches face: the pressures from outside the church and the pressures from inside, and it is the latter that are the more dangerous. Satan has never destroyed the church from outside. The more he hits it from the outside, the bigger and stronger it gets. This is why, during the first three centuries of Christianity, when Christians were being thrown to the lions, the church grew very rapidly. This is also why today you can go to China – a nation where Christians are persecuted – and find villages where most of the population are born again. So whereas hostility was the problem in the first letter, it's heresy that is being faced in the second.

CONTRASTS BETWEEN 1 AND 2 PETER

1 Peter (AD 64)	2 Peter (AD 67)
'suffering' 16 times	'knowledge' 16 times
Danger	
Simple External Persecution	Subtle Internal Heresy
Weakness	
Compromise Anxiety	Corruption Apostasy
Status	
Birth Milk	Growth Maturity
Tone	
Comfort Wooing	Caution Warning
Hope of Christ's return	
To save The godly	To judge The ungodly

AN OUTLINE OF 2 PETER

Chapter 1: maturity to be attained
Chapter 2: morality to be maintained
Chapter 3: morale to be sustained

Peter's second letter follows exactly the same pattern as his first, which is a further proof to me that it is from the same author. There is a section on salvation, then a section on the danger. He then draws out the implications and prepares them to cope with the persecution that he knew would come.

Chapter 1: maturity to be attained

The first letter talks about new birth and the need to desire 'the milk of the word'. But in the second letter he addresses them as adults, urging them to growth and maturity. Immature Christians crave novelty; mature believers desire knowledge. He wants them to be among the second category, believing that knowledge leads to maturity.

He uses the word 'knowledge' 16 times, but never in an academic sense. He is concerned that they might have an experiential knowledge of God, based on the Scriptures. He is keen, too, that they should bring to mind all that they know about God and their faith. He uses words such as 'forgotten', 'remind', 'refresh your memory' and 'remember'. The Christian life requires constant recall of truth. This is seen supremely, of course, in eating bread and drinking wine at Communion – an ordinance designed so that we might remember Christ.

Peter's description of the mature life that every believer should seek can be summarized with a diagram showing the household of faith:

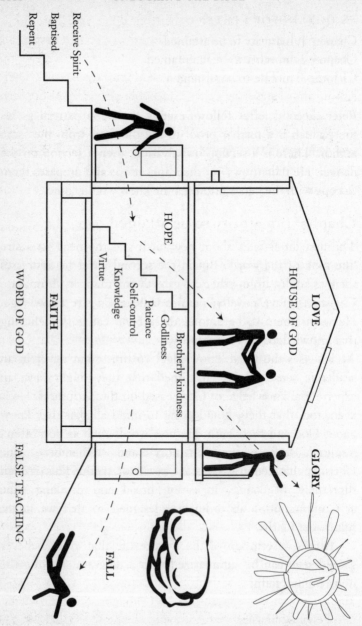

Note the steps of faith up to the front door, which are not in 2 Peter but are in Peter's sermon in Acts 2:38. The first step is 'Repent'; the second is 'Be baptized'; the third is 'Receive the Holy Spirit'. These are all steps of faith into the 'house'. There are no more steps than that. My book, *The Normal Christian Birth* (Hodder & Stoughton, 1989), gives further explanation of why these should be part of every believer's entrance into the Kingdom. We must make sure we don't raise the front door higher than we need to. Too many Bible teachers make additions that are not necessary for someone to be part of the household.

But having taken the first three steps into the household, there is a staircase. Peter says that we should add to our faith a number of qualities: virtue, knowledge, self-control, patience, godliness, brotherly kindness, and love.

In climbing the staircase of these qualities, we are building up our hope, for they help to make our calling and election sure. Indeed, this assurance can't be gained any other way. Our certainty about what God is going to do will get stronger and stronger as we progress.

So the church is founded on faith, grows in hope and is filled with love. The triad of his first letter and other parts of the Bible reappears.

There is a balcony upstairs and from that balcony you take off for glory, and you make a grand entrance into heaven. So Peter is urging his readers to progress. Don't sit down on the sofa on the ground floor. Climb the stairs, live in the upper room, get up there as quickly as you can.

So the answer to heresy is maturity. People who make little progress are vulnerable to false teaching on the ground floor. If they listen to false teaching they will find themselves going out the back door and slipping down a slippery slope and falling.

Peter emphasizes that the truth that he preached was not

his own idea. Rather, he and the other apostles and prophets had received it from God. Indeed, the prophets were often unaware of the full implications of what they were saying, serving generations to come rather than their immediate audience.

Chapter 2: morality to be maintained

This chapter in 2 Peter is almost word for word the same as the Letter of Jude. It is not, of course, the only place in the Bible where this is the case. Isaiah 2 and Micah 4 also include identical text, but questions have inevitably been raised as to how this can be.

When you come across this phenomenon in Scripture, there are five possibilities. Here they are:

1   Peter borrowed it from Jude.
2   Jude borrowed it from Peter.
3   Peter and Jude borrowed it from somewhere else.
4   Peter and Jude got together and discussed the problem and agreed on the solution, and sent it in different letters.
5   The Holy Spirit gave both of them exactly the same words.

All are possible, though I am inclined to rule out the fifth option, because the Holy Spirit doesn't use people as word processors. Our doctrine of the inspiration of Scripture must not suggest that the writers were just human typewriters. This is not how the Bible tells us that it was written. Indeed, it is unlikely that the Holy Spirit would give exactly the same words to two different people.

I prefer to say that there was collaboration. Peter was one of the inner circle of disciples and Jude was one of the Lord's own brothers, so it is highly likely that they knew each other.

In any case, the overlap material is relatively small. Jude is very short – it is the same length as 2 Peter chapter 2. The material that overlaps with Jude concerns the four corruptions that were in the church.

1. A CORRUPT CREED

Just as there were false prophets in Israel, so there were false prophets in the church. We are not told their precise message, but it is clear from the way Peter deals with the problem that two beliefs in particular were being changed. They had moved to a syncretistic view of the person of Christ and a sentimental view of the grace of God.

(a) A syncretistic view of the person of Christ

Some of the church were saying that Jesus was not the only Lord, but just one among others. He was a way to God, but there were many others. It was the word 'only' which caused offence. They were thus corrupting the person of Christ, making a Jesus of their own imagination rather than the one of the Gospels. It was not an uncommon teaching in the early church. For example, the church at Colosse was affected by such Gnostic teaching, with devastating effects.

(b) A sentimental view of the grace of God

Some professing believers thought it didn't really matter how they lived, as long as they had their ticket to heaven. Their attitude was that God loves to forgive, and will go on forgiving, no matter what you do. This is sheer sentiment and is a view preached widely today. But, of course, it means that Christians go on sinning, and take advantage of God's mercy. Such a view perverts the grace of God and leads inevitably to immorality, for there is no perception that God is concerned about how Christians live.

2. CORRUPT CONDUCT

What you believe affects your behaviour. So if individuals change or adjust the Christian faith, they will inevitably introduce error into the church. Peter describes the sins of speech that characterize their lives. He says they are bold and arrogant, slanderers, blasphemers, mouthing empty and boastful words.

Not only was their speech corrupt, but so was their behaviour. They weren't coming under the lordship of Christ. They were ignoring the commandments.

Both Peter and Jude were writing to help churches that had fallen into error. So, alas, there are some people who come into the household of faith in the correct way, but they leave by the back door. Then there are those who climb the stairs, get stronger in hope, reach the room of love and take off for glory. The former go back under the wrath and judgement of God. The latter enjoy the sunshine of his grace and favour.

3. CORRUPT CHARACTER

Corrupt character flows from corrupt conduct. There is a description of the effects of this wrong teaching on the character of people. It says that they become more animal than human, operating by base instincts rather than the Spirit of God. They become greedy and lustful and no longer reliable, for they are more driven by mood than by principle. They are like 'clouds driven by the wind', like 'waves of the sea' – vivid depictions of weak character.

4. CORRUPT CONVERSATION

Inevitably, corrupt conduct and character is seen in the kind of conversation that goes on within the church. Grumblers and complainers rebelled against the leadership, and there was the kind of unrest that leads to disunity. People not previously affected become engulfed in the gathering fire of discontent, in a manner that denies the uniting power of the gospel.

Both Peter and Jude write about this train of corruptions in order to fight them, for they knew they would finish off the church. Persecution wouldn't finish the church, because it would collapse from within. And so when persecution did come, it would be unable to stand.

Peter was thus concerned about the state of the believers within the churches. He issues some severe warnings about apostasy. He says it would be better for believers never to have known the way of righteousness than to know it, only to fall back into sin. He uses crude language to describe someone who falls away – they are like a dog going back to lick its own vomit. They came from sin and are now going back to it. Or they are like a pig that is going back to wallow in the mud after having been bathed and washed.

God is as concerned about sin in believers as he is about sin in those who are outside the church. Indeed, the person who falls away will be punished more severely than the one who never repented. It is a stark and solemn warning for those who believe they are 'safe' because they have trusted in Christ, even though their life gives a lie to their profession of faith.

Chapter 3: morale to be sustained

The final chapter in 2 Peter looks at hope for the future. Again the teaching is motivated by the concerns of the churches. Some were claiming that talk about the second coming was empty. Christ had not returned. Where was he?

So Peter replies to the scoffers. He reminds them that time is different to God. To him one day is as a thousand years. Every day that the coming is delayed is an example of God's patience. The delay is 'their salvation'. He says that one day all the universe will be dissolved in fire. There is to be another holocaust, and this time it will be not a flood of water, but a flood of fire. I don't imagine that it will be a nuclear war; I think God will release all the energy in every atom. He packed the energy into the atom, so all he would need to do would be to unlock it, and the whole world would go up in smoke.

But Peter concludes the section by reminding his readers that out of the fire, like a phoenix rising from the flames, there will be a new heaven and a new earth. I love preaching about the new earth. Don't leave it to the Jehovah's Witnesses – it is a Christian truth, it is in the Bible! But I am afraid Christians only want to hear about going to heaven – which is, after all, just a waiting-room we go to before we enter into all that God has for us.

The theme of the new earth coming is developed by John at the end of Revelation. This earth is going to be the centre of the future. Christians are the only ones who know this. Everybody is panicking about the ozone layer and the polluted oceans and the dying forests. They are concerned because they think this is the only planet we will ever have to live on. We know better than that; we look for a new heaven and a new earth. We know there is going to be something that will be different from this planet we have known, for it will be a new heaven and earth in which righteousness will dwell. There will be no vice, no crime, no sin, nothing dirty, nothing filthy.

Peter says that if we keep our hope fixed on this, we will live the way that we will be living in that new world. We won't listen to the false teaching and won't get caught up in it and tainted by it. We will keep ourselves unspotted from the apostate church, never mind the world.

So a godly hope is his real defence against the immorality that can get into the church through false teaching. Keep your eyes fixed on that new world, a world of righteousness which will keep you living right, because you know that if you don't, you won't be part of that new world. It is as we live in faith, hope and love that we get ready for glory. When you hear the sound of the trumpet, you will have your first free flight to the Holy Land!

On my grandfather's tombstone in Newcastle there are three words from an old Methodist hymn. There is his name, 'David Ledger Pawson', and underneath, 'What a Meeting'. If you don't like noisy worship, don't be around then, for the archangel will be shouting and trumpets will be blowing. It will be enough to raise the dead, which is exactly what it will do. Those who have died will get front seats, so don't worry if you die first.

Peter finishes with a stark choice. We can either ignore his teaching and be among those who fall away, or we can be those who continue to grow in the grace of Christ. Peter said God was able to keep Lot even in Sodom and Gomorrah. And so he can keep you too.

56.

JUDE

Introduction

A neglected book

Jude has been called 'the most neglected book in the New Testament'. There are a number of reasons for this:

1. IT'S SMALL

Along with Philemon and 2 and 3 John, it is one of the smallest books in the New Testament.

2. IT'S STRANGE

Readers are puzzled by the reference to the Archangel Michael arguing with Satan over Moses' body. What does that refer to? The references to 'the sons of Korah' and to angels locked in a dungeon seem similarly obscure. What did the sons do and why are angels locked up in a dungeon?

3. IT'S SUSPECT

Some people take exception to the way Jude quotes the Apocrypha. The Apocrypha is the name given to the Jewish books written in the 400 years between the end of Malachi and the beginning of Matthew – books included in the Catholic version of the Bible but not in the Protestant Bible. These

writings never claim to be the word of God, for they do not
include the phrase, 'Thus says the Lord', which occurs 3,808
times in the Old Testament – hence their omission from the
Protestant Bible. God didn't speak during the 400 years
between the Testaments. There were no prophets to speak for
him. These writings are not prophetic, but this does not mean
that they do not have value or do not contain true statements.
So Jude's quotations from the Apocrypha need not cast doubt
on Jude, just because apocryphal writings are not canonical.
The writings were well known and so proved valuable to back
up his point.

4. IT'S SEVERE

Jude comes across as negative and intolerant, as he seeks to
warn the believers and challenge them to action.

5. IT'S SHARP

Jude is like a surgeon wielding a knife to cut out the cancer in
the body of Christ. Hence some of the language is strong, as he
condemns evil teaching.

PRESSURES

Jude's sharp tone is necessary on occasion, especially as internal
pressures from errant teachers can create such havoc among
the people of God. Churches face danger from two sources:

External

Pressure from persecution will always be possible, though at
different levels. Today the church is undergoing what may be
termed 'persecution' in 225 countries. But during external
pressure, the church continues to thrive.

Internal

Pressure from within is the greater cause for concern. Paul's Letter to the Galatians explains how legalism and liberalism within the church gave great concern in the early years of its life. Jesus condemned both the legalism of the Pharisees and the liberalism of the Sadducees. Yet these dangers are all too evident in churches, especially in second-generation ones. They can become too narrow-minded, imposing standards of discipline that go beyond the requirements of the Bible. Or they can become too lax, failing to impose any discipline on behaviour that is contrary to apostolic practice.

The different views can be summed up like this. Legalism says you are *not free to sin*, and we are going to see that you don't. Licence says you are *free to sin* and it is OK now that you are a Christian – you have your ticket to heaven, so you needn't worry. But the true liberty of Christianity says, 'You are *free not to sin*. Sin does matter in the life of the believer, but Christ has freed you from its power.' So Jude's concerns are no different from those of Jesus and the apostle Paul. Jude is a profound epistle with a message that is vital for the church today.

But having explained some of its difficulties, there is no doubt that it is a challenging book to understand. I've paraphrased it to bring out its meaning a little more clearly.

A paraphrase

This letter comes from Judas – Jude for short – one of the slaves bought by King Jesus, and a brother of the James you know well.

It is addressed to those who have been called out of the world, who are now loved ones in the family of God, their Father, and who are being kept for presentation to King Jesus. May you have more and more of the mercy, peace and love you have already experienced.

Loved ones, I was fully intending to correspond with you about the wonderful salvation we share, but found that I had to write quite a different kind of letter. I must urge you to keep up the painful struggle for the preservation of the true faith that was passed on to the early saints once and for all. I've heard that certain persons, who shall be nameless, have sneaked in among you – godless men whose sentence of doom was pronounced long ago. They twist the free grace of God into an excuse for blatant immorality, and they deny that King Jesus is our only Master and Lord.

Now I want to remind you of some of those absolute truths which you already know perfectly well, particularly that God is not someone to be trifled with. You will recall that the Lord brought a whole nation safely out of Egypt, but the next time he intervened, they were all exterminated for not trusting him.

Nor were his angels any more exempt than his people. When some of them deserted their rank and abandoned their proper station, he took them into custody and is keeping them permanently chained in the lowest and darkest dungeon until their trial on the great Day of Judgement.

And in the same way, the inhabitants of Sodom and Gomorrah, together with those from two neighbouring towns, glutted themselves with gross debauchery, craving for unnatural intercourse, just as the angels had done. And the fate they suffered in the fire that burned for ages is a solemn warning to us all.

In spite of such examples in history, these people who have wormed their way into your fellowship pollute their own bodies in exactly the same manner. They belittle divine authority and smear angels in glory. Yet even the chief of all angels – Michael, whose very name means 'godlike' – did not dare to accuse Satan directly of blasphemy when they were arguing about who owned the body of Moses, and he was content to leave accusations to God himself and said simply, 'The Lord rebuke you.'

But these men among you don't hesitate to malign whatever they don't understand, and the only things they do understand will prove their undoing in the end, for their knowledge of life comes only from their animal instincts, like brute beasts without any capacity for reason. Woe betide them! They've gone down the same road as Cain. They have rushed headlong into the same mistake as Balaam, and for the same motivation – money. They will come to the same end as Korah did in his rebellion.

These people have the cheek to eat with you at your fellowship meals of love, though they are only looking for pasture for themselves. Like submerged rocks, they could wreck everything. They're like clouds driven past so hard by the wind that they give no rain. They are like uprooted trees in autumn, with neither leaves nor fruit, doubly dead. They are like wild waves of the sea, stirring up the filthy foam of their own odious disgrace. They are like shooting stars falling out of orbit, destined to disappear down a black hole forever.

Enoch, who lived only seven generations after the first man, Adam, saw all this coming. He was referring to these very people when he made his prophetic announcement, 'Look out! The Lord has arrived with ten thousand of his angels to put all human beings on trial and convict all godless people of all the godless deeds they have committed in their godless lives, and of the hard things they have spoken against him.' These people are discontented grumblers, always complaining and finding fault. Their mouths are full of big talk about themselves, but they're not above flattering others when it is to their advantage.

Now, loved ones, you should have remembered what the apostles of our Lord Jesus Christ said would happen. They predicted that in the final age there are bound to be those who pour scorn on godliness, whose lives will only be governed by their own godless cravings. People like this can only create divisions among you, since they only have their natural instincts to go by and they lack the guidance of the Spirit.

As for you, loved ones, be sure to go on building yourselves up on the solid foundation of your most holy faith, praying in the way the Spirit gives you. Stay in love with God, waiting patiently for the time when our Lord Jesus Christ in his sheer mercy will bring you into immortal living. As regards the others, here is my advice. To those who are still wavering, be especially kind and gentle. Those who have already been led into error must be snatched from the fire before they are badly burned. And those who have been thoroughly contaminated should be treated better than they deserve, though you must never lose a healthy fear of being infected yourself, even by their stained underwear. Let's just praise the one Person who is able to keep you from stumbling and to make you stand upright in his glorious presence without any imperfection, but with great jubilation – the only God there is, and he's our Saviour too, through Jesus Christ our Lord. For to him alone belongs all glory, all majesty, all power and all authority, before history began, now in this present time, and for all ages to come. So it will be. [That's what the word 'Amen' means.]

WHO IS JUDE?

Jude was the second youngest brother of Jesus. His real name is Judas, shortened to Jude, to distinguish him from the apostle who betrayed Jesus.

When we examined the letter written by James, one of his other brothers, we noted that the brothers of Jesus didn't believe in him during his lifetime. This is made clear by their scepticism about his claims to messiahship recorded in John's Gospel (John 7:4). It was at the time of the Feast of

Tabernacles in Jerusalem, and they teased him about his claims to be sent by God. Everyone knew that if the Messiah came, it would be during the Festival, so they said he had better go and show himself. Jesus told them that the time was not right to say who he was publicly, but he did go to the Feast secretly.

But after the resurrection, the situation changed and his brothers became missionaries for Jesus. James and Jude wrote two letters and were both careful to play down their family relationship with Jesus, preferring to focus on their spiritual relationship. They both refer to themselves as 'a slave of Jesus'.

Content

Moral pollution

It is clear that Jude intended to write a quite different letter. In the early part of the letter he says, 'I wanted to write about the salvation we enjoy in Jesus.' But when he heard what was happening in the churches he was writing to, he changed his mind. So he adds, 'I'm pleading with you to keep up the painful struggle for the faith that was once delivered to the saints' (my translation).

The word 'painful' indicates the intensity of the struggle. Indeed, it is the most painful struggle that they will ever have. It is especially painful because it is their own brothers and sisters they have to deal with. The struggle concerns heretical teachers who were leading the church astray. Jude knew they would continue to pollute the membership if they were not checked.

The first half of the letter is about a very dangerous corruption that has crept into the churches to which he is writing. Then the second half tells them how to deal with that situation in a delicate way. We shall look first at the four phases whereby the corruption affects the church.

1. CREED

Jude outlines how people have secretly wormed their way into the fellowship. The implication is that their actions were underhand, and their intentions evil. They poisoned the fellowship with their teaching and their behaviour, and so must be dealt with. False teaching was like a cancer spreading throughout the body, and would result in death if it wasn't dealt with. It is clear that the false teaching was similar to that which Peter wrote against in his second letter, which is why the two letters share an identical section. I believe Jude used 2 Peter as part of his research and was happy to include part of it word for word.

There were two areas in particular in which the false teachers were errant. They had a sentimental view of God and a syncretistic view of Jesus.

(a) A sentimental view of God

Their sentimental view of God made God's grace an excuse for immorality. They saw God as a 'nice old boy' who pats you on the head and says, 'Let's forgive and forget. All I want you to be is happy.' That's the caricature of God that is too often preached on TV – a nice, comfortable God who wouldn't harm a fly. It's a sentimental view of God, but not a scriptural one. God doesn't overlook sin, he deals with it. We need to recover that non-sentimental but scriptural view of God.

(b) A syncretistic view of Jesus

They also had a syncretistic view of Jesus. They no longer believed that Jesus was the only Master and Lord, and sought to put him on a level with others – a situation all too common in the present day. Once you put Jesus in a pantheon with Mohammed and Buddha and all the rest, he is no longer the only way to God. He is no longer 'the way, the truth and the life' but 'a way, a truth and a life'.

2. CONDUCT

Once you've corrupted a church's creed, it's not long before their conduct goes haywire as well. Ultimately belief determines behaviour, so Jude comes to the severest part of his warning. He reminds the believers of what had happened to three groups in history.

(a) Israel in the wilderness

Jude recalls the story from Exodus 32 of the children of Israel in the wilderness, who made a golden calf and quickly fell into immorality and idolatry. Their view of God departed from the one given by Moses in the Ten Commandments and subsequent teaching. As a consequence, they developed a wrong view of each other and started mistreating each other, rather than loving each other in the way they had been taught. The result was that none of them got into Canaan. They had been redeemed from Egypt but they didn't get into the Promised Land. They started out but none of them finished.

This incident is used three times in the New Testament by three different writers to warn Christians that it's not those who start but those who finish who will inherit all that God has for them. Paul uses it, the writer to the Hebrews uses it, and here Jude uses it.

So the warning is clear: if the children of Israel were redeemed from Egypt but didn't make it to the Promised Land, that can also happen to the believer today. It's not just what you've left behind, it's what's still ahead. It's not yours yet – you need to persevere if you are not to perish in the wilderness.

(b) The angels at Mount Hermon

Jude looks at what happened to the angels at Mount Hermon. We know details of this from the Book of Enoch in the Apocrypha (though, as we have noted, the Apocrypha is not part of the Bible).

In the region of Mount Hermon about 200 angels seduced women and impregnated them. This horrible intercourse between angels and humans spawned ghastly hybrid creatures called the Nephilim – thankfully, they have all died out. We can't be sure what they were like – they are known as 'giants' in some translations. God has his order of life, and angels having sex with human beings is as offensive to him as human beings having sex with animals.

The result of this behaviour was that violence filled the earth, and perverted sex and occultism were rampant. We even read in Genesis that God was grieved that he had ever made humankind – in my view, that is one of the saddest verses in the Bible.

So Jude is saying that if God's people Israel didn't escape judgement and the angels didn't escape judgement, how do you think you will as Christians?

(c) Sodom and Gomorrah

The third example concerns Sodom and Gomorrah. These cities are well known, but there were also Admah and Zeboiim, making four cities at the southern end of the Dead Sea. In due course they have all been engulfed by an earthquake. The Dead Sea is like a figure-of-eight. The cities are under the most southerly part which is now drying up. So Sodom and Gomorrah could reappear in our lifetime. What a symbolic event that would be!

We know from the Jewish historian Josephus that the fire that destroyed Sodom and Gomorrah 2,000 years before Jesus was still burning in Jesus' day. When Jesus spoke of it in his talks, the hearers could just walk for 30 minutes outside Jerusalem and see the smoke.

These two cities were punished because they went against God's laws. Homosexual relationships became tolerated, just as today the criticism of same-sex unions is regarded as politically incorrect and a form of sex discrimination.

Jude is warning the Christians that God will judge them if they follow the same pattern. God is not to be trifled with. He loathes idolatry (which hurts him) and immorality (which hurts those he has made). He may not deal with them immediately, but ultimately all moral pollution of his creation must be punished.

3. CHARACTER

When your creed is corrupted, your conduct will soon follow. When your conduct is corrupted, your character will go the same way. Character is the result of conduct – an act reaps a habit, a habit reaps a character, a character reaps a destiny. So the third phase in the moral pollution of the church is that their character becomes increasingly worldly. Jude focuses next on the characters of the false teachers and their similarity to the characters of three people in the Old Testament.

(a) Cain

He starts with Cain, who killed his brother out of jealousy (Genesis 4). He tells the readers that the false teachers are motivated in part by jealousy, just like Cain, and so are bound to affect those who listen.

(b) Balaam

He continues with Balaam the prophet, who was offered money to prophesy against Israel (Numbers 22). The love of money had so taken hold of Balaam that God had to speak to him through his donkey! Balaam was a man of avarice, as Cain was a man of anger.

(c) Korah

Korah was a man of ambition who was jealous of Moses and wanted to set up his own show (Numbers 16). He completes a rather depressing triad. There are modern parallels to Korah. New churches can be great, but it is clear that some are being set up for the wrong reasons. They are set up because a man wants his own show – a modern 'son of Korah' who doesn't accept God-given leadership and wants his own way. In the end Korah was swallowed up in judgement with 250 others who perished because of their defiance of the authority that God had invested in Moses.

All three of these characters were governed by self, and all three caused death to others. They depict the kind of characters that will emerge in the church if it doesn't deal with false teaching. Anger, avarice and ambition will all be prominent.

4. CONVERSATION

But these weren't the only problems they faced. Once character is corrupted, conversation will also be corrupted, because conversation flows out of character. Jude describes the sort of speaking which characterizes the people who have wormed their way into the fellowship. Sure signs of inner decay are constant grumbling and complaining, muttering and moaning, contempt for inferiors, flattery for superiors, scorn and ridicule for whatever is not understood and, above all, rejection of anyone else's authority. Beware of people who join your fellowship because they are dissatisfied with another fellowship – in six months' time they'll be dissatisfied with yours! Grumblers and fault-finders on the move are always looking for the perfect fellowship. The old saying is true:

'If you're looking for the perfect fellowship, don't join it, because you're bound to spoil it!'

A puzzling passage

Perhaps the most puzzling verses in Jude concern an angel arguing with the devil about the body of Moses. It refers back to an extraordinary statement at the end of Deuteronomy, where we are told that Moses died on Mount Nebo but 'no one knows where his grave is to this day.' So if no one was with him and nobody knows where his grave is – who buried him? The answer is that God sent the angel Michael to bury Moses. Angels are very practical people. They're good cooks (Elijah found out that angels can cook a jolly good meal) and they can ride chariots (as Elijah also discovered). In the modern day I have heard of angels in Afghanistan riding bicycles, protecting a missionary who was on his bike! Angels don't come with shiny white nightdresses, wings, harps and long blond hair. Hebrews 13 speaks of 'entertaining angels unawares', which certainly wouldn't be possible if their appearance was that strange. They look like normal humans.

So this angel was sent with a spade to bury the body of Moses, but when he got there the devil was standing over the body and told him that the body was his. It is instructive to note that in the confrontation that follows Michael didn't even rebuke Satan. We can be very cheeky with Satan and we are very foolish if we are. He's far cleverer than we are. It worries me when I hear young people say, 'We rebuke you, Satan.' Michael actually said, 'The Lord rebuke you', and the devil went and Michael buried Moses properly.

Dealing with corruption

Having looked at the four areas of Jude's concern – creed, conduct, character and conversation – we next need to ask how we should face similar difficulties today.

1. WE SHOULD EXPECT PROBLEMS

The first thing is not to be surprised when things go wrong in the church. Some Christians are over-alarmed, but both the Old Testament prophets and the New Testament apostles told us to expect things to go wrong. Jesus himself warned us about wolves in sheep's clothing. Why are we so surprised when their predictions come true? After all, we're not yet entirely saved and so there are bound to be problems in the church. It's the way we deal with them that is important. We should be unshockable, take them in our stride and deal with them.

2. WE MUST RESIST WHAT IS HAPPENING

It is intriguing to note that Jude does not indict Satan for this havoc. He places the blame firmly at the door of 'these men' who are responsible for causing trouble. And he makes it quite clear that some in the church will have the job of speaking out against error. Man must deal with it – it's not God's job. Jude mentions the ministry of Enoch, the very first prophet in the Bible – the first man to get a message from the Lord for other people. It was a warning that God was going to come in judgement and deal with that whole generation. He was 65 years old when he had a son, and he asked God what he should call him. God gave him an extraordinary name for the son. He said, 'Call him "When he dies it will happen"' – though we know him as Methuselah. It's clear that he lived longer than anybody else, because God is so patient that he waited almost a millennium before judgement came. On the day that Methuselah died, it began to rain. But by that time Methuselah's grandson

Noah had built a boat. God waited 969 years before judging that generation. It was Martin Luther who said, 'If I was God I'd have kicked the whole world to bits long ago.'

Jude was especially keen to point out that the behaviour of the false teachers was 'godless'. He uses the word five times in all. Godliness had become an object of their scorn. The New Testament apostles warned us that in the last days there will be scoffers and godliness will be a joke. There are times when Christians are a laughing-stock because they want to be godly and it goes against the grain. Godlessness is the 'in' thing, and anyone who thinks otherwise is regarded as odd.

3. WE CAN REDUCE THE EXTENT OF THE DAMAGE

Jude next gives practical advice on how the believers should protect themselves and others.

(a) Themselves

The first way to deal with it was for the believers to make sure they were right with God and to build themselves up in faith, hope and love.

The stronger we are, the more likely we are to stand firm. The best way to avoid sickness is to foster health. Jude urges the strengthening of the familiar triad of faith, hope and love. Healthy living includes praying in the Spirit, keeping God's commandments and living for the future, realizing that God intends that we should be holy, not necessarily happy. After all, compared to the 'happiness' we will enjoy in eternity, we shouldn't be concerned if life is tough. It is crucial to note that we are responsible for looking after ourselves and building ourselves up. God won't do it for us.

(b) Others
There were three categories of people who needed help.

(i)   Those with mental doubts. Jude urges the believers to help those who are wavering. They are wondering whether to follow these teachers or not, and are in mental doubt. They must be talked to, even argued with, but always in a tender rather than a tough way. Harshness could drive them further into error.

(ii) Those in mortal danger. Next, there will be others who have been led further into mortal danger because they have already started to believe the new ideas. Jude says the believers should 'snatch them from the fire' – they should regard them as being in a house on fire and should get them out any way they can! The phrase 'snatch them from the fire' has been used in evangelism to mean snatching people from the fire of hell, although these verses have nothing to do with that. Yes, it's snatching people from the fire of hell, but not because they're unsaved, but because they're Christians who are going to be led astray. Even those who were spreading the falsehood must not be written off but given a chance to repent.

(iii) Those morally defiled. The third category of people concerns those who are defiled. The Greek says we should be very, very wary of being infected by them, even by their stained underwear! It seems a strange phrase to use, but it's obvious that there are diseases that are introduced through sexual perversion and promiscuity that we need to be afraid of.

4. WE CAN AVOID WHAT IS HAPPENING

Jude's message is that we should not be surprised by attacks on the faith, but should deal with them and remember all the time that God is able to keep us from falling. It's important, however, that we strike a balance when reading verses that speak of God's keeping power. There are a series of texts in the Bible which affirm God's keeping power, but they are invariably close to ones which emphasize our need to remain close to him. So the penultimate verse of Jude doesn't say, 'God is certain to keep you from falling', but says, 'he is *able* to help you to keep yourself in him.' It's not all on us and it's not all on him – it's 'Keep yourself in him, for he is able to keep you. Go on trusting him and you won't fall.'

We can say that he has the ability to keep us and present us before God, providing we remain faithful. He also has the authority, for he is the only God and only Saviour.

So Jude finishes with a note of praise. In spite of the evil teaching and the attendant dangers, God is able to keep us and present us faultless before him on the Last Day. There's no question about it. If God is on our side (the real meaning of the name Immanuel, 'God with us'), we can fight and win. So be it!

Conclusion

There's one clear message from studying the letters of the New Testament. The biggest danger to the church is from the inside. We've got to watch it all the time and in truth and love contend for the gospel that was 'once delivered' to the saints. There's a big battle on right now in the Western world to do just that. We must be clear about the truth. If you don't believe that my writing fits with what your Bible says, then forget it. But if you do find it there, then cling to it and fight for it and contend for the faith once delivered to the saints! It may not sound like glamorous work, but it's crucial if church fellowships are going to remain strong.

So although Jude is one of the most neglected books in the New Testament, its message is ever relevant and needs to be heard by the church today if it is not to be increasingly riddled with the same problems.

57.

 1, 2, AND 3 JOHN

Introduction

There are two sorts of letter in the New Testament. Some are general or circular letters with no specific recipients – rather like tracts. Others are personal, reflecting what the readers needed to hear.

John's letters are a mixture of the two. His first is general and, at five chapters, is much longer than the others, as John addresses particular concerns that he has for the believers. The second and third are more personal and are the shortest books in the New Testament. In these John addresses two separate individuals, using just one sheet of papyrus for each.

The letters are warm and personal, reflecting the character of this saint, who is now probably in his eighties. Some call them 'fatherly letters', but given his age, 'grandfatherly' might be a more appropriate description.

They were written at a time when the church was being affected for good or ill by travelling Bible teachers. John is very concerned about the damage that some are causing, but is too elderly to travel – unlike the false teachers who, it seems, are able to promote their heresy with considerable vigour. Hence these letters were his best way of addressing the problem.

John was one of the twelve apostles called by Jesus during his earthly ministry, and the only one to live to an old age. Extra-biblical records state that he looked after Mary, the mother of Jesus, in Ephesus until she died. He too died there. His letters breathe with the authority not just of an elder, but of *the* elder. For here is one who has had personal contact with Christ (see 1:2; 2:1; 4:6, 14).

Some Bible scholars argue that the apostle John did not write the letters. It is certainly a surprise that there are not more references to the Old Testament than his single reference to Cain killing Abel – especially as the Book of Revelation, also by John, has over 300 allusions. But when you compare the letters to John's Gospel, they have the same style and vocabulary. Expressions found in the Gospel, such as 'eternal life', 'new commandment' and 'remain in Christ', which are special to John, are also in the letters, and in some cases identical phrases are found – for example, 'walking in darkness' and 'that your joy may be full'.

Furthermore, both the Gospel and the letters describe the Christian life with absolute contrasts. John's assessment of the world is in sharp contrast to the modern vogue of relativism, which believes that distinctions are inappropriate – nothing is true or false – everything is just an opinion. John, and the rest of the Bible, stand against this view. John draws a number of contrasts: life and death, light and darkness, truth and lies, love and hate, righteousness and lawlessness, children of God and children of Satan, love of the Father and love of the world, Christ and antichrist and – the biggest contrast of all – heaven and hell. Such opposites give no room for a 'third way'. You are either one or the other, and there are no further options.

So although there is no name on the manuscripts, internal evidence points strongly to John as the author. Furthermore,

Irenaeus and Papias, two early church fathers, confirm that the letters came from John's pen.

There is no date given, but it seems likely that the letters were written after John's Gospel, and before John's exile on Patmos, where he wrote the Book of Revelation. There is no reference to Domitian's terrible attacks on the church, which came in AD 95, so a date of around AD 90 is likely.

1 John

John's readers

We have noted that the first letter is a general letter with no specific destination as such. But there are clear categories of reader that John has in mind. These come in 2:12–14, where John addresses his letter to three groups of people: 'little children', 'young men' and 'fathers'.

It is not physical ages but spiritual ages that are in view. The 'little children' are the recent converts, who need to be given milk rather than meat to help them grow. John says the little children have experienced two things: they know forgiveness, and they know God is the Father, but they know little else.

The 'young men' are those who have grown up and matured. John says three things about them: they have grown a bit stronger than weak babies, they have digested Scripture, and they have known victory in battles with Satan.

John is also writing to much older Christians whom he calls 'fathers'. Their experience has both length and depth. Here are people whose experience of God is very rich.

Modern eyes will notice that John puts the groups into a male form. This is not unusual, for the whole New Testament is addressed to 'brothers', not 'brothers and sisters'. We need to explain this male emphasis, especially in a day of 'non-sexist' or 'inclusivist' Bibles and confusion about the appropriate gender to give to God.

The main reason for the male focus of Scripture is that the strength and character of the church can be seen in its men. Men have the responsibility of leadership in the church as well as in the home, and it is their character that will determine the strength of the whole church. This is one reason why I have spent so much time setting up and speaking at 'Men for God' conferences. Most of the letters I have received have been from women delighted at the change in their husbands! Sadly, I would be a wealthy man if I had a £10 note for every family in the church where the wife is ahead of the husband spiritually. It's healthy where the husband is ahead of the wife, for the husband can't be a head unless he's ahead. But, of course, this is not to imply that women are inferior in any way, merely that the roles are complementary.

John's reasons for writing

It is clear that John's first concern in writing is pastoral. He refers to the readers as his 'little children'. He has great affection for them, but is unable to visit them all. There are hints in the text that he may have particular concerns in mind. There are two ways of examining John's reasons for writing:

LIST 1

He wants his readers to be:

> *Satisfied* (1:4). He writes 'that their joy may be full', implying that they are dissatisfied with life.
> *Sinless* (2:1). He is concerned that they should live blameless lives.
> *Safe* (2:26). He wants them to be safe from all the wiles of the devil, especially false teaching, which is the devil's

particular approach to church life and which was affecting the believers he wrote to.

Sure (5:13). Above all, he wants the readers to be sure of what they believe. Christians need to be assured. There's a doctrine of assurance in these little letters that is very important. We don't want to be waking up every morning insecure, but to be sure of who we are in Christ. We need to 'know' (a key word here) that we are in God's hands.

LIST 2

On the other hand, an alternative way of examining the motives would be as follows. He is writing:

to promote harmony among them (1:3);
to produce happiness (1:4):
to protect holiness (2:1);
to prevent heresy (2:26);
to provide hope (5:13).

What is clear is that he is writing about 60 years after he first heard Jesus say 'Follow me.' He is an old man, and I can imagine him with a long beard saying, 'I'm your grandfather in the faith. I want you to be satisfied and sure of who you are, and I want you to be holy, and in harmony and full of hope.' So there is a very tender pastoral heart writing these letters.

An outline of 1 John

Although we can discern John's motives in writing, it is not so easy to find any pattern in the way he has arranged his material. The letter is almost impossible to analyse because he seems to go round in circles. His thinking is cyclic rather than linear. I'm a linear man – I like to see the progress of an argument and to analyse. The apostle Paul, with his legal mind, writes that way. So I find myself a little lost when I come to a man who thinks in circles and goes round the same themes. John's circular style can be explained by his profession, his age and his nationality.

1. HIS PROFESSION

John is a fisherman, not a lawyer like Paul, and so is apt to move from one subject to the next as if he's having a conversation. He wasn't an educated man and so hadn't been taught to think in linear patterns.

2. HIS AGE

Old men tend to become garrulous – they talk round and round things – it is characteristic of age. Listeners need to concentrate to pick up the wisdom they impart.

3. HIS NATIONALITY

But I think the major reason is that John follows the fashion of the Jews, who tend to talk like the book reads. Both the Book of Proverbs in the Old Testament and James in the New visit and revisit a number of subjects. Anyone seeking a systematic study on an area in these books needs to hunt all the way through. There's no real structure in them.

WORLD OR WORD?

One way of looking at 1 John is to focus upon a theme which John develops throughout the epistle, using the diagram opposite.

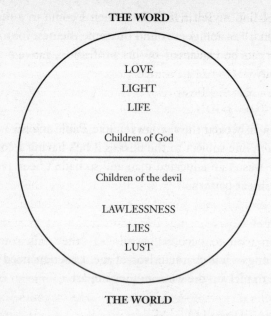

THE WORD

LOVE

LIGHT

LIFE

Children of God

Children of the devil

LAWLESSNESS

LIES

LUST

THE WORLD

The diagram shows a world with two hemispheres. The one half is governed by the word of God – it is a sphere of life, love and light. The other half is governed by the world – lawlessness, lies and lust. John is urging his readers to live by the word of God. He is telling them that he wants them to focus on the word of God and not be tempted to listen to the world. Every Christian has to make this choice. If you love the world, you will soon be living that kind of life. If you love the word, you will be living in an altogether different kind of way.

This simple framework helps us to see that there is some shape to the letter. It begins positive, then turns negative, and then turns positive again – a pleasing sandwich with twice as much positive as negative. We need both; we need to know what to believe and what not to, how to behave and how not to.

So the 'sandwich' structure of 1 John can be summarized as follows:

Life – 1:1–4 } Positive
Light – 1:5–2:11 }
Lust, lies and lawlessness – 2:15–3:10 } Negative
Love – 3:11–4:21 } Positive
Life – 5:1–21 } Positive

We will now look at the themes to be found in 1 John.

Love

John is the only person in the Bible to make the statement, 'God is love.' It may sound like a 'normal' statement to the well-taught Christian, but it is actually a revolutionary statement. No other religion in the world has ever said it, nor could they. Judaism can say, 'God loves us', but that's a different thing. To say, 'God is love' means that God is understood to be more than one Person. You cannot *be* 'love' by yourself. So it is because we know that God is three Persons – Father, Son and Holy Spirit – that we can say, 'God is love.' Before the world came into being, there were the Father, the Son and the Holy Spirit, who all loved each other.

People sometimes ask, 'Why did God make us?' At the simplest level, God had one Son, and he loved him so much that he wanted a bigger family. He wanted to share the love he already had with a larger circle – that's why he wanted to have many sons.

Heresy

As well as general concern for the readers' spiritual well-being, John is also facing specific problems, and writes to counter the false teaching that he knows is affecting them. At different points in the letter he refers to 'they' (as opposed to 'we' and 'you'), meaning a group of teachers known to the church.

The false teachers taught Greek philosophy, which included

a number of elements that contradicted the biblical worldview. Crucially, they taught that there was a necessary separation between the physical and the spiritual.

We imbibe this disintegrated outlook on life, even today. For example, you will never find the distinction between 'sacred' and 'secular' in the Bible, and yet even Christians say to me, 'I'm in a secular job.' I always reply that they are in no such thing. Unless a job is immoral or illegal, it is not secular. There is nothing secular except sin. Indeed, I made this point once in the North of England, and a nationally known pop singer was converted. He thought he was in a secular job, part of which was making the jingles for advertisements on TV. My words helped him to realize that he could do his work for the glory of God.

Those promoting Greek philosophy also believed that the physical was evil, and only the spiritual was good. So the body was evil, and the soul good. They gave people the impression that anything physical was somehow dirty or sinful. This underlying philosophy had repercussions for what the church believed and the way she behaved. Let us look at belief first.

1. BELIEF

John's biggest concern was that the false teachers applied this thinking to Jesus. They found it impossible to accept that God could be a man. They reasoned that God is eternal and man is in time. God is spiritual and man is physical. So how could God be a man on earth?

This belief took many different forms. One was the belief that Jesus didn't come in the flesh but only appeared to. It is a heresy called 'docetism', which means simply 'to put on a mask, 'to appear'. John says in this letter that if you hear someone say that Jesus hasn't come in the flesh, you know that view is inspired by the devil. John was at pains to point out that he had seen and touched Jesus himself. He was flesh and bones, and indeed still is. The so-called New Age philosophy is teaching something similar when it separates the human Jesus from the divine Christ.

Another heresy said that Jesus was a human being until his baptism at the age of 30, when 'the Christ' came upon him. Then, at his death, 'the Christ' went away again, and it was 'Jesus' who died and was buried. So in this theory, 'Jesus' and 'the Christ' are actually two different entities.

In the same way, the New Age teachers talk about Christ but don't like the name Jesus. They say that everyone can have the Christ come upon them. It is very subtle and it fools a lot of people, who believe that because the New Age is using biblical language, it is with biblical meaning. One of the favourite statements of New Age teachers is that God is outside time, that he is timeless – a belief not uncommon amongst Christians. Actually the Bible never says that God is timeless. It says that God is everlasting, which is quite a different thing. Time is real to God. God is the God who was and who is and who is to come. God isn't in time; rather, time is in God.

The Greeks also separated God entirely from time, and this belief is still around today. You would be amazed how many Christians think that when we go to heaven, we go outside time. We don't – we go into everlasting life. Time is extended infinitely. Time is real in God, and time is real in the Bible, and therefore history is 'his story'.

But, of course, these teachers believed they were 'in the know'. Their knowledge was superior to the church. It was a form of Gnosticism, which was to dog the church for centuries, and is still around in different guises today.

So John had to fight heresy on a number of counts. This is why he begins by emphasizing that when the Christ came, he

was a real human being. The three strongest physical senses –
sight, hearing and touch – were all used. He says, 'We saw him,
we touched him, we heard him.'

For John, the Incarnation is fundamental – ultimately
everything boils down to what we think of Jesus. We must
realize that he is totally divine and totally human – that in him
the physical and the spiritual are totally integrated. The other
world and this world have totally met, and the Greek idea that
there is a separation between time and eternity, between spiritual and physical, was proven false when the Word became
flesh and lived among us. As Archbishop Temple said,
'Christianity is the most materialist of all world religions.'

2. BEHAVIOUR

The Greeks' separation of the physical from the spiritual not
only affected their belief about Jesus, but also coloured their
behaviour. The Greeks believed that salvation (however this
was understood) had nothing to do with what a person did with
their body, and this was becoming a normal view inside the
church. Some were living quite immoral lives but claiming to
be spiritual, because they believed that their body had nothing
to do with their soul.

It is a small step from thinking like this to saying that sin
doesn't matter in Christians. They say, 'I've got my ticket to
heaven – sin doesn't matter.' Indeed, some go even further and
say, 'Sin doesn't exist in Christians', suggesting a kind of per-
fectionism – as far as God is concerned, they are sinless.

One of the biggest mistakes people make when they come
to Christ is to think that their future sins are forgiven. But only
past sins are forgiven when someone comes to Christ. They
need to go on receiving forgiveness for later sins. John has
to say, 'If we go on confessing our sins, he is faithful and just to
go on forgiving our sins, and the blood of Jesus will go on

cleansing us from all unrighteousness.' If I come to Christ, I do not have a blank cheque to sin. My past sins are now forgiven, but I must keep short accounts with God. As I confess them, he goes on forgiving, but only as I go on confessing.

John's emphasis is very much needed in the church today. Greek thinking leads to lawlessness in the church, immorality and spiritual elitism that thinks that Christians are above the normal rules of right and wrong. God is absolutely fair; he doesn't overlook sin in unbelievers or believers. But he is waiting to forgive if there is true repentance.

In John's day such teaching wreaked havoc in the church. It left people confused and bewildered, unsure about what they should believe and where they stood with God. They were uncertain about salvation and unconcerned about sin. The teachers seemed to have little regard for the 'ordinary Christians' whom they deemed to be unenlightened.

Assurance

But with great pastoral heart, John is concerned that Christians should be sure that they are Christians, and so he tells them to examine themselves with respect to four areas, and they are quite severe tests. He goes through them very carefully and in great detail.

1. THE DOCTRINAL TEST

The first is the doctrinal test. Every true Christian must pass this test. It concerns how they think of Christ. If someone has a shaky understanding and is not sure if the human Jesus is the divine Christ, they don't pass the test. On 25 occasions in the three letters John uses the verb 'to know'. He believed knowledge was important for the believers, especially in view of the so-called 'higher knowledge' claimed by the Gnostic teachers. There are plenty of people in churches who think of Jesus as a great human being who responded to God better than any other, but they fail to believe that he is fully God and fully man, as the Bible teaches.

2. THE SPIRITUAL TEST

John says, 'We know we are sons of God because he has given us his Spirit.' There is a witness between God's Spirit and our spirit that we are sons of God. So without the Holy Spirit we don't pass the second test, because it's the Spirit who tells us whether we are children of God. Some people try to find assurance from Scripture – they try to deduce that they are Christians from the Bible by arguing that the Bible says it, they believe it, so that settles it. But the Bible never encourages us to do so. Assurance actually comes from the Spirit rather than the Scripture in the New Testament. You can't try to prove you're a Christian by quoting texts. It's the Spirit who tells you that you're a Christian, not the Scriptures. Hence this is a spiritual test, and a crucial one, for if you don't have the Spirit, then you're still a possession of the devil.

3. THE MORAL TEST

The third test is the moral test. If you are living rightly before God, then your conscience tells you that you belong to the Father. Conscience was given as part of our assurance. In biblical terms, if we are practising righteousness and find ourselves keeping the laws of God, then we have a confirmation that we are his children. But if we are rebelling against his laws, and kicking against the way he wants us to live, then we don't pass the third test.

4. THE SOCIAL TEST

The final test is a social test. We are told that we cannot say we love Christ if we don't love Christians, because Christ is in the other Christians. If you love Christ, then you will love the Christ in your brothers. If you hate your brothers, you certainly don't love your Father, because he loves them.

Another proof is the love we have for the Jewish people. They're not lovable. At the human level, I believe I would get on better with Arabs than Jews. But the Spirit can give us a great love for the Jewish people. It's not a natural thing at all, but a supernatural thing. Jesus called them his 'brethren', and God still loves them, in spite of all they've done to him.

In particular, John says that it's our love and our prayers that prove that the love of the Father is in us. You find yourself loving people you would not normally like, because they're children of the Father and the love of the Father is in you.

Once a believer has an assurance of fellowship with God, they have tremendous confidence to set out each day knowing that they are a child of God. This confidence is shown in their attitude towards God. They can say, 'Dad, I am asking you in the name of Jesus for this,' knowing that God is able and willing to respond.

It also gives confidence before men and women. When you are sure you are a child of the royal family of heaven, you are literally part of the royal family on earth, which gives you confidence to speak more boldly to others.

Sin

By the same token, it is also important to identify those who are not real Christians. The church was old enough in John's day to include nominal Christians – people who pretended to be part of God's family but were not actually trusting Christ. One acid test was the presence or absence of sin, and John has a lot to say in his letter about this theme. Indeed, he said some very strange things about this, which seem to contradict one another at times. In some statements he assumes the believers will sin, but in others he says they cannot sin, and this has puzzled many people.

We need to be clear about what John understands by 'sin'. He defines sin as 'lawlessness', meaning that the individual believes he or she is not responsible or accountable to anyone but themselves. John reminds the readers that Christ came to take away our sins and destroy the works of the devil. Sin is normal for the children of the devil, but abnormal for the children of God.

1. THE POSSIBILITIES

But it is the presence of sin within believers that is the biggest concern for John, and this is where the controversy arises. There are a number of possible statements. For believers sin is:

Indisputable – we do sin.
Inevitable – we will sin.
Incompatible – we should not sin.
Intolerable – we must not sin.
Indefensible – we need not sin.
Inapplicable – we do not sin.
Inconceivable – we cannot sin.

The controversy centres on the statements in John's letters that appear to contradict one another. Compare, for example, John's statement in 1 John 1:8 with ones later in the epistle:

If we claim to be without sin, we deceive ourselves and the truth is not in us (1:8).

No-one who is born of God will continue to sin, because God's seed remains in him; he cannot go on sinning, because he has been born of God (3:9).

We know that anyone born of God does not continue to sin; the
one who was born of God keeps him safe, and the evil one does
not touch him (5:18).

The first verse suggests that sin is inevitable, and the latter two
suggest that those who are born of God cannot sin. Yet few
would dare to claim that this was true of them. So how should
these verses be interpreted?

2. A KEY VERSE EXAMINED
Let's look at the problems with 1 John 3:9.

(a) Major problems
The verse suggests that anyone born of God (i.e. out of water
and Spirit, John 3:5) 1. doesn't sin and 2. cannot sin. There are
many interpretations:

(i)   It is literally true – the verse means exactly what it says.
      But this would contradict 1:8 and 5:16, which both imply
      that sin is possible.
(ii) The sin referred to is only crude and blatant sins: vices,
      crimes and sins against love. Some of the great theologians,
      such as Augustine, Luther and Wesley, take this view.
(iii) If believers do wrong, God doesn't call it sin. So there are
      effectively two standards of morality.
(iv) The word only refers to our new nature. The 'old man'
      still misbehaves, but the 'new man' never does. However, a
      Christian is not a divided person, but a unity!
(v)   The verse describes the ideal, without ever believing that
      it is actually possible. So this reflects a goal we are to
      desire, without ever imagining that we will achieve it.
(vi) The verse only refers to habitual, persistent sin. The tense
      suggests someone who goes on sinning.

(b) Minor problems

(i)   The reason the believer doesn't sin is that they are 'born of God'. Regeneration is said to lead to righteousness. But who would claim to be righteous this side of heaven?

(ii) Secondly, we are told that God's seed remains in the believer. The word literally means 'sperm', which is a very potent metaphor! But how should the word be interpreted? It can be used literally as referring to human sperm, or even animal or vegetable sperm. But it is not clear what 'his seed' refers to. Does it refer to God or the believer?

(iii) Then there's a third problem. Is this a categorical statement or a conditional statement? The use of the phrase 'abide/remain in Christ' also seems open to interpretation. Is this categorical as in verse 9, true of everyone who was once 'born of God'? Or is it conditional as in verse 6, true only of those who '*live* in him'? A categorical statement is a statement that will always be true. A conditional statement is one that will be true, if certain conditions follow.

How then should we understand the verse?

First, we need to ask why John is making this statement. He is not discussing the 'once saved, always saved' conundrum. He is dealing with those who call themselves disciples, but continue to sin and accept it, almost as if it doesn't matter!

So John says we can't sin because we are born of God. The clear implication is that regeneration leads to righteousness. Sin has no place in the believer's life.

Secondly, we should note the tense of 'no one who lives in him keeps on sinning.' The verbs here are in a special Greek tense called the continuous present. So the verbs don't just refer to something done at the time, but something you continue doing.

So, for example, Jesus didn't actually say 'Ask, and you'll receive; seek, and you'll find; knock, and the door will be opened.' He said, 'Keep on asking, and you will receive; keep on seeking, and you will find; keep on knocking, and the door will be opened.' Take the famous verse, John 3:16, which is generally totally misunderstood. This is also in the present continuous tense: 'For God so loved the world that he gave his only-begotten Son, that whoever goes on believing in him will never perish but will go on having eternal life.' It is not that those who believe once have eternal life, but it's those who go on believing who go on having life.

So to return to this verse, it says, 'No one who goes on living in Christ will go on sinning.' The word 'lives' is the same as the word 'abides'. John 15 says: 'I am the true vine – remain in me', which means 'stay in me', 'go on living in me'. The verse is therefore conditioned by the context. You go on living in Christ, and the statement then becomes true. Whoever goes on living in Christ doesn't go on sinning and can't go on sinning.

People who are not continuing in Christ will not show any progress spiritually. They will not be moving into this promise.

The third verse quoted earlier (1 John 5:18) backs this up: 'We know that anyone born of God does not continue to sin; the one who was born of God keeps him safe, and the evil one does not touch him.'

So whoever is born of God 'does not continue to sin' – they cannot go on sinning, because if they're living in Christ they will make progress and will have victory. It's the relationship with Christ that determines the truth of this promise. This whole letter assumes that Christians will fall into sin – there will be no one perfect this side of heaven – but not that they will go on sinning.

For our understanding we must add the perspective of the Letter to the Hebrews, which says that if you receive forgiveness but deliberately go on sinning, there remains no more sacrifice for sin. It's not saying Christians will never sin but that they have a way of dealing with it, and if they are living in Christ they will want to deal with it. One of the proofs that you're a Christian is that when you sin you hate it. You don't love sin and you want to be rid of it. Those who go on living in Christ cannot go on sinning. It is incompatible with the new life within.

Having dealt with this problem, chapter 5 suggests something else which is very serious. We are told that when we see a brother sinning, we should do everything we can to help him and convert him from his evil ways. If we do, we have 'saved' a brother. But, John adds, there is a 'sin unto death'. There is no point in praying for a brother who's sinned unto death!

All the way through Scripture we find that backsliders can reach a point of no return. There is a sin unto death, and we need to take these warnings very seriously. They are most prominent in the Letter to the Hebrews. There comes a point where repentance is impossible. John says that a brother can so sin that it's no use praying for him any more. This means, of course, that he is not living in Christ, that he has lost his link with the true vine, and is no longer abiding.

So if we synthesize all that John says about sin and believers, we will have a beautiful balance. We will not become neurotic on the one hand or complacent on the other. There will be a healthy fear of the Lord that will keep us in Christ. But if we take just one verse out of its context, we can create havoc.

God

In the light of his concerns about sin, John wants his readers to understand what God is like. He reminds them that God is 'light' – God is pure and holy and morally separate from the world. God is also 'life'. Sin leads to death, but life comes from God – it is his gift to us. The God whom John describes wants fellowship with us. The word 'fellowship' literally means 'sharing' or 'partnership'. John explains the conditions for fellowship with such a God:

1. WALK IN LIGHT

We must embrace the light and shun the darkness. We cannot have fellowship with God or his people if we have hidden lives – our lives should be transparent.

2. WALK IN LOVE

The imperative is to love God and our new brothers. Indeed, if we don't love them, we can't love him – it's as simple as that. The command to love one another is described as an 'old command', even though Jesus described it as a 'new commandment'. The reason is simple – it was now 60 years since it was first given.

3. WALK IN LIFE

Christ has provided all that is necessary for living the new life; therefore the believers are encouraged to live in the good of it.

It is clear that John's passion is that the readers might experience the joy of fellowship with Christ, and that nothing should get in the way of that.

2 and 3 John

Introduction

For our study of these two letters, we are going to look first at the difference between men and women. It may seem an unusual way to begin, but it provides a helpful foundation for grasping the outline and purpose of each book. When God made us in his image, he made us male and female, and therefore complementary to one another. It's astonishing how the strengths of maleness correspond to the weaknesses of femaleness, and vice versa. We need each other.

The diagram overleaf looks at the difference between men and women – that is, between the average man, represented by one circle, and the average woman, represented by the other – though, clearly, there will be men and women who show these characteristics to a greater or lesser measure. There are effeminate men and masculine women.

The humanist tends to assume that there is just one spectrum – a male end and a female end, with a mixture in the middle, as if we're all really one. But we are separately male and female, and the two spectrums overlap.

This helps us to understand the differences between 2 John and 3 John. 2 John is the only letter in the New Testament addressed to a woman, and 3 John is an almost identical letter addressed to a man. They say opposite things and yet they have the same subject.

The obvious visual difference is that men are angular to look at while women are curved. Men have an analytical brain, whereas women are more intuitive. It's quite irritating when my wife comes to the same conclusion as myself, especially when she reaches it six weeks earlier! Intuition is much stronger in most women, whereas men like to sit down and think it through.

Men can think in more abstract terms, and women can think in more concrete terms. Men think of general things, women think of particular things. So whereas men are goal-orientated and live for the future, women are need-orientated. A man is fulfilled if he has a goal to aim for; a woman is fulfilled if she has a need to meet. Men therefore tend to be more interested in things and women tend to be more interested in people.

This is reflected in conversation. A male gathering is likely to talk about motorbikes and cars, whereas women will get together and talk about people and relationships.

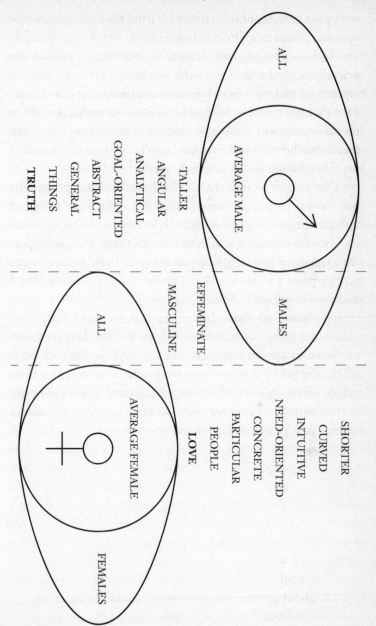

ALL

AVERAGE MALE

TALLER
ANGULAR
ANALYTICAL
GOAL-ORIENTED
ABSTRACT
GENERAL
THINGS
TRUTH

MASCULINE

EFFEMINATE

MALES

SHORTER
CURVED
INTUITIVE
NEED-ORIENTED
CONCRETE
PARTICULAR
PEOPLE
LOVE

ALL

AVERAGE FEMALE

FEMALES

A man can separate his thoughts from his feelings, whereas a woman thinks as a whole person. This is why a man can be in love with more than one woman at once, but a woman can generally only be in love with one man. Women need to understand that men face different temptations for this reason. If a wife finds that her husband has gone off with a woman at the office, she will assume he doesn't love her any more. His claims that he does still love her aren't understood because of this difference. It is still wrong, however.

This ability to be cold and analytical is one reason why men have a particular responsibility for discipline. They can separate their feelings from their thoughts and be more objective about a situation that needs confronting and punishing. I happen to believe in capital punishment. People ask whether I could press the button. I reply that I think I could, but I would never ask my wife to.

It's because of these differences that men are more concerned with truth and women with love. But the danger of men is to have too much emphasis on truth and too little on love, and the danger of women is to have too little emphasis on truth and too much on love. John's second and third epistles perfectly fit this pattern. They are very similar, but the differences correspond to these gender characteristics.

An outline of 2 and 3 John

2 JOHN ♀	3 JOHN ♂
HOSPITALITY	**– TRUTH AND LOVE**
To a lady	To a man
Danger:	Danger:
too much love	too much truth
Attitude:	Attitude:
too soft-hearted	too hard-headed
Door open too wide	Door shut too tightly
Welcome wrong people	Refuse right people
Neglect truth	Neglect love
Wrong belief	Wrong behaviour
We need both ...	
Female	Male
Love	Truth
Love *and* truth	Truth *and* love
in women	in men

The letters are very short. They would each have fitted onto one sheet of papyrus, probably A4 size. They are both concerned with the subject of hospitality and were probably written together.

Hospitality was especially important in the early church because Christians weren't by and large welcome anywhere else. There were no church buildings, and so they met in each other's homes. Futhermore, the inns often doubled as brothels, so they weren't suitable for travelling preachers. Most would have depended upon believers for financial support.

The church needs both travelling ministries and local ministries. Some churches are locked into their own local ministry and don't listen enough to other ministries. Others live on visiting preachers all the time, but don't have enough of their own. But in the New Testament there were local ministries – pastors and teachers – and travelling ministries – apostles, prophets and evangelists. One of the earliest Christian writings, The Didache, warns that if a prophet stays more than three days with you, he's a false prophet. Prophets get too intense if they're permanent. If you have a resident prophet, then you are in trouble, because they come on heavy week after week!

Prophets and evangelists need to travel; pastors and teachers need to stay put. Servants of the church need to choose whether they prefer to be the pastor of a church or a travelling preacher. It's unfair on a church if they try to do both. I've seen many churches wrecked because they never knew whether the pastor would be there or not.

John writes these two letters because he believes the attitude to hospitality has been inappropriate. Each reflects the weakness common to their gender – the lady was throwing the door open too wide and the man was keeping it too tightly shut. They represent the typical responses that we can learn from.

The lady's danger was that she had too much love and not enough truth. She was welcoming people she ought not to have welcomed. She was giving hospitality, but her attitude was that she was too soft-hearted and accommodating to anyone who wanted to stay. She was unwittingly being used to introduce bad teaching to the church. John had to rebuke her mildly that in doing this she was neglecting the truth.

Many heresies have been promoted within the church through women. The woman's heart goes with the teacher, but she needs to spend time evaluating the teaching as well. Paul's second letter to Timothy shows us that heretical teachers were especially successful in deceiving widows and weak-willed women. Paul had to urge Timothy to protect them from being misled. This is one reason why Paul tells Timothy that women should not be involved in teaching. He points out that Eve was deceived, though we must add that Eve was fooled in the presence of Adam, who kept his mouth shut.

The opposite danger is found in John's third letter. He is writing about a man who is too jealous for his own ministry and not welcoming to any other teacher. Good teachers were being refused entrance who could bring some real help to the fellowship. His danger is that he's so focused on truth that he's forgotten love. He thinks he has everything 100 per cent doctrinally correct and nobody else has. So he shuts the door, and his attitude is too hard-hearted.

The two letters emphasize the importance of teamwork between men and women. God made us for each other, though it doesn't mean we can only find this partnership in marriage. Jesus is a perfect example of a single man who had perfect relationships with women. He appreciated them, ministered to them and allowed them to minister to him. But he still made clear distinctions between the roles and responsibilities of men and women. Both are equally made in the image of God and are equal in dignity, depravity and destiny. We need love and truth in the woman, and we need truth and love in the man.

An analysis of 2 and 3 John

	2 John		3 John
1–3	Love in truth	1	Love in truth
4	Following truth	2–4	Following truth
5–6	Following love	5–8	Following love
7–9	Some reject truth	9–10	Some refuse love
10–11	Don't invite them	11–12	Don't imitate them
12–13	Our joy	13–15	Your peace

These letters were clearly written at the same time and follow exactly the same pattern. The 'second' letter is addressed to Kyria, which means 'lady', but we don't know if this is the title of a prominent lady or not. The 'children' referred to could be the spiritual children who meet in her home. The analysis shows that the same outline is followed in each letter, and yet the emphasis for the man and the woman is totally different.

The 'third' letter is addressed to Gaius, but contains a warning about a man called Diotrephes. The description of him is not positive. He was a man guilty of being too tight. He was talkative, over-bearing, headstrong and power-hungry. He was jealous for his little fellowship and didn't want other teachers coming in and distracting people away from his leadership. He refused to allow the apostle John to visit, even tearing up a letter he had written.

Here was a man who excommunicated anyone not on his side and who was malicious against those who didn't agree with him – even the apostles. There is no record that he was not orthodox in his beliefs, but he was certainly stifling the teaching gifts that others would bring.

So John had to urge Gaius to welcome Demetrius – a respected teacher who shouldn't have been turned away. It is not clear whether Demetrius was a local or travelling preacher. He may even have been the postman who took the letters to the church. He was certainly known to them.

The elderly apostle

There are two stories about John in his old age which we know from church records. They reveal John's balance of truth and love. He stood firmly for the truth, refusing to compromise, especially concerning the Person of Christ. But at the same time he was the most loving old man.

An early church writer, Jerome, tells a story about John from the AD 90s. By this time John was very old, and used to be carried into church every week on a chair with poles through it. The church members would often ask him to speak. He would sit in the chair at the front and he'd just say, 'Little children, love one another!'

The next Sunday they would carry him into church and ask if he had a word for them. 'Yes,' he'd say, 'I've got a word for you today.' They would carry the chair to the front and he'd say, 'Little children, love one another!'

The next Sunday they brought him in and exactly the same thing happened. They began to think he was getting senile. Didn't he realize that he kept repeating the same words? They finally went to the old man and said, 'Master, why do you always say, "Little children, love one another"?' He said: 'Because it is the Lord's command, and if this only is done, it is enough.'

Another tale demonstrates that John's concern for truth was no less strong. He made frequent visits to the Roman baths to bathe. Once he was lowered into the water, and at the other end of the pool he saw a man called Cerinthus. He was the leading false teacher who was going round the churches. John said, 'Let us fly! let us fly! lest even the bath-house fall down because Cerinthus, the enemy of the truth, is within!'

So they had to lift him out and take him home unwashed that day. John was the most loving man, but truth was all-important too.

When Jesus met him he was one of the most bad-tempered men around. Jesus called John and his brother James 'Boanerges', which meant 'sons of thunder' – not a flattering nickname! John's reaction to the Samaritans was not untypical. When the Samaritans spat on them as they walked through Samaria, he said, 'I'm going to call fire down from heaven, if you give me permission, Jesus, and we'll burn up the whole lot of them!'

Later on he and James were persuaded by their mother to request a higher position than the other apostles when Jesus entered his Kingdom.

Some suggest that his later, milder manner came because he mellowed with age. But not everyone mellows with age! This was the man whom Jesus loved, and bit by bit his character was made like his Master's.

These letters display none of the less pleasant characteristics of a former period in his life. Here is a man who is now full of love and truth, and longs that others should be too. Jesus has changed him, and he is concerned in these letters that his readers should come to know and value the Saviour in the way that he does.

58.

REVELATION

Differences of opinion

Opinions about the Book of Revelation cover a huge spectrum. When put together, it seems impossible that they all refer to the same piece of literature.

Human Opinion

Human opinion varies enormously. The reaction of unbelievers is understandable, since it is not intended for them. It is probably the worst book to use as an introduction to Christian Scriptures. The world assumes it is the result of 'indigestion at best or insanity at worst', to quote a typical comment.

Yet even among Christians there are diverse attitudes, ranging from the fearful who can't get into the book to the fanatical who can't get out of it! Bible scholars have made many negative comments: 'as many riddles as there are words'; 'haphazard accumulation of weird symbols'; 'either finds a man mad or leaves him mad'.

Surprisingly, most of the Protestant Reformers (the 'magisterial' ones, so called because they used the civic authorities to achieve their objectives) had an extremely low view:

Luther: 'neither apostolic nor prophetic ... everyone thinks of the book whatever his spirit suggests ... there are many nobler books to be retained ... my spirit cannot acquiesce in this book.'

Calvin: omitted it from his New Testament commentary!

Zwingli: said its testimony can be rejected because 'it is not a book of the Bible'.

This down-grading has influenced many denominations which sprang from the Reformation.

There had, as we know, been some debate in the early Church about its inclusion in the 'canon' (rule or standard) of Scripture; but by the fifth century it was confidently and universally included.

Some commentators are very positive in their assessment: 'the only masterpiece of pure art in the New Testament; 'beautiful beyond description'. Even William Barclay, who collected these varied comments but was himself inclined to a 'liberal' view of Scripture, told his readers that it was 'infinitely worthwhile to wrestle with it until it gives its blessings and opens its riches'.

Satanic opinion

Satanic opinion is consistently negative. The devil hates the first few pages of the Bible (which reveal how he gained control of our planet) and the last few pages (which reveal how he will lose control of it). If he can convince humans that Genesis is composed of impossible myths and Revelation of impenetrable mysteries, he is content.

The author has remarkable proof of Satan's particular hatred of Revelation 20. Many cassette recordings of an exposition of this chapter have been damaged between despatch and receipt. In some cases the section dealing with the devil's doom has been wiped clean before reaching its destination; in others a screaming voice using a foreign language has been superimposed, rendering the original words unintelligible!

The book calls his bluff. He is only prince and ruler of this world by God's permission. And that has only been given temporarily.

Divine opinion

Divine opinion is consistently positive. It is the only book in the Bible to which divine sanctions of reward and punishment have been directly attached. On the one hand, a special blessing will rest upon those who read it aloud, both to themselves and others (1:3) and who 'keep the words', by meditation and application (22:7). On the other, a special curse will rest on those who tamper with its text. If this is done by addition, or by insertions, the plagues described in the book will be added to the culprit's experience. If it is done by subtraction, by deletions, the culprit's share of eternal life in the new Jerusalem will be taken away.

Such a blessing and curse tell us how seriously God regards the facts and truths revealed here. He could hardly have made its importance clearer.

From these opinions about the book, we turn to look at the book itself.

Consider first its position in the Bible. Just as Genesis could be nowhere else but at the beginning, Revelation could be nowhere else but at the end. In so many ways it completes the 'story'.

If the Bible is simply regarded as the history of our world, Revelation is needed to round it off. Of course, biblical history is different from all other such publications. It starts earlier, before there were any observers to record events. It finishes later, by predicting events that cannot yet be observed and recorded.

This, of course, raises the question as to whether we are dealing with works of human imagination or divine inspiration. The answer depends on faith. It is a simple choice: to believe or not to believe. While going beyond reason, faith is not contrary to reason. The biblical accounts of the origin and destiny of our universe can be shown to be the best explanation of its present state. To know how it will end is of profound significance to the way we live now.

But the interest of the Bible is in the human race rather than the environment and in God's chosen people in particular. With them he has a 'covenant' relationship, analogous to marriage. From one point of view, the Bible is the story of a romance, a heavenly Father seeking an earthly bride for his Son. Like every good romance, they 'get married and live happily ever after'. But this climax is only reached in the Book of Revelation, without which we would never know whether the engagement (or 'betrothal'; 2 Corinthians 11:2) ever came to anything or was broken off!

Indeed, it is quite difficult to imagine what it would be like to have a Bible without the Book of Revelation, even if we don't use it much. Imagine a New Testament that closed with the little Letter of Jude addressed to a second-generation church that was being corrupted in its creed, conduct, character and conversation. So is that how it will all end? What a depressing anticlimax!

So most Christians are glad that the Book of Revelation is there, even if they are not very well acquainted with it. They can usually cope with the first few chapters and the last few, but feel out of their depth in the central bulk of it (chapters 6–18). That is largely because this portion is so unlike anything else. It is difficult because it is different. Just what makes it so?

The nature of apocalyptic writing

Revelation is not only different from other New Testament books in content. It is also unique in origin.

All the others were intended to be written. Each author decided to put pen to paper, either himself or through an 'amanuensis' (i.e. a secretary; e.g. Romans 16:22). He considered what he wanted to say before it was put down. The result bore the marks of his own temperament, character, outlook and experience – even though he was 'inspired' by the Holy Spirit, prompting his thoughts and feelings.

Scholars have noted many differences between Revelation and the other writings of the apostle John (one Gospel and three Epistles). The style, grammar and vocabulary are so unusual for him that they have concluded that it must come from another 'John'. They have actually found a somewhat vague reference to an obscure elder of that name in Ephesus to fit the bill. But the man who wrote Revelation simply introduces himself as 'I, John' (1:9), which indicates that he was well and widely known.

There is a simpler explanation for the contrast, even apart from the obvious difference of subject. He never intended to write Revelation. He never even thought about it. It came to him as a totally unexpected 'revelation' in verbal annd visual form. As he 'heard' and 'saw' this astonishing series of voices and visions, he was repeatedly told to 'write' it all down (1:11, 19; 2:1, 8, 12, 18; 3:1; 7:14; 14:13; 19:9; 21:5). The reiterated command suggests that he became so absorbed in what was happening to him that he forgot to record it from time to time.

This explains the 'inferior Greek', compared to his normal fluency. It was written hurriedly in very distracting circumstances. Imagine watching a film and being told to 'get it all down on paper', while it was being shown. College students will understand the 'scrappy' style by looking at their lecture notes. Why, then, did John not write it up afterwards from his scribbled précis, so that its permanent form might be rather more polished? He was hardly likely to when the last dictated words contained a curse on anyone who tampered with what he had written!

All this means that John was not the author of Revelation. He was merely the 'amanuensis' who took it down. So who was the 'author'? The message was often communicated to him by angels. But it was also what the Spirit was saying to the churches; and it was the revelation of Jesus Christ. But it was given to Jesus by God. So a complex chain of communication was involved – God, Jesus, Spirit, angels, John. More than once, poor John was confused about who should get the glory for what he was experiencing (19:10; 22:8–9). Only the first two links in the chain are worshipped in this book.

More directly than any other book in the New Testament, this deserves the name of 'Revelation'. The Greek word so translated in the first sentence is *apokalypsis*, from which came the noun 'Apocalypse' and the adjective 'apocalyptic', which is now more widely used of other literature similar in style and content. The root word means 'unveiling'.

It is the pulling back of a curtain to reveal what has been hidden (as in the unveiling of a picture or plaque).

In the context of Scripture, it is the unveiling of that which is hidden from man, but is known to God. There are some things which man cannot know unless God chooses to inform him. In particular, he cannot know what is happening in heaven and he cannot know what will happen in the future. His recording and interpreting of events is therefore strictly limited in both time and space. It can only be, at best, a partial account of the flow of history.

When God writes history, he gives a total picture, not least because he orders as well as observes the events. 'History is his story.' He 'makes known the end from the beginning, from ancient times, what is still to come' (Isaiah 46:10). Past, present and future are interrelated in him.

So are heaven and earth. There is an interaction between what goes on up there and what goes on down here. One of the disturbing features in Revelation is the constant shift of scene from earth to heaven and back again. That is because of the connection between events above and below (e.g. war in heaven leads to war on earth; 12:7; 13:7).

'Apocalyptic' is history written from God's point of view. It gives the total picture. It enlarges our understanding of world events by seeing them in the light of what is above and beyond our limited perception. This gives us both insight and foresight, enlarging our comprehension of what is going on around us, far beyond that of the normal historian.

Patterns and purposes emerge to which he is blind. History is not just a haphazard accumulation of happenings. Coincidence gives way to providence. History is going somewhere.

Time is eternally significant. Time and eternity are interrelated. God is not outside time, as Greek philosophy imagined. He is inside time; or rather, time is inside God. He is the God who was, is and is to come. Even God himself cannot change the past, once it has happened! The death and resurrection of Jesus can never be changed or cancelled.

God is working out his plans and purposes within time (the classic book on this is *Christ and Time* by Oscar Cullmann, SCM Press, 1950). He is the Lord of history. But it is his pattern, which can only be discerned when he has revealed the missing pieces of the jigsaw. Things hidden from human observation and which God reveals are called 'mysteries' in the New Testament.

The direction of events in the past and present becomes apparent in the light of the future. The shape of history cannot be seen in the short term, only in the long term. For time is relative as well as real to God. 'A thousand years are like a day' to him (Psalm 90:4, quoted in 2 Peter 3:8). His amazing patience with us makes him appear 'slow' to us (2 Peter 3:9).

The Bible contains a 'philosophy of history' quite different from those which man's unaided reason has adopted. The contrast is clear when we compare it with the four most commonly held ideas:

1. *Cyclic*. 'History repeats itself'. It simply goes round in endless circles, or cycles. Sometimes the world gets better, then worse, then better, then worse again ... and so on. This was the Greek idea.

2. *Rhythmic*. This is a variation on the cyclic. The world still alternates between better and worse, but never repeats itself in exactly the same way. It is always moving on, but whether it will end on an 'up' or a 'down' is anyone's guess!

3. *Optimistic*. The world is getting better and better. As one British Prime Minister said at the beginning of the twentieth century: 'up and up and up and on and on and on'. The word on everyone's lips then was 'progress'. History was an ascending escalator.

4. *Pessimistic*. The word on everyone's lips at the end of the twentieth century was 'survival'. The 'doom and gloom' experts believe we are on a descending escalator. It might be slowed down, but cannot be stopped. The world will get worse until life becomes impossible (current estimates are around 2040!).

The biblical pattern is quite different from all of these, combining both pessimism and optimism in a realism based on all the facts.

5. *Apocalyptic*. The world will get steadily worse, then suddenly better than it has ever been – and will stay that way.

This last belief is shared by Jews, Christians and Communists. They all got it from the same source: the Hebrew prophets (Karl Marx had a Jewish mother and a Lutheran father). The basic difference between them is what they believe will bring about the sharp change of direction. Communists believe it will be by human revolution. Jews believe it will be by divine intervention. Christians believe it will be by the return of the God-man Jesus to planet earth.

Those who have read through the book of Revelation will now realize that it is actually structured on this very basis. After dealing with the present in its earlier chapters, it turns to the future course of history, which gets steadily worse (in chapters 6–18), then suddenly better (in chapters 20–22), the change coinciding with the Second Coming of Christ (in chapter 19).

There are two more characteristics of 'apocalyptic' history that we must talk about before moving on.

The first feature is that the pattern is basically *moral*. Since history is ordered by God and he is perfectly good and all-powerful, we would expect to see his justice administered in the encouragement of good and the punishment of evil.

But this does not seem to be the case, either in international or individual experience. Life seems to be terribly unjust. History seems indifferent to morality. The righteous suffer and the wicked prosper. The constant cry is: 'Why does a good God allow such things to go on?' The Bible is honest enough to record the bewilderment of Job, David (Psalm 73:1–4), Jesus himself (Mark 15:34, the words of Psalm 22:1), and the Christians who were martyred for him (Revelation 6:10).

All such doubts spring from a short-term view focused main-ly on the present and partly on the past. A long-term view takes the future, the ultimate outcome, into account. This can totally change the understanding (Job 42; Psalm 73:15–28; Hebrews 12:2; Revelation 20:4; Paul sums it up in Romans 8:18).

'Apocalyptic' portions of the Bible all encourage this long-term view which reveals that history does uphold morality (Daniel 7–12, with which Revelation has much in common, is an excellent example). We do live in a moral universe. The good God is still on the throne. He will bring it all to the right conclusion. He will punish the wicked and reward the right-eous. He will put the world right again and give it to those who have been willing to be put right themselves. There will be a 'happy ever after' ending to the story.

'Apocalyptic' literature, including Revelation, therefore concentrates on such themes as reward, retribution and restora-tion. Above all, it pictures God reigning on a throne, in perfect control of world affairs. Notice that word 'pictures', which introduces the other quality.

The second feature is that the presentation is often *symbol-ical*. It has to be, since the unfamiliar is being communicated. As every teacher knows, the unknown has somehow to be related to the known, usually by analogy ('well, it's like this'). Most of Jesus' parables about the Kingdom of Heaven use earthly situations to assist understanding ('the Kingdom of Heaven is like …').

Helping people to comprehend something involves imagination as much as information. If they can 'picture' it in their mind, it will be much easier to grasp. Significantly, the response is usually: 'Now I see'.

Revelation is full of pictorial language. Through the constant use of 'symbols' we can visualize what would otherwise be incomprehensible. It cannot be too strongly emphasized that this is intended to help our understanding, not hinder it. Too many have used the 'highly symbolic' nature of the book to ignore or even dismiss its teaching, as if the symbols are too obscure to convey a clear message. That is simply not the case, as is apparent when they are listed in four categories:

Some are *obvious* in their meaning. The 'dragon' or 'serpent' is the devil. The 'lake of fire' is hell. The 'great white throne' is the Lord's judgement seat.

Some are *explained* in the context. The 'stars' are angels. The 'lampstands' are churches. The 'seals', 'trumpets' and 'bowls' are disasters. The 'incense' represents prayers ascending. The 'ten horns' are kings.

Some are *paralleled* elsewhere in scripture. In the Old Testament may be found the tree of life, the rainbow, the morning star, the rod of iron, horsemen, tyrannical regimes pictured as wild 'beasts'. It may safely be assumed that these emblems have retained their original meaning.

Some are *obscure*, but very few. One example is the 'white stone', for which scholars have offered an amazing number of interpretations. A declaration of innocence? A sign of approval? A badge of excellence? Maybe we won't know what it signifies until we receive one!

Numbers are also used as symbols. There are many 'sevens' in Revelation – stars, lampstands, lamps, seals, trumpets, bowls. It is the 'round' number of the Bible, the complete, the perfect figure. 'Twelve' is associated with the old people of God (their tribes) and the new (their apostles); 'twenty-four' brings them together. 'One thousand' is the largest number. 'Twelve thousand' from each tribe of Israel brings the total to 'one hundred and forty-four thousand'.

'666' is the one that captures attention. It is made up of sixes, a figure which always points to the human failure to reach the seven of 'complete perfection'. It is used here as a clue to the identity of the last world dictator before Jesus reigns for a thousand years (in Latin, a *millennium*). Is it significant that '666' is the total of all the Roman numerals (I=1 + V=5 + X=10 + L=50 +C=100 + D=500) except one (M=1000)? But all attempts to name him from this figure will fail until his appearing makes it perfectly clear.

There is so much in Revelation that is quite clear that we can cope with a few obscurities now, believing that they will be clarified by future events when the information is really needed. Meanwhile, we can thank God that he has told us so much.

Of course, he speaks through human voices, through the mouths of his 'prophets'. John realized that the message he delivered was not his. He calls his writing 'this prophecy' (1:3; 22:7, 10, 18, 19). He is therefore a prophet as well as an apostle. This is the only 'prophetic' book in the New Testament.

Prophecy is both 'forthtelling' (a word of God about the present) and 'foretelling' (a word of God about the future). Revelation is both, the greater part being predictions of events yet to happen.

When will they be fulfilled? Have they happened already? Are they happening right now? Or have they still to happen? We must now consider the various answers being given to these questions.

Schools of interpretation

Nearly one third of the verses in the book of Revelation contain a prediction. Between them, some 56 separate events are foretold. Exactly half of these are in plain language and the other half are in symbolic picture form.

Most of them occur after chapter 4, which opens with a marked change in perspective – from earth to heaven and from present to future ('come up here and I will show you what must take place after this'; 4:1).

Clearly, this refers to happenings that are future to the original writer and readers in the first century AD. But how far ahead of them did the forecast stretch? Are the predicted events past, present or future to us who live 19 centuries later? Do we look behind, around or ahead for their fulfilment?

This is where the differences begin. Over the intervening years between then and now, four major opinions have arisen, leading to four 'schools of interpretation'. Most commentaries are written from only one point of view. It is important to look at them all before assuming that one is right. It is too easy and risky to follow the first that has been heard or read about.

The four are now so well established, they have been given familiar labels: preterist, historicist (of which there are two distinct varieties), futurist and idealist. Don't be put off by this rather technical jargon. It is important to be able to identify the very different approaches you may encounter.

1. Preterist

This school regards the predictions as fulfilled during the decline and fall of the Roman Empire, when the church was under the pressures of imperial persecutions. It was written for Christians of the first century, to prepare them for what would happen in the second and third. The 'great city' of Babylon, sitting on 'seven hills' (17:9) is identified as Rome (Peter seems to make the same comparison; 1 Peter 5:13).

Though the bulk of Revelation is thus 'past' to us, that does not mean it is of limited value. We can learn lessons from all the historical narrative in scripture. Indeed, it constitutes the major part of the Bible. We can draw inspiration and instruction from what has gone before.

The strength of this view is that all Bible study should begin with the original context of writer and readers. What did this mean to them? What the writer intended and what the readers would understand in their situation are vital steps towards a true interpretation and application.

But there are a number of weaknesses. For one thing, very few if any of the specific predictions actually came true in the Roman Empire. Only a few general trends can be identified but no particular correspondence (some have tried to distil '666' from the letters of 'Nero Caesar', though Revelation was probably written 30 years after his death!). It also means that after Rome fell, the major part of the book lost its direct relevance and really said little to the later church. Since nearly all scholars accept that the last few chapters cover the end of the world, which is still future to us, a huge gap is left between the beginning and end of church history, with no direct guidance for the many intervening centuries. This deficiency is met by the second approach.

2. Historicist

This school believes the predictions cover the entire 'church age' between the First and Second Comings of Christ. It is a coded history of 'anno domini' in symbolic form, covering the major phases and crises of the entire period. So the fulfilment is past, present and future to us. We are right in there and from what has already come to pass we can know what is next on the programme.

One scholar produced a cross-reference index between every section of Revelation and the many volumes of the *Cambridge Ancient and Modern History*. It is generally held that we are living somewhere in chapter 16 or 17!

At least this theory has made the book relevant to every generation of Christians. It has also stimulated interest. But this is more than outweighed by its drawbacks.

One is that many details are rather forced to fit known events, which appears somewhat artificial. But the main problem is that no two 'historicists' seem to agree on the correlation of Scripture and history! Were they using the right method, there would surely be a greater degree of unanimity in their conclusions. And they still finish up with many unfulfilled details.

So far we have only considered one type of 'historicism'. We will call it *linear*, because it believes that the central part of Revelation goes in one straight line of events from the first to the Second Advent of Christ.

There is another type, which we will call the *cyclical*, which believes that it covers the whole church history more than once, constantly returning to the beginning and 'recapitulating' the events from another angle. One popular volume (*More than Conquerors* by William Hendiksen, Baker, 1960) claims to have discovered seven such cycles, each covering the whole church age (in chapters 1–3, 4–7, 8–11, 12–14, 15–16, 17–19, 20–22)! This enables him to place the 'Millennium' (in chapter 20) before the Second Coming (chapter 19) and therefore hold the 'post-millennial' view. But this 'progressive parallelism', as it is called, seems to be forced onto the text, rather than found within it. In particular, the radical separation of chapters 19 and 20 is totally unwarranted.

The historicist interpretation is probably the least satisfactory and the least convincing, in either linear or cyclical form.

3. Futurist

This school believes that the central block of predictions applies to the last few years leading up to the Second Coming. It is therefore still future to us today, hence the label. It concerns the climax of evil control in the world, which will be the 'Great Tribulation' for the people of God (Revelation 7:14; also referred to by Jesus in Matthew 24:12–22).

All the events will be compressed into quite a short time – three and a half years, to be exact (explicitly referred to as 'a time, times and half a time' or 'forty-two months' or 'one thousand, two hundred and sixty days'; 11:2–3; 12:6, 14, quoting Daniel 12:7).

Since the events are still future, the predictions tend to be taken more literally, as an accurate description of what will happen. There is no longer any need to tailor them to fit past history. Certainly, the series of disasters seems to lead straight into the end of the world.

What, then, is the message for the church through the ages? Most of the book would only be relevant to the very last generation of believers in this case. Surprisingly, many futurists also believe that the church will be 'raptured' to heaven before the troubles start, so even the last Christians don't need to know these things either!

A further weakness is that futurists are prone to treat Revelation as an 'almanac', leading to an excessive interest in charts, schedules of the future. The fact that they do not always agree suggests that Revelation was not primarily written for such speculative purposes.

4. Idealist

This approach removes all specific time references and discourages correlation with particular events. Revelation pictures the 'eternal' struggle between good and evil and the 'truths' contained in its narratives can be applied to any century. The battle between God and Satan is ongoing, but the divine victory can be experienced by an 'overcoming' church at any time. The 'essential message' can be universally applied throughout time and space.

The main and perhaps only merit of this view is that the message of the book becomes directly relevant to all who read it. They are in the struggle that is described and are assured that 'the one who is in you is greater than the one who is in the world' (1 John 4:4). It is possible to be 'more than conquerors' (Romans 8:37).

This, however, is to treat Revelation as 'myth'. It is spiritually true, but not historically true. These are fictional events, but the stories contain truths – as in Aesop's fables or *Pilgrim's Progress*. The truths must be dug out of the narrative before being applied. The cost of this 'demythologizing' process is to jettison a great deal of material, dismissing it as poetic licence which belongs to the package rather than the content.

Behind all this is the Greek philosophy which separated spiritual and physical, sacred and secular, eternity and time. God, they said, is timeless. So truth is timeless, though it is also therefore timely. But it is not in 'the times'. Their notion of history as cyclical cut out the concept of the 'end-time', the idea that time would reach a climax or conclusion.

This has serious consequences for 'eschatology' (the study of 'the last things', from the Greek word *eschatos* = 'end' or 'last'). Events like the Second Coming and the Day of Judgement are transferred from the future to the present, from then to now. Eschatology becomes 'existential' (i.e. concerned with the present moment of existence, or it is said to be 'realized' (as in 'realizing investments' – having the money to spend now).

Of course, radical changes have to be made to the 'predictions' to make them fit the present – usually by 'spiritualizing' them (a 'Platonic' way of thinking). For example, the 'New Jerusalem' (in chapter 21) becomes the description of a people rather than a place, an 'idealized' (note the word) picture of the church, the architectural details conveniently forgotten!

It is time to summarize this survey. There are four different answers to the question: what period of time does Revelation cover?

The preterist replies: the first few centuries AD.

The historicist replies: all the centuries AD from the First to the Second Advent.

The futurist replies: the last years of the last century AD.

The idealist replies: any century AD, none in particular.

So which is right? There are pros and cons for each. Do we have to choose between them? Could they all be right? Could they all be wrong?

The following observations may help the reader to reach a conclusion.

First, it seems obvious that no one key unlocks the whole book. Each 'school' has seen some truths, but none has released all. When only one approach is used there is always some manipulation of the text.

Second, there is no reason why more than one may not be used. Texts have different meanings and applications. But some control is needed to avoid the arbitrary use of different approaches to bolster an opinion already decided upon before studying the scripture. This restraint is provided by the context and by constantly asking the question: was this the meaning intended by the divine author for the human reader?

Third, parts of each of the four methods can help understanding. Some elements from all four are compatible and can be used in conjunction with each other, though it must be added that other elements are quite incompatible and cannot be combined.

Fourth, the emphasis may change in different sections of the book. At each stage, the most appropriate method or methods of interpretation must be chosen and used. In the remainder of this section we shall illustrate this in practical terms by considering the three major divisions of the book:

THE BEGINNING (CHAPTERS 1–3)

This section is not very controversial, so is more frequently and confidently expounded than the rest (see, for example, *What Christ thinks of the Church* by John Stott, Lutterworth Press, 1958). Most are comfortable with the traditional interpretation (though uncomfortable with the application!). The problem with this section is that we *do* understand it, only too well. There are a few problems with details (the angels) and symbols (white stones and hidden manna). But the letters to the seven churches in Asia are not unlike other New Testament epistles. So which 'school' is appropriate?

The 'preterist' is surely right in directing our attention to the first century. Any true exegesis must *begin* with what this meant to them then. But need it end there?

The 'historicist' believes that the seven churches represent the whole church in *time*, seven consecutive epochs in church history. Ephesus covers the early church, Smyrna the Roman persecutions, Pergamum the time of Constantine, Thyatira the Middle Ages, Sardis the Reformation, Philadelphia the worldwide missionary movement and Laodicea the twentieth century. But the parallels are forced (Western churches may look 'Laodicean', but the Third-World ones are anything but!). This scheme simply doesn't fit.

The 'futurist' is even more bizarre, believing that the seven churches will be re-established in the very same cities of Asia just before Jesus returns, based on the mistaken assumption that 'I will come' (2:5, 16; 3:4) refers to the Second Advent. Actually, these churches have long since disappeared, their 'lampstands removed'.

The 'idealist' usually shares the 'preterist' view of this section, but adds the belief that the seven historical churches represent the whole Church in *space*. Ephesus represents the orthodox but loveless fellowships, Smyrna the suffering, Pergamum the enduring, Thyatira the corrupt, Sardis the dead, Philadelphia the feeble but evangelistic, Laodicea the lukewarm.

Whether they cover the entire range of church character between them is debatable. But the comfort and challenge of their example can be applied anywhere and any time.

So the preterist with a dash of idealist seems the right mixture for the first section.

THE MIDDLE (CHAPTERS 4–18)

This is where the differences are most acute. The opening vision of God's throne presents few problems and has inspired worship through the ages. It is when Jesus the Lion/Lamb releases disasters on the world and suffering on the church that the debate begins. When does this happen? It must be some-time between the second century (which was 'hereafter' to the seven churches; 4:1) and the Second Coming (in chapter 19).

The 'preterist' limits this section to the 'decline and fall of the Roman Empire'. But the fact remains that most predicted events, particularly the 'natural' catastrophes, simply did not happen during that period. Much of the text has to be treated as 'poetic licence', rather vaguely hinting at what might happen.

The 'historicist' has much the same problem when attempting to fit the whole of church history into these chapters, either as one continuous narrative or in repeated 'recapitulations'. The details will not fit.

The 'futurist' is, of course, free to believe in the literal fulfilment of the detailed forecast, since none of it has happened yet. Two features seem to confirm that this is nearer the correct application. First, the 'troubles' are clearly worse than anything the world has yet seen (as Jesus predicted in Matthew 24:21). Second, they seem to lead directly into the events at the end of history. But is that all? Has this section no relevance before then?

The 'idealist' is wrong to 'demythologize' this section, divorcing it from time altogether. But it is right to look for a message that can apply to any phase of church history. The clue lies in Scripture itself, which clearly teaches that future events cast their shadows ahead in time. Jesus is 'foreshadowed' in many ways in the Old Testament (as the letter to the Hebrews explains). The coming antichrist is preceded by 'many antichrists' (1 John 2:18); the coming false prophet by many false prophets (Matthew 24:11). The coming universal persecution is already experienced in many local regions. The 'Great Tribulation' is only different in scale from the 'much tribulation' which is normal at all times (John 16:33; Acts 14:22). So these chapters can help us to understand current trends as well as their ultimate climax.

So the futurist and a measure of idealist open up this section in the best way.

THE END (CHAPTERS 19–22)

Revelation seems to get clearer towards the end, but there are still some areas of controversy. Most take these chapters to refer to the ultimate future, the very 'last things' to happen, beginning with the return of Christ (in chapter 19).

The 'preterist' drops out here. Very few attempt to fit these chapters into the days of the early Church.

The 'historicist' school divides sharply in two. The 'linear' variety invariably see this section as the 'end-times', following the 'church age'. But the 'cyclical' find 'recapitulations' even here. Some see the Millennium in chapter 20 as a description of the church before the Second Coming in chapter 19! Others see the 'New Jerusalem' in chapter 21 as a description of the Millennium before the final judgement in chapter 20! Such radical dislocation of events are not justified by the text itself and suggest manipulation in the interests of theological systems and dogma.

The 'futurist' has few opponents in this section. The Second Coming, the Day of Judgement, and the new heaven and earth have clearly not yet arrived.

The 'idealist' has few proponents in this section. These tend to overlook the new earth altogether and talk about 'heaven' as the timeless sphere into which believers are transferred at death. The 'New Jerusalem' pictures this eternal realm (the 'heavenly Zion' of Hebrews 12:22), which is never expected to come 'down out of heaven' (in spite of Revelation 21:2, 10!).

So the futurist can be given a monopoly in handling this section.

In a later section we shall be sharing an 'introduction' to the text of Revelation itself, using the tools we have considered appropriate (which do not include the historicist). However, before we do that, there is one other important matter to consider.

The four 'schools' of interpretation share one common assumption: that the most important question is – WHEN? That is, when are the predictions fulfilled in time?

This is to start with the supposition that Revelation is primarily concerned with forecasting the future, to satisfy our curiosity or reduce our anxiety by revealing what is going to happen, both in the immediate and ultimate future.

But this is highly questionable. The New Testament never indulges in idle speculation, even warns against it. Every 'unveiling' of what lies ahead has a practical, indeed a moral purpose. The future is only revealed so that the present may be influenced by it.

So the fundamental question is not 'when'? but WHY? Why was Revelation written? Why was it revealed to John? Why was he told to pass it on? Why do we need to read and 'keep' these words?

Not just to tell us what is going to happen but to get us *ready* for what is going to happen. How do we arrive at that answer?

Sense of purpose

Why was the Book of Revelation written? The answer is readily accessible by asking another question: For whom was it written?

It was never intended to be a university textbook for theological staff or students. It is often they who have made it appear so complex that simple folk have been intimidated. Let one of them confess this:

> *We boldly affirm that the study of this book would present absolutely no possibility of error if the inconceivable, often ridiculous, prejudice of theologians in all ages had not so trammelled it and made it bristle with difficulties, that most readers shrink from it in alarm. Apart from these preconceptions, the Revelation would be the most simple, most transparent book that prophet ever penned* (Reuss, *in 1884, quoted in* The Prophecy Handbook, *World Bible Publishers, 1991*).

The situation has hardly improved since then, as a recent comment reveals:

> *It is one of the misfortunes of our expertise-oriented culture that when anything seems difficult it is sent off to the university to be figured out (Eugene Peterson, writing on Revelation in* Reversed Thunder, *HarperCollins, 1988, p. 200).*

This has led to a widespread notion that this book will not be understood by the 'layman' (whether that label is used in its ecclesiastical or educational sense).

Ordinary readers

It cannot be too strongly emphasized that Revelation was written for very ordinary people. It was addressed to the members of seven churches at a time when 'not many were wise by human standards; not many were influential; not many were of noble birth' (1 Corinthians 1:26).

It was said of Jesus that 'the common people heard him gladly' (Mark 12:37, Authorized Version). This was a tribute to them as well as to him. They recognized that he 'spoke with authority', that he knew what he was talking about. It is much easier to fool the highly educated!

The Book of Revelation yields its treasures to those who read it with a simple faith, an open mind and a tender heart.

A story has circulated in America which highlights the point, though it sounds like an apocryphal preacher's tale (as the pastor's little boy said: 'Daddy, was that story true, or was you just preaching?')! Apparently some theological students were tired and confused by lectures on 'apocalyptic' so decided to have a game of basketball in the campus gymnasium. While playing, they noticed the black janitor reading his Bible while waiting to lock up. They asked which part he was studying and were surprised to find he was going through Revelation. 'You don't understand that, do you?'

'Sure do.'

'What's it about, then?'

With eyes lit up and a broad smile came the reply: 'Simple! Jesus wins!!'

Of course, there's more to be said than that. But it's not a bad summary of the message. Plenty have studied the contents and missed the message. Common sense is a basic requirement. No one takes the whole book literally. No one takes it all symbolically. But where is the line to be drawn between the literal and the symbolical? This will have a profound effect on interpretation. Common sense will be a great help. The four horsemen are symbols, but the wars, bloodshed, famine and disease they represent clearly literal. The 'lake of fire' is a symbol of hell, but the unending 'torment' in it is literal (Revelation 20:10).

The rules of common speech may be usefully employed. Words should be taken in their plainest, simplest sense, unless clearly indicated otherwise. It should be assumed that speakers (including Jesus) and writers (including John) mean what they say. Their communications should be taken at face value.

Another such rule is that the same word in the same context is presumed to have the same meaning, again unless clearly indicated otherwise. To change the meaning of a word suddenly and without warning would be as confusing as changing the pronunciation or spelling. This rule directly affects the two 'resurrections' in Revelation 20.

Having said all this, we must add the necessary qualification that Revelation was written for ordinary folk in a very different time and place from ours. It is not surprising if some things obvious to them are obscure to us 2,000 years later and a similar number of miles away.

They were Gentiles of mixed race who lived in a Roman province, spoke Greek, read Jewish scriptures and were held together by a shared Christian faith. So we need to use as much knowledge of their background, culture and language as we can. The object of the exercise is to discover what *they* would have understood when they heard Revelation read aloud to them, perhaps at one sitting. That could be quite different from what we perceive as we read it silently, a short portion each day.

But the book is clearly for us in our day as well, or it would not be in the New Testament. The Lord must have intended this when he gave it to John. So we can assume that our distance in time and space is not an insuperable handicap.

A much more important factor than the cultural gap is the difference of circumstances. It is vital to ask what situation required the writing of this book. This is the master key required to unlock the whole volume. Behind every other book in the New Testament there is a reason for its being written, a need which it is designed to meet. Revelation is no exception.

Practical reasons

We have already said that its primary purpose was not to reveal a schedule of future events but to prepare people for what would happen. So what is coming for which, without this book, they would not be ready? The answer comes on the first page (1:9–10).

John, the writer, is already suffering for his faith. He is in prison, but not for any crime. He is a 'political' prisoner on the island of Patmos in the Aegean Sea (the modern equivalent would be Alcatraz or Robben Island). He has been arrested and exiled for religious reasons. His exclusive devotion to 'the word of God and the testimony of Jesus' is seen as treason by the authorities, a threat to the *pax Romana* based on polytheistic tolerance and an imperial cult. Citizens were expected to believe in many gods and the Emperor was one of them.

Towards the end of the first century, this situation came to a head, creating a crisis of conscience for Christians. Julius Caesar had been the first to proclaim himself divine. His successor, Augustus, had encouraged the building of temples in his honour; a number of these had been erected in Asia (now western Turkey). While Nero had begun the persecution of Christians (daubing them with pitch and burning them alive as torches for his nightly garden parties or sewing them in the skins of wild animals to be hunted by dogs), this was limited in duration and location.

It was the advent of Domitian in the last decade of the first century that inaugurated the fiercest attacks on Christians which would continue intermittently for 200 years. He demanded universal worship of himself, on pain of death. Once a year incense had to be thrown on an altar fire before his bust with an acclamation: 'Caesar is Lord.' The appointed day on which this had to be done was designated 'the Lord's Day'.

This was the very day on which Revelation began to be written. Modern readers may be forgiven for thinking it was a Sunday. Actually, it could have been, but Sunday was called 'the first day of the week' in the early church. Two elements in the Greek text indicate the annual imperial festival. One is the definite article (on '*the* Lord's day' not 'a Lord's day'). The other is the fact that 'Lord' is in the form of an adjective, not a noun ('the Lordy or Lordly day'), the very name given to it by Domitian, who also claimed the title: 'Lord and our God'.

Tough times lay ahead. For those who refused to say anything but 'Jesus is Lord', it would be a matter of life and death. The word 'witness' (in Greek: *martur*) would take on a new, deadly meaning. The church was facing its fiercest test so far. How many would remain loyal under such pressure?

After all, John was the only one of the 12 apostles left. All the others had already suffered a martyr's death. Christian tradition records that Andrew died on an X-shaped cross in Patras of Achaia, Bartholomew (Nathaniel) was flayed alive in Armenia, James (brother of John) was beheaded by Herod Agrippa in Jerusalem, James (son of Cleopas and Mary) was stoned, Jude (Thaddeus) was shot with arrows in Armenia, Matthew was slain by the sword in Parthia, Peter was crucified upside down in Rome, Philip was hanged on a pillar in Hieropolis in Phrygia, Simon (Zelotes) was crucified in Persia, Thomas was slain with a spear in India, Matthias was stoned and beheaded. Paul also had been beheaded in Rome. So the writer of Revelation was only too aware of the cost of loyalty to Jesus. He did not then know that he would be the only apostle to die a natural death.

Revelation is a 'manual for martyrdom'. It calls believers to 'be faithful, even to the point of death' (2:10). Martyrs figure largely in its pages.

Believers are encouraged to 'stick it out'. One frequent exhortation is to 'endure', a passive attitude. Right in the middle of the biggest trouble comes the plea: 'This calls for patient endurance on the part of the saints who obey God's commandments and remain faithful to Jesus' (14:12). This may be said to be the key verse in the whole book.

But there is also a call to an active attitude in suffering for Jesus: to 'overcome'. This verb is used even more frequently than 'endure' and may be said to be the key word in the whole book.

Each letter to the seven churches concludes with a call to each member to be an 'overcomer', that is, to overcome all temptations and pressures, both inside and outside the church. To lapse from truly Christian belief and behaviour is to be unfaithful to Jesus.

The message is not just that Christ wins, but that Christians must also win through. They are to follow the Lord who said: 'Take heart! I have overcome the world' (John 16:33) and who now says in Revelation: 'You also must overcome the world.'

Of course, that is why this book becomes so much more meaningful to Christians under persecution. Maybe this is also why Western Christians in comfortable churches fail to find it relevant. It has to be read through tears.

The book offers two incentives to encourage the persecuted to 'overcome'. One is positive: *reward*. Many prizes are offered to those who persevere – the right to eat of the tree of life in the paradise of God; never to be hurt by the second death; to eat the hidden manna and be given a white stone with a secret new name on it; to have authority to rule the nations; to sit with Jesus on his throne; to be dressed in white and made a pillar in the temple of God bearing his name and never to leave it. Above all, and beyond all the suffering, the overcoming believer is promised a place in the new heaven and earth, enjoying God's presence for ever and ever. The prospect is glorious.

But there is a negative motivation as well: *punishment*. What is the fate of believers who are unfaithful under pressure? In a word, they will have none of the above blessings. Worse than that, they will share the fate of unbelievers in the 'lake of fire'. Two verses alone, taken from first and last sections, confirm this awful possibility.

'He who overcomes ... I will never erase his name from the book of life' (3:5). If language means anything at all, it means that those who do not overcome are in danger of having their names erased (literally, 'scraped off' the parchment with a knife). The 'book of life' appears in four books of the Bible (Exodus 32:32; Psalm 69:28; Philippians 4:3; Revelation 3:5).

Three of these contexts mention names of the people of God being blotted out after they have sinned against the Lord. To read the verse in Revelation as if it could include 'he who doesn't overcome' in the promise as well is to make the reward meaningless.

'He who overcomes will inherit all this [the new heaven and earth, with the New Jerusalem] and I will be his God and he will be my son. But the cowardly, the faithless, the immoral … their place will be in the fiery lake of burning sulphur. This is the second death' (21:7–8). It needs to be remembered that the whole of Revelation is directed to believers, not unbelievers. Throughout, it is addressed to 'the saints' and 'his servants'. The reference here is to cowardly and faithless believers. This is confirmed by the word 'but', directly contrasting those deserving such a fate with the believers who 'overcome'.

In other words, Revelation sets two destinies before *Christians*. They will either be raised with Christ and share his reign, ending up in the new universe. Or they will lose their inheritance in the Kingdom and end up in hell.

This alternative is confirmed elsewhere in the New Testament. The Gospel of Matthew is a 'manual for discipleship' containing five major discourses addressed to 'sons of the Kingdom'. Yet most of Jesus' teaching on hell is to be found here and all but two of his warnings are addressed to his disciples. The Sermon on the Mount (in chapters 5–7), which blesses those who are persecuted because of Jesus, goes on to speak of hell and concludes with a reminder that there are two destinies. The missionary commissioning (in chapter 10) includes the charge: 'Do not be afraid of those who kill the body but cannot kill the soul. Rather be afraid of the one who can destroy both body and soul in hell' (verse 28) and 'whoever disowns me before men, I will disown him before my Father in heaven' (verse 33). The Olivet discourse (in chapters

24–25) condemns slothful and careless servants of the master to being 'assigned a place with the hypocrites' (24:51) and 'thrown outside into the darkness, where there will be weeping and gnashing of teeth' (25:30).

Paul takes the same line when reminding Timothy of a 'trustworthy saying':

> If we died with him,
>   we will also live with him;
> If we endure,
>   we will also reign with him.
> If we disown him,
>   He will also disown us … (2 Timothy 2:11–12)

Many Christians deny the implications of all this. Certainly there is more to be said (the author has dealt more fully with this vital question in a volume entitled *Once Saved, Always Saved?* Hodder & Stoughton, 1996). Meanwhile, the position in Revelation seems very clear. It is even possible for believers to lose their 'share in the tree of life and in the holy city' simply by tampering with the text of the book (22:19), thus changing its message.

We could summarize the aim of Revelation by saying it was written to exhort Christians facing immense pressures to 'endure' and 'overcome' and thus avoid the 'second death' by keeping their names in the 'book of life'. We shall find that every chapter and verse fits easily into this overall purpose, as we look at the shape or structure of the whole book.

The structure of Revelation

If we have been right in defining the purpose of Revelation as the preparation of believers to face persecution and even martyrdom, it should be possible to relate this to every part of the book. Moreover, the overall structure should reveal a development of this theme.

We shall construct a number of outlines by analysing the contents from different perspectives and for different purposes, starting with the simplest. The most obvious division occurs at 4:1, with the radical shift in viewpoint from earth to heaven and from the present situation to the future prospects:

1–3	Present
4–22	Future

The larger second part also divides neatly between the bad news and the good news. The change from one to the other comes in 19. So now we have:

1–3	Present
4–22	Future
	4–18 *Bad news*
	20–22 *Good news*

Now we consider how each section relates to the main purpose of the book. That is, how does each section prepare believers for the coming 'Big Trouble'? We can expand the outline thus:

1–3	Present
	Things must be put right now.
4–22	Future

4–18   *Bad news:* things will get much worse before they get better.

20–22   *Good news:* things will get much better after they get worse.

Only one more item remains to be added, namely, chapter 19. What occurs in this chapter to change the whole situation? The Second Coming of Jesus to planet earth! This is really the framework of the whole book, according to the prologue and epilogue (1:7 and 22:20). We can now insert '19 Jesus returns' between the bad and good news (rather than repeat the outline unnecessarily, readers are invited to write it themselves in the gap left above).

If this simple outline is kept in mind when reading through the book, many things will become clearer. Above all, the unity of the whole book will become apparent. Its objective is achieved in three phases.

First, Jesus tells the churches that they must deal with internal problems if they are to face external pressures. Compromise in belief or behaviour, tolerance of idolatry or immorality, weaken the church from within.

Second, Jesus, who was always noted for his honesty, shows them the worst that can happen to them. They will never have to go through anything worse! And the very worst time ahead will be at most only a few years.

Third, Jesus reveals the wonders that will follow. To throw away such eternal prospects for the sake of avoiding temporary troubles would be the greatest tragedy of all.

In all three ways, Jesus is encouraging his followers to 'endure' and 'overcome' until he gets back. One verse sums it all up: 'Only hold on to what you have until I come' (2:25). Then he can say: 'Come and share your master's happiness' (Matthew 25:21).

Of course, there are other ways of analysing the book. A 'topical' outline is more like an index of subjects and will assist us to 'find our way around' the book.

Such an outline will ignore the switch from earth to heaven and back again. We can work with three periods of time:

A. What is already happening in the present (1–5).
B. What will happen in the nearer future (6–19).
C. What will happen in the further future (20–22).

We will then note the main features of each period and seek to list these in a way that can easily be memorized. Here is one example of such a 'catalogue' of events:

A.   The present
    1–3   One ascended Lord
              Seven assorted lampstands
    4–5   Creator and creatures
              Lion and Lamb
B.   The near future
    6–16   Seals, trumpets, bowls
              Devil, antichrist, false prophet
    17–19 Babylon – last capital
              Armageddon – last battle
C.   The far future
    20   Millennial reign
              Judgement Day
    21–22 New heaven and earth
              New Jerusalem

Note that chapters 4–5 are now in the first division. That is because the 'action' leading to the 'Big Trouble' actually begins with chapter 6. Chapter 19 is now in the second division because the 'Big Trouble' ends here, with Christ defeating the 'unholy trinity'.

This kind of outline is easily memorized and provides a useful 'ready reference' when looking up particular subjects.

It is important to do this kind of exercise before getting down to a closer look at the several sections. There is an over-used proverb about 'not being able to see the wood for the trees'! Revelation is one of the easiest books in which to get so interested in the details that the overall thrust is lost sight of.

However, it is now time to exchange the telescope for a microscope – or at least for a magnifying glass!

The contents of Revelation

In a book this size it is impossible to include a full commentary. What we intend to do is give an introduction to each section that will enable the Bible student to 'read, mark, learn and in-wardly digest the same', as the Book of Common Prayer puts it.

We shall highlight the major features, tackle some of the problems and generally help the reader to keep on course through some of the hazards. Many questions will have to be left unanswered, but these can be followed up in some of the published commentaries (George Eldon Ladd's is one of the best; Eerdmans, 1972).

The suggestion is that each part of Revelation is read before and after the relevant section in this chapter.

Chapters 1–3: The Church on Earth

This is by far the most straightforward, easy to read and under-stand. It is like paddling at the edge of the sea, after which you may find yourself out of your depth and in the grip of an undertow, swirling around in a panic!

Though frequently describing itself as a 'prophecy', Revelation is actually in the form of a letter (compare 1:4–6 with the opening 'address' of other epistles). However, it is sent to seven churches rather than one. While containing a particular message for each, it is clearly intended that all should hear each other's.

After the usual Christian greeting ('grace and peace'), the main theme is announced: 'he is coming', an event which will cause unhappiness to the world but joy to the Church. This event is absolutely certain ('Amen').

The 'sender' of the letter is God himself, the Lord of time, who is, was and is to come, the Alpha and Omega (the first and the last letters of the Greek alphabet, symbolizing the beginning and end of everything). The same titles will be given to Jesus, by himself (1:17; 22:13), proof that he believed in his own deity.

The 'secretary' who writes the letter down is the apostle John, exiled to the eight-miles-by-four island of Patmos in the Dodecanese of the Aegean Sea, a political prisoner for religious reasons.

The contents were given in verbal and visual form. Note that he 'heard' something before he 'saw' anything. The voice commanding him to write was followed by an overwhelming vision of Jesus as John had never seen him before: snow-white hair, blazing eyes, thundering voice, sharp tongue, glowing feet. Even on the Mount of Transfiguration, he had never looked like this. No wonder John swooned, until he heard some very familiar words: 'Don't be afraid'.

Every other great figure of history was alive and is dead. Jesus alone was dead and is alive, 'for ever and ever' (1:18; literally 'to the ages of the ages').

John is told to write 'what is now' (chapters 1–3) and 'what will take place later' (chapters 4–22). The word for the present is the state of the seven churches of Asia, each of which has a 'guardian angel' and for which Jesus has oversight (as well as insight and foresight!). They were represented in the original vision by seven stars (the angels) and seven lampstands (the churches). Note that Jesus characteristically 'walks' around them, as John must have done when he was free. In the Gospels, most of Jesus' messages were delivered and miracles were done as he walked 'in the way', both before his death and after his resurrection.

The seven letters to the seven churches are best studied together and compared with each other. It is very illuminating when they are written out side by side, which emphasizes both their similarities and differences.

It becomes immediately obvious that their form is identical, comprising seven elements (yet another 'seven'):

1. Address:
      'To the angel of the church in ...'
2. Attribute:
      'These are the words of him who ...'
3. Approval:
      'I know your deeds ...'
4. Accusation:
      'Yet I hold this against you'
5. Advice:
      '... or else I will come and ...'
6. Assurance:
      'To him who overcomes, I will ...'
7. Appeal:
      '... let him hear what the Spirit says ...'

The only variation from this order is in the last four letters, where the final two items are reversed (the reason for this is not apparent). We shall now compare and contrast the letters.

THE ADDRESS

This is exactly the same in all seven, except for the named destination. The cities are on a circular route, starting in the major port of Ephesus (a church of which we have more information than any other of those days), heading north up the coast, then inland to the east and finally south to the rich valley of the river Meander.

The only point of debate is whether the word *angelos* (literally 'messenger') refers to a heavenly or human person. Since everywhere else in Revelation it is rightly translated as 'angel', the strong presumption is that it is the same here. Angels are very much involved with churches (even noting hairstyles of worshippers! 1 Corinthians 11:10). Since John is totally isolated, heavenly 'messengers' would have to deliver the letters. It is only modern scepticism about the existence of angels that has led to the translation: 'minister' (presumably with the title 'Rev.'!).

THE ATTRIBUTE

It is noticeable that Jesus never refers to himself by name, only by titles, many of them quite new. In fact, he has over 250 titles, the largest number of any historical personage (it is a useful devotional exercise to list them). In each letter, the title of Jesus is carefully chosen to describe an aspect of his character which that church has tended to forget or needs to consider. Some are to be found in John's original vision of him. All are very significant. The 'key of David' points to his fulfilment of the messianic hopes of Israel. 'Ruler of God's creation' signifies his universal authority (Matthew 28:18).

THE APPROVAL

This opens the most intimate part of each letter, switching from the third person ('him') to the first ('I'). Is this the same person? The 'him' certainly refers to Christ, but the 'I' could be the Spirit, the 'Spirit of Christ', of course. Later comments (e.g. 'I have received authority from my Father' in 2:27) favour the former.

'I know' is a claim to be totally aware, both of their internal state and external situation. His knowledge, and therefore his understanding, is total. His judgement is accurate, his opinion crucial and his honesty transparent.

Above all, he knows their 'works', that is, their deeds, their actions. This emphasis on works runs right through Revelation. That is because its theme is judgement. Jesus is coming again – to judge the living and the dead. We are justified by faith, but we shall be judged by works (2 Corinthians 5:10). Jesus approves good works and encourages their continuance.

When the letters are viewed side by side, it is immediately apparent that Jesus has nothing good to say about two of them, Sardis and Laodicea. Yet these are both 'successful' to human eyes. Jesus' opinion may be very different from ours. Large congregations, big collections and full programmes are not necessarily signs of spiritual health.

Five of the churches are commended: Ephesus for effort, patience, persistence and discernment (rejecting false apostles); Smyrna for its courage in the face of opposition and depriva-tion (though adjacent to a 'synagogue of Satan', possibly an occult form of Judaism); Pergamum for not denying the faith under pressure, even when one member was martyred (though under the shadow of the 'throne of Satan', a gigantic temple now re-erected in an East Berlin museum); Thyatira for its love, faith, patience and progress; Philadelphia for its costly fidelity (with another 'synagogue of Satan' nearby).

In passing we note that Jesus frequently speaks of Satan, who is behind all hostility towards the churches. He is also responsible for the looming crisis they will face, 'the hour of trial that is going to come upon the whole world to test those who live on the earth' (3:10).

Finally, how characteristic of Jesus to commend before he criticizes, an example followed by the apostles. Paul thanked God that the Corinthians had all the 'spiritual gifts' (1 Corinthians 1:4–7) before he corrected their abuse of them. Of course, he also encountered church situations where this was not possible, as in Galatia. But the principle is one to be emulated by all Christians.

THE ACCUSATION

Again, two are exempt from criticism, Smyrna and Philadelphia. What a relief they must have felt when their letters were read out! They are weaker than the others and already suffering, but they have remained faithful, which pleases Jesus more than anything else (Matthew 25:21, 23).

What was wrong with the others? Ephesus had forsaken its 'first love' (for the Lord, each other or lost sinners? Probably all three, since they are interconnected); Pergamum was into idolatry and immorality (syncretism and permissiveness are the modern counterparts); Thyatira was guilty of the same things (as a result of listening to 'Jezebel', a false prophetess); Sardis was for ever starting new ventures, giving it the reputation of being a 'live' church, but they were not kept up or seen through to the finish (does that strike a chord?); Laodicea was sick, but didn't know it.

This last letter is perhaps the best known and most striking. They prided themselves on being a warm fellowship, with a warm welcome for the many visitors. But 'lukewarm' churches make Jesus feel sick. He can handle icy-cold or piping-hot ones more easily! This is a reference to the salty hot springs covering a hillside outside the city (the 'white castle' of Pamukkale is still a popular 'spa' for health seekers); by the time the stream reached Laodicea it was 'lukewarm' and acted as an emetic, causing its drinkers to vomit.

Jesus has stopped attending services here! He cannot be found inside – but stands just outside. 3:20 is probably the most abused text in Scripture and has been almost universally used as an evangelistic invitation and in counselling enquirers. It has nothing to do with becoming a Christian. Indeed, it gives quite a wrong impression when used in this way (actually, it is the sinner who is on the outside needing to knock and enter the Kingdom, of which Jesus is the door; Luke 11:5–10; John 3:5; 10:7). The 'door' in 3:20 is the church door in Laodicea. The verse is a prophetic message to a church which has lost Christ and it is full of hope. It only takes one member who wants to sit at his table with him to get Christ back inside! For a fuller treatment of this verse and the New Testament way to become a Christian, see my book *The Normal Christian Birth* (Hodder and Stoughton, 1989).

Before we leave this section, it needs to be pointed out that these accusations stem from the love of Jesus for the churches. He says this himself: 'as many as I love I reprove and chasten' (3:19). In fact, the absence of such discipline could be a sign of not belonging to his family at all (Hebrews 12:7–8)!

He is not wanting to put them down, but lift them up. Above all, he seeks to get them ready for pending pressure, which will 'test' them (3:10). If they compromise now, they will surrender then. That could cost them their inheritance.

THE ADVICE

There is a word of counsel for all seven churches. Even the two of which he thoroughly approves are exhorted to keep up the good work, to 'hold on to what you have until I come' (2:25).

The other five are cautioned with two words: 'remember' and 'repent'. They are to call to mind what they once were and what they ought to be. And true repentance involves much more than regret or remorse; it requires confession and correction.

He warns those that spurn his appeal that he 'will come' and deal with them. There will be a time when it will be too late to put things right. Sometimes this refers to his Second Coming, when the 'crown of life' will be given to those who have been 'faithful, even to the point of death' (2:10; compare 2 Timothy 4:6–8), but those who are not ready will hear the dreadful words: 'I don't know you' (Matthew 25:12).

Usually, 'I will come' refers to an earlier 'visitation' to a single church, to remove its 'lampstand' (2:5). Jesus has a ministry of closing churches down! A compromised church that is not willing to be corrected is worse than useless to the Kingdom of God. It is better to remove such a poor advertisement for the gospel altogether.

We could summarize this part of the letters: 'put it right, keep it up or I will close it down'.

THE ASSURANCE

It is noticeable that the call to 'overcome' is not addressed to a church as a whole, but to each individual member. Judgement is always individual, whether for the purpose of reward or punishment, never corporate (note 'each one' in 2 Corinthians 5:10). There is no suggestion of leaving a corrupt church and catching a chariot to a better one down the road! Neither is a person excused compromise because their whole church is slipping. The wrong trends in a fellowship are not to be followed. In other words, a Christian may have to learn to resist pressures in the church first before facing them in the world. If we cannot 'overcome' the former, we are unlikely to 'overcome' the latter.

Jesus has no hesitation in offering rewards as incentives (5:12). He himself endured the cross, scorning its shame, 'for the joy set before him' (Hebrews 12:2). In each of the letters he encourages 'overcomers' to think of the prizes awaiting those who 'press on toward the goal' (Philippians 3:14).

Just as his title in each letter is taken from the first chapter, the rewards he offers are taken from the last chapters. They will come in the ultimate future rather than the immediate present. Only those who have faith that he keeps his promises will be motivated by distant compensations.

Once again, we must realize that the joys of the new heaven and earth are not for all believers, but only for those who overcome the pressures of temptation and persecution (21:7–8 makes this abundantly clear). It is those who remain obedient and faithful 'to the end' (2:26) who will be saved (compare Matthew 10:22; 24:13; Mark 13:13; Luke 21:19).

THE APPEAL

The final call, 'he that has an ear, let him hear', is a familiar conclusion to Jesus' words (Matthew 13:9, for example). Its meaning becomes clear in the light of one of the most frequently quoted texts from the Old Testament in the New: 'You will be ever hearing, but never understanding ... they hardly hear with their ears ... otherwise they might ... hear with their ears, understand with their hearts and turn, and I would heal them' (Isaiah 6:9–10, quoted in Matthew 13:13–15; Mark 4:12; Luke 8:10; Acts 28:26–27).

Jesus knew that this would be the general response from the Jews. Now he is challenging Christians not to have the same reaction. He is highlighting the difference between hearing and heeding a message. It is a question of how much notice is taken of what he says. His words in Revelation will only be a blessing if they are read and 'kept', that is, not just taken into the ear but 'taken to heart' (1:3). A parent whose child has ignored the order to 'put that down' will say, 'Did you hear what I said?', knowing full well that it was heard, but was not heeded.

Quite simply, the closing remark in each of the letters to the seven churches means that Jesus expects a reply, in the form of a positive response of obedience. He has the right to expect this. He is Lord.

Chapters 4–5: God in Heaven

This section is relatively straightforward and needs little introduction. In particular, chapter 4 is probably familiar in the context of worship; it is often read to stimulate praise and has provided the content for many hymns and choruses. It gives a glimpse of that heavenly adoration of which all earthly worship is an echo.

John has been invited to 'come up here' (4:1) and see what heaven looks like, a privilege shared by few during their lifetime (Paul had a similar experience; 2 Corinthians 12:1–6). It is the place where God reigns and from which he rules. 'Throne' is the keyword and it occurs 16 times. Notice the emphasis on 'sitting' (4:2, 9, 10; 5:1). This is the control centre of the 'Kingdom of Heaven'.

The scene is breathtakingly beautiful, almost defying description. Green rainbows (!), golden crowns, thunder and lightning, blazing lamps – one can almost imagine John's eyes darting from one striking feature to another as he gazes in awe and wonder. In trying to describe what he can see of God himself, he can only compare this with two of the most brilliant gemstones he has ever seen before (jasper and carnelian).

Above all, there is a peaceful aspect to the whole scene, expressed as a 'sea of glass', stretching to the horizon. The sharp contrast with profound disturbances on earth (from chapter 6 onwards) is clearly intentional. God reigns supreme above all the battles between good and evil. He does not have to struggle; even Satan has to ask his permission before he can touch a human being (Job 1). He is not even surprised by anything. He knows exactly how to deal with whatever arises, since that also can only be what he allows.

He is God, not man. He is therefore worthy of worship (the word derives from 'worth-ship', telling someone how much they are worth to you). The Creator receives non-stop praise from the creatures he has made. The four 'living' ones are only 'like' a lion, ox, man and eagle; together they may represent all creatures from the four corners of the earth (though there are 20 other interpretations!). Their praise is vaguely 'trinitarian': 'holy' three times and God in three dimensions of time – past, present and future.

Twenty-four elders comprise the 'council' of heaven (Jeremiah 23:18). Almost certainly they represent the two covenant peoples of God, Israel and the Church (notice the 24 names on the New Jerusalem's gates and foundations; 21:12–14). They have 'crowns' and 'thrones', but only delegated authority.

There is no action in chapter 4, other than unceasing worship. It is a permanent scene with no time reference. With chapter 5 the action begins – with the search for someone 'in heaven and earth', someone 'worthy to break the seals and open the scroll'.

The significance of the scroll becomes apparent in the light of events. On it must be written the programme which will bring to an end the age of earthly history in which we live. Breaking its seals begins the countdown.

Until this happens, the world must continue in its present state. The 'present evil age' must be closed before the 'age to come' can open. There must be a decisive termination of the 'kingdoms of the world' if the 'Kingdom of God' is to be universally established on the earth. That is why John 'wept and wept' in frustration and grief when no one was found 'worthy' to set this in motion.

But why was this a problem? God himself had released many judgements on the earth through history. Why not the final ones? Either he does not choose to do so or does not feel he is qualified to do so! This last thought is not so bizarre or even blasphemous as some might think, in the light of what is said about the one Person who is found to be 'worthy'.

Who is it? Someone who is both a 'Lion' and a 'Lamb'! Actually, the contrast between the two is not as great as many assume. The Lamb is male and fully mature, as was every lamb used in sacrifice ('one year old'; Exodus 12:5). In this case, the 'Ram', as we should really say, has seven horns (one more than Jacob sheep), signifying perfect power and seven eyes, signifying perfect oversight. Yet it has been 'slain' as a sacrifice.

The lion is king of the jungle, but here of the tribe of Judah and rooted in the Davidic dynasty. So we have a unique combination of the sovereign Lion and the sacrificial Lamb, which corresponds to the coming king and suffering servant predicted by the Hebrew prophets (e.g. Isaiah 9–11 and 42–53).

But it is not just what he is, but what he has done, that fits him to release the troubles that will bring the world to an end, for 'end' can mean two things: termination and consummation. He will bring it to the latter.

He has prepared a people to take over the government of the world. He has purchased them, at the price of his own blood, out of every ethnic group in the human race. He has trained them in royal and priestly duties in God's service and thus prepared them for the responsibility of *reigning on the earth* (this is fully developed in Revelation 20:4–6).

Only someone who has done all this is able to begin the series of disasters that will bring all other regimes down. To destroy a bad system without having a good one ready to replace it can only lead to anarchy.

And he himself is a worthy sovereign over the government he has prepared, precisely because he was willing to give his all to make it possible. It was because he became 'obedient to death – even death on a cross!' that 'God exalted him to the highest place' (Philippians 2:8–9).

No wonder thousands of angels agree, in musical acclamation, that it is only right to give him power, wealth, wisdom, strength, honour, glory and praise. Then all the creatures in the universe join the choir's anthem, though with one significant addition. The power, honour, glory and praise should be shared between the one sitting on the throne and the one standing in the centre in front of him, the Father and the Son together. For it was a joint effort. They were both involved. They both suffered to make it all possible, though in very different ways.

Nothing reveals more clearly the divinity of our Lord Jesus Christ as the offering of unqualified praise and worship to both him and God together.

Chapters 6–16: Satan on Earth

This section is the heart of the book and the most difficult to understand and apply.

We are into the bad news. Things will get much worse before they get better. At least there is the comfort of knowing that the situation cannot ever be worse than that foretold in these chapters. But that's bad enough!

There are three major problems for interpreters.

First, what is the *order* of events? It is quite difficult to put them all on a time chart, as those who attempt this soon discover.

Second, what do all the *symbols* mean? Some are clear. Some are explained. But some are a problem (the 'pregnant woman' in chapter 12 is a case in point).

Third, when is the *fulfilment* of the predictions? In our past, our present or our future? Have they already happened, are they happening right now or are they yet to happen?

We shall concentrate on the order of events, which is far from clear at the first reading, looking at the symbols as we come to them. The task is complicated by the insertion of three features which are out of order, scattered seemingly at random through these chapters.

First, there are *digressions*. In the form of 'interludes' or parentheses, these deal with subjects that seem to be outside the main stream of events.

Second, there are *recapitulations*. From time to time the narrative seems to go back on its track, recalling events already mentioned.

Third, there are *anticipations*. Events are mentioned without explanation until later in the story (for example, 'Armageddon' first appears in 16:16, but does not happen until chapter 19).

These have led to misunderstanding and speculation, notably in the 'cyclical historicist' interpretation already discussed. We shall follow a simpler route, working from the obvious to the obscure.

Reading through these chapters at one sitting, the most striking features are the three sequences of seals, trumpets and bowls. The symbolism in these is comparatively easy to decode.

Seals:
1. White horse – military aggression
2. Red horse – bloodshed
3. Black horse – famine
4. Green horse – disease, epidemics

* * *

5. Persecution and prayer
6. Tremor and terror

* * *

           7. Silence in heaven, listening to prayers which
              are then answered in a final catastrophe:
              severe earthquake

Trumpets: 1. Scorched earth
           2. Polluted sea
           3. Contaminated water
           4. Reduced sunlight

* * *

           5. Insects and plague (five months)
           6. Oriental invasion (200 million)

* * *

           7. The Kingdom comes, the world is taken over
              by God and Christ after a severe earthquake

Bowls: 1. Boils on the skin
           2. Blood in the sea
           3. Blood from the springs
           4. Burning by the sun

* * *

           5. Darkness
           6. Armageddon

* * *

           7. Hailstorm and severe earthquake, leading to
              international collapse

As soon as they are laid out like this a number of things
become clear:

The events are not totally unfamiliar. They are vaguely
reminiscent of the plagues in Egypt when Moses confronted
Pharaoh, even down to frogs and locusts (Exodus 7–11). They
are also happening today on a local or regional scale. For
example, the sequence of four horses can be observed in many

parts of the world, each a result of the previous one. The major novelty is the universal scale on which they happen here, as if the troubles have spread worldwide.

Each series divides into three parts. The first four belong together, the most notable example being the 'four horsemen of the Apocalypse' as they have become known since the artist Albrecht Dürer portrayed them. The next two are not quite so closely related and the last one stands on its own. The last three in each are labelled 'woes', a word indicating curses.

Looking at the three series together, there appears to be an *intensification* in the severity of events. While a quarter of mankind perish in the 'seals', one third of the remainder fail to survive the 'trumpets'. Furthermore, there is a progression in the causes of disaster. The 'seals' are of human origin; the 'trumpets' seem to be a natural deterioration of the environment; the 'bowls' are directly poured out by angelic agents.

There is also an *acceleration* of events. The 'seals' seem quite spread out in time, but the later series appear to be measured in months or even days.

All this suggests a progression in the three series, which brings us to the question of the relation between them. The most obvious answer is that they are *successive*, which may be represented thus: Seals: 1234567, then trumpets: 1234567, then bowls: 1234567. In other words, the series simply follow each other, 21 events in all.

But it is not quite as simple as this! A careful study reveals that the seventh in each case seems to refer to the same event (a severe earthquake on a world scale is the common factor; 8:5; 11:19; 16:18). This has led to an alternative theory, beloved by the 'cyclical historicist' school, which believes the series are *simultaneous*, thus:

Seals:	1 2 3 4 5 6 7
Trumpets:	1 2 3 4 5 6 7
Bowls:	1 2 3 4 5 6 7

In other words, they cover the same period (usually held to be the whole time between the First and Second Advents) from different angles.

A more convincing, but more complicated pattern combines these two insights, treating the first six as successive and the seventh as simultaneous:

Seals:	1 2 3 4 5 6			7
Trumpets:		1 2 3 4 5 6		7
Bowls:			1 2 3 4 5 6 7	

In other words, each series advances on the previous one but all climax in the same catastrophic end. This seems to best fit the evidence and is mainly held by the 'futurist' school who believe all three series still lie ahead in history.

All three concentrate on what will happen to the world. In passing, the reaction of human beings should be noted. While recognizing that these terrible tragedies are evidence of the wrath of God (and the Lamb's!), the human response is one of terror (6:15–17) and curses on God (16:21) rather than repentance (9:20–21), even though the gospel of forgiveness is still available (14:6). It is a sad comment on the hardness of the human heart, but it is true to life. In disasters we either turn towards God or against him (the last words of crashing airline pilots often curse God; they are usually edited out of the 'black box' recording before it is played at the enquiry).

It is time to look at the chapters inserted between the three series of seals, trumpets and bowls – or rather, within them, as we shall see. There are three such insertions: chapter 7, chapters

10–11 and chapters 12–14. The first two sections are put between the sixth and seventh seals and trumpets, but the third is put before the first bowl, as if there is no time-scale for it between the sixth and seventh bowls. We can put this in diagram form, using the previous illustration:

Seals: 1 2 3 4 5 6 (ch. 7)   7
Trumpets: 1 2 3 4 5 6 (chs. 10–11)   7
Bowls: (chs. 12–14)   1 2 3 4 5 6 7

We now have a complete outline of chapters 6–16.

Whereas the three series of seals, trumpets and bowls are primarily concerned with what will happen to the *world*, the three insertions deal with what will happen to the *Church*. Here we are given information about God's people during this terrible upheaval. How will they be affected? Since Revelation aims to prepare the 'saints' for what is to come, these insertions are more relevant and important for them.

Chapter 7: the two groups

Between the sixth and seventh seals, we catch a glimpse of two distinct kinds of people in two very different places.

On the one hand, *a limited number of Jews are protected on earth* (verses 1–8). God has not rejected Israel (Romans 11:1, 11). He made an unconditional promise that they would survive as long as the universe lasted (Jeremiah 31:35–37). He will keep his word. They have a future.

The numbers seem somewhat arbitrary, even artificial. Perhaps they are 'round' numbers or maybe symbolic in some way. What is clear is that it will be a very limited proportion of a nation now numbered in millions. And the total will be equally divided between the 12 tribes, without favouring any. This means that the 10 tribes taken to Assyria were not 'lost' to

God and that he will preserve the survivors of each tribe that are known to him. There is one lost tribe, Dan, which rebelled against God's will for it and was replaced – in much the same way as Judas Iscariot among the 12 apostles. Both are warnings against taking our place in God's purposes for granted.

On the other hand, *an uncountable number of Christians are protected in heaven* (verses 8–17). The international crowd stand in an honoured place before the King, joining with the elders and living creatures in their songs of praise. But they add one new note of praise: for their 'salvation'.

John does not realize their significance and confesses ignorance of their qualifications for such honour. One of the elders enlightens him: 'These are they who are coming out of the Great Tribulation' (verse 14; the tense of the verb clearly indicates a continuing procession of individuals and groups through the whole time of trouble). How are they escaping? Not by one sudden and secret 'rapture', but by death, most by martyrdom, which figures so prominently in these very chapters (we have already heard the cries of their 'souls' for vengeance; 6:9–11).

But it is the shedding of the Lamb's blood rather than their own that has rescued them. It was his suffering, not theirs, a sacrifice that atoned for their sins and made them clean enough to stand in God's presence and offer their service.

But God is mindful of what they have suffered for his Son's sake and he will make sure that they will 'never again' experience such pain. The scorching sun will not burn them (16:8–9). They will be looked after by the 'good shepherd' (Psalm 23; John 10). They will be refreshed with water, 'living' (fizzy!) rather than 'still' (John 4:14; 7:38; Revelation 21:6; 21:1, 17). And God, like every parent with a weeping child, will 'wipe away every tear from their eyes' (21:4). Note that being in heaven now is a foretaste of life on the new earth.

Chapters 10–11: the two witnesses

Between the sixth and seventh trumpets, attention is focused on the human channels through which the divine revelations are communicated. The keyword in both chapters is 'prophesy' (10:11; 11:3, 6). At the beginning of the Church age, John in Patmos is the prophet; at the end there will be two 'witnesses' who will prophesy in the city of Jerusalem.

There is a sense of impending disaster in the spectacular appearance of two 'mighty' angels. The terrible truths uttered by the first in a thunderous voice are for John alone and must not be communicated to anyone else (compare 2 Corinthians 12:4). The second announces that there will be no more delay in the build-up of events – the seventh trumpet will be the climax (confirming our conclusion that the seventh seal, trumpet and bowl all refer to the same 'end').

The last and worst part of the 'bad news' is about to be given. It is on a 'little scroll' (an expanded, more detailed, version of part of the larger one already opened?). John is told to 'eat it' (we would say: 'digest it'). It will taste 'sweet and sour', sweet at first but sour when it begins to sink in (a reaction that many have to the whole Book of Revelation when they begin to grasp its message).

John is told to 'prophesy again', to continue his work of foretelling the future of the world. Then he is 'shown' around the city of Jerusalem and its temple. He measures its courts, but not the outermost one for Gentile worshippers, since they will be coming to 'trample' on the city rather than pray in it. They will, however, encounter two extraordinary persons who will preach to them about the God they despise.

The result will be death for preachers and hearers alike! The two witnesses will have miraculous power, to stop the rain (like Elijah; 1 Kings 17:1; James 5:17) and to bring fire upon their enemies (like Moses; Leviticus 10:1–3). But they will be killed when their testimony is concluded. Their bodies will lie in the streets for just over three days, while the multi-national crowd, 'tormented' in conscience by their words, gloat over and celebrate their removal. The relief will turn to terror when the two are resurrected in full view of all. A loud voice from heaven 'Come up here' will result in their ascension. At the moment of their departure, a severe earthquake will destroy one-tenth of the city's buildings and 7,000 of its population.

The similarity between the fate of the two witnesses and 'the prophet' Jesus is striking. It will be impossible not to recall his crucifixion, resurrection and ascension in this very same city. Of course, there are differences: in his case, the earthquake coincided with his death (Matthew 27:51) and neither his resurrection after three days nor his ascension were witnessed by the general public. But it will still be a vivid reminder, especially to the Jewish inhabitants, of those far-off days. It will result in fear of, and glory to, God.

Who these two witnesses are, we are not told. All attempts to identify them are sheer speculation. There is no suggestion that they are 'reincarnate' figures from previous times, so they are not Moses and Elijah, even though they are like them in some ways, any more than they are two Jesuses, though they are like him in others. We must 'wait and see' who they are, but it obviously does not really matter. What they do and what is done to them are the important things.

Before leaving this section, two 'anticipations' need to be noted. For one thing, there is the first mention of a time period of 1,260 days, which is 42 months, which is three and a half years. We shall come across this figure in succeeding chapters, where it seems to indicate the duration of the 'Big Trouble'. Many link it with the 'half week' predicted by Daniel (Daniel 9:27; the New International Version rightly translates 'week' as 'seven'). It is quite a brief time and recalls Jesus' own prediction that it would be kept short (Matthew 24:22).

For another thing, this is the first mention of the 'beast', who figures so largely in the next parentheses in the ongoing narrative.

Chapters 12–14: the two beasts

To follow the literary pattern so far, this section should have come between the sixth and seventh bowls, but these follow each other so closely that there is neither time nor space between them for other events. So these three chapters are inserted before the seven bowls are poured out as the final expression of God's wrath on a rebellious world (see the diagram on page 1292).

Six seals and six trumpets are over. The very last series of disasters is about to happen. It will be the worst for the world – and the toughest for the church. Evil powers will gain a tighter grip on society than they have ever had before, though their hold is about to be broken.

The section introduces three persons who form an alliance to rule the world themselves. One is angelic in origin and nature: a 'great dragon' and 'ancient serpent', otherwise known as 'Satan', or 'the devil' (12:9). The other two are human in origin and nature: 'beasts', otherwise known as 'the antichrist' (1 John 2:18; also 'the man of lawlessness' in 2 Thessalonians 2:3) and 'the false prophet' (16:13; 19:20; 20:10). Together they form a kind of 'unholy trinity' in a ghastly mimicry of God, Christ and the Holy Spirit.

Satan is introduced into the 'troubles' for the first time. He has not been mentioned in Revelation since the letters to the seven churches (2:9, 13, 24; 3:9). Seals and trumpets have loosed their burdens on the earth, while Satan has been in heaven. As an angel he has access to 'the heavenly realms'

(Ephesians 6:12; compare Job 1:6–7). That is where the real battle between good and evil is being fought out, as anyone entering these realms through prayer will discover.

This battle, between good and bad angels in heaven, will not last for ever. For one thing, the forces are unequal in number. The devil's side comprises one third of the heavenly host (12:4); the two thirds are led by the archangel Michael, who will lead his forces to victory (a sculpture portraying this conquest adorns the east wall of Coventry Cathedral).

The devil will be 'hurled' down to the earth. Later he will again be defeated and thrown into the 'abyss' (20:3). Meanwhile, in the few years he has left, his fury and frustration are concentrated on our planet. Unable to challenge God directly in heaven any more, he declares war on God's people below. It is a rearguard action, undertaken in the hope of retaining his kingdom on earth, through puppet rulers, one political and the other religious.

So far the message of chapter 12 is quite clear, even if it stretches the imagination. But we have overlooked (deliberately) the other major figure in the drama – a pregnant woman, bathed in sunshine, standing on the moon and wearing a crown of 12 stars on her head.

Who is she? Is she an individual person at all, or perhaps a 'personification' of a place or a people (as are the other 'women' in Revelation; for example, the 'prostitute' representing Babylon in chapters 17–18)?

Certainly, this figure has been the source of much debate and many differences among Bible students. For some, the matter is settled by the fact that the devil wanted to 'devour her child the moment it was born' (verse 4) and the statement that 'she gave birth to a son, a male child, who will rule all the nations with an iron sceptre' (verse 5). Surely, they say, this is an unmistakable reference to the birth of Jesus and Herod's immediate but abortive attempt to destroy him. The woman is therefore his mother, Mary (the usual Catholic interpretation); or a personification of Israel, from whom the Messiah came (a common Protestant interpretation to exclude Mary).

But it is not quite so simple as this. Why should there be a sudden and unexpected return to the very beginning of the Christian era in the middle of a passage describing the end times? Why bring Mary into the picture (after Acts 1 she disappears from the New Testament, her work completed)? Of course, the 'cyclical historicists' see this as proof of yet another 'recapitulation' of the entire cycle of Church history, this time starting with the nativity, Satan being defeated and exiled from heaven at that time.

There are still problems. Apparently the child is 'snatched up to God and to his throne' almost immediately after his birth. This could be a 'telescoping' of the incarnation and ascension, but the absence of any reference to the ministry, death and resurrection of Jesus in between is at least striking. And if the woman is his mother, who are 'the rest of her offspring' to whom the frustrated dragon turns his attention (verse 17)? We know she had other children, including four boys and some girls (Mark 6:3), but they are unlikely candidates. Nor is it certain that 'ruling the nations with an iron sceptre' necessarily points to Jesus; it is applied to him (19:15, in fulfilment of Psalm 2:9), but it is also promised to his faithful followers (2:27). Then there is the preservation of the woman in 'the desert' for 1,260 days (12:6), a period which has already emerged as the duration of greatest distress at the end of the Church age.

The interpretation which best fits all this data sees the woman as a personification representing the Church in the end times, preserved outside urban areas during the worst troubles. Her man-child is also a personification, representing the martyred believers at this time, safe in heaven, out of Satan's reach. They will return to the earth one day and rule it with Christ (20:4 emphatically declares this). The 'rest of her offspring' are those who survive the holocaust, yet 'obey God's commandments and hold to the testimony of Jesus' (verse 17; compare 1:9; 14:12). There are still some tensions with the text in this view, but far fewer than with any other explanation.

Once again, there seems to be an implied comparison between the experience of Christ at the beginning of the Christian era and his followers at the end of it (as we saw earlier). In particular, as he 'overcame' (John 16:33) his followers will 'overcome', not 'loving their lives so much as to shrink from death' (12:11). Their victory demonstrates 'the kingdom of our God, and the authority of his Christ' (12:10; compare 11:15 and Acts 28:31).

The two 'beasts' arrive in chapter 13. The first and foremost is a political figure, a world dictator wielding a totalitarian regime over all known ethnic groupings. He is 'the antichrist' (1 John 2:18; note that *anti*- in Greek means 'instead of' rather than 'against', indicating a counterfeit rather than a competitor), 'the man of lawlessness' (2 Thessalonians 2:3–4) acknowledging no higher law than his own will and therefore claiming divinity and demanding worship. The beast is a human individual who accepts the satanic offer which Jesus refused (Matthew 4:8–9; had he accepted he would have become Jesus Antichrist!).

But he is also 'anti-Christian' in the other sense of that prefix. He has the power to 'make war against the saints and to *overcome* them' (13:7; he overcomes them temporarily, but they overcome him eternally, 12:11).

His characteristics are those of other fierce beasts – leopard, bear and lion (see pages 658–9). He seems to arise from a federation of political rulers, gaining the attention of the world through an astonishing recovery from a fatal wound, presumably in an attempted assassination. His blasphemous egotism is broadcast for 42 months.

His position is bolstered by the second beast, a religious colleague with supernatural power who focuses the world's worship on his superior. His miracles will deceive the nations as he commands fire to fall down from the sky and images of the dictator to speak.

His appearance will be 'like a lamb', a young sheep with only 'two horns'. This would seem to indicate mildness rather than Christlikeness, since it is contrasted with his dragon-like speech.

His master-stroke will not be his display of miracles but his domination of markets. Only those bearing a special number on a visible part of their body (hand or forehead) will be allowed to trade and the number will only be marked on those who engage in imperial idolatry. Jews and Christians will therefore be excluded from all commerce, even to the purchase of bare necessities of life.

The number '666' is the coded name of the dictator. We have already discussed its meaning (see page 1252). Until he arrives, when his identity with this figure will be only too obvious, all attempts to decode it are useless speculation. One thing is clear, he will fall short of perfection (7) in every regard.

Chapter 14 seems to compensate for these horrific scenes by turning our attention to a group of people standing (literally) in sharp contrast to those who have allowed themselves to be entrapped in the system. Instead of the cryptic name of the beast, they carry the Lamb's Father's name on their foreheads (another feature picked up in 22:4). Instead of the arrogant lies, they are known for integrity of speech, as well as pure sexual relations.

There is a little uncertainty about their location, whether in heaven or on earth, but the context favours the former, because of the songs of praise from living creatures and elders (14:3 seems to repeat 4:4–11), songs which only the redeemed can 'learn', much less sing. The number (144,000) is puzzling. It is not to be confused with the same number in chapter 7. There it referred to Jews on earth, here to Christians in heaven. There it was made up from 12 tribes, here it is not. Neither can it be equated with the 'great multitude that no one could count' in that same chapter. Again, it may be a 'round' number. But the clue probably lies in their being 'purchased from among men and offered as *firstfruits* to God and the Lamb' (verse 4). They are only the small foretaste of a very large harvest. So the point may be that what is the total number of Jews preserved on earth is only a partial number of Christians praising in heaven.

The rest of the chapter has a procession of angels bringing various messages from God to men:

The first calls for the fear and worship of God, with a reminder that the gospel is still available to save anyone from the 'coming wrath' (Luke 3:7).

The second announces the fall of Babylon. Here is another 'anticipation', since this is the first time such a place has been mentioned. All will be made clear in the next section (chapters 16–17).

The third warns believers of the terrible consequences of giving in to the pressures of the final totalitarian system. The language is that of hell: unceasing 'torment' (the same word describing the experience of the devil, the antichrist and the false prophet in the 'lake of fire'; 20:10). In other words, they will share the fate of those to whom they have surrendered. The fact that 'saints' could find themselves in this dreadful destiny is underlined by a call to 'patient endurance' immediately after the warning (verse 12, which repeats 13:10). Both contexts recognize that some will pay for their loyalty with their lives. For them a special beatitude is written: 'Blessed are the dead who die in [the sense is almost 'for'] the Lord from now on' (verse 13). The blessing is twofold: they can now rest from travail and, since the record of their loyalty has been kept, look forward to a reward. Even those who die of natural causes at that time will enjoy this blessing. But this verse should not yet be used at funerals; the promise is qualified by 'from now on', which refers to the reign of the 'beast'.

The fourth shouts to someone 'like a son of man on the clouds' (a clear reference to Daniel 7:13), telling him it is high time for harvest time. Whether this is to gather tares for burning or wheat for storing (Matthew 13:40–43) is not immediately clear.

The fifth simply appears with a sickle in his hand.

The sixth directs the sickle to 'grapes' which are to be trampled on in the 'great winepress of God's wrath', which is 'outside the city'. That this refers to a mass slaughter of human beings is indicated by the massive pool of blood (a metre deep over 180 square miles – surely a touch of hyperbole?). This is probably an anticipation of the battle of Armageddon, where vultures will clean up the corpses (19:17–21). In passing, we note this link between blood, wine and God's wrath, which occurs quite frequently. This throws a flood of light on the cross and particularly on the agonizing prayer in 'Gethsemane', which means 'crushing'. The metaphorical use of 'cup' in Scripture invariably refers to God's wrath (Isaiah 51:21–22; Mark 14:36; Revelation 16:19).

These six angels are followed by seven more who act out rather than speak about the outpoured wrath of God. They carry seven bowls, not just cups, of wrath to tip on the earth. This is accompanied by a song of triumph from the martyrs in heaven, consciously echoing the rejoicing of Moses after the Egyptian forces were drowned in the Red Sea (15:2–4). The theme is the justice and righteousness of God, expressed in great and marvellous deeds which vindicate his holiness by punishing the oppressors. The 'King of the Ages' may take his time to judge the guilty, but judgement is certain to come – and at last has come.

Before we leave this major middle section of Revelation, two further observations must be made.

The first concerns the *order* of events. An attempt has been made to fit the seals, trumpets and bowls, together with the inserted parentheses, into some kind of consecutive schedule. Whether this has been successful must be judged by the reader, who may have already worked out a different scheme.

The fact is that it is extremely difficult, if not impossible, to fit all the predicted events into a coherent pattern. But Jesus is too good a teacher to hide his essential message in such a complex narrative. What does this tell us?

Simply this: *the order is not the primary thrust* in this section. It is far more concerned with what will happen than with when anything will happen. The purpose of it all is not to enable us to become accurate soothsayers, able to forecast the future, but to be faithful servants of the Lord, ready to face the worst that can happen to us. But will it happen to us?

The second concerns the *fulfilment* of predictions. If the 'Big Trouble' only covers the last few years, it may be that we shall not have to face it in our lifetime. So could it be a waste of time for all but the last generation of saints to prepare for it?

One answer is that the current trend and speed of world events makes it an increasing possibility in the near future.

But the main response to this kind of thinking must be the reminder that future events cast their shadows before them. 'Dear children, this is the last hour; and as you have heard that the antichrist is coming, even now many antichrists have come'

(1 John 2:18). The false prophet is coming, but even now many false prophets have come (Matthew 24:11; Acts 13:6; Revelation 2:20).

In other words, what will one day be experienced by the whole church on a universal scale ('hated by all nations'; Matthew 24:9) is already happening in local and regional settings. Any Christian can go through much tribulation before all go through the 'Great Tribulation'. We must all be ready for the kind of troubles that reach a climax then, but can come now.

This section (chapters 6–16) is therefore directly relevant to all believers, whatever their contemporary situation. The church is already under pressure in the majority of countries and the number of those where this is not the case diminishes annually.

And beyond all this lies the return of the Lord Jesus Christ, for which every believer needs to be ready. The main motive for preparing to be faithful under pressure is to be able to face him without shame. Perhaps that explains the following reminder inserted between the sixth and seventh bowls of wrath (incidentally, confirming that some Christians will still be on earth at that time): 'Behold, I come like a thief! Blessed is he who stays awake and keeps his clothes with him, so that he may not go naked and be shamefully exposed' (16:15; note the same emphasis on attire in Matthew 22:11; Luke 12:35; Revelation 19:7–8).

Chapters 17–18: Man on Earth

This section is still part of the 'Big Trouble', but only just. It concerns the very end, at the time of the severe earthquake in the seventh seal, trumpet and bowl (see 16:17–19).

World history is hastening to an end. The final denouement is at hand. In spite of all the warnings, whether in divine word or deed, human beings still refuse to repent and curse God for all their troubles (16:9, 11, 21).

The remainder of Revelation is dominated by two female figures, one a filthy prostitute and the other a pure bride. Neither is a person; both are personifications. They represent cities.

We could use the title: 'A tale of two cities'. They are Babylon and Jerusalem, the city of man and the city of God. In this section we consider the former, which has been mentioned already (14:8; 16:19).

Cities are generally regarded as bad places in the Bible. The first mention (which is usually significant) associates them with the line of Lamech and the manufacture of weapons for mass destruction. They concentrate people, therefore sinners, therefore sin. With less community and more anonymity, vice and crime flourish. There is more lust (prostitution) and anger (violence) in urban than rural communities.

The two sins that are singled out here are greed and pride. Both are related to the idolatry of money. Since it is impossible to worship both God and Mammon (Luke 16:13), it is easier to forget the Maker of heaven and earth in a prosperous city. Self-made men worship their own creator! Arrogance shows in architecture; buildings are often monuments to human ambition and achievement.

Such was the tower of Babel by the Euphrates river, sitting on the route between Asia, Africa and Europe. Founded by Nimrod the mighty hunter (of animals) and warrior (among men), it was founded on the belief that might is right, that the fittest survive.

Typically, the tower was to be the tallest man-made structure in the world, as an impressive statement both to men and God. The expressed intention to 'make a name for ourselves' (Genesis 11:4) marks the beginning of humanism, man's self-deification. God judged this presumption by granting its inhabitants the gift of tongues! But the simultaneous removal of their common speech brought unintelligible bedlam, from which we derive the verb 'babble' (note that at Pentecost this did not happen, for the same gift brought unity; Acts 2:44).

This city later became the capital of a large and powerful empire, especially under Nebuchadnezzar, a ruthless tyrant who destroyed babies, animals and even trees when conquering new territory (Habakkuk 2:17; 3:17).

Meanwhile, King David of Israel had established Jerusalem as his capital. By contrast, it was not in a strategic position for trade, since it was not by the sea, a major river or a main road. It was, however, the 'city of God', the place where he put his name and chose to live among his people – at first in the tent Moses assembled, later in the temple Solomon built.

Babylon became the greatest threat to Jerusalem. Nebuch-adnezzar ultimately destroyed the holy city, with its temple, transporting its treasures and deporting its people into 70 years of exile. God allowed this to happen because the inhabitants had made it an 'unholy' city like all others.

But this was a temporary chastisement rather than a perma-nent punishment. Through the prophets God promised both the restoration of Jerusalem and the ruin of Babylon (for exam-ple, Isaiah 13:19–20; Jeremiah 51:6–9, 45–48). Sure enough, that evil city became a desolate heap of rubble, totally uninhab-ited, except by wild creatures of the desert, exactly as foretold.

It is no coincidence that there are profound similarities between the books of Daniel and Revelation. Both contain visions of the end times that are in remarkable agreement. Yet the revelations were given to Daniel during the time of Nebuchadnezzar (he had been a young man in the first of three deportations). He had 'seen' the future course of world empires right up to the time of Christ and then beyond, to the very end of history, the reign of antichrist, the millennial rule, the resurrection of the dead and the Day of Judgement.

Both books talk about a city called 'Babylon'. But are they talking about the same place?

If so, it will have to be rebuilt. Those who take the Revelation 'Babylon' as the very same are quite excited that parts of it have already been rebuilt by the then President of Iraq, Saddam Hussein. But he seems to have had no intention of restoring it as a living city; it was more a showcase for his own prestige (laser lights were projecting his profile, alongside Nebuchadnezzar's, on to the clouds!). It is highly unlikely that ancient Babylon, even fully rebuilt, could ever become a strategic centre again.

The 'preterist' school of interpretation applies 'Babylon' to the metropolis of Rome. There is some ground for doing so, not least because this was probably the way original readers of Revelation would take it. One of Peter's letters, written for a very similar purpose (to prepare saints for suffering), may already have made this coded link (1 Peter 5:13). And the reference to 'seven hills' would probably clinch it (17:9, though note that the 'hills' represent kings).

Rome's decadent character would also fit the description in Revelation. Her seductive attraction of goods and finance in return for favours rendered and her domination of petty kings fit the picture well.

Yet it is doubtful if this is the total fulfilment. Rome was certainly *a* Babylon. But it was only a foreshadowing of *the* Babylon which dominates the end of history, which is where Revelation firmly places it.

Some have resolved the problem by postulating a revived Roman Empire. Their pulses quickened when 10 nations (17:12) signed the 'Treaty of Rome' as the basis for a new superpower, the European Community. Interest has subsided with the addition of other states; there are now too many 'horns'! But the flag has the 12 stars of Revelation 12.

The reluctance to let go of Rome as the main candidate is also apparent in the 'historicist' school of interpretation. Taking Revelation as an overview of the whole of Church history, Protestants invariably fastened on the papacy and the Vatican, with their claims to political as well as religious power, as the 'scarlet woman' of Babylon (this identification has created havoc in the 'troubles' of Northern Ireland). Catholics returned the compliment and regarded the Protestant Reformers in a similar light!

Actually, there is no hint in Revelation that 'Babylon' is in any way a religious centre. The emphasis is on business and pleasure as the primary occupations of its inhabitants.

The 'futurist' school seems to be nearer the truth in seeing the city as a new metropolis rising to dominate others during the 'end time'. Since it is designated a 'mystery' (i.e. a secret now revealed), it would appear to be a fresh creation of man rather than the re-establishment of a former city (whether ancient Babylon or Rome).

It is clearly going to be a, even the, centre of commerce, a place for getting and spending money (note how the traders are affected by its downfall; 18:11–16). Culture will not be neglected (note the music in 18:22).

But it will be corrupt and corrupting, characterized by materialism without morality, pleasure without purity, wealth without wisdom, lust without love. The simile of the harlot is peculiarly appropriate, giving anyone what they want in exchange for money.

So far we have only considered the 'woman', but she rides a 'beast' with seven heads and ten horns, which clearly represent a federation of political figures. We are not told who they are, nor are we given many details about them. They are powerful men but without territory to rule. Their authority derives from the 'beast', presumably the antichrist, to whom they will devote absolute allegiance. Above all, they will be blatantly anti-Christian, making 'war against the Lamb' and those 'with him' (17:14), presumably because their consciences will be pricked.

But Babylon is doomed. She and they will fall. Their days will be numbered. The astonishing way in which this is brought about is entirely credible in the modern world.

The woman rides the beast. A queen is riding on the backs of kings (a reversal of gender contrary to creation). It is another way of saying that economics will rule politics, that the power of money will override other authority. Since by the year AD 2000 the bulk of the world's business was in the hands of 300 colossal corporations, this scenario is not difficult to imagine.

Amtibious politicians, hungry for power, resent this financial clout. They are even prepared to bring about economic disaster if that will enable them to take over. One thinks of Hitler's treatment of the Jews, who controlled many banks in Germany.

The 'kings' will be jealous of the 'woman' who rides them and will resolve to destroy her. The city will be razed by fire. It will be the biggest economic disaster the world will have seen. Many, many people will 'weep and mourn' over the ruins.

God will have caused the catastrophe, but not by any physical action. He will have 'put it into their hearts to accomplish his purpose' (17:17). He will have encouraged them to make an alliance with the beast against the city. The antichrist will have political control and the false prophet religious control; the 'kings' will now offer them economic control in return for delegated powers for themselves. But their enjoyment of such privileges will be extremely brief ('one hour'; 17:12).

So sure is Babylon's downfall that it is pictured in Revelation as already having happened. Christians can be absolutely certain of this. But there are practical reasons why they are being told about it. What is the relation between God's people and this last 'Babylon'? Three guidelines are given:

First, there will be many martyrs in the city. The whore is 'drunk with the blood of the saints, the blood of those who bore testimony to Jesus'. This last phrase again indicates the presence of Christians and occurs throughout Revelation (1:9; 12:17; 14:12; 17:6; 19:10; 20:4). There is no place for holy people in a city devoted to immorality. The community does not want a conscience.

Second, the Christians are told to 'come out of her, my people, so that you will not share in her sins, so that you will not receive any of her plagues, for her sins are piled up to heaven, and God has remembered her crimes' (18:4–5). This is almost identical to Jeremiah's plea to Jews in ancient Babylon (Jeremiah 51:6). Note that they have to 'come out'; the Lord does not take them out. Clearly, not all believers will be martyred; some will escape with their lives, though they may have to leave their money and possessions behind.

Third, when Babylon falls, a celebration is commanded: 'Rejoice over her, O heaven! Rejoice, saints and apostles and prophets! God has judged her for the way she treated you' (18:20). This is done in 19:1–5. Very few realize that the famous 'Hallelujah' chorus in Handel's *Messiah* oratorio is a celebration of the collapse of the world economy, the closure of stock exchanges, the bankruptcy of banks and the disruption of trade and commerce! Only God's people will be singing 'Hallelujah' (which means: 'Praise the Lord') on that day!

The prostitute disappears and the bride appears. The 'wedding supper of the Lamb' is about to take place. Jesus is going to get married – rather, he's coming to get married (Matthew 25:1–13). The bride has 'made herself ready' by acquiring a dress of pure white linen (note the 'clothes' reference again); this is explained as a symbol of 'the righteous acts of the saints' (19:8). The guest list is completed and 'blessed' are those on it.

We have already strayed into chapter 19, which leads into the next section, while rounding off this one. But then the chapter divisions were not part of the original text and often come in the wrong places, putting asunder what God has joined together, never more so than in the penultimate section of Revelation.

Chapters 19–20: Christ on Earth

This series of events brings history, as we know it, to a close. Our world is brought to an end at last. We are now dealing with the ultimate future.

Alas, this section has given rise to more controversy than any other in the whole book, mainly centred on the Millennium, the repeated mention of a 'thousand years'. This is such an important issue that it will be dealt with as a separate subject. That treatment will include an exhaustive exegesis of the text, so no more than a summary will be given here (see p. 1333).

It is vital to note the change from verbal to visual revelations. Throughout the previous section John says: 'I heard' (18:4; 19:1, 6). Then the phrase becomes a repeated: 'I saw', until it changes back to 'I heard' again (in 21:3).

When the visual part is analysed, a series of seven visions is clearly discerned. But for the unwarranted intrusion of chapter divisions ('20' and '21'), this sevenfold revelation would have been noticed by most readers. As it is, few have marked it. Yet it is the final 'seven' in Revelation. As with previous sevens, the first four belong together, the next two are less closely related and the last stands on its own (we shall postpone study of it until we look at chapters 21–22). They may be listed as follows:

1. Parousia (19:11–16)
   King of kings, Lord of lords (and *logos* = 'word')
   White horses, blood-stained robes

2. Supper (19:17–18)
   Angelic invitation to birds …
   … to gorge on corpses

3. Armageddon (19:19–21)
   Kings and armies destroyed (by 'word' = *logos*)
   Two beasts thrown into the lake of fire

4. Satan (20:1–3)
   Bound and banished to 'abyss'
   But for limited time

5. Millennium (20:4–10)
   Saints and martyrs reign (first resurrection)
   Satan released and thrown into the lake of fire

6. Judgement (20:11–15)
   General resurrection of 'the rest'
   Books and 'book of life' opened

7. Re-creation (21:1–2)
   New heaven and earth
   New Jerusalem

Clearly this indicates a consecutive series of events, beginning with the Second Coming and ending with the new creation. This is confirmed by internal cross-references (e.g. 20:10 refers back to 19:20). Unfortunately, commentators have tried to disrupt the sequence in the interests of a theological system (by claiming that chapter 20 precedes chapter 19, for example). But the order in these last chapters is far clearer than the middle of Revelation – and it is very significant.

For example, the enemies of the people of God are expelled from the scene in reverse order to their introduction. Satan appears in chapter 12, the two 'beasts' in chapter 13 and Babylon in chapter 17. Babylon disappears in chapter 18, the two 'beasts' in chapter 19 and Satan in chapter 20. The city falls before the return of Christ, but he is needed on earth to deal with the 'unholy trinity' of devil, antichrist and false prophet.

The opening vision is acknowledged to be a picture of the Second Coming by almost all scholars (only a few, for vested theological interests, say it refers to his First). But Jesus' return to earth will cause consternation in the powers-that-be. Shocked by his reappearance, they will plan a second assassination. But this time a small platoon of guards will be totally inadequate, since millions of his devoted followers will have met him in Jerusalem (1 Thessalonians 4:14–17). A huge military force will gather some miles north in the valley of Esdraelon at the foot of the 'mountain of Megiddo' (in Hebrew, Har-mageddon): it is the crossroads of the world, overlooked by Nazareth. Many battles have been fought here; many kings have died here (Saul and Josiah among them).

Jesus only needs a 'word' to raise the dead or kill the living. It is more a sentence than a struggle. Vultures deal with the bodies, too many to bury.

At this point, there are a number of surprising developments. The two 'beasts' are not killed but 'thrown alive' into hell, the first human beings to go there. The devil is not sent there, but taken into custody – to be released again later!

Above all, Jesus does not then bring this world to an end, but takes over the government himself, filling the political vacuum left by the 'unholy trinity' with his own faithful followers, especially the martyrs. They will, of course, have to be raised from the dead to fulfil this responsibility. This 'Kingdom' will last for a thousand years but come to an end when a paroled devil deceives the nations into a final but abortive rebellion, put down by fire from heaven. This interim between Jesus' return and the Day of Judgement is widely rejected in the Church today, yet it was the accepted view of the early Church.

There is widespread agreement on what follows. A final day of reckoning is clearly taught throughout the New Testament. It is heralded by two remarkable portents. The earth and sky disappear. We know (from 2 Peter 3:10) that both will be 'razed' by fire. The dead, including those lost at sea, reappear. This is the second, or 'general' resurrection (20:5) and confirms that the wicked as well as the righteous will be re-embodied before entering their eternal destiny (Daniel 12:2; John 5:29; Acts 24:15). Both 'soul and body' will be thrown into the lake of fire (Matthew 10:28; Revelation 19:20). The 'torment' will be physical as well as mental (Luke 16:23–24). Therefore, both 'death', which separates body from spirit, and 'hades', the abode of disembodied spirits, are now abolished (20:14). The 'second death', which neither separates body and soul nor annihilates either, takes over from then on.

All that is now visible are the judge sitting on a throne, the judged standing before it and an enormous pile of books. The throne is large and white, representing absolute power and purity. It is probably not the same throne as the one John saw in heaven (4:2–4). That was not described as 'great' or 'white'. Furthermore, it is most unlikely that the resurrected wicked would be allowed anywhere near heaven. Indeed, there is no hint that the scene in chapter 20 has shifted back to heaven; it is more likely to be located where the earth has been, the earth having disappeared leaving only its past and present inhabitants. Above all, the person sitting on this throne is not identified as God (as in 4:8–11). It is, in fact, not God. From other scriptures, we know that he has delegated the task of judging the human race to his Son, Jesus: 'For he has set a day when he will judge the world with justice by the man he has appointed' (Acts 17:31; compare Matthew 25:31–32; 2 Corinthians 5:10). Human beings will be judged by a human being.

This will be no long drawn-out trial. All the evidence has already been gathered and examined by the judge. It is contained in 'books', volumes truly deserving the title: 'This is Your Life'! They will not be a selection of the commendable occasions for a television presentation, but a complete record of the deeds (and words; Matthew 5:22; 12:36) of a whole lifetime, from birth to death. We may be justified by faith, but we shall be judged by works.

If this was all the evidence to be considered, it would damn us all to the 'second death'. What hope would there be for any? Thank God, one other book will be opened on that terrible day. It is the record of the judge's own life on earth, both absolving him and qualifying him to judge others. It is the 'Lamb's book of life' (21:27). But it contains other names besides his. Those who are 'in Christ' are listed there, those who have lived and died in him, those who have been joined to and have remained in this 'true vine' (John 15:1–8). They have thus borne the fruit that attests their continuing union with him (Philippians 4:3; contrast Matthew 7:16–20). The fruitfulness is proof of their faithfulness.

Their names have been put into this book when they came to be in Christ, when they repented and believed (the phrase 'from the creation of the world' in 17:8 refers to those whose names are *not* written in the book and simply means 'through the whole of human history'; likewise in 13:8 though the phrase there may be linked to the slaying of the Lamb). Their names have not been 'erased' from the book of life because they have 'overcome' (3:5).

Only those whose names are still in this book escape the 'second death' in the 'lake of fire'. In other words, outside of Christ there is no hope whatsoever, since 'all have sinned and fall short of the glory of God' (Romans 3:23). The gospel is therefore *exclusive:* 'Salvation is found in no one else, for there is no other name [except 'Jesus'] under heaven given to men by which we must be saved' (Acts 4:12). But it must also therefore be *inclusive:* 'Go into all the world and preach the good news to all creation' (Mark 16:15; compare Matthew 28:19; Luke 24:47).

The human race will then be permanently divided into two groups (Matthew 13:41–43, 47–50; 25:32–33). For one, their destination has already been 'prepared' (Matthew 25:41). The lake (or 'sea') of fire has been in existence for at least a thousand years (Revelation 19:20). For the other, a new metropolis has been 'prepared' (John 14:2), but there is no earth on which it may be sited, much less a sky above it. A new universe is needed.

Chapters 21–22: Heaven on Earth

It is with great relief that we enter this final section. The atmosphere has changed dramatically. The dark clouds have rolled away and the sun is shining again – except that the sun has also disappeared, to be replaced by the much more brilliant glory of God (21:23).

This is the final act of redemption, bringing salvation to the entire universe. This is the 'cosmic' work of Christ (Matthew 19:28; Acts 3:21; Romans 8:18–25; Colossians 1:20; Hebrews 2:8), the renewal of heaven and earth (note that 'heaven' means 'sky', what we call 'space'; it is the same word in

20:11 and 21:1). Christians have already received new bodies, when Jesus came back to the old earth. Now they are to be given a new environment corresponding to their new bodies.

The first two verses cover the last vision in the sequence of seven which John 'saw' (19:11 to 21:2), the climax to the final events of history. There is more than a new universe here. Within the 'general' creation is a 'special' creation. Just as within the first universe God 'planted a garden' (Genesis 2:8), so here he has designed and built a 'garden city', which even Abraham knew about and looked forward to (Hebrews 11:10).

Just as the new 'heaven and earth' are recognizably similar enough to the old to bear the same names, this city is given the same name as David's capital. Jerusalem has a place in the New Testament as well as the Old. Jesus called it 'the city of the Great King' (Matthew 5:35; compare Psalm 48:2). It was just 'outside a city wall' that he died, rose again and ascended to heaven. It is to this city that he will return to sit on the throne of David. In the Millennium it will be 'the camp of God's people, the city he loves' (20:9).

Of course, the earthly city was in a sense a temporary replica of 'the heavenly Jerusalem, the city of the living God', of which all believers in Jesus are already citizens, together with Hebrew saints and angels (Hebrews 12:22–23). But that does not mean that the original is somehow less real than the copy, that one is material and the other 'spiritual'. The main difference between them is one of location. And that will change.

The heavenly city will come 'down out of heaven' and be sited on the new earth. It will be a real city, a material construction, though of rather different materials! Unfortunately, ever since Augustine's Platonic separation of the physical and spiritual realms, the Church has had real difficulties in accepting the concept of a new earth, never mind a new city on it.

The equation of 'spiritual' and 'intangible' has done immense damage to Christian hopes for the future. This new universe and its metropolis will not be less 'material' than the old.

Verses 3–8 are an explanatory comment on this final vision. The attention is immediately diverted from the new creation to its Creator. Note the transition from what John 'saw' to what he 'heard'. But whose 'loud voice' did he hear? It speaks of God in the third person, then in the first. This is surely Christ speaking (compare 1:15). The phrase 'seated on' the throne is the same as in the previous chapter (compare 20:11 with 21:5). In both contexts judgement is expressed and the 'lake of fire' mentioned (compare 20:15 with 21:8). Above all, the identical claim is made by this 'voice' as Jesus makes in the epilogue (compare 21:6 with 22:13). However, the 'throne of God and of the Lamb' are later seen as one (22:1).

Three startling statements follow:

The first is the most remarkable revelation about the future in the whole book. God himself is changing his residence from heaven to earth! He will come to live with human beings at their address, no longer 'our Father in heaven' (Matthew 6:9), but 'our Father on earth', leading to the most intimate relationship ever between human and divine persons. Since all death, sorrow and pain are contrary to his nature, they will have no place. There will be no more separation, no more tears. In passing, we recall the only other mention of God on earth in the Bible: his evening stroll in the garden of Eden (Genesis 3:8). Once again, the Bible has come full circle.

The second is the announcement that 'I am making everything new' (Revelation 21:5). Here the carpenter of Nazareth claims to be the Creator of the new universe, as he was of the old (John 1:3; Hebrews 1:2). His work is not limited to regenerating people, though that also is 'the new creation' (2 Corinthians 5:17). He is restoring all things as well.

There is considerable debate about the word 'new'. How new is 'new'? Is this 'new' universe simply the old one 'renovated' or a brand new manufacture? There certainly are two Greek words for 'new' (*kainos* and *eos*), but they are somewhat synonymous and the use of the former here does not settle the issue. References to the old universe as being 'destroyed by fire' (2 Peter 3:10) and having 'passed away' (Revelation 21:1) suggest eradication rather than transformation. But the process has already begun – with the resurrection of Jesus. His 'old' body dissolved inside the graveclothes and he came from death with a new 'glorious' body (Philippians 3:21); see also my book *Explaining the Resurrection* (Sovereign World, 1993). The exact 'connection' between the two bodies is hidden in the darkness of the tomb, but what happened there will one day happen on a universal scale.

The third spells out the practical implications of this new creation for the readers of Revelation (note that John has had to be reminded to keep writing down what he is hearing because 'these words are trustworthy and true'; 21:5). On the positive side is the promise to satisfy the thirst of those seeking 'the water of life' (21:6; 22:1, 17). But this must lead on to an 'overcoming' life, in order to inherit a place in the new earth and enjoy the family relationship with God in it.

On the negative side is the warning that those who do not overcome, but are cowardly, faithless, immoral and deceitful, will never be part of all this, but end up in 'the fiery lake of burning sulphur. This is the second death' (21:8). It needs to be pointed out that this warning is given to wayward believers, not unbelievers, as is the whole book. Most of Jesus' earlier warnings about hell were addressed, not to sinners, but to his own disciples (see my book *The Road to Hell*, Hodder and Stoughton, 1992).

At this point an angel takes John on a conducted tour of the New Jerusalem and its life (the idea that what follows is actually a 'recapitulation' of the 'old' Jerusalem in the Millennium is so bizarre we shall not consider it; verse 10 clearly expands verse 2). The description is breathtaking, straining vocabulary to the limit, which raises a fundamental question: how much is literal and how much is symbolical?

On the one hand, taking it entirely literally seems wrong. Clearly, John is describing the indescribable (Paul had the same difficulty when shown heavenly realities; 2 Corinthians 12:4). Notice how often he can only use a comparison ('like' or 'as' in 21:11, 18, 21; 22:1), yet all analogies are only approximate and ultimately inadequate. But the realities imperfectly portrayed here must be more wonderful than this, not less.

On the other hand, taking it entirely symbolically also seems wrong. Taken to this extreme, the whole picture dissolves into 'spiritual' unreality, which fails to do justice to the 'new earth' as the clear location.

To highlight the problem, we may ask the question: does the New Jerusalem represent a place or a people? The question arises because she is called a 'bride', which previously indicated a people, the Church (in 19:7–8). At first, this is only an analogy (in 21:3; '*as* a bride') and anyone who has seen a Semitic wedding will understand the likeness of the highly coloured clothes bedecked with jewellery. Later, however, the city is specifically designated 'the bride, the wife of the Lamb' (21:9). The angel, promising to *show* 'the bride' to John, *shows* him the city (21:10), though the vision moves on to reveal the life of its inhabitants (21:24–22:5).

The answer to the dilemma is much more obvious to a Jew than a Christian. 'Israel', the bride of Yahweh, was always a people *and* a place, inextricably involved with each other, hence all the prophetic promises of the ultimate restoration of the people to their own land. By comparison, Christians are a people without a place here, strangers, pilgrims, sojourners passing through, the new 'diaspora' or dispersed and exiled people of God (James 1:1; 1 Peter 1:1). Heaven is our 'home'. But heaven is coming down to earth at the last. Jew and Gentile will together be the people with a place. That is why the names on the city are the 12 tribes and the 12 apostles (21:12–14).

This dual unifying of Jew and Gentile, heaven and earth, is fundamental to God's eternal purpose 'to bring all things ... together under one head, even Christ' (Ephesians 1:10; Colossians 1:20). So the 'bride', who becomes one both in herself and with her husband, is a people and a place. And what a place!

The measurements are clearly important, all multiples of 12. The *size* is enormous: over 2,000 kilometres in each of three dimensions; the city would cover most of Europe or just fit into the moon if it were hollow. In other words, big enough to accommodate all God's people. The *shape* is also significant, more like a cube than a pyramid, indicating a 'holy' city like the cubed 'holy of holies' in tabernacle and temple. The walls define the outside rather than defend the inside, since the gates are always open. There is no threatened danger so its inhabitants can freely leave and return at any time.

The materials used in its construction are already known to us, but only as rare and precious gemstones which give us a tiny glimpse of heaven. The list here is one of the most remarkable proofs of the divine inspiration of this book. Now that we can produce 'purer' light (polarized and laser), a hitherto unknown quality of precious stones has been revealed. When thin sections are exposed to cross-polarized light (as when two lenses from sun-glasses are superimposed at right angles), they fall into two very distinct categories. 'Isotropic' stones lose all their colour, for they depend on random rays for their brilliance (e.g. diamonds, rubies and garnets). 'Anisotropic' stones produce all the colours of the rainbow in dazzling patterns, whatever their original colour. *All* the stones in the New Jerusalem belong to this latter category! No one could possibly have known this when Revelation was written – except God himself!

Another striking feature of this description is that in just 32 verses there are over 50 allusions to the Old Testament (mainly from Genesis, Psalms, Isaiah, Ezekiel and Zechariah). Every major feature is, in fact, the fulfilment of Jewish hopes expressed in prophecy. This also indicates that Old and New Testament prophecies all spring from the same source (1 Peter 1:11; 2 Peter 1:21). Revelation is the climax and conclusion to the whole Bible.

When the angelic demonstration moves on to the life enjoyed by the inhabitants of the city, there are some surprises. Perhaps the biggest contrast to the 'old' Jerusalem is the absence of a dominating temple to focus worship at a particular place (or at a particular time?). The whole city *is* his temple, in which the redeemed 'serve him day and night' (Revelation 7:15), which suggests that work and worship have been blended together again, as they were for Adam (Genesis 2:15; Adam was not told to have one day in seven for worship).

The city will be enriched with international culture (Revelation 21:24, 26). It will never be polluted with immoral behaviour (21:27). That is why compromised believers are in danger of having their names erased from 'the Lamb's book of life' (3:5; 21:7–8).

The river and tree of life will ensure continuous health. As at the beginning, the diet will be fruit rather than meat (Genesis 1:29), though there is no obligation to be vegetarian before then (Genesis 9:3; Romans 14:2; 1 Timothy 4:3).

Above all, the saints will live in the presence of God. They will actually see his face, a privilege given to few before (Genesis 32:30; Exodus 33:11) but then to all (1 Corinthians 13:12). They will reflect him in their own faces, his name on their foreheads, as once others bore the number of the 'beast' (Revelation 13:16). They will 'reign for ever and ever', presumably over the new creation rather than each other, as was originally intended (Genesis 1:28). In this way they will 'serve' the Creator.

Once again, it needs to be emphasized that human beings have not gone to heaven to be with the Lord for ever; he has come to earth to be with them for ever. The New Jerusalem is at once the eternal divine and human 'dwelling-place', their permanent residence.

As before, John has to be reminded to write it all down. His distraction from the task is understandable!

The 'epilogue' (Revelation 22:7–21) has much in common with the 'prologue' (1:1–8). The same title is applied to God in one and Christ in the other (1:8; 22:13). This concluding exhortation is thoroughly trinitarian: God, the Lamb and the Spirit are all present.

There is a strong emphasis on the fact that time is short. Jesus is coming 'soon' (22:7, 12, 20). The fact that many centuries have elapsed since this was said and written should not lead to complacency; we must be much nearer 'the things that must soon take place' (22:6).

The day of opportunity is still here. The thirsty may still drink the water of life as a free gift (22:17). But choices must be made now. The time is coming when the moral direction of our lives will be fixed for ever (22:11). Pharaoh hardened his heart against the Lord seven times, so then God hardened it for him three times (Exodus 7–11; Romans 9:17–18). There will come a point when this happens to all who defy and disobey his will.

There are only two categories of people in the end: those who 'go on washing their robes' (Revelation 22:17; compare 7:14) and thus enter the city – and those kept outside it (22:15), like the wild curs of the Middle East today. This is now the third time a list of disqualifying offences has been included in this sublime finale (21:8, 27; 22:15), as if the readers must never be allowed to forget that the glories of the future will not come to them automatically because they have believed in Jesus and belong to a church, but to those who 'press on towards the goal to win the prize for which God has called us heavenwards in Christ Jesus' (Philippians 3:14) and who 'make every effort ... to be holy, for without holiness no one will see the Lord' (Hebrews 12:14).

Another way in which believers can forfeit the future is by tampering with this Book of Revelation, either by addition or subtraction. Since it is a 'prophecy', God speaking through his servant, to alter it in any way is to commit sacrilege, incurring the severest penalty. It is unlikely that unbelievers would even bother to do this. It is much more likely to be done by those who take upon themselves the task of explaining and interpreting it to others. May God have mercy on this poor author if he has offended in this way!

But the final note is positive, not negative, and is summed up in one word: 'Come!'

On the one hand, this invitation on the lips of the Church is addressed to the world, to 'whoever' will respond to the gospel (Revelation 22:17; compare John 3:16). On the other hand, it is addressed to the Lord: 'Amen. Come, Lord Jesus' (22:10).

This dual plea is characteristic of the true bride who is moved by the Spirit (22:17) and is experiencing the grace of the Lord Jesus (22:21). All the saints cry: 'Come!', both to the renegade world and its returning Lord.

The centrality of Christ

This last book of the Bible is 'the revelation of Jesus Christ' (1:1). The genitive ('of') can be understood in two ways: It is *from* him or *about* him. Perhaps the double meaning is intended. Either way he is central to its message.

If the theme is the end of the world, he is 'the end', as he was 'the beginning' (22:13). God's plan is 'to bring all things in heaven and on earth together under one head, even Christ' (Ephesians 1:10).

The prologue and epilogue both focus on his return to planet earth (1:7; 22:20). The hinge on which future history swings from getting worse to getting better is that second coming (19:11–16).

It is 'this same Jesus' (Acts 1:11) who will return. He is the Lamb of God who came the first time to take away 'the sin of the world' (John 1:29). Throughout Revelation the Lamb looks 'as if it had been slain' (5:6). Presumably the scars will still be visible on his head, side, back, hands and feet (John 20:25–27). There are frequent reminders that he shed his blood to redeem human beings of every type (5:9; 7:14; 12:11).

Yet the Jesus of Revelation is also very different from the man of Galilee. His first appearance to John was so awesome that this disciple who had been closest to him (John 21:20) fell in a dead faint. We have already mentioned his snow-white hair, blazing eyes, sharp tongue, shining face and burnished feet.

Though there are brief glimpses of the angry Jesus in the Gospels (Mark 3:5; 10:14; 11:15), his sustained 'wrath' in

Revelation strikes terror in the hearts of all kinds of people, who would rather be crushed by falling rocks than look into his eyes (6:16–17). This is no 'gentle Jesus, meek and mild'. Though that would be a doubtful description of him at any time, it is particularly inappropriate here.

Many believe Jesus preached and practised pacificism, despite his assertion to the contrary: 'Do not suppose that I have come to bring peace to the earth. I did not come to bring peace, but a sword' (Matthew 10:34; Luke 12:51). Of course, his words can be 'spiritualized', but it is far less easy to explain them away in Revelation, where the most natural understanding of the final conflict is physical.

Jesus rides down from heaven on a horse of war rather than a donkey of peace (Zechariah 9:9; Revelation 19:11; compare 6:2). His robe is 'dipped in blood' (19:13), but not his own. Though the only 'sword' he wields is his tongue, the effect of using it is to slaughter thousands of kings, generals and mighty men (both volunteering and conscripted), as once that same tongue dealt death to a fig-tree (Mark 11:20–21).

Jesus is clearly depicted here as a mass killer, the vultures cleaning up the mess afterwards! This graphic portrayal comes as a shock to respectable worshippers used to seeing him gazing benignly from stained-glass windows. It will be an even greater surprise to those who use the weeks of Advent in the Church calendar to present him in nativity plays as a helpless baby. He will never be that again.

Has Jesus changed? We know that old age mellows some but others become cantankerous and even malicious. Has this happened to him during the intervening centuries? God forbid!

It is not his character or personality that have changed, but his mission. His first visit was 'to seek and save what was lost' (Luke 19:10). He did not come 'into the world to condemn the world, but to save the world' (John 3:17). He came to give human beings the opportunity to be separated from their sins before all sin has to be destroyed. His second visit is for the opposite purpose – to destroy rather than to save, to punish sin rather than pardon it, 'to judge the quick [living] and the dead', as the Apostles' Creed and Nicene Creed put it.

It has become a cliché that Jesus 'loves the sinner but hates the sin'. The former was clearly seen in his first coming; the latter will be just as apparent at his second. Those who cling to their sins must face the consequences. At that time 'the Son of man will send out his angels and they will weed out of his kingdom everything that causes sin and all who do evil' (Matthew 10:41). This 'weeding' will be as thorough as it will be fair. But if it is to be totally fair, it must be applied to believers as well as unbelievers (as Paul clearly teaches in Romans 2:1–11, concluding that 'God does not show favouritism').

Once again, we need to remember that the Book of Revelation is addressed exclusively to 'born-again' believers. The descriptions of his fierce opposition to sinning are intended to induce a wholesome fear in 'saints' as an incentive to 'obey God's commandments and remain faithful to Jesus' (14:12).

It is all too easy for those who have experienced the grace of our Lord Jesus Christ, to forget that he will still be their Judge (2 Corinthians 5:10). Those who have known him as friend and brother (John 15:15; Hebrews 2:11) are apt to overlook his more challenging attributes. At the least, he is worthy of 'praise and honour and glory and power, for ever and ever' (5:13).

Of the 250 names and titles given to Jesus in Scripture, a considerable number are used in this book and some are unique to it, found nowhere else. He is the first and the last, the beginning and the end, the Alpha and the Omega. He is the ruler of God's creation. That is *his relation to our universe*. He was involved in its creation, is responsible for its continuation and will bring it to its consummation (John 1:3; Colossians 1:15–17; Hebrews 1:1–2).

He is the lion of the tribe of Judah, the root (and offspring) of David. That is *his relation to God's chosen people Israel*. He was, is and always will be, the Jewish Messiah.

He is holy and true, faithful and true, the faithful and true witness. He is the living one, who was dead and is alive for evermore, who holds the keys of death and Hades. That is *his relation to the Church*. They need to remember his passion for truth, which means for reality and integrity, as opposed to hypocrisy.

He is King of kings, and Lord of lords. He is the bright morning star, the one still shining when all others (pop and film stars included!) have disappeared. That is *his relation to the world*. One day his authority will be universally recognized.

So many of these titles are introduced with a formula familiar from the Gospel of John: 'I am'. This is not just a personal claim. The phrase sounds so much like the name by which God revealed himself that using it directly led to assassination attempts and ultimate execution for Jesus (John 8:58–59; Mark 14:62–63). That it was intended to indicate shared divinity and equality with God is confirmed in Revelation by Father and Son claiming exactly the same titles: for example, 'Alpha and Omega' (1:8 and 22:13).

The world is coming to an end, but that end is personal rather than impersonal. In fact, the end is a person. Jesus is the end.

To study Revelation primarily to discover *what* the world is coming to is to miss the point. The essential message is about *who* the world is coming to or, rather, who is coming to the world.

Christians are really the only ones who are longing for 'the end' to come, every generation hoping that this will happen during their lifetime. For them 'the end' is not an event, but a person. They are eagerly awaiting 'him', not 'it'.

The penultimate verse (22:20) contains a very personal summary of the whole book: 'He who testifies to these things says, "Yes, I am coming soon".' There can be only one response from those who have understood: 'Amen. Come, Lord Jesus.'

The rewards of study

We have already noted that Revelation is the only biblical book to carry both a blessing on those who read it and a curse on those who tamper with it (1:3; 22:18–19). By way of summary, we shall now list 10 benefits that result from mastering its message, all of which assist authentic Christian living.

1. The completion of the Bible

The student will begin to share God's knowledge of 'the end from the beginning' (Isaiah 46:10). The story is complete. The happy ending is revealed. The romance ends in the wedding and the real relationship begins. Without this, the Bible would be incomplete. It would have to be known as the 'Amputated Version'! The striking resemblances between the first and last pages of Holy Scripture (e.g. the tree of life) make sense of all that lies between.

2. A defence against heresy

So often the cults and sects, whose representatives come knocking at our doors, major on Revelation. Their apparent knowledge of it deeply impresses churchgoers who have never grasped it, largely through lack of teaching (and lack of teachers who know it). They are unable to challenge the interpretation offered, which can be quite bizarre. The only real defence is a superior knowledge.

3. An interpretation of history

A superficial awareness of current affairs can leave anyone baffled as to any discernible direction. Since future events cast their shadows before them, the student of Revelation will find an astonishing correspondence with world events, as they clearly head towards a world government and a world economy. Any preacher who systematically expounds the book is likely to be given many relevant newspaper cuttings by his hearers.

4. A ground for hope

Everything is going according to plan, God's plan. He is still on the throne, directing affairs towards the end, Jesus. Revelation assures us that good will triumph over evil, Christ will conquer Satan and the saints will one day rule the world. Our planet will be cleared of all pollution, physical and moral. Even the universe will be recycled. The hope of all this is 'an anchor for the soul' in the storms of life (Hebrews 6:19). Paganism, secularism and humanism only appear to gain ground. Their days are numbered.

5. A motive for evangelism

There is no clearer presentation of the alternative destinies placed before the human race – the new heaven and earth or the lake of fire, everlasting joy or everlasting torment. The opportunity to choose will not last indefinitely. The Day of Judgement must come, with every member of the human race accountable. But the day of salvation is still here: 'Whoever is thirsty, let him come; and whoever wishes, let him take the free gift of the water of life' (22:17). The invitation to 'Come!' is issued jointly by the 'Spirit and the bride [i.e. the Church]'.

6. A stimulus to worship

Revelation is full of worship, sung and shouted by many voices. There are 11 major songs, which have inspired many other hymns down the ages, from Handel's *Messiah* to the 'Battle Hymn of the Republic' ('Mine eyes have seen the glory of the coming of the Lord'). Worship is directed towards God and the Lamb, not the Spirit; and never to the angels. 'Therefore, with angels and archangels, we laud and magnify your holy name ...'

7. An antidote to worldliness

It is so easy to be 'earthly minded'. As William Wordsworth reminds us:

> *The world is too much with us, late and soon,*
> *getting and spending, we lay waste our powers,*
> *little we see in Nature that is ours.*

Revelation teaches us to think more about our eternal home than a temporary 'Ideal Home', more about our new resurrection body than our old ageing frame.

8. An incentive to godliness

God's will for us is holiness here and happiness hereafter, not vice versa, as many would wish. Holiness is essential if we are going to survive present troubles, overcoming internal temptation and external persecution. Revelation shakes us out of slackness, complacency and indifference by reminding us that God is 'holy, holy, holy' (4:8) and that only 'holy' people will share in the first resurrection when Jesus returns (20:6). The whole book, but especially the seven letters at the beginning, confirms the principle that 'without holiness no-one will see the Lord' (Hebrews 12:14).

9. A preparation for persecution

This, of course, is the fundamental purpose for Revelation being written. Its message comes across loud and clear to Christians who are suffering for their faith, encouraging them to 'endure' and 'overcome', thus keeping their names in the book of life and their inheritance in the new creation. Jesus predicted universal hatred of his followers before the end (Matthew 24:9). So we all need to be prepared.

Reader, if this is not already happening in your country, it will certainly come. And so will Jesus, before whom cowards will be 'shamefully exposed' (16:15) and condemned to hell (22:8).

10. An understanding of Christ

With Revelation, the picture of our Lord and Saviour is completed. Without it, the portrait is unbalanced, even distorted. If the Gospels present him in his role as prophet and the Epistles cover his role as priest, Revelation clarifies his role as King, the King of kings and the Lord of lords. Here is the Christ the world has never seen, yet will one day see; the Christ the Christian sees now by faith and will one day meet in the flesh.

After studying Revelation, no one can ever be quite the same again. Yet its message can be forgotten. That is why its blessing is not just for those who read it, even aloud to others, but for those who 'keep' what is written. This means that we 'take it to heart' (1:3; New International Version) as well as mind, but also that we put it into practice. 'Do not merely listen to the word, and so deceive yourselves. Do what it says' (James 1:22).

59.

THE MILLENNIUM

Sadly, chapter 20 has led to deep divisions among Christians. So different are the interpretations that there is an unwritten agreement not to discuss them for the sake of unity.

Readers may well have heard about the three major views – *a*millennial, *pre*millennial and *post*millennial – but there are other variations.

Some are inclined to treat the whole issue as academic, speculative and irrelevant (a friend of mine called it 'a pre-post-erous question'!) and have coined a new label: *pan*millennial (the vague belief that everything will pan out all right in the end, whatever we think now).

But hope is as integral to the Christian life as faith and love. What we are sure will happen in the future profoundly affects our behaviour in the present. Our 'millennial' convictions influence our evangelism and our social action.

In particular, our hopes for *this* world are crucial. Will it only get worse or ever get better? Will Jesus' return to this planet have any beneficial effect or simply write it off? Is he coming to judge the nations or reign over them? And why is he bringing all departed Christians back here with him (1 Thessalonians 4:14)?

The Lord does not reveal the future to satisfy our curiosity or give us superior knowledge but so that we may prepare ourselves for our part in it. If we were convinced that we were going to share his reign over this world, we would behave rather more responsibily now.

We need to look at the passage itself, in its own context; then ask when and why such widely divergent interpretations of it have arisen; and finally make some evaluation and hopefully reach a conclusion.

The biblical exposition

Verses 1–10 of chapter 20 in Revelation are the focus of the whole debate. It is important to review what is stated clearly before attempting to draw inferences from the passage.

The most striking feature is the repeated phrase 'a thousand years' – six times, twice with the definite article '*the* thousand years'. The emphasis is unmistakable. Whether the figure is taken literally or metaphorically, it clearly means an extended period of time, as most commentators agree. It is an era, an epoch.

Surprisingly little information is given here about this whole time. Indeed, only three things are told us. One single event at the beginning, another at the end and a continuous situation in between. The opening and concluding happenings both concern Satan, while the state in between is about the saints.

The 'millennium' starts with the removal of the devil from the earthly scene altogether. A descending angel with a huge chain seizes, binds, throws, locks and seals him. The five verbs emphasize the complete helplessness of the devil, which is confirmed by the plain statement that his career of brilliant deception is over – though only for the duration of the millennium. He is not thrown into the lake of fire (yet!) but is securely imprisoned in the 'Pit' or 'Abyss', usually thought of as under the earth, out of reach of and out of touch with its living inhabitants.

This banishment of Satan, together with the previous consignment of his two henchmen, Antichrist and the False Prophet (the two 'beasts' of Revelation 13), to the 'lake of fire' (19:20), will leave the world without a government, in a political vacuum.

In the second part of this millennial vision, John sees 'thrones' (only plural here and in 4:4), occupied by those given authority to 'judge' (ie. settle disputes, maintain law and order, apply justice). Within this larger group he notices particularly those who were martyred for refusing to worship the Antichrist or be branded with his number (666). What an amazing reversal of their former situation!

Obviously, both this small group and the larger one of which they are part have come back from the dead. They have 'come to life' again to reign with Christ during the millennium. This is specifically described as a 'resurrection', a noun only used throughout scripture with reference to physical bodies. We know that those who belong to Christ are thus raised at his coming (1 Corinthians 15:23). They are 'blessed and holy' to be raised then and become royal priests in the millennium and will never again run the risk of being consigned to 'the second death' (the 'lake of fire', i.e. hell).

There is in this passage a very clear distinction between this 'first resurrection' of the saints and the resurrection of 'the rest' of the human race. The two events are separated by the entire 'millennium'. And the two resurrections have two entirely different objectives. One is to reign with Christ, the other is to be judged (20:12).

The third section of this vision takes us to the very end of the millennium – Satan removed (1–3), saints reigning (4–6), and Satan released (7–10). This is an astonishing development, easier to attribute to divine revelation than human imagination! Who would have guessed that the devil would be allowed back on earth for a second (and final) attempt to claim it as his kingdom! Yet he is able again to deceive multitudes into thinking he can give them liberty, and so enlist a vast army to march on 'the camp of God's people, the *city* he loves' (surely a reference to Jerusalem). The forces are labelled 'Gog and Magog' (from Ezekiel we know this refers to an attack on the restored throne of David) and this assault is therefore to be distinguished from Armageddon (19:19–21). There is no battle. The forces are destroyed by fire from heaven and the devil finally joins the Antichrist and the False Prophet in hell to be tormented for ever (the Greek phrase 'to the ages of the ages' cannot mean less).

No reason is given for allowing the devil to have his final fling after such a long period of a godly government and all its benefits. But it will serve to underline the truth that the rebellion of sin comes from within the heart and not from the environment and to justify the immediate division of the human race into two groups – those who want to live under the divine rule and those who don't. The 'millennium' leads straight into the final day of judgement when this final separation takes place.

Two questions remain to be answered and they are crucial to understanding why there is such controversy over this 'millennium'. They are:

WHERE does all this happen?
WHEN does all this happen?

'The revelation of Jesus Christ' recorded in this book, consisting of verbal ('I heard') and visual ('I saw') elements, alternates settings between heaven and earth, relating events in both. But changes of scene are clearly indicated (4:1; 12:13).

The entire passage from 19:11 to 20:11 is clearly set on earth. The King of kings rides out of an open heaven to 'strike down the nations' on earth; the battle against the forces of Antichrist and the False Prophet takes place on earth; the angel comes 'down out of heaven' to banish Satan from earth; the martyrs 'reign with Christ' who is now on earth; Satan finally gathers his 'Gog and Magog' forces 'from the four corners of the earth'; the earth finally 'flees from the presence of the one on the great white throne'.

It is perverse to avoid the conclusion that the 'millennium' takes place on earth. 'Heaven' is only mentioned when someone comes 'out of' there to come here. That answers the question: 'Where?'

The question 'When?' would have an equally clear answer had not God's word been divided into chapters in the Middle Ages. This arrangement may be convenient (together with verse numbers, a separate but uninspired development) but the division is sometimes in the wrong place, setting asunder what God had joined together. This is especially true here. The bishop who inserted '20' into the text was clearly not afraid of the curse on those who 'add anything to the words of' the prophecy of this book (22:18). Little did he realize what damage it would do, though it probably reflected his own view, as we shall see.

If the three chapters 19, 20 and 21 are read as one continuous revelation, as the Lord intended, the sequence of *seven* visions (from 'I saw' in 19:11 to 21:1) becomes clear. They reveal the final events of world history, in the order with which they follow each other (for example, 20:10 refers back to 19:20

as having already happened). Dividing the visions between three chapters has meant that they are rarely read, much less studied, together. The sequence is lost. The events can then be juggled into a quite different order – and have been.

Anyone reading through Revelation, without any pre-conditioning of their minds and without letting chapter divisions have any influence, would naturally assume that the 'millennium' *follows* the return of Christ and the battle of Armageddon and *precedes* the day of judgement and the new heaven and earth. That is the simple and plain meaning of the text.

So the passage appears to reveal a lengthy period of Christian government on this earth after Christ returns and raises his own from the dead but before he finally judges the world. Why don't all Christians believe this – and look forward to sharing in the transformation it will bring?

The historical interpretation

For the first five centuries the church apparently agreed on the above interpretation. Over a dozen of the 'Fathers', as early theologians are called, mention what Papias, bishop of Hiero-polis, referred to as 'the corporeal (i.e. bodily) reign of Christ on the earth'. There is not a hint of any other view, much less any debate about it. They assumed that scripture was to be taken as it stood, on this as on other matters.

This position, seemingly universal in the early church, is better known as pre-millennial, because it holds that Jesus will return *before* (i.e. 'pre') the 'millennium' describes in Revelation 20.

All this was to change through a North African bishop called Augustine, who has had more influence on 'Western' theology, Catholic and Protestant, than anyone else. He began with pre-millennial views, but later allowed his Greek education (neo-Platonic) to change his thinking on this and many other aspects of Christian belief and behaviour.

The basic problem was that Greek thought, unlike the Hebrew mind in scripture, separated the spiritual and physical realms, tending to identify the former as holy and the latter as sinful. Sex, even within marriage, came under suspicion and clerical celibacy followed.

Inevitably, the bodily return of Jesus to reign over a physical earth became difficult to handle and there may have been a reaction to over-indulgent preaching of physical pleasures on the millennial earth. Suffice it to say that even the 'new' earth tended to disappear and Christians only looked forward to 'going to heaven'. Jesus' second coming was reduced to judging the 'quick and the dead' and destroying the earth (actually, Revelation 20 puts these in reverse order). The Council of Ephesus in AD 531 was so heavily influenced by this new approach that it condemned pre-millennialism as heresy, which has caused it to be under suspicion ever since!

What should we do with Revelation 20? It is still part of God's Word and we cannot afford to ignore it. The simple solution is to transfer the millennium from after to before Christ's return, to claim that chapter 20 comes before chapter 19 in history, even if it doesn't in scripture! Chapter 20 marks a 'recapitulation' of events leading up to the second coming. It belongs to church history in the present, not the future.

Strictly speaking, this shifted the church from a pre-millennial to a post-millennial position, because it holds that Jesus will return *after* (ie 'post') the 'millennium' described in Revelation 20!

But there was an ambiguity in all this, that was to lead to a further major division of views. Augustine did not spell out clearly whether this new 'millennium' was a purely *spiritual* reign of the saints with Christ (which in a sense could be applied to the whole church history, from the first to the second coming of Christ) or whether it would be *political* as well (when the church would have become strong enough to take over the government of the nations in the name of Christ). His book *The City of God*, written when the Roman empire was collapsing, does not make it clear whether he expected the 'Kingdom of God' to take over from Rome (which it virtually did) or merely survive and grow in spite of the catastrophe. This paved the way for two schools of thought, both claiming roots in Augustine.

On the one hand are those who believe the church will 'Christianize' the world, not by converting everyone but by gaining political power to apply God's laws – and thus introduce a lengthy period (even literally a thousand years) of universal peace and prosperity, incidentally relegating the second coming to the distant future, since this 'millennium' hasn't even started yet and, indeed, seems to be further off than ever. But this idea has often resurfaced – in Victorian missionary hymns coinciding with the expansion of a 'Christian' British Empire, for example; and more recently under labels like Restoration, Reconstruction and even Revival. This optimistic outlook has claimed exclusive use of the adjective 'post-millennial'.

On the other hand those who believe the 'reign' of Jesus and his saints is purely spiritual and began at the first advent and will continue to the second, have had to find a new title for themselves and have chosen 'a-millennial'. This is both inaccurate and misleading, since the prefix 'a-' means 'non' (as in 'a-theist'). It is still post-millennial in believing the 'millennium' is a period of time *before* Christ returns, but only differs from other 'post-millennials' in believing that we are *already* in the millennium and have been for two thousand years!

This view, going back through the Protestant Reformers to Augustine, is probably the most common view in Europe, though not in America, as we shall see. It is worth pausing to note how Revelation 20 is handled by those espousing it.

Many subtle changes have to be made. The 'angel' dealing with Satan becomes Jesus himself, the 'binding' taking place either at his temptations or crucifixion. Satan is bound but not banished. He is merely put on a long chain, so only limited in his movements (thrown, locked and sealed are dismissed as meaningless). Usually the 'limit' on his activities is solely an inability to prevent the gospel spreading and the church being built. He is left on earth, not shut up in a pit or 'abyss'. Those martyred under Antichrist represent all saints throughout the ages reigning in heaven with Jesus. Their 'coming to life' in the 'first resurrection' was either their conversion (raised from the 'death' of sin) or their going to heaven at their death – but nothing to do with their bodies. However, the 'rest' 'coming to life' (the same word in the same context) *does* mean raised bodies! And all six times, a 'thousand years' means at least two thousand so far.

And so it goes on. The reader's common sense is left to judge whether all this is good *ex*egesis (reading out of scripture what is clearly there) or bad *eis*egesis (reading into scripture what one wants to find there). This author finds such interpretation totally unconvincing.

There has been one other major development in the millennial debate which needs to be noted, not least because it is widely held on the other side of the Atlantic, though it originated over here, in the teaching of John Nelson Darby, founder of the Brethren movement. It was popularized by his pupil, an American lawyer called Dr C. I. Scofield, who produced the 'Scofield' Bible, and by a seminary in Dallas, Texas, especially through a former student, Hal Lindsay.

The positive side is that, from the early nineteenth century, many were led back to the pre-millennial conviction of the early church. It had never entirely disappeared (Isaac Newton was a supporter of this view) and others would rediscover it including Anglican bishops like Ryle, Westcott and Hort, but the major influence came through the Brethren.

The negative side is that Darby combined this ancient belief with some quite novel notions in a complete theological system now known as Dispensationalism, after the seven eras, or dispensations, into which he divided history, in each of which God dispensed his grace on a different basis. He taught that the church was in a state of irrecoverable ruin; that the Jews were God's 'earthly' and Christians his 'heavenly' people, kept separate for all eternity; and, above all, that Christ would come again *twice*, once secretly to take his church away before the Great Tribulation and then publicly, to rule the world. His detailed schedule of the future also included four separate judgements.

Tragically, all this was so tightly integrated that it is widely thought that a pre-millennial belief must be 'dispensational'. To reject the latter is to reject the former! But that is to throw away the baby with the bathwater (a saying dating from the days when a whole extended family used the same tin bath and by the turn of the youngest the water was so muddy that it's final occupant could be overlooked!).

It is therefore necessary to make a very clear distinction between the 'classical' pre-millennialism of the early church and the 'dispensational' premillennialism of many modern Evangelicals and Pentecostals. A small but growing number of biblical scholars are realizing this (the names of George Eldon Ladd and Merrill Tenney spring to mind).

A personal conclusion

I will close this Appendix with the reasons why I am a 'classic pre-millennialist' in interpreting Revelation 20.

1 It is the most natural interpretation, without any forcing of the text.
2 It gives the most satisfying explanation of why Jesus needs to come back and bring us with him.
3 It is the view that gives greatest emphasis to the hopeful expectancy of his return.
4 It explains why God would want to vindicate his Son in the eyes of the whole world.
5 It 'earths' our future, as does the whole New Testament, heaven being a waiting-room until we return.
6 It is realistic, avoiding the post-optimism and the a-pessimism, as regards this world.
7 It has fewer problems than the other views, though it still leaves some questions unanswered.
8 It is what the early church unanimously believed and they were nearer to the apostles.

For these reasons, I am able to pray, with real meaning and longing: 'Your kingdom come on earth … as it is in heaven'.

Note: This whole issue is dealt with in greater depth and detail in 'The Millennium Muddle', the fourth section of my book *When Jesus Returns* (Hodder and Stoughton, 1995).

Ezekiel.